OPERATIONS MANAGEMENT FOR COMPETITIVE ADVANTAGE

THE MCGRAW-HILL/IRWIN SERIES

Operations and Decision Sciences

OPERATIONS MANAGEMENT

Bowersox, Closs, and Cooper
Supply Chain Logistics Management
First Edition

Burt and Dobler
World Class Supply Management
Seventh Edition

Cachon and Terwiesch
Matching Supply with Demand: An Introduction
to Operations Management
First Edition

Chase, Jacobs, and Aquilano
Operations Management for Competitive
Advantage
Eleventh Edition

Davis and Heineke
Managing Services
First Edition

Davis and Heineke
Operations Management: Integrating
Manufacturing and Services
Fifth Edition

Finch
Operations Now: Profitability, Processes,
Performance
Second Edition

Fitzsimmons and Fitzsimmons
Service Management
Fifth Edition

Flaherty
Global Operations Management
First Edition

Gehrlein
Operations Management Cases
First Edition

Gray and Larson
Project Management
Third Edition

Harrison and Samson
Technology Management
First Edition

Hill
Manufacturing Strategy: Text & Cases
Third Edition

Hopp and Spearman
Factory Physics
Second Edition

Jacobs and Whybark
Why ERP?
First Edition

Knod and Schonberger
Operations Management
Seventh Edition

Lambert and Stock
Strategic Logistics Management
Third Edition

Leenders, Johnson, Flynn, and Fearon
Purchasing and Supply Management
Thirteenth Edition

Melnyk and Swink
Value-Driven Operations Management
First Edition

Moses, Seshadri, and Yakir
HOM Operations Management Software
First Edition

Nahmias
Production and Operations Analysis
Fifth Edition

Nicholas
Competitive Manufacturing Management
First Edition

Olson
Introduction to Information Systems Project
Management
Second Edition

Pinto and Parente
SimProject: A Project Management Simulation
for Classroom Instruction
First Edition

Schroeder
Operations Management: Contemporary
Concepts and Cases
Second Edition

Seppanen, Kumar, and Chandra
Process Analysis and Improvement
First Edition

Simchi-Levi, Kaminsky, and Simchi-Levi
Designing and Managing the Supply Chain
Second Edition

Stevenson
Operations Management
Eighth Edition

Vollmann, Berry, Whybark, and Jacobs
Manufacturing Planning & Control for Supply
Chain Management Systems
Fifth Edition

Zipkin
Foundations of Inventory Management
First Edition

BUSINESS STATISTICS

Aczel and Sounderpandian
Complete Business Statistics
Sixth Edition

ALEKS Corporation
ALEKS for Business Statistics
First Edition

Alwan
Statistical Process Analysis
First Edition

Bowerman and O'Connell
Business Statistics in Practice
Third Edition

Bowerman, O'Connell, and Orris
Essentials of Business Statistics
First Edition

Bryant and Smith
Practical Data Analysis: Case Studies in Business
Statistics, Volumes I, II, and III*

Cooper and Schindler
Business Research Methods
Eighth Edition

Delurgio
Forecasting Principles and Applications
First Edition

Doane
LearningStats CD Rom
First Edition, 1.2

Doane, Mathieson, and Tracy
Visual Statistics
Second Edition, 2.0

Gitlow, Oppenheim, Oppenheim, and Levine
Quality Management
Third Edition

Kutner, Nachtsheim, and Neter
Applied Linear Regression Models
Fourth Edition

Kutner, Nachtsheim, Neter, and Li
Applied Linear Statistical Models
Fifth Edition

Lind, Marchal, and Wathen
Basic Statistics for Business and Economics
Fifth Edition

Lind, Marchal, and Wathen
Statistical Techniques in Business and Economics
Twelfth Edition

Merchant, Goffinet, and Koehler
Basic Statistics Using Excel for Office XP
Third Edition

Sahai and Khurshid
Pocket Dictionary of Statistics
First Edition

Siegel
Practical Business Statistics
Fifth Edition

Wilson, Keating, and John Galt Solutions, Inc.
Business Forecasting
Fourth Edition

Zagorsky
Business Information
First Edition

QUANTITATIVE METHODS AND MANAGEMENT SCIENCE

Hillier and Hillier
Introduction to Management Science
Second Edition

OPERATIONS MANAGEMENT FOR COMPETITIVE ADVANTAGE

eleventh edition

RICHARD B. CHASE
University of Southern California

F. ROBERT JACOBS
Indiana University

NICHOLAS J. AQUILANO
University of Arizona

Available in MHE (India) Edition

McGraw-Hill Irwin

Boston   Burr Ridge, IL   Dubuque, IA   Madison, WI   New York   San Francisco   St. Louis
Bangkok   Bogotá   Caracas   Kuala Lumpur   Lisbon   London   Madrid   Mexico City
Milan   Montreal   New Delhi   Santiago   Seoul   Singapore   Sydney   Taipei   Toronto

OPERATIONS MANAGEMENT FOR COMPETITIVE ADVANTAGE

To our wives
Harriet, Jeanne, and Nina
and to our children
Laurie, Andy, Glenn, Rob, Christine, and Batsheva
Jennifer and Suzy
Don, Kara, and Mark

PREFACE

Operations management (OM) has been a key element in the improvement in productivity in businesses around the world. Creating a *competitive advantage* through operations requires an understanding of how the operations function contributes to productivity growth. However, our intent in this book is to do more than just show you what companies are doing to create competitive advantage through OM. Our overriding goal is to create a competitive advantage for you in the marketplace by conveying a set of skills and tools that you can actually apply.

Service

Global

Cross Functional

Excel: Project Management

Three hot topics in business today are Supply Chain Management, Six Sigma, and Enterprise Resource Planning Systems. These topics are studied in the book from the view of the operations function with up-to-date high-level managerial material to clarify the "big picture" of what these topics are and why they are so important to business today. Applications that range from high-tech manufacturing to high-touch service are used in the balanced treatment of the traditional topics of the field. Operations management requires a global perspective for many of the topics. Operations management is best done with significant cross-functional integration. Accounting, finance, marketing, human resources management, purchasing, logistics, and engineering impact how firms are run operationally. To highlight our emphasis on services, globalization, and cross-functional integration, we've used the logos you see here in the text margin next to these discussions.

Technical Notes detail how operations-related problems are solved. These are concise treatments of the many decisions that need to be made in designing, planning, and managing the operations of a business. Many spreadsheets are included on the DVD to help clarify how these problems are quickly solved. We've indicated those spreadsheets with the spreadsheet logo shown here in the margin.

A Managerial Briefing section starts Section Four and provides an executive summary-style introduction to the concepts of Enterprise Resource Planning.

Operations Management should appeal to individuals who want to be directly involved in making products or providing services. The entry-level operations specialist is the person who determines how best to design, supply, and run the processes. Senior operations managers are responsible for setting the strategic direction of the company from an operations standpoint, deciding what technologies should be used, where facilities should be located, and managing the facilities that make the products or provide the services. Operations Management is an interesting mix of managing people and applying sophisticated technology. The goal is to efficiently create wealth by supplying quality goods and services.

Features to aid in your understanding of the material include the following:

- Solved problems at the end of chapters to serve as models that can be reviewed prior to attempting problems.
- Key terms highlighted in the chapter outline and their definitions at the end of each chapter.
- Answers to selected problems in Appendix A.
- The student DVD that includes PowerPoint slide outlines of each chapter, Excel® spreadsheets for many of the solved problems and other examples, practice exams, electronic ScreenCam tutorials, Internet links, and video segments and clips that illustrate the application of operations concepts in companies such as Honda, Disney, BP, Ford, and many more.
- Breakthrough Boxes and boxed inserts provide short overviews of how leading-edge companies are applying OM concepts today.

Our aim is to cover the latest and the most important issues facing OM managers, as well as the basic tools and techniques. We supply many examples of leading-edge companies and practices. We have done our best to make the book interesting reading and, as we said at the outset, give you a competitive advantage in your career.

We hope you enjoy it.

Plan of This Book

This book is about methods to effectively produce and distribute the goods and services sold by a company. To develop a better understanding of the field, this book is organized into four major sections: Operations Strategy and Managing Change, Process Selection and Design, Supply Chain Design, and Planning and Controlling the Supply Chain. In the following, we quickly describe the major topics in the book.

Strategy is an important and recurring topic in the book. Any company must have a comprehensive business plan that is supported by a marketing strategy, operations strategy, and financial strategy. It is essential for a company to ensure that the three strategies support each other. Strategy is covered from a high-level view in Chapter 2 (Operations Strategy and Competitiveness) and more details are covered in three chapters: Chapter 10 (Supply Chain Strategy), Chapter 11 (Strategic Capacity Management), and Chapter 12 (Lean Production). Our reason for spreading the strategy material throughout the book is to make things a bit more interesting. In general, we try to give you the "big picture" and then fill in the details with following chapters.

Businesses have to change to remain competitive. The first section of the book is titled Operations Strategy and Managing Change. The idea is to get you thinking early in your course about how to organize projects that are needed to manage change. As a company's strategy changes in response to market demand and new technology, change is needed. Working on a project is a common assignment in any company. The success of a project is invariably measured by our ability to complete the project on time and within budget. How can we be confident we will meet the objectives? Becoming proficient in managing projects is important to success in operations management. Project Management is covered in Chapter 3. In Chapter 4, we discuss possibly the most complex project that most firms face, the design of products.

The second section of the book, titled Process Selection and Design, focuses on the design of internal processes. Chapter 5, Process Analysis, is a nuts-and-bolts chapter on process flow charting and static process analysis using some easily understood "real-life" examples. Chapters 6 and 7 cover the unique characteristics of manufacturing (Manufacturing Process Selection and Design) and service (Service Process Selection and Design) processes. Important technical material that relates to these design activities is covered in two technical notes (Facility Layout and Waiting Line Management).

An essential element of process design is quality. Quality Management is the topic of Chapter 8. Here we cover Total Quality Management concepts, Six-Sigma Tools, and ISO 9000. A technical note covering all the statistical aspects of quality is titled Process Capability and Statistical Quality Control and follows the Quality Management chapter.

Chapter 9 (Operations Consulting and Reengineering) is designed to show how consultants package the material that is covered in the book. Many students who major in operations end up working for consulting companies, so this information is particularly valuable. Synchronous Manufacturing and Theory of Constraints, the focus of Chapter 18, is also used by consultants, as well as being very popular among practitioners. The basic idea is to add resources to production bottlenecks that are constraints or obstacles to producing more profit. It is fairly complex material, so we positioned this at the end of the book so that you would have the background to better understand the ideas.

The third section of the book, titled Supply Chain Design, expands our focus to the entire distribution system from the sourcing of material and other resources to the distribution of our products and services. Many critical decisions need to be made. Where should we locate our facility? What equipment should we buy or lease? How many people should we hire? We need the skills to make important financial decisions related to the capacity of resources that we use.

Making fact-based decisions is what operations management is all about, so this book features extensive coverage of decision-making approaches and tools. One useful way to categorize decisions is by the length of the planning horizon, or the period of time, that the decision maker must consider. For example, building a new plant would be a long-term decision that a firm would need to be happy with for 10 to 15 years into the future. At the other extreme, a decision about how much inventory for a particular item should be ordered for tomorrow typically has a much shorter planning horizon of a few months or, in many cases, only a few days. Such short-term decisions are usually automated using computer programs. In the intermediate term are decisions that a company needs to live with for only 3 to 12 months. Often these decisions would correspond to yearly model changes for seasonal business cycles.

A typical initial decision is the nature of a firm's operations strategy. This comes from the mission of the firm itself and is tied to the notion of achieving competitive advantage through operations—the broad goal of this book. We introduce linear programming and the important product mix problem in Technical Note 2 to get students thinking quantitatively about strategic decisions. Later we use linear programming in plant and warehouse location decisions, manpower planning, and scheduling.

Many different transformation processes are needed to put together a supply chain. In Chapter 12, we discuss the concepts behind Lean Manufacturing and Just-in-Time processes. These ideas are used by companies throughout the world and are key to efficient and quick-responding supply systems.

Section Four (Planning and Controlling the Supply Chain) covers the techniques required to actually run the system. This is at the heart of operations management. The basic building blocks are Forecasting (Chapter 13), Aggregate Sales and Operations Planning (Chapter 14), Inventory Control and Material Requirements Planning (Chapters 15 and 16), and Operations Scheduling (Chapter 17). These daily processes are often partially automated with computer information systems. Coverage of enterprise resource planning systems is included in a managerial briefing that starts this section.

As you can see from this discussion, this material is all interrelated. A company's strategy dictates how operations are designed. The design of the operation dictates how it needs to be managed. Finally, because businesses are constantly being presented with new opportunities through new markets, products, and technologies, a business needs to be very good at managing change.

ACKNOWLEDGMENTS

Many very talented scholars have made major contributions to specific chapters in the book. We are pleased to thank the following individuals:

G. Peter Zhang, Georgia State University, for his many ideas for improving material in various chapters.

Chris Albright, Indiana University, for his advice on notation and statistics.

John R. M. Gordon, Professor, Queens University, for his ideas on the bullwhip effect.

Luca Bencini, Rath & Strong, for providing case studies and feedback on Six Sigma materials.

Kennedy Information Inc., www.ConsultingCentral.com, for providing current employment data on the consulting industry.

Mark Ippolito of Indiana University/Purdue University Indianapolis for the Pizza USA case.

Gilvan Souza of University of Maryland for editing the queuing approximation formulas.

Tatikonda Mohan of Indiana University/Purdue University Indianapolis for his ideas on the product development process.

Urban Wemmerlöv of the University of Wisconsin–Madison for his ideas on cell design and efficient factories.

Michael Maggard of Northeastern University for his ideas on Service Design.

Louis R. Chase, editor extraordinaire and Shakespeare expert, for ideas in several chapters.

"Raj" Rajagopalan, Tom Housel, Yahuda Bassok, Jon Yormark, and Ram Challappa of the University of Southern California for their input on E-Ops.

Greys Sosic, Bill Edstrom, Jay Ghosh, Sriram Dasu, Richard McBride, and Constantin Vaitsos, also at USC, for their suggestions on a variety of topics in the book.

Jim Patterson, Doug Blocher, Vince Mabert, Ken Schultz, Kurt Bretthauer, Chris Albright, Wayne Winston, Ash Soni, Venkat, Carl Briggs, and Rex Cutshall of Indiana University for their unselfish sharing of time to discuss ideas.

Barb Flynn and Tim Smunt of Wake Forest University, Dan Bragg of Bowling Green State University, and E. Powell Robinson of Texas A&M for all the suggestions for improving the book.

Special thanks to John Muth of Cudjoe Key, Florida, for sharing his wisdom.

Clay Whybark of the University of North Carolina for the countless hours spent discussing OM issues.

Special thanks to John McClain of Cornell University for contributing the spreadsheet simulations titled Cell.xls and LineSim.xls.

Rex Cutshall of Indiana University prepared the PowerPoint slides and several ScreenCam tutorials. Rene Ordonez of Southern Oregon University revised the Excel spreadsheets. Bill Berry of Queens College wrote the test bank. Marilyn Helms of Dalton State University revised the Student Study and Lecture Guide. Charlie Watts of John Carroll University authored the Solutions Manual. These supplements are a great deal of work to write, and we appreciate their efforts that make teaching the course easier for everyone who uses the text. Craig Hill and G. Peter Zhang of Georgia State University checked the text for accuracy.

We also wish to thank the following reviewers and focus group participants for their many thoughtful suggestions for this edition: Yasemin Aksoy, *Tulane University;* Saba Bahouth, *University of Central Oklahoma;* Frank Barnes, *University of North Carolina–Charlotte;* Uttarayan Bagchi, *University of Texas;* Ravi Behara, *Florida Atlantic University;* Injazz J. Chen, *Cleveland State University;* Susan Cholette, *San Francisco State University;* Bruce Christensen, *Weber State University;* David Cook, *Old Dominion University;* Bill Cosgrove, *California Polytechnic State University;* Henry Crouch, *Pittsburg State University;* Dinesh Dave, *Appalachian State University;* Eddie Davila, *Arizona State University;* Renato DeMatta, *University of Iowa;* Steven Dickstein, *Ohio State University;* Chris Ellis, *Florida International University;* Farzaneh Fazel, *Illinois State University;* Mark Ferguson, *Georgia Institute of Technology;* Joy Field, *Boston College;* Jonathan Furdek, *Purdue University–Calumet;* Marijane Hancock, *University of Nebraska–Lincoln;* Daniel Heiser, *DePaul University;* Paul Hong, *University of Toledo;* Seung-Lae Kim, *Drexel University;* Vinod Lall, *Minnesota State University–Moorhead;* Dennis Krumwiede, *Idaho State University;* Rhonda Lummis, *Iowa State University;* Buchi Felix Offodile, *Kent State University;* Özgür Özlük, *San Francisco State University;* Shrikant S. Panwalkar, *Purdue University;* Eddy Patuwo, *Kent State University;* Andru Peters, *San Jose State University;* Sharma Pillutla, *Towson University;* Anita Lee Post, *University of Kentucky;* Fred Raaafat, *San Diego State University;* Drew Rosen, *University of North Carolina–Wilmington;* Edie K. Schmidt, *Purdue University;* Sue Siferd, *Arizona State University;* Ronald Tibben-Lembke, *University of Nevada–Reno;* Vera Tilson, *Case Western Reserve University;* Jay Varzandeh, *California State University–San Bernadino;* Lori Cook, *DePaul University;* Helio Yang, *San Diego State University;* Scott Young, *DePaul University;* G. Peter Zhang, *Georgia State University.*

We once again thank those individuals whose input over past editions has helped the book to evolve to its present form: Robert F. Conti, *Bryant College;* Vicente A. Vargas, *University of San Diego;* Daniel R. Heiser, *DePaul University;* Susan Perrott Siferd, *Arizona State University;* Antonio Arreola-Risa, *Texas A&M University;* Uday Apte, *Southern Methodist University;* Scott Young, *University of Utah–Salt Lake City;* John Aloysius, *University of Arkansas;* David Levy, *Bellevue University;* Gregory Stock, *Northern Illinois University;* Ruth Seiple, *University of Cincinnati;* Joao Neves, *College of New Jersey;* Donna

H. Stewart, *University of Wisconsin–Stout;* David Alexander, *Angelo State University;* Alysse Morton, *University of Utah–Salt Lake City;* Carl Steiner, *University of Illinois–Chicago;* Michael R. Godfrey, *University of Wisconsin–Oshkosh;* Dennis Krumwiede, *Idaho State University;* Patrick McDonald, *University of Arizona;* Sunder Kekre, *Carnegie Mellon University;* Chen-Hua Chung, *University of Kentucky;* Craig Hill, *Georgia State University;* Rohit Verma, *University of Utah;* Bill L. Ward, *University of Western Alabama;* D. M. Halemane, *Erasmus University, Rotterdam;* Frank Montabon, *Iowa State University;* John Jensen, *University of Southern Maine;* Marc J. Schniederjans, *University of Nebraska–Lincoln;* Bruce P. Christensen, *Weber State University;* Robert H. Greinier, *Augustana College;* Gilvan C. Souza, *University of Maryland;* Paul J. Kuzdrall, *University of Akron.*

We also want to thank former doctoral students who have contributed to the book over the years, including Mahesh Nagarajan, Hiroshi Ochiumi, and Wayne Johannson, *USC;* Douglas Stewart, *Michigan State University;* Andreas Soteriou, *University of Cyprus;* Arvinder Loomba, *University of Northern Iowa;* Deborah Kellogg, *University of Colorado–Denver;* Blair Berkeley, *California State University–Los Angeles;* and Bill Youngdahl, *Thunderbird American Graduate School of International Management.*

We sincerely appreciate the amazing dedication of our executive editor, Dick Hercher. Over the years his brilliant guidance and all-out support have provided the solid foundation on which the entire team associated with this book is built.

Christina Sanders, our development editor, has done a great job editing our scribbling and nudging us to hit those due dates. Thanks for the patience.

Thanks to the McGraw-Hill/Irwin marketing and production team who make this possible—Douglas Reiner, marketing manager; Brent Gordon, editorial director; Laura Griffin, project manager; Michael McCormick, production supervisor; Artemio Ortiz, designer; Lori Kramer, photo research coordinator; Becky Szura, supplement producer; and Gregory Bates, media producer.

Last but certainly not least, we thank our families, who for the eleventh time let the life cycle of the book disrupt theirs.

Richard B. Chase
F. Robert Jacobs
Nicholas J. Aquilano

Contents in Brief

CONTENTS

SECTION ONE

OPERATIONS STRATEGY AND MANAGING CHANGE

SECTION TWO

PROCESS SELECTION AND DESIGN

Section Four

Planning and Controlling
the Supply Chain

SUPPLEMENTS

APPENDICES

OPERATIONS MANAGEMENT FOR COMPETITIVE ADVANTAGE

section

OPERATIONS STRATEGY AND MANAGING CHANGE

1

GAINING COMPETITIVE ADVANTAGE

HOW WE MANAGE PRODUCTIVE RESOURCES IS CRITICAL to strategic growth and competitiveness. Operations management is the managing of these productive resources. It entails the design and control of systems responsible for the productive use of raw materials, human resources, equipment, and facilities in the development of a product or service. This section addresses the issues of operations strategy and competitiveness and how the field of operations management can provide direction in gaining and maintaining competitive advantage.

chapter

INTRODUCTION TO THE FIELD

1

AUTOMATED INVENTORY CONTROL, CONSTANT CUSTOMER FEEDBACK, CUSTOMIZED PRODUCTS, AND PERSONAL SERVICE

 Predicting the future of operations is not easy, but it is interesting to speculate. Consider what is happening with smart tags, such as radio frequency identification (RFID). Large companies already use these wireless microchips to track products in real time. Wal-Mart, the gigantic U.S. retailer, is requiring its top 100 vendors to employ the technology. Other retailers are using RFID to track

containers moving from seaport to seaport. Microchip tags will give companies the ability to monitor the location and condition of individual products anytime, anywhere in the world.

Specialization and outsourcing are here to stay. Nimble, highly focused companies are taking advantage of short production cycles and global markets to create new products and new business models. Dell, the innovative personal computer (PC) maker, is the best-known example. Its dynamic connections to roughly 60 core suppliers allow the PC maker to cycle inventory through assembly facilities in just six hours.

Project these realities a few decades into the future—say, to the year 2020. RFID chips will become ubiquitous, providing unprecedented information

Source: Adapted from "The World of Business in 2020," *Business* 2.0, April 2004, pp. 119–26.

about manufacturing processes and consumer behavior. Meanwhile, as specialization becomes the order of the day, vertically integrated companies may be supplanted by net-worked constellations of business partners. Just how might these new partnerships work?

- *Outsourcing everything*—A firm will focus on its core competencies and nothing more. One electronics firm may focus on product management and marketing, while design and manufacturing are farmed out to a constellation of partner firms. Another firm may focus on the design and manufacturing of electronic products and partner with the firm specializing in product management and marketing.
- *Smart factories*—Contract manufacturers around the world work from Web-based computer-aided design drawings, adaptive injection-molding tools, and self-reconfiguring assembly machines. These technologies allow factories to profitably produce small component runs for niche markets.
- *Talking inventory*—Tiny RFID tags attached to parts and components ensure that suppliers have just enough inventory to fill orders. Each tag emits a faint radio signal that provides the network with real-time information about inventory status and location. Manufacturers monitor these data to coordinate with vendors and suppliers.
- *An industrial army of robots*—Adaptive manufacturing robots scan component RFIDs to figure out which model to assemble. Coordinated by intelligent production control software, the robots develop assembly routines automatically. Built-in vibration alerts and diagnostic infrared sensors allow technicians to anticipate assembly-line failures before they actually occur.
- *What's in the box*—Smart tags and a special container satellite transmitter allow every item being shipped to be monitored by buyers with detailed information about the location of containers and the condition of each product inside.
- *Unloading zones*—Containers are taken off ships by robotic gantry cranes. Gamma-ray machines scan for nuclear material or bioterror agents, while RFID receivers automatically route goods to waiting trucks. All this dramatically reduces manual labor and cuts unloading time to hours.
- *The lonely road*—Long-haul trucks travel in pods, with a single human driver commanding a column of automated drone trucks linked by wireless remote control. Using flexible subcontracting arrangements and precision route management software, trucks are full nearly 100 percent of the time. Local deliveries are made by fuel cell–powered parcel vans.
- *Have it your way*—Each unit is tailored to local tastes, with final paint, styling, and design touches added at local distribution centers. Customization machines are programmed to add splashy colors, special logos, and silk screen images to the exterior of each unit.
- *Main Street chain store*—"Regional experience" stores designed to attract shoppers who are nostalgic for mom-and-pop retailing use RFID tags and inventory management algorithms to help these small stores quickly adapt to changing customer demand.

- *Personalized recommendations*—Shopping carts detect RFID tags to identify products placed within. Subtotals are shown on an LCD screen as a recommendation engine suggests additional items based on current selections and past buying habits.

- *Sign here, please*—The shopping cart beams the merchandise total to a transaction station, and the customer signs the screen to pay. Identity is verified by tracking the pressure, vector, and velocity of the signature script. →

OPERATIONS MANAGEMENT: A CRITICAL RESPONSIBILITY OF EVERY MANAGER

If you have an interest in becoming a great manager, the topics in this book are important for your achieving this goal. Whether the economy is booming or in a recession, delivering a firm's goods and services in the most effective manner is critical to its survival. And if you think this book is just about manufacturing and relevant only for people working in a factory, you are in for some surprises about this fascinating field.

At the most fundamental level, operations management is about getting the day-to-day work done quickly, efficiently, without errors, and at low cost. Actually, at the level of day-to-day processes, we are all experts already. Think of how quickly you can get ready for the day when the pressure is really on. You have your morning routine of showering, brushing your teeth, and so on down to a science. You know exactly how long it will take and can execute that routine without much thought.

The day-to-day processes that make up a firm's activities should be done in the same efficient manner. Alas, as you know, this is not always true. How many times have you had to wait at a checkout counter because an error in pricing of an item is discovered when you try to check out? The cause of the problem may not be as straightforward as you initially think. Perhaps the item was not marked when it was stocked in the store, or the proper label was not applied when the product was manufactured. With today's integrated information systems, it is even possible that the item was not properly entered in the system to begin with. The disruption this mistake causes can be extensive, with delays occurring every time someone attempts to purchase the item at this store and possibly at all the other stores run by the company. How would you approach fixing the problem? What would you do to minimize the chance that it will recur?

In addition to making processes work right, an essential feature of operations management is helping companies create dramatic improvements in customer service and reductions in cost. Whether you are a marketing, accounting, finance, or operations specialist, being the innovator who spearheads such changes is where you can have a real impact. This book is about the concepts and tools you need to craft innovative ways to deliver a firm's goods and services.

Consider Progressive Insurance, an automobile insurer based in Mayfield Village, Ohio. In 1991, the company had approximately $1.3 billion in sales. By 2002, that figure had grown to $9.5 billion. What trendy strategies did Progressive employ to achieve sevenfold growth in just over a decade? Was it positioned in a high-growth industry? Did it come up with a new insurance product? Did it diversify into new businesses? Did it go global? Did it hire a new, aggressive sales force? Did it grow through acquisitions or clever marketing schemes? It did none of these things. For years Progressive did little advertising, and some of its campaigns were notably unsuccessful. It did not unveil a slew of new products, nor did it grow at the expense of its profit margins, even when it set low prices.

A key measure that sheds light on what Progressive did is the combined ratio (expenses plus claims payouts, divided by insurance premiums), the measure of financial performance in the insurance industry. Most auto insurers have a combined ratio that fluctuates around 102 percent; that is, they run a 2 percent loss on their underwriting activities and recover the loss with investment income. By contrast, Progressive's combined ratio fluctuates around 96 percent. The company has not only seen dramatic growth but it is now the country's third largest auto insurer—and it also has been profitable.

The secret of Progressive's success is simple: It out-operated its competitors. By offering lower prices and better service than its rivals, it simply took their customers away. What enabled Progressive to have better prices and service was innovations in operations, new and better ways of doing the day-to-day work of providing automobile insurance.

Progressive realized that possibly the only way to compete with much larger companies was to actually change the rules for how to play the insurance game. The company introduced what it calls Immediate Response claims handling: A claimant can reach a Progressive representative by phone 24 hours a day, and the representative then schedules a time when an adjuster will inspect the vehicle. Adjusters no longer work out of offices from 9 to 5 but out of mobile claims vans. Instead of taking between 7 and 10 days for an adjuster to see the vehicle, Progressive's target is now just 9 hours. The adjuster not only examines the vehicle but also prepares an on-site estimate of the damage and, if possible, writes a check on the spot.

The approach has many benefits. Claimants get faster service with less hassle, which means they are less likely to abandon Progressive because of an unsatisfactory claims experience. The shortened cycle time has reduced Progressive's costs dramatically. The cost of storing a damaged vehicle or renting a replacement car for one day, around $28, is roughly equal to the expected underwriting profit on a six-month policy. It's not hard to calculate the saving this translates into for a company that handles more than 10,000 claims each day. Other benefits for Progressive are an improved ability to detect fraud (because it is easier to conduct an accident investigation before skid marks wash away and witnesses leave the scene), lower operating costs (because fewer people are involved in handling claims), and a reduction in claim payouts (because claimants often accept less money if it's given sooner and with less hassle).

No single innovation conveys a lasting advantage, however. In addition to Immediate Response, Progressive has introduced a system that allows customers to call an 800 number or visit its Web site and, by providing a small amount of information, compare Progressive's rates with those of three competitors. Because insurance is a regulated industry, rates are on file with state insurance commissioners. The company also has devised even better ways to assess an applicant's risk profile to calculate the right rate to quote. When Progressive realized that an applicant's credit rating was a good proxy for responsible driving behavior, it changed its application process. Now its computer systems automatically contact a credit agency, and the applicant's credit score is factored into its pricing calculation. More accurate pricing translates into increased underwriting profit. Put all these improvements together and Progressive's remarkable growth becomes comprehensible.

Compared with most of the other ways managers try to stimulate growth—technology investments, acquisitions, and major market campaigns, for example—innovations in operations are relatively reliable and low cost. As a business student, you are perfectly positioned to come up with innovative operations-related ideas. You understand the big picture of all the processes that generate the costs and support the cash flow essential to the firm's long-term viability.

Efficiency

Effectiveness

Service

Value

Through this book, you will become aware of the concepts and tools now being employed by companies around the world as they craft efficient and effective operations. **Efficiency** means doing something at the lowest possible cost. Later in the book we define this more thoroughly, but roughly speaking the goal of an efficient process is to produce a good or provide a service by using the smallest input of resources. **Effectiveness** means doing the right things to create the most value for the company. Often maximizing effectiveness and efficiency at the same time creates conflict between the two goals. We see this trade-off every day in our lives. At the customer service counter at a local store or bank, being efficient means using the fewest people possible at the counter. Being effective, though, means minimizing the amount of time customers need to wait in line. Related to efficiency and effectiveness is the concept of **value**, which can be metaphorically defined as quality divided by price. If you can provide the customer with a better car without changing price, value has gone up. If you can give the customer a better car at a *lower* price, value goes way up. A major objective of this book is to show how smart management can achieve high levels of value.

Besides its importance to corporate competitiveness, reasons for studying OM are as follows:

1. **A business education is incomplete without an understanding of modern approaches to managing operations.** Every organization produces some product

or service, so students must be exposed to modern approaches for doing this effectively. Moreover, hiring organizations now expect business graduates to speak knowledgeably about many issues in the field. While this has long been true in manufacturing, it is becoming equally important in services, both public and private. For example, "reinventing government" initiatives draw heavily on supply chain management, total quality management, business process reengineering, and just-in-time delivery—concepts that fall under the OM umbrella.

Service

2. **Operations management provides a systematic way of looking at organizational processes.** OM uses analytical thinking to deal with real-world problems. It sharpens our understanding of the world around us, whether we are talking about how to expand globally or how many lines to have at the bank teller's window.

3. **Operations management presents interesting career opportunities.** These can be in direct supervision of operations or in staff positions in OM specialties such as supply chain management, purchasing, and quality assurance. In addition, consulting firms regularly recruit individuals with strong OM capabilities to work in such areas as process reengineering and enterprise resource planning systems.

Cross Functional

4. **The concepts and tools of OM are widely used in managing other functions of a business.** All managers have to plan work, control quality, and ensure productivity of individuals under their supervision. Other employees must know how operations work to effectively perform their jobs.

WHAT IS OPERATIONS MANAGEMENT?

 Operations management (OM) is defined as the design, operation, and improvement of the systems that create and deliver the firm's primary products and services. Like marketing and finance, OM is a functional field of business with clear line management responsibilities. This point is important because operations management is frequently confused with operations research and management science (OR/MS) and industrial engineering (IE). The essential difference is that OM is a field of management, whereas OR/MS is the application of quantitative methods to decision making in all fields and IE is an engineering discipline. Thus, while operations managers use the decision-making tools of OR/MS (such as critical path scheduling) and are concerned with many of the same issues as IE (such as factory automation), OM's distinct management role distinguishes it from these other disciplines.

Operations management (OM)

As Exhibit 1.1 shows, OM is concerned with the management of the entire system that produces a good or delivers a product. Producing a product such as a cell phone, or providing a service such as a cellular phone account, involves a complex series of transformation processes. Exhibit 1.1 is a supply network for an original equipment manufacturer (OEM), such as Nokia, the Finnish maker of cell phones. To actually produce the phones and get them to the customer, many transformations must take place. For example, the suppliers purchase raw materials and produce the parts for the phone. The Nokia manufacturing plant takes these parts and assembles the various popular cell phone models. Orders for the phones are taken over the Internet from all the distributor, dealer, and warehouse sites around the world. Local retailers work directly with customers in setting up and managing the cell phone accounts. OM is concerned with managing all of these individual processes as effectively as possible.

Within the operations function, management decisions can be divided into three broad areas:

Global

Strategic (long-term) decisions.

Tactical (intermediate-term) decisions.

Operational planning and control (short-term) decisions.

The strategic issues are usually broad, addressing such questions as these: How will we make the product? Where do we locate the facility or facilities? How much capacity do we need? When should we add more capacity? Thus, by necessity, the time frame for strategic

exhibit 1.1
Supply Chain of a Typical Original Equipment Manufacturer

As this schematic suggests, a value chain is not a simple linear series of connections. It typically involves a complex series of business interactions and channel configurations. The Web is a key technology enabling efficient communication throughout the chain.

THE PURCHASING MANAGERS INDEX (PMI)

During the first week of every month, headlines on the front page of *The Wall Street Journal* announce the current reading of the purchasing managers index (PMI). What is the PMI? Why is it so important to economists? How does it relate to the study of operations management?

The Institute for Supply Management (ISM, http://www.ism.ws) has been calculating this index since 1931. The index is like the Dow Jones Industrial Average, but instead of measuring the rise and fall of a set of stocks, the PMI measures the rise and fall of manufacturing in the United States. The index is calculated using a set of measures of new manufacturing orders, production volume, supplier deliveries, inventory levels, and employment. The data are collected from a monthly survey conducted by ISM.

The PMI is a leading indicator of economic activity. A PMI above 44.5 percent, over a period of time, indicates the overall economy, or gross domestic product (GDP), is generally expanding; a PMI below 44.5 percent indicates the GDP is generally declining. The distance from 44.5 percent indicates the strength of the expansion or decline.

The indicator is calculated from the activity levels for functions we study in operations management. We will study how manufacturing orders are processed, how decisions related to the volume that can be processed are made, coordination of supplier deliveries, management of inventory, and scheduling of employees.

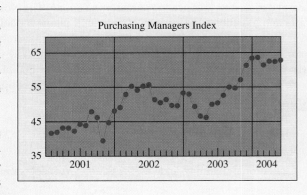

decisions is typically long—usually several years or more, depending on the specific industry. (Chapter 2 discusses operations strategy in depth.)

Operations management decisions at the strategic level affect the company's long-range effectiveness in terms of how it can address its customers' needs. Thus, for the firm to succeed, these decisions must be in alignment with the corporate strategy. Decisions made at the strategic level become the fixed conditions or operating constraints under which the firm must operate in both the intermediate and short term.

At the next level in the decision-making process, tactical planning primarily addresses how to efficiently schedule material and labor within the constraints of previously made strategic decisions. Issues on which OM concentrates on this level include these: How many workers do we need? When do we need them? Should we work overtime or put on a second shift? When should we have material delivered? Should we have a finished goods inventory? These tactical decisions, in turn, become the operating constraints under which operational planning and control decisions are made.

Management decisions with respect to operational planning and control are narrow and short term by comparison. Issues at this level include these: What jobs do we work on today or this week? Whom do we assign to what tasks? What jobs have priority?

TRANSFORMATION PROCESSES

Transformation processes are used in all types of businesses. A **transformation process** uses resources to convert inputs into some desired output. Inputs may be raw material, a customer, or a finished product from another system. Exhibit 1.2 shows examples of

Transformation process

Q #1

Input–Transformation–Output Relationships for Typical Systems

exhibit 1.2

System	Primary Inputs	Resources	Primary Transformation Function(s)	Typical Desired Output
Hospital	Patients	MDs, nurses, medical supplies, equipment	Health care (physiological)	Healthy individuals
Restaurant	Hungry customers	Food, chef, wait staff, environment	Well-prepared, well-served food; agreeable environment (physical and exchange)	Satisfied customers
Automobile factory	Sheet steel, engine parts	Tools, equipment, workers	Fabrication and assembly of cars (physical)	High-quality cars
College or university	High school graduates	Teachers, books, classrooms	Imparting knowledge and skills (informational)	Educated individuals
Department store	Shoppers	Displays, stocks of goods, sales clerks	Attract shoppers, promote products, fill orders (exchange)	Sales to satisfied customers
Distribution center	Stockkeeping units (SKUs)	Storage bins, stockpickers	Storage and redistribution	Fast delivery, availability of SKUs
Airline	Travelers	Airplanes, crews, scheduling/ ticketing systems	Move to destination	On-time, safe delivery to destination

different types of transformation processes in such varied areas as health care, education, and retail stores. In general, transformation processes can be categorized as follows:

- Physical (as in manufacturing).
- Location (as in transportation).
- Exchange (as in retailing).
- Storage (as in warehousing).
- Physiological (as in health care).
- Informational (as in telecommunications).

These transformations are not mutually exclusive. For example, a department store can (1) allow shoppers to compare prices and quality (informational), (2) hold items in inventory until needed (storage), and (3) sell goods (exchange).

Service

DIFFERENCES BETWEEN SERVICES AND GOODS

The essential difference between services and goods is that a service is an intangible process, while a good is the physical output of a process. To put it another way, a service is something that "can be dropped on your foot without hurting you." Other differences are that in services, location of the service facility and direct customer involvement in creating the output are often essential factors; in goods production, they usually are not. There are many shades of gray here. Manufacturers provide many services as part of their product, and many services often manufacture the physical products they deliver to their customers or consume goods in creating the service. McDonald's manufactures a tangible product, but because it is designed to have some contact with the customer to complete the service production process, the firm is in the service category.

Also, from an operations perspective, customers are on the "shop floor" when consuming many services. The shop floor may be called the front office, dining area, operating room, or passenger cabin, depending on the industry. There are also many behind-the-scenes activities with tangible inputs and outputs. For example, major airlines, banks, and insurance companies have large back offices that support customer contact operations. As Chapter 7 on service process selection and design relates, such back-office operations process items and information (e.g., tickets, checks, and claims) and so can be run much like a factory. See the box below titled "Taco Bell's Transformation."

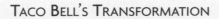

TACO BELL'S TRANSFORMATION

In the 1980s, Taco Bell transformed its restaurant operations by reconsidering them in manufacturing rather than in fast-food terms. The restaurant chain reduced the amount of on-site food preparation by outsourcing to its suppliers, centralizing the production of key components, and concentrating on assembly rather than fabrication in the restaurants. The new approach lowered Taco Bell's costs and increased customer satisfaction by ensuring consistency and allowing restaurant personnel to focus on customers rather than production.

OM IN THE ORGANIZATIONAL CHART

Exhibit 1.3 locates operations activities within a manufacturing organization and two service organizations. Aside from differences in terminology, the service organizations differ from the manufacturing firm in structure. The manufacturing company typically groups operations activities to produce its products in one department. Service firms scatter operations activities throughout the organization. For example, reservations scheduling in an airline is part of the production process for airline travel, even though it is carried out by a

Service

OM in the Organization Chart

exhibit 1.3

SOURCE FOR CHART C: F. OSTROFF, *THE HORIZONTAL ORGANIZATION* (NEW YORK: OXFORD UNIVERSITY PRESS, 1999), P. 34.

nonoperations department. This is seen even more clearly in banking, where there is often a retail operations department and a check-processing operations department. Note that Chart C, based on Ford's Customer Service Division, reflects the recent trend in many organizations to organize around cross-functional core processes managed by teams. This focuses more directly on the needs of the customer, enriches the work of employees, and generally enhances coordination. Note also that in both types of organization, operations activities typically account for the lion's share of capital investment and workforce.

OPERATIONS AS SERVICE

Service

Core services

Value-added services

Cross Functional

The emerging model in industry is that every organization is in the service business. This is true whether the organization makes big planes or Big Macs. From this we must recognize that manufacturing operations, as well as every other part of the organization, are also in the service business even if the customer is an internal one. In manufacturing, such services can be divided into core and value-added services that are provided to internal and external customers of the factory.

The **core services** customers want are products that are made correctly, customized to their needs, delivered on time, and priced competitively. These are commonly summarized as the classic performance objectives of the operations function: *quality, flexibility, speed,* and *price* (or cost of production). Achieving these services is the focus of this book and is discussed in detail in Chapter 2.

Value-added services simply make the external customer's life easier or, in the case of internal customers, help them to better carry out their particular function. Value-added factory services can be classified into four broad categories: information, problem solving, sales support, and field support.

1. **Information** is the ability to furnish critical data on product performance, process parameters, and cost to internal groups (such as R&D) and to external customers, who then use the data to improve their own operations or products. For example, Hewlett-Packard's Fort Collins quality department provides quality data sheets and videotapes documenting actual product testing and field quality performance to field sales and service personnel.
2. **Problem solving** is the ability to help internal and external groups solve problems, especially in quality. For example, Raritan Corporation, a metal rod fabricator, sends factory workers out with salespeople to troubleshoot quality problems. Those factory workers then return to the factory and join with shop-floor personnel on remedial efforts.
3. **Sales support** is the ability to enhance sales and marketing efforts by demonstrating the technology, equipment, or production systems the company is trying to sell. Sometimes sales are enhanced by the factory showing off its workforce's skills. For example, to demonstrate its products' quality, Sara Lee has visitors observe the artistic skills of its "meringue fluffers" on its pie line.
4. **Field support** is the ability to replace defective parts quickly (for example, Caterpillar promises to make repair parts available anywhere in the world within 48 hours) or to replenish stocks quickly to avoid downtime or stockouts (for example, The Limited, a retail chain, is linked to its Hong Kong textile mills via a sophisticated computer system that signals factories to begin producing fast-selling items as soon as weekly sales figures are collected).

Value-added services provided to external customers yield two benefits. First, they differentiate the organization from the competition. Indeed, in many cases it is easier to copy a firm's product than to create the value-added service infrastructure to support it. Second, these services build relationships that bind customers to the organization in a positive way.

The design and ongoing management of a firm's operations have a significant if not crucial impact on the financial success of the firm. The firm's strategy is implemented with a design that is portrayed financially in the assets of the firm. Each asset, be it a plant, a warehouse, an operations center, or the inventory carried in these facilities, is owned by the firm and requires a significant investment. The firm's owners and shareholders want a return on this investment.

Decisions such as how big a plant should be, how many plants there should actually be and where to locate them, and whether or not certain operations should be outsourced are major topics of operations management. Other decisions, such as how much inventory will be needed to meet required service levels, relate directly to the asset investment required to deliver the firm's products and services.

On the other side of the balance sheet, many of the costs that affect the firm's profitability are incurred by the operations of the firm. Deciding on an appropriate number of workers, scheduling these workers, and deciding whether overtime or multiple work shifts should be employed are decisions directly related to the material in this book. Further, deciding how much inventory to purchase and what quantities are fundamental topics of operations management.

WHY IS OPERATIONS NOT PERCEIVED AS IMPORTANT?

Many senior executives do not really understand operations. Many of them entered the organization through finance, strategy, or marketing and built their reputations on work in these domains. When they moved into their first general management role, they relied on others—plant managers, engineers, customer service leaders—to mind the details of the actual work. Times have changed dramatically over the past few years, however. Organization structures are now flat and, rather than functionally organized, companies are now organized by customer and product groups. Today's manager cannot ignore how the organization's real work is done.

We have heard students argue that operations is not glamorous, but deals are. Making acquisitions, planning mergers, and buying and selling divisions will get the company's name and the chief executive officer's picture in business magazines. Redesigning procurement or transforming product development will not, even if it is much more important to the company's performance. Deals are easily explained to and understood by boards, shareholders, and the media. They offer the prospect of nearly immediate gratification, and the deal is consistent with the modern image of the executive as someone who focuses on grand strategy and leaves operational details to others. Unfortunately, the great majority of deals are unsuccessful. The devil is in the operational details.

Really successful deals happen when there is a synergy that allows major operational processes to be shared. Sharing of customer service processes, purchasing, distribution, manufacturing, and other processes can lead to great success. Operations account for 60 to 80 percent of the direct expenses that burden a firm's profit. Without these synergies, companies are often left with an expensive appendage and a drag on their earnings potential.

Unfortunately, only a few companies have a vice president of operations or a chief operating officer, so a focus on operations is not owned by anyone in the organization. It does not fit into research and development, where product innovation is based. Functional line managers are too focused on meeting deadlines to have time for or interest in finding new ways of doing things. Furthermore, the most significant operational innovations are not limited to individual departments but involve end-to-end processes that cross departmental boundaries.

Firms today often have hundreds of different types of small improvement projects. Some projects are technologically based, such as the implementation of an enterprise resource planning system, customer relationship management software, or supply chain management software. Others are centered on specific improvement techniques such as Six-Sigma quality or lean manufacturing. Each project typically has a narrow scope, a group of experts dedicated to it, and a sponsor whose enthusiasm is tolerated as long as it is kept within bounds. These projects are worthwhile but can drain the firm of its capacity for change. It is important that they be coordinated with a view of the big picture and a goal of making significant operational improvements. Improvements that result in major reductions in cost and improvements in service are essential to the competitiveness of the firm.

HISTORICAL DEVELOPMENT OF OM

 Exhibit 1.4 gives a timeline of OM's history. Our purpose in this section is not to go through all the details of OM; that would require us to recount the entire Industrial Revolution. Rather, the focus is on major operations-related concepts that have been popular since the 1980s. Where appropriate, how a supposedly new idea relates to an older idea is discussed. (We seem to keep rediscovering the past.)

In the late 1950s and early 1960s, scholars began to deal specifically with operations management as opposed to industrial engineering or operations research. Writers such as Edward Bowman and Robert Fetter (*Analysis for Production and Operations Management,* 1957) and Elwood S. Buffa (*Modern Production Management,* 1961) noted the commonality of problems faced by all production systems and emphasized the importance of viewing production operations as a system. They also stressed the useful application of waiting-line theory, simulation, and linear programming, which are now standard topics in the field. In 1973, Chase and Aquilano's first edition of this book stressed the need "to put the management back in operations management." Bob Jacobs joined the book team in 1997.

JIT AND TQC

The 1980s saw a revolution in the management philosophies and technologies by which production is carried out. Just-in-time (JIT) production was the major breakthrough in manufacturing philosophy. Pioneered by the Japanese, JIT is an integrated set of activities

designed to achieve high-volume production using minimal inventories of parts that arrive at the workstation exactly when they are needed. The philosophy—coupled with total quality control (TQC), which aggressively seeks to eliminate causes of production defects—is now a cornerstone in many manufacturers' production practices. Chapter 12 covers this topic.

Of course, the Japanese were not the first to develop a highly integrated, efficient production system. In 1913, Henry Ford developed an assembly line to make the Model-T automobile. Ford developed a system for making the Model-T that was constrained only by the capabilities of the workforce and existing technology. Quality was a critical prerequisite for Ford: The line could not run steadily at speed without consistently good components. On-time delivery was also critical for Ford; the desire to keep workers and machines busy with materials flowing constantly made scheduling critical. Product, processes, material, logistics, and people were well integrated and balanced in the design and operation of the plant.[1]

MANUFACTURING STRATEGY PARADIGM

The late 1970s and early 1980s saw the development of the manufacturing strategy paradigm by researchers at the Harvard Business School. This work by professors William Abernathy, Kim Clark, Robert Hayes, and Steven Wheelwright (built on earlier efforts by Wickham Skinner) emphasized how manufacturing executives could use their factories' capabilities as strategic competitive weapons. Central to their thinking was the notion of factory focus and

Historical Summary of OM   Q #2

exhibit 1.4

YEAR	CONCEPT	TOOL	ORIGINATOR
1910s	Principles of scientific management	Formalized time-study and work-study concepts	Frederick W. Taylor (United States)
	Industrial psychology	Motion study	Frank and Lillian Gilbreth (United States)
	Moving assembly line	Activity scheduling chart	Henry Ford and Henry L. Gantt (United States)
	Economic lot size	EOQ applied to inventory control	F. W. Harris (United States)
1930s	Quality control	Sampling inspection and statistical tables for quality control	Walter Shewhart, H. F. Dodge, and H. G. Romig (United States)
	Hawthorne studies of worker motivation	Activity sampling for work analysis	Elton Mayo (United States) and L. H. C. Tippett (England)
1940s	Multidisciplinary team approaches to complex system problems	Simplex method of linear programming	Operations research groups (England) and George B. Dantzig (United States)
1950s–60s	Extensive development of operations research tools	Simulation, waiting-line theory, decision theory, mathematical programming, project scheduling techniques of PERT and CPM	Many researchers in the United States and Western Europe
1970s	Widespread use of computers in business	Shop scheduling, inventory control, forecasting, project management, MRP	Led by computer manufacturers, in particular, IBM; Joseph Orlicky and Oliver Wight were the major MRP innovators (United States)
	Service quality and productivity	Mass production in the service sector	McDonald's restaurants
1980s	Manufacturing strategy paradigm	Manufacturing as a competitive weapon	Harvard Business School faculty (United States)
	JIT, TQC, and factory automation	Kanban, poka-yokes, CIM, FMS, CAD/CAM, robots, etc.	Tai-Ichi Ohno of Toyota Motors (Japan), W. E. Deming and J. M. Juran (United States), and engineering disciplines (United States, Germany, and Japan)
	Synchronous manufacturing	Bottleneck analysis, OPT, theory of constraints	Eliyahu M. Goldratt (Israel)
1990s	Total quality management	Baldrige quality award, ISO 9000, quality function development, value and concurrent engineering, continuous improvement paradigm	National Institute of Standards and Technology, American Society of Quality Control (United States), and International Organization for Standardization (Europe)
	Business process reengineering	Radical change paradigm	Michael Hammer and major consulting firms (United States)
	Electronic enterprise	Internet, World Wide Web	U.S. government, Netscape Communication Corporation, and Microsoft Corporation
	Supply chain management	SAP/R3, client/server software	SAP (Germany), Oracle (United States)
2000s	E-commerce	Internet, World Wide Web	Amazon, eBay, America Online, Yahoo!

manufacturing trade-offs. They argued that because a factory cannot excel on all performance measures, its management must devise a focused strategy, creating a focused factory that performs a limited set of tasks extremely well. This required trade-offs among such performance measures as low cost, high quality, and high flexibility in designing and managing factories. Ford seems to have realized this about 60 years before the Harvard professors.

SERVICE QUALITY AND PRODUCTIVITY

The great diversity of service industries—ranging from airlines to zoos, with many different types in between—precludes identifying any single pioneer or developer that has made a major impact in these areas. However, McDonald's unique approach to quality and productivity has

Service

been so successful that it stands as a reference point in thinking about how to deliver high-volume standardized services.

TOTAL QUALITY MANAGEMENT AND QUALITY CERTIFICATION

Global

Another major development was the focus on total quality management (TQM) in the late 1980s and 1990s. All operations executives are aware of the quality message put forth by the so-called quality gurus: W. Edwards Deming, Joseph M. Juran, and Philip Crosby. It's interesting that these individuals were students of Shewhart, Dodge, and Romig in the 1930s (sometimes it takes a generation for things to catch on). Helping the quality movement along is the Baldrige National Quality Award, which was started in 1987 under the direction of the National Institute of Standards and Technology. The Baldrige Award recognizes companies each year for outstanding quality management systems.

The ISO 9000 certification standards, created by the International Organization for Standardization, now plays a major role in setting quality standards for global manufacturers. Many European companies require that their vendors meet these standards as a condition for obtaining contracts.

BUSINESS PROCESS REENGINEERING

The need to become lean to remain competitive in the global economic recession in the 1990s pushed companies to seek innovations in the processes by which they run their operations. The flavor of business process reengineering (BPR) is conveyed in the title of Michael Hammer's influential article in *Harvard Business Review:* "Reengineering Work: Don't Automate, Obliterate." The approach seeks to make revolutionary changes as opposed to evolutionary changes (which are commonly advocated in TQM). It does this by taking a fresh look at what the organization is trying to do in all its business processes, and then eliminating non–value-added steps and computerizing the remaining ones to achieve the desired outcome.

Hammer actually was not the first consultant to advocate eliminating non–value-added steps and reengineering processes. In the early 1900s, Frederick W. Taylor developed principles of scientific management that applied scientific analysis to eliminating wasted effort from manual labor. Around the same time, Frank and Lillian Gilbreth used the new technology of the time, motion pictures, to analyze such diverse operations as bricklaying and medical surgery procedures. Many of the innovations this husband-and-wife team developed, such as time and motion study, are widely used today.

To cause to disappear or collapse

SUPPLY CHAIN MANAGEMENT

The central idea of supply chain management is to apply a total system approach to managing the flow of information, materials, and services from raw material suppliers through factories and warehouses to the end customer. Recent trends such as outsourcing and **mass customization** are forcing companies to find flexible ways to meet customer demand. The focus is on optimizing core activities to maximize the speed of response to changes in customer expectations.

Mass customization

ELECTRONIC COMMERCE

The quick adoption of the Internet and the World Wide Web during the late 1990s was remarkable. The term *electronic commerce* refers to the use of the Internet as an essential element of business activity. The Internet is an outgrowth of a government network called ARPANET, which was created in 1969 by the Defense Department of the U.S. government. The use of Web pages, forms, and interactive search engines has changed the way people collect information, shop, and communicate. It has changed the way operations managers coordinate and execute production and distribution functions.

CURRENT ISSUES IN OPERATIONS MANAGEMENT

Operations management is a dynamic field, and challenges presented by global enterprise present exciting new issues for operations managers. Looking forward to the future, we believe the major challenges in the field will be as follows:

1. **Coordinating the relationships between mutually supportive but separate organizations.** Recently there has been a dramatic surge in the outsourcing of parts and services that had previously been produced internally. This has been encouraged by the availability of fast, inexpensive communications. A whole new breed of *contract manufacturers* that specialize in performing focused manufacturing activities now exists. The success of this kind of traditional outsourcing has led companies to consider outsourcing other major corporate functions such as information systems, product development and design, engineering services, packaging, testing, and distribution. The ability to coordinate these activities is a significant challenge for the operations manager of the future.

2. **Optimizing global supplier, production, and distribution networks.** The implementation of global enterprise resource planning systems, now common in large companies, has challenged managers to use all of this information. This requires a careful understanding of where control should be centralized and where autonomy is important, among other issues. Companies have only begun to truly take advantage of the

BREAKTHROUGH

CMAX.COM—SOLEMATES, INC.

Would you like to start a business quickly? How about selling custom shoes to your classmates? They can be in the style and color of your choice and include custom logos of your school. It's easier to do than you might think.

CMAX.com is the global leader in customized athletic footwear and specializes in promotional footwear products. A team of ex-Adidas "shoe dogs" has revolutionized the athletic footwear industry by allowing anyone anywhere in the world at any time of day to design his or her own shoes. The shoes are produced one at a time in a purpose-built, state-of-the-art manufacturing facility in Shenzhen, China, and delivered within two to four weeks of order direct to your door through a unique partnership with UPS Worldwide.

CMAX expanded into the promotional footwear business almost by accident. Kimberly Page, an executive from

Microsoft's new gaming console division, XBOX, contacted CMAX about producing shoes with its XBOX logo and graphics to be used as an incentive for its employees. The idea was born. Since that time, CMAX has produced footwear products for a variety of clients, including the cast of the highly acclaimed (USA) CBS television series *The King of Queens* and international companies such as Germany's software giant SAP.

With minimums of just 30 pairs per design (over any size range), CMAX also has carved a niche within the grassroot market of small companies, events, and promotions, including orders for professional motor racing teams, advertising agencies, corporate sales meetings, and restaurants. You can order a batch of shoes online and have your business up and running in only six to eight weeks.

CMAX is a great example of a company that has leveraged the power of the Internet to efficiently communicate with customers. This, in combination with the mass customization manufacturing facility located in China, is an innovative platform for leveraging the ideas of entrepreneurs like you around the world.

Any shoe, any logo, any graphic, any country in the world. Delivered in as little as two weeks.

information from these systems to optimally control such resources as inventory, transportation, and production equipment.

3. **Increased co-production of goods and services.** The Internet has opened new ways for the customer to interact directly with a firm. Simple direct entry and monitoring of orders is only the first step in the progression of value-added services made possible through information sharing. Intelligent use of information technology will allow the shedding of entire layers of inefficient customer-oriented functions within a firm, resulting in dramatic reductions in cost while actually improving service to the customer.

4. **Managing customer touch points.** As companies strive to become superefficient, they often scrimp on customer support personnel (and training) required to effectively staff service departments, help lines, and checkout counters. This leads to the frustrations we have all experienced such as being placed in call-center limbo seemingly for hours, getting bad advice when finally interacting with a company rep, and so on. The issue here is to recognize that making resource utilization decisions must capture the implicit costs of lost customers as well as the direct costs of staffing.

5. **Raising senior management awareness of operations as a significant competitive weapon.** As we stated earlier, many senior executives entered the organization through finance, strategy, or marketing and built their reputations on work in these areas, and as a result often take operations for granted. As we will demonstrate in this book, this is can be a critical mistake when we realize how profitable companies such as Toyota, Dell, Taco Bell, and Southwest Airlines are. These are companies where executives have creatively used operations management for competitive advantage.

KEY TERMS

Efficiency Doing something at the lowest possible cost.

Effectiveness Doing the right things to create the most value for the company.

Value Ratio of quality to price paid. Competitive "happiness" is being able to increase quality and reduce price while maintaining or improving profit margins. (This is a way that operations can directly increase customer retention and gain market share.)

Operations management (OM) Design, operation, and improvement of the systems that create and deliver the firm's primary products and services.

Transformation process System by which resources are used to convert inputs into desired output.

Core services Basic things that customers want from the products they purchase—for example, to be made correctly, customized to their needs, delivered on time, and priced competitively.

Value-added services Services that differentiate the organization from competitors and build relationships that bind customers to the firm in a positive way.

Mass customization Producing products to order in lot sizes of one.

REVIEW AND DISCUSSION QUESTIONS

1 What is the difference between OM and OR/MS? Between OM and IE?

2 How would you distinguish OM from management and organizational behavior as taught at your university?

3 Look at the want ads in *The Wall Street Journal* and evaluate the opportunities for an OM major with several years of experience.

4 What factors account for the resurgence of interest in OM today?

5 Using Exhibit 1.2 as a model, describe the input–transformation–output relationships in the following systems:
   a. An airline.
   b. A state penitentiary.
   c. A branch office of a bank.
   d. The home office of a major banking firm.

6 Sketch the production–delivery system used by CMAX.com–Solemates, Inc., in providing custom tennis shoes. Could this approach be applied to other consumer goods? Give examples.

7 Suppose *Rolling Stone* presented the following headlines relating to OM. To what particular historical events or individuals would they refer?
- OVER 5 BAZILLION SOLD TO DATE
- BEANTOWN B-SCHOOL DISCOVERS YOU CAN'T HAVE IT ALL
- INVENTORY—OH NO!
- BUSINESSES USE A BIG HAMMER TO FORCE CHANGE
- FAST HENRY BECOMES MARVEL OF MOTOWN
- EXECS FOLLOW GURU'S RECIPE FOR BIG Q STEW
- 10 BILLION FAX MACHINES DUMPED IN THE OCEAN
- "THE CHAIN GANG" MOVES TO TOP OF THE CHARTS

C A S E : FAST-FOOD FEAST

Visit at least two different fast-food restaurants that make hamburgers. For example, in the United States McDonald's, Wendy's, and Burger King are good choices. For some of you fast-food junkies, this will not be difficult; vegans may have to take a friend for product testing. Observe the basic operational differences between these stores. Note the differences in the following processes:

Q U E S T I O N S

1 How are in-store orders taken?
2 Are the hamburgers prepared to order, or are they prepared ahead of time and delivered from a storage bin?
3 How are special orders handled?
4 How are the hamburgers cooked?
5 How are the hamburgers assembled?
6 Is a microwave oven used in the process?
7 How are other common items, such as french fries and drinks, handled?

S E L E C T E D B I B L I O G R A P H Y

Chase, Richard B., and David A. Garvin. "The Service Factory." *Harvard Business Review,* July–August 1989, pp. 61–69.

Feld, William M. *Lean Manufacturing: Tools, Techniques, and How to Use Them.* Boca Raton, FL: CRC Press, 2000.

Journal of Operations Management. Washington, DC: American Production and Inventory Control Society, 1980–current.

Manufacturing & Service Operations Management: M&SOM. Linthicum, MD: Institute for Operations Research and the Management Sciences, 1999–current.

Nersesian, R. L. *Trends and Tools for Operations Management: An Updated Guide for Executives and Managers.* Westport, CT: Quorum, 2000.

Operations Management Review. Austin, TX: Operations Management Association, 1982–current.

Production and Operations Management: An International Journal of the Production and Operations Management Society/POMS. Baltimore: Production and Operations Management Society, 1992–current.

Slack, N., ed. *The Blackwell Encyclopedia Dictionary of Operations Management.* Cambridge, MA: Blackwell, 1996.

Sower, V. E.; J. Motwani; and M. J. Savoie, eds. *Classic Readings in Operations Management.* Fort Worth: Dryden Press, 1995.

Womak, J. P.; D. T. Jones; and D. Roos. *The Machine That Changed the World.* New York: Rawson Associates, 1990.

Wyzalek J., ed. *Handbook of Enterprise Operations Management, 1999.* Boca Raton, FL: Auerbach, 1999.

F O O T N O T E

1 See J. Wilson, "Henry Ford: A Just-in-Time Pioneer," *Production & Inventory Management Journal* 37 (1996), pp. 26–31.

chapter

OPERATIONS STRATEGY AND COMPETITIVENESS

2

Competitive strategy is about being different. It means deliberately choosing a different set of activities to deliver a unique mix of value. Southwest Airlines Company, for example, offers low-cost, point-to-point service between midsize cities and secondary airports in large cities. Southwest avoids large airports and, for the most part, does not fly long distances. Southwest's frequent departures and low fares attract price-sensitive customers who otherwise would travel by bus or car, as well as convenience-oriented travelers who would choose a full-service airline on other routes.

Most managers describe strategic positioning in terms of their customers: "Southwest Airlines serves price- and convenience-sensitive travelers," for example. But the essence of strategy is in business activities—choosing to

perform activities differently than rivals. Otherwise, a strategy is nothing more than a marketing slogan that will not withstand competition.

A full-service airline is configured to get passengers from almost any point A to any point B. To reach many destinations and serve passengers with connecting flights, full-service airlines employ a hub-and-spoke system centered on major airports. To attract passengers who desire more comfort, they offer first-class or business-class service. To accommodate passengers who must change planes, they coordinate schedules and check and transfer baggage. And because some passengers will be traveling for many hours, full-service airlines serve meals.

Southwest, in contrast, tailors all its activities to delivering low-cost, convenient service on its particular type of route. Through fast turnarounds at the gate of only 15 minutes, it is able to keep planes flying longer hours than rivals and provide frequent departures with fewer aircraft. Southwest does not offer meals, assigned seats, interline baggage checking, or premium classes of service. Automated ticketing at the gate encourages customers to bypass

Source: Reprinted by permission of the *Harvard Business Review.* From "What Is Strategy?" by M. E. Porter, November–December 1996. Copyright © 1996 by the President and Fellows of Harvard College; all rights reserved.

travel agents, allowing Southwest to avoid their commissions. A standardized fleet of 737 aircraft boosts the efficiency of maintenance.

Southwest has staked out a unique and valuable strategic position based on a tailored set of activities. →

Global

Strategy should describe how a firm intends to create and sustain value for its shareholders. Typically a strategy breaks down into three major components: operations effectiveness, customer management, and product innovation. It is important that a firm's strategy aligns with its mission of serving the customer. Complicating the situation is the fact that the needs of customers change over time, thus requiring continuous changes to strategy.

① Operations effectiveness relates to the core business processes needed to run the business. Business processes span all the business functions from taking customer orders, handling returns, manufacturing, managing the updating of Web sites, to shipping products. Operational effectiveness is reflected directly in the costs associated with doing business. Strategies associated with operational effectiveness, such as quality initiatives, process redesign, and technology investments, can show quick near-term (12 to 24 months) results.

② Customer management relates to better understanding and leveraging customer relationships. A strategy that involves segmenting customers, for example, may take a little longer to realize, perhaps two to three years.

③ Product innovation involves the development of new products, markets, and relationships to sustain growth. Service companies may be able to implement a product innovation in as few as two to three years, while manufacturers may take three to five years. Pharmaceutical firms may take as many as 10 years to reap benefits from a new product.

Operations management is significant since it relates to all three components of strategy. A world-class company recognizes that its ability to compete in the marketplace depends on developing an operations strategy that is properly aligned with its mission of serving the customer. A company's *competitiveness* refers to its relative position in comparison to other firms in the local or global marketplace.

In this chapter, we first define what operations strategy is and how it relates to competitive priorities. In our discussion of priorities, we explain how company priorities change over time. We then address how to develop an operations strategy in manufacturing and services. We conclude with a discussion of productivity performance measures.

OPERATIONS STRATEGY

WHAT IS OPERATIONS STRATEGY?

Operations strategy

Operations strategy is concerned with setting broad policies and plans for using the resources of a firm to best support its long-term competitive strategy. A firm's operations strategy is comprehensive through its integration with corporate strategy. The strategy involves a long-term process that must foster inevitable change. An operations strategy involves decisions that relate to the design of a process and the infrastructure needed to support the process. Process design includes the selection of appropriate technology, sizing the process over time, the role of inventory in the process, and locating the process. The infrastructure decisions involve the logic associated with the planning and control systems, quality assurance and control approaches, work payment structures, and organization of the operations function.

Operations strategy can be viewed as part of a planning process that coordinates operational goals with those of the larger organization. Since the goals of the larger organization change over time, the operations strategy must be designed to anticipate future needs. A firm's operations capabilities can be viewed as a portfolio best suited to adapt to the changing product and/or service needs of the firm's customers.

Looking at operations strategy from a historical perspective, for example in the post–World War II era, U.S. companies experienced tremendous consumer demand that had been pent up during the war. As a result, manufacturing in the United States emphasized turning out high volumes of products to satisfy this demand. In contrast, during the same period, Japanese manufacturing companies focused on the quality of their products. Priorities needed to remain competitive differed for companies in the different countries. Keys to success in operations strategy lie in identifying what the priority choices are, understanding the consequences of each choice, and navigating the ensuing trade-offs.

OPERATIONS COMPETITIVE DIMENSIONS

COMPETITIVE DIMENSIONS

Q. # 2

Given the choices customers face today, how do they decide which product or service to buy? Different customers are attracted by different attributes. Some customers are interested primarily in the cost of a product or service and, correspondingly, some companies attempt to position themselves to offer the lowest prices. The major competitive dimensions that form the competitive position of a firm include the following.

Cost or Price: "Make the Product or Deliver the Service Cheap"   Within every industry, there is usually a segment of the market that buys solely on the basis of low cost. To successfully compete in this niche, a firm must be the low-cost producer, but even this does not always guarantee profitability and success. Products and services sold strictly on the basis of cost are typically commoditylike; in other words, customers cannot distinguish the product or service of one firm from those of another. This segment of the market is frequently very large, and many companies are lured by the potential for significant profits, which they associate with the large unit volumes. As a consequence, however, competition in this segment is fierce—and so is the failure rate. After all, there can be only one low-cost producer, who usually establishes the selling price in the market.

Price, however, is not the only basis on which a firm can compete (although many economists appear to assume it is!). Other companies, such as BMW, seek to attract those who want *higher quality*—in terms of performance, appearance, or features—than that available in competing products and services, even though accompanied by a higher price.

Quality: "Make a Great Product or Deliver a Great Service"   There are two characteristics of a product or service that define quality: design quality and process quality. Design quality relates to the set of features the product or service contains. This relates directly to the design of the product or service. Obviously a child's first two-wheel bicycle is of significantly different quality than the bicycle of a world-class cyclist. The use of special aluminum alloys and special lightweight sprockets and chains is important to the performance needs of the advanced cyclist. These two types of bicycle are designed for different customers' needs. The higher-quality cyclist product commands a higher price in the marketplace due to its special features. The goal in establishing the proper level of design quality is to focus on the requirements of the customer. Overdesigned products and services with too many or inappropriate features will be viewed as prohibitively expensive. In comparison, underdesigned products and services will lose customers to products that cost a little more but are perceived by customers as offering greater value.

Greater value product wins

Process quality, the second characteristic of quality, is critical because it relates directly to the reliability of the product or service. Regardless of whether the product is a child's first two-wheeler or a bicycle for an international cyclist, customers want products without defects. Thus, the goal of process quality is to produce defect-free products and services. Product and service specifications, given in dimensional tolerances and/or service error rates, define how the product or service is to be made. Adherence to these specifications is critical to ensure the reliability of the product or service as defined by its intended use.

Delivery Speed: "Make the Product or Deliver the Service Quickly" In some markets, a firm's ability to deliver more quickly than its competitors may be critical. A company that can offer an on-site repair service in only 1 or 2 hours has a significant advantage over a competing firm that guarantees service only within 24 hours.

Delivery Reliability: "Deliver It When Promised" This dimension relates to the firm's ability to supply the product or service on or before a promised delivery due date. For an automobile manufacturer, it is very important that its supplier of tires provide the needed quantity and types for each day's car production. If the tires needed for a particular car are not available when the car reaches the point on the assembly line where the tires are installed, the whole assembly line may have to be shut down until they arrive. For a service firm such as Federal Express, delivery reliability is the cornerstone of its strategy.

Coping with Changes in Demand: "Change Its Volume" In many markets, a company's ability to respond to increases and decreases in demand is important to its ability to compete. It is well known that a company with increasing demand can do little wrong. When demand is strong and increasing, costs are continuously reduced due to economies of scale, and investments in new technologies can be easily justified. But scaling back when demand decreases may require many difficult decisions about laying off employees and related reductions in assets. The ability to effectively deal with dynamic market demand over the long term is an essential element of operations strategy.

Flexibility and New-Product Introduction Speed: "Change It" Flexibility, from a strategic perspective, refers to the ability of a company to offer a wide variety of products to its customers. An important element of this ability to offer different products is the time required for a company to develop a new product and to convert its processes to offer the new product.

Other Product-Specific Criteria: "Support It" The competitive dimensions just described are certainly the most common. However, other dimensions often relate to specific products or situations. Notice that most of the dimensions listed next are primarily service in nature. Often special services are provided to augment the sales of manufactured products.

Service

1. **Technical liaison and support.** A supplier may be expected to provide technical assistance for product development, particularly during the early stages of design and manufacturing.
2. **Meeting a launch date.** A firm may be required to coordinate with other firms on a complex project. In such cases, manufacturing may take place while development

work is still being completed. Coordinating work between firms and working simultaneously on a project will reduce the total time required to complete the project.

3. **Supplier after-sale support.**   An important competitive dimension may be the ability of a firm to support its product after the sale. This involves availability of replacement parts and, possibly, modification of older, existing products to new performance levels. Speed of response to these after-sale needs is often important as well.

4. **Other dimensions.**   These typically include such factors as colors available, size, weight, location of the fabrication site, customization available, and product mix options.

THE NOTION OF TRADE-OFFS

Central to the concept of operations strategy is the notion of operations focus and trade-offs. The underlying logic is that an operation cannot excel simultaneously on all competitive dimensions. Consequently management has to decide which parameters of performance are critical to the firm's success and then concentrate the resources of the firm on these particular characteristics.

For example, if a company wants to focus on speed of delivery, it cannot be very flexible in its ability to offer a wide range of products. Similarly, a low-cost strategy is not compatible with either speed of delivery or flexibility. High quality is also viewed as a trade-off to low cost. For firms with large existing manufacturing facilities, Skinner suggests the creation of a **plant-within-a-plant (PWP)** concept, in which different locations within the facility are allocated to different product lines, each with their own operations strategy. Under the PWP concept, even the workers are separated to minimize the confusion associated with shifting from one type of strategy to another.[1]

Plant-within-a-plant (PWP)

A strategic position is not sustainable unless there are compromises with other positions. Trade-offs occur when activities are incompatible so that more of one thing necessitates less of another. An airline can choose to serve meals—adding cost and slowing turnaround time at the gate—or it can choose not to, but it cannot do both without bearing major inefficiencies.[2]

Straddling occurs when a company seeks to match the benefits of a successful position while maintaining its existing position. It adds new features, services, or technologies onto the activities it already performs. A good case study is how Continental Airlines reacted to the strategy of Southwest Airlines, described at the beginning of this chapter. While maintaining its position as a full-service airline, Continental set out to match Southwest on a number of point-to-point routes. The airline dubbed the new service Continental Lite. It eliminated meals and first-class service, increased departure frequency, lowered fares, and shortened gate turnaround time. Because Continental remained a full-service airline on other routes, it continued to use travel agents and its mixed fleet of planes and to provide baggage checking and seat assignments.

Straddling

Trade-offs ultimately grounded Continental Lite. The airline lost hundreds of millions of dollars, and the chief executive officer lost his job. Its planes were delayed leaving congested hub cities or slowed at the gate by baggage transfers. Late flights and cancellations generated a thousand complaints a day. Continental Lite could not afford to compete on price and still pay standard travel agent commissions, but neither could it do without agents for its full-service business. The airline compromised by cutting commissions for all Continental flights. Similarly, it could not afford to offer the same frequent-flier benefits to travelers paying the much lower ticket prices for Lite service. It compromised again by lowering the rewards of Continental's entire frequent-flier program. The results: angry travel agents and full-service customers. Continental tried to compete in two ways at once and paid an enormous straddling penalty.

ORDER WINNERS AND QUALIFIERS: THE MARKETING–OPERATIONS LINK

An interface between marketing and operations is necessary to provide a business with an understanding of its markets from both perspectives. Terry Hill, a professor at Oxford University, has coined the terms *order winner* and *order qualifier* to describe

Cross Functional

Order winner

Order qualifier

Global

marketing-oriented dimensions that are key to competitive success.[3] An **order winner** is a criterion that differentiates the products or services of one firm from another. Depending on the situation, the order-winning criterion may be the cost of the product (price), product quality and reliability, or any of the other dimensions developed earlier. An **order qualifier** is a screening criterion that permits a firm's products to even be considered as possible candidates for purchase. Professor Hill states that a firm must requalify the order qualifiers every day it is in business.

It is important to remember that the order-winning and order-qualifying criteria may change over time. For example, when Japanese companies entered the world automobile markets in the 1970s, they changed the way these products won orders, from predominantly price to product quality and reliability. American automobile producers were losing orders through quality to the Japanese companies. By the late 1980s, product quality was raised by Ford, General Motors, and Chrysler (now DaimlerChrysler); today they are "qualified" to be in the market. Consumer groups continually monitor the quality and reliability criteria, thus requalifying the top-performing companies. Today the order winners for automobiles vary greatly depending on the model. Customers know the set of features they want (such as reliability, design features, and gas mileage), and they want to purchase a particular combination at the lowest price, thus maximizing value.

THE CORPORATE STRATEGY DESIGN PROCESS[4]

Cross Functional

The task of developing a comprehensive strategy for a firm that integrates the finance, marketing, and operations functions is complex. Robert Kaplan and David Norton in *The Strategy Focused Organization* have developed a generic strategy map template that they use in consulting work. The template is a starting point for the strategy design process and is tailored for a particular firm.

Kaplan and Norton claim the template helps executive teams describe their strategies and dramatically improve the quality of their insights. The template facilitates great precision in defining the customer value proposition and increases awareness that internal processes, competencies, and technologies must be linked to that value proposition. The purpose is to foster a cause-and-effect mentality that encourages more innovative approaches to strategy implementation.

The template is also useful to analyze or reverse-engineer an existing strategy. Mapping what a firm is currently doing into the template should tell the story of the strategy. Starting with the structure of the template, you should be able to reverse the logic and deduce the current strategy.

Exhibit 2.1 is the template proposed by Kaplan and Norton. It's very important to keep in mind that the positioning of a perspective on the template in no way indicates the importance of the idea. For example, the "Learning and Growth Perspective" at the bottom of the template is just as important as the "Financial Perspective" at the top. When properly constructed, the strategy map should portray an integrated and logical description of how the strategy will be accomplished.

THE *FINANCIAL* PERSPECTIVE

Whether companies use return on investment, return on capital employed (ROCE), economic value added (EVA), or some other value-based metric as the high-level *financial* objective, they have two basic strategies for driving financial performance: growth and productivity. The revenue growth strategy focuses on developing new sources of revenue and profitability. It generally has two components:

1. **Build the franchise.**   Develop new sources of revenue from new markets, new products, or new customers. This dimension of the strategy implies the greatest amount of change and requires the longest time to execute.

Kaplan and Norton's Generic Strategy Map

exhibit 2.1

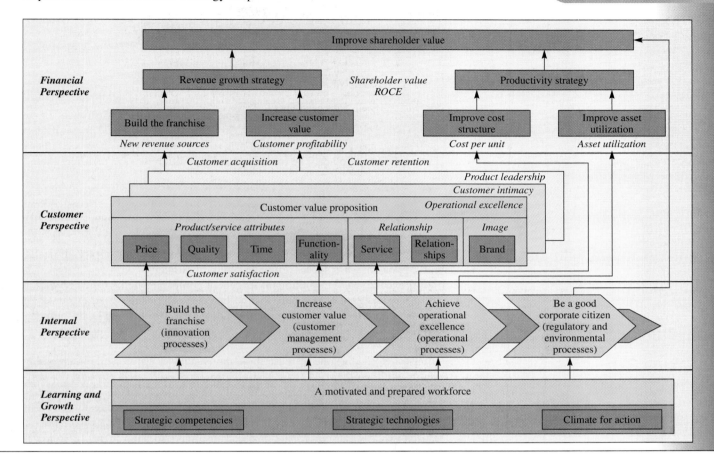

2. **Increase customer value.** Work with existing customers to expand their relationship with the company. This component tends to be intermediate term in duration and focuses on processes that integrate the firm's systems with the customer's to make processes more efficient.

The productivity strategy features the efficient execution of operational activities in support of existing customers. Productivity strategies focus on cost reduction and efficiency. Like the revenue growth strategy, the productivity strategy generally has two components:

1. **Improve cost structure.** Lower the direct costs of products and services, reduce indirect costs, and share common resources with other business units.
2. **Improve asset utilization.** Reduce the working and fixed capital needed to support a given level of business by more efficient utilization, more careful acquisition, or disposal of parts of the current and fixed asset base.

The productivity strategy generally yields results sooner than the growth strategy. Kaplan and Norton stress a balanced approach to ensure that cost and asset reductions do not compromise a company's growth opportunities. They argue that companies that are in early-stage start-up mode see opportunity for rapid growth and will emphasize objectives from the revenue growth side. Cost and productivity will be less emphasized as these organizations spend heavily to develop and introduce new products and services and to extend into new markets and applications. Companies in the mature end of their life cycle will emphasize the cost reduction and asset utilization components, as limited opportunities remain to find new customers or expand into new markets. Most companies are in the middle of their life cycle and employ a "profitable growth" strategy that requires a balance of the contributions from revenue growth and from cost reduction and productivity.

THE *CUSTOMER* PERSPECTIVE

The *customer* perspective is the heart of the strategy and defines how growth will be achieved. The value proposition defines the specific strategy to compete for new customers or an increased share of existing customer businesses. A clear definition of this value proposition is the most important single step in the development of a strategy map. This is how a company differentiates itself in the marketplace. The following are three different ways to differentiate:[5]

Service

1. **Product leadership.**   A product leadership company pushes its products into the realm of the unknown, the untried, or the highly desirable. Sony Corporation and Intel Corporation epitomize this strategy.
2. **Customer intimacy.**   A customer-intimate company builds bonds with its customers: it knows the *people* to whom it sells and the products and services it needs. The Home Depot, Inc., has successfully executed this strategy.
3. **Operational excellence.**   Operationally excellent companies deliver a combination of quality, price, and ease of purchase that no one else can match. Good examples of these companies are McDonald's Corporation, Southwest Airlines, and Dell Computer Corporation.

Successful companies excel at one of these three dimensions of value while maintaining "threshold standards" on the other two. This is similar to Terry Hill's concept of order winners and qualifiers described in the previous section. For example, The Home Depot differentiates itself through the knowledge and helpfulness of its sales staff. The company must still have excellent product selection, high-quality inventory management, and reasonable prices, but these are not the primary reasons for its targeted customers to shop there. In contrast, Intel, Sony, and many pharmaceutical companies succeed by offering the best product for their customers' needs. Prices of product leadership companies are generally high, and service is adequate but not necessarily exceptional. Companies such as McDonald's Corporation that stress operational excellence excel at being competitive on prices, customer-perceived quality, and lead-time response.

THE *INTERNAL* PERSPECTIVE

The *internal* perspective defines the business processes and the specific activities the organization must master to support the customer value proposition. It is important that strategy not only specify the desired outcomes but also describe how these outcomes will be achieved. As Michael Porter states, "The essence of strategy is in the activities—choosing to perform activities differently or to perform different activities than rivals."[6]

The activities of an organization are embedded in the internal business processes that comprise its value chain. Kaplan and Norton's template segments the value chain into four sets of business processes. These processes align with the three customer-value perspectives just introduced and add a fourth perspective: regulatory and environmental considerations.

Here it is important to stress the importance of operations management. Operations management is all about the design of effective business processes. Whether we are talking about the management of a sales force executing a marketing plan, a group of finance wizards managing an investment portfolio, or a factory making jet aircraft, these processes must be designed to operate effectively. Operations management is all about designing and managing these processes.

A *product leadership* strategy would require a leading-edge innovation process that creates new products with best-in-class functionality and brings them to market rapidly.

Customer management processes might focus on rapid acquisition of new customers to consolidate the early-mover advantage that a product leader creates.

A *customer intimacy* strategy requires excellent customer management processes such as relationship management and solution development. The innovation process would be motivated by the needs of targeted customers, focusing on those new-product developments and service enhancements that contribute to better customer solutions.

A strategy of *operational excellence* emphasizes cost, quality, quickness of operating processes, excellent supplier relationships, and speed and efficiency of supply and distribution processes.

It is not uncommon to see companies that claim to have a strategy of innovation or value-adding customer relationships but choose an internal business process that focuses on cost minimization. Cost minimization implies an emphasis on efficiency, high labor productivity, and standardization. These companies have a complete disconnect between the internal and customer perspectives of their strategy.

A strategy of *regulatory and environmental excellence* is important for companies such as telecommunications and utilities, whose prices and operations are regulated to some extent by the government. Companies whose operations entail significant environment, health, and safety (EHS) risks need to comply with regulations in the communities where they operate. Beyond compliance, these companies may even seek to achieve a reputation as a leader to enhance their ability to recruit and retain employees, and to maintain and expand their physical presence in communities. When such regulatory and EHS considerations are important for a successful strategy, companies may include several objectives in a "good corporate citizen" theme in the internal perspective.

THE *LEARNING AND GROWTH* PERSPECTIVE

The *learning and growth perspective* defines the intangible assets needed to enable activities and customer relationships to be conducted at high levels of performance. There are three principal categories:

1. *Strategic competencies* are the strategic skills and knowledge required by the workforce to support the strategy.
2. *Strategic technologies* are the materials and process technologies, information systems, databases, tools, and network required to support the strategy.
3. *Climate for action* provides the cultural shifts needed to motivate, empower, and align the workforce behind the strategy.

Learning and growth strategies are important for the firm's long-term development. It is vital that a firm align human resources, information technology, corporate climate, and research activities with requirements from the strategic business processes and customer differentiation strategy.

Kaplan and Norton have developed their concept of "The Balanced Scorecard" to describe how well an integrated strategy is being executed. They propose that an integrated set of measures be developed to track performance from financial, customer, internal, and learning and growth perspectives. Cause-and-effect linkages in strategy maps describe a path by which improvements in the capabilities of intangible assets get translated in tangible customer and financial outcomes.

Kaplan and Norton use the example of Rockwater, a division of Brown & Root Energy Services. Rockwater is an undersea contractor that does projects with major oil companies around the world. Rockwater developed a strategy to improve its return-on-capital financial performance through two strategic themes: (1) operations excellence, reducing costs and improving quality; and (2) customer management, developing long-term partnerships with targeted (Tier I) customers. Both themes required new capabilities and attitudes on the part of the workforce (see Exhibit 2.2).

For the operational excellence theme, improved attitude and morale among employees led to a higher frequency of suggestions (linkage A1 in Exhibit 2.2). The suggestions, in turn, led

exhibit 2.2   Rockwater's Strategy Map

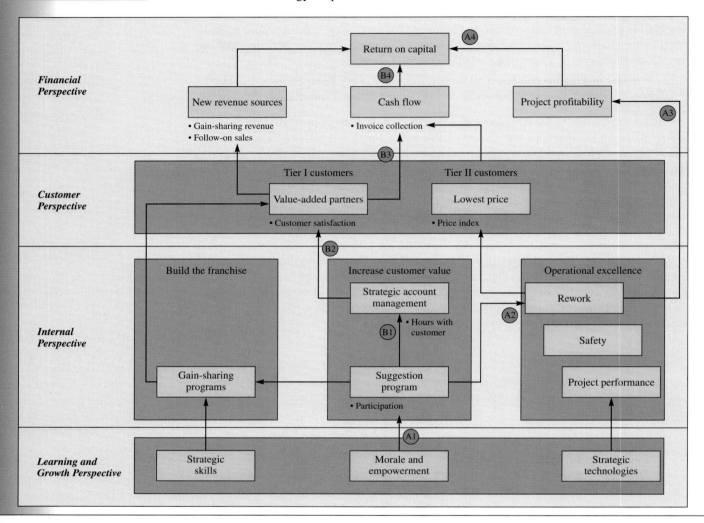

to many improvements in work practices that significantly reduced the incidence of costly rework (linkage A2). The lower incidence of rework translated directly into lower project costs (A3), higher profitability, and a higher return on capital (A4). The project teams also could leverage their cost reduction experiences into lower prices for future work for price-sensitive (Tier II) customers.

For the customer management strategic theme, the company observed that its most satisfied value-seeking (Tier I) customers were serviced by employees who had scored highest on measures of attitude and alignment with Rockwater's strategy (linkages B1 and B2). These satisfied customers paid outstanding invoices with the shortest delays (linkage B3), 30 to 90 days faster than dissatisfied customers paid. The short collection period led to lower levels of working capital and higher cash flows leading directly (linkage B4) to an increased return on capital.

The linkages in strategy maps provide the recipes for transformation and value creation over time. Near term, value creation can focus on operational excellence; medium term, increasing customer value is important; long term, building the business through loyalty and new customers is the main focus. Collectively, these perspectives ensure the short- and long-term performance of the firm.

STRATEGIC FIT: FITTING OPERATIONAL ACTIVITIES TO STRATEGY

All of the activities that make up a firm's operation relate to one another. Making these activities efficient means minimizing their total cost. On the other hand, making them effective means making the combined set of activities support the firm's strategy. Exhibit 2.3 shows how Southwest Airlines' strategy is implemented through a set of activities designed to deliver it.[7] Southwest's rapid gate turnaround, which allows frequent departures and greater use of aircraft, is essential to its high-convenience, low-cost positioning. But how does Southwest achieve this? Part of the answer lies in the company's well-paid gate and ground crews, whose productivity in turnarounds is enhanced by flexible union rules. But the bigger part of the answer lies in how Southwest performs (or avoids) other activities. With no meals, no seat assignments, and no interline baggage transfers, Southwest avoids having to perform activities that slow down other airlines. It selects airports and routes to avoid congestion that introduces delays. Southwest's strict limits on the type and length of routes make standardized aircraft possible: Southwest uses only Boeing 737s.

Activity-system maps, such as the one for Southwest, show how a company's strategy is delivered through a set of tailored activities. In companies with a clear strategy, a number of higher-order strategic themes (in green) can be identified and implemented through clusters of tightly linked activities. This type of map can be useful in understanding how good the fit is between the system of activities and the company's strategy. Competitive advantage comes from the way a firm's activities fit and reinforce one another.

Activity-system maps

Activity Map Showing How Southwest's Strategy Is Implemented

exhibit 2.3

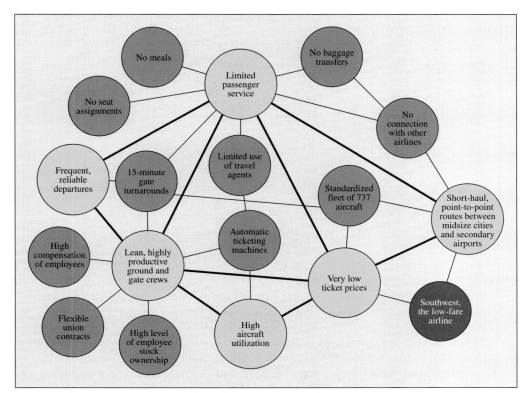

SOURCE: M. E. PORTER, "WHAT IS STRATEGY?" *HARVARD BUSINESS REVIEW*, NOVEMBER–DECEMBER 1996, P. 73.

A FRAMEWORK FOR OPERATIONS STRATEGY IN MANUFACTURING

Operations strategy cannot be designed in a vacuum. It must be linked vertically to the customer and horizontally to other parts of the enterprise. Exhibit 2.4 shows these linkages among customer needs, their performance priorities and requirements for manufacturing operations, and the operations and related enterprise resource capabilities to satisfy those needs. Overlying this framework is senior management's strategic vision of the firm. The vision identifies, in general terms, the target market, the firm's product line, and its core enterprise and operations capabilities.

The choice of a target market can be difficult, but it must be made. Indeed, it may lead to turning away business—ruling out a customer segment that would simply be unprofitable or too hard to serve given the firm's capabilities. An example here is clothing manufacturers not making half-sizes in their dress lines. **Core capabilities** (or competencies) are the skills that differentiate the service or manufacturing firm from its competitors.

Core capabilities

Possibly the most difficult thing for a firm to do is part with tradition. Top-level managers often made their mark based on innovations made 15 to 20 years ago. These managers are often too comfortable with just tinkering with the current system.[8] All the new advanced technologies present themselves as quick fixes. It is easy to patch these technologies into the current system with great enthusiasm. While doing this may be exciting to managers and engineers working for the firm, they may not be creating a distinctive core competence—a competence that wins future customers. What companies need in this world of intense global competition is not more techniques but a way to structure a whole new product realization system differently and better than any competitor. In the next section, we give guidelines for how to accomplish this.

exhibit 2.4

Operations Strategy Framework: From Customer Needs to Order Fulfillment

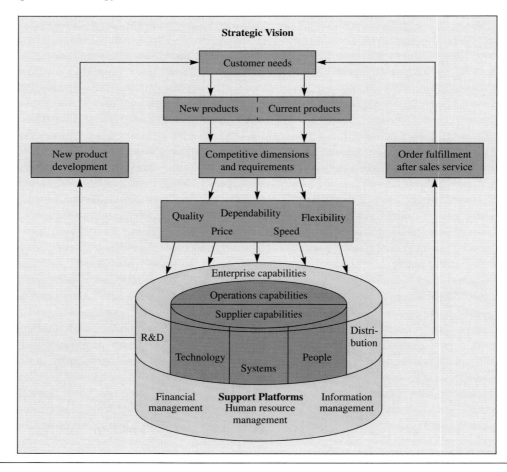

DEVELOPING A MANUFACTURING STRATEGY

The main objectives of manufacturing strategy development are (1) to translate required competitive dimensions (typically obtained from marketing) into specific performance requirements for operations and (2) to make the plans necessary to ensure that operations (and enterprise) capabilities are sufficient to accomplish them. The steps for prioritizing these dimensions are as follows:

1. Segment the market according to the product group.
2. Identify the product requirements, demand patterns, and profit margins of each group.
3. Determine the order winners and order qualifiers for each group.
4. Convert order winners into specific performance requirements.

The process of achieving a satisfactory manufacturing segmentation that maintains focus is often a matter of deciding which products or product groups fit together in the sense that they have similar market performance characteristics or place similar demands on the manufacturing system. For example, Exhibit 2.5 shows how two product groups manufactured by one

A Comparison of How Two Product Groups Differ in Their Manufacturing Requirements   **exhibit 2.5**

MANUFACTURING REQUIREMENTS DIFFERENCES	PRODUCT GROUP 1	PRODUCT GROUP 2
Products	Standard medical equipment	Electronic measuring devices
Customers	Hospitals/clinics	Medical and other OEMs
Product specs	Not high-tech, but periodic updates	Varies; some high specs and others less so
Product range	Narrow—4 variants	Wide; many types and variants; some customization
Design changes	Infrequent	Continuous process
Delivery	Customer lead time important—ship directly from stock on hand	On-time delivery important
Quality	Conformance/reliability	Performance/conformance
Demand variation	Financial year–related but predictable	Lumpy and unpredictable
Volume/line	High	Medium to low
Margins	Low	Low to very high
EXTERNAL PERFORMANCE DIMENSIONS		
Order winners	Price Product reliability	Product specification Product range
Qualifiers	Delivery lead time Product specification Quality conformance	Delivery dependability Delivery lead time Price
MAIN OPERATIONS PERFORMANCE DIMENSIONS		
	Cost Quality	New-product flexibility Range flexibility Dependability

SOURCE: N. SLACK, *THE MANUFACTURING ADVANTAGE* (LONDON: MANAGEMENT BOOKS 2000 LTD., 1992), PP. 14–15.

instrument manufacturer differ in their manufacturing requirements. The first product group is a range of standard electronic medical equipment sold "off the shelf" directly to hospitals and clinics. The second product group is a wider range of measuring devices sold to original equipment manufacturers and often have to be customized to individual customer requirements. The analysis of the two product groups in the exhibit shows they have very different market competitive characteristics. Therefore, different external performance objectives are required from the manufacturing operation. Each product group also has different priorities for its internal performance objectives. Product group 1 needs to concentrate on cost and quality performance. All other internal performance objectives should be bent to achieving this. Product group 2 needs the flexibility to cope with a wide product range and considerable design turbulence. Such diverse competitive needs will almost certainly require two separate focused manufacturing processes, each devoted to providing the things that are important in their separate markets.

Service

OPERATIONS STRATEGY IN SERVICES

Operations strategy in service firms is generally inseparable from the corporate strategy. For most services, the service delivery system is the business, and hence any strategic decision must include operations considerations. However, operations executives do not always have a voice equal to other functions of the firm. A marketing decision to add a new route for an airline or to add new in-flight services may be made despite operations' protests about feasibility (just as in manufacturing).

Although we will discuss service strategy in Chapter 7, we should note that many of the strategy concepts discussed relative to manufacturing also apply to services. For example, service firms may use the plant-within-a-plant (PWP) structure to achieve focus. Hospitals using the PWP focus may have separate units for distinct patient services such as cardiac units, oncology units, labor and delivery units, and rehabilitation units. Major department stores group products and services into separate units or "departments," each with a separate customer focus, ordering, product arrangement, flow, and strategy. Each department—women's sportswear, customer service, children's apparel, housewares, and men's clothing—focuses on specific customer niches with unique needs, particularly if the organization serves a variety of customers and markets with distinct needs. Likewise, order winners and qualifiers have service applications. For a bank, qualifiers might be a good location, availability of tellers and loan officers, and ATMs. Order winners might be relationship banking and customer-oriented banking hours.

INTERNET COMPLEMENTS STRATEGY

It has been widely assumed that the Internet is cannibalistic and will replace conventional ways of doing business and overturn traditional advantages. In many cases, however, the Internet complements, rather than cannibalizes, companies' traditional activities and ways of competing.[9] Walgreens, the most successful pharmacy chain in the United States, introduced a Web site that provides customers with extensive information and allows them to order prescriptions online. Far from cannibalizing the company's stores, the Web site has underscored their value. Fully 90 percent of customers who place orders over the Web prefer to pick up their prescriptions at a nearby store rather than have them shipped to their homes. Walgreens has found that its extensive network of stores remains a potent advantage, even as some ordering shifts to the Internet.

Strategies that employ online activities do not eliminate the need for physical activities; in fact, they often amplify their importance. Direct ordering, for example, makes warehousing and shipping more important. Sometimes using the Internet in one activity can require new or enhanced physical activities that may be difficult to anticipate. Internet-based job-posting services, for example, have greatly reduced the cost of reaching potential job applicants, but they also have flooded employers with electronic résumés. By making it easier for job seekers to distribute résumés, the Internet forces employers to sort through many more unsuitable candidates. The added back-end costs, often for physical activities, can end up outweighing the up-front savings.

Ultimately, strategies that integrate the Internet and traditional ways of competing should win in many industries. On the demand side, most buyers will value a combination of online services and physical locations over stand-alone Web distribution. They will want a choice of channels, delivery options, and ways of dealing with companies. On the supply side, production and procurement will be more effective if they involve a combination of Internet and traditional methods, tailored to strategy.

ATTACKING THROUGH OPERATIONS[10]

Consider the following story about how Wal-Mart became the dominant discount retailer in the United States.

Wal-Mart became a public corporation in 1972. At the time it operated 30 discount stores in rural Arkansas, Missouri, and Oklahoma.[11] It had to go public to get the money needed to build its first warehouse. Then, following an unwavering strategy, it steadily expanded from that base. A little over 10 years later, it had about 650 stores and almost $4.7 billion in sales. By the 1980s (even though most Americans had never seen a Wal-Mart store or even a Wal-Mart advertisement), one would think that larger rivals such as Sears and Kmart would have been aware of its stunning progress and alert to the potential threat it posed. By 1987, only five years later, Wal-Mart had almost 1,200 stores, just over half as many as Kmart (its $16 billion in sales were now about 60 percent of Kmart's); the industry's "country bumpkin" had taken the lead in applying computer technology to track sales and coordinate replenishment of its stores. Yet, as Wal-Mart steadily approached the large cities where Kmart was entrenched, rather than prepare for the predictable head-to-head confrontation, Kmart turned its energies to diversification and building a more upscale image.

By 1993 the battle was essentially over. Wal-Mart's sales had surpassed Kmart's two years earlier and now, with $67 billion, were over half again as large. Over 80 percent of Kmart stores now faced direct competition from Wal-Mart (while only slightly over half of Wal-Mart stores competed directly with Kmart), and Kmart—so financially strapped that it could barely cover its annual dividend—was hamstrung in its attempts to renovate its old stores. By then, of course, it was a case of too little, too late. Why didn't it react sooner? What should it have done while it still had a chance to change the course of events?

Kmart did finally attempt to react to Wal-Mart's attack by pouring money into new computerized scanners and new product procurement and inventory control systems. It found that its employees lacked the skills necessary to use the new systems effectively and that the data being entered into them were full of errors. Instilling the organizational discipline required to ensure the accuracy of data and then providing the training required to make the most effective use of its sophisticated systems had taken Wal-Mart many years. In 2004, Kmart merged with Sears.

In this example, we see three different ways Wal-Mart created a competitive operations advantage that differentiates Wal-Mart from the competition. First, Wal-Mart created significant advantage through the systems it developed to manage its warehouses and stores. These systems are the envy of the retailing industry. Next, Wal-Mart created a location advantage. Initially Wal-Mart chose locations without direct competition from the large chains—rural areas in Arkansas, Missouri, and Oklahoma. Once Wal-Mart had developed the infrastructure to compete, it could exploit this great system and compete head to head in large urban areas while enjoying a significant operating cost advantage. Finally, in developing its efficient system, Wal-Mart created a culture of supporting values, skills, technologies, supplier–customer relationships, human resources, and approaches to motivation that are neither easily copied nor transferable to other organizations.

Capabilities such as those Wal-Mart developed are nurtured over a long time. In thinking about how to develop such capabilities, it is useful to break them up into three types:

- *Process-based* capabilities are derived from activities that transform material or information and tend to provide advantages along such standard competitive dimensions as low cost and high quality.

BREAKTHROUGH

RACING BARNES & NOBLE FOR SAME-DAY DELIVERY IN NEW YORK

Amazon.com has thrived by delivering many of its Web orders free of shipping charges. Now it's delivering some of them faster—even the same day.

For the past several months, teams of couriers have used luggage carts to deliver books, CDs and movies that were ordered online just that morning to offices and residences in Manhattan. The move matches a service by rival **Barnes & Noble** Inc., which has offered same-day delivery for some time in New York. But Amazon hasn't promoted the service, and some customers have been surprised when their goods arrive so fast.

Such same-day shipping leaves little room for error. It wasn't a viable business for Kozmo, Urbanfetch Inc. and other dot-com companies that tried to ship online orders, from ice cream to videos, within hours. Amazon was the largest investor in Kozmo, sinking $60 million into the Web courier before it went belly-up.

That explains why Amazon is testing the new service on a modest basis. The current test is only in Manhattan, and it isn't informing customers whether they'll receive their items the same day. For now at least, Amazon is charging the same for same-day service as for standard delivery. The deliveries are handled by Choice Logistics Inc., a New York–based service.

Shipping has long been a deal breaker for hesitant online shoppers. Customers generally don't like paying for delivery and they are impatient for orders to arrive. Amazon in past years has concentrated on the first hurdle, doing away with shipping fees on certain orders to encourage people to buy more. But its newer emphasis on fast shipping reflects a belief that there's still a sizable audience willing to pay for more immediate gratification.

While the company won't say whether it plans to expand same-day shipping outside of New York City, Amazon has been speeding delivery elsewhere. Late last year, it quietly introduced a shipping option for U.S. customers called "guaranteed accelerated delivery," in which it promises to deliver an order the next business day if it is placed in the morning. Although Amazon has long offered overnight delivery, it often wouldn't pack orders for a day, so customers would get their overnight-delivery goodies two days after buying them.

Many items on Amazon now display a ticking clock that counts the time left for an order to make it to a customer by the next day. The software is sophisticated enough to figure in the customer's location and where within Amazon's network of warehouses the product is stored. A customer in Hawaii, for instance, may have less time left to get a next-day order for an item warehoused on the East Coast than for those stored in Nevada.

A courier makes a same-day Amazon delivery.

SOURCE: NICK WINGFIELD, "RACING BARNES & NOBLE FOR SAME-DAY DELIVERY IN NEW YORK," *THE WALL STREET JOURNAL*, JUNE 3, 2004, P. B1. USED WITH PERMISSION. © 2004 DOW JONES COMPANY INC.

- *Systems (coordination)-based* operating capabilities underpin such competitive advantages as short lead times, a broad range of products or services, the ability to customize on demand, and fast new-product development. Such capabilities require broad involvement throughout the entire operating system.
- *Organization-based* operating capabilities involve the ability to master new technologies, design and introduce new products, and bring new plants online significantly faster than competitors. Since they are even more difficult to replicate, such capabilities are among the most powerful in the firm's operating arsenal.

To sustain an operations-based competitive advantage, operations-based strategies must be dynamic and change over time. Ongoing invention is at the core of today's most effective operations organizations; they cannot stand still while their competitors try to catch up. Those that can consistently create new, more effective ways to deliver value to customers will stay ahead of the pack. Although individuals (at least some) learn and adapt easily, organizations rarely do. They must be structured and shaped in a way that facilitates learning and change.

The technical note on learning curves that follows Chapter 4 discusses organizational and individual learning. This is an important topic, and, as you will see, the steady improvement in operating efficiency has been studied over the years. Strategies that combine existing and new operating capabilities in novel ways can be powerful, but the most sustainable advantages are those based on a firm's ability to learn. A company can easily replicate a competitor's equipment and operating policies within a few years. Learning to use them effectively usually takes much longer. A company that continually invents practices that innovatively use new technologies and methods is difficult to catch.

PRODUCTIVITY MEASUREMENT

The Breakthrough Box titled "The Balanced Scorecard" found on p. 41 describes a popular approach for organizing a firm's **key performance indicators (KPI)**. KPIs should be structured to help managers predict the company's economic performance and spot the need for changes in operations. Financial measures such as days' cash on hand and operating income by unit or division are used together with nonfinancial metrics such as average time to respond to service calls, lead time to fill customer orders, and percentage of sales from new products. Evaluating how productively a firm uses its resources is the basis for important KPIs.

Key performance indicators (KPI)

Productivity is a common measure of how well a country, industry, or business unit is using its resources (or factors of production). Since operations management focuses on making the best use of the resources available to a firm, productivity measurement is fundamental to understanding operations-related performance. In this section, we define various measures of productivity. Throughout the rest of the book, many other performance measures will be defined as they relate to the material.

Productivity

In its broadest sense, productivity is defined as

$$\text{Productivity} = \frac{\text{Outputs}}{\text{Inputs}}$$

To increase productivity, we want to make this ratio of outputs to inputs as large as practical.

Productivity is what we call a *relative measure.* In other words, to be meaningful, it needs to be compared with something else. For example, what can we learn from the fact that we operate a restaurant and that its productivity last week was 8.4 customers per labor hour? Nothing!

Productivity comparisons can be made in two ways. First, a company can compare itself with similar operations within its industry, or it can use industry data when such data are available (e.g., comparing productivity among the different stores in a franchise). Another approach is to measure productivity over time within the same operation. Here we would compare our productivity in one time period with that of the next.

As Exhibit 2.6 shows, productivity may be expressed as partial measures, multifactor measures, or total measures. If we are concerned with the ratio of output to a single input, we have a *partial productivity measure.* If we want to look at the ratio of output to a group of inputs (but not all inputs), we have a *multifactor productivity measure.* If we want to express the ratio of all outputs to all inputs, we can use a *total factor measure of productivity* to describe the productivity of an entire organization or even a nation.

A numerical example of productivity appears in Exhibit 2.7. The data reflect quantitative measures of input and output associated with the production of a certain product. Notice that

exhibit 2.6

Examples of Productivity Measures

Partial measure	$\dfrac{\text{Output}}{\text{Labor}}$ or $\dfrac{\text{Output}}{\text{Capital}}$ or $\dfrac{\text{Output}}{\text{Materials}}$ or $\dfrac{\text{Output}}{\text{Energy}}$
Multifactor measure	$\dfrac{\text{Output}}{\text{Labor} + \text{Capital} + \text{Energy}}$ or $\dfrac{\text{Output}}{\text{Labor} + \text{Capital} + \text{Materials}}$
Total measure	$\dfrac{\text{Output}}{\text{Inputs}}$ or $\dfrac{\text{Goods and services produced}}{\text{All resources used}}$

SOURCE: D. J. SUMANTH AND K. TANG, "A REVIEW OF SOME APPROACHES TO THE MANAGEMENT OF TOTAL PRODUCTIVITY IN A COMPANY/ORGANIZATION," *INSTITUTE OF INDUSTRIAL ENGINEERING CONFERENCE PROCEEDINGS*, FALL 1984, P. 305. COPYRIGHT INSTITUTE OF INDUSTRIAL ENGINEERS, 25 TECHNOLOGY PARK/ATLANTA, NORCROSS, GEORGIA 30092.

exhibit 2.7

Numerical Example of Productivity Measures

Excel

INPUT AND OUTPUT PRODUCTION DATA ($)		PRODUCTIVITY MEASURE EXAMPLES
OUTPUT		Total measure:
1. Finished units	$10,000	$\dfrac{\text{Total output}}{\text{Total input}} = \dfrac{13,500}{15,193} = .89$
2. Work in process	2,500	
3. Dividends	1,000	
4. Bonds		Multifactor measures:
5. Other income	————	$\dfrac{\text{Total output}}{\text{Human} + \text{Material}} = \dfrac{13,500}{3,153} = 4.28$
Total output	$13,500	$\dfrac{\text{Finished units}}{\text{Human} + \text{Material}} = \dfrac{10,000}{3,153} = 3.17$
INPUT		
1. Human	$ 3,000	Partial measures:
2. Material	153	$\dfrac{\text{Total output}}{\text{Energy}} = \dfrac{13,500}{540} = 25$
3. Capital	10,000	
4. Energy	540	$\dfrac{\text{Finished units}}{\text{Energy}} = \dfrac{10,000}{540} = 18.52$
5. Other expenses	1,500	
Total input	$15,193	

NOTE: FIND THE SPREADSHEET ON THE CD INCLUDED WITH THE TEXT.

for the multifactor and partial measures, it is not necessary to use total output as the numerator. Often it is desirable to create measures that represent productivity as it relates to some particular output of interest. For example, as in Exhibit 2.7, total units might be the output of interest to a production control manager, whereas total output may be of key interest to the plant manager. This process of aggregation and disaggregation of productivity measures provides a means of shifting the level of the analysis to suit a variety of productivity measurement and improvement needs.

Exhibit 2.7 shows all units in dollars. Often, however, management can better understand how the company is performing when units other than dollars are used. In these cases, only partial measures of productivity can be used, as we cannot combine dissimilar units such as labor hours and pounds of material. Examples of some commonly used partial measures of productivity are presented in Exhibit 2.8. Such partial measures of productivity give managers information in familiar units, allowing them to easily relate these measures to the actual operations.

BREAKTHROUGH

The Balanced Scorecard

The Balanced Scorecard concept is an outgrowth of the so-called value-based management techniques that first appeared in the late 1980s. It helps you highlight the cause-and-effect relationships among performance drivers and identify the links to strategic outcomes. David P. Norton, who together with Robert Kaplan developed the concept, insists that a Balanced Scorecard is not strategic planning; rather, "It's a tool that forces you to articulate your strategy. You should be able to look at your scorecard and reverse-engineer it to see what the underlying strategy is."

In addition to traditional financial measures, a Balanced Scorecard includes metrics that help your company answer three critical performance questions:

- **How do customers see us?** Metrics for this category include customer satisfaction, price relative to the competition, and market share.
- **What must we excel at?** That is, what internal business processes will ensure that we continually meet customers' expectation? Typical measures here have to do with cycle time, productivity, and quality.
- **How can we continue to improve and create value?** Metrics such as the percentage of sales from new products or the rate of improvement in on-time delivery assess your firm's ability to learn and innovate.

Norton contends that many firms do their strategic planning backward. Their strategic plan lists initiatives and uses internal business measures—time and cost metrics—as milestones. But a strategic plan should not be about managing initiatives. Your strategy should describe how your firm intends to create and sustain value for its shareholders.

Source: Loren Gary, "How to Think about Performance Measures Now," *Harvard Management Update*, February 2002.

Partial Measures of Productivity

exhibit 2.8

Business	Productivity Measure
Restaurant	Customers (meals) per labor hour
Retail store	Sales per square foot
Chicken farm	Lb. of meat per lb. of feed
Utility plant	Kilowatts per ton of coal
Paper mill	Tons of paper per cord of wood

How Does Wall Street Evaluate Operations Performance?

Comparing firms from an operations view is important to investors since the relative cost of providing a good or service is essential to high earnings growth. When you think about it, earnings growth is largely a function of the firm's profitability and profit can be increased through higher sales and/or reduced cost. Highly efficient firms usually shine when demand drops during recession periods since they often can continue to make a profit due to their low cost structure. These operations-savvy firms may even see a recession as an opportunity to gain market share as their less-efficient competitors struggle to remain in business.

Exhibit 2.9 compares some companies that make personal computer systems using some of the common management efficiency measures.

exhibit 2.9

Efficiency Measures Used by Wall Street: A Comparison of Personal Computer Makers

MANAGEMENT EFFICIENCY MEASURE	APPLE COMPUTER	DELL COMPUTER	GATEWAY	INDUSTRY	S&P 500
Income per employee	$15,000	$60,000	$66,000	$37,000	$24,000
Revenue per employee	$658,000	$945,000	$463,000	$832,000	$323,000
Receivable turnover	11.5	14.0	14.5	13.3	5.6
Inventory turnover	98.2	106.3	20.6	88.3	8.0
Asset turnover	1.1	2.5	1.5	2.0	0.3

Here we can see that Dell Computer is a very efficient company, at least compared to Apple and Gateway. At the time of this comparison (May 2004), Gateway is struggling to make a profit and its revenue per employee is only about half that of Dell. Receivable turnover is a measure of how quickly a company is paid for products sold (a higher number is better), and Gateway does pretty well. Inventory turnover measures how much inventory a company carries relative to its yearly cost of sales (higher numbers are better), and this is where Dell is strong compared to the competition, although Apple is very good too. Finally, asset turnover evaluates how much money a company makes relative to the money invested in plant, equipment, and other company assets (higher numbers are better). Once again, Dell is very strong on this measure, explaining why investors perceive Dell as an outstanding long-term investment.

Each summer, *USA Today* publishes annual reports of productivity gains by the largest U.S. firms. Productivity has been on the rise for the past few years, which is very good for the economy. Productivity often increases in times of recession; as workers are fired, those remaining are expected to do more. Increases also come from technological advances. Think of what the tractor did for farm productivity.

When evaluating the largest productivity winners and losers, it is important to look for unusual explanations. For example, energy companies have had big productivity gains due almost exclusively to higher oil prices, which boosted the companies' revenue without forcing them to add employees. Pharmaceutical companies such as Merck and Pfizer have not done well recently. Their productivity plunges were due primarily to one-time events, Merck because it spun off a company and Pfizer because it bought a company. Such one-time quirks create a lot of noise for anybody who wants to know how well companies are run. It is best to examine multiyear productivity patterns.

CONCLUSION

Nonoperations students often view operations strategy and competitiveness as not being particularly relevant to their specialty areas. We hope this chapter conveys the importance of the link between operations and the competitive success of the firm. The concepts of competitive dimensions, order winners and qualifiers, and capabilities apply to virtually any business and are critical to the firm's ability to sustain a competitive advantage.

For a firm to remain competitive, all of the activities that make up the operations' core must buttress the firm's strategy. Many new technologies, and especially the Internet, have an impact on operations capabilities. The firm must actively explore changes in operations strategy to take advantage of these new technologies. Productivity measures provide the benchmarks for how well a company is doing and are useful for measuring improvement. These are important terms that make up the new language of operations strategy—and the language of business.

KEY TERMS

Operations strategy Setting broad policies and plans for using the resources of a firm to best support the firm's long-term competitive strategy.

Plant-within-a-plant (PWP) A concept in which different locations within a facility are dedicated to different product lines. Each location is operated according to its own strategy to minimize the confusion associated with shifting from one type of strategy to another.

Straddling Occurs when a company seeks to match what a competitor is doing by adding new features, services, or technologies to existing activities. This often creates problems if certain trade-offs need to be made.

Order winner A dimension that differentiates the products or services of one firm from those of another.

Order qualifier A dimension used to screen a product or service as a candidate for purchase.

Activity-system map A diagram that shows how a company's strategy is delivered through a set of supporting activities.

Core capabilities Skills that differentiate a manufacturing or service firm from its competitors.

Key performance indicators (KPI) A set of measures that help managers evaluate a company's economic performance and spot the need for changes in operations. KPIs include financial measures such as days' cash on hand and operating income by unit or division, as well as nonfinancial metrics such as average time to respond to service calls, lead time, or percentage of sales from new products.

Productivity A measure of how well resources are used.

SOLVED PROBLEM

A furniture manufacturing company has provided the following data. Compare the labor, raw materials and supplies, and total productivity of 2004 and 2005.

		2004	2005
Output:	Sales value of production	$22,000	$35,000
Input:	Labor	10,000	15,000
	Raw materials and supplies	8,000	12,500
	Capital equipment depreciation	700	1,200
	Other	2,200	4,800

Solution

	2004	2005
Partial productivities		
Labor	2.20	2.33
Raw materials and supplies	2.75	2.80
Total productivity	1.05	1.04

REVIEW AND DISCUSSION QUESTIONS

1 Can a factory be fast, dependable, and flexible; produce high-quality products; and still provide poor service from a customer's perspective?

2 Why should a service organization worry about being world-class if it does not compete outside its own national border? What impact does the Internet have on this?

3 What are the major priorities associated with operations strategy? How has their relationship to one another changed over the years?

4 For each priority in question 3, describe the unique characteristics of the market niche with which it is most compatible.

5 A few years ago, the dollar showed relative weakness with respect to foreign currencies such as the yen, euro, and pound. This stimulated exports. Why would long-term reliance on a lower-valued dollar be at best a short-term solution to the competitiveness problem?

6 In your opinion, do business schools have competitive priorities?

7 Why does the "proper" operations strategy keep changing for companies that are world-class competitors?

8 What is meant by the expressions *order winners* and *order qualifiers*? What was the order winner(s) for your last major purchase of a product or service?

9 What do we mean when we say productivity is a "relative" measure?

10   What are the typical performance measures for quality, speed of delivery, and flexibility?

11   What should be the criteria for management to adopt a particular performance measure?

PROBLEMS *

1   Two types of cars (Deluxe and Limited) were produced by a car manufacturer in 2005. Quantities sold, price per unit, and labor hours follow. What is the labor productivity for each car? Explain the problem(s) associated with the labor productivity.

	QUANTITY	$/UNIT
Deluxe car	4,000 units sold	$8,000/car
Limited car	6,000 units sold	$9,500/car
Labor, Deluxe	20,000 hours	$12/hour
Labor, Limited	30,000 hours	$14/hour

2   A U.S. manufacturing company operating a subsidiary in an LDC (less developed country) shows the following results:

	U.S.	LDC
Sales (units)	100,000	20,000
Labor (hours)	20,000	15,000
Raw materials (currency)	$20,000	FC 20,000
Capital equipment (hours)	60,000	5,000

   a. Calculate partial labor and capital productivity figures for the parent and subsidiary. Do the results seem misleading?

   b. Compute the multifactor productivity figures for labor and capital together. Are the results better?

   c. Calculate raw material productivity figures (units/$ where $1 = FC 10). Explain why these figures might be greater in the subsidiary.

3   Various financial data for 2004 and 2005 follow. Calculate the total productivity measure and the partial measures for labor, capital, and raw materials for this company for both years. What do these measures tell you about this company?

		2004	2005
Output:	Sales	$200,000	$220,000
Input:	Labor	30,000	40,000
	Raw materials	35,000	45,000
	Energy	5,000	6,000
	Capital	50,000	50,000
	Other	2,000	3,000

4   An electronics company makes communications devices for military contracts. The company just completed two contracts. The navy contract was for 2,300 devices and took 25 workers two weeks (40 hours per week) to complete. The army contract was for 5,500 devices that were produced by 35 workers in three weeks. On which contract were the workers more productive?

5   A retail store had sales of $45,000 in April and $56,000 in May. The store employs eight full-time workers who work a 40-hour week. In April the store also had seven part-time workers at 10 hours per week, and in May the store had nine part-timers at 15 hours per week (assume four weeks in each month). Using sales dollars as the measure of output, what is the percentage change in productivity from April to May?

6   A parcel delivery company delivered 103,000 packages in 2004, when its average employment was 84 drivers. In 2005 the firm handled 112,000 deliveries with 96 drivers. What was the percentage change in productivity from 2004 to 2005?

7   A fast-food restaurant serves hamburgers, cheeseburgers, and chicken sandwiches. The restaurant counts a cheeseburger as equivalent to 1.25 hamburgers and chicken sandwiches as 0.8 hamburger. Current employment is five full-time employees who work a 40-hour week. If the restaurant sold 700 hamburgers, 900 cheeseburgers, and 500 chicken sandwiches in one week, what is its productivity? What would its productivity have been if it had sold the same number of sandwiches (2,100) but the mix was 700 of each type?

*Special thanks to Bill Ruck of Arizona State University for the problems in this section.

CASE: CUSTOM FABRICATORS, INC.—FROM LEAN MANUFACTURING PARTNER TO CONTRACT MANUFACTURER

⦿⦿⦿ As Ben Lawson, CEO of Custom Fabricators, Inc., drove back to his home in South Indianapolis, he thought about the day.

I've done a lot of business with Orleans Elevator in Bloomington over the years, but just wonder how long this will continue. I have much invested in my manufacturing plant located right next to their plant, but now that United Technologies [the parent company of Orleans] is all into this FreeMarkets Internet purchasing system, I just wonder how long they are going to be interested in keeping me in the supply chain loop.

It's been a good business over the past few years. I was in the right place at the right time when Orleans got into just-in-time and lean manufacturing in the late 1980s. Initially I was just making the control panels for the elevators. It was interesting to walk into a new building, get on the elevator, and see my company's handiwork in that beautiful stainless steel panel that houses the buttons for the floors on the building. I could take a lot of pride in the craftsmanship even though it was largely a technology thing. That new numerically controlled machine tool that I purchased in 1985 made making the holes in those custom panels easy. We are still making beautiful panels.

Since that time, my company has gotten a lot of other business from Orleans. We now make all kinds of special brackets and panels for the plant. This has been great for us over the years. We have set up a very efficient process for fabricating exactly what the plant needs in these parts with very little lead time. For most items, Orleans simply gives us the production schedule for elevators being shipped over the next month, and we make the required parts automatically. We know exactly what they need based on their schedule. Of course, it is easy to modify things for the specific needs of a particular elevator order.

The business has changed over the past few years, though. "Outsourcing" is now the big game. Orleans is much more interested in whole subassemblies than just the parts. We now make that entire control panel, complete with the buttons and the wiring harness. One of our biggest money makers is the elevator motor housing. This is a massive box that contains the motor and control electronics for the elevator. The motor housing electronically connects to our control panel. We custom fabricate each of these in our shop and ship them directly to the site where the elevator is being assembled. The Orleans plant never even sees them.

There is not much left there at the Orleans plant site. In 1985 they were running a massive operation with over 400,000 square feet of production space spread over two buildings. Now all the production takes place in only 150,000 square feet. They still make some of the large sheet metal parts and fabricate some of the lighting fixtures for the elevators. The engineers still are located on the site. It's still a pretty big job to engineer the elevators for a large building. Everything associated with the design of the elevator is modular, so it's a matter of sizing the modules to the needs of the building and fitting them all together.

It is companies like mine that really represent the backbone of the U.S. manufacturing system. I was lucky to hook up with a major company like Orleans, since I never had to go public with my company. Orleans has always bought the raw materials that I

need, so all I have needed to worry about is the lease on my land, my investment in the plant and equipment, and paying my employees. I was lucky to find that plant site. It was an old distribution center. After the tax breaks given to me by the county, the building is really inexpensive. I can easily maintain profit margins close to 30 percent of revenue.

I have a loyal group of employees; many had worked for Orleans and been part of the union. We are a lean shop and I pay my employees well. There has never been any interest in joining the union. My employees often joke about how much they produce compared to what they did at the Orleans plant. So far, I have never had to lay anyone off. We have just been able to pick up more and more business from Orleans as they continued to outsource manufacturing.

I am really getting concerned, though, with the future. This morning was interesting. Orleans is now trying to further reduce costs associated with its elevators. Now they are working on reducing the cost of the raw materials. What they did was contract with a company known as FreeMarkets, now a part of Ariba, located in Pittsburgh, to conduct an auction for nearly $20 million worth of raw materials and parts. The idea was to contract with Mexican suppliers. The thinking is that with the lower labor cost in Mexico, costs should be much lower. Orleans did not feel it knew enough about Mexican suppliers to try to contract with the companies on their own. FreeMarkets has developed considerable experience with this type of activity over the past few years, and has developed the contacts needed to attract Mexican companies to the opportunity presented by Orleans.

Orleans invited me to the FreeMarkets bidding event this morning. We sat in a conference room at the Orleans plant and watched the bidding from the Mexican suppliers. The 20 auctions took over five hours to conduct. The auctions were each started at different times with some overlap in the times. As one auction was ending, another was just starting and a second was about 10 minutes from completion. Auctions were scheduled to take 20 minutes, but if any bidding took place in the last 3 minutes, the auction was automatically extended an extra 3 minutes. One auction took over an hour to complete. Exhibit 2.10 is a screen from one of the auctions. In this auction, the winning bid was more than 27 percent lower than Orleans' current contract for these parts. Today's event was just one step in a process for auctioning off the contracts.

Working with FreeMarkets, Orleans had identified approximately 50 potential suppliers. Orleans ran a prebid conference in Mexico six weeks ago for the group. Most of the potentials attended the conference where Orleans discussed the parts that were being bid and the process that would be used in the auction. Orleans even brought many of the parts so that the attendees could see the wide range of parts. There was a healthy exchange of information.

The auction involved 20 different "lots" of materials. Each lot consisted of about $1 million worth of material for each year and had from 50 to approximately 100 different items. The lots were designed based on what Orleans felt might be groups of parts that would be attractive to produce for a particular company. One lot included all types of fasteners: nuts, bolts, screws, washers, and the like. Another lot had different kinds of brackets that could be

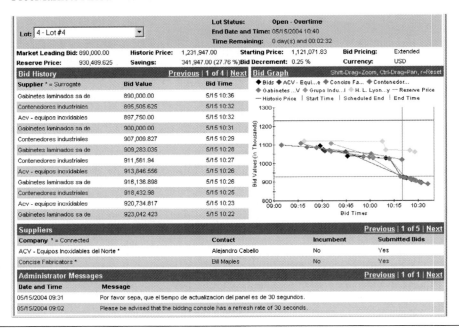

exhibit 2.10   FreeMarkets Ariba Inc. Auction Bid Screen

fabricated by cutting and drilling holes. A few lots included some more complex parts that required welding some pieces together.

For Ben Lawson, what was most interesting was to observe the auction for some parts that he used at his plant. The parts in this lot included some brackets that Orleans currently had made at a manufacturing plant located in Bedford, Indiana, a town about 20 miles out of Bloomington. These brackets have been made by the Bedford plant for over 15 years. The Bedford plant purchased the bar stock for the brackets and fabricated the parts with some simple machining operations. The Bedford plant also heat-treated the brackets to make them very strong. The finished parts were sent to Ben's plant, where they are used in the motor housing.

Ben was concerned about how well a Mexican plant, one located in central Mexico near Monterrey, could supply these parts. Over the years, Ben had some problems with the Bedford plant. Sometimes the quality was just not up to par due to poor welds, and the heat-treating process not being completed properly. When these problems occurred, it was easy for Ben to run down to Bedford and get things straightened out. Things simply could not be the same with the Mexican supplier. It would take at least a week just to transport the parts to Bloomington, and Ben did not even know Spanish, so there might be some major problems even communicating with the managers.

Of course, Ben realized that the production might not even move to Mexico, even if the bid was lower than the Bedford deal. Orleans had indicated a minimum or "reserve" price for the lot, but the Bedford plant would be given the opportunity to negotiate its price. In addition, pricing in the auction was specifically set up to exclude

shipping costs, so there was some spread in what the Bedford plant might be able to offer due to its close proximity. There was no guarantee to the Mexican bidders that the contract would go to the lowest bidder. FreeMarkets indicated to Orleans, though, that if a pattern were developed where Orleans simply used the FreeMarkets system to "leverage" its current suppliers, those companies might have little interest in Orleans auctions in the future.

Ben also was concerned about some bigger issues. What will Orleans do next? Might it begin seeking additional suppliers for his business? Ben knew it would be very difficult to reduce his labor costs, and there would be no way he could compete with the Mexican labor market on that dimension. He could see that one reason things worked so well in Bloomington was his proximity to the Bedford plant supplying him parts. Might difficulty with his working with the Mexican supplier give someone at Orleans or possibly in Mexico the idea of taking over his business and sourcing totally from Mexico?

QUESTIONS

1 How does Ben Lawson's Custom Fabricators, Inc., create value for Orleans?
2 In the past, what has been Ben Lawson's competitive advantage in keeping the Orleans business?
3 Have Orleans' priorities changed?
4 Should Ben change his business model?
5 How should Ben position his company in the value chain?
6 What should Ben do to ensure his company's future success?

CASE: LASIK VISION CORPORATION

At its peak in late 2000, Lasik Vision Corporation had over 30 clinics operating in North America, second only to TLC Laser Eye Centers of Toronto, Ontario, which had 62 clinics. Dr. Hugo Sutton, an eye surgeon and a clinical associate professor at the University of British Columbia, and Michael Henderson founded Lasik Vision in 1997. Since 1978 Sutton had been operating his own eye clinic, initially specializing in cataract surgery. In the intervening years, technological advances such as the excimer laser had transformed refractive surgery (the process of correcting myopia, hyperopia, or astigmatism by altering the contours of the cornea) from a low-tech risky procedure using lathes and sutures into a viable proposition for patients who could spend $5,000. After the surgery, they could discard their glasses or contacts. The efficient new procedure allowed surgeons to eventually reduce the fees for this service, thus making it even more attractive for patients. In 1991, in partnership with two other surgeons, Sutton set up his own refractive surgery clinic. By 1996, the Lasik technique, sparing patients the months of healing that came with older procedures, became the vogue.

It was at that time that Michael Henderson, a business executive and husband to one of Sutton's patients, approached him. Sutton

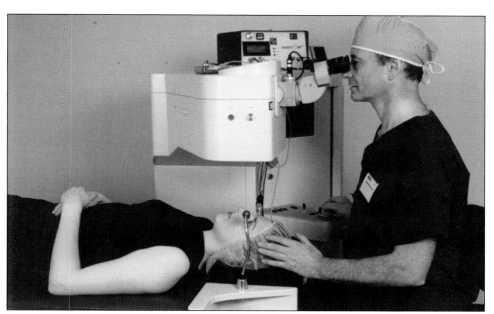

remembers that "Henderson felt that this was a very powerful technology, a technology that he could take much further. He thought that we were rather pedestrian, slow, and old-fashioned." As Sutton was tiring of doing all the surgeries with little help, the proposal sounded very appealing. So in June 1997, Michael Henderson joined Sutton's company, TMX Laser Vision Canada Inc., as vice president.

Soon it was clear that Henderson was on an efficiency drive. He felt that the way to fortune was to reengineer the traditional model of the refractive surgery process. He let a few employees go, increasing the workload for the remainder. To improve efficiency,

he tried not to use expensive equipment. For example, he opposed installing an ultrasound scanner to measure the individual layers of each cornea. This scanner improves the Lasik technique's success ratio. Sutton overruled him on this idea, but many of Henderson's ideas were implemented.

The traditional model involved acquiring patients through optometrist referrals. These optometrists also provided the postoperative care and received a portion of the $4,000 to $5,000 fee. In the reengineered model, the optometrists were cut out of the loop. Also, every step in the care delivery system was standardized. Patients were attracted directly with aggressive advertising and a price well below competitors', initially $2,995. Henderson's vision of mass volume with low margins was launched in February 1998. Traditionally other competitors, such as TLC, ran higher-priced, lower-volume operations (TLC has continued with its model of including the optometrists).

At the same time, Sutton believed in aggressive treatment. According to one of his colleagues, Dr. Dan Reinstein, "Hugo's nature is pioneering. And so by definition, he is more likely to have less conservative, uh, outcomes." Unfortunately, many patients were not properly informed that they were less than ideal candidates for the surgery. In a competitive medical environment, patients emerging from surgery with unsatisfactory results led to lawsuits. As a result, in August 1998, a rare public statement from the B.C. College of Physicians and Surgeons said that Sutton "has agreed to a modification of his practice and he has voluntarily agreed not to perform these surgical procedures on patients in the higher risk categories."

In light of Sutton's troubles, Henderson became president and CEO in April 1999 and began pushing the company into massive expansion and a public offering. This expansion actually started with Toronto in September 1998, followed by Calgary two months later. Henderson continued expansion until eight more sites had been added in September 1999. Henderson insisted that pricing was the key. In TV advertisements, Henderson personally extolled the Lasik Vision message—Why pay more?—standing next to a large graphic proclaiming "$1,475 per eye." By early 1999, the price was dropped to $1,598 for both eyes, but Henderson preferred to see it even lower. One advertisement he initiated proclaimed a cost of $999 with an asterisk listing another $599 in additional fees in fine print. This prompted Advertising Standards Canada to demand a change.

In December 1999, Henderson announced his intention to step up the pace of expansion. Beginning in March 2000, Lasik Vision would start expanding at the rate of one new site per week to open about 20 clinics in the United States. The whole delivery process would be standardized, from the decor of the waiting rooms to the approach in which patients were counseled and corneas were lasered. This was the only way large volumes of patients could be treated with a high level of care. The medical doctors responded to the challenge by devising a hiring and training system that Sutton and the other doctors felt would enable reliable quality across the company.

All this development and expansion took place while trouble was brewing between the doctors and Henderson over financial and managerial improprieties. Henderson was aggressively skimming profits off the company for himself. The last straw came in the spring in 2000 when PriceWaterhouseCoopers, while auditing Lasik's financial statements, grew concerned about Henderson's "unfettered" activities. Thus, in June 2000, Henderson was fired from the company.

Henderson subsequently sued Lasik Vision and Sutton for negligence during an eye surgery performed on his eyes in March 1998, which he claims damaged his vision. Reinstein admits that Henderson had a complication. Henderson's problem, Reinstein insists, is that he does not understand the difference between complication and negligence. "Well, maybe you shouldn't expect him to," he sniffs. "He is not a doctor." Still, you have to hand it to him, says Reinstein, "He is an amazing guy. I did learn a lot about doing business from him."

By 2001 the industry was mired in the ugly price war initiated by Lasik Vision (not to mention an advertising war with many companies spending 10 to 13 percent of revenue on advertising—TLC even signed professional golfer Tiger Woods to a multiyear contract to endorse his surgery at TLC). Lasik's own stock slid from $6 in April 1999 to about a tenth that amount by December 2000. As a result of all this, a consolidation spree ensued.

The January 31, 2001, edition of Toronto's *Globe and Mail* reported that Lasik Vision was acquired by another discounter, Icon Laser Eye Centers. At that time Lasik called itself the Dell Computer of laser vision correction: "We offer a high-quality product direct to customers and we cut distribution costs without compromising patient care." However, TLC disagreed: "Clearly it's the utter failure of both their business and clinical models that has forced them into such dire financial circumstances and their marriage of desperation in the first place." At about the same time, Aris Vision of Los Angeles acquired control of Gimbel Vision International of Calgary.

The August 28, 2001, issue of the the *Toronto Globe* reported that the number 1 and number 2 laser eye surgery companies, TLC Laser Centers and St. Louis–based Laser Vision Centers Inc., were merging. It also mentioned that these two companies had refused to participate in the price war initiated by Lasik Vision, which ironically had resulted in both Lasik Vision and its acquirer, Icon, going bankrupt.

QUESTIONS

1 What was Lasik Vision's competitive priority?
2 Is it an appropriate approach in this industry? What repercussions, actual or perceived, might occur with this priority?
3 Given that a company has chosen this priority, what would it have to do to achieve success?

SOURCE: THIS CASE WAS ADAPTED BY JAYDEEP BALAKRISHNAN FROM AN ARTICLE WRITTEN BY TREVOR COLE IN *ROB MAGAZINE*, JANUARY 2001, AND IS FOR DISCUSSION PURPOSES ONLY. IT IS NOT INTENDED TO ILLUSTRATE THE PROPER OR IMPROPER MANAGEMENT OF A SITUATION.

SELECTED BIBLIOGRAPHY

Chase, R. B., and D. A. Garvin. "The Service Factory." *Harvard Business Review,* July–August 1989, pp. 61–69.

Hayes, R. H., and G. P. Pisano. "Beyond World Class: The New Manufacturing Strategy." *Harvard Business Review,* January–February 1994, pp. 77–86.

Hayes, Robert; Gary Pisano; David Upton; and Steven Wheelwright. *Operations, Strategy, and Technology: Pursuing the Competitive Edge.* New York: John Wiley & Sons, 2004.

Hill, T. J. *Manufacturing Strategy—Text and Cases.* Burr Ridge; IL: Irwin/McGraw-Hill, 2000.

Hopp, W., and M. Spearman. *Factory Physics: A New Approach to Manufacturing Management.* Burr Ridge, IL: Irwin/McGraw-Hill, 2000.

Kaplan, Robert S., and David P. Norton. *The Strategy Focused Organization.* Cambridge, MA: Harvard Business School Press, 2001.

Skinner, W. (ed.). "Special Issue on Manufacturing Strategy." *Production and Operations Management* 5, no. 1 (Spring 1996).

Slack, N., and M. Lewis. *Operations Strategy.* Harlow, England, and New York: Prentice Hall, 2002.

FOOTNOTES

1 C. W. Skinner, "The Focused Factory," *Harvard Business Review,* May–June 1974, pp. 113–22.

2 See M. E. Porter, "What Is Strategy?" *Harvard Business Review,* November–December 1996, p. 68.

3 T. Hill, *Manufacturing Strategy—Text and Cases,* 3rd ed. (Burr Ridge, IL: Irwin/McGraw-Hill, 2000).

4 This material is an edited version of Chapter 3, "Building Strategy Maps," Robert S. Kaplan and David P. Norton, *The Strategy Focused Organization* (Cambridge, MA: Harvard Business School Press, 2001), pp. 69–105.

5 M. Treacy and F. Wiersema, *The Discipline of Market Leaders: Choose Your Customers, Narrow Your Focus, Dominate Your Market* (Reading, MA: Addison-Wesley, 1995), pp. 31–38.

6 Porter, "What Is Strategy?" p. 77.

7 Ibid., pp. 70–71.

8 W. Skinner, "Three Yards and a Cloud of Dust: Industrial Management at Century End," *Production and Operations Management,* Spring 1996, pp. 15–41.

9 Michael E. Porter, "Strategy and the Internet," from *Harvard Business Review on Advances in Strategy* (Cambridge, MA: Harvard Business School Press, 2002), pp. 28–35.

10 This section is adapted from R. H. Hayes and D. M. Upton, "Operations Based Strategy," *California Management Review,* Summer 1998, pp. 11–12.

11 "Wal-Mart Stores, Inc.," Harvard Business School Case #9-794-024.

technical note two
LINEAR PROGRAMMING USING THE EXCEL SOLVER

⭕⭕⭕⭕   The key to profitable operations is making the best use of available resources of people, material, plant and equipment, and money. Today's manager has a powerful mathematical modeling tool available for this purpose with linear programming. In this note, we will show how the use of the Microsoft Excel Solver to solve LP problems opens a whole new world to the innovative manager and provides an invaluable addition to the technical skill set for those who seek careers in consulting. In this technical note, we introduce the use of this tool using a product-planning problem. Here we find the optimal mix of products that have different costs and resource requirements. This problem is certainly relevant to today's competitive market. Truly successful companies provide a mix of products, from standard to high-end luxury models. All these products compete for the use of limited production and other capacity. Maintaining the proper mix of these products over time can significantly bolster earnings and the return on a firm's assets.

We begin with a quick introduction to linear programming and conditions under which the technique is applicable. Then we solve a simple product-mix problem. Other linear programming applications appear throughout the rest of the book. →

INTRODUCTION

⟨⟨⟨○○ **Linear programming** (or simply **LP**) refers to several related mathematical techniques used to allocate limited resources among competing demands in an optimal way. LP is the most popular of the approaches falling under the general heading of mathematical optimization techniques and has been applied to many operations management problems. The following are typical applications:

Linear programming (LP)

Aggregate sales and operations planning: Finding the minimum-cost production schedule. The problem is to develop a three- to six-month plan for meeting expected demand given constraints on expected production capacity and workforce size. Relevant costs considered in the problem include regular and overtime labor rates, hiring and firing, subcontracting, and inventory carrying cost.

Service/manufacturing productivity analysis: Comparing how efficiently different service and manufacturing outlets are using their resources compared to the best-performing unit. This is done using an approach called data envelopment analysis.

Product planning: Finding the optimal product mix where several products have different costs and resource requirements. Examples include finding the optimal blend of chemicals for gasoline, paints, human diets, and animal feeds. Examples of this problem are covered in this technical note.

Product routing: Finding the optimal way to produce a product that must be processed sequentially through several machine centers, with each machine in the center having its own cost and output characteristics.

Vehicle/crew scheduling: Finding the optimal way to use resources such as aircraft, buses, or trucks and their operating crews to provide transportation services to customers and materials to be moved between different locations.

Process control: Minimizing the amount of scrap material generated by cutting steel, leather, or fabric from a roll or sheet of stock material.

Inventory control: Finding the optimal combination of products to stock in a network of warehouses or storage locations.

Distribution scheduling: Finding the optimal shipping schedule for distributing products between factories and warehouses or between warehouses and retailers.

Plant location studies: Finding the optimal location of a new plant by evaluating shipping costs between alternative locations and supply and demand sources.

Material handling: Finding the minimum-cost routings of material handling devices (such as forklift trucks) between departments in a plant, or hauling materials from a supply yard to work sites by trucks, for example. Each truck might have different capacity and performance capabilities.

Linear programming is gaining wide acceptance in many industries due to the availability of detailed operating information and the interest in optimizing processes to reduce cost. Many software vendors offer optimization options to be used with enterprise resource planning systems. Some firms refer to these as *advanced planning option, synchronized planning,* and *process optimization.*

There are five essential conditions in a problem situation for linear programming to pertain. First, there must be *limited resources* (such as a limited number of workers, equipment, finances, and material); otherwise there would be no problem. Second, there must be an *explicit objective* (such as maximize profit or minimize cost). Third, there must be *linearity* (two is twice as much as one; if it takes three hours to make a part, then two parts would take six hours and three parts would take nine hours). Fourth, there must be *homogeneity* (the products produced on a machine are identical, or all the hours available from a worker are equally productive). Fifth, there must be *divisibility:* Normal linear programming assumes products and resources can be subdivided into fractions. If this subdivision is not possible (such as flying half an airplane or hiring one-fourth of a person), a modification of linear programming, called *integer programming,* can be used.

When a single objective is to be maximized (like profit) or minimized (like costs), we can use linear programming. When multiple objectives exist, *goal programming* is used. If a problem is best solved in stages or time frames, *dynamic programming* is employed. Other restrictions on the nature of the problem may require that it be solved by other variations of the technique, such as *nonlinear programming* or *quadratic programming.*

THE LINEAR PROGRAMMING MODEL

Stated formally, the linear programming problem entails an optimizing process in which nonnegative values for a set of decision variables $X_1, X_2, \ldots, X_n$ are selected so as to maximize (or minimize) an objective function in the form

$$\text{Maximize (minimize) } Z = C_1 X_1 + C_2 X_2 + \cdots + C_n X_n$$

subject to resource constraints in the form

$$A_{11}X_1 + A_{12}X_2 + \cdots + A_{1n}X_n \leq B_1$$
$$A_{21}X_1 + A_{22}X_2 + \cdots + A_{2n}X_n \leq B_2$$
$$\vdots$$
$$A_{m1}X_1 + A_{m2}X_2 + \cdots + A_{mn}X_n \leq B_m$$

where C_n, A_{mn}, and B_m are given constants.

Depending on the problem, the constraints also may be stated with equal signs ($=$) or greater-than-or-equal-to signs ($\geq$).

EXAMPLE TN2.1: Puck and Pawn Company

We describe the steps involved in solving a simple linear programming model in the context of a sample problem, that of Puck and Pawn Company, which manufactures hockey sticks and chess sets. Each hockey stick yields an incremental profit of $2, and each chess set, $4. A hockey stick requires 4 hours of processing at machine center A and 2 hours at machine center B. A chess set requires 6 hours at machine center A, 6 hours at machine center B, and 1 hour at machine center C. Machine center A has a maximum of 120 hours of available capacity per day, machine center B has 72 hours, and machine center C has 10 hours.

If the company wishes to maximize profit, how many hockey sticks and chess sets should be produced per day?

SOLUTION

Formulate the problem in mathematical terms. If H is the number of hockey sticks and C is the number of chess sets, to maximize profit the objective function may be stated as

$$\text{Maximize } Z = \$2H + \$4C$$

The maximization will be subject to the following constraints:

$$4H + 6C \leq 120 \quad \text{(machine center A constraint)}$$
$$2H + 6C \leq 72 \quad \text{(machine center B constraint)}$$
$$1C \leq 10 \quad \text{(machine center C constraint)}$$
$$H, C \geq 0 \; \bullet$$

This formulation satisfies the five requirements for standard LP stated in the first section of this note:

1. There are limited resources (a finite number of hours available at each machine center).
2. There is an explicit objective function (we know what each variable is worth and what the goal is in solving the problem).
3. The equations are linear (no exponents or cross-products).
4. The resources are homogeneous (everything is in one unit of measure, machine hours).
5. The decision variables are divisible and nonnegative (we can make a fractional part of a hockey stick or chess set; however, if this were deemed undesirable, we would have to use integer programming).

GRAPHICAL LINEAR PROGRAMMING

Though limited in application to problems involving two decision variables (or three variables for three-dimensional graphing), **graphical linear programming** provides a quick insight into the nature of linear programming. We describe the steps involved in the graphical method in the context of Puck and Pawn Company. The following steps illustrate the graphical approach:

Graphical linear programming

1. **Formulate the problem in mathematical terms.** The equations for the problem are given above.

2. **Plot constraint equations.** The constraint equations are easily plotted by letting one variable equal zero and solving for the axis intercept of the other. (The inequality portions of the restrictions are disregarded for this step.) For the machine center A constraint equation, when $H = 0$, $C = 20$, and when $C = 0$, $H = 30$. For the machine center B constraint equation, when $H = 0$, $C = 12$, and when $C = 0$, $H = 36$. For the machine center C constraint equation, $C = 10$ for all values of H. These lines are graphed in Exhibit TN2.1.

Graph of Hockey Stick and Chess Set Problem

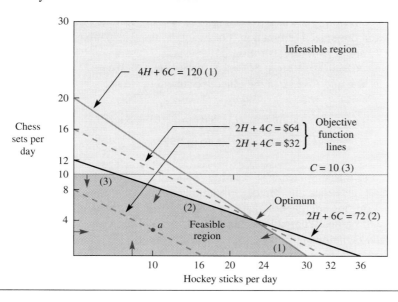

3.   **Determine the area of feasibility.**   The direction of inequality signs in each constraint determines the area where a feasible solution is found. In this case, all inequalities are of the less-than-or-equal-to variety, which means it would be impossible to produce any combination of products that would lie to the right of any constraint line on the graph. The region of feasible solutions is unshaded on the graph and forms a convex polygon. A convex polygon exists when a line drawn between any two points in the polygon stays within the boundaries of that polygon. If this condition of convexity does not exist, the problem is either incorrectly set up or is not amenable to linear programming.

4.   **Plot the objective function.**   The objective function may be plotted by assuming some arbitrary total profit figure and then solving for the axis coordinates, as was done for the constraint equations. Other terms for the objective function when used in this context are the *iso-profit* or *equal contribution line,* because it shows all possible production combinations for any given profit figure. For example, from the dotted line closest to the origin on the graph, we can determine all possible combinations of hockey sticks and chess sets that yield $32 by picking a point on the line and reading the number of each product that can be made at that point. The combination yielding $32 at point *a* would be 10 hockey sticks and three chess sets. This can be verified by substituting $H = 10$ and $C = 3$ in the objective function:

$$\$2(10) + \$4(3) = \$20 + \$12 = \$32$$

H	C	EXPLANATION
0	$120/6 = 20$	Intersection of Constraint (1) and C axis
$120/4 = 30$	0	Intersection of Constraint (1) and H axis
0	$72/6 = 12$	Intersection of Constraint (2) and C axis
$72/2 = 36$	0	Intersection of Constraint (2) and H axis
0	10	Intersection of Constraint (3) and C axis
0	$32/4 = 8$	Intersection of $32 iso-point line (objective function) and C axis
$32/2 = 16$	0	Intersection of $32 iso-profit line and H axis
0	$64/4 = 16$	Intersection of $64 iso-profit line and C axis
$64/2 = 32$	0	Intersection of $64 iso-profit line and H axis

5.   **Find the optimum point.**   It can be shown mathematically that the optimal combination of decision variables is always found at an extreme point (corner point) of the convex polygon. In Exhibit TN2.1 there are four corner points (excluding the origin), and we can determine which one is the optimum by either of two approaches. The first approach is to find the values of the various corner solutions algebraically. This entails simultaneously solving the equations of various pairs of intersecting lines and substituting the quantities of the resultant variables in the objective function. For example, the calculations for the intersection of $2H + 6C = 72$ and $C = 10$ are as follows:

Substituting $C = 10$ in $2H + 6C = 72$ gives $2H + 6(10) = 72$, $2H = 12$, or $H = 6$. Substituting $H = 6$ and $C = 10$ in the objective function, we get

$$\text{Profit} = \$2H + \$4C = \$2(6) + \$4(10)$$
$$= \$12 + \$40 = \$52$$

A variation of this approach is to read the *H* and *C* quantities directly from the graph and substitute these quantities into the objective function, as shown in the previous calculation. The drawback in this approach is that in problems with a large number of constraint equations, there will be many possible points to evaluate, and the procedure of testing each one mathematically is inefficient.

The second and generally preferred approach entails using the objective function or iso-profit line directly to find the optimum point. The procedure involves simply drawing a straight line *parallel* to any arbitrarily selected initial iso-profit line so the iso-profit line is farthest from the origin of the graph. (In cost minimization problems, the objective would be to draw the line through the point closest to the origin.) In Exhibit TN2.1, the dashed line labeled $2H + $4C = $64 intersects the most extreme point. Note that the initial arbitrarily selected iso-profit line is necessary to display the slope of the objective function for the particular problem.[1] This is important since a different objective function (try profit = 3H + 3C) might indicate that some other point is farthest from the origin. Given that $2H + $4C = $64 is optimal, the amount of each variable to produce can be read from the graph: 24 hockey sticks and four chess sets. No other combination of the products yields a greater profit.

LINEAR PROGRAMMING USING MICROSOFT EXCEL

Spreadsheets can be used to solve linear programming problems. Microsoft Excel has an optimization tool called *Solver* that we will demonstrate by solving the hockey stick and chess problem. We invoke the Solver from the Tools menu. A dialogue box requests information required by the program. The following example describes how our sample problem can be solved using Excel.

If the Solver option does not appear in your Tools menu, click on Add-Ins, select the Solver Add-In, and then click OK. Solver should then be available directly from the Tools menu for future use.

In the following example, we work in a step-by-step manner, setting up a spreadsheet and then solving our Puck and Pawn Company problem. Our basic strategy is to first define the problem within the spreadsheet. Following this, we invoke the Solver and feed it required information. Finally, we execute the Solver and interpret results from the reports provided by the program.

Step 1: Define Changing Cells A convenient starting point is to identify cells to be used for the decision variables in the problem. These are H and C, the number of hockey sticks and number of chess sets to produce. Excel refers to these cells as changing cells in Solver. Referring to our Excel screen (Exhibit TN2.2), we have designated B4 as the location for the number of hockey sticks to produce and C4 for the number of chess sets. Note that we have set these cells equal to 2 initially. We could set these cells to anything, but it is good to use some value other than zero to help verify that our calculations are correct.

Step 2: Calculate Total Profit (or Cost) This is our objective function and is calculated by multiplying profit associated with each product by the number of units produced. We have placed the profits in cells B5 and C5 ($2 and $4), so the profit is calculated by the following equation: B4*B5 + C4*C5, which is calculated in cell D5. Solver refers to this as the Target Cell, and it corresponds to the objective function for a problem.

Step 3: Set Up Resource Usage Our resources are machine centers A, B, and C as defined in the original problem. We have set up three rows (9, 10, and 11) in our spreadsheet, one for each resource constraint. For machine center A, 4 hours of processing time are used for each hockey stick produced (cell B9) and 6 hours for each chess set (cell C9). For a particular solution, the total amount of the machine center A resource used is calculated in D9 (B9*B4 + C9*C4). We have indicated in cell E9 that we want this value to be less than the 120-hour capacity of machine center A, which is entered in F9. Resource usage for machine centers B and C are set up in the exact same manner in rows 10 and 11.

Microsoft Excel Screen for Puck and Pawn Company

Microsoft Excel - Solver_LP.xls

File Edit View Insert Format Tools Data Window Help

D5   *fx* =+B4*B5+C4*C5

	A	B	C	D	E	F
1						
2						
3		Hockey Sticks	Chess Sets	Total		
4	Changing Cells	2	2			
5	Profit	$2	$4	$12		
6						
7				Resources		
8		Hockey Sticks	Chess Sets	Used		Capacity
9	Machine A	4	6	20	<=	120
10	Machine B	2	6	16	<=	72
11	Machine C	0	1	2	<=	10
12						
13						
14						

Hockey Stocks and Chess Sets

Ready   NUM

Step 4: Set Up Solver   Go to the Tools menu and select the Solver option.

Solver Parameters

Set Target Cell: $D$5

Equal To: ⦿ Max   ○ Min   ○ Value of: 0

By Changing Cells:

$B$4:$C$4   Guess

Subject to the Constraints:

$D$10 <= $F$10
$D$11 <= $F$11
$D$9 <= $F$9

Add
Change
Delete

Solve
Close
Options
Reset All
Help

1. Set Target Cell: is set to the location where the value that we want to optimize is cal-culated. This is the profit calculated in D5 in our spreadsheet.

2. Equal To: is set to Max since the goal is to maximize profit.

3. By Changing Cells: are the cells that Solver can change to maximize profit. Cells B4 through C4 are the changing cells in our problem.

4. Subject to the Constraints: correspond to our machine center capacity. Here we click on Add and indicate that the total used for a resource is less than or equal to the capacity avail-able. A sample for machine center A follows. Click OK after each constraint is specified.

Add Constraint

Cell Reference: Constraint:

$D$9   <=   =$F$9

OK   Cancel   Add   Help

5.   Clicking on Options allows us to tell Solver what type of problem we want it to solve and how we want it solved. Solver has numerous options, but we will need to use only a few. The screen is shown below.

Most of the options relate to how Solver attempts to solve nonlinear problems. These can be very difficult to solve and optimal solutions difficult to find. Luckily our problem is a linear problem. We know this since our constraints and our objective function are all calculated using linear equations. Click on Assume Linear Model to tell Solver that we want to use the linear programming option for solving the problem. In addition, we know our changing cells (decision variables) must be numbers that are greater than or equal to zero since it makes no sense to make a negative number of hockey sticks or chess sets. We indicate this by selecting Assume Non-Negative as an option. We are now ready to actually solve the problem. Click OK to return to the Solver Parameters box.

Step 5: Solve the Problem   Click Solve. We immediately get a Solver Results acknowledgment like that show below.

Solver acknowledges that a solution was found that appears to be optimal. On the right side of this box are options for three reports: an Answer Report, a Sensitivity Report, and a Limits Report. Click on each report to have Solver provide these. After highlighting the reports, click OK to exit back to the spreadsheet. Three new tabs have been created that correspond to these reports.

exhibit TN2.3   Excel Solver Answer and Sensitivity Reports

Answer Report

TARGET CELL (MAX)

CELL	NAME	ORIGINAL VALUE	FINAL VALUE
$D$5	Profit Total	$12	$64

ADJUSTABLE CELLS

CELL	NAME	ORIGINAL VALUE	FINAL VALUE
$B$4	Changing Cells Hockey Sticks	2	24
$C$4	Changing Cells Chess Sets	2	4

CONSTRAINTS

CELL	NAME	CELL VALUE	FORMULA	STATUS	SLACK
$D$11	Machine C Used	4	$D$11<=$F$11	Not Binding	6
$D$10	Machine B Used	72	$D$10<=$F$10	Binding	0
$D$9	Machine A Used	120	$D$9<=$F$9	Binding	0

Sensitivity Report

ADJUSTABLE CELLS

CELL	NAME	FINAL VALUE	REDUCED COST	OBJECTIVE COEFFICIENT	ALLOWABLE INCREASE	ALLOWABLE DECREASE
$B$4	Changing Cells Hockey Sticks	24	0	2	0.666666667	0.666666667
$C$4	Changing Cells Chess Sets	4	0	4	2	1

CONSTRAINTS

CELL	NAME	FINAL VALUE	SHADOW PRICE	CONSTRAINT R.H. SIDE	ALLOWABLE INCREASE	ALLOWABLE DECREASE
$D$11	Machine C Used	4	0	10	1E+30	6
$D$10	Machine B Used	72	0.333333333	72	18	12
$D$9	Machine A Used	120	0.333333333	120	24	36

The most interesting reports for our problem are the Answer Report and the Sensitivity Report, both of which are shown in Exhibit TN2.3. The Answer Report shows the final answers for the total profit ($64) and the amounts produced (24 hockey sticks and 4 chess sets). In the constraints section of the Answer Report, the status of each resource is given. All of machine A and machine B are used, and there are six units of slack for machine C.

The Sensitivity Report is divided into two parts. The first part, titled "Adjustable Cells," corresponds to objective function coefficients. The profit per unit for the hockey sticks can be either up or down $.67 (between $2.67 and $1.33) without having an impact on the solution. Similarly, the profit of the chess sets could be between $6 and $3 without changing the solution. In the case of machine A, the right-hand side could increase to 144 (120 + 24) or decrease to 84 with a resulting $.33 increase or decrease per unit in the objective function. The right-hand side of machine B can increase to 90 units or decrease to 60 units with the same $.33 change for each unit in the objective function. For machine C, the right-hand side could increase to infinity (1E+30 is scientific notation for a very large number) or decrease to 4 units with no change in the objective function.

GENETIC SOLVER OPTION

⚬⚬⚬⚬ On the DVD-ROM that is packaged with the book, we have included a great product from Frontline Systems called the *Premium Solver.* The package installs on top of Microsoft's Solver and adds many new features to the Microsoft product. All of the old Solver capabilities are retained, but in Premium Solver mode new capabilities include

- A new evolutionary solver for doing genetic searches. This can be very useful for solving problems that are not linear.
- A linearity report for finding where the calculations in a spreadsheet violate the linearity conditions needed to use a standard linear programming algorithm.
- A feasibility report to help identify why it is not possible to find a feasible solution to your problem.
- A population report to help explain solutions generated with the new genetic search capability.

If you are interested in the latest tricks for solving problems with spreadsheets, install the Premium Solver.

KEY TERMS

Linear programming (LP) Refers to several related mathematical techniques used to allocate limited resources among competing demands in an optimal way.

Graphical linear programming Provides a quick insight into the nature of linear programming.

SOLVED PROBLEMS

SOLVED PROBLEM 1

A furniture company produces three products: end tables, sofas, and chairs. These products are processed in five departments: the saw lumber, fabric cutting, sanding, staining, and assembly departments. End tables and chairs are produced from raw lumber only, and the sofas require lumber and fabric. Glue and thread are plentiful and represent a relatively insignificant cost that is included in operating expense. The specific requirements for each product are as follows:

RESOURCE OR ACTIVITY (QUANTITY AVAILABLE PER MONTH)	REQUIRED PER END TABLE	REQUIRED PER SOFA	REQUIRED PER CHAIR
Lumber (4,300 board feet)	10 board feet @ $10/foot = $100/table	7.5 board feet @ $10/foot = $75	4 board feet @ $10/foot = $40
Fabric (2,500 yards)	None	10 yards @ $17.50/yard = $175	None
Saw lumber (280 hours)	30 minutes	24 minutes	30 minutes
Cut fabric (140 hours)	None	24 minutes	None
Sand (280 hours)	30 minutes	6 minutes	30 minutes
Stain (140 hours)	24 minutes	12 minutes	24 minutes
Assemble (700 hours)	60 minutes	90 minutes	30 minutes

The company's direct labor expenses are $75,000 per month for the 1,540 hours of labor, at $48.70 per hour. Based on current demand, the firm can sell 300 end tables, 180 sofas, and 400 chairs per month. Sales prices are $400 for end tables, $750 for sofas, and $240 for chairs. Assume that labor cost is fixed and the firm does not plan to hire or fire any employees over the next month.

a. What is the most limiting resource to the furniture company?

b. Determine the product mix needed to maximize profit at the furniture company. What is the optimal number of end tables, sofas, and chairs to produce each month?

Solution

Define X_1 as the number of end tables, X_2 as the number of sofas, and X_3 as the number of chairs to produce each month. Profit is calculated as the revenue for each item minus the cost of materials (lumber and fabric), minus the cost of labor. Since labor is fixed, we subtract this out as a total sum. Mathematically we have $(400 - 100) + (750 - 75 - 175) + (240 - 40) - 75{,}000$. Profit is calculated as follows:

$$\text{Profit} = 400X_1 + 750X_2 + 240X_3 - 75{,}000$$

Constraints are the following:

Lumber:	$10X_1 + 7.5X_2 + 4X_3 \le 4{,}350$
Fabric:	$10X_2 \le 2{,}500$
Saw:	$.5X_1 + .4X_2 + .5X_3 \le 280$
Cut:	$.4X_2 \le 140$
Sand:	$.5X_1 + .1X_2 + .5X_3 \le 280$
Stain:	$.4X_1 + .2X_2 + .4X_3 \le 140$
Assemble:	$1X_1 + 1.5X_2 + .5X_3 \le 700$
Demand:	
Table:	$X_1 \le 300$
Sofa:	$X_2 \le 180$
Chair:	$X_3 \le 400$

Step 1: Define changing cells   These are B3, C3, and D3. Note that these cells have been set equal to zero.

Step 2: Calculate total profit   This is E4 (this is equal to B3 times the $300 revenue associated with each end table, plus C3 times the $500 revenue for each sofa, plus D3 times the $200 revenue associated with each chair). Note the $75,000 fixed expense that has been subtracted from revenue to calculate profit.

Step 3: Set up resource usage   In cells E6 through E15, the usage of each resource is calculated by multiplying B3, C3, and D3 by the amount needed for each item and summing the product (for example, E6 = B3*B6 + C3*C6 + D3*D6). The limits on these constraints are entered in cells F6 to F15.

Step 4: Set up Solver   Go to Tools and select the Solver option.

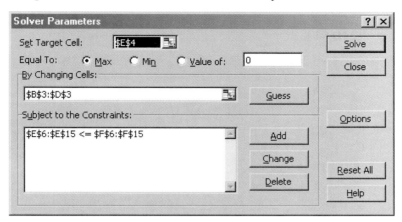

a. Set Target Cell: is set to the location where the value that we want to optimize is calculated. This is the profit calculated in E4 in this spreadsheet.

b. Equal To: is set to Max since the goal is to maximize profit.

c. By Changing Cells: are the cells that Solver can change to maximize profit (cells B3 through D3 in this problem).

d. Subject to the Constraints: is where a constraint set is added; we indicate that the range E6 to E15 must be less than or equal to F6 to F15.

Step 5: Set Options   There are many options here, but for our purposes we just need to indicate Assume Linear Model and Assume Non-Negative. Assume Linear Model means all of our formulas are simple linear equations. Assume Non-Negative indicates that changing cells must be greater than or equal to zero. Click OK and we are ready to solve our problem.

Step 6: Solve the Problem   Click Solve. We can see the solution and two special reports by highlighting items on the Solver Results acknowledgment that is displayed after a solution is

found. Note that in the following report, Solver indicates that it has found a solution and all constraints and optimality conditions are satisfied. In the Reports box on the right, the Answer, Sensitivity, and Limits options have been highlighted, indicating that we would like to see these items. After highlighting the reports, click OK to exit back to the spreadsheet.

Note that three new tabs have been created: an Answer Report, a Sensitivity Report, and a Limits Report. The Answer Report indicates in the Target Cell section that the profit associated with this solution is $93,000 (we started at −$75,000). From the Target Cell section, we should make 260 end tables, 180 sofas, and no chairs. From the Constraints section, notice that the only constraints limiting profit are the staining capacity and the demand for sofas. We can see this from the column indicating whether a constraint is binding or nonbinding. Nonbinding constraints have slack, as indicated in the last column.

TARGET CELL (MAX)

CELL	NAME	ORIGINAL VALUE	FINAL VALUE
$E$4	Profit Total	−$75,000	$93,000

ADJUSTABLE CELLS

CELL	NAME	ORIGINAL VALUE	FINAL VALUE
$B$3	Changing cells End Tables	0	260
$C$3	Changing cells Sofas	0	180
$D$3	Changing cells Chairs	0	0

CONSTRAINTS

CELL	NAME	CELL VALUE	FORMULA	STATUS	SLACK
$E$6	Lumber Total	3950	$E$6<=$F$6	Not Binding	400
$E$7	Fabric Total	1800	$E$7<=$F$7	Not Binding	700
$E$8	Saw Total	202	$E$8<=$F$8	Not Binding	78
$E$9	Cut fabric Total	72	$E$9<=$F$9	Not Binding	68
$E$10	Sand Total	148	$E$10<=$F$10	Not Binding	132
$E$11	Stain Total	140	$E$11<=$F$11	Binding	0
$E$12	Assemble Total	530	$E$12<=$F$12	Not Binding	170
$E$13	Table Demand Total	260	$E$13<=$F$13	Not Binding	40
$E$14	Sofa Demand Total	180	$E$14<=$F$14	Binding	0
$E$15	Chair Demand Total	0	$E$15<=$F$15	Not Binding	400

Of course, we may not be too happy with this solution since we are not meeting all the demand for tables, and it may not be wise to totally discontinue the manufacturing of chairs.

The Sensitivity Report (shown below) gives additional insight into the solution. The Adjustable Cells section of this report shows the final value for each cell and the reduced cost. The reduced cost indicates how much the target cell value would change if a cell that was currently set to zero were brought into the solution. Since the end tables (B3) and sofas (C3) are in the current solution, their reduced cost is zero. For each chair (D3) that we make, our target cell would be reduced $100 (just round these numbers for interpretation purposes). The final three columns in the adjustable cells section of the report are the Objective Coefficient from the original spreadsheet and columns titled

Allowable Increase and Allowable Decrease. Allowable Increase and Decrease show by how much the value of the corresponding coefficient could change so there would not be a change in the changing cell values (of course, the target cell value would change). For example, revenue for each end table could be as high as $1,000 ($300 + $700) or as low as $200 ($300 − $100), and we would still want to produce 260 end tables. Keep in mind that these values assume nothing else is changing in the problem. For the allowable increase value for sofas, note the value 1E+30. This is a very large number, essentially infinity, represented in scientific notation.

ADJUSTABLE CELLS

CELL	NAME	FINAL VALUE	REDUCED COST	OBJECTIVE COEFFICIENT	ALLOWABLE INCREASE	ALLOWABLE DECREASE
$B$3	Changing cells End Tables	260	0	299.9999997	700.0000012	100.0000004
$C$3	Changing cells Sofas	180	0	500.0000005	1E+30	350.0000006
$D$3	Changing cells Chairs	0	−100.0000004	199.9999993	100.0000004	1E+30

CONSTRAINTS

CELL	NAME	FINAL VALUE	SHADOW PRICE	CONSTRAINT R.H. SIDE	ALLOWABLE INCREASE	ALLOWABLE DECREASE
$E$6	Lumber Total	3950	0	4350	1E+30	400
$E$7	Fabric Total	1800	0	2500	1E+30	700
$E$8	Saw Total	202	0	280	1E+30	78
$E$9	Cut fabric Total	72	0	140	1E+30	68
$E$10	Sand Total	148	0	280	1E+30	132
$E$11	Stain Total	140	749.9999992	140	16	104
$E$12	Assemble Total	530	0	700	1E+30	170
$E$13	Table Demand Total	260	0	300	1E+30	40
$E$14	Sofa Demand Total	180	350.0000006	180	70	80
$E$15	Chair Demand Total	0	0	400	1E+30	400

For the Constraints section of the report, the actual final usage of each resource is given in Final Value. The Shadow Price is the value to our target cell for each unit increase in the resource. If we could increase staining capacity, it would be worth $750 per hour. The Constraint Right-Hand Side is the current limit on the resource. Allowable Increase is the amount the resource could be increased while the shadow price is still valid. Another 16 hours' work of staining capacity could be added with a value of $750 per hour. Similarly, the Allowable Decrease column shows the amount the resource could be reduced without changing the shadow price. There is some valuable information available in this report.

The Limits Report provides additional information about our solution.

CELL	TARGET NAME	VALUE
$E$4	Profit Total	$93,000

CELL	ADJUSTABLE NAME	VALUE	LOWER LIMIT	TARGET RESULT	UPPER LIMIT	TARGET RESULT
$B$3	Changing cells End Tables	260	0	15000	260.0000002	93000
$C$3	Changing cells Sofas	180	0	3000	180	93000
$D$3	Changing cells Chairs	0	0	93000	0	93000

Total profit for the current solution is $93,000. Current value for B3 (end tables) is 260 units. If this were reduced to 0 units, profit would be reduced to $15,000. At an upper limit of 260, profit is $93,000 (the current solution). Similarly, for C3 (sofas), if this were reduced to 0, profit would be reduced to $3,000. At an upper limit of 180, profit is $93,000. For D3 (chairs), if this were reduced to 0, profit is $93,000 (current solution), and in this case the upper limit on chairs is also 0 units.

Acceptable answers to the questions are as follows:

a. *What is the most limiting resource to the furniture company?*

In terms of our production resources, staining capacity is really hurting profit at this time. We could use another 16 hours of capacity.

b. *Determine the product mix needed to maximize profit at the furniture company.*

The product mix would be to make 260 end tables, 180 sofas, and no chairs.

Of course, we have only scratched the surface with this solution. We could actually experiment with increasing staining capacity. This would give insight into the next most limiting resource. We also could run scenarios where we are required to produce a minimum number of each product, which is probably a more realistic scenario. This could help us determine how we could possibly reallocate the use of labor in our shop.

SOLVED PROBLEM 2

It is 2:00 on Friday afternoon and Joe Bob the head chef (grill cook) at Bruce's Diner is trying to decide the best way to allocate the available raw material to the four Friday night specials. The decision has to be made in the early afternoon because three of the items must be started now (Sloppy Joes, Tacos, and Chili). The Table below contains the information on the food in inventory and the amounts required for each item.

FOOD	CHEESE BURGER	SLOPPY JOES	TACO	CHILI	AVAILABLE
Ground Beef (lbs.)	0.3	0.25	0.25	0.4	100 lbs.
Cheese (lbs.)	0.1	0	0.3	0.2	50 lbs.
Beans (lbs.)	0	0	0.2	0.3	50 lbs.
Lettuce (lbs.)	0.1	0	0.2	0	15 lbs.
Tomato (lbs.)	0.1	0.3	0.2	0.2	50 lbs.
Buns	1	1	0	0	80 buns
Taco Shells	0	0	1	0	80 shells

There is one other fact relevant to Joe Bob's decision. That is the estimated market demand and selling price.

	CHEESE BURGER	SLOPPY JOES	TACO	CHILI
Demand	75	60	100	55
Selling Price	$2.25	$2.00	$1.75	$2.50

Joe Bob wants to maximize revenue since he has already purchased all the materials that are sitting in the cooler.

Required:

1   What is the best mix of the Friday night specials to maximize Joe Bob's revenue?
2   If a supplier offered to provide a rush order of buns at $1.00 a bun, is it worth the money?

Solution

Define X_1 as the number of Cheese Burgers, X_2 as the number of Sloppy Joes, X_3 as the number of Tacos, and X_4 as the number of bowls of chili made for the Friday night specials.

$$\text{Revenue} = \$2.25\, X_1 + \$2.00\, X_2 + \$1.75\, X_3 + \$2.50\, X_4$$

Constraints are the following:

Ground Beef:	$0.30\, X_1 + 0.25\, X_2 + 0.25\, X_3 + 0.40\, X_4 \leq 100$
Cheese:	$0.10\, X_1 + 0.30\, X_3 + 0.20\, X_4 \leq 50$
Beans:	$0.20\, X_3 + 0.30\, X_4 \leq 50$
Lettuce:	$0.10\, X_1 + 0.20\, X_3 \leq 15$
Tomato:	$0.10\, X_1 + 0.30\, X_2 + 0.20\, X_3 + 0.20\, X_4 \leq 50$
Buns:	$X_1 + X_2 \leq 80$
Taco Shells:	$X_3 \leq 80$

Demand

Cheese Burger	$X_1 \leq 75$
Sloppy Joes	$X_2 \leq 603$
Taco	$X_3 \leq 100$
Chili	$X_4 \leq 55$

Step 1: Define the changing cells—These are B3, C3, D3, and E3. Note the values in the changing cell are set to 10 each so the formulas can be checked.

Step 2: Calculate total revenue—This is in cell F7 (this is equal to B3 times the $2.25 for each cheese burger, plus C3 times the $2.00 for a Sloppy Joe, plus D3 times the $1.75 for each taco, plus E3 times the $2.50 for each bowl of chili, the SUMPRODUCT function in excel was used to make this calculation faster). Note that the current value is $85 which is a result of selling 10 of each item.

Step 3: Setup the usage of the food—In cells F11 to F17 the usage of each food is calculated by multiplying the changing cells row times the per item use in the table and then summing the result. The limits on each of these food types are given in H11 through H17.

Step 4: Set up Solver and select the Solver option.

a. Set Target Cell to the location where the value that we want to optimize is calculated. The revenue is calculated in F7 in this spreadsheet.
b. Equal to: is set to Max since the goal is to maximize revenue.
c. By Changing Cells: are the cells that tell how many of each special to produce.
d. Subject to the Constraints: here we added two separate constraints, one for demand and one for the usage of food.

Step 5: Set Options: clicking on "Options" we wil leave all the settings as the default values and we only need to make sure of two changes: (1) we need to make sure that there is a check under the Assume Linear Model option and (2) we must check the Assume Non-Negative option. These two options make sure that Solver knows that this is a linear programming problem and that all changing cells should be non-negative. Click OK to return to the Solver Parameters screen.

Step 6: Solve the Problem—Click Solve. We will get a solver results box. Make sure it says that it has the following statement; "Solver found a solution. All constraints and optimality conditions are satisfied."

On the right-hand side of the box there is an option for three reports: Answer, Sensitivity, and Limit. Click on all three reports and then click OK, and this will exit you back to the spreadsheet, but you will have three new worksheets on your work book.

The answer report indicates that the target cell has a final solution of $416.50 and started at $85. From the adjustable cells area we can see that we should make 20 cheese burgers, 60 Sloppy Joes, 65 tacos and 55 bowls of chili. This answers the first requirement from the problem of what the mix of Friday night specials should be.

TARGET CELL (MAX)

CELL	NAME	ORIGINAL VALUE	FINAL VALUE
$F$7	Revenue Total	$85.00	$416.25

ADJUSTABLE CELLS

CELL	NAME	ORIGINAL VALUE	FINAL VALUE
$B$3	Changing Cells Cheese Burger	10	20
$C$3	Changing Cells Sloppy Joes	10	60
$D$3	Changing Cells Taco	10	65
$E$3	Changing Cells Chili	10	55

CONSTRAINTS

CELL	NAME	CELL VALUE	FORMULA	STATUS	SLACK
$F$11	Ground Beef (lbs.) Total	59.25	$F$11<=$H$11	Not Binding	40.75
$F$12	Cheese (lbs.) Total	32.50	$F$12<=$H$12	Not Binding	17.5
$F$13	Beans (lbs.) Total	29.50	$F$13<=$H$13	Not Binding	20.5
$F$14	Lettuce (lbs.) Total	15.00	$F$14<=$H$14	Binding	0
$F$15	Tomato (lbs.) Total	44.00	$F$15<=$H$15	Not Binding	6
$F$16	Buns Total	80.00	$F$16<=$H$16	Binding	0
$F$17	Taco Shells Total	65.00	$F$17<=$H$17	Not Binding	15
$B$3	Changing Cells Cheese Burger	20	$B$3<=$B$5	Not Binding	55
$C$3	Changing Cells Sloppy Joes	60	$C$3<=$C$5	Binding	0
$D$3	Changing Cells Taco	65	$D$3<=$D$5	Not Binding	35
$E$3	Changing Cells Chili	55	$E$3<=$E$5	Binding	0

The second required answer was whether it is worth it to pay a rush supplier $1 a bun for additional buns. The answer report shows us that the buns constraint was binding. This means that if we had more buns we could make more money. However, the answer report does not tell us whether a rush order of buns at $1 a bun is worthwhile. In order to answer that question we have to look at the sensitivity report.

ADJUSTABLE CELLS

CELL	NAME	FINAL VALUE	REDUCED COST	OBJECTIVE COEFFICIENT	ALLOWABLE INCREASE	ALLOWABLE DECREASE
$B$3	Changing Cells Cheese Burger	20	0	2.25	0.625	1.375
$C$3	Changing Cells Sloppy Joes	60	0.625	2	1E+30	0.625
$D$3	Changing Cells Taco	65	0	1.75	2.75	1.25
$E$3	Changing Cells Chili	55	2.5	2.5	1E+30	2.5

CONSTRAINTS

CELL	NAME	FINAL VALUE	SHADOW PRICE	CONSTRAINT R.H. SIDE	ALLOWABLE INCREASE	ALLOWABLE DECREASE
$F$11	Ground Beef (lbs.) Total	59.25	0.00	100	1E+30	40.75
$F$12	Cheese (lbs.) Total	32.50	0.00	50	1E+30	17.5
$F$13	Beans (lbs.) Total	29.50	0.00	50	1E+30	20.5
$F$14	Lettuce (lbs.) Total	15.00	8.75	15	3	13
$F$15	Tomato (lbs.) Total	44.00	0.00	50	1E+30	6
$F$16	Buns Total	80.00	1.38	80	55	20
$F$17	Taco Shells Total	65.00	0.00	80	1E+30	15

We have highlighted the buns row to answer the question. We can see that buns have a shadow price of $1.38. This shadow price means that each additional bun will generate $1.38 of profit. We can also see that other foods such as ground beef have a shadow price of $0. The items with a shadow price add nothing to profit since there we are currently not using all that we have now. The other important piece of information that we have on the buns is that they are only worth $1.38 up until the next 55 buns and that is why the allowable increase is 55. We can also see that a pound of lettuce is worth $8.75. It might be wise to also look for a rush supplier of lettuce so we can increase our profit on Friday nights.

Acceptable answers to the questions are as follows:

1   *What is the best mix of the Friday night specials to maximize Joe Bob's revenue?*
    20 cheese burgers, 60 Sloppy Joes, 65 tacos and 55 bowls of chili.
2   *If a supplier offered to provide a rush order of buns at $1.00 a bun is it worth the money?*
    Yes, each additional bun brings in $1.38 so if they cost us $1 then we will net $.38 per bun.
    However, this is only true up to 55 addtional buns.

PROBLEMS

1   Solve the following problem with Excel Solver:

$$\text{Maximize } Z = 3X + Y.$$
$$12X + 14Y \leq 85$$
$$3X + 2Y \leq 18$$
$$Y \leq 4$$

2   Solve the following problem with Excel Solver:

$$\text{Minimize } Z = 2A + 4B.$$
$$4A + 6B \geq 120$$
$$2A + 6B \geq 72$$
$$B \geq 10$$

3   A manufacturing firm has discontinued production of a certain unprofitable product line. Considerable excess production capacity was created as a result. Management is considering devoting this excess capacity to one or more of three products: X_1, X_2, and X_3.

Machine hours required per unit are

		PRODUCT	
MACHINE TYPE	X_1	X_2	X_3
Milling machine	8	2	3
Lathe	4	3	0
Grinder	2	0	1

The available time in machine hours per week is

	MACHINE HOURS PER WEEK
Milling machines	800
Lathes	480
Grinders	320

The salespeople estimate they can sell all the units of X_1 and X_2 that can be made. But the sales potential of X_3 is 80 units per week maximum.

Unit profits for the three products are

	UNIT PROFITS
X_1	$20
X_2	6
X_3	8

a. Set up the equations that can be solved to maximize the profit per week.
b. Solve these equations using the Excel Solver.
c. What is the optimal solution? How many of each product should be made, and what should the resultant profit be?
d. What is this situation with respect to the machine groups? Would they work at capacity, or would there be unused available time? Will X_3 be at maximum sales capacity?
e. Suppose that an additional 200 hours per week can be obtained from the milling machines by working overtime. The incremental cost would be $1.50 per hour. Would you recommend doing this? Explain how you arrived at your answer.

4   A diet is being prepared for the University of Arizona dorms. The objective is to feed the students at the least cost, but the diet must have between 1,800 and 3,600 calories. No more than 1,400 calories can be starch, and no fewer than 400 can be protein. The varied diet is to be made of two foods: A and B. Food A costs $0.75 per pound and contains 600 calories, 400 of which are protein and 200 starch. No more than two pounds of food A can be used per resident. Food B costs $0.15 per pound and contains 900 calories, of which 700 are starch, 100 are protein, and 100 are fat.

a. Write the equations representing this information.
b. Solve the problem graphically for the amounts of each food that should be used.

5   Do Problem 4 with the added constraint that not more than 150 calories shall be fat and that the price of food has escalated to $1.75 per pound for food A and $2.50 per pound for food B.

6   Logan Manufacturing wants to mix two fuels, A and B, for its trucks to minimize cost. It needs no fewer than 3,000 gallons to run its trucks during the next month. It has a maximum fuel storage capacity of 4,000 gallons. There are 2,000 gallons of fuel A and 4,000 gallons of fuel B available. The mixed fuel must have an octane rating of no less than 80.

When fuels are mixed, the amount of fuel obtained is just equal to the sum of the amounts put in. The octane rating is the weighted average of the individual octanes, weighted in proportion to the respective volumes.

The following is known: Fuel A has an octane of 90 and costs $1.20 per gallon. Fuel B has an octane of 75 and costs $0.90 per gallon.

   a. Write the equations expressing this information.

   b. Solve the problem using the Excel Solver, giving the amount of each fuel to be used. State any assumptions necessary to solve the problem.

7   You are trying to create a budget to optimize the use of a portion of your disposable income. You have a maximum of $1,500 per month to be allocated to food, shelter, and entertainment. The amount spent on food and shelter combined must not exceed $1,000. The amount spent on shelter alone must not exceed $700. Entertainment cannot exceed $300 per month. Each dollar spent on food has a satisfaction value of 2, each dollar spent on shelter has a satisfaction value of 3, and each dollar spent on entertainment has a satisfaction value of 5.

   Assuming a linear relationship, use the Excel Solver to determine the optimal allocation of your funds.

8   C-town brewery brews two beers: Expansion Draft and Burning River. Expansion draft sells for $20 per barrel while Burning River sells for $8 per barrel. Producing a barrel of Expansion Draft takes 8 pounds of corn and 4 pounds of hops. Producing a barrel of Burning River requires 2 pounds of corn, 6 pounds of rice, and 3 pounds of hops. The brewery has 500 pounds of corn, 300 pounds of rice, and 400 pounds of hops. Assume a linear relationship, use Excel solver to determine the optimal mix of Expansion Draft and Burning River that maximizes C-town's revenue.

9   BC Petrol manufactures three chemicals at their chemical plant in Kentucky: BCP1, BCP2, and BCP3. These chemicals are produced in two production processes known as zone and man. Running the zone process for an hour costs $48 and yields three units of BCP1, one unit of BCP2, and one unit of BCP3. Running the man process for one hour costs $24 and yields one unit of BCP1 and one unit of BCP2. To meet customer demands, at least twenty units of BCP1, ten units of BCP2, and six units of BCP3 must be produced daily. Assuming a linear relationship, use Excel solver to determine the optimal mix of processes zone and man to minimize costs and meet BC Petrol daily demands.

10 A farmer in Wood County has 900 acres of land. She is going to plant each acre with corn, soybeans, or wheat. Each acre planted with corn yields a $2,000 profit; each with soybeans yields $2,500 profit; and each with wheat yields $3,000 profit. She has 100 workers and 150 tons of fertilizer. The table below shows the requirement per acre of each of the crops. Assuming a linear relationship, use Excel solver to determine the optimal planting mix of corn, soybeans, and wheat to maximize her profits.

	CORN	SOYBEANS	WHEAT
Labor (workers)	0.1	0.3	0.2
Fertilizer (tons)	0.2	0.1	0.4

SELECTED BIBLIOGRAPHY

Anderson, D. R.; D. J. Sweeney; and T. A. Williams. *An Introduction to Management Science*. 10th ed. Cincinnati: South-Western, 2002.

Winston, W. L., and S. C. Albright. *Practical Management Science*. 3rd ed. Belmont, CA: Duxbury Press, 2002.

FOOTNOTE

1 The slope of the objective function is -2. If P = profit, $P = \$2H + \$4C$; $\$2H = P - \$4C$; $H = P/2 - 2C$. Thus the slope is -2.

chapter

PROJECT MANAGEMENT

PROJECT MANAGEMENT:
THE VIEW FROM 30,000 FEET

The long-term competitiveness of any company depends ultimately on the success of its product development capabilities. New product development holds hope for improving market position and financial performance, creating new industry standards and new niche markets, and even renewing the organization. Yet few development projects fully deliver on their early promises. Wheelwright and Clark report that often problems arise from the way companies approach the development process or how the projects are actually coordinated.[1]

Wheelwright and Clark studied a large scientific instruments company and found that senior management became alarmed about a rash of late product-development projects. For some months, the development budget had been rising even as the number of completed projects declined. To make matters worse they found that many of the projects in the development pipeline no longer seemed to reflect the needs of the market. To get to the root of the problem, the chief executive first asked senior managers to compile a list of all the current development projects. They discovered that 30 projects were under way—far more than anticipated, and, they suspected, far more than the organization could support. Further analysis revealed that the company had two to three times more development work than it was capable of completing over its three-year development planning horizon.

With such a strain on resources, delays were inevitable. When a project ran into trouble, engineers from other projects were reassigned or, more commonly, asked to add the crisis project to their already long list of active projects. The more projects they added, the more their productivity dropped. The reshuffling caused delays in other projects, and the effects cascaded.

Furthermore, as deadlines slipped and development costs rose, project managers faced pressure to cut corners and compromise quality just to keep their projects moving forward.

This company's story is not unique. Most organizations spend their time putting out fires and pursuing projects aimed at catching up to their competitors. They have far too many projects going at once and all too often seriously overcommit their development resources. They spend too much time dealing with short-term pressures and not enough time on the strategic mission of product development so essential to the long-term success of the firm. →

"The high-impact project is the gem . . . the fundamental nugget . . . the fundamental atomic particle from which the new white collar world will be constructed and/or reconstructed. Projects should be, well WOW!"—Tom Peters

Although most of the material in this chapter focuses on the technical aspects of project management (structuring project networks and calculating the critical path), as we see in the opening vignette, the management aspects are certainly equally important. Success in project management is very much an activity that requires careful control of critical resources. We spend much of the time in this book focused on the management of nonhuman resources such as machine and material; for projects, however, the key resource is often our employees' time. Human resources are often the most expensive and those people involved in the projects critical to the success of the firm are often the most valuable managers, consultants, and engineers.

At the highest levels in an organization, management often involves juggling a portfolio of projects. There are many different types of projects ranging from the development of totally new products, revisions to old products, new marketing plans, and a vast array of projects for better serving customers and reducing cost.

Most companies deal with projects individually—pushing each through the pipeline as quickly and cost-effectively as possible. Many of these same companies are very good at applying the techniques described in this chapter in a manner where the myriad of tasks are executed flawlessly, but the projects just do not deliver the expected results. Worse, what often happens is the projects consuming the most resources have the least connection to the firm's strategy.

The vital big-picture decision is what mix of projects is best for the organization. Steven Wheelwright and Kim Clark argue that a firm should have the right mix of projects that best support a company's strategy.[2] Projects should be selected from the following types: derivative (incremental changes such as new product packaging or no-frills versions), breakthrough (major changes that create entirely new markets), platform (fundamental improvements to existing products), research and development, and alliances and partnerships (see Exhibit 3.1).

In this chapter we only scratch the surface in our introduction to the topic of project management. Professional project managers are individuals skilled at not only the technical aspects of calculating such things as early start and early finish time but, just as important, the people skills related to motivation. In addition, the ability to resolve conflicts as key decision points occur in the project is a critical skill. Without a doubt, leading successful projects is the best way to prove your promotability to the people who make promotion decisions. Virtually all project work is team work and leading a project involves leading a team. Your success at

Mapping the Five Types of Development Projects

exhibit 3.1

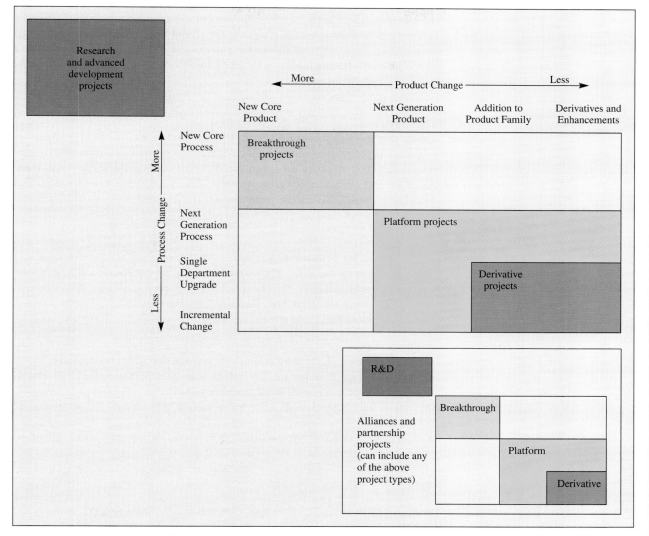

leading a project will spread quickly through the individuals in the team. As organizations flatten (though reengineering, downsizing, outsourcing), more will depend on projects and project leaders to get work done, work that previously was handled within departments.

WHAT IS PROJECT MANAGEMENT?

⊂⊃⊂⊃ A **project** may be defined as a series of related jobs usually directed toward some major output and requiring a significant period of time to perform. **Project management** can be defined as planning, directing, and controlling resources (people, equipment, material) to meet the technical, cost, and time constraints of the project.

Project

Project management

Although projects are often thought to be one-time occurrences, the fact is that many projects can be repeated or transferred to other settings or products. The result will be another project output. A contractor building houses or a firm producing low-volume products such as supercomputers, locomotives, or linear accelerators can effectively consider these as projects.

STRUCTURING PROJECTS

Cross Functional

Pure project

Before the project starts, senior management must decide which of three organizational structures will be used to tie the project to the parent firm: pure project, functional project, or matrix project. Management also must consider the characteristics of the project leader. (See the box titled "Selecting the Right Project Leader.") We next discuss the strengths and weaknesses of the three main forms.

PURE PROJECT

Tom Peters predicts that most of the world's work will be "brainwork," done in semipermanent networks of small project-oriented teams, each one an autonomous, entrepreneurial center of opportunity, where the necessity for speed and flexibility dooms the hierarchical management structures we and our ancestors grew up with.[3] Thus, out of the three basic project organizational structures, Peters favors the **pure project** (nicknamed *skunk works*), where a self-contained team works full time on the project.

ADVANTAGES
- The project manager has full authority over the project.
- Team members report to one boss. They do not have to worry about dividing loyalty with a functional-area manager.
- Lines of communication are shortened. Decisions are made quickly.
- Team pride, motivation, and commitment are high.

DISADVANTAGES
- Duplication of resources. Equipment and people are not shared across projects.
- Organizational goals and policies are ignored, as team members are often both physically and psychologically removed from headquarters.
- The organization falls behind in its knowledge of new technology due to weakened functional divisions.
- Because team members have no functional area home, they worry about life-after-project, and project termination is delayed.

FUNCTIONAL PROJECT

Functional project

At the other end of the project organization spectrum is the **functional project,** housing the project within a functional division.

```
                          ┌───────────────┐
                          │   President   │
                          └───────┬───────┘
        ┌─────────────────────────┼─────────────────────────┐
┌───────────────┐         ┌───────────────┐         ┌───────────────┐
│  Research     │         │  Engineering  │         │ Manufacturing │
│     and       │         │               │         │               │
│  Development  │         │               │         │               │
└───┬───┬───┬───┘         └───┬───┬───┬───┘         └───┬───┬───┬───┘
 Project Project Project   Project Project Project   Project Project Project
   A     B     C             D     E     F             G     H     I
```

ADVANTAGES
- A team member can work on several projects.
- Technical expertise is maintained within the functional area even if individuals leave the project or organization.
- The functional area is a home after the project is completed. Functional specialists can advance vertically.
- A critical mass of specialized functional-area experts creates synergystic solutions to a project's technical problems.

SELECTING THE RIGHT PROJECT LEADER

Senior management must exercise judgment and initiative in finding, selecting, hiring, and training the specific people who will fulfill a project's charter. At Toyota, for example, senior managers explicitly choose a project leader whose personality is consistent with the type of product they intend to introduce. Thus, for a sporty car targeted to a young, aggressive customer, they looked for a "fighter-pilot" type. When the project was to develop a luxurious sedan, they selected an "executive" type. The aim is to select project leaders who, by identifying with both the project and the customer, can internalize much of what counts in the product's total system performance.

SOURCE: S. C. WHEELWRIGHT AND K. B. CLARK, *LEADING PRODUCT DEVELOPMENT* (NEW YORK: THE FREE PRESS, 1995), p. 91.

DISADVANTAGES
- Aspects of the project that are not directly related to the functional area get shortchanged.
- Motivation of team members is often weak.
- Needs of the client are secondary and are responded to slowly.

MATRIX PROJECT

The classic specialized organizational form, "the **matrix project**," attempts to blend properties of functional and pure project structures. Each project utilizes people from different functional areas. The project manager (PM) decides what tasks and when they will be performed, but the functional managers control which people and technologies are used. If the matrix form is chosen, different projects (rows of the matrix) borrow resources from functional areas (columns). Senior management must then decide whether a weak, balanced, or strong form of a matrix is to be used. This establishes whether project managers have little, equal, or more authority than the functional managers with whom they negotiate for resources.

Matrix project

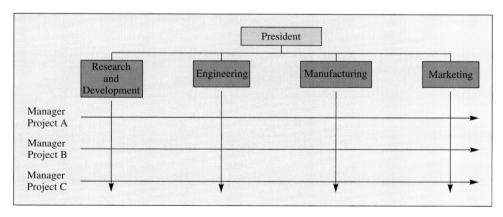

ADVANTAGES
- Communication between functional divisions is enhanced.
- A project manager is held responsible for successful completion of the project.
- Duplication of resources is minimized.
- Team members have a functional "home" after project completion, so they are less worried about life-after-project than if they were a pure project organization.
- Policies of the parent organization are followed. This increases support for the project.

DISADVANTAGES
- There are two bosses. Often the functional manager will be listened to before the project manager. After all, who can promote you or give you a raise?
- It is doomed to failure unless the PM has strong negotiating skills.
- Suboptimization is a danger, as PMs hoard resources for their own project, thus harming other projects.

Note that regardless of which of the three major organizational forms is used, the project manager is the primary contact point with the customer. Communication and flexibility are greatly enhanced because one person is responsible for successful completion of the project.

WORK BREAKDOWN STRUCTURE

A project starts out as a *statement of work* (SOW). The SOW may be a written description of the objectives to be achieved, with a brief statement of the work to be done and a proposed schedule specifying the start and completion dates. It also could contain performance measures in terms of budget and completion steps (milestones) and the written reports to be supplied.

A *task* is a further subdivision of a project. It is usually not longer than several months in duration and is performed by one group or organization. A *subtask* may be used if needed to further subdivide the project into more meaningful pieces.

A *work package* is a group of activities combined to be assignable to a single organizational unit. It still falls into the format of all project management; the package provides a description of what is to be done, when it is to be started and completed, the budget, measures of performance, and specific events to be reached at points in time. These specific events are called **project milestones.** Typical milestones might be the completion of the design, the production of a prototype, the completed testing of the prototype, and the approval of a pilot run.

Project milestones

Work breakdown structure

The **work breakdown structure** (WBS) defines the hierarchy of project tasks, subtasks, and work packages. Completion of one or more work packages results in the completion of a subtask; completion of one or more subtasks results in the completion of a task; and finally, the completion of all tasks is required to complete the project. A representation of this structure is shown in Exhibit 3.2.

Exhibit 3.3 shows the WBS for an optical scanner project. The WBS is important in organizing a project because it breaks the project down into manageable pieces. The number of levels will vary depending on the project. How much detail or how many levels to use depends on the following:

- The level at which a single individual or organization can be assigned responsibility and accountability for accomplishing the work package.
- The level at which budget and cost data will be collected during the project.

There is not a single correct WBS for any project, and two different project teams might develop different WBSs for the same project. Some experts have referred to project

exhibit 3.2

An Example of a Work Breakdown Structure

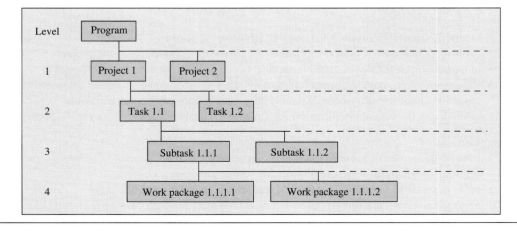

Work Breakdown Structure, Large Optical Scanner Design

exhibit 3.3

Level 1	2	3	4		
X				1	Optical simulator design
	X			1.1	Optical design
		X		1.1.1	Telescope design/fab
		X		1.1.2	Telescope/simulator optical interface
		X		1.1.3	Simulator zoom system design
		X		1.1.4	Ancillary simulator optical component specification
	X			1.2	System performance analysis
		X		1.2.1	Overall system firmware and software control
			X	1.2.1.1	Logic flow diagram generation and analysis
			X	1.2.1.2	Basic control algorithm design
		X		1.2.2	Far beam analyzer
		X		1.2.3	System inter- and intra-alignment method design
		X		1.2.4	Data recording and reduction requirements
	X			1.3	System integration
	X			1.4	Cost analysis
		X		1.4.1	Cost/system schedule analysis
		X		1.4.2	Cost/system performance analysis
	X			1.5	Management
		X		1.5.1	System design/engineering management
		X		1.5.2	Program management
	X			1.6	Long lead item procurement
		X		1.6.1	Large optics
		X		1.6.2	Target components
		X		1.6.3	Detectors

management as an art rather than a science, because there are so many different ways that a project can be approached. Finding the correct way to organize a project depends on experience with the particular task.

Activities are defined within the context of the work breakdown structure and are pieces of work that consume time. Activities do not necessarily require the expenditure of effort by people, although they often do. For example, waiting for paint to dry may be an activity in a project. Activities are identified as part of the WBS. From our sample project in Exhibit 3.3, activities would include telescope design and fabrication (1.1.1), telescope/simulator optical interface (1.1.2), and data recording (1.2.4). Activities need to be defined in such a way that when they are all completed, the project is done.

Activities

PROJECT CONTROL CHARTS

The U.S. Department of Defense (one of the earliest large users of project management) has published a variety of helpful standard forms. Many are used directly or have been modified by firms engaged in project management. Computer programs are available to quickly generate the charts described in this section. Charts are useful because their visual presentation is easily understood. Exhibit 3.4 shows a sample of the available charts.

Exhibit 3.4A is a sample **Gantt chart,** sometimes referred to as a *bar chart,* showing both the amount of time involved and the sequence in which activities can be performed. The chart is named after Henry L. Gantt, who won a presidential citation for his application of this type of chart to shipbuilding during World War I. In the example in Exhibit 3.4A, "long lead procurement" and "manufacturing schedules" are independent activities and can occur simultaneously. All other activities must be done in the sequence from top to bottom. Exhibit 3.4B graphs the amounts of money spent on labor, material, and overhead. Its value is its clarity in identifying sources and amounts of cost.

Exhibit 3.4C shows the percentage of the project's labor hours that comes from the various areas of manufacturing, finance, and so on. These labor hours are related to the proportion of the project's total labor cost. For example, manufacturing is responsible for

Gantt chart

exhibit 3.4   A Sample of Graphic Project Reports

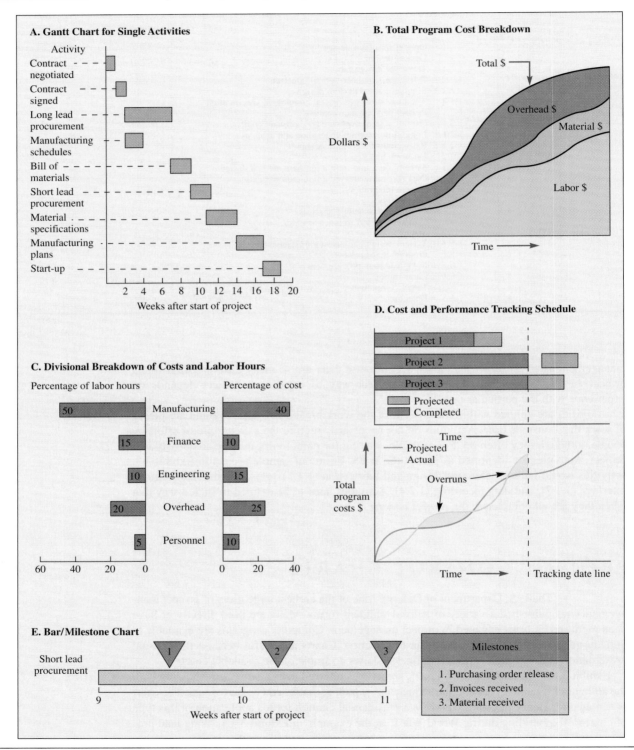

A. Gantt Chart for Single Activities

Activity

Contract negotiated
Contract signed
Long lead procurement
Manufacturing schedules
Bill of materials
Short lead procurement
Material specifications
Manufacturing plans
Start-up

2 4 6 8 10 12 14 16 18 20
Weeks after start of project

B. Total Program Cost Breakdown

Total $
Overhead $
Material $
Labor $

Dollars $

Time

C. Divisional Breakdown of Costs and Labor Hours

Percentage of labor hours   Percentage of cost

50   Manufacturing   40
15   Finance   10
10   Engineering   15
20   Overhead   25
5   Personnel   10

60 40 20 0   0 20 40

D. Cost and Performance Tracking Schedule

Project 1
Project 2
Project 3

Projected
Completed

Time

Projected
Actual

Overruns

Total program costs $

Time   Tracking date line

E. Bar/Milestone Chart

Short lead procurement

1   2   3

9   10   11
Weeks after start of project

Milestones

1. Purchasing order release
2. Invoices received
3. Material received

50 percent of the project's labor hours, but this 50 percent has been allocated just 40 percent of the total labor dollars charged.

The top half of Exhibit 3.4D shows the degree of completion of these projects. The dotted vertical line signifies today. Project 1, therefore, is already late because it still has work to be done. Project 2 is not being worked on temporarily, so there is a space before the projected work. Project 3 continues to be worked on without interruption. The bottom of Exhibit 3.4D compares actual total costs and projected costs. As we see, two cost overruns occurred, and the current cumulative costs are over projected cumulative costs.

Exhibit 3.4E is a milestone chart. The three milestones mark specific points in the project where checks can be made to see if the project is on time and where it should be. The best place to locate milestones is at the completion of a major activity. In this exhibit, the major activities completed were "purchase order release," "invoices received," and "material received."

Other standard reports can be used for a more detailed presentation comparing cost to progress (such as cost schedule status report—CSSR) or reports providing the basis for partial payment (such as the earned value report).

NETWORK-PLANNING MODELS

 The two best-known network-planning models were developed in the 1950s. The Critical Path Method (CPM) was developed for scheduling maintenance shutdowns at chemical processing plants owned by Du Pont. Since maintenance projects are performed often in this industry, reasonably accurate time estimates for activities are available. CPM is based on the assumptions that project activity times can be estimated accurately and that they do not vary. The Program Evaluation and Review Technique (PERT) was developed for the U.S. Navy's Polaris missile project. This was a massive project involving over 3,000 contractors. Because most of the activities had never been done before, PERT was developed to handle uncertain time estimates. As years passed, features that distinguished CPM from PERT have diminished, so in our treatment here we just use the term CPM.

In a sense, the CPM techniques illustrated here owe their development to the widely used predecessor, the Gantt chart. Although the Gantt chart is able to relate activities to time in a usable fashion for small projects, the interrelationship of activities, when displayed in this form, becomes extremely difficult to visualize and to work with for projects that include more than 25 activities. Also, the Gantt chart provides no direct procedure for determining the critical path, which is of great practical value to identify.

The **critical path** of activities in a project is the sequence of activities that form the longest chain in terms of their time to complete. If any one of the activities in the critical path is delayed, then the entire project is delayed. Determining scheduling information

Interactive Operations Management

Critical path

A NOMINEE FOR THE PROJECT MANAGEMENT INSTITUTE 2003 PMI PROJECT OF THE YEAR AWARD, THE PENTAGON PHOENIX PROJECT (PENTAGON RENOVATION PROGRAM), RUN BY THE OFFICE OF THE SECRETARY OF DEFENSE, WAS COMPLETED BEFORE SCHEDULED. THE RECONSTRUCTION OF TWO MILLION SQUARE FEET COST $526 MILLION, WHICH WAS APPROXIMATELY $200 MILLION LESS THAN ORIGINAL ESTIMATES.

about each activity in the project is the major goal of CPM techniques. The techniques calculate when an activity must start and end, together with whether the activity is part of the critical path.

CPM WITH A SINGLE TIME ESTIMATE

Here is a procedure for scheduling a project. In this case, a single time estimate is used because we are assuming that the activity times are known. Later this will be expanded to the case where there is uncertainty in the activity times. A very simple project will be scheduled to demonstrate the basic approach.

Consider that you have a group assignment that requires a decision on whether you should invest in a company. Your instructor has suggested that you perform the analysis in the following four steps:

A   Select a company.
B   Obtain the company's annual report and perform a ratio analysis.
C   Collect technical stock price data and construct charts.
D   Individually review the data and make a team decision on whether to buy the stock.

Your group of four people decides that the project can be divided into four activities as suggested by the instructor. You decide that all the team members should be involved in selecting the company and that it should take one week to complete this activity. You will meet at the end of the week to decide what company the group will consider. During this meeting you will divide your group: two people will be responsible for the annual report and ratio analysis, and the other two will collect the technical data and construct the charts. Your group expects it to take two weeks to get the annual report and perform the ratio analysis, and a week to collect the stock price data and generate the charts. You agree that the two groups can work independently. Finally, you agree to meet as a team to make the purchase decision. Before you meet, you want to allow one week for each team member to review all the data.

This is a simple project, but it will serve to demonstrate the approach. The following are the appropriate steps.

1. Identify each activity to be done in the project and estimate how long it will take to complete each activity.   This is simple, given the information from your instructor. We identify the activities as follows: A(1), B(2), C(1), D(1). The number is the expected duration of the activity.

Immediate predecessors

2. Determine the required sequence of activities and construct a network reflecting the precedence relationships.   An easy way to do this is to first identify the **immediate predecessors** associated with an activity. The immediate predecessors are the activities that need to be completed immediately before an activity. Activity A needs to be completed before activities B and C can start. B and C need to be completed before D can start. The following table reflects what we know so far:

ACTIVITY	DESIGNATION	IMMEDIATE PREDECESSORS	TIME (WEEKS)
Select company	A	None	1
Obtain annual report and perform ratio analysis	B	A	2
Collect stock price data and perform technical analysis	C	A	1
Review data and make a decision	D	B and C	1

Here is a diagram that depicts these precedence relationships:

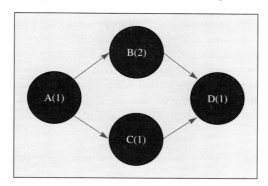

3. **Determine the critical path.**   Consider each sequence of activities that runs from the beginning to the end of the project. For our simple project there are two paths: A–B–D and A–C–D. The critical path is the path where the sum of the activity times is the longest. A–B–D has a duration of four weeks and A–C–D, a duration of three weeks. The critical path, therefore, is A–B–D. If any activity along the critical path is delayed, then the entire project will be delayed.

4. **Determine the early start/finish and late start/finish schedule.**   To schedule the project, find when each activity needs to start and when it needs to finish. For some activities in a project there may be some leeway in when an activity can start and finish. This is called the **slack time** in an activity. For each activity in the project, we calculate four points in time: the early start, early finish, late start, and late finish times. The early start and early finish are the earliest times that the activity can start and be finished. Similarly, the late start and late finish are the latest times the activities can start and finish. The difference between the late start time and early start time is the slack time. To help keep all of this straight, we place these numbers in special places around the nodes that represent each activity in our network diagram, as shown here.

Slack time

To calculate numbers, start from the beginning of the network and work to the end, calculating the early start and early finish numbers. Start counting with the current period, designated as period 0. Activity A has an early start of 0 and an early finish of 1. Activity B's early start is A's early finish or 1. Similarly, C's early start is 1. The early finish for B is 3, and the early finish for C is 2. Now consider activity D. D cannot start until both B and C are done. Because B cannot be done until 3, D cannot start until that time. The early start for D, therefore, is 3, and the early finish is 4. Our diagram now looks like this.

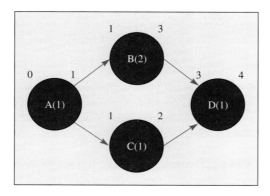

To calculate the late finish and late start times, start from the end of the network and work toward the front. Consider activity D. The earliest that it can be done is at time 4; and if we do not want to delay the completion of the project, the late finish needs to be set to 4. With a duration of 1, the latest that D can start is 3. Now consider activity C. C must be done by time 3 so that D can start, so C's late finish time is 3 and its late start time is 2. Notice the difference between the early and late start and finish times: This activity has one week of slack time. Activity B must be done by time 3 so that D can start, so its late finish time is 3 and late start time is 1. There is no slack in B. Finally, activity A must be done so that B and C can start. Because B must start earlier than C, and A must get done in time for B to start, the late finish time for A is 1. Finally, the late start time for A is 0. Notice there is no slack in activities A, B, and D. The final network looks like this. (Hopefully the stock your investment team has chosen is a winner!)

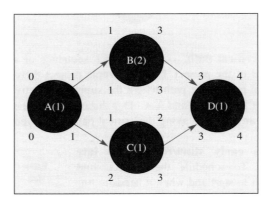

EXAMPLE 3.1: Single Time Estimate

Many firms that have tried to enter the notebook computer market have failed. Suppose your firm believes that there is a big demand in this market because existing products have not been designed correctly. They are too heavy, too large, or too small to have standard-size keyboards. Your intended computer will be small enough to carry inside a jacket pocket if need be. The ideal size will be no larger than 5 inches × 9½ inches × 1 inch with a folding keyboard. It should weigh no more than 15 ounces and have an LCD display, a micro disk drive, and an ethernet port. This should appeal to traveling businesspeople, but it could have a much wider market, including students. It should be priced in the $175–$200 range.

The project, then, is to design, develop, and produce a prototype of this small computer. In the rapidly changing computer industry, it is crucial to hit the market with a product of this sort in less than a year. Therefore, the project team has been allowed approximately eight months (35 weeks) to produce the prototype.

SOLUTION

The first charge of the project team is to develop a project network chart and estimate the likelihood of completing the prototype computer within the 35 weeks. Let's follow the steps in the development of the network.

1. **Activity identification.** The project team decides that the following activities are the major components of the project: design of the computer, prototype construction, prototype testing, methods specification (summarized in a report), evaluation studies of automatic assembly equipment, an assembly equipment study report, and a final report summarizing all aspects of the design, equipment, and methods.

2. **Activity sequencing and network construction.** On the basis of discussion with staff, the project manager develops the precedence table and sequence network shown in Exhibit 3.5. When constructing a network, take care to ensure that the activities are in the proper order and that the logic of their relationships is maintained. For example, it would be illogical to have a situation where Event A precedes Event B, B precedes C, and C precedes A.

CPM Network for Computer Design Project

exhibit 3.5

CPM ACTIVITY DESIGNATIONS AND TIME ESTIMATES

ACTIVITY	DESIGNATION	IMMEDIATE PREDECESSORS	TIME (WEEKS)
Design	A	–	21
Build prototype	B	A	5
Evaluate equipment	C	A	7
Test prototype	D	B	2
Write equipment report	E	C, D	5
Write methods report	F	C, D	8
Write final report	G	E, F	2

3. **Determine the critical path.** The critical path is the longest sequence of connected activities through the network and is defined as the path with zero slack time. This network has four different paths: A–C–F–G, A–C–E–G, A–B–D–F–G, and A–B–D–E–G. The lengths of these paths are 38, 35, 38, and 35 weeks. Note that this project has two different critical paths; this might indicate that this would be a fairly difficult project to manage. Calculating the early start and late start schedules gives additional insight into how difficult this project might be to complete on time. ●

Early Start and Late Start Schedules   An **early start schedule** is one that lists all of the activities by their early start times. For activities not on the critical path, there is slack time between the completion of each activity and the start of the next activity. The early start schedule completes the project and all its activities as soon as possible.

Early start schedule

A **late start schedule** lists the activities to start as late as possible without delaying the completion date of the project. One motivation for using a late start schedule is that savings are realized by postponing purchases of materials, the use of labor, and other costs until necessary. These calculations are shown in Exhibit 3.6. From this we see that the only activity that has slack is activity E. This certainly would be a fairly difficult project to complete on time.

Late start schedule

CPM WITH THREE ACTIVITY TIME ESTIMATES

If a single estimate of the time required to complete an activity is not reliable, the best procedure is to use three time estimates. These three times not only allow us to estimate the activity time but also let us obtain a probability estimate for completion time for the entire network. Briefly, the procedure is as follows: The estimated activity time is calculated using a weighted average of a minimum, maximum, and most likely time estimate. The expected completion time of the network is computed using the procedure described above. Using estimates of variability for the activities on the critical path, the probability of completing the project by particular times can be estimated. (Note that the probability calculations are a distinguishing feature of the classic PERT approach.)

exhibit 3.6

CPM Network for Computer Design Project

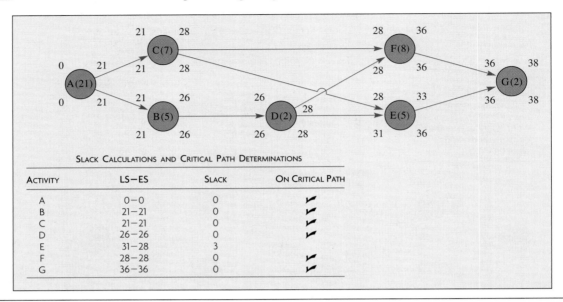

SLACK CALCULATIONS AND CRITICAL PATH DETERMINATIONS

ACTIVITY	LS−ES	SLACK	ON CRITICAL PATH
A	0−0	0	✔
B	21−21	0	✔
C	21−21	0	✔
D	26−26	0	✔
E	31−28	3	
F	28−28	0	✔
G	36−36	0	✔

EXAMPLE 3.2: Three Time Estimates

We use the same information as in Example 3.1 with the exception that activities have three time estimates.

SOLUTION

1. Identify each activity to be done in the project.
2. Determine the sequence of activities and construct a network reflecting the precedence relationships.
3. The three estimates for an activity time are

    $a =$ Optimistic time: the minimum reasonable period of time in which the activity can be completed. (There is only a small probability, typically assumed to be 1 percent, that the activity can be completed in less time.)

    $m =$ Most likely time: the best guess of the time required. Since m would be the time thought most likely to appear, it is also the mode of the beta distribution discussed in step 4.

    $b =$ Pessimistic time: the maximum reasonable period of time the activity would take to be completed. (There is only a small probability, typically assumed to be 1 percent, that it would take longer.)

    Typically, this information is gathered from those people who are to perform the activity.
4. Calculate the expected time (ET) for each activity. The formula for this calculation is

    [3.1]
    $$ET = \frac{a + 4m + b}{6}$$

    This is based on the beta statistical distribution and weights the most likely time (m) four times more than either the optimistic time (a) or the pessimistic time (b). The beta distribution is extremely flexible. It can take on the variety of forms that typically arise; it has finite end points (which limit the possible activity times to the area between a and b); and, in the simplified version, it permits straightforward computation of the activity mean and standard deviation.

5. Determine the critical path. Using the expected times, a critical path is calculated in the same way as the single time case.

6. Calculate the variances (σ^2) of the activity times. Specifically, this is the variance, σ^2, associated with each ET and is computed as follows:

[3.2]
$$\sigma^2 = \left(\frac{b-a}{6} \right)^2$$

As you can see, the variance is the square of one-sixth the difference between the two extreme time estimates. Of course, the greater this difference, the larger the variance.

7. Determine the probability of completing the project on a given date, based on the application of the standard normal distribution. A valuable feature of using three time estimates is that it enables the analyst to assess the effect of uncertainty on project completion time. (If you are not familiar with this type of analysis, see the box titled "Probability Analysis.") The mechanics of deriving this probability are as follows:

    a. Sum the variance values associated with each activity on the critical path.

    b. Substitute this figure, along with the project due date and the project expected completion time, into the Z transformation formula. This formula is

[3.3]
$$Z = \frac{D - T_{\mathrm{E}}}{\sqrt{\sum \sigma^2_{cp}}}$$

where

$D =$ Desired completion date for the project
$T_{\mathrm{E}} =$ Expected completion time for the project
$\sum \sigma^2_{cp} =$ Sum of the variances along the critical path

    c. Calculate the value of Z, which is the number of standard deviations (of a standard normal distribution) that the project due date is from the expected completion time.

    d. Using the value of Z, find the probability of meeting the project due date (using a table of normal probabilities such as Appendix E). The *expected completion time* is the starting time plus the sum of the activity times on the critical path.

Following the steps just outlined, we developed Exhibit 3.7 showing expected times and variances. The project network was created the same as we did previously. The only difference is that the activity times are weighted averages. We determine the critical path as before, using these values as if they were single numbers. The difference between the single time estimate and the three times (optimistic, most likely, and pessimistic) is in computing probabilities of completion. Exhibit 3.8 shows the network and critical path.

Activity Expected Times and Variances

exhibit 3.7

ACTIVITY	ACTIVITY DESIGNATION	TIME ESTIMATES a	m	b	EXPECTED TIMES (ET) $\frac{a + 4m + b}{6}$	ACTIVITY VARIANCES (σ^2) $\left(\frac{b-a}{6}\right)^2$
Design	A	10	22	28	21	9
Build prototype	B	4	4	10	5	1
Evaluate equipment	C	4	6	14	7	$2\frac{7}{9}$
Test prototype	D	1	2	3	2	$\frac{1}{9}$
Write report	E	1	5	9	5	$1\frac{7}{9}$
Write methods report	F	7	8	9	8	$\frac{1}{9}$
Write final report	G	2	2	2	2	0

Excel: Project Management

PROBABILITY ANALYSIS

The three-time-estimate approach introduces the ability to consider the probability that a project will be completed within a particular amount of time. The assumption needed to make this probability estimate is that the activity duration times are independent random variables. If this is true, the central limit theorem can be used to find the mean and the variance of the sequence of activities that form the critical path. The central limit theorem says that the sum of a group of independent, identically distributed random variables approaches a normal distribution as the number of random variables increases. In the case of project management problems, the random variables are the actual times for the activities in the project. (Recall that the time for each activity is assumed to be independent of other activities, and to follow a beta statistical distribution.) For this the expected time to complete the critical path activities is the sum of the activity times.

Likewise, because of the assumption of activity time independence, the sum of the variances of the activities along the critical path is the variance of the expected time to complete the path. Recall that the standard deviation is equal to the square root of the variance.

To determine the actual probability of completing the critical path activities within a certain amount of time, we need to find where on our probability distribution the time falls. Appendix E shows the areas of the cumulative standard normal distribution for different values of Z. Z measures the

number of standard deviations either to the right or to the left of zero in the distribution. Referring to Appendix E, the $G(z)$ values are the area under the curve representing the distribution. The values correspond to the cumulative probability associated with each value of Z. For example, the first value in the table, -4.00, has a $G(z)$ equal to .00003. This means that the probability associated with a Z value of -4.0 is only .003 percent. Similarly, a Z value of 1.50 has a $G(z)$ equal to .93319 or 93.319 percent. The Z values are calculated using Equation (3.3) given in Step 7b of the "Three Time Estimates" example solution. These cumulative probabilities also can be obtained by using the NORMSDIST (Z) function built into Microsoft Excel.

exhibit 3.8   Computer Design Project with Three Time Estimates

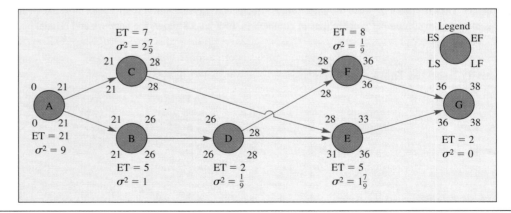

Because there are two critical paths in the network, we must decide which variances to use in arriving at the probability of meeting the project due date. A conservative approach dictates using the path with the largest total variance to focus management's attention on the activities most likely to exhibit broad variations. On this basis, the variances associated with activities A, C, F, and G would be used to find the probability of completion. Thus $\sum \sigma_{cp}^2 = 9 + 2\frac{7}{9} + \frac{1}{9} + 0 = 11.89$. Suppose management asks for the probability of completing the project in 35 weeks. D, then, is 35. The expected completion time was found to be 38. Substituting into the Z equation and solving, we obtain

$$Z = \frac{D - T_E}{\sqrt{\sum \sigma_{cp}^2}} = \frac{35 - 38}{\sqrt{11.89}} = -0.87$$

Looking at Appendix E we see that a Z value of –0.87 yields a probability of 0.1922, which means that the project manager has only about a 19 percent chance of completing the project in 35 weeks. Note that this probability is really the probability of completing the critical path A–C–F–G. Because there is another critical path and other paths that might become critical, the probability of completing the project in 35 weeks is actually less than 0.19. ●

MAINTAINING ONGOING PROJECT SCHEDULES

It is important to keep a project schedule accurate and current. The schedule tracks progress and identifies problems as they occur while corrective time may still be available. It also monitors the progress of cost and is often the basis for partial payments. Yet schedules are often sloppily kept or even totally abandoned.

A 1996 study that surveyed project managers indicates that there are many potential roadblocks to success. See the box titled "Project Managers, Challenges."

TIME–COST MODELS

In practice, project managers are as much concerned with the cost to complete a project as with the time to complete the project. For this reason, **time–cost models** have been devised. These models—extensions of the basic critical path method—attempt to develop a minimum-cost schedule for an entire project and to control expenditures during the project.

Time–cost models

MINIMUM-COST SCHEDULING (TIME–COST TRADE-OFF)

The basic assumption in minimum-cost scheduling is that there is a relationship between activity completion time and the cost of a project. On one hand, it costs money to expedite an activity; on the other, it costs money to sustain (or lengthen) the project. The costs associated with expediting activities are termed *activity direct costs* and add to the project direct cost. Some may be worker-related, such as overtime work, hiring more workers, and transferring workers from other jobs; others are resource-related, such as buying or leasing additional or more efficient equipment and drawing on additional support facilities.

The costs associated with sustaining the project are termed *project indirect costs:* overhead, facilities, and resource opportunity costs, and, under certain contractual situations, penalty costs or lost incentive payments. Because *activity direct costs* and *project indirect costs* are opposing costs dependent on time, the scheduling problem is essentially one of finding the project duration that minimizes their sum, or in other words, finding the optimum point in a time–cost trade-off.

The procedure for finding this point consists of the following five steps. It is explained by using the simple four-activity network shown in Exhibit 3.9. Assume that the indirect costs remain constant for eight days and then increase at the rate of $5 per day.

1. **Prepare a CPM-type network diagram.**   For each activity this diagram should list
    a. Normal cost (NC): the lowest expected activity costs. (These are the lesser of the cost figures shown under each node in Exhibit 3.9.)
    b. Normal time (NT): the time associated with each normal cost.
    c. Crash time (CT): the shortest possible activity time.
    d. Crash cost (CC): the cost associated with each crash time.

PROJECT MANAGERS, CHALLENGES

Despite the fact that 84 percent of project managers are responsible for staying within a project budget, only 15 percent of the time are they faced with direct ramifications for not doing so. In fact, 16 percent of project managers don't always know the budget of their jobs, according to a survey of project managers conducted by Zweig White & Associates, of Natick, Massachusetts.

The survey showed that project managers consider meeting schedules and budgets to be the greatest challenge that they face (19 percent). This may be partially attributed to the areas they rated as their two top complaints—insufficient or inadequate staff support (10 percent) and responsibility without authority (9 percent).

Project managers cited several reasons for not performing their best. Seventeen percent said that all team members are rarely or never allowed to see their own portion of the scope of services for a project. Also, they do not receive much training. Just 26 percent of firms have mandatory formal training for project managers, while 40 percent have optional training, and 29 percent have no training. For the firms that do offer training, the level is inadequate. Fewer than half of project managers are trained to perform basic tasks such as opening a job number, charging time, and budgeting.

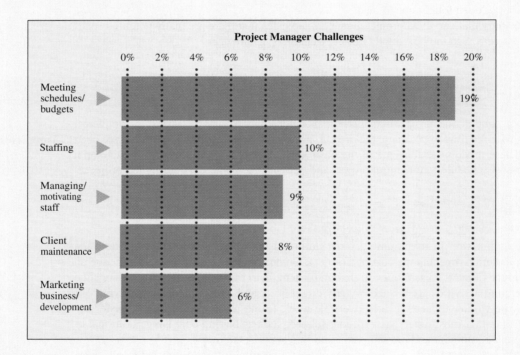

SOURCE: "PROJECT MANAGERS, CHALLENGES," *IIE SOLUTIONS*, DECEMBER 1996, p. 9. REPRINTED WITH PERMISSION OF THE INSTITUTE OF INDUSTRIAL ENGINEERS, 25 TECHNOLOGY PARK, NORCROSS, GA 30092, 770-449-0461. COPYRIGHT © 1996.

2. **Determine the cost per unit of time (assume days) to expedite each activity.** The relationship between activity time and cost may be shown graphically by plotting CC and CT coordinates and connecting them to the NC and NT coordinates by a concave, convex, or straight line—or some other form, depending on the actual cost structure of activity performance, as in Exhibit 3.9. For activity A, we assume a linear relationship between time and cost. This assumption is common in practice and helps us derive the cost per day to expedite because this value may be found directly by taking the slope of the line using the formula Slope = (CC − NC) ÷ (NT − CT). (When the assumption of linearity cannot be made, the cost of expediting must be determined graphically for each day the activity may be shortened.)

Example of Time–Cost Trade-Off Procedure

exhibit 3.9

Excel: Project Management

Calculation of Cost per Day to Expedite Each Activity

exhibit 3.10

ACTIVITY	CC − NC	NT − CT	$\dfrac{CC − NC}{NT − CT}$	COST PER DAY TO EXPEDITE	NUMBER OF DAYS ACTIVITY MAY BE SHORTENED
A	$10 − $6	2 − 1	$\dfrac{\$10 − \$6}{2 − 1}$	$4	1
B	$18 − $9	5 − 2	$\dfrac{\$18 − \$9}{5 − 2}$	$3	3
C	$8 − $6	4 − 3	$\dfrac{\$8 − \$6}{4 − 3}$	$2	1
D	$9 − $5	3 − 1	$\dfrac{\$9 − \$5}{3 − 1}$	$2	2

The calculations needed to obtain the cost of expediting the remaining activities are shown in Exhibit 3.10.

3. **Compute the critical path.**   For the simple network we have been using, this schedule would take 10 days. The critical path is A–B–D.

4. **Shorten the critical path at the least cost.**   The easiest way to proceed is to start with the normal schedule, find the critical path, and reduce the path time by one day using the lowest-cost activity. Then recompute and find the new critical path and reduce it by one day also. Repeat this procedure until the time of completion is satisfactory, or until there can be no further reduction in the project completion time. Exhibit 3.11 shows the reduction of the network one day at a time.

Working though Exhibit 3.11 might initially seem difficult. In the first line, all activities are at their normal time and costs are at their lowest value. The critical path is A–B–D, cost for completing the project is $26, and the project completion time 10 days.

exhibit 3.11

Reducing the Project Completion Time One Day at a Time

CURRENT CRITICAL PATH	REMAINING NUMBER OF DAYS ACTIVITY MAY BE SHORTENED	COST PER DAY TO EXPEDITE EACH ACTIVITY	LEAST-COST ACTIVITY TO EXPEDITE	TOTAL COST OF ALL ACTIVITIES IN NETWORK	PROJECT COMPLETION TIME
ABD	All activity times and costs are normal.			$26	10
ABD	A–1, B–3, D–2	A–4, B–3, D–2	D	28	9
ABD	A–1, B–3, D–1	A–4, B–3, D–2	D	30	8
ABD	A–1, B–3	A–4, B–3	B	33	7
ABCD	A–1, B–2, C–1	A–4, B–3, C–2	A*	37	6
ABCD	B–2, C–1	B–3, C–2	B&C†	42	5
ABCD	B–1	B–3	B‡	45	5

*To reduce the critical path by one day, reduce either A alone or B and C together at the same time (either B or C by itself just modifies the critical path without shortening it).

†B&C must be crashed together to reduce the path by one day.

‡Crashing activity B does not reduce the length of the project, so this additional cost would not be incurred.

The goal in line two is to reduce the project completion time by one day. We know it is necessary to reduce the time for one or more of the activities on the critical path. In the second column we note that activity A can be reduced one day (from two to one day), activity B can be reduced three days (from five to two days), and activity D can be reduced two days (from three to one day). The next column tracks the cost to reduce each of the activities by a single day. For example, for activity A, it normally costs $6 to complete in two days. It could be completed in one day at a cost of $10, a $4 increase. So we indicate the cost to expedite activity A by one day is $4. For activity B, it normally costs $9 to complete in five days. It could be completed in two days at a cost of $18. Our cost to reduce B by three days is $9, or $3 per day. For C, it normally costs $5 to complete in three days. It could be completed in one day at a cost of $9; a two-day reduction would cost $4 ($2 per day). The least expensive alternative for a one-day reduction in time is to expedite activity D at a cost of $2. Total cost for the network goes up to $28 and the project completion time is reduced to nine days.

Our next iteration starts in line three, where the goal is to reduce the project completion time to eight days. The nine-day critical path is A–B–D. We could shorten activity A by one day, B by three days, and D by one day (note D has already been reduced from three to two days). Cost to reduce each activity by one day is the same as in line two. Again, the least expensive activity to reduce is D. Reducing activity D from two to one day results in the total cost for all activities in the network going up to $30 and the project completion time coming down to eight days.

Line four is similar to line three, but now only A and B are on the critical path and can be reduced. B is reduced, which takes our cost up $3 to $33 and reduces the project completion time to seven days.

In line five (actually our fifth iteration in solving the problem), activities A, B, C, and D are all critical. D cannot be reduced, so our only options are activities A, B, and C. Note that B and C are in parallel, so it does not help to reduce B without reducing C. Our options are to reduce A alone at a cost of $4 or B and C together at a cost of $5 ($3 for B and $2 for C), so we reduce A in this iteration.

In line six, we take the B and C option that was considered in line five. Finally, in line seven, our only option is to reduce activity B. Since B and C are in parallel and we cannot reduce C, there is no value in reducing B alone. We can reduce the project completion time no further.

5. **Plot project direct, indirect, and total-cost curves and find the minimum-cost schedule.** Exhibit 3.12 shows the indirect cost plotted as a constant $10 per day for eight

Plot of Costs and Minimum-Cost Schedule

exhibit 3.12

days and increasing $5 per day thereafter. The direct costs are plotted from Exhibit 3.11, and the total project cost is shown as the total of the two costs.

Summing the values for direct and indirect costs for each day yields the project total cost curve. As you can see, this curve is at its minimum with an eight-day schedule, which costs $40 ($30 direct + $10 indirect).

MANAGING RESOURCES

In addition to scheduling each task, we must assign resources. Modern software quickly highlights overallocations—situations in which allocations exceed resources.

To resolve overallocations manually, you can either add resources or reschedule. Moving a task within its slack can free up resources.

Mid- to high-level project management information systems (PMIS) software can resolve overallocations through a "leveling" feature. Several rules of thumb can be used. You can specify that low-priority tasks should be delayed until higher-priority ones are complete, or that the project should end before or after the original deadline.

TRACKING PROGRESS

The real action starts after the project gets under way. Actual progress will differ from your original, or baseline, planned progress. Software can hold several different baseline plans, so you can compare monthly snapshots.

A *tracking Gantt chart* superimposes the current schedule onto a baseline plan so deviations are easily noticed. If you prefer, a spreadsheet view of the same information could be output. Deviations between planned start/finish and newly scheduled start/finish also appear, and a "slipping filter" can be applied to highlight or output only those tasks that are scheduled to finish at a later date than the planned baseline.

Management by exception also can be applied to find deviations between budgeted costs and actual costs. (See the Breakthrough box titled "Project Management Information Systems.")

CAUTIONS ON CRITICAL PATH ANALYSIS

Several assumptions need to be made to use project critical path analysis. This section summarizes some significant assumptions and their criticisms. One particularly difficult point for operating personnel is understanding the statistics when three time estimates are

BREAKTHROUGH

PROJECT MANAGEMENT INFORMATION SYSTEMS

Interest in the techniques and concepts of project management has exploded in the past 10 years. This has resulted in a parallel increase in project management software offerings. Now there are over 100 companies offering project management software. For the most up-to-date information about software available, check out the Web site of the Project Management Institute (www.pmi.org). Two of the leading companies are Microsoft, with Microsoft Project, and Primavera, with Primavera Project Planner. The following is a brief review of these two programs:

The Microsoft Project program comes with an excellent online tutorial, which is one reason for its overwhelming popularity with project managers tracking midsized projects. This package is compatible with the Microsoft Office Suite, which opens all the communications and Internet integration capability that Microsoft offers. The program includes features for scheduling, allocating and leveling resources, as well as controlling costs and producing presentation-quality graphics and reports.

Finally, for managing very large projects or programs having several projects, Primavera Project Planner is often the choice. Primavera was the first major vendor of this type of software and has possibly the most sophisticated capability.

Included on the DVD that comes with this book is SureTrack Project Management. This program is a streamlined version of Primavera Project Planner that has full capability for smaller projects. The program has a full tutorial and the Project KickStart Wizard makes setting up your initial project very easy. The screen shown is for a project for starting a new radio station. On the left are each of the tasks needed to complete the project. On the right is a Gantt chart that graphically depicts the timing of each activity.

The SureTrack program is very easy to use and we encourage you to experiment with it on your computer.

used. The beta distribution of activity times, the three time estimates, the activity variances, and the use of the normal distribution to arrive at project completion probabilities are all potential sources of misunderstandings, and with misunderstanding comes distrust and obstruction. Thus, management must be sure that the people charged with monitoring and controlling activity performance understand the statistics.

1. **Assumption:** Project activities can be identified as entities. (There is a clear beginning and ending point for each activity.)
   Criticism: Projects, especially complex ones, change in content over time, so a network made at the beginning may be highly inaccurate later. Also, the very fact that activities are specified and a network is formalized tends to limit the flexibility that is required to handle changing situations as the project progresses.
2. **Assumption:** Project activity sequence relationships can be specified and networked.
   Criticism: Sequence relationships cannot always be specified beforehand. In some projects, in fact, ordering certain activities is conditional on previous activities. (Critical path analysis, in the basic form shown here, has no provision for treating this problem, although some other techniques have been proposed that allow the project manager several contingency paths, given different outcomes from each activity.)
3. **Assumption:** Project control should focus on the critical path.
   Criticism: It is not necessarily true that the longest time-consuming path (or the path with zero slack) obtained from summing activity expected time values ultimately determines project completion time. What often happens as the project progresses is that some activity not on the critical path becomes delayed to such a degree that it extends the entire project. For this reason it has been suggested that a "critical activity" concept replace the critical path concept as the focus of managerial control. Under this approach, attention would center on those activities that have a high potential variation and lie on the critical path or on a "near-critical path." A near-critical path is one that does not share any activities with the critical path and, though it has slack, could become critical if one or a few activities along it become delayed. Obviously, the more parallelism in a network, the more likely that one or more near-critical paths exist. Conversely, the more a network approximates a single series of activities, the less likely it is to have near-critical paths.
4. **Assumption:** The activity time estimates, when using the three-time approach, follow the beta distribution, with the variance of the project assumed to equal the sum of the variances along the critical path.
   Criticism: Although originally the beta distribution was selected for a variety of good reasons, each component of the statistical treatment has been brought into question. First, the formulas are in reality a modification of the beta distribution mean and variance, which, when compared to the basic formulas, could be expected to lead to absolute errors on the order of 10 percent for the entire project and 5 percent for the individual activity variances. Second, given that the activity-time distributions have the properties of unimodality, continuity, and finite positive end points, other distributions with the same properties would yield different means and variances. Third, obtaining three "valid" time estimates to put into the formulas presents operational problems; it is often difficult to arrive at one activity time estimate, let alone three, and the subjective definitions of the optimistic and pessimistic times do not help the matter.

Finally, the cost of applying critical path methods to a project is sometimes used as a basis for criticism. However, the cost of applying critical path techniques rarely exceeds 2 percent of total project cost. When used with added features of a work breakdown structure and various reports, it is more expensive but rarely exceeds 5 percent of total project costs. Thus, this added cost is generally outweighed by the savings from improved scheduling and reduced project time.

CONCLUSION

Although much of this chapter has dealt with networking techniques, we would like to again emphasize the importance of teamwork. Effective project management involves much more than simply setting up a CPM schedule; it also requires clearly identified project responsibilities, a simple and timely progress reporting system, and good people-management practices.

Projects fail for a number of reasons. The most important reason is insufficient effort in the planning phase. In addition, the implementation of a project will fail unless the team has the commitment of top management and has a talented project manager.

KEY TERMS

Project A series of related jobs usually directed toward some major output and requiring a significant period of time to perform.

Project management Planning, directing, and controlling resources (people, equipment, material) to meet the technical, cost, and time constraints of a project.

Pure project A structure for organizing a project where a self-contained team works full time on the project.

Functional project A structure where team members are assigned from the functional units of the organization. The team members remain a part of their functional units and typically are not dedicated to the project.

Matrix project A structure that blends the functional and pure project structures. Each project uses people from different functional areas. A dedicated project manager decides what tasks need to be performed and when, but the functional managers control which people to use.

Project milestone A specific event in a project.

Work breakdown structure The hierarchy of project tasks, subtasks, and work packages.

Activities Pieces of work within a project that consume time. The completion of all the activities of a project marks the end of the project.

Gantt chart Shows in a graphic manner the amount of time involved and the sequence in which activities can be performed. Often referred to as a *bar chart*.

Critical path The sequence of activities in a project that forms the longest chain in terms of their time to complete. This path contains zero slack time. Techniques used to find the critical path are called CPM or Critical Path Method techniques.

Immediate predecessor Activity that needs to be completed immediately before another activity.

Slack time The time that an activity can be delayed; the difference between the late and early start times of an activity.

Early start schedule A project schedule that lists all activities by their early start times.

Late start schedule A project schedule that lists all activities by their late start times. This schedule may create savings by postponing purchases of material and other costs associated with the project.

Time–cost models Extension of the critical path models that considers the trade-off between the time required to complete an activity and cost. This is often referred to as "crashing" the project.

FORMULA REVIEW

Expected Time

[3.1]
$$ET = \frac{a + 4m + b}{6}$$

Variance (σ^2) of the activity times

[3.2]
$$\sigma^2 = \left(\frac{b - a}{6}\right)^2$$

Z transformation formula

[3.3]
$$Z = \frac{D - T_E}{\sqrt{\sum \sigma_{cp}^2}}$$

SOLVED PROBLEMS

SOLVED PROBLEM 1

A project has been defined to contain the following list of activities, along with their required times for completion:

ACTIVITY	TIME (DAYS)	IMMEDIATE PREDECESSORS
A	1	—
B	4	A
C	3	A
D	7	A
E	6	B
F	2	C, D
G	7	E, F
H	9	D
I	4	G, H

Excel: PM_solved problem.xls

a. Draw the critical path diagram.
b. Show the early start and early finish times.
c. Show the critical path.
d. What would happen if activity F was revised to take four days instead of two?

Solution

The answers to *a*, *b*, and *c* are shown in the following diagram.

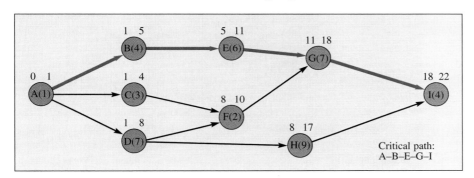

d. New critical path: A–D–F–G–I. Time of completion is 23 days.

SOLVED PROBLEM 2

A project has been defined to contain the following activities, along with their time estimates for completion,

ACTIVITY	TIME ESTIMATES (WK)			IMMEDIATE PREDECESSOR
	a	*m*	*b*	
A	1	4	7	—
B	2	6	7	A
C	3	4	6	A, D
D	6	12	14	A
E	3	6	12	D
F	6	8	16	B, C
G	1	5	6	E, F

a. Calculate the expected time and the variance for each activity.
b. Draw the critical path diagram.

c. Show the early start, early finish times and late start, late finish times.
d. Show the critical path.
e. What is the probability that the project can be completed in 34 weeks?

Solution

a.

ACTIVITY	EXPECTED TIME $\dfrac{a + 4m + b}{6}$	ACTIVITY VARIANCE $\left(\dfrac{b - a}{6}\right)^2$
A	4.00	1
B	5.50	$\frac{25}{36}$
C	4.17	$\frac{1}{4}$
D	11.33	$1\frac{7}{9}$
E	6.50	$2\frac{1}{4}$
F	9.00	$2\frac{7}{9}$
G	4.50	$\frac{25}{36}$

b.

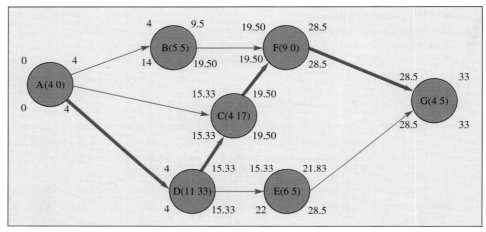

c. Shown on diagram.
d. Shown on diagram.

e. $Z = \dfrac{D - T_E}{\sqrt{\sum \sigma_{cp}^2}} = \dfrac{34 - 33}{\sqrt{1 + 1\frac{7}{9} + \frac{1}{4} + 2\frac{7}{9} + \frac{25}{36}}} = \dfrac{1}{2.5495} = .3922$

Look up that value in Appendix E and we see that there is about a 65 percent chance of completing the project by that date.

SOLVED PROBLEM 3

Here are the precedence requirements, normal and crash activity times, and normal and crash costs for a construction project:

ACTIVITY	PRECEDING ACTIVITIES	REQUIRED TIME (WEEKS)		COST	
		NORMAL	CRASH	NORMAL	CRASH
A	—	4	2	$10,000	$11,000
B	A	3	2	6,000	9,000
C	A	2	1	4,000	6,000
D	B	5	3	14,000	18,000
E	B, C	1	1	9,000	9,000
F	C	3	2	7,000	8,000
G	E, F	4	2	13,000	25,000
H	D, E	4	1	11,000	18,000
I	H, G	6	5	20,000	29,000

a. What are the critical path and the estimated completion time?

b. To shorten the project by three weeks, which tasks would be shortened and what would the final total project cost be?

Solution

The construction project network is shown below:

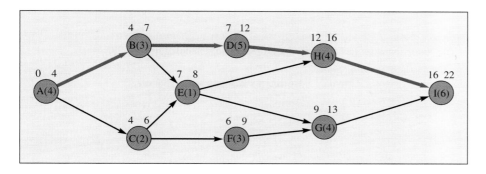

a. Critical path A–B–D–H–I.
Normal completion time is 22 weeks.

b.

ACTIVITY	CRASH COST	NORMAL COST	NORMAL TIME	CRASH TIME	COST PER WEEK	WEEKS
A	$11,000	$10,000	4	2	$ 500	2
B	9,000	6,000	3	2	3,000	1
C	6,000	4,000	2	1	2,000	1
D	18,000	14,000	5	3	2,000	2
E	9,000	9,000	1	1		0
F	8,000	7,000	3	2	1,000	1
G	25,000	13,000	4	2	6,000	2
H	18,000	11,000	4	1	2,333	3
I	29,000	20,000	6	5	9,000	1

(1) 1st week: CP = A–B–D–H–I. Cheapest is A at $500. Critical path stays the same.
(2) 2nd week: A is still the cheapest at $500. Critical path stays the same.
(3) 3rd week: Because A is no longer available, the choices are B (at $3,000), D (at $2,000), H (at $2,333), or I (at $9,000). Therefore, choose D at $2,000.

Total project cost shortened three weeks is

A	$ 11,000
B	6,000
C	4,000
D	16,000
E	9,000
F	7,000
G	13,000
H	11,000
I	20,000
	$97,000

REVIEW AND DISCUSSION QUESTIONS

1   What was the strangest project that you have been involved in? Give examples of the following as they pertain to the project: the work breakdown structure, tasks, subtasks, and work package. Were you on the critical path? Did it have a good project manager?

2   What are some reasons project scheduling is not done well?

3   Discuss the graphic presentations in Exhibit 3.4. Are there any other graphic outputs you would like to see if you were project manager?

4   Which characteristics must a project have for critical path scheduling to be applicable? What types of projects have been subjected to critical path analysis?
5   What are the underlying assumptions of minimum-cost scheduling? Are they equally realistic?
6   "Project control should always focus on the critical path." Comment.
7   Why would subcontractors for a government project want their activities on the critical path? Under what conditions would they try to avoid being on the critical path?

PROBLEMS

1   The following activities are part of a project to be scheduled using CPM:

ACTIVITY	IMMEDIATE PREDECESSOR	TIME (WEEKS)
A	—	6
B	A	3
C	A	7
D	C	2
E	B, D	4
F	D	3
G	E, F	7

a. Draw the network.
b. What is the critical path?
c. How many weeks will it take to complete the project?
d. How much slack does activity B have?

2   Schedule the following activities using CPM:

ACTIVITY	IMMEDIATE PREDECESSOR	TIME (WEEKS)
A	—	1
B	A	4
C	A	3
D	B	2
E	C, D	5
F	D	2
G	F	2
H	E, G	3

a. Draw the network.
b. What is the critical path?
c. How many weeks will it take to complete the project?
d. Which activities have slack, and how much?

3   The R&D department is planning to bid on a large project for the development of a new communication system for commercial planes. The accompanying table shows the activities, times, and sequences required:

ACTIVITY	IMMEDIATE PREDECESSOR	TIME (WEEKS)
A	—	3
B	A	2
C	A	4
D	A	4
E	B	6
F	C, D	6
G	D, F	2
H	D	3
I	E, G, H	3

a. Draw the network diagram.

b. What is the critical path?

c. Suppose you want to shorten the completion time as much as possible, and you have the option of shortening any or all of B, C, D, and G each one week. Which would you shorten?

d. What is the new critical path and earliest completion time?

4   A construction project is broken down into the following 10 activities:

ACTIVITY	IMMEDIATE PREDECESSOR	TIME (WEEKS)
1	—	4
2	1	2
3	1	4
4	1	3
5	2, 3	5
6	3	6
7	4	2
8	5	3
9	6, 7	5
10	8, 9	7

a. Draw the network diagram.

b. Find the critical path.

c. If activities 1 and 10 cannot be shortened, but activities 2 through 9 can be shortened to a minimum of one week each at a cost of $10,000 per week, which activities would you shorten to cut the project by four weeks?

5   The following represents a project that should be scheduled using CPM:

		TIMES (DAYS)		
ACTIVITY	IMMEDIATE PREDECESSORS	*a*	*m*	*b*
A	—	1	3	5
B	—	1	2	3
C	A	1	2	3
D	A	2	3	4
E	B	3	4	11
F	C, D	3	4	5
G	D, E	1	4	6
H	F, G	2	4	5

a. Draw the network.

b. What is the critical path?

c. What is the expected project completion time?

d. What is the probability of completing this project within 16 days?

6   Here is a CPM network with activity times in weeks:

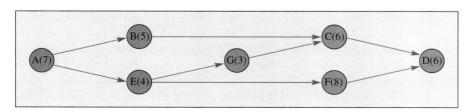

a. Determine the critical path.

b. How many weeks will the project take to complete?

c. Suppose F could be shortened by two weeks and B by one week. How would this affect the completion date?

7 The following table represents a plan for a project:

		TIMES (DAYS)		
JOB NO.	PREDECESSOR JOB(S)	a	m	b
1	—	2	3	4
2	1	1	2	3
3	1	4	5	12
4	1	3	4	11
5	2	1	3	5
6	3	1	2	3
7	4	1	8	9
8	5, 6	2	4	6
9	8	2	4	12
10	7	3	4	5
11	9, 10	5	7	8

a. Construct the appropriate network diagram.

b. Indicate the critical path.

c. What is the expected completion time for the project?

d. You can accomplish any one of the following at an additional cost of $1,500:

(1) Reduce job 5 by two days.

(2) Reduce job 3 by two days.

(3) Reduce job 7 by two days.

If you will save $1,000 for each day that the earliest completion time is reduced, which action, if any, would you choose?

e. What is the probability that the project will take more than 30 days to complete?

8 Here is a network with the activity times shown in days:

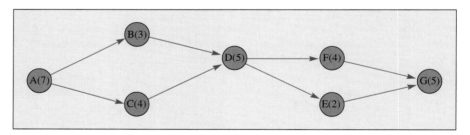

a. Find the critical path.

b. The following table shows the normal times and the crash times, along with the associated costs for each activity.

ACTIVITY	NORMAL TIME	CRASH TIME	NORMAL COST	CRASH COST
A	7	6	$7,000	$ 8,000
B	3	2	5,000	7,000
C	4	3	9,000	10,200
D	5	4	3,000	4,500
E	2	1	2,000	3,000
F	4	2	4,000	7,000
G	5	4	5,000	8,000

If the project is to be shortened by four days, show which activities, in order of reduction, would be shortened and the resulting cost.

9 The home office billing department of a chain of department stores prepares monthly inventory reports for use by the stores' purchasing agents. Given the following information, use the critical path method to determine

a. How long the total process will take.

b. Which jobs can be delayed without delaying the early start of any subsequent activity.

JOB AND DESCRIPTION		IMMEDIATE PREDECESSORS	TIME (HOURS)
a	Start	—	0
b	Get computer printouts of customer purchases	a	10
c	Get stock records for the month	a	20
d	Reconcile purchase printouts and stock records	b, c	30
e	Total stock records by department	b, c	20
f	Determine reorder quantities for coming period	e	40
g	Prepare stock reports for purchasing agents	d, f	20
h	Finish	g	0

10 For the network shown:

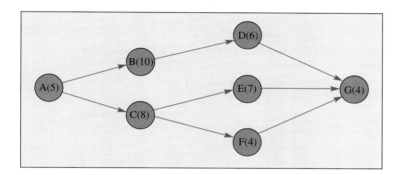

a. Determine the critical path and the early completion time in weeks for the project.
b. For the data shown, reduce the project completion time by three weeks. Assume a linear cost per week shortened, and show, step by step, how you arrived at your schedule.

ACTIVITY	NORMAL TIME	NORMAL COST	CRASH TIME	CRASH COST
A	5	$ 7,000	3	$13,000
B	10	12,000	7	18,000
C	8	5,000	7	7,000
D	6	4,000	5	5,000
E	7	3,000	6	6,000
F	4	6,000	3	7,000
G	4	7,000	3	9,000

11 The following CPM network has estimates of the normal time in weeks listed for the activities:

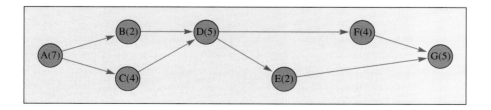

a. Identify the critical path.
b. What is the length of time to complete the project?
c. Which activities have slack, and how much?

d. Here is a table of normal and crash times and costs. Which activities would you shorten to cut two weeks from the schedule in a rational fashion? What would be the incremental cost? Is the critical path changed?

ACTIVITY	NORMAL TIME	CRASH TIME	NORMAL COST	CRASH COST	POSSIBLE NUMBER OF WEEKS DECREASE	COST/WEEK TO EXPEDITE
A	7	6	$7,000	$ 8,000		
B	2	1	5,000	7,000		
C	4	3	9,000	10,200		
D	5	4	3,000	4,500		
E	2	1	2,000	3,000		
F	4	2	4,000	7,000		
G	5	4	5,000	8,000		

12 A project has been defined to contain the following activities, along with their time estimates for completion.

ACTIVITY	TIME ESTIMATES (WK) a	m	b	IMMEDIATE PREDECESSOR
A	2	5	8	—
B	1	5	9	—
C	4	6	9	A
D	2	2	2	B
E	1	2	9	A
F	2	4	5	C, D
G	3	8	10	C, E
H	1	2	3	F, G

a. Calculate the expected time and the variance for each activity.
b. Draw the critical path diagram. Show the early start, early finish times and late start, late finish times.
c. Show the critical path.
d. What is the probability that the project can be completed in 19 weeks?

13 Hungry Henry's is building a new restaurant. In order complete the project the following activities, along with their time estimates, are given below.

ACTIVITY	TIME ESTIMATES (WK) a	m	b	IMMEDIATE PREDECESSOR
A	2	4	7	—
B	1	4	9	A
C	3	6	9	A
D	2	3	5	B, C
E	1	3	9	B
F	2	4	5	C, D
G	3	8	10	E
H	1	2	3	F, E
I	3	5	7	G, H

a. Calculate the expected time and the variance for each activity.
b. Draw the critical path diagram. Show the early start, early finish times and late start, late finish times.

c. Show the critical path.
d. What is the probability that the project can be completed in 26 weeks? What is the probability it will take longer than 26 weeks?
e. Are there any other paths that can interfere with completing this project on time?

14 Bragg's Bakery is building a new automated bakery in downtown Sandusky. Here are the activities that need to be completed to get the new bakery built and the equipment installed.

ACTIVITY	PREDECESSOR	NORMAL TIME (WEEKS)	CRASH TIME (WEEKS)	EXPEDITING COST/WEEK
A	—	9	6	$3,000
B	A	8	5	$3,500
C	A	15	10	$4,000
D	B, C	5	3	$2,000
E	C	10	6	$2,500
F	D, E	2	1	$5,000

a. Draw the project diagram.
b. What is the normal project length?
c. What is the project length if all activities are crashed to their minimum?
d. Bragg's loses $3,500 in profit per week for every week the bakery is not completed. How many weeks will the project take if we are willing to pay crashing cost as long as it is less than $3,500?

ADVANCED PROBLEM

15 Assume the network and data that follow:

ACTIVITY	NORMAL TIME (WEEKS)	NORMAL COST	CRASH TIME (WEEKS)	CRASH COST	IMMEDIATE PREDECESSORS
A	2	$50	1	$70	—
B	4	80	2	160	A
C	8	70	4	110	A
D	6	60	5	80	A
E	7	100	6	130	B
F	4	40	3	100	D
G	5	100	4	150	E, F

a. Construct the network diagram.
b. Indicate the critical path when normal activity times are used.
c. Compute the minimum total direct cost for each project duration based on the cost associated with each activity. Consider durations of 13, 14, 15, 16, 17, and 18 weeks.
d. If the indirect costs for each project duration are $400 (18 weeks), $350 (17 weeks), $300 (16 weeks), $250 (15 weeks), $200 (14 weeks), and $150 (13 weeks), what is the total project cost for each duration? Indicate the minimum total project cost duration.

CASE: THE CAMPUS WEDDING (A)

On March 31 of last year, Mary Jackson burst into the family living room and announced that she and Larry Adams (her college boyfriend) were going to be married. After recovering from the shock, her mother hugged her and asked, "When?" The following conversation resulted:

Mary: April 22.

Mother: What!

Father: The Adams–Jackson wedding will be the social hit of the year. Why so soon?

Mary: Because on April 22 the cherry blossoms on campus are always in full bloom! The wedding pictures will be beautiful.

Mother: But honey, we can't possibly finish all the things that need to be done by then. Remember all the details that were involved in your sister's wedding? Even if we start tomorrow, it takes a day to reserve the church and reception hall, and they need at least 17 days' notice. That has to be done before we can start decorating the church, which takes three days. An extra $100 contribution on

Sunday would probably cut that 17-day notice to 10 days, though.

Father: Ugh!

Mary: I want Jane Summers to be my maid of honor.

Father: But she's in the Peace Corps, in Guatemala, isn't she? It would take her 10 days to get ready and drive up here.

Mary: But we could fly her up in two days, and it would cost only $500. She would have to be here in time to have her dress fitted.

Father: Ugh!

Mother: And catering! It takes two days to choose the cake and table decorations, and Jack's Catering wants at least 10 days' notice prior to the rehearsal dinner (the night before the wedding).

Mary: Can I wear your wedding dress, Mom?

Mother: Well, we'd have to replace some lace, but you could wear it, yes. We could order the lace from New York when we order the material for the bridesmaids' dresses. It takes eight days to order and receive the material. The pattern needs to be chosen first, and that would take three days.

Father: We could get the material here in five days if we paid an extra $25 to airfreight it.

Mary: I want Mrs. Watson to work on the dresses.

Father: But she charges $120 a day!

Mother: If we did all the sewing, we could finish the dresses in 11 days. If Mrs. Watson helped, we could cut that down to six days, at a cost of $120 for each day less than 11 days.

Mary: I don't want anyone but her.

Mother: It would take another two days to do the final fitting. It normally takes two days to clean and press the dresses, but that new cleaner downtown could do them in one day if we pay the $30 charge for express service.

Father: Everything should be completed by rehearsal night, and that's only 21 days from now. I bet that will be a busy day.

Mother: We've forgotten something. The invitations.

Father: We should order the invitations from Bob's Printing Shop, and that usually takes 12 days. I'll bet he would do it in five days if we slipped him an extra $35.

Mother: It would take us three days to choose the invitation style before we could order them, and we want the envelopes printed with our return address.

Mary: Oh! That will be elegant.

Mother: The invitations should go out at least 10 days before the wedding. If we let them go any later, some of the relatives would get theirs too late to come, and that would make them mad. I'll bet that if we didn't get them out until eight days before the wedding, Aunt Ethel couldn't make it, and she would reduce her wedding gift by $200.

Father: Ugh!

Mother: We'll have to take them to the post office to mail them, and that takes a day. Addressing would take four days unless we hired some part-time help, and we can't start until the printer is finished. If we hired someone, we could probably save two days by spending $25 for each day saved.

Mary: We need to get gifts to give to the bridesmaids at the rehearsal dinner. I can spend a day and do that.

Mother: Before we can even start to write out those invitations, we need a guest list. Heavens, that will take four days to get in order, and only I can understand our address file.

Mary: Oh, Mother, I'm so excited. We can start each of the relatives on a different job.

Mother: Honey, I don't see how we can do it. Why, we've got to choose the invitations and patterns and reserve the church and . . .

Father: Why don't you just take $1,500 and elope. Your sister's wedding cost me $1,200, and she didn't have to fly people up from Guatemala, hire extra people, use airfreight, or anything like that.

QUESTIONS

1 Given the activities and precedence relationships described in the (A) case, develop a network diagram for the wedding plans.
2 Identify the paths. Which are critical?
3 What is the minimum-cost plan that meets the April 22 date?

CASE: THE CAMPUS WEDDING (B)

⊙⊙⊙ Several complications arose during the course of trying to meet the deadline of April 21 for the Adams–Jackson wedding rehearsal. Because Mary Jackson was adamant about having the wedding on April 22 (as was Larry Adams, because he wanted her to be happy), the implications of each of these complications had to be assessed.

1 On April 1 the chairman of the Vestry Committee at the church was left unimpressed by the added donation

and said he wouldn't reduce the notice period from 17 to 10 days.
2 A call to Guatemala revealed that the potential bridesmaid had several commitments and could not possibly leave the country until April 10.
3 Mother came down with the four-day flu just as she started on the guest list.
4 The lace and dress materials were lost in transit. Notice of the loss was delivered to the Jackson home early on April 10.

5   There was a small fire at the caterer's shop on April 8. It was estimated that the shop would be closed two or three days for repairs.

Mary Jackson's father, in particular, was concerned about expense and kept offering $1,500 to Mary and Larry for them to elope.

QUESTION

1   Given your answers to the (A) case, describe the effects on the wedding plans of each incident noted in the (B) case.

SOURCE: ADAPTED FROM A CASE ORIGINALLY WRITTEN BY PROFESSOR D. C. WHYBANK, UNIVERSITY OF NORTH CAROLINA, CHAPEL HILL, NORTH CAROLINA.

CASE: PRODUCT DESIGN AT FORD

Ford Motor Company is ranked second on the Fortune 500 list of the largest U.S. industrial corporations, based on sales. Ford currently sells over 60 different models of cars. Product design is a major activity critical to the creation of the innovative products that ensure the ongoing success of the firm.

Ford has developed the Ford Product Development System (FPDS) that is used to organize the activities required to develop and deliver a new car. The firm has great experience in developing new cars, but the pressure to develop them quicker presents an ongoing challenge. The automobile market is fast changing, with the desire of consumers quickly shifting. Ford's current process requires nearly four years to develop a totally new car, one that involves a new body style and powertrain combination.

In this case, our goal is to give you a good idea of the issues related to planning the development of new vehicles at a company like Ford. The data in the case are roughly based on how Ford actually approaches the problem, but due to the amazing details associated with developing a real car, we have considerably simplified things.

A major challenge in planning the development of a car relates to the timing of the major events that must occur in order to meet the launch date. The launch date refers to the date when the car is available for ordering by dealers. Consider the fact that for a company like Ford virtually all of 60 different models that are offered are "launched" each year. Usually the year-to-year changes are minor with small changes to body style and minor engine/drivetrain changes. Approximately, every four or five years a totally new car is introduced.

In the lingo of Ford, changes are categorized in two major ways: "vehicle" changes and "powertrain" changes. "Vehicle" changes relate to the exterior, interior, and frame. These changes involve everything except the engine, transmission, and items related to moving the car. The engine, transmission, and items related to moving the car are categorized as "powertrain" changes.

The significance of a vehicle and powertrain change for a particular vehicle is evaluated on a 1–6 scale where 1 represents minor or no change and 6 represents something totally new. Above is a table where the scale parameters are defined.

In making plans for each model, Ford's product development group, while working with top-level management, marketing, and engineering, plan a strategy for each model car in each year's line-up. Developing totally new cars every year is not possible, so management works to develop an interesting mix of new and revised models that keep costs within reason while generating excitement in the market.

SCALE	VEHICLE CHANGE(S)	POWERTRAIN CHANGE(S)
6	All new vehicle	New engine, new transmission
5	New exterior, modified lower structure (floor pan, chassis, dashboard)	Major engine, major transmission upgrade
4	New exterior, use existing lower structure	New use for an existing engine, new use of an existing transmission
3	Moderate freshening	Minor engine/transmission change
2	Minor freshening	Use existing engine/transmission
1	Trim changes only	Use existing engine/transmission

Each project is organized into sets of major activities that must be completed. Keep in mind that within each activity, literally hundreds of individual tasks may need to be completed. For the purposes of this case, we consider these groups of tasks as a single activity that can be scheduled for the project.

The following is a list of the activities required to develop a car:

1   Kick off (KO)—This is the beginning of work on a model. A program "black book" is compiled that contains historic information that relates to the model and a statement of the anticipated scope of the project.

2   Prestrategic intent activities I (PS1)—A mission, vision, and initial strategy are developed. Customer profile is established together with the definition of customer and market requirements. Regulatory issues also are identified. Predecessor activity: KO.

3   Prestrategic intent activities II (PS2)—Preliminary functional design strategy is proposed. Preliminary alternatives are developed. Preliminary manufacturing and program work plan are established. A parts/components sourcing council is established for make/buy studies. Predecessor activity: PS1.

4   Strategic intent (SI)—Strategies for product, market, manufacturing, supply, and design are developed. Major customer and regulatory requirements plans are made. Comparable cars are analyzed and target performance ranges established. Appearance image is developed. New

powertrain and vehicle technologies are identified. Program timing is confirmed (work plan, resources, and facilities). Predecessor activity: PS2.

5   Strategic confirmation (SC)—Vehicle subsystem performance targets are confirmed. Powertrain is selected. The manufacturing and assembly locations for each subsystem are confirmed. All major suppliers are selected and become part of the team. Prototype plan is developed. Predecessor activity: SI.

6   Proportions and hardpoints (PH)—Basic configuration of the vehicle including size, people, and cargo space is finalized. Appearance themes are reviewed and subjected to market research (interior and exterior). Predecessor activity: SC.

7   Program approval (PA)—Interior and exterior appearance themes are approved. All performance targets become goals. Program facilities and manufacturing tooling investments are approved. Marketing commits to net revenue goal. Initial dealer ordering guide developed. Parts lists are completed. Powertrain design is complete. Final prototype plan is developed. Predecessor activity: PH.

8   Surface transfer (ST)—Interior and exterior designs are approved. Predecessor activity: PA.

9   Powertrain design complete (PT)—Powertrain analytical design verification and calibration are complete. Powertrain prototype manufacturing plan is developed. Prototype powertrain assembly starts. Sign-off on powertrain manufacturing feasibility. Predecessor activity: PA.

10   Product readiness (PR)—Computer-aided design (CAD) files are all verified for accuracy. Sign-off that objectives can be met. Launch plan is confirmed and issued. Predecessor activities: ST and PT.

11   Confirmation prototype (CP)—"Make like production" prototype made using parts, product tools, and process plans to the extent feasible. First prototypes are available for testing. Accuracy of prototype items (interior, exterior, etc.) is verified using computerized dimensioning equipment. Powertrain manufacturing capability is verified (assembly, fabrication, and parts). Predecessor activity: PR.

12   Change cut-off (CC)—Preliminary engineering sign-off is completed. Decision to support lifetime requirements for replacement parts, tooling, and so forth is made. Predecessor activity: CP.

13   Launch readiness (LR)—Final engineering sign-off (functional objectives met, final road tests completed, other testing completed). Production assembly tools are functional. Sign-off of interior and exterior colors/textures/gloss. Parts

are verified for meeting specifications and being available. Predecessor activity: CC.

14   Launch sign-off (LS)—CAD models are correlated with prototype test results. Tool try-out is complete and assembly plant processes are verified. Overall vehicle audit on manufacturing-controlled items. Manufacturing verifies full production feasibility. Predecessor activity: LR.

15   Vehicle launch (VL)—Operator training is complete and continuing through ramp-up. In-process and final quality indicators meet program objectives. Powertrain manufacturing capability is validated. In-field evaluation of units is completed. CAD models are correlated and archived. Predecessor activity: LS.

At the bottom of the page is a table with the times in weeks that are allowed for the various activities. The activity duration depends on the "scale" of the vehicle and powertrain change. This table gives the number of weeks that must be reserved to complete each activity given the scale of vehicle and powertrain changes. For example, if there is a "moderate freshening" of the vehicle (a V3 change) combined with "minor engine/transmission change" (a P3 change) the strategic intent (SI) activity is scheduled to take eight weeks to complete. For our purposes, only the times associated with vehicle and powertrain changes that are the same are given, since these are the types of changes that usually occur.

APPLYING FPDS TO THE FORD THUNDERBIRD

The new Ford Thunderbird is a great reminder of the past. The 2002 model blends 50 years of Thunderbird history, yet is a thoroughly modern car. Ford intends the car to set the stylistic tone

SCALE: VEHICLE (V), POWERTRAIN (P)	TIME TO COMPLETE ACTIVITIES (WEEKS)														
	KO	PS1	PS2	SI	SC	PH	PA	ST	PT	PR	CP	CC	LR	LS	VL
V6/P6	4	12	12	24	10	14	18	24	26	44	26	14	5	13	12
V5/P5	4	12	12	20	10	14	18	24	26	40	26	14	5	13	12
V4/P4	4	8	8	12	2	14	14	18	26	40	24	14	5	13	8
V3/P3	4	4	8	8	0	12	0	12	26	32	24	14	5	13	2
V2/P2	4	4	4	8	0	8	0	0	26	32	16	10	5	9	2
V1/P1	4	4	4	8	0	8	0	0	12	24	12	6	5	9	2

for the rest of the Ford line. The T-bird shares some of its components, including the design of its powerful engine and transmission, with the Lincoln LS and the Jaguar S-Type, two other Ford luxury cars.

The product development team at Ford has developed the following plan for new models of the Ford Thunderbird over the next five years. Due to the long duration of the projects associated with developing the new models, it is easy to see that coordinating all of the tasks associated with future models can be complex. Answer the following questions by analyzing the Thunderbird model development projects using the critical path methods discussed in the chapter. It is important to recognize that in a particular year multiple projects will be going on at the same time.

MODEL	2004	2005	2006	2007	2008
Ford Thunderbird	V1/P1	V1/P1	V3/P3	V1/P1	V5/P5

QUESTIONS

1 Using the project planning data from the FPDS, develop a plan that shows what car projects will be happening during the first week of January each year. Assume that the launch date for new models is the first week of August (week 33) each year. Also, assume that the division operates only 50 weeks each year (the division is idle during Christmas and New Year's each year).

2 How are these data useful to the Thunderbird team?

3 What additional data would be useful to the team? How would these data be used?

4 Given the very dynamic nature of the luxury automobile market, and the complex engineering and design issues associated with building new cars, what would you consider the most important features of a product development system for the Thunderbird product planning group?

SELECTED BIBLIOGRAPHY

Devaux, S. A. *Total Project Control: A Manager's Guide to Integrated Project Planning, Measuring, and Tracking.* New York: Wiley, 1999.

Gray, C. F., and E. W. Larson. *Project Management: The Managerial Process.* New York: Irwin/McGraw-Hill, 2002.

Kerzner, H. *Project Management: A Systems Approach to Planning, Scheduling, and Controlling.* 8th ed. New York: Wiley, 2002.

Lewis, James P. *The Project Manager's Desk Reference.* New York: McGraw-Hill Professional Publishing, 1999.

Smith-Daniels, D. E., and N. J. Aquilano. "Constrained Resource Project Scheduling." *Journal of Operations Management* 4, no. 4 (1984), pp. 369–87.

Smith-Daniels, D. E., and V. Smith-Daniels. "Optimal Project Scheduling with Materials Ordering." *IIE Transactions* 19, no. 2 (June 1987), pp. 122–29.

Williams, P. B. *Getting a Project Done on Time: Managing People, Time, and Results.* New York: The American Management Association, 1996.

FOOTNOTES

1 Steven C. Wheelwright and Kim B. Clark, "Creating Project Plans to Focus Product Development," *Harvard Business Review,* September 2003.

2 Ibid., p. 1.

3 T. Peters, *Liberation Management* (New York: Alfred A. Knopf, 1992), p. 5 and cover flyleaf.

chapter

PRODUCT DESIGN

IDEO PRODUCT DEVELOPMENT—CAN YOU LEARN CREATIVITY?

IDEO Product Development is the world's most celebrated design firm. Its ultimate creation is the process of creativity itself. For founder David M. Kelley and his colleagues, work is play, brainstorming is a science, and the most important rule is to break the rules (www.ideo.com).

"IDEO is a zoo—oh, lovely metaphor for this age of the nanosecond! Experts of all flavors commingle in 'offices' that look more like cacophonous kindergarten classrooms than home to one of America's (and the world's) most successful design firms. Desks are littered with works-in-progress and the remains of midnight fast food binges. Models of futuristic lamps and movie special-effects devices and high-tech blood-chemistry analyzers, in all stages of development, lie about here and there—and are the cause of nonstop kibitzing. The planet's most advanced software programs, running on the world's most advanced workstations, networked with heaven-knows-whom from heaven-knows-where, hum 24 hours a day.

"Clients and other outsiders pop in and out without ado. Chatter is ceaseless. Brainstorming sessions, pitting a dozen minds from different disciplines against one another in raucous pursuit of zany ideas, are called on a moment's notice. Bikes line the halls. Joke prizes, along with impressive awards, hang on every wall. The bottom line: IDEO gets the job done on time, on budget, and with exceptional imagination."[1]

IDEO's novel design process centers on two activities that are repeated over and over:

1. **Brainstorming.**   IDEO enforces some strict rules during these sessions.
   a. Defer judgment so that the flow of ideas is not interrupted.
   b. Build on the ideas of others because this is far more productive than hogging the glory for your own insights.
   c. Stay focused on the topic; tangents are not allowed.
   d. One person at a time so that you do not drown out that quiet, brilliant mumbler in the corner of the room.
   e. Go for quantity—150 in 30–45 minutes is good.
   f. Encourage wild ideas.
   g. Be visual; for example, sketch ideas to help others understand them.
2. **Rapid prototyping.**   The idea is that it is easier to discuss a model of something, no matter how primitive, than to talk about a bunch of abstract ideas. Rapid prototyping consists of three R's: rough, rapid, and right. The first two R's are fairly self-explanatory—make your models rough and make them rapidly. In the early stages, perfecting a model is a waste of time. Right does not mean your model needs to work. Instead, it refers to building lots of small models that focus on specific problems. For example, when a group at IDEO designed a phone, they cut out dozens of pieces of foam and cradled them between their heads and shoulders to find the best shape for a handset. →

Designing new products and getting them to market quickly is the challenge facing manufacturers in industries as diverse as computer chips and potato chips. Customers of computer chip manufacturers, such as computer companies, need ever-more-powerful semiconductors for their evolving product lines. Food producers need to provide their grocery store customers new taste sensations to sustain or enlarge their retail market share. How manufactured products are designed and how the process to produce them is selected are the topics of this chapter.

THE PRODUCT DESIGN PROCESS

In today's world, companies often outsource major functions rather than support these functions in-house. Companies that specialize in manufacturing products for other companies have become very successful. These companies are called **contract manufacturers** and they have become successful in industries such as electronic products, clothing, drug, plastics, and custom manufacturing. A simple definition of a contract manufacturer is an organization capable of manufacturing and/or purchasing all the components needed to produce a finished product or device.

Contract manufacturer

The use of contract manufacturers has dramatically changed the way traditional manufacturing companies now operate. Depending on the situation, contract manufacturers will take various roles for a company. For example, in the automobile industry, contract manufacturers produce many of the parts and subassemblies such as the seats and other interior parts, the headlight and taillight assemblies, and the electronic equipment such as radio/CD and GPS navigation systems. The actual automobiles are often built regionally in the countries where the products will be sold to reduce transportation cost and manage currency exchange risk. Close coordination is required to manage the network of assembly plants and contract manufacturing partners for success.

Similar to the outsourcing of manufacturing, many companies outsource the product design function. Product design differs significantly depending on the industry. For consumer products, understanding consumer preferences and market testing prospective products are very important activities. For pharmaceuticals, extensive clinical tests are often required that involve carefully controlled experiments to test both the safety and the effectiveness of a potential product. Companies that specialize in the design of products have highly developed processes to support the activities needed for an industry.

Given the potential advantages of using contract manufacturers for producing products and specialized design firms for designing their products, a firm must decide what their core competency should be. A company's **core competency** is the one thing that it can do better than its competitors. A core competency can be anything from product design to sustained dedication of a firm's employees. The goal is to have a core competency that yields a long-term competitive advantage to the company.

Core competency

As an example, consider Honda's expertise in engines. Honda has been able to exploit this core competency to develop a variety of quality products from lawn mowers and snow blowers to trucks and automobiles. To take another example from the automotive industry, it has been claimed that Volvo's core competency is safety.

A core competency has three characteristics:

1. It provides potential access to a wide variety of markets.
2. It increases perceived customer benefits.
3. It is hard for competitors to imitate.

A good example is Black and Decker, the U.S. manufacturer of tools. Black and Decker's core technological competency is in 200- to 600-watt electric motors. All of their products are modifications of this basic technology (with the exception of their work benches, flashlights, battery-charging systems, toaster ovens, and coffee percolators). They produce products for three markets:

1. The home workshop market. In the home workshop market, small electric motors are used to produce drills, circular saws, sanders, routers, rotary tools, polishers, and drivers.
2. The home cleaning and maintenance market. In the home cleaning and maintenance market, small electric motors are used to produce dust busters, vacuum cleaners, hedge trimmers, edge trimmers, lawn mowers, leaf blowers, and pressure sprayers.
3. Kitchen appliance market. In the kitchen appliance market, small electric motors are used to produce can openers, food processors, blenders, bread makers, and fans.

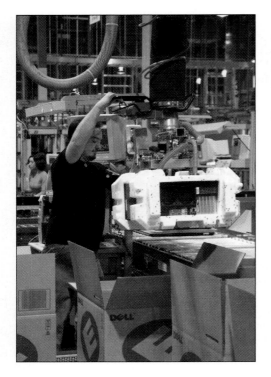

The real challenge for a firm is to decide exactly how the various functions critical to success will be handled. At one extreme is the fully vertically integrated firm where all activities from the design to the fabrication of the individual parts are handled in-house. At the other extreme is a company that only sells products and outsources all the design and manufacturing functions.

The following are a few examples of what some highly successful companies are doing:

- Sun Microsystems designs the SPARC chips used in its high-performance workstations but subcontracts the fabrication of those chips to specialized chip makers (while maintaining ownership of the intellectual property).
- A pharmaceutical company may purchase information on genetic targets from a genomics company, contract with a specialist in combinatorial chemistry for rapid synthesis and screening of candidate compounds, and even utilize a contract research organization to conduct clinical trials but retain ownership of the intellectual property (patents, experimental data, trademarks, etc.) of the drug that eventually comes to market.
- Dell has developed a set of highly specialized systems that support its make-to-order operating strategy. Dell has created a set of proprietary logistical processes that range from the design of its Web page through its information systems infrastructure (a process that has proven difficult for others to imitate). Dell owns the data about what people are buying and in which combinations. It also has been vertically integrated into final assembly facilities that are designed to efficiently produce in lot sizes of one. Finally, while it outsources components, Dell uses longer-term relationships with its suppliers and links them into its information system to support quick response.

In this chapter we first discuss a generic product design process. Here we develop a generic process and show how this can be adapted to various types of common products. Next, we show how the economic impact of new products can be evaluated. Later in the chapter we discuss how customer preferences are considered in product design. Then we show how the design of the product impacts manufacturing and assembly processes. Finally, we discuss measures of product development performance.

THE PRODUCT DEVELOPMENT PROCESS[2]

We begin by defining a generic product development process that describes the basic steps needed to design a product. This process represents the basic sequence of steps or activities that a firm employs to conceive, design, and bring a product to market. Many of these tasks involve intellectual rather than physical activities. Some firms define and follow a precise and detailed development process, while others may not even be able to describe their processes. Every organization employs a process that is different from that of every other organization; in fact, the same organization may follow different processes for different product groups.

Our generic product development process consists of six phases, as illustrated in Exhibit 4.1. The process begins with a planning phase, which is the link to advanced research and technology development activities. The output of the planning phase is the project's mission statement, which is the input required to begin the concept development phase and serves as a guide to the development team. The conclusion of the product development process is the product launch, at which time the product becomes available for purchase in the marketplace. Exhibit 4.1 identifies the key activities and responsibilities of the different functions of the firm during each development phase. Because of their continuous involvement in the process, we articulate the roles of marketing, design, and manufacturing. Representatives from other functions, such as research, finance, field service, and sales, also play key roles at points in the process.

The Generic Product Development Process.
Six phases are shown, including the tasks and responsibilities of the key functions of the
organization for each phase.

exhibit 4.1

	PHASE 1: CONCEPT DEVELOPMENT	PHASE 2: SYSTEM-LEVEL DESIGN	PHASE 3: DETAIL DESIGN	PHASE 4: TESTING AND REFINEMENT	PHASE 5: PRODUCTION RAMP-UP
PHASE 0: PLANNING					
MARKETING					
• Articulate market opportunity. • Define market segments.	• Collect customer needs. • Identify lead users. • Identify competitive products.	• Develop plan for product options and extended product family. • Set target sales price point(s).	• Develop marketing plan.	• Develop promotion and launch materials. • Facilitate field testing.	• Place early production with key customers.
DESIGN					
• Consider product platform and architecture. • Assess new technologies.	• Investigate feasibility of product concepts. • Develop industrial design concepts. • Build and test experimental prototypes.	• Generate alternative product architectures. • Define major subsystems and interfaces. • Refine industrial design.	• Define part geometry. • Choose materials. • Assign tolerances. • Complete industrial design control documentation.	• Reliability testing. • Life testing. • Performance testing. • Obtain regulatory approvals. • Implement design changes.	• Evaluate early production output.
MANUFACTURING					
• Identify production constraints. • Set supply chain strategy.	• Estimate manufacturing cost. • Assess production feasibility.	• Identify suppliers for key components. • Perform make-buy analysis. • Define final assembly scheme. • Set target costs.	• Define piece-part production processes. • Design tooling. • Define quality assurance processes. • Begin procurement of long-lead tooling.	• Facilitate supplier ramp-up. • Refine fabrication and assembly processes. • Train work force. • Refine quality assurance processes.	• Begin operation of entire production system.
OTHER FUNCTIONS					
• Research: Demonstrate available technologies. • Finance: Provide planning goals. • General Management: Allocate project resources.	• Finance: Facilitate economic analysis. • Legal: Investigate patent issues.	• Finance: Facilitate make-buy analysis. • Service: Identify service issues.		• Sales: Develop sales plan.	

The six phases of the generic development process are

Phase 0: Planning. The planning activity is often referred to as "phase zero" since it precedes the project approval and launch of the actual product development process. This phase begins with corporate strategy and includes assessment of technology developments and market objectives. The output of the planning phase is the project mission statement, which specifies the target market for the product, business goals, key assumptions, and constraints.

Phase 1: Concept development. In this phase the needs of the target market are identified, alternative product concepts are generated and evaluated, and one or more concepts are selected for further development and testing. A concept is a description of the form, function, and features of a product and is usually accompanied by a set of specifications, an analysis of competitive products, and an economic justification of the project.

Phase 2: System-level design. The system-level design phase includes the definition of the product architecture and the decomposition of the product into subsystems and components. The final assembly scheme (which we discuss later in the chapter) for the production system is usually defined during this phase as well. The output of this phase usually includes a geometric layout of the product, a functional specification of each of the product's subsystems, and a preliminary process flow diagram for the final assembly process.

Phase 3: Design detail. This phase includes the complete specification of the geometry, materials, and tolerances of all the unique parts in the product and the identification of all the standard parts to be purchased from suppliers. A process plan is established and tooling is designed for each part to be fabricated within the production system. The output of this phase is the drawings or computer files describing the geometry of each part and its production tooling, the specifications of purchased parts, and the process plans for the fabrication and assembly of the product.

Phase 4: Testing and refinement. The testing and refinement phase involves the construction and evaluation of multiple preproduction versions of the product. Early prototypes are usually built with parts with the same geometry and material properties as the production version of the product but not necessarily fabricated with the actual processes to be used in production. Prototypes are tested to determine whether the product will work as designed and whether the product satisfies customer needs.

Phase 5: Production ramp-up: In the production ramp-up phase, the product is made using the intended production system. The purpose of the ramp-up is to train the workforce and to work out any remaining problems in the production processes. Products produced during production ramp-up are sometimes supplied to preferred customers and are carefully evaluated to identify any remaining flaws. The transition from production ramp-up to ongoing production is usually gradual. At some point in the transition, the product is *launched* and becomes available for widespread distribution.

The development process described in Exhibit 4.1 is generic, and particular processes will differ in accordance with a firm's unique context. The generic process is most like the process used in a *market-pull* situation. This is when a firm begins product development with a market opportunity and then uses whatever available technologies are required to satisfy the market need (i.e., the market "pulls" the development decisions). In addition to the generic market-pull processes, several variants are common and correspond to the following: *technology-push* products, *platform* products, *process-intensive* products, *customized* products, *high-risk* products, *quick-build* products, and *complex systems*. Each of these situations is described below. The characteristics of these situations and the resulting deviations from the generic process are summarized in Exhibit 4.2.

Technology-Push Products   In developing technology-push products, a firm begins with a new proprietary technology and looks for an appropriate market in which to apply this technology (that is, the technology "pushes" development). Gore-Tex, an expanded Teflon sheet manufactured by W. L. Gore Associates, is a good example of technology push. The company has developed dozens of products incorporating Gore-Tex, including artificial

Summary of Variants of Generic Product Development Process

exhibit 4.2

PROCESS TYPE	DESCRIPTION	DISTINCT FEATURES	EXAMPLES
Generic (market-pull products)	The team begins with a market opportunity and selects appropriate technologies to meet customer needs	Process generally includes distinct planning, concept development, system-level design, detail design, testing and refinement, and production ramp-up phases	Sporting goods, furniture, tools
Technology-push products	The team begins with a new technology, then finds an appropriate market	Planning phase involves matching technology and market; concept development assumes a given technology	Gore-Tex rainwear, Tyvek envelopes
Platform products	The team assumes that the new product will be built around an established technological subsystem	Concept development assumes a proven technology platform	Consumer electronics, computers, printers
Process-intensive products	Characteristics of the product are highly constrained by the production process	Either an existing production process must be specified from the start or both product and process must be developed together from the start	Snack foods, breakfast cereals, chemicals, semiconductors
Customized products	New products are slight variations of existing configurations	Similarity of projects allows for a streamlined and highly structured development process	Motors, switches, batteries, containers
High-risk products	Technical or market uncertainties create high risks of failure	Risks are identified early and tracked throughout the process Analysis and testing activities take place as early as possible	Pharmaceuticals, space systems
Quick-build products	Rapid modeling and prototyping enables many design–build–test cycles	Detail design and testing phases are repeated a number of times until the product is completed or time/budget runs out	Software, cellular, phones
Complex systems	System must be decomposed into several subsystems and many components	Subsystems and components are developed by many teams working in parallel, followed by system integration and validation	Airplanes, jet engines, automobiles

veins for vascular surgery (see photo this page), insulation for high-performance electric cables, fabric for outerwear, dental floss, and liners for bagpipe bags.

Platform Products A platform product is built around a preexisting technological subsystem (a technology *platform*). Examples include the tape transport mechanism in the Sony Walkman, the Apple Macintosh operating system, and the instant film used in Polaroid cameras. Huge investments were made in developing these platforms, and therefore every attempt is made to incorporate them into several different products. In some sense, platform products are very similar to technology-push products in that the team begins the development effort with an assumption that the product concept will embody a particular technology. The primary difference is that a technology platform has already demonstrated its usefulness in the marketplace in meeting customer needs. The firm, in many cases, can assume that the technology also will be useful in related markets. Products built on technology platforms are much simpler to develop than if the technology were developed from scratch. For this reason, and because of the possible sharing of costs across several products, a firm may be able to offer a platform product in markets that could not justify the development of a unique technology.

Process-intensive Products   Examples of process-intensive products include semiconductors, foods, chemicals, and paper. For these products, the production process has an impact on properties of the product so that product design cannot be separated from the production process design. In many cases, process-intensive products are produced at very high volumes and are bulk, rather than discrete, goods. Often, the new product and new process are developed simultaneously. For example, creating a new shape of breakfast cereal or snack food requires both product and process development activities. In other cases, the existing process will constrain the product design by the capabilities of the process. This might be true of a new paper product to be made in a particular paper mill or a new semi-conductor device to be made in an existing wafer fabrication facility, for example.

Customized Products   Customized products are slight variations of standard configurations and are typically developed in response to a specific order by a customer. Examples include switches, motors, batteries, and containers. Developing these products consists primarily of setting values of design variables such as physical dimensions and materials. Companies can become very good at quickly producing these custom products using a highly structured design and development process structured around the capabilities of the process to be used.

High-Risk Products   High-risk products are those that entail unusually large uncertainties related to the technology or market so that there is substantial technical or market risk. The generic product development process is modified to face high-risk situations by taking steps to address the largest risks in the early stages of product development. This usually requires completing some design and test activities earlier in the process. For example, if there is high uncertainty related to the technical performance of the product, it makes sense to build working models of the key features and to test these earlier in the process. Multiple solution paths may be explored in parallel to ensure that one of the solutions succeeds. Design reviews must assess levels of risk on a regular basis, with the expectation that risk is being reduced over time and not postponed.

Quick-Build Products   For the development of some products, such as software and many electronic products, building and testing prototype models has become such a rapid process that the design–build–test cycle can be repeated many times. Following concept development in this process, the system-level design phase entails decomposition of the product into high-, medium-, and low-priority features. This is followed by several cycles of design, build, integrate, and test activities, beginning with the highest-priority items. This process takes advantage of the fast prototyping cycle by using the result of each cycle to learn how to modify the priorities for the next cycle. Customers may even be involved in the testing process. When time or budget runs out, usually all of the high- and medium-priority features have been incorporated into the evolving product, and the low-priority features may be omitted until the next product generation.

Complex Systems   Larger-scale products such as automobiles and airplanes are complex systems comprised of many interacting subsystems and components. When developing complex systems, modifications to the generic product development process address a number of system-level issues. The concept development phase considers the architecture of the entire system, and multiple architectures may be considered as competing concepts for the overall system. The system-level design becomes critical. During this phase, the system is decomposed into subsystems and these further into many components. Teams are assigned to develop each component. Additional teams are assigned the special challenge of integrating components into the subsystems and these into the overall system. Detail design of the components is a highly parallel process, often referred to as **concurrent engineering,** with many separate development teams working at once. System engineering specialists manage the interactions across the components and subsystems. The testing and refinement phase includes not only system integration but extensive testing and validation of the product.

Concurrent engineering

ECONOMIC ANALYSIS OF PRODUCT DEVELOPMENT PROJECTS[3]

A product development team at Polaroid Corporation was in the midst of developing a new photograph printer, the CI-700. The CI-700 would produce instant full-color photographs from digital images stored in a computer. The primary markets for the product are the graphic arts, insurance, and real estate industries. During the CI-700's development, the Polaroid team was faced with several decisions that it knew could have a significant impact on the product's profitability:

- Should the team take more time for development in order to make the product available on multiple computer "platforms" or would a delay in bringing the CI-700 to market be too costly?
- Should the product use print media (instant film) from Polaroid's consumer camera business or new and specialized premium-quality print media?
- Should the team increase development spending in order to increase the reliability of the CI-700?

It is important to remember that economic analysis can only capture those factors that are measurable and that projects often have both positive and negative implications that are difficult to quantify. Also, it is difficult for an economic analysis to capture the characteristics of a dynamic and competitive environment. Economic analysis is useful in at least two different circumstances:

1. Go/no-go milestones. For example, should we try to develop a product to address a new market opportunity? Should we proceed with the implementation of a selected concept? Should we launch the product we have developed? These decisions typically arise at the end of each phase of development.
2. Operational design and development decisions. Operational decisions involve questions such as: Should we spend $100,000 to hire an outside firm to develop this component in order to save two months of development time? Should we launch the product in four months at a unit cost of $450 or wait six months when we can reduce the cost to $400?

We recommend that a base-case financial model be initially built to understand the financial implications of a product development project. In the following, we describe how to construct this model.

BUILD A BASE-CASE FINANCIAL MODEL

Constructing the base-case model consists of estimating the timing and magnitude of future cash flows and then computing the net present value (NPV) of those cash flows. The timing and magnitude of the cash flows are estimated by merging the project schedule with the project budget, sales volume forecasts, and estimated production costs. The level of detail of cash flows should be coarse enough to be convenient to work with, yet contain enough detail to facilitate effective decision making. The most basic categories of cash flow for a typical new product development project are

Cross Functional

- Development cost (all remaining design, testing, and refinement costs up to production ramp-up).
- Ramp-up cost.
- Marketing and support cost.
- Production cost.
- Sales revenue.

The financial model we use is simplified to include only the major cash flows that are typically used in practice, but conceptually it is identical to more complex models. The numerical values of the cash flows come from budgets and other estimates obtained from the development team, the manufacturing organization, and the marketing organization. We will illustrate the approach by using data similar to what might have been used by the Polaroid team developing the CI-700.

exhibit 4.3

CI-700 Project Schedule from Inception through Market Withdrawal

	Year 1				Year 2				Year 3				Year 4			
CI-700 Project Schedule	Q1	Q2	Q3	Q4	Q1	Q2	Q3	Q4	Q1	Q2	Q3	Q4	Q1	Q2	Q3	Q4
Development																
Ramp-up																
Marketing and support																
Production and sales																

The following are cost estimates that we will use for our sample model:

Development cost	$5 million
Ramp-up cost	$2 million
Marketing and support cost	$1 million/year
Unit production cost	$400/unit
Sales and production volume	20,000 units/year
Unit price	$800/unit

For our model, we assume that all revenue and expenses that have occurred prior to today are sunk costs and are irrelevant to NPV calculations. For those of you not familiar with NPV calculations, see Supplement A at the end of the book.

To complete the model, the financial estimates must be merged with timing information. This can be done by considering the project schedule and sales plan. Exhibit 4.3 shows the project timing information in Gantt chart form for the CI-700. For most projects, a time increment of months or quarters is most appropriate. The remaining time to market is estimated to be five quarters, and the product sales are anticipated to last 11 quarters.

A simple method of organizing project cash flow is with a spreadsheet. The rows of the spreadsheet are the different cash flow categories, while the columns represent successive time periods. To keep things simple, we assume that the rate of cash flow for any category is constant across any time period. For example, total development spending of $5 million over one year is allocated equally to each of the four quarters. In practice, of course, the values can be arranged in any way that best represents the team's forecast of the cash flows. We multiply the unit sales quantity by the unit price to find the total product revenues in each period. We also multiply the unit production quantity by the unit production cost to find the total production cost in each period. Exhibit 4.4 illustrates the resulting spreadsheet.

Computing the NPV requires that the net cash flow for each period be determined, and then that this cash flow be converted to its present value (its value in today's dollars), as shown in the last few rows of Exhibit 4.5. Consider, for example, the calculations for year 3, first quarter:

1. The period cash flow is the sum of inflows and outflows.

Marketing cost	$ −250,000
Product revenues	4,000,000
Production cost	−2,000,000
Period cash flow	$1,750,000

2. The present value of this period cash flow discounted at 10 percent per year (2.5 percent per quarter) back to the first quarter of year 1 (a total of nine quarters) is $1,401,275. (The concepts and spreadsheet functions for calculating present value, net present value, and discount rate are reviewed in Supplement A.)

$$\frac{\$1,750,000}{1.025^9} = \$1,401,275$$

3. The project NPV is the sum of the discounted cash flows for each of the periods, or $8,002,819. (Note that in the spreadsheet we have rounded the numbers to the nearest $1,000.)

The NPV of this project, according to the base-case model, is positive, so the model supports and is consistent with the decision to proceed with development. Such modeling also can be used to support major investment decisions. Say, for example, that Polaroid were deciding between two different production facilities with different ramp-up, production, and support

Merging the Project Financials and Schedule into a Cash Flow Report

exhibit 4.4

	A	B	C	D	E	F	G	H	I	J	K	L	M	N	O	P	Q
			Year 1				Year 2				Year 3				Year 4		
2	CI-700 Project Schedule	Q1	Q2	Q3	Q4	Q1	Q2	Q3	Q4	Q1	Q2	Q3	Q4	Q1	Q2	Q3	Q4
3	Development																
4	Ramp-up																
5	Marketing and support																
6	Production and sales																
7																	
8				Year 1				Year 2				Year 3				Year 4	
9	($ values in thousands)	Q1	Q2	Q3	Q4	Q1	Q2	Q3	Q4	Q1	Q2	Q3	Q4	Q1	Q2	Q3	Q4
10																	
11	Development cost	-1,250	-1,250	-1,250	-1,250												
12	Ramp-up cost				-1,000	-1,000											
13	Marketing and support cost					-250	-250	-250	-250	-250	-250	-250	-250	-250	-250	-250	-250
14	Production volume						5,000	5,000	5,000	5,000	5,000	5,000	5,000	5,000	5,000	5,000	5,000
15	Unit production cost						-0.4	-0.4	-0.4	-0.4	-0.4	-0.4	-0.4	-0.4	-0.4	-0.4	-0.4
16	Production cost						-2,000	-2,000	-2,000	-2,000	-2,000	-2,000	-2,000	-2,000	-2,000	-2,000	-2,000
17	Sales volume						5,000	5,000	5,000	5,000	5,000	5,000	5,000	5,000	5,000	5,000	5,000
18	Unit price						0.8	0.8	0.8	0.8	0.8	0.8	0.8	0.8	0.8	0.8	0.8
19	Sales revenue						4,000	4,000	4,000	4,000	4,000	4,000	4,000	4,000	4,000	4,000	4,000
20																	
21	Period cash flow	-1,250	-1,250	-1,250	-2,250	-1,250	1,750	1,750	1,750	1,750	1,750	1,750	1,750	1,750	1,750	1,750	1,750
22	PV Year 1, r = 10%	-1,220	-1,190	-1,161	-2,038	-1,105	1,509	1,472	1,436	1,401	1,367	1,334	1,301	1,269	1,239	1,208	1,179
23																	
24	Project NPV	8,003															

Microsoft Excel - Ch5 - Economic Analysis.xls

File Edit View Insert Format Tools Data Window Help   Type a question for help

Economic Analysis

CI-700 Development Cost Sensitivity

exhibit 4.5

CHANGE IN DEVELOPMENT COST (%)	DEVELOPMENT COST ($ THOUSANDS)	CHANGE IN DEVELOPMENT COST ($ THOUSANDS)	CHANGE IN NPV (%)	NPV ($ THOUSANDS)	CHANGE IN NPV ($ THOUSANDS)
50	7,500	2,500	−29.4	5,791	−2,412
20	6,000	1,000	−11.8	7,238	−964
10	5,500	500	−5.9	7,721	−482
Base case	5,000	Base case	0.0	8,203	0
−10	4,500	−500	5.9	8,685	482
−20	4,000	−1,000	11.8	9,167	964
−30	2,500	−2,500	29.4	10,615	2,412

costs. The team could develop a model for each of the two scenarios and then compare the NPVs. The scenario with the higher NPV would better support the investment decision. We now consider sensitivity analysis as a technique for studying multiple scenarios for ongoing product development decisions.

SENSITIVITY ANALYSIS TO UNDERSTAND PROJECT TRADE-OFFS

Sensitivity analysis uses the financial model to answer "what if" questions by calculating the change in NPV corresponding to a change in the factors included in the model. As an example, consider the sensitivity of NPV to changes in development cost. By making incremental changes to develop cost while holding other factors constant, we can see the incremental impact on project NPV. For example, what will be the change in NPV if the development cost is decreased by 20 percent? A 20 percent decrease would lower the total development spending form $5 million to $4 million. If development time remains one year, then the spending per quarter would decrease from $1.25 million to $1 million. This change is simply entered in the model and the resulting NPV calculated.

A 20 percent decrease in development cost will increase NPV to $9,167,000. This represents a dollar increase of $964,000 and a percentage increase of 11.8 in NPV. This is an extremely simple case: we assume we can achieve the same project goals by spending $1 million less on development and we therefore have increased the project value by the present value of $1 million in savings accrued over a one-year period of time. The CI-700 development cost sensitivity analysis for a range of changes is shown in Exhibit 4.5.

Many other scenarios can be developed for the project including the following:

1. **Project development time.**   Consider the impact of a 25 percent increase in the project development time. This would raise the development time from four to five quarters and delay the start of the production ramp-up, marketing efforts, and product sales.
2. **Sales volume.**   Increasing sales is a powerful way to increase profit. Of course, a decrease in sales can result in significant loss. Consider, for example, the impact of a 25 percent increase and a 25 percent decrease on the profitability of the new product.
3. **Product cost or sales price.**   Consider that a $1 increase in price or a $1 decrease in cost results in a $1 increase in profit. Of course, the $1 increase in price may have a significant impact on demand. Scenarios relating to these parameters are often useful to study.
4. **Development cost.**   A dollar spent or saved on development cost is worth the present value of that dollar to the value of the project.

Financial modeling and sensitivity analysis are powerful tools for supporting product development decisions, but these techniques have important limitations. Many argue that rigorous financial analyses are required to bring discipline and control to the product development process. Others argue that financial analysis only focuses on measurable quantities and that it is often extremely difficult to predict these values accurately. The analysis is only as good as the assumptions built into the model, so these limitations must be considered. Possibly more significant are those that argue that activities associated with economic modeling can be very expensive and may significantly reduce the productivity associated with the real product development activities. Their point is that potentially productive development time is devoted to preparation of analyses and meetings and the cumulative effect of this planning and review time can significantly increase development costs.

Development teams must understand the strengths and limitations of the techniques and refrain from developing a stifling bureaucracy around the development of new products. New product development should be a process that nurtures innovation and creativity. The purpose of economic modeling is simply to ensure that the team is making decisions that are economically sound.

DESIGNING FOR THE CUSTOMER

⬭⬭⬭⬭   Before we detail the hows and whys of designing and producing products, it is useful to reflect (or, perhaps more accurately, to editorialize) on the issue of product design from the user's standpoint. In recent years, companies have been so caught up with technological efforts and advances—especially in the field of electronics—that somewhere along the line, consumers were forgotten. Designing for aesthetics and for the user is generally termed *industrial design*. IDEO is one of the most successful industrial design firms in the world. The unique process used at the company is described in the chapter's opening vignette titled "IDEO Product Development—Can You Learn Creativity?"

Industrial design is probably the area most abused by manufacturers. When frustrated with products—setting the VCR, working on the car, adjusting a computerized furnace thermostat, or operating a credit card telephone at the airport—most of us have said to ourselves, "The blankety-blank person who designed this should be made to use it!" Often parts are inaccessible, operation is too complicated, or there is no logic to setting or controlling the unit. Sometimes even worse conditions exist: metal edges are sharp and consumers cut their hands trying to reach for adjustment or repairs. Many products have too many technological features—far more than necessary. Most purchasers of electronic products cannot fully operate them and use only a small number of the available features. This has occurred because computer chips are inexpensive and adding more controls has negligible cost. Including an alarm clock or a calculator on a microwave oven costs little. But do you need it? What happens when you lose the operator's manual to any of these complex devices? Why is it that the "Help" icon on your computer provides so little help? Where is the voice of the customer?

QUALITY FUNCTION DEPLOYMENT

One approach to getting the voice of the customer into the design specification of a product is **quality function deployment (QFD)**.[4] This approach, which uses interfunctional teams from marketing, design engineering, and manufacturing, has been credited by Toyota Motor Corporation for reducing costs on its cars by more than 60 percent by significantly shortening design times.

Quality function deployment (QFD)

The QFD process begins with studying and listening to customers to determine the characteristics of a superior product. Through market research, the consumers' product needs and preferences are defined and broken down into categories called *customer requirements*. One example is an auto manufacturer that would like to improve the design of a car door. Through customer surveys and interviews, it determines that two important customer requirements in a car door are that it "stays open on a hill" and is "easy to close from the outside." After the customer requirements are defined, they are weighted based on their relative importance to the customer. Next the consumer is asked to compare and rate the company's products with the products of competitors. This process helps the company determine the product characteristics that are important to the consumer and to evaluate its product in relation to others. The end result is a better understanding and focus on product characteristics that require improvement.

Customer requirement information forms the basis for a matrix called the **house of quality** (see Exhibit 4.6). By building a house of quality matrix, the cross-functional QFD team can use customer feedback to make engineering, marketing, and design decisions. The matrix helps the team to translate customer requirements into concrete operating or engineering goals. The important product characteristics and goals for improvement are jointly agreed on and detailed in the house. This process encourages the different departments to work closely together, and it results in a better understanding of one another's goals and issues. However, the most important benefit of the house of quality is that it helps the team to focus on building a product that satisfies customers.

House of quality

The first step in building the house of quality is to develop a list of customer requirements for the product. These requirements should be ranked in order of importance. Customers are then asked to compare the company's product to the competition. Next a set of technical characteristics of the product is developed. These technical characteristics should relate directly to customer requirements. An evaluation of these characteristics should support or refute customer perception of the product. These data are then used to evaluate the strengths and weaknesses of the product in terms of technical characteristics.

VALUE ANALYSIS/VALUE ENGINEERING

Another way to consider the customer in designing products is by analyzing the "value" they see in the end product. Because it is so important that value be designed into products, we briefly describe value analysis and value engineering. The purpose of **value analysis/value engineering (VA/VE)** is to simplify products and processes. Its objective is to achieve equivalent or better performance at a lower cost while maintaining all functional requirements defined by the customer. VA/VE does this by identifying and eliminating unnecessary cost. Technically, VA deals with products already in production and is used to analyze product specifications and requirements as shown in production documents and purchase requests. Typically, purchasing departments use VA as a cost reduction technique. Performed before the production stage, value engineering is considered a cost-avoidance method. In practice, however, there is a looping back and forth between the two for a given product. This occurs because new materials, processes, and so forth require the application of VA techniques to products that have previously undergone VE. The VA/VE analysis approach involves brainstorming such questions as

Value analysis/value engineering (VA/VE)

Does the item have any design features that are not necessary?

Can two or more parts be combined into one?

How can we cut down the weight?

Are there nonstandard parts that can be eliminated?

In the following section we describe a more formal approach that is often used to guide the process of designing and improving the design of products.

exhibit 4.6 Completed House of Quality Matrix for a Car Door

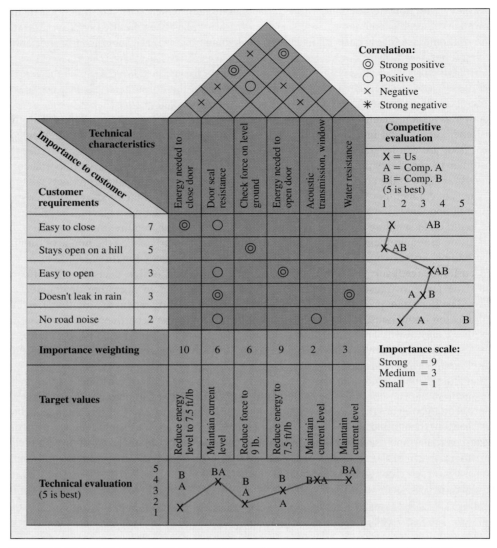

SOURCE: BASED ON J. R. HAUSER AND D. CLAUSING. "THE HOUSE OF QUALITY," *HARVARD BUSINESS REVIEW*, MAY–JUNE 1988, PP. 62–73.

DESIGNING PRODUCTS FOR MANUFACTURE AND ASSEMBLY

The word *design* has many different meanings. To some it means the aesthetic design of a product, such as the external shape of a car or the color, texture, and shape of the casing of a can opener. In another sense, design can mean establishing the basic parameters of a system. For example, before considering any details, the design of a power plant might mean establishing the characteristics of the various units such as generators, pumps, boilers, connecting pipes, and so forth.

Yet another interpretation of the word *design* is the detailing of the materials, shapes, and tolerance of the individual parts of a product. This is the concern of this section. It is an activity that starts with sketches of parts and assemblies and then progresses to the computer-aided design (CAD) workstation (described in the supplement on Operations Technology at the end of the book), where assembly drawings and detailed part drawings are produced. Traditionally, these drawings are then passed to the manufacturing and assembly engineers, whose job it is to optimize the processes used to produce the final product. Frequently, at this stage manufacturing and assembly problems are encountered and requests are made for design changes. Often these design changes are major and result in considerable additional expense and delays in the final product release.

Traditionally, the attitude of designers has been "We design it; you build it." This has now been termed the "over-the-wall approach," where the designer is sitting on one side of the wall and throwing the design over the wall to the manufacturing engineers. These manufacturing engineers then have to deal with the problems that arise because they were not involved in the design effort. One way to overcome this problem is to consult the manufacturing engineers during the design stage. The resulting teamwork avoids many of the problems that will arise. These concurrent engineering teams require analysis tools to help them study proposed designs and evaluate them from the point of view of manufacturing difficulty and cost.

How Does Design for Manufacturing and Assembly (DFMA) Work?

Let's follow an example from the conceptual design stage.[5] Exhibit 4.7 represents a motor drive assembly that is required to sense and control its position on two steel guide rails. This might be the motor that controls a power window in a drive-through window at McDonald's, for example. The motor must be fully enclosed and have a removable cover for access to adjust the position sensor. A major requirement is a rigid base designed to slide up and down the guide rails, which will both support the motor and locate the sensor. The motor and sensor have wires connecting to a power supply and control unit.

A proposed solution is shown in Exhibit 4.8. The base has two bushing inserts so that the holes will not wear out. The motor is secured to the base with two screws and a hole accepts the cylindrical sensor, which is held in place with a set screw. To provide the required covers, an end plate is screwed to two stand-offs, which are screwed into the base. To keep the wires from shorting out on the metal cover, should they become worn, a plastic bushing is fitted to the end plate, through which the wires pass. Finally, a box-shaped cover slides

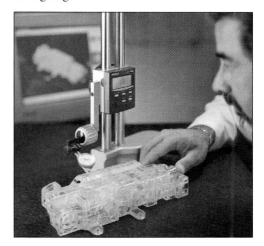

RAPID PROTOTYPING COMBINED WITH **DFMA** TOOLS NOT ONLY CAN DETERMINE IF A PRODUCT WILL PERFORM ITS DESIGNED FUNCTIONS, BUT HOW WELL AND FOR HOW LONG. USED EARLY IN THE DESIGN CYCLE, IT LEADS TO MORE ROBUST DESIGNS FOR MANUFACTURE, ASSEMBLY, AND PRODUCT USE, AND ALLOWS CRITICAL CHANGES TO BE MADE BEFORE EXPENSIVE TOOLING IS APPLIED. A PRODUCT'S ESTHETICS AND FUNCTIONALITY ARE CONSIDERED JOINTLY AND RESULT IN PRODUCTS CONSTRUCTED WITH OPTIMAL FUNCTIONALITY, CORRECT MATERIALS, AND EFFICIENT ASSEMBLY.

Configuration of Required Motor Drive Assembly   **exhibit 4.7**

exhibit 4.8   Proposed Motor Drive Design

Cover screw (4)
0.12 dia × 0.3

Bush (2)
brass, impregnated
powder metal
0.5 dia × 0.8

End plate
l.c. steel, painted
4.5 × 2.5 × 1.3

Plastic bushing
0.7 dia 0.4

Cover 16 gauge
steel, painted
soldered seams
4.5 × 2.75 × 24

Motor
2.75 dia × 4.75

Motor screw (2)
0.2 dia × 0.6

Set screw
0.06 × 0.12

Base
aluminum, machined
4 × 21.2 × 1

Sensor
0.187 × 1

Stand-off
l.c. steel, machined
0.5 dia × 2

End plate screw (2)
0.2 dia × 0.5

over the whole assembly from below the base and is held in place by four screws, two passing into the base and two passing into the end cover.

The current design has 19 parts that must be assembled to make the motor drive. These parts consist of the two subassemblies—the motor and the sensor—an additional eight main parts (cover, base, two bushings, two stand-offs, a plastic bushing, and the end plate), and nine screws.

The greatest improvements related to DFMA arise from simplification of the product by reducing the number of separate parts. In order to guide the designer in reducing the part count, the methodology provides three criteria against which each part must be examined as it is added to the product during assembly:

1. During the operation of the product, does the part move relative to all other parts already assembled?
2. Must the part be of a different material than or be isolated from other parts already assembled?
3. Must the part be separate from all other parts to allow the disassembly of the product for adjustment or maintenance?

Application of these criteria to the proposed design would proceed as follows:

1. **Base.**   Because this is the first part to be assembled, there are no other parts with which to combine, so it is theoretically a necessary part.
2. **Bushings (2).**   These do not satisfy the second criterion. Theoretically, the base and bushings could be of the same material.
3. **Motor.**   The motor is a subassembly purchased from a supplier. The criteria do not apply.
4. **Motor screws (2).**   In most cases, separate fasteners are not needed, because a fastening arrangement integral to the design (for example, snapping the part into place) is usually possible.
5. **Sensor.**   This is another standard subassembly.
6. **Set screw.**   Similar to 4, this should not be necessary.
7. **Standoffs (2).**   These do not meet the second criterion; they could be incorporated into the base.
8. **End plate.**   This must be separate to allow disassembly (apply criterion three).
9. **End plate screws (2).**   These should not be necessary.

exhibit 4.9

Redesign of Motor Drive Assembly Following Design for Assembly (DFA) Analysis

10. **Plastic bushing.**   Could be of the same material as, and therefore combined with, the end plate.
11. **Cover.**   Could be combined with the end plate.
12. **Cover screws (4).**   Not necessary.

From this analysis, it can be seen that if the motor and sensor subassemblies could be arranged to snap or screw into the base, and if a plastic cover could be designed to snap on, only 4 separate items would be needed instead of 19. These four items represent the theoretical minimum number needed to satisfy the constraints of the product design.

At this point, it is up to the design team to justify why the parts above the minimum should be included. Justification may be due to practical, technical, or economic considerations. In this example, it could be argued that two screws are needed to secure the motor and that one set screw is needed to hold the sensor, because any alternatives would be impractical for a low-volume product such as this. However, the design of these screws could be improved by providing them with pilot points to facilitate assembly.

Exhibit 4.9 is a drawing of a redesigned motor drive assembly that uses only seven separate parts. Notice how the parts have been eliminated. The new plastic cover is designed to snap onto the base plate. This new product is much simpler to assemble and should be much less expensive due to the reduced number of parts.

MEASURING PRODUCT DEVELOPMENT PERFORMANCE

There is strong evidence that generating a steady stream of new products to market is extremely important to competitiveness. To succeed, firms must respond to changing customer needs and the moves of their competitors. The ability to identify opportunities, mount the development effort, and bring to market new products and processes quickly is critical. Firms also must bring new products and processes to market efficiently. Because the number of new products and new process technologies has increased while model lives and life cycles have shrunk, firms must mount more development projects than previously, and these projects must use substantially fewer resources per project.

In the U.S. automobile market, for example, the growth of models and market segments over the last 25 years has meant that an auto firm must initiate close to four times as many development projects simply to maintain its market share position. But smaller volumes per model and shorter design lives mean resource requirements must drop dramatically. Remaining competitive requires efficient engineering, design, and development activities.

Measures of product development success can be categorized into those that relate to the speed and frequency of bringing new products online, to the productivity of the actual development process, and to the quality of the actual products introduced (see Exhibit 4.10). Taken

Performance Measures for Development Projects

PERFORMANCE DIMENSION	MEASURES	IMPACT ON COMPETITIVENESS
Time to market	Frequency of new product introductions	Responsiveness to customers/competitors
	Time from initial concept to market introduction	Quality of design—close to market
	Number started and number completed	Frequency of projects—model life
	Actual versus plan	
	Percentage of sales coming from new products	
Productivity	Engineering hours per project	Number of projects—freshness and breadth of line
	Cost of materials and tooling per project	
	Actual versus plan	Frequency of projects—economics of development
Quality	Conformance—reliability in use	Reputation—customer loyalty
	Design—performance and customer satisfaction	Relative attractiveness to customers—market share
	Yield—factory and field	
		Profitability—cost of ongoing service

together, time, quality, and productivity define the performance of development, and in combination with other activities—sales, manufacturing, advertising, and customer service—determine the market impact of the project and its profitability.

CONCLUSION

Product development is a major challenge that directly impacts the long-range success of a firm. Effectively managing the process requires an integrated effort involving all the functional areas of the firm. In this chapter, a generic process for developing products has been discussed. How this generic process is modified for various types of products is considered. An economic plan that ties the timing of the various product development activities to the project budget is essential for making good decisions as the process progresses. In the chapter, we also gave some insight into how the customer view may be incorporated into the product design process. Designing a product that can be produced efficiently is an interesting engineering exercise that we briefly introduced in the chapter. Finally, we considered various measures that are useful for monitoring a firm's product design activities.

KEY TERMS

Contract manufacturer An organization capable of manufacturing and/or purchasing all the components needed to produce a finished product or device.

Core competency The one thing that a firm can do better than its competitors. The goal is to have a core competency that yields a long-term competitive advantage to the company.

Concurrent engineering Emphasizes cross-functional integration and concurrent development of a product and its associated processes.

Quality function deployment (QFD) A process that helps a company determine the product characteristics important to the consumer and to evaluate its own product in relation to others.

House of quality A matrix that helps a product design team translate customer requirements into operating and engineering goals.

Value analysis/value engineering (VA/VE) Analysis with the purpose of simplifying products and processes by achieving equivalent or better performance at a lower cost.

SOLVED PROBLEM

VidMark, a manufacturer of cell phones, is currently developing a new model (VidPhone X70) that will be released on the market when development is complete. This phone will be revolutionary in that it will allow the user to place video phone calls. VidMark is concerned about the development cost and time. They are also worried about market estimates of the sales of the new VidPhone X70. The cost estimates and forecast are given in the table below.

Development Cost	$2,00,000
Development Time	2 years
Ramp-up Cost	$750,000
Marketing and Support Cost	$500,000/year
Unit Production Cost	$75
Unit Price	$135
Sales and Production Volume	
Year 3	40,000
Year 4	50,000
Year 5	40,000

Use the data above to develop a base-case analysis. The project schedule is shown below with timings of the cash flows.

PROJECT SCHEDULE VIDPHONE X70	YEAR 1	YEAR 2	YEAR 3	YEAR 4	YEAR 5
Development					
Ramp-up					
Marketing and Support					
Production and Sales					

There are several questions that need to be answered for VidMark on this project:

a. What are the yearly cash flows and their present value (discounted at 12%) of this project? What is the net present value?
b. What is the impact on VidMark if their sales estimates are off by 20%?
c. What is the impact on VidMark if their unit production cost is $85?
d. VidMark thinks that they can cut the development time in half if they spend an extra $1,500,000 on development for this project. If the product is launched a year earlier, then the product will still have a 3-year life but the forecast starting in year 2 will be 48,000, 60,0000, and 50,000. Is it worth it to VidMark to spend the extra money on development?

Solution

a. Start by building the base case scenario (analysis is in 000).

PROJECT SCHEDULE VIDPHONE X 70	YEAR 1	YEAR 2	YEAR 3	YEAR 4	YEAR 5
Development	−$1,000	−$1,000			
Ramp-up		−$750			
Marketing and Support		−$500	−$500	−$500	-$500
Production Volume			40	50	40
Unit Production Cost (dollars)			−$75	−$75	−$75
Production Costs			−$3,000	−$3,750	−$3,000
Sales Volume			40	50	40
Unit Price (dollars)			$135	$135	$135
Sales Revenue			$5,400	$6,750	$5,400
Period Cash Flow	−$1,000	−$2,250	$1,900	$2,500	$1,900
PV Year 1 r = 12%	−$1,000	−$2,009	$1,515	$1,779	$1,207
Project NPV	$1,493				

The cash flows and present value of the cash flows are shown in the bolded rows above. The project NPV under the base case is $1.493 million.

b. If sales are reduced by 20% then project NPV drops to $378,000.

PROJECT SCHEDULE VIDPHONE X70	YEAR 1	YEAR 2	YEAR 3	YEAR 4	YEAR 5
Period Cash Flow	−$1,000	−$2,250	$1,420	$1,900	$1,420
PV Year 1 r = 12	−$1,000	−$2,009	$1,132	$1,352	$902
Project NPV	$378				

If sales are increased by 20% then project NPV goes up to $2.607 million. A change of 20% either way has a large impact on the NPV.

PROJECT SCHEDULE VIDPHONE X70	YEAR 1	YEAR 2	YEAR 3	YEAR 4	YEAR 5
Period Cash Flow	−$1,000	−$2,250	$2,380	$3,100	$2,380
PV Year 1 r = 12	−$1,000	−$2,009	$1,897	$2,207	$1,513
Project NPV	$2,607				

c. Increased unit production costs.

PROJECT SCHEDULE VIDPHONE X70	YEAR 1	YEAR 2	YEAR 3	YEAR 4	YEAR 5
Period Cash Flow	−$1,000	−$2,250	$1,500	$2,000	$1,500
PV Year 1 r = 12	−$1,000	−$2,009	$1,196	$1,424	$953
Project NPV	$564				

The cash flows are severely affected by the increased unit production cost. Increased future cash outflow of $1.3 million (130,000 units * $10 increase) causes a decrease in net present value of $929,000 ($1.493 million − $.564 million). However, it still appears to be worth developing the new phone.

d. Here are the changes proposed by VidMark:

Development Cost	$3,500,000
Development Time	1 year
Ramp-up Cost	$750,000
Marketing and Support Cost	$500,000/year
Unit Production Cost	$75
Unit Price	$135
Sales and Production Volume	
Year 2	48,000
Year 3	60,000
Year 4	50,000

Use the data above to develop a base-case analysis. The project schedule is shown below with timings of cash flows.

PROJECT SCHEDULE VIDPHONE X70	YEAR 1	YEAR 2	YEAR 3	YEAR 4
Development				
Ramp-up				
Marketing and Support				
Production and Sales				

It appears that VidMark is better off to take 2 years to develop their new VidPhone X70 because the NPV of the base case is $1.493 million versus the fast development NPV of $733,000 (see table on the next page).

PROJECT SCHEDULE VIDPHONE X70	YEAR 1	YEAR 2	YEAR 3	YEAR 4
Development	−$3,500			
Ramp-up	−$750			
Marketing and Support	−$500	−$500	−$500	−$500
Production Volume		48	60	50
Unit Production Cost (dollars)		−$75	−$75	−$75
Production Costs		−$3,600	−$4,500	−$3,750
Sales Volume		48	60	50
Unit Price (dollars)		$135	$135	$135
Sales Revenue		$6,480	$8,100	$6,750
Period Cash Flow	−$4,750	$2,380	$3,100	$2,500
PV Year 1 r = 12	−$4,750	$2,125	$2,471	$1,779
Project NPV	$1,625			

REVIEW AND DISCUSSION QUESTIONS

1 Describe the generic product development process described in the chapter. How does the process change for "technology-push" products?
2 Discuss the product design philosophy behind industrial design and design for manufacture and assembly. Which one do you think is more important in a customer-focused product development?
3 Discuss design-based incrementalism, which is frequent product redesign throughout the product's life. What are the pros and cons of this idea?
4 What factors must be traded off by product development before introducing a new product?
5 How does the QFD approach help? What are some limitations of the QFD approach?

PROBLEMS

1 The Tuff Wheels was getting ready to start their development project for a new product to be added to its small motorized vehicle line for children. The new product is called the Kiddy Dozer. It will look a miniature bulldozer, complete with caterpillar tracks and a blade. Tuff Wheels has forecasted the demand and the cost to develop and produce the new Kiddy Dozer. The table below contains the relevant information for this project.

Development Cost	$1,000,000
Estimated Development time	9 months
Pilot Testing	$200,000
Ramp-up Cost	$400,000
Marketing and Support Cost	$150,000 per year
Sales and Production Volume	60,000 per year
Unit Production Cost	$100
Unit Price	$170
Interest rate	8%

Tuff Wheels has also provided the project plan shown below. As can be seen in the project plan the company thinks that the product life will be three years until a new product must be created.

PROJECT SCHEDULE KIDDY DOZER	YEAR 1				YEAR 2				YEAR 3				YEAR 4			
	Q1	Q2	Q3	Q4	Q1	Q2	Q3	Q4	Q1	Q2	Q3	Q4	Q1	Q2	Q3	Q4
Development																
Pilot Testing																
Ramp-up																
Marketing and Support																
Production and Sales																

a. What are the yearly cash flows and their present value (discounted at 8%) of this project? What is the net present value?
b. What is the impact on NPV for the Kiddy Dozer if the actual sales are 50,000 per year or 70,000 per year?
c. What is the effect caused by changing the discount rate to 9%, 10%, or 11%?

2   Perot Corporation is developing a new CPU chip based on a new type of technology. Their new chip, the Patay2 chip, will take 2 years to develop. However, because chip manufacturers will be able to copy the technology it will have a market life of 2 years after it is introduced. Perot expects to be able to price the chip higher in the first year and they anticipate a significant production cost reduction after the first year as well. The relevant information for developing and selling the Patay2 is given below.

PATAY2 CHIP PRODUCT ESTIMATES

Development Cost	$20,000,000
Pilot Testing	$5,000,000
Debug	$3,000,000
Ramp-up Cost	$3,000,000
Advance Marketing	$5,000,000
Marketing and Support Cost	$1,000,000 per year
Unit Production Cost Year 1	$655.00
Unit Production Cost Year 2	$545.00
Unit Price Year 1	$820.00
Unit Price Year 2	$650.00
Sales and Production Volume Year 1	250,000
Sales and Production Volume Year 2	150,000
Interest rate	10%

PATAY2 CHIP PROJECT TIMING

PROJECT SCHEDULE	YEAR 1		YEAR 2		YEAR 3		YEAR 4	
	1ST HALF	2ND HALF	1ST HALF	2ND HALF	1ST HALF	2ND HALF	1ST HALF	2ND HALF
PATAY2 CHIP								
Development								
Pilot Testing								
Debug								
Ramp-up								
Advance Marketing								
Marketing and Support								
Production and Sales								

a. What are the yearly cash flows and their present value (discounted at 10%) of this project? What is the net present value?

b. Perot's engineers have determined that if they spend $10 million more on development it will allow them to add even more advanced features. Having a more advanced chip will allow them to price the chip $50 higher in both years ($870 for year 1 and $700 for year 2). Is it worth the additional investment?

c. If sales are only 200,000 the first year and 100,000 the second year would Perot still do the project?

3   Pick a product and list issues that need to be considered in its design and manufacture. The product can be something like a stereo, telephone, desk, or kitchen appliance. Consider the functional and aesthetic aspects of design as well as the important concerns for manufacturing.

4   The following is a partial house of quality for a golf country club. Provide an importance weighting from your perspective (or that of a golfing friend) in the unshaded areas. If you can, using the QFD approach, compare it to a club where you or your friends play.

5   The purpose of this system design exercise is to gain experience in setting up a manufacturing process. (We suggest that this be done as a team project.) Assignment:

a. Get one Ping-Pong paddle.

b. Specify the type of equipment and raw materials you would need to manufacture that paddle, from the receipt of seasoned wood to packaging for shipment.

c. Assume that one unit of each type of equipment is available to you. Further assume that you have a stock of seasoned wood and other materials needed to produce and box 100 paddles. Making reasonable assumptions about times and distances where necessary,

(1) Develop an assembly drawing for the paddle.
(2) Prepare an assembly chart for the paddle.
(3) Develop a process flowchart for the paddle.
(4) Develop a route sheet for the paddle.

WHATs versus HOWs Strong Relationship: ● Medium Relationship: ○ Weak Relationship: △	Physical Aspects	Course location	Grounds maintenance	Landscaping	Pin placement	Course tuning	Tee placement	Service Facilities	Customer-trained attendants	Top-quality food	Highly rated chefs	Attractive restaurant	Tournament Activities	Calloway handicapping	Exciting door prizes	Perception Issues	Invitation only	Types of guests	Income level	Celebrity
Physical Aspects																				
Manicured grounds																				
Easy access																				
Challenging																				
Service Facilities																				
Restaurant facilities																				
Good food																				
Good service																				
Good layout																				
Plush locker room																				
Helpful service attendants																				
Tournament Facilities																				
Good tournament prize																				
Types of players																				
Fair handicapping system																				
Perception Issues																				
Prestigious																				

CASE: NEW PRODUCT DEVELOPMENT AT HPM*

INTRODUCTION

To compete in today's business environment, HPM Industries must deal with the most competitive and hostile marketplace that it has faced in the company's entire history. Improvements in technology and an increasingly globalised market mean that competitors are now causing severe pressure in markets where HPM has traditionally held dominance.

The company's strategy to overcome this threat is to use innovation and technology to differentiate itself in the marketplace. Over the last two decades HPM has concentrated on developing a strong innovation culture within the organisation, and this is now successfully demonstrated in many areas throughout the company. This, combined with the company's strong focus on using the latest technology in both its products and manufacturing processes, has positioned the company in an excellent position to be able to adapt to market changes.

This case therefore describes how HPM is positioning itself in the marketplace and details some of the ways that the company is utilising technology and innovation to differentiate itself. It also details an example of how the company conducted a comparison between the conventional engineering path from product design to marketing introduction, with two "rapid" development alternatives. One alternative demonstrated the advantages gained by introducing stereolithography models while the other identified the further gains made by utilising the models to produce "rapid tooling" through a cold metal spray process.

COMPANY BACKGROUND

HPM Industries is a privately owned company established in 1925. Its core business is in the design, manufacture, and distribution of electrical wiring accessories such as electrical power plugs, power outlets, and light switches. HPM has traditionally marketed and sold its products through the electrical wholesale market, and although this area still forms the backbone of the company's success, more recently the company has also been successful in developing and marketing many products for the retail market sector.

For electrical products HPM has been the dominant player in the Australian domestic market for many years, and internationally the company has also managed to break into a number of special niches. Although the company is widely recognised as a leading electrical accessory manufacturer in Australia, the company could not be considered a "household" name. This is despite the fact that almost every home in Australia would contain one or more product lines that HPM manufactures.

The company had its origins in button production, when Ruth Simons's parents (Ruth is the wife of the current chief executive officer, Peter Simons) started HPM in the button-moulding business. In 1948 they bought a tool at auction to make plug-tops and started turning out about 20 products.

Today the business employs more than 1,100 employees working in its various factory sites, warehouses, and sales offices around the country, from which it supplies over 3,500 product lines. In Sydney alone, there are approximately 800 employees engaged in manufacturing, with over 200 staff in sales, administration, finance, and distribution around the country.

The Darlinghurst site in Sydney contains the operations of design, engineering, manufacture, and also distribution, while the 500 employees at the newer Waterloo factory are mainly involved in assembly and distribution. There are nine factories in Sydney which supply every part of HPM's manufactured product range. The seven sites average around 200 employees, with each managed by a single engineer plant manager qualified in moulding, materials, processing, and the latest technology.

As an Australian company, HPM has a strong philanthropic ethic and sense of corporate responsibility and each year contributes in various ways to the Australian community. As well as sponsoring the annual HPM Award for Excellence in Design, the company supports a number of Australian community organisations such as the National Trust, the Australian Chamber Orchestra, Kidsafe, and the Lord Mayor's Bush Fire Appeal. In 1994, HPM also committed to fund a three-year scientific research project through the Australian Koala Foundation and James Cook University.

COMPETING IN A CHANGING ENVIRONMENT

HPM has enjoyed a strong position in the Australian electrical market for almost half a century, and through its attention to quality and strong product development the company still continues to enjoy steady growth. In the pursuit of this growth, however, the company now faces many different challenges to those which existed when the company first began.

One of the most notable changes that has taken place in the market over the last two decades is in the length of product life cycles. In the 1970s and 1980s HPM's products generally had a life cycle of around 8–10 years. However, in today's market the company now must contend with product life cycles of two years and less.

Impact of Technology   The company's Managing Director Stuart Romm attributes much of the reason for this reduction to the impact of new technology on the market. This is not only because competitors are able to develop alternative products on a much more frequent basis, but also because competitors are now able to reengineer exact duplicates of HPM's products and saturate the market with cheap copies.

In the past, the quality of the cheaper, generally imported, products was very poor, thereby providing HPM with a competitive advantage on quality. However, recent improvements in technology mean that the quality of the imported product coming into Australia is now very good. Competitors can optically scan a product, reverse engineer it, and then produce a product with all the same characteristics as the HPM product.

These products are on the market today, and although they have not been very successful in gaining market share up to now, they are causing severe price pressure in the marketplace. Technology, in this sense, is therefore creating a lot of extra competition in HPM's traditional market areas.

Impact of Cheap Imports   In contrast to the recent trend for companies to outsource and/or move offshore for their manufacturing requirements, HPM has for many years held a unique "in-house" manufacturing philosophy and sourcing structure. The company has been fully committed to manufacturing in Australia, and this "Australian Made" philosophy has contributed greatly to the company's marketing success. As CEO Peter Simons remarks, "We made a conscious decision a few years ago to continue to manufacture our components locally."

The logic behind this domestic manufacturing strategy was that the company would be able to overcome the cheap labour and the lower setup costs of overseas competitors by investing in more automated manufacturing technology, and by utilising the superior engineering skills that exist within the company.

Today, however, the market pressure facing the company, particularly on standard products, is fast becoming overwhelming. Stuart Romm recognises this and attributes much of the pressure to low-cost Chinese sourcing. He comments that low-cost overseas sourcing has now reached the point where HPM can source a packaged finished product out of China for less than the cost of the raw material in Australia.

This kind of market pressure is no longer forcing HPM to increase its automation; it is forcing the company to totally reposition its manufacturing strategy. Management has come to the realisation that the domestic manufacture of standard, low-technology products has now become uncompetitive against low-cost imports coming from Southeast Asia. In recognition of this, from the year 2000 onward, the company's manufacturing strategy will change dramatically, and the manufacture of high volume, and particularly low-technology, products will probably be forced offshore.

Still concious of its commitment to Australian manufacturing, however, HPM is expanding its manufacturing capability in Australia in higher technology areas, and the company's acquisition of a large electronics factory in Sydney is a good example of this. This factory is larger than currently needed by the company; however, the acquisition forms part of the company's longer term strategy for developing its electronics capabilities.

STRATEGIC DIRECTION: USING TECHNOLOGY AND INNOVATION TO DIFFERENTIATE

To achieve its goals, the company's main strategy is to differentiate itself from low-cost competitors through innovation. Management's aim is to build on the company's strong tradition of product development and to position the company such that the marketplace is constantly looking toward HPM for refreshing new products all the time.

Innovation at HPM   Similar to the way in which 3M operates, HPM has for many years tried to instill a culture of innovation within the company. This approach is still as strong as ever in the way that the company operates, and it continues to bear fruit.

Developing a Culture of Innovation

Organisational   HPM's culture for innovation has historically been embedded in its free-thinking process. The company structure involves very few rules and regulations, with a deliberate exclusion of set policies, and no job or position descriptions. "We don't like anything formal," comments the managing director, working instead with clear directional indicators and understood limits. There is no formal vision, mission, goals, or strategic objectives set down. They exist in broad terms, but are kept as fuzzy as possible to ensure that necessary changes and resources can be drafted as needed. The only documentation is in the form of a pictorial diagram of the business objectives. This is represented as a roof with five supporting product line pillars. To have a formalised corporate planning process would be too bureaucratic, totally alien to the company, and would destroy its family culture.

Remuneration is highly graded, with executives highly paid and tradespeople drawing 30 to 40 percent over the MTIA award. Design and engineering staff are given the necessary resources, freedom of action, full responsibility, and opportunity to exhibit initiative and creativity—there are no rules to inhibit performance.

The enterprise agreement that HPM has been able to develop with its factory employees over the last five to six years also provides the company with the flexibility it requires and reinforces the company's desire for flexibility, employee contribution, and new ideas. Features of the agreements that have been struck are as follows:

- Workplace flexibility; related to flexible starting and stopping times for specified periods, staggering start and finish times for auxiliary staff, continuity of operation, and coverage of additional machines due to absences.
- Quality assurance for continuous improvement, with future progress motivated by employees taking responsibility for quality within their workstations and diversifying the responsibility of quality to each employee rather than to inspectors only.
- Responsibility for control and work planning taken by operational staff for their own stock at their workstation, rather than relying upon auxiliary or indirect labour.
- A consultative committee to continuously monitor and review training for new technology, multiskilling and job sharing, shop-floor training for new/transferred staff, English in the workplace programs, and shop-floor training for QA procedures and requirements.

To emphasise the importance of innovation and new ideas, the company has also set up a separate research and development organisation that is constantly looking for new product ideas and better ways to progress from concept to marketplace. R & D is given so much credibility in the organisation because it is seen as the key to the future success of the company.

External Influences   Some of the ways in which HPM encourages innovation through its external relationships are as follows:

1   HPM has made a significant commitment to the federal government's Intelligent Manufacturing Systems (IMS) consortium agreement for R & D projects. This program gives the company an insight into tertiary-level research and development and provides it with a network of contacts around the world. Through this program the company has been able to develop strong relationships with other facilitating companies, including Daimler-Benz (Europe), Pratt and Whitney (Canada), and United Technologies in the United States. Participating institutions also include the Fraunhoffer Institute in Germany and MIT in the United States.

    Wherever there is research going on within this international consortium, HPM is in an excellent position to tap into that knowledge and intellectual property. It is the company's strategy to utilise the latest in processing technology, and by maintaining strong links with other leading companies and tertiary institutions the company can be confident that it will have the inside information on any new developments in processing technology.

2   The company is also heavily involved with a number of Australian universities; for example, the company provides the funds for an annual engineering co-op scholarship with the University of NSW, and they are also governors of the Warren Centre, which is Sydney University's commercial arm.

New Product Innovation   The company's approach to product development is very much marketing-led, as Stuart Romm remarks: "The strategy to start with has to be to find the problems in the marketplace, and create the solutions. That's innovation."

At HPM innovation inputs come from four different directions.

1   Management think tank. Every morning there is an executive think tank for 45 minutes to one hour. Executives who know the industry get together to play around with ideas and discuss the progress of different issues. There is also a formal meeting with the R & D executives once per week for about two hours.

2   Inventors. The company encourages these, and there are probably around two to three per week who "knock on the door" with some idea that they are looking to develop. These people are embraced and encouraged.

3   Salespeople. All of the salespeople are strategically aligned with the end user, which is the electrical contractor, rather than the commercial customer, who is the electrical wholesaler. Salespeople are encouraged to spend 70–80 percent of their time with the end installer, the electrician, who actually makes the purchasing decision.

    The issue here is that the user knows the problems with the HPM or competitive products, and he/she knows the problems on installation. This feedback generally provides simple and practical ideas which are then fed back through the salespeople to the designers and engineers.

This is the area responsible for the majority of the company's new innovation ideas.

4   International study tours. The innovation process is also supported by attendance at a number of the international conferences that are held around the world each year. The idea here is not to copy the products shown at the fairs but to stimulate thought and generate ideas.

Technology in New Products   HPM's strategy is to concentrate on highly innovative products, particularly focusing on those that hold the following characteristics:

1   Where there is added value.
2   Where the company has some intellectual property in the product.
3   Where the product can't be copied or will take a long time to copy.

In satisfying these criteria the company is increasingly moving toward new electronics technology in an effort to:

1   Increase the product life cycle of their products.
2   Differentiate the HPM product in the marketplace.

Placing electronics into products is allowing the company to do things that could never be done before. A typical example of this is the way in which HPM now offers dimmers and time switches in a lot of its products. This patented technology works off a single wire (there is no neutral required), giving the company an advantage that competitors have as yet been unable to match.

The technology means that an electrical contractor can now take out a light switch (which just has a wire in and a wire out), and without having to bring a neutral wire into it, he/she can replace it with an HPM digital time switch. This allows the user to set the time for whenever he/she wants it to go on or off.

The company is not only using electronics in existing products but is also moving into the area of providing complete electronic systems. The company's "smart house" product, OSCAR, is an example of this. This product is designed for the normal domestic residence, and provides home automation to the consumer for security, light control, power control, and home entertainment.

Management's vision is that tomorrow's consumer will want increased functionality within the home. Consumers will want to be able to plug their computer into any room in the house, to be able to turn on the video downstairs and watch it on the television upstairs. They will also want the ability for remote operation of these facilities, the ability to log in to the network and have total control of the system from anywhere in the world. In a similar style, HPM's continuing focus will be on providing total electronic systems for commercial and industrial applications.

It can clearly be seen that although technology is in one sense causing the company increased competition, on the flip side it is also allowing the company to differentiate itself from the competition and move into other areas.

Increased Market Servicing   Coinciding with the development of higher technology products, HPM is also looking to increase the number of support services that they offer in the field. In the future the company will offer services such as systems installation, commissioning, and upgrades to support their products.

The premise for this is that the electrical contracting industry tends to be quite conservative, and HPM believes that without this support they will not move at the rate that the company wants to move. The concern therefore is that the momentum of the penetration of electronic systems (like OSCAR) into the marketplace will be limited by a conservative installation industry.

Developing New Distribution Channels   The existing OSCAR system is sold through traditional distribution channels (i.e., the same as powerpoints, etc.). It goes on the shelf of the electrical wholesaler, and is then sold to the electrical contractor.

Future systems will not be sold via this channel, however, as they will need to be programmed on-site by someone with the appropriate programming skills. It is not envisaged that the normal electrical contractor will have these skills and hence new distribution channels and a new style of contractor will be required.

Technology in New Processes   HPM's main manufacturing strategy in the 1960s, 1970s, and 1980s was vertical integration, and this is clearly shown in the way the company operates today. It makes its own mouldings, screws, pressed metal parts, production tools and equipment, and robots.

The flexibility of designing and making their own equipment gives the company an advantage in creating a fit between the technology it introduces and the goals of the technology introduction. The focus is on the unique requirements of the situation, rather than what is available, and will this work.

New technology flows through the company to all areas, and the direction of the company is for complete computer control. The following describes how technology currently impacts the production of the company's core products, such as powerpoints and light switches.

1   Design is done on CAD [computer aided design] electronically. The tools are made via a direct download from the CAD workstations to either wire-cutting or spark erosion equipment.
2   Component warehousing is computerised with radio frequency control.
3   The components are then all fully automatically made, whether it be metal or plastic, which are all computer controlled.
4   The material handling between these processes is all manual.
5   Assembly and subassembly of products to the lowest common denominator is then done on PLC-controlled robots.
6   Final assembly of these products is then manual or semiautomatic to configure the product to the customer's requirements (e.g., colour).
7   Fully automatic testing.
8   Automatically packaged.
9   Finished goods warehousing is not computerised yet, but will be in the near future.

ADOPTING NEW PROCESS TECHNOLOGY

When a new technology is developed or introduced into the marketplace HPM prides itself on being an "early adopter." Introducing new technology when it is early in its life cycle can bring many benefits, as it may let the early adopter get the jump on its competition. However, because decisions must be made without proven evidence of the benefits that the technology can bring, the implementing company must be very thorough in its decision-making process.

Investment decisions at HPM are carefully evaluated, and any major capital purchases must comply with two primary criteria:

- Strategic fit: Investments must be aligned within the company's overall business strategy, which is to satisfy the needs of consumers in terms of their electrical requirements.
- Financial payback: Previously HPM used a two-year payback period as a guide for deciding whether an investment decision was financially viable. This has now changed, however, and financial decisions are made on a more ad-hoc basis. For example, for investment decisions involving a product that has an "electronic" type long-term focus, the company may approve a purchase with a five-plus year payback. However, if it is a copyable product, and especially if it is low-tech, then the company would be looking for well less than one year.

RAPID PRODUCT DEVELOPMENT

HPM recognises the importance of getting new products to market quickly and therefore pays particular attention to new developments in the area of rapid prototyping technology.

The case that follows is typical of the type of investment decision that the company often finds itself in. It describes how the company was able to evaluate the benefits and costs of using:

1 The stereolithography rapid prototyping technique.
2 A technique to produce rapid tooling for "first off" production samples.

STEREOLITHOGRAPHY

Stereolithography is a process that has the potential for dramatically reducing product development lead times and their associated costs. Stereolithography was discovered in the early 1980s and patented in 1986.

Traditional prototyping and hard tooling processes rely on the removal of material for the formation of prototype parts and the subsequent manufacture of their tooling for production. Stereolithography and other rapid prototyping techniques are the complete opposite. Using layer-building processes, they deposit only the required material for each particular layer, gradually building an exact replica of the part, regardless of its complexity.

DEVELOPMENT OF A NEW LIGHT SWITCH PRODUCT

During mid-1993 HPM perceived a strategic threat to one of its light switch products in the marketplace. It was anticipated that the product could suffer serious damage from inferior but inexpensive import competition by early 1994. The key strategic objective, therefore, was to "fast track" a product development that would produce a new model that was considerably cost reduced and yet maintained the traditional product's superior performance and market appeal.

In developing the new product, HPM also wished to test and quantify the benefits of the rapid product development approach. The decision was therefore made to carry out the product development using three concurrent but different methods, and to monitor the progress of each method. These three product development paths were:

Case 1: Employing conventional engineering.

Case 2: Employing a rapid prototype model.

Case 3: Employing a rapid prototype model plus rapid tooling.

The critical component of the new model light switch to be developed was the switch cover, a highly accurate polycarbonate moulding that would house and locate all the metal components of the product and would be used as an assembly jig during the manufacturing process. The development of this component therefore forms the basis of this case.

Project Management For each new product, a project management plan is constructed for the design, tooling, and production stages. Milestones are set to resolve problems and these are continually reviewed in relation to manufacturing processes, functions, and testing requirements.

The company uses the Microsoft Project software to keep track of the various projects that are occurring concurrently at any one time. The main projects and some of the smaller ones are monitored on a weekly basis, against theoretical timescales. Product comparisons and cost estimates are also made at every stage of the project to ensure that the project remains within its boundaries.

At one time there are typically around 40 projects in the pipeline around the company. Of these, around 10 are given priority as they are believed to be the main ones.

Comparative Analysis of RPD Options In order to make an accurate comparison between the various methods for developing the new switch cover product, the projects were all measured from a point where the overall product design had been completed and confirmed.

Case 1: In the case of the conventional engineering path, the injection mould tool design was then commenced.

Cases 2 and 3: For both the cases utilising the rapid prototype development technique, the injection moulded component data was processed using INPROTO faceting. These data files, in STL format, were then passed to the Queensland Manufacturing Institute (QMI) for the production of stereolithography models on their SLA 250 machine. For additional security, four complete sets of stereolithography models were produced.

The stereolithography models were produced within a couple of days by QMI and, once received, the components were then assembled to evaluate form and fit. One error and two tolerance problems were discovered when the components were assembled and these changes were incorporated into the design of the production tooling.

The stereolithography models were then measured in all major dimensions and these results are shown in Figure 1.

Once the production of the models was shown to have been successful, no further work was carried out to monitor the conventional engineering path. However, Figure 2 has been extrapolated from results recorded over the last six years to obtain a reasonably accurate comparison with the other two methods.

Cases 2 and 3: For both these cases, the tooling design was completed on the Intergraph CAD/CAM System, and the tool design data transferred to a Sodick A 3CR spark erosion machine for production of the injection mould tool.

Figure 1

DIM NUMBER	CAD DIMENSION	STEREOLITHOGRAPHY	COLD METAL SPRAY TOOL	POLYCARBONATE MOULDING
1	39.78	39.86	39.89	39.77
2	29.15	29.16	29.01	28.88
3	45.66	46.06	46.09	45.78
4	45.12	45.23	45.26	44.73
5	31.65	31.72	31.50	31.24

Figure 2

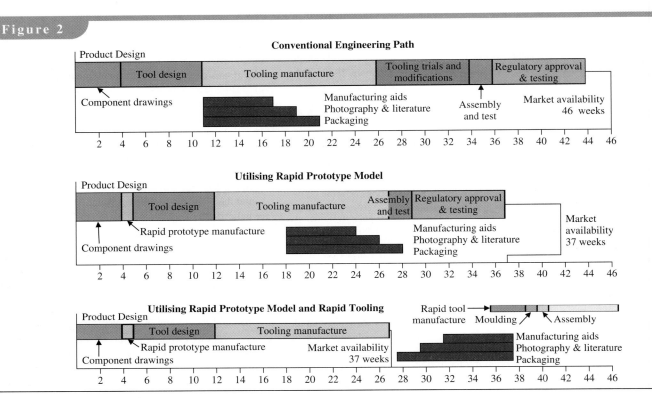

Case 3: For the case utilising rapid tooling, at the same time as the production tooling was being designed and manufactured, one of the four stereolithography models was passed to QMI. The rapid tooling was created using a cold metal spray process known as the HEK process. This process combines the use of zinc alloy wires which are melted under a plasma arc and "blown" by an air blast onto the model. By the time the molten metal reaches the stereolithography model, the metal is almost at room temperature and thus causes no distortion to the photopolymer model. The thickness of the cold metal spray is then built up gradually layer by layer, until a thickness of approximately 4 mm is achieved.

Once this was completed, the stereolithography model was then physically removed from the metal backing. This is a difficult process, as the model must be carefully broken into small parts and removed piece by piece.

The cold metal spray mould was then "backed" in epoxy resin, and with a hand-made metal core, the tool was then inserted into an Engel 150 ton injection moulding machine. The injection moulding was carried out by the Plastics & Rubber Technical Education Centre (PARTEC) in Queensland. Initially, the mould trials were carried out by injecting polypropylene material at the lowest possible clamp pressure, deliberately "flashing" the mould. The clamp pressure was then gradually increased until the flashing was eliminated and the minimum clamp pressure noted. After this trial, the polypropylene was replaced with polycarbonate, this being the engineering plastic required in the final product and essential as part of the Regulatory Approval testing procedures.

For comparison purposes, the cold metal spray tool and the final polycarbonate moulding were both measured and the results are shown in Figure 1. Both were well within the tolerances limits required for prototype performance.

Comparative Improvements Figure 2 displays the steps and time taken by each of the different development methods to bring the product to the point where it is ready for release into the marketplace.

Conventional Engineering Model With the conventional engineering approach, it can be seen that the market availability (elapsed time) was 46 weeks from the time of confirming the product design until the product was available for mass production and distribution.

The photography and production of literature and brochures is normally conditional on the availability of the finished product, or highly accurate models, and it is therefore shown that, using the conventional development method, this process cannot commence until the product is physically available. It is also conventional practice not to complete manufacture of production jigs and fixtures until the final product or models are available. Packaging design, particularly any blister packaging and drop testing, are also not normally finalised until the product or models are available.

Rapid Prototype Model In the second case, where a stereolithography model was used, it can be seen that the minimum time from product design to market availability was reduced to 37 weeks, compared to the 46 weeks for conventional methodology. This reduction of 9 weeks represents a 19.5 percent reduction in development lead time.

The availability of the stereolithography model at week five meant that the production of manufacturing aids and jigs, photography, and product literature, as well as packaging, could commence at week five, although not critically required until week 37. However, even though the stereolithography model was available at week five, the product could not be submitted for the Regulatory Approval tests until week 29, when the product was available in its specified material form. Stereolithography polymers are not suitable for Approval Testing since they are not representative of the final product's electrical insulation, physical strength, and fire retardant properties.

By using RPD processes, a physical appreciation of any redesign to improve functionality or manufacture related to tooling, moulding, or testing can be given early attention.

Rapid Prototype and Rapid Tooling Method As can be seen from Figure 2, the major advantage that this approach had on the development project was that it enabled HPM to obtain Government Regulatory Approval for the product prior to the completion of the production moulding tool.

The Approval Testing delay was regarded as one of the obvious strategic areas for improvement, but one that industry generally has little or no control over. The process typically takes eight weeks to meet the requirements for Government Regulatory Approval testing of electrical products in Australia.

Because Regulatory Approval could be carried out in parallel with the manufacture of production tooling, the minimum development lead time was reduced down to 27 weeks. When compared to the conventional engineering path, this methodology saves 19 weeks (or 41.3 percent) compared to the orthodox process.

Cost-Benefit Evaluation The development savings from this comparative analysis were clearly identifiable and relatively easy to quantify. Compared to the conventional engineering path, the path employing both the rapid prototype model plus rapid tooling produced an estimated saving of 19 weeks in development time.

An historical analysis conducted by the company's accountants and engineers of the costs incurred in typical tool trials with tooling modifications and rework indicated a saving of approximately A\$20,000.

In addition to the operational efficiencies calculated above, the more significant financial gains were achieved through the early introduction of the product into the marketplace. The financial and commercial gains cited below represent the gross profit generated in the first 19 weeks of the product's release onto the market. (N.B.—These figures exclude any commercial overheads associated with the marketing of the product.)

WEEK	GROSS PROFIT (A\$)
1–4	\$28,550
5–8	71,375
9–12	99,925
13–16	142,750
17–19	71,275
Total: 19 weeks	\$413,975

The direct development costs of the series of experimental trials, excluding management time overviewing and recording the trial, were calculated as:

4 stereolithography models	A\$2,000
Cold metal spray cavity and die production	A\$2,200
Low pressure injection moulding of 20 components	A\$ 500

The relationship between cost savings in development and the cost of the RPD models was found to be typical of case studies reported in the rapid product development literature, that is, savings are approximately 10 times the cost of the models.

It is recognised that there are a number of costs that have not been quantified in this analysis, such as the increased project management costs resulting from the new development method. However, there are also significant additional benefits that have not been specifically valued in this costing. These concern the strategic benefits of bringing a new and unique product into the marketplace, which strengthens both the product range and the company's commercial market presence.

These benefits are of paramount importance to HPM, particularly in HPM's retail market sector, where major retail stores are constantly seeking to reduce the number of suppliers in order to reduce their own administrative costs. Ability to fill orders with new products ahead of competitors is the company's key competitive advantage.

CHANGES IN OPERATIONAL PROCESSES
The introduction of change initiatives into any organisation is never easy and there are always some difficulties that must be overcome. Listed below are a number of the experiences and insights that HPM was able to gain through the assessment of the new product development process.

Quality Assurance The need for a separate and unique quality assurance process for rapid prototype development was evident from the delays caused by the formalities required by the company's adherence to ISO 9002. While every effort was made to gather all the required approvals and signatures as the product design progressed from research and development through to production engineering, the procedure was far too bureaucratic for "fast tracking" a new product development, and the company lost its agility as it introduced ISO 9002.

Compliance with procedures imposed restrictions, particularly when introducing new technology in days and not as part of a six-month project. "If we find something we do it tomorrow, we don't plan it, we get it in, let's try it," says the GM. Following ISO documentation meant the company couldn't short-circuit the design, the R & D, the production engineering, and manufacture of the product, if they were to gain compliance. A form of short-circuit documentation was trialed to avoid these restrictions, finally resulting in a ". . . controlled short-circuit, quick control mechanism that works within ISO 9002" and is mutually acceptable.

Politics of Change   The need for the company's senior executives and management to support the cultural change necessary to successfully implement rapid product development was certainly one of the key issues. Changing the way of thinking of traditional engineers and designers was a difficult but rewarding process. It was necessary to convince the company engineers and tool designers that an entirely new set of rules and standards for simple rapid tool design was required, where tool longevity and short moulding cycles are no longer acceptable. Prototype tooling design only has a requirement for 1,000–2,000 shots, and if components have to be removed by hand for expediency, then this is perfectly acceptable.

Project Management Resources   The experiment confirmed current experience of a heavy demand on management resources when introducing rapid product development projects. In this particular case study, involving extensive use of subcontractors, the amount of project management resources virtually had to be doubled for the short period of implementation. Without any doubt, one of the most crucial factors in the implementation of successful rapid product development is the allocation of dedicated project management resources.

Skills Acquisition   Before RPD was introduced, the CAD skills of the design group were used to incorporate tool-making skills into the drawing office as tool quality was believed to be the way to ensure a quality product. The company now employs highly skilled industrial design engineers with design and tool-making skills, supported by electronic technology and quality engineers. A wide range of new skills have been added to support RPD, where those long-time middle managers who could not accept the changes or reorient themselves to the new process responsibilities were relocated or retrenched.

CURRENT USE OF RAPID PROTOTYPING

The success of this and other projects has reinforced the company's commitment to using rapid prototype techniques in order to improve product development. The company today uses the latest technology in this area, working in 3-D CAD with direct connection to computerised spark erosion and wire-cutting equipment.

The company now almost always produces rapid prototypes for a wide variety of products:

- For metal products, these are created directly from the CAD screen, downloaded, and produced by the wire cutter.
- For plastic products, prototypes are generally produced using the stereolithography process with QMI. Numerous other alternatives are also available depending on the requirements of the prototype.
- Once the product is designed, the company uses the latest technology to produce rapid tooling. In conjunction with IMS (intelligent manufacturing systems), HPM shares technology on an international basis (mainly in R & D) and hence it has access to leading edge developments in this area.

*THIS CASE WAS DEVELOPED FOR USE IN CLASSROOM DISCUSSION AND IS NOT INTENDED TO NECESSARILY ILLUSTRATE APPROPRIATE OR INAPPROPRIATE MANAGEMENT PRACTICES. CASE INFORMATION WAS GATHERED THROUGH INTERVIEWS WITH STUART ROMM, MANAGING DIRECTOR OF HPM, VISITS TO THE HPM SITE, AND REVIEWS OF VARIOUS DOCUMENTS PROVIDED BY HPM. THE CASE AUTHOR OF THE ORIGINAL CASE (1996) WAS GRAEME SHEATHER, UNIVERSITY OF TECHNOLOGY, SYDNEY. SCOTT CAMERON WAS THE RESEARCH ASSOCIATE ON THE PROJECT IN THE GRADUATE SCHOOL OF MANAGEMENT AT MACQUARIE UNIVERSITY AND UPDATED THE CASE IN 2000. WE WISH TO THANK STUART ROMM AND HIS HPM ASSOCIATES FOR THEIR CONTRIBUTIONS. THE FUNDING FOR THIS CASE PRODUCTION WAS PROVIDED BY THE AUSTRALIAN FEDERAL GOVERNMENT'S DEPARTMENT OF INDUSTRY, SCIENCE AND RESOURCES.

SELECTED BIBLIOGRAPHY

Adler, P. S.; A. Mandelbaum; V. Nguyen; and Elizabeth Schwerer. "Getting the Most Out of Your Product Development Process." *Harvard Business Review,* March–April 1996, pp. 134–52.

Boothroyd, G.; P. Dewhurst; and W. Knight. *Product Design for Manufacture and Assembly,* 2nd ed. New York: Marcel Dekker, 2002.

Cooper, R. G. *Winning at New Products: Accelerating the Process from Idea to Launch.* Reading, MA: Perseins Books, 2001.

Huthwaite, B. *Design for Competitiveness: A Concurrent Engineering Handbook.* Institute for Competitive Design, 530 N. Pine, Rochester, Michigan, 1991.

Petroski, H. *Invention by Design: How Engineers Get from Thought to Thing.* Cambridge, MA: Harvard University Press, 1996.

Ulrich, Karl T., and Steven D. Eppinger. *Product Design and Development.* New York: McGraw-Hill/Irwin, 2004.

Wheelwright, S. C., and K. B. Clark. *Revolutionizing Product Development.* New York: The Free Press, 1992.

————. *Leading Product Development.* New York: The Free Press, 1995.

FOOTNOTES

1 Excerpt from T. Peters, "Beating the Great Blight of Dullness," *Forbes ASAP* (undated).

2 Adapted from Karl T. Ulrich and Steven D. Eppinger, *Product Design and Development,* 3rd ed. (New York: McGraw-Hill/Irwin, 2004), pp. 12–25.

3 Adapted from ibid., pp. 308–19.

4 The term *quality* is actually a mistranslation of the Japanese word for qualities, because QFD is widely used in the context of quality management.

5 Example adapted from G. Boothroyd, P. Dewhurst, and W. Knight, *Product Design for Manufacture and Assembly* (New York: Marcel Dekker, 1994), pp. 5–10.

technical note four
LEARNING CURVES

APPLICATION OF LEARNING CURVES

   A **learning curve** is a line displaying the relationship between unit production time and the cumulative number of units produced. Learning (or experience) curve theory has a wide range of application in the business world. In manufacturing, it can be used to estimate the time for product design and production, as well as costs. Learning curves are important and are sometimes overlooked as one of the trade-offs in just-in-time (JIT) systems, where sequencing and short runs achieve lower inventories by forfeiting some benefits of experience from long product runs. Learning curves are also an integral part in planning corporate strategy, such as decisions concerning pricing, capital investment, and operating costs based on experience curves.

Learning curve

Learning curves can be applied to individuals or organizations. **Individual learning** is improvement that results when people repeat a process and gain skill or efficiency from their own experience. That is, "practice makes perfect." **Organizational learning** results from practice as well, but it also comes from changes in administration, equipment, and product design. In organizational settings, we expect to see both kinds of learning occurring simultaneously and often describe the combined effect with a single learning curve.

Individual learning

Organizational learning

Learning curve theory is based on three assumptions:

1. The amount of time required to complete a given task or unit of a product will be less each time the task is undertaken.
2. The unit time will decrease at a decreasing rate.
3. The reduction in time will follow a predictable pattern.

Each of these assumptions was found to hold true in the airplane industry, where learning curves were first applied.[1] In this application, it was observed that, as output doubled, there was a 20 percent reduction in direct production worker-hours per unit between doubled units. Thus, if it took 100,000 hours for Plane 1, it would take 80,000 hours for Plane 2, 64,000 hours for Plane 4, and so forth. Because the 20 percent reduction meant that, say, Unit 4 took only 80 percent of the production time required for Unit 2, the line connecting the coordinates of output and time was referred to as an "80 percent learning curve." (By convention, the percentage learning rate is used to denote any given exponential learning curve.)

A learning curve may be developed from an arithmetic tabulation, by logarithms, or by some other curve-fitting method, depending on the amount and form of the available data.

There are two ways to think about the improved performance that comes with learning curves: time per unit (as in Exhibit TN4.1A) or units of output per time period (as in TN4.1B). *Time per unit* shows the decrease in time required for each successive unit. *Cumulative average time* shows the cumulative average performance times as the total number of units increases. Time per unit and cumulative average times are also called *progress curves* or

**Interactive
Operations
Management**

Learning Curves Plotted as Times and Numbers of Units

A.

Time per unit

Cumulative average time

Observed data

Fitted line

Unit number →

A Progress Curve

B.

Output per time period

Average output during a time period in the future

Time →

Industrial Learning

product learning and are useful for complex products or products with a longer cycle time. *Units of output per time period* is also called *industry learning* and is generally applied to high-volume production (short cycle time).

Note in Exhibit TN4.1A that the cumulative average curve does not decrease as fast as the time per unit because the time is being averaged. For example, if the time for Units 1, 2, 3, and 4 were 100, 80, 70, and 64, they would be plotted that way on the time per unit graph, but would be plotted as 100, 90, 83.3, and 78.5 on the cumulative average time graph.

PLOTTING LEARNING CURVES

There are many ways to analyze past data to fit a useful trend line. We will use the simple exponential curve first as an arithmetic procedure and then by a logarithmic analysis. In an arithmetical tabulation approach, a column for units is created by doubling, row by row, as 1, 2, 4, 8, 16 . . . . The time for the first unit is multiplied by the learning percentage to obtain the time for the second unit. The second unit is multiplied by the learning percentage for the fourth unit, and so on. Thus, if we are developing an 80 percent learning curve, we would arrive at the figures listed in column 2 of Exhibit TN4.2. Because it is often desirable for planning purposes to know the cumulative direct labor hours, column 4, which lists this information, is also provided. The calculation of these figures is straightforward; for example, for Unit 4, cumulative average direct labor hours would be found by dividing cumulative direct labor hours by 4, yielding the figure given in column 4.

Exhibit TN4.3 shows three curves with different learning rates: 90 percent, 80 percent, and 70 percent. Note that if the cost of the first unit was $100, the 30th unit would cost $59.63 at the 90 percent rate and $17.37 at the 70 percent rate. Differences in learning rates can have dramatic effects.

In practice, learning curves are plotted using a graph with logarithmic scales. The unit curves become linear throughout their entire range and the cumulative curve becomes linear after the first few units. The property of linearity is desirable because it facilitates extrapolation and permits a more accurate reading of the cumulative curve. This type of scale is an option in Microsoft Excel. Simply generate a regular scatter plot in your spreadsheet and then select each axis and format the axis with the logarithmic option. Exhibit TN4.4 shows the 80 percent unit cost curve and average cost curve on a logarithmic scale. Note that the cumulative average cost is essentially linear after the eighth unit.

Although the arithmetic tabulation approach is useful, direct logarithmic analysis of learning curve problems is generally more efficient because it does not require a complete enumeration

---

exhibit TN4.2

Excel: Learning Curves

Unit, Cumulative, and Cumulative Average Direct Labor Worker-Hours Required for an 80 Percent Learning Curve

(1) UNIT NUMBER	(2) UNIT DIRECT LABOR HOURS	(3) CUMULATIVE DIRECT LABOR HOURS	(4) CUMULATIVE AVERAGE DIRECT LABOR HOURS
1	100,000	100,000	100,000
2	80,000	180,000	90,000
4	64,000	314,210	78,553
8	51,200	534,591	66,824
16	40,960	892,014	55,751
32	32,768	1,467,862	45,871
64	26,214	2,392,453	37,382
128	20,972	3,874,395	30,269
256	16,777	6,247,318	24,404

TN4.3—Arithmetic Plot of 70, 80, and 90 Percent Learning Curves

TN4.4—Logarithmic Plot of an 80 Percent Learning Curve

Excel: Learning Curves

of successive time–output combinations. Moreover, where such data are not available, an analytical model that uses logarithms may be the most convenient way of obtaining output estimates.

LOGARITHMIC ANALYSIS

The normal form of the learning curve equation is[2]

[TN4.1]
$$Y_x = Kx^n$$

where

> x = Unit number
> Y_x = Number of direct labor hours required to produce the xth unit
> K = Number of direct labor hours required to produce the first unit
> n = log b/log 2 where b = Learning percentage

We can solve this mathematically or by using a table, as shown in the next section. Mathematically, to find the labor-hour requirement for the eighth unit in our example (Exhibit TN4.2), we would substitute as follows:

$$Y_8 = (100,000)(8)^n$$

Using logarithms:

$$Y_8 = 100,000(8)^{\log 0.8/\log 2}$$

$$= 100,000(8)^{-0.322} = \frac{100,000}{(8)^{0.322}}$$

$$= \frac{100,000}{1.9535} = 51,192$$

Therefore, it would take 51,192 hours to make the eighth unit. (See the spreadsheet "Learning Curves.")

LEARNING CURVE TABLES

When the learning percentage is known, Exhibits TN4.5 and TN4.6 can be easily used to calculate estimated labor hours for a specific unit or for cumulative groups of units. We need only multiply the initial unit labor hour figure by the appropriate tabled value.

Excel: Learning Curves

Improvement Curves: Table of Unit Values

Excel: Learning Curves

| UNIT | \multicolumn{8}{c}{UNIT IMPROVEMENT FACTOR} |
	60%	65%	70%	75%	80%	85%	90%	95%
1	1.0000	1.0000	1.0000	1.0000	1.0000	1.0000	1.0000	1.0000
2	.6000	.6500	.7000	.7500	.8000	.8500	.9000	.9500
3	.4450	.5052	.5682	.6338	.7021	.7729	.8462	.9219
4	.3600	.4225	.4900	.5625	.6400	.7225	.8100	.9025
5	.3054	.3678	.4368	.5127	.5956	.6857	.7830	.8877
6	.2670	.3284	.3977	.4754	.5617	.6570	.7616	.8758
7	.2383	.2984	.3674	.4459	.5345	.6337	.7439	.8659
8	.2160	.2746	.3430	.4219	.5120	.6141	.7290	.8574
9	.1980	.2552	.3228	.4017	.4930	.5974	.7161	.8499
10	.1832	.2391	.3058	.3846	.4765	.5828	.7047	.8433
12	.1602	.2135	.2784	.3565	.4493	.5584	.6854	.8320
14	.1430	.1940	.2572	.3344	.4276	.5386	.6696	.8226
16	.1290	.1785	.2401	.3164	.4096	.5220	.6561	.8145
18	.1188	.1659	.2260	.3013	.3944	.5078	.6445	.8074
20	.1099	.1554	.2141	.2884	.3812	.4954	.6342	.8012
22	.1025	.1465	.2038	.2772	.3697	.4844	.6251	.7955
24	.0961	.1387	.1949	.2674	.3595	.4747	.6169	.7904
25	.0933	.1353	.1908	.2629	.3548	.4701	.6131	.7880
30	.0815	.1208	.1737	.2437	.3346	.4505	.5963	.7775
35	.0728	.1097	.1605	.2286	.3184	.4345	.5825	.7687
40	.0660	.1010	.1498	.2163	.3050	.4211	.5708	.7611
45	.0605	.0939	.1410	.2060	.2936	.4096	.5607	.7545
50	.0560	.0879	.1336	.1972	.2838	.3996	.5518	.7486
60	.0489	.0785	.1216	.1828	.2676	.3829	.5367	.7386
70	.0437	.0713	.1123	.1715	.2547	.3693	.5243	.7302
80	.0396	.0657	.1049	.1622	.2440	.3579	.5137	.7231
90	.0363	.0610	.0987	.1545	.2349	.3482	.5046	.7168
100	.0336	.0572	.0935	.1479	.2271	.3397	.4966	.7112
120	.0294	.0510	.0851	.1371	.2141	.3255	.4830	.7017
140	.0262	.0464	.0786	.1287	.2038	.3139	.4718	.6937
160	.0237	.0427	.0734	.1217	.1952	.3042	.4623	.6869
180	.0218	.0397	.0691	.1159	.1879	.2959	.4541	.6809
200	.0201	.0371	.0655	.1109	.1816	.2887	.4469	.6757
250	.0171	.0323	.0584	.1011	.1691	.2740	.4320	.6646
300	.0149	.0289	.0531	.0937	.1594	.2625	.4202	.6557
350	.0133	.0262	.0491	.0879	.1517	.2532	.4105	.6482
400	.0121	.0241	.0458	.0832	.1453	.2454	.4022	.6419
450	.0111	.0224	.0431	.0792	.1399	.2387	.3951	.6363
500	.0103	.0210	.0408	.0758	.1352	.2329	.3888	.6314
600	.0090	.0188	.0372	.0703	.1275	.2232	.3782	.6229
700	.0080	.0171	.0344	.0659	.1214	.2152	.3694	.6158
800	.0073	.0157	.0321	.0624	.1163	.2086	.3620	.6098
900	.0067	.0146	.0302	.0594	.1119	.2029	.3556	.6045
1,000	.0062	.0137	.0286	.0569	.1082	.1980	.3499	.5998
1,200	.0054	.0122	.0260	.0527	.1020	.1897	.3404	.5918
1,400	.0048	.0111	.0240	.0495	.0971	.1830	.3325	.5850
1,600	.0044	.0102	.0225	.0468	.0930	.1773	.3258	.5793
1,800	.0040	.0095	.0211	.0446	.0895	.1725	.3200	.5743
2,000	.0037	.0089	.0200	.0427	.0866	.1683	.3149	.5698
2,500	.0031	.0077	.0178	.0389	.0806	.1597	.3044	.5605
3,000	.0027	.0069	.0162	.0360	.0760	.1530	.2961	.5530

Improvement Curves: Table of Cumulative Values

UNIT	CUMULATIVE IMPROVEMENT FACTOR							
	60%	65%	70%	75%	80%	85%	90%	95%
1	1.000	1.000	1.000	1.000	1.000	1.000	1.000	1.000
2	1.600	1.650	1.700	1.750	1.800	1.850	1.900	1.950
3	2.045	2.155	2.268	2.384	2.502	2.623	2.746	2.872
4	2.405	2.578	2.758	2.946	3.142	3.345	3.556	3.774
5	2.710	2.946	3.195	3.459	3.738	4.031	4.339	4.662
6	2.977	3.274	3.593	3.934	4.299	4.688	5.101	5.538
7	3.216	3.572	3.960	4.380	4.834	5.322	5.845	6.404
8	3.432	3.847	4.303	4.802	5.346	5.936	6.574	7.261
9	3.630	4.102	4.626	5.204	5.839	6.533	7.290	8.111
10	3.813	4.341	4.931	5.589	6.315	7.116	7.994	8.955
12	4.144	4.780	5.501	6.315	7.227	8.244	9.374	10.62
14	4.438	5.177	6.026	6.994	8.092	9.331	10.72	12.27
16	4.704	5.541	6.514	7.635	8.920	10.38	12.04	13.91
18	4.946	5.879	6.972	8.245	9.716	11.41	13.33	15.52
20	5.171	6.195	7.407	8.828	10.48	12.40	14.61	17.13
22	5.379	6.492	7.819	9.388	11.23	13.38	15.86	18.72
24	5.574	6.773	8.213	9.928	11.95	14.33	17.10	20.31
25	5.668	6.909	8.404	10.19	12.31	14.80	17.71	21.10
30	6.097	7.540	9.305	11.45	14.02	17.09	20.73	25.00
35	6.478	8.109	10.13	12.72	15.64	19.29	23.67	28.86
40	6.821	8.631	10.90	13.72	17.19	21.43	26.54	32.68
45	7.134	9.114	11.62	14.77	18.68	23.50	29.37	36.47
50	7.422	9.565	12.31	15.78	20.12	25.51	32.14	40.22
60	7.941	10.39	13.57	17.67	22.87	29.41	37.57	47.65
70	8.401	11.13	14.74	19.43	25.47	33.17	42.87	54.99
80	8.814	11.82	15.82	21.09	27.96	36.80	48.05	62.25
90	9.191	12.45	16.83	22.67	30.35	40.32	53.14	69.45
100	9.539	13.03	17.79	24.18	32.65	43.75	58.14	76.59
120	10.16	14.11	19.57	27.02	37.05	50.39	67.93	90.71
140	10.72	15.08	21.20	29.67	41.22	56.78	77.46	104.7
160	11.21	15.97	22.72	32.17	45.20	62.95	86.80	118.5
180	11.67	16.79	24.14	34.54	49.03	68.95	95.96	132.1
200	12.09	17.55	25.48	36.80	52.72	74.79	105.0	145.7
250	13.01	19.28	28.56	42.05	61.47	88.83	126.9	179.2
300	13.81	20.81	31.34	46.94	69.66	102.2	148.2	212.2
350	14.51	22.18	33.89	51.48	77.43	115.1	169.0	244.8
400	15.14	23.44	36.26	55.75	84.85	127.6	189.3	277.0
450	15.72	24.60	38.48	59.80	91.97	139.7	209.2	309.0
500	16.26	25.68	40.58	63.68	98.85	151.5	228.8	340.6
600	17.21	27.67	44.47	70.97	112.0	174.2	267.1	403.3
700	18.06	29.45	48.04	77.77	124.4	196.1	304.5	465.3
800	18.82	31.09	51.36	84.18	136.3	217.3	341.0	526.5
900	19.51	32.60	54.46	90.26	147.7	237.9	376.9	587.2
1,000	20.15	31.01	57.40	96.07	158.7	257.9	412.2	647.4
1,200	21.30	36.59	62.85	107.0	179.7	296.6	481.2	766.6
1,400	22.32	38.92	67.85	117.2	199.6	333.9	548.4	884.2
1,600	23.23	41.04	72.49	126.8	218.6	369.9	614.2	1001
1,800	24.06	43.00	76.85	135.9	236.8	404.9	678.8	1116
2,000	24.83	44.84	80.96	144.7	254.4	438.9	742.3	1230
2,500	26.53	48.97	90.39	165.0	296.1	520.8	897.0	1513
3,000	27.99	52.62	98.90	183.7	335.2	598.9	1047	1791

Excel: Learning Curves

To illustrate, suppose we want to double-check the figures in Exhibit TN4.2 for unit and cumulative labor hours for Unit 16. From Exhibit TN4.5, the unit improvement factor for Unit 16 at 80 percent is .4096. This multiplied by 100,000 (the hours for Unit 1) gives 40,960, the same as in Exhibit TN4.2. From Exhibit TN4.6, the cumulative improvement factor for cumulative hours for the first 16 units is 8.920. When multiplied by 100,000, this gives 892,000, which is reasonably close to the exact value of 892,014 shown in Exhibit TN4.2.

The following is a more involved example of the application of a learning curve to a production problem.

EXAMPLE TN4.1: Sample Learning Curve Problem

Captain Nemo, owner of the Suboptimum Underwater Boat Company (SUB), is puzzled. He has a contract for 11 boats and has completed 4 of them. He has observed that his production manager, young Mr. Overick, has been reassigning more and more people to torpedo assembly after the construction of the first four boats. The first boat, for example, required 225 workers, each working a 40-hour week, while 45 fewer workers were required for the second boat. Overick has told them that "this is just the beginning" and that he will complete the last boat in the current contract with only 100 workers!

Overick is banking on the learning curve, but has he gone overboard?

SOLUTION

Because the second boat required 180 workers, a simple exponential curve shows that the learning percentage is 80 percent (180 ÷ 225). To find out how many workers are required for the 11th boat, we look up unit 11 for an 80 percent improvement ratio in Exhibit TN4.5 and multiply this value by the number required for the first sub. By interpolating between Unit 10 and Unit 12 we find the improvement ratio is equal to .4629. This yields 104.15 workers (.4269 interpolated from table × 225). Thus, Overick's estimate missed the boat by four people. ●

EXAMPLE TN4.2: Estimating Cost Using Learning Curves

SUB has produced the first unit of a new line of minisubs at a cost of $500,000—$200,000 for materials and $300,000 for labor. It has agreed to accept a 10 percent profit, based on cost, and it is willing to contract on the basis of a 70 percent learning curve. What will be the contract price for three minisubs?

SOLUTION

Cost of first sub		$ 500,000
Cost of second sub		
Materials	$200,000	
Labor: $300,000 × .70	210,000	410,000
Cost of third sub		
Materials	200,000	
Labor: $300,000 × .5682	170,460	370,460
Total cost		1,280,460
Markup: $1,280,460 × .10		128,046
Selling price		$1,408,506

If the operation is interrupted, then some relearning must occur. How far to go back up the learning curve can be estimated in some cases. ●

ESTIMATING THE LEARNING PERCENTAGE

If production has been under way for some time, the learning percentage is easily obtained from production records. Generally speaking, the longer the production history, the more accurate the estimate. Because a variety of other problems can occur during the early stages of production, most companies do not begin to collect data for learning curve analysis until some units have been completed.

If production has not started, estimating the learning percentage becomes enlightened guesswork. In such cases the analyst has these options:

1. Assume that the learning percentage will be the same as it has been for previous applications within the same industry.
2. Assume that it will be the same as it has been for the same or similar products.
3. Analyze the similarities and differences between the proposed start-up and previous start-ups and develop a revised learning percentage that appears to best fit the situation.

The following guidelines are useful for estimating the impact of learning on manufacturing tasks.[3] These guidelines use estimates of the percentage of time spent on manual work (i.e., hand assembly) versus the time spent on machine-controlled work (i.e., machining).

- 75 percent hand assembly/25 percent machining = 80 percent learning
- 50 percent hand assembly/50 percent machining = 85 percent
- 25 percent hand assembly/75 percent machining = 90 percent

Another set of guidelines based on what is seen in specific industries is the following:

- Aerospace, 85 percent
- Shipbuilding, 80–85 percent
- Complex machine tools for new models, 75–85 percent
- Repetitive electronics manufacturing, 90–95 percent
- Repetitive machining or punch-press operations, 90–95 percent
- Repetitive electrical operations (wiring and circuit board fabrication), 75–85 percent
- Repetitive welding operations, 90 percent
- Raw materials manufacturing, 93–96 percent
- Purchased parts fabrication, 85–88 percent

There are two reasons for disparities between a firm's learning rate and that of its industry. First, there are the inevitable differences in operating characteristics between any two firms, stemming from the equipment, methods, product design, plant organization, and so forth. Second, procedural differences are manifested in the development of the learning percentage itself, such as whether the industry rate is based on a single product or on a product line, and the manner in which the data were aggregated.

HOW LONG DOES LEARNING GO ON?

Does output stabilize, or is there continual improvement? Some areas can be shown to improve continually even over decades (radios, computers, and other electronic devices; and, if we allow for the effects of inflation, also automobiles, washing machines, refrigerators, and most other manufactured goods). If the learning curve has been valid for several hundreds or thousands of units, it will probably be valid for several hundreds or thousands more. On the other hand, highly automated systems may have a near-zero learning curve because, after installation, they quickly reach a constant volume.

GENERAL GUIDELINES FOR LEARNING

In this section we offer guidelines for two categories of "learners": individuals and organizations.

INDIVIDUAL LEARNING

A number of factors affect an individual's performance and rate of learning. Remember that there are two elements involved: the rate of learning and the initial starting level. To explain this more clearly, compare the two learning curves in Exhibit TN4.7. Suppose these were

Test Results of Two Job Applicants

the times for two individuals who performed a simple mechanical test administered by the personnel department as part of their application for employment in the assembly area of manufacturing.

Which applicant would you hire? Applicant A had a much lower starting point but a slower learning rate. Applicant B, although starting at a much higher point, is clearly the better choice. This points out that performance times are important—not just the learning rate by itself.

Some general guidelines to improve individual performance based on learning curves include the following:

1. **Proper selection of workers.**   A test should be administered to help choose the workers. These tests should be representative of the planned work: a dexterity test for assembly work, a mental ability test for mental work, tests for interaction with customers for front office work, and so on.
2. **Proper training.**   The more effective the training, the faster the learning rate.
3. **Motivation.**   Productivity gains based on learning curves are not achieved unless there is a reward. Rewards can be money (individual or group incentive plans) or nonmonetary (employee of the month awards, etc.).
4. **Work specialization.**   As a general rule, the simpler the task, the faster the learning. Be careful that boredom doesn't interfere; if it does, redesign the task.
5. **Do one or very few jobs at a time.**   Learning is faster on each job if completed one at a time, rather than working on all jobs simultaneously.
6. **Use tools or equipment that assists or supports performance.**
7. **Provide quick and easy access for help.**   The benefits from training are realized and continue when assistance is available.
8. **Allow workers to help redesign their tasks.**   Taking more performance factors into the scope of the learning curve can, in effect, shift the curve downward.

ORGANIZATIONAL LEARNING

Organizations learn as well. It has been argued that organizational learning is critical to sustaining a competitive advantage. For the individual, it is easy to conceptualize how knowledge is acquired and retained and how this results in an individual learning effect. Certainly, a main source of organizational learning is the individual learning of the employees. An organization also acquires knowledge in its technology, its structure, documents that it retains, and standard operating procedures.[4] For example, as a manufacturing unit becomes experienced, knowledge is embedded in software and in tooling used for production. Knowledge also can be embedded in the organization's structure. For example, when an organization shifts its industrial engineering group from a functional organization centralized in one area to a decentralized organization where individuals are deployed to particular parts of the plant floor, knowledge about how to become more productive is embedded in the organization's structure.

Knowledge can depreciate if individuals leave the organization. When Lockheed had problems in the production of the L-1011, it was blamed on the fact that the company hired 2,000 inexperienced employees to quickly ramp up production. These employees were put through a four-week training program in aircraft construction. Initial costs rose rather than fell during the initial production of the plane due to the inexperienced workers.

Knowledge also can depreciate if technologies become inaccessible or difficult to use. An example of this is the difficulty in accessing data collected by Landsat, an earth surveillance program. Ninety percent of the data collected before 1979 is now inaccessible because the data were recorded by equipment that no longer exists or cannot be operated. Knowledge can also depreciate if a company's records and routine processes are lost. When Steinway Piano Company decided to put a discontinued piano back into production, the plant discovered it no longer had records or blueprints for the piano.

LEARNING CURVES APPLIED TO HEART TRANSPLANT MORTALITY

Learning curves provide an excellent means to examine performance. The best comparison for one's performance would be the learning rates for competitors in the industry. Even when a standard or expected level is unknown, much can still be learned by simply using and plotting data in a learning curve fashion. As an illustration of this ability to learn about one's performance, we present the experience of a heart transplant facility in a hospital.[5]

Service

The learning curve model in the heart transplant analysis was of the form

$$Y_i = B_0 + B_1 x^{-B_2}$$

where Y_i is the cumulative average resource consumption (the total number of deaths, costs, and so on divided by the number of transplants), B_0 is the asymptote (the minimum), B_1 is the maximum possible reduction (the difference between the first unit and minimum B_0), x is the total number of units produced, and B_2 is the rate of change for each successive unit as it moves toward the lower bound.

Exhibit TN4.8 shows the coefficients that were obtained for the model. Exhibit TN4.9 shows the cumulative death rate. This seems to follow an industrial learning curve with a rate just over 80 percent. Seven of the first 23 transplant patients died within a year after transplant surgery. Only 4 of the next 39 patients died within a year. For the cumulative average length of stay, shown in Exhibit TN4.10, the reduction rate is approximately 9 percent.

exhibit TN4.8

Consumption Coefficients for Heart Transplant Learning Model

	B_0 (ASYMPTOTE)	B_1 (RANGE)	B_2 (RATE)	PERCENTAGE DECREASE
Death rate	.2329	.8815	.2362	21.04%
Length of stay	28.26	23.76	.0943	9.00
Units of service	1,282.84	592.311	.0763	7.35
Adjusted charges	$96,465.90	$53,015.80	.0667	6.45

exhibit TN4.9

Death Rates, Less than One Year Survival

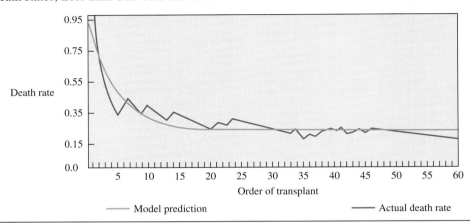

exhibit TN4.10

Average Length of Stay (ALOS) for Heart Transplant Survivors

The least sloping curve (the lowest learning rate) is the cost of heart transplants. Exhibit TN4.11 shows that the initial costs were in the vicinity of $150,000. After 51 surviving patients (62 procedures, 11 died), the average cost was still close to $100,000. (A learning rate of 80 percent would result in an average cost of $40,000; a 90 percent rate would result in a cost of $80,000.)

Why are learning rates high in death rate reduction and low in average length of stay, with the lowest rate in cost reduction? Smith and Larsson question whether the low learning rates

Cost for Heart Transplant Survivors   **exhibit TN4.11**

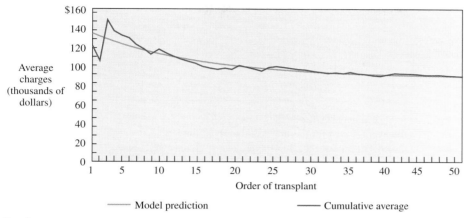

Order of transplant

——— Model prediction   ——— Cumulative average

NOTE: FOR TRANSPLANT ADMISSION ONLY, ACTUAL COSTS ARE APPROXIMATELY 50 PERCENT OF CHARGES.

may be related to conservatism in dealing with human lives. Or could it be due to the power and insulation of the heart transplant team from pressure to reduce cost? The purpose of this study on learning curves was to make institutions and administrators aware of learning. Institutions need to behave according to learning curve logic—that is, in pricing as well as in motivation for continuous improvement.

KEY TERMS

Learning curve A line displaying the relationship between unit production time and the cumulative number of units produced.

Individual learning Improvement that results when people repeat a process and gain skill or efficiency from their own experience.

Organizational learning Improvement that comes both from experience and from changes in administration, equipment, and product design.

FORMULA REVIEW

Logarithmic curve:

[TN4.1] $$Y_x = Kx^n$$

SOLVED PROBLEMS

SOLVED PROBLEM 1

A job applicant is being tested for an assembly line position. Management feels that steady-state times have been approximately reached after 1,000 performances. Regular assembly line workers are expected to perform the task within four minutes.

a. If the job applicant performed the first test operation in 10 minutes and the second one in 9 minutes, should this applicant be hired?

b. What is the expected time that the job applicant would take to finish the 10th unit?

c. What is a significant limitation of this analysis?

Solution

a. Learning rate = 9 minutes/10 minutes = 90%
From Exhibit TN4.5, the time for the 1,000th unit is .3499 × 10 minutes = 3.499 minutes. Yes, hire the person.

b. From Exhibit TN4.5, unit 10 at 90% is .7047. Therefore, the time for the 10th unit = .7047 × 10 = 7.047 minutes.

c. More data should be collected on the job applicant's performance.

SOLVED PROBLEM 2

Boeing Aircraft collected the following cost data on the first 8 units of their new business jet.

Excel: Learning Curves

UNIT NUMBER	COST ($ MILLIONS)	UNIT NUMBER	COST ($ MILLIONS)
1	$100	5	60
2	83	6	57
3	73	7	53
4	62	8	51

a. Estimate the learning curve for the new business jet.
b. Estimate the average cost for the first 1,000 units of the jet.
c. Estimate the cost to produce the 1,000th jet.

Solution

a. First, estimate the learning curve rate by calculating the average learning rate with each doubling of production.

$$\text{Units 1 to 2} = 83/100 = 83\%$$
$$\text{Units 2 to 4} = 62/83 = 74.7\%$$
$$\text{Units 4 to 8} = 51/62 = 82.26\%$$
$$\text{Average} = (83 + 74.4 + 82.6)/3 = 80\%$$

b. The average cost of the first 1,000 units can be estimated using Exhibit TN4.6. The cumulative improvement factor for the 1,000th unit at 80 percent learning is 158.7. The cost to produce the first 1,000 units is

$$\$100M \times 158.7 = \$15,870M$$

The average cost for each of the first 1,000 units is

$$\$15,870M/1,000 = \$15.9M$$

c. To estimate the cost to produce the 1,000th unit use Exhibit TN4.5.
The unit improvement factor for the 1,000th unit at 80 percent is .1082.
The cost to produce the 1,000th unit is

$$\$100M \times .1082 = \$10.82M$$

REVIEW AND DISCUSSION QUESTIONS

1   If you kept any of your old exam grades from last semester, get them out and write down the grades. Use Exhibits TN4.5 and TN4.6, use log-log graph paper, or use a spreadsheet to find whether the exponential curve fits showing that you experienced learning over the semester (insofar as your exam performance is concerned). If not, can you give some reasons why not?

2   How might the following business specialists use learning curves: accountants, marketers, financial analysts, personnel managers, and computer programmers?

3   As a manager, which learning percentage would you prefer (other things being equal), 110 percent or 60 percent? Explain.

4   What difference does it make if a customer wants a 10,000-unit order produced and delivered all at one time or in 2,500-unit batches?

PROBLEMS

1   A time standard was set as 0.20 hour per unit based on the 50th unit produced. If the task has a 90 percent learning curve, what would be the expected time of the 100th, 200th, and 400th units?

2   You have just received 10 units of a special subassembly from an electronics manufacturer at a price of $250 per unit. A new order has also just come in for your company's product that uses these subassemblies, and you wish to purchase 40 more to be shipped in lots of 10 units each. (The subassemblies are bulky, and you need only 10 a month to fill your new order.)

   a. Assuming a 70 percent learning curve by your supplier on a similar product last year, how much should you pay for each lot? Assume that the learning rate of 70 percent applies to each lot of 10 units, not each unit.

    b. Suppose you are the supplier and can produce 20 units now but cannot start production on the second 20 units for two months. What price would you try to negotiate for the last 20 units?

3   Johnson Industries received a contract to develop and produce four high-intensity long-distance receiver/transmitters for cellular telephones. The first took 2,000 labor hours and $39,000 worth of purchased and manufactured parts; the second took 1,500 labor hours and $37,050 in parts; the third took 1,450 labor hours and $31,000 in parts; and the fourth took 1,275 labor hours and $31,492 in parts.

     Johnson was asked to bid on a follow-on contract for another dozen receiver/transmitter units. Ignoring any forgetting factor effects, what should Johnson estimate time and parts costs to be for the dozen units? (Hint: There are two learning curves—one for labor and one for parts.)

4   Lambda Computer Products competed for and won a contract to produce two prototype units of a new type of computer that is based on laser optics rather than on electronic binary bits.

     The first unit produced by Lambda took 5,000 hours to produce and required $250,000 worth of material, equipment usage, and supplies. The second unit took 3,500 hours and used $200,000 worth of materials, equipment usage, and supplies. Labor is $30 per hour.

    a. Lambda was asked to present a bid for 10 additional units as soon as the second unit was completed. Production would start immediately. What would this bid be?

    b. Suppose there was a significant delay between the contracts. During this time, personnel and equipment were reassigned to other projects. Explain how this would affect the subsequent bid.

5   You've just completed a pilot run of 10 units of a major product and found the processing time for each unit was as follows:

UNIT NUMBER	TIME (HOURS)
1	970
2	640
3	420
4	380
5	320
6	250
7	220
8	207
9	190
10	190

    a. According to the pilot run, what would you estimate the learning rate to be?

    b. Based on *a*, how much time would it take for the next 190 units, assuming no loss of learning?

    c. How much time would it take to make the 1,000th unit?

6   Lazer Technologies Inc. (LTI) has produced a total of 20 high-power laser systems that could be used to destroy any approaching enemy missiles or aircraft. The 20 units have been produced, funded in part as private research within the research and development arm of LTI, but the bulk of the funding came from a contract with the U.S. Department of Defense (DoD).

     Testing of the laser units has shown that they are effective defense weapons, and through redesign to add portability and easier field maintenance, the units could be truck-mounted.

     DoD has asked LTI to submit a bid for 100 units.

     The 20 units that LTI has built so far cost the following amounts and are listed in the order in which they were produced:

UNIT NUMBER	COST ($ MILLIONS)	UNIT NUMBER	COST ($ MILLIONS)
1	$12	11	$3.9
2	10	12	3.5
3	6	13	3.0
4	6.5	14	2.8
5	5.8	15	2.7
6	6	16	2.7
7	5	17	2.3
8	3.6	18	3.0
9	3.6	19	2.9
10	4.1	20	2.6

a. Based on past experience, what is the learning rate?

b. What bid should LTI submit for the total order of 100 units, assuming that learning continues?

c. What is the cost expected to be for the last unit under the learning rate you estimated?

7   Jack Simpson, contract negotiator for Nebula Airframe Company, is currently involved in bidding on a follow-up government contract. In gathering cost data from the first three units, which Nebula produced under a research and development contract, he found that the first unit took 2,000 labor hours, the second took 1,800 labor hours, and the third took 1,692 hours.

In a contract for three more units, how many labor hours should Simpson plan for?

8   Honda Motor Company has discovered a problem in the exhaust system of one of its automobile lines and has voluntarily agreed to make the necessary modifications to conform with government safety requirements. Standard procedure is for the firm to pay a flat fee to dealers for each modification completed.

Honda is trying to establish a fair amount of compensation to pay dealers and has decided to choose a number of randomly selected mechanics and observe their performance and learning rate. Analysis demonstrated that the average learning rate was 90 percent, and Honda then decided to pay a $60 fee for each repair (3 hours × $20 per flat-rate hour).

Southwest Honda, Inc., has complained to Honda Motor Company about the fee. Six mechanics, working independently, have completed two modifications each. All took 9 hours on the average to do the first unit and 6.3 hours to do the second. Southwest refuses to do any more unless Honda allows at least 4.5 hours. The dealership expects to perform the modification to approximately 300 vehicles.

What is your opinion of Honda's allowed rate and the mechanics' performance?

9   United Research Associates (URA) had received a contract to produce two units of a new cruise missile guidance control. The first unit took 4,000 hours to complete and cost $30,000 in materials and equipment usage. The second took 3,200 hours and cost $21,000 in materials and equipment usage. Labor cost is charged at $18 per hour.

The prime contractor has now approached URA and asked to submit a bid for the cost of producing another 20 guidance controls.

a. What will the last unit cost to build?

b. What will be the average time for the 20 missile guidance controls?

c. What will the average cost be for guidance control for the 20 in the contract?

10 United Assembly Products (UAP) has a personnel screening process for job applicants to test their ability to perform at the department's long-term average rate. UAP has asked you to modify the test by incorporating learning theory. From the company's data, you discovered that if people can perform a given task in 30 minutes or less on the 20th unit, they achieve the group long-run average. Obviously, all job applicants cannot be subjected to 20 performances of such a task, so you are to determine whether they will likely achieve the desired rate based on only 2 performances.

a. Suppose a person took 100 minutes on the first unit and 80 minutes on the second. Should this person be hired?

b. What procedure might you establish for hiring (i.e., how to evaluate the job applicant's two performances)?

c. What is a significant limitation of this analysis?

11 A potentially large customer offered to subcontract assembly work that is profitable only if you can perform the operations at an average time of less than 20 hours each. The contract is for 1,000 units.

You run a test and do the first one in 50 hours and the second one in 40 hours.

a. How long would you expect the third one to take?

b. Would you take the contract? Explain.

12 Western Turbine, Inc., has just completed the production of the 10th unit of a new high-efficiency turbine/generator. Its analysis showed that a learning rate of 85 percent existed over the production of the 10 units. If the 10th unit contained labor costs of $2.5 million, what price should Western Turbine charge for labor on units 11 and 12 to make a profit of 10 percent of the selling price?

13 FES Auto has recently hired Meg the mechanic to specialize in front-end alignments. Although she is a trained auto mechanic, she has not used FES's brand of equipment before taking this job. The standard time allocated for a front-end alignment is 30 minutes. Her first front-end alignment took 50 minutes and her second 47.5 minutes.

a. What is the expected time for Meg's 10th front-end alignment?

b. What is the expected time for Meg's 100th front-end alignment?

14   An initial pilot run of 10 units produces the following times:

Unit Number	Time (minutes)
1	39
2	29
3	23
4	19
5	17
6	16
7	15
8	13
9	13
10	12

   a. According to this pilot run, what is your estimate of the learning rate?
   b. How much time will it take for the next 90 units?
   c. How much time will it take to make the 2,000th unit?

15   A new bank clerk needed an hour to encode his first 500 checks, 51 minutes for the second 500, and 46 minutes for the third 500. After how many batches of 500 checks will he be able to work at the standard rate of 1,000 checks per hour?

16   A fast-food trainee takes an hour to prepare his first 20 sandwiches, 45 minutes for the second 20, and 38 minutes for the third 20. What will his production rate be after 24 hours of experience?

SELECTED BIBLIOGRAPHY

Argote, L. "Organizational Learning Curves: Persistence, Transfer and Turnover." *International Journal of Technology Management* 11, nos. 7/8 (1996), pp. 759–69.

Argote, L., and D. Epple. "Learning Curves in Manufacturing." *Science* 247 (February 1990), pp. 920–24.

Bailey, C. D. "Forgetting and the Learning Curve: A Laboratory Study." *Management Science* 35, no. 3 (March 1989), pp. 340–52.

Smunt, T. L. "A Comparison of Learning Curve Analysis and Moving Average Ratio Analysis for Detailed Operational Planning." *Decision Sciences* 17, no. 4 (Fall 1986), pp. 475–95.

Wright, T. P. "Factors Affecting the Cost of Airplanes." *Journal of Aeronautical Sciences,* February 1936, pp. 122–28.

Yelle, L. E. "The Learning Curves: Historical Review and Comprehensive Survey." *Decision Sciences* 10, no. 2 (April 1979), pp. 302–28.

FOOTNOTES

1 See the classic paper by T. P. Wright, "Factors Affecting the Cost of Airplanes," *Journal of the Aeronautical Sciences,* February 1936, pp. 122–28.

2 This equation says that the number of direct labor hours required for any given unit is reduced exponentially as more units are produced.

3 Rodney D. Stewart, Richard M. Wyskida, and James D. Johannes (eds.), *Cost Estimator's Reference Manual,* 2nd ed. (New York: John Wiley & Sons, 1995).

4 See L. Argote, "Organizational Learning Curves: Persistence, Transfer and Turnover," *International Journal of Technology Management* 11, nos. 7/8 (1996), pp. 759–69.

5 D. B. Smith, and J. L. Larsson, "The Impact of Learning on Cost: The Case of Heart Transplantation," *Hospital and Health Sciences Administration* 34, no. 1 (Spring 1989), pp. 85–97.

section

PROCESS SELECTION AND DESIGN

2

HOW TO BECOME AN EFFICIENCY EXPERT

 MAYBE BECOMING AN EFFICIENCY EXPERT IS NOT YOUR dream, but it is important to learn the fundamentals. Have you ever wondered why you always have to wait in line at one store, but another one seems to be on top of the crowds? The key to serving customers well, whether with products or services, is having a great process. We use processes to do most things. You probably have a regular process that you use every morning. What are the tasks associated with your process? Do you brush your teeth, take a shower, dress, make coffee, and read the paper? Have you ever thought about how the tasks should be ordered or what is the best way to execute each task? This section is about designing efficient processes—all kinds of processes. Companies also need to develop a quality philosophy and integrate it into their processes. Actually, quality and process efficiency are closely related. Have you ever done something, but then had to do it again because it was not done properly the first time? This section considers these subjects in both manufacturing and service industries.

chapter

PROCESS ANALYSIS

5

CUSTOMER-DRIVEN SERVICE FOR McDONALD'S

SELF-ORDERING KIOSKS AND ENVIRONMENT

IDEO collaborated with McDonald's on the first generation of a new service system in their Lone Tree restaurant, south of Denver. The new system allows McDonald's customers to place their orders without assistance, providing improved flexibility, speed, accuracy, and convenience to both McDonald's customers as well as its crews. The system consists of touch-screen self-order kiosks at the front counter and in the children's PlayPlace area that have been fully integrated into the McDonald's physical environment, operational flow, and brand message.

Customers place their orders using an icon-based system and pay at the kiosk or at the pick-up counter. After placing their orders, customers pick up their food at the counter by showing the order number on their printed receipts. In the PlayPlace area, parents can place and pay for their orders while supervising their children. A McDonald's crewmember then delivers the food to their table.

This new model needed to work within the popular and highly efficient system in use today. The completed design spanned the entire ordering experience and not just the kiosks themselves. The team updated the restaurant's graphics, signage, counters, and crew uniforms, and created nine self-order kiosks with a fully developed icon-based menu system. All design elements plus the in-store layout of the new service experience were arranged to complement the traditional experience of ordering at the counter.

The work began with a national survey of all kinds of quick-serve and self-serve experiences and distilled behavioral patterns of McDonald's customers to guide the design work. Since its launch and after thousands of transactions, the new service has had a high customer adoption rate with virtually no lines. →

PROCESS ANALYSIS

Process

Understanding how processes work is essential to ensuring the competitiveness of a company. A process that does not match the needs of the firm will punish the firm every minute that the firm operates. Take, for example, two fast-food restaurants. If one restaurant can deliver a quarter-pound hamburger to the customer for $.50 in direct costs and a second restaurant costs $.75, no matter what the second restaurant does, it will lose $.25 in profit for every hamburger it sells compared to the first restaurant. Many factors need to be considered when one sets up the process to make those hamburgers. These factors include the cost of the raw materials, the costs associated with how the hamburger is prepared, and the cost of taking the order and delivering it to the customer.

What is a process? A **process** is any part of an organization that takes inputs and transforms them into outputs that, it is hoped, are of greater value to the organization than the original inputs. Consider some examples of processes. Honda Motors assembles the Accord in a plant in Marysville, Ohio. The assembly plant takes in parts and components that have been fabricated for the plant. Using labor, equipment along an assembly line, and energy, these parts and components are transformed into automobiles. McDonald's, at each of its restaurants, uses inputs such as hamburger meat, lettuce, tomatoes, and potatoes. To these inputs, trained labor is added in the form of cooks and order takers, and capital equipment is used to transform the inputs into hamburgers, french fries, and other foods.

In both of these examples, the process produces products as output. However, the outputs of many processes are services. In a hospital, for example, specialized equipment and highly trained doctors, nurses, and technicians are combined with another input, the patient. The

Service

patient is transformed through proper treatment and care into a healthy patient. An airline is another example of a service organization. The airline uses airplanes, ground equipment, flight crews, ground crews, reservation personnel, and fuel to transport customers between locations all over the world.

This chapter describes how to analyze a process. Analyzing a process allows some important questions to be answered, such as these: How many customers can the process handle per hour? How long will it take to serve a customer? What change is needed in the process to expand capacity? How much does the process cost? A difficult, but important, first step in process analysis is to clearly define the purpose of the analysis. Is the purpose to solve a problem? Is it to better understand the impact of a change in how business will be done in the future?

Clearly understanding the purpose of the analysis is critical to setting the level of detail in modeling the process. The analysis must be kept as simple as possible. The following sections of this chapter discuss the details of constructing flowcharts and measures that are appropriate for different types of processes. But first, consider a simple example.

ANALYZING A LAS VEGAS SLOT MACHINE

The slot machine is common in casinos around the world. Let's use this machine to illustrate how a simple process is analyzed.

Assume that we work for the casino and management is considering a new type of electronic slot machine that is much faster than the current mechanical machine. Management has asked how much we can expect to make from the new electronic machine over a 24-hour period compared to the old mechanical machine.

Service

Begin by analyzing a mechanical slot machine. The slot machine is activated when the customer puts one or more coins in the machine and then pulls the arm on the machine (slot machines are often called "one-armed bandits"). Three wheels spin, and after a time each wheel stops and displays a particular symbol. The machine pays money when certain combinations of symbols simultaneously appear. For those not familiar with how a slot machine works, we have included a slot machine simulation program on the CD included with the book. Sorry, but it does not pay real money.

Slot machines are designed to pay back a certain percentage of what they take in. Typical paybacks would be 90 to 95 percent of what is taken in; the casino keeps 5 to 10 percent. These payback percentages are a function of the number of different symbols that are on each wheel. Each symbol is repeated on each wheel a certain number of times. For example, if a

SLOT MACHINES IN A CASINO IN RENO, NEVADA, HAVE A MAJOR IMPACT ON THE CASINO'S PROFITS. AN ELECTRONIC VERSION VERSUS A MECHANICAL VERSION IMPACTS CYCLE TIME, WHICH IN TURN AFFECTS REVENUES.

wheel has 10 symbols, one might be a single bar, one a double bar, and one a lemon; two might be cherries, three lucky sevens, and two liberty bells. Because the wheels stop on a random symbol, the probability of lucky sevens coming up on all three wheels is $\frac{3}{10} \times \frac{3}{10} \times \frac{3}{10} = 0.027$ or 2.7 percent of the time. The probability of certain combinations of symbols coming up, combined with the payout for each combination, sets the average percentage that the machine is expected to pay out.

Cycle time

Consider a mechanical slot machine that pays out 95 percent of the coins played. With this machine, assume the average player feeds coins into the machine at a pace of one coin each 15 seconds. This 15-second interval is called the *cycle time* of the process. The cycle time of a repetitive process is the average time between completions of successive units. In the case of the slot machine, the unit is a silver dollar. With a 15-second cycle time, our mechanical slot machine can process $4 (60 seconds/15 seconds) per minute or $240 ($4/minute × 60 minutes) per hour. Because our slot machine has a payout of 95 percent, we would expect the machine to give the customer 228 (240 × 0.95) of the silver dollars that it took in and keep $12 for the casino for each hour that it is in operation. If we started with $100, we could expect to play for about 8.3 hours ($100/$12 per hour) before we would run out of silver dollars. We might be lucky and win the jackpot, or we might be unlucky and lose it all in the first hour; but on average we would expect to lose the entire $100 in 8.3 hours.

Now consider the new electronic slot machine. It operates in exactly the same manner; the only difference is that it processes coins in 10 seconds. With a 10-second cycle time, the machine processes $6 (60 seconds/10 seconds) per minute or $360 ($6/minute × 60 minutes) per hour. With a 95 percent payout, the machine would give the customer back 342 (360 × 0.95) silver dollars and keep $18 for the casino each hour. This machine would take our $100 in only 5.5 hours ($100/$18 per hour).

Utilization

So how much does the electronic slot machine make for the casino in 24 hours compared to the mechanical slot machine? One more critical piece of information is needed to answer this question: How long will the slot machine operate over the 24 hours? The casino feels that the machine will be used 12 out of the 24 hours; this 12 out of 24 hours is the expected utilization of the machine. Utilization is the ratio of the time that a resource is actually activated relative to the time that it is available for use. Adjusting for utilization, the expected revenue from the mechanical machine is $144/day ($12/hour × 24 hours × 0.5) compared to revenue of $216/day ($18/hour × 24 hours × 0.5) for the electronic machine. When an analysis is performed, it is important to qualify the analysis with the assumptions made. In this comparison, we assumed that the operator puts only one silver dollar in the machine at a time and that the utilization would be the same for the mechanical and electronic slot machines.

The speed of the slot machine can have a major impact on the casino's revenue. The single slot machine is only a small part of the casino. To really understand how much revenue the casino can generate, we need to consider all of the other revenue-generating processes such as the blackjack and poker tables, keno games, craps, and the other games in the casino. Many times analyzing an enterprise involves evaluating a number of independent activities, like our slot machine. The aggregate performance of each individual activity may be all that is needed to understand the overall process. On the other hand, often there is significant interaction between individual activities or processes that must be considered.

Think about our gambling casino. Many casinos offer great deals on food, which is served right in the casino. What do you think would be the main priority of the food operation manager in one of these casinos? Would great-tasting food be important? How important is the cost of the food? Is speed of service important? Good food certainly is important. If the food is unpleasant, the customer will not even consider eating at the casino. This is bad for the casino because if the customers leave, they take their money with them. Remember, the casino makes money based on how long the customers gamble. The more time spent gambling, the more money the casino makes. What about cost? If the customers think the meals are too expensive, they might leave. So it is important to keep the cost of the meals down so that they can be priced inexpensively. Many casinos even give meals away. How important is it to serve the customer quickly? Think about it this way: Every minute that the customers are sitting in the restaurant, they are not feeding silver dollars into a slot machine. So speed is important because it impacts the revenue generated at the games in the casino.

PROCESS FLOWCHARTING

Often the activities associated with a process affect one another so that it is important to consider the simultaneous performance of a number of activities, all operating at the same time. A good way to start analyzing a process is with a diagram showing the basic elements of a process—typically tasks, flows, and storage areas. Tasks are shown as rectangles, flows as arrows, and the storage of goods or other items as inverted triangles. Sometimes flows through a process can be diverted in multiple directions depending on some condition. Decision points are depicted as a diamond with the different flows running from the points on the diamond. Exhibit 5.1 displays examples of these symbols. It sometimes is useful to separate a diagram into different horizontal or vertical bands. This allows the separation of tasks that are part of the process. For example, with the slot machine, the tasks performed by the customer can be separated from the tasks performed by the slot machine.

In the slot machine example, the level of abstraction considers the slot machine as a simple black box that takes in silver dollars and either keeps them or returns some of them during each cycle. Viewing the slot machine as a black box might be fine if the purpose is just to analyze how much the machine is expected to make for the casino each hour. In reality, more activities are required to support the slot machine. Inside the slot machine are two buckets of silver dollars. One bucket stores coins needed for internal use by the slot machine. When a customer wins, the payout comes from this payout bucket. The slot machine is designed to

Process Flowchart Example

exhibit 5.1

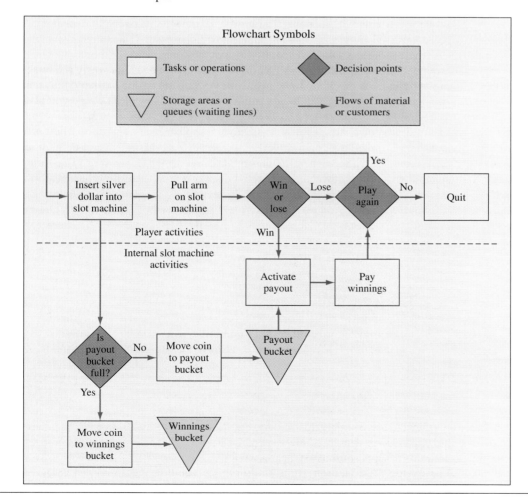

automatically keep this payout bucket filled during play. When the payout bucket is full, the silver dollars are deposited in a second winnings bucket. The winnings bucket must be periodically emptied to claim the winnings for the casino. The flowchart in Exhibit 5.1 depicts the external activities of the player and the internal movement of the coins within the machine.

Probably the most interesting thing about the payout bucket is how big it should be. The slot machine is programmed so that if the payout bucket empties, the machine stops and lights on the top of the machine flash, thus notifying casino personnel that a lucky customer has emptied the machine. The payout bucket would be sized to keep this a rare occurrence. Think of the payout bucket as a buffer or intermediate storage area for silver dollars that allows the slot machine to operate on its own. The smaller the payout bucket, the more the casino personnel need to attend to the machine, and the more time the machine is idle for lack of silver dollars. On the other hand, with a larger bucket more money is tied up.

The situation with the winnings bucket in the machine is similar. A small winnings bucket will need to be emptied more often. On the other hand, a large winnings bucket means that the casino does not deposit the money into its bank account as quickly. It is easy to see the advantage of buffering operations with the slot machine. Large buffers allow the process to operate independently, whereas small buffers require more attention. In the case of the slot machine, the buffer is composed of the silver dollars. In other situations, where the buffer is other items such as a raw material, these items have a value, so they also represent money.

Consider a slot machine that we expect to deposit $12 into the winnings bucket every hour. If our winnings bucket can hold 1,000 silver dollars, then we expect to need to empty the winnings bucket every 83.3 hours ($1,000/$12 per hour) if the slot machine is used 100 percent of the time. It is interesting to think about what happens when the winnings bucket fills up. If the slot machine is smart enough to know that the winnings bucket is full, it might be programmed to just stop working with its lights flashing as they do when the payout bucket empties. This would cause downtime on the machine and might upset a customer using the machine because the customer would have to move to another slot machine. If the slot machine were not programmed to stop working, the silver dollars would fill the cavity where the bucket is located in the base of the machine. Imagine the mess when the casino worker opens that overflowed machine and all those silver dollars come pouring out. How often would you plan on emptying the winnings bucket?

An easy way to draw flowcharts is to use the Drawing toolbar available in the Microsoft Office programs (i.e., Word, Excel, and PowerPoint). To access this toolbar, go to View → Toolbars and click on "Drawing". The Drawing menu should then appear. Use the Auto-Shapes button and then select "Flowchart". This will display a number of flowchart symbols to use to create your flowchart. Text can be added by selecting a symbol and then clicking on the right mouse button. Select "Add text" to insert text in the symbol. The symbols can be connected by using "Connectors" available from the AutoShapes button. Nice flowcharts can be made using these tools.

TYPES OF PROCESSES

It is useful to categorize processes to describe how a process is designed. By being able to quickly categorize a process, we can show the similarities and differences between processes.

The first way to categorize a process is to determine whether it is a *single-stage* or a *multiple-stage* process. If the slot machine were viewed as a simple black box, it would be categorized as a single-stage process. In this case, all of the activi-

ties that are involved in the operation of the slot machine would be collapsed and analyzed using a single cycle time to represent the speed of the slot machine. A multiple-stage process has multiple groups of activities that are linked through flows. The term *stage* is used to indicate that multiple activities have been pulled together for analysis purposes.

A multiple-stage process may be buffered internally. **Buffering** refers to a storage area between stages where the output of a stage is placed prior to being used in a downstream stage. Buffering allows the stages to operate independently. If one stage feeds a second stage with no intermediate buffer, then the assumption is that the two stages are directly linked. When a process is designed this way, the most common problems that can happen are blocking and starving. **Blocking** occurs when the activities in the stage must stop because there is no place to deposit the item just completed. **Starving** occurs when the activities in a stage must stop because there is no work.

Consider a two-stage process where the first stage has a cycle time of 30 seconds and the second a cycle time of 45 seconds. If this process needs to produce 100 units, then for each unit produced, the first stage would be blocked for 15 seconds.

What would happen if an inventory buffer were placed between the two stages? In this case, the first stage would complete the 100 units in 3,000 seconds (30 seconds/unit × 100 units). During these 3,000 seconds, the second stage would complete only 66 units ((3,000 − 30) seconds/45 seconds/unit). The 30 seconds are subtracted from the 3,000 seconds because the second stage is starved for the first 30 seconds. This would mean that the inventory would build to 34 units (100 units − 66 units) over that first 3,000 seconds. All of the units would be produced in 4,530 seconds. The second stage in this case is called a **bottleneck** because it limits the capacity of the process.

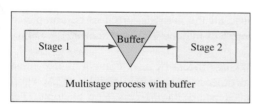

Multistage process with buffer

What would happen if the first stage required 45 seconds and the second stage had the 30-second cycle time? In this case the first stage would be the bottleneck, and each unit would go directly from the first stage to the second. The second stage would be starved for 15 seconds waiting for each unit to arrive; however, it would still take 4,530 seconds to complete all 100 units. All of this assumes that there is no variability in the cycle time. With the relatively low 67 percent utilization on the second stage, variability would have little impact on the performance of this system, but if the cycle times were closer, some inventory might collect in the buffer.

Often activities, stages, and even entire processes are operated in parallel. For example, operating two identical activities in parallel would theoretically double capacity. Or perhaps two different sets of activities can be done at the same time on the unit being produced. In analyzing a system with parallel activities or stages, it is important to understand the context. In the case where parallel processes represent alternatives, for example, a diamond should show that flows divert and what percentage of the flow moves in each direction. Sometimes two or more processes terminate in a common inventory buffer. This normally indicates that

$\dfrac{3000}{4500}$ = Utilization for stage 2 = 67%

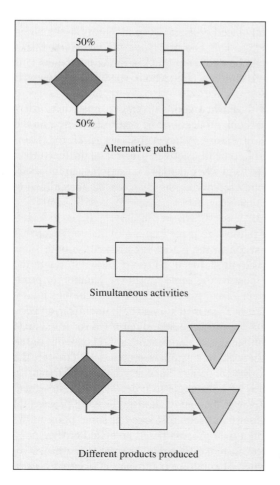

Alternative paths

Simultaneous activities

Different products produced

the two processes make identical items that are going into this inventory. Separate inventories should be used in the diagram if the outputs of the parallel processes are different.

Another useful way to characterize a process is whether the process *makes to stock* or *makes to order*. To illustrate these concepts, consider the processes used to make hamburgers at the three major fast-food restaurant chains in the United States: McDonald's, Burger King, and Wendy's. In the case of McDonald's, in 1999 the company converted to a new make-to-order process, but the company has now revised that into a "hybrid" system. We begin our tour of the approaches used by the top fast-food restaurants by first reviewing the traditional approach.

Consider a traditional restaurant making hamburgers. Before the era of fast food, hamburgers were always made to order. In the traditional process, the customer places an order specifying the degree of doneness (medium or well done) and requests specific condiments (pickles, cheese, mustard, onions, catsup). Using this specification, the cook takes raw hamburger meat from inventory (typically this inventory is refrigerated and the patties have already been made), cooks the hamburger, and warms the bun. The hamburger is then assembled and delivered to the customer. The quality of the hamburger is highly dependent on the skill of the cook.

This **make-to-order** process is activated only in response to an actual order. Inventory (both work-in-process and finished goods) is kept to a minimum. Theoretically, one would expect that response time would be slow because all the activities need to be completed before the product is delivered to the customer. Services by their very nature often use make-to-order processes.

McDonald's revolutionized the hamburger-making process by developing a high-volume approach. A diagram of McDonald's traditional process is shown in Exhibit 5.2A. Until recently, hamburgers were grilled in batches. Standard hamburgers (for example, the "Big Mac" consists of two beef patties, sauce, lettuce, cheese, pickles, and onion on a sesame seed bun) were then prepared and stored in a holding bin for immediate delivery to the customer. A person that judged current demand and placed orders to keep inventory in the bin at an appropriate level controlled the whole process. This is a highly efficient **make-to-stock** process that produces standard products that can be delivered quickly to the customer. This quick process appeals to families with small children, for whom speed of delivery is important.

In general, a make-to-stock process ends with finished goods inventory; customer orders are then served from this inventory. A make-to-stock process can be controlled based on the actual or anticipated amount of finished goods inventory. A target stocking level, for example, might be set, and the process would be periodically activated to maintain that target stocking level. Make-to-stock processes are also used when demand is seasonal. In this case, inventory can be built during the slow season and used during the peak season, thus allowing the process to run at a constant rate throughout the year.

The unique feature of the Burger King process, shown in Exhibit 5.2B, is a highly specialized conveyor–broiler. Raw hamburger patties are placed on a moving conveyor that runs through a flaming broiler. In exactly 90 seconds, the patties are cooked on both sides with a unique broiler taste. Due to the fixed time for a patty to move through the conveyor–broiler, the thickness of the patties must be the same for all the hamburger products. The buns are also warmed on a conveyor. This system results in a unique, highly consistent product. The cooked patties are stored in a warmed storage container. During periods of high demand, some standard hamburgers are prepared and inventoried for immediate delivery. Custom hamburgers with unique combinations of condiments are prepared to order. This *hybrid* process provides flexibility to respond to customer preferences through the assemble-to-order backend process—thus, the Burger King "have it your way" slogan. In general, **hybrid** processes combine the features of both make-to-order and make-to-stock. Here two types of process are parallel alternatives at the end of the Burger King process. In the most common hybrid form, a generic product is made and stocked at some point in the process. These generic units are then finished in a final process based on actual orders.

Continuing with our tour, Wendy's uses a make-to-order process (as shown in Exhibit 5.2C) that is in full view of the customer. Hamburger patties are cooked on a grill.

Service

Make-to-order

Make-to-stock

Hybrid

Making Hamburgers at McDonald's, Burger King, and Wendy's

exhibit 5.2

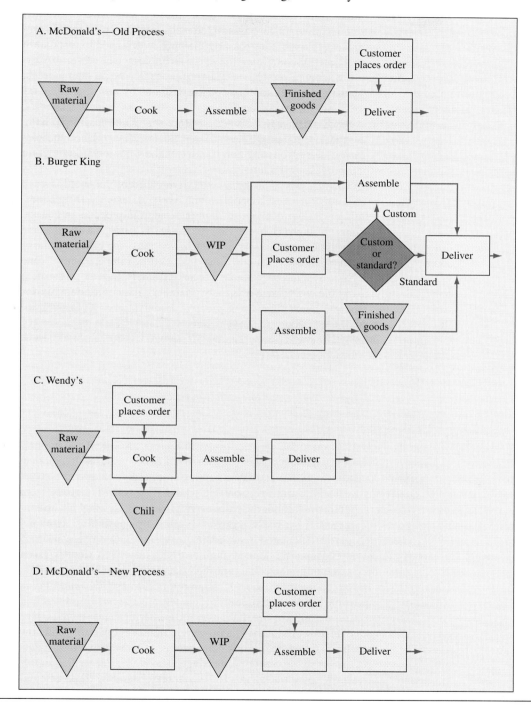

During high-volume times, the cook tries to get a little ahead and anticipates the arrival of customers. Patties that are on the grill too long are used in the chili soup. On arrival of a customer order, a patty is taken from the grill and the hamburger is assembled to the exact specifications of the customer. Because the process starts with the cooking of the patty, it is a little slower. The customer can see what is going on, and the perception is of a high-quality custom product.

Finally, the new McDonald's process introduced in 1999 (Exhibit 5.2D) is a hybrid process. Cooked hamburger patties are inventoried in a special storage device that maintains the moistness of the cooked patties for up to 30 minutes. The process makes extensive use of the latest cooking technologies. Hamburger patties are cooked in less than 45 seconds. Buns are toasted in only eleven seconds. Individual items on each customer order are transmitted immediately to the area where the hamburgers are assembled using a specially designed computer system. The assembly process that includes toasting the buns is designed to respond to a customer order in only 15 seconds. By combining the latest technology and clever process engineering, McDonald's has developed a very quick response process. The product is fresh, delivered quickly, and made to the exact specifications of the customer.

Each of the processes used by these companies has its strengths and weaknesses. McDonald's is the high-volume leader, catering to families with young children. Burger King has its unique taste. Wendy's appeals to those who want their hamburgers prepared the old-fashioned way. Each company focuses advertising and promotional efforts toward attracting the segment of the market their process characteristics best support.

Pacing

One final method for categorizing a process is by whether it is paced or nonpaced. Recall that Burger King uses the conveyor–broiler to cook hamburgers in exactly 90 seconds. **Pacing** refers to the fixed timing of the movement of items through the process. In a serial process, the movement of items through each activity (or stage) is often paced in some mechanical way in order to coordinate the line. An assembly line may, for example, move every 45 seconds. Another mechanism used is a clock that counts down the amount of time left in each cycle. When the clock reaches zero, the parts are manually moved to the next activity. Dividing the time available to produce a certain product by customer demand for the product calculates the required cycle time for a process. For example, if an automobile manufacturer needs to produce 1,000 automobiles during a shift where the assembly line operates 420 minutes, the cycle time is 25.2 seconds (420 minutes/1,000 automobiles × 60 seconds/minute = 25.2 seconds/automobile).

MEASURING PROCESS PERFORMANCE

There is much variation in the way performance metrics are calculated in practice. This section defines metrics in a manner consistent with the most common use in practice. It is vital, though, to understand exactly how a metric coming from a particular company or industry is calculated prior to making any decisions. It would be easier if metrics were calculated more consistently, but this just is not the case. So if a manager says that his utilization is 90 percent or her efficiency is 115 percent, a standard follow-up question is "How did you calculate that?" Metrics often are calculated in the context of a particular process. Metrics used in cases that you are studying may be defined slightly differently from what is given here. It is important to understand, within the context of the case, how a term is being used.

Comparing the metrics of one company to another, often referred to as *benchmarking,* is an important activity. Metrics tell a firm if progress is being made toward improvement. Similar to the value of financial measures to accountants, process performance metrics give the operations manager a gauge on how productively a process currently is operating and how productivity is changing over time. Often operations managers need to improve the performance of a process or project the impact of a proposed change. The metrics described in this section are important for answering these questions. To help in understanding these calculations, Exhibit 5.3 shows how these metrics relate to one another.

Possibly the most common process metric is utilization. As discussed earlier in the chapter, utilization is the ratio of the time that a resource is actually being used relative to the time that it is available for use. Utilization is always measured in reference to some resource—for example, the utilization of direct labor or the utilization of a machine resource. The distinction between productivity and utilization is important. **Productivity** is the ratio of output to input. Total factor productivity is usually measured in monetary units, dollars for example, by taking the dollar value of the output (such as goods and services sold) and dividing by the cost of all the inputs (that is, material, labor, and capital investment). Alternatively, *partial factor productivity* is measured based on an individual input, labor being the most common. Partial

Productivity

Process Performance Metrics

exhibit 5.3

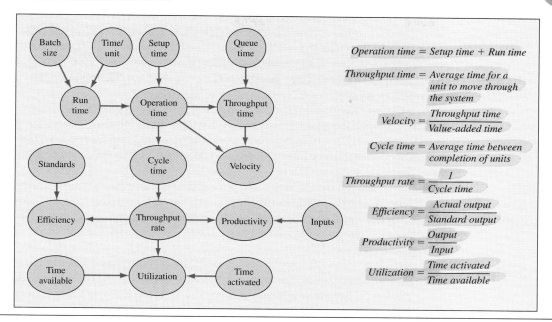

$$\text{Operation time} = \text{Setup time} + \text{Run time}$$

$$\text{Throughput time} = \text{Average time for a unit to move through the system}$$

$$\text{Velocity} = \frac{\text{Throughput time}}{\text{Value-added time}}$$

$$\text{Cycle time} = \text{Average time between completion of units}$$

$$\text{Throughput rate} = \frac{1}{\text{Cycle time}}$$

$$\text{Efficiency} = \frac{\text{Actual output}}{\text{Standard output}}$$

$$\text{Productivity} = \frac{\text{Output}}{\text{Input}}$$

$$\text{Utilization} = \frac{\text{Time activated}}{\text{Time available}}$$

factor productivity answers the question of how much output we can get from a given level of input; for example, how many computers are made per employee working in the computer manufacturing plant? (See Chapter 2 for additional information about productivity.) Utilization measures the actual activation of the resource. For example, what is the percentage of time that an expensive machine is actually operating?

Efficiency is a ratio of the actual output of a process relative to some standard. For example, consider a machine designed to package cereal at a rate of 30 boxes per minute. If during a shift the operators actually produce at a rate of 36 boxes per minute, then the efficiency of the machine is 120 percent (36/30). An alter-

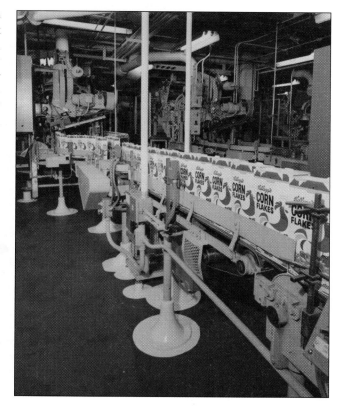

Efficiency

native way that the term *efficiency* is used is to measure the loss or gain in a process. For example, if 1,000 units of energy are put into a process designed to convert that energy to some alternative form, and the process produces only 800 units of energy in the new form, then the process is 80 percent efficient.

Run time is the time required to produce a batch of parts. This is calculated by multiplying the time required to produce each unit by the batch size. The **setup time** is the time

Run time
Setup time

Operation time

required to prepare a machine to make a particular item. Machines that have significant setup time will typically run parts in batches. The **operation time** is the sum of the setup time and run time for a batch of parts that are run on a machine. Consider the cereal-boxing machine (on page 163) that is designed to produce at a rate of 30 boxes per minute. The run time for each box is 2 seconds. To switch the machine from 16-ounce boxes to 12-ounce boxes requires a setup time of 30 minutes. The operation time to make a batch of 10,000 12-ounce boxes is 21,800 seconds (30 minutes' setup × 60 seconds/minute + 2 seconds/box × 10,000 boxes) or 363.33 minutes.

In practice, often setup time is not included in the utilization of the process. In essence, setup time is categorized like the downtime caused by repair or some other disruption to the process. This assumption can vary from company to company, so it is important when comparing the utilization of a machine or other resource to understand exactly how the company categorizes setup time.

Throughput time

The cycle time (also defined earlier in this chapter) is the elapsed time between starting and completing a job.[1] Another related term is **throughput time.** Throughput time includes the time that the unit spends actually being worked on together with the time spent waiting in a queue. As a simple example, consider a paced assembly line that has six stations and runs with a cycle time of 30 seconds. If the stations are located one right after another and every 30 seconds parts move from one station to the next, then the throughput time is three minutes (30 seconds × 6 stations/60 seconds per minute). The **throughput rate** is the output rate that the process is expected to produce over a period of time. The throughput rate of the assembly line is 120 units per hour (60 minutes/hour × 60 seconds/minute ÷ 30 seconds/unit). In this case, the throughput rate is the mathematical inverse of the cycle time.

Throughput rate

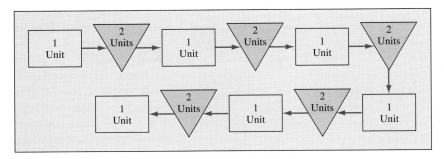

Often units are not worked on 100 percent of the time as they move through a process. Because there often is some variability in the cycle time of a process, buffers are incorporated in the process to allow individual activities to operate independently, at least to some extent. In the six-station assembly line just described, consider the impact of having 10 additional buffer positions along the line. Assume that two of these positions are between the first and second workstation, two are between stations 2 and 3, and so forth. If these positions are always occupied, then the throughput time would be eight minutes (assuming a total of 16 positions along the assembly line and an average cycle time of 30 seconds).

Process velocity (throughput ratio)

Value-added time

Process velocity (also known as **throughput ratio**) is the ratio of the total throughput time to the value-added time. **Value-added time** is the time in which useful work is actually being done on the unit. Assuming that all of the activities that are included in the process are value-added activities, value-added time should be the sum of the activity operation times in the process. The process velocity (or throughput ratio) for our assembly line with the 10 additional buffer positions, assuming the positions are used 100 percent of the time, is 2.66 (8 minutes/3 minutes).

Little's Law

Interactive Operations Management

Little's Law[2] states a mathematical relationship between throughput rate, throughput time, and the amount of work-in-process inventory. Little's Law estimates the time that an item will spend in work-in-process inventory, which can be useful for calculating the total throughput time for a process. Using the terminology defined in this section, Little's Law is defined as follows:

$$\text{Throughput time} = \frac{\text{Work-in-process}}{\text{Throughput rate}}$$

Notice how this law holds for the example of the assembly line without the buffer inventory. If the assembly line has six stations with one unit of work-in-process at each station, and the throughput rate is two units per minute (60 seconds/30 seconds per unit), then the throughput time is three minutes (6 units/2 units per minute). In general, this equation is useful when two of the three quantities are known. For example, if the throughput time and throughput rate are known, the work-in-process can be calculated. This formula holds for any process that is operating at a steady rate.

By *steady rate* we mean that work is entering and exiting the system at the same rate over the time period being analyzed. Our assembly line has 120 units entering and 120 units exiting the process each hour. If, for example, 150 units were entering the system each hour but only 120 units were exiting, then the system would not be operating at a steady rate since 30 additional units would be accumulating in the system each hour. These 30 units add to work-in-process, which would cause the throughput time to increase each hour. The actual increase in throughput time would be 15 minutes per hour (30 units/120 units per hour = 0.25 hour). Another example of how Little's Law can be applied is in the following section relative to diagnosing the performance of a process.

PROCESS ANALYSIS EXAMPLES

In this section the concepts described thus far in the chapter are illustrated with three examples. These examples are typical of the types of analysis that are performed in manufacturing, services, and logistics businesses. Keep in mind that the analysis used in each example can be applied to many different contexts. Be creative in applying something that you have seen in another context to the problem at hand. The first example analyzes a bread-making process. Following this, a restaurant operation is evaluated. Finally, a typical logistics operation is appraised.

A BREAD-MAKING OPERATION[3]

EXAMPLE 5.1: Bread Making

For the manager of a bakery, a first priority is to understand the products that are made and the process steps required. Exhibit 5.4A is a simplified diagram of the bread-making process. There are two steps required to prepare the bread. The first is preparing the dough and baking the loaves, here referred to as bread making. The second is packaging the loaves. Due to the size of the mixers

Bread-Making Processes   **exhibit 5.4**

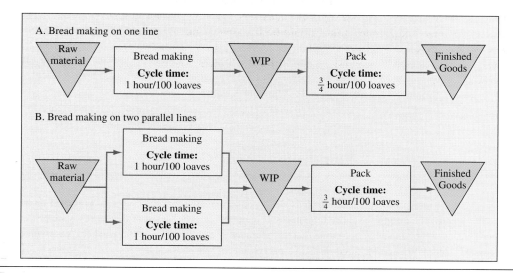

in the bakery, bread is made in batches of 100 loaves. Bread making completes a batch of 100 loaves every hour, which is the cycle time for the activity. Packaging needs only 0.75 hour to place the 100 loaves in bags.

From this we see that bread making is the bottleneck in the process. A bottleneck is the activity in a process that limits the overall capacity of the process. So if we assume that the bread-making and packaging activities both operate the same amount of time each day, then the bakery has a capacity of 100 loaves per hour. Notice that over the course of the day the packaging operation will be idle for quarter-hour periods in which the next batch of bread is still being made but packaging has already completed bagging the previous batch. One would expect that the packaging operation would be utilized only 75 percent of the time under this scenario.

Suppose that instead of having only one bread-making operation we now have two, as shown in Exhibit 5.4B. The cycle time for each individual bread-making operation is still one hour per 100 loaves. The cycle time for the two bread-making lines operating together is half an hour. Because the packaging operation takes 0.75 hour to bag 100 loaves, the packaging operation now is the bottleneck. If both bread making and packaging were operated the same number of hours each day, it would be necessary to limit how much bread was made because we do not have the capacity to package it. However, if we operated the packaging operation for three eight-hour shifts and bread making for two shifts each day, then the daily capacity of each would be identical at 3,200 loaves a day (this assumes that the packaging operation starts up one hour after the bread-making operation). Doing this requires building up a shift's worth of inventory each day as work-in-process. Packaging would bag this during the third shift. So what is the throughput time of our bakery?

SOLUTION

In the original operation with just the single bread-making process, this is easy to calculate because inventory would not build between the bread-making and packaging processes. In this case the throughput time would be 1.75 hours. In the case where we operate the packaging operation for three shifts, the average wait in work-in-process inventory needs to be considered. If both bread-making operations start at the same time, then at the end of the first hour the first 100 loaves move immediately into packaging while the second 100 loaves wait. The waiting time for each 100-loaf batch increases until the baking is done at the end of the second shift.

This is a case where Little's Law can estimate the time that the bread is sitting in work-in-process. To apply Little's Law we need to estimate the average work-in-process between bread making and packaging. During the first two shifts inventory builds from 0 to 1,200 loaves. We can estimate the average work-in-process over this 16-hour period to be 600 loaves (half the maximum). Over the last eight-hour shift inventory drops from the 1,200-loaf maximum down to 0. Again the average work-in-process is 600 loaves. Given this, the overall average over the 24-hour period is simply 600 loaves of bread. The packing process limits the cycle time for the process to 0.75 hour per 100 loaves (assume that the loaves are packaged in a batch), and this is equivalent to a throughput rate of 133.3 loaves/hour (100/0.75 = 133.3). Little's Law calculates that the average time that loaves are in work-in-process is 4.5 hours (600 loaves/133.3 loaves/hour).

The total throughput time is the time that the loaves are in work-in-process plus the operations time for the bread-making and packaging processes. The total throughput time then is 6.25 hours (1 hour for bread making + 4.5 hours in inventory + 0.75 hour packaging). ●

A RESTAURANT OPERATION

Service

EXAMPLE 5.2: A Restaurant

Our bakery operates in what is referred to as *steady state,* meaning that the operation is started up and runs at a steady rate during the entire time that it is in operation. The output of this steady state process is adjusted by setting the amount of time that the operation is run. In the case of the bakery, we assumed that bread making worked for three shifts and packaging for two shifts.

A restaurant cannot run in this manner. The restaurant must respond to varying customer demand throughout the day. During some peak times, it may be impossible to serve all customers immediately, and some customers may have to wait to be seated. The restaurant, because of this varying demand, is a *non–steady state* process. Keep in mind that many of the menu items in a restaurant can be pre-prepared. The pre-prepared items, salads and desserts for example, help speed the processes that must be performed when customers are at the restaurant being served.

Consider the restaurant in the casino that we discussed earlier. Because it is important that customers be served quickly, the managers have set up a buffet arrangement where customers serve themselves. The buffet is continually replenished to keep items fresh. To further speed service, a fixed amount is charged for the meal, no matter what the customer eats. Assume that we have designed our buffet so customers take an average of 30 minutes to get their food and eat. Further, assume that they typically eat in groups (or customer parties) of two or three to a table. The restaurant has 40 tables. Each table can accommodate four people. What is the maximum capacity of this restaurant?

SOLUTION

It is easy to see that the restaurant can accommodate 160 people seated at tables at a time. Actually, in this situation it might be more convenient to measure the capacity in terms of customer parties because this is how the capacity will be used. If the average customer party is 2.5 individuals, then the average seat utilization is 62.5 percent (2.5 seats/party ÷ 4 seats/table) when the restaurant is operating at capacity. The cycle time for the restaurant, when operating at capacity, is 0.75 minute (30 minutes/table ÷ 40 tables). So on average a table would become available every 45 seconds. The restaurant could handle 80 customer parties per hour (60 minutes ÷ 0.75 minute/party).

The problem with this restaurant is that everyone wants to eat at the same time. Management has collected data and expects the following profile for customer parties arriving during lunch, which runs from 11:30 A.M. until 1:30 P.M. Customers are seated only until 1:00 P.M.

TIME	PARTIES ARRIVING
11:30–11:45	15
11:45–12:00	35
12:00–12:15	30
12:15–12:30	15
12:30–12:45	10
12:45–1:00	5
Total parties	110

Because the restaurant operates for two hours for lunch and the capacity is 80 customer parties per hour, it does not appear that the restaurant has a problem. In reality, though, there is a problem due to the uneven flow of customers into the restaurant. A simple way to analyze the situation is to calculate how we expect the system to look in terms of number of customers being served and number waiting in line at the end of each 15-minute interval. Think of this as taking a snapshot of the restaurant every 15 minutes.

The key to understanding the analysis is to look at the cumulative numbers. The difference between cumulative arrivals and cumulative departures gives the number of customer parties in the restaurant (those seated at tables and those waiting). Because there are only 40 tables, when the cumulative difference through a time interval is greater than 40, a waiting line forms. When all 40 tables are busy, the system is operating at capacity; and, from the previous calculation, we know the cycle time for the entire restaurant is 45 seconds per customer party at this time (this means that on average a table empties every 45 seconds or 20 tables empty during each 15-minute interval). The last party will need to wait for all of the earlier parties to get a table, so the expected waiting time is the number of parties in line multiplied by the cycle time.

TIME PERIOD	PARTIES ARRIVING DURING PERIOD (CUMULATIVE)	PARTIES DEPARTING DURING PERIOD (CUMULATIVE)	PARTIES EITHER AT TABLE OR WAITING TO BE SERVED (AT END OF PERIOD)	TABLES USED (AT END OF PERIOD)	CUSTOMER PARTIES WAITING (AT END OF PERIOD)	EXPECTED WAITING TIME (AT END OF PERIOD)
11:30–11:45	15	0	15	15		
11:45–12:00	35(50)	0	50	40	10	7.5 minutes
12:00–12:15	30(80)	15	65	40	25	18.75 minutes
12:15–12:30	15(95)	20(35)	60	40	20	15 minutes
12:30–12:45	10(105)	20(55)	50	40	10	7.5 minutes
12:45–1:00	5(110)	20(75)	35	35		
1:00–1:30	0(110)	35(110)				

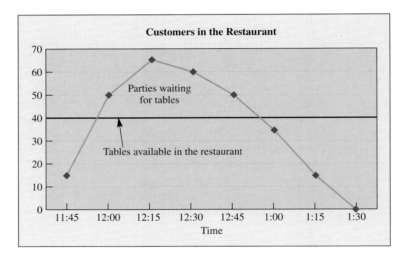

The analysis shows that by 12 noon, 10 customer parties are waiting in line. This line builds to 25 parties by 12:15. The waiting line shortens to only 10 parties by 12:45.

So what can we do to solve our waiting line problem? One idea might be to shorten the cycle time for a single table, but customers are unlikely to be rushed through their lunch in less than 30 minutes. Another idea would be to add tables. If the restaurant could add 25 tables, then a wait would not be expected. Of course, this would eat into the space used for slot machines, so this alternative might not be attractive to casino management. A final idea might be to double up parties at the tables, thus getting a higher seat utilization. Doubling up might be the easiest thing to try. If 25 out of the 40 tables were doubled up, our problem would be solved. ●

PLANNING A TRANSIT BUS OPERATION

EXAMPLE 5.3: Transit Bus Operation

The final example involves a *logistics* system. The term *logistics* refers to the movement of things such as materials, people, or finished goods. Our example involves a bus route that would be typical of one used on campus or in a metropolitan area. A similar analysis could be used for analyzing plane routes, truck routes, or ships. Similar to the restaurant, a bus transit route does not operate in steady state. There are definite peaks in demand during the day and evening. A good approach to take, the same as was done with the restaurant, is to analyze distinct periods of time that represent the different types of demand patterns placed on the service. These distinct analyses can be referred to as *scenarios*. Depending on the situation, it might be reasonable to develop either a single solution that covers all the relevant scenarios or a set of solutions for the different scenarios.

A great bus route is the Balabus, or "tourist bus," in Paris. This route loops past all the major attractions in Paris. Some of the sights along the route include Notre-Dame, the Louvre, Concorde, Champs-Elysées, the Arc de Triomphe, the Eiffel Tower, and others.

Service

Global

Consider the problem of planning the number of buses needed to service this route. A number of factors need to be considered. Let's assume that a single bus takes exactly two hours to traverse the route during peak traffic. The bus company has designed delays in the route so that even though traffic is busy the bus can keep on schedule. The route has 60 stops, although the bus stops only when passengers on the bus request a stop or when the driver sees customers waiting to board at a stop. Each bus has seating capacity of about 50 passengers, and another 30 passengers can stand. This route is busy much of the day because visitors to the city tend to start visiting the sites early and continue until dark. Finally, the transit authority wants to give good service and have enough capacity to handle peak customer loads. The following is an analysis of the situation.

SOLUTION

A key measure of service is how long a customer must wait prior to the arrival of a bus. Consider initially the case of only a single bus serving the route. If a person at a random time comes to a bus stop, we know that the maximum time that the customer needs to wait is two hours. Here we assume that the bus is able to cover the route in exactly two hours. If there is significant variability in this cycle time, the waiting time goes up. We discuss the impact of variability in Technical Note 6. This would be the case when the unlucky customer just missed the bus. If the bus was halfway through the route (relative to where the customer is waiting), then the customer needs to wait one hour. Continuing with this logic, we can estimate the average wait time for the customer to be one hour. In general, we can say that the average wait time would be half the cycle time of the process. If two buses are used, the cycle time is one hour and the average wait is 30 minutes. If we want the average wait to be two minutes, then the required cycle time is four minutes, and 30 buses are needed (120 minutes ÷ 4 minutes/bus = 30 buses).

The next issue relates to the capacity of the system. If we have 30 buses on the route and each bus seats 50 passengers with another 30 standing, we know that we can accommodate 1,500 seated or 2,400 passengers in total at one point in time.

Assume that the following table is an estimate of the number of passengers that travel the route during a typical tourist season day. The table shows calculations of the amount of bus capacity required during each hour. If a customer rides the bus for 45 minutes, then one seat is needed for 45 minutes, or 0.75 hour, to handle that passenger. Of course, 60 minutes, or a full hour's worth, of capacity is available for each seat that we have. At maximum utilization including standing, each bus can handle 80 passenger-hours' worth of load. Dividing the expected passenger load during the hour by the maximum load for a single bus calculates the minimum number of buses needed. Similarly, dividing the expected passenger load by the number of seats on each bus calculates the number of buses needed so that all passengers can be seated.

Time	Number of Customers	Average Time on Bus	Load (Passenger Hours)	Minimum Number of Buses Needed	Buses Needed for All Passengers to Be Seated
8:00–9:00 A.M.	2,000	45 minutes	1,500	18.75	30
9:00–10:00 A.M.	4,000	30 minutes	2,000	25	40
10:00–11:00 A.M.	6,000	30 minutes	3,000	37.5	60
11:00 A.M.–12:00 NOON	5,000	30 minutes	2,500	31.25	50
12:00–1:00 P.M.	4,000	30 minutes	2,000	25	40
1:00–2:00 P.M.	3,500	30 minutes	1,750	21.875	35
2:00–3:00 P.M.	3,000	45 minutes	2,250	28.125	45
3:00–4:00 P.M.	3,000	45 minutes	2,250	28.125	45
4:00–5:00 P.M.	3,000	45 minutes	2,250	28.125	45
5:00–6:00 P.M.	4,000	45 minutes	3,000	37.5	60
6:00–7:00 P.M.	3,000	45 minutes	2,250	28.125	45
7:00–8:00 P.M.	1,500	45 minutes	1,125	14.0625	22.5
TOTALS	42,000		25,875		

From the analysis, if the Paris transit authority uses only 30 buses throughout the day, many people will need to stand. Further, during the morning rush between 10 and 11 A.M. and the evening rush between 5 and 6 P.M., not all of the customers can be accommodated. It would seem reasonable that at least 40 buses should be used between 9 A.M. and 7 P.M. Even with this number of buses, one would expect passengers to be standing most of the time.

If the transit authority decided to use 40 buses between the extended hours of 8 A.M. through 8 P.M., what would be the average utilization of the buses in terms of seats occupied? Over this 12-hour period, 24,000 seat-hours of capacity would be available (40 buses $\times$ 12 hours $\times$ 50 seats/bus). The table indicates that 25,875 seat-hours are needed. The utilization would be 107.8 percent (25,875/24,000 $\times$ 100). What this means is that on average 7.8 percent of the customers must stand. Of course, this average value significantly understates the severe capacity problem that occurs during the peak times of the day. ●

Consider in the preceding example how useful this type of analysis is to the Paris transit authority. Data can be collected for each day of the week and the analysis performed. Interesting questions concerning the design of the route or the capacity of the buses can be evaluated. Consider, for example, what would happen if the route were split into two parts. What if larger buses that could carry 120 passengers were put into service? The analysis can be extended to include the cost of providing the service by considering the wages paid the operators, the cost to maintain and operate the vehicles, and depreciation of the buses. As seen from the above example, designing a transit system involves a trade-off between the convenience of the service, or how frequently buses arrive at each stop, and the capacity utilization of the buses.

PROCESS THROUGHPUT TIME REDUCTION

⬯⬯◯   Critical processes are subject to the well-known rule that time is money. For example, the longer a customer waits, the more likely it is that the customer will switch to a different vendor. The longer material is kept in inventory, the higher the investment cost. Unfortunately, critical processes often depend on specific limited resources, resulting in bottlenecks. Throughput time can sometimes be reduced without purchasing additional equipment. The following are some suggestions for reducing the throughput time of a process that do not require the purchase of new equipment. Often a combination of ideas is appropriate.[4]

1. **Perform activities in parallel.**   Most of the steps in an operations process are performed in sequence. A serial approach results in the throughput time for the entire process being the sum of the individual steps plus transport and waiting time between steps. Using a parallel approach can reduce throughput time by as much as 80 percent and produces a better result.

   A classic example is product development, where the current trend is toward concurrent engineering. Instead of forming a concept, making drawings, creating a bill of materials, and mapping processes, all activities are performed in parallel by integrated teams. Development time is reduced dramatically, and the needs of all those involved are addressed during the development process.

2. **Change the sequence of activities.**   Documents and products are often transported back and forth between machines, departments, buildings, and so forth. For instance, a document might be transferred between two offices a number of times for inspection and signing. If the sequence of some of these activities can be altered, it may be possible to perform much of the document's processing when it comes to a building the first time.

3. **Reduce interruptions.**   Many processes are performed with relatively large time intervals between each activity. For example, purchase orders may be issued only every other day. Individuals preparing reports that result in purchase orders should be aware of deadlines to avoid missing them, because improved timing in these processes can save many days of throughput time.

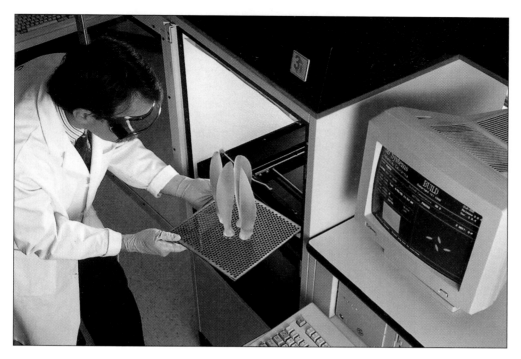

To illustrate these ideas, consider an electronics manufacturer that has been receiving customer complaints about a long order lead time of 29 days. As assessment of the order-processing system revealed 12 instances where managers had to approve employees' work. It was determined that the first 10 approvals were not needed. This saved an average of seven to eight days in the order processing.

Many subsystems—each performing the same or similar tasks—had interfered with the process. The logical step was to eliminate redundancy, and a detailed flowchart of the process was created. At close inspection, 16 steps proved very similar to one another. Changing the sequence of activities and creating one companywide order document removed 13 of these steps.

Over four months, the order system was totally redesigned to allow information to be entered once and become available to the entire organization. Due to this adjustment, activities could be handled in a parallel manner. After a value-added analysis (focused on eliminating the non–value-adding activities), the manufacturer was able to reduce the customer order lead time from 29 days to 9 days, save cost and employee time per order, and increase customer satisfaction.

CONCLUSION

Process analysis is a basic skill needed to understand how a business operates. Great insight is obtained by drawing a simple flowchart showing the flow of materials or information through an enterprise. The diagram should include all the operating elements and show how they fit together. Be sure to indicate where material is stored or where orders are queued. Often 90 percent or more of the time that is required to serve a customer is spent just waiting. Hence, merely eliminating the waiting time can dramatically improve the performance of the process.

Remember this fundamental concept when analyzing a process: What goes into the process must come out of the process. A process taken as a whole is like the funnel shown in Exhibit 5.5. The outlet of the funnel restricts the amount that can flow through. In a real business process, certain resources limit output. If liquid is poured into the funnel at a rate greater than it can exit, the level in the funnel will continue to grow. As the level of liquid in the exhibit 5.5   What Goes into a Process Must Come Out of the Process. Input Rate Must Be Less than or Equal to the Output Rate; otherwise, the System Will Overflow.

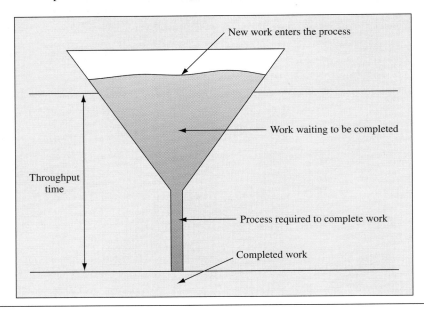

funnel grows, the time that it takes the liquid to flow through the funnel increases. If too much liquid is poured into the funnel, it just spills over the top and never flows through.

The same is true of a real process. If too many jobs are pumped into the process, the time that it takes to complete a job will increase because the waiting time will increase. At some point, customers will go somewhere else and the business will be lost. When a process is operating at capacity, the only way to take on more work without increasing the waiting time is to add more capacity. This requires finding what activity is limiting the output of the process and increasing the capacity of that activity. In essence, the tube leading out of the funnel needs to be made larger.

KEY TERMS

Process Any set of activities performed by an organization that takes inputs and transforms them into outputs ideally of greater value to the organization than the original inputs.

Cycle time The average time between completions of successive units in a process (this is the definition used in this book). The term is sometimes used to mean the elapsed time between starting and completing a job.

Utilization The ratio of the time that a resource is actually activated relative to the time that it is available for use.

Buffering A storage area between stages where the output of a stage is placed prior to being used in a downstream stage. Buffering allows the stages to operate independently.

Blocking The activities in the stage must stop because there is no place to deposit the item just completed.

Starving The activities in a stage must stop because there is no work.

Bottleneck A resource that limits the capacity or maximum output of the process.

Make-to-order A process that is activated only in response to an actual order.

Make-to-stock A process that produces standard products that are stored in finished goods inventory. The product is delivered quickly to the customer from the finished goods inventory.

Hybrid Combines the features of both make-to-order and make-to-stock. Typically, a generic product is made and stocked at some point in the process. These generic units are customized in a final process to meet actual orders.

Pacing Movement of items through a process is coordinated through a timing mechanism. Most processes are not paced, but assembly lines usually are paced.

Productivity The ratio of output to input. Taking the dollar value of the output and dividing by the dollar value of the inputs usually measures total factor productivity. Alternatively, *partial factor productivity* is measured based on an individual input and often is not calculated using dollar values (an example would be units/person).

Efficiency A ratio of the actual output of a process relative to some standard.

Run time The time required to produce a batch of parts.

Setup time The time required to prepare a machine to make a particular item.

Operation time The sum of the setup time and run time for a batch of parts that are run on a machine.

Throughput time The average time that it takes a unit to move through an entire process. Usually the term *lead time* is used to refer

to the total time that it takes a customer to receive an order (includes time to process the order, throughput time, and delivery time).

Throughput rate The output rate that the process is expected to produce over a period of time.

Process velocity or **throughput ratio** The ratio of the total throughput time to the value-added time.

Value-added time The time in which useful work is actually being done on the unit.

Little's Law States a mathematical relationship between throughput rate, throughput time, and the amount of work-in-process inventory. Throughput time is equal to work-in-process divided by the throughput rate.

SOLVED PROBLEM

Daffy Dave's Sub Shop makes custom submarine sandwiches to order. They are analyzing the processes at their shop. The general flow of the process is shown below. There is a separate person working at each of the steps in the process.

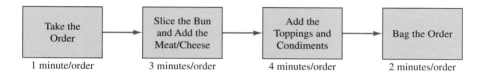

Take the Order	Slice the Bun and Add the Meat/Cheese	Add the Toppings and Condiments	Bag the Order
1 minute/order	3 minutes/order	4 minutes/order	2 minutes/order

Daffy Dave wants to figure out the following for a typical 8-hour work day.
a. What is the current maximum output of the process?
b. If we add another person where would we add him or her and what is the benefit?
c. Is there a benefit if we can shift 1 minute from Bun and Meat to Order Taking? Assume we do not make the change in part *b* above.
d. Is there a benefit if we shift 1 minute of work from Condiments to Bagging? Assume we do not make the changes in parts *b* and *c* above.

Solution

a. Maximum output is 120 subs per day.

OPERATION	OUTPUT
Take Orders	(60 min. per hour/1 min. per order) * 8 hours = 480 subs per day
Bun and Meat	(60 min. per hour/3 min. per order) * 8 hours = 160 subs per day
Toppings/Condiments	**(60 min. per hour/4 min. per order) * 8 hours = 120 subs per day**
Bag the Order	(60 min. per hour/2 min. per order) * 8 hours = 240 subs per day

Output per day is determined by the slowest station; therefore we can only produce 120 per day because that is the limit of the Toppings/Condiments station.

b. Dave should add the person to the slowest station (Condiments/Toppings) since it is the bottleneck.

OPERATION	OUTPUT
Take Orders	480 subs per day
Bun and Meat	**160 subs per day**
Toppings/Condiments	120 * 2 = 240 subs per day
Bag the Order	240 subs per day

The impact is not a very big one. Even though the Toppings/Condiments station now can do 240 subs per day, the Bun and Meat station can only do 160 so that is the maximum output.

c. Order Taking station will go from 1 minute to 2 minutes and Bun and Meat goes from 3 minutes to 2 minutes.

Operation	Output
Take Orders	(60 min. per hour/2 min. per order) * 8 hours = 240 subs per day
Bun and Meat	(60 min. per hour/2 min. per order) * 8 hours = 240 subs per day
Toppings/Condiments	**(60 min. per hour/4 min. per order) * 8 hours = 120 subs per day**
Bag the Order	(60 min. per hour/2 min. per order) * 8 hours = 240 subs per day

There is no benefit to this change. Dave can still only make 120 subs per day since we can only produce 120 per day because that is the limit of the Toppings/Condiments station.

d. Toppings/Condiments station will go from 4 minutes to 3 minutes and Bagging goes from 2 minutes to 3 minutes.

Operation	Output
Take Orders	(60 min. per hour/1 min. per order) * 8 hours = 480 subs per day
Bun and Meat	**(60 min. per hour/3 min. per order) * 8 hours = 160 subs per day**
Toppings/Condiments	**(60 min. per hour/3 min. per order) * 8 hours = 160 subs per day**
Bag the Order	**(60 min. per hour/3 min. per order) * 8 hours = 160 subs per day**

There is a benefit to this change. Dave can now make 160 subs per day. This will provide the same benefit as hiring another worker. However, if Dave wants to increase output further he will have to hire some additional staff.

Review and Discussion Questions

1   Compare McDonald's old and new processes for making hamburgers. How valid is McDonald's claim that the new process will produce fresher hamburgers for the customer? Comparing McDonald's new process to the processes used by Burger King and Wendy's, which process would appear to produce the freshest hamburgers?

2   State in your own words what Little's Law means. Describe an example that you have observed where Little's Law applies.

3   Explain how having more work-in-process inventory can improve the efficiency of a process. How can this be bad?

4   Recently some operations management experts have begun insisting that simply minimizing process velocity, which actually means minimizing the time that it takes to process something through the system, is the single most important measure for improving a process. Can you think of a situation in which this might not be true?

Problems [5]

1   An enterprising student has set up an internship clearinghouse for business students. Each student that uses the service fills out a form and lists up to 10 companies that he or she would like to have contacted. The clearinghouse has a choice of two methods to use for processing the forms. The traditional method requires about 20 minutes to review the form and arrange the information in the proper order for processing. Once this setup is done, it takes only two minutes per company requested to complete the processing. The other alternative uses an optical scan/retrieve system, which takes only a minute to prepare but requires five minutes per company for completing the processing. If it costs about the same amount per minute for processing with either of the two methods, when should each be used?

2 Rockness Recycling refurbishes rundown business students. The process uses a moving belt, which carries each student through the five steps of the process in sequence. The five steps are as follows:

STEP	DESCRIPTION	TIME REQUIRED PER STUDENT
1	Unpack and place on belt	1.0 minute
2	Strip off bad habits	1.5 minutes
3	Scrub and clean mind	0.8 minute
4	Insert modern methods	1.0 minute
5	Polish and pack	1.2 minutes

One faculty member is assigned to each of these steps. Faculty members work a 40-hour week and rotate jobs each week. Mr. Rockness has been working on a contract from General Eclectic, which requires delivery of 2,000 refurbished students per week. A representative of the human resources department has just called complaining that the company hasn't been receiving the agreed-upon number of students. A check of finished goods inventory by Mr. Rockness reveals that there is no stock left. What is going on?

3 The bathtub theory of operations management is being promoted as the next breakthrough for global competitiveness. The factory is a bathtub with 50 gallons of capacity. The drain is the outlet to the market and can output three gallons per hour when wide open. The faucet is the raw material input and can let material in at a rate of four gallons per hour. Now, to test your comprehension of the intricacies of operations (assume the bathtub is empty to begin with):

a. Draw a diagram of the factory and determine the maximum rate at which the market can be served if all valves are set to maximum. What happens to the system over time?

b. Suppose that instead of a faucet, a five-gallon container is used for filling the bathtub (assume a full container is next to the tub to begin with); it takes two hours to refill the container and return it to the bathtub. What happens to the system over time?

4 A local market research firm has just won a contract for several thousand small projects involving data gathering and statistical analysis. In the past the firm has assigned each project to a single member of its highly trained professional staff. This person would both gather and analyze the data. Using this approach an experienced person can complete an average of 10 such projects in an eight-hour day.

The firm's management is thinking of assigning two people to each project in order to allow them to specialize and become more efficient. The process would require the data gatherer to fill out a matrix on the computer, check it, and transmit it to the statistical analysis program for the analyst to complete. Data can be gathered on one project while the analysis is being completed on another, but the analysis must be complete before the statistical analysis program can accept the new data. After some practice, the new process can be completed with a standard time of 20 minutes for the data gathering and 30 minutes for the analysis.

a. What is the production (output per hour) for each alternative? What is the productivity (output per labor hour)?

b. How long would it take to complete 1,000 projects with each alternative? What would be the labor content (total number of labor hours) for 1,000 projects for each alternative?

5 A processor makes two components, A and B, which are then packaged together as the final product (each product sold contains one A and one B). The processor can do only one component at a time: either it can make As or it can make Bs. There is a setup time when switching from A to B.

Current plans are to make 100 units of component A, then 100 units of component B, then 100 units of component A, then 100 units of component B, and so forth, where the setup and run times for each component are given below.

COMPONENT	SETUP/CHANGEOVER TIME	RUN TIME/UNIT
A	5 minutes	0.2 minute
B	10 minutes	0.1 minute

Assume the packaging of the two components is totally automated and takes only two seconds per unit of the final product. This packaging time is small enough that you can ignore it. What is the average hourly output, in terms of the number of units of packaged product (which includes one component A and one component B)?

6. The following represents a process used to assemble a chair with an upholstered seat. Stations A, B, and C make the seat; stations J, K, and L assemble the chair frame; station X is where the two subassemblies are brought together; and some final tasks are completed in stations Y and Z. One worker is assigned to each of the stations. Generally there is no inventory kept anywhere in the system, although there is room for one unit between each of the stations that might be used for a brief amount of time.

Given the following amount of work in seconds required at each station:

A	38	J	32	X	22
B	34	K	30	Y	18
C	35	L	34	Z	20

a. What is the possible daily output of this "process" if 8 hours of processing time is available each day?
b. Given your output rate in part *a*, what is the efficiency of the process?
c. What is the throughput time of the process?

7. Wally's Widget Warehouse takes orders from 7 A.M. to 7 P.M. The manager wants to analyze the process and has provided the process flow diagram shown below. There are three steps required to ship a customer order. The first step is to take the order from a customer. The second step is to pick the order for the customer and then they have to pack the order ready for shipping. Wally promises that every order placed today gets shipped tomorrow. That means that the picking and packing operation must finish all orders before they go home.

Wally wants to figure out the following.
a. What is the current maximum output of the process?
b. How long will the picking and packing operations have to work if we have a day with the maximum orders?
c. What is the maximum number of orders waiting to be picked?
d. What is the maximum number of orders waiting to be packed?
e. If we double the packing capacity (from 60 to 120 orders per hour), what impact does this have on your answers in parts *b*, *c*, and *d*?

8. The National State Bank is trying to make sure that they have enough tellers to handle the Friday afternoon rush of workers wanting to cash their paychecks. They are only concerned with the last hour of the day from 4:00 to 5:00 P.M. It takes 5 minutes per customer to be processed by the tellers. The average customer arrivals are shown in the table below.

TIME	CUSTOMERS ARRIVING
4:00–4:05	2
4:05–4:10	5
4:10–4:15	6
4:15–4:20	8
4:20–4:25	10 2
4:25–4:30	12 4
4:30–4:35	16 8
4:35–4:40	12 4
4:40–4:45	10 2 – 20
4:45–4:50	6 – 2
4:50–4:55	4 – 4
4:55–5:00	2 – 6
5:00–5:05	0 – 8
Total	93

The bank currently has 8 teller stations and all are staffed during the Friday afternoon rush hour.
a. What is the current maximum output at the bank during rush hour?
b. Can the bank process all the customers by 5:00 P.M.?
c. What is the maximum waiting time for customers and what time period does it occur in?

Excel:
Bottleneck
Simulation

ADVANCED PROBLEM

9 Remember Mr. Rockness in Problem 2? He now retrains college professors. It is a much more challenging task but still involves five steps. He has worked hard to balance the line; however, there is a lot of variability. Each stage in the process now handles between one and six faculty members per hour depending on how bad the case is. If there is some inventory available for every position (do not worry about the start-up), what is the expected output per hour? (Assume that each stage is independent and that it is equally likely that one, two, three, four, five, or six faculty members get processed each hour at each stage.)[6]

CASE: ANALYZING CASINO MONEY-HANDLING PROCESSES

Retrieving money from a slot machine is referred to as the *drop process.* The drop process begins with a security officer and the slot drop team leader obtaining the slot cabinet keys from the casino cashier's cage. Getting the keys takes about 15 minutes. The slot drop team consists of employees from the hard count coin room, security, and accounting. The slot drop leader, under the observation of a security officer and a person from accounting, actually removes the drop bucket from the slot machine cabinet. When the drop bucket is pulled from the slot cabinet, a tag with the proper slot machine number is placed on top of the coins to identify where that bucket came from when the weigh process begins. Retrieving the drop bucket takes about 10 minutes per slot machine. Once a cart is filled with buckets from 20 different slot machines, the drop team leader and security and accounting people deliver the buckets to the hard count room. The buckets are securely locked in the hard count room to await the start of the hard count process. Delivering and securing the buckets takes about 30 minutes per cart.

The hard count process is performed at a designated time known to gaming regulatory authorities. The hard count team first tests the weigh scale, which takes 10 minutes. The scale determines the dollar value, by denomination, for set weights of 10 and 25 pounds. These results are compared to calibration results, calculated when the scale was last serviced, to determine if a significant variance exists. If one does exist, the hard count supervisor must contact the contractor responsible for maintaining the scale and the controller's office. If no significant variance is found, the weigh process can continue.

Following the scale check, each drop bucket is emptied into the weigh scale holding hopper. Using information from the identification tag, the specific slot machine number from which the bucket originated is entered into the weigh scale computer. The weigh scale computer is programmed to convert the weight of coins, by denomination, into specific dollar values, which are recorded in the weigh journal along with the slot machine number. This weighing and recording process takes seven minutes per bucket. Once the scale has weighed the contents of the drop bucket, the coins automatically drop onto a conveyor belt, which transports them to wrapping machines. As the coins are wrapped, the rolls of coins drop onto another conveyor belt, which takes them to a canning station. Twenty-five silver dollars are wrapped in each roll at a rate of 10 rolls per minute.

At the canning station, the coin rolls are placed in metal or plastic cans that hold specific dollar amounts based on coin denomination. The cans are stacked to facilitate counting the wrapped coins.

Silver dollar cans hold $1,000, or 40 rolls, and take five minutes to fill and stack. When the weigh process is completed, the weigh scale computer runs a summary report totaling the weight by denomination. These totals are recorded on the weigh/wrap verification report, which takes five minutes to produce.

When the wrap portion of the count is completed and all of the rolled coins have been canned and stacked, they are manually counted by denomination. These totals are also recorded on the weigh/wrap verification report. The variance in both dollar amounts and percentages, for each denomination, is calculated. Variances that exceed plus or minus 2 percent or are $1,000 or greater (whichever is less) must be investigated by the hard count supervisor, who writes an explanatory report. If no significant variances exist, all members of the hard count team sign the weigh/wrap verification report. To complete the hard count process, the casino cashier's cage is then notified that the slot drop is ready to be transferred into cage accountability. Manually counting and verifying the counts take on average two minutes per can.

In a process separate from the hard count, a cage cashier performs an independent count and verification, by denomination, of the wrap. If everything balances, the main bank cashier signs the weigh/wrap verification report, accepting the slot drop into cage accountability. It is at this point that the actual slot gross gaming revenue is recognized.

QUESTIONS

1   Draw a diagram of the drop process. How long should it take to empty 300 silver dollar slot machines?
2   Draw a diagram of the hard count process. How long should this process take to complete for 300 silver dollar slot machines? Assume that each slot machine has an average of 750 silver dollars when it is emptied.
3   The casino is considering the purchase of a second coin-wrapping machine. What impact would this have on the hard count process? Is this the most desirable machine to purchase?

CASE: KRISTEN'S COOKIE COMPANY (A)

You and your roommate are preparing to start Kristen's Cookie Company in your on-campus apartment. The company will provide fresh cookies to starving students late at night. You need to evaluate the preliminary design for the company's production process to figure out many variables, including what prices to charge, whether you will be able to make a profit, and how many orders to accept.

BUSINESS CONCEPT

Your idea is to bake fresh cookies to order, using any combination of ingredients that the buyer wants. The cookies will be ready for pickup at your apartment within an hour.

Several factors will set you apart from competing products such as store-bought cookies. First, your cookies will be completely fresh. You will not bake any cookies before receiving the order; therefore, the buyer will be getting cookies that are literally hot out of the oven.

Second, like Steve's Ice Cream,[7] you will have a variety of ingredients available to add to the basic dough, including chocolate chips, M&M's, chopped Heath bars, coconut, walnuts, and raisins. Buyers will telephone in their orders and specify which of these ingredients they want in their cookies. You guarantee completely fresh cookies. In short, you will have the freshest, most exotic cookies anywhere, available right on campus.

THE PRODUCTION PROCESS

Baking cookies is simple: mix all the ingredients in a food processor; spoon out the cookie dough onto a tray; put the cookies into the oven; bake them; take the tray of cookies out of the oven; let the cookies cool; and, finally, take the cookies off the tray and carefully pack them in a box. You and your roommate already own all the necessary capital equipment: one food processor, cookie trays, and spoons. Your apartment has a small oven that will hold one tray at a time. Your landlord pays for all the electricity. The variable costs, therefore, are merely the cost of the ingredients (estimated to be $.60/dozen), the cost of the box in which the cookies are packed

($.10 per box; each box holds a dozen cookies), and your time (what value do you place on your time?).

A detailed examination of the production process, which specifies how long each of the steps will take, follows. The first step is to take an order, which your roommate has figured out how to do quickly and with 100 percent accuracy. (Actually, you and your roommate devised a method using the campus electronic mail system to accept orders and to inform customers when their orders will be ready for pickup. Because this runs automatically on your personal computer, it does not take any of your time.) Therefore, this step will be ignored in further analysis.

You and your roommate have timed the necessary physical operations. The first physical production step is to wash out the mixing bowl from the previous batch, add all of the ingredients, and mix them in your food processor. The mixing bowls hold ingredients for up to 3 dozen cookies. You then dish up the cookies, one dozen at a time, onto a cookie tray. These activities take six minutes for the washing and mixing steps, regardless of how many cookies are being made in the batch. That is, to mix enough dough and ingredients for two dozen cookies takes the same six minutes as one dozen cookies. However, dishing up the cookies onto the tray takes two minutes per tray.

The next step, performed by your roommate, is to put the cookies in the oven and set the thermostat and timer, which takes about one minute. The cookies bake for the next nine minutes. So total baking time is 10 minutes, during the first minute of which your roommate is busy setting the oven. Because the oven holds only one tray, a second dozen takes an additional 10 minutes to bake.

Your roommate also performs the last steps of the process by first removing the cookies from the oven and putting them aside to cool for 5 minutes, then carefully packing them in a box and accepting payment. Removing the cookies from the oven takes only a negligible amount of time, but it must be done promptly. It takes two minutes to pack each dozen and about one minute to accept payment for the order.

That is the process for producing cookies by the dozen in Kristen's Cookie Company. As experienced bakers know, a few simplifications were made in the actual cookie production process. For example, the first batch of cookies for the night requires pre-heating the oven. However, such complexities will be put aside for now. Begin your analysis by developing a process flow diagram of the cookie-making process.

KEY QUESTIONS TO ANSWER BEFORE YOU LAUNCH THE BUSINESS
To launch the business, you need to set prices and rules for accepting orders. Some issues will be resolved only after you get started and try out different ways of producing the cookies. Before you start, however, you at least want a preliminary plan, with as much as possible specified, so that you can do a careful calculation of how much time you will have to devote to this business each night, and how much money you can expect to make. For example, when you conduct a market survey to determine the likely demand, you will want to specify exactly what your order policies will be. Therefore, answering the following operational questions should help you:

1. How long will it take you to fill a rush order?
2. How many orders can you fill in a night, assuming you are open four hours each night?
3. How much of your own and your roommate's valuable time will it take to fill each order?
4. Because your baking trays can hold exactly one dozen cookies, you will produce and sell cookies by the dozen. Should you give any discount for people who order two dozen cookies, three dozen cookies, or more? If so, how much? Will it take you any longer to fill a two-dozen cookie order than a one-dozen cookie order?
5. How many food processors and baking trays will you need?

6. Are there any changes you can make in your production plans that will allow you to make better cookies or more cookies in less time or at lower cost? For example, is there a bottleneck operation in your production process that you can expand cheaply? What is the effect of adding another oven? How much would you be willing to pay to rent an additional oven?

PROBLEMS FOR FURTHER THOUGHT

1. What happens if you are trying to do this by yourself without a roommate?
2. Should you offer special rates for rush orders? Suppose you have just put a tray of cookies into the oven and someone calls up with a "crash priority" order for a dozen cookies of a different flavor. Can you fill the priority order while still fulfilling the order for the cookies that are already in the oven? If not, how much of a premium should you charge for filling the rush order?
3. When should you promise delivery? How can you look quickly at your order board (list of pending orders) and tell a caller when his or her order will be ready? How much of a safety margin for timing should you allow?
4. What other factors should you consider at this stage of planning your business?
5. Your product must be made to order because each order is potentially unique. If you decide to sell standard cookies instead, how should you change the production system? The order-taking process?

SELECTED BIBLIOGRAPHY

Anupindai, R.; S. Chopra; S. D. Deshmukh; J. A. van Mieghem; and E. Zemel. *Managing Business Process Flows.* Upper Saddle River, NJ: Prentice Hall, 1999.

Gray, A. E., and J. Leonard. "Process Fundamentals." Harvard Business School 9-696-023.

Hopp, J. W., and M. L. Spearman. *Factory Physics: Foundations of Manufacturing Management.* New York: Irwin/McGraw-Hill, 2000.

Smith, Howard, and Peter Fingar. *Business Process Management (BPM): The Third Wave.* Tampa, FL: Meghan-Kiffer Press, 2003.

Suri, R. *Quick Response Manufacturing: A Companywide Approach to Reducing Lead Times.* Portland, OR: Productivity Press, 1998.

FOOTNOTES

1. Often the term *cycle time* is used to mean *throughput time.* It is important to carefully determine how the term is being used in the context of the process being studied.
2. J. D. C. Little, "A Proof for the Queuing Formula: $L = \lambda W$," *Operations Research* 9, no. 3 (1961), pp. 383–87. Special thanks to J. F. Muth, Indiana University.
3. This example is similar to one given by A. E. Gray in "Capacity Analysis: Sample Problems," Harvard Business School 9-696-058.
4. B. Andersen, "Process Cycle Time Reduction," *Quality Progress,* July 1999, p. 120. For some additional guidelines for improving process, also see Chapter 17.
5. The authors are indebted to D. Clay Whybark of the University of North Carolina for contributing Problems 1–4 and Problem 9.
6. The idea for this problem came from an exercise developed by Dr. Eli Goldratt titled "The Great Manufacturing Crapshoot."
7. Steve's Ice Cream was started in the Boston area by a young entrepreneur to provide make-to-order ice cream, using mix-ins.

technical note five

JOB DESIGN AND WORK MEASUREMENT

The operations manager's job, by definition, deals with managing the personnel that create a firm's products and services. To say that this is a challenging job in today's complex environment is an understatement. The diversity of the workforce's cultural and educational background, coupled with frequent organization restructuring, calls for a much higher level of people management skills than has been required in even the recent past.

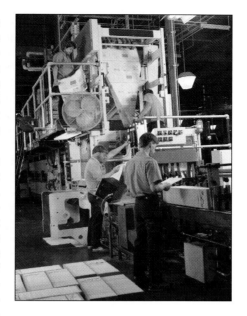

The objective in managing personnel is to obtain the highest productivity possible without sacrificing quality, service, or responsiveness. The operations manager uses job design techniques to structure the work so that it will meet both the physical and psychological needs of the human worker. Work measurement methods are used to determine the most efficient means of performing a given task, as well as to set reasonable standards for performing it. People are motivated by many things, only one of which is financial reward. Operations managers can structure such rewards not only to motivate consistently high performance but also to reinforce the most important aspects of the job.

JOB DESIGN DECISIONS

Job design may be defined as the function of specifying the work activities of an individual or group in an organizational setting. Its objective is to develop job structures that meet the requirements of the organization and its technology and that satisfy the jobholder's personal and individual requirements. Exhibit TN5.1 summarizes the decisions involved. These decisions are affected by the following trends:

Job design

1. **Quality control as part of the worker's job.** Now often referred to as "quality at the source" (see Chapter 8), quality control is linked with the concept of empowerment.

Job Design Decisions

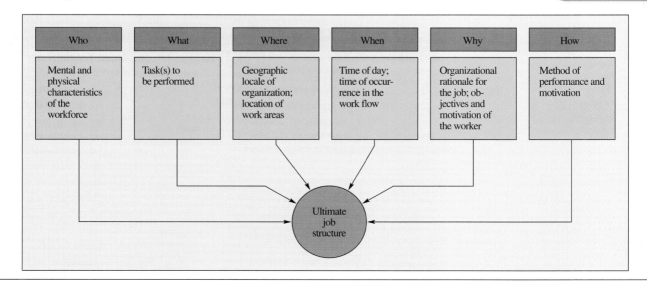

Who	What	Where	When	Why	How
Mental and physical characteristics of the workforce	Task(s) to be performed	Geographic locale of organization; location of work areas	Time of day; time of occurrence in the work flow	Organizational rationale for the job; objectives and motivation of the worker	Method of performance and motivation

Ultimate job structure

Empowerment, in turn, refers to workers being given authority to stop a production line if there is a quality problem, or to give a customer an on-the-spot refund if service was not satisfactory.

2. **Cross-training of workers to perform multiskilled jobs.**   As companies downsize, the remaining workforce is expected to do more and different tasks.

3. **Employee involvement and team approaches to designing and organizing work.** This is a central feature in total quality management (TQM) and continuous improvement efforts. In fact, it is safe to say that virtually all TQM programs are team based.

4. **"Informating" of ordinary workers through e-mail and the Internet, thereby expanding the nature of their work and their ability to do it.**   In this context, informating is more than just automating work—it is revising work's fundamental structure. Northeast Utilities' computer system, for example, can pinpoint a problem in a service area before the customer service representative answers the phone. The rep uses the computer to troubleshoot serious problems, to weigh probabilities that other customers in the area have been affected, and to dispatch repair crews before other calls are even received.

5. **Extensive use of temporary workers.**   Manpower, a company specializing in providing temporary employees, has over 1.9 million temporary employees worldwide on its payroll.

6. **Creation of "alternative workplaces" such as shared offices, telecommuting, and virtual offices to supplement or replace traditional office settings.**   These are used to increase productivity, reduce travel and real estate costs, and aid in recruiting and retaining employees. IBM, AT&T, and American Express are major proponents of the approach.[1]

7. **Automation of heavy manual work.**   Examples abound in both services (one-person trash pickup trucks) and manufacturing (robot spray painting on auto lines). These changes are driven by safety regulations as well as economics and personnel reasons.

8. **Most important of all, organizational commitment to providing meaningful and rewarding jobs for all employees.**   Companies featured on *Fortune* magazine's "100 Best Companies to Work For" use creative means to keep employees satisfied, and offer generous severance and compassion when cuts must be made (see www.fortune.com for the current list of companies).

BEHAVIORAL CONSIDERATIONS IN JOB DESIGN

DEGREE OF LABOR SPECIALIZATION

Specialization of labor

Specialization of labor is the two-edged sword of job design. On one hand, specialization has made possible high-speed, low-cost production, and from a materialistic standpoint, it has greatly enhanced our standard of living. On the other hand, extreme specialization (as we see in mass-production industries) often has serious adverse effects on workers, which in turn are passed on to management. In essence, the problem is to determine how much specialization is enough. At what point do the disadvantages outweigh the advantages? (See Exhibit TN5.2.)

Recent research suggests that the disadvantages dominate the advantages much more commonly than was thought in the past. However, simply stating that, for purely humanitarian reasons, specialization should be avoided is risky. The reason, of course, is that people differ in what they want from their work and what they are willing to put into it. Some workers prefer not to make decisions about their work, some like to daydream on the job, and others are simply not capable of performing more complex work. To improve the quality of jobs, leading organizations try different approaches to job design. Two popular contemporary approaches are job enrichment and sociotechnical systems.

Advantages and Disadvantages of Specialization of Labor

ADVANTAGES OF SPECIALIZATION	
TO MANAGEMENT	TO LABOR
1. Rapid training of the workforce	1. Little or no education required to obtain work
2. Ease in recruiting new workers	2. Ease in learning job
3. High output due to simple, repetitive work	
4. Low wages due to ease of substitutability of labor	
5. Close control over work flow and workloads	

DISADVANTAGES OF SPECIALIZATION	
TO MANAGEMENT	TO LABOR
1. Difficulty in controlling quality because no one has responsibility for entire product	1. Boredom stemming from repetitive nature of work
2. Worker dissatisfaction leading to hidden costs arising from turnover, absenteeism, tardiness, grievances, and intentional disruption of production process	2. Little gratification from work itself because of small contribution to each item
3. Reduced likelihood of improving the process because of workers' limited perspective	3. Little or no control over the work pace, leading to frustration and fatigue (in assembly-line situations)
4. Limited flexibility to change the production process to produce new or improved products	4. Little opportunity to progress to a better job because significant learning is rarely possible on fractionated work

JOB ENRICHMENT

Job enlargement generally entails adjusting a specialized job to make it more interesting to the job holder. A job is said to be enlarged *horizontally* if the worker performs a greater number or variety of tasks, and it is said to be enlarged *vertically* if the worker is involved in planning, organizing, and inspecting his or her own work. Horizontal job enlargement is intended to counteract oversimplification and to permit the worker to perform a "whole unit of work." Vertical enlargement (traditionally termed *job enrichment*) attempts to broaden workers' influence in the transformation process by giving them certain managerial powers over their own activities. Today, common practice is to apply both horizontal and vertical enlargement to a given job and refer to the total approach as **job enrichment.**

Job enrichment

The organizational benefits of job enrichment occur in both quality and productivity. Quality in particular improves dramatically because when individuals are responsible for their work output, they take ownership of it and simply do a better job. Also, because they have a broader understanding of the work process, they are more likely to catch errors and make corrections than if the job is narrowly focused. Productivity improvements also occur from job enrichment, but they are not as predictable or as large as the improvements in quality. The reason is that enriched work invariably contains a mix of tasks that (for manual labor) causes interruptions in rhythm and different motions when switching from one task to the next. Such is not the case for specialized jobs.[2]

SOCIOTECHNICAL SYSTEMS

Consistent with the job enrichment philosophy but focusing more on the interaction between technology and the work group is the **sociotechnical systems** approach. This approach attempts to develop jobs that adjust the needs of the production process technology to the needs of the worker and work group. The term was developed from studies of weaving mills in India and of coal mines in England in the early 1950s. These studies revealed that work groups could effectively handle many production problems better than management if they were permitted to make their own decisions on scheduling, work allocation among members, bonus sharing, and so forth. This was particularly true when variations in the production process required quick reactions by the group or when one shift's work overlapped with other shifts' work.

Sociotechnical systems

Since those pioneering studies, the sociotechnical approach has been applied in many countries—often under the heading of "autonomous work groups," "Japanese-style work groups," or employee involvement (EI) teams. Most major American manufacturing companies use work teams as the basic building block in so-called high employee involvement plants. They are now becoming common in service organizations as well. The benefits of teams are similar to those of individual job enrichment: They provide higher quality and greater productivity (they often set higher production goals than general management), do their own support work and equipment maintenance, and have increased chances to make meaningful improvements.[3]

One major conclusion from these applications is that the individual or work group requires a logically integrated pattern of work activities that incorporates the following job design principles:

1. **Task variety.**   An attempt must be made to provide an optimal variety of tasks within each job. Too much variety can be inefficient for training and frustrating for the employee. Too little can lead to boredom and fatigue. The optimal level is one that allows the employee to rest from a high level of attention or effort while working on another task or, conversely, to stretch after periods of routine activity.
2. **Skill variety.**   Research suggests that employees derive satisfaction from using a number of skill levels.
3. **Feedback.**   There should be some means for informing employees quickly when they have achieved their targets. Fast feedback aids the learning process. Ideally, employees should have some responsibility for setting their own standards of quantity and quality.
4. **Task identity.**   Sets of tasks should be separated from other sets of tasks by some clear boundary. Whenever possible, a group or individual employee should have responsibility for a set of tasks that is clearly defined, visible, and meaningful. In this way, work is seen as important by the group or individual undertaking it, and others understand and respect its significance.
5. **Task autonomy.**   Employees should be able to exercise some control over their work. Areas of discretion and decision making should be available to them.

PHYSICAL CONSIDERATIONS IN JOB DESIGN

Beyond the behavioral components of job design, another aspect warrants consideration: the physical side. Indeed, while motivation and work group structure strongly influence job performance, they may be of secondary importance if the job is too demanding

THE ERGONOMICS PROGRAM AT BOEING HAS PROFESSIONALS AVAILABLE TO MAKE "HOUSE CALLS" AT BOEING SITES. THEY ANALYZE RISKS IN THE SHOP OR OFFICE AND SUGGEST NEW PROCESSES, TOOLS OR PROTECTIVE EQUIPMENT. THIS WORKER APPLYING SEALANT TO ENGINE MOUNT SURFACES IN WICHITA REQUIRED THE MECHANIC, IN THE PAST, TO REACH OVER HER HEAD FROM AN AWKWARD SEATED POSITION. A HEIGHT-ADJUSTABLE BELT ROTATOR NOW HOLDS AND POSITIONS THE STRUT.

Calorie Requirements for Various Activities

TYPE OF ACTIVITY	TYPICAL ENERGY COST IN CALORIES PER MINUTE*	REQUIRED MINUTES OF REST FOR EACH MINUTE OF WORK
Sitting at rest	1.7	—
Writing	2.0	—
Typing on a computer	2.0	—
Medium assembly work	2.9	—
Shoe repair	3.0	—
Machining	3.3	—
Ironing	4.4	—
Heavy assembly work	5.1	—
Chopping wood	7.5	1
Digging	8.9	2
Tending furnace	12.0	3
Walking upstairs	12.0	3

*Five calories per minute is generally considered the maximum sustainable level throughout the workday.

from a physical (or "human factors") standpoint. One approach to incorporating the physical costs of moderate to heavy work in job design is **work physiology.** Pioneered by Eastman Kodak in the 1960s, work physiology sets work–rest cycles according to the energy expended in various parts of the job. For example, if a job entails caloric expenditure above five calories per minute (the rough baseline for sustainable work), the required rest period must equal or exceed the time spent working. Obviously, the harder the work, the more frequent and longer the rest periods. (Exhibit TN5.3 shows caloric requirements for various activities.)

Work physiology

Ergonomics is the term used to describe the study of the physical arrangement of the work space together with the tools used to perform a task. In applying ergonomics, we strive to fit the work to the body rather than forcing the body to conform to the work. As logical as this may sound, it is actually a recent point of view.

Ergonomics

WORK METHODS

⌒⌒⌒⌒ In contemporary industry, responsibility for developing work methods in large firms is typically assigned either to a staff department designated *methods analysis* or to an industrial engineering department. In small firms, this activity is often performed by consulting firms that specialize in work methods design.

The principal approach to the study of work methods is the construction of charts, such as operations charts, worker–machine charts, simo (simultaneous motion) charts, and activity charts, in conjunction with time study or standard time data. The choice of which charting method to use depends on the task's activity level—that is, whether the focus is on (1) a production process, (2) the worker at a fixed workplace, (3) a worker interacting with equipment, or (4) a worker interacting with other workers (see Exhibit TN5.4). (These charting techniques were introduced in Chapter 5, where they were used to aid in process analysis. Chapter 7 introduces the service blueprint that accounts for customer interactions.)

A PRODUCTION PROCESS

The objective in studying a production process is to identify delays, transport distances, processes, and processing time requirements to simplify the entire operation. The underlying

Work Methods Design Aids

ACTIVITY	OBJECTIVE OF STUDY	STUDY TECHNIQUES
Production process	Eliminate or combine steps; shorten transport distance; identify delays	Flow diagram, service blueprint, process chart
Worker at fixed workplace	Simplify method; minimize motions	Operations charts, simo charts; apply principles of motion economy
Worker's interaction with equipment	Minimize idle time; find number or combination of machines to balance cost of worker and machine idle time	Activity chart, worker–machine charts
Worker's interaction with other workers	Maximize productivity; minimize interference	Activity charts, gang process charts

philosophy is to eliminate any step in the process that does not add value to the product. The approach is to flowchart the process and then ask the following questions:

What is done? Must it be done? What would happen if it were not done?

Where is the task done? Must it be done at that location or could it be done somewhere else?

When is the task done? Is it critical that it be done then or is there flexibility in time and sequence? Could it be combined with some other step in the process?

How is the task done? Why is it done this way? Is there another way?

Who does the task? Can someone else do it? Should the worker be of a higher or lower skill level?

These thought-provoking questions usually help eliminate much unnecessary work and simplify the remaining work by combining processing steps and changing the order of performance.

The process chart is valuable in studying an overall system, though care must be taken to - follow the same item throughout the process. The subject may be a product being manufactured, a service being created, or a person performing a sequence of activities. Exhibit TN5.5 shows a process chart (and flow diagram) for a clerical operation. Exhibit TN5.6 shows common notation in process charting. Can you suggest any ways to improve this process? (See Problem 2.)

WORKER AT A FIXED WORKPLACE

Many jobs require the worker to remain at a specified workstation. When the nature of the work is primarily manual (such as sorting, inspecting, making entries, or assembly operations), the focus of work design is on simplifying the work method and making the required operator motions as few and as easy as possible.

There are two basic ways to determine the best method when a methods analyst studies a single worker performing an essentially manual task. The first is to search among the workers and find the one who performs the job best. That person's method is then accepted as the standard, and others are trained to perform it in the same way. This was basically F. W. Taylor's approach, though after determining the best method, he searched for "first-class men" to perform according to the method. (A first-class worker possessed the natural ability to do much more productive work in a particular task than the average. Workers who were not first class were transferred to other jobs.) The second way is to

Flow Diagram and Process Chart of an Office Procedure—Present Method

Note: Requisition is written by a supervisor, typed by a secretary, approved by a superintendent, and approved by a purchasing agent. Then a purchase order is prepared by a stenographer.

observe the performance of a number of workers, analyze in detail each step of their work, and pick out the superior features of each worker's performance. This results in a composite method that combines the best elements of the group studied. Frank Gilbreth, the father of motion study, used this procedure to determine the "one best way" to perform a work task.

Taylor observed actual performance to find the best method; Frank Gilbreth and his wife Lillian studied movie film. Through micromotion analysis—observing the filmed work

exhibit TN5.6   Notation for the Process Chart in Exhibit TN5.5

> Operation. Something is actually being done. This may be work on a product, some support activity, or anything that is directly productive in nature.
>
> Transportation. The subject of the study (product, service, or person) moves from one location to another.
>
> Inspection. The subject is observed for quality and correctness.
>
> Delay. The subject of the study must wait before starting the next step in the process.
>
> Storage. The subject is stored, such as finished products in inventory or completed papers in a file. Frequently, a distinction is made between temporary storage and permanent storage by inserting a T or P in the triangle.

PACIFIC NORTHWEST NATIONAL LABORATORY'S REMOTELY OPERATED PIT VIPER RADIOACTIVE CLEANUP TECHNOLOGY RESULTS IN 50–75 PERCENT REDUCTION IN WORKER EXPOSURE. THE REMOTE CAPABILITY ALLOWS WORKERS TO PERFORM OPERATIONS IN MORE THAN 600 EQUIPMENT PITS ON THE HANFORD SITE NEAR RICHLAND, WASHINGTON.

performance frame by frame—the Gilbreths studied work very closely and defined its basic elements, which were termed *therbligs* ("Gilbreth" spelled backward, with the *t* and *h* transposed). As part of his work, Gilbreth constructed wire representations of the path of motion. Their study led to the rules or principles of motion economy, such as "The hands should begin and complete the motions at the same time" and "Work should be arranged to permit natural rhythm."

Once the motions for performing the task have been identified, an *operations chart* may be made, listing the operations and their sequence of performance. For greater detail, a *simo* (simultaneous motion) *chart* may be constructed, listing not only the operations but also the times for both left and right hands. This chart may be assembled from the data collected with a stopwatch, from analysis of a film of the operation, or from predetermined motion–time data (discussed later in the technical note). Many aspects of poor design are immediately obvious: a hand being used as a holding device (rather than a jig or fixture), an idle hand, or an exceptionally long time for positioning.

WORKER INTERACTING WITH EQUIPMENT

When a person and equipment operate together to perform a productive process, interest focuses on the efficient use of the person's time and equipment time. When the operator's working time is less than the equipment run time, a worker–machine chart is a useful device in analysis. If the operator can operate several pieces of equipment, the problem is to find

Worker–Machine Chart for a Gourmet Coffee Store

	Person				Machine	
	Customer	Time in sec.	Clerk	Time in sec.	Coffee Grinder	Time in sec.
0	1. Ask grocer for 1 pound of coffee (brand and grind)	5	Listen to order	5	Idle	5
10	2.		Get coffee and put in machine, set grind, and			
20	Wait	15	start grinder	15	Idle	15
30	3. Wait	21	Idle while machine grinds	21	Grind coffee	21
40 50	4. Wait	12	Stop grinder, place coffee in package, and close it	12	Idle	12
60 70	5. Receive coffee from grocer, pay grocer, and receive change	17	Give coffee to customer, wait for customer to pay for coffee, receive money, and make change	17	Idle	17

Time in Seconds

Summary

	Customer	Clerk	Coffee Grinder
Idle time	48 sec.	21 sec.	49 sec.
Working time	22	49	21
Total cycle time	70	70	70
Utilization percentage	Customer utilization = $\frac{22}{70} = 31\%$	Clerk utilization = $\frac{49}{70} = 70\%$	Machine utilization = $\frac{21}{70} = 30\%$

The customer, the clerk, and the coffee grinder (machine) are involved in this operation. It required 1 minute 10 seconds for the customer to purchase a pound of coffee in this store. During this time the customer spent 22 seconds, or 31 percent of the time, giving the clerk his order, receiving the ground coffee, and paying the clerk. He was idle the remaining 69 percent of the time. The clerk worked 49 seconds, or 70 percent of the time, and was idle 21 seconds, or 30 percent of the time. The coffee grinder was in operation 21 seconds, or 30 percent of the time, and was idle 70 percent of the time.

the most economical combination of operator and equipment, when the combined cost of the idle time of a particular combination of equipment and the idle time for the worker is at a minimum.

Worker–machine charts are always drawn to scale, the scale being time as measured by length. Exhibit TN5.7 shows a worker–machine chart in a service setting. The question here is, whose utilization use is most important?

WORKERS INTERACTING WITH OTHER WORKERS

The degree of interaction among teams may be as simple as one operator handing a part to another, or as complex as a cardiovascular surgical team of doctors, nurses, anesthesiologist, operator of an artificial heart machine, X-ray technician, standby blood donors, and pathologist (and perhaps a minister to pray a little).

An activity or a gang process chart is useful in plotting each individual's activities on a time scale similar to that of the worker–machine chart. A *gang process chart* is usually employed to trace the interaction of a number of workers with machines in a specified operating cycle to find the best combination of workers and machines. An *activity chart* is less restrictive and may be used to follow the interaction of any group of operators, with or without equipment being involved. Such charts are often used to study and define each operation in an ongoing repetitive process, and they are extremely valuable in developing a

exhibit TN5.8 Activity Chart of Emergency Tracheotomy

Time	NURSE	FIRST DOCTOR	ORDERLY	SECOND DOCTOR	NURSE SUPERVISOR	SCRUB NURSE	Time
0							0
1	Detects problem Notifies doctor						1
2							2
3	Gets mobile cart	Makes diagnosis					3
4							4
5							5
6	Notifies nurse supervisor	Helps patient to breathe			Opens OR Calls scrub nurse		6
7	Notifies second doctor			Assures availability of laryngoscope and endotracheal tube			7
8	Notifies orderly	Moves to OR					8
9	Moves patient to OR	Scrubs	Moves patient to OR			Moves to OR Sets up equipment	9
10		Dons gown and gloves					10
11				Operates laryngoscope and inserts endotracheal tube			11
12		Performs tracheotomy		Calls for IPPB machine			12
13							13
14							14
15							15
16							16

SOURCE: DATA TAKEN FROM H. E. SMALLEY AND J. FREEMAN, *HOSPITAL INDUSTRIAL ENGINEERING* (NEW YORK: REINHOLD, 1966), P. 409.

standardized procedure for a specific task. Exhibit TN5.8, for example, shows an activity chart for a hospital's emergency routine in performing a tracheotomy (opening a patient's throat surgically to allow the patient to breathe), where detailed activity analysis is critical and any delay could be fatal.

WORK MEASUREMENT AND STANDARDS

Work measurement

The fundamental purpose of **work measurement** is to set time standards for a job. Such standards are necessary for four reasons:

1. **To schedule work and allocate capacity.** All scheduling approaches require some estimate of how much time it takes to do the work being scheduled.
2. **To provide an objective basis for motivating the workforce and measuring workers' performance.** Measured standards are particularly critical where output-based incentive plans are employed.
3. **To bid for new contracts and to evaluate performance on existing ones.** Questions such as "Can we do it?" and "How are we doing?" presume the existence of standards.
4. **To provide benchmarks for improvement.** In addition to internal evaluation, benchmarking teams regularly compare work standards in their company with those of similar jobs in other organizations.

Work measurement and its resulting work standards have been controversial since Taylor's time. Much of this criticism has come from unions, which argue that management often sets standards that cannot be regularly achieved. (To counter this, in some contracts, the industrial engineer who sets the standard must demonstrate that he or she can do the job over a representative period of time at the rate that was set.) There is also the argument that workers who find a better way of doing the job get penalized by having a revised rate set. (This is commonly called *rate cutting*.)

With the widespread adoption of W. Edwards Deming's ideas, the subject has received renewed criticism. Deming argued that work standards and quotas inhibit process improvement and tend to focus the worker's efforts on speed rather than quality.

Despite these criticisms, work measurement and standards have proved effective. Much depends on sociotechnical aspects of the work. Where the job requires work groups to function as teams and create improvements, worker-set standards often make sense. On the other hand, where the job really boils down to doing the work quickly, with little need for creativity (such as delivering packages for UPS as the box on page 192 relates), tightly engineered, professionally set standards are appropriate.

WORK MEASUREMENT TECHNIQUES

There are four basic techniques for measuring work and setting standards. These consist of two direct observational methods and two indirect methods: The direct methods are **time study**, which uses a stopwatch to time the work, and **work sampling**, which entails recording random observations of a person or teams at work. The two indirect methods are **predetermined motion-time data systems (PMTS)**, which sum data from tables of generic movement times developed in the laboratory to arrive at a time for the job (the most widely used are proprietary systems—Methods Time Measurement [MTM] and Most Work Measurement System [MOST]), and **elemental data**, which sums times from a database of similar combinations of movements to arrive at job time. The choice of techniques depends on the level of detail desired and the nature of the work itself. Highly detailed, repetitive work usually calls for time study and predetermined motion-time data analysis. When work is done in conjunction with fixed-processing-time equipment, elemental data are often used to reduce the need for direct observation. When work is infrequent or entails a long cycle time, work sampling is the tool of choice. (See box "What the Pros Say . . . About Work Measurement Applications in Retailing" for an example of how the different techniques are used in a service setting.)

We now turn to a discussion of the technical details of time study and work sampling. A time study is generally made with a stopwatch, either on the spot or by analyzing a videotape for the job. The job or task to be studied is separated into measurable parts or elements, and each element is timed individually.

Some general rules for breaking down the elements are

1. Define each work element to be short in duration but long enough so that it can be timed with a stopwatch and the time can be written down.

Time study

Work sampling

Predetermined motion-time data systems (PMTS)

Elemental data

WHAT THE PROS SAY . . . ABOUT WORK MEASUREMENT APPLICATIONS IN RETAILING

"We use the predetermined motion time system, MOST, to set standards in retail stores, such as the Gap. In addition to MOST, we use work sampling and some automated time study in the standards development process. MOST is used for the majority of the manual tasks—receiving product, stocking product, conditioning the store, checking a person out, etc.

Work sampling is used to determine frequencies, understand customer shopping behaviors and for standards validation. Time study is used for process related activities such as response time on a credit card or POS machine, and for customer engagement/sales activities."

SOURCE: JEFF PERETIN OF H. B. MAYNARD (ONE OF THE WORLD'S LEADING CONSULTING FIRMS IN WORK MEASUREMENT).

WORK MEASUREMENT AT UNITED PARCEL SERVICE

Grabbing a package under his arm, Joseph Polise, a driver for United Parcel Service (UPS), bounds from his brown delivery truck toward an office building. A few paces behind him, Marjorie Cusack, a UPS industrial engineer, clutches a digital timer.

Her eyes fixed on him, Cusack counts Polise's steps and times his contact with customers. Scribbling on a clipboard, Cusack records every second taken up by stoplights, traffic, detours, doorbells, walkways, stairways, and coffee breaks.

Eighty thousand UPS drivers travel 1.2 billion miles per year and deliver more than 13 million packages a day. On average, UPS drivers move in and out of the truck 200 times a day. An unnecessary step or indirect travel path reduces the effectiveness of the driver and impacts service to the customer. One minute saved each day saves the company $5 million annually. For this reason, UPS spends millions each year to train its drivers in proper, efficient, and safe work methods.

Approximately 1,118 industrial engineers at UPS ensure efficient and reliable customer service by conducting time studies on drivers' routes to provide job method instruction. They have measured even the finest details of the drivers' job, including determining on which finger drivers should consistently carry their key rings to avoid losing them.

In addition to developing specific job methods, UPS provides drivers with custom-built package vehicles with features including

- Domed seats that allow the driver to slide on and off easily at each delivery stop.
- A drop floor well located behind the rear wheel housing, making the rear of the vehicle only a short step from the ground for easy entry.
- Bulkhead doors that allow easy access to the package compartment and save the driver steps in selecting parcels for delivery.

SOURCE: ABSTRACTED FROM D. MACHALABA, "UP TO SPEED: UNITED PARCEL SERVICE GETS DELIVERIES DONE BY DRIVING ITS WORKERS," *THE WALL STREET JOURNAL,* APRIL 22, 1986, P. 1. INFORMATION PROVIDED BY UPS, 1999.

2. If the operator works with equipment that runs separately (meaning the operator performs a task and the equipment runs independently), separate the actions of the operator and of the equipment into different elements.
3. Define any delays by the operator or equipment into separate elements.

After a number of repetitions, the collected times are averaged. (The standard deviation may be computed to give a measure of variance in the performance times.) The averaged times for each element are added, yielding the performance time for the operator. However, to make this operator's time usable for all workers, a measure of speed or *performance rating* must be included to "normalize" the job. The application of a rating factor gives what is called **normal time**. For example, if an operator performs a task in two minutes and the time-study analyst estimates her to be performing about 20 percent faster than normal, the operator's performance rating would be 1.2, or 120 percent of normal. The normal time would be computed as 2 minutes × 1.2, or 2.4 minutes. In equation form,

Normal time = Observed performance time per unit × Performance rating

In this example, denoting normal time by NT,

$$NT = 2(1.2) = 2.4 \text{ minutes}$$

When an operator is observed for a period of time, the number of units produced during this time, along with the performance rating, gives

$$NT = \frac{\text{Time worked}}{\text{Number of units produced}} \times \text{Performance rating}$$

Normal time

Standard time is derived by adding to normal time allowances for personal needs (such   **Standard time**
as washroom and coffee breaks), unavoidable work delays (such as equipment breakdown or
lack of materials), and worker fatigue (physical or mental). Two such equations are

$$\text{Standard time} = \text{Normal time} + (\text{Allowances} \times \text{Normal time})$$

or

[TN5.1]
$$ST = NT\,(1 + \text{Allowances})$$

and

[TN5.2]
$$ST = \frac{NT}{1 - \text{Allowances}}$$

Equation (TN5.1) is most often used in practice. If one presumes that allowances should
be applied to the total work period, then equation (TN5.2) is the correct one. To illustrate, suppose that the normal time to perform a task is one minute and that allowances for personal
needs, delays, and fatigue total 15 percent; then by equation (TN5.1)

$$ST = 1(1 + 0.15) = 1.15 \text{ minutes}$$

In an eight-hour day, a worker would produce $8 \times 60/1.15$, or 417 units. This implies 417
minutes working and $480 - 417$ (or 63) minutes for allowances.
With equation (TN5.2),

$$ST = \frac{1}{1 - 0.15} = 1.18 \text{ minutes}$$

In the same eight-hour day, $8 \times 60/1.18$ (or 408) units are produced with 408 working
minutes and 72 minutes for allowances. Depending on which equation is used, there is a difference of nine minutes in the daily allowance time.

EXAMPLE TN5.1: Time Study for a Four-Element Job

Exhibit TN5.9 shows a time study of 10 cycles of a four-element job. For each element, there is a space
for the watch readings that are recorded in 100ths of a minute. Space also is provided for summarizing
the data and applying a performance rating.

Time-Study Observation Sheet

Time Study Observation Sheet

Identification of Operation	ASSEMBLE 24" × 36" CHART BLANKS		Date *10/9*

Began Timing: 9:26
Ended Timing: 9:32 — Operator 109 — Approval *BgR* — Observer *FDT.*

Element Description and Breakpoint		1 0.00	2	3	4	5	6	7	8	9	10	ΣT	T̄	PR	NT
1	Fold over end (grasp stapler)	.07	.07	.05	.07	.09	.06	.05	.08	.08	.06	.68	.07	.90	.06
		.07	.61	.14	.67	.24	.78	.33	.88	.47	.09				
2	Staple five times (drop stapler)	.16	.14	.14	.15	.16	.16	.14	.17	.14	.15	1.51	.15	1.05	.16
		.23	.75	.28	.82	.40	.94	.47	.05	.61	.24				
3	Bend and insert wire (drop pliers)	.22	.25	.22	.25	.23	.23	.21	.26	.25	.24	2.36	.24	1.00	.24
		.45	.00	.50	.07	.63	.17	.68	.31	.86	.48				
4	Dispose of finished chart (touch next sheet)	.09	.09	.10	.08	.09	.11	.12	.08	.17	.08	1.01	.10	.90	.09
		.54	.09	.60	.15	.72	.28	.80	.39	.03	.56			0.55	
5														normal minute for cycle	
6															
10															

Normal cycle time __0.55__ + Allowance *(0.55 × 0.143) or 0.08* = Std. time __0.63 min./pc.__

SOLUTION

The value of $\overline{T}$ is obtained by averaging the observed data. *PR* denotes the performance rating and is multiplied with $\overline{T}$ to obtain the normal time (*NT*) for each element. The normal time for the job is the sum of the element normal times. The standard time, calculated according to equation (TN5.1), is given at the bottom of Exhibit TN5.9. ●

Service

How many observations are enough? Time study is really a sampling process; that is, we take relatively few observations as being representative of many subsequent cycles to be performed by the worker. Based on a great deal of analysis and experience, Benjamin Niebel's table shown in Exhibit TN5.10 indicates that "enough" is a function of cycle length and number of repetitions of the job over a one-year planning period.

A second common technique for measuring a job is called work sampling. As the name suggests, work sampling involves observing a portion or sample of the work activity. Then, based on the findings in this sample, statements can be made about the activity. For example, if we were to observe a fire department rescue squad at 100 random times during the day and found it was involved in a rescue mission for 30 of the 100 times (en route, on site, or returning from a call), we would estimate that the rescue squad spends 30 percent of its time directly on rescue mission calls. (The time it takes to make an observation depends on what is being observed. Many times, only a glance is needed to determine the activity, and the majority of studies require only several seconds' observation.)

Observing an activity even 100 times may not, however, provide the accuracy desired in the estimate. To refine this estimate, three main issues must be decided. (These points are discussed later in this section, along with an example.)

1. What level of statistical confidence is desired in the results?
2. How many observations are necessary?
3. Precisely when should the observations be made?

exhibit TN5.10

Guide to Number of Cycles to Be Observed in a Time Study

WHEN TIME PER CYCLE IS MORE THAN	MINIMUM NUMBER OF CYCLES OF STUDY (ACTIVITY)		
	OVER 10,000 PER YEAR	1,000–10,000	UNDER 1,000
8 hours	2	1	1
3	3	2	1
2	4	2	1
1	5	3	2
48 minutes	6	3	2
30	8	4	3
20	10	5	4
12	12	6	5
8	15	8	6
5	20	10	8
3	25	12	10
2	30	15	12
1	40	20	15
.7	50	25	20
.5	60	30	25
.3	80	40	30
.2	100	50	40
.1	120	60	50
Under .1	140	80	60

SOURCE: B. W. NIEBEL, *MOTION AND TIME STUDY*, 9TH ED. (BURR RIDGE, IL: RICHARD D. IRWIN, 1993), P. 390. THE MCGRAW-HILL COMPANIES, INC. USED WITH PERMISSION.

The three primary applications for work sampling are

1. Ratio delay to determine the activity-time percentage for personnel or equipment. For example, management may be interested in the amount of time a machine is running or idle.
2. Performance measurement to develop a performance index for workers. When the amount of work time is related to the quantity of output, a measure of performance is developed. This is useful for periodic performance evaluation.
3. Time standards to obtain the standard time for a task. When work sampling is used for this purpose, however, the observer must be experienced because he or she must attach a performance rating to the observations.

The number of observations required in a work-sampling study can be fairly large, ranging from several hundred to several thousand, depending on the activity and desired degree of accuracy. Although the number can be computed from formulas, the easiest way is to refer to a table such as Exhibit TN5.11, which gives the number of observations needed for a 95 percent confidence level in terms of absolute error. *Absolute error* is the actual range of the observations. For example, if a clerk is idle 10 percent of the time and the designer of the study is satisfied with a 2.5 percent range (meaning that the true percentage lies between 7.5 and 12.5 percent), the number of observations required for the work sampling is 576. A 2 percent error (or an interval of 8 to 12 percent) would require 900 observations.

Five steps are involved in making a work-sampling study:

1. Identify the specific activity or activities that are the main purpose for the study. For example, determine the percentage of time that equipment is working, idle, or under repair.
2. Estimate the proportion of time of the activity of interest to the total time (e.g., that the equipment is working 80 percent of the time). These estimates can be made from the analyst's knowledge, past data, reliable guesses from others, or a pilot work-sampling study.
3. State the desired accuracy in the study results.
4. Determine the specific times when each observation is to be made.
5. At two or three intervals during the study period, recompute the required sample size by using the data collected thus far. Adjust the number of observations if appropriate.

The number of observations to be taken in a work-sampling study is usually divided equally over the study period. Thus, if 500 observations are to be made over a 10-day period, observations are usually scheduled at 500/10, or 50 per day. Each day's observations are then assigned a specific time by using a random number table.

EXAMPLE TN5.2: Work Sampling Applied to Nursing

There has been a long-standing argument that a large amount of nurses' hospital time is spent on nonnursing activities. This, the argument goes, creates an apparent shortage of well-trained nursing personnel, wastes talent, hinders efficiency, and increases hospital costs because nurses' wages are the highest single cost in the operation of a hospital. Further, pressure is growing for hospitals and hospital administrators to contain costs. With that in mind, let us use work sampling to test the hypothesis that a large portion of nurses' time is spent on nonnursing duties.

Service

SOLUTION

Assume at the outset that we have made a list of all the activities that are part of nursing and will make our observations in only two categories: nursing and nonnursing activities. Actually, there is much debate on what constitutes nursing activity. For instance, is talking to a patient a nursing duty? (An

Number of Observations Required for a Given Absolute Error at Various Values of p, with 95 Percent Confidence Level

**Excel:
Sample-size**

PERCENTAGE OF TOTAL TIME OCCUPIED BY ACTIVITY OR DELAY, P	ABSOLUTE ERROR					
	±1.0%	±1.5%	±2.0%	±2.5%	±3.0%	±3.5%
1 or 99	396	176	99	63	44	32
2 or 98	784	348	196	125	87	64
3 or 97	1,164	517	291	186	129	95
4 or 96	1,536	683	384	246	171	125
5 or 95	1,900	844	475	304	211	155
6 or 94	2,256	1,003	564	361	251	184
7 or 93	2,604	1,157	651	417	289	213
8 or 92	2,944	1,308	736	471	327	240
9 or 91	3,276	1,456	819	524	364	267
10 or 90	3,600	1,600	900	576	400	294
11 or 89	3,916	1,740	979	627	435	320
12 or 88	4,224	1,877	1,056	676	469	344
13 or 87	4,524	2,011	1,131	724	503	369
14 or 86	4,816	2,140	1,204	771	535	393
15 or 85	5,100	2,267	1,275	816	567	416
16 or 84	5,376	2,389	1,344	860	597	439
17 or 83	5,644	2,508	1,411	903	627	461
18 or 82	5,904	2,624	1,476	945	656	482
19 or 81	6,156	2,736	1,539	985	684	502
20 or 80	6,400	2,844	1,600	1,024	711	522
21 or 79	6,636	2,949	1,659	1,062	737	542
22 or 78	6,864	3,050	1,716	1,098	763	560
23 or 77	7,084	3,148	1,771	1,133	787	578
24 or 76	7,296	3,243	1,824	1,167	811	596
25 or 75	7,500	3,333	1,875	1,200	833	612
26 or 74	7,696	3,420	1,924	1,231	855	628
27 or 73	7,884	3,504	1,971	1,261	876	644
28 or 72	8,064	3,584	2,016	1,290	896	658
29 or 71	8,236	3,660	2,059	1,318	915	672
30 or 70	8,400	3,733	2,100	1,344	933	686
31 or 69	8,556	3,803	2,139	1,369	951	698
32 or 68	8,704	3,868	2,176	1,393	967	710
33 or 67	8,844	3,931	2,211	1,415	983	722
34 or 66	8,976	3,989	2,244	1,436	997	733
35 or 65	9,100	4,044	2,275	1,456	1,011	743
36 or 64	9,216	4,096	2,304	1,475	1,024	753
37 or 63	9,324	4,144	2,331	1,492	1,036	761
38 or 62	9,424	4,188	2,356	1,508	1,047	769
39 or 61	9,516	4,229	2,379	1,523	1,057	777
40 or 60	9,600	4,266	2,400	1,536	1,067	784
41 or 59	9,676	4,300	2,419	1,548	1,075	790
42 or 58	9,744	4,330	2,436	1,559	1,083	795
43 or 57	9,804	4,357	2,451	1,569	1,089	800
44 or 56	9,856	4,380	2,464	1,577	1,095	804
45 or 55	9,900	4,400	2,475	1,584	1,099	808
46 or 54	9,936	4,416	2,484	1,590	1,104	811
47 or 53	9,964	4,428	2,491	1,594	1,107	813
48 or 52	9,984	4,437	2,496	1,597	1,109	815
49 or 51	9,996	4,442	2,499	1,599	1,110	816
50	10,000	4,444	2,500	1,600	1,111	816

Note: Number of observations is obtained from the formula $E = Z \sqrt{\dfrac{p(1-p)}{N}}$ and the required sample (N) is $N = \dfrac{Z^2 p(1-p)}{E^2}$
where E = Absolute error
   p = Percentage occurrence of activity or delay being measured
   N = Number of random observations (sample size)
   Z = Number of standard deviations to give desired confidence level (e.g., for 90 percent confidence, Z = 1.65; for 95 percent, Z = 1.96; for 99 percent, Z = 2.23). In this table Z = 2.

expanded study could list all nursing activities to determine the portion of time spent in each.) Therefore, when we observe during the study and find the nurse performing one of the duties on the nursing list, we simply place a tally mark in the nursing column. If we observe anything besides nursing activities, we place a tally mark in the nonnursing column.

We can now plan the study. Assume that we (or the nursing supervisor) estimate that nurses spend 60 percent of their time in nursing activities. Assume that we would like to be 95 percent confident that findings of our study are within the absolute error range of ±3 percent; that is, if our study shows nurses spend 60 percent of their time on nursing duties, we want to be 95 percent confident that the true percentage lies between 57 and 63 percent. From Exhibit TN5.11, we find that 1,067 observations are required for 60 percent activity time and ±3 percent error. If our study is to take place over 10 days, we start with 107 observations per day.

To determine when each day's observations are to be made, we assign specific numbers to each minute and use a random number table to set up a schedule. If the study extends over an eight-hour shift, we can assign numbers to correspond to each consecutive minute. For this study it is likely the night shift would be run separately because nighttime nursing duties are considerably different from daytime duties. Exhibit TN5.12A shows the assignment of numbers to corresponding minutes. For simplicity, because each number corresponds to one minute, a three-number scheme is used, with the second and third numbers corresponding to the minute of the hour. A number of other schemes would also be appropriate. If a number of studies are planned, a computer program may be used to generate a randomized schedule for the observation times.

If we refer to a random number table and list three-digit numbers, we can assign each number to a time. The random numbers in Exhibit TN5.12B demonstrate the procedure for seven observations.

Sampling Plan for Nurses' Activities
A. Assignment of Numbers to Corresponding Minutes
B. Determination of Observation Times
C. Observation Schedule

A.

Time	Assigned Numbers
7:00–7:59 A.M.	100–159
8:00–8:59 A.M.	200–259
9:00–9:59 A.M.	300–359
10:00–10:59 A.M.	400–459
11:00–11:59 A.M.	500–559
12:00–12:59 P.M.	600–659
1:00–1:59 P.M.	700–759
2:00–2:59 P.M.	800–859

B.

Random Number	Corresponding Time from the List in TN5.12A
669	Nonexistent
831	2:31 P.M.
555	11:55 A.M.
470	Nonexistent
113	7:13 A.M.
080	Nonexistent
520	11:20 A.M.
204	8:04 A.M.
732	1:32 P.M.
420	10:20 A.M.

C.

Observation	Schedule Time	Nursing Activity(✓)	Nonnursing Activity(✓)
1	7:13 A.M.		
2	8:04 A.M.		
3	10:20 A.M.		
4	11:20 A.M.		
5	11:55 A.M.		
6	1:32 P.M.		
7	2:31 P.M.		

This procedure is followed to generate 107 observation times, and the times are rearranged chronologically for ease in planning. Rearranging the times determined in Exhibit TN5.12B gives the total observations per day shown in Exhibit TN5.12C (for our sample of seven).

To be perfectly random in this study, we should also "randomize" the nurse we observe each time. (The use of various nurses minimizes the effect of bias.) In the study, our first observation is made at 7:13 A.M. for Nurse X. We walk into the nurse's area and, on seeing the nurse, check either a nursing or a nonnursing activity. Each observation need be only long enough to determine the class of activity—in most cases only a glance is needed. At 8:04 A.M. we observe Nurse Y. We continue in this way to the end of the day and the 107 observations. At the end of the second day (and 214 observations), we decide to check for the adequacy of our sample size.

Let us say we made 150 observations of nurses working and 64 of them not working, which gives 70.1 percent working. From Exhibit TN5.11, this corresponds to 933 observations. Because we have already taken 214 observations, we need take only 719 over the next eight days, or 90 per day.

When the study is half over, another check should be made. For instance, if days 3, 4, and 5 showed 55, 59, and 64 working observations, the cumulative data would give 328 working observations of a total 484, or a 67.8 percent working activity. For a ±3 percent error, Exhibit TN5.11 shows the sample size to be about 967, leaving 483 to be made—at 97 per day—for the following five days. Another computation should be made before the last day to see if another adjustment is required. If after the 10th day several more observations are indicated, these can be made on day 11.

If at the end of the study we find that 66 percent of nurses' time is involved with what has been defined as nursing activity, there should be an analysis to identify the remaining 34 percent. Approximately 12 to 15 percent is justifiable for coffee breaks and personal needs, which leaves 20 to 22 percent of the time that must be justified and compared to what the industry considers ideal levels of nursing activity. To identify the nonnursing activities, a more detailed breakdown could have been originally built into the sampling plan. Otherwise, a follow-up study may be in order. ●

As mentioned earlier, work sampling can be used to set time standards. To do this, the analyst must record the subject's performance rate (or index) along with working observations. Exhibit TN5.13 gives a manufacturing example that demonstrates how work sampling can be used for calculating standard time.

---

exhibit TN5.13

Deriving a Time Standard Using Work Sampling

INFORMATION	SOURCE OF DATA	DATA FOR ONE DAY
Total time expended by operator (working time and idle time)	Computer payroll system	480 min.
Number of parts produced	Inspection department	420 pieces
Working time in percent	Work sampling	85%
Idle time in percent	Work sampling	15%
Average performance index	Work sampling	110%
Total allowances	Company time-study manual	15%

$$\text{Standard time per piece} = \frac{\left(\begin{array}{c}\text{Total time}\\\text{in minutes}\end{array}\right) \times \left(\begin{array}{c}\text{Working time}\\\text{proportion}\end{array}\right) \times \left(\begin{array}{c}\text{Performance}\\\text{index}\end{array}\right)}{\text{Total number of pieces produced}} \times \frac{1}{1 - \text{Allowances}}$$

$$= \left(\frac{480 \times 0.85 \times 1.10}{420}\right) \times \left(\frac{1}{1 - 0.15}\right) = 1.26 \text{ minutes}$$

WORK SAMPLING COMPARED TO TIME STUDY

Work sampling offers several advantages:

1. Several work-sampling studies may be conducted simultaneously by one observer.
2. The observer need not be a trained analyst unless the purpose of the study is to determine a time standard.
3. No timing devices are required.
4. Work of a long cycle time may be studied with fewer observer hours.
5. The duration of the study is longer, which minimizes effects of short-period variations.
6. The study may be temporarily delayed at any time with little effect.
7. Because work sampling needs only instantaneous observations (made over a longer period), the operator has less chance to influence the findings by changing his or her work method.

When the cycle time is short, time study is more appropriate than work sampling. One drawback of work sampling is that it does not provide as complete a breakdown of elements as time study. Another difficulty with work sampling is that observers, rather than following a random sequence of observations, tend to develop a repetitive route of travel. This may allow the time of the observations to be predictable and thus invalidate the findings. A third factor—a potential drawback—is that the basic assumption in work sampling is that all observations pertain to the same static system. If the system is in the process of change, work sampling may give misleading results.

FINANCIAL INCENTIVE PLANS

The third piece of the job design equation is the paycheck. This section briefly reviews common methods for setting financial incentives.

BASIC COMPENSATION SYSTEMS

The main forms of basic compensation are hourly pay, straight salary, piece rate, and commissions. The first two are based on time spent on the job, with individual performance rewarded by an increase in the base rate. Piece rate plans reward on the basis of direct daily output. (A worker is paid $5 a unit; thus, by producing 10 units per day, the worker earns $50.) Sometimes a guaranteed base is included in a piece-rate plan; a worker would receive this base amount regardless of output, plus a piece-rate bonus. (For example, the worker's hourly base pay is $8, so this coupled with $50 piece-rate earnings gives the worker $114 for an eight-hour day.) Commissions may be thought of as sales-based piece rates and are calculated in the same general way.

The two broad categories of financial incentive plans are individual or small-group incentive plans and organizationwide plans.

INDIVIDUAL AND SMALL-GROUP INCENTIVE PLANS

Individual and work group plans traditionally have rewarded performance by using output (often defined by piece rates) and quality measures. Quality is accounted for by a quality adjustment factor, say, a percentage of rework. (For example: Incentive pay = Total output × [1 − Percent deduction for rework].) In recent years, skill development also has been rewarded. Sometimes called *pay for knowledge,* this means a worker is compensated for learning new tasks. This is particularly important in job shops using group technology, as well as in banking, where supervisors' jobs require knowledge of new types of financial instruments and selling approaches.

AT&T, for example, instituted incentive programs for its managers—an Individual Incentive Award (IIA) and a Management Team Incentive Award (MTIA). The IIA provides lump-sum bonuses to outstanding performers. These outstanding performers are determined by individual performance ratings accompanied by extensive documentation. The lump-sum bonus can range between 15 and 30 percent of base pay.

MTIAs are granted to members of specific divisions or units. Appropriate division or unit goals are established at the beginning of the year. The goals include department service objectives and interdepartmental goals. A typical MTIA could call for a standard amount equivalent to 1.5 percent of wages plus overtime for the next three years based on performance in the current year.

ORGANIZATIONWIDE PLANS

Profit sharing and gain sharing are the major types of organizationwide plans. Profit sharing simply distributes a percentage of corporate profits across the workforce. In the United States, at least one-third of all organizations have profit sharing. In Japan, most major companies give profit-based bonuses twice a year to all employees. Such bonuses may range from 50 percent of salaries, in good years, to nothing in bad years.

Gain sharing also involves giving organizationwide bonuses, but it differs from profit sharing in two important respects. First, it typically measures controllable costs or units of output, not profits, in calculating a bonus. Second, gain sharing is always combined with a participative approach to management. The original and best-known gainsharing plan is the Scanlon Plan.

In the late 1930s, the Lapointe Machine and Tool Company was on the verge of bankruptcy, but through the efforts of union president Joseph Scanlon and company management, the Scanlon Plan was devised to save the company by reducing labor costs. In essence, this plan started with the normal labor cost within the firm. Workers as a group were rewarded for any reductions in labor cost below this base cost. The plan's success depended on committees of workers throughout the firm whose purpose was to search out areas for cost saving and to devise ways of improvement. There were many improvements, and the plan did, in fact, save the company.

The basic elements of the Scanlon Plan are

1. **The ratio.** The ratio is the standard that serves as a measure for judging business performance. It can be expressed as

$$\text{Ratio} = \frac{\text{Total labor cost}}{\text{Sales value of production}}$$

2. **The bonus.** The amount of bonus depends on the reduction in costs below the preset ratio.
3. **The production committee.** The production committee is formed to encourage employee suggestions to increase productivity, improve quality, reduce waste, and so forth. The purpose of a production committee is similar to that of a quality circle.
4. **The screening committee.** The screening committee consists of top management and worker representatives who review monthly bonuses, discuss production problems, and consider improvement suggestions.

Though originally established in small companies such as Lapointe, Lincoln Electric Company, and Herman Miller, gain sharing has been installed by large firms such as TRW, General Electric, Motorola, and Firestone. These companies apply gain sharing to organizational units. Motorola, for example, has virtually all its plant employees covered by gain sharing. These plans are increasing because "they are more than just pay incentive plans; they are a participative approach to management and are often used as a way to install

Comparison of Common Reward/Incentive Plans

TYPE OF PLAN	APPLICATION	ADVANTAGES	DISADVANTAGES
Merit pay	Individual	• Allows management to target specific behavior and to easily evolve criteria over time.	• Can be arbitrary and unbiased when incorrectly administered. • Often not clearly tied to business goals.
Profit sharing	Group	• Ties business performance to employee reward.	• Often individual or group behavior is not correlated to business performance.
Gain sharing	Group	• Specific group performance directly tied to employee reward.	• Often focuses excessively on cost control. • More applicable for tactical improvements than strategic changes.
Lump-sum bonuses and individual bonuses	Either	• Allows management to vary criteria and magnitude of reward; able to target specific actions and behavior.	• Often used for and seen as deferred compensation. • Not always a tie to business goals or performance.
Pay-for-knowledge	Individual	• Allows management to target specific types of skills and personal growth.	• May not impact business performance unless management targets correct skills and applies new skills effectively.
Piece rate	Either	• Allows management to target specific output goals.	• May lead to undesirable competition among workers. • Standards must be kept up to date.

SOURCE: MODIFIED FROM C. GIFFI, A. ROTH, AND G. SEAL, *COMPETING IN WORLD-CLASS MANUFACTURING, AMERICA'S 21ST CENTURY CHALLENGE* (HOMEWOOD, IL: BUSINESS ONE IRWIN, 1990). © 1990 MCGRAW-HILL COMPANIES, INC. USED BY PERMISSION.

participative management."[4] The typical applications of the plans are discussed, along with merit pay, in Exhibit TN5.14.

CONCLUSION

At the outset of this technical note we identified current trends in job design. What will the future hold? One thing is clear: Globalization and the successful application of sophisticated process technologies will make the human element even more important to operations competitiveness than before. Giffi, Roth, and Seal speculate that "the 21st century will be marked by the human resource renaissance." In their view, this renaissance will be characterized by companies actively cultivating their human resources through careful selection and training of the best and brightest employees, implementing innovative team-based employee involvement programs, developing genuinely participative management approaches, and continually retraining their employees.[5] What is the future of the time study techniques also addressed in this technical note? In our opinion, they will always have application to analyzing work methods, to setting work standards, and to structuring incentive plans. (See the Breakthrough box "Linking Standards and Incentives at the Gap Distribution Centers.")

BREAKTHROUGH

LINKING STANDARDS AND INCENTIVES AT THE GAP DISTRIBUTION CENTERS

Fashion retailer The Gap, Inc., believes strongly in the value of engineered labor standards, which have been implemented in some Gap distribution centers for more than a decade. The retailer has engineered labor standards in place for receiving, stocking, order filling, and shipping. These standards "are our number one means of communication" with warehouse associates, explains Jay Ninah, senior planning engineer for The Gap. Reports on individual and group performance are posted weekly and associates meet with their supervisors on a monthly basis to discuss their performance. As a result, associates always know what level of performance is expected of them and how their individual performance compares to the standard.

Posting individual as well as group performance data keeps with The Gap's open-book policy, Ninah says. "It's not there to intimidate anyone, but to share our findings. It also creates an expectation that the standards are correctly set. If 85 percent to 90 percent are achieving the standard, those not meeting the standard can determine whether they're using a method that's not the best one." The Gap coaches based on its standards. Ninah states, "As we identify lower-performing individuals, we have a structured coaching process," whereby supervisors work with associates on the areas they need to improve. Associates have an extra push to improve their work, thanks to an incentive program tied to performance. The program was pioneered last year, Ninah says, and is getting a good response from associates. "Instead of giving an across-the-board increase, we give it based on performance," he says.

GLOBAL STANDARDS, LOCAL APPLICATION

The Gap's distribution network is made up of 18 facilities that range from brand-new warehouses with the latest technology to others that are 20 years old. To make sure that the labor standards are appropriate for each facility, The Gap's central engineering group in Erlanger, Kentucky, creates global standards. These are then localized to fit each distribution center by engineers that work in that facility. Most of The Gap's labor standards are derived largely by using predetermined labor standards using the MOST system developed by H. B. Maynard Co., Ninah says. They are then validated with stopwatch studies. A handful of standards not included in the predetermined time measures have to be completely developed by the engineering staff.

STANDARDS TO BUILD ON

The standards are a key planning and scheduling tool for The Gap and have proven to be very valuable when setting up new distribution centers. "It gives us a good gauge of how many people we need to hire," Ninah reports. They also use the labor standards to track a new facility's learning curve. "We're able to see how long it takes a new distribution center to get up to speed," he says, and for associates to learn their jobs. The standards have proven to be a powerful communication tool for new facilities. The engineering staff develops labor standards for a new distribution center before it opens. The measures enable associates to "understand what's expected of them, and where they are with respect to where they should be," Ninah says. "We used to expect a six- to eight-month learning curve. Now, it's about half that."

SOURCE: MODIFIED FROM DISTRIBUTION CENTER MANAGEMENT 2002, ALEXANDER COMMUNICATIONS GROUP, INC., WWW.DISTRIBUTIONGROUP.COM.

KEY TERMS

Job design The function of specifying the work activities of an individual or group in an organizational setting.

Specialization of labor Simple, repetitive jobs are assigned to each worker.

Job enrichment Specialized work is made more interesting by giving the worker a greater variety of tasks or by getting a worker involved in planning, organization, and inspection.

Sociotechnical systems A philosophy that focuses more on the interaction between technology and the work group. The approach attempts to develop jobs that adjust the production process technology to the needs of the worker and work group.

Work physiology Considers the physical demands of a job. Work–rest cycles are set according to the energy expended on the job.

Ergonomics Study of the physical arrangement of the work space together with the tools used to perform a task.

Work measurement Job analysis for the purpose of setting time standards.

Time study Separation of a job into measurable parts, with each element timed individually. The individual times are then combined, and allowances are added to calculate a standard time.

Work sampling Analyzing a work activity by observing an activity at random times. Statements about how time is spent during the activity are made from these observations.

Predetermined motion-time data systems (PMTS) Systems for deriving a time for a job by summing data from tables of generic movement times developed in the laboratory.

Elemental data Used to derive a job time by summing times from a database of similar combinations of movements.

Normal time The time that a normal operator would be expected to take to complete a job without the consideration of allowances.

Standard time Calculated by taking the normal time and adding allowances for personal needs, unavoidable work delays, and worker fatigue.

FORMULA REVIEW

Standard time

[TN5.1]
$$ST = NT(1 + \text{Allowances})$$

Assumes that allowances are added to normal time.

[TN5.2]
$$ST = \frac{NT}{1 - \text{Allowances}}$$

Assumes that allowances are applied to the total work period.

SOLVED PROBLEMS

SOLVED PROBLEM 1

Brandon is very organized and wants to plan his day perfectly. To do this, he has his friend Kelly time his daily activities. Here are the results of her timing Brandon on polishing two pairs of black shoes using the snapback method of timing. What is the standard time for polishing two pairs? (Assume a 5 percent allowance factor for Brandon to put something mellow on the CD player. Account for noncyclically recurring elements by dividing their observed times by the total number of cycles observed.)

	OBSERVED TIMES					
ELEMENT	1	2	3	4	PERFORMANCE RATING	NT
Get shoeshine kit	0.50				125%	
Polish shoes	0.94	0.85	0.80	0.81	110	
Put away kit				0.75	80	

Solution

	ΣT	$\bar{T}$	PERFORMANCE RATING	NT
Get shoeshine kit	.50	.50/2 = .25	125%	.31
Polish shoes (2 pairs)	3.40	3.40/2 = 1.70	110	1.87
Put away kit	.75	.75/2 = .375	80	.30
Normal time for one pair of shoes				2.48

Standard time for the pair $= 2.48 \times 1.05 = 2.60$ minutes.

SOLVED PROBLEM 2

A total of 15 observations has been taken on a head baker for a school district. The numerical breakdown of the baker's activities is

MAKE READY	DO	CLEAN UP	IDLE
2	6	3	4

Based on this information, how many work-sampling observations are required to determine how much of the baker's time is spent in "doing"? Assume a 5 percent desired absolute accuracy and 95 percent confidence level.

Solution

To calculate the number of observations, use the formula at the bottom of Exhibit TN5.11 because the 95 percent confidence is required (that is, $Z \cong 2$).

$$p = \text{"Doing"} = 6/15 = 40\%$$

$E = 5\%$ (given)

$$N = \frac{4p(1 - p)}{E^2} = \frac{4(.4)(1 - .4)}{(.05)(.05)} = \frac{.96}{.0025} = 384$$

REVIEW AND DISCUSSION QUESTIONS

1. Why might practicing managers and industrial engineers be skeptical about job enrichment and sociotechnical approaches to job design?
2. Professors commonly complain to their families that book writing is hard work and that they should be excused from helping out with the housework so that they can rest. Which exhibit in this technical note should they never let their families see?
3. Is there an inconsistency when a company requires precise time standards and encourages job enlargement?
4. Match the following techniques to their most appropriate application:

   Worker–machine chart   Washing clothes at laundromat
   Process chart   Tracing your steps in getting a parking permit
   Work sampling   Faculty office hours kept

5. You have timed your friend, Lefty, assembling widgets. His time averaged 12 minutes for the two cycles you timed. He was working very hard, and you believe that none of the nine other operators doing the same job can beat his time. Are you ready to put forth this time as the standard for making an order of 5,000 widgets? If not, what else should you do?
6. Comment on the following:
   a. "Work measurement is old hat. We have automated our office, and now we run every bill through our computer (after our 25 clerks have typed the data into our computer database)."
   b. "It's best that our workers don't know that they are being time studied. That way, they can't complain about us getting in the way when we set time standards."
   c. "Once we get everybody on an incentive plan, then we will start our work measurement program."
   d. "Rhythm is fine for dancing, but it has no place on the shop floor."
7. Organizationwide financial incentive plans cover all the workers. Some units or individuals may have contributed more to corporate profits than others. Does this detract from the effectiveness of the incentive plan system? How would your incentive scheme for a small software development firm compare to an established auto manufacturing firm?

PROBLEMS

1. Use the following form to evaluate a job you have held relative to the five principles of job design given in the technical note. Develop a numerical score by summing the numbers in parentheses.

	POOR (0)	ADEQUATE (1)	GOOD (2)	OUTSTANDING (3)
Task variety				
Skill variety				
Feedback				
Task identity				
Task autonomy				

    a. Compute the score for your job. Does the score match your subjective feelings about the job as a whole? Explain.

    b. Compare your score with the scores generated by your classmates. Is there one kind of job that everybody likes and one kind that everybody dislikes?

2   Examine the process chart in Exhibit TN5.5. Can you recommend some improvements to cut down on delays and transportation? (Hint: The research laboratory can suggest changes in the requisition form.)

3   A time study was made of an existing job to develop new time standards. A worker was observed for 45 minutes. During that period, 30 units were produced. The analyst rated the worker as performing at a 90 percent performance rate. Allowances in the firm for rest and personal time are 12 percent.

    a. What is the normal time for the task?

    b. What is the standard time for the task?

    c. If the worker produced 300 units in an eight-hour day, what would be the day's pay if the basic rate was $6 per hour and the premium payment system paid on a 100 percent basis?

4   The Bullington Company wants a time standard established on the painting operation of souvenir horseshoes for the local Pioneer Village. Work sampling is to be used. It is estimated that working time averages 95 percent of total time (working time plus idle time). A co-op student is available to do the work sampling between 8:00 A.M. and 12:00 noon. Sixty working days are to be used for the study. Use Exhibit TN5.11 and an absolute error of 2.5 percent. Use the table of random numbers (Appendix B) to calculate the sampling schedule for the first day (that is, show the times of day that an observation of working/idle should be made). Hint: Start random number selection with the first tour.

5   The final result of the study in Problem 4 estimated working time at 91.0 percent. In a 480-minute shift, the best operator painted 1,000 horseshoes. The student's performance index was estimated to be 115 percent. Total allowances for fatigue, personal time, and so on are 10 percent. Calculate the standard time per piece.

6   Suppose you want to set a time standard for the baker making her specialty, square doughnuts. A work-sampling study of her on "doughnut day" yielded the following results:

Time spent (working and idle)	320 minutes
Number of doughnuts produced	5,000
Working time	280 minutes
Performance rating	125%
Allowances	10%

    What is the standard time per doughnut?

7   In an attempt to increase productivity and reduce costs, Rho Sigma Corporation is planning to install an incentive pay plan in its manufacturing plant. In developing standards for one operation, time-study analysts observed a worker for 30 minutes. During that time the worker completed 42 parts. The analysts rated the worker as producing at 130 percent. The base wage rate of the worker is $5 per hour. The firm has established 15 percent as a fatigue and personal time allowance.

    a. What is the normal time for the task?

    b. What is the standard time for the task?

    c. If the worker produced 500 units during an eight-hour day, what wages would the worker have earned?

8   Because new regulations will greatly change the products and services offered by savings and loan associations, time studies must be performed on tellers and other personnel to determine the number and types of personnel needed and incentive wage payment plans that might be installed. As an example of the studies that the various tasks will undergo, consider the following problem and come up with appropriate answers.

A hypothetical case was set up in which the teller (to be retitled later as an *account advisor*) was required to examine a customer's portfolio and determine whether it was more beneficial for the customer to consolidate various CDs into a single issue currently offered, or to leave the portfolio unaltered. A time study made of the teller yielded the following findings:

Time of study	90 minutes
Number of portfolios examined	10 portfolios
Performance rating	130 percent
Rest for personal time	15 percent
Teller's proposed new pay rate	$12 per hour

    a. What is the normal time for the teller to do a portfolio analysis for the CDs?

    b. What is the standard time for the analysis?

    c. If the S&L decides to pay the new tellers on a 100 percent premium payment plan, how much would a teller earn for a day in which he or she analyzed 50 customer portfolios?

9   Based on a manager's observations, a milling machine appears to be idle approximately 30 percent of the time. Develop a work-sampling plan to determine the percentage of idle time, accurate within a 3 percent error ($\pm 3\%$) with a 95 percent confidence level. Use the random numbers from Appendix B to derive the first day's sampling schedule (assume that the sample will take place over 60 days and that an eight-hour shift is used from 8:00 to 12:00 and 1:00 to 5:00).

CASE: JEANS THERAPY—LEVI'S FACTORY WORKERS ARE ASSIGNED TO TEAMS, AND MORALE TAKES A HIT

In an industry notorious for low wages and lousy working conditions, Levi's has prided itself on being a grand exception. It offered generous pay plus plenty of charity support in factory towns—all financed by the phenomenal profitability of its brilliantly marketed brand name. It clung to a large U.S. manufacturing base long after other apparel firms began moving offshore, and it often was ranked among the best companies to work for.

But to many of Levi's workers, the company's image has not fit for some time. In 1992 the company directed its U.S. plants to abandon the old piecework system, under which a worker repeatedly performed a single, specialized task (like sewing zippers or attaching belt loops) and was paid according to the amount of work he or she completed. In the new system, groups of 10 to 35 workers would share the tasks and be paid according to the total number of trousers the group completed. Levi's figured that this would cut down on the monotony of the old system and enable stitchers to do different tasks, thus reducing repetitive-stress injuries.

At the time, the team concept was a much-touted movement designed to empower factory workers in many industries, and Levi's unions agreed to the effort. But there was more to it than that for Levi's. Faced with low-cost competitors manufacturing overseas, the San Francisco–based company did not feel it could keep many of its U.S. plants open unless it could raise productivity and reduce costs, particularly those incurred by injured workers pushing to make piecework goals. Teamwork, Levi's felt, would be more humane, safe, and profitable.

Instead, the new system led to a quagmire in which skilled workers found themselves pitted against slower colleagues, damaging morale and triggering corrosive infighting. Many top performers said the first thing they noticed about teams was that their pay shrank—and some of them decided to throttle back. They felt cheated because they were making less. Whenever a team member was absent, inexperienced, or just slow, the rest of the team had to make up for it. That infuriated some team members who felt they were carrying subpar workers. With limited supervision from coaches, groups were forced to resolve most workflow and personality issues themselves.

The fundamental problem arises from the nature of work at Levi's factories. Unlike an assembly line for cars or copiers, speed in garment-making relates directly to a worker's skill and stamina for grueling, repetitive motions of joining and stitching fabric. The workers in Levi's plants operate machines that perform specific tasks: pocket setter, belt looper, and fly stitcher, among others. Some employees work much faster than others.

In 1993 Levi's hired a consulting firm to analyze the problems. Its conclusion was simply that the company should start from scratch and involve all parties in a redesign of pay structures and work processes. As they began discussing the changes, some plant managers complained that the sessions were "at times too touchy-feely and not business-based enough." Some managers just did not like the idea of having sewing machine operators challenge their authority. Costs mounted, and in April 1994 plant managers were warned that they must cut costs by 28 percent on average by the end of 1997 or face an uncertain future.

By early 1997, Levi's share of the domestic men's denim jeans market fell to 26 percent from a high of 48 percent in 1990. Burdened by new debt, Levi's in February 1997 announced plans to cut its salaried workforce by 20 percent over 12 months. Later in November 1997, the firm announced the closing of 11 U.S. plants and layoffs of 6,395 workers. The company said that none of these jobs were transferred overseas. Still, over the years the company shifted much of its work abroad. Industrywide in 1991, approximately 15 percent of the jeans for the U.S. market were manufactured abroad. Approximately 45 percent of the jeans were produced in foreign plants by the end of 1997.

Levi's says the team approach was the company's attempt to ensure long-term survival for as many U.S. plants as possible. Plant closures might have come sooner, and job losses might have been heavier, had teams never been adopted, company officials say. Levi's vows to persevere with the team strategy at its remaining U.S. plants. But unofficially, much of the approach is being scrapped as individual managers seek ways to improve productivity. People in the plants are gradually going back to the old way of doing things.

QUESTIONS

1   What went wrong with Levi's move to teams in their plants?
2   What could Levi's have done differently to avert the problems?
3   Devise a team incentive plan that you think might work.
4   Do you think the need to move jeans production offshore was inevitable? Could Levi's have done anything to avert the problem of increasing labor costs?

SOURCE: R. T. KING JR., "JEANS THERAPY," *THE WALL STREET JOURNAL*, MAY 20, 1998, P. A1. © 1998 DOW JONES AND COMPANY, INC. ALL RIGHTS RESERVED WORLDWIDE. USED WITH PERMISSION.

SELECTED BIBLIOGRAPHY

Aft, Lawrence S. *Work Measurement and Methods Improvement (Engineering Design and Automation).* New York: Wiley-Interscience, 2000.

Meyers, F. E., and J. R. Stewart. *Time and Motion Study: For Lean Manufacturing.* 3rd ed. Upper Saddle River, NJ: Prentice Hall, 2001.

Niebel, B. W., and A. Freivalds. *Methods, Standards, and Work Design.* New York: WCB/McGraw-Hill, 1998.

Parker, S., and T. Hall. *Job and Work Design: Organizing Work to Promote Well-Being and Effectiveness.* Thousand Oaks, CA: Sage, 1998.

Ramsey, G. F., Jr. "Using Self-Administered Work Sampling in a State Agency." *Industrial Engineering,* February 1993, pp. 44–45.

Rutter, R. "Work Sampling: As a Win/Win Management Tool." *Industrial Engineering,* February 1994, pp. 30–31.

Sasser, W. E., and W. E. Fulmer. "Creating Personalized Service Delivery Systems." In *Service Management Effectiveness,* ed. D. Bowen, R. Chase, and T. Cummings. San Francisco: Jossey-Bass, 1990, pp. 213–33.

FOOTNOTES

1   M. Apgar IV, "The Alternative Workplace: Changing Where and How People Work," *Harvard Business Review* 76, no. 3 (May–June 1998), pp. 121–36.

2   E. E. Lawler III, *The Ultimate Advantage: Creating the High Involvement Organizations* (San Francisco: Jossey-Bass, 1992), pp. 85–86.

3   Ibid., pp. 98–99.

4   E. E. Lawler III, "Paying for Organizational Performance," Report G87-1(92) (Los Angeles: Center for Effective Organizations, University of Southern California, 1987).

5   C. Giffi, A. Roth, and G. M. Seal, *Competing in World-Class Manufacturing: America's 21st Century Challenge* (Homewood, IL: Richard D. Irwin, 1990), p. 299.

chapter

MANUFACTURING PROCESS SELECTION AND DESIGN

AN EFFICIENCY GURU REFITS
HONDA TO FIGHT AUTO GIANTS

The car-racing enthusiasts who design its engines have long dominated Honda Motor Company. But lately, a motor for change has been humming at the company, a hard-charging industrial engineer named Masaki Iwai. Iwai, an efficiency expert and cost-cutting fanatic, is betting Honda can reap economies of scale by doubling its speed and efficiency in manufacturing cars. He scoffs at the idea that the company will have to bulk up through a merger or takeover. "Honda will never have to go after volume," says the senior managing director, an influential member of Honda's inner management circle. "We'll

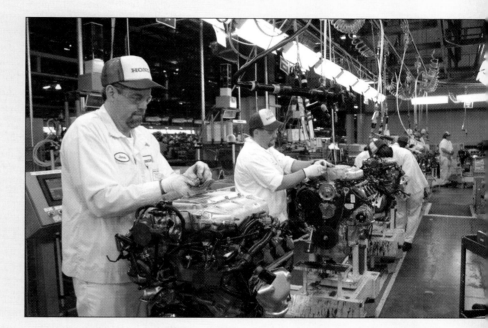

be able to make the kind of profits only an industry Goliath can make, with half their volume."

Iwai has set the bar high. He wants to refit Honda's assembly lines so that they can produce any model in the company's lineup, ranging from the minimalist Civic to the luxurious Acura. He aims to make the final assembly line shorter—half the Honda average of 3,300 feet—to slash the time and money required to put new products and models into production. Eventually, he wants each assembly line to have about 20 off-line branches, up from just a few today. One of them would not just install engines but also actually produce them, work now handled in most cases at specialized plants. Honda's goal is to synchronize engine production and final assembly so that hardly any engines will sit in inventory, representing tied-up money. →

Source: "An Efficiency Guru Refits Honda to Fight Auto Giants," *The Wall Street Journal,* September 15, 1999, p. B1. Republished by permission of Dow Jones, Inc., via Copyright Clearance Center, Inc. © 1999 Dow Jones and Company, Inc. All Rights Reserved Worldwide.

PROCESS SELECTION

⊂⊂⊂⊃ *Process selection* refers to the strategic decision of selecting which kind of production processes to have in the manufacturing plant. For example, in the case of the Honda motors, if the volume is very low, we might just have a worker manually assemble each motor by hand. On the other hand, if the volume is very high, setting up an assembly line might be appropriate.

TYPES OF PROCESSES

Recall from Chapter 5 that processes are categorized based on how they are designed. There we defined terms such as single- and multiple-stage, and make-to-stock and make-to-order processes. Another way to categorize processes is based on what they do.

At the most basic level, the types of processes do the following things:

- Conversion processes include examples such as changing iron ore into steel sheets or making all the ingredients listed on the box of toothpaste into toothpaste.
- Fabrication processes include examples such as changing raw materials into some specific form (for example, making sheet metal into a car fender or forming gold into a crown for a tooth).
- Assembly processes include examples such as assembling a fender to a car, putting toothpaste tubes into a box, or fastening a dental crown in somebody's mouth.
- Testing processes are not, strictly speaking, fundamental processes, but they are so widely mentioned as a stand-alone major activity that they are included here for completeness.

PROCESS FLOW STRUCTURES

A *process flow structure* refers to how a factory organizes material flow using one or more of the process technologies just listed.

Hayes and Wheelwright have identified four major process flow structures:

Job shop

Job shop.   Production of small batches of a large number of different products, most of which require a different set or sequence of processing steps. Commercial printing firms, airplane manufacturers, machine tool shops, and plants that make custom-designed printed circuit boards are examples of this type of structure.

Batch shop

Batch shop.   Essentially, a somewhat standardized job shop. Such a structure is generally employed when a business has a relatively stable line of products, each of which is produced in periodic batches, either to customer order or for inventory. Most of these items follow the same flow pattern through the plant. Examples include heavy equipment, electronic devices, and specialty chemicals.

JOB SHOP

BATCH SHOP

Assembly line. Production of discrete parts moving from workstation to workstation at a controlled rate, following the sequence needed to build the product. Examples include manual assembly of toys and appliances, and automatic assembly (called *insertion*) of components on a printed circuit board. When other processes are employed in a line fashion along with assembly, it is commonly referred to as a *production line*. (See Exhibit 6.1.)

Assembly line

Continuous flow. Conversion or further processing of undifferentiated materials such as petroleum, chemicals, or beer, as the photo below (right) shows. As on assembly lines, production follows a predetermined sequence of steps, but the flow is continuous rather than discrete. Such structures are usually highly automated and, in effect, constitute one integrated "machine" that must be operated 24 hours a day to avoid expensive shutdowns and start-ups.

Continuous flow

The choice of which flow structure to select, with the exception of continuous flow structures, is generally a function of the volume requirements for each product.

PRODUCT–PROCESS MATRIX

The relationship between process structures and volume requirements is often depicted on a **product–process matrix** (Exhibit 6.2). The way to interpret this matrix is that as volume increases and the product line (the horizontal dimension) narrows, specialized equipment and standardized material flows (the vertical dimension) become economically feasible. Because this evolution in process structure is frequently related to the product's life cycle stage (introduction, growth, or maturity), it is very useful in linking marketing and manufacturing strategies.

Product–process matrix

The industries listed within the matrix are presented as ideal types that have found their structural niche. (Sample food service systems are included to help readers get a gut feel for the dimensions.) It is certainly possible for an industry member to choose another position on the matrix, however. For example, the opening vignette describes Honda Motor Company's redesign of its assembly lines so that any model can be produced. Honda recognizes that with the more flexible lines, it will not be able to produce at the high volumes common at Ford or General Motors. This recognition of lower volume paired with the production of a higher variety of products corresponds to a horizontal move from stage III to stage II. From the product–process matrix, one might also think that Honda would move from a pure assembly line to a batch process structure. In the case of Honda, cars will still be made using a modified assembly-line structure, but batches of each model will be made; at least that is what our framework would suggest. It will be interesting to learn how successful Honda's new approach is in the future.

ASSEMBLY LINE

CONTINUOUS FLOW

exhibit 6.1

How to Make a Car: The Production Process in a Modern Car Plant Includes Lots of Checks on Quality and Extensive Treatment to Prevent Corrosion

SOURCE: MITCHELL J. FRUMKIN, "DRIVE COMMUNICATIONS," *CHICAGO SUN-TIMES*, SEPTEMBER 17, 1999.

Matching Major Stages of Product and Process Life Cycles

exhibit 6.2

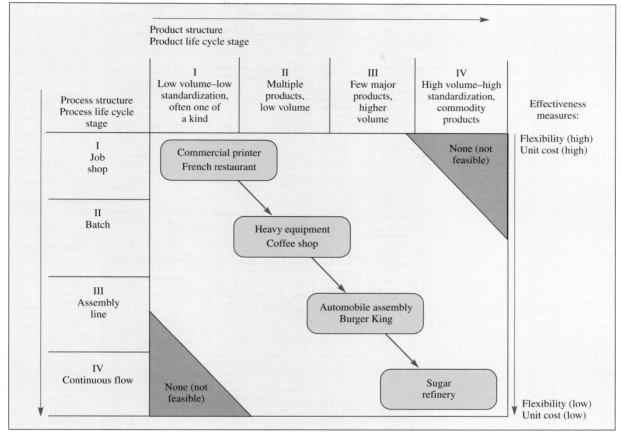

SOURCE: MODIFIED FROM R. HAYES AND S. WHEELWRIGHT, *RESTORING OUR COMPETITIVE EDGE: COMPETING THROUGH MANUFACTURING*, P. 209. COPYRIGHT © 1984 JOHN WILEY & SONS. THIS MATERIAL IS USED BY PERMISSION.

BREAK-EVEN ANALYSIS

SPECIFIC PROCESS EQUIPMENT SELECTION

The choice of specific equipment naturally follows the selection of the general type of process structure. Exhibit 6.3 shows some key factors to consider in the selection and investment decision. Firms may have both general-purpose equipment and special-purpose equipment. For example, a machine shop would have lathes and drill presses (general-purpose) and could have transfer machines (special-purpose). An electronics firm may have a single-function test module to perform only one test at a time (general-purpose) and may have a multifunction test unit to perform multiple tests at the same time (special-purpose). As computer-based technology evolves, however, the general-purpose/special-purpose distinction becomes blurred because a general-purpose machine has the capability to produce just as efficiently as many special-purpose ones.

A standard approach to choosing among alternative processes or equipment is *break-even analysis*. A break-even chart visually presents alternative profits and losses due to the number of units produced or sold. The choice obviously depends on anticipated demand. The method is most suitable when processes and equipment entail a large initial investment and fixed cost, and when variable costs are reasonably proportional to the number of units produced.

**Interactive
Operations
Management**

exhibit 6.3

Major Decision Variables in Equipment Selection

DECISION VARIABLE	FACTORS TO CONSIDER
Initial investment	Price Manufacturer Availability of used models Space requirements Need for feeder/support equipment
Output rate	Actual versus rated capacity
Output quality	Consistency in meeting specs Scrap rate
Operating requirements	Ease of use Safety Human factors impact
Labor requirements	Direct to indirect ratio Skills and training
Flexibility	General-purpose versus special-purpose equipment Special tooling
Setup requirements	Complexity Changeover speed
Maintenance	Complexity Frequency Availability of parts
Obsolescence	State of the art Modification for use in other situations
In-process inventory	Timing and need for supporting buffer stocks
Systemwide impacts	Tie-in with existing or planned systems Control activities Fit with manufacturing strategy

EXAMPLE 6.1: Break-Even Analysis

Suppose a manufacturer has identified the following options for obtaining a machined part: It can buy the part at $200 per unit (including materials); it can make the part on a numerically controlled semiautomatic lathe at $75 per unit (including materials); or it can make the part on a machining center at $15 per unit (including materials). There is negligible fixed cost if the item is purchased; a semiautomatic lathe costs $80,000; and a machining center costs $200,000.

The total cost for each option is

$$\text{Purchase cost} = \$200 \times \text{Demand}$$

$$\text{Produce-using-lathe cost} = \$80,000 + \$75 \times \text{Demand}$$

$$\text{Produce-using-machining-center cost} = \$200,000 + \$15 \times \text{Demand}$$

SOLUTION

Whether we approach the solution to this problem as cost minimization or profit maximization really makes no difference as long as the relationships remain linear: that is, variable costs and revenue are the same for each incremental unit. Exhibit 6.4 shows the break-even point for each process. If demand is expected to be more than 2,000 units (point A), the machine center is the best choice because this would result in the

Break-Even Chart of Alternative Processes

exhibit 6.4

Excel: Breakeven Analysis

lowest total cost. If demand is between 640 (point B) and 2,000 units, the semiautomatic lathe is the cheapest. If demand is less than 640 (between 0 and point B), the most economical course is to buy the product.

The break-even point A calculation is

$$\$80,000 + \$75 \times \text{Demand} = \$200,000 + \$15 \times \text{Demand}$$

$$\text{Demand (point A)} = 120,000/60 = 2,000 \text{ units}$$

if demand < 640 buy

The break-even point B calculation is

$$\$200 \times \text{Demand} = \$80,000 + \$75 \times \text{Demand}$$

$$\text{Demand (point B)} = 80,000/125 = 640 \text{ units}$$

Consider the effect of revenue, assuming the part sells for $300 each. As Exhibit 6.4 shows, profit (or loss) is the distance between the revenue line and the alternative process cost. At 1,000 units, for example, maximum profit is the difference between the $300,000 revenue (point C) and the semiautomatic lathe cost of $155,000 (point D). For this quantity the semiautomatic lathe is the cheapest alternative available. The optimal choices for both minimizing cost and maximizing profit are the lowest segments of the lines: origin to B, to A, and to the right side of Exhibit 6.4 as shown in red. ●

MANUFACTURING PROCESS FLOW DESIGN

⊙⊙⊙⊙ Manufacturing process flow design is a method to evaluate the specific processes that raw materials, parts, and subassemblies follow as they move through the plant. The most common production management tools used in planning and designing the process flow are assembly drawings, assembly charts, route sheets, and flow process charts. Each of these charts is a useful diagnostic tool and can be used to improve operations during the steady state of the productive system. Indeed, the standard first step in analyzing any production system is to map the flows and operations using one or more of these techniques. These are the "organization charts" of the manufacturing system.

An *assembly drawing* (Exhibit 6.5) is simply an exploded view of the product showing its component parts. An *assembly chart* (Exhibit 6.6) uses the information presented in the assembly drawing and defines (among other things) how parts go together, their order of

exhibit 6.5

Plug Assembly Drawing

exhibit 6.6

Assembly (or Gozinto) Chart for Plug Assembly

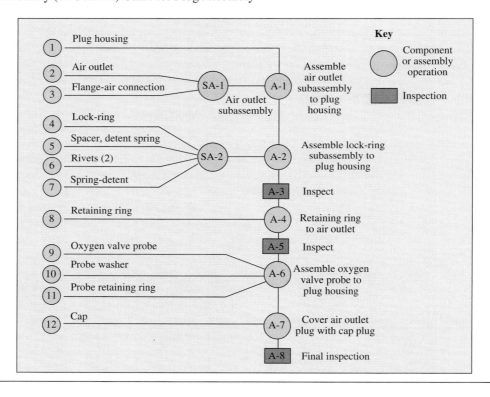

assembly, and often the overall material flow pattern.[1] An *operation and route sheet* (Exhibit 6.7), as its name implies, specifies operations and process routing for a particular part. It conveys such information as the type of equipment, tooling, and operations required to complete the part.

A *process flowchart* such as Exhibit 6.8 denotes what happens to the product as it progresses through the productive facility. Recall, process flowcharting was covered in Chapter 5. The focus in analyzing a manufacturing operation should be the identification of activities that can be minimized or eliminated, such as movement and storage within the process. As a rule, the fewer the moves, delays, and storages in the process, the better the flow.

Operation and Route Sheet for Plug Assembly

exhibit 6.7

Material Specs _____ Purchased Stock Size _____ Pcs. Per Pur Size _____ Weight _____		Part Name __ Plug Housing Usage __ Plug Assembly Assy. No. __ TA 1279 Sub.Assy. No. _____		Part No. __ TA 1274 Date Issued _____ Date Supplied _____ Issued By _____		

Oper. No.	Operation Description	Dept.	Machine	Setup Hr.	Rate Pc. Hr.	Tools
20	Drill hole .32 $^{+.015}_{-.005}$	Drill	Mach. 513 Drill	1.5	254	Drill fixture L-76 Jig # 10393
30	Deburr .312 $^{+.015}_{-.005}$ dia. hole	Drill	Mach. 510 Drill	.1	424	Multitooth burring tool
40	Chamfer .009/875. bore .878/.875 dia (2 passes). bore .7600/7625 (1 pass)	Lathe	Mach. D 109 lathe	1.0	44	Ramet-1, TPG 221, chamfer tool
50	Tap hole as designated 1/4 min. full thread	Tap	Mach. 517 drill tap	2.0	180	Fixture #CR-353 tap. 4 Flute sp.
60	Bore hole 1.33 to 1.138 dia.	Lathe	H&H E107	3.0	158	L44 turret fixture Hartford
						Superspacer, pl. #45 holder #L46
						FDTW-100, insert #21 chk. fixture
70	Deburr .005 to.010 both sides, hand feed to hard stop	Lathe	E162 lathe	.3	175	Collect CR #179 1327 RPM
80	Broach keyway to remove thread burrs	Drill	Mach. 507 drill	.4	91	B87 fixture, L59 broach tap. .875120 G-H6
90	Hone thread I.D. .822/ .828	Grind	Grinder	1.5	120	
95	Hone .7600/ .7625	Grind	Grinder	1.5	120	

Process Flowchart for the Plug Housing (partial)

exhibit 6.8

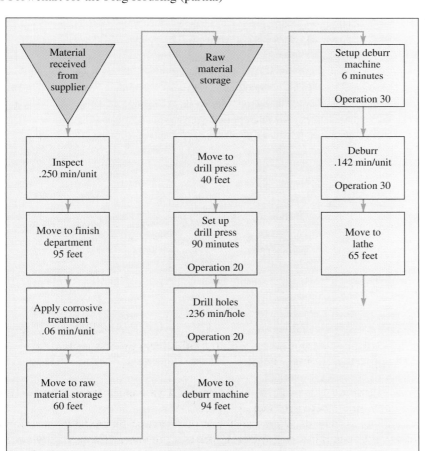

Example 6.2: Manufacturing Process Analysis

Recall from Chapter 5 that a process usually consists of (1) a set of *tasks,* (2) a *flow* of material and information that connects the set of tasks, and (3) *storage* of material and information.

1. Each task in a process accomplishes, to a certain degree, the transformation of input into the desired output.
2. The flow in a process consists of material flow as well as flow of information. The flow of material transfers a product from one task to its next task. The flow of information helps in determining how much of the transformation has been done in the previous task and what exactly remains to be completed in the present task.
3. When neither a task is being performed nor a part is being transferred, the part has to be stored. Goods in storage, waiting to be processed by the next task, are often called *work-in-process inventory.*

Process analysis involves adjusting the capacities and balance among different parts of the process to maximize output or minimize the costs with available resources. Our company supplies a component to several large auto manufacturers.[2] This component is assembled in a shop by 15 workers working an eight-hour shift on an assembly line that moves at the rate of 150 components per hour. The workers receive their pay in the form of a group incentive amounting to 30 cents per completed good part. This wage is distributed equally among the workers. Management believes that it can hire 15 more workers for a second shift if necessary.

Parts for the final assembly come from two sources. The molding department makes one very critical part and the rest come from outside suppliers. There are 11 machines capable of molding the one part done in-house; but historically, one machine is being overhauled or repaired at any given time. Each machine requires a full-time operator. The machines could each produce 25 parts per hour, and the workers are paid on an individual piece rate of 20 cents per good part. The workers will work overtime at a 50 percent increase in rate, or for 30 cents per good part. The workforce for molding is flexible; currently, only six workers are on this job. Four more are available from a labor pool within the company. The raw materials for each part molded cost 10 cents per part; a detailed analysis by the accounting department has concluded that 2 cents of electricity is used in making each part. The parts purchased from the outside cost 30 cents for each final component produced.

This entire operation is located in a rented building costing $100 per week. Supervision, maintenance, and clerical employees receive $1,000 per week. The accounting department charges depreciation for equipment against this operation at $50 per week.

The process flow diagram just below describes the process. The tasks have been shown as rectangles and the storage of goods (inventories) as triangles.

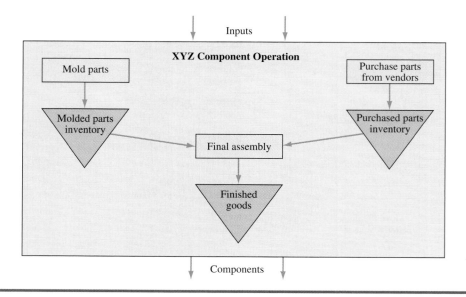

SOLUTION

a. Determine the capacity (number of components produced per week) of the entire process. Are the capacities of all the processes balanced?

Capacity of the molding process:

Only six workers are employed for the molding process, each working as a full-time operator for one machine. Thus, only 6 of the 11 machines are operational at present.

$$\text{Molding capacity} = \frac{6 \text{ machines} \times 25 \text{ parts per hour per machine} \times 8 \text{ hours per day} \times 5 \text{ days per week}}{}$$

$$= 6{,}000 \text{ parts per week}$$

Capacity of the assembly process:

$$\text{Assembly capacity} = \frac{150 \text{ components per hour} \times 8 \text{ hours per day} \times 5 \text{ days per week}}{}$$

$$= 6{,}000 \text{ components per week}$$

Because capacity of both the tasks is 6,000 units per week, they are balanced.

b. If the molding process were to use 10 machines instead of 6, and no changes were to be made in the final assembly task, what would be the capacity of the entire process?

Molding capacity with 10 machines:

$$\text{Molding capacity} = \frac{10 \text{ machines} \times 25 \text{ parts per hour per machine} \times 8 \text{ hours per day} \times 5 \text{ days per week}}{}$$

$$= 10{,}000 \text{ parts per week}$$

Because no change has been made in the final assembly task, the capacity of the assembly process remains 6,000 components per week. Thus, even though the molding capacity is 10,000 per week, the capacity of the entire process is only 6,000 per week because in the long run the overall capacity cannot exceed the slowest task.

c. If our company went to a second shift of eight more hours on the assembly task, what would be the new capacity?

A second shift on the assembly task:

As calculated in the previous section, the molding capacity is 10,000.

$$\text{Assembly capacity} = \frac{150 \text{ components per hour} \times 16 \text{ hours per day} \times 5 \text{ days per week}}{}$$

$$= 12{,}000 \text{ components per week}$$

Here, even though the assembly capacity is 12,000 per week, the capacity of the entire process remains at 10,000 per week because now the slowest task is the molding process, which has a capacity of 10,000 per week. Thus, we can note here that capacity of a process is not a constant factor; it depends on the availability of inputs and the sequence of tasks. In fact, it depends on several other factors not covered here.

d. Determine the cost per unit output when the capacity is (1) 6,000 per week or (2) 10,000 per week.

(1) Cost per unit when output per week = 6,000

First, we calculate the cost of producing all the 6,000 parts per week:

ITEM	CALCULATION	COST
Raw material for molding	$0.10 per part × 6,000 =	$ 600
Parts purchased from outside	$0.30 per component × 6,000 =	1,800
Electricity	$0.02 per part × 6,000 =	120
Molding labor	$0.20 per part × 6,000 =	1,200
Assembly labor	$0.30 per part × 6,000 =	1,800
Rent	$100 per week	100
Supervision	$1,000 per week	1,000
Depreciation	$50 per week	50
Total cost		$6,670

$$\text{Cost per unit} = \frac{\text{Total cost per week}}{\text{Number of units produced per week}} = \frac{\$6{,}670}{6{,}000} = \$1.11$$

(2) Cost per unit when output per week = 10,000

Next, we calculate the cost of producing all the 10,000 parts per week:

ITEM	CALCULATION	COST
Raw material for molding	$0.10 per part × 10,000 =	$ 1,000
Parts purchased from outside	$0.30 per component × 10,000 =	3,000
Electricity	$0.02 per part × 10,000 =	200
Molding labor	$0.20 per part × 10,000 =	2,000
Assembly labor	$0.30 per part × 10,000 =	3,000
Rent	$100 per week	100
Supervision	$1,000 per week	1,000
Depreciation	$50 per week	50
Total cost		$10,350

$$\text{Cost per unit} = \frac{\text{Total cost per week}}{\text{Number of units produced per week}} = \frac{\$10,350}{10,000} = \$1.04$$

As you can see, our cost per unit has been reduced by spreading the fixed cost over a greater number of units.

Such process analysis calculations are required for many production decisions discussed throughout this book. ●

CONCLUSION

Designing a customer-pleasing product is an art. Building the product is a science. Moving the product from design to the customer is management. World-class manufacturers excel at the speedy and flexible integration of these processes. A key to this is teamwork, not only on the part of marketing, product development, manufacturing, and distribution, but on the part of the supplier and customer as well.

Effective process planning requires clear understanding of what the factory can and cannot do relative to process structures. Many plants use a combination of the structures identified in this chapter—job shops for some parts, batch or assembly operations for others. Frequently a choice exists as to when demand seems likely to favor a switch from one to the other. Making such decisions also requires understanding the nuances of each production process to determine if the process really fits new product specifications. On a day-to-day basis, it requires the ability to systematically analyze capacity capabilities of each processing step, as was done in this chapter.

Finally, there is the issue of technology. Although the details of manufacturing processes constitute the world of the engineer, awareness of modern technologies—particularly computer-integrated manufacturing—is now seen as an essential part of a business education. CIM, along with other operations technologies, is discussed in Supplement B, "Operations Technology."

KEY TERMS

Job shop A process structure suited for low-volume production of a great variety of nonstandard products.

Batch shop A process structure that produces a variety of standard products at relatively low volumes. The products are produced periodically in batches to reduce the impact of setup time on equipment.

Assembly line A process structure designed to make discrete parts. Parts are moved through a set of specially designed workstations at a controlled rate.

Continuous flow An often automated process structure that converts raw materials into finished product in one continuous process.

Product–process matrix Shows the relationship between process structures and product volume and variety characteristics.

SOLVED PROBLEMS

SOLVED PROBLEM 1

A company is considering adding a new feature that will increase unit sales by 6 percent and product cost by 10 percent. Profit is expected to increase by 16 percent of the increased sales. Initially the product cost incurred by the company was 63 percent of the sales price. Should the new feature be added?

Solution

Let the sales be $100 M.

Sales increase by 6% = $100 M × 6% = $6 M.

    Benefits: Profits increase by 16% of the increased sales = $6 M × 16% = $0.96 M.

    Cost: Increase product cost by 10% = ($100 M × 63%) × 10% = $6.3 M.

Because costs exceed benefits, the new feature should not be added.

SOLVED PROBLEM 2

An automobile manufacturer is considering a change in an assembly line that should save money due to a reduction in labor and material cost. The change involves the installation of four new robots that will automatically install windshields. The cost of the four robots, including installation and initial programming, is $400,000. Current practice is to amortize the initial cost of robots over two years on a straight-line basis. The process engineer estimates that one full-time technician will be needed to monitor, maintain, and reprogram the robots on an ongoing basis. This person will cost approximately $60,000 per year. Currently, the company uses four full-time employees on this job and each makes about $52,000 per year. One of these employees is a material handler, and this person will still be needed with the new process. To complicate matters, the process engineer estimates that the robots will apply the windshield sealing material in a manner that will result in a savings of $0.25 per windshield installed. How many automobiles need to be produced over the next two years to make the new robots an attractive investment? Due to the relatively short horizon, do not consider the time value of money.

Solution

Cost of the current process over the next two years is just the cost of the four full-time employees.

$$\$52,000/\text{employee} \times 4 \text{ employees} \times 2 \text{ years} = \$416,000$$

The cost of the new process over the next two years, assuming the robot is completely costed over that time, is the following:

$$(\$52,000/\text{material handler} + \$60,000/\text{technician}) \times 2 + \$400,000/\text{robots} - \$0.25 \times \text{autos}$$

Equating the two alternatives:

$$\$416,000 = \$624,000 - \$0.25 \times \text{autos}$$

Solving for the break-even point:

$$-\$208,000/-\$0.25 = 832,000 \text{ autos}$$

This indicates that to break even, 832,000 autos would need to be produced with the robots over the next two years.

REVIEW AND DISCUSSION QUESTIONS

1. What does the product–process matrix tell us? Where would you place a Chinese restaurant on the matrix?
2. It has been noted that during World War II Germany made a critical mistake by having its formidable Tiger tanks produced by locomotive manufacturers, while the less formidable U.S. Sherman tank was produced by American car manufacturers. Use the product–process matrix to explain that mistake and its likely result.
3. How does the production volume affect break-even analysis?
4. What is meant by a process? Describe its important features.

PROBLEMS

1 Consider the construction of a simple $8'' \times 10''$ wood picture frame. The picture frame consists of four wood pieces that are cut from the wood molding, four staples to hold the frame together, a piece of glass, a backing board made of cardboard, six points to hold the glass and backing board to the frame, and a clip for hanging the picture frame from the wall.

   a. Construct an assembly chart for the picture frame.

   b. Construct a flowchart for the entire process from receiving materials to final inspection.

2 The purpose of this system design exercise is to gain experience in setting up a manufacturing process. (We suggest that this be done as a team project.) Assignment:

   a. Get one Ping-Pong paddle.

   b. Specify the type of equipment and raw materials you would need to manufacture that paddle, from the receipt of seasoned wood to packaging for shipment.

   c. Assume that one unit of each type of equipment is available to you. Further assume that you have a stock of seasoned wood and other materials needed to produce and box 100 paddles. Making reasonable assumptions about times and distances where necessary,

   (1) Develop an assembly drawing for the paddle.

   (2) Prepare an assembly chart for the paddle.

   (3) Develop a process flowchart for the paddle.

   (4) Develop a route sheet for the paddle.

3 The Goodparts Company produces a component that is subsequently used in the aerospace industry. The component consists of three parts (A, B, and C) that are purchased from outside and cost 40, 35, and 15 cents per piece, respectively. Parts A and B are assembled first on assembly line 1, which produces 140 components per hour. Part C undergoes a drilling operation before being finally assembled with the output from assembly line 1. There are in total six drilling machines, but at present only three of them are operational. Each drilling machine drills part C at a rate of 50 parts per hour. In the final assembly, the output from assembly line 1 is assembled with the drilled part C. The final assembly line produces at a rate of 160 components per hour. At present, components are produced eight hours a day and five days a week. Management believes that if need arises, it can add a second shift of eight hours for the assembly lines.

   The cost of assembly labor is 30 cents per part for each assembly line; the cost of drilling labor is 15 cents per part. For drilling, the cost of electricity is 1 cent per part. The total overhead cost has been calculated as $1,200 per week. The depreciation cost for equipment has been calculated as $30 per week.

   a. Draw a process flow diagram and determine the process capacity (number of components produced per week) of the entire process.

   b. Suppose a second shift of eight hours is run for assembly line 1 and the same is done for the final assembly line. In addition, four of the six drilling machines are made operational. The drilling machines, however, operate for just eight hours a day. What is the new process capacity (number of components produced per week)? Which of the three operations limits the capacity?

   c. Management decides to run a second shift of eight hours for assembly line 1 plus a second shift of only four hours for the final assembly line. Five of the six drilling machines operate for eight hours a day. What is the new capacity? Which of the three operations limits the capacity?

   d. Determine the cost per unit output for questions *b* and *c*.

   e. The product is sold at $4.00 per unit. Assume that the cost of a drilling machine (fixed cost) is $30,000 and the company produces 8,000 units per week. Assume that four drilling machines are used for production. If the company had an option to buy the same part at $3.00 per unit, what would be the break-even number of units?

4 A book publisher has fixed costs of $300,000 and variable costs per book of $8.00. The book sells for $23.00 per copy.[3]

   a. How many books must be sold to break even?

   b. If the fixed cost increased, would the new break-even point be higher or lower?

   c. If the variable cost per unit decreased, would the new break-even point be higher or lower?

5 A manufacturing process has a fixed cost of $150,000 per month. Each unit of product being produced contains $25 worth of material and takes $45 of labor. How many units are needed to break even if each completed unit has a value of $90?

6 Assume a fixed cost of $900, a variable cost of $4.50, and a selling price of $5.50.

   a. What is the break-even point?

   b. How many units must be sold to make a profit of $500.00?

   c. How many units must be sold to average $0.25 profit per unit? $0.50 profit per unit? $1.50 profit per unit?

7   Aldo Redondo drives his own car on company business. His employer reimburses him for such travel at the rate of 36 cents per mile. Aldo estimates that his fixed costs per year such as taxes, insurance, and depreciation are $2,052. The direct or variable costs such as gas, oil, and maintenance average about 14.4 cents per mile. How many miles must he drive to break even?

8   A firm is selling two products, chairs and bar stools, each at $50 per unit. Chairs have a variable cost of $25 and bar stools $20. Fixed cost for the firm is $20,000.
   a. If the sales mix is 1:1 (one chair sold for every bar stool sold), what is the break-even point in dollars of sales? In units of chairs and bar stools?
   b. If the sales mix changes to 1:4 (one chair sold for every four bar stools sold), what is the break-even point in dollars of sales? In units of chairs and bar stools?

9   How would you characterize the most important difference for the following issues when comparing a job shop and a flow shop?

ISSUE	JOB SHOP	FLOW SHOP
Number of changeovers		
Labor content of product		
Flexibility		

10   The diagram below represents a process where two components are made at stations A1 and A2 (one component is made at A1 and the other at A2). These components are then assembled at station B and moved through the rest of the process, where some additional work is completed at stations C, D, and E.

   Assume that one and only one person is allowed at each station. Assume that the times given below for each station represent the amount of work that needs to be done at that station by that person, with no processing time variation. Assume that inventory is not allowed to build in the system.

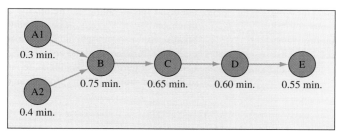

   What is the average hourly output of the process when it is in normal operation?

11   A certain custom engraving shop has traditionally had orders for between 1 and 50 units of whatever a customer orders. A large company has contacted this shop about engraving "reward" plaques (which are essentially identical to each other). It wants the shop to place a bid for this order. The expected volume is expected to be 12,000 units per year and will most likely last four years. To successfully bid (low enough price) for such an order, what will the shop likely have to do?

12   The product–process matrix is a convenient way of characterizing the relationship between product volumes (one-of-a-kind to continuous) and the processing system employed by a firm at a particular location. In the boxes presented below, describe the nature of the intersection between the type of shop (column) and process dimension (row).

	JOB SHOP	FLOW SHOP
Engineering emphasis		
General workforce skill		
Statistical process control		
Facility layout		
WIP inventory level		

13   For each of the following variables, explain the differences (in general) as one moves from a job shop to a flow shop environment.
   a. Throughput time (time to convert raw material into product).
   b. Capital/labor intensity.
   c. Bottlenecks.

CASE: CIRCUIT BOARD FABRICATORS, INC.

Circuit Board Fabricators, Inc. (CBF), is a small manufacturer of circuit boards located in California near San Jose. Companies such as Apple Computer and Hewlett-Packard use the company to make boards for prototypes of new products. It is important that CBF give quick and very-high-quality service. The engineers working on the new products are on a tight schedule and have little patience with sloppy work or missing delivery dates.

Circuit boards are a rigid flat surface where electronic components are mounted. Electronic components such as integrated circuits, resistors, capacitors, and diodes are soldered to the boards. Lines called "traces" are etched on the board and electronically connect the components. Since the electronic traces cannot cross, holes through the circuit board are used to connect traces on both sides of the boards, thus allowing complex circuits to be implemented. These boards often are designed with 40–50 components that are connected through hundreds of traces on a small four- by six-inch board.

CBF has developed a good business plan. They have four standard-size board configurations and have automated much of their process for making these standard boards. Fabricating the boards requires CBF's numerically controlled (NC) equipment to be programmed. This is largely an automated process that works directly from engineering drawings that are formatted using industry standard codes.

Currently, the typical order is for 60 boards. Engineers at customer companies prepare a computer-aided design (CAD) drawing of the board. This CAD drawing precisely specifies each circuit trace, circuit pass-through holes, and component mounting points on the board. An electronic version of the drawing is used by a CBF process engineer to program the NC machines used to fabricate the boards.

Due to losses in the system, CBF has a policy of increasing the size of an order by 25 percent. For example, for a typical order consisting of 60 boards, 75 boards would be started through the process. Fifteen percent of the boards are typically rejected during an inspection that occurs early in the manufacturing process and another 5 percent of the remaining boards are rejected in final test.

BOARD FABRICATION PROCESS

CBF purchases circuit board blanks from a vendor. These boards are made from woven fiberglass cloth that is impregnated with epoxy. A layer of copper is laminated onto each side to form a blank board. The blank board comes from the vendor trimmed to the standard sizes that CBF's numerically controlled equipment can handle.

The following is a description of the steps involved in processing an order at CBF:

1 **Order acceptance.** Check to verify that the order fits within the specification of boards that can be produced with CBF equipment. The process engineer at CBF works with the customer engineer to resolve any problems with the order.
2 **NC machine programming.** CAD information is used to program the machines to produce the order.
3 **Board fabrication.**
   a. **Clean.** Each board is manually loaded into this machine by an operator. The machine then cleans the boards with a special chemical. Each board is then automatically transferred to the coating machine.
   b. **Coat.** A liquid plastic coating is deposited on both sides of the board. Following this process, an operator places the

exhibit 6.9

Circuit Board Fabricators—Process Data

Required output per shift	1,000
Average job size (boards)	60
Production hours per day	7.5
Working days per week	5

Excel: Circuit Board Fabricators

PROCESS/MACHINE	NUMBER OF MACHINES	NUMBER OF EMPLOYEES	SETUP (MINUTES PER JOB)	RUN (MINUTES PER PART)
Load	1	1	5	0.33
Clean	1			0.5
Coat	1			0.5
Unload	1	1		0.33
Expose	5	5	15	1.72
Load	1	1	5	0.33
Develop	1			0.33
Inspect	2	2		0.5
Bake	1			0.33
Unload	1	1		0.33
Drilling	6	3	15	1.5
Copper plate	1	2	5	0.2
Final test	6	6	15	2.69

boards on a cart. Each cart, with a complete order of boards, is then moved immediately to the "clean room."

c. **Expose.**   This photographic process makes the exposed plastic coating resistant to dissolving in the areas where the copper traces are needed. An operator must attend to this machine 100 percent of the time, and load and unload each individual board.

d. **Develop.**   Each board is manually loaded onto this machine. The boards are dipped by the machine, one-at-a-time, in a chemical bath that dissolves the plastic and the underlying copper in the proper areas. After dipping, the machine places each board on a conveyor.

e. **Inspect.**   Each board is picked from the conveyor as it comes from the developer. The board is optically checked for defects using a machine similar to a scanner. Approximately 15 percent of the boards are rejected at this point. Boards that pass inspection are placed back on the conveyor that feeds the bake oven. Two inspectors are used at this station.

f. **Bake.**   Boards travel through a bake oven that hardens the plastic coating, thus protecting the traces. Boards are then manually unloaded and placed on a cart. When all the boards for an order are on the cart, it is moved to the drilling machines.

g. **Drilling.**   Holes are drilled using an NC machine to connect circuits on both sides of the board. The boards are manually loaded and unloaded. The machines are arranged so that one person can keep two machines going simultaneously. The cart is used to move the boards to the copper plate bath.

h. **Copper plate.**   Copper is deposited inside the holes by running the boards through a special copper plating bath. This copper connects the traces on both sides of the board. Each board is manually loaded on a conveyor that passes through the plating bath. Two people are needed for this process, one loading and a second unloading the conveyor.

On completion of plating, boards are moved on the cart to the final test machines.

i. **Final test.**   Using a special NC machine, a final electrical test of each board is performed to check the integrity of the circuits. On average, approximately 5 percent of the boards fail this test. The boards are manually loaded and unloaded. One person is needed to operate each machine and sort the good and bad boards. The cart is used to move the good boards to the shipping area. The bad boards are scrapped.

4 **Shipping.**   The completed order is packed and shipped to the customer.

The plant was designed to run 1,000 boards per day when running five days a week and one eight-hour shift per day. Unfortunately, to date they have not come near that capacity and on a good day are only able to produce about 700 boards. Data concerning the standard setup and run times for the fabrication process are given in Exhibit 6.9. These times include allowances for morning and afternoon breaks, but do not include time for the half-hour lunch period. In addition, data on current staffing levels also are provided. The CBF process engineer insists that the capacity at each process is sufficient to run 1,000 boards per day.

In order to help understand the problem, CBF hired a consulting company to help solve the problem.

ASSIGNMENT

CBF has hired you to help determine why they are not able to produce the 1,000 boards per day.

1 What type of process flow structure is CBF using?
2 Diagram the process in a manner similar to Exhibit 6.7.
3 Analyze the capacity of the process.
4 What is the impact of losses in the process in Inspection and Final Test?
5 What recommendations would you make for a short-term solution to CBF's problems?
6 What long-term recommendations would you make?

SELECTED BIBLIOGRAPHY

Hammer, M. "Reengineering Work: Don't Automate, Obliterate." *Harvard Business Review,* July–August 1990, pp. 104–12.

Hill, T. *Manufacturing Strategy.* 3rd ed. New York: Irwin/McGraw-Hill, 2000.

Hyer, N., and U. Wemmerlöv. *Reorganizing the Factory: Competing through Cellular Manufacturing.* Portland, OR: Productivity Press, 2002.

Schniederjans, M. J., and J. R. Olsen. *Advanced Topics in Just-in-Time Management.* Westport, CT: Quorum Books, 1999.

Womack, J. P., and D. T. Jones. *Lean Thinking: Banish Waste and Create Wealth in Your Corporation.* New York: Simon and Schuster, 1996.

FOOTNOTES

1 Also called a *Gozinto chart,* named, so the legend goes, after the famous Italian mathematician Zepartzat Gozinto.

2 This section is modified from P. W. Marshall et al., *Operations Management: Text and Cases* (Homewood, IL: Richard D. Irwin, 1975), pp. 12–16.

3 Special thanks to Professor W. Ruch of Arizona State University for his contribution of problems 4 through 8.

technical note six
FACILITY LAYOUT

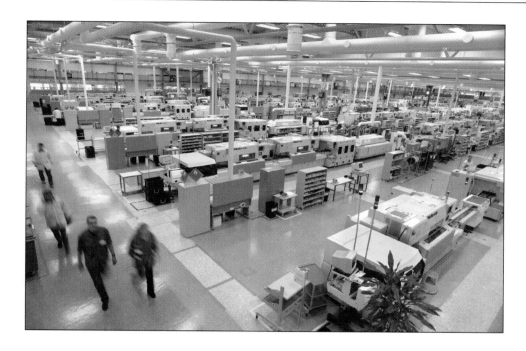

THIS SALO OPERATION IN MERIKAARI, FINLAND, IS ONE OF NINE NOKIA MOBILE FACTORIES WORLDWIDE. THE TOTAL FACTORY AREA IS OVER 15,000 SQUARE METERS AND IT EMPLOYS OVER 1,200.

Layout decisions entail determining the placement of departments, work groups within the departments, workstations, machines, and stock-holding points within a production facility. The objective is to arrange these elements in a way that ensures a smooth work flow (in a factory) or a particular traffic pattern (in a service organization). In general, the inputs to the layout decision are as follows:

1. Specification of the objectives and corresponding criteria to be used to evaluate the design. The amount of space required and the distance that must be traveled between elements in the layout are common basic criteria.
2. Estimates of product or service demand on the system.
3. Processing requirements in terms of number of operations and amount of flow between the elements in the layout.
4. Space requirements for the elements in the layout.
5. Space availability within the facility itself, or if this is a new facility, possible building configurations.

In our treatment of layout, we examine how layouts are developed under various formats (or work-flow structures). Our emphasis is on quantitative techniques, but we also show examples of how qualitative factors are important in the design of the layout. Both manufacturing and service facilities are covered in this technical note.

BASIC PRODUCTION LAYOUT FORMATS

The formats by which departments are arranged in a facility are defined by the general pattern of work flow; there are three basic types (process layout, product layout, and fixed-position layout) and one hybrid type (group technology or cellular layout).

A **process layout** (also called a *job-shop* or *functional layout*) is a format in which similar equipment or functions are grouped together, such as all lathes in one area and all stamping machines in another. A part being worked on then travels, according to the established sequence of operations, from area to area, where the proper machines are located for each operation. This type of layout is typical of hospitals, for example, where areas are dedicated to particular types of medical care, such as maternity wards and intensive care units.

A **product layout** (also called a *flow-shop layout*) is one in which equipment or work processes are arranged according to the progressive steps by which the product is made. The

Process layout

Service

Product layout

path for each part is, in effect, a straight line. Production lines for shoes, chemical plants, and car washes are all product layouts.

Group technology (cellular) layout

A **group technology (cellular) layout** groups dissimilar machines into work centers (or cells) to work on products that have similar shapes and processing requirements. A group technology (GT) layout is similar to a process layout in that cells are designed to perform a specific set of processes, and it is similar to a product layout in that the cells are dedicated to a limited range of products. (*Group technology* also refers to the parts classification and coding system used to specify machine types that go into a cell.)

Fixed-position layout

In a **fixed-position layout,** the product (by virtue of its bulk or weight) remains at one location. Manufacturing equipment is moved to the product rather than vice versa. Construction sites and movie lots are examples of this format.

Many manufacturing facilities present a combination of two layout types. For example, a given production area may be laid out by process, while another area may be laid out by product. It is also common to find an entire plant arranged according to product layout—for example, a parts fabrication area followed by a subassembly area, with a final assembly area at the end of the process. Different types of layouts may be used in each area, with a process layout used in fabrication, group technology in subassembly, and a product layout used in final assembly.

PROCESS LAYOUT

The most common approach to developing a process layout is to arrange departments consisting of like processes in a way that optimizes their relative placement. For example, the departments in a low-volume toy factory might consist of the shipping and

DESIGN STYLING STUDIO 1, PRODUCTION LINE, PAINT SHOP, AND PRODUCTION LINE 3 FOR LOTUS ELISE FACILITY IN HETHEL, UNITED KINGDOM.

receiving department, the plastic molding and stamping department, the metal forming department, the sewing department, and the painting department. Parts for the toys are fabricated in these departments and then sent to assembly departments where they are put together. In many installations, optimal placement often means placing departments with large amounts of interdepartment traffic adjacent to one another.

Suppose that we want to arrange the eight departments of a toy factory to minimize the interdepartmental material handling cost. Initially, let us make the simplifying assumption that all departments have the same amount of space (say, 40 feet by 40 feet) and that the building is 80 feet wide and 160 feet long (and thus compatible with the department dimensions). The first things we would want to know are the nature of the flow between departments and how the material is transported. If the company has another factory that makes similar products, information about flow patterns might be abstracted from the records. On the other hand, if this is a new product line, such information would have to come from routing sheets or from estimates by knowledgeable personnel such as process or industrial engineers. Of course, these data, regardless of their source, will have to be modified to reflect the nature of future orders over the projected life of the proposed layout.

Let us assume that this information is available. We find that all material is transported in a standard-size crate by forklift truck, one crate to a truck (which constitutes one "load"). Now suppose that transportation costs are $1 to move a load between adjacent departments and $1 extra for each department in between. The expected loads between departments for the first year of operation are tabulated in Exhibit TN6.1; available plant space is depicted in Exhibit TN6.2. Note that in our example, diagonal moves are permitted so that departments 2 and 3, and 3 and 6, are considered adjacent.

Interdepartmental Flow

Flow between Departments (Number of Moves)

	1	2	3	4	5	6	7	8
1		175	50	0	30	200	20	25
2			0	100	75	90	80	90
3				17	88	125	99	180
4					20	5	0	25
5						0	180	187
6							374	103
7								7
8								

Department	Activity
1	Shipping and receiving
2	Plastic molding and stamping
3	Metal forming
4	Sewing department
5	Small toy assembly
6	Large toy assembly
7	Painting
8	Mechanism assembly

Building Dimensions and Departments

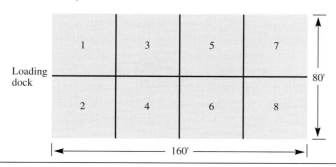

Interdepartmental Flow Graph with Number of Annual Movements

Cost Matrix—First Solution

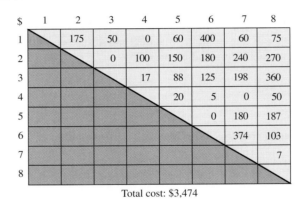

$	1	2	3	4	5	6	7	8
1		175	50	0	60	400	60	75
2			0	100	150	180	240	270
3				17	88	125	198	360
4					20	5	0	50
5						0	180	187
6							374	103
7								7
8								

Total cost: $3,474

Given this information, our first step is to illustrate the interdepartmental flow by a model, such as Exhibit TN6.3. This provides the basic layout pattern, which we will try to improve.

The second step is to determine the cost of this layout by multiplying the material handling cost by the number of loads moved between each pair of departments. Exhibit TN6.4 presents this information, which is derived as follows: The annual material handling cost between Departments 1 and 2 is $175 ($1 × 175 moves), $60 between Departments 1 and 5 ($2 × 30 moves), $60 between Departments 1 and 7 ($3 × 20 moves), $240 between diagonal Departments 2 and 7 ($3 × 80), and so forth. (The "distances" are taken from Exhibit TN6.2 or TN6.3, not Exhibit TN6.4.)

The third step is a search for departmental changes that will reduce costs. On the basis of the graph and the cost matrix, it seems desirable to place Departments 1 and 6 closer together to reduce their high move-distance costs. However, this requires shifting several other departments, thereby affecting their move-distance costs and the total cost of the second solution. Exhibit TN6.5 shows the revised layout resulting from relocating Department 6 and an adjacent department. (Department 4 is arbitrarily selected for this purpose.) The revised cost matrix for the exchange, showing the cost changes, is given in Exhibit TN6.6. Note the total cost is $262 *greater* than in the initial solution. Clearly, doubling the distance between Departments 6 and 7 accounted for the major part of the cost increase. This points out the fact that, even in a small problem, it is rarely easy to decide the correct "obvious move" on the basis of casual inspection.

Thus far, we have shown only one exchange among a large number of potential exchanges; in fact, for an eight-department problem, there are 8! (or 40,320) possible arrangements.

Excel: Process Layout

Revised Interdepartmental Flow Chart (Only interdepartmental flow with effect on cost is depicted.)

Cost Matrix—Second Solution

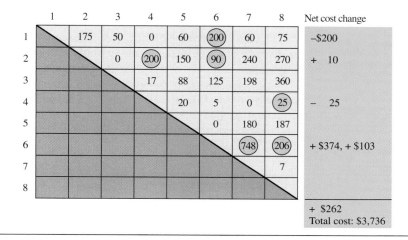

A Feasible Layout

Small toy assembly	Mechanism assembly	Shipping and receiving	Large toy assembly
5	8	1	6
Metal forming	Plastic molding and stamping	Sewing	Painting
3	2	4	7

Therefore, the procedure we have employed would have only a remote possibility of achieving an optimal combination in a reasonable number of tries. Nor does our problem stop here.

Suppose that we *do* arrive at a good solution solely on the basis of material handling cost, such as that shown in Exhibit TN6.7 (whose total cost is $3,550). We would note, first of all, that our shipping and receiving department is near the center of the factory—an arrangement that probably would not be acceptable. The sewing department is next to the painting department, introducing the hazard that lint, thread, and cloth particles might drift onto painted items. Further, small toy assembly and large toy assembly are located at opposite ends of the plant, which would increase travel time for assemblers (who very likely would be needed in both departments at various times of the day) and for supervisors (who might otherwise supervise both departments simultaneously). Often factors other than material handling cost need to be considered in finalizing a layout.

COMPUTERIZED LAYOUT TECHNIQUES—CRAFT

A number of computerized layout programs have been developed since the 1970s to help devise good process layouts. Of these, the most widely applied is the Computerized Relative Allocation of Facilities Technique (**CRAFT**).[1]

CRAFT

The CRAFT method follows the same basic idea that we developed in the layout of the toy factory, but with some significant operational differences. Like the toy factory example, it requires a load matrix and a distance matrix as initial inputs, but in addition, it requires a cost per unit distance traveled, say, $.10 per foot moved. (Remember, we made the simplifying assumption that cost doubled when material had to jump one department, tripled when it had to jump two departments, and so forth.) With these inputs and an initial layout in the program, CRAFT then tries to improve the relative placement of the departments as measured by total material handling cost for the layout. (Material handling cost between departments = Number of loads × Rectilinear distance between department centroids × Cost per unit distance.) It makes improvements by exchanging pairs of departments iteratively until no further cost reductions are possible. That is, the program calculates the effect on total cost of exchanging departments; if this yields a reduction, the exchange is made, which constitutes an iteration. As we saw in the manual method, the departments are part of a material flow network, so even a simple pairwise exchange generally will affect flow patterns among many other departments.

EXAMPLE TN6.1: Applying CRAFT to the Toy Factory

This example shows how CRAFT is applied to the toy factory problem defined in Exhibits TN6.4–TN6.7.

SOLUTION

A CRAFT layout solution to the toy factory problem is shown in Exhibit TN6.8. It provides a higher-cost layout than the manual one ($3,497 versus $3,244). Note, however, that these costs are not precisely comparable because CRAFT uses rectilinear distances as opposed to Euclidean (straight-line) distances, and links centroids of departments instead of "entrances." Because we were not given cost-per-unit distances in this example, CRAFT simply broke the stated $1-per-unit cost of movement between

---

exhibit TN6.8   CRAFT Solution to Toy Factory Layout

Shipping and receiving	Large toy assembly	Painting	Metal forming
50¢	50¢ 50¢ 50¢		
Sewing	Plastic molding and stamping	Small toy assembly	Mechanism assembly
50¢	50¢		

Material handling cost between departments	1 and 2 = $2 × 175 = $350
	6 and 7 = $1 × 374 = $374

departments into 50¢ segments. Exhibit TN6.8 shows two example calculations of the CRAFT movement costs. (Having square departments in the toy factory makes this calculation method a reasonable one for example purposes.) Also note that we fixed the location of the shipping and receiving department in the CRAFT solution so that it would be adjacent to the loading dock. ●

Distinguishing features of CRAFT and issues relating to it are as follows:

1. It is a heuristic program. It uses a simple rule of thumb in making evaluations: "Compare two departments at a time and exchange them if it reduces the total cost of the layout." This type of rule is obviously necessary to analyze even a modest-size layout.
2. It does not guarantee an optimal solution.
3. CRAFT is biased by its starting conditions: where you start (that is, the initial layout) will determine the final layout.
4. Starting with a reasonably good solution is more likely to yield a lower-cost final solution, but it does not always. This means that a good strategy for using CRAFT is to generate a variety of different starting layouts to expose the program to different pairwise exchanges.
5. It can handle up to 40 departments and rarely exceeds 10 iterations in arriving at a solution.
6. CRAFT departments consist of combinations of square modules (typically representing floor areas 10 feet by 10 feet). This permits multiple departmental configurations, but often results in strange departmental shapes that have to be modified manually to obtain a realistic layout.
7. A modified version called SPACECRAFT has been developed to handle multistory layout problems.[2]
8. CRAFT assumes the existence of variable-path material handling equipment such as forklift trucks. Therefore, when computerized fixed-path equipment is employed, CRAFT's applicability is greatly reduced.

SYSTEMATIC LAYOUT PLANNING

In certain types of layout problems, numerical flow of items between departments either is impractical to obtain or does not reveal the qualitative factors that may be crucial to the placement decision. In these situations, the venerable technique known as **systematic layout planning (SLP)** can be used.[3] It involves developing a relationship chart showing the degree of importance of having each department located adjacent to every other department. From this chart, an activity relationship diagram, similar to the flow graph used for illustrating material handling between departments, is developed. The activity relationship diagram is then adjusted by trial and error until a satisfactory adjacency pattern is obtained. This pattern, in turn, is modified department by department to meet building space limitations. Exhibit TN6.9 illustrates the technique with a simple five-department problem involving laying out a floor of a department store.

Systematic layout planning (SLP)

The SLP approach has been quantified for ease of evaluating alternative layouts. This entails assigning numerical weights to the closeness preferences and then trying different layout arrangements. The layout with the highest total closeness score is selected. For example, weights of 16 for "A," 8 for "E," 4 for "I," 2 for "O," 0 for "U," and −80 for "X" could be assigned. The choice of this weight structure is rather ad hoc, but the logic is that the most undesirable preference weighting (−80 for "X") is five times worse than the most desirable weighting of 16 for "A." Applying this weighting scheme using the software gives a score of 40 to the final layout in Exhibit TN6.9. (The score is the summation of the preference scores for each pair—in this case, 10 pairs. Exchanges may be made randomly, by user choice, or by pairs in this software program.)

Systematic Layout Planning for a Floor of a Department Store

A. Relationship Chart (based on Tables B and C)

From	To				Area (sq. ft.)
	2	3	4	5	
1. Credit department	I / 6	U / —	E / 4	U / —	100
2. Toy department		U / —	I / 1	A / 1,6	400
3. Wine department			U / —	X / 1	300
4. Camera department				X / 1	100
5. Candy department					100

Letter	Closeness rating
Number	Reason for rating

B.

CODE	REASON*
1	Type of customer
2	Ease of supervision
3	Common personnel
4	Contact necessary
5	Share same space
6	Psychology

*Others may be used.

C.

VALUE	CLOSENESS	LINE CODE*	NUMERICAL WEIGHTS
A	Absolutely necessary	≡	16
E	Especially important	≡	8
I	Important	=	4
O	Ordinary closeness OK	—	2
U	Unimportant		0
X	Undesirable	∧∧	−80

*Used for example purposes only.

Initial relationship diagram (based on Tables A and C)

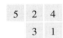

Initial layout based on relationship diagram (ignoring space and building constraints)

Final layout adjusted by square footage and building size

PRODUCT LAYOUT

The basic difference between product layout and process layout is the pattern of work flow. As we have seen in process layout, the pattern can be highly variable because material for any given job may have to be routed to the same processing department several times during its production cycle. In product layout, equipment or departments are dedicated to a particular product line, duplicate equipment is employed to avoid backtracking, and a straight-line flow of material movement is achievable. Adopting a product layout makes sense when the batch size of a given product or part is large relative to the number of different products or parts produced.

ASSEMBLY LINES

Assembly lines are a special case of product layout. In a general sense, the term *assembly line* refers to progressive assembly linked by some material handling device. The usual assumption is that some form of pacing is present and the allowable processing time is equivalent for all workstations. Within this broad definition, there are important differences among line types.

A few of these are material handling devices (belt or roller conveyor, overhead crane); line configuration (U-shape, straight, branching); pacing (mechanical, human); product mix (one product or multiple products); workstation characteristics (workers may sit, stand, walk with the line, or ride the line); and length of the line (few or many workers). For many readers, their first exposure to assembly lines is in the *I Love Lucy* episode where Lucy and Ethel are putting candies in paper wrappings on a fast-moving line and in order to keep up, they resort to sticking them in their pockets and finally in their mouths. While this clearly overstates the pressure of assembly line work, there is no doubt that speed and dexterity are of the essence in real situations such as automobile lines. For worker insight, see the box titled "What's It Like Working on an Assembly Line?"

The range of products partially or completely assembled on lines includes toys, appliances, autos, planes, guns, garden equipment, clothing, and a wide variety of electronic components. In fact, it is probably safe to say that virtually any product that has multiple parts and is produced in large volume uses assembly lines to some degree. Clearly, lines are an important technology; to really understand their managerial requirements, we should have some familiarity with how a line is balanced.

ASSEMBLY-LINE BALANCING

Though primarily a scheduling issue, assembly-line balancing often has implications for layout. This would occur when, for balance purposes, workstation size or the number used would have to be physically modified.

The most common assembly line is a moving conveyor that passes a series of workstations in a uniform time interval called the **workstation cycle time** (which is also the time between successive units coming off the end of the line). At each workstation, work is performed on a product either by adding parts or by completing assembly operations. The work performed at each station is made up of many bits of work, termed *tasks, elements,* and *work units.* Such tasks are described by motion–time analysis. Generally, they are groupings that cannot be subdivided on the assembly line without paying a penalty in extra motions.

Workstation cycle time

The total work to be performed at a workstation is equal to the sum of the tasks assigned to that workstation. The **assembly-line balancing** problem is one of assigning all tasks to a series of workstations so that each workstation has no more than can be done in the workstation cycle time, and so that the unassigned (that is, idle) time across all workstations is minimized. The problem is complicated by the relationships among tasks imposed by product design and process technologies. This is called the **precedence relationship,** which specifies the order in which tasks must be performed in the assembly process.

Assembly-line balancing

Precedence relationship

WHAT'S IT LIKE WORKING ON AN ASSEMBLY LINE?

Ben Hamper, the infamous "Rivethead" working for General Motors, describes his new job on the Chevy Suburban assembly line with the following:

> The whistle blew and the Rivet Line began to crawl. I took a seat up on the workbench and watched the guy I was replacing tackle his duties. He'd grab one end of a long rail and, with the help of the worker up the line from him, flip it over on its back. CLAAAANNNNNNGGGG! He then raced back to the bench and grabbed a four-wheel-drive spring casting and a muffler hanger. He would rivet the pieces onto the rail. With that completed, he'd jostle the rail back into an upright position and grab a cross member off the overhanging feeder line that curled above the bench. Reaching up with his spare arm, he'd grab a different rivet gun while fidgeting to get the cross member firmly planted so that it aligned with the proper set of holes. He then inserted the rivets and began

> squashing the cross member into place. Just watching this guy go at it made my head hurt.

> "How about takin' a stab at it?" the guy asked me after a while. "You're not gonna get the feel of the job sittin' up there on the bench."

> I politely declined. I didn't want to learn any portion of this monster maze before it was absolutely necessary. Once the bossman thought you had a reasonable grasp of the setup, he was likely to step in and turn you loose on your own. I needed to keep delaying in order to give Art some time to reel me back up to Cab Shop.

> "Well, you've got three days," the guy replied. "After that, this baby's all yours."

EXCERPT FROM B. HAMPER'S *RIVETHEAD: TALES FROM THE ASSEMBLY LINE* (NEW YORK: WARNER BOOKS, 1992), P. 90.

Interactive Operations Management

The steps in balancing an assembly line are straightforward:

1. Specify the sequential relationships among tasks using a precedence diagram. The diagram consists of circles and arrows. Circles represent individual tasks; arrows indicate the order of task performance.
2. Determine the required workstation cycle time (C), using the formula

$$C = \frac{\text{Production time per day}}{\text{Required output per day (in units)}}$$

3. Determine the theoretical minimum number of workstations (N_t) required to satisfy the workstation cycle time constraint using the formula (note that this must be rounded up to the next highest integer)

$$N_t = \frac{\text{Sum of task times } (T)}{\text{Cycle time } (C)}$$

4. Select a primary rule by which tasks are to be assigned to workstations, and a secondary rule to break ties.
5. Assign tasks, one at a time, to the first workstation until the sum of the task times is equal to the workstation cycle time, or no other tasks are feasible because of time or sequence restrictions. Repeat the process for Workstation 2, Workstation 3, and so on until all tasks are assigned.
6. Evaluate the efficiency of the balance derived using the formula[4]

$$\text{Efficiency} = \frac{\text{Sum of task times } (T)}{\text{Actual number of workstations } (N_a) \times \text{Workstation cycle time } (C)}$$

7. If efficiency is unsatisfactory, rebalance using a different decision rule.

EXAMPLE TN6.2: Assembly-Line Balancing

The Model J Wagon is to be assembled on a conveyor belt. Five hundred wagons are required per day. Production time per day is 420 minutes, and the assembly steps and times for the wagon are given in Exhibit TN6.10. Assignment: Find the balance that minimizes the number of workstations, subject to cycle time and precedence constraints.

SOLUTION

1. Draw a precedence diagram. Exhibit TN6.11 illustrates the sequential relationships identified in Exhibit TN6.10. (The length of the arrows has no meaning.)
2. Determine workstation cycle time. Here we have to convert to seconds because our task times are in seconds.

$$C = \frac{\text{Production time per day}}{\text{Output per day}} = \frac{60 \text{ sec.} \times 420 \text{ min.}}{500 \text{ wagons}} = \frac{25{,}200}{500} = 50.4$$

Assembly Steps and Times for Model J Wagon

TASK	TASK TIME (IN SECONDS)	DESCRIPTION	TASKS THAT MUST PRECEDE
A	45	Position rear axle support and hand fasten four screws to nuts.	—
B	11	Insert rear axle.	A
C	9	Tighten rear axle support screws to nuts.	B
D	50	Position front axle assembly and hand fasten with four screws to nuts.	—
E	15	Tighten front axle assembly screws.	D
F	12	Position rear wheel #1 and fasten hubcap.	C
G	12	Position rear wheel #2 and fasten hubcap.	C
H	12	Position front wheel #1 and fasten hubcap.	E
I	12	Position front wheel #2 and fasten hubcap.	E
J	8	Position wagon handle shaft on front axle assembly and hand fasten bolt and nut.	F, G, H, I
K	9	Tighten bolt and nut.	J
	195		

Precedence Graph for Model J Wagon

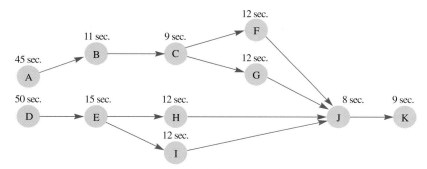

3. Determine the theoretical minimum number of workstations required (the actual number may be greater):

$$N_t = \frac{T}{C} = \frac{195 \text{ seconds}}{50.4 \text{ seconds}} = 3.87 = 4 \text{ (rounded up)}$$

4. Select assignment rules. Research has demonstrated that some rules are better than others for certain problem structures. In general, the strategy is to use a rule assigning tasks that either have many followers or are of long duration because they effectively limit the balance achievable. In this case, we use the following as our primary rule:
    a. Prioritize tasks in order of the largest number of following tasks.

TASK	NUMBER OF FOLLOWING TASKS
A	6
B or D	5
C or E	4
F, G, H, or I	2
J	1
K	0

Our secondary rule, to be invoked where ties exist from our primary rule, is
    b. Prioritize tasks in order of longest task time (shown in Exhibit TN6.12). Note that D should be assigned before B, and E assigned before C due to this tiebreaking rule.

5. Make task assignments to form Workstation 1, Workstation 2, and so forth until all tasks are assigned. The actual assignment is given in Exhibit TN6.12A and is shown graphically in Exhibit TN6.12B. It is important to meet precedence and cycle time requirements as the assignments are made.

6. Calculate the efficiency. This is shown in Exhibit TN6.12C.

7. Evaluate the solution. An efficiency of 77 percent indicates an imbalance or idle time of 23 percent (1.0 − .77) across the entire line. From Exhibit TN6.12A we can see that there are 57 total seconds of idle time, and the "choice" job is at Workstation 5.

Is a better balance possible? In this case, yes. Try balancing the line with rule *b* and breaking ties with rule *a*. (This will give you a feasible four-station balance.) ●

SPLITTING TASKS

Often the longest required task time forms the shortest workstation cycle time for the production line. This task time is the lower time bound unless it is possible to split the task into two or more workstations.

Consider the following illustration: Suppose that an assembly line contains the following task times in seconds: 40, 30, 15, 25, 20, 18, 15. The line runs for $7\frac{1}{2}$ hours per day and demand for output is 750 per day.

The workstation cycle time required to produce 750 per day is 36 seconds ($[7\frac{1}{2}$ hours × 60 minutes × 60 seconds]/750). Our problem is that we have one task that takes 40 seconds. How do we deal with this task?

There are several ways that we may be able to accommodate the 40-second task in a 36-second cycle. Possibilities are

1. **Split the task.** Can we split the task so that complete units are processed in two workstations?

2. **Share the task.** Can the task somehow be shared so an adjacent workstation does part of the work? This differs from the split task in the first option because the adjacent station acts to assist, not to do some units containing the entire task.

A. Balance Made According to Largest-Number-of-Following-Tasks Rule

	TASK	TASK TIME (IN SECONDS)	REMAINING UNASSIGNED TIME (IN SECONDS)	FEASIBLE REMAINING TASKS	TASK WITH MOST FOLLOWERS	TASK WITH LONGEST OPERATION TIME
Station 1	A	45	5.4 idle	None		
Station 2	D	50	0.4 idle	None		
Station 3	B	11	39.4	C, E	C, E	E
	E	15	24.4	C, H, I	C	
	C	9	15.4	F, G, H, I	F, G, H, I	F, G, H, I
	F*	12	3.4 idle	None		
Station 4	G	12	38.4	H, I	H, I	H, I
	H*	12	26.4	I		
	I	12	14.4	J		
	J	8	6.4 idle	None		
Station 5	K	9	41.4 idle	None		

*Denotes task arbitrarily selected where there is a tie between longest operation times.

B. Precedence Graph for Model J Wagon

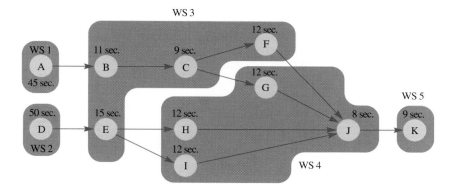

C. Efficiency Calculation

$$\text{Efficiency} = \frac{T}{N_a C} = \frac{195}{(5)(50.4)} = .77, \text{ or } 77\%$$

3. **Use parallel workstations.** It may be necessary to assign the task to two workstations that would operate in parallel.
4. **Use a more skilled worker.** Because this task exceeds the workstation cycle time by just 11 percent, a faster worker may be able to meet the 36-second time.
5. **Work overtime.** Producing at a rate of one every 40 seconds would create 675 per day, 75 short of the needed 750. The amount of overtime required to produce the additional 75 is 50 minutes (75 × 40 seconds/60 seconds).
6. **Redesign.** It may be possible to redesign the product to reduce the task time slightly.

Other possibilities to reduce the task time include an equipment upgrade, a roaming helper to support the line, a change of materials, and multiskilled workers to operate the line as a team rather than as independent workers.

Flexible Line Layouts

Bad: Operators caged. No chance
to trade elements of work
between them.
(Subassembly line layout
common in American plants.)

Better: Operators can trade elements of
work. Can add and subtract
operators. Trained ones can
nearly self-balance at different
output rates.

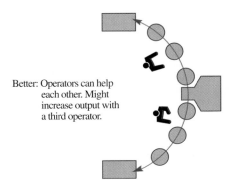

Bad: Operators birdcaged. No chance
to increase output with a
third operator.

Better: Operators can help
each other. Might
increase output with
a third operator.

Bad: Straight line difficult to balance.

Better: One of several advantages
of U-line is better operator
access. Here, five operators
were reduced to four.

SOURCE: R. W. HALL, *ATTAINING MANUFACTURING EXCELLENCE* (HOMEWOOD, IL: DOW JONES-IRWIN, 1987), P. 125. COPYRIGHT
© 1987 MCGRAW-HILL COMPANIES INC.

FLEXIBLE AND U-SHAPED LINE LAYOUTS

As we saw in the preceding example, assembly-line balances frequently result in unequal work-station times. Flexible line layouts such as those shown in Exhibit TN6.13 are a common way of dealing with this problem. In our toy company example, the U-shaped line with work sharing at the bottom of the figure could help resolve the imbalance.

MIXED-MODEL LINE BALANCING

This approach is used by JIT manufacturers such as Toyota. Its objective is to meet the demand for a variety of products and to avoid building high inventories. Mixed-model line balancing involves scheduling several different models to be produced over a given day or week on the same line in a cyclical fashion.

EXAMPLE TN6.3: Mixed-Model Line Balancing

To illustrate how this is done, suppose our toy company has a fabrication line to bore holes in its Model J wagon frame and its Model K wagon frame. The time required to bore the holes is different for each wagon type.

Assume that the final assembly line downstream requires equal numbers of Model J and Model K wagon frames. Assume also that we want to develop a cycle time for the fabrication line that is balanced for the production of equal numbers of J and K frames. Of course, we could produce Model J frames for several days and then produce Model K frames until an equal number of frames have been produced. However, this would build up unnecessary work-in-process inventory.

If we want to reduce the amount of in-process inventory, we could develop a cycle mix that greatly reduces inventory buildup while keeping within the restrictions of equal numbers of J and K wagon frames.

Process times: 6 minutes per J and 4 minutes per K.

The day consists of 480 minutes (8 hours × 60 minutes).

SOLUTION

$$6J + 4K = 480$$

Because equal numbers of J and K are to be produced (or J = K), produce 48J and 48K per day, or 6J and 6K per hour.

The following shows one balance of J and K frames.

Balanced Mixed-Model Sequence

Model sequence	J J	K K K	J J	J J	K K K	
Operation time	6 6	4 4 4	6 6	6 6	4 4 4	Repeats 8 times per day
Minicycle time	12	12	12	12	12	
Total cycle time			60			

This line is balanced at 6 frames of each type per hour with a minicycle time of 12 minutes.

Another balance is J K K J K J, with times of 6, 4, 4, 6, 4, 6. This balance produces 3J and 3K every 30 minutes with a minicycle time of 10 minutes (JK, KJ, KJ). ●

The simplicity of mixed-model balancing (under conditions of a level production schedule) is seen in Yasuhiro Mondon's description of Toyota Motor Corporation's operations:

> Final assembly lines of Toyota are mixed product lines. The production
> per day is averaged by taking the number of vehicles in the monthly

production schedule classified by specifications, and dividing by the number of working days.

In regard to the production sequence during each day, the cycle time of each different specification vehicle is calculated. To have all specification vehicles appear at their own cycle time, different specification vehicles are ordered to follow each other.[5]

CURRENT THOUGHTS ON ASSEMBLY LINES

It is true that the widespread use of assembly-line methods in manufacturing has dramatically increased output rates. Historically, the focus has almost always been on full utilization of human labor—that is, to design assembly lines minimizing human idle time. Equipment and facility utilization stood in the background as much less important. Past research has tried to find optimal solutions as if the problem stood in a never-changing world.

Newer views of assembly lines take a broader perspective. The intentions are to incorporate greater flexibility in products produced on the line, more variability in workstations (such as size and number of workers), improved reliability (through routine preventive maintenance), and high-quality output (through improved tooling and training). The Breakthrough box on Dell Computer describes how a combination of assembly lines and manufacturing cells (the topic of the next section) can be used when product demand changes quickly.

BREAKTHROUGH

DELL COMPUTER'S SERVER PLANT USES CELLS

The one-person build cells that populate the heart of the plant enhance flexibility—a critical element of Dell Computer's direct build-to-order model. Assisted by Web-based online work instructions, an experienced operator in a standard cell can assemble any of the 10 basic server platforms in various configurations.

"With the old-style progressive-build approach, you pretty much batched your build every day," notes Mark Lozano, senior production control manager. "You couldn't change what was

going down the line. But here, you can build whatever you want when you want. In one cell we can have a high-end machine following a low-end machine. That kind of flexibility allows us a much shorter cycle time for all of our platforms."

Server components begin their journey through the plant at one of two locations. In one area, motherboards are prepped and installed into the computer chassis. In the second, a kitting area, other components are pulled from storage racks with the aid of a computerized "pick to light" system and placed into totes. From there, intelligent conveyors—linked to a manufacturing execution system—deliver the materials to an open build cell using a pull process.

In the cell the operator does the rest, including putting in the screws. "The next person who can open it up is the customer," says Kris Vorm, director of server engineering. No downstream quality inspector examines the innards of the unit, unless subsequent electronic tests indicate a pesky quality problem. Under a buddy system, a builder will ask another operator to make a visual inspection before he or she screws the cover onto the box. Next stop is the extended test rack, where detailed diagnostics are conducted prior to downloading and testing the operating system and application software—all based on customer specifications.

GROUP TECHNOLOGY (CELLULAR) LAYOUT

Group technology (or cellular) layout allocates dissimilar machines into cells to work on products that have similar shapes and processing requirements. Group technology (GT) layouts are now widely used in metal fabricating, computer chip manufacture, and assembly work. The overall objective is to gain the benefits of product layout in job-shop kinds of production. These benefits include

1. **Better human relations.**   Cells consist of a few workers who form a small work team; a team turns out complete units of work.
2. **Improved operator expertise.**   Workers see only a limited number of different parts in a finite production cycle, so repetition means quick learning.
3. **Less in-process inventory and material handling.**   A cell combines several production stages, so fewer parts travel through the shop.
4. **Faster production setup.**   Fewer jobs mean reduced tooling and hence faster tooling changes.

DEVELOPING A GT LAYOUT

Shifting from process layout to a GT cellular layout entails three steps:

1. Grouping parts into families that follow a common sequence of steps. This step requires developing and maintaining a computerized parts classification and coding system. This is often a major expense with such systems, although many companies have developed shortcut procedures for identifying parts families.
2. Identifying dominant flow patterns of parts families as a basis for location or relocation of processes.
3. Physically grouping machines and processes into cells. Often there will be parts that cannot be associated with a family and specialized machinery that cannot be placed in any one cell because of its general use. These unattached parts and machinery are placed in a "remainder cell."

Exhibit TN6.14 illustrates the cell development process for four part families. Part A shows the original process layout. Part B shows a routing matrix based on flow of parts. Part C illustrates the final organization of cells, with equipment organized in the traditional U shape. The example assumes that there are multiple lathes, mills, and so forth, so that each cell will have the requisite number of each type physically located within it.

VIRTUAL GT CELLS

When equipment is not easily movable, many companies dedicate a given machine out of a set of identical machines in a process layout. A virtual GT cell for, say, a two-month production run for the job might consist of Drill 1 in the drills area, Mill 3 in the mill area, and Assembly Area 1 in the machine assembly area. To approximate a GT flow, all work on the particular part family would be done only on these specific machines.

FIXED-POSITION LAYOUT

Fixed-position layout is characterized by a relatively low number of production units in comparison with process and product layout formats. In developing a fixed-position layout, visualize the product as the hub of a wheel with materials and equipment arranged concentrically around the production point in their order of use and movement difficulty. Thus, in building custom yachts, for example, rivets that are used throughout construction would be placed close to or in the hull; heavy engine parts, which must travel to the hull only

Development of GT Cells

A. Original process layout

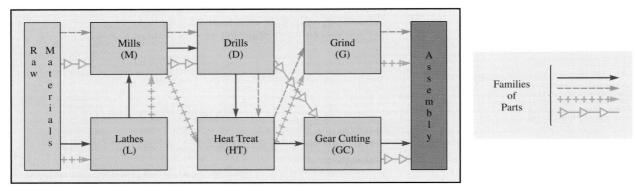

ADAPTED FROM D. FOGARTY AND T. HOFFMAN, *PRODUCTION AND INVENTORY MANAGEMENT* (CINCINNATI: SOUTH-WESTERN PUBLISHING, 1983), P. 472.

B. Routing matrix based upon flow of parts

Raw Materials	Part Family	Lathes	Mills	Drills	Heat Treating	Grinders	Gear Cutting	To	Assembly
	– – >	X		X		X	X	– – >	
	⊳–▷–	X		X	X	X		⊳–▷–	
	→	X	X	X	X			→	
	+ + >		X	X			X	+ + >	

C. Reallocating machines to form cells according to part family processing requirements

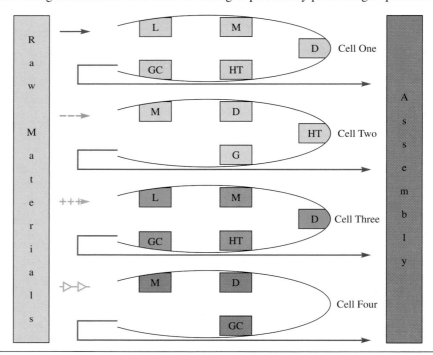

once, would be placed at a more distant location; and cranes would be set up close to the hull because of their constant use.

In fixed-position layout, a high degree of task ordering is common, and to the extent that this precedence determines production stages, a fixed-position layout might be developed by arranging materials according to their technological priority. This procedure would be expected in making a layout for a large machine tool, such as a stamping machine, where manufacture follows a rigid sequence; assembly is performed from the ground up, with parts being added to the base in almost a building-block fashion.

As far as quantitative layout techniques are concerned, there is little in the literature devoted to fixed-position formats, even though they have been utilized for thousands of years. In certain situations, however, it may be possible to specify objective criteria and develop a fixed-position layout through quantitative means. For instance, if the material handling cost is significant and the construction site permits more or less straight-line material movement, the CRAFT process layout technique might be advantageously employed.

RETAIL SERVICE LAYOUT

The objective of a *retail service layout* (as is found in stores, banks, and restaurants) is to maximize net profit per square foot of store space. A company that has been very successful in leveraging every inch of its layout space to achieve this objective is Taco Bell Restaurants. Exhibit TN6.15 illustrates Taco Bell store layouts used in 1986 and from 1991 to the present. The nature of the layout changes reflects actions required to support the company's value strategy of speed and low prices. Key operational modifications include elimination of many on-site food preparation steps, which simultaneously increased the speed

Service

Taco Bell Restaurant Floor Plans

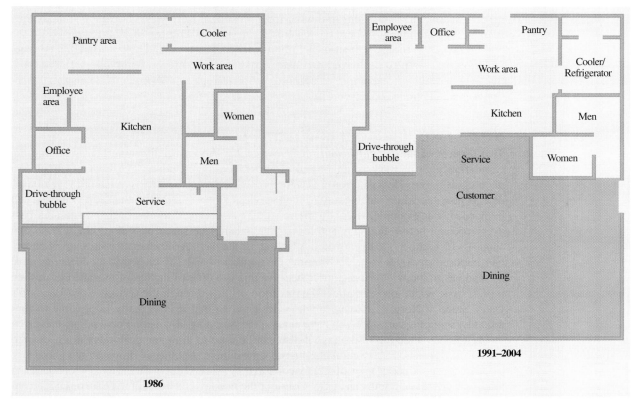

1986

1991–2004

of service while reducing the amount of working space needed. For example, the chopping and bagging of lettuce and the precooking and seasoning of meats, beans, and hard tortilla products are now done at central kitchens or by suppliers. The restaurant kitchens are now heating and assembly units only. In addition to such outsourcing, changes were made in queue structures, such as moving from a single line running parallel to the counter, to a double line running perpendicular to it. This improved product flow facilitated serving drive-through windows, increased capacity, and allowed customers to see assembly workers' faces (as opposed to just their backs, as was the case before).

SERVICESCAPES

As previously noted, the broad objective of layout in retail services is generally to maximize net profit per square foot of floor space. Operationally, this goal is often translated into such criteria as "minimize handling cost" or "maximize product exposure." However, as Sommers and Kernan observed more than 30 years ago, employing these and similar criteria in service layout planning "results in stores that look like warehouses and requires shoppers to approach the task like order pickers or display case stockers."[6] Of course, Wal-Mart and Home Depot customers gladly accept such arrangements for price savings.

There are other, more humanistic aspects of the service that also must be considered in the layout. Bitner coined the term *servicescape* to refer to the physical surroundings in which the service takes place and how these surroundings affect customers and employees. An understanding of the servicescape is necessary to create a good layout for the service firm (or the service-related portions of the manufacturing firm). The servicescape has three elements that must be considered: the ambient conditions; the spatial layout and functionality; and the signs, symbols, and artifacts.[7]

AMBIENT CONDITIONS

The term *ambient conditions* refers to background characteristics such as the noise level, music, lighting, temperature, and scent that can affect employee performance and morale as well as customers' perceptions of the service, how long they stay, and how much money they spend. Although many of these characteristics are influenced primarily by the design of the building (such as the placement of light fixtures, acoustic tiles, and exhaust fans), the layout within a building also can have an effect. Areas near food preparation will smell like food, lighting in a hallway outside a theater must be dim, tables near a stage will be noisy, and locations near an entrance will be drafty.

SPATIAL LAYOUT AND FUNCTIONALITY

Two aspects of the *spatial layout and functionality* are especially important: planning the circulation path of the customers and grouping the merchandise. The goal of circulation planning is to provide a path for the customers that exposes them to as much of the merchandise as possible while placing any needed services along this path in the sequence they will be needed. For example, IKEA furniture stores are designed to ensure that customers pass every product before they pay and leave. They also place snack bars along the way so that shoppers can grab a bite to eat without getting off the path. Aisle characteristics are of particular importance. Aside from determining the number of aisles to be provided, decisions must be made as to the width of the aisles because this is a direct function of expected or desired traffic. Aisle width also can affect the direction of flow through the service. Stew Leonard's Dairy Store in Norwalk, Connecticut, is designed so that it is virtually impossible to turn around a shopping cart once you have entered the shopping flow path. Focal points that catch the customers' attention in the layout also can be used to draw the customers in the desired direction. The famous blue light at Kmart is an example. Another is shown in the photo.

To enhance shoppers' view of merchandise as they proceed down a main aisle, secondary and tertiary aisles may be set at an angle. Consider the two layouts in Exhibit TN6.16. The rectangular layout would probably require less expensive fixtures and contain more display space. If storage considerations are important to the store management, this would be the more desirable

STEW LEONARD'S DESIGNS STORES TO MOVE CUSTOMERS ALONG A SHOPPING FLOW PATH. ENTERTAINING CHARACTERS SCATTERED THROUGHOUT THE STORE ARE USED TO CATCH CUSTOMERS' ATTENTION AND DRAW THEM INTO VARIOUS AREAS IN THE STORE.

Alternative Store Layouts

exhibit TN6.16

Merchandise Counters

layout. On the other hand, the angular layout provides the shopper with a much clearer view of the merchandise and, other things being equal, presents a more desirable selling environment.

It is common practice now to base merchandise groupings on the shopper's view of related items, as opposed to the physical characteristics of the products or shelf space and servicing requirements. This grouping-by-association philosophy is seen in boutiques in department stores and gourmet sections in supermarkets.

Special mention is in order for a few guidelines derived from marketing research and relating to circulation planning and merchandise grouping:

1. People in supermarkets tend to follow a perimeter pattern in their shopping behavior. Placing high-profit items along the walls of a store will enhance their probability of purchase.
2. Sale merchandise placed at the end of an aisle in supermarkets almost always sells better than the same sale items placed in the interior portion of an aisle.
3. Credit and other nonselling departments that require customers to wait for the completion of their services should be placed either on upper floors or in "dead" areas.
4. In department stores, locations nearest the store entrances and adjacent to front-window displays are most valuable in terms of sales potential.

SIGNS, SYMBOLS, AND ARTIFACTS

Signs, symbols, and artifacts refer to the parts of the service that have social significance. As with the ambiance, these are often a characteristic of the design of the building, although the orientation, location, and size of many objects and areas can carry special meaning. As examples,

- In the old days, bank loan officers were easily identified because their desks were located on a raised section of the bank floor called the platform.
- A person seated at the desk closest to the entrance is usually in charge of greeting customers and directing them to their destination.
- In a department store, the tiled areas indicate the aisles for travel, while carpeted areas indicate departments for browsing.
- Some car salespeople have blackboards installed in their offices because a person writing on a blackboard symbolizes someone who should be listened to and trusted (such as a teacher).

As you might have gathered from these examples, the influence of behavioral factors makes the development of hard and fast rules for servicescape layout rather difficult. Suffice it to say that making the layout choice is not simply a matter of choosing between display space and ease of operation.

OFFICE LAYOUT

Service

Global

The trend in *office layout* is toward more open offices, with personal work spaces separated only by low divider walls. Companies have removed fixed walls to foster greater communication and teamwork. (See, for example, the Breakthrough box titled "In New Drug Labs, 'Porches' and 'Huddle Zones.' ") Signs, symbols, and artifacts, as discussed in the section on service layout, are possibly even more important in office layout than in retailing. For instance, size and orientation of desks can indicate the importance or professionalism of the people behind them.

Central administration offices are often designed and laid out so as to convey the desired image of the company. For example, Scandinavian Airlines System's (SAS) administrative office complex outside Stockholm is a two-story collection of glass-walled pods that provide the feeling of the open communication and flat hierarchy (few levels of organization) that characterize the company's management philosophy.

Service-Master (the highly profitable janitorial management company) positions its "Know-How Room" at the center of its headquarters. This room contains all of the physical products, operations manuals, and pictorial displays of career paths and other symbols for the key knowledge essential to the business. "From this room, the rest of the company can be seen as a big apparatus to bring the knowledge of the marketplace to its employees and potential customers."[8]

CONCLUSION

Facility layout is where the rubber meets the road in the design and operation of a production system. A good factory (or office) layout can provide real competitive advantage by facilitating material and information flow processes. It also can enhance employees' work life. A good service layout can be an effective "stage" for playing out the service encounter. In conclusion, here are some marks of a good layout in these environments:

MARKS OF A GOOD LAYOUT FOR MANUFACTURING AND BACK-OFFICE OPERATIONS
1. Straight-line flow pattern (or adaptation).
2. Backtracking kept to a minimum.
3. Production time predictable.
4. Little interstage storage of materials.
5. Open plant floors so everyone can see what is happening.
6. Bottleneck operations under control.
7. Workstations close together.
8. Orderly handling and storage of materials.
9. No unnecessary rehandling of materials.
10. Easily adjustable to changing conditions.

MARKS OF A GOOD LAYOUT FOR FACE-TO-FACE SERVICES
1. Easily understood service flow pattern.
2. Adequate waiting facilities.
3. Easy communication with customers.
4. Easily maintained customer surveillance.
5. Clear exit and entry points with adequate checkout capabilities.
6. Departments and processes arranged so that customers see only what you want them to see.
7. Balance between waiting areas and service areas.
8. Minimum walking and material movement.
9. Lack of clutter.
10. High sales volume per square foot of facility.

KEY TERMS

Process layout Also called a *job-shop* or *functional layout;* a format in which similar equipment or functions are grouped together.

Product layout Also called a *flow-shop layout;* equipment or work processes are arranged according to the progressive steps by which the product is made.

Group technology (cellular) layout Groups dissimilar machines into work centers (or cells) to work on products that have similar shapes and processing requirements.

Fixed-position layout The product remains at one location and equipment is moved to the product.

CRAFT (Computerized Relative Allocation of Facilities Technique) A method to help devise good process layouts. The technique is designed to minimize material handling costs in the facility and works by iteratively exchanging pairs of departments until no further cost reductions are possible.

Systematic layout planning (SLP) A technique for solving process layout problems when the use of numerical flow data between departments is not practical. The technique uses an activity relationship diagram that is adjusted by trial and error until a satisfactory adjacency pattern is obtained.

Workstation cycle time The time between successive units coming off the end of an assembly line.

Assembly-line balancing The problem of assigning all the tasks to a series of workstations so that each workstation has no more than can be done in the workstation cycle time, and so that idle time across all workstations is minimized.

Precedence relationship The order in which tasks must be performed in the assembly process.

SOLVED PROBLEMS

SOLVED PROBLEM 1

A university advising office has four rooms, each dedicated to specific problems: petitions (Room A), schedule advising (Room B), grade complaints (Room C), and student counseling (Room D). The office is 80 feet long and 20 feet wide. Each room is 20 feet by 20 feet. The present location of rooms is A, B, C, D—that is, a straight line. The load summary shows the number of contacts that each adviser in a room has with other advisers in the other rooms. Assume that all advisers are equal in this value.

$$\text{Load summary: } AB = 10, AC = 20, AD = 30,$$
$$BC = 15, BD = 10, CD = 20.$$

a. Evaluate this layout according to the material handling cost method.

b. Improve the layout by exchanging functions within rooms. Show your amount of improvement using the same method as in *a.*

Solution

a.

Using the material handling cost method shown in the toy company example, we obtain the following costs, assuming that every nonadjacency doubles the initial cost/unit distance:

$$AB = 10 \times 1 = 10$$
$$AC = 20 \times 2 = 40$$
$$AD = 30 \times 3 = 90$$
$$BC = 15 \times 1 = 15$$
$$BD = 10 \times 2 = 20$$
$$CD = 20 \times 1 = 20$$
$$\text{Current cost} = 195$$

b. A better layout would be *BCDA*.

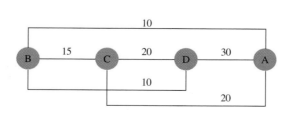

$$AB = 10 \times 3 = 30$$
$$AC = 20 \times 2 = 40$$
$$AD = 30 \times 1 = 30$$
$$BC = 15 \times 1 = 15$$
$$BD = 10 \times 2 = 20$$
$$CD = 20 \times 1 = 20$$
$$\text{Improved cost} = 155$$

SOLVED PROBLEM 2

The following tasks must be performed on an assembly line in the sequence and times specified:

TASK	TASK TIME (SECONDS)	TASKS THAT MUST PRECEDE
A	50	—
B	40	—
C	20	A
D	45	C
E	20	C
F	25	D
G	10	E
H	35	B, F, G

a. Draw the schematic diagram.
b. What is the theoretical minimum number of stations required to meet a forecast demand of 400 units per eight-hour day?
c. Use the longest-task-time rule and balance the line in the minimum number of stations to produce 400 units per day.

Solution

a.

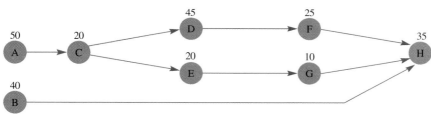

b. The theoretical minimum number of stations to meet $D = 400$ is

$$N_t = \frac{T}{C} = \frac{245 \text{ seconds}}{\left(\dfrac{60 \text{ seconds} \times 480 \text{ minutes}}{400 \text{ units}} \right)} = \frac{245}{72} = 3.4 \text{ stations}$$

c.

	TASK	TASK TIME (SECONDS)	REMAINING UNASSIGNED TIME	FEASIBLE REMAINING TASK
Station 1	A	50	22	C
	C	20	2	None
Station 2	D	45	27	E, F
	F	25	2	None
Station 3	B	40	32	E
	E	20	12	G
	G	10	2	None
Station 4	H	35	37	None

SOLVED PROBLEM 3

The manufacturing engineers at Suny Manufacturing were working on a new remote controlled toy Monster Truck. They hired a production consultant to help them determine the best type of production process to meet the forecasted demand for this new product. The consultant recommended that they use an assembly line. He told the manufacturing engineers that the line must be able to produce

600 Monster Trucks per day to meet the demand forecast. The workers in the plant work eight hours per day. The task information for the new monster truck is given below:

TASK	TASK TIME (SECONDS)	TASK THAT MUST PRECEDE
A	28	—
B	13	—
C	35	B
D	11	A
E	20	C
F	6	D,E
G	23	F
H	25	F
I	37	G
J	11	G,H
K	27	I,J
Total	236	

a. Draw the schematic diagram.

b. What is the required cycle time to meet the forecasted demand of 600 trucks per day based on an eight hour work day?

c. What is the theoretical minimum number of workstations given the answer in part *b*?

d. Use longest task time with alphabetical order as the tie breaker and balance the line in the minimum number of stations to produce 600 trucks per day.

e. Use shortest task time with largest number of following task as the tie breaker and balance the line in the minimum number of stations to produce 600 trucks per day.

Solution

a.

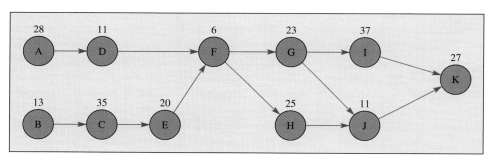

b. $C = \dfrac{\text{Production time per day}}{\text{Output per day}} = \dfrac{60 \text{ seconds} \times 480 \text{ minutes}}{600 \text{ trucks}} = \dfrac{28{,}800}{600} = 48 \text{ seconds}$

c. $N_t = \dfrac{T}{C} = \dfrac{236 \text{ seconds}}{48 \text{ seconds}} = 4.92 = 5 \text{ (rounded up)}$

d.

	FEASIBLE TASKS	TASK	TASK TIME (SECONDS)	REMAINING UNASSIGNED TIME
Station 1	A,B	A	28	20
	B,D	B	13	7
Station 2	C,D	C	35	13
	D	D	11	2

	FEASIBLE TASKS	TASK	TASK TIME (SECONDS)	REMAINING UNASSIGNED TIME
Station 3	E	E	20	28
	F	F	6	22
Station 4	G,H	H	25	23
	G	G	23	0
Station 5	I,J	I	37	11
	J	J	11	0
Station 6	K	K	27	21

e.

TASK	NUMBER OF FOLLOWING TASK
A	7
B	8
C	7
D	6
E	6
F	5
G	3
H	2
I	1
J	1
K	0

	FEASIBLE TASKS	TASK	TASK TIME (SECONDS)	REMAINING UNASSIGNED TIME
Station 1	A,B	B	13	35
	A,C	A	28	7
Station 2	C,D	D	11	37
	C	C	35	2
Station 3	E	E	20	28
	F	F	6	22
Station 4	G,H	G	23	25
	H,I	H	25	0
Station 5	I,J	J	11	37
	I	I	37	0
Station 6	K	K	27	21

REVIEW AND DISCUSSION QUESTIONS

1 What kind of layout is used in a physical fitness center?
2 What is the key difference between SLP and CRAFT?
3 What is the objective of assembly-line balancing? How would you deal with the situation where one worker, although trying hard, is 20 percent slower than the other 10 people on a line?
4 How do you determine the idle time percentage from a given assembly-line balance?

5   What information of particular importance do route sheets and process charts (discussed in Technical Note 5) provide to the layout planner?

6   What is the essential requirement for mixed-model lines to be practical?

7   Why might it be difficult to develop a GT layout?

8   In what respects is facility layout a marketing problem in services? Give an example of a service system layout designed to maximize the amount of time the customer is in the system.

9   Consider a department store. Which departments probably should not be located near each other? Would any departments benefit from close proximity?

10 How would a flowchart help in planning the servicescape layout? What sorts of features would act as focal points or otherwise draw customers along certain paths through the service? In a supermarket, what departments should be located first along the customers' path? Which should be located last?

PROBLEMS

1   The Cyprus Citrus Cooperative ships a high volume of individual orders for oranges to northern Europe. The paperwork for the shipping notices is done in the accompanying layout. Revise the layout to improve the flow and conserve space if possible.

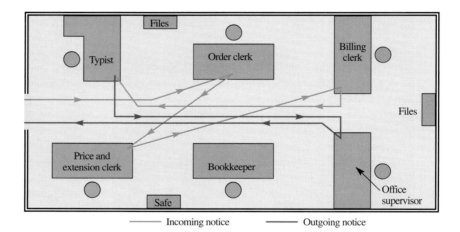

——— Incoming notice   ——— Outgoing notice

2   An assembly line makes two models of trucks: a Buster and a Duster. Busters take 12 minutes each and Dusters take 8 minutes each. The daily output requirement is 24 of each per day. Develop a perfectly balanced mixed-model sequence to satisfy demand.

3   An assembly line is to operate eight hours per day with a desired output of 240 units per day. The following table contains information on this product's task times and precedence relationships:

TASK	TASK TIME (SECONDS)	IMMEDIATE PREDECESSOR
A	60	—
B	80	A
C	20	A
D	50	A
E	90	B, C
F	30	C, D
G	30	E, F
H	60	G

a. Draw the precedence diagram.

b. What is the workstation cycle time?

c. Balance this line using the longest task time.

d. What is the efficiency of your line balance?

4   The desired daily output for an assembly line is 360 units. This assembly line will operate 450 minutes per day. The following table contains information on this product's task times and precedence relationships:

TASK	TASK TIME (SECONDS)	IMMEDIATE PREDECESSOR
A	30	—
B	35	A
C	30	A
D	35	B
E	15	C
F	65	C
G	40	E, F
H	25	D, G

a. Draw the precedence diagram.
b. What is the workstation cycle time?
c. Balance this line using the largest number of following tasks. Use the longest task time as a secondary criterion.
d. What is the efficiency of your line balance?

5   Some tasks and the order in which they must be performed according to their assembly requirements are shown in the following table. These are to be combined into workstations to create an assembly line. The assembly line operates $7\frac{1}{2}$ hours per day. The output requirement is 1,000 units per day.

TASK	PRECEDING TASKS	TIME (SECONDS)	TASK	PRECEDING TASKS	TIME (SECONDS)
A	—	15	G	C	11
B	A	24	H	D	9
C	A	6	I	E	14
D	B	12	J	F, G	7
E	B	18	K	H, I	15
F	C	7	L	J, K	10

a. What is the workstation cycle time?
b. Balance the line using the longest task time based on the 1,000-unit forecast, stating which tasks would be done in each workstation.
c. For *b*, what is the efficiency of your line balance?
d. After production was started, Marketing realized that they understated demand and must increase output to 1,100 units. What action would you take? Be specific in quantitative terms, if appropriate.

6   An initial solution has been given to the following process layout problem. Given the flows described and a cost of $2.00 per unit per foot, compute the total cost for the layout. Each location is 100 feet long and 50 feet wide as shown on the following figure. Use the centers of departments for distances and measure distance using metropolitan-rectilinear distance.

DEPARTMENT

		A	B	C	D
	A	0	10	25	55
DEPARTMENT	B		0	10	5
	C			0	15
	D				0

7 An assembly line is to be designed to operate $7\frac{1}{2}$ hours per day and supply a steady demand of 300 units per day. Here are the tasks and their performance times:

TASK	PRECEDING TASKS	PERFORMANCE TIME (SECONDS)	TASK	PRECEDING TASKS	PERFORMANCE TIME (SECONDS)
a	—	70	g	d	60
b	—	40	h	e	50
c	—	45	i	f	15
d	a	10	j	g	25
e	b	30	k	h, i	20
f	c	20	l	j, k	25

a. Draw the precedence diagram.
b. What is the workstation cycle time?
c. What is the theoretical minimum number of workstations?
d. Assign tasks to workstations using the longest operating time.
e. What is the efficiency of your line balance?
f. Suppose demand increases by 10 percent. How would you react to this? Assume that you can operate only $7\frac{1}{2}$ hours per day.

8 S. L. P. Craft would like your help in developing a layout for a new outpatient clinic to be built in California. From analysis of another recently built clinic, she obtains the data shown in the following diagram. This includes the number of trips made by patients between departments on a typical day (shown above the diagonal line) and the numbered weights (defined in Exhibit TN6.9) between departments as specified by the new clinic's physicians (below the diagonal). The new building will be 60 feet by 20 feet.
a. Develop an interdepartmental flow graph that minimizes patient travel.
b. Develop a "good" relationship diagram using systematic layout planning.
c. Choose either of the layouts obtained in *a* or *b* and sketch the departments to scale within the building.
d. Will this layout be satisfactory to the nursing staff? Explain.

DEPARTMENTS	2	3	4	5	6	AREA REQUIREMENT (SQ. FT.)
1 Reception	2 / A	5 / O	200 / E	0 / U	10 / O	100
2 X-ray		10 / E	300 / I	0 / U	8 / O	100
3 Surgery			100 / I	0 / U	4 / A	200
4 Examining rooms (5)				0 / U	15 / I	500
5 Lab					3 / O	100
6 Nurses' station						100

9 The following tasks are to be performed on an assembly line:

TASK	SECONDS	TASKS THAT MUST PRECEDE
A	20	—
B	7	A
C	20	B
D	22	B
E	15	C
F	10	D
G	16	E, F
H	8	G

The workday is seven hours long. Demand for completed product is 750 per day.

a. Find the cycle time.

b. What is the theoretical number of workstations?

c. Draw the precedence diagram.

d. Balance the line using sequential restrictions and the longest-operating-time rule.

e. What is the efficiency of the line balanced as in *d*?

f. Suppose that demand rose from 750 to 800 units per day. What would you do? Show any amounts or calculations.

g. Suppose that demand rose from 750 to 1,000 units per day. What would you do? Show any amounts or calculations.

10 The Dorton University president has asked the OM department to assign eight biology professors (A, B, C, D, E, F, G, and H) to eight offices (numbered 1 to 8 in the diagram) in the new biology building.

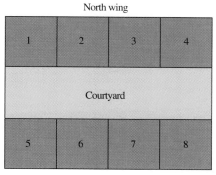

The following distances and two-way flows are given:

DISTANCES BETWEEN OFFICES (FEET)									TWO-WAY FLOWS (UNITS PER PERIOD)								
	1	2	3	4	5	6	7	8		A	B	C	D	E	F	G	H
1	—	10	20	30	15	18	25	34	A	—	2	0	0	5	0	0	0
2		—	10	20	18	15	18	25	B		—	0	0	0	3	0	2
3			—	10	25	18	15	18	C			—	0	0	0	0	3
4				—	34	25	18	15	D				—	4	0	0	0
5					—	10	20	30	E					—	1	0	0
6						—	10	20	F						—	1	0
7							—	10	G							—	4
8								—	H								—

a. If there are no restrictions (constraints) on the assignment of professors to offices, how many alternative assignments are there to evaluate?

b. The biology department has sent the following information and requests to the OM department:

> Offices 1, 4, 5, and 8 are the only offices with windows.
>
> A must be assigned Office 1.
>
> D and E, the biology department co-chairpeople, must have windows.
>
> H must be directly across the courtyard from D.
>
> A, G, and H must be in the same wing.
>
> F must *not* be next to D or G or directly across from G.

Find the optimal assignment of professors to offices that meets all the requests of the biology department and minimizes total material handling cost. You may use the path flow list as a computational aid.

PATH	FLOW	PATH	FLOW	PATH	FLOW	PATH	FLOW	PATH	FLOW
A–B	2	B–C	0	C–D	0	D–E	4	E–F	1
A–C	0	B–D	0	C–E	0	D–F	0	E–G	0
A–D	0	B–E	0	C–F	0	D–G	0	E–H	0
A–E	5	B–F	3	C–G	0	D–H	0	F–G	1
A–F	0	B–G	0	C–H	3			F–H	0
A–G	0	B–H	2					G–H	4
A–H	0								

11 The flow of materials through eight departments is shown in the table below. Even though the table shows flows into and out of the different departments, assume that the direction of flow is not important. In addition, assume that the cost of moving material depends only on the distance moved.

DEPARTMENTS

	1	2	3	4	5	6	7	8
1	—	20						
2	15	—	25				4	
3		5	—	40	5			
4			5	—	10			
5	1			20	—	30		
6						—	20	
7				3			—	10
8							5	—

a. Construct a schematic layout where the departments are arranged on a 2 × 4 grid with each cell representing a 10 × 10-meter square area.

b. Evaluate your layout using a distance-times-flow measure. Assume that distance is measured rectilinearly (in this case departments that are directly adjacent are 10 meters apart and those that are diagonal to one another are 20 meters apart).

12 A firm uses a serial assembly system and needs answers to the following:

a. A desired output of 900 units per shift (7.5 hours) is desired for a new processing system. The system requires product to pass through four stations where the work content at each station is 30 seconds. What is the required cycle time for such a system?

b. How efficient is your system with the cycle time you calculated?

c. Station 3 changes and now requires 45 seconds to complete. What will need to be done to meet demand (assume only 7.5 hours are available)? What is the efficiency of the new system?

13 A sheet metal shop was in moving to a new facility and wanted to create a layout for their new factory. The new building was 60 feet by 20 feet. The operations manager had looked into different methods for developing a layout and decided to try Systematic Layout Planning (SLP). He has worked with the project team to put together the information given below.

	2	3	4	5	6	AREA (SQ. FT.)
1. Cutting	A	E	I	U	U	200
2. Stamping		U	O	U	U	300
3. Welding			U	O	U	200
4. Etching				E	I	100
5. Sanding					X	200
6. Painting						200

a. Construct the initial relationship diagram based on the information given above and table C in exhibit TN6.9.

b. Use the answer in part *a* to create an initial layout for the sheet metal shop assuming all departments are of equal size.

c. Create a final layout by adjusting your answer in part *b* to account for square footage and building size.

ADVANCED PROBLEM

14 Francis Johnson's plant needs to design an efficient assembly line to make a new product. The assembly line needs to produce 15 units per hour and there is room for only four workstations. The tasks and the order in which they must be performed are shown in the following table. Tasks cannot be split, and it would be too expensive to duplicate any task.

TASK	TASK TIME (MINUTES)	IMMEDIATE PREDECESSOR
A	1	—
B	2	—
C	3	—
D	1	A, B, C
E	3	C
F	2	E
G	3	E

  a. Draw the precedence diagram.
  b. What is the workstation cycle time?
  c. Balance the line so that only four workstations are required. Use whatever method you feel is appropriate.
  d. What is the efficiency of your line balance?

CASE: VIRTUAL CELL AT ALAN GROUP, U.K.*

SYNOPSIS

Following a turbulent history of rapid growth followed by restructuring over the past 20 years the Company, now employing 57 people, is stable and successful. It is recognised as a "world class" operation in high precision engineer-to-order products and in high volume component manufacturing. It enjoys an outstanding employee skills/loyalty profile.

However, it is not meeting certain business goals nor generating the opportunity to grow both the business and the employees, which it desires. Organisational development through the introduction of a special form of cellular operation was proposed.

The challenge is to introduce a self-sustaining culture of organisational development alongside established technical excellence. The cellular working processes threaten established methods and certain employees, and have far-reaching consequences that cannot easily be tested in an incremental way before widespread introduction or perhaps total rejection. This case study describes the processes adopted by this small company in the crucial pilot phases of a special form of cellular operation.

THE COMPANY

Alan Group has 57 employees, all based in the U.K. The Company specialises in the design and manufacture of precision mould tools for the plastic injection moulding industry. Alan Group has the production capability to carry out high volume injection moulding; its main customers are in the communications and IT (information technology) sectors.

The Group has been identified as "world class" in surveys carried out by IBM Consultants and by the London Business School. They were presented with the Queen's Award for Export Achievement in 1994, and were competing in the 1995 Sussex Business Awards.

The Company's statement of purpose is:

The Alan Group is dedicated to the design and manufacture of "World Class" precision engineered products and, through its commitment to continuous improvement and unsurpassed quality, to providing lifetime support, superior value, and competitive advantage.

History

1973	Founded by Alan Mason and a partner, they were initially involved in the manufacture of interchangeable spare parts for die tools. Customers suggested that they should make complete tools. The Company was split into two divisions, with spares having five employees and the tooling division having one.
1980/1981	The Company bought its first injection moulding machine and started to concentrate on tooling for the plastics industry, alongside the production die side.
Mid-1980s	Embarked on rapid growth via a venture into Scotland, taking advantage of regional financial incentives. Initially, it was successful, but when a major customer reneged on a gentleman's agreement to place a very large order, they faced potentially enormous losses. Alan Group spent the next two years rebuilding the Scottish operation, and eventually sold it to an American company.

1988   The Company was bought out by venture capitalists, who were in the process of building a portfolio of companies. In addition to being given cash and shares in the Group, the partners were allowed to run the Company without outside interference. However, due to business practices by the venture capitalist, the Group went into receivership. With the help of the Receiver, Alan Mason was able to secure temporary financial backing to allow the preparation of a management buyout scheme.

It was at this time that Alan Mason's partner of 19 years wanted to end the partnership. The Company was bought back with the help of money from directors and employees of the firm. Eighty percent of the current employees are also shareholders, many with a significant vested interest in seeing the firm do well. These employees have had to wait until 1995 to see the first dividends being paid out.

Structure   The Company comprises three divisions:

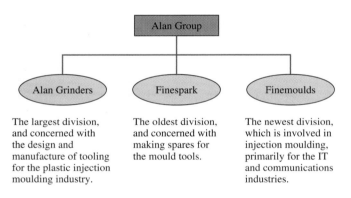

Alan Grinders and Finespark are further subdivided into sections, which cover each of the processes involved in their operations. These sections can have up to seven people, or as few as one. In charge of each section is a section leader, who besides normal duties as an operator, allocates particular jobs to others in the section. The main criteria used are the ability of the particular operator and the difficulty of the job. The section leader must sequence jobs to get them through their own section on time for final customer delivery. The section leaders do not deal directly with the customers.

Employee Skill Levels/Training   Everyone in the Company, with the exception of three office staff, is an apprentice-trained engineer. Therefore, all have a full appreciation of the work carried out on the shop floor, and indeed the directors are sometimes to be found working on the machines.

It is a point of pride that the Company trains its own apprentices, and operators' skills continue to be updated and added to long after their apprenticeship is finished. The labour turnover in the Alan Group is virtually zero.

The directors are engineers first, and managers second, largely due to their lack of formal management education. This is in the

process of being addressed and all of the directors have now undergone a training course in basic management theory.

Business Plan   In 1995, the Board devised an updated business plan. It covers their high-level plans for the growth of the business up to the year 2000, during which time they intend to increase turnover. They undertook a SWOT (Strengths, Weaknesses, Opportunities, and Threats) analysis of their current position, and identified issues that need to be addressed. These included:

- *Space for expansion.* The current premises are already cramped.
- *The availability of a skilled work force.* The planned rate of expansion is too fast for the Company to fill all of the vacancies with its own apprentices—and suitably skilled labour is scarce.
- *Management.* All levels in the Company will need education and training to manage the projected growth.

THE NEED TO CHANGE
Realisation of the need for change was the result of increasing awareness of influence, internally within the Company, and externally in the marketplace in which it operates. Alan Mason was the driving force. The catalyst was the formal recognition of the Company's status through the Queen's Award. This led to exposure to alternative practice and new business structures from government agencies, practitioners, and academics. The Company engaged The CIM Institute, Cranfield, U.K., to review its strategy options.[†]

Internal Influences   The primary internal indication of the need for change was the profit performance of the Company. Although Alan Group enjoys World Class status, a happy work force, and satisfied customers, it has not reaped the level of profit it could be reasonably expected to.

Alan Mason is, by his own admission, a perfectionist. As a result, the priority of the Company has always been quality. Prior to starting the Alan Group, he had established a reputation for excellence, and his initial customers were looking for the quality of work that they knew he could produce. As the group grew, the unwritten technical strategy has always been the need to maintain the technical capability required to cater to the increasingly exacting demands of the customer. Consequently the Company has invested in new machinery and computer systems and updated the skills of the operators working in the plant ahead of market demand.

Company strategy appraisal carried out in 1994 for the Alan Group recognised the basis of competition and envisioned a development path. It identified that operational efficiency, talent, and the energy in the work force were not being properly utilised. The work force is fully committed, heavily loaded, highly trained, and proud to work for the Company. A need was identified for a method of harnessing latent human potential and channeling it toward making more money for the Company and for its owners, many of whom are the employees. This potential could be realised through organisational development.

A need was identified therefore for something alongside "hard" technology to provide the platform the Company needed to improve its profit performance and maximise employee development. Directors of the Group recently devised a five-year Business Plan, part of which is a financial objective. The main aims of this are:

A 10 percent profit margin

Turnover to grow at 25 percent per annum

To attain this, there will need to be a radical restructuring of the Company. One of the biggest changes will be in the work force. The Company trains its own apprentices, and most people working for the Company were trained there. In 1994, for example, there were eight apprentices at varying levels of training, out of a total work force of 57. (This is an exceptional statistic, way outside normal U.K. practice.) To achieve the 25 percent growth target, however, they will need to look outside of the Company for personnel, which will inevitably impact the Company's culture.

Current informal communication channels work reasonably well in the present setup, but as the Company grows, there will be a need for more formalised methods of information transfer.

The Company is thought of, by most of those within it, as one big team. It would be highly unlikely, however, that this could be maintained with the expected influx of new employees without special attention to this issue.

External Influences The study carried out into the Alan Group's business strategy in 1994 also examined the Company's customer base, and identified the major customer demands. It was found that the main customers were delighted with the quality of product and the quality of service they received. Although the procurement pricing was not considered to be competitive, the initial cost of the tooling was justified by the total life cycle costs and realised product performance. The major complaint was the customer perception of unreliability in quoted delivery dates.

In late 1994 at the invitation of the U.K. government but at the cost of Alan Group, Alan Mason went on a trade mission to Japan. This was organised by the U.K. Department of Trade and Industry, and included a number of other British companies involved in the electronics industry. As a result Alan has initiated a major drive to supply certain of the European subsidiaries of the Japanese multinationals he visited. This represents a change in the marketplace. The demands of these customers differ from the established client base. These companies demand exceptional delivery performance from their suppliers, and are unforgiving of those that let them down. If Alan Group is to be successful in this environment, it will have to improve its delivery performance beyond what may be traditionally regarded as good in this industry sector.

Directors see organisational development affecting every member of the work force as a strategic priority. The introduction of cellular working is a part of an empowerment initiative and a way of highlighting the importance of delivery performance to all the employees.

THE CONTEXT OF CHANGE

Factors that determined the Company's decision to move toward cellular manufacturing methods are grouped under two headings.

External Until recently the Company has adopted a very low profile. The media attention resulting from the presentation of the Queen's Award for Export Achievement, and the acknowledgment

of its World Class status, have put pressure on the Company to live up to its reputation and even exceed it.

The Company's marketplace is truly international, but the majority of its work is for a handful of major customers. This relatively small client base enables the Company to establish and maintain a collaborative learning relationship with each customer over a long period.

The drive to improve delivery dependability results from the demands of new customers. However, a successful outcome should also be increasingly valued by Alan Group's existing customers, both domestic and international. The opportunity exists to extend the breadth of the company's existing business through a more integrated role in the product development process of its customers.

Internal Engineers at Alan Group are some of the best in their trade, and they are rewarded accordingly.

Human resource issues do not centre around unions, and strikes are an unknown phenomenon at Alan Group. Issues do arise and there was some minor discontent recently over the decision to limit overtime payments and provide a better quality of life for employees. Traditionally the Company has worked very high levels of overtime and this became a cultural issue not always related to best operational practice. The issue was resolved through discussion focusing on achieving corporate and business goals.

Organisational culture is one of mutual respect. Around 80 percent of the work force are shareholders in the Company, and there is a widespread culture of pride. It is also a point of pride that Alan Group trains its own apprentices who can and do progress to the highest levels in the organisation. The lack of visible hierarchy within the Company adds to the informality within the organisation, and the operators are allowed to do a job in the way they see fit, another sign of the respect accorded to the work force.

The Company's products, mould tools, mould tool spares, and moulded components have to fulfill the demanding specifications of the communications and IT industries, so the machinery and the operator training need to be and are of a very high standard. The technology used is the best available. Due to the tolerances required, leading-edge technologies, such as wire erosion and spark erosion, are used alongside the more common precision tool shop processes.

In the U.K., a major study was undertaken during 1995 on the technology issues affecting Small and Medium Sized Manufacturing Enterprises. Opportunities for growth and the characteristics of SMEs with manageable risk growth potential were examined.[‡] These findings suggest that Alan Group is well positioned to use AMT in the process of business growth.

THE PROCESS OF TRANSITION

Planning and implementation of the proof-of-concept at Alan Group followed a logical sequence of steps over a period of more than a year.

First, the specific strategic objectives that needed to be addressed were identified. There were two such objectives for the Alan Grinders tooling business:

- Improvement of delivery performance.
- Improvement of profit performance.

The next stage was concerned with reviewing the type of change required to accomplish the strategic objectives. The main influences on the choice of cellular working were:

- The Strategy Review carried out in 1994, which identified cellular working as a way of tapping and developing the potential of the work force. This gave operator teams the opportunity to take responsibility for a complete order—including delivery, eventually with the potential to interface directly with customers operating in an Extended Enterprise mode.
- Alan Mason attended a seminar on the subject of Kaizen. He came away with the conviction that cells were the way to empower the work force at Alan Group, and that it was the best way to improve the firm's delivery performance.

Alan Mason set about justifying organisational development through cells to the other directors of the firm. Justification is concerned solely with how empowerment through manufacturing cells would help the firm to achieve the strategic objectives: delivery and profit performance.

Cells might achieve the first objective, of improving delivery performance, by giving responsibility for complete orders to cross-functional teams. Each team would have a particular interest in getting their tool to the customer on time, rather than the present objective of getting work done to be passed on to the next section. It would then be a matter of pride for the team to meet the customer delivery date. It might also be reasonable to expect this increased motivation to translate into increased productivity and more importantly enhanced customer perception of values. This would help the Company achieve the objective of improving profit performance by further reducing the significance of first cost as an order winning criterion.

There was some scepticism about whether cells were appropriate to the Alan Group, and this is examined more deeply in the section on the politics of change. The majority board decision, however, was to go ahead and evaluate the cellular method of working in a pilot study.

In most companies that have introduced cellular working, the machinery has been physically moved to form distinct cells. The reason for this is that families of products can flow around the cell, without excessive work in progress, or the need for minimum batch sizes.

In the Alan Group, however, no two tools produced are identical, and there are hundreds of man-hours spent on machine stations. The transport time between different tool processes is the minutes it takes to carry the part to the next room, or down the stairs. Since the tools cannot be split into distinct families, each requiring similar processing times on the same machines, it would not make sense to form distinct physical cells of machinery.

Manufacturing Cells in the Alan Group are order-based virtual cells. Fully implemented, each cell would be a group of people in different sections all working on the same order. There are no product families; as such, the cell would last for the duration of a particular order, and then disband. Operators would then be assigned to new cells. This is a virtual transient cell system. The time frame for the introduction of cells would therefore have to be long, with a gradual introduction into the factory.

It was decided that there would be great danger in going for the "big bang" approach, and introducing multiple virtual cells all at once. Initially, there would be one cell running at a time, so that:

- Its degree of success could be measured.
- Lessons learned from problems encountered by the first one could be passed on to subsequent cells in a continuous improvement process.
- Sceptics within the work force could be won over by being able to see the difference made by cellular working.

Planning   Planning of the implementation was recognised as crucial, as the success of the project would largely depend on how well the pilot was planned. To increase the chances of success, the Company waited until a suitable order came along. The main criteria for suitability were:

- The job should not be particularly complicated, although none of the tools the Company makes could be described as simple.
- There should be plenty of time to make the product; there should not be an unrealistically tight deadline.

Once a suitable order was identified, the technical director selected a team of people to form the cell. Personalities were chosen with the hope that the sceptics among them would adjust their views once they saw the cell was working. It did not comprise a group of cell "enthusiasts." There was an initial briefing meeting where the cell members were given the design of the tool and the delivery date. It was not known at that stage what exactly the cell would make of the opportunity, because none of the firm's employees had worked in a cellular environment before. The work force knew in outline the theory about how virtual cells were supposed to function, but there was no formal training as such.

Possibly the most crucial function was that of cell leader. The operator chosen had no real leadership experience within the firm. He was chosen because it was felt that he could make a good attempt at the job, even though nobody knew exactly what that role would be. It was hoped that he would take hold of the opportunity and develop the leadership needed to get the job done. This risk-taking illustrates the level of trust placed on all employees in Alan Group.

Although the cell changed the way in which the order progressed through the factory, the jobs done by the cell members did not really alter. As one cell member put it:

> Everyone knows what they are doing anyway, so it is not as if somebody's started something new. It is a job we do every day, we are all fairly good at it, so we all know what we are doing.

So implementing the changes affected how the tool progressed within the Company, rather than what individuals did while working on the tool. The usual method of getting tools through the factory depends on the supervisor in each section getting work through the section in order of priority. They assign a job to a particular operator primarily because of the operator's abilities and the difficulty of the job. Some orders need the involvement of several operators, and this would also be organised by the supervisor.

The virtual cell processes the job without the supervisor deciding who in their section would work on it. This might be seen as threatening to the supervisors, but no resistance was met once it was realised that they were working on the cell job.

There were difficulties encountered and issues that needed to be resolved. One mentioned by the cell concerned noncell members trying to work on the cell job.

> Two people decided they were going to pick up the job to work on, so it had to be pointed out basically, "keep your nose out"—politely, because it would disrupt what was happening within the cell. (quoted from a cell member)

Another anticipated problem was with the section leaders. These supervisors have their list of priorities, which are the Company's priorities. If a cell member works on the cell job while there is more pressing work to be done, the section fails to meet its targets. It had to be pointed out, therefore, both to cell members and to section leaders, that the Company priorities were more important than the cell priorities. It was clear that if the section leader asked a cell member to work on another, more urgent job, it would be done. To date no problems have arisen with this issue.

Implementation Cell 01   At the time of writing this case study, the first cell order has been delivered and the second cell order is nearing completion, so the process has been trialed but it is still novel.

At launch, the cell members were called together for an initial meeting, at which they were given the design for the tool, and a deadline. The major change from normal working, therefore, was that people knew which individual in the sections would be working on the job. Usually, nobody would know or be concerned with who would end up working on a specific order, as scheduling in each section is done by that section's leader. It is interesting to note that, because the design was completed before the cell was assembled, it only consisted of the operators who would work on it. The tool designer was outside of the virtual cell system.

Roles for the cell members were not predefined, and it was not known or preplanned how they would work. It was hoped that the cell leader would take advantage of the opportunity. The operator chosen for the position was not the leader in his section, so this was his first real leadership role within the Company. He made it his business to know where the job was at any point in time, and kept in touch with the other cell members. He greatly enjoyed the extra responsibility, and found it to be a very good motivator and process for personal development.

> Because I have got no real position here . . . it does generate for the like of me, a little bit more responsibility. You are not just "the man upstairs that did that," you are a little bit more. It gives you a sense of achievement as well. (virtual cell leader)

While the tool was making its way through the various processes, the work carried out by the cell members did not differ from what they would normally do. One significant change, however, was that the section leaders (as opposed to the team leaders) played no part in scheduling the progress of the order through the factory. The section leader still has the overriding authority, however, and if there is a conflict between the cell's needs and those of the Company, they can ensure that the Company comes first.

The pilot job went through smoothly, and the cell members were all anxious to see how good the first mouldings would be. There was a serious problem with the finished tool, which would require a significant amount of rework. It was a bitter disappointment to the virtual cell team, who had taken particular pride in the fact that the order had progressed so well. It became apparent that the root cause of the problem was a fundamental design fault, and the cell members were concerned that their work would be remembered as a failure, even though the error was outside of the cell's control. The consensus of opinion is that the problem would also have occurred if the order had been processed normally, and that it would not have been identified any earlier than it was.

Significant amounts of remedial action were required to rectify the problems in the tool's performance. There has been discussion, both inside and outside the cell, about the need to prevent such errors in future. Currently, there is no formal checking of designs before they are launched onto the shop floor, because there is no time allocated for this. The problem was there previously, but the cell has highlighted a problem that the Company needs to address.

THE SUBSTANCE OF CHANGE

The substance of the change at Alan Group was the introduction of a special form of cellular type working. Giving a small group of individuals the overall responsibility for an order, from inception to delivery, is seen as an effective way of improving delivery performance, while also tapping the reservoir of talent on the shop floor. It is crucial to realising the company's strategic plan.

Cells have proven very successful in other industry sectors. In the tooling engineer-to-order industry, all orders are unique, processes are measured in 10s or 100s of hours, and there is negligible "idle" work in progress. So the formation of physical cells might be expected to have minimal positive influence on performance.

A cell in the Alan Group sense is a group of operators from each of the major process sections, a virtual cell. They are made "owners" of a complete order from design to the first moulds being made. The Company is taking a step-by-step approach to this project seeking to learn cellurisation from the cells themselves.

THE POLITICS OF CHANGE

The Company's CEO Alan Mason is the kingpin of the operation, and although he is not by any means dictatorial, he commands respect from all levels in the Company. The Alan Group has pulled through several major crises in recent years, and much of this is attributed to the CEO. The work force has faith in his abilities. It was Alan who suggested that the Company move toward cellular manufacture, and although there was scepticism from some quarters, the Board decided to back the idea.

There were conflicts at various stages in the planning, running, and reflection stages of the cell's operation:

- One director was sceptical about the applicability of cellular working to the Alan Group. In particular, he saw the Company as one big cell anyway, and did not believe that using cells would bring any significant extra benefit to the firm. This is a view shared with some others at Alan Group, but as one cell member said:

  > . . . It is only true if everybody was to work the same way. They do not. If everybody communicated and everybody [was] motivated in the same way, then that would be perfectly true. We would have one big cell.

- Once, two people picked up the cell job to work on it. It was pointed out to them that it was the cell job, and that they should leave it alone.
- When the problems with the tool became apparent toward the end of the project, there was disappointment within the cell, as they believed they had done a good job. As a result, there is some resentment felt toward the designer.

> It is unfortunate that this has happened because you are going to get a situation, as is possibly happening at the moment, in that everybody that worked on it, worked hard on it and achieved the delivery date. And when something goes wrong, you want to blame somebody, it's human nature. (cell member)

There is also a possibility that the section leaders might start to suspect a hidden agenda, because cellular working removes the need for them to allocate and sequence jobs in their section. There was no evidence of this during the running of this particular cell, but if cells are to become more numerous, the worries of the section leaders must be addressed.

The majority of the board were in agreement with the cells idea so the sceptical director went along with their decision. Although he still maintains that cells, even virtual ones, are not designed to work in the Alan Group's environment, his objections were not so forceful as to cause any major rifts.

Employees within the firm know that the Board is not unanimously in support of the cells idea, and they might, as a result, have reservations themselves. To have the best chance of success, any change effort needs the full support of the work force. So, if the sceptical director could be persuaded that cells can work, it would send a very strong positive signal to the work force. The Company is considering trying to identify small companies who have successfully implemented virtual cells, and arrange to visit them. They could also be good sources of advice about how to overcome implementation problems.

Some cell members have identified feelings of resentment directed at the designer of the tool, because had there been no design errors, the cell would probably have been seen as a great success by others within the Company. Now, however, there is a danger that it will be seen to have failed as an idea. They also realise, however, that it is destructive to point the finger of blame at an individual, without analysing the root causes of the problem.

> The cell has shown a weakness, which is very basic tool design. That is not incriminating, that is showing a weakness, because it is a problem that we had. (cell member)

The designer himself feels that he would have benefited from being in the cell, and having direct feedback from the cell members during the project. He would particularly have liked to have had input from the cell at the start, before the designs were finished.

> The buck stops here, but it would be nice to get some feedback, which doesn't always happen. (designer)

How the Company deals with the present situation is important to the chances of successful organisational development. If blame is allotted, without addressing the fundamental causes of the problem, it will:

- Be repeated.
- Serve to back up the perception that cells do not work in Alan Group.

There have been difficulties in the introduction of cells into Alan Group. Problems originating from scepticism will only be really solved by proving the success of cellularisation. The perception that "cells do not work," arising from the difficulties that occurred because of a design error, might be even more difficult to overcome if left unchallenged and unresolved.

THE OPERATION OF NEW PRACTICES

Major rework required on the job, as a result of the design fault, was an unexpected outcome. This particular job had been chosen because it was simple in comparison to the majority of the work they undertake. Possibly because it was considered to be simple, it was assumed that design errors were inconceivable. The cell team was understandably disappointed to find that all of its hard work, in producing the tool to tight time estimates, came to nothing because of a problem that was outside of its control. There is some bitterness felt toward the designer, and the issue was confronted.

A review meeting was planned and set to take place after the job had successfully been completed. Its purpose was to resolve the issues arising. The interviews conducted with cell members indicate agreement on the major point: that the designer should have been in the cell from the start. There was some difference of opinion as to how the problems of design faults are tackled. The two schools of thought were:

1. Have the design reviewed by a toolmaker and/or fitter prior to launching it onto the shop floor. They would not pick up all the errors, but since there isn't the time to get the designs fully checked, they would at least be able to correct the most obvious problems.

   > It's much better to spend an hour at the beginning of it, because if there are any mistakes on the job and they aren't picked up until the end, the job is already late at that stage. (designer)

2. Develop a comprehensive feedback channel to the designers, so that errors made on the job will not be made again.

   > Obvious problems, design faults or things which have actually physically changed, usually get marked on the drawings and get back. But a lot of things don't. (designer)

It was expected that at this meeting, the cell will suggest a number of refinements to the cell structure. These will help to form the template for subsequent cells. The cellularisation of Alan Group is still in the initial stages: there has been no stable state reached, although a feedback loop in the form of a review meeting at the end of the cell is in place.

Evaluation of the degree of success of the cell would depend greatly upon who was asked. Those people outside of the cell could come to the conclusion that the project was less than a resounding success:

- There were problems when the tool was tested.
- There has been a significant amount of rework.
- There has been criticism of individuals, from people within the team, which might be seen as scapegoating to those not directly involved.

Cell members found the cell to be a good motivator:

> Giving somebody ownership of an idea, helping them, encourage them to get on and do it, they have a goal. It's great. I like that idea. (cell member)

There is also a willingness to take part in future cells:

> I've enjoyed it . . . To generate that throughout the firm, it gives people that little bit of responsibility that they did not have before. Rather than being just an operator on a machine, it does generate a bit more interest. (cell member)

VIRTUAL CELL REVIEW MEETING

When the tool had been completed, and rework virtually finished, the cell members held an end-of-project meeting to:

- Identify the problems encountered by individuals.
- Identify successes during the project.
- Devise a list of recommended actions for solving the problems encountered.

This meeting used external guidance from The CIM Institute, Cranfield University, on its process of working. All the cell members were invited to the meeting, along with others who had expressed an interest in attending. Among these were the designers of the tool, and the fitter who had been working with the tool in the mould shop.

Problems were initially brainstormed and formed a list that was visible to all participants. The problems were discussed in some detail, and suggested actions were put forward by various individuals.

Outputs from the meeting were in the form of three lists:

- *Stops.* Actions and practices that hindered the work of the cell and should therefore be discontinued.
- *Starts.* Actions that the cell believes would have helped them attain their objective, and that they would like to see started.
- *Continues.* Actions and practices that the cell found useful and helpful and that they believe should be continued.

Main problems identified by the cell were:

- The initial cell meeting was held too late, drawings had already been finalised, and not everyone who would be involved had been invited.
- The cell members were not aware of some important information from the customer, regarding technical difficulties they might face.
- With the need for early planning, problems can arise due to the large number of jobs, which management needs to consider simultaneously.
- Some major decisions were taken out of the hands of the cell.
- In estimating the time to do a job, no allowance is made for any difficulties that may be encountered.
- Inflexible values of estimated working hours at each process might hinder the smooth progress of the tool.
- There is some conflict between sections, which results in a breakdown in communications, and individuals passing the buck when decisions need to be made.
- Trying to cut corners at an early stage leads to more time being spent in total.

Main improvements suggested were:

- The initial cell meeting needs to be held much earlier in the process, with all cell members present, including someone from the mould shop.

- Rather than leave all of the important technical decisions to management, they should be made by the cell as a whole, and discussed with management.
- There is a need for a more flexible attitude throughout the production of the tool, and there should be a willingness to listen to ideas that might prove beneficial.
- More time needs to be allowed at the initial planning stage, where discussions within the cell may save time and money later in the process.
- There needs to be an allowance in the time estimates for some rework and adjustment, which are almost inevitable when producing such high precision tooling.
- Cell members need to be supportive of their team mates and be open to constructive criticism as individuals.

Plus points were mentioned by cell members, the main ones of which were:

- The hours spent in the initial production of the tool were within budget, and the tool was finished by the due date.
- "The few problems which we came across, we solved together and with better results."
- There was greater cooperation, and a real willingness to work as a team.
- Working as a cell, the members found that their personal interest had increased, and that involvement extended to cover the whole production process.

CONCLUSION

The virtual cell-based organisational development pilot at Alan Group primarily served as a test-bed for the empowerment process idea. Lessons that the Company learned are:

- The Alan Group is atypical of companies that introduce cellularisation. They are not an assembly operation, they do not have multiple batch sizes, and they do not have product families that would justify physical cells. This does not mean that special virtual cells are inappropriate to the Company, but it does mean that issues need to be confronted and addressed through a clear process.
- The work force needs more education about the idea of organisational development via cells and how they are supposed to work. This could serve to dispel any feelings of mistrust, or any misunderstanding there may be about why cells are being implemented.
- Section leaders might lose from cellularisation; it removes some of their authority. The question of what exactly their role will be needs to be addressed. They are a vital resource to the Company, especially in enabling growth through their expertise.
- Cells have delivered organisational development. Those benefits identified by the cell members include:
  - Greater responsibility.
  - Increased motivation.
  - More "ownership" of the project.
  - Team spirit.
  - Sense of achievement.
  - Job satisfaction and enjoyment.

By increasing the involvement and ownership felt by the cell members, the resulting positive attitude benefits delivery performance on other jobs, as well as the particular cell order.

- There needs to be a recognition of the need for flexibility in the design and implementation of cells.

  . . . Some of the management have looked into these cells, and they have read one book on it, got this one idea of it. I don't think they realise that you should tailor the cell to the way we work a little bit, as well as trying to make our work fit this one cellular system. They are trying to stick to the letter of the law, and you need a bit more flexibility. They should go and see the way other firms work it. (cell member)

- Cell members suggested a number of possible solutions to the problems they encountered during this project. They also identified possible improvements to the cell structure as it currently stands. Team members understand cells within the Alan Group; they are the best people to design the framework of operation for the next phase in cell implementation.

- The cell served to highlight a problem within the Company by focusing attention on shortcomings in the design process. Responsibility for the order had been given to a group of people, and when an error was detected, they wanted to know what had gone wrong. In the normal mode of working, no individual has the overall responsibility for a particular order, so there is nobody to ask questions when something goes awry. If these difficulties are not fully investigated, they may be repeated.

Following the pilot the cell leader wrote a report and presented it to the Board of Directors. This direct data capture of ideas from the cell members influenced the future working of AMT in the Alan Group. It was made possible by the organisational development achieved during the period of the case study. The tremendous potential business performance improvements available through this organisational change were directly illustrated by this single action.

In 1998 the Company has significantly advanced its strategy of becoming a World Class, worldwide supplier to international players. A key support element in this process has been the further adoption of the cell-based product system described.

The Company is approaching the 21st century with confidence. Global operation is being achieved and staff development needed to support the growth is being sustained through a widening of the cell-based operation to all aspects of the business. According to Alan Mason it's just common sense!

*THIS CASE WAS DEVELOPED FOR USE IN CLASSROOM DISCUSSION AND IS NOT INTENDED TO NECESSARILY ILLUSTRATE APPROPRIATE OR INAPPROPRIATE MANAGEMENT PRACTICES. THE CASE AUTHOR WAS PETER J. SACKETT, CRANFIELD UNIVERSITY, OCTOBER 1995. THE FUNDING FOR THIS CASE PRODUCTION WAS PROVIDED BY THE AUSTRALIAN FEDERAL GOVERNMENT'S DEPARTMENT OF INDUSTRY, SCIENCE AND RESOURCES. THE AUTHORS WOULD LIKE TO THANK THE ALAN GROUP FOR ITS HELP IN COMPILING THE DATA FOR THIS EXCITING CASE STUDY, IN PARTICULAR, ALAN MASON, THE BOARD OF DIRECTORS, AND THE CELL MEMBERS.

†P. WEST. "MANUFACTURING STRATEGY REVIEW IN A SPECIALISED APPLICATION," CIM INSTITUTE, CRANFIELD UNIVERSITY, BEDFORD, U.K., 1994.

‡P. J. SACKETT AND G. NELDER, "MANAGING MANUFACTURING CHANGE IN SMEs: A UNITED KINGDOM POSITION STUDY," PROCEEDINGS AUTOFACT '95, CHICAGO, NOV. 14, 1995, PP. 129–144.

SELECTED BIBLIOGRAPHY

Bitner, M. J. "Servicescapes: The Impact of Physical Surroundings on Customers and Employees." *Journal of Marketing* 56 (April 1992), pp. 57–71.

Bollinger, S. *Fundamentals of Plant Layout*. Society of Manufacturing Engineers in Association with Richard Muther and Associates, 1998.

Ghosh, S., and R. Gagnon. "A Comprehensive Literature Review and Analysis of the Design, Balancing and Scheduling of Assembly Systems." *International Journal of Production Research* 27, no. 4 (1989), pp. 637–70.

Heragu, S. *Facilities Design*. Boston, MA: PWS Publishing Company, 1997.

Hyer, N., and U. Wemmerlöv. *Reorganizing the Factory: Competing through Cellular Manufacturing*. Portland, OR: Productivity Press, 2002.

Love, J. F. *McDonald's: Behind the Arches*. New York: Bantam, 1986.

Meyers, F. E. *Manufacturing Facilities Design and Material Handling*. Upper Saddle River, NJ: Prentice Hall, 2000.

Sule, D. R. *Manufacturing Facilities: Location, Planning, and Design*. Boston: PWS Publishing Company, 1994.

Tompkins, J. A., and J. A. White. *Facilities Planning*. New York: John Wiley & Sons, 2003.

Underhill, P. *Why We Buy: The Science of Shopping*. New York: Simon & Schuster, 1999.

FOOTNOTES

1 For a discussion of CRAFT and other methods, see J. A. Tompkins and J. A. White, *Facilities Planning* (New York: John Wiley & Sons, 2003).

2 R. Johnson, "Spacecraft for Multi-Floor Layout Planning," *Management Science* 28, no. 4 (April 1982), pp. 407–17.

3 See R. Muther and J. D. Wheeler, "Simplified Systematic Layout Planning," *Factory* 120, nos. 8, 9, 10 (August, September, October 1962), pp. 68–77, 111–19, 101–13.

4 The workstation cycle time used in this calculation should be the actual cycle time used by the assembly line.

5 Y. Monden, *Toyota Production System: Practical Approach to Production Management* (Atlanta, GA: Industrial Engineering and Management Press, Institute of Industrial Engineers, 1983), p. 208.

6 M. S. Sommers and J. B. Kernan, "A Behavioral Approach to Planning, Layout and Display," *Journal of Retailing,* Winter 1965–66, pp. 21–27.

7 M. J. Bitner, "Servicescapes: The Impact of Physical Surroundings on Customers and Employees," *Journal of Marketing* 56 (April 1992), pp. 57–71.

8 R. Norman, *Service Management,* 2nd ed. (New York: John Wiley & Sons, 1991), p. 28.

chapter

SERVICE PROCESS SELECTION AND DESIGN

7

MY WEEK AS A ROOM-SERVICE WAITER AT THE RITZ

This was to be my first real test. After completing a two-day orientation program and spending the same number of days shadowing Stephen Posner, a veteran Ritz-Carlton room-service waiter, I was going to take the lead on delivering a dinner order. As we headed up the service elevator with a light meal for two—a cheeseburger, a salad, a beer, and a bottle of mineral water—I again went over in my head Steve's instruction on what to say and do. He noticed my furrowed brow. "Don't be so serious," he said, as I awkwardly maneuvered the room-service cart down the hall. "Feel out the guests and try to match their mood."

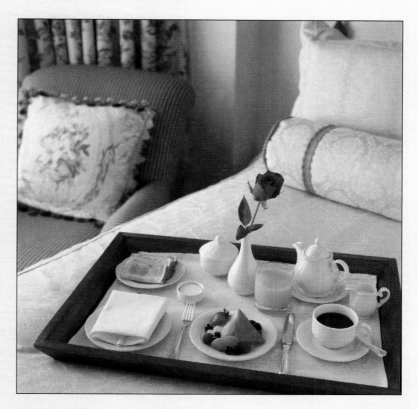

I knocked on the door of Room 1036 and swallowed: "Good evening. In-room dining." A cheerful woman opened the door and I pushed, rather than pulled, the jiggling and tinkling cart over the threshold—nearly tipping over the bottle of San Pellegrino in the process. When the woman, who was watching a game show on television with her husband, learned from Steve that I was in training, she tried to put me at ease with some conversation about the program. But I didn't have the excess mental capacity required for casual banter. I was focused on my task.

"Would you like me to open the water for you?" I asked.

"Oh, sure, if you'd like to," said the woman.

Then I stood there, slightly slack jawed, hands behind my back, surveying the cart and trying to recall what my checklist said to do next. The woman stood there looking at me expectantly. Steve stood there looking at me quizzically. Ah, I know! Explain what I've brought for them. "You have a Caesar salad and a grilled beef burger with cheese, medium rare," I said, lifting up the warming cover. "And I brought some extra mustard and ketchup, in case you need it." Steve, having finally despaired of my ever opening the San Pellegrino, deftly stepped forward and did it himself. "Please don't hesitate to call us if you need anything else," I said, as we prepared to leave. The woman smiled. I forgot to offer to open the Heineken. As Steve and I stepped into the hallway, he closed the door behind us and said: "We have a few things to talk about on the way downstairs." →

Service

The delivery of food at the Ritz-Carlton is just the visible portion of a series of service design decisions that emanate from their service strategy. The best service companies, like the Ritz-Carlton, understand that how well they manage the details of every stage of their operations determines the success of the business.

In this chapter, after some preliminary comments about services, we address the issue of service delivery system design, starting with the notion of customer contact as a way of classifying service operations. Next we discuss service organization design, service strategy, and service focus, and describe how marketing and operations interrelate to achieve (or fail to achieve) competitive advantage. We also look at a service-system design matrix that can define the broad features of a service process, and at service blueprints as a way of designing the precise steps of a process. In the latter part of the chapter, we present three service designs used in service industries and discuss how service guarantees can be used as "design drivers." The chapter ends with two service organization case studies.

THE NATURE OF SERVICES

Our study of the nature of services leads to seven generalizations:

1. Everyone is an expert on services. We all think we know what we want from a service organization and, by the very process of living, we have a good deal of experience with the service creation process.
2. Services are idiosyncratic: What works well in providing one kind of service may prove disastrous in another. For example, consuming a restaurant meal in less than half an hour may be exactly what you want at Jack-in-the-Box but would be totally unacceptable at an expensive French restaurant.
3. Quality of work is not quality of service. An auto dealership may do good work on your car, but it may take a week to get the job done.
4. Most services contain a mix of tangible and intangible attributes that constitute a *service package*. This package requires different approaches to design and management than the production of goods.
5. High-contact services (described later) are *experienced*, whereas goods are *consumed*.
6. Effective management of services requires an understanding of marketing and personnel, as well as operations.
7. Services often take the form of cycles of encounters involving face-to-face, telephone, electromechanical, and/or mail interactions. (The term *encounter*, by the way, is defined as "meeting in conflict or battle" and hence is often apt as we make our way through the service economy.)

Cross Functional

SERVICE BUSINESSES AND INTERNAL SERVICES

Service operations management issues exist in two broad organizational contexts:

1. **Service businesses.** Organizations whose primary business requires interaction with the customer to produce the service. These include such familiar services as banks,

airlines, hospitals, law firms, retail stores, and restaurants. Within this category, we can make a further major distinction: **facilities-based services,** where the customer must go to the service facility; and **field-based services,** where production and consumption of the service take place in the customer's environment (for example, cleaning and home repair services).

Facilities-based services

Field-based services

Technology has allowed for the transfer of many facility-based services to field-based services. Dental vans bring the dentist to your home; some auto repair services have repair-mobiles; and telemarketing brings the shopping center to your TV screen.

2. **Internal services.** Services required to support the activities of the larger organization. These services include such functions as data processing, accounting, engineering, and maintenance. Their customers are the various departments within the organization that require such services. Incidentally, it is not uncommon for an internal service to start marketing its services outside the parent organization and become a service business itself.

Our emphasis in this chapter is on service businesses, but most of the ideas apply equally well to internal services.

A Customer-Centered View of Service Management

A glance at the management book section in your local bookstore gives ample evidence of the concern for service among practitioners. The way we now view service parallels the way we view quality: The *customer* is (or should be) the focal point of all decisions and actions of the service organization. This philosophy is captured nicely in the service triangle in Exhibit 7.1. Here the customer is the center of things—the service strategy, the systems, and the employees who serve him or her. From this view, the organization exists to serve the customer, and the systems and the employees exist to facilitate the process of service. Some suggest that the service organization also exists to serve the workforce because they generally determine how the service is perceived by the customers. Relative to the latter point, the customer gets the kind of service that management deserves; in other words, how management treats the worker is how the worker will treat the public. If the workforce is well trained and well motivated by management, they will do good jobs for their customers.

The role of operations in the triangle is a major one. Operations is responsible for service systems (procedures, equipment, and facilities) and is responsible for managing the work of the service workforce, who typically make up the majority of employees in large service organizations. But before we discuss this role in depth, it is useful to classify services to show how the customer affects the operations function.

The Service Triangle

exhibit 7.1

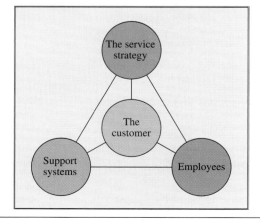

AN OPERATIONAL CLASSIFICATION OF SERVICES

⊙⊙⊙⊙   Service organizations are generally classified according to who the customer is, for example, individuals or other businesses, and to the service they provide (financial services, health services, transportation services, and so on). These groupings, though useful in presenting aggregate economic data, are not particularly appropriate for OM purposes because they tell us little about the process. Manufacturing, by contrast, has fairly evocative terms to classify production activities (such as intermittent and continuous production); when applied to a manufacturing setting, they readily convey the essence of the process. Although it is possible to describe services in these same terms, we need one additional item of information to reflect the fact that the customer is involved in the production system. That item, which we believe operationally distinguishes one service system from another in its production function, is the extent of customer contact in the creation of the service.

Customer contact refers to the physical presence of the customer in the system, and *creation of the service* refers to the work process involved in providing the service itself.

exhibit 7.2

Major Differences between High- and Low-Contact Systems in a Bank

DESIGN DECISION	HIGH-CONTACT SYSTEM (A BRANCH OFFICE)	LOW-CONTACT SYSTEM (A CHECK PROCESSING CENTER)
Facility location	Operations must be near the customer.	Operations may be placed near supply, transport, or labor.
Facility layout	The facility should accommodate the customer's physical and psychological needs and expectations.	The facility should focus on production efficiency.
Product design	Environment as well as the physical product define the nature of the service.	The customer is not in the service environment, so the product can be defined by fewer attributes.
Process design	Stages of production process have a direct, immediate effect on the customer.	The customer is not involved in the majority of processing steps.
Scheduling	The customer is in the production schedule and must be accommodated.	The customer is concerned mainly with completion dates.
Production planning	Orders cannot be stored, so smoothing production flow will result in loss of business.	Both backlogging and production smoothing are possible.
Worker skills	The direct workforce constitutes a major part of the service product and so must be able to interact well with the public.	The direct workforce need only have technical skills.
Quality control	Quality standards are often in the eye of the beholder and, thus, are variable.	Quality standards are generally measurable and, thus, fixed.
Time standards	Service time depends on customer needs, so time standards are inherently loose.	Work is performed on customer surrogates (such as forms), so time standards can be tight.
Wage payment	Variable output requires time-based wage systems.	"Fixable" output permits output-based wage systems.
Capacity planning	To avoid lost sales, capacity must be set to match peak demand.	Storable output permits capacity at some average demand level.

Extent of contact here may be roughly defined as the percentage of time the customer must be in the system relative to the total time it takes to perform the customer service. Generally speaking, the greater the percentage of contact time between the service system and the customer, the greater the degree of interaction between the two during the production process.

From this conceptualization, it follows that service systems with a **high degree of customer contact** are more difficult to control and more difficult to rationalize than those with a **low degree of customer contact.** In high-contact systems, the customer can affect the time of demand, the exact nature of the service, and the quality, or perceived quality, of service because the customer is involved in the process.

Exhibit 7.2 describes the implications of this distinction. Here we see that each design decision is impacted by whether the customer is present during service delivery. We also see that when work is done behind the scenes (in this case, in a bank's processing center), it is performed on customer surrogates—reports, databases, and invoices. We can thus design it according to the same principles we would use in designing a factory—to maximize the amount of items processed during the production day.

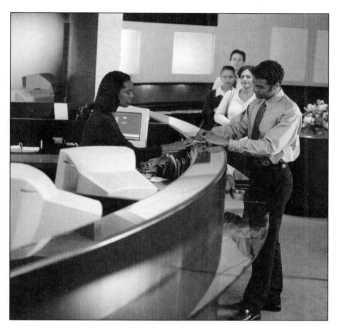

High and low degree of customer contact

There can be tremendous diversity of customer influence and, hence, system variability within high-contact service systems. For example, a bank branch offers both simple services such as cash withdrawals that take just a minute or so and complicated services such as loan application preparation that can take in excess of an hour. Moreover, these activities may range from being self-service through an ATM, to coproduction where bank personnel and the customer work as a team to develop the loan application.

DESIGNING SERVICE ORGANIZATIONS

 In designing service organizations we must remember one distinctive characteristic of services: We cannot inventory services. Unlike manufacturing, where we can build up inventory during slack periods for peak demand and thus maintain a relatively stable level of employment and production planning, in services we must (with a few exceptions) meet demand as it arises. Consequently, in services capacity becomes a dominant issue. Think about the many service situations you find yourself in—for example, eating in a restaurant or going to a Saturday night movie. Generally speaking, if the restaurant or the theater is full, you will decide to go someplace else. So, an important design parameter in services is "What capacity should we aim for?" Too much capacity generates excessive costs. Insufficient capacity leads to lost customers. In these situations, of course, we seek the assistance of marketing. This is one reason we have discount airfares, hotel specials on weekends, and so on. This is also a good illustration of why it is difficult to separate the operations management functions from marketing in services.

Waiting line models, which are discussed in the technical note to this chapter, provide a powerful mathematical tool for analyzing many common service situations. Questions such as how many tellers we should have in a bank or how many telephone lines we need in an Internet service operation can be analyzed with these models. These models can be easily implemented using spreadsheets.

Designing a service organization involves four major elements.[1] The first element is identification of the target market (Who is our customer?); the second is the service concept (How do we differentiate our service in the market?); the third is the service strategy (What is our service package and the operating focus of our service?); and the fourth is the service delivery system (What are the actual processes, staff, and facilities by which the service is created?).

Choosing a target market and developing the service package are top management decisions setting the stage for the direct operating decisions of service strategy and delivery system design.

Cross Functional

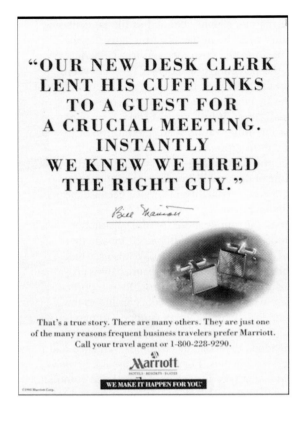

Several major factors distinguish service design and development from typical manufactured product development. First, the process and the product must be developed simultaneously; indeed, in services, the process is the product. (We say this with the general recognition that many manufacturers are using such concepts as concurrent engineering and DFM [design for manufacture] as approaches to more closely link product design and process design.)

Second, although equipment and software that support a service can be protected by patents and copyrights, a service operation itself lacks the legal protection commonly available to goods production. Third, the service package, rather than a definable good, constitutes the major output of the development process. Fourth, many parts of the service package are often defined by the training individuals receive before they become part of the service organization. In particular, in professional service organizations (PSOs) such as law firms and hospitals, prior certification is necessary for hiring. Fifth, many service organizations can change their service offerings virtually overnight. Routine service organizations (RSOs) such as barbershops, retail stores, and restaurants have this flexibility.

SERVICE STRATEGY: FOCUS AND ADVANTAGE

Service strategy begins by selecting the operating focus—the performance priorities—by which the service firm will compete. These include

1. Treatment of the customer in terms of friendliness and helpfulness.
2. Speed and convenience of service delivery.
3. Price of the service.
4. Variety of services (essentially a one-stop shopping philosophy).
5. Quality of the tangible goods that are central to or accompany the service. Examples include a "world-class" corned-beef sandwich, eyeglasses made while you wait, or an understandable insurance policy.
6. Unique skills that constitute the service offering, such as hair styling, brain surgery, or piano lessons.

Operations Focus of Selected Service Firms   exhibit 7.3

	TREATMENT	SPEED/ CONVENIENCE	PRICE	VARIETY	QUALITY	UNIQUE SKILLS/ TANGIBLES
Nordstrom Department Stores*	×				×	
Federal Express Corporation	×	×				
Merrill Lynch & Company (Cash Management Account)		×		×[a]		
eBay		×	×	×		×
Wal-Mart Stores	×		×[b]	×		
Monster.com		×				×[c]
Disneyland*	×				×	×
American Express Company	×	×				
McDonald's Corporation*		×	×		×	
Domino's Pizza		×[d]	×			
Marriott Corporation	×					
Club Med Resorts	×[e]		×			
American Airlines		×[f]		×		
Singapore Airlines	×					
Southwest Airlines			×[g]			
Riverside Methodist Hospital (Columbus, Ohio)	×[h]					
H & R Block		×	×			
American Automobile Association		×[i]				

[a] A cash management account includes checkbook, credit card, money market fund, and other services in one account.
[b] Wal-Mart controls cost of inventory by driving tough bargains with suppliers.
[c] World's leading Internet job placement company brings applicants and employers together in cyberspace.
[d] First to use the automated pizza maker where an attendant puts a raw pie in one side and pulls out a cooked pie on the other.
[e] All-inclusive, low-cost resorts where staff known as *Gentils Organisateurs* (GOs) coproduce a fun vacation with the guests, *Gentils Membres* (GMs).
[f] Sabre reservation system makes it easy for travel agents to book seats and for the company to instantaneously change prices to counter competitors' rates.
[g] No-frills service (that is, no interline baggage transfer, no assigned seating, and no meals) allows lowest prices in the industry.
[h] Riverside Hospital treats patients and their families like customers—gives adult heart patients teddy bears to hold and colorful smocks with hearts imprinted on them. Holding a teddy bear feels good and helps the healing process.
[i] The AAA phone/computer network uses the number of the phone a customer is calling from anywhere in the United States to pinpoint the nearest AAA garage.
* Nordstrom—high quality, personalized service. Disneyland—all employees are cast members who help stage customers' experience. McDonald's—consistency of preparation.

Exhibit 7.3 presents what we view as the operating service focus choices of a number of well-known companies. If our interpretation is correct, it shows that most companies choose to compete on relatively few dimensions—that trade-offs have been made. What best practices are being emphasized by service executives? Although most people often think that service quality or service consistency might lead the list, a survey of executives at 181 service firms showed that accessibility to the service provider was number one. Exhibit 7.4 suggests that accessibility (defined in the study as the ability to get in touch with a service provider, any time, by multiple communication channels) is the "location, location, location" of service industries.

The interesting question for 21st century service companies is what location means in light of outsourcing, particularly of knowledge work, not just simple service jobs. (See the box "Outsourcing of Knowledge Work.")

Integrating Marketing and Operations to Achieve Competitive Advantage   Achieving competitive advantage in services requires integration of service marketing with service delivery to meet or exceed customer expectations. This holds true no matter which competitive dimensions are emphasized.

Exhibit 7.5 gives an overview of the elements leading to service advantage and service oblivion. As it shows, marketing typically has responsibility for communicating the service

Cross Functional

Best Practices Emphasized by Service Executives

ITEMS "MOST" EMPHASIZED	ITEM MEAN*
Accessibility	4.02
Openness to employees	3.91
Leadership	3.87
Listening to the customer	3.82
Service tangibles	3.79
Employee handling of service failures	3.79
Competitive positioning	3.72
Quality values	3.68
Consistently meeting customers' needs	3.68
Customer orientation	3.66
Management involvement in quality	3.66

Scale: 1 = Little emphasis, 3 = Moderate emphasis, 5 = High emphasis.
*Top 10 most emphasized practices out of 55 best practice items listed in the survey.

SOURCE: A. V. ROTH, R. B. CHASE, AND C. VOSS, "SERVICE IN THE U.S.: A STUDY OF SERVICE PRACTICE AND PERFORMANCE IN THE UNITED STATES," SUPPORTED BY SEVERN TRENT PLC, U.K. GOVERNMENT'S DEPARTMENT OF TRADE AND INDUSTRY, DEPARTMENT OF NATIONAL HERITAGE, 1997.

OUTSOURCING OF KNOWLEDGE WORK

Outsourcing of knowledge work is the next wave in the globalization of work. The first wave started in the 1980s with the outsourcing of jobs making shoes, cheap electronics, and toys to developing countries. The second is outsourcing of simple service work, such as processing credit-card receipts and writing software code. Now, enabled by digitization, the Internet, and high-speed data networks, all kinds of knowledge tasks such as drawing up detailed architectural blueprints, preparing a company's financial disclosures, or reading X-rays can be done almost anywhere. A Forrester Research Inc. analyst predicts at least 3.3 million white-collar jobs and $136 billion in wages will shift from the United States to low-cost countries by 2015. Europe is joining the trend, too. Should the West panic? It's too early to tell. Obviously, the bursting

of the tech bubble and Wall Street's woes are chiefly behind the layoffs. Also, any impact of offshore hiring is hard to measure, since so far a tiny portion of U.S. white-collar work has jumped overseas. For security and practical reasons, corporations are likely to keep crucial R&D and the bulk of back-office operations close to home. In a recent Gartner Inc. survey of 900 big U.S. companies that outsource IT work offshore, a majority complained of difficulty communicating and meeting deadlines. Many jobs can't go anywhere because they require face-to-face contact with customers. Americans will continue to deliver medical care, negotiate deals, audit local companies, and wage legal battles. Talented, innovative people will adjust as they always have.

SUMMARIZED FROM STEPHEN BAKER AND MANJEET KRIPALANI, "SOFTWARE: WILL OUTSOURCING HURT AMERICA'S SUPREMACY?" *BUSINESSWEEK*, MARCH 1, 2004, PP. 85–94.

promise to the customer and thereby creating customer expectations about service outcomes. Operations is responsible for the actions executing the promise and managing the customer experience. The feedback loop indicates that if outcomes are not satisfactory or do not create service advantage, management may alter either the service marketing strategy or the delivery system. The need to monitor and control the execution phase and have a recovery plan to defuse negative reactions before the customer leaves the system is also indicated.

Monitoring and controlling involve the standard managerial actions of reassigning workers to deal with short-run demand variations (such as Von's Supermarkets opening up another checkout stand when there are more than three people in line); checking with customers and employees as to how things are going; and, for many services, simply being available to customers. (Customers like the idea that they can talk to the manager . . . and few people want to talk to the assistant manager.)

Service Measurement Monitoring and Recovery Process

exhibit 7.5

SOURCE: THE MAC GROUP: BUILDING VALUE THROUGH CREATING A SERVICE ADVANTAGE. 1 MONTGOMERY ST., TELESIS TOWER. SUITE 1700, SAN FRANCISCO, CA 94104, JUNE 1990.

Recovery planning involves training frontline workers to respond to such situations as overbooking, lost luggage, or a bad meal.

One approach to measuring the economic value of customer satisfaction is to survey your customers. Ask them to rate each of a list of service and quality dimension items on two scales: importance and satisfaction. The point is to focus your attention on factors that are most important to your customers. In particular, focus on factors where their satisfaction rating is below their importance rating. (SERVQUAL, a widely applied questionnaire for measuring customer satisfaction, is discussed in Chapter 8.)

A company that clearly understands what drives customer satisfaction is Harrah's Casinos. (See the box "Service Strategy at Harrah's Casinos.")

STRUCTURING THE SERVICE ENCOUNTER: SERVICE-SYSTEM DESIGN MATRIX

Service encounters can be configured in a number of different ways. The service-system design matrix in Exhibit 7.6 identifies six common alternatives.

The top of the matrix shows the degree of customer/server contact: the *buffered core,* which is physically separated from the customer; the *permeable system,* which is penetrable by the customer via phone or face-to-face contact; and the *reactive system,* which is both penetrable and reactive to the customer's requirements. The left side of the matrix shows what we believe to be a logical marketing proposition, namely, that the greater the amount of contact, the greater the sales opportunity; the right side shows the impact on production efficiency as the customer exerts more influence on the operation.

The entries within the matrix list the ways in which service can be delivered. At one extreme, service contact is by mail; customers have little interaction with the system. At the other extreme, customers "have it their way" through face-to-face contact. The remaining four entries in the exhibit contain varying degrees of interaction.

As one would guess, production efficiency decreases as the customer has more contact (and therefore more influence) on the system. To offset this, the face-to-face contact provides high sales opportunity to sell additional products. Conversely, low contact, such as mail, allows the system to work more efficiently because the customer is unable to significantly affect (or disrupt) the system. However, there is relatively little opportunity for additional product sales.

SERVICE STRATEGY AT HARRAH'S CASINOS

In 1998, Harrah's was facing a big problem. How could it compete with the architectural splendor of its competitors on the Vegas Strip, given the company's aging, undistinguished Las Vegas hotel and run-of-the-mill casino facilities? Of course, they could invest millions in an effort to create their own Bellagio, Paris, or Caesar's Palace, but at best about all they could do was just catch up. In analyzing the situation, a new management team headed by its current CEO, Gary Loveman, hit upon a novel idea for the gaming industry: How about competing based on service? Why service? Analysis showed that what was important to gamblers in the way of service was not having to wait in lines, as well as employee friendliness and helpfulness. Making sure that the customer doesn't have to wait for service to check in to the hotel, to get chips, or to get into the restaurants signals to customers that the company respects the value of their time. Today, if you win a jackpot at Harrah's, you'll have someone there to help within 90 seconds. At other "Strip" hotels, you can easily wait 10 minutes or more. To further reduce waiting, Harrah's has invested heavily in self-service technology, such as $125,000 counting machines that allow players to convert their coins into bills without having to wait in line at the cashier's cage. Friendliness and helpfulness create a pleasant overall experience even when losing money. Employees are encouraged to talk to guests and are measured internally by supervisors and externally by mystery shoppers as a part of their "Spotlight on Success" program. Each department supervisor holds five-minute buzz sessions at the start of each shift to communicate knowledge and reinforce elements of Harrah's service culture. Senior management is required to attend at least three departmental buzz sessions per day. To reward good

service, Harrah's introduced a bonus program in which every employee receives a bonus of $75 to $200 for each quarter in which the measured level of services goes up by 3 percent or more. After crunching data, taking surveys, and conducting focus groups, Harrah's management discovered that gamblers who were more satisfied with their service experience also increased their gaming expenditures by 10 percent and that those who were extremely satisfied increased their gaming expenditures by 24 percent! The results of these efforts are high levels of customer loyalty and profitability that are the envy of the industry!

SOURCE: PRAVEEN NAYAR, "HARRAH'S CUSTOMER SATISFACTION PROGRAM," 2003 CASE STUDY, AND INTERVIEWS WITH GARY LOVEMAN AND JOHN BRUNS, HARRAH'S CASINOS.

There can be some shifting in the positioning of each entry. For our first example, consider the "Internet and on-site technology" entry in the matrix. The Internet clearly buffers the company from the customer, but interesting opportunities are available to provide relevant information and services to the customer. Because the Web site can be programmed to intelligently react to the inputs of the customer, significant opportunities for new sales may be possible. In addition, the system can be made to interface with real employees when the customer needs assistance that goes beyond the programming of the Web site. The Internet is truly a revolutionary technology when applied to the services that need to be provided by a company.

Another example of shifting in the positioning of an entry can be shown with the "face-to-face tight specs" entry in Exhibit 7.6. This entry refers to those situations where there is little variation in the service process—neither customer nor server has much discretion in creating the service. Fast-food restaurants and Disneyland come to mind. Face-to-face loose specs refers to situations where the service process is generally understood but there are options in how it will be performed or in the physical goods that are part of it. A full-service restaurant and a car sales agency are examples. Face-to-face total customization refers to

Service-System Design Matrix

exhibit 7.6

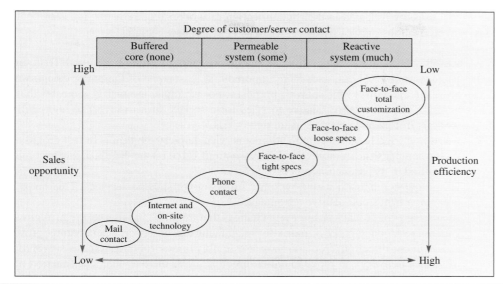

Characteristics of Workers, Operations, and Innovations Relative to the Degree of Customer/Service Contact

exhibit 7.7

| | | Degree of customer/server contact | | | | |
	Low ←					→ High
Worker requirements	Clerical skills	Helping skills	Verbal skills	Procedural skills	Trade skills	Diagnostic skills
Focus of operations	Paper handling	Demand management	Scripting calls	Flow control	Capacity management	Client mix
Technological innovations	Office automation	Routing methods	Computer databases	Electronic aids	Self-serve	Client/worker teams

service encounters whose specifications must be developed through some interaction between the customer and server. Legal and medical services are of this type, and the degree to which the resources of the system are mustered for the service determines whether the system is reactive, possibly to the point of even being proactive, or merely permeable. Examples would be the mobilization of an advertising firm's resources in preparation for an office visit by a major client, or an operating team scrambling to prepare for emergency surgery.

Exhibit 7.7 extends the design matrix. It shows the changes in workers, operations, and types of technical innovations as the degree of customer/service system contact changes. For worker requirements, the relationships between mail contact and clerical skills, Internet technology and helping skills, and phone contact and verbal skills are self-evident. Face-to-face tight specs require procedural skills in particular, because the worker must follow the routine in conducting a generally standardized, high-volume process. Face-to-face loose specs frequently call for trade skills (bank teller, draftsperson, maitre d', dental hygienist) to finalize the design for the service. Face-to-face total customization tends to call for diagnostic skills of the professional to ascertain the needs or desires of the client.

STRATEGIC USES OF THE MATRIX

The matrices in Exhibit 7.6 and Exhibit 7.7 have both operational and strategic uses. The operational uses are reflected in their identification of worker requirements, focus of operations, and innovations previously discussed. The strategic uses include

Cross Functional

1. Enabling systematic integration of operations and marketing strategy. Trade-offs become more clear-cut, and, more important, at least some of the major design variables are crystallized for analysis purposes. For example, the matrix indicates that it would make little sense relative to sales for a service firm to invest in high-skilled workers if it plans to operate using tight specs.
2. Clarifying exactly which combination of service delivery the firm is in fact providing. As the company incorporates the delivery options listed on the diagonal, it is becoming diversified in its production process.
3. Permitting comparison with how other firms deliver specific services. This helps to pinpoint a firm's competitive advantage.
4. Indicating evolutionary or life cycle changes that might be in order as the firm grows. Unlike the product–process matrix for manufacturing, however, where natural growth moves in one direction (from job shop to assembly line as volume increases), evolution of service delivery can move in either direction along the diagonal as a function of a sales–efficiency trade-off.

---

exhibit 7.8   Fail-Safing an Automotive Service Operation

FAILURE: CUSTOMER FORGETS THE NEED FOR SERVICE.
POKA-YOKE: SEND AUTOMATIC REMINDERS WITH A 5 PERCENT DISCOUNT.

FAILURE: CUSTOMER CANNOT FIND SERVICE AREA, OR DOES NOT FOLLOW PROPER FLOW.
POKA-YOKE: CLEAR AND INFORMATIVE SIGNAGE DIRECTING CUSTOMERS.

FAILURE: CUSTOMER HAS DIFFICULTY COMMUNICATING PROBLEM.
POKA-YOKE: JOINT INSPECTION—SERVICE ADVISER REPEATS HIS/HER UNDERSTANDING OF THE PROBLEM FOR CONFIRMATION OR ELABORATION BY THE CUSTOMER.

FAILURE: CUSTOMER DOES NOT UNDERSTAND THE NECESSARY SERVICE.
POKA-YOKE: PREPRINTED MATERIAL FOR MOST SERVICES, DETAILING WORK, REASONS, AND POSSIBLY A GRAPHIC REPRESENTATION.

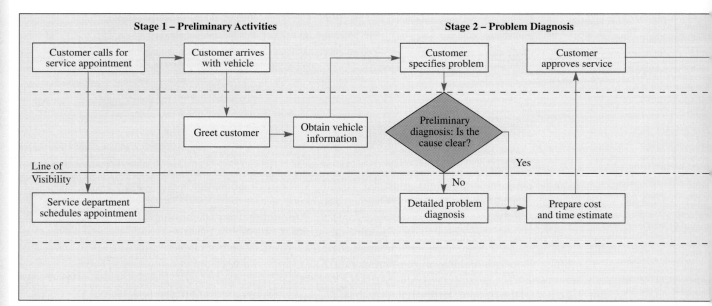

FAILURE: CUSTOMER ARRIVAL UNNOTICED.
POKA-YOKE: USE A BELL CHAIN TO SIGNAL ARRIVALS.

FAILURE: CUSTOMERS NOT SERVED IN ORDER OF ARRIVAL.
POKA-YOKE: PLACE NUMBERED MARKERS ON CARS AS THEY ARRIVE.
FAILURE: VEHICLE INFORMATION INCORRECT AND PROCESS IS TIME-CONSUMING.
POKA-YOKE: MAINTAIN CUSTOMER DATABASE AND PRINT FORMS WITH HISTORICAL INFORMATION.

FAILURE: INCORRECT DIAGNOSIS OF THE PROBLEM.
POKA-YOKE: HIGH-TECH CHECKLISTS, SUCH AS EXPERT SYSTEMS AND DIAGNOSTIC EQUIPMENT.

FAILURE: INCORRECT ESTIMATE.
POKA-YOKE: CHECKLISTS ITEMIZING COSTS BY COMMON REPAIR TYPES.

SERVICE BLUEPRINTING AND FAIL-SAFING

Just as is the case with manufacturing process design, the standard tool for service process design is the flowchart. Recently, the service gurus have begun calling the flowchart a **service blueprint** to emphasize the importance of process design. A unique feature of the service blueprint is the distinction made between the high customer contact aspects of the service (the parts of the process that the customer sees) and those activities that the customer does not see. This distinction is made with a "line of visibility" on the flowchart.

Service blueprint

Exhibit 7.8 is a blueprint of a typical automobile service operation. Each activity that makes up a typical service encounter is mapped into the flowchart. To better show the entity that controls the activities, levels are shown in the flowchart. The top level consists of activities that are under the control of the customer. Next are those activities performed by the service manager in handling the customer. The third level is the repair activities performed in the garage; the lowest level is the internal accounting activity.

Basic blueprinting describes the features of the service design but does not provide any direct guidance for how to make the process conform to that design. An approach to this problem is the application of **poka-yokes**—procedures that block the inevitable mistake from becoming a service defect.[2] Poka-yokes (roughly translated from the Japanese as "avoid mistakes") are common in factories (see Chapter 8, "Quality Management," for examples)

Poka-yokes

FAILURE: CUSTOMER NOT LOCATED.
POKA-YOKE: ISSUE BEEPERS TO CUSTOMERS WHO WISH TO LEAVE FACILITY.

FAILURE: BILL IS ILLEGIBLE.
POKA-YOKE: TOP COPY TO CUSTOMER, OR PLAIN PAPER BILL.

FAILURE: FEEDBACK NOT OBTAINED.
POKA-YOKE: CUSTOMER SATISFACTION POSTCARD GIVEN TO CUSTOMER WITH KEYS TO VEHICLE.

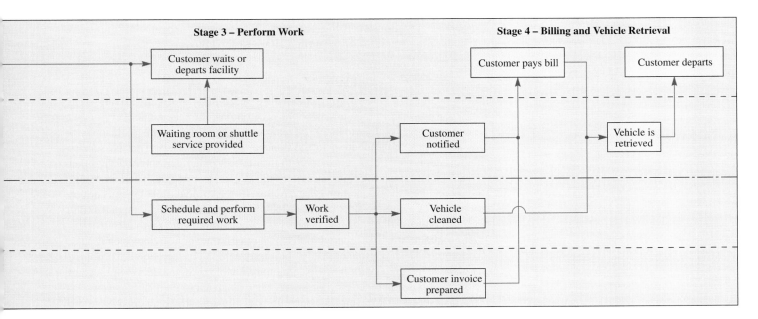

FAILURE: SERVICE SHUTTLE IS INCONVENIENT.
POKA-YOKE: SEATING IN AVAILABLE SHUTTLES IS ALLOCATED WHEN SCHEDULING APPOINTMENTS. LACK OF FREE SPACE INDICATES THAT CUSTOMERS NEEDING SHUTTLE SERVICE SHOULD BE SCHEDULED FOR ANOTHER TIME.
FAILURE: PARTS ARE NOT IN STOCK.
POKA-YOKE: LIMIT SWITCHES ACTIVATE SIGNAL LAMPS WHEN PART LEVEL FALLS BELOW ORDER POINT.

FAILURE: VEHICLE NOT CLEANED CORRECTLY.
POKA-YOKE: PERSON RETRIEVING VEHICLE INSPECTS, ORDERS A TOUCH-UP IF NECESSARY, AND REMOVES FLOOR MAT IN PRESENCE OF CUSTOMER.

FAILURE: VEHICLE TAKES TOO LONG TO ARRIVE.
POKA-YOKE: WHEN CASHIER ENTERS CUSTOMER'S NAME TO PRINT THE BILL, INFORMATION IS ELECTRONICALLY SENT TO RUNNERS WHO RETRIEVE VEHICLE WHILE THE CUSTOMER IS PAYING.

and consist of such things as fixtures to ensure that parts can be attached only in the right way, electronic switches that automatically shut off equipment if a mistake is made, kitting of parts prior to assembly to make sure the right quantities are used, and checklists to ensure that the right sequence of steps is followed.

There are many applications of poka-yokes to services as well. These can be classified into warning methods, physical or visual contact methods, and by what we call the *Three T's*— the Task to be done (Was the car fixed right?), the Treatment accorded to the customer (Was the service manager courteous?), and the Tangible or environmental features of the service facility (Was the waiting area clean and comfortable?). Finally (unlike in manufacturing), service poka-yokes often must be applied to fail-safing the actions of the customer as well as the service worker.

Poka-yoke examples include height bars at amusement parks; indented trays used by surgeons to ensure that no instruments are left in the patient; chains to configure waiting lines; take-a-number systems; turnstiles; beepers on ATMs to warn people to take their cards out of the machine; beepers at restaurants to make sure customers do not miss their table calls; mirrors on telephones to ensure a "smiling voice"; reminder calls for appointments; locks on airline lavatory doors that activate lights inside; small gifts in comment card envelopes to encourage customers to provide feedback about a service; and pictures of what "a clean room" looks like for kindergarten children.

Exhibit 7.8 illustrates how a typical automobile service operation might be fail-safed using poka-yokes. As a final comment, although these procedures cannot guarantee the level of error protection found in the factory, they still can reduce such errors in many service situations.

THREE CONTRASTING SERVICE DESIGNS

Three contrasting approaches to delivering on-site service are the production-line approach, made famous by McDonald's Corporation; the self-service approach, made famous by ATMs and gas stations; and the personal-attention approach, made famous by Nordstrom Department Stores and the Ritz-Carlton Hotel Company.

THE PRODUCTION-LINE APPROACH

The production-line approach pioneered by McDonald's refers to more than just the steps required to assemble a Big Mac. Rather, as Theodore Levitt notes, it treats the delivery of fast food as a manufacturing process rather than a service process.[3] The value of this philosophy is that it overcomes many problems inherent in the concept of service itself. That is, service implies subordination or subjugation of the server to the served; manufacturing, on the other hand, avoids this connotation because it focuses on things rather than people. Thus, in manufacturing and at McDonald's, "the orientation is toward the efficient production of results not on the attendance on others." Levitt notes that besides McDonald's marketing and financial skills, the company carefully controls "the execution of each outlet's central function—the rapid delivery of a uniform, high-quality mix of prepared foods in an environment of obvious cleanliness, order, and cheerful courtesy. The systematic substitution of equipment for people, combined with the carefully planned use and positioning of technology, enables McDonald's to attract and hold patronage in proportions no predecessor or imitator has managed to duplicate."

Levitt cites several aspects of McDonald's operations to illustrate the concepts. Note the extensive use of what we term poka-yokes.

- The McDonald's french fryer allows cooking of the optimum number of french fries at one time.
- A wide-mouthed scoop is used to pick up the precise amount of french fries for each order size. (The employee never touches the product.)
- Storage space is expressly designed for a predetermined mix of prepackaged and premeasured products.

INFORMATION PRODUCTION LINE

In a recent *Harvard Business Review* article, Uday Karmarkar discusses a different kind of production line made possible by technology. "Forget about the information highway, Moore's Law, and the wonders of wirelessness. Rather think of technology as creating an information assembly line—information today can be standardized, built to order, assembled from components, picked, packed, stored, and shipped, all using processes resembling manufacturing." As an example, he describes how the process of diagnostic imaging can be entirely reconfigured from one involving extensive manual activities with a patient being moved through a hospital to one where "a patient can be scanned at a convenient location by a technologist operating a machine out of a storefront or even a mobile trailer. The images can be sent electronically to the diagnosing radiologist, who may be in a clinic many miles away, or directly to the referring physician. Voice recognition software transcribes the diagnosis, or the transcriptions can be performed offshore. Intelligent software tools are being developed to aid in the actual diagnosis, and one day they may even supplant the radiologist for certain problems."

SOURCE: UDAY KARMARKAR, "WILL YOU SURVIVE THE SERVICES REVOLUTION?" *HARVARD BUSINESS REVIEW*, MAY–JUNE 2004, P. 102.

- Cleanliness is pursued by providing ample trash cans in and outside each facility. (Larger outlets have motorized sweepers for the parking area.)
- Hamburgers are wrapped in color-coded paper.
- Through painstaking attention to total design and facilities planning, everything is built integrally into the (McDonald's) machine itself—into the technology of the system. The only choice available to the attendant is to operate it exactly as the designers intended. Using our service-system design matrix (Exhibit 7.6), we would categorize this as a face-to-face tight spec service.

THE SELF-SERVICE APPROACH

In contrast to the production-line approach, C. H. Lovelock and R. F. Young propose that the service process can be enhanced by having the customer take a greater role in the production of the service.[4] Company Web sites, automatic teller machines, self-service gas stations, salad bars, and e-tickets are approaches that shift the service burden to the consumer. Based on our service-system design matrix, these are great examples of the use of Internet and on-site technology. Many customers like self-service because it puts them in control. For others, this philosophy requires some selling on the part of the service organization to convince customers that it helps them. To this end, Lovelock and Young propose a number of steps, including developing customer trust; promoting the benefits of cost, speed, and convenience; and following up to make sure that the procedures are being effectively used. In essence, this turns customers into "partial employees" who must be trained in what to do and, as noted earlier, must be "fail-safed" in case of mistake.

THE PERSONAL-ATTENTION APPROACH

An interesting contrast in the way personal attention is provided can be seen in Nordstrom Department Stores and the Ritz-Carlton Hotel Company.

At Nordstrom, a rather loose, unstructured process relies on developing a relationship between the individual salesperson

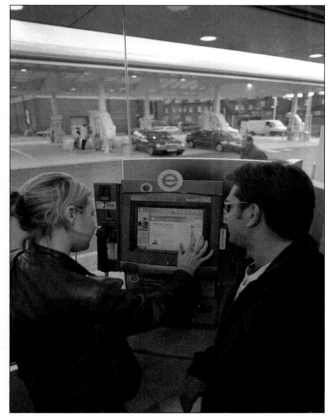

BP AMOCO PROVIDES PAY AT THE PUMP SERVICES AS WELL AS THE NEW "BP ATTENDANT." CUSTOMERS CAN USE TOUCH SCREENS TO LOG ONTO THE INTERNET TO VIEW LOCAL WEATHER REPORTS AND TRAFFIC INFORMATION WHILE FILLING UP.

and the customer (this is a face-to-face with total customization service). At the Ritz-Carlton, the process is virtually scripted, and the information system rather than the employee keeps track of the guest's (customer's) personal preferences (this is a face-to-face loose spec example). Tom Peters describes Nordstrom's approach here:

> After several visits to a store's men's clothing department, a customer's suit still did not fit. He wrote the company president, who sent a tailor to the customer's office with a new suit for fitting. When the alterations were completed, the suit was delivered to the customer—free of charge.
>
> This incident involved the $1.3 billion, Seattle-based Nordstrom, a specialty clothing retailer. Its sales per square foot are about five times that of a typical department store. Who received the customer's letter and urged the extreme (by others' standards) response? Co-chairman John Nordstrom.
>
> The frontline providers of this good service are well paid. Nordstrom's salespersons earn a couple of bucks an hour more than competitors, plus a 6.75 percent commission. Its top salesperson moves over $1 million a year in merchandise. Nordstrom lives for its customers and salespeople. Its only official organization chart puts the customer at the top, followed by sales and sales support people. Next come department managers, then store managers, and the board of directors at the very bottom.
>
> Salespersons religiously carry a "personal book," where they record voluminous information about each of their customers; senior, successful salespeople often have three or four bulging books, which they carry everywhere, according to Betsy Sanders, the vice president who orchestrated the firm's wildly successful penetration of the tough southern California market. "My objective is to get one new personal customer a day," says a budding Nordstrom star. The system helps him do just that. He has a virtually unlimited budget to send cards, flowers, and thank-you notes to customers. He also is encouraged to shepherd his customer to any department in the store to assist in a successful shopping trip.
>
> He also is abetted by what may be the most liberal returns policy in this or any other business: Return *anything,* no questions asked. Sanders says that "trusting customers," or "our bosses" as she repeatedly calls them, is vital to the Nordstrom philosophy. President Jim Nordstrom told the *Los Angeles Times,* "I don't care if they roll a Goodyear tire into the store. If they say they paid $200, give them $200 (in cash) for it." Sanders acknowledges that a few customers rip the store off—"rent hose from us," to use a common insider's line. But this is more than offset by goodwill from the 99 percent-plus who benefit from the "No Problem at Nordstrom" logo that the company lives up to with unmatched zeal.
>
> No bureaucracy gets in the way of serving the customer. Policy? Sanders explains to a dumbfounded group of Silicon Valley executives, "I know this drives the lawyers nuts, but our whole 'policy manual' is just one sentence, 'Use your own best judgment at all times.' " One store manager offers a translation: "Don't chew gum. Don't steal from us."[5]

The Ritz-Carlton approach is described in the following excerpts from the company's Baldrige Award Application Summary and discussions with Scott Long of Ritz-Carlton's Huntington Hotel in Pasadena, California. Exhibit 7.9 shows the formalized service procedure (the Three Steps of Service). Exhibit 7.10 displays the information system used to capture data about guests ("The Ritz-Carlton Repeat Guest History Program"). Note that the three steps of service are integrated into the guest history information system.

> Systems for the collection and utilization of customer reaction and satisfaction are widely deployed and extensively used throughout the organization. Our efforts are centered on various customer segments and product lines.

The Ritz-Carlton Hotel Company (Three Steps of Service)

exhibit 7.9

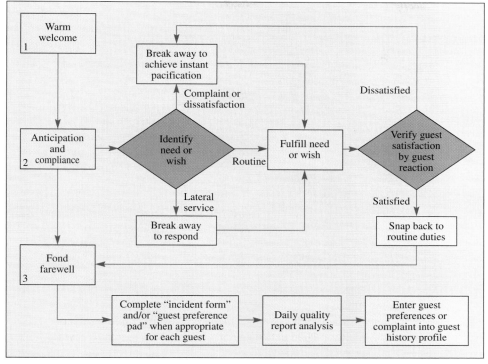

SOURCE: *RITZ-CARLTON MALCOLM BALDRIGE NATIONAL QUALITY AWARD APPLICATION SUMMARY*, 1993, P. 11.

The Ritz-Carlton Repeat Guest History Program (An Aid to Highly Personalized Service Delivery)

exhibit 7.10

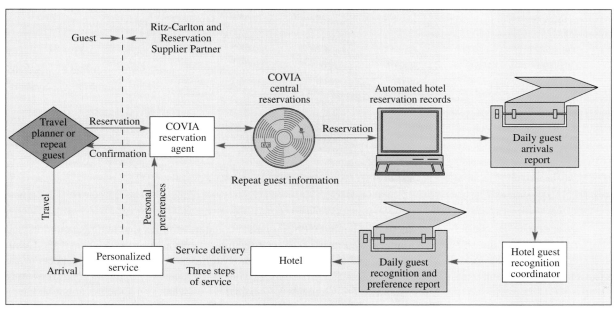

SOURCE: *RITZ-CARLTON MALCOLM BALDRIGE NATIONAL QUALITY AWARD APPLICATION SUMMARY*, 1993, P. 6.

SEVEN CHARACTERISTICS OF A WELL-DESIGNED SERVICE SYSTEM

1 **Each element of the service system is consistent with the operating focus of the firm.** For example, when the focus is on speed of delivery, each step in the process should help foster speed.

2 **It is user-friendly.** This means that the customer can interact with it easily—that is, it has good signage, understandable forms, logical steps in the process, and service workers available to answer questions.

3 **It is robust.** That is, it can cope effectively with variations in demand and resource availability. For example, if the computer goes down, effective backup systems are in place to permit service to continue.

4 **It is structured so that consistent performance by its people and systems is easily maintained.** This means the tasks required of the workers are doable, and the supporting technologies are truly supportive and reliable.

5 **It provides effective links between the back office and the front office so that nothing falls between the cracks.** In football parlance, there should be "no fumbled handoffs."

6 **It manages the evidence of service quality in such a way that customers see the value of the service provided.** Many services do a great job behind the scenes but fail to make this visible to the customer. This is particularly true where a service improvement is made. Unless customers are made aware of the improvement through explicit communication about it, the improved performance is unlikely to gain maximum impact.

7 **It is cost-effective.** There is minimum waste of time and resources in delivering the service. Even if the service outcome is satisfactory, customers are often put off by a service company that appears inefficient.

Our approach is the use of systems which allow every employee to collect and utilize quality-related data on a daily basis. These systems provide critical, responsive data which include:
(1) On-line guest preference information;
(2) Quantity of error free products and services;
(3) Opportunities for quality improvement.

Our automated property management systems enable the on-line access and utilization of guest preference information at the individual customer level. All employees collect and input this data, and use the data as part of their service delivery with individual guests.

Our quality production reporting system is a method of aggregating hotel level data from nearly two dozen sources into a summary format. It serves as an early warning system and facilitates analysis. The processes employees use to identify quality opportunities for improvement are standardized in a textbook, and available throughout our organization.[6]

No matter what approach is taken to design a service, the need for the service characteristics shown in the box titled "Seven Characteristics of a Well-Designed Service System" should be evident.

APPLYING BEHAVIORAL SCIENCE TO SERVICE ENCOUNTERS

Effective management of service encounters requires that managers understand customer perceptions as well as the technical features of service processes. Chase and Dasu[7] suggest applying behavioral concepts to enhance customer perceptions of three aspects of the encounter: *the flow of the service experience* (what's happening), *the flow of time* (how long it seems to take), and *judging encounter performance* (what you thought about it later). Looking at the service encounter from this perspective has led to the following six behaviorally based principles for service encounter design and management.

1. **The front-end and the back-end of the encounter are not created equal.** It is widely believed that the start and finish of a service or the so-called service bookends are equally weighted in the eyes of the customer. A good deal of research indicates that this is not the case. While it is essential to achieve a base level of satisfactory performance at the beginning so that the customer remains throughout the service, a company is likely to be better off with a relatively weak start and a modest upswing on the end than having a great start and a so-so ending. This ties in with two important findings from behavioral decision theory: the preference for improvement and the dominant effect of the ending in our recollections. The disproportionate influence of the ending gives rise to a corollary principle—that is, end on an up note. Examples of companies that "finish strong": Malaysian Airlines, which lavishes attention on baggage collection and ground transportation, in order to leave the customer with a good feeling; a kitchen cabinet company that ties bright bows on all the installed work, and leaves behind a vase of flowers; cruise lines that end each day with raffles, contests, and shows, end the cruise with the captain's dinner, and pass out keepsakes or bottles of wine upon reaching the home port. All of these strategies are designed to make the final interaction a good one. In a similar vein, relative to unpleasant experiences, researchers have found that prolonging of a colonoscopy by painlessly leaving the colon scope for about a minute after the procedure was completed produced significant improvements in how patients perceived the procedure. (Note here that we are actually extending the duration of discomfort, yet the overall perception is superior to immediate cessation of the procedure!)

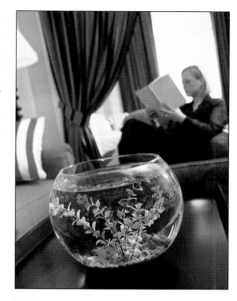

THE HOTEL MONACO IN CHICAGO AIMS TO IMPRESS ITS GUESTS THROUGHOUT THEIR STAY. GUESTS ARE GIVEN THEIR OWN PET GOLDFISH TO MAKE THEM FEEL AT HOME.

2. **Segment the pleasure; combine the pain.** Breaking up may be hard to do, but depending upon the type of encounter, it might be the best thing to do. Events seem longer when they are segmented. This suggests that we want to break pleasant experiences into multiple stages and combine unpleasant ones into a single stage. Thus, it makes sense to, say, reduce the number of stages in a visit to a clinic, even if it extends the time of the visit somewhat, and to provide two 90-second rides at Disneyland rather than one three-minute ride.

3. **Let the customer control the process.** Giving people control over how a process is to be conducted enhances their satisfaction with it. In the medical area, allowing people to choose which arm a blood sample is drawn from reduces the perceived pain of the procedure. For certain repair jobs, allowing people to select a future date they want it to be scheduled may be preferred to doing it right away.

4. **Pay attention to norms and rituals.** Deviations from norms are likely to be overly blamed for failures. This is particularly true for professional services whose processes and outcomes are not clearly ascertainable by the client, and hence adherence to norms is the central basis for evaluation. Consulting firms are expected to make presentations to the boss, even if he or she has little or nothing to do with the problem being studied. At such presentations, all members of the client team are to be lauded for their assistance even if they were less than helpful in accomplishing the work.

5. **People are easier to blame than systems.** When things go wrong, people's gut reaction is to blame the server rather than the system. We want to put a human face on the problem. This is seen especially in complex services where what goes on behind the scenes or in the system is difficult for the customer to untangle. The gate agent is frequently blamed for not allowing a late arrival to get on the plane, even though it is a rule of the airline association that no one can board 15 minutes before departure. (A corollary to this principle is that "a miss is worse than a mile." That is, if someone arrives late for a service, it's better not to say, "too bad, you just missed it.")

6. **Let the punishment fit the crime in service recovery.** How do you make up for an encounter error? Research suggests that the most appropriate recovery action depends upon whether it is a task (outcome) error or a treatment (interpersonal process) error. A botched task calls for material compensation, while poor treatment from a server

exhibit 7.11   The New Service Development Process Cycle

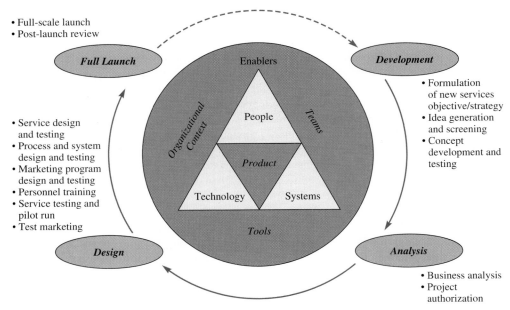

- Full-scale launch
- Post-launch review

Full Launch

Enablers

Organizational Context

People

Teams

Product

Technology   Systems

Tools

Development

- Formulation of new services objective/strategy
- Idea generation and screening
- Concept development and testing

- Service design and testing
- Process and system design and testing
- Marketing program design and testing
- Personnel training
- Service testing and pilot run
- Test marketing

Design

Analysis

- Business analysis
- Project authorization

SOURCE: REPRINTED WITH PERMISSION FROM S. P. JOHNSON, L. J. MENOR, A. V. ROTH, AND R. B. CHASE, "A CRITICAL EVALUATION OF THE NEW SERVICE DEVELOPMENT PROCESS," IN J. A. FITZSIMMONS AND M. J. FITZSIMMONS (EDS.), *NEW SERVICE DEVELOPMENT* (THOUSAND OAKS, CA: SAGE PUBLICATIONS, 2000), P. 18.

calls for an apology. Reversing these recovery actions is unlikely to be effective. For example, having a copying job done poorly at a copy store, of course, calls for a quick apology, but more important for quick rework and perhaps some compensation for the customer's inconvenience. On the other hand, if the copying job is done correctly, but the clerk is rude, a sincere apology from the store manager and the clerk is far more likely to result in a satisfied customer than a free coupon or other minor tangible form of compensation.

NEW SERVICE DEVELOPMENT PROCESS

The new service development process can be viewed as a cycle of activities as depicted in Exhibit 7.11. The development and analysis stages represent the planning phase where the strategic fit and market viability are determined. The Design and Launch stages represent the implementation phase. The enablers are the teams, tools, and organizational context that facilitate the process. The resultant service product is defined by its people, technology, and systems elements.

SERVICE GUARANTEES AS DESIGN DRIVERS

The phrase "Positively, absolutely, overnight" is an example of a service guarantee most of us know by heart. Hiding behind such marketing promises of service satisfaction is a set of actions that must be taken by the operations organization to fulfill these promises.

Service guarantees

Thousands of companies have launched **service guarantees** as a marketing tool designed to provide peace of mind for customers unsure about trying their service. From an operations perspective, a service guarantee can be used not only as an improvement tool but also at the design stage to focus the firm's delivery system squarely on the things it must do well to satisfy the customer.

Even professional service firms such as Rath and Strong Consulting have service guarantees. (Theirs allows the client to choose from a menu of payouts if they do not—for example—cut lead time by *x* percent. Menu options include refunds and no charge for overtime work to get the job done.)

The elements of a good service guarantee are that it is unconditional (no small print); meaningful to the customer (the payoff fully covers the customer's dissatisfaction); easy to understand and communicate (for employees as well as customers); and painless to invoke (given proactively).[8]

Recent research on service guarantees has provided the following conclusions about them:[9]

1. Any guarantee is better than no guarantee. The most effective guarantees are big deals. They put the company at risk in the eyes of the customer.
2. Involve the customer as well as employees in the design.
3. Avoid complexity or legalistic language. Use big print, not small print.
4. Do not quibble or wriggle when a customer invokes the guarantee.
5. Make it clear that you are happy for customers to invoke the guarantee.

An issue of growing importance in service relates to the ethical and possibly legal responsibility of a company to actually provide the service that is promised. For example, is an airline responsible for transporting a passenger with a guaranteed reservation, even though the flight has been overbooked? Or consider the Internet service provider's responsibility to provide enough telephone lines so that customers do not receive busy signals when they try to connect to the service. These are difficult issues because having excess capacity is expensive. Demand can be nearly impossible to predict with great accuracy, thus making the estimates of needed capacity difficult.

A very powerful tool—waiting line analysis—is available to help better understand the relationships between the factors that drive a service system. These factors include the average number of customers that arrive over a period of time, the average time that it takes to serve each customer, the number of servers, and information about the size of the customer population. Waiting line models have been developed that allow the estimation of expected waiting time and expected resource utilization. This is the topic of the technical note to this chapter.

CONCLUSION

In this chapter, we have shown how service businesses are in many ways very similar to manufacturing businesses. Likewise is the need for trade-offs in developing a focus. Focus, for example, is important to success, just as it was with the design of manufacturing systems.

The service-system design matrix is in many ways similar to the product–process matrix we used to categorize manufacturing operations. Further, the tools of flow diagrams and capacity analysis are similar as well.

Services are, however, very different compared to manufacturing when we consider the high degree of personalization often required, the speed of delivery needed, the direct customer contact, and the inherent variability of the service encounter. The buffering and scheduling mechanisms that we have available to smooth the demand placed on a manufacturing operation are often not available to the service operation. Services generally require much higher levels of capacity relative to demand. In addition, they place a greater need for flexibility on the part of the workers involved in providing the services.

KEY TERMS

Facilities-based services Customers must go to the place of business.

Field-based services Production and consumption take place in the customer's environment.

High and low degree of customer contact The physical presence of the customer in the system and the percentage of time the customer must be in the system relative to the total time it takes to perform the service.

Service blueprint The flowchart of a service process, emphasizing what is visible and what is not visible to the customer.

Poka-yokes Procedures that prevent mistakes from beginning defects. They are commonly found in manufacturing but also can be used in service processes.

Service guarantee A promise of service satisfaction backed up by a set of actions that must be taken to fulfill the promise.

REVIEW AND DISCUSSION QUESTIONS

1   Who is the "customer" in a jail? A cemetery? A summer camp for children?
2   How have price and variety competition changed McDonald's basic formula for success?
3   Could a service firm use a production-line approach or self-serve design and still keep a high customer focus (personal attention)? Explain and support your answer with examples.
4   Why should a manager of a bank home office be evaluated differently than a manager of a bank branch?
5   Identify the high-contact and low-contact operations of the following services:
    a. A dental office.
    b. An airline.
    c. An accounting office.
    d. An automobile agency.
    e. Amazon.com
6   Are there any service businesses that won't be affected by knowledge outsourcing?
7   Relative to the behavioral science discussion, what practical advice do you have for a hotel manager to enhance the ending of a guest's stay in the hotel?
8   List some occupations or sporting events where the ending is a dominant element in evaluating success.
9   Behavioral scientists suggest that we remember events as snapshots, not movies. How would you apply this to designing a service?
10 Some suggest that customer expectation is the key to service success. Give an example from your own experience to support or refute this assertion.
11 Where would you place a drive-in church, a campus food vending machine, and a bar's automatic mixed drink machine on the service-system design matrix?
12 Can a manufacturer have a service guarantee in addition to a product guarantee?
13 Suppose you were the manager of a restaurant and you were told honestly that a couple eating dinner had just seen a mouse. What would you say to them? How would you recover from this service crisis?

PROBLEMS

1   Place the following functions of a department store on the service-system design matrix: mail order (that is, catalog), phone order, hardware, stationery, apparel, cosmetics, customer service (such as taking complaints).
2   Do the same as in the previous problem for a hospital with the following activities and relationships: physician/patient, nurse/patient, billing, medical records, lab tests, admissions, diagnostic tests (such as X-rays).
3   Perform a quick service audit the next time you go shopping at a department store. Evaluate the three T's of service: the Task, the Treatment, and the Tangible features of the service on a scale of 1 (poor), 3 (average), and 5 (excellent). Remember that the tangible features include the environment, layout, and appearance of the store, not the goods you purchased.
4   SYSTEM DESCRIPTION EXERCISE
    The beginning step in studying a productive system is to develop a description of that system. Once a system is described, we can better determine why the system works well or poorly and recommend production-related improvements. Because most of us are familiar with fast-food

restaurants, try your hand at describing the production system employed at, say, a McDonald's. In doing so, answer the following questions:

a. What are the important aspects of the service package?

b. Which skills and attitudes are needed by the service personnel?

c. How can customer demand be altered?

d. Provide a rough-cut blueprint of the delivery system. (It is not necessary to provide execution times. Just diagram the basic flow through the system.) Critique the blueprint. Are there any unnecessary steps or can failure points be eliminated?

e. Can the customer/provider interface be changed to include more technology? More self-serve?

f. Which measures are being used to evaluate the service? Which could be used?

5 What are the differences between high and low customer contact service (CCS) businesses, in general, for the dimensions listed below? (Example—Facility Layout: in a high CCS, the facility would be designed to enhance the feelings and comfort of the customer while in a low CCS, the facility would be designed for efficient processing.)

	Low CCS Businesses	High CCS Businesses
Worker skill		
Capacity utilization		
Level of automation		

CASE: PIZZA USA: AN EXERCISE IN TRANSLATING CUSTOMER REQUIREMENTS INTO PROCESS DESIGN REQUIREMENTS

A central theme of contemporary operations management is *focus on the customer.* This is commonly understood to mean that if a company does focus on its customers and if it is able to consistently deliver what the customer wants in a cost-effective manner, then the company should be successful. The hard part is to be able to truly understand what the customer wants. Translating what the customer wants into a deliverable product (meaning some combination of goods and services) and designing a set of processes that will consistently deliver the product in a cost-effective manner are every bit as difficult. Finally, connecting the management of these products and processes to obtain desired business outcomes of the organization is a further challenge.

The following exercise will try to illustrate how difficult all of this can be.

THE SETTING

Pizza USA is a chain of pizza restaurants that currently offers sit-down and take-out service. Many customers have said that they would buy more pizzas from Pizza USA if it offered a delivery service. This exercise is in two parts. In Part I, you play the customer. In Part II, you play the manager at Pizza USA who is responsible for developing the pizza delivery process design requirements.

PART I

To start with, you have to think *like* a customer. This should be easy since you probably have experience with *ordering pizza to be delivered.* Put that experience to work! Make a list of the attributes of *pizza delivery* that are important to you *AS A CUSTOMER!*

As we said, this should be easy. Right? Or is it? In devising your list, consider the following:

What must a pizza delivery service accomplish so that you are reasonably satisfied? Beyond your being reasonably satisfied, what could a pizza delivery service do that would make it really unique and create a differential advantage? In other words, what could a pizza delivery service do that might cause you to ALWAYS order from one particular service (and, perhaps, to pay more for the privilege)?

As you develop your list, remember that you are considering *only the delivery service* and NOT the pizza itself. Assume that this pizza restaurant can make whatever kind of pizza (and side items) that you want.

PART II

Now, put on your *"Pizza USA manager's hat."* For this part of the exercise, you will be teamed with some other students. First, using the lists of all of your team members, create a master list. Next, try to group the items on your list under a series of major headings; for example, "condition of the delivered pizza" or "quick, on-time delivery" or "order accuracy," and so on. Finally, make a list of the "pizza delivery process design requirements" that your pizza delivery process will have to meet. As you do this, think about measurable standards; in other words, what would you measure in order to ensure that your process is operating effectively and efficiently? Why do you think that these measures will be useful?

Here's an example of how a part of this analysis could go. One customer requirement may be that *the pizza should be hot when it is delivered.* The fact is that as soon as the pizza comes out of the oven, it starts to cool. So, how could you keep the pizza from dropping below some minimum temperature before you hand it to your customer?

ASSIGNMENT

1 Make a list of pizza delivery attributes that are important to you as a customer.

2 Combine your list with the list of a few other class members and categorize the items under a series of major headings.

3 Make a list of pizza delivery process design requirements. Associate with each requirement a measure that would ensure that the process meets the requirement.

4 Design a process that meets your requirements. Describe it by using a flowchart similar to those shown in Exhibits 7.8, 7.9, and 7.10.

SOURCE: SPECIAL THANKS TO MARK IPPOLITO OF INDIANA UNIVERSITY–PURDUE UNIVERSITY INDIANAPOLIS FOR CONTRIBUTING THIS EXERCISE.

CASE: CONTACT CENTERS SHOULD TAKE A LESSON FROM LOCAL BUSINESSES

There are now three bagel shops in my hometown, two of which are fairly rudimentary in nature: They sell bagels, cream cheese, and coffee. Good bagels, but nothing fancy.

The third store is part of a large, Boston-area chain, and the bagels there are also good. The store often has children's entertainment and has a large seating area with games, free newspapers, and room to spread out and relax. Last, and most important, it has a system that consists of a conveyor belt running across the length of the counter—between the register and the "schmearing" operation—with a huge circular saw in the center. As bagels are ordered, they are tossed onto the conveyor, sliced in half by the saw, and travel at high speed to the end of the conveyor. In other words, store number three isn't just a bagel store; it's entertainment as well.

But that store has lost my business . . . At least 30 percent of the time we order from this store, the order is wrong. And the schmearers at store number three are probably the most stressed cream cheese–appliers ever. The look of terror on their faces from the constant pressure of the sliced bagels whizzing down the conveyor toward them is similar to the look I've seen on the faces of customer service reps in oh-so-many call centers.

Does this happen in your call center? Think about it. The system that makes store number three so very profitable just cost it what I'd argue is a pretty profitable customer.

There's also a hardware store in my hometown (actually, two). In the next town, there is a Home Depot, which I've frequented many a weekend, but not anymore. Our kitchen sink had been leaking on and off for six months, though the leak had been patched. The prospect of standing in line at Home Depot yet again, waiting for service and searching through what seemed like thousands of O-rings to find the right one, was not what I had planned for the weekend.

So I changed my plan and went to my local hardware store. As expected, the prices were at least two times what Home Depot charges, but the service was fabulous, particularly the part when the plumbing department manager suggested a little trick that would prevent the O-ring from failing. I took my expensive O-ring, went home, tried his suggestion, and five minutes later was finished. Not a drop since.

QUESTIONS

1 What lessons are there from these two examples for contact (call) center managers?

2 What are the dilemmas posed in solving these problems in the context of a call center?

SOURCE: MODIFIED FROM CHRIS SELLAND, *CUSTOMER RELATIONSHIP MANAGEMENT* 8, NO. 4 (APRIL 2004), P. 22.

SELECTED BIBLIOGRAPHY

Baker, S., and M. Kripalani. "Software: Will Outsourcing Hurt America's Supremacy?" *BusinessWeek,* March 1, 2004, pp. 85–94.

Bitran, G. R., and J. Hoech. "The Humanization of Service: Respect at the Moment of Truth." *Sloan Management Review,* Winter 1990, pp. 89–96.

Chase, R. B. "The Customer Contact Approach to Services: Theoretical Bases and Practical Extensions." *Operations Research* 21, no. 4 (1981), pp. 698–705.

———. "The Mall Is My Factory: Reflections of a Service Junkie." *Production and Operations Management,* Winter 1996, pp. 298–308.

Chase, R. B., and S. Dasu. "Want to Perfect Your Company's Service? Use Behavioral Science." *Harvard Business Review* 72, no. 6 (May–June 2001), pp. 78–84.

Chase, R. B., and D. M. Stewart. "Make Your Service Fail-Safe." *Sloan Management Review,* Spring 1994, pp. 35–44.

Cleveland, B., and J. Mayben. "Call Center Management on Fast Forward: Succeeding in Today's Dynamic Inbound Environment." Call Center Press, 1997.

Collier, D. A. *The Service/Quality Solution.* Burr Ridge, IL: Irwin Professional Publishing, 1993.

Finsthal, T. W. "My Employees Are My Service Guarantee." *Harvard Business Review,* July–August 1989, pp. 28–33.

Fitzsimmons, J. A., and M. J. Fitzsimmons. *Service Management: Operations, Strategy, and Information Technology.* 4th ed. New York: Irwin/McGraw-Hill, 2004.

Heskett, J. L.; W. E. Sasser; and L. A. Schlesinger. *The Service Profit Chain: How Leading Companies Link Profit and Growth to Loyalty, Satisfaction, and Value.* New York: Free Press, 1997.

Karmarkar, U. "Will You Survive the Services Revolution?" *Harvard Business Review,* May–June 2004, pp. 99–107.

Metters, R.; K. King-Metters; and M. Pullman. *Successful Service Operations Management.* Cincinnati, OH: Thomson South-Western Publishing, 2003.

Poisant, J. *Creating and Sustaining a Superior Customer Service Organization: A Book about Taking Care of the People Who Take Care of the Customers.* Westport, CT: Quorum Books, 2002.

Roth, A. V.; R. B. Chase; and C. Voss. "Service in the U.S.: A Study of Service Practice and Performance in the United States," supported by Severn Trent Plc, U.K. Government's Department of Trade and Industry, Department of National Heritage, 1997.

Sawhney, M.; S. Balasubramanian; and V. V. Krishnan. "Creating Growth with Services." *MIT Sloan Management Review,* Winter 2004, pp. 34–43.

Schmenner, R. W. *Service Operations Management.* Englewood Cliffs, NJ: Prentice Hall, 1995.

Zemke, R., and C. Bell. *Service Magic: The Art of Amazing Your Customers.* Chicago: Dearborn, 2003.

FOOTNOTES

1 J. Heskett, "Lessons from the Service Sector," *Harvard Business Review*, March–April 1987.

2 R. B. Chase and D. M. Stewart, "Make Your Service Fail-Safe," *Sloan Management Review*, Spring 1994, pp. 35–44.

3 T. Levitt, "Production-Line Approach to Service," *Harvard Business Review* 50, no. 5 (September–October 1972), pp. 41–52.

4 C. H. Lovelock and R. F. Young, "Look to Customers to Increase Productivity," *Harvard Business Review* 57, no. 2 (March–April 1979), pp. 168–78.

5 T. Peters, *Quality!* (Palo Alto, CA: TPC Communications, 1986), pp. 10–12.

6 *Ritz-Carlton Malcolm Baldrige National Quality Award Application Summary*, 1993, p. 6.

7 Richard B. Chase and Sriram Dasu, "Want to Perfect Your Company's Service? Use Behavioral Science." *Harvard Business Review* 72, no. 6 (May–June 2001), pp. 78–84.

8 C. W. L. Hart, "The Power of Unconditional Service Guarantees," *Harvard Business Review* 56, no. 4 (July–August 1988), p. 55.

9 Gordon H. G. McDougall, T. Levesque, and P. VanderPlaat, "Designing the Service Guarantee: Unconditional or Specific?" *The Journal of Service Marketing* 12, no. 4 (1998), pp. 278–93.

technical note seven
WAITING LINE MANAGEMENT

Understanding waiting lines or **queues** and learning how to manage them is one of the most important areas in operations management. It is basic to creating schedules, job design, inventory levels, and so on. In our service economy we wait in line every day, from driving to work to checking out at the supermarket. We also encounter waiting lines at factories—jobs wait in lines to be worked on at different machines, and machines themselves wait their turn to be overhauled. In short, waiting lines are pervasive.

Queues

In this technical note we discuss the basic elements of waiting line problems and provide standard steady-state formulas for solving them. These formulas, arrived at through queuing theory, enable planners to analyze service requirements and establish service facilities appropriate to stated conditions. Queuing theory is broad enough to cover such dissimilar delays as those encountered by customers in a shopping mall or aircraft in a holding pattern awaiting landing slots. Recently, Internet access providers have had problems providing enough modem telephone lines for subscribers dialing into the Internet. This problem can also be analyzed by queuing models.

ECONOMICS OF THE WAITING LINE PROBLEM

The central problem in virtually every waiting line situation is a trade-off decision. The manager must weigh the added cost of providing more rapid service (more traffic lanes, additional landing strips, more checkout stands) against the inherent cost of waiting.

Service

Frequently, the cost trade-off decision is straightforward. For example, if we find that the total time our employees spend in the line waiting to use a copying machine would otherwise be spent in productive activities, we could compare the cost of installing one additional machine to the value of employee time saved. The decision could then be reduced to dollar terms and the choice easily made.

On the other hand, suppose that our waiting line problem centers on demand for beds in a hospital. We can compute the cost of additional beds by summing the costs for building construction, additional equipment required, and increased maintenance. But what is on the other side of the scale? Here we are confronted with the problem of trying to place a dollar figure on a patient's need for a hospital bed that is unavailable. While we can estimate lost hospital income, what about the human cost arising from this lack of adequate hospital care?

Service

COST-EFFECTIVENESS BALANCE

Exhibit TN7.1 shows the essential trade-off relationship under typical (steady-state) customer traffic conditions. Initially, with minimal service capacity, the waiting line cost is at a maximum. As service capacity is increased, there is a reduction in the number of customers in the line and in their waiting times, which decreases waiting line cost. The variation in this function is often represented by the negative exponential curve. The cost of installing service capacity is shown simplistically as a linear rather than step function. The aggregate or total cost is shown as a U-shaped curve, a common approximation in such equilibrium problems. The idealized optimal cost is found at the crossover point between the service capacity and waiting line curves.

Service

THE PRACTICAL VIEW OF WAITING LINES

Before we proceed with a technical presentation of waiting line theory, it is useful to look at the intuitive side of the issue to see what it means. Exhibit TN7.2 shows arrivals at a service facility (such as a bank) and service requirements at that facility (such as tellers and loan officers). One important variable is the number of arrivals over the hours that the service system is open. From the service delivery viewpoint, customers demand varying amounts of service, often exceeding normal capacity. We can control arrivals in a variety of ways. For example, we can have a short line (such as a drive-in at a fast-food restaurant with only several spaces), we can establish specific hours for specific customers, or we can run specials. For the server,

exhibit TN7.1

Service Capacity versus Waiting Line Trade-Off

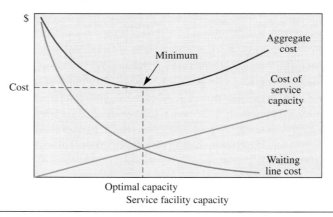

exhibit TN7.2

Arrival and Service Profiles

SUGGESTIONS FOR MANAGING QUEUES

The following are some useful suggestions for managing queues that go beyond the quantitative waiting line models.

1   **Determine an acceptable waiting time for your customers.** How long do your customers expect to wait? Set operational objectives based on what is acceptable.

2   **Try to divert your customers' attention when waiting.** Providing music, a video, or some other form of entertainment may help to distract the customers from the fact they are waiting.

3   **Inform your customers of what to expect.** This is especially important when the waiting time will be longer than normal. Tell them why the waiting time is longer than normal and what you are doing to alleviate the queue.

4   **Keep employees not serving the customers out of sight.** Nothing is more frustrating to someone waiting in line than to see employees, who potentially could be serving those in line, working on other activities.

5   **Segment customers.** If a group of customers needs something that can be done very quickly, give them a special line so they do not have to wait for the slower customers.

6   **Train your servers to be friendly.** Greeting the customer by name, or providing some other special attention, can go a long way toward overcoming the negative feeling of a long wait. [Hint: Rather than servers being told to just "be friendly," psychologists suggest they be told when to invoke specific friendly actions such as smiling—when greeting customers, when taking orders, and when giving change (in a convenience store). Tests using such specific behavioral actions have shown significant increases in perceived friendliness of the servers in the eyes of the customer.]

7   **Encourage customers to come during the slack periods.** Inform customers of times when they usually would not have to wait; also tell them when the peak periods are—this may help to smooth the load.

8   **Take a long-term perspective toward getting rid of the queues.** Develop plans for alternative ways to serve your customers. Where appropriate, develop plans for automating or speeding up the process in some manner. This is not to say you want to eliminate personal attention; some customers expect this.

SOURCE: BASED ON K. KATZ, B. M. LARSON, AND R. C. LARSON, "PRESCRIPTION FOR THE WAITING-IN-LINE BLUES," *SLOAN MANAGEMENT REVIEW,* WINTER 1991, PP. 51–52.

we can affect service time by using faster or slower servers, faster or slower machines, different tooling, different material, different layout, faster setup time, and so on.

The essential point is waiting lines are *not* a fixed condition of a productive system but are to a very large extent within the control of the system management and design. Professor Richard Larson (the famous "wait-watcher") and his colleagues offer useful suggestions for managing queues based on their research in the banking industry. (See the box titled "Suggestions for Managing Queues.")

THE QUEUING SYSTEM

The **queuing system** consists essentially of three major components: (1) the source population and the way customers arrive at the system, (2) the servicing system, and (3) the condition of the customers exiting the system (back to source population or not?), as seen in Exhibit TN7.3. The following sections discuss each of these areas.

Queuing system

Service

CUSTOMER ARRIVALS

Arrivals at a service system may be drawn from a *finite* or an *infinite* population. The distinction is important because the analyses are based on different premises and require different equations for their solution.

Finite Population   A *finite population* refers to the limited-size customer pool that will use the service and, at times, form a line. The reason this finite classification is important is that when a customer leaves its position as a member for the population (a machine breaking down and requiring service, for example), the size of the user group is reduced by one, which reduces the probability of the next occurrence. Conversely, when a customer is serviced and

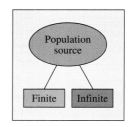

Components of a Queuing System

**Interactive
Operations
Management**

returns to the user group, the population increases and the probability of a user requiring service also increases. This finite class of problems requires a separate set of formulas from that of the infinite population case.

As an example, consider a group of six machines maintained by one repairperson. When one machine breaks down, the source population is reduced to five, and the chance of one of the remaining five breaking down and needing repair is certainly less than when six machines were operating. If two machines are down with only four operating, the probability of another breakdown is again changed. Conversely, when a machine is repaired and returned to service, the machine population increases, thus raising the probability of the next breakdown. A finite population model with one server that can be used in such cases is presented in Exhibits TN7.8 and TN7.10.

Infinite Population   An *infinite population* is large enough in relation to the service system so that the population size caused by subtractions or additions to the population (a customer needing service or a serviced customer returning to the population) does not significantly affect the system probabilities. If, in the preceding finite explanation, there were 100 machines instead of six, then if one or two machines broke down, the probabilities for the next breakdowns would not be very different and the assumption could be made without a great deal of error that the population (for all practical purposes) was infinite. Nor would the formulas for "infinite" queuing problems cause much error if applied to a physician with 1,000 patients or a department store with 10,000 customers.

DISTRIBUTION OF ARRIVALS

When describing a waiting system, we need to define the manner in which customers or the waiting units are arranged for service.

Waiting line formulas generally require an **arrival rate**, or the number of units per period (such as an average of one every six minutes). A *constant* arrival distribution is periodic, with exactly the same time between successive arrivals. In productive systems, the only arrivals that truly approach a constant interval period are those subject to machine control. Much more common are *variable* (random) arrival distributions.

In observing arrivals at a service facility, we can look at them from two viewpoints: First, we can analyze the time between successive arrivals to see if the times follow some statistical distribution. Usually we assume that the time between arrivals is exponentially distributed. Second, we can set some time length (T) and try to determine how many arrivals might enter the system within T. We typically assume that the number of arrivals per time unit is Poisson distributed.

SIX FLAGS' FAST LANE USERS PURCHASE LOW-TECH, GO-TO-THE-HEAD-OF-THE-LINE PAPER TICKETS OR A HIGH-TECH, ELECTRONIC "Q-BOT" DEVICE. Q-BOTS ARE BEEPERS THAT SERVE AS VIRTUAL PLACEHOLDERS. THEY VIBRATE AND FLASH A TEXT MESSAGE WHEN IT'S TIME TO REPORT TO THE RIDE.

Arrival rate

Exponential Distribution

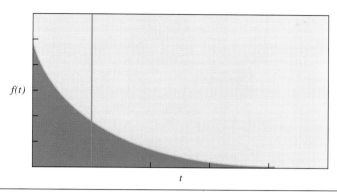

Exponential Distribution In the first case, when arrivals at a service facility occur in a purely random fashion, a plot of the interarrival times yields an **exponential distribution** such as that shown in Exhibit TN7.4. The probability function is

Exponential distribution

[TN7.1] $$f(t) = \lambda e^{-\lambda t}$$

where λ is the mean number of arrivals per time period.

The cumulative area beneath the curve in Exhibit TN7.4 is the summation of equation (TN7.1) over its positive range, which is $e^{-\lambda t}$. This integral allows us to compute the probabilities of arrivals within a specified time. For example, for the case of single arrivals to a waiting line ($\lambda = 1$), the following table can be derived either by solving $e^{-\lambda t}$ or by using Appendix F. Column 2 shows the probability that it will be more than t minutes until the next arrival. Column 3 shows the probability of the next arrival within t minutes (computed as 1 minus column 2)

(1) t (MINUTES)	(2) PROBABILITY THAT THE NEXT ARRIVAL WILL OCCUR IN t MINUTES OR MORE (FROM APPENDIX F OR SOLVING e^{-t})	(3) PROBABILITY THAT THE NEXT ARRIVAL WILL OCCUR IN t MINUTES OR LESS [1 − COLUMN (2)]
0	1.00	0
0.5	0.61	0.39
1.0	0.37	0.63
1.5	0.22	0.78
2.0	0.14	0.86

Poisson Distribution In the second case, where one is interested in the number of arrivals during some time period T, the distribution appears as in Exhibit TN7.5 and is obtained by finding the probability of exactly n arrivals during T. If the arrival process is random, the distribution is the **Poisson**, and the formula is

Poisson distribution

[TN7.2] $$P_T(n) = \frac{(\lambda T)^n e^{-\lambda T}}{n!}$$

Equation (TN7.2) shows the probability of exactly n arrivals in time T.[1] For example, if the mean arrival rate of units into a system is three per minute ($\lambda = 3$) and we want to find the probability that exactly five units will arrive within a one-minute period ($n = 5, T = 1$), we have

$$P_1(5) = \frac{(3 \times 1)^5 e^{-3 \times 1}}{5!} = \frac{3^5 e^{-3}}{120} = 2.025 e^{-3} = 0.101$$

That is, there is a 10.1 percent chance that there will be five arrivals in any one-minute interval.

Poisson Distribution for $\lambda T = 3$

Customer Arrivals in Queues

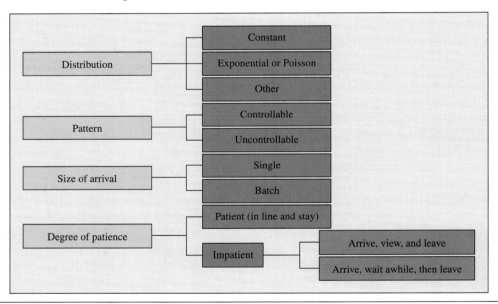

Although often shown as a smoothed curve, as in Exhibit TN7.5, the Poisson is a discrete distribution. (The curve becomes smoother as n becomes large.) The distribution is discrete because n refers, in our example, to the number of arrivals in a system, and this must be an integer. (For example, there cannot be 1.5 arrivals.)

Also note that the exponential and Poisson distributions can be derived from one another. The mean and variance of the Poisson are equal and denoted by λ. The mean of the exponential is $1/\lambda$ and its variance is $1/\lambda^2$. (Remember that the time between arrivals is exponentially distributed and the number of arrivals per unit of time is Poisson distributed.)

Other arrival characteristics include arrival patterns, size of arrival units, and degree of patience. (See Exhibit TN7.6.)

Arrival patterns. The arrivals at a system are far more controllable than is generally recognized. Barbers may decrease their Saturday arrival rate (and supposedly shift it to other days of the week) by charging an extra $1 for adult haircuts or charging adult prices for children's haircuts. Department stores run sales during the off-season or hold one-day-only sales in part for purposes of control. Airlines offer excursion and off-season rates for similar reasons. The simplest of all arrival-control devices is the posting of business hours.

Some service demands are clearly uncontrollable, such as emergency medical demands on a city's hospital facilities. But even in these situations, arrivals at emergency rooms in specific hospitals are controllable to some extent by, say, keeping ambulance drivers in the service region informed of the status of their respective host hospitals.

Size of arrival units.   A *single arrival* may be thought of as one unit. (A unit is the smallest number handled.) A single arrival on the floor of the New York Stock Exchange (NYSE) is 100 shares of stock; a single arrival at an egg-processing plant might be a dozen eggs or a flat of 2½ dozen; a single arrival at a restaurant is a single person.

A *batch arrival* is some multiple of the unit, such as a block of 1,000 shares on the NYSE, a case of eggs at the processing plant, or a party of five at a restaurant.

Degree of patience.   A *patient* arrival is one who waits as long as necessary until the service facility is ready to serve him or her. (Even if arrivals grumble and behave impatiently, the fact that they wait is sufficient to label them as patient arrivals for purposes of waiting line theory.)

There are two classes of *impatient* arrivals. Members of the first class arrive, survey both the service facility and the length of the line, and then decide to leave. Those in the second class arrive, view the situation, join the waiting line, and then, after some period of time, depart. The behavior of the first type is termed *balking,* while the second is termed *reneging.*

THE QUEUING SYSTEM: FACTORS

The queuing system consists primarily of the waiting line(s) and the available number of servers. Here we discuss issues pertaining to waiting line characteristics and management, line structure, and service rate. Factors to consider with waiting lines include the line length, number of lines, and queue discipline.

Length.   In a practical sense, an infinite line is simply one that is very long in terms of the capacity of the service system. Examples of *infinite potential length* are a line of vehicles backed up for miles at a bridge crossing and customers who must form a line around the block as they wait to purchase tickets at a theater.

Gas stations, loading docks, and parking lots have *limited line capacity* caused by legal restrictions or physical space characteristics. This complicates the waiting line problem not only in service system utilization and waiting line computations but also in the shape of the actual arrival distribution. The arrival denied entry into the line because of lack of space may rejoin the population for a later try or may seek service elsewhere. Either action makes an obvious difference in the finite population case.

Number of lines.   A single line or single file is, of course, one line only. The term *multiple lines* refers to the single lines that form in front of two or more servers or to single lines that converge at some central redistribution point. The disadvantage of multiple lines in a busy facility is that arrivals often shift lines if several previous services have been of short duration or if those customers currently in other lines appear to require a short service time.

Queue discipline.   A queue discipline is a priority rule or set of rules for determining the order of service to customers in a waiting line. The rules selected can have a dramatic effect on the system's overall performance. The number of customers in line, the average waiting time, the range of variability in waiting time, and the efficiency of the service facility are just a few of the factors affected by the choice of priority rules.

Probably the most common priority rule is first come, first served (FCFS). This rule states that customers in line are

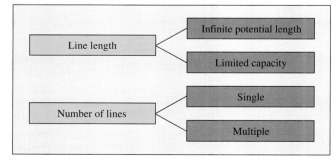

served on the basis of their chronological arrival; no other characteristics have any bearing on the selection process. This is popularly accepted as the fairest rule, although in practice it discriminates against the arrival requiring a short service time.

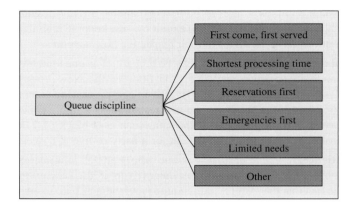

Reservations first, emergencies first, highest-profit customer first, largest orders first, best customers first, longest waiting time in line, and soonest promised date are other examples of priority rules. There are two major practical problems in using any rule: One is ensuring that customers know and follow the rule. The other is ensuring that a system exists to enable employees to manage the line (such as take-a-number systems).

Service Time Distribution   Another important feature of the waiting structure is the time the customer or unit spends with the server once the service has started. Waiting line formulas generally specify **service rate** as the capacity of the server in number of units per time period (such as 12 completions per hour) and *not* as service time, which might average five minutes each. A constant service time rule states that each service takes exactly the same time. As in constant arrivals, this characteristic is generally limited to machine-controlled operations.

Service rate

When service times are random, they can be approximated by the exponential distribution. When using the exponential distribution as an approximation of the service times, we will refer to μ as the average number of units or customers that can be served per time period.

Line Structures   As Exhibit TN7.7 shows, the flow of items to be serviced may go through a single line, multiple lines, or some mixtures of the two. The choice of format depends partly on the volume of customers served and partly on the restrictions imposed by sequential requirements governing the order in which service must be performed.

1.   **Single channel, single phase.**   This is the simplest type of waiting line structure, and straightforward formulas are available to solve the problem for standard distribution patterns of arrival and service. When the distributions are nonstandard, the problem is easily solved by computer simulation. A typical example of a single-channel, single-phase situation is the one-person barbershop.

2.   **Single channel, multiphase.**   A car wash is an illustration because a series of services (vacuuming, wetting, washing, rinsing, drying, window cleaning, and parking) is performed in a fairly uniform sequence. A critical factor in the single-channel case with service in series is the amount of buildup of items allowed in front of each service, which in turn constitutes separate waiting lines.

3.   **Multichannel, single phase.**   Tellers' windows in a bank and checkout counters in high-volume department stores exemplify this type of structure. The difficulty with this format is that the uneven service time given each customer results in unequal speed or flow among the lines. This results in some customers being served before others who arrived earlier, as well as in some degree of line shifting. Varying this structure to ensure the servicing of arrivals in chronological order would require forming a single line, from which, as a server becomes available, the next customer in the queue is assigned.

Line Structures

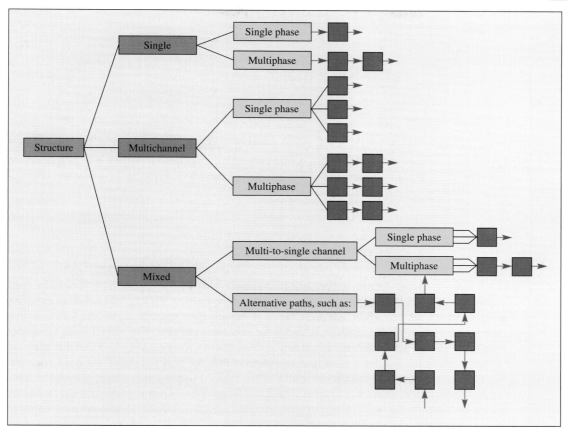

The major problem of this structure is that it requires rigid control of the line to maintain order and to direct customers to available servers. In some instances, assigning numbers to customers in order of their arrival helps alleviate this problem.

4. **Multichannel, multiphase.** This case is similar to the preceding one except that two or more services are performed in sequence. The admission of patients in a hospital follows this pattern because a specific sequence of steps is usually followed: initial contact at the admissions desk, filling out forms, making identification tags, obtaining a room assignment, escorting the patient to the room, and so forth. Because several servers are usually available for this procedure, more than one patient at a time may be processed.

5. **Mixed.** Under this general heading we consider two subcategories: (1) multiple-to-single channel structures and (2) alternative path structures. Under (1), we find either lines that merge into one for single-phase service, as at a bridge crossing where two lanes merge into one, or lines that merge into one for multiphase service, such as subassembly lines feeding into a main line. Under (2), we encounter two structures that differ in directional flow requirements. The first is similar to the multichannel–multiphase case, except that (a) there may be switching from one channel to the next after the first service has been rendered and (b) the number of channels and phases may vary—again—after performance of the first service.

EXIT

Once a customer is served, two exit fates are possible: (1) The customer may return to the source population and immediately become a competing candidate for service again or (2) there may be a low probability of reservice. The first case can be illustrated by a machine that has been routinely repaired and returned to duty but may break down again; the second can be illustrated by a machine that has been overhauled or modified and has a low probability of reservice over the near future. In a lighter vein, we might refer to the first as the "recurring-common-cold case" and to the second as the "appendectomy-only-once case."

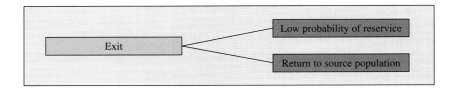

It should be apparent that when the population source is finite, any change in the service performed on customers who return to the population modifies the arrival rate at the service facility. This, of course, alters the characteristics of the waiting line under study and necessitates reanalysis of the problem.

WAITING LINE MODELS

Excel: Queue

In this section we present four sample waiting line problems followed by their solutions. Each has a slightly different structure (see Exhibit TN7.8) and solution equation (see Exhibit TN7.10). There are more types of models than these four, but the formulas and solutions become quite complicated, and those problems are generally solved using computer simulation (see Technical Note 17). Also, in using these formulas, keep in mind that they are steady-state formulas derived on the assumption that the process under study is ongoing. Thus, they may provide inaccurate results when applied to processes where the arrival rates and/or service rates change over time. The Excel Spreadsheet QueueModel.xls, developed by John McClain of Cornell University and included on the DVD-ROM, can be used to solve these problems.

Here is a quick preview of our four problems to illustrate each of the four waiting line models in Exhibits TN7.8 and TN7.10. Exhibit TN7.9 defines the notations used in Exhibit TN7.10.

Problem 1: Customers in line. A bank wants to know how many customers are waiting for a drive-in teller, how long they have to wait, the utilization of the teller, and what the service rate would have to be so that 95 percent of the time there will not be more than three cars in the system at any time.

Problem 2: Equipment selection. A franchise for Robot Car Wash must decide which equipment to purchase out of a choice of three. Larger units cost more but wash cars faster. To make the decision, costs are related to revenue.

Properties of Some Specific Waiting Line Models

MODEL	LAYOUT	SERVICE PHASE	SOURCE POPULATION	ARRIVAL PATTERN	QUEUE DISCIPLINE	SERVICE PATTERN	PERMISSIBLE QUEUE LENGTH	TYPICAL EXAMPLE
1	Single channel	Single	Infinite	Poisson	FCFS	Exponential	Unlimited	Drive-in teller at bank; one-lane toll bridge
2	Single channel	Single	Infinite	Poisson	FCFS	Constant	Unlimited	Roller coaster rides in amusement park
3	Multichannel	Single	Infinite	Poisson	FCFS	Exponential	Unlimited	Parts counter in auto agency
4	Single channel	Single	Finite	Poisson	FCFS	Exponential	Unlimited	Machine breakdown and repair in a factory

Notations for Equations (Exhibit TN7.10)

INFINITE QUEUING NOTATION: MODELS 1–3

λ = Arrival rate

μ = Service rate

$\dfrac{1}{\mu}$ = Average service time

$\dfrac{1}{\lambda}$ = Average time between arrivals

ρ = Ratio of total arrival rate to service rate for a single server $\left(\dfrac{\lambda}{\mu}\right)^{*}$

L_q = Average number waiting in line

L_s = Average number in system (including any being served)

W_q = Average time waiting in line

W_s = Average total time in system (including time to be served)

n = Number of units in the system

S = Number of identical service channels

P_n = Probability of exactly n units in system

P_w = Probability of waiting in line

FINITE QUEUING NOTATION: MODEL 4

D = Probability that an arrival must wait in line

F = Efficiency factor, a measure of the effect of having to wait in line

H = Average number of units being serviced

J = Population source less those in queuing system ($N - n$)

L = Average number of units in line

S = Number of service channels

n = Average number of units in queuing system (including the one being served)

N = Number of units in population source

P_n = Probability of exactly n units in queuing system

T = Average time to perform the service

U = Average time between customer service requirements

W = Average waiting time in line

X = Service factor, or proportion of service time required

*For single-server queues, this is equivalent to utilization.

Equations for Solving Four Model Problems

Model 1

$$L_q = \frac{\lambda^2}{\mu(\mu - \lambda)} \qquad W_q = \frac{L_q}{\lambda} \qquad P_n = \left(1 - \frac{\lambda}{\mu}\right)\left(\frac{\lambda}{\mu}\right)^{n} \qquad P_0 = \left(1 - \frac{\lambda}{\mu}\right)$$

$$L_s = \frac{\lambda}{\mu - \lambda} \qquad W_s = \frac{L_s}{\lambda} \qquad \rho = \frac{\lambda}{\mu}$$

(TN7.3)

Model 2

$$L_q = \frac{\lambda^2}{2\mu(\mu - \lambda)} \qquad W_q = \frac{L_q}{\lambda}$$

$$L_s = L_q + \frac{\lambda}{\mu} \qquad W_s = \frac{L_s}{\lambda}$$

(TN7.4)

(Exhibit TN7.11 provides the value of L_q given λ/μ and the number of servers S.)

Model 3

$$L_s = L_q + \lambda/\mu \qquad W_s = L_s/\lambda$$

$$W_q = L_q/\lambda \qquad P_w = L_q\left(\frac{S_\mu}{\lambda} - 1\right)$$

(TN7.5)

Model 4 is a finite queuing situation that is most easily solved by using finite tables. These tables, in turn, require the manipulation of specific terms.

Model 4

$$X = \frac{T}{T + U} \qquad H = FNX \qquad L = N(1 - F) \qquad n = L + H$$

$$P_n = \frac{N!}{(N - n)!} X^n P_0 \qquad J = NF(1 - X)$$

$$W = \frac{L(T + U)}{N - L} = \frac{LT}{H} \qquad F = \frac{T + U}{T + U + W}$$

(TN7.6)

Problem 3: Determining the number of servers. An auto agency parts department must decide how many clerks to employ at the counter. More clerks cost more money, but there is a savings because mechanics wait less time.

Problem 4: Finite population source. Whereas the previous models assume a large population, finite queuing employs a separate set of equations for those cases where the calling customer population is small. In this last problem, mechanics must service four weaving machines to keep them operating. Based on the costs associated with machines being idle and the costs of mechanics to service them, the problem is to decide how many mechanics to use.

Service

EXAMPLE TN7.1: Customers in Line

Western National Bank is considering opening a drive-through window for customer service. Management estimates that customers will arrive at the rate of 15 per hour. The teller who will staff the window can service customers at the rate of one every three minutes.

Part 1   Assuming Poisson arrivals and exponential service, find

1. Utilization of the teller.
2. Average number in the waiting line.
3. Average number in the system.
4. Average waiting time in line.
5. Average waiting time in the system, including service.

Excel:
Queue.xls

SOLUTION—Part 1

1. The average utilization of the teller is (using Model 1)

$$\rho = \frac{\lambda}{\mu} = \frac{15}{20} = 75 \text{ percent}$$

2. The average number in the waiting line is

$$L_q = \frac{\lambda^2}{\mu(\mu - \lambda)} = \frac{(15)^2}{20(20 - 15)} = 2.25 \text{ customers}$$

3. The average number in the system is

$$L_s = \frac{\lambda}{\mu - \lambda} = \frac{15}{20 - 15} = 3 \text{ customers}$$

4. Average waiting time in line is

$$W_q = \frac{L_q}{\lambda} = \frac{2.25}{15} = 0.15 \text{ hour, or 9 minutes}$$

5. Average waiting time in the system is

$$W_s = \frac{L_s}{\lambda} = \frac{3}{15} = 0.2 \text{ hour, or 12 minutes}$$

EXAMPLE TN7.1 (Continued)

Part 2   Because of limited space availability and a desire to provide an acceptable level of service, the bank manager would like to ensure, with 95 percent confidence, that no more than three cars will be in the system at any time. What is the present level of service for the three-car limit? What level of teller use must be attained and what must be the service rate of the teller to ensure the 95 percent level of service?

SOLUTION—Part 2

The present level of service for three or fewer cars is the probability that there are 0, 1, 2, or 3 cars in the system. From Model 1, Exhibit TN7.10,

$$P_n = \left(1 - \frac{\lambda}{\mu}\right)\left(\frac{\lambda}{\mu}\right)^n$$

at $n = 0$, $P_0 = (1 - 15/20)$ $(15/20)^0 = 0.250$

at $n = 1$, $P_1 = (1/4)$ $(15/20)^1 = 0.188$

at $n = 2$, $P_2 = (1/4)$ $(15/20)^2 = 0.141$

at $n = 3$, $P_3 = (1/4)$ $(15/20)^3 = \underline{0.105}$

 0.684   or   68.5 percent

The probability of having more than three cars in the system is 1.0 minus the probability of three or fewer cars ($1.0 - 0.685 = 31.5$ percent).

For a 95 percent service level of three or fewer cars, this states that $P_0 + P_1 + P_2 + P_3 = 95$ percent.

$$0.95 = \left(1 - \frac{\lambda}{\mu}\right)\left(\frac{\lambda}{\mu}\right)^0 + \left(1 - \frac{\lambda}{\mu}\right)\left(\frac{\lambda}{\mu}\right)^1 + \left(1 - \frac{\lambda}{\mu}\right)\left(\frac{\lambda}{\mu}\right)^2 + \left(1 - \frac{\lambda}{\mu}\right)\left(\frac{\lambda}{\mu}\right)^3$$

$$0.95 = \left(1 - \frac{\lambda}{\mu}\right)\left[1 + \frac{\lambda}{\mu} + \left(\frac{\lambda}{\mu}\right)^2 + \left(\frac{\lambda}{\mu}\right)^3\right]$$

We can solve this by trial and error for values of λ/μ. If $\lambda/\mu = 0.50$,

$$0.95 \overset{?}{=} 0.5(1 + 0.5 + 0.25 + 0.125)$$

$$0.95 \neq 0.9375$$

With $\lambda/\mu = 0.45$,

$$0.95 \overset{?}{=} (1 - 0.45)(1 + 0.45 + 0.203 + 0.091)$$

$$0.95 \neq 0.96$$

With $\lambda/\mu = 0.47$,

$$0.95 \overset{?}{=} (1 - 0.47)(1 + 0.47 + 0.221 + 0.104) = 0.9512$$

$$0.95 \approx 0.95135$$

Therefore, with the utilization $\rho = \lambda/\mu$ of 47 percent, the probability of three or fewer cars in the system is 95 percent.

To find the rate of service required to attain this 95 percent service level, we simply solve the equation $\lambda/\mu = 0.47$, where $\lambda =$ number of arrivals per hour. This gives $\mu = 32$ per hour. That is, the teller must serve approximately 32 people per hour (a 60 percent increase over the original 20-per-hour capability) for 95 percent confidence that not more than three cars will be in the system. Perhaps service may be speeded up by modifying the method of service, adding another teller, or limiting the types of transactions available at the drive-through window. Note that with the condition of 95 percent confidence that three or fewer cars will be in the system, the teller will be idle 53 percent of the time. ●

EXAMPLE TN7.2: Equipment Selection

The Robot Company franchises combination gas and car wash stations throughout the United States. Robot gives a free car wash for a gasoline fill-up or, for a wash alone, charges $0.50. Past experience shows that the number of customers that have car washes following fill-ups is about the same as for a wash alone. The average profit on a gasoline fill-up is about $0.70, and the cost of the car wash to Robot is $0.10. Robot stays open 14 hours per day.

Robot has three power units and drive assemblies, and a franchisee must select the unit preferred. Unit I can wash cars at the rate of one every five minutes and is leased for $12 per day. Unit II, a larger unit, can wash cars at the rate of one every four minutes but costs $16 per day. Unit III, the largest, costs $22 per day and can wash a car in three minutes.

The franchisee estimates that customers will not wait in line more than five minutes for a car wash. A longer time will cause Robot to lose the gasoline sales as well as the car wash sale.

Service

Excel: Queue.xls

If the estimate of customer arrivals resulting in washes is 10 per hour, which wash unit should be selected?

SOLUTION

Using unit I, calculate the average waiting time of customers in the wash line (μ for unit I $= 12$ per hour). From the Model 2 equations (Exhibit TN7.10),

$$L_q = \frac{\lambda^2}{2\mu(\mu - \lambda)} = \frac{10^2}{2(12)(12 - 10)} = 2.08333$$

$$W_q = \frac{L_q}{\lambda} = \frac{2.08333}{10} = 0.208 \text{ hour, or } 12\tfrac{1}{2} \text{ minutes}$$

For unit II at 15 per hour,

$$L_q = \frac{10^2}{2(15)(15 - 10)} = 0.667$$

$$W_q = \frac{0.667}{10} = 0.0667 \text{ hour, or 4 minutes}$$

If waiting time is the only criterion, unit II should be purchased. But before we make the final decision, we must look at the profit differential between both units.

With unit I, some customers would balk and renege because of the $12\tfrac{1}{2}$-minute wait. And, although this greatly complicates the mathematical analysis, we can gain some estimate of lost sales with unit I by increasing $W_q = 5$ minutes or $\frac{1}{12}$ hour (the average length of time customers will wait) and solving for λ. This would be the effective arrival rate of customers:

$$W_q = \frac{L_q}{\lambda} = \left(\frac{\lambda^2/2\mu(\mu - \lambda)}{\lambda}\right)$$

$$W_q = \frac{\lambda}{2\mu(\mu - \lambda)}$$

$$\lambda = \frac{2W_q \mu^2}{1 + 2W_q \mu} = \frac{2\left(\frac{1}{12}\right)(12)^2}{1 + 2\left(\frac{1}{12}\right)(12)} = 8 \text{ per hour}$$

Therefore, because the original estimate of λ was 10 per hour, an estimated 2 customers per hour will be lost. Lost profit of 2 customers per hour $\times$ 14 hours $\times \frac{1}{2}$ ($0.70 fill-up profit $+$ $0.40 wash profit) $=$ $15.40 per day.

Because the additional cost of unit II over unit I is only $4 per day, the loss of $15.40 profit obviously warrants installing unit II.

The original five-minute maximum wait constraint is satisfied by unit II. Therefore unit III is not considered unless the arrival rate is expected to increase. ●

Service

**Excel:
Queue.xls**

EXAMPLE TN7.3: Determining the Number of Servers

In the service department of the Glenn-Mark Auto Agency, mechanics requiring parts for auto repair or service present their request forms at the parts department counter. The parts clerk fills a request while the mechanic waits. Mechanics arrive in a random (Poisson) fashion at the rate of 40 per hour, and a clerk can fill requests at the rate of 20 per hour (exponential). If the cost for a parts clerk is $6 per hour and the cost for a mechanic is $12 per hour, determine the optimum number of clerks to staff the counter. (Because of the high arrival rate, an infinite source may be assumed.)

SOLUTION

First, assume that three clerks will be used because having only one or two clerks would create infinitely long lines (since $\lambda = 40$ and $\mu = 20$). The equations for Model 3 from Exhibit TN7.10 will be used here. But first we need to obtain the average number in line using the table of Exhibit TN7.11. Using the table and values $\lambda/\mu = 2$ and $S = 3$, we obtain $L_q = 0.8888$ mechanic.

At this point, we see that we have an average of 0.8888 mechanic waiting all day. For an eight-hour day at \$12 per hour, there is a loss of mechanic's time worth 0.8888 mechanic $\times$ \$12 per hour $\times$ 8 hours = \$85.32.

Our next step is to reobtain the waiting time if we add another parts clerk. We then compare the added cost of the additional employee with the time saved by the mechanics. Again, using the table of Exhibit TN7.11 but with $S = 4$, we obtain

$L_q = 0.1730$ mechanic in line

$0.1730 \times \$12 \times 8$ hours = \$16.61 cost of a mechanic waiting in line

Value of mechanics' time saved is \$85.32 − \$16.61   = \$68.71

Cost of an additional parts clerk is 8 hours $\times$ \$6/hour =   48.00

Cost of reduction by adding fourth clerk   = \$20.71

This problem could be expanded to consider the addition of runners to deliver parts to mechanics; the problem then would be to determine the optimal number of runners. This, however, would have to include the added cost of lost time caused by errors in parts receipts. For example, a mechanic would recognize a wrong part at the counter and obtain immediate correction, whereas the parts runner might not. ●

EXAMPLE TN7.4: Finite Population Source

Studies of a bank of four weaving machines at the Loose Knit textile mill have shown that, on average, each machine needs adjusting every hour and that the current servicer averages $7\frac{1}{2}$ minutes per adjustment. Assuming Poisson arrivals, exponential service, and a machine idle time cost of \$40 per hour, determine if a second servicer (who also averages $7\frac{1}{2}$ minutes per adjustment) should be hired at a rate of \$7 per hour.

Service

SOLUTION

This is a finite queuing problem that can be solved by using finite queuing tables. (See Exhibit TN7.12.) The approach in this problem is to compare the cost of machine downtime (either waiting in line or being serviced) and of one repairer, to the cost of machine downtime and two repairers. We do this by finding the average number of machines that are in the service system and multiply this number by the downtime cost per hour. To this we add the repairers' cost.

Before we proceed, we first define some terms:

N = Number of machines in the population

S = Number of repairers

T = Time required to service a machine

U = Average time a machine runs before requiring service

X = Service factor, or proportion of service time required for each machine ($X = T/(T + U)$)

L = Average number of machines waiting in line to be serviced

H = Average number of machines being serviced

Excel: Queue.xls

The values to be determined from the finite tables are

D = Probability that a machine needing service will have to wait

F = Efficiency factor, which measures the effect of having to wait in line to be serviced

The tables are arranged according to three variables: N, population size; X, service factor; and S, the number of service channels (repairers in this problem). To look up a value, first find the table for the correct N size, then search the first column for the appropriate X, and finally find the line for S. Then

exhibit TN7.11 — Expected Number of People Waiting in Line (L_q) for Various Values of S and λ/μ

λ/μ	NUMBER OF SERVICE CHANNELS, S														
	1	2	3	4	5	6	7	8	9	10	11	12	13	14	15
0.10	0.0111														
0.15	0.0264	0.0006													
0.20	0.0500	0.0020													
0.25	0.0833	0.0039													
0.30	0.1285	0.0069													
0.35	0.1884	0.0110													
0.40	0.2666	0.0166													
0.45	0.3681	0.0239	0.0019												
0.50	0.5000	0.0333	0.0030												
0.55	0.6722	0.045	0.0043												
0.60	0.9090	0.0593	0.0061												
0.65	1.2071	0.0767	0.0084												
0.70	1.6333	0.0976	0.0112												
0.75	2.2500	0.1227	0.0147												
0.80	3.2000	0.1523	0.0189												
0.85	4.8165	0.1873	0.0239	0.0031											
0.90	8.1000	0.2285	0.0300	0.0041											
0.95	18.0500	0.2767	0.0371	0.0053											
1.0		0.3333	0.0454	0.0067											
1.2		0.6748	0.0940	0.0158											
1.4		1.3449	0.1778	0.0324	0.0059										
1.6		2.8441	0.3128	0.0604	0.0121										
1.8		7.6731	0.5320	0.1051	0.0227	0.0047									
2.0			0.8888	0.1730	0.0390	0.0090									
2.2			1.4907	0.2770	0.066	0.0158									
2.4			2.1261	0.4205	0.1047	0.0266	0.0065								
2.6			4.9322	0.6581	0.1609	0.0425	0.0110								
2.8			12.2724	1.0000	0.2411	0.0659	0.0180								
3.0				1.5282	0.3541	0.0991	0.0282	0.0077							
3.2				2.3855	0.5128	0.1452	0.0427	0.0122							
3.4				3.9060	0.7365	0.2085	0.0631	0.0189							
3.6				7.0893	1.0550	0.2947	0.0912	0.0283	0.0084						
3.8				16.9366	1.5181	0.4114	0.1292	0.0412	0.0127						
4.0					2.2164	0.5694	0.1801	0.0590	0.0189						
4.2					3.3269	0.7837	0.2475	0.0827	0.0273	0.0087					
4.4					5.2675	1.0777	0.3364	0.1142	0.0389	0.0128					
4.6					9.2885	1.4857	0.4532	0.1555	0.0541	0.0184					
4.8					21.6384	2.0708	0.6071	0.2092	0.0742	0.0260					
5.0						2.9375	0.8102	0.2785	0.1006	0.0361	0.0125				
5.2						4.3004	1.0804	0.3680	0.1345	0.0492	0.0175				
5.4						6.6609	1.4441	0.5871	0.1779	0.0663	0.0243	0.0085			
5.6						11.5178	1.9436	0.6313	0.2330	0.0683	0.0330	0.0119			
5.8						26.3726	2.6481	0.8225	0.3032	0.1164	0.0443	0.0164			
6.0							3.6878	1.0707	0.3918	0.1518	0.0590	0.0224			
6.2							5.2979	1.3967	0.5037	0.1964	0.0775	0.0300	0.0113		
6.4							8.0768	1.8040	0.6454	0.2524	0.1008	0.0398	0.0153		
6.6							13.7992	2.4198	0.8247	0.3222	0.1302	0.0523	0.0205		
6.8							31.1270	3.2441	1.0533	0.4090	0.1666	0.0679	0.0271	0.0105	
7.0								4.4471	1.3471	0.5172	0.2119	0.0876	0.0357	0.0141	
7.2								6.3133	1.7288	0.6521	0.2677	0.1119	0.0463	0.0187	
7.4								9.5102	2.2324	0.8202	0.3364	0.1420	0.0595	0.0245	0.0097
7.6								16.0379	2.9113	1.0310	0.4211	0.1789	0.0761	0.0318	0.0129
7.8								35.8956	3.8558	1.2972	0.5250	0.2243	0.0966	0.0410	0.0168
8.0									5.2264	1.6364	0.6530	0.2796	0.1214	0.0522	0.0220
8.2									7.3441	2.0736	0.8109	0.3469	0.1520	0.0663	0.0283
8.4									10.9592	2.6470	1.0060	0.4288	0.1891	0.0834	0.0361
8.6									18.3223	3.4160	1.2484	0.5236	0.2341	0.1043	0.0459
8.8									40.6824	4.4805	1.5524	0.6501	0.2885	0.1208	0.0577
9.0										6.0183	1.9366	0.7980	0.3543	0.1603	0.0723
9.2										8.3869	2.4293	0.9788	0.4333	0.1974	0.0899
9.4										12.4183	3.0732	1.2010	0.5267	0.2419	0.1111
9.6										20.6160	3.9318	1.4752	0.5437	0.2952	0.1367
9.8										45.4769	5.1156	1.8165	0.7827	0.3699	0.16731
10										6.8210	2.2465	0.9506	0.4352	0.2040	

Finite Queuing Tables

POPULATION 4

X	S	D	F	X	S	D	F	X	S	D	F
.015	1	.045	.999		1	.479	.899	.400	3	.064	.992
.022	1	.066	.998	.180	2	.088	.991		2	.372	.915
.030	1	.090	.997		1	.503	.887		1	.866	.595
.034	1	.102	.996	.190	2	.098	.990	.420	3	.074	.990
.038	1	.114	.995		1	.526	.874		2	.403	.903
.042	1	.126	.994	.200	3	.008	.999		1	.884	.572
.046	1	.137	.993		2	.108	.988	.440	3	.085	.986
.048	1	.143	.992	.200	1	.549	.862		2	.435	.891
.052	1	.155	.991	.210	3	.009	.999		1	.900	.551
.054	1	.161	.990		2	.118	.986	.460	3	.097	.985
.058	1	.173	.989		1	.572	.849		2	.466	.878
.060	1	.179	.988	.220	3	.011	.999		1	.914	.530
.062	1	.184	.987		2	.129	.984	.480	3	.111	.983
.064	1	.190	.986		1	.593	.835		2	.498	.864
.066	1	.196	.985	.230	3	.012	.999	.480	1	.926	.511
.070	2	.014	.999		2	.140	.982	.500	3	.125	.980
	1	.208	.984		1	.614	.822		2	.529	.850
.075	2	.016	.999	.240	3	.014	.999		1	.937	.492
	1	.222	.981		2	.151	.980	.520	3	.141	.976
.080	2	.018	.999		1	.634	.808		2	.561	.835
	1	.237	.978	.250	3	.016	.999		1	.947	.475
.085	2	.021	.999		2	.163	.977	.540	3	.157	.972
	1	.251	.975		1	.654	.794		2	.592	.820
.090	2	.023	.999	.260	3	.018	.998		1	.956	.459
	1	.265	.972		2	.175	.975	.560	3	.176	.968
.095	2	.026	.999		1	.673	.780		2	.623	.805
	1	.280	.969	.270	3	.020	.998		1	.963	.443
.100	2	.028	.999		2	.187	.972	.580	3	.195	.964
	1	.294	.965		1	.691	.766		2	.653	.789
.105	2	.031	.998	.280	3	.022	.99s8		1	.969	.429
	1	.308	.962		2	.200	.968	.600	3	.216	.959
.110	2	.034	.998		1	.708	.752		2	.682	.774
	1	.321	.958	.290	3	.024	.998		1	.975	.415
.115	2	.037	.998		2	.213	.965	.650	3	.275	.944
	1	.335	.954		1	.725	.738		2	.752	.734
.120	2	.041	.997	.300	3	.027	.997		1	.985	.384
	1	.349	.950		2	.226	.962	.700	3	.343	.926
.125	2	.044	.997		1	.741	.724		2	.816	.695
	1	.362	.945	.310	3	.030	.997		1	.991	.357
.130	2	.047	.997		2	.240	.958	.750	3	.422	.905
	1	.376	.941		1	.756	.710		2	.871	.657
.135	2	.051	.996	.320	3	.033	.997		1	.996	.333
	1	.389	.936		2	.254	.954	.800	3	.512	.880
.140	2	.055	.996		1	.771	.696		2	.917	.621
	1	.402	.931	.330	3	.036	.996		1	.998	.312
.145	2	.058	.995		2	.268	.950	.850	3	.614	.852
	1	.415	.926		1	.785	.683		2	.954	.587
.150	2	.062	.995	.340	3	.039	.996		1	.999	.294
	1	.428	.921		2	.282	.945	.900	3	.729	.821
.155	2	.066	.994		1	.798	.670		2	.979	.555
	1	.441	.916	.360	3	.047	.994	.950	3	.857	.786
.160	2	.071	.994		2	.312	.936		2	.995	.526
	1	.454	.910		1	.823	.644				
.165	2	.075	.993	.380	3	.055	.993				
	1	.466	.904		2	.342	.926				
.170	2	.079	.993		1	.846	.619				

A Comparison of Downtime Costs for Service and Repair of Four Machines

NUMBER OF REPAIRERS	NUMBER OF MACHINES DOWN $(H + L)$	COST PER HOUR FOR MACHINES DOWN $[(H + L) \times \$40/\text{HOUR}]$	COST OF REPAIRERS ($7/HOUR EACH)	TOTAL COST PER HOUR
1	0.597	$23.88	$ 7.00	$30.88
2	0.451	18.04	14.00	32.04

read off D and F. (In addition to these values, other characteristics about a finite queuing system can be found by using the finite formulas.)

To solve the problem, consider Case I with one repairer and Case II with two repairers.

Case I: One repairer. From problem statement,

$N = 4$

$S = 1$

$T = 7\frac{1}{2}\text{minutes}$

$U = 60\text{ minutes}$

$$X = \frac{T}{T + U} = \frac{7.5}{7.5 + 60} = 0.111$$

From Exhibit TN7.12, which displays the table for $N = 4$, F is interpolated as being approximately 0.957 at $X = 0.111$ and $S = 1$.

The number of machines waiting in line to be serviced is L, where

$$L = N(1 - F) = 4(1 - 0.957) = 0.172 \text{ machine}$$

The number of machines being serviced is H, where

$$H = FNX = 0.957(4)(0.111) = 0.425 \text{ machine}$$

Exhibit TN7.13 shows the cost resulting from unproductive machine time and the cost of the repairer.

Case II: Two repairers. From Exhibit TN7.12, at $X = 0.111$ and $S = 2$, $F = 0.998$.

The number of machines waiting in line, L, is

$$L = N(1 - F) = 4(1 - 0.998) = 0.008 \text{ machine}$$

The number of machines being serviced, H, is

$$H = FNX = 0.998(4)(0.111) = 0.443 \text{ machine}$$

The costs for the machines being idle and for the two repairers are shown in Exhibit TN7.13. The final column of that exhibit shows that retaining just one repairer is the best choice. ●

APPROXIMATING CUSTOMER WAITING TIME[2]

⊙⊙⊙◯   Good news for managers. All you need is the mean and standard deviation to compute average waiting time! Some good research has led to a "quick and dirty" mathematical approximation to the queuing models illustrated earlier in the technical note. What's nice about the approximation is that it does not assume a particular arrival rate or service distribution. All that is needed is the mean and standard deviation of the interarrival time and the service time. We will not burden you with all the details of how the approximations were derived, just how to use the formulas.

First, you will need to collect some data on your service time. The service time is the amount of time that it takes to serve each customer. Keep in mind that you want to collect your data during a period of time that fairly represents what you expect to happen during the period that you are concerned about. For example, if you want to know how many bank tellers you should have to service customers on Friday around the lunch period, collect your data during that period. This will ensure that the transactions being performed are similar to those that you expect in the future. You can use a stop watch to time how long it takes to serve each customer. Using these data, calculate the mean and standard deviation of the service time.

Recall from your statistics that the mean is

[TN7.7]
$$\overline{X} = \sum_{i=1}^{N} x_i / N$$

where x_i = observed value and N = total number of observed values.

The standard deviation is

$$s = \sqrt{\frac{\sum_{i=1}^{N}(x_i - \overline{X})^2}{N - 1}}$$

Next, capture data on the amount of time between the arrivals of each new customer during the period of time you are studying. This is called the interarrival time. From the data, calculate the mean and standard deviation of the interarrival time. From these calculations, we have

$$\overline{X}_s = \text{Mean service time}$$
$$\overline{X}_a = \text{Mean interarrival time}$$
$$S_s = \text{Standard deviation of the service time sample}$$
$$S_a = \text{Standard deviation of the interarrival time sample}$$

Next, define the following:

$$C_s = \text{Coefficient of variation of service time} = \frac{S_s}{\overline{X}_s}$$

$$C_a = \text{Coefficient of variation of interarrival time} = \frac{S_a}{\overline{X}_a}$$

$$\lambda = \text{Customer arrival rate} = \frac{1}{\overline{X}_a}$$

$$\mu = \text{Customer service rate} = \frac{1}{\overline{X}_s}$$

Now, we can calculate some statistics about our system. First, define S as the number of servers that we intend to use. Then,

$$\rho = \text{Utilization of the servers} = \frac{\lambda}{S\mu}$$

$$L_q = \text{Expected length of the waiting line} = \frac{\rho^{\sqrt{2(S+1)}}}{1 - \rho} \times \frac{C_a^2 + C_s^2}{2}$$

$$L_s = \text{Expected number of people in the system} = L_q + S\rho$$

$$W_q = \text{Expected time waiting in line} = \frac{L_q}{\lambda}$$

$$W_s = \text{Expected time in the system} = \frac{L_s}{\lambda}$$

The utilization (ρ) is the percentage of time that the servers are expected to be busy. Often companies that provide high service target this number at between 70 and 80 percent depending on the amount of variance there is in the customer arrival and service rates. L_q is how long the queue is expected to be, and W_q is how long a customer is expected to have to wait in the queue. L_s and W_s are the expected number of customers in the system and the expected time that a customer is in the system. These statistics consider that the total number of customers and the total waiting time must include those that are actually being served.

EXAMPLE TN7.5: Waiting Line Approximation

Let's consider an example of a call center that takes orders for a mail order business. During the peak period, the average time between call arrivals ($\overline{X}_a$) is 0.5 minute with a standard deviation (S_a) of 0.203 minute. The average time to service a call ($\overline{X}_s$) is 4 minutes and the standard deviation of the service time (S_s) is 2.5 minutes. If the call center is using 9 operators to service calls, how long would you expect customers to wait before being serviced? What would be the impact of adding an additional operator?

**Excel:
Queue.xls**

SOLUTION

W_q is the time that we expect a customer to wait before being served. The best way to do these calculations is with a spreadsheet. The spreadsheet "Queue_Models.xls" on the DVD-ROM can be easily used. The following steps are needed for the calculation of the customer wait time.

Step 1. Calculate expected customer arrival rate (λ), service rate per server (μ), coefficient of variation for the interarrival time (C_a) and service time (C_s).

$$\lambda = \frac{1}{\overline{X}_a} = \frac{1}{.5} = 2 \text{ customers per minute}$$

$$\mu = \frac{1}{\overline{X}_s} = \frac{1}{4} = .25 \text{ customer per minute}$$

$$C_a = \frac{S_a}{\overline{X}_a} = \frac{.203}{.5} = .406$$

$$C_s = \frac{S_s}{\overline{X}_s} = \frac{2.5}{4} = .625$$

Step 2. Calculate the expected server utilization (σ).

$$\rho = \frac{\lambda}{S\mu} = \frac{2}{9 \times .25} = .888889 \qquad \text{(Operators are expected to be busy 89 percent of the time.)}$$

Step 3. Calculate the expected number of people waiting (L_q) and the length of the wait (W_q).

$$L_q = \frac{\rho^{\sqrt{2(S+1)}}}{1-\rho} \times \frac{C_a^2 + C_s^2}{2} = \frac{.888889^{\sqrt{2(9+1)}}}{1-.888889} \times \frac{.406^2 + .625^2}{2} = 1.476064 \text{ customers}$$

(This is the number of customers that we expect to be waiting on hold.)

$$W_q = \frac{L_q}{\lambda} = \frac{1.476064}{2} = .738032 \text{ minute}$$

On average, we expect customers to wait 44 seconds (.738032 × 60) before talking to an operator.

For 10 operators, the calculations are as follows:

$$\rho = \frac{\lambda}{S\mu} = \frac{2}{10 \times .25} = .8 \qquad \text{(Operators are expected to be busy 80 percent of the time.)}$$

$$L_q = \frac{\rho^{\sqrt{2(S+1)}}}{1-\rho} \times \frac{C_a^2 + C_s^2}{2} = \frac{.8^{\sqrt{2(10+1)}}}{1-.8} \times \frac{.406^2 + .625^2}{2} = .487579 \text{ customer}$$

$$W_q = \frac{L_q}{\lambda} = \frac{0.487579}{2} = 0.24379 \text{ minute}$$

With 10 operators, the waiting time is cut one-third to 14.6 seconds. If you add two operators (bringing the total to 11), the waiting time in queue is 6.4 seconds. Adding the first additional operator has a significant impact on customer wait time. ●

This approximation is useful for many typical queuing situations. It is easy to implement using a spreadsheet such as the "Queue_Models.xls" spreadsheet on the DVD-ROM included with the book. Keep in mind that the approximation assumes that the population to be served is large and customers arrive one at a time. The approximation can be useful for a quick analysis of a queuing situation.

COMPUTER SIMULATION OF WAITING LINES

Some waiting line problems that seem simple on first impression turn out to be extremely difficult or impossible to solve. Throughout this supplement we have been treating waiting line situations that are independent; that is, either the entire system consists of a single phase, or else each service that is performed in a series is independent. (This could happen if the output of one service location is allowed to build up in front of the next one so that this, in essence, becomes a calling population for the next service.) When a series of services is performed in sequence where the output rate of one becomes the input rate of the next, we can no longer use the simple formulas. This is also true for any problem where conditions do not meet the requirements of the equations, as specified in Exhibit TN7.9. The technique best suited to solving this type of problem is computer simulation. We treat the topic of modeling and simulation in Technical Note 17.

CONCLUSION

Waiting line problems both challenge and frustrate those who try to solve them. The basic objective is to balance the cost of waiting with the cost of adding more resources. For a service system this means that the utilization of a server may be quite low to provide a short waiting time to the customer. One main concern in dealing with waiting line problems is which procedure or priority rule to use in selecting the next product or customer to be served.

Many queuing problems appear simple until an attempt is made to solve them. This technical note has dealt with the simpler problems. When the situation becomes more complex, when there are multiple phases, or where services are performed only in a particular sequence, computer simulation is necessary to obtain the optimal solution.

KEY TERMS

Queue A line of waiting persons, jobs, things, or the like.

Queuing system Consists of three major components: (1) the source population and the way customers arrive at the system, (2) the serving systems, and (3) how customers exit the system.

Arrival rate The expected number of customers that arrive each period.

Exponential distribution A probability distribution often associated with interarrival times.

Poisson distribution Probability distribution often used to describe the number of arrivals during a given time period.

Service rate The capacity of a server measured in number of units that can be processed over a given time period.

FORMULA REVIEW

Exponential distribution

[TN7.1]
$$f(t) = \lambda e^{-\lambda t}$$

Poisson distribution

[TN7.2]
$$P_T(n) = \frac{(\lambda T)^n e^{-\lambda T}}{n!}$$

Model 1 (See Exhibit TN7.10.)

$$L_q = \frac{\lambda^2}{\mu(\mu - \lambda)} \qquad W_q = \frac{L_q}{\lambda} \qquad P_n = \left(1 - \frac{\lambda}{\mu}\right)\left(\frac{\lambda}{\mu}\right)^n \qquad P_o = \left(1 - \frac{\lambda}{\mu}\right)$$

[TN7.3]

$$L_s = \frac{\lambda}{\mu - \lambda} \qquad W_s = \frac{L_s}{\lambda} \qquad \rho = \frac{\lambda}{\mu}$$

Model 2

$$L_q = \frac{\lambda^2}{2\mu(\mu - \lambda)} \qquad W_q = \frac{L_q}{\lambda}$$

[TN7.4]

$$L_s = L_q + \frac{\lambda}{\mu} \qquad W_s = \frac{L_s}{\lambda}$$

Model 3

$$L_s = L_q + \lambda/\mu \qquad W_s = L_s/\lambda$$

[TN7.5]

$$W_q = L_q/\lambda \qquad P_w = L_q\left(\frac{S_\mu}{\lambda} - 1\right)$$

Model 4

$$X = \frac{T}{T + U} \qquad H = FNX \qquad L = N(1 - F) \qquad n = L + H$$

[TN7.6]

$$P_n = \frac{N!}{(N - n)!} X^n P_0 \qquad J = NF(1 - X)$$

$$W = \frac{L(T + U)}{N - L} = \frac{LT}{H} \qquad F = \frac{T + U}{T + U + W}$$

Waiting time approximation

$$\overline{X} = \sum_{i=1}^{N} x_i \Big/ N \qquad s = \sqrt{\frac{\sum_{i=1}^{N}(x_i - \overline{X})^2}{N - 1}}$$

$$C_s = \frac{S_s}{\overline{X}_s} \qquad C_a = \frac{S_a}{\overline{X}_a} \qquad \lambda = \frac{1}{\overline{X}_a} \qquad \mu = \frac{1}{\overline{X}_s}$$

[TN7.7]

$$\rho = \frac{\lambda}{S\mu}$$

$$L_q = \frac{\rho^{\sqrt{2(S+1)}}}{1 - \rho} \times \frac{C_a^2 + C_s^2}{2}$$

$$L_s = L_q + S\rho$$

$$W_q = \frac{L_q}{\lambda}$$

$$W_s = \frac{L_s}{\lambda}$$

**Excel:
Queue.xls**

SOLVED PROBLEMS

SOLVED PROBLEM 1

Quick Lube Inc. operates a fast lube and oil change garage. On a typical day, customers arrive at the rate of three per hour, and lube jobs are performed at an average rate of one every 15 minutes. The mechanics operate as a team on one car at a time.

Assuming Poisson arrivals and exponential service, find

    a. Utilization of the lube team.
    b. The average number of cars in line.
    c. The average time a car waits before it is lubed.
    d. The total time it takes to go through the system (that is, waiting in line plus lube time).

Solution

$\lambda = 3, \mu = 4$

    a. Utilization $\rho = \dfrac{\lambda}{\mu} = \dfrac{3}{4} = 75\%$.

    b. $L_q = \dfrac{\lambda^2}{\mu(\mu - \lambda)} = \dfrac{3^2}{4(4 - 3)} = \dfrac{9}{4} = 2.25$ cars in line.

    c. $W_q = \dfrac{L_q}{\lambda} = \dfrac{2.25}{3} = .75$ hour, or 45 minutes.

    d. $W_s = \dfrac{L_s}{\lambda} = \dfrac{\lambda}{\mu - \lambda} \Big/ \lambda = \dfrac{3}{4 - 3} \Big/ 3 = 1$ hour (waiting + lube).

SOLVED PROBLEM 2

American Vending Inc. (AVI) supplies vended food to a large university. Because students often kick the machines out of anger and frustration, management has a constant repair problem. The machines break down on an average of three per hour, and the breakdowns are distributed in a Poisson manner. Downtime costs the company $25/hour per machine, and each maintenance worker gets $4 per hour. One worker can service machines at an average rate of five per hour, distributed exponentially; two workers working together can service seven per hour, distributed exponentially; and a team of three workers can do eight per hour, distributed exponentially.

    What is the optimal maintenance crew size for servicing the machines?

Excel:
Queue.xls

Solution

Case I—One worker:
  $\lambda = 3$/hour Poisson, $\mu = 5$/hour exponential
There is an average number of machines in the system of

$$L_s = \frac{\lambda}{\mu - \lambda} = \frac{3}{5 - 3} = \frac{3}{2} = 1\tfrac{1}{2} \text{ machines}$$

Downtime cost is $25 \times 1.5 = 37.50$ per hour; repair cost is $4.00 per hour; and total cost per hour for 1 worker is $37.50 + $4.00 = $41.50.

$$\begin{array}{lr}
\text{Downtime } (1.5 \times \$25) = & \$37.50 \\
\text{Labor } (1 \text{ worker} \times \$4) = & \underline{4.00} \\
& \$41.50
\end{array}$$

Case II—Two workers:
  $\lambda = 3, \mu = 7$

$$L_s = \frac{\lambda}{\mu - \lambda} = \frac{3}{7 - 3} = .75 \text{ machine}$$

$$\begin{array}{lr}
\text{Downtime } (.75 \times \$25) & = \$18.75 \\
\text{Labor } (2 \text{ workers} \times \$4.00) = & \underline{8.00} \\
& \$26.75
\end{array}$$

Case III—Three workers:
  $\lambda = 3, \mu = 8$

$$L_s = \frac{\lambda}{\mu - \lambda} = \frac{3}{8 - 3} = \frac{3}{5} = .60 \text{ machine}$$

$$\begin{array}{lr}
\text{Downtime } (.60 \times \$25) & = \$15.00 \\
\text{Labor } (3 \text{ workers} \times \$4) = & \underline{12.00} \\
& \$27.00
\end{array}$$

Comparing the costs for one, two, or three workers, we see that Case II with two workers is the optimal decision.

**Excel:
Queue.xls**

SOLVED PROBLEM 3

American Bank has a single automated teller machine (ATM) located in a shopping center. Data were collected during a period of peak usage on Saturday afternoon and it was found that the average time between customer arrivals is 2.1 minutes with a standard deviation of .8 minute. It also was found it takes an average of 1.9 minutes for a customer to complete a transaction with a standard deviation of 2 minutes. Approximately how long will customers need to wait in line during the peak usage period?

Solution

Step 1. Calculate expected customer arrival rate (λ), service rate per server (μ), coefficient of variation for the arrival distribution (C_a), and service distribution (C_s).

$$\lambda = \frac{1}{\overline{X}_a} = \frac{1}{2.1} = .47619 \text{ customer per minute}$$

$$\mu = \frac{1}{\overline{X}_s} = \frac{1}{1.9} = .526316 \text{ customer per minute}$$

$$C_a = \frac{S_a}{\overline{X}_a} = \frac{.8}{2.1} = .380952$$

$$C_s = \frac{S_s}{\overline{X}_s} = \frac{2}{1.9} = 1.052632$$

Step 2. Calculate the expected server utilization (σ).

$$\rho = \frac{\lambda}{S\mu} = \frac{.47619}{1 \times .526316} = .904762 \qquad \text{(Operators are expected to be busy 90.5 percent of the time.)}$$

Step 3. Calculate the expected number of people waiting (L_q) and the length of the wait (W_q).

$$L_q = \frac{\rho^{\sqrt{2(S+1)}}}{1-\rho} \times \frac{C_a^2 + C_s^2}{2} = \frac{.904762^{\sqrt{2(1+1)}}}{1-.904762} \times \frac{.380952^2 + 1.052632^2}{2}$$

$$= 5.385596 \text{ customers}$$

(This is the number of customers that we expect to be waiting on hold.)

$$W_q = \frac{L_q}{\lambda} = \frac{5.385596}{.47619} = 11.30975 \text{ minutes}$$

On average we expect customers to wait 11 minutes and 19 seconds (.30975 × 60) before having access to the ATM.

REVIEW AND DISCUSSION QUESTIONS

1 Cultural factors affect waiting lines. For example, fast checkout lines (e.g., 10 items or less) are uncommon in Japan. Why do you think this is so?
2 How many waiting lines did you encounter during your last airline flight?
3 Distinguish between a *channel* and a *phase.*
4 What is the major cost trade-off that must be made in managing waiting line situations?
5 Which assumptions are necessary to employ the formulas given for Model 1?
6 In what way might the first-come, first-served rule be unfair to the customer waiting for service in a bank or hospital?
7 Define, in a practical sense, what is meant by an *exponential service time.*
8 Would you expect the exponential distribution to be a good approximation of service times for
    a. Buying an airline ticket at the airport?
    b. Riding a merry-go-round at a carnival?
    c. Checking out of a hotel?
    d. Completing a midterm exam in your OM class?
9 Would you expect the Poisson distribution to be a good approximation of
    a. Runners crossing the finish line in the Boston Marathon?
    b. Arrival times of the students in your OM class?
    c. Arrival times of the bus to your stop at school?

PROBLEMS

1   Students arrive at the Administrative Services Office at an average of one every 15 minutes, and their requests take on average 10 minutes to be processed. The service counter is staffed by only one clerk, Judy Gumshoes, who works eight hours per day. Assume Poisson arrivals and exponential service times.

    a. What percentage of time is Judy idle?

    b. How much time, on average, does a student spend waiting in line?

    c. How long is the (waiting) line on average?

    d. What is the probability that an arriving student (just before entering the Administrative Services Office) will find at least one other student waiting in line?

2   The managers of the Administrative Services Office estimate that the time a student spends waiting in line costs them (due to goodwill loss and so on) $10 per hour. To reduce the time a student spends waiting, they know that they need to improve Judy's processing time (see Problem 1). They are currently considering the following two options:

    a. Install a computer system, with which Judy expects to be able to complete a student request 40 percent faster (from 2 minutes per request to 1 minute and 12 seconds, for example).

    b. Hire another temporary clerk, who will work at the same rate as Judy.

    If the computer costs $99.50 to operate per day, while the temporary clerk gets paid $75 per day, is Judy right to prefer the hired help? Assume Poisson arrivals and exponential service times.

3   Sharp Discounts Wholesale Club has two service desks, one at each entrance of the store. Customers arrive at each service desk at an average of one every six minutes. The service rate at each service desk is four minutes per customer.

    a. How often (what percentage of time) is each service desk idle?

    b. What is the probability that both service clerks are busy?

    c. What is the probability that both service clerks are idle?

    d. How many customers, on average, are waiting in line in front of each service desk?

    e. How much time does a customer spend at the service desk (waiting plus service time)?

4   Sharp Discounts Wholesale Club is considering consolidating its two service desks (see Problem 3) into one location, staffed by two clerks. The clerks will continue to work at the same individual speed of four minutes per customer.

    a. What is the probability of waiting in line?

    b. How many customers, on average, are waiting in line?

    c. How much time does a customer spend at the service desk (waiting plus service time)?

    d. Do you think the Sharp Discounts Wholesale Club should consolidate the service desks?

5   Burrito King (a new fast-food franchise opening up nationwide) has successfully automated burrito production for its drive-up fast-food establishments. The Burro-Master 9000 requires a constant 45 seconds to produce a batch of burritos. It has been estimated that customers will arrive at the drive-up window according to a Poisson distribution at an average of one every 50 seconds. To help determine the amount of space needed for the line at the drive-up window, Burrito King would like to know the expected average time in the system, the average line length (in cars), and the average number of cars in the system (both in line and at the window).

6   The Bijou Theater in Hermosa Beach, California, shows vintage movies. Customers arrive at the theater line at the rate of 100 per hour. The ticket seller averages 30 seconds per customer, which includes placing validation stamps on customers' parking lot receipts and punching their frequent watcher cards. (Because of these added services, many customers don't get in until after the feature has started.)

    a. What is the average customer waiting time in the system?

    b. What would be the effect on system waiting time of having a second ticket taker doing nothing but validations and card punching, thereby cutting the average service time to 20 seconds?

    c. Would system waiting time be less than you found in *b* if a second window was opened with each server doing all three tasks?

7   To support National Heart Week, the Heart Association plans to install a free blood pressure testing booth in El Con Mall for the week. Previous experience indicates that, on the average, 10 persons per hour request a test. Assume arrivals are Poisson from an infinite population. Blood pressure measurements can be made at a constant time of five minutes each. Assume the queue length can be infinite with FCFS discipline.

    a. What average number in line can be expected?

    b. What average number of persons can be expected to be in the system?

    c. What is the average amount of time that a person can expect to spend in line?

    d. On the average, how much time will it take to measure a person's blood pressure, including waiting time?

    e. On weekends, the arrival rate can be expected to increase to over 12 per hour. What effect will this have on the number in the waiting line?

8   A cafeteria serving line has a coffee urn from which customers serve themselves. Arrivals at the urn follow a Poisson distribution at the rate of three per minute. In serving themselves, customers take about 15 seconds, exponentially distributed.

    a. How many customers would you expect to see on the average at the coffee urn?

    b. How long would you expect it to take to get a cup of coffee?

    c. What percentage of time is the urn being used?

    d. What is the probability that three or more people are in the cafeteria?

    e. If the cafeteria installs an automatic vendor that dispenses a cup of coffee at a constant time of 15 seconds, how does this change your answers to *a* and *b*?

9   An engineering firm retains a technical specialist to assist four design engineers working on a project. The help that the specialist gives engineers ranges widely in time consumption. The specialist has some answers available in memory; others require computation, and still others require significant search time. On the average, each request for assistance takes the specialist one hour.

    The engineers require help from the specialist on the average of once each day. Because each assistance takes about an hour, each engineer can work for seven hours, on the average, without assistance. One further point: Engineers needing help do not interrupt if the specialist is already involved with another problem.

    Treat this as a finite queuing problem and answer the following questions:

    a. How many engineers, on average, are waiting for the technical specialist for help?

    b. What is the average time that an engineer has to wait for the specialist?

    c. What is the probability that an engineer will have to wait in line for the specialist?

10   L. Winston Martin (an allergist in Tucson) has an excellent system for handling his regular patients who come in just for allergy injections. Patients arrive for an injection and fill out a name slip, which is then placed in an open slot that passes into another room staffed by one or two nurses. The specific injections for a patient are prepared, and the patient is called through a speaker system into the room to receive the injection. At certain times during the day, patient load drops and only one nurse is needed to administer the injections.

    Let's focus on the simpler case of the two—namely, when there is one nurse. Also assume that patients arrive in a Poisson fashion and the service rate of the nurse is exponentially distributed. During this slower period, patients arrive with an interarrival time of approximately three minutes. It takes the nurse an average of two minutes to prepare the patients' serum and administer the injection.

    a. What is the average number you would expect to see in Dr. Martin's facilities?

    b. How long would it take for a patient to arrive, get an injection, and leave?

    c. What is the probability that there will be three or more patients on the premises?

    d. What is the utilization of the nurse?

    e. Assume three nurses are available. Each takes an average of two minutes to prepare the patients' serum and administer the injection. What is the average total time of a patient in the system?

11   The Judy Gray Income Tax Service is analyzing its customer service operations during the month prior to the April filing deadline. On the basis of past data it has been estimated that customers arrive according to a Poisson process with an average interarrival time of 12 minutes. The time to complete a return for a customer is exponentially distributed with a mean of 10 minutes. Based on this information, answer the following questions:

    a. If you went to Judy, how much time would you allow for getting your return done?

    b. On average, how much room should be allowed for the waiting area?

    c. If Judy stayed in the office 12 hours per day, how many hours on average, per day, would she be busy?

    d. What is the probability that the system is idle?

    e. If the arrival rate remained unchanged but the average time in system must be 45 minutes or less, what would need to be changed?

12   A graphics reproduction firm has four units of equipment that are automatic but occasionally become inoperative because of the need for supplies, maintenance, or repair. Each unit requires service roughly twice each hour, or, more precisely, each unit of equipment runs an average of 30 minutes before needing service. Service times vary widely, ranging from a simple service (such as pressing a restart switch or repositioning paper) to more involved equipment disassembly. The average service time, however, is five minutes.

Equipment downtime results in a loss of $20 per hour. The one equipment attendant is paid $6 per hour.

Using finite queuing analysis, answer the following questions:

a. What is the average number of units in line?

b. What is the average number of units still in operation?

c. What is the average number of units being serviced?

d. The firm is considering adding another attendant at the same $6 rate. Should the firm do it?

13 Benny the Barber owns a one-chair shop. At barber college, they told Benny that his customers would exhibit a Poisson arrival distribution and that he would provide an exponential service distribution. His market survey data indicate that customers arrive at a rate of two per hour. It will take Benny an average of 20 minutes to give a haircut. Based on these figures, find the following:

a. The average number of customers waiting.

b. The average time a customer waits.

c. The average time a customer is in the shop.

d. The average utilization of Benny's time.

14 Benny the Barber (see Problem 13) is considering the addition of a second chair. Customers would be selected for a haircut on a FCFS basis from those waiting. Benny has assumed that both barbers would take an average of 20 minutes to give a haircut, and that business would remain unchanged with customers arriving at a rate of two per hour. Find the following information to help Benny decide if a second chair should be added:

a. The average number of customers waiting.

b. The average time a customer waits.

c. The average time a customer is in the shop.

15 Customers enter the camera department of a store at the average rate of six per hour. The department is staffed by one employee, who takes an average of six minutes to serve each arrival. Assume this is a simple Poisson arrival exponentially distributed service time situation.

a. As a casual observer, how many people would you expect to see in the camera department (excluding the clerk)? How long would a customer expect to spend in the camera department (total time)?

b. What is the utilization of the clerk?

c. What is the probability that there are more than two people in the camera department (excluding the clerk)?

d. Another clerk has been hired for the camera department who also takes an average of six minutes to serve each arrival. How long would a customer expect to spend in the department now?

16 Cathy Livingston, bartender at the Tucson Racquet Club, can serve drinks at the rate of one every 50 seconds. During a hot evening recently, the bar was particularly busy and every 55 seconds someone was at the bar asking for a drink.

a. Assuming that everyone in the bar drank at the same rate and that Cathy served people on a first-come, first-served basis, how long would you expect to have to wait for a drink?

b. How many people would you expect to be waiting for drinks?

c. What is the probability that three or more people are waiting for drinks?

d. What is the utilization of the bartender (how busy is she)?

e. If the bartender is replaced with an automatic drink dispensing machine, how would this change your answer in part *a*?

17 An office employs several clerks who originate documents and one operator who enters the document information in a word processor. The group originates documents at a rate of 25 per hour. The operator can enter the information with average exponentially distributed time of two minutes. Assume the population is infinite, arrivals are Poisson, and queue length is infinite with FCFS discipline.

a. Calculate the percentage utilization of the operator.

b. Calculate the average number of documents in the system.

c. Calculate the average time in the system.

d. Calculate the probability of four or more documents being in the system.

e. If another clerk were added, the document origination rate would increase to 30 per hour. What would this do to the word processor workload? Show why.

18 A study-aid desk staffed by a graduate student has been established to answer students' questions and help in working problems in your OM course. The desk is staffed eight hours per day. The dean wants to know how the facility is working. Statistics show that students arrive at a rate of four per hour, and the distribution is approximately Poisson. Assistance time averages

10 minutes, distributed exponentially. Assume population and line length can be infinite and queue discipline is FCFS.

   a. Calculate the percentage utilization of the graduate student.

   b. Calculate the average number of students in the system.

   c. Calculate the average time in the system.

   d. Calculate the probability of four or more students being in line or being served.

   e. Before a test, the arrival of students increases to six per hour on the average. What does this do to the average length of the line?

19   At the California border inspection station, vehicles arrive at the rate of 10 per minute in a Poisson distribution. For simplicity in this problem, assume that there is only one lane and one inspector, who can inspect vehicles at the rate of 12 per minute in an exponentially distributed fashion.

   a. What is the average length of the waiting line?

   b. What is the average time that a vehicle must wait to get through the system?

   c. What is the utilization of the inspector?

   d. What is the probability that when you arrive there will be three or more vehicles ahead of you?

20   The California border inspection station (see Problem 19) is considering the addition of a second inspector. The vehicles would wait in one lane and then be directed to the first available inspector. Arrival rates would remain the same (10 per minute) and the new inspector would process vehicles at the same rate as the first inspector (12 per minute).

   a. What would be the average length of the waiting line?

   b. What would be the average time that a vehicle must wait to get through the system?

   If a second lane was added (one lane for each inspector):

   c. What would be the average length of the waiting line?

   d. What would be the average time that a vehicle must wait to get through the system?

21   During the campus Spring Fling, the bumper car amusement attraction has a problem of cars becoming disabled and in need of repair. Repair personnel can be hired at the rate of $20 per hour, but they only work as one team. Thus, if one person is hired, he or she works alone; two or three people work together on the same repair.

     One repairer can fix cars in an average time of 30 minutes. Two repairers take 20 minutes, and three take 15 minutes. While these cars are down, lost income is $40 per hour. Cars tend to break down at the rate of two per hour.

     How many repairers should be hired?

22   A toll tunnel has decided to experiment with the use of a debit card for the collection of tolls. Initially, only one lane will be used. Cars are estimated to arrive at this experimental lane at the rate of 750 per hour. It will take exactly four seconds to verify the debit card.

   a. In how much time would you expect the customer to wait in line, pay with the debit card, and leave?

   b. How many cars would you expect to see in the system?

23   You are planning a bank. You plan for six tellers. Tellers take 15 minutes per customer with a standard deviation of 7 minutes. Customers arrive one every three minutes according to an exponential distribution (recall that the standard deviation is equal to the mean). Every customer that arrives eventually gets serviced.

   a. On average how many customers would be waiting in line?

   b. On average how long would a customer spend in the bank?

   c. If a customer arrived, saw the line, and decided not to get in line, that customer has _____.

   d. A customer who enters the line but decides to leave the line before getting service is said to have _____.

24   You are planning the new layout for the local branch of the Sixth Ninth Bank. You are considering separate cashier windows for the three different classes of service. Each class of service would be separate with its own cashiers and customers. Oddly enough, each class of service, while different, has exactly the same demand and service times. People for one class of service arrive every four minutes and arrival times are exponentially distributed (the standard deviation is equal to the mean). It takes seven minutes to service each customer and the standard deviation of the service times is three minutes. You assign two cashiers to each type of service.

   a. On average, how long will each line be at each of the cashier windows?

   b. On average how long will a customer spend in the bank (assume they enter, go directly to one line, and leave as soon as service is complete).

You decide to consolidate all the cashiers so they can handle all types of customers without increasing the service times.

c. What will happen to the amount of time each cashier spends idle? (increase, decrease, stay the same, depends on _____)

d. What will happen to the average amount of time a customer spends in the bank? (increase, decrease, stay the same, depends on _____)

SELECTED BIBLIOGRAPHY

Davis, M. M., and M. J. Maggard. "An Analysis of Customer Satisfaction with Waiting Times in a Two-Stage Service Process." *Journal of Operations Management* 9, no. 3 (August 1990), pp. 324–34.

Fitzsimmons, J. A., and M. J. Fitzsimmons. *Service Management,* 4th ed. New York: Irwin/McGraw-Hill, 2003.

Gross, D., and C. M. Harris. *Fundamentals of Queuing Theory.* New York: Wiley, 1997.

Hillier, F. S., et al. *Queuing Tables and Graphs.* New York: Elsevier–North Holland, 1981.

Katz, K. L.; B. M. Larson; and R. C. Larson. "Prescription for the Waiting-in-Line Blues: Entertain, Enlighten, and Engage." *Sloan Management Review* 32, no. 2 (Winter 1991), pp. 44–53.

Kleinrock, L., and R. Gail. *Queuing Systems: Problems and Solutions.* New York: Wiley, 1996.

Winston, W. L., and S. C. Albright. *Practical Management Science: Spreadsheet Modeling and Application.* New York: Duxbury, 2000.

FOOTNOTES

1 $n!$ is defined as $n(n - 1)(n - 2) \cdots (2)(1)$.

2 We are indebted to Gilvan Souza of the Robert H. Smith School of Business, University of Maryland, for his help with this section.

chapter

QUALITY MANAGEMENT: FOCUS ON SIX SIGMA

8

General Electric (GE) has been a major promoter of Six Sigma for over 10 years. Jack Welch, the legendary and now retired CEO, declared that "the big myth is that Six Sigma is about quality control and statistics. It is that—but it's much more. Ultimately, it drives leadership to be better by providing tools to think through tough issues. At Six Sigma's core is an idea that can turn a company inside out, focusing the organization outward on the customer." GE's commitment to quality centers on Six Sigma. Six Sigma is defined on the GE Web site as follows:

> **First, What is Six Sigma?** First, what it is not. It is not a secret society, a slogan or a cliché. Six Sigma is a highly disciplined process that helps us focus on developing and delivering near-perfect products

> and services. Why "Sigma"? The word is a statistical term that measures how far a given process deviates from perfection. The central idea behind Six Sigma is that if you can measure how many "defects" you have in a process, you can systematically figure out how to eliminate them and get as close to "zero defects" as possible. To achieve Six Sigma Quality, a process must produce no more than 3.4 defects per million opportunities. An "opportunity" is defined as a chance for nonconformance, or not meeting the required specifications. This means we need to be nearly flawless in executing our key processes.
>
> At its core, Six Sigma revolves around a few key concepts.

> | Critical to Quality: | Attributes most important to the customer |
> |---|---|
> | Defect: | Failing to deliver what the customer wants |
> | Process Capability: | What your process can deliver |
> | Variation: | What the customer sees and feels |
> | Stable Operations: | Ensuring consistent, predictable processes to improve what the customer sees and feels |
> | Design for Six Sigma: | Designing to meet customer needs and process capability → |

In this chapter, we first review the general subject of total quality management and the quality movement. We then develop the basic features and concepts of the Six Sigma approach to TQM. We then describe the Shingo system, which takes a unique approach to quality by focusing on preventing mistakes. This is followed by a review of ISO 9000 standards for quality certification used by many companies throughout the world. We then provide the major steps of external benchmarking for quality improvement. We conclude with a presentation of SERVQUAL, a tool designed expressly for measuring quality in service delivery.

TOTAL QUALITY MANAGEMENT

Total quality management   **Total quality management** may be defined as "managing the entire organization so that it excels on all dimensions of products and services that are important to the customer." It has two fundamental operational goals, namely

1. Careful design of the product or service.
2. Ensuring that the organization's systems can consistently produce the design.

These two goals can only be achieved if the entire organization is oriented toward them—hence the term *total* quality management. TQM became a national concern in the United States in the 1980s primarily as a response to Japanese quality superiority in manufacturing automobiles and other durable goods such as room air conditioners. A widely cited study of Japanese and U.S. air-conditioning manufacturers showed that the best-quality American products had *higher* average defect rates than those of the poorest Japanese manufacturers.[1] So severe was the quality shortfall in the United States that improving it throughout industry

BREAKTHROUGH

BALDRIGE QUALITY AWARD

The Baldrige Quality Award is given to organizations that have demonstrated outstanding quality in their products and processes. Four awards may be given annually in each of these categories: manufacturing, service, small business, education and health care, and not-for-profit.

Candidates for the award must submit an application of up to 75 pages that details the approach, deployment, and results of their quality activities under seven major categories: Leadership, Strategic Planning, Customer and Market Focus, Information and Analysis, Human Resource Focus, Process Management, and Business Results. These applications are scored on total points out of 1,000 by examiners and judges. Those who score above roughly 650 are selected for site visits. Winners selected from this group are then honored at an annual meeting in Washington, DC. A major benefit to all applicants is feedback from the examiners, which is essentially an audit of their practices. Many states have used the Baldrige Criteria as the basis of their own quality award programs. A report, *Building on Baldrige: American Quality for the 21st Century*, by the private Council on

Competitiveness, said, "More than any other program, the Baldrige Quality Award is responsible for making quality a national priority and disseminating best practices across the United States."

became a national priority, with the Department of Commerce establishing the **Malcolm Baldrige National Quality Award** in 1987 to help companies review and structure their quality programs. Also gaining major attention at this time was the requirement that suppliers demonstrate that they are measuring and documenting their quality practices according to specified criteria, called ISO standards, if they wished to compete for international contracts. We will have more to say about this later.

The philosophical leaders of the quality movement, notably Philip Crosby, W. Edwards Deming, and Joseph M. Juran—the so-called Quality Gurus—had slightly different definitions of what quality is and how to achieve it (see Exhibit 8.1), but they all had the same general message: To achieve outstanding quality requires quality leadership from senior management, a customer focus, total involvement of the workforce, and continuous improvement based upon rigorous analysis of processes. Later in the chapter, we will discuss how these precepts are applied in the latest approach to TQM—Six Sigma. We will now turn to some fundamental concepts that underlie any quality effort: quality specifications and quality costs.

Malcolm Baldrige National Quality Award

The Quality Gurus Compared

exhibit 8.1

	CROSBY	DEMING	JURAN
Definition of quality	Conformance to requirements	A predictable degree of uniformity and dependability at low cost and suited to the market	Fitness for use (satisfies customer's needs)
Degree of senior management responsibility	Responsible for quality	Responsible for 94% of quality problems	Less than 20% of quality problems are due to workers
Performance standard/ motivation	Zero defects	Quality has many "scales"; use statistics to measure performance in all areas; critical of zero defects	Avoid campaigns to do perfect work
General approach	Prevention, not inspection	Reduce variability by continuous improvement; cease mass inspection	General management approach to quality, especially human elements
Structure	14 steps to quality improvement	14 points for management	10 steps to quality improvement
Statistical process control (SPC)	Rejects statistically acceptable levels of quality [wants 100% perfect quality]	Statistical methods of quality control must be used	Recommends SPC but warns that it can lead to tool-driven approach
Improvement basis	A process, not a program; improvement goals	Continuous to reduce variation; eliminate goals without methods	Project-by-project team approach; set goals
Teamwork	Quality improvement teams; quality councils	Employee participation in decision making; break down barriers between departments	Team and quality circle approach
Costs of quality	Cost of nonconformance; quality is free	No optimum; continuous improvement	Quality is not free; there is not an optimum
Purchasing and goods received	State requirements; supplier is extension of business; most faults due to purchasers themselves	Inspection too late; sampling allows defects to enter system; statistical evidence and control charts required	Problems are complex; carry out formal surveys
Vendor rating	Yes; quality audits useless	No, critical of most systems	Yes, but help supplier improve

QUALITY SPECIFICATION AND QUALITY COSTS

⊙⊙⊙◯ Fundamental to any quality program is the determination of quality specifications and the costs of achieving (or *not* achieving) those specifications.

DEVELOPING QUALITY SPECIFICATIONS

Design quality

The quality specifications of a product or service derive from decisions and actions made relative to the quality of its design and the quality of its conformance to that design. **Design quality** refers to the inherent value of the product in the marketplace and is thus a strategic decision for the firm. The dimensions of quality are listed in Exhibit 8.2. These dimensions refer to features of the product or service that relate directly to design issues. A firm designs a product or service to address the need of a particular market.

A firm designs a product or service with certain performance characteristics and features based on what the intended market expects. Materials and manufacturing process attributes can greatly impact the reliability and durability of a product. Here the company attempts to design a product or service that can be produced or delivered at reasonable cost. The serviceability of the product may have a great impact on the cost of the product or service to the customer after the initial purchase is made. It also may impact the warranty and repair cost to the firm. Aesthetics may greatly impact the desirability of the product or service, in particular consumer products. Especially when a brand name is involved, the design often represents the next generation of an ongoing stream of products or services. Consistency in the relative performance of the product compared to the state of the art, for example, may have a great impact on how the quality of the product is perceived. This may be very important to the long-run success of the product or service.

Conformance quality

Conformance quality refers to the degree to which the product or service design specifications are met. The activities involved in achieving conformance are of a tactical, day-to-day nature. It should be evident that a product or service can have high design quality but low conformance quality, and vice versa.

Quality at the source

Quality at the source is frequently discussed in the context of conformance quality. This means that the person who does the work takes responsibility for making sure that his or her output meets specifications. Where a product is involved, achieving the quality specifications is typically the responsibility of manufacturing management; in a service firm, it is usually the responsibility of the branch operations management. Exhibit 8.3 shows two examples of the **dimensions of quality.** One is a laser printer that meets the pages-per-minute and print density standards; the second is a checking account transaction in a bank.

Dimensions of quality

Both quality of design and quality of conformance should provide products that meet the customer's objectives for those products. This is often termed the product's *fitness for use,* and it entails identifying the dimensions of the product (or service) that the customer wants (that is, the voice of the customer) and developing a quality control program to ensure that these dimensions are met.

exhibit 8.2

The Dimensions of Design Quality

DIMENSION	MEANING
Performance	Primary product or service characteristics
Features	Added touches, bells and whistles, secondary characteristics
Reliability/durability	Consistency of performance over time, probability of failing, useful life
Serviceability	Ease of repair
Aesthetics	Sensory characteristics (sound, feel, look, and so on)
Perceived quality	Past performance and reputation

Examples of Dimensions of Quality

exhibit 8.3

| | MEASURES | |
DIMENSION	PRODUCT EXAMPLE: LASER PRINTER	SERVICE EXAMPLE: CHECKING ACCOUNT AT A BANK
Performance	Pages per minute Print density	Time to process customer requests
Features	Multiple paper trays Color capability	Automatic bill paying
Reliability/durability	Mean time between failures Estimated time to obsolescence Expected life of major components	Variability of time to process requests Keeping pace with industry trends
Serviceability	Availability of authorized repairs centers Number of copies per print cartridge Modular design	Online reports Ease of getting updated information
Aesthetics	Control button layout Case style Courtesy of dealer	Appearance of bank lobby Courtesy of teller
Perceived quality	Brand name recognition Rating in *Consumer Reports*	Endorsed by community leaders

COST OF QUALITY

Although few can quarrel with the notion of prevention, management often needs hard numbers to determine how much prevention activities will cost. This issue was recognized by Joseph Juran, who wrote about it in 1951 in his *Quality Control Handbook*. Today, **cost of quality (COQ)** analyses are common in industry and constitute one of the primary functions of QC departments.

There are a number of definitions and interpretations of the term *cost of quality*. From the purist's point of view, it means all of the costs attributable to the production of quality that is not 100 percent perfect. A less stringent definition considers only those costs that are the difference between what can be expected from excellent performance and the current costs that exist.

How significant is the cost of quality? It has been estimated at between 15 and 20 percent of every sales dollar—the cost of reworking, scrapping, repeated service, inspections, tests, warranties, and other quality-related items. Philip Crosby states that the correct cost for a well-run quality management program should be under 2.5 percent.[2]

Three basic assumptions justify an analysis of the costs of quality: (1) failures are caused, (2) prevention is cheaper, and (3) performance can be measured.

The costs of quality are generally classified into four types:

1. **Appraisal costs.** Costs of the inspection, testing, and other tasks to ensure that the product or process is acceptable.
2. **Prevention costs.** The sum of all the costs to prevent defects, such as the costs to identify the cause of the defect, to implement corrective action to eliminate the cause, to train personnel, to redesign the product or system, and to purchase new equipment or make modifications.

Cost of quality

A GOODYEAR ASSOCIATE INSPECTS A RADIAL TIRE AT THE SAO PAULO, BRAZIL, FACTORY BEFORE MOUNTING IT ON THE WHEEL. GOODYEAR PRACTICES BOTH VISUAL AND INTERNAL INSPECTIONS OF TIRES, EVEN PULLING SOME TIRES FROM THE PRODUCTION LINE TO BE X-RAYED. QUALITY CONTROL ENGINEERS ALSO REGULARLY CUT APART RANDOMLY CHOSEN TIRES TO STUDY VARIOUS DETAILS THAT MAY AFFECT PERFORMANCE, RIDE, OR SAFETY.

exhibit 8.4

Quality Cost Report

	CURRENT MONTH'S COST	PERCENTAGE OF TOTAL
Prevention costs		
Quality training	$ 2,000	1.3%
Reliability consulting	10,000	6.5
Pilot production runs	5,000	3.3
Systems development	8,000	5.2
Total prevention	25,000	16.3
Appraisal costs		
Materials inspection	6,000	3.9
Supplies inspection	3,000	2.0
Reliability testing	5,000	3.3
Laboratory testing	25,000	16.3
Total appraisal	39,000	25.5
Internal failure costs		
Scrap	15,000	9.8
Repair	18,000	11.8
Rework	12,000	7.8
Downtime	6,000	3.9
Total internal failure	51,000	33.3
External failure costs		
Warranty costs	14,000	9.2
Out-of-warranty repairs and replacement	6,000	3.9
Customer complaints	3,000	2.0
Product liability	10,000	6.5
Transportation losses	5,000	3.3
Total external failure	38,000	24.9
Total quality costs	$153,000	100.0

3. **Internal failure costs.** Costs for defects incurred within the system: scrap, rework, repair.
4. **External failure costs.** Costs for defects that pass through the system: customer warranty replacements, loss of customers or goodwill, handling complaints, and product repair.

Exhibit 8.4 illustrates the type of report that might be submitted to show the various costs by categories. Prevention is the most important influence. A rule of thumb says that for every dollar you spend in prevention, you can save $10 in failure and appraisal costs.

Often increases in productivity occur as a by-product of efforts to reduce the cost of quality. A bank, for example, set out to improve quality and reduce the cost of quality and found that it had also boosted productivity. The bank developed this productivity measure for the loan processing area: the number of tickets processed divided by the resources required (labor cost, computer time, ticket forms). Before the quality improvement program, the productivity index was 0.2660 [2,080/($11.23 × 640 hours + $0.05 × 2,600 forms + $500 for systems costs)]. After the quality improvement project was completed, labor time fell to 546 hours and the number of forms rose to 2,100, for a change in the index to 0.3088, an increase in productivity of 16 percent.

Service

FUNCTIONS OF THE QC DEPARTMENT

Although the focus of this chapter is on corporatewide quality programs, it is useful to comment on the functions of QC departments.

THE THEORY BEHIND SIX SIGMA

Six Sigma reflects the goal of having the customer's specification limits of the items produced by a process be twice the natural variation ($\pm 3\sigma$) of the process outputs (or, to put it another way, the process variation to be half the specification limits). For example, suppose the outputs of a process are normally distributed as shown above line A in Exhibit 8.5. By the definition of $\pm 3\sigma$ (σ is the standard deviation), 99.73 percent of the outputs are within $\pm 3\sigma$ of the mean and, therefore, .27 percent are outside $\pm 3\sigma$ of the mean. Thus, if the specification limits of the product are set equal to $\pm 3\sigma$ for the process, we could expect .27 percent of the outputs to be out of specification. That is, we could expect 2.7 units per thousand or 2,700 units or parts per million (ppm) to be out of specification. Now suppose that we decide that a defect rate of 2,700 ppm is too high. If the specification limits are kept at the same place and the process is improved so the output variation is much less, the probability of producing a unit out of specification will go down. This is shown below line B in the exhibit. In particular, suppose the process is improved to the point where the interval of natural variation ($\pm 3\sigma$) of the process is half of the interval of the specification limits (which then, by definition, will be $\pm 6\sigma$ for the process outputs). Then, the probability of producing a unit outside the $\pm 3\sigma$ interval remains .0027 (by definition of $\pm 3\sigma$), but the probability of having a part produced out of the specification interval is an order of magnitude less—about two parts per billion (by the definition of $\pm 6\sigma$). Details about the statistical characteristics of Six Sigma are covered in Technical Note 8.

Comparison of Three Sigma and Six Sigma Distributions

exhibit 8.5

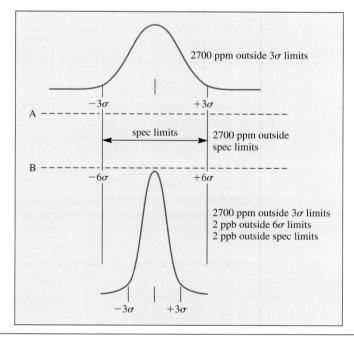

The typical manufacturing QC department has a variety of functions to perform. These include testing designs for their reliability in the lab and the field; gathering performance data on products in the field and resolving quality problems in the field; planning and budgeting the QC program in the plant; and, finally, designing and overseeing quality control systems and inspection procedures, and actually carrying out inspection activities requiring special technical knowledge to accomplish. The tools of the QC department fall under the heading of statistical quality control (SQC) and consist of two main sections: acceptance sampling and process control. These topics are covered in the technical note to this chapter.

SIX-SIGMA QUALITY

Six Sigma

Six Sigma refers to the philosophy and methods companies such as General Electric and Motorola use to eliminate defects in their products and processes. A defect is simply any component that does not fall within the customer's specification limits. Each step or activity in a company represents an opportunity for defects to occur and Six-Sigma programs seek to reduce the variation in the processes that lead to these defects. Indeed, Six-Sigma advocates see variation as the enemy of quality, and much of the theory underlying Six Sigma is devoted to dealing with this problem. A process that is in Six-Sigma control will produce no more than two defects out of every billion units. Often, this is stated as four defects per million units, which is true if the process is only running somewhere within one sigma of the target specification.

One of the benefits of Six-Sigma thinking is that it allows managers to readily describe the performance of a process in terms of its variability and to compare different processes using a common metric. This metric is **defects per million opportunities (DPMO)**. This calculation requires three pieces of data:

DPMO

1. **Unit.**   The item produced or being serviced.
2. **Defect.**   Any item or event that does not meet the customer's requirements.
3. **Opportunity.**   A chance for a defect to occur.

A straightforward calculation is made using the following formula:

$$\text{DPMO} = \frac{\text{Number of defects}}{\text{Number of opportunities for error per unit} \times \text{Number of units}} \times 1{,}000{,}000$$

EXAMPLE 8.1

The customers of a mortgage bank expect to have their mortgage applications processed within 10 days of filing. This would be called a *critical customer requirement,* or CCR, in Six-Sigma terms. Suppose all defects are counted (loans in a monthly sample taking more than 10 days to process), and it is determined that there are 150 loans in the 1,000 applications processed last month that don't meet this customer requirement. Thus, the DPMO = 150/1000 × 1,000,000, or 150,000 loans out of every million processed that fail to meet a CCR. Put differently, it means that only 850,000 loans out of a million are approved within time expectations. Statistically, 15 percent of the loans are defective and 85 percent are correct. This is a case where all the loans processed in less than 10 days meet our criteria. Often there are upper and lower customer requirements rather than just a single upper requirement as we have here. ●

There are two aspects to Six-Sigma programs: the methodology side and the people side. We will take these up in order.

SIX-SIGMA METHODOLOGY

DMAIC

PDCA cycle

Continuous improvement

Kaizen

While Six Sigma's methods include many of the statistical tools that were employed in other quality movements, here they are employed in a systematic project-oriented fashion through the define, measure, analyze, improve, and control (**DMAIC**) cycle. The DMAIC cycle is a more detailed version of the Deming **PDCA cycle**, which consists of four steps—plan, do, check, and act—that underly **continuous improvement**. (Continuous improvement, also called **kaizen**, seeks continual improvement of machinery, materials, labor utilization, and production methods through applications of suggestions and ideas of company teams.) Like Six Sigma, it also emphasizes the scientific method, particularly hypothesis testing about the relationship between process inputs (X's) and outputs (Y's) using design of experiments (DOE) methods. The availability of modern statistical software has reduced the drudgery of analyzing and displaying data and is now part of the Six-Sigma tool kit. The overarching focus of the methodology, however, is understanding and achieving what the customer wants, since that is seen as the key to profitability of a production process. In fact, to get across this point, some use the DMAIC as an acronym for "Dumb Managers Always Ignore Customers."

The standard approach to Six-Sigma projects is the DMAIC methodology developed by General Electric, described below:[3]

1. Define (D)
    - Identify customers and their priorities.
    - Identify a project suitable for Six-Sigma efforts based on business objectives as well as customer needs and feedback.
    - Identify CTQs (critical-to-quality characteristics) that the customer considers to have the most impact on quality.
2. Measure (M)
    - Determine how to measure the process and how it is performing.
    - Identify the key internal processes that influence CTQs and measure the defects currently generated relative to those processes.
3. Analyze (A)
    - Determine the most likely causes of defects.
    - Understand why defects are generated by identifying the key variables that are most likely to create process variation.
4   Improve (I)
    - Identify means to remove the causes of defects.
    - Confirm the key variables and quantify their effects on the CTQs.
    - Identify the maximum acceptance ranges of the key variables and a system for measuring deviations of the variables.
    - Modify the process to stay within an acceptable range.
5. Control (C)
    - Determine how to maintain the improvements.
    - Put tools in place to ensure that the key variables remain within the maximum acceptance ranges under the modified process.

ANALYTICAL TOOLS FOR SIX SIGMA AND CONTINUOUS IMPROVEMENT

The analytical tools of Six Sigma have been used for many years in traditional quality improvement programs. What makes their application to Six Sigma unique is the integration of these tools in a corporatewide management system. The tools common to all quality efforts, including Six Sigma, are flowcharts, run charts, Pareto charts, histograms, checksheets, cause-and-effect diagrams, and control charts. Examples of these, along with an opportunity flow diagram, are shown in Exhibit 8.6 arranged according to DMAIC categories where they commonly appear.

Flowcharts.   There are many types of flow charts. The one shown in Exhibit 8.6 depicts the process steps as part of a SIPOC (supplier, input, process, output, customer) analysis. SIPOC in essence is a formalized input-output model, used in the define stage of a project.

Run charts.   They depict trends in data over time, and thereby help to understand the magnitude of a problem at the define stage. Typically, they plot the median of a process.

Pareto charts.   These charts help to break down a problem into the relative contributions of its components. They are based on the common empirical finding that a large percentage of problems are due to a small percentage of causes. In the example, 80 percent of customer complaints are due to late deliveries, which are 20 percent of the causes listed.

Checksheets.   These are basic forms that help standardize data collection. They are used to create histograms such as shown on the Pareto chart.

Cause-and-effect diagrams.   Also called *fishbone diagrams,* they show hypothesized relationships between potential causes and the problem under study. Once the C & E diagram is constructed, the analysis would proceed to find out which of the potential causes were in fact contributing to the problem.

exhibit 8.6

Analytical Tools for Six Sigma and Continuous Improvement

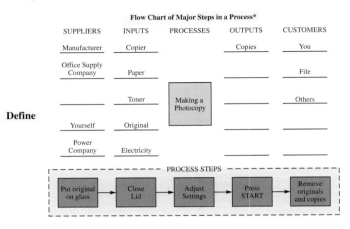

Flow Chart of Major Steps in a Process*

SUPPLIERS	INPUTS	PROCESSES	OUTPUTS	CUSTOMERS

Define

Manufacturer — Copier — Copies — You

Office Supply Company — Paper — File

Toner — Making a Photocopy — Others

Yourself — Original

Power Company — Electricity

PROCESS STEPS

Put original on glass → Close Lid → Adjust Settings → Press START → Remove originals and copies

Run Chart**

Average monthly volume of deliveries
(per shop)

1,951 deliveries

Measure

Pareto Chart**

Types of customer complaints
Total = 2520 October–December
(across 6 shops)

(1890) (220) (206) (117) (87)

Late deliveries · Wrong order · Cold food · Taste · Other

Illustration note: Delivery time was defined
by the total time from when the order was
placed to when the customer received it.

DATA COLLECTION FORMS*

Checksheets are basic forms that help standardize data collection
by providing specific spaces where people should record data.

Defines what data → **Machine Downtime**
are being collected   **(Line 13)**

Operator: Wendy		Date: May 19
Reason	Frequency	Comments
Carton Transport	‖‖‖ ‖‖‖ II	
Metal Check	IIII	
No Product	‖‖‖ I	←
Sealing Unit	II	
Barcoding	III	
Conveyor Belt		
Bad Product	‖‖‖	Burned flakes III / Low weight II
Other	II	

Lists the characteristics or conditions of interest

Includes place to put the data

May want to add space for tracking stratification factors

Has room for comments

*SOURCE: RATH & STRONG, *RATH & STRONG'S SIX SIGMA POCKET GUIDE*, 2001.
**SOURCE: RAYTHEON SIX SIGMA, *THE MEMORY JOGGER*™II, 2001.

Analyze

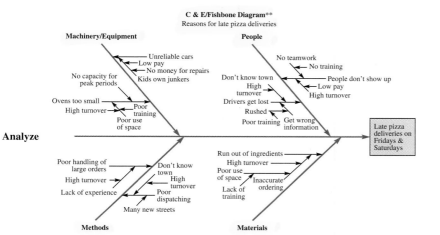

C & E/Fishbone Diagram**
Reasons for late pizza deliveries

Improve

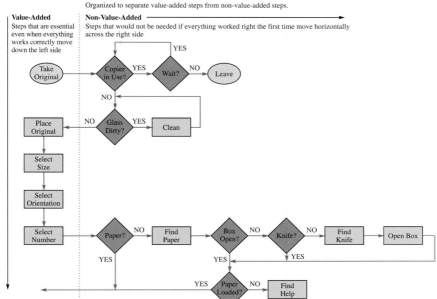

Opportunity Flow Diagram*
Organized to separate value-added steps from non-value-added steps.

Control

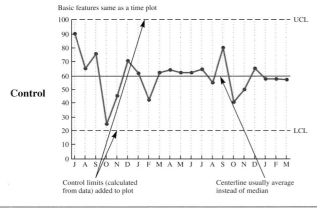

Control Chart Features*
Basic features same as a time plot

exhibit 8.7

FMEA Form

FMEA Analysis

Project: _____

Team: _____

Date: _____(original)

_____(revised)

Item or Process Step	Potential Failure Mode	Potential Effects of Failure	Severity	Potential Cause(s)	Occurrence	Current Controls	Detection	RPN	Recommended Action	Responsibility and Target Date	"After" → Action Taken	Severity	Occurrence	Detection	RPN
					Total Risk Priority Number:					"After" Risk Priority Number:				

SOURCE: RATH & STRONG, *RATH & STRONG'S SIX SIGMA POCKET GUIDE:* 2001, P. 31.

Opportunity flow diagram.   This is used to separate value-added from non-value-added steps in a process.

Control charts.   These are time-sequenced charts showing plotted values of a statistic including a centerline average and one or more control limits. It is used here to assure that changes introduced are in statistical control. See the technical note following this chapter for a discussion of the various types and uses of charts for process control.

Other tools that have seen extensive use in Six-Sigma projects are failure mode and effect analysis (FMEA) and design of experiments (DOE).

Failure mode and effect analysis.   This is a structured approach to identify, estimate, prioritize, and evaluate risk of possible failures at each stage of a process. It begins with identifying each element, assembly, or part of the process and listing the potential failure modes, potential causes, and effects of each failure. A risk priority number (RPN) is calculated for each failure mode. It is an index used to measure the rank importance of the items listed in the FMEA chart. See Exhibit 8.7. These conditions include the probability that the failure takes place (occurrence), the damage resulting from the failure (severity), and the probability of detecting the failure in-house (detection). High RPN items should be targeted for improvement first. The FMEA suggests a recommended action to eliminate the failure condition by assigning a responsible person or department to resolve the failure by redesigning the system, design, or process and recalculating the RPN.

Design of experiments (DOE).   DOE, sometimes referred to as *multivariate testing,* is a statistical methodology used for determining the cause-and-effect relationship between process variables (X's) and the output variable (Y). In contrast to standard statistical tests, which require changing each individual variable to determine the most influential one, DOE permits experimentation with many variables simultaneously through carefully selecting a subset of them.

SIX-SIGMA ROLES AND RESPONSIBILITIES

Successful implementation of Six Sigma is based on using sound personnel practices as well as technical methodologies. The following is a brief summary of the personnel practices that are commonly employed in Six-Sigma implementation.

1. ***Executive leaders,* who are truly committed to Six Sigma and who promote it throughout the organization, and *champions,* who take ownership of the processes that are to be improved.**   Champions are drawn from the ranks of the executives and managers are expected to identify appropriate metrics early in the project

BREAKTHROUGH

WHAT MAKES A GOOD CHAMPION?

At a manufacturing company implementing Six Sigma, a designated champion regularly met with his black belts. At one report-out meeting, a black belt informed him that she needed to purchase and install a table for sorting defects off-line. It would cost about $17,000, but it would provide an alternative to shutting down the entire line, which would cost far more. The controller told her to go through the normal requisition process and she'd have her table in about four months. That delay would have killed the project right

then and there: to submit the project to "business as usual" would have shown little real commitment to supporting Six Sigma. So the champion asked for the data that backed up her request, analyzed it, agreed with it, and then got immediate executive sign-off on securing a table the following week.

This is the stuff of a good champion: removing barriers and sending a clear signal that he and upper management are aligned and committed to Six Sigma. The champion does whatever it takes to support the black belts.

SOURCE: GREG BRUE, *SIX SIGMA FOR MANAGERS* (NEW YORK: McGRAW-HILL, 2002), P. 84.

Organizing the Roles Needed to Support Six-Sigma Efforts

exhibit 8.8

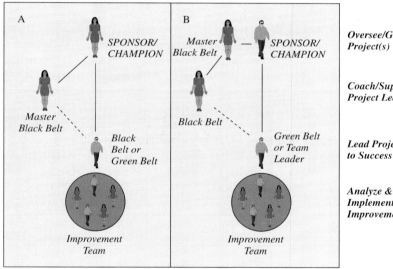

SOURCE: PETER S. PANDE, ROBERT P. NEUMAN, AND ROLAND R. CAVANAGH, *THE SIX SIGMA WAY TEAM FIELDBOOK* (NEW YORK: McGRAW-HILL, 2002), P. 31.

---

and make certain that the improvement efforts focus on business results. (See the Breakthrough box "What Makes a Good Champion?")

2. **Corporatewide training in Six-Sigma concepts and tools.** GE spent over a billion dollars training its professional workforce in the concepts. Now, virtually every professional in the organization is qualified in Six-Sigma techniques. To convey the need to vigorously attack problems, professionals are given martial arts titles reflecting their skills and roles: **black belts,** who coach or actually lead a Six-Sigma improvement team; **master black belts,** who receive in-depth training on statistical tools and process improvement (they perform many of the same functions as black belts but for a larger number of teams); and **green belts,** who are employees who have received enough Six-Sigma training to participate in a team or, in some companies, to work individually on a small-scale project directly related to their own job. Different companies use these "belts" in different combinations with sponsors and champions to guide teams. Several options are shown in Exhibit 8.8.

Black belts

Master black belts

Green belts

3. **Setting of stretch objectives for improvement.**
4. **Continuous reinforcement and rewards.** At GE, before any savings from a project are declared, the black belt in charge must provide proof that the problems are fixed permanently.

---

exhibit 8.9

Sources of Defects

What Are the Sources of Defects?
There are various types of defects. In order of importance these are

1. Omitted processing
2. Processing errors
3. Errors setting up workpieces
4. Missing parts
5. Wrong parts
6. Processing wrong workpiece
7. Misoperation
8. Adjustment error
9. Equipment not set up properly
10. Tools and jigs improperly prepared

What are the connections between these defects and the mistakes people make?

☆ Causal connections between defects and human errors

◉ Strongly connected   ○ Connected

CAUSES OF DEFECTS \ HUMAN ERRORS	INTENTIONAL	MIS-UNDERSTANDING	FORGETFUL	MIS-IDENTIFICATION	AMATEURS	WILLFULL	INADVERTENT	SLOWNESS	NON-SUPERVISION	SURPRISE
Omitted processing	◉	○	◉	○	○	○	◉	○	○	
Processing errors	◉	◉	○	○	○	◉	◉	◉	◉	
Errors setting up workpieces	○	○	◉	○	○		◉	○	○	
Missing parts	◉	○			○	◉	◉		○	
Wrong parts	◉	◉	◉	◉	◉	◉	◉		◉	
Processing wrong workpiece	◉	◉	◉	○	○	◉	◉		○	
Misoperation			○				○		○	◉
Adjustment error	○	○	○	○	○	○	○	○	○	○
Improper equipment setup			○				◉			◉
Improper tools and jigs			○				◉			○

THE SHINGO SYSTEM: FAIL-SAFE DESIGN

The Shingo system developed in parallel and in many ways in conflict with the statistically based approach to quality control. As we discussed in Chapter 7 relating to service applications, this system—or, to be more precise, philosophy of production management—is named after the codeveloper of the Toyota just-in-time system, Shigeo Shingo. Two aspects of the Shingo system in particular have received great attention. One is how to accomplish drastic cuts in equipment setup times by *single-minute exchange of die* (SMED) procedures. The other, the focus of this section, is the use of source inspection and the poka-yoke system to achieve zero defects.

Shingo has argued that SQC methods do not prevent defects. Although they provide information to tell us probabilistically when a defect will occur, they are after the fact. The way to prevent defects from coming out at the end of a process is to introduce controls within the process. Central to Shingo's approach is the difference between errors and defects. Defects arise because people make errors. Even though errors are inevitable, defects can be prevented if feedback leading to corrective action takes place immediately after the errors are made. Such feedback and action require inspection, which should be done on 100 percent of the items produced. This inspection can be one of three types: successive check, self-check, and source inspection. *Successive check* inspection is performed by the next person in the process or by an objective evaluator such as a group leader. Information on defects is immediate feedback for the worker who produced the product, who then makes the repair. *Self-check* is done by the individual worker and is appropriate by itself on all but items that require sensory judgment (such as existence or severity of scratches, or correct matching of shades of paint). These require successive checks. *Source inspection* is also performed by the individual worker, except instead of checking for defects, the worker checks for the errors that will cause defects. (See Exhibit 8.9 for sources of defects attributable to the worker.) This prevents the defects from ever occurring and, hence, requiring rework. All three types of inspection rely on controls consisting of **fail-safe procedures** or devices (called **poka-yoke**). Poka-yoke includes such things as checklists or special tooling that (1) prevents the worker from making an error that leads to a defect before starting a process or (2) gives rapid feedback of abnormalities in the process to the worker in time to correct them.

Fail-safe procedures

Poka-yoke

There are a wide variety of poka-yokes, ranging from kitting parts from a bin (to ensure that the right number of parts are used in assembly) to sophisticated detection and electronic signaling devices. An example taken from the writings of Shingo is shown in Exhibit 8.10.

There is a good deal more to say about the work of Shingo. Blasting industry's preoccupation with control charts, Shingo states they are nothing but a mirror reflecting current conditions. When a chemical plant QC manager proudly stated that it had 200 charts in a plant of 150 people, Shingo asked him if "they had a control chart for control charts."[4]

ISO 9000

ISO 9000 is a series of international quality standards that have been developed by the International Organization for Standardization. More than 100 countries now recognize the 9000 series. The idea behind the standards is defects can be prevented through the planning and application of *best practices* at every stage of business—from design through manufacturing and then installation and servicing. These standards focus on identifying criteria by which any organization, regardless of whether it is manufacturing or service oriented, can ensure that product leaving its facility meets the requirements of its customers. These standards ask a company to first document and implement its systems for quality management,

ISO 9000

Global
www.iso.ch

exhibit 8.10   Poka-Yoke Example (Placing labels on parts coming down a conveyor)

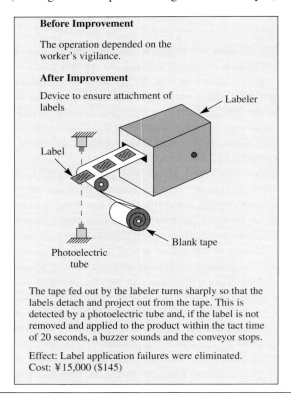

Before Improvement

The operation depended on the worker's vigilance.

After Improvement

Device to ensure attachment of labels

Labeler

Label

Blank tape

Photoelectric tube

The tape fed out by the labeler turns sharply so that the labels detach and project out from the tape. This is detected by a photoelectric tube and, if the label is not removed and applied to the product within the tact time of 20 seconds, a buzzer sounds and the conveyor stops.

Effect: Label application failures were eliminated.
Cost: ¥15,000 ($145)

and then to verify, by means of an audit conducted by an independent accredited third party, the compliance of those systems to the requirements of the standards.

Fundamentally these standards can be grouped into two categories:

- **Requirements**—These mandatory standards dictate what a company *shall* do. Companies become registered to or compliant with one of the requirements standards. There are four requirements standards:
    - ISO 9001 Model for quality assurance: design, development, production, installation and servicing
    - ISO 9002 Model for quality assurance: production, installation and servicing
    - ISO 9003 Model for quality assurance: final inspection and test
    - ISO 10012 Requirements for measuring equipment
- **Guidelines**—These assist a company to interpret the requirements standards, suggesting what a company *should* do. There are also four guidelines:
    - ISO 8402 Quality management and quality assurance vocabulary
    - ISO 9000 Guidelines for selection and use
    - ISO 9004 Quality management and quality system elements
    - ISO 10011 Guidelines for auditing quality systems
    - ISO 10013 Guidelines for quality manuals

Regardless of whether an organization is involved in a total manufacturing operation, including design, or only inspection and testing process, it can develop a quality management system based on one of the ISO 9000 requirements standards. By design, these standards can accommodate variation from company to company and between economic sectors. It is simply up to each individual business to interpret the appropriate requirements standard in light of its own processes.

The principal standards within the group are ISO 9001, 9002 and 9003. These are the requirements standards, and all of the other standards within the series are related to these three. Of the three, ISO 9001 is the most comprehensive. Divided into 20 specific elements, it provides a foundation for basic quality management and continuous improvement practices. Each of its 20 elements covers a particular area of an organization's business processes:

1. Management Responsibility
2. Quality Planning
3. Contract Review
4. Design Control
5. Document and Data Control
6. Purchasing
7. Control of Customer-Supplied Product
8. Identification and Traceability
9. Process Control
10. Inspection and Testing
11. Control of Inspection, Measuring and Test Equipment
12. Inspection and Test Status
13. Control of Nonconforming Product
14. Corrective and Preventive Action
15. Storage, Handling, Packaging, Preservation and Delivery
16. Control of Quality Records
17. Internal Quality Audits
18. Training
19. Servicing
20. Statistical Techniques

ISO 9002 and ISO 9003 are derivatives of the 9001 requirements standard. Much work and expense may be needed to be accredited at the highest level, which is 9001. Furthermore, some firms may not need ISO 9001 accreditation. For example, note that in Exhibit 8.11, ISO 9003 covers quality in production's final inspection and testing. A firm can be accredited at this level of final production only. This would essentially guarantee the firm's quality of final output and be attractive to customers. A broader accreditation would be ISO 9002, which extends from purchasing and production through installation.

ISO 9000 CERTIFICATION

Why is it important to become ISO 9000 certified? For one reason, it is essential from a purely competitive standpoint. Consider the situation where you need to purchase parts for your firm,

ISO 9000 Standards: Areas of Application in Production Flow, and Guidelines for Use   **exhibit 8.11**

and several suppliers offer similar parts at similar prices. Assume that one of these firms has been ISO 9000 certified and the others have not. From whom would you purchase? There is no doubt that the ISO 9000–certified company would have the inside track in your decision making. Why? Because ISO 9000 specifies the way the supplier firm operates as well as its quality standards, delivery times, service levels, and so on.

There are three forms of certification:

1. First party: A firm audits itself against ISO 9000 standards.
2. Second party: A customer audits its supplier.
3. Third party: A "qualified" national or international standards or certifying agency serves as auditor.

The best certification of a firm is through a third party. Once passed by the third-party audit, a firm is certified and may be registered and recorded as having achieved ISO 9000 status, and it becomes part of a registry of certified companies. This third-party certification also has legal advantages in the European Community. For example, a manufacturer is liable for injury to a user of the product. The firm, however, can free itself from any liability by showing that it has used the appropriate standards in its production process and carefully selected its suppliers as part of its purchasing requirement. For this reason, there is strong motivation to choose ISO 9000–certified suppliers.

EXTERNAL BENCHMARKING FOR QUALITY IMPROVEMENT

External benchmarking

The quality improvement approaches described so far are more or less inward looking. They seek to make improvements by analyzing in detail the current practices of the company itself. **External benchmarking**, however, goes outside the organization to examine what industry competitors and excellent performers outside of industry are doing. Benchmarking typically involves the following steps:

Identify processes needing improvement. Identify a firm that is the world leader in performing the process. For many processes, this may be a company that is not in the same industry. Examples would be Procter & Gamble using L.L Bean as the benchmark in evaluating its order entry system, or ICL (a large British computer maker) benchmarking Marks and Spencer (a large U.K. clothing retailer) to improve its distribution system.

A McKinsey study cited a firm that measured pit stops on a motor racing circuit as a benchmark for worker changes on its assembly line.[5] *Contact the managers of that company and make a personal visit to interview managers and workers.* Many companies select a team of workers from that process as part of the team of visitors.

Analyze data. This entails looking at gaps between what your company is doing and what the benchmarking company is doing. There are two aspects of the study: one is comparing the actual processes; the other is comparing the performance of these processes according to a set of measures. The processes are often described using flowcharts and subjective evaluations of how workers relate to the process. In some cases, companies permit videotaping, although there is a tendency now for benchmarked companies to keep things under wraps for fear of giving away process secrets.

THE NEW BMW MINI-COOPER SET STANDARDS AS THE FIRST LUXURY COMPACT CAR, THUS ACTING AS A BENCHMARK IN THE AUTO INDUSTRY.

Perceived Service Quality

exhibit 8.12

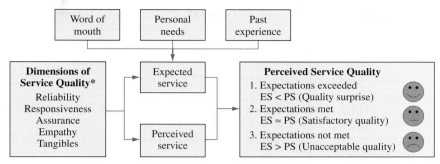

Reliability: the ability to perform service as promised, both dependably and accurately.

Responsiveness: willingness to help customers promptly.

Assurance: knowledge and courtesy of employees, as well as their ability to convey trust.

Empathy: caring and individualized attention.

Tangibles: the appearance of physical facilities, equipment, and personnel, as well as other factors affecting the senses such as noise and temperature.

SOURCE: ADAPTED WITH PERMISSION FROM THE *JOURNAL OF MARKETING*, PUBLISHED BY THE AMERICAN MARKETING ASSOCIATION, A. PARASURAMAN, V. A. ZEITHHAML, AND L. L. BERRY, "A CONCEPTUAL MODEL OF SERVICE QUALITY AND ITS IMPLICATIONS FOR FUTURE RESEARCH," FALL 1985/49, P. 48.

SERVICE QUALITY MEASUREMENT: SERVQUAL

Although the approaches to improving product quality are equally applicable to services, identifying what should be improved requires tapping the customer's satisfaction with the service process as well as the outcome from that process. A standard approach to making this determination is to measure the gap between what customers expected and their perceptions of the service provided in a service encounter (see Exhibit 8.12). The size of the gap indicates where improvements should be made. The measurement is done by having customers fill out the **SERVQUAL** questionnaire[6] (contained on the DVD-ROM that accompanies this book). The questionnaire consists of 22 expectation and matching perception questions relating to the five statistically derived dimensions of service quality listed in Exhibit 8.12. Each item is scored on a 1 to 7 scale, from strongly disagree (1) to strongly agree (7). For example, expectation question 1 states that the company under study "should have up-to-date equipment"; and perception question 1 states that the company "has up-to-date equipment." Thus, if the customer assigns a 6 to expectation and 4 to perception, the gap score is -2. (By convention, expectations are subtracted from perceptions.) Typically, tangibles have the lowest gap score because physical features of a service are easier to control.

SERVQUAL

SERVQUAL

Weighted SERVQUAL   The SERVQUAL procedure also permits assignment of importance weightings to each of the five dimensions. This is done by allocating 100 points across the dimensions and then multiplying the dimension gap score by points assigned to it. All five weighted dimension scores are then added to derive an overall weighted service quality score. Bank customers, for example, usually weight reliability heavily and tangibles lightly.

e-SERVICE QUALITY   A new version of SERVQUAL, e-SERVICE QUALITY, has been developed to evaluate service on the Internet. e-SQ is defined as the extent to which a Web site facilitates efficient and effective shopping, purchasing, and delivery. Its dimensions are shown in Exhibit 8.13.

e-SERVICE QUALITY

exhibit 8.13   Dimensions of Perceived e-SQ

1. **Reliability** involves the correct technical functioning of the site and the accuracy of service promises (having items in stock, delivering when promised), billing, and product information.

2. **Responsiveness** means quick response and the ability to get help if there is a problem or question.

3. **Access** is the ability to get on the site quickly and to reach the company when needed.

4. **Flexibility** involves choice of ways to pay, ship, buy, search for, and return items.

5. **Ease of navigation** means that a site contains functions that help customers find what they need without difficulty, possesses a good search engine, and allows the customer to maneuver easily and quickly back and forth through the pages.

6. **Efficiency** means that a site is simple to use, is structured properly, and requires a minimum of information to be input by the customer.

7. **Assurance trust** involves the confidence the customer feels in dealing with the site and is due to the reputation of the site and the products or services it sells as well as clear and truthful information presented.

8. **Security privacy** involves the degree to which the customer believes the site is safe from intrusion and personal information is protected.

9. **Price knowledge** is the extent to which the customer can determine shipping price, total price, and comparative prices during the shopping process.

10. **Site aesthetics** relates to the appearance of the site.

11. **Customization/personalization** is how much and how easily the site can be tailored to individual customers' preferences, histories, and ways of shopping.

SOURCE: VALARIE A. ZEITHAML, A. PARASURAMAN, AND ARVIND MALHOTRA, "A CONCEPTUAL FRAMEWORK FOR UNDERSTANDING e-SERVICE QUALITY: IMPLICATIONS FOR FUTURE RESEARCH AND MANAGERIAL PRACTICE," *MARKETING SCIENCE INSTITUTE*, REPORT SUMMARY 00-115, 2001, P. 14.

CONCLUSION

How to achieve TQM is no secret anymore. The challenge is to make certain that a quality program really does have a customer focus and is sufficiently agile to be able to make improvements quickly without losing sight of the real-time needs of the business. The quality system must be analyzed for its own quality. There is also a need for sustaining a quality culture over the long haul. Some companies (who will remain nameless) that gained a great reputation for quality in the 1980s and 90s simply ran out of gas in their quality efforts—their managers just couldn't sustain the level of enthusiasm necessary for quality to remain a top priority goal. As Tom Peters has said, "Most Quality programs fail for one of two reasons: they have system without passion, or passion without system."[7]

KEY TERMS

Total quality management (TQM) Managing the entire organization so that it excels on all dimensions of products and services that are important to the customer.

Malcolm Baldrige National Quality Award An award established by the U.S. Department of Commerce given annually to companies that excel in quality.

Design quality The inherent value of the product in the marketplace.

Conformance quality The degree to which the product or service design specifications are met.

Quality at the source The person who does the work is responsible for ensuring that specifications are met.

Dimensions of quality Criteria by which quality is measured.

Cost of quality Expenditures related to achieving product or service quality, such as the costs of prevention, appraisal, internal failure, and external failure.

Six Sigma A statistical term to describe the quality goal of no more than four defects out of every million units. Also refers to a quality improvement philosophy and program.

DPMO (defects per million opportunities) A metric used to describe the variability of a process.

DMAIC An acronym for the **D**efine, **M**easure, **A**nalyze, **I**mprove, and **C**ontrol improvement methodology followed by companies engaging in Six-Sigma programs.

PDCA cycle Also called "The Deming cycle or wheel"; refers to the plan–do–check–act cycle of continuous improvement.

Continuous improvement The philosophy of continually seeking improvements in processes through the use of team efforts.

Kaizen Japanese term for continuous improvement.

Black belts, master black belts, green belts Terms used to describe different levels of personal skills and responsibilities in Six-Sigma programs.

Fail-safe or **poka-yoke procedures** Simple practices that prevent errors or provide feedback in time for the worker to correct errors.

ISO 9000 Formal standards used for quality certification, developed by the International Organization for Standardization.

External benchmarking Looking outside the company to examine what excellent performers inside and outside the company's industry are doing in the way of quality.

SERVQUAL A service quality questionnaire that measures the gap between customer expectations and perceptions of performance after a service encounter.

e-SERVICE QUALITY A version of SERVQUAL designed to evaluate service on the Internet.

REVIEW AND DISCUSSION QUESTIONS

1   Is the goal of Six Sigma realistic for services such as Blockbuster Video stores?
2   "If line employees are required to work on quality improvement activities, their productivity will suffer." Discuss.
3   "You don't inspect quality into a product; you have to build it in." Discuss the implications of this statement.
4   "Before you build quality in, you must think it in." How do the implications of this statement differ from those in question 3?
5   Business writer Tom Peters has suggested that in making process changes, we should "Try it, test it, and get on with it." How does this square with the DMAIC/continuous improvement philosophy?
6   Shingo told a story of a poka-yoke he developed to make sure that the operators avoided the mistake of putting fewer than the required four springs in a push-button device. The existing method involved assemblers taking individual springs from a box containing several hundred, and then placing two of them behind an ON button and two more behind an OFF button. What was the poka-yoke Shingo created?
7   A typical word processing package is loaded with poka-yokes. List three. Are there any others you wish the packages had?

PROBLEMS

1   A manager states that his process is really working well. Out of 1,500 parts, 1,477 were produced free of a particular defect and passed inspection. Based upon Six-Sigma theory, how would you rate this performance, other things being equal?
2   Professor Chase is frustrated by his inability to make a good cup of coffee in the morning. Show how you would use a fishbone diagram to analyze the process he uses to make a cup of his evil brew.
3   Use the benchmarking process and as many DMAIC/CI analytical tools as you can to show how you can improve your performance in your weakest course in school.
4   Consider a simple repair job that you performed that did not turn out particularly well. Analyze the mistakes or defects you made using the Sources of Defects table presented in Exhibit 8.9. Which errors were your fault?
5   Evaluate the service quality of your bank using the perceptions of performance portion of the SERVQUAL questionnaire contained on the student DVD-ROM. Compute the score for each of the five SERVQUAL dimensions. On which dimensions does your bank score the highest? Lowest?
6   Evaluate the service quality of your bank's Web site using the Dimensions of Perceived e-SQ given in Exhibit 8.13.
7   Prepare a SIPOC flowchart of the major steps in the process of boarding a commercial flight. Start the process with the passenger arriving curbside at your local airport.
8   Prepare an opportunity flow diagram for the same process of boarding a commercial flight.

www.quality.nist.gov

Internet

INTERNET ENRICHMENT EXERCISES

1   Visit the Baldrige Award Web site and see who won this year. What quality ideas did the winner demonstrate? What did the winner do that was particularly creative?
2   Visit the Six Sigma Web site to see how companies are applying the concept.

www.isixsigma.com

CASE: HANK KOLB, DIRECTOR OF QUALITY ASSURANCE

Hank Kolb was whistling as he walked toward his office, still feeling a bit like a stranger since he had been hired four weeks before as director of quality assurance. All that week he had been away from the plant at a seminar given for quality managers of manufacturing plants by the corporate training department. He was now looking forward to digging into the quality problems at this industrial products plant employing 1,200 people.

Kolb poked his head into Mark Hamler's office, his immediate subordinate as the quality control manager, and asked him how things had gone during the past week. Hamler's muted smile and an "Oh, fine," stopped Kolb in his tracks. He didn't know Hamler very well and was unsure about pursuing this reply any further. Kolb was still uncertain of how to start building a relationship with him since Hamler had been passed over for the promotion to Kolb's job; Hamler's evaluation form had stated "superb technical knowledge; managerial skills lacking." Kolb decided to inquire a little further and asked Hamler what had happened; he replied, "Oh, just another typical quality snafu. We had a little problem on the Greasex line last week [a specialized degreasing solvent packed in a spray can for the high-technology sector]. A little high pressure was found in some cans on the second shift, but a supervisor vented them so that we could ship them out. We met our delivery schedule!" Because Kolb was still relatively unfamiliar with the plant and its products, he asked Hamler to elaborate; painfully, Hamler continued:

> We've been having some trouble with the new filling equipment and some of the cans were pressurized beyond the upper specification limit.
>
> The production rate is still 50 percent of standard, about 14 cases per shift, and we caught it halfway into the shift. Mac Evans [the inspector for that line] picked it up, tagged the cases "hold," and went on about his duties. When he returned at the end of the shift to write up the rejects, Wayne Simmons, first-line supervisor, was by a pallet of finished goods finishing sealing up a carton of the rejected Greasex; the reject "hold" tags had been removed. He told Mac that he had heard about the high pressure from another inspector at coffee break, had come back, taken off the tags, individually turned the cans upside down and vented every one of them in the eight rejected cartons. He told Mac that production planning was really pushing for the stuff and they couldn't delay by having it sent through the rework area. He told Mac that he would get on the operator to run the equipment right next time. Mac didn't write it up but came in about three days ago to tell me about it. Oh, it happens every once in a while and I told him to make sure to check with maintenance to make sure the filling machine was adjusted; and I saw Wayne in the hall and told him that he ought to send the stuff through rework next time.

Kolb was a bit dumbfounded at this and didn't say much—he didn't know if this was a big deal or not. When he got to his office he thought again what Morganthal, general manager, had said when he had hired him. He warned Kolb about the "lack of quality attitude" in the plant, and said that Kolb "should try and do something about this." Morganthal further emphasized the quality problems in the plant: "We have to improve our quality; it's costing us a lot of money, I'm sure of it, but I can't prove it! Hank, you have my full support in this matter; you're in charge of these quality problems. This downward quality–productivity–turnover spiral has to end!"

The incident had happened a week before; the goods were probably out in the customers' hands by now, and everyone had forgotten about it (or wanted to). There seemed to be more pressing problems than this for Kolb to spend his time on, but this continued to nag him. He felt that the quality department was being treated as a joke, and he also felt that this was a personal slap from manufacturing. He didn't want to start a war with the production people, but what could he do? Kolb was troubled enough to cancel his appointments and spend the morning talking to a few people. After a long and very tactful morning, he learned the following information:

1   **From personnel.**   The operator for the filling equipment had just been transferred from shipping two weeks ago. He had no formal training in this job but was being trained by Wayne, on the job, to run the equipment. When Mac had tested the high-pressure cans, the operator was nowhere to be found and had only learned of the rejected material from Wayne after the shift was over.

2   **From plant maintenance.**   This particular piece of automated filling equipment had been purchased two years ago for use on another product. It had been switched to the Greasex line six months ago and maintenance completed 12 work orders during the last month for repairs or adjustments on it. The equipment had been adapted by plant maintenance for handling the lower viscosity of Greasex, which it had not originally been designed for. This included designing a special filling head. There was no scheduled preventive maintenance for this equipment, and the parts for the sensitive filling head, replaced three times in the last six months, had to be made at a nearby machine shop. Nonstandard downtime was 15 percent of actual running time.

3   **From purchasing.**   The plastic nozzle heads for the Greasex can, designed by a vendor for this new product on a rush order, were often found to have slight burrs on the inside rim, and this caused some trouble in fitting the top to the can. An increase in application pressure at the filling head by maintenance adjustment had solved the burr application problem or had at least forced the nozzle heads on despite burrs. Purchasing agents said that they were going to talk to the sales representative of the nozzle head supplier about this the next time he came in.

4   **From product design and packaging.**   The can, designed especially for Greasex, had been contoured to allow better gripping by the user. This change, instigated by marketing research, set Greasex apart from the appearance of its competitors and was seen as significant by the designers. There had been no test of the effects of the contoured can on filling speed or filling hydrodynamics from a high-pressured filling head. Kolb had a hunch that the new design was acting as a venturi (carrier creating suction) when being filled, but the packaging designer thought that was unlikely.

5   **From the manufacturing manager.**   He had heard about the problem; in fact, Simmons had made a joke about it, bragging about how he beat his production quota to the other foremen and shift supervisors. The manufacturing manager thought Simmons was one of the "best foremen we have . . .

he always got his production out." His promotion papers were actually on the manufacturing manager's desk when Kolb dropped by. Simmons was being strongly considered for promotion to shift supervisor. The manufacturing manager, under pressure from Morganthal for cost improvements and reduced delivery times, sympathetized with Kolb but said that the rework area would have vented with their pressure gauges what Wayne had done by hand. "But I'll speak with Wayne about the incident," he said.

6 **From marketing.** The introduction of Greasex had been rushed to market to beat competitors, and a major promotional advertising campaign was under way to increase consumer awareness. A deluge of orders was swamping the order-taking department and putting Greasex high on the back-order list. Production had to turn the stuff out; even being a little off spec was tolerable because "it would be better to have it on the shelf than not there at all. Who cares if the label is a little crooked or the stuff comes out with a little too much pressure? We need market share now in that high-tech segment."

What bothered Kolb most was the safety issue of the high pressure in the cans. He had no way of knowing how much of a hazard the high pressure was or if Simmons had vented them enough to effectively reduce the hazard. The data from the can manufacturer, which Hamler had showed him, indicated that the high pressure found by the inspector was not in the danger area. But, again, the inspector had used only a sample testing procedure to reject the eight cases. Even if he could morally accept that there was no product safety hazard, could Kolb make sure that this would never happen again?

Skipping lunch, Kolb sat in his office and thought about the morning's events. The past week's seminar had talked about the role of quality, productivity and quality, creating a new attitude, and the quality challenge; but where had they told him what to do when this happened? He had left a very good job to come here because he thought the company was serious about the importance of quality, and he wanted a challenge. Kolb had demanded and received a salary equal to the manufacturing, marketing, and R&D directors, and he was one of the direct reports to the general manager. Yet he still didn't know exactly what he should or shouldn't do, or even what he could or couldn't do under these circumstances.

QUESTIONS

1 What are the causes of the quality problems on the Greasex line? Display your answer on a fishbone diagram.
2 What general steps should Hank follow in setting up a continuous improvement program for the company? What problems will he have to overcome to make it work?

SOURCE: COPYRIGHT 1981 BY PRESIDENT AND FELLOWS OF HARVARD COLLEGE, HARVARD BUSINESS SCHOOL. CASE 681.083. THIS CASE WAS PREPARED BY FRANK S. LEONARD AS THE BASIS FOR CLASS DISCUSSION RATHER THAN TO ILLUSTRATE EITHER EFFECTIVE OR INEFFECTIVE HANDLING OF AN ADMINISTRATIVE SITUATION. REPRINTED BY PERMISSION OF THE HARVARD BUSINESS SCHOOL.

CASE: SHORTENING CUSTOMERS' TELEPHONE WAITING TIME

This case illustrates how a bank applied some of the basic tools shown in Exhibit 8.6 and storyboard concepts to improve customer service. It is the story of a quality circle (QC) program implemented in the main office of a large bank. An average of 500 customers call this office every day. Surveys indicated that callers tended to become irritated if the phone rang more than five times before it was answered, and often would not call the company again. In contrast, a prompt answer after just two rings reassured the customers and made them feel more comfortable doing business by phone.

SELECTION OF A THEME

Telephone reception was chosen as a QC theme for the following reasons: (1) Telephone reception is the first impression a customer receives from the company; (2) this theme coincided with the company's telephone reception slogan, "Don't make customers wait, and avoid needless switching from extension to extension"; and (3) it also coincided with a companywide campaign being promoted at that time that advocated being friendly to everyone one met.

First, the staff discussed why the present method of answering calls made callers wait. Exhibit 8.14 illustrates a frequent situation

Why Customers Had to Wait

exhibit 8.14

exhibit 8.15   Cause-and-Effect Diagram

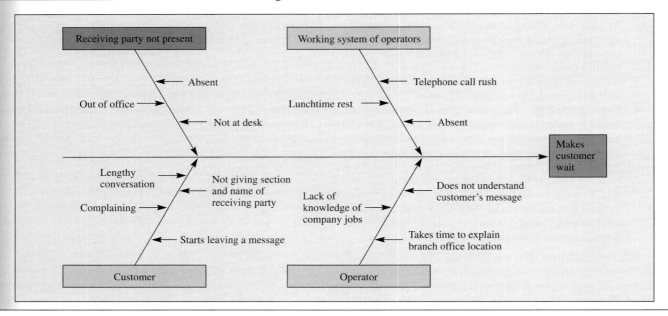

exhibit 8.16   Causes of Callers' Waits

A. Checksheet—Designed to Identify the Problems

Date	NO ONE PRESENT IN SECTION RECEIVING THE CALL	RECEIVING PARTY NOT PRESENT	ONLY ONE OPERATOR (PARTNER OUT OF THE OFFICE)	TOTAL
June 4	\\\\	ЖҤ \	ЖҤ ЖҤ \	24
June 5	ЖҤ	ЖҤ \\\	ЖҤ ЖҤ \\\\	32
June 6	ЖҤ \	\\\\	ЖҤ ЖҤ \\	28
June 15	ЖҤ	ЖҤ	ЖҤ \\\	25

B. Reasons Why Callers Had to Wait

		DAILY AVERAGE	TOTAL NUMBER
A	One operator (partner out of the office)	14.3	172
B	Receiving party not present	6.1	73
C	No one present in the section receiving the call	5.1	61
D	Section and name of receiving party not given	1.6	19
E	Inquiry about branch office locations	1.3	16
F	Other reasons	0.8	10
	Total	29.2	351

Period: 12 days from June 4 to 16, 1980

C. Reasons Why Callers Had to Wait (Pareto Diagram)

A B C D E F

in which a call from customer B comes in while the operator is talking with customer A. Let's see why the customer has to wait.

At (1), the operator receives a call from the customer but, due to lack of experience, does not know where to connect the call. At (2), the receiving party cannot answer the phone quickly, perhaps because he or she is unavailable, and no one else can take the call. The result is that the operator must transfer the call to another extension while apologizing for the delay.

CAUSE-AND-EFFECT (FISHBONE) DIAGRAM AND SITUATION ANALYSIS

To fully understand the situation, the quality circle members decided to conduct a survey regarding callers who waited for more than five rings. Circle members itemized factors at a brainstorming discussion and arranged them in a cause-and-effect diagram. (See Exhibit 8.15.) Operators then kept checksheets on several points to tally the results spanning 12 days from June 4 to 16. (See Exhibit 8.16.)

RESULTS OF THE CHECKSHEET SITUATION ANALYSIS

The data recorded on the checksheets unexpectedly revealed that "one operator (partner out of the office)" topped the list by a big margin, occurring a total of 172 times. In this case, the operator on duty had to deal with large numbers of calls when the phones were busy. Customers who had to wait a long time averaged 29.2 daily, which accounted for 6 percent of the calls received every day. (See Exhibits 8.16B and 8.16C.)

SETTING THE TARGET

After an intense but productive discussion, the staff decided to set a QC program goal of reducing the number of waiting callers to zero. That is to say that all incoming calls would be handled promptly, without inconveniencing the customer.

MEASURES AND EXECUTION

1 **Taking lunches on three different shifts, leaving at least two operators on the job at all times.**   Until this resolution was made, a two-shift lunch system had been employed, leaving only one operator on the job while the other was taking a lunch break. However, because the survey revealed that this was a major cause of customers waiting on the line, the company brought in a helper operator from the clerical section.

2 **Asking all employees to leave messages when leaving their desks.**   The objective of this rule was to simplify the operator's chores when the receiving party was not at his desk. The new program was explained at the employees' regular morning meetings, and companywide support was

---

Effects of QC

exhibit 8.17

A. Effects of QC (Comparison of before and after QC)

	REASON WHY CALLERS HAD TO WAIT	TOTAL NUMBER BEFORE	TOTAL NUMBER AFTER	DAILY AVERAGE BEFORE	DAILY AVERAGE AFTER
A	One operator (partner out of the office)	172	15	14.5	1.2
B	Receiving party not present	73	17	6.1	1.4
C	No one present in the section receiving the call	61	20	5.1	1.7
D	Section and name of receiving party not given	19	4	1.6	0.3
E	Inquiry about branch office locations	16	3	1.3	0.2
F	Others	10	0	0.8	0
	Total	351	59	29.2	4.8

Period: 12 days from Aug. 17 to 30.

Problems are classified according to cause and presented in order of the amount of time consumed. They are illustrated in a bar graph. 100% indicates the total number of time-consuming calls.

B. Effects of QC (Pareto Diagram)

Interactive Operations Management

requested. To help implement this practice, posters were placed around the office to publicize the new measures.

3 **Compiling a directory listing the personnel and their respective jobs.** The notebook was specially designed to aid the operators, who could not be expected to know the details of every employee's job. The notebook would help properly route calls.

CONFIRMING THE RESULTS

Although the waiting calls could not be reduced to zero, all items presented showed a marked improvement as shown in Exhibits 8.17A and 8.17B. The major cause of delays, "one operator (partner out of the office)," plummeted from 172 incidents during the control period to 15 in the follow-up survey.

SOURCE: FROM "THE QUEST FOR HIGHER QUALITY—THE DEMING PRIZE AND QUALITY CONTROL," RICOH COMPANY, LTD., IN MASAAKI IMAI, *KAIZEN: THE KEY TO JAPAN'S COMPETITIVE SUCCESS* (NEW YORK: RANDOM HOUSE, 1986), PP. 54–58.

CASE: "HEY, IS ANYBODY THERE?" AN EXAMPLE OF DMAIC AT AMERICAN EXPRESS

In this case the *customer* is using Six Sigma to reduce defects in a service.

THE GENERAL SITUATION

A number of merchants that accept American Express cards fail to place point-of-purchase materials (e.g., decals) that notify customers that they can use these cards at these establishments while displaying competing (e.g., Visa, Mastercard, etc.) point-of-purchase materials. American Express defines these merchants as "passive suppressors." In an effort to increase visibility, an external vendor that placed point-of-purchase material in the marketplace, identified passive suppressors, and measured placement and passive suppression rates was hired by American Express. However, the vendor had a significant rate of failure to contact or meet with the merchants. The leading reason for not meeting with the merchant was that the store was closed when the vendor stopped by.

DEFINE AND MEASURE

The objective was to reduce closed store uncallables (failures to contact), which represented 27.4 percent of total uncallables and 8.0 percent of the annualized attempted visits. The process represented a 2.9 sigma level and 80,000 defects per million opportunities.

ANALYZE

A Pareto chart pointed to the "closed store" category as the number one reason for uncallables. By shadowing the vendor on merchant visits, American Express learned that the visits took place between 8:00 A.M. and 6:00 P.M. Of the closed stores, 45 percent were retail establishments and 16 percent were restaurants. Typically, these two types of establishments are not open before 10:00 A.M. Therefore, American Express hypothesized that the hours the vendor was calling on the merchant contributed to the high uncallable rate. It also was determined that if an establishment was closed, the inspection process was terminated with the merchant being reported as

uncallable without first checking to see if any point-of-purchase materials were visible from the outside. This resulted in merchants who displayed point-of-purchase material being visited multiple times—leading to rework.

IMPROVE

American Express then tested and validated their hypotheses. The call hours for all visits were changed to begin after 10:00 A.M. The vendor was required to continue the inspection process with respect to external placement of point-of-purchase material. The first change, revised call hours, resulted in a decrease to 4.5 percent from 8.0 percent in the defect rate. The second change, continued inspection, indicated that 35.4 percent of the remaining 4.5 percent closed stores actually had external point-of-purchase material displayed. Combined, these two changes had the following effects: the defect rate decreased to 2.8 percent, the number of defects per million decreased to 28,000, and the sigma level increased to 3.2.

CONTROL

In order to achieve control, American Express uses a p control chart to track the proportion of closed stores over time and the vendor call report was revised to reflect the uncallable rate by reason.

QUESTIONS

1 In terms of "design quality" and "conformance quality," explain how using the Six-Sigma approach helped American Express.

2 In the case, American Express uncovered the two primary causes of the uncallable rate by "shadowing" the vendor. What Six-Sigma/continuous improvement tools might the vendor have used to uncover the same information and revise the process?

3 What are some of the limitations of the Six-Sigma approach when there is subjectivity in the metrics used?

SOURCE: SAI KIM, "SERVICE QUALITY SIX SIGMA CASE STUDIES," *ANNUAL QUALITY CONGRESS PROCEEDINGS* 54 (MAY 2000).

SELECTED BIBLIOGRAPHY

Bemowski, K., and B. Stratton, eds. *101 Good Ideas: How to Improve Just About Any Process.* Washington, DC: American Society for Quality, 1999.

Blakeslee, Jerome A., Jr. "Implementing the Six Sigma Solution." *Quality Progress,* July 1999, pp. 77–85.

Brue, Greg. *Six Sigma for Managers.* New York: McGraw-Hill, 2002.

Chowdhury, Subir. *Design for Six Sigma.* Chicago: Dearborn Trade Publishing, 2002.

Chowdhury, S., and K. Zimmer. *QS-9000 Pioneers—Registered Companies Share Their Strategies for Success.* Burr Ridge, IL: Richard D. Irwin, 1996.

Crosby, P. B. *Quality Is Free.* New York: McGraw-Hill, 1979 (reissue 1992).

————. *Quality Is Still Free.* New York: McGraw-Hill, 1996.

Deming, W. E. *Quality, Productivity and Competitive Position.* Cambridge, MA: MIT Center for Advanced Engineer Study, 1982.

Eckes, George. *Six Sigma Revolution: How General Electric and Others Turned Process into Profits.* New York: John Wiley & Sons, 2001.

Evans, James R., and William M. Lindsay. *The Management and Control of Quality.* Cincinnati: South-Western/Thomson Learning, 2002.

Feigenbaum, A. V. *Total Quality Control.* New York: McGraw-Hill, 1991.

Gitlow, H.; A. Oppenheim; and R. Oppenheim. *Quality Management: Tools and Methods for Improvement.* 2nd ed. New York: Irwin/McGraw-Hill, 1995.

Juran, J. M. *Quality Control Handbook.* 3rd ed. New York: McGraw-Hill, 1979.

Juran, J. M., and F. M. Gryna. *Quality Planning and Analysis.* 2nd ed. New York: McGraw-Hill, 1980.

Pande, Peter S.; Robert P. Neuman; and Roland R. Cavanagh. *The Six Sigma Way.* New York: McGraw-Hill, 2000.

————. *The Six Sigma Way Team Fieldbook.* New York: McGraw-Hill, 2002.

Robinson, A. *Modern Approaches to Manufacturing Improvement: The Shingo System.* Cambridge, MA: Productivity Press, 1990.

Shingo, S. *Zero Quality Control: Source Inspection and the Poka-Yoke System.* Stamford, CT: Productivity Press, 1986.

Taormina, T. *Virtual Leadership and the ISO 9000 Imperative.* Englewood Cliffs, NJ: Prentice Hall, 1996.

Welch, Jack. *Jack: Straight from the Gut.* New York: Warner Business Books, 2001.

FOOTNOTES

1 D. A. Garvin, *Managing Quality* (New York: Free Press, 1988).

2 P. B. Crosby, *Quality Is Free* (New York: New American Library, 1979), p. 15.

3 S. Walleck, D. O'Halloran, and C. Leader, "Benchmarking World-Class Performance," *McKinsey Quarterly,* no. 1 (1991), p. 7.

4 A. Robinson, *Modern Approaches to Manufacturing Improvement: The Shingo System* (Cambridge, MA: Productivity Press, 1990), p. 234.

5 Walleck, O'Halloran, and Leader, "Benchmarking World-Class Performance," p. 7.

6 A. Parasuraman, V. A. Zeithaml, and L. L. Berry, "SERVQUAL: A Multiple-Item Scale for Measuring Customer Perceptions of Service Quality," *Journal of Retailing* 64, no. 1 (Spring 1988), pp. 12–40.

7 Tom Peters, *Thriving on Chaos* (New York: Knopf, 1987), p. 74.

technical note eight

PROCESS CAPABILITY AND STATISTICAL QUALITY CONTROL

This technical note on statistical quality control (SQC) covers the quantitative aspects of quality management. In general, SQC is a number of different techniques designed to evaluate quality from a conformance view. That is, how well are we doing at meeting the specifications that have been set during the design of the parts or services that we are providing? Managing quality performance using SQC techniques usually involves periodic sampling of a process and analysis of these data using statistically derived performance criteria.

As you will see, SQC can be applied to both manufacturing and service processes. Here are some examples of the types of situations where SQC can be applied:

- How many paint defects are there in the finish of a car? Have we improved our painting process by installing a new sprayer?
- How long does it take to execute market orders in our Web-based trading system? Has the installation of a new server improved the service? Does the performance of the system vary over the trading day?
- How well are we able to maintain the dimensional tolerance on our three-inch ball bearing assembly? Given the variability of our process for making this ball bearing, how many defects would we expect to produce per million bearings that we make?
- How long does it take for customers to be served from our drive-through window during the busy lunch period?

Processes that provide goods and services usually exhibit some variation in their output. This variation can be caused by many factors, some of which we can control and others that are inherent in the process. Variation that is caused by factors that can be clearly identified and possibly even managed is called **assignable variation.** For example, variation caused by workers not being equally trained or by improper machine adjustment is assignable variation. Variation that is inherent in the process itself is called **common variation.** Common variation is often referred to as *random variation* and may be the result of the type of equipment used to complete a process, for example.

As the title of this technical note implies, this material requires an understanding of very basic statistics. Recall from your study of statistics involving numbers that are normally distributed the definition of the mean and standard deviation. The mean ($\overline{X}$) is just the average value of a set of numbers. Mathematically this is

Service

Assignable variation

Common variation

[TN8.1]
$$\overline{X} = \sum_{i=1}^{N} x_i / N$$

where:

x_i = Observed value
N = Total number of observed values

The standard deviation is

[TN8.2]

$$\sigma = \sqrt{\dfrac{\displaystyle\sum_{i=1}^{N}(x_i - \overline{X})^2}{N}}$$

In monitoring a process using SQC, samples of the process output would be taken and sample statistics calculated. The distribution associated with the samples should exhibit the same kind of variability as the actual distribution of the process, although the actual variance of the sampling distribution would be less. This is good because it allows the quick detection of changes in the actual distribution of the process. The purpose of sampling is to find when the process has changed in some nonrandom way, so that the reason for the change can be quickly determined.

In SQC terminology, *sigma* is often used to refer to the sample standard deviation. As you will see in the examples, sigma is calculated in a few different ways, depending on the underlying theoretical distribution (i.e., a normal distribution or a Poisson distribution).

VARIATION AROUND US

It is generally accepted that as variation is reduced, quality is improved. Sometimes that knowledge is intuitive. If a train is always on time, schedules can be planned more precisely. If clothing sizes are consistent, time can be saved by ordering from a catalog. But rarely are such things thought about in terms of the value of low variability. With engineers, the knowledge is better defined. Pistons must fit cylinders, doors must fit openings, electrical components must be compatible, and boxes of cereal must have the right amount of raisins—otherwise quality will be unacceptable and customers will be dissatisfied.

However, engineers also know that it is impossible to have zero variability. For this reason, designers establish specifications that define not only the target value of something but also acceptable limits about the target. For example, if the aim value of a dimension is 10 inches, the design specifications might then be 10.00 inches ±0.02 inch. This would tell the manufacturing department that, while it should aim for exactly 10 inches, anything between 9.98 and 10.02 inches is OK. These design limits are often referred to as the **upper and lower specification limits** or the **upper and lower tolerance limits.**

Upper and lower specification or tolerance limits

A traditional way of interpreting such a specification is that any part that falls within the allowed range is equally good, whereas any part falling outside the range is totally bad. This is illustrated in Exhibit TN8.1. (Note that the cost is zero over the entire specification range, and then there is a quantum leap in cost once the limit is violated.)

Genichi Taguchi, a noted quality expert from Japan, has pointed out that the traditional view illustrated in Exhibit TN8.1 is nonsense for two reasons:

1. From the customer's view, there is often practically no difference between a product just inside specifications and a product just outside. Conversely, there is a far greater difference in the quality of a product that is the target and the quality of one that is near a limit.
2. As customers get more demanding, there is pressure to reduce variability. However, Exhibit TN8.1 does not reflect this logic.

Taguchi suggests that a more correct picture of the loss is shown in Exhibit TN8.2. Notice that in this graph the cost is represented by a smooth curve. There are dozens of illustrations of this notion: the meshing of gears in a transmission, the speed of photographic film, the temperature in a workplace or department store. In nearly anything that can be measured, the customer sees not a sharp line, but a gradation of acceptability away from the "Aim" specification. Customers see the loss function as Exhibit TN8.2 rather than Exhibit TN8.1.

A Traditional View of the Cost of Variability

Taguchi's View of the Cost of Variability

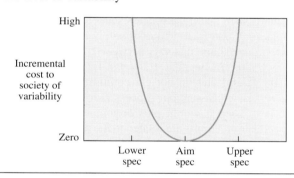

Of course, if products are consistently scrapped when they are outside specifications, the loss curve flattens out in most cases at a value equivalent to scrap cost in the ranges outside specifications. This is because such products, theoretically at least, will never be sold so there is no external cost to society. However, in many practical situations, either the process is capable of producing a very high percentage of product within specifications and 100 percent checking is not done, or if the process is not capable of producing within specifications, 100 percent checking is done and out-of-spec products can be reworked to bring them within specs. In any of these situations, the parabolic loss function is usually a reasonable assumption.

PROCESS CAPABILITY

Taguchi argues that being within tolerance is not a yes/no decision, but rather a continuous function. The Motorola quality experts, on the other hand, argue that the process used to produce a good or deliver a service should be so good that the probability of generating a defect should be very, very low. Motorola made process capability and product design famous by adopting Six-Sigma limits. When we design a part, we specify that certain dimensions should be within the upper and lower specification limits.

As a simple example, assume that we are designing a bearing for a rotating shaft—say an axle for the wheel of a car. There are many variables involved for both the bearing and the axle—for example, the width of the bearing, the size of the rollers, the size of the axle, the length of the axle, how it is supported, and so on. The designer specifies tolerances for each of these variables to ensure that the parts will fit properly. Suppose that initially a design is selected and the diameter of the bearing is set at 1.250 inches ±0.005 inch. This means that acceptable parts may have a diameter that varies between 1.245 and 1.255 inches (which are the lower and upper tolerance limits).

DOW CHEMICAL COMPANY HAS ADOPTED SIX-SIGMA PROCESSES TO ACHIEVE EXCELLENCE BY REDUCING DEFECTS IN PRODUCTS, PROCESSES, AND SERVICES.

Next, consider the process in which the bearing will be made. Consider that we can select many different processes for making the bearing. Usually there are trade-offs that need to be considered when designing a process for making a part. The process, for example, might be very fast but not very consistent, or alternatively it might be very slow but very consistent. The consistency of a process for making our bearing can be measured by the standard deviation of the diameter measurement. We can run a test by making, say, 100 bearings and measuring the diameter of each bearing in the sample.

Let's say that, after running our test, we find that the average or mean diameter is 1.250 inches. Another way to say this is that the process is "centered" right in the middle of the upper and lower specification limits. In reality it may be very difficult to have a perfectly centered process like our example. Let's say that the diameter values have a standard deviation or sigma equal to 0.002 inch. What this means is that our process does not make each bearing exactly the same size.

As we will see later in this technical note, normally we monitor a process using control charts such that if the process starts making bearings that are more than three standard deviations ($\pm$ 0.006 inch) above or below 1.250 inches, we stop the process. This means that we will produce parts that vary between 1.244 (this is $1.250 - 3 \times .002$) and 1.256 (this is $1.250 + 3 \times .002$) inches. The 1.244 and 1.256 are referred to as the upper and lower process limits. Be careful and do not get confused with the terminology here. The "process" limits relate to how consistent our process is for making the bearing. Our goal in managing the process is to keep it within plus or minus three standard deviations of the process mean. The "specification" limits are related to the design of the part. Recall that, from a design view, acceptable parts have a diameter between 1.245 and 1.255 inches (which are the lower and upper specification limits).

As we can see, our process limits are slightly greater than the specification limits given to us by the designer. This is not good because we will produce some parts that do not meet specifications. Companies with Six-Sigma processes insist that a process making a part be capable of operating so that the design specification limits are six standard deviations away from the process mean. For our bearing process, how small would the process standard deviation need to be for it to be Six-Sigma capable? Recall that our design specification was 1.250 inches plus or minus 0.005 inch. When you think about it, that 0.005 inch must relate to the variation in the process. By dividing 0.005 inch by 6, which equals 0.00083, we can determine our process standard deviation for a Six-Sigma process. So for our process to be Six-Sigma capable, the mean diameter produced by the process would need to be exactly 1.250 inches and the process standard deviation would need to be less than or equal to 0.00083 inch.

We can imagine that some of you are really confused at this point with the whole idea of Six Sigma. Why doesn't our company, for example, just check the diameter of each bearing and throw out the ones with a diameter less than 1.245 or greater than 1.255? This could certainly be done and for many, many parts 100 percent testing is done. The problem is for a company that is making thousands of parts each hour, testing each critical dimension of each part made can be very expensive. For our bearing, there could easily be 10 or more additional critical dimensions in addition to the diameter. These would all need to be checked. Using a 100 percent testing approach, the company would spend more time testing than it takes to actually make the part! This is why a company uses small samples to periodically check that the process is in statistical control. We discuss exactly how this statistical sampling works later in the technical note.

We say that a process is *capable* when the mean and standard deviation of the process are operating such that the upper and lower control limits are acceptable relative to the upper and lower specification limits. Consider diagram A in Exhibit TN8.3. This represents the distribution of the bearing diameter dimension in our original process. The average or mean value is 1.250 and the lower and upper design specifications are 1.245 and 1.255 respectively. Process control limits are plus and minus three standard deviations (1.244 and 1.256). Notice that there is a probability (the red areas) of producing defective parts.

Diagram A

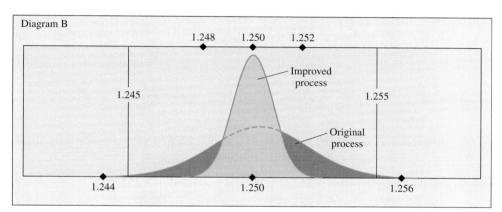

Diagram B

Process Capability

If we can improve our process by reducing the standard deviation associated with the bearing diameter, the probability can be reduced. Diagram B in Exhibit TN8.3 shows a new process where the standard deviation has been reduced to 0.00083 (the orange area). Even though we cannot see it in the diagram, there is some probability that a defect could be produced by this new process, but that probability is very, very small.

Suppose that the central value or mean of the process shifts away from the mean. Exhibit TN8.4 shows the mean shifted one standard deviation closer to the upper specification limit. This, of course, causes a slightly higher number of expected defects, but we can see that this is still very, very good. We use the *capability index* to measure how well our process is capable of producing relative to the design tolerances. We describe how to calculate this index in the next section.

CAPABILITY INDEX (C_{pk})

The **capability index** (C_{pk}) shows how well the parts being produced fit into the range specified by the design limits. If the design limits are larger than the three sigma allowed in the process, then the mean of the process can be allowed to drift off-center before readjustment, and a high percentage of good parts will still be produced.

Referring to Exhibits TN8.3 and TN8.4, the capability index (C_{pk}) is the position of the mean and tails of the process relative to design specifications. The more off-center, the greater the chance to produce defective parts.

Because the process mean can shift in either direction, the direction of shift and its distance from the design specification set the limit on the process capability. The direction of shift is toward the smaller number.

Capability index (C_{pk})

Excel: SPC.xls

Process Capability with a Shift in the Process Mean

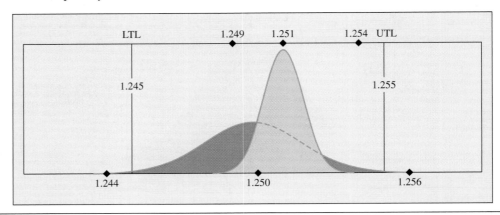

Formally stated, the capability index (C_{pk}) is calculated as the smaller number as follows:

[TN8.3]
$$C_{pk} = \min\left[\frac{\overline{X} - \text{LTL}}{3\sigma} \quad \text{or} \quad \frac{\text{UTL} - \overline{X}}{3\sigma}\right]$$

Working with our example in Exhibit TN8.4, let's assume our process is centered at 1.251 and $\sigma = 0.00083$ (σ is the symbol for standard deviation).

$$C_{pk} = \min\left[\frac{1.251 - 1.245}{3(.00083)} \quad \text{or} \quad \frac{1.255 - 1.251}{3(.00083)}\right]$$

$$= \min\left[\frac{.006}{.00249} \quad \text{or} \quad \frac{.004}{.00249}\right]$$

$$C_{pk} = \min[2.4 \quad \text{or} \quad 1.6]$$

$C_{pk} = 1.6$, which is the smaller number.

This tells us that the process mean has shifted to the right similar to Exhibit TN8.4, but parts are still well within design limits.

At times it is useful to calculate the actual probability of producing a defect. Assuming that the process is producing with a consistent standard deviation, this is a fairly straightforward calculation, particularly when we have access to a spreadsheet. The approach to use is to calculate the probability of producing a part outside the lower and upper design limits given the mean and standard deviation of the process.

Working with our example, where the process is not centered, with a mean of 1.251 inch, $\sigma = .00083$, LTL = 1.245, and UTL = 1.255, we first need to calculate the Z score associated with the upper and lower tolerance (specification) limits. Recall from your study of statistics that the Z score is the standard deviations either to the right or to the left of zero in a probability distribution.

$$Z_{\text{LTL}} = \frac{\text{LTL} - \overline{X}}{\sigma} \qquad Z_{\text{UTL}} = \frac{\text{UTL} - \overline{X}}{\sigma}$$

For our example,

$$Z_{\text{LTL}} = \frac{1.245 - 1.251}{.00083} = -7.2289 \qquad Z_{\text{UTL}} = \frac{1.255 - 1.251}{.00083} = 4.8193$$

An easy way to get the probabilities associated with these Z values is to use the NORMS-DIST function built into Excel (you also can use the table in Appendix G). The format for this function is NORMSDIST(Z), where Z is the Z value calculated above. Excel returns the following values. (We have found that you might get slightly different results from those given here, depending on the version of Excel you are using.)

$$\text{NORMSDIST}(-7.2289) = 2.43461\text{E-}13 \quad \text{and} \quad \text{NORMSDIST}(4.8193) = .99999928$$

Interpreting this information requires understanding exactly what the NORMSDIST function is providing. NORMSDIST is giving the cumulative probability to the left of the given Z value. Since $Z = -7.2289$ is the number of standard deviations associated with the lower specification limit, the fraction of parts that will be produced lower than this is 2.43461E-13. This number is in scientific notation and that E-13 at the end means we need to move the decimal over thirteen places to get the real fraction defective. So the fraction defective is .00000000000024361, which is a very small number! Similarly, we see that approximately .99999928 of our parts will be below our upper specification limit. What we are really interested in is the fraction that will be above this limit since these are the defective parts. This fraction defective above the upper spec is $1 - .99999928 = .00000082$ of our parts.

Adding these two fraction defective numbers together we get .00000082000024361. We can interpret this to mean that we only expect about .82 parts per million to be defective. Clearly, this is a great process. You will discover as you work the problems at the end of the chapter that this is not always the case.

EXAMPLE TN8.1:

The quality assurance manager is assessing the capability of a process that puts pressurized grease in an aerosol can. The design specifications call for an average of 60 pounds per square inch (psi) of pressure in each can with an upper tolerance limit of 65 psi and a lower tolerance limit of 55 psi. A sample is taken from production and it is found that the cans average 61 psi with a standard deviation of 2 psi. What is the capability of the process? What is the probability of producing a defect?

SOLUTION

Step 1—Interpret the data from the problem

$$\text{LTL} = 55 \quad \text{ULT} = 65 \quad \bar{X} = 61 \quad \sigma = 2$$

Step 2—Calculate the C_{pk}

$$C_{pk} = \min \left[\frac{\bar{X} - \text{LTL}}{3\sigma}, \frac{\text{UTL} - \bar{X}}{3\sigma} \right]$$

$$C_{pk} = \min \left[\frac{61 - 55}{3(2)}, \frac{65 - 61}{3(2)} \right]$$

$$C_{pk} = \min [1, .6667] = .6667$$

Step 3—Calculate the probability of producing a defect
Probability of a can with less than 55 psi

$$Z = \frac{X - \bar{X}}{\sigma} = \frac{55 - 61}{2} = -3$$

$$\text{NORMSDIST}(-3) = 0.001349898$$

Probability of a can with more than 65 psi

$$Z = \frac{X - \bar{X}}{\sigma} = \frac{65 - 61}{2} = 2$$

$$1 - \text{NORMSDIST}(2) = 1 - 0.977249868 = 0.022750132$$

Probability of a can less than 55 psi or more than 65 psi

$$Probability = 0.001349898 + 0.022750132 = .024100030$$

Or approximately 2.4% of the cans will be defective. ●

The following table is a quick reference for the fraction of defective units for various design limits (expressed in standard deviations). This table assumes that the standard deviation is constant and that the process is centered exactly between the design limits.

DESIGN LIMITS	DEFECTIVE PARTS	FRACTION DEFECTIVE
$\pm 1\sigma$	317 per thousand	.3173
$\pm 2\sigma$	45 per thousand	.0455
$\pm 3\sigma$	2.7 per thousand	.0027
$\pm 4\sigma$	63 per million	.000063
$\pm 5\sigma$	574 per billion	.000000574
$\pm 6\sigma$	2 per billion	.000000002

Motorola's design limit of six sigma with a shift of the process off the mean by 1.5σ ($C_{pk} = 1.5$) gives 3.4 defects per million. If the mean is exactly in the center ($C_{pk} = 2$), then 2 defects per *billion* are expected, as the table above shows.

PROCESS CONTROL PROCEDURES

Process control is concerned with monitoring quality *while the product or service is being produced.* Typical objectives of process control plans are to provide timely information on whether currently produced items are meeting design specifications and to detect shifts in the process that signal that future products may not meet specifications. **Statistical process control (SPC)** involves testing a random sample of output from a process to determine whether the process is producing items within a preselected range.

The examples given so far have all been based on quality characteristics (or *variables*) that are measurable, such as the diameter or weight of a part. **Attributes** are quality characteristics that are classified as either conforming or not conforming to specification. Goods or services may be observed to be either good or bad, or functioning or malfunctioning. For example, a lawnmower either runs or it doesn't; it attains a certain level of torque and horsepower or it doesn't. This type of measurement is known as sampling by attributes. Alternatively, a lawnmower's torque and horsepower can be measured as an amount of deviation from a set standard. This type of measurement is known as sampling by variables. The following section describes some standard approaches to controlling processes: first an approach useful for attribute measures and then an approach for variable measures. Both of these techniques result in the construction of control charts. Exhibit TN8.5 shows some examples for how control charts can be analyzed to understand how a process is operating.

Statistical process control (SPC)

Attributes

Interactive Operations Management

PROCESS CONTROL WITH ATTRIBUTE MEASUREMENTS: USING *p* CHARTS

Measurement by attributes means taking samples and using a single decision—the item is good or it is bad. Because it is a yes or no decision, we can use simple statistics to create a *p* chart with an upper control limit (UCL) and a lower control limit (LCL). We can draw these control limits on a graph and then plot the fraction defective of each individual sample tested. The process is assumed to be working correctly when the samples, which are taken periodically during the day, continue to stay between the control limits.

[TN8.4]

$$\bar{p} = \frac{\text{Total number of defects from all samples}}{\text{Number of samples} \times \text{Sample size}}$$

Control Chart Evidence for Investigation

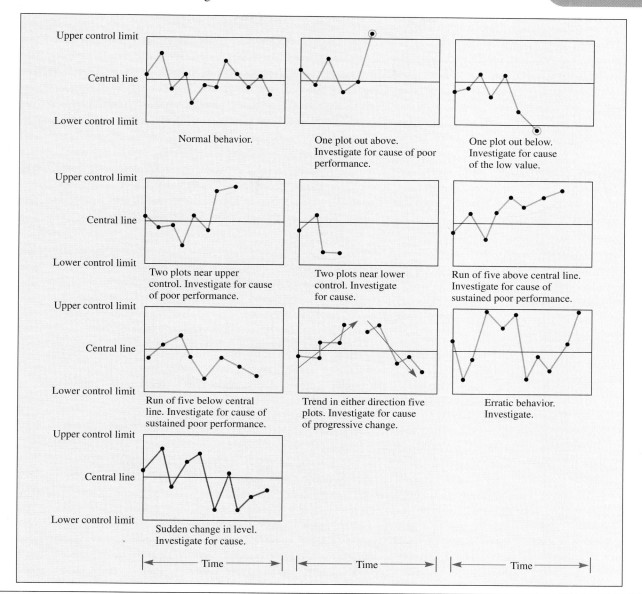

[TN8.5]
$$s_p = \sqrt{\frac{\bar{p}(1 - \bar{p})}{n}}$$

[TN8.6]
$$\text{UCL} = \bar{p} + z s_p$$

[TN8.7]
$$\text{LCL} = \bar{p} - z s_p$$

where $\bar{p}$ is the fraction defective, s_p is the standard deviation, n is the sample size, and z is the number of standard deviations for a specific confidence. Typically, $z = 3$ (99.7 percent confidence) or $z = 2.58$ (99 percent confidence) is used.

Size of the Sample   The size of the sample must be large enough to allow counting of the attribute. For example, if we know that a machine produces 1 percent defects, then a sample size of five would seldom capture a defect. A rule of thumb when setting up a p chart is to make the sample large enough to expect to count the attribute twice in each sample. So an

Insurance Company Claim Form

SAMPLE	NUMBER INSPECTED	NUMBER OF FORMS COMPLETED INCORRECTLY	FRACTION DEFECTIVE
1	300	10	0.03333
2	300	8	0.02667
3	300	9	0.03000
4	300	13	0.04333
5	300	7	0.02333
6	300	7	0.02333
7	300	6	0.02000
8	300	11	0.03667
9	300	12	0.04000
10	300	8	0.02667
Totals	3000	91	0.03033
Sample standard deviation			0.00990

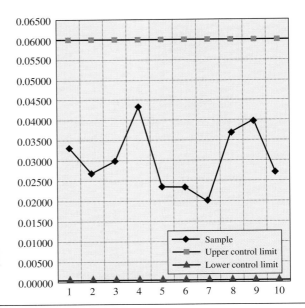

appropriate sample size if the defect rate were approximately 1 percent would be 200 units. One final note: In the calculations shown in equations TN8.4–8.7, the assumption is that the sample size is fixed. The calculation of the standard deviation depends on this assumption. If the sample size varies, the standard deviation and upper and lower control limits should be recalculated for each sample.

EXAMPLE TN8.2: Control Chart Design

Service

An insurance company wants to design a control chart to monitor whether insurance claim forms are being completed correctly. The company intends to use the chart to see if improvements in the design of the form are effective. To start the process, the company collected data on the number of incorrectly completed claim forms over the past 10 days. The insurance company processes thousands of these forms each day, and due to the high cost of inspecting each form, only a small representative sample was collected each day. The data and analysis are shown in Exhibit TN8.6.

SOLUTION

To construct the control chart, first calculate the overall fraction defective from all samples. This sets the centerline for the control chart.

$$\bar{p} = \frac{\text{Total number of defects from all samples}}{\text{Number of samples} \times \text{Sample size}} = \frac{91}{3000} = .03033$$

Next calculate the sample standard deviation:

$$s_p = \sqrt{\frac{\bar{p}(1 - \bar{p})}{n}} = \sqrt{\frac{.03033(1 - .03033)}{300}} = .00990$$

Excel: SPC.xls

Finally, calculate the upper and lower control limits. A z-value of 3 gives 99.7 percent confidence that the process is within these limits.

$$\text{UCL} = \bar{p} + 3s_p = .03033 + 3(.00990) = .06003$$

$$\text{LCL} = \bar{p} - 3s_p = .03033 - 3(.00990) = .00063$$

The calculations in Exhibit TN8.6, including the control chart, are included in the spreadsheet SPC.xls. ●

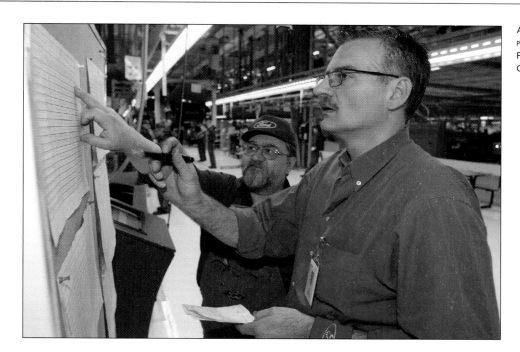

PROCESS CONTROL WITH VARIABLE MEASUREMENTS: USING $\overline{X}$ AND R CHARTS

$\overline{X}$ and R (range) charts are widely used in statistical process control.

In attribute sampling, we determine whether something is good or bad, fits or doesn't fit— it is a go/no-go situation. In **variables** sampling, however, we measure the actual weight, volume, number of inches, or other variable measurements, and we develop control charts to determine the acceptability or rejection of the process based on those measurements. For example, in attribute sampling, we might decide that if something is over 10 pounds we will reject it and under 10 pounds we will accept it. In variable sampling, we measure a sample and may record weights of 9.8 pounds or 10.2 pounds. These values are used to create or modify control charts and to see whether they fall within the acceptable limits.

Variables

There are four main issues to address in creating a control chart: the size of the samples, number of samples, frequency of samples, and control limits.

Size of Samples   For industrial applications in process control involving the measurement of variables, it is preferable to keep the sample size small. There are two main reasons. First, the sample needs to be taken within a reasonable length of time; otherwise, the process might change while the samples are taken. Second, the larger the sample, the more it costs to take.

Sample sizes of four or five units seem to be the preferred numbers. The *means* of samples of this size have an approximately normal distribution, no matter what the distribution of the parent population looks like. Sample sizes greater than five give narrower control limits and thus more sensitivity. For detecting finer variations of a process, it may be necessary, in fact, to use larger sample sizes. However, when sample sizes exceed 15 or so, it would be better to use $\overline{X}$ charts with standard deviation σ rather than $\overline{X}$ charts with the range R as we use in Example TN8.3.

Number of Samples   Once the chart has been set up, each sample taken can be compared to the chart and a decision can be made about whether the process is acceptable. To set up the charts, however, prudence and statistics suggest that 25 or so samples be taken.

Frequency of Samples   How often to take a sample is a trade-off between the cost of sampling (along with the cost of the unit if it is destroyed as part of the test) and the benefit of adjusting the system. Usually, it is best to start off with frequent sampling of a process and taper off as confidence in the process builds. For example, one might start with a sample of five units every half hour and end up feeling that one sample per day is adequate.

Control Limits   Standard practice in statistical process control for variables is to set control limits three standard deviations above the mean and three standard deviations below. This means that 99.7 percent of the sample means are expected to fall within these control limits (that is, within a 99.7 percent confidence interval). Thus, if one sample mean falls outside this obviously wide band, we have strong evidence that the process is out of control.

How to Construct $\overline{X}$ and R Charts

If the standard deviation of the process distribution is known, the $\overline{X}$ chart may be defined:

[TN8.8] $$\text{UCL}_{\overline{X}} = \overline{\overline{X}} + zs_{\overline{X}} \quad \text{and} \quad \text{LCL}_{\overline{X}} = \overline{\overline{X}} - zs_{\overline{X}}$$

where

$s_{\overline{X}} = s/\sqrt{n} =$ Standard deviation of sample means
$s =$ Standard deviation of the process distribution
$n =$ Sample size
$\overline{\overline{X}} =$ Average of sample means or a target value set for the process
$z =$ Number of standard deviations for a specific confidence level (typically, $z = 3$)

An $\overline{X}$ chart is simply a plot of the means of the samples that were taken from a process. $\overline{\overline{X}}$ is the average of the means.

In practice, the standard deviation of the process is not known. For this reason, an approach that uses actual sample data is commonly used. This practical approach is described in the next section.

An R chart is a plot of the range within each sample. The range is the difference between the highest and the lowest numbers in that sample. R values provide an easily calculated measure of variation used like a standard deviation. An $\overline{R}$ chart is the average of the range of each sample. More specifically defined, these are

[Same as TN8.1] $$\overline{X} = \frac{\sum\limits_{i=1}^{n} X_i}{n}$$

where

$\overline{X} =$ Mean of the sample
$i =$ Item number
$n =$ Total number of items in the sample

[TN8.9] $$\overline{\overline{X}} = \frac{\sum\limits_{j=1}^{m} \overline{X}_j}{m}$$

where

$\overline{\overline{X}} =$ The average of the means of the samples
$j =$ Sample number
$m =$ Total number of samples

[TN8.10] $$\overline{R} = \frac{\sum\limits_{j=1}^{m} R_j}{m}$$

where

$R_j =$ Difference between the highest and lowest measurement in the sample
$\overline{R} =$ Average of the measurement differences R for all samples

Factor for Determining from $\bar{R}$ the Three-Sigma Control Limits for $\bar{X}$ and R Charts

NUMBER OF OBSERVATIONS IN SUBGROUP	FACTOR FOR $\bar{X}$ CHART	FACTORS FOR R CHART	
		LOWER CONTROL LIMIT	UPPER CONTROL LIMIT
n	A_2	D_3	D_4
2	1.88	0	3.27
3	1.02	0	2.57
4	0.73	0	2.28
5	0.58	0	2.11
6	0.48	0	2.00
7	0.42	0.08	1.92
8	0.37	0.14	1.86
9	0.34	0.18	1.82
10	0.31	0.22	1.78
11	0.29	0.26	1.74
12	0.27	0.28	1.72
13	0.25	0.31	1.69
14	0.24	0.33	1.67
15	0.22	0.35	1.65
16	0.21	0.36	1.64
17	0.20	0.38	1.62
18	0.19	0.39	1.61
19	0.19	0.40	1.60
20	0.18	0.41	1.59

Excel: SPC.xls

Upper control limit for $\bar{X} = \text{UCL}_{\bar{X}} = \bar{\bar{X}} + A_2\bar{R}$
Lower control limit for $\bar{X} = \text{LCL}_{\bar{X}} = \bar{\bar{X}} - A_2\bar{R}$
Upper control limit for $R = \text{UCL}_R = D_4\bar{R}$
Lower control limit for $R = \text{LCL}_R = D_3\bar{R}$

Note: All factors are based on the normal distribution.

E. L. Grant and R. Leavenworth computed a table (Exhibit TN8.7) that allows us to easily compute the upper and lower control limits for both the $\bar{X}$ chart and the R chart.[1] These are defined as

[TN8.11]   Upper control limit for $\bar{X} = \bar{\bar{X}} + A_2\bar{R}$

[TN8.12]   Lower control limit for $\bar{X} = \bar{\bar{X}} - A_2\bar{R}$

[TN8.13]   Upper control limit for $R = D_4\bar{R}$

[TN8.14]   Lower control limit for $R = D_3\bar{R}$

EXAMPLE TN8.3: $\bar{X}$ and R Charts

We would like to create $\bar{X}$ and R charts for a process. Exhibit TN8.8 shows measurements for all 25 samples. The last two columns show the average of the sample $\bar{X}$ and the range R.
    Values for A_2, D_3, and D_4 were obtained from Exhibit TN8.7.

Based on # of samples in each sample → 5

Total 25 samples and 5 observations in each sample.

Upper control limit for $\bar{X} = \bar{\bar{X}} + A_2\bar{R} = 10.21 + .58(.60) = 10.56$

Lower control limit for $\bar{X} = \bar{\bar{X}} - A_2\bar{R} = 10.21 - .58(.60) = 9.86$

Upper control limit for $R = D_4\bar{R} = 2.11(.60) = 1.27$

Lower control limit for $R = D_3\bar{R} = 0(.60) = 0$

exhibit TN8.8

Measurements in Samples of Five from a Process

SAMPLE NUMBER	EACH UNIT IN SAMPLE					AVERAGE $\overline{X}$	RANGE R
1	10.60	10.40	10.30	9.90	10.20	10.28	.70
2	9.98	10.25	10.05	10.23	10.33	10.17	.35
3	9.85	9.90	10.20	10.25	10.15	10.07	.40
4	10.20	10.10	10.30	9.90	9.95	10.09	.40
5	10.30	10.20	10.24	10.50	10.30	10.31	.30
6	10.10	10.30	10.20	10.30	9.90	10.16	.40
7	9.98	9.90	10.20	10.40	10.10	10.12	.50
8	10.10	10.30	10.40	10.24	10.30	10.27	.30
9	10.30	10.20	10.60	10.50	10.10	10.34	.50
10	10.30	10.40	10.50	10.10	10.20	10.30	.40
11	9.90	9.50	10.20	10.30	10.35	10.05	.85
12	10.10	10.36	10.50	9.80	9.95	10.14	.70
13	10.20	10.50	10.70	10.10	9.90	10.28	.80
14	10.20	10.60	10.50	10.30	10.40	10.40	.40
15	10.54	10.30	10.40	10.55	10.00	10.36	.55
16	10.20	10.60	10.15	10.00	10.50	10.29	.60
17	10.20	10.40	10.60	10.80	10.10	10.42	.70
18	9.90	9.50	9.90	10.50	10.00	9.96	1.00
19	10.60	10.30	10.50	9.90	9.80	10.22	.80
20	10.60	10.40	10.30	10.40	10.20	10.38	.40
21	9.90	9.60	10.50	10.10	10.60	10.14	1.00
22	9.95	10.20	10.50	10.30	10.20	10.23	.55
23	10.20	9.50	9.60	9.80	10.30	9.88	.80
24	10.30	10.60	10.30	9.90	9.80	10.18	.80
25	9.90	10.30	10.60	9.90	10.10	10.16	.70

$$\overline{\overline{X}} = 10.21$$

$$\overline{R} = .60$$

Excel: SPC.xls

exhibit TN8.9

$\overline{X}$ Chart and R Chart

Excel: SPC.xls

SOLUTION

Exhibit TN8.9 shows the $\overline{X}$ chart and R chart with a plot of all the sample means and ranges of the samples. All the points are well within the control limits, although sample 23 is close to the $\overline{X}$ lower control limit. ●

ACCEPTANCE SAMPLING

DESIGN OF A SINGLE SAMPLING PLAN FOR ATTRIBUTES

Acceptance sampling is performed on goods that already exist to determine what percentage of products conform to specifications. These products may be items received from another company and evaluated by the receiving department, or they may be components that have passed through a processing step and are evaluated by company personnel either in production or later in the warehousing function. Whether inspection should be done at all is addressed in the following example.

Acceptance sampling is executed through a sampling plan. In this section we illustrate the planning procedures for a single sampling plan—that is, a plan in which the quality is determined from the evaluation of one sample. (Other plans may be developed using two or more samples. See J. M. Juran and F. M. Gryna's *Quality Planning and Analysis* for a discussion of these plans.)

EXAMPLE TN8.4: Costs to Justify Inspection

Total (100 percent) inspection is justified when the cost of a loss incurred by not inspecting is greater than the cost of inspection. For example, suppose a faulty item results in a $10 loss and the average percentage defective of items in the lot is 3 percent.

SOLUTION

If the average percentage of defective items in a lot is 3 percent, the expected cost of faulty items is $0.03 \times \$10$, or $0.30 each. Therefore, if the cost of inspecting each item is less than $0.30, the economic decision is to perform 100 percent inspection. Not all defective items will be removed, however, because inspectors will pass some bad items and reject some good ones.

The purpose of a sampling plan is to test the lot to either (1) find its quality or (2) ensure that the quality is what it is supposed to be. Thus, if a quality control supervisor already knows the quality (such as the 0.03 given in the example), he or she does not sample for defects. Either all of them must be inspected to remove the defects or none of them should be inspected, and the rejects pass into the process. The choice simply depends on the cost to inspect and the cost incurred by passing a reject. ●

Excel: SPC.xls

A single sampling plan is defined by n and c, where n is the number of units in the sample and c is the acceptance number. The size of n may vary from one up to all the items in the lot (usually denoted as N) from which it is drawn. The acceptance number c denotes the maximum number of defective items that can be found in the sample before the lot is rejected. Values for n and c are determined by the interaction of four factors (AQL, α, LTPD, and β) that quantify the objectives of the product's producer and its consumer. The objective of the producer is to ensure that the sampling plan has a low probability of rejecting good lots. Lots are defined as high quality if they contain no more than a specified level of defectives, termed the *acceptable quality level (AQL).*[2] The objective of the consumer is to ensure that the sampling plan has a low probability of accepting bad lots. Lots are defined as low quality if the percentage of defectives is greater than a specified amount, termed *lot tolerance percent defective (LTPD).* The probability associated with rejecting a high-quality lot is denoted by the Greek letter alpha (α) and is termed the *producer's risk*. The probability associated with accepting a low-quality lot is denoted by the letter beta (β) and is termed the *consumer's risk*. The selection of particular values for AQL, α, LTPD, and β is an economic decision based on a cost trade-off or, more typically, on company policy or contractual requirements.

There is a humorous story supposedly about Hewlett-Packard during its first dealings with Japanese vendors, who place great emphasis on high-quality production. HP had insisted on 2 percent AQL in a purchase of 100 cables. During

ALUMINUM SHEETS ARE EXAMINED UNDER QUALITY CONTROL LIGHTS ON THE ALUMINUM PRODUCTION LINE AT THE ALCOA SZÉKESFEHÉRVÁR, HUNGARY, EXTRUSION PLANT.

Excerpt from a Sampling Plan Table for $\alpha = 0.05$, $\beta = 0.10$

c	LTPD ÷ AQL	$n \cdot$ AQL	c	LTPD ÷ AQL	$n \cdot$ AQL
0	44.890	0.052	5	3.549	2.613
1	10.946	0.355	6	3.206	3.286
2	6.509	0.818	7	2.957	3.981
3	4.890	1.366	8	2.768	4.695
4	4.057	1.970	9	2.618	5.426

the purchase agreement, some heated discussion took place wherein the Japanese vendor did not want this AQL specification; HP insisted that they would not budge from the 2 percent AQL. The Japanese vendor finally agreed. Later, when the box arrived, there were two packages inside. One contained 100 good cables. The other package had 2 cables with a note stating: "We have sent you 100 good cables. Since you insisted on 2 percent AQL, we have enclosed 2 defective cables in this package, though we do not understand why you want them."

The following example, using an excerpt from a standard acceptance sampling table, illustrates how the four parameters—AQL, α, LTPD, and β—are used in developing a sampling plan.

EXAMPLE TN8.5: Values of *n* and *c*

Hi-Tech Industries manufactures Z-Band radar scanners used to detect speed traps. The printed circuit boards in the scanners are purchased from an outside vendor. The vendor produces the boards to an AQL of 2 percent defectives and is willing to run a 5 percent risk (α) of having lots of this level or fewer defectives rejected. Hi-Tech considers lots of 8 percent or more defectives (LTPD) unacceptable and wants to ensure that it will accept such poor-quality lots no more than 10 percent of the time (β). A large shipment has just been delivered. What values of *n* and *c* should be selected to determine the quality of this lot?

SOLUTION

The parameters of the problem are AQL $= 0.02$, $\alpha = 0.05$, LTPD $= 0.08$, and $\beta = 0.10$. We can use Exhibit TN8.10 to find *c* and *n*.

First, divide LTPD by AQL ($0.08 \div 0.02 = 4$). Then, find the ratio in column 2 that is equal to or just greater than that amount (4). This value is 4.057, which is associated with $c = 4$.

Finally, find the value in column 3 that is in the same row as $c = 4$, and divide that quantity by AQL to obtain *n* ($1.970 \div 0.02 = 98.5$).

The appropriate sampling plan is $c = 4$, $n = 99$. ●

OPERATING CHARACTERISTIC CURVES

While a sampling plan such as the one just described meets our requirements for the extreme values of good and bad quality, we cannot readily determine how well the plan discriminates between good and bad lots at intermediate values. For this reason, sampling plans are generally displayed graphically through the use of operating characteristic (OC) curves. These curves, which are unique for each combination of *n* and *c*, simply illustrate the probability of accepting lots with varying percentages of defectives. The procedure we have followed in developing the plan, in fact, specifies two points on an OC curve: one point defined by AQL and $1 - \alpha$ and the other point defined by LTPD and β. Curves for common values of *n* and *c* can be computed or obtained from available tables.[3]

Shaping the OC Curve   A sampling plan discriminating perfectly between good and bad lots has an infinite slope (vertical) at the selected value of AQL. In Exhibit TN8.11, any percentage defective to the left of 2 percent would always be accepted, and those to the

Operating Characteristic Curve for AQL = 0.02, α = 0.05, LTPD = 0.08, β = 0.10

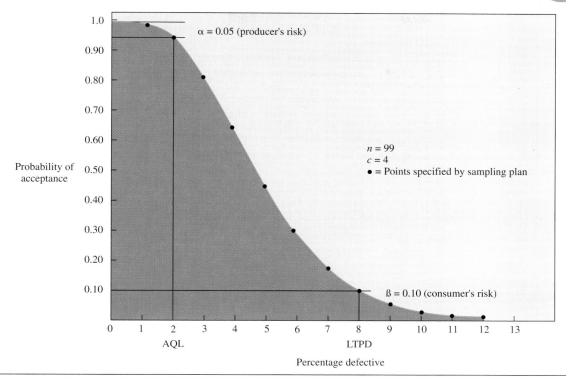

right, always rejected. However, such a curve is possible only with complete inspection of all units and thus is not a possibility with a true sampling plan.

An OC curve should be steep in the region of most interest (between the AQL and the LTPD), which is accomplished by varying n and c. If c remains constant, increasing the sample size n causes the OC curve to be more vertical. While holding n constant, decreasing c (the maximum number of defective units) also makes the slope more vertical, moving closer to the origin.

The Effects of Lot Size   The size of the lot that the sample is taken from has relatively little effect on the quality of protection. Consider, for example, that samples—all of the same size of 20 units—are taken from different lots ranging from a lot size of 200 units to a lot size of infinity. If each lot is known to have 5 percent defectives, the probability of accepting the lot based on the sample of 20 units ranges from about 0.34 to about 0.36. This means that as long as the lot size is several times the sample size, it makes little difference how large the lot is. It seems a bit difficult to accept, but statistically (on the average in the long run) whether we have a carload or box full, we'll get about the same answer. It just seems that a carload should have a larger sample size. Of course, this assumes that the lot is randomly chosen and that defects are randomly spread through the lot.

CONCLUSION

Statistical quality control is a vital topic. Quality has become so important that statistical quality procedures are *expected* to be part of successful firms. Sampling plans and statistical process control are taken as given with the emphasis shifting to broader aspects (such as eliminating dockside acceptance sampling because of reliable supplier quality, and employee empowerment transforming much of the process control). World-class manufacturing companies expect people to understand the basic concepts of the material presented in this technical note.

KEY TERMS

Assignable variation Deviation in the output of a process that can be clearly identified and managed.

Common variation Deviation in the output of a process that is random and inherent in the process itself.

Upper and lower specification or **tolerance limits** The range of values in a measure associated with a process that are allowable given the intended use of the product or service.

Capability index (C_{pk}) The ratio of the range of values produced by a process divided by the range of values allowed by the design specification.

Statistical process control (SPC) Techniques for testing a random sample of output from a process to determine whether the process is producing items within a prescribed range.

Attributes Quality characteristics that are classified as either conforming or not conforming to specification.

Variables Quality characteristics that are measured in actual weight, volume, inches, centimeters, or other measure.

FORMULA REVIEW

Mean or average

[TN8.1]
$$\overline{X} = \sum_{i=1}^{N} x_i / N$$

Standard deviation

[TN8.2]
$$\sigma = \sqrt{\frac{\sum_{i=1}^{N}(x_i - \overline{X})^2}{N}}$$

Capability index

[TN8.3]
$$C_{pk} = \min\left[\frac{\overline{X} - \text{LTL}}{3\sigma}, \frac{\text{UTL} - \overline{X}}{3\sigma}\right]$$

Process control charts using attribute measurements

[TN8.4]
$$\overline{p} = \frac{\text{Total number of defects from all samples}}{\text{Number of samples} \times \text{Sample size}}$$

[TN8.5]
$$s_p = \sqrt{\frac{\overline{p}(1 - \overline{p})}{n}}$$

[TN8.6]
$$\text{UCL} = \overline{p} + zs_p$$

[TN8.7]
$$\text{LCL} = \overline{p} - zs_p$$

[TN8.8]
$$\text{UCL}_{\overline{X}} = \overline{\overline{X}} + zs_{\overline{x}} \quad \text{and} \quad \text{LCL}_{\overline{X}} = \overline{\overline{X}} - zs_{\overline{X}}$$

Process control $\overline{X}$ and R charts

[TN8.9]
$$\overline{\overline{X}} = \frac{\sum_{j=1}^{m} \overline{X}_j}{m}$$

[TN8.10]
$$\overline{R} = \frac{\sum_{j=1}^{m} R_j}{m}$$

[TN8.11]	Upper control limit for $\overline{X} = \overline{\overline{X}} + A_2\overline{R}$
[TN8.12]	Lower control limit for $\overline{X} = \overline{\overline{X}} - A_2\overline{R}$
[TN8.13]	Upper control limit for $R = D_4\overline{R}$
[TN8.14]	Lower control limit for $R = D_3\overline{R}$

SOLVED PROBLEMS

SOLVED PROBLEM 1

Completed forms from a particular department of an insurance company were sampled daily to check the performance quality of that department. To establish a tentative norm for the department, one sample of 100 units was collected each day for 15 days, with these results:

Excel: SPC.xls

SAMPLE	SAMPLE SIZE	NUMBER OF FORMS WITH ERRORS	SAMPLE	SAMPLE SIZE	NUMBER OF FORMS WITH ERRORS
1	100	4	9	100	4
2	100	3	10	100	2
3	100	5	11	100	7
4	100	0	12	100	2
5	100	2	13	100	1
6	100	8	14	100	3
7	100	1	15	100	1
8	100	3			

a. Develop a *p* chart using a 95 percent confidence interval ($1.96s_p$).
b. Plot the 15 samples collected.
c. What comments can you make about the process?

Solution

a. $\overline{p} = \dfrac{46}{15(100)} = .0307$

$$s_p = \sqrt{\frac{\overline{p}(1 - \overline{p})}{n}} = \sqrt{\frac{.0307(1 - .0307)}{100}} = \sqrt{.0003} = .017$$

UCL $= \overline{p} + 1.96s_p = .031 + 1.96(.017) = .064$

LCL $= \overline{p} - 1.96s_p = .031 - 1.96(.017) = -.00232$ or zero

b. The defectives are plotted below.

c. Of the 15 samples, 2 were out of the control limits. Because the control limits were established as 95 percent, or 1 out of 20, we would say that the process is out of control. It needs to be examined to find the cause of such widespread variation.

SOLVED PROBLEM 2

Management is trying to decide whether Part A, which is produced with a consistent 3 percent defective rate, should be inspected. If it is not inspected, the 3 percent defectives will go through a product assembly phase and have to be replaced later. If all Part A's are inspected, one-third of the defectives will be found, thus raising the quality to 2 percent defectives.

a. Should the inspection be done if the cost of inspecting is $0.01 per unit and the cost of replacing a defective in the final assembly is $4.00?

b. Suppose the cost of inspecting is $0.05 per unit rather than $0.01. Would this change your answer in a?

Solution

Should Part A be inspected?

.03 defective with no inspection.

.02 defective with inspection.

a. This problem can be solved simply by looking at the opportunity for 1 percent improvement.

Benefit = .01($4.00) = $0.04

Cost of inspection = $0.01

Therefore, inspect and save $0.03 per unit.

b. A cost of $0.05 per unit to inspect would be $0.01 greater than the savings, so inspection should not be performed.

REVIEW AND DISCUSSION QUESTIONS

1   The capability index allows for some drifting of the process mean. Discuss what this means in terms of product quality output.

2   Discuss the purposes of and differences between p charts and $\overline{X}$ and R charts.

3   In an agreement between a supplier and a customer, the supplier must ensure that all parts are within tolerance before shipment to the customer. What is the effect on the cost of quality to the customer?

4   In the situation described in Question 3, what would be the effect on the cost of quality to the supplier?

5   Discuss the trade-off between achieving a zero AQL (acceptable quality level) and a positive AQL (such as an AQL of 2 percent).

PROBLEMS

1   A company currently using an inspection process in its material receiving department is trying to install an overall cost reduction program. One possible reduction is the elimination of one inspection position. This position tests material that has a defective content on the average of 0.04. By inspecting all items, the inspector is able to remove all defects. The inspector can inspect 50 units per hour. The hourly rate including fringe benefits for this position is $9. If the inspection position is eliminated, defects will go into product assembly and will have to be replaced later at a cost of $10 each when they are detected in final product testing.

a. Should this inspection position be eliminated?

b. What is the cost to inspect each unit?

c. Is there benefit (or loss) from the current inspection process? How much?

2   A metal fabricator produces connecting rods with an outer diameter that has a 1 ± .01 inch specification. A machine operator takes several sample measurements over time and determines the sample mean outer diameter to be 1.002 inches with a standard deviation of .003 inch.

a. Calculate the process capability index for this example.

b. What does this figure tell you about the process?

3   Ten samples of 15 parts each were taken from an ongoing process to establish a *p* chart for control. The samples and the number of defectives in each are shown in the following table:

SAMPLE	*n*	NUMBER OF DEFECTS IN SAMPLE	SAMPLE	*n*	NUMBER OF DEFECTS IN SAMPLE
1	15	3	6	15	2
2	15	1	7	15	0
3	15	0	8	15	3
4	15	0	9	15	1
5	15	0	10	15	0

a. Develop a *p* chart for 95 percent confidence (1.96 standard deviations).

b. Based on the plotted data points, what comments can you make?

4   Output from a process contains 0.02 defective units. Defective units that go undetected into final assemblies cost $25 each to replace. An inspection process, which would detect and remove all defectives, can be established to test these units. However, the inspector, who can test 20 units per hour, is paid $8 per hour, including fringe benefits. Should an inspection station be established to test all units?

a. What is the cost to inspect each unit?

b. What is the benefit (or loss) from the inspection process?

5   There is a 3 percent error rate at a specific point in a production process. If an inspector is placed at this point, all the errors can be detected and eliminated. However, the inspector is paid $8 per hour and can inspect units in the process at the rate of 30 per hour.

   If no inspector is used and defects are allowed to pass this point, there is a cost of $10 per unit to correct the defect later on.

   Should an inspector be hired?

6   Resistors for electronic circuits are manufactured on a high-speed automated machine. The machine is set up to produce a large run of resistors of 1,000 ohms each.

   To set up the machine and to create a control chart to be used throughout the run, 15 samples were taken with four resistors in each sample. The complete list of samples and their measured values are as follows:

SAMPLE NUMBER	READINGS (IN OHMS)			
1	1010	991	985	986
2	995	996	1009	994
3	990	1003	1015	1008
4	1015	1020	1009	998
5	1013	1019	1005	993
6	994	1001	994	1005
7	989	992	982	1020
8	1001	986	996	996
9	1006	989	1005	1007
10	992	1007	1006	979
11	996	1006	997	989
12	1019	996	991	1011
13	981	991	989	1003
14	999	993	988	984
15	1013	1002	1005	992

   Develop an $\overline{X}$ chart and an *R* chart and plot the values. From the charts, what comments can you make about the process? (Use three-sigma control limits as in Exhibit TN8.7.)

7   In the past, Alpha Corporation has not performed incoming quality control inspections but has taken the word of its vendors. However, Alpha has been having some unsatisfactory experience recently with the quality of purchased items and wants to set up sampling plans for the receiving department to use.

   For a particular component, X, Alpha has a lot tolerance percentage defective of 10 percent. Zenon Corporation, from which Alpha purchases this component, has an acceptable quality level in its production facility of 3 percent for component X. Alpha has a consumer's risk of 10 percent and Zenon has a producer's risk of 5 percent.

a. When a shipment of Product X is received from Zenon Corporation, what sample size should the receiving department test?

b. What is the allowable number of defects in order to accept the shipment?

8 You are the newly appointed assistant administrator at a local hospital, and your first project is to investigate the quality of the patient meals put out by the food-service department. You conducted a 10-day survey by submitting a simple questionnaire to the 400 patients with each meal, asking that they simply check off that the meal was either satisfactory or unsatisfactory. For simplicity in this problem, assume that the response was 1,000 returned questionnaires from the 1,200 meals each day. The results are as follows:

	NUMBER OF UNSATISFACTORY MEALS	SAMPLE SIZE
December 1	74	1,000
December 2	42	1,000
December 3	64	1,000
December 4	80	1,000
December 5	40	1,000
December 6	50	1,000
December 7	65	1,000
December 8	70	1,000
December 9	40	1,000
December 10	75	1,000
	600	10,000

a. Construct a *p* chart based on the questionnaire results, using a confidence interval of 95.5 percent, which is two standard deviations. ← 2

b. What comments can you make about the results of the survey?

9 Large-scale integrated (LSI) circuit chips are made in one department of an electronics firm. These chips are incorporated into analog devices that are then encased in epoxy. The yield is not particularly good for LSI manufacture, so the AQL specified by that department is 0.15 while the LTPD acceptable by the assembly department is 0.40.

a. Develop a sampling plan.

b. Explain what the sampling plan means; that is, how would you tell someone to do the test?

10 The state and local police departments are trying to analyze crime rates so they can shift their patrols from decreasing-rate areas to areas where rates are increasing. The city and county have been geographically segmented into areas containing 5,000 residences. The police recognize that not all crimes and offenses are reported: people do not want to become involved, consider the offenses too small to report, are too embarrassed to make a police report, or do not take the time, among other reasons. Every month, because of this, the police are contacting by phone a random sample of 1,000 of the 5,000 residences for data on crime. (Respondents are guaranteed anonymity.) Here are the data collected for the past 12 months for one area:

MONTH	CRIME INCIDENCE	SAMPLE SIZE	CRIME RATE
January	7	1,000	0.007
February	9	1,000	0.009
March	7	1,000	0.007
April	7	1,000	0.007
May	7	1,000	0.007
June	9	1,000	0.009
July	7	1,000	0.007
August	10	1,000	0.010
September	8	1,000	0.008
October	11	1,000	0.011
November	10	1,000	0.010
December	8	1,000	0.008

Construct a *p* chart for 95 percent confidence (1.96) and plot each of the months. If the next three months show crime incidences in this area as

January = 10 (out of 1,000 sampled)

February = 12 (out of 1,000 sampled)

March = 11 (out of 1,000 sampled)

what comments can you make regarding the crime rate?

11 Some citizens complained to city council members that there should be equal protection under the law against the occurrence of crimes. The citizens argued that this equal protection should be interpreted as indicating that high-crime areas should have more police protection than low-crime areas. Therefore, police patrols and other methods for preventing crime (such as street lighting or cleaning up abandoned areas and buildings) should be used proportionately to crime occurrence.

In a fashion similar to Problem 10, the city has been broken down into 20 geographic areas, each containing 5,000 residences. The 1,000 sampled from each area showed the following incidence of crime during the past month:

AREA	NUMBER OF CRIMES	SAMPLE SIZE	CRIME RATE
1	14	1,000	0.014
2	3	1,000	0.003
3	19	1,000	0.019
4	18	1,000	0.018
5	14	1,000	0.014
6	28	1,000	0.028
7	10	1,000	0.010
8	18	1,000	0.018
9	12	1,000	0.012
10	3	1,000	0.003
11	20	1,000	0.020
12	15	1,000	0.015
13	12	1,000	0.012
14	14	1,000	0.014
15	10	1,000	0.010
16	30	1,000	0.030
17	4	1,000	0.004
18	20	1,000	0.020
19	6	1,000	0.006
20	30	1,000	0.030
	300		

Suggest a reallocation of crime protection effort, if indicated, based on a *p* chart analysis. To be reasonably certain in your recommendation, select a 95 percent confidence level (that is, $Z = 1.96$).

12 The following table contains the measurements of the key length dimension from a fuel injector. These samples of size five were taken at one-hour intervals.

| SAMPLE NUMBER | OBSERVATIONS | | | | |
	1	2	3	4	5
1	.486	.499	.493	.511	.481
2	.499	.506	.516	.494	.529
3	.496	.500	.515	.488	.521
4	.495	.506	.483	.487	.489
5	.472	.502	.526	.469	.481

(continued)

	OBSERVATIONS				
SAMPLE NUMBER	1	2	3	4	5
6	.473	.495	.507	.493	.506
7	.495	.512	.490	.471	.504
8	.525	.501	.498	.474	.485
9	.497	.501	.517	.506	.516
10	.495	.505	.516	.511	.497
11	.495	.482	.468	.492	.492
12	.483	.459	.526	.506	.522
13	.521	.512	.493	.525	.510
14	.487	.521	.507	.501	.500
15	.493	.516	.499	.511	.513
16	.473	.506	.479	.480	.523
17	.477	.485	.513	.484	.496
18	.515	.493	.493	.485	.475
19	.511	.536	.486	.497	.491
20	.509	.490	.470	.504	.512

Construct a three-sigma $\overline{X}$ chart and R chart (use Exhibit TN8.7) for the length of the fuel injector. What can you say about this process?

13   C-Spec, Inc., is attempting to determine whether an existing machine is capable of milling an engine part that has a key specification of $4 \pm .003$ inches. After a trial run on this machine, C-Spec has determined that the machine has a sample mean of 4.001 inches with a standard deviation of .002 inch.

     a. Calculate the C_{pk} for this machine.

     b. Should C-Spec use this machine to produce this part? Why?

ADVANCED PROBLEM

14   Design specifications require that a key dimension on a product measure 100 ± 10 units. A process being considered for producing this product has a standard deviation of four units.

     a. What can you say (quantitatively) regarding the process capability?

     b. Suppose the process average shifts to 92. Calculate the new process capability.

     c. What can you say about the process after the shift? Approximately what percentage of the items produced will be defective?

SELECTED BIBLIOGRAPHY

Alwan, L. *Statistical Process Analysis.* New York: Irwin/McGraw-Hill, 2000.

Aslup, F., and R. M. Watson. *Practical Statistical Process Control: A Tool for Quality Manufacturing.* New York: Van Nostrand Reinhold, 1993.

Feigenbaum, A. V. *Total Quality Control.* New York: McGraw-Hill, 1991.

Grant, E. L., and R. S. Leavenworth. *Statistical Quality Control.* New York: McGraw-Hill, 1996.

Ledolter, J., and C. Burrill. *Statistical Quality Control: Strategies and Tools for Continual Improvement.* New York: Wiley, 1999.

Rath & Strong. *Rath & Strong's Six Sigma Pocket Guide.* Rath & Strong, Inc., 2000.

Small, B. B. (with committee). *Statistical Quality Control Handbook.* Western Electric Co., Inc., 1956.

Taguchi, G. *On-Line Quality Control during Production.* Tokyo: Japanese Standards Association, 1987.

Zimmerman, S. M., and M. L. Icenogel. *Statistical Quality Control; Using Excel.* 2nd ed. Milwaukee, WI: ASQ Quality Press, 2002.

FOOTNOTES

1 E. L. Grant and R. S. Leavenworth, *Statistical Quality Control* (New York: McGraw-Hill, 1996).

2 There is some controversy surrounding AQLs. This is based on the argument that specifying some acceptable percentage of defectives is inconsistent with the philosophical goal of zero defects. In practice, even in the best QC companies, there is an acceptable quality level. The difference is that it may be stated in parts per million rather than in parts per hundred. This is the case in Motorola's Six-Sigma quality standard, which holds that no more than 3.4 defects per million parts are acceptable.

3 See, for example, H. F. Dodge and H. G. Romig, *Sampling Inspection Tables—Single and Double Sampling* (New York: John Wiley & Sons, 1959); and *Military Standard Sampling Procedures and Tables for Inspection by Attributes* (MIL-STD-105D) (Washington, DC: U.S. Government Printing Office, 1983).

chapter

OPERATIONS CONSULTING AND REENGINEERING

McKinsey & Company: Operations Consulting Practice

 Just a few years ago, seduced by visions of limitless growth, many companies gave limited attention to operational excellence. Acquisitions, alliances, and Web-based strategies were far more alluring. Today, with a focus on fundamental strength and bottom-line results, 60 percent of CEOs surveyed by McKinsey & Company say that achieving operational excellence is their top priority.

LEARNING TO EXECUTE

Of course, manufacturers of steel, paper, and other basic materials have long stressed operations (even if the industry struggled to improve them). But for

most service industries, including retail, telecom, insurance, and financial services, CEOs' attention to the nuts and bolts of their business infrastructure marks a turning point.

"A lot of companies made promises to customers during the dot-com era, and found they couldn't deliver," says Philippe Bideau, a director in the Paris office. "Those were failures of execution, not of strategy. What drives bottom-line performance in most industries is quality, cost, and service—and those are all operational issues."

Adapted from: McKinsey & Company, www.mckinsey.com, statement relating to operations consulting practice.

FORCES FOR CHANGE

In a changing economic environment, three forces have led companies to rethink their operational capabilities:

- **Customer sophistication.** Customers in every market have become better informed, more demanding, and more selective. They can readily compare prices and assess many aspects of vendors' performance before they buy. The Internet, which once diverted attention from operations, now has underscored their importance. With greater transparency, companies that cannot leverage their operations to provide superior service or value will lose.

- **Competitive pressure.** As globalization brings low-cost competitors to the market, incumbents have squeezed obvious inefficiency from their systems—often by restructuring, outsourcing, or offshoring pieces of the business. Significant performance-improvement opportunities remain, but are harder to achieve. Retailers, for instance, could cut inventory costs by up to 50 percent, and boost sales volume by 14 percent, by reducing overstocks and stock-outs, respectively. Likewise, consumer electronics makers, whose products may have less than a six-month life cycle, can improve their returns by reducing their time to market.

- **The move to services.** Lean manufacturing techniques, which have helped automotive and other manufacturers reduce costs by 30–40 percent, are now showing similar results in other sectors. But there are no silver bullets; lean transformation affects almost every business activity, the management systems that support those activities, and the mindsets and behaviors of the people who perform them.

"Executives are trying to understand the limits of operational performance, and are pushing those limits," says Raimund Deiderichs, a director in the Vienna office. "Many healthcare and telecom providers, for instance, are for the first time developing standard operating procedures—benchmarks for every service they provide—rather than responding to problems on an ad hoc basis. Every company has a production system, and cracks in that system can be disastrous—operationally and strategically." →

Operations consulting has become one of the major areas of employment for business school graduates. The above page from the McKinsey & Company Web site nicely summarizes the importance of operations on bottom-line performance. In this chapter, we discuss how one goes about consulting for operations, as well as the nature of the consulting business in general. We also survey the tools and techniques used in operations consulting and provide an overview of business process reengineering since much OM consulting entails this activity.

WHAT IS OPERATIONS CONSULTING?

Operations consulting   ⬤⬤⬤◯ **Operations consulting** deals with assisting clients in developing operations strategies and improving production processes. In strategy development, the focus is on analyzing the capabilities of operations in light of the firm's competitive strategy. By way of example, Treacy and Wiersema suggest that market leadership can be attained in one of three ways: through product leadership, through operational excellence, or through customer intimacy.[1] Each of these strategies may well call for different operations capabilities and focus. The operations consultant must be able to assist management in understanding these differences and be able to define the most effective combination of technology and systems to execute the strategy. In process improvement, the focus is on employing analytical tools and methods to help operating managers enhance performance of their departments. Deloitte & Touche Consulting lists the actions to improve processes as follows: refine/revise processes, revise activities, reconfigure flows, revise policies/procedures, change outputs, and realign structure. We say more about both strategy issues and tools later. Regardless of where one focuses, *an effective job of operations consulting results in an alignment between strategy and process dimensions that enhances the business performance of the client.*

THE NATURE OF THE MANAGEMENT CONSULTING INDUSTRY

⦿⦿⦾ Frederick W. Taylor, "the father of scientific management," is also credited as "the father of management consulting." Taylor, a young engineer, devised a philosophy and system of production management at the turn of the century. His book, *The Principles of Scientific Management,* converted what had been an art into a systematic, teachable approach to the study of work. Since Taylor's time, management consulting has reached far beyond the shop floor. Today management consulting is booming, as can be seen by the revenue figures from *Consultants News* given in Exhibit 9.1A. The reasons for this boom include the following: market pressures on clients to reengineer their core processes and eliminate their noncore processes; globalization requiring companies to seek expert advice on entering foreign markets and defending local ones against new competitors; and the need to better manage information technology, including systems integration, packaged software solutions, and, of course, Internet applications.

The management consulting industry can be categorized in three ways: by size, by specialization, and by in-house and external consultants. Most consulting firms are small, generating less than $500,000 in annual billings. But as David J. Collis notes in his article "The Management Consulting Industry," the typical consultant works for a large firm, with three-quarters working for firms employing more than 100 professionals.[2] Relative to specialization, although all large firms provide a variety of services, they may also specialize by function, such as operations management, or by industry, such as manufacturing (see Exhibit 9.1B and 9.1C). Most large consulting companies are built on information technology (IT) and accounting work. The third basis for segmentation, in-house versus external, refers to whether a company maintains its own consulting organization or buys consulting services from the outside. Collis observes that internal consulting arms are common in large companies and are often affiliated with planning departments.

Cross Functional

Consulting firms are also frequently characterized according to whether their primary skill is in strategic planning or in tactical analysis and implementation. McKinsey & Company and the Boston Consulting Group are standard examples of strategy-type companies, whereas Gemini Consulting and A. T. Kearney focus rather extensively on tactical and implementation projects. The big accounting firms and Accenture are known for providing a wide range of services. The major new players in the consulting business are the large information technology firms such as Computer Sciences Corporation (CSC), Electronic Data Systems (EDS), and IBM. Consultancies are faced with problems similar to those of their clients: the need to provide a global presence, the need to computerize to coordinate activities, and the need to continually recruit and train their workers. This has led consultancies to make the hard choice of being very large or being a boutique firm. Being in the middle creates problems of lack of scale economies on the one hand and lack of focus and flexibility on the other.

exhibit 9.1   Consulting Industry Data

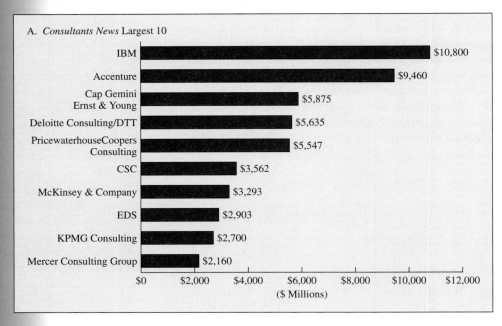

A. *Consultants News* Largest 10

IBM — $10,800
Accenture — $9,460
Cap Gemini Ernst & Young — $5,875
Deloitte Consulting/DTT — $5,635
PricewaterhouseCoopers Consulting — $5,547
CSC — $3,562
McKinsey & Company — $3,293
EDS — $2,903
KPMG Consulting — $2,700
Mercer Consulting Group — $2,160

($ Millions)

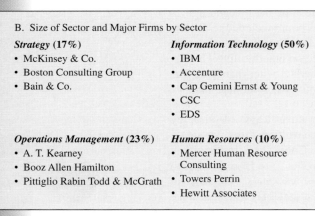

B. Size of Sector and Major Firms by Sector

Strategy (17%)
- McKinsey & Co.
- Boston Consulting Group
- Bain & Co.

Information Technology (50%)
- IBM
- Accenture
- Cap Gemini Ernst & Young
- CSC
- EDS

Operations Management (23%)
- A. T. Kearney
- Booz Allen Hamilton
- Pittiglio Rabin Todd & McGrath

Human Resources (10%)
- Mercer Human Resource Consulting
- Towers Perrin
- Hewitt Associates

C. Consulting Market Segmentation by Vertical Industry

Other 29%
Government 17%
Financial Services 18%
Manufacturing 16%
Retail/Wholesale 10%
Communications 10%

SOURCE: KENNEDY INFORMATION, www.kennedyinfo.com.

The hierarchy of the typical consulting firm can be viewed as a pyramid. At the top of the pyramid are the partners or seniors, whose primary function is sales and client relations. In the middle are managers, who manage consulting projects or "engagements." At the bottom are juniors, who carry out the consulting work as part of a consulting team. There are gradations in rank within each of these categories (such as senior partners). The three categories are frequently referred to colloquially as the **"finders"** (of new business), the **"minders"** (or managers) of the project teams, and the **"grinders"** (the consultants who do the work). Consulting firms typically work in project teams, selected according to client needs and the preferences of the project managers and the first-line consultants themselves. Getting oneself assigned to interesting, high-visibility projects with good co-workers is an important career strategy of most junior consultants. Being in demand for team membership and obtaining quality consulting experiences are critical for achieving long-term success with a consulting firm (or being attractive to another firm within or outside of consulting).

"Finders"

"Minders"

"Grinders"

ECONOMICS OF CONSULTING FIRMS

⟨⟨⟨⟩⟩ The economics of consulting firms have been written about extensively by David H. Maister. In his classic article "Balancing the Professional Service Firm,"[3] he draws the analogy of the consulting firm as a job shop, where the right kinds of "machines" (professional staff) must be correctly allocated to the right kinds of jobs (consulting projects). As in any job shop, the degree of job customization and attendant complexity is critical. The most complex projects, which Maister calls *brain surgery* projects, require innovation and creativity. Next come *gray hair* projects, which require a great deal of experience but little in the way of innovation. A third type of project is the *procedures* project, where the general nature of the problem is well known and the activities necessary to complete it are similar to those performed on other projects.

Because consulting firms are typically partnerships, the goal is to maximize profits for the partners. This, in turn, is achieved by leveraging the skills of the partners through the effective use of midlevel and junior consultants. This is often presented as a ratio of partners to midlevel to junior consultants for the average project. (See Exhibit 9.2 for a numerical example of how profitability is calculated for a hypothetical consulting firm, Guru Associates.) Because most consulting firms are engaged in multiple projects simultaneously, the percentage of billable employee hours assigned to all projects (target utilization) will be less than 100 percent. A practice that specializes in cutting-edge, high-client risk (brain surgery) work must be staffed with a high partner-to-junior ratio because lower-level people will not be able to deliver the quality of services required. In contrast, practices that deal with more procedural, low-risk work will be inefficient if they do not have a lower ratio of partners to juniors because high-priced staff should not be doing low-value tasks.

The most common method for improving efficiency is the use of uniform approaches to each aspect of a consulting job. Accenture, the company most famous for this approach, sends its new consultants through a boot camp at its St. Charles, Illinois, training facility. At this boot camp, it provides highly refined, standardized methods for such common operations work as systems design, process reengineering, and continuous improvement, and for the project management and reporting procedures by which such work is carried out. Of

---

The Economics of Guru Associates

exhibit 9.2

LEVEL	No.	TARGET UTILIZATION	TARGET BILLABLE HOURS @ 2,000 HOURS PER PERSON PER YEAR	BILLING RATE	FEES	SALARY PER INDIVIDUAL	TOTAL SALARIES
Partner (senior)	4	75%	6,000	$200	$1,200,000	(see calculations below)	
Middle	8	75%	12,000	$100	$1,200,000	$75,000	$600,000
Junior	20	90%	36,000	$50	$1,800,000	$32,000	$640,000
Totals					$4,200,000		$1,240,000

Fees	$4,200,000
Salaries	(1,240,000)
Contributions	$2,960,000
Overhead*	$1,280,000
Partner profits	$1,680,000
Per partner	$ 420,000

*Assume overhead costs of $40,000 per professional.

SOURCE: D. H. MAISTER, *MANAGING THE PROFESSIONAL SERVICE FIRM* (NEW YORK: THE FREE PRESS, 1993), P. 11. COPYRIGHT 1993 BY SLOAN MANAGEMENT REVIEW ASSOCIATION. ALL RIGHTS RESERVED.

course, other large consulting firms have their own training methods and step-by-step procedures for selling, designing, and executing consulting projects.

WHEN OPERATIONS CONSULTING IS NEEDED

 The following are some of the major strategic and tactical areas where companies typically seek operations consulting. Looking first at manufacturing consulting areas (grouped under what could be called *the 5 Ps of production*), we have

- *Plant:* Adding and locating new plants; expanding, contracting, or refocusing existing facilities.
- *People:* Quality improvement, setting/revising work standards, learning curve analysis.
- *Parts:* Make or buy decisions, vendor selection decisions.
- *Processes:* Technology evaluation, process improvement, reengineering.
- *Planning and control systems:* Supply chain management, MRP, shop-floor control, warehousing, distribution.

Obviously, many of these issues are interrelated, calling for systemwide solutions. Examples of common themes reflecting this are developing manufacturing strategy; designing and implementing JIT systems; implementing MRP or proprietary ERP software such as SAP; and systems integration involving client–server technology. Typical questions addressed are "How can the client cut lead times? How can inventory be reduced? How can better control be maintained over the shop floor?" Among the hot areas of manufacturing strategy consulting are developing factory focus; outsourcing; supply chain management; and global manufacturing networks. At the tactical level, there is a huge market for consulting in E-operations, product development, ISO 9000 quality certification, six-sigma training, and designing and implementing decentralized production control systems.

Turning to services, while consulting firms in manufacturing may have broad specialties in process industries on the one hand and assembly or discrete product manufacture on the other, service operations consulting typically has a strong industry or sector focus. A common consulting portfolio of specialties in services (and areas of consulting need) would include the following:

Financial services (staffing, automation, quality studies).

Health care (staffing, billing, office procedures, phone answering, layout).

Transportation (route scheduling and shipping logistics for goods haulers, reservation systems and baggage handling for airlines).

Hospitality (reservations, staffing, cost containment, quality programs).

Without question, however, the major area of operations consulting emphasis in most service industries is process improvement, particularly in the management of call centers.

WHEN ARE OPERATIONS CONSULTANTS NEEDED?

Companies typically seek out operations consultants when they are faced with major investment decisions or when they believe that they are not getting maximum effectiveness from their productive capacity. As an example of the first type of situation, consider the following:

> A national pie restaurant chain retained consultants to determine if a major addition to its freezer storage capacity was needed at its pie-making plant. Its lease had run out on a nearby freezer warehouse, so the firm had to make

Service

a decision rather quickly. The pie plant manager wanted a $500,000 increase in capacity. After analysis of the demand for various types of pies, the distribution system, and the contractual arrangement with the shipper, the consultant concluded that management could avoid all but a $30,000 investment in capacity if they did the following: Run a mixed-model production schedule for pies according to a forecast for each of 10 kinds of pies (for example, 20 percent strawberry, 30 percent cherry, 30 percent apple, and 20 percent other pies each two-day pie production cycle). To do this, more timely information about pie demand at each of the chain restaurants had to be obtained. This in turn required that information links for pie requirements go directly to the factory. (Previously the distributor bought the pies and resold them to the restaurants.) Finally, the company renegotiated pickup times from the pie plant to enable just-in-time delivery at the restaurants. The company was in a much stronger bargaining situation than they were five years previously, and the distributor was willing to make reasonable adjustments.

The lesson from this is that few investment decisions in operations are all or nothing, and good solutions can be obtained by simply applying standard OM concepts of production planning, forecasting, and scheduling. The solution recognized that the problem must be viewed at a systemwide level to see how better planning and distribution could substitute for brick-and-mortar capacity.

THE OPERATIONS CONSULTING PROCESS

The broad steps in the operations consulting process (see Exhibit 9.3) are roughly the same as for any type of management consulting. The major differences exist in the nature of the problem to be analyzed and the kinds of analytical methods to be employed. Like general management consulting, operations consulting may focus on the strategic level or tactical level, and the process itself generally requires extensive interviewing of employees, managers, and, frequently, customers. If there is one large difference, it is that operations consulting leads to changes in physical or information processes whose results are measurable immediately. General management consulting usually calls

Stages in the Operations Consulting Process

exhibit 9.3

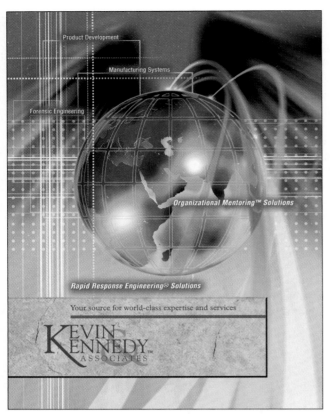

OPERATIONS CONSULTING FIRMS SUCH AS KEVIN KENNEDY AND ASSOCIATES INC. HELP COMPANIES FOCUS ON THE STRATEGIC OR TACTICAL LEVEL OF DECISIONS.

for changes in attitudes and culture, which take longer to yield measurable results. The roles in which consultants find themselves range from an *expert,* to a *pair of hands,* to a *collaborative or process consultant.* Generally, the collaborative or process consultation role is most effective in operations management consulting projects. Some consulting firms now provide the expert role online.

The steps in a typical operations consulting process are summarized in Exhibit 9.3. A book by Ethan M. Rasiel on the McKinsey & Company approach[4] offers some practical guidelines for conducting consulting projects:

- Be careful what you promise in structuring an engagement. *Underpromise and overdeliver* is a good maxim.
- Get the team mix right. You can't just throw four random people at a problem and expect them to solve it. Think about what sorts of skill and personalities work best for the project at hand, and choose your teammates accordingly.
- The 80–20 rule is a management truth. Eighty percent of sales come from 20 percent of the sales force; 80 percent of your time is taken up with 20 percent of your job; and so on.
- Don't boil the ocean. Don't try to analyze everything—be selective in what you investigate.
- Use the elevator test. If you know your solution so well that you can explain it clearly and precisely to your client in a 30-second elevator ride, you are doing well enough to sell it to the client.
- Pluck the low-hanging fruit. If you can make an immediate improvement even though you are in the middle of a project, do it. It boosts morale and gives credibility to your analysis.
- Make a chart every day. Commit your learning to paper; it will help push your thinking and assure that you won't forget it.
- Hit singles. You can't do everything, so don't try. It's better to get to first base consistently than to try to hit a home run and strike out 9 times out of 10.
- Don't accept "I have no idea." Clients and their staff always know something, so probe them for some educated guesses.
- Engage the client in the process. If the client doesn't support you, the project will stall. Keep your clients engaged by keeping them involved.
- Get buy-in throughout the organization. If your solution is to have lasting impact on your client, you have to get support for it throughout the organization.
- Be rigorous about implementation. Making change happen takes a lot of work. Be rigorous and thorough. Make sure someone takes responsibility for getting the job done.

OPERATIONS CONSULTING TOOL KIT

Operations consulting tools can be categorized as tools for *problem definition, data gathering, data analysis and solution development, cost impact and payoff analysis,* and *implementation.* These—along with some tools from strategic management, marketing, and information systems that are commonly used in OM consulting—are noted in Exhibit 9.4 and are described next. (Note that several of these tools are used in more than one stage of a project.)

Operations Consulting Tool Kit

exhibit 9.4

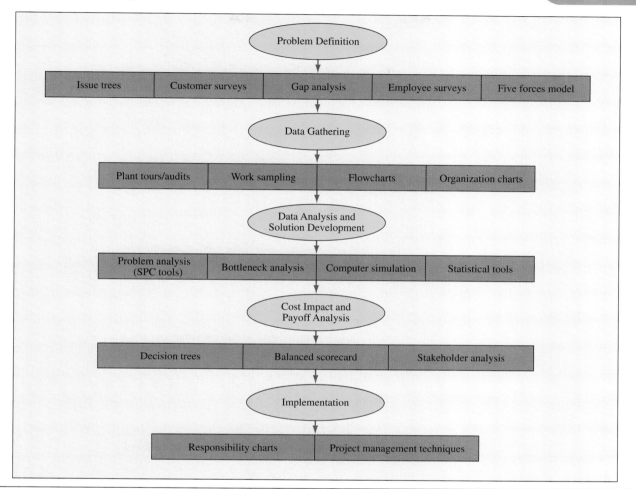

PROBLEM DEFINITION TOOLS

Issue Trees   Issue trees are used by McKinsey to structure or map the key problems to be investigated and provide a working initial hypothesis as to the likely solution to these problems. As can be seen in Exhibit 9.5, a tree starts with the general problem (increase widget sales) and then goes level by level until potential sources of the problem are identified. Once the tree is laid out, the relationships it proposes and possible solutions are debated, and the project plan is then specified.

Customer Surveys   Frequently OM consultants are called in to address problems identified by customer surveys performed by marketing consultants or marketing staff. Often, however, these are out of date or are in a form that does not separate process issues from advertising or other marketing concerns. Even if the surveys are in good form, calling customers and soliciting their experience with the company is a good way to get a feel for process performance. A key use of customer surveys is *customer loyalty analysis,* although in reality customers are not so much "loyal" (your dog, Spot, is loyal) as "earned" through effective performance. Nevertheless, the term *loyalty* captures the flavor of how well an organization is performing according to three critical market measures: customer retention, share of wallet, and price sensitivity relative to competitors. Having such information available helps the OM consultant drill down into the organization to find what operational factors are directly linked to customer retention. Although loyalty studies are usually performed by marketing groups, OM consultants should be aware of their importance.

Cross Functional

exhibit 9.5   Issue Tree for Acme Widgets

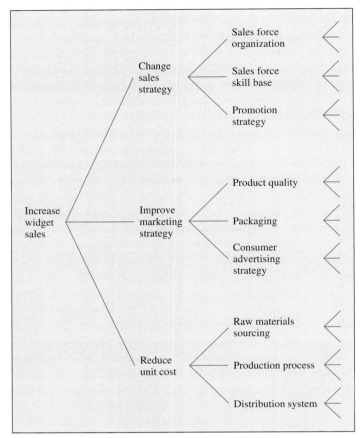

SOURCE: E. M. RASIEL, *THE MCKINSEY WAY* (NEW YORK, MCGRAW-HILL, 1998), P. 12. USED WITH PERMISSION.

Gap Analysis   Gap analysis is used to assess the client's performance relative to the expectations of its customers, or relative to the performance of its competitors. An example is shown in Exhibit 9.6.

Another form of gap analysis is benchmarking particular client company processes against exemplars in the process and measuring the differences. For example, if one is interested in billing process accuracy and problem resolution, American Express would be the benchmark; for timeliness and efficiency in railway transportation, Japanese Railways; for order entry in catalog sales, it would be L. L. Bean.

Employee Surveys   Such surveys range from employee satisfaction surveys to suggestion surveys. A key point to remember is if the consultant requests employee suggestions, such information must be carefully evaluated and acted upon by management. A few years ago, Singapore Airlines distributed a questionnaire to its flight personnel, but made the mistake of not following through to address their concerns. As a result, the employees were more critical of the company than if the survey had not been taken, and to this day the company does not use this form of evaluation.

Five Forces Model   This is one of the better-known approaches to evaluating a company's competitive position in light of the structure of its industry. The five forces are buyer power, potential entrants, suppliers, substitute products, and industry rivals. The consultant applies the model by developing a list of factors that fit under each of these headings.

Gap Analysis

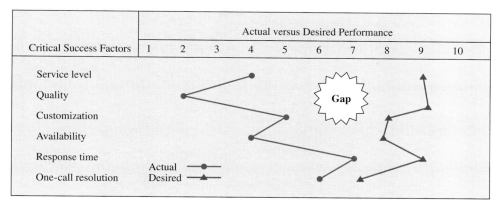

SOURCE: DELOITTE & TOUCHE CONSULTING GROUP.

Value Chain

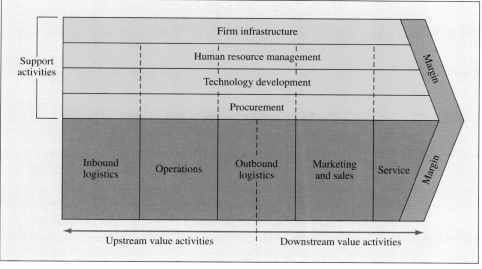

SOURCE: REPRINTED BY PERMISSION OF HARVARD BUSINESS SCHOOL PRESS. FROM *COMPETITION IN GLOBAL INDUSTRIES* BY M. E. PORTER. BOSTON, MA, 1986, P. 24. COPYRIGHT 1986 BY THE PRESIDENT AND FELLOWS OF HARVARD COLLEGE; ALL RIGHTS RESERVED.

Some examples of where a client's competitive position might be strong are when buyers have limited information, there are major barriers to potential entrants, there are many alternative suppliers, there are few substitute products (or services), and there are few industry rivals.

Often used with the five forces model is the *value chain,* such as shown in Exhibit 9.7. The value chain provides a structure to capture the linkage of organizational activities that create value for the customer and profit for the firm. It is particularly useful to get across the notion that operations and the other activities must work cross-functionally for optimal organizational performance (and avoid the dreaded "functional silo" syndrome).

A tool similar to the five forces model is *SWOT analysis.* This is a somewhat more general method of evaluating an organization, and has the advantage of being easy to remember: *S*trengths of the client, *W*eaknesses of the client, *O*pportunities for the client in the industry, and *T*hreats from competitors or the economic and market environment.

DATA GATHERING

Plant Tours/Audits   These can be classified as manufacturing tours/audits and service facility tours/audits. Full manufacturing audits are a major undertaking, entailing measurement of all aspects of the production facility and processes, as well as support activities such as maintenance and inventory stockkeeping. Frequently these require several weeks, utilizing checklists developed explicitly for the client's industry. Plant tours, on the other hand, are usually much less detailed and can be done in a half day. The purpose of the tour is to get a general understanding of the manufacturing process before focusing on a particular problem area. Tours use generic checklists or general questions such as given in the rapid plant assessment method.[5]

The rapid plant assessment (RPA) tour is designed to enable a study team to determine the "leanness" of a plant in just 30 minutes. The approach uses a 20-item questionnaire and an 11-category item rating sheet (see Exhibits 9B.1 and 9B.2 in Appendix B to this chapter). During the tour, team members talk with workers and managers and look for evidence of best practices. RPA's developer, R. Eugene Goodson, suggests that each member of the team focus on a few categories and not take notes since this interferes with conversations with the workers and picking up visual cues. At the end of the tour, members discuss their impressions and fill out the work sheets. The categories are key to the tour. Their features are summarized in the Breakthrough box, "Rapid Plant Assessment."

BREAKTHROUGH

RAPID PLANT ASSESSMENT

1   **Customer satisfaction.**   A customer-oriented workforce will take pride in satisfying both external and internal customers. The extent of this orientation should be apparent even in a brief plant tour. For example, when asked about the next step in the process, customer-aware employees will respond by giving a person's name or product, rather than saying that they just put it on the pallet and it's moved later. Cordiality to the touring group and posted quality and customer satisfaction ratings are other signs of a customer-oriented workforce. (Questions 1, 2, and 20 on the RPA questionnaire relate to this measure. This questionnaire is included in the appendix at the end of this chapter.)

2   **Safety, environment, cleanliness, and order.**   The physical environment of a plant is important to operating effectiveness. Cleanliness, low noise levels, good lighting, and air quality are obvious things to look for. Labeling and tracking of all inventory items, not just expensive ones, should be in evidence. (Not having the required nuts and bolts can be as disruptive to production as lacking a major component.) (Questions 3–5 and 20.)

3   **Visual management system.**   Production management tools such as work instructions, kanban schedules, and quality and productivity charts should be easily visible. Posted workflow diagrams linking each stage of a process

(such as found in chemical plants) are particularly effective visual cues. (Questions 2, 4, 6–10, and 20.)

The next three categories are intertwined. Rating a plant quickly on these three is straightforward from obvious visual clues.

4   **Scheduling system.**   Scheduling involves pacing of the workflow. Goodson suggests that there should be a single "pacing process" for each product line and its suppliers. This process, usually at the end of the line, controls speed and production for all the upstream activities, much as a pace car sets the speed at a racetrack. Demand for product at each work center is triggered by demand at the next. This keeps inventory from building up, improves quality, and reduces downtime because production lines aren't kept waiting for parts. Such is usually not the case in plants that use a central scheduling system; in these plants, production orders come from a central computer, not from the production area or line that uses the part. Other things to look for: visual and verbal communication among operators on the same line; inventory buildup at one work center indicating lack of coordination. (Questions 11 and 20.)

5   **Use of space, movement of materials, and product line flow.**   Good indicators of efficient space utilization are minimum material movement over short distances, use of

Service

Goodson reports that based upon tours of 150 companies, the typical scores for the sum of the ratings of the 11 categories, 11 points possible for each category, range between 30 and 90, with an average of 55. Categories 4, 5, and 6 (scheduling, space and materials flow, and inventory) in the rating sheet consistently receive the lowest ratings. The reason for this, according to Goodson, is that few plants have an obvious strategy for how they move materials, resulting in inefficient use of space and equipment. One of the major strengths of the RPA method is that it tends to give very consistent results among raters, since it is very hard to "fake leanness." As Goodson says, "if an operation looks good to a trained eye, it usually is."

Complete service facility audits are also a major undertaking, but they differ from manufacturing audits in that, when properly done, they focus on the customer's experience as much as on the utilization of resources. Typical questions in a service audit address time to get service, the cleanliness of the facility, staff sizing, and customer satisfaction. A service facility tour or walk-through can often be done as a mystery shopper, where the consultant actually partakes of the service and records his or her experiences. (In consulting with the Peninsula Hotel in Beverly Hills 90210, one of the authors went through the grueling ordeal of staying the night in a $2,500-per-night villa and reporting to management on the quality of the experience.)

Work Sampling   Work sampling entails random sampling observations of work activities, designed to give a statistically valid picture of how time is spent by a worker or the

---

efficient containers; materials stored at the point of use, not in separate inventory storage areas; tooling kept near the machines; and product flow layout rather than process layout. (Questions 7, 12, 13, and 20.)

6. **Levels of inventory and work in process.** Counting the number of items coming off a line provides a quick gauge of how much inventory is required. If a line produces 60 units an hour, then an inventory of two or three times that amount sitting by the machine is a sign of scheduling problems. (Questions 7, 11, and 20.)

7. **Teamwork and motivation.** Discussions with workers and visible indicators of teamwork such as names of teams over a work area and productivity award banners are quick ways of determining how the workforce feels about their jobs, the company, and their co-workers. (Questions 6, 9, 14, 15, and 20.)

8. **Condition and maintenance of equipment and tools.** Purchase dates and equipment costs should be stenciled on the side of machinery, and maintenance records should be posted nearby. Asking people on the factory floor how things are working and whether they are involved in purchasing tools and equipment is also indicative of the extent to which workers are encouraged to address these issues. (Questions 16 and 20.)

9. **Management of complexity and variability.** This depends greatly on the type of industry. Obviously, industries with narrow product lines have less difficulty handling complexity and variability. Indicators to watch

for in general are the number of people manually recording data and the number of keyboards available for data entry. (Questions 8, 17, and 20.)

10. **Supply chain integration.** It is generally desirable to work closely with a relatively small number of dedicated and supportive suppliers. A rough estimate of the number of suppliers can be ascertained by looking at container labels to see what supplier names appear on containers. Containers that appear to be designed and labeled specifically for customized parts shipped to a plant indicate the extent to which a strong supplier partnership exists. A sign of poor supply chain integration is lots of paperwork on the receiving dock. This indicates lack of a smooth pull system where plants pull the materials from their suppliers as if it was just another link in the pull system for each product line. (Questions 18 and 20.)

11. **Commitment to quality.** Attention to quality is evidenced in many ways, including posting of quality awards, quality scorecards, and quality goal statements. One that we found to be particularly interesting was a door panel hung on a wall at the Toyota plant in Paramount, California, which had a large circle painted around a nonexistent scratch with the inscription: "An acceptable paint scratch." Asking what people do with scrap also sheds light on quality practices. Quality is reflected in many of the other plant activities such as product development and start-ups. (Questions 15, 17, 19, and 20.)

FORD MOTOR COMPANY'S COMMITMENT TO EMPLOYEE INVOLVEMENT HAS IMPROVED COMPANY COMPETITIVENESS. TRAINING PROGRAMS, SUCH AS CERTIFICATION TRAINING FOR QUALITY, HAVE IMPROVED OVERALL AWARENESS AND PRODUCT RELIABILITY.

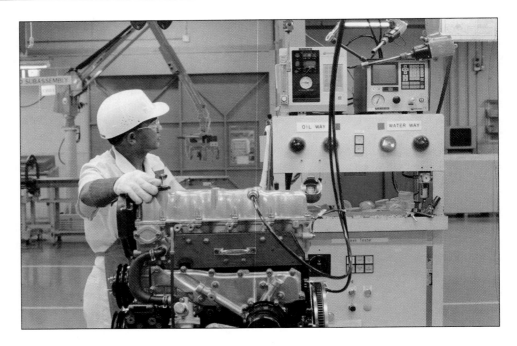

utilization of equipment. Diary studies are another way to collect activity data. These are used by consultants to get an understanding of very specific tasks being performed by the workforce. In these, the employee simply writes down the activities he or she performs during the week as they occur. This avoids the problem of having analysts look over a worker's shoulder to gather data. Examples of where these studies are used include library front desks, nursing, and knowledge work.

Service

Flowcharts   Flowcharts can be used in both manufacturing and services to track materials, information, and people flows. Workflow software, such as Optima! and BPR Capture, are widely used for process analysis. In addition to providing capabilities for defining a process, most workflow software provides four other basic functions: work assignment and routing, scheduling, work list management, and automatic status and process metrics. Flowcharts used in services—service blueprints—are basically the same thing, but add the important distinction of the line of visibility to clearly differentiate activities that take place with the customer versus those that are behind the scenes. In our opinion, the service blueprint is not used to its full potential by consulting firms, perhaps because relatively few consultants are exposed to them in their training.

Organization Charts   Organization charts are often subject to change, so care must be taken to see who really reports to whom. Some companies are loath to share organization charts externally. Several years ago a senior manager from a large electronics firm told us that a detailed organization chart gives free information to the competition.

DATA ANALYSIS AND SOLUTION DEVELOPMENT

Interactive Operations Management

Problem Analysis (SPC Tools)   Pareto analysis, fishbone diagrams, run charts, scatter diagrams, and control charts are fundamental tools in virtually every continuous improvement project. *Pareto analysis* is applied to inventory management under the heading of ABC analysis. Such ABC analysis is still the standard starting point of production control consultants when examining inventory management problems. *Fishbone diagrams* (or cause-and-effect diagrams) are a great way to organize one's first cut at a consulting problem (and they make a great impression when used to analyze, for example, a case study as part of the employment selection process for a consulting firm). *Run charts, scatter diagrams,* and *control charts* are tools that one is simply expected to know when doing operations consulting.

Bottleneck Analysis   Resource bottlenecks appear in most OM consulting projects. In such cases the consultant has to specify how available capacity is related to required capacity for some product or service in order to identify and eliminate the bottleneck. This isn't always evident, and abstracting the relationships calls for the same kind of logical analysis used in the classic "word problems" you loved in high school algebra.

Computer Simulation   Computer simulation analysis has become a very common tool in OM consulting. The most common general-purpose simulation packages are Extend and Crystal Ball. SimFactory and ProModel (for manufacturing systems), MedModel (hospital simulation), and Service Model are examples of specialized packages. For smaller and less complex simulation, consultants often use Excel. Technical Note 17 introduces the topic of simulation in this book.

A growing interest in simulation is in the analysis of "system dynamics." System dynamics is a language that helps us see the patterns that underlie complex situations. These complex situations are modeled using causal loop diagrams that are useful when factors either enhance or degrade system performance. Causal loops are of two types: reinforcing loops and balancing loops. *Reinforcing loops* are positive feedback loops driving positive values in criteria important to the system. *Balancing loops* reflect the mechanisms that counter reinforcing loops, thereby driving the system toward equilibrium. By way of example, with reference to Exhibit 9.8, suppose you have a quality goal that is reflected in a quality standard. The reinforcing loop (R) indicates that the standard, if left unmodified, would yield an ever-increasing (or decreasing) level of actual quality. In reality, what happens is that the balancing loop (B) comes into play. Effective time required to meet the standard determines time pressure (on the workers), which, in turn, modifies the actual quality achieved and ultimately achievement of the quality standard itself. An obvious use of the system shown here would be to hypothesize the consequences of raising the quality goal, or raising or lowering the values of the other variables in the system. In addition to its use in problem analysis, causal loop analysis simulations are often used by consultants to help client companies become more effective learning organizations.[6]

For more information about system dynamics and causal loop analysis, take a look at Appendix A, "Systems Thinking," included at the end of this chapter.

Statistical Tools   *Correlation analysis* and *regression analysis* are expected skills for consulting in OM. The good news is that these types of analyses are easily performed with spreadsheets. *Hypothesis testing* is mentioned frequently in the consulting firm methodology manuals, and one should certainly be able to perform Chi-square and *t*-tests in analyzing data. Two other widely used tools that use statistical analysis are *queuing theory* and *forecasting*. Consultants frequently use queuing theory to investigate how many service channels are needed to handle customers in person or on the phone. Forecasting problems likewise arise continually in OM consulting (such as forecasting the incoming calls to a call center).

Causal Loop Analysis   **exhibit 9.8**

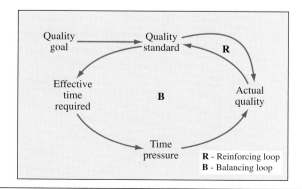

R - Reinforcing loop
B - Balancing loop

A newly emerging tool (not shown on our exhibit) is *data envelopment analysis.* DEA is a linear programming technique used to measure the relative performance of branches of multi-site service organizations such as banks, franchise outlets, and public agencies. A DEA model compares each branch with all other branches and computes an efficiency rating based on the ratio of resource inputs to product or service outputs. The key feature of the approach is that it permits using multiple inputs such as materials and labor hours, and multiple outputs such as products sold and repeat customers, to get an efficiency ratio. This feature provides a more comprehensive and reliable measure of efficiency than a set of operating ratios or profit measures.[7]

COST IMPACT AND PAYOFF ANALYSIS

Decision Trees   Decision trees represent a fundamental tool from the broad area of risk analysis. They are widely used in examining plant and equipment investments and R&D projects. Decision trees are built into various software packages such as @ Risk (*Risk Analysis for Spreadsheets,* Palisade Publications, 2000), which in addition to tree-type analysis has simulation capability.

Stakeholder Analysis   Most consulting projects impact in some way each of five types of stakeholders: customers, stockholders, employees, suppliers, and the community. The importance of considering the interest of all stakeholders is reflected in the mission statements of virtually all major corporations and, as such, provides guidance for consultants in formulating their recommendations.

Balanced Scorecard   In an attempt to reflect the particular needs of each stakeholder group in a performance measurement system, accountants have developed what is termed a *balanced scorecard.* (Balance refers to the fact that the scorecard looks at more than just the bottom line or one or two other performance measures.) Atkinson et al. note how the Bank of Montreal has used the balanced scorecard notion in setting specific goals and measures for customer service, employee relations, return to owners, and community relations. A key feature of the system is that it is tailored to what senior management and branch-level management can control.[8]

Process Dashboards   In contrast to the balanced scorecard, which focuses on organizationwide performance data, process dashboards are designed to provide summary performance updates for specific processes. Dashboards consist of a selection of performance metrics presented in graphical form with color-coding of trend lines, alarms in the form of exclamation marks, and so forth, to show when key indicators are nearing a problem level. For example, three different dials on a dashboard for suppliers are shown in Exhibit 9.9.

IMPLEMENTATION

Responsibility Charts   A responsibility chart is used in planning the task responsibilities for a project. It usually takes the form of a matrix with tasks listed across the top and project team members down the side. The goal is to make sure that a checkmark exists in each cell to assure that a person is assigned to each task.

exhibit 9.9   Dashboard for Suppliers

Project Management Techniques   Consulting firms use the project management techniques of CPM/PERT and Gantt charts to plan and monitor the entire portfolio of consulting engagements of the firm, as well as individual consulting projects. Microsoft Project and Primavera Project Planner are examples of commonly used software to automate such tools. Evolve Software has developed a software suite for professional service firms, modeled on ERP for manufacturing, that allows management to integrate opportunity management (the selling process), resource management, and delivery management. It should be emphasized that these planning tools are very much secondary to the people management skills needed to successfully execute a consulting project. This admonition is likewise true for all of the tools we have discussed in this section.

BUSINESS PROCESS REENGINEERING (BPR)

⦾⦾⦾⦾   Michael Hammer, the management expert who initiated the reengineering movement, defines **reengineering** as "the fundamental rethinking and radical redesign of business processes to achieve dramatic improvements in critical, contemporary measures of performance, such as cost, quality, service, and speed."[9] It uses many of the tools just discussed to achieve these goals.

Reengineering

The concept of reengineering has been around for nearly two decades and was implemented in a piecemeal fashion in organizations. Production organizations have been in the vanguard without knowing it. They have undertaken reengineering by implementing concurrent engineering, lean production, cellular manufacturing, group technology, and pull-type production systems. These represent fundamental rethinking of the manufacturing process.

Reengineering is often compared to total quality management (TQM), a topic covered in Chapter 8. Some people have said that the two are, in fact, the same, while others have even argued that they are incompatible. Michael Hammer says that the two concepts are compatible and actually complement one another. Both concepts are centered on a customer focus. The concepts of teamwork, worker participation and empowerment, cross-functionality, process analysis and measurement, supplier involvement, and benchmarking are significant contributions from quality management. In addition, the need for a "total" view of the organization has been reemphasized by quality management in an era of extensive functionalization of business. Quality management has also influenced company culture and values by exposing organizations to the need for change. The basic difference between the two is that quality management has emphasized continuous and incremental improvement of processes that are in control, whereas reengineering is about radical, discontinuous change through process innovation. Thus, a given process is enhanced by TQM until its useful lifetime is over, at which point it is reengineered. Then enhancement is resumed and the entire cycle starts again. Hammer points out that this is not a once-in-a-lifetime endeavor. As business circumstances change in major ways, so must process designs.

PRINCIPLES OF REENGINEERING

⦾⦾⦾⦾   Reengineering is about achieving a significant improvement in processes so that contemporary customer requirements of quality, speed, innovation, customization, and service are met. Hammer has proposed seven principles or rules for reengineering and integration.[10]

Rule 1. Organize around Outcomes, Not Tasks   Several specialized tasks previously performed by different people should be combined into a single job. This could be performed by an individual "case worker" or by a "case team." The new job created should involve all the steps in a process that creates a well-defined outcome. Organizing around outcomes eliminates the need for handoffs, resulting in greater speed, productivity, and customer responsiveness. It also provides a single knowledgeable point of contact for the customer.

Cross Functional

Rule 2. Have Those Who Use the Output of the Process Perform the Process   In other words, work should be carried out where it makes the most sense to do it. This results in people closest to the process actually performing the work, which shifts work across traditional intra- and interorganizational boundaries. For instance, employees can make some of their own purchases without going through purchasing, customers can perform simple repairs themselves, and suppliers can be asked to manage parts inventory. Relocating work in this fashion eliminates the need to coordinate the performers and users of a process.

Rule 3. Merge Information-Processing Work into the Real Work That Produces the Information   This means that people who collect information should also be responsible for processing it. It minimizes the need for another group to reconcile and process that information, and greatly reduces errors by cutting the number of external contact points for a process. A typical accounts payable department that reconciles purchase orders, receiving notices, and supplier invoices is a case in point. By eliminating the need for invoices by processing orders and receiving information online, much of the work done in the traditional accounts payable function becomes unnecessary.

Rule 4. Treat Geographically Dispersed Resources as Though They Were Centralized   Information technology now makes the concept of hybrid centralized/decentralized operations a reality. It facilitates the parallel processing of work by separate organizational units that perform the same job, while improving the company's overall control. For instance, centralized databases and telecommunication networks now allow companies to link with separate units or individual field personnel, providing them with economies of scale while maintaining their individual flexibility and responsiveness to customers.

Rule 5. Link Parallel Activities Instead of Integrating Their Results   The concept of integrating only the outcomes of parallel activities that must eventually come together is the primary cause for rework, high costs, and delays in the final outcome of the overall process. Such parallel activities should be linked continually and coordinated during the process.

TEXAS INSTRUMENTS REENGINEERING STAFF, THE STRATEGIC SERVICES GROUP, HAS ONGOING PROJECTS IN HUMAN RESOURCES, SUPPLY CHAIN IMPROVEMENT, PRODUCT AND STRATEGY DESIGN. MEMBERS OF THE GROUP ACT AS BUSINESS ADVOCATES TO LOOK FOR PROCESS IMPROVEMENT OPPORTUNITIES.

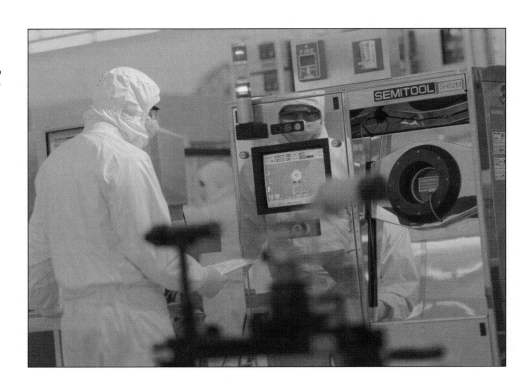

Rule 6. Put the Decision Point Where the Work Is Performed, and Build Control into the Process   Decision making should be made part of the work performed. This is possible today with a more educated and knowledgeable workforce plus decision-aiding technology. Controls are now made part of the process. The vertical compression that results produces flatter, more responsive organizations.

Rule 7. Capture Information Once—at the Source   Information should be collected and captured in the company's online information system only once—at the source where it was created. This approach avoids erroneous data entries and costly reentries.

GUIDELINES FOR IMPLEMENTATION

The principles of business process reengineering just enumerated are based on a common platform of the innovative use of information technology. But creating a new process and sustaining the improvement requires more than a creative application of information technology. A recent study of reengineering applications in 765 hospitals[11] yielded the following three managerial guidelines that apply to almost every organization contemplating reengineering:

1. **Codification of reengineering.**   Organizationwide change programs such as reengineering are complex processes whose implementation may be separated by space and time. Middle managers are often left to implement significant portions of reengineering proposals. Codifying provides guidance and direction for consistent, efficient implementation.

2. **Clear goals and consistent feedback.**   Goals and expectations must be clearly established, preapplication baseline data gathered, and the results monitored and fed back to employees. Without clear feedback, employees often became dissatisfied, and their perceptions of reengineering success can be quite different from actual outcomes. For example, the hospital researchers found that at 10 hospitals they studied in depth, most employees in four of them felt that the reengineering program had done little to change costs, even though their costs had actually dropped 2 to 12 percent relative to their competitors'. On the other hand, four hospitals in which most felt that reengineering had lowered costs actually experienced an increase in relative costs and a deterioration of their cost position.

3. **High executive involvement in clinical changes.**   A high level of involvement by the chief executive officer in major process changes (clinical changes in hospitals) improves reengineering outcomes. Bogue et al. found that CEOs in unsuccessful applications tended to be more involved in reductions of managers and employees and less engaged in activities surrounding clinical changes.

CONCLUSION

Consulting opportunities abound for individuals with OM skills. This is true not only for the major consulting firms but also for the smaller niche firms, particularly those with capabilities in supply chain management and Internet applications. The profitability to partners of a consulting firm depends on their being able to effectively leverage their time with that of their junior consultants. For beginning consultants the goal is to get involved in high-visibility projects where they can demonstrate their skills and increase their skill sets. Companies such as Accenture and McKinsey & Company have developed special approaches to consulting that are part art and part procedure. Much of the success of a consulting engagement depends on the people-handling skills of the consultants and their ability to make their work visible (see box "The Challenge and Reward of OM Consulting"). This is especially true for reengineering, where changing not just practices and procedures but also work cultures is often necessary if the reengineering is to succeed.

THE CHALLENGE AND REWARD OF OM CONSULTING

The scene: Arnold's Drive-In in *Happy Days:* Richie is being harassed by a bully, and he scurries over to the booth where Fonzie is sitting. Richie asks Fonzie for advice about what he should do.

The Fonze: Don't let him push you around! Act tough and he will back off.

Richie: (*swaggering back to the bully*) I'm warning you, I'm going to take you apart if you give me any more guff!

The Bully: Oh yeah. Put up your dukes, wise guy!

With this, Richie calls "time out" and goes back to Fonzie.

Richie: Fonzie, he isn't backing down! Now what?

Fonzie: Uh, Richie, one thing I forgot to tell you is that to get a reputation as a tough guy, sometime or other, you have to be seen actually hitting somebody!!! I suggest you run.

The moral is that for OM consulting, you actually have to make positive visible changes with a measurable impact on performance to be successful. More than any other type of consulting, OM consultants need to make recommendations that result in real improvements in the physical aspects of a manufacturing process or in the subjective experience of customers in services. This is the challenge and the reward of operations consulting.

SOURCE: R. B. CHASE AND K. R. KUMAR, "OPERATIONS CONSULTING," CHAPTER 7 IN L. GREINER AND F. POULFELT, *THE CONTEMPORARY CONSULTANT: INSIGHTS FROM WORLD EXPERTS* (CANADA: SOUTH-WESTERN, THOMSON, 2005).

KEY TERMS

Operations consulting Assisting clients in developing operations strategies and improving production processes.

"Finders" Partners or senior consultants whose primary function is sales and client relations.

"Minders" Managers of a consulting firm whose primary function is managing consulting projects.

"Grinders" Junior consultants whose primary function is to do the work.

Reengineering (or business process reengineering) The fundamental rethinking and radical redesign of business processes to achieve dramatic improvements in cost, quality, service, and speed.

REVIEW AND DISCUSSION QUESTIONS

Internet

1   Check the Web sites of the consulting companies listed in the chapter. Which ones impressed you most as a potential client and as a potential employee?
Boston Consulting Group (www.bcg.com)
Deloitte Touche Tohmatsu (www.deloitte.com)
McKinsey & Co. (www.McKinsey.com)

2   What does it take to be a good consultant? Is this the career for you?

3   Think about the registration process at your university. Develop a flowchart to understand it. How would you radically redesign this process?

4   Have you driven any car lately? Try not to think of the insurance claim settlement process while you drive! How would you reengineer your insurance company's claim process?

5   Identify the typical processes in manufacturing firms. Discuss how the new product development process interacts with the traditional functions in the firm.

6   In discussing characteristics of efficient plants, Goodson, developer of rapid plant assessments (see the Breakthrough Box), suggests that numerous forklifts are a sign of poor space utilization. What do you think is behind this observation?

PROBLEMS

1   You have been asked to bid on a consulting job to increase the profitability of a golf course company. It owns three courses in Cleveland, Ohio. Prepare a proposal to find out why other companies are more profitable and what to do about it.

2 Work with two other students to develop a two-page prospectus describing the particular features of an OM consulting practice you would start after graduation. (Hint: Identify a target market and unique skills your team possesses that fit that market.)

3 Sketch a typical materials procurement process that exists in functional organizations. Using reengineering principles, challenge the status quo and redesign this process.

4 An equipment manufacturer has the following steps in its order entry process:
   a. Take the order and fax it to order entry.
   b. Enter the order into the system (10 percent unclear or incorrect).
   c. Check stock availability (stock not available for 15 percent of orders).
   d. Check customer credit (10 percent of orders have credit questions).
   e. Send bill of materials to warehouse.

   The order receipt to warehouse cycle time is typically 48 hours; 80 percent of the orders are handled without error; and order handling costs are 6 percent of order revenue. Should you reengineer this process, or is continuous improvement the appropriate approach? If you choose to reengineer, how would you go about it?

5 Rapid plant assessment leanness exercise: Form a team of four to five people and take a 30-minute tour of a plant or service business. At the conclusion of the tour, rate the leanness of the operation using the RPA questionnaire given in the appendix to this chapter. (According to the questionnaire's developer, the average number of yeses for over 400 plant tours was seven, and the standard deviation was 2.) In class, discuss those areas where leanness is generally lacking across all companies visited.

6 Advanced analysis:
   a. Use the results from filling out the leanness questionnaire and your team's observations to develop a consensus score for each item in the RPA rating sheet. (There are many quantifiable factors by which to assess performance in the rating sheet's 11 categorises. They are presented on Goodson's Web site: www.bus.umich.edu/rpa.)
   b. Prioritize targets of opportunity for management.
   c. Develop a two-page action plan that you would present to management to help them make improvements.

C A S E : REENGINEERING AT SAMWON PRECISION MACHINES COMPANY*

INTRODUCTION

Mr. Yang Yong Sik, age 48, an executive director of Samwon Precision Company who has played an important role in the company's innovative growth, described how he saw the company situation in the business environment in which there are increasing cost and quality demands from buyers, both domestic and overseas. He argued that:

> I can see that Korean products are losing their competitive edge from everywhere, but why is this happening? . . . I have traveled to many countries in Southeast Asia and I see that our products are in good shape, in the matter of design and quality, but the problems lie in their cost. . . . Why is our cost higher compared to other countries?

He then explained:

> In the last few years, our labour and manufacturing overhead cost have been rising constantly, but we are not adding enough value to cope with this rising cost. . . . That is to say, in the past, we worked for 1,000 wons of wages and produced 1,100 wons of value, but we now get paid 3,000 wons but produce only 2,000 wons of value.

He further asked:

> What shall we do now? . . . We must reduce our costs by 2–3 percent a year, and produce more value than our costs. . . . In every part of our company, I can see so many areas of waste where we could be adding value. Our opportunity cost is much higher than before and we cannot afford to waste time and resources when we are working.

He continued:

> Now that I have explained this to my company, we have really seen what we can do, if we just realize what we are doing. . . . It is us who must realize what is in front of us.

According to Mr. Yang, it is going to be two or three years before the Korean economy is going to either prosper again or fall behind other rapidly rising countries. (Appendixes 1 and 2 illustrate some financial data that show the cost increases.)

BACKGROUND OF THE COMPANY

The Samwon Precision Machines Company was first established in 1974 producing springs for ballpoint pens, and expanded quietly until 1980. In 1975, the company started to develop auto parts and became a member of the Korea Auto Association. It joined the Korea Metal Industry Association in September 1976. In 1978, the company established a technical coalition with Murada Hatchizo Co. of Japan.

In 1980, Samwon was designated as an auto parts factory by the Korean Ministry of Commerce and Industry and, in 1983, was designated as a supplying company for the Ministry of National Defence. In 1986, Samwon was designated by the government as a promising small to medium company and, in 1987, became a member of the Korea Electronics Association. In 1990, just after Samwon was designated as an outstanding small to medium company, they established a new factory in Kyung Ki Do.

Figure 1   The Organizational Structure

The company now produces about 1,800 different kinds of springs and manufactures 100 million springs per month. From about 2,000 spring makers in Korea, Samwon became one of the largest suppliers after Daewon, which is now the largest company in the industry by size. The organizational structure is shown in Figure 1. However, for cold coil springs, Samwon was the largest in size and supplies various companies ranging from auto to ballpoint pen manufacturers.

Though there had been evidence of growth, it was in the 1980s that the company needed some changes to cope with the hostile business environment. The economic environment of that time was not very pleasant for managers of any industry in Korea. The executive director, Mr. Yang Yong Sik, worked with the owner, Mr. Mun Hak Moo, CEO, who is now 75 years old. Mr. Mun worked in the company from its beginnings as a line foreman. He learned his own managerial skills while managing the growing company with expanding managerial boundaries. It is interesting that Mr. Yang, while he was only a line foreman and never had regular school education beyond the six years of public school and a short term in a vocational institution, could manage to propel the reformation of the company. This is very unusual for Korean companies that traditionally have a top-down management structure.

FACTORS SETTING THE CONTEXT OF CHANGE
Due to the Korean government's growth-oriented policy of that era, Samwon had expanded rapidly to evolve as a well-balanced company, but problems arose as the company expanded. In the 1980s, just like other Korean companies, Samwon faced many problems such as rising wages and worker resistance while their customers' requests for lower costs was the strongest pressure on Samwon.

RECOGNITION OF THE NEED TO CHANGE AND CONTENT OF CHANGE
The hostile conditions of the 1980s were the driving force to adopt the 5S program. Samwon adopted 5S just before the crisis was felt at the company.

While Mr. Yang was a line foreman at Samwon, he visited Japan. During his visit, he figured that a crisis would soon come to the Korean industry and he wanted Samwon to be prepared. He met with the licensor of Samwon in Osaka and learned from the Japanese that productivity increases could only be achieved by

workers and at the place of production. He felt that his company had to change quickly to compete with the competitors in Japan. Hence, Mr. Yang's mission was to implement the 5S program in Samwon. He took a risk in that he received a six-month window of opportunity from Mr. Mun the CEO, and if the program did not succeed, he was to leave the company. "5S" is Japanese which stands for *seri* (determine which equipment is necessary and which is not), *seiton* (have the necessary equipment in reach and in the right place), *seiso* (clean), *seiketsu* (maintain the above 3S), and *sitsuke* (mental discipline and readiness).

PROCESS OF TRANSITION
After his return to Korea, Mr. Yang, with the owner Mr. Mun's permission, launched this 5S project in Samwon without knowing precisely what the consequences would be.

Implementation of the 5S Program   The adaptation of 5S was the hardest part for the company, just like any other innovation process, reflected in the old Korean aphorism "the start is when half of the work is done." The 5S program was first adopted in 1980 and failed in the first and second attempts because of the resistance of the workers and other managers; however, it finally came to fruition in 1988. When it was fully embraced by the workers, they took six months of pre-educational programs to establish the cultural background before actually adopting the fundamental principles of 5S. This was when Samwon's culture was formed, based on the following forces that drive the culture:

- "I am the owner of the company"; "Do it myself first."
- "I get what I earn."
- "I am evaluated by my work for the company, not by my school diploma."

Senior management were encouraged to take the initiative of setting an example to subordinates and were encouraged to arrive at work earlier than their subordinates. General managers would arrive at 6:30 A.M. 30 minutes earlier than regular workers, and chief executives would arrive at 6:00 A.M. No office meeting would occur during office hours; they would meet before the office hours that normally started at 8:00 A.M.

After Mr. Yang's venture turned out to be successful, Samwon became a lean company with employee support of the new company direction. It took eight years of downsizing to make the company slim and fit enough to cope with the environment. In fact,

Samwon was ahead of the downsizing trend that was carried out in Korea. Mr. Yang is proud of the fact that the 5S program was originally adopted from Japan and has been attempted by almost every Korean company, but no other company succeeded in setting up the system.

The core part of the change was the new culture of the workers where everyone believed that he/she was the owner of the company. This is shown in the company's payments, where every increased profit was reinvested or paid to the workers and even more importantly the company kept its word when implementing the project. In order for Samwon to prosper, the 5S program had to be successful. The success was due to many factors peculiar to small companies like Samwon (such as no shift in politics and no changes of CEO). The successful adaptation of 5S from their Japanese licensor company gave Samwon the structure for other campaigns to be successfully implemented.

The Initiation of the Program Cho Kwan Ri   Once management of the 5S was found to be mature and the results had become well established, Mr. Yang wanted to introduce the next action program to increase the productivity and sophistication of the company by utilizing the 5S foundation. Mr. Yang thought the market pressures on price and quality would increase at a greater rate than they could manage.

The next program was named "cho kwan ri" (CKR: *cho* stands for a second of time; *kwan ri* refers to management), a time-based management system. Unlike the Japanese 5S campaign, CKR was exclusively invented by Samwon. In the process of waste analysis, Mr. Yang wanted to investigate the amount of time wasted during work both on the factory floor and at office desks, and measure these in some monetary terms. In other words, establish how much money the company actually lost due to wasted time.

While Samwon successfully adopted the 5S program after eight years of difficult work, the environment around Samwon had also grown more adversarial than before. Their main problem was with manufacturing cost. Since the material cost was over 80 percent of the manufacturing cost, it was not easy for Samwon to reduce the manufacturing cost while the wages and other overheads increased due to social pressure. They needed something more than just 5S. As was the case with other Korean manufacturers, the material cost as a proportion of the total manufacturing cost actually surpassed the labour cost (which accounted for around 15 percent of total manufacturing cost) in competition with other foreign competing partners. This was in contrast to Korean managers' perceptions that the labour cost was actually the worst factor.

In establishing cho kwan ri, Mr. Yang thought that the 60-minute hour was not accurate enough to measure the wasted time. He took the "second" as the measuring scale to count the time as accurately as possible. Mr. Yang calculated the value of "each second" represented by workers and managers by dividing their average annual salaries by the total number of seconds for the actual annual working days. Hence, one second of floor workers' time and managers' time have a different worth.

Cho kwan ri calculated all work activity, including futile team meetings, chatting time, smoking, coffee breaks, etc., into monetary value in an attempt to publicly identify the wasted time in the company. Figure 2 shows the wage table. For example, if it took 10 seconds to make one spring, then, since it cost 2 wons per second for wages, it has cost 20 wons in wages. It would get more expensive when it is calculated for top managers. If it took 600 seconds to write a report by a manager and it cost 3 wons per second, then it would cost 1,800 wons in wages.[†]

Cho kwan ri initially looked like a way of squeezing time from the workers. On the other hand, it reflected what the workers wanted. The workers would get more days off than at other companies if the factory was run 359 days a year. The main purpose was to concentrate on working hours and use the saved time to good purpose regardless if it is for personal use or for the company. Samwon started cho kwan ri in 1990 and this time was easier than before, because the new company culture had already been established from the 5S program.

Once the cost measuring system was developed, everyone was equipped in calculating cost information on wasted time and its effect on productivity as well as the value creation by individual workers, departments, and the whole company. This enabled workers to manage their own ways of working in order to be as efficient as possible themselves, without any supervision or direction from the top. Many programs to get rid of wasted time have been automatically created by the employees for themselves. The employees suggested themselves that any business meeting should be called before the workday starts at 8:00 A.M. The company saw that meetings during the working day caused the most waste of working hours and they did not want the company operations being interrupted by workers being called away for the meetings.

As a result of CKR, employees have shifted team meetings to 7:00 A.M. to discuss and find problems that lie ahead. This was quickly supported by everyone. As a result, it encouraged an

Cho Kwan Ri

Figure 2

YOU CANNOT SAVE TIME; LET'S DO OUR BEST WHILE WE HAVE IT!		
	MANAGERS	WORKERS
1 second	3 wons	2 wons
1 minute	180 wons	120 wons
1 hour	10,800 wons	7,200 wons
8 hours	86,400 wons	57,600 wons
12 hours	129,600 wons	86,400 wons

efficient flow of communication and feedback improvements and the team leaders could then be well aware of what was going on in the company. The information flow between departments was sufficient to ensure that any team leader could answer simple phone calls or questions from external parties.

Some of the effects that cho kwan ri has achieved for the company are listed below:

1 **Wasted time reduction.** A new system for morning meetings usually commenced at 7:00 A.M. in order to reduce wasted time during the day. The best part of this was that all the participants were eager to have the meeting and it was very productive. A suggestion system in fact changed the way R & D efforts were conducted in such a way that workers on the floor supported the work of R & D members, resulting in teamwork between workers and R & D personnel. In an attempt to get rid of the waste, all workers were asked to develop or improve their work, which was very effective in process development. The machines were customized to the workers so that they could run the machines with the knowledge of the processes going on inside the machine. The workers saved a lot of time due to time-based management. They spent this time with the machines and suggested improvements every week. Every worker kept a self-management checksheet by seconds for a month and salaries were set based upon their performance, not by seniority.

According to Mr. Yang, most of the machines produced four times more springs than when they were imported from Japan and the U.S. Some machines that made long coil springs were redesigned to make short coil springs and replaced the imported machines so that they did not have to import those machines again. They also had a custom-made quality checking machine made by the manufacturing department, which would be very expensive if imported.

2 **Welfare was enhanced.**
   a. Pay was 30 percent more than any other company in Korea.
   b. Bonuses were up 6 times previous levels.
   c. The company paid all the employees' children's educational fees up to college level.
   d. The company supported overseas training.
   e. All the company-owned cars were air-conditioned for efficiency of the work force.
   f. The suggestion system worked without any intervention from upper management.

The CKR system was nationally acknowledged as "best practice" and was also recognized as a benchmark model for other companies. Samsung Group, the national representative business conglomerate, benchmarked Samwon to add the basics of the CKR program to its own operation. Samsung's early office hour system (7:00 A.M. to 4:00 P.M.) started in 1994 after Samwon's CKR system.

Boosting the Phase: Saryuk 0.01 Campaign As part of the company's "continuous improvement" program, Samwon then adopted the Saryuk 0.01 campaign after the CKR and 5S programs were successfully implemented. The reason for the Saryuk 0.01 campaign (*saryuk* means to make a desperate or frantic effort for the ultimate goal) was a goal-oriented campaign to improve by even 1 percent. Externally, it was the buyer companies' pressure on price reduction and adversarial economic conditions for small-sized supplying companies. In an effort to reduce cost, they focused on reducing the waste. The principle of cho kwan ri was to reduce waste that is invisible, whereas the principle of Saryuk 0.01 was to reduce waste that is visible. Mr. Yang wished to continue to seek out any waste in the company in order to meet the competitive situation. The Saryuk 0.01 program was introduced into the company in order to get rid of the visible waste in every aspect of the company's operations.

Samwon's motto was:

Saryuk for 0.01 of productivity improvement.

Saryuk for 0.01 of waste.

Saryuk for 0.01 of profit.

Its specific objective was to reach a total of two million wons of waste for the whole corporation. It was calculated that if each member of the company saves 10 thousand wons of waste this would result in 2 million wons of waste for the company. It is natural that this process would be impossible to implement if they did not have 5S and cho kwan ri in place beforehand. Mr. Yang insisted that "a company always has to prepare itself to be a wave rider instead of a victim of environmental change." Buyers always impose their own cost and quality pressures on their suppliers. For the last contract the major automakers wanted a 5 percent price cut while Samwon's profit rate was only about 4 percent. This meant that if Samwon was not prepared for the cost reduction pressures from buyers, there would not be any chance of surviving from such pressure.

Samwon targeted nine waste categories as follows:

1 **Waste from defects.** It is important to keep in mind that quality control is important for all, even in managerial work. In fact, defects in managerial work bring more damage to the company. To prevent these wastes, we must be accurate and sensitive in every operation.

2 **Waste from clumsy work.** We should know that no matter how precise the plan is, there is a chance that it cannot be completed at the right time. It is better to take time in this case, rather than poorly finishing the work.

3 **Waste from inventories.** Inventory is money, whether it is product or material. Any inventories over the minimum required level not only cause stagnation in cash flow, but also a waste in managing the inventories. This can be managed as part of a JIT [just-in-time] program.

4 **Waste of motions.** Every motion of the work can be a process of creating value. We have to keep in mind that we should watch every motion of our work and machines so that it can be improved and add more value.

5 **Waste of waiting.** For example, waiting for service in a bank is a waste of a lot of time. Every member of the company must be organized and information flow should be comprehensive so that we can reduce the waste of time in places such as the bank or taxation office.

6 **Waste of transporting.** Usage of mass transportation in the company and outside the company can reduce a large waste.

7 **Waste of process.** We should use suggestion systems so that any waste in the process can be found and the improved work situation should be communicated to all workers.

8 **Waste of industrial accident.** This brings most of the waste for the company and for the person, not to mention all of the pain that he or she will suffer. These kinds of accidents are almost always from carelessness of the workers (90 percent of the time). It is only ourselves who can prevent these kinds of wastes.

9 **Waste of managerial work.** This is invisible waste. The most important thing to reduce this kind of waste is to have good information flow in the company, both vertically and horizontally.

The company saved W 49,000,000 and W 59,896,719 for the 24 months from June 1993 when it started the Saryuk 0.01 campaign. There are weekly and monthly schedules in Samwon to reduce waste and keep up the above three campaigns. Mr. Yang asserted that the management systems operate not by order and supervision, issued every time something has to be done as is usually seen in other companies, but by the predesigned "time-work schedule." He says,

> We even care about the waste caused by making schedules about what we do today and this week and who should do this and that every time. . . . Instead, we tried to make ourselves used to the jobs done regularly by whom and by when.

The time-work schedule in Table 1 shows how each department is scheduled to do what at which day of the week and in which week. For instance, on Tuesday, everybody is supposed to carry out the 5S campaign tasks from 7:55 to 8:15 A.M. Specifically, in Week 1 of the month, office cleaning is the work to do. Everyone has to clean up the personal drawers, files, computers, etc., by 5S system rules. Each one has a designated area to clean if it is for a companywide cleaning.

Some of the Achievements of Saryuk 0.01 Campaign One of the striking examples of reducing waste was the way in which workers innovated the way of serving meals in the cafeteria. The workers used to be served their meals from a fixed menu and amount by cafeteria workers at the meal stands, which resulted in the workers throwing away any leftover food. That wasted food needed containers and the related activities to abandon the waste and caused workers to be involved in cleaning the containers. The workers' committee recommended a self-service system by which workers select the amount of food to as much as 80 percent that they need at the first trip to the serving stand. This system eventually eliminated 20 percent of cafeteria overhead costs by getting rid of wasted food, waste containers, and the cleaning work. The workers took seats from the first row of tables in arrival sequence so that unoccupied seats were not mixed up with the used dirty seats. They saved cleaning work of the dining room by 20 percent. Trash cans were sorted by items like bottles, metal cans, paper cups, and others. The workers reduced the number of dumping trash cans by crushing the metal cans and piling the paper cups in columns in order to save space in the trash cans. They decided not to put bottled drinks in the vending machines because the empty bottles need more storage room.

Another example was a reduction in the electricity bills by switching the lights in the restroom on and off as needed and indicating the occupancy by using O and X signs on the outside of the door. As such, the ideas were actually suggested by workers themselves. Each worker was committed to report 15 or more cases of removing waste per month. The company called the suggestions a "guaranteed cheque," meaning that the ideas make money by reducing waste. The suggestion system was successfully operated along with an incentive system. The suggesters were paid by a certain ratio of total income gained from the specific ideas plus a compensation reward in terms of promotion and wage increases based on the company evaluation scheme.

Mr. Yang wondered how the office staff determines their workload and identifies the waste in office work. He considered the production workers to be more effectively measurable than the office workers. He finally decided to utilize the CKR technique to analyze their work in seconds for each job for a period of one month. The monthly job analysis sheets gave them important information on which jobs were more important than others in terms of time requirement and then they could easily determine

The Pre-designed "Time-Work" Schedule

Table 1

WORKS	TIME	DAY	WEEK 1	WEEK 2	WEEK 3	WEEK 4
Presentation: Process, technology	7:55–8:15	Monday	Production I	Process	Marketing	Accounting
5S	7:55–8:15	Tuesday	Cleaning: Office	Cleaning: Factory	Cleaning: Factory	Cleaning: Total
Education, suggestions	7:55–8:15	Wednesday	Education: About the company	Education: Technology	Education: Production, quality	Education: Mental preparation
Organization development	7:55–8:15	Thursday	Related department	Related department	Related department	Related department
Team meeting	7:55–8:15	Friday	Inspection	Education	Inspection	Education
Meeting—Each department	7:55–8:15	Saturday	Meeting—each department		Meeting—each department	

Figure 3   Sand Cone of the Campaigns

how to improve the way of doing jobs and the kind of jobs that could be eliminated. This process provided the company with very reasonable ways of optimizing the manpower level in the office. As shown in Figure 3, the series of campaigns are depicted as a sand cone.

POLITICS OF CHANGE

When the 5S program was first adopted, it seemed that it would be successful. However, just when the work was showing a positive outcome, resistance came not from the workers but from the higher managers. They could not bear to see that this new approach, implemented by only a line foreman, was working out well. They refused to embrace 5S and naturally the workers refused also. Samwon showed its difference from other companies with the owner backing Mr. Yang and supporting him with the power to sack employees, even managers, if they were not embracing this new program. Ten percent of the employees were fired and many of them were managers rather than workers. Consequently, this had a downsizing effect and flattened the organizational structure making it simple, single-pathed, and cross-functional with a lot of power held by Mr. Yang. This was a totally new concept at that time in Korea, as traditionally, there were managers for each department and it became a multiple-path structure.

After eight years of the cultural change within the company, there was little, if any, functional politics during the development and implementation of cho kwan ri programs and the Saryuk 0.01 campaign.

OPERATIONS OF NEW PRACTICES

The series of campaigns eventually brought in a broad range of changes in the managerial system assisting to resolve the fundamental operational problems. The typical problems included layoff of people, which was inevitable after downsizing, capital investment that was required for replacing the old equipment and updating the technologies, and wage increases that surpassed productivity increases and the like.

Layoffs were not generally accepted by the public in Korea and were usually subject to very emotional resistance by the labour unions. Unless a natural decrease of manpower exists, the company should depend on some other way of utilizing the excess manpower realized by a reduction of unproductive work time. Samwon Precision Company expanded the plant capacity without extra capital investment by adding a third work shift to the existing two-shift

system. The plants were then operated on a 24-hour per day basis, absorbing the excess manpower available from the innovation campaigns. The company also extended the annual working days to as many as 359 days with only six days unutilized per year, which was significantly different from the average working days of 300 or less for other Korean companies. This system utilized the factory at the maximum capacity in such a way as to save extra capital investment otherwise required for increasing production capacity. This maximum machine utilization system, combined with automation of the production process, allowed the company to let their workers free from work for 94 days per capita per year. This holiday benefit was much longer than that of other average Korean companies while keeping the factories working for more days at three full shifts.

The company created its own working calendar with the workers scheduled into two groups, A and B. According to the calendar, employees in group A did not need to work on Sundays while the employees of group B did not work on Tuesdays. The company kept the production lines in full operation throughout the year without shutdowns. It reduced factory overhead by one-fourth and increased overall productivity to four times higher than other similar companies in Korea. This unique operational system coupled with the automation of the process resulted in a reduction of production cost by 30 percent and at the same time, wages increased by 20 percent over the 18 months since the Saryuk 0.01 program was launched. On top of that, the workers benefited by 900 percent of the annual flat bonus instead of 400 percent that used to be the amount a year ago.

The company accelerated the automation of production lines through the innovative activities of the machine workers and R & D staff. Many production processes were automated with the help of the innovative efforts through the Saryuk 0.01 waste banishment program. Nowadays a line consisting of 50 machines is operated by just one worker.

As an example of a typical success story, an automatic sorting machine was designed by Mr. Kim T. S., the operator who wanted to drive out the waste of man-hours required in sorting the oversized springs from the good ones. He spent about one and a half months in developing an electrical sensor to sort the over-sized springs. Mr. Kim won a grade A reward of W 500,000 as one of the "innovative performances of the month," which was an incentive system to encourage the line workers to improve the automation level.

Another was Mr. Lee S. C., who wondered if he could reduce the man-hours to pack the products. He tried to automate the process, by reducing the need for manual packing. He eventually automated the whole process by which the company saved 24 percent of the work time and cut inventory by 20 percent. In the process, 50 machines in that particular line were managed only by one worker. Another example was the simple adjustment of the machine rack that resulted in import substitution of Japanese machines. Mr. Cho C. R. developed it in three weeks and he was subsequently awarded a W 1,500,000 reward.

The main characteristic of these successes was that the R & D activities were cross-functional among the development engineers and line workers who work 24 hours a day on a three-shift system, providing prompt reaction to the floor problems and new product development.

The company motivated its employees to participate in the programs by reinforcing their trust in the company policy. The policy was to reinvest the profits back into the company operations, and for employees' welfare so that the employees were confident that they worked on behalf of themselves, and believed that they could manage their wage increases, not by the CEO. It was not surprising that there was no labour union. The line managers rotated as superintendent every month, so that every line manager and worker had to know about the problems and issues faced in the factories. The company kept its organization exceptionally flat, flexible, and cross-functional so that communication barriers were removed. Training was also considered an important communication device to share the vision, value of the operation, technique, and skill. Management submitted the model to the subordinates and encouraged them to accept the idea "to work for themselves."

CONCLUSION

This case sheds light on a general proposition that the sustained innovation of a company can only be realized if top management is committed to the vision that everyone in the company shares and is involved in the process of improvement. Mr. Mun, the owner, became a winner of the game by implementing this proposition. He believed in the process by empowering his employees, especially Mr. Yang, initially only a line foreman.

The point of the proposition is to run a company to achieve aggregate effectiveness of the total organization. It encourages the company to integrate all levels of the organization and all functional areas of the company. Motivation, communication, and empowerment are critical foundations for total innovation of the

APPENDIX 1

APPENDIX 2

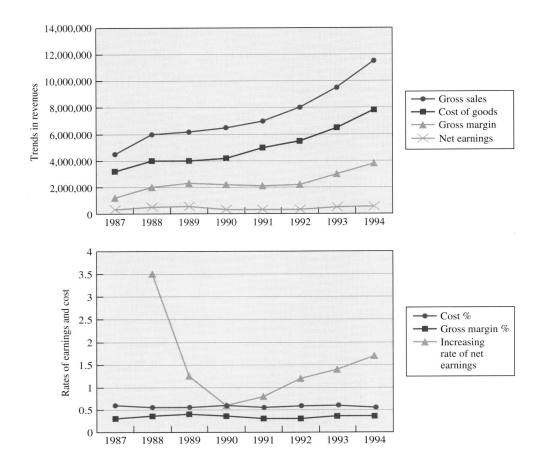

company. This means that production and the process technologies are considered as only part of the total management process. The overall measure of innovation is the aggregate effectiveness of the whole company operation, not the simple sum of the efficiencies of each operation of the individual functions such as production lines, marketing, finance, the information network, etc.

Another point is that the managerial system needs to have a specific prescription rather than a panacea for all companies. This case demonstrates that the Samwon Precision Company discovered their own innovation process and system. Education and training were considered as most important tools for the company in order to keep everyone informed of what their vision and targets were, and also to provide them with updated skills and ideas. The Samwon Precision Company showed how an organization should be oriented for the future, and why the organization should be flexible and motivated to continually improve.

*THIS CASE WAS DEVELOPED FOR USE IN CLASSROOM DISCUSSION AND IS NOT INTENDED TO NECESSARILY ILLUSTRATE APPROPRIATE OR INAPPROPRIATE MANAGEMENT PRACTICES. CASE AUTHOR: KEE YOUNG KIM, YONSEI UNIVERSITY, 1996. SIMON POON, A DOCTORAL STUDENT IN THE GRADUATE SCHOOL OF MANAGEMENT AT MACQUARIE UNIVERSITY, WAS THE RESEARCH ASSOCIATE WHO REWROTE THE CASE IN 2000. THE FUNDING FOR THIS CASE PRODUCTION WAS PROVIDED BY THE AUSTRALIAN FEDERAL GOVERNMENT'S DEPARTMENT OF INDUSTRY, SCIENCE AND RESOURCES.

†THE AVERAGE WORKING YEAR WAS ASSUMED TO BE 250 DAYS, I.E., 7,200,000 SECONDS. IF WORKERS WERE PAID 14 MILLION WON PER YEAR, THEN IT WOULD COST 2 WONS PER SECOND AND IF MANAGERS WERE PAID 20 MILLION WON PER YEAR, THEN IT WOULD COST 3 WONS PER SECOND.

SELECTED BIBLIOGRAPHY

Bogue, E. M.; M. J. Schwartz; and S. L. Watson. "The Effects of Reengineering: Fad or Competitive Factor?" *Journal of Healthcare Management* 44, no. 6 (November–December 1999), pp. 456–76.

Davenport, T. H. *Process Innovation: Reengineering Work through Information Technology.* Boston: Harvard Business School Press, 1993.

George, M. L. *Lean Six Sigma: Combining Six Sigma Quality with Lean Speed.* New York: McGraw-Hill, 2002.

Goodson, R. E. "Read a Plant—Fast." *Harvard Business Review* 80, no. 5 (May 2002), pp. 105–13.

Greiner, L., and F. Poulfelt. *The Contemporary Consultant: Insights from World Experts.* Canada: South-Western, Thomson, 2005.

Greiner, L., and R. Savich. *Consulting to Management.* New York: Prentice Hall, 1998.

Hammer, M. "Reengineering Work: Don't Automate, Obliterate." *Harvard Business Review* 90, no. 4 (July–August 1990), pp. 104–12.

Hammer, M., and J. Champy. *Reengineering the Corporation: A Manifesto for Business Revolution.* New York: Harper Business, 1993.

Hammer, M., and S. Stanton. "How Process Enterprises Really Work." *Harvard Business Review* 99, no. 6 (November–December 1999), pp. 108–18.

Maister, D. H. *Managing the Professional Service Firm.* New York: The Free Press, 1993.

Mango, P. D., and L. A. Shapiro. "Hospitals Get Serious about Operations." *The McKinsey Quarterly,* no. 2 (2001), pp. 74–85.

Rasiel, E. M. *The McKinsey Way: Using the Techniques of the World's Top Strategic Consultants to Help You and Your Business.* New York: McGraw-Hill, 1998.

Rohleder, T. R., and E. A. Silver. "A Tutorial on Business Process Improvement." *Journal of Operations Management* 15, no. 2 (May 1997), pp. 139–54.

Upton, D., and S. Macadam. "Why (and How) to Take a Plant Tour." *Harvard Business Review,* May–June 1997, pp. 97–106.

FOOTNOTES

1   M. Treacy and F. Wiersema, *The Discipline of Market Leaders* (Reading, MA: Addison-Wesley, 1997).

2   D. J. Collis, "The Management Consulting Industry," *Internet Class Notes,* Harvard Business School, 1996.

3   D. H. Maister, "Balancing the Professional Service Firm," *Sloan Management Review* 24, no. 1 (Fall 1982), pp. 15–29.

4   E. M. Rasiel, *The McKinsey Way: Using the Techniques of the World's Top Strategic Consultants to Help You and Your Business* (New York: McGraw-Hill, 1998).

5   R. E. Goodson, "Read a Plant—Fast," *Harvard Business Review* 80, no. 5 (May 2002), pp. 105–13.

6   See J. D. Sterman, "System Dynamics Modeling: Tools for Learning in a Complex World," *California Management Review* 43, no. 4 (Summer 2002), pp. 8–26.

7   J. Fitzsimmons and M. Fitzsimmons, *Service Management, Operations, Strategy, and Information Technology,* 2nd ed. (New York: Irwin/McGraw-Hill, 1998), p. 74.

8   A. Atkinson, R. Banker, R. Kaplan, and M. Young, *Management Accounting* (Englewood Cliffs, NJ: Prentice Hall, 1995), p. 446.

9   M. Hammer and J. Champy, *Reengineering the Corporation: A Manifesto for Business Revolution* (New York: Harper Business, 1993), p. 30.

10 M. Hammer, "Reengineering Work: Don't Automate, Obliterate," *Harvard Business Review* 90, no. 4 (July–August 1990), pp. 104–12.

11 E. M. Bogue, M. J. Schwartz, and S. L. Watson, "The Effects of Reengineering: Fad or Competitive Factor?" *Journal of Healthcare Management* 44, no. 6 (November–December 1999), pp. 456–76.

APPENDIX A: SYSTEMS THINKING[1]

Key issues in operations management such as mass customization, global supply chains, achievement of a service factory to deliver personalized services, and integration of Internet and wireless technologies into operations all conspire to increase the complexity of operations. Complexity, however, is of two types: detailed complexity (dealing with many variables) and dynamic complexity (seeing patterns and relationships over time). Nearly all of the methods and tools of operations management (with the exception of some simulation approaches) have been developed to address detailed complexity and provide little assistance to deal with dynamic complexity. Dynamic complexity arises when cause and effect are distant in time and location and when many consequences of actions are subtle, especially over longer time horizons, and unintended. Peter Senge, a leading systems thinking expert, emphasizes that "the real leverage in most management situations lies in understanding dynamic complexity, not detailed complexity."[2] Along similar lines, Russell Ackoff, the management guru, also reminds us that the job of management today is one of managing interactions.

Systems thinking provides us with a language to understand, analyze, and communicate situations that involve dynamic complexity. It is considered to be one of the core disciplines (see *The Fifth Discipline* by Peter Senge) on which learning organizations are built. A *system* is typically defined as a collection of parts that interact with each other to function as a whole. It is derived from the Greek verb *sunistanai,* which means "to cause to stand together." The field consists of a diverse set of theories and methods such as cybernetics, sociotechnical systems, and chaos theory. System dynamics (usually misspelt as *systems dynamics*) is one such methodology in systems thinking formulated by Jay Forrester at the Massachusetts Institute of Technology in the 1960s. It has since become a valuable language to address organizational issues and will be the focus of this section.

CAUSAL LOOP DIAGRAMMING

System dynamics is a language that helps us see the patterns underlying complex situations. But our perceptions are limited by spoken languages such as English that have a subject-verb-object linear structure. So we tend to think of cause and effect as being linear. However, cause and effect are circular in nature, with effects being causes of the next interaction, and all causes eventually being effects. Such relationships can be better understood using the tool called *causal loop diagramming.* Feedback loops form the basis of such diagrams. There are two types of feedback loops: positive and negative feedback loops. For instance, greater sales efforts lead to a larger number of customers, and a larger customer base spurs on further sales efforts (positive feedback loop), but a large number of customers eventually result in poor quality service, which then results in fewer customers (negative feedback loop). The former is also called a *reinforcing loop* (R) and the latter a *balancing loop* (B). Taken together, they give a picture of the behavior of customer populations over time (Exhibit 9A.1). The plus (+) sign on the arrows in the diagram indicates that the two related variables move in the same direction, and a minus (−) indicates that the two related variables move in opposite directions. One other important characteristic of feedback loops is usually overlooked. That is the concept of a *delay.* In many complex systems, the effect of an action is sometimes delayed in time. Here, service quality deteriorates with the increasing number of customers, but the effects are not felt immediately.

The causal loop diagram is further illustrated in Exhibit 9A.2 with some typical dynamics seen in operational settings and includes the following loops:

- The productivity loop is a balancing loop in which the greater the pending work, the more overtime is needed to complete it in a timely fashion, the higher the completion rate, and so the lower the pending work. This in turn requires less overtime, a lower completion rate, so higher pending work. This oscillation is a main characteristic of the balancing loop.
- The burnout loop is a reinforcing loop in which higher overtime, over time (delay), results in burnout, which in turn affects completion rate.
- The cost-of-poor-quality loop is also a reinforcing loop in which higher pending work reduces time per task, which in turn leads to increased error rates. Completion rates ultimately reduce putting further pressure on reducing time per task.

---

exhibit 9A.1   Reinforcing and Balancing Loops

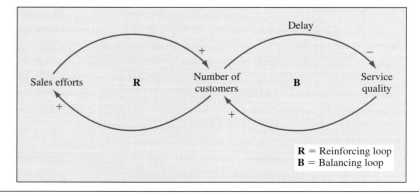

R = Reinforcing loop
B = Balancing loop

Causal Loop Diagram of Typical Operational Dynamics

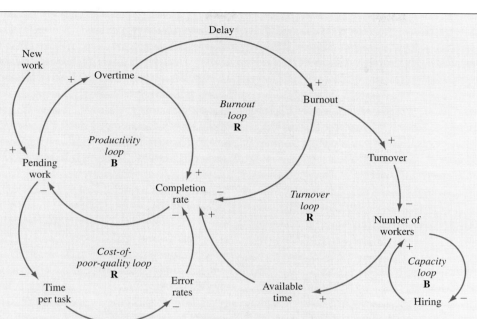

- The turnover loop is a reinforcing loop in which burnout leads to turnover, which reduces the number of workers, which reduces available time and then reduces completion rate, which eventually contributes to further burnout.
- Finally there is the capacity loop, which is a balancing loop. Here, the reduced number of workers increases hiring, which increases the number of workers, which then reduces hiring.

ARCHETYPES

"If reinforcing and balancing feedback (loops) and delays are like the nouns and verbs of systems thinking, then the systems archetypes are analogous to basic sentences or simple stories that get retold again and again."[3] Archetypes are the patterns that repeat themselves in various situations in entirely different industries. Recognizing them and their underlying structures helps in understanding the complex systems being evaluated. All archetypes are made up of feedback loops and delays. Some of the well-recognizable systems archetypes are discussed below (Exhibit 9A.3).

Limits-to-Growth or Limits-to-Success Archetype   Here continued efforts lead to improved performance or growth, but also lead to unintended secondary effects that cause the performance to eventually slow down or decline. Working long hours to meet a deadline will accomplish that objective but also would create fatigue, which is detrimental to the quality of work, negating what was achieved by the long hours to start with. One suggestion when faced with this archetype is to not push growth but to relieve the pressures being developed as a result of growth.

Shifting-the-Burden/Addiction Archetype   When the underlying problem is difficult to address, the problem is "solved" by symptomatic solutions. This may alleviate the symptoms, but the underlying problem goes unattended (and worse) until it cannot be solved. Further, the "shifting of the burden" degrades into an addictive pattern in which the side effects overwhelm the original problem. Cellular phone customers leave the company at the end of the contract period due to poor service; firms expend a lot of resources to gain

Systems Archetypes

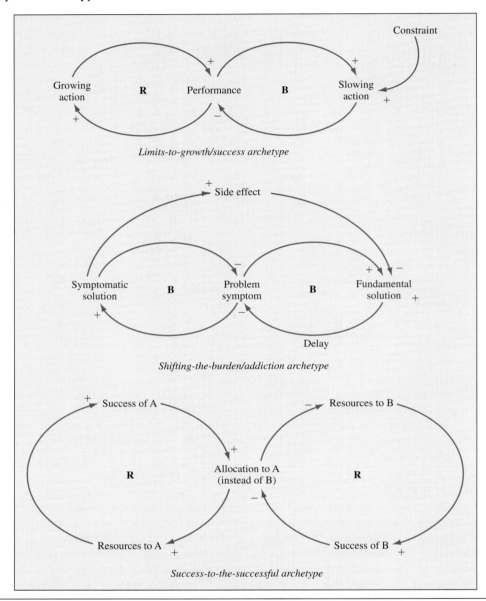

Limits-to-growth/success archetype

Shifting-the-burden/addiction archetype

Success-to-the-successful archetype

new customers instead of trying to retain existing customers. In that process, they provide new customers more incentives than they give their existing customers. This provides a symptomatic solution in that it increases the customer base, but it does not address the retention issue. In addition, it creates a side effect of unfairness that further alienates the current customers, affecting their retention. Exploring the problem from different perspectives could help avoid responding to the easily recognizable symptoms and facilitate defining the underlying issues.

Success-to-the-Successful Archetype   When one of two equally competent persons or groups gets a higher allocation of a common resource, that person or group has a greater chance of being successful. This in turn leads to the successful person or group being given more resources at the expense of the other person or group, thereby perpetuating the pattern of success. This is typically the resource allocation method used among competing groups in many product development or process redesign efforts. The less successful are starved of resources, ensuring their ultimate failure. The system has to be evaluated to see why the "winner takes all" and why the system is set up to create only one winner.

MODELING AND SIMULATION

The limitation of the popular and near-omnipresent spreadsheet is obvious as it would return a circular logic error in the case of feedback loops. Hence, a more appropriate set of tools is needed to articulate system dynamics models on computers. A more complex problem situation requires an appropriate level of complexity of the solution; a simple solution to a complex problem is usually the wrong one! Causal loop diagrams are implemented in software to facilitate computer modeling and simulation efforts through the use of stock-and-flow diagrams. Further, such diagrams help clearly represent the flow of entities (e.g., people, materials, money) in a system. Stocks are state variables or buffers, while flows are rates or throughput in any system. A simple causal stock-and-flow diagram describing the relationships among awareness of a product, the number of customers, and potential customers is constructed in an online tutorial at www.vensim.com/documentation/html/usr05.htm by Ventana Systems (see below).

There are three dominant software products for system dynamics simulation. Typically, such simulations are used to gain insights and evaluate different scenarios. Ventana Systems' (www.vensim.com) *Vensim* is capable of integrating both managerial and technical elements to solve difficult problems. It is used for constructing models of business, scientific, environmental, and social systems. These products have graphical user interfaces that facilitate model development as well as the building of simulators that managers can use in scenario gaming. *Vensim PLE* (Personal Learning Edition, www.vensim.com/venple.html) is a software tool that can be used initially to get started in system dynamics modeling and is free for educational use. The software *ithink,* from *isee systems* (www.iseesystems.com), is designed for managers and business consultants. Powersim Solutions (www.powersimsolutions.com) has an application platform called *ExPlan* to create risk-free simulation environments for strategic and scenario planning, decision support, and management training. A wide variety of organizations such as the U.S. Navy, the World Bank, Ford Motor Company, Nestlé, and Microsoft and industries such as pharmaceutical, petrochemical, government, manufacturing, and transportation use system dynamics simulation models. This highlights the universal nature of the underlying principles.

Interactive simulation games based on computer models that are developed using the tools are called management flight simulators (MFSs). They provide managers a safe environment to "fly" the firm or a specific policy decision, and reflect and learn in the process. We learn best through failure, but neither the dominant culture nor the way simulation is usually implemented allows us to learn this way. MFSs allow us in operations management to reclaim the essence of simulation—learning through failure in a safe environment! MIT's popular Peoples Express MSF and other newer MFSs such as those based on mobile phones and professional services are available at www.strategydynamics.com.

INDUSTRY EXAMPLES

Two industry examples, in manufacturing and services, are briefly discussed below to highlight the scope and commercial application of the system dynamics approach.

GM Strategic Initiatives (GMSI) staff at General Motors Corporation are responsible for analyzing major strategic initiatives for the company. GMSI often develops system dynamics models of the automotive industry or specific aspects of it in order to more accurately assess the likely impact of potential new strategies. Recent topics range from internal cost driver studies to projections about the hydrogen economy and the transition to fuel cell vehicles. They also developed an enterprise model to take a broad look at the corporation and its marketplace, combining internal activities such as engineering, manufacturing, and marketing with external factors such as competition in the new and used vehicle marketplaces. In addition, they developed models to look at the design of new vehicles and the constraints inherent in managing a portfolio of expensive, long-lead-time projects, and senior management adopted a key policy recommendation derived from the model.

OLM Consulting (www.OLMgroup.com) undertakes a wide range of system dynamics consulting in health and social care in the United Kingdom for local government. Typical issues include the extent of community services to manage chronic disease and avoid the need for hospitalization, the use of intermediate care to avoid unnecessary hospitalizations, minimization of the use of tertiary and out-of-area services, configuration of post-acute services to maximize the independence of patients, modeling of alternate forms of sustainable care, and workforce planning.

APPENDIX A REVIEW AND DISCUSSION QUESTIONS

1 Identify and discuss operational situations that exemplify any two systems thinking archetypes presented in this chapter.

2 Develop a causal loop diagram for the operational situation presented in the article "Calling JetBlue," by Chuck Salter, *Fast Company* 82 (May 2004). This article is available on-line in the *OM Articles* section of the *OM Center* at www.mhhe.com/omc/index.html

APPENDIX A BIBLIOGRAPHY

Ackoff, Russell L. *The Democratic Corporation.* New York: Oxford University Press, 1994.

Forrester, Jay. *Industrial Dynamics.* Waltham, MA: Pegasus Communications, 1961.

Senge, Peter M. *The Fifth Discipline: The Art and Practice of the Learning Organization.* New York: Currency Doubleday, 1990.

Sterman, John D. *Business Dynamics: Systems Thinking and Modeling for a Complex World.* New York: McGraw-Hill, 2000.

APPENDIX A FOOTNOTES

1 Contributed by Ravi S. Behara, Florida Atlantic University.

2 Peter M. Senge, *The Fifth Discipline: The Art and Practice of the Learning Organization* (New York: Currency Doubleday, 1990).

3 Ibid.

APPENDIX B: RPA QUESTIONNAIRE AND RATING SHEET

exhibit 9B.1   RPA Questionnaire

The total number of yeses on this questionnaire is an indicator of a plant's leanness: the more yeses, the leaner the plant. Each question should be answered yes only if the plant obviously adheres to the principle implied by the question. In case of doubt, answer no.

		YES	NO
1	Are visitors welcomed and given information about plant layout, workforce, customers, and products?	O	O
2	Are ratings for customer satisfaction and product quality displayed?	O	O
3	Is the facility safe, clean, orderly, and well lit? Is the air quality good, and are noise levels low?	O	O
4	Does a visual labeling system identify and locate inventory, tools, processes, and flow?	O	O
5	Does everything have its own place, and is everything stored in its place?	O	O
6	Are up-to-date operational goals and performance measures for those goals prominently posted?	O	O
7	Are production materials brought to and stored at line side rather than in separate inventory storage areas?	O	O
8	Are work instructions and product quality specifications visible at all work areas?	O	O
9	Are updated charts on productivity, quality, safety, and problem solving visible for all teams?	O	O
10	Can the current state of the operation be viewed from a central control room, on a status board, or on a computer display?	O	O
11	Are production lines scheduled off a single pacing process, with appropriate inventory levels at each stage?	O	O
12	Is material moved only once and as short a distance as possible? Is material moved efficiently in appropriate containers?	O	O
13	Is the plant laid out in continuous product line flows rather than in "shops"?	O	O
14	Are work teams trained, empowered, and involved in problem solving and ongoing improvements?	O	O
15	Do employees appear committed to continuous improvement?	O	O
16	Is a timetable posted for equipment preventive maintenance and ongoing improvement of tools and processes?	O	O
17	Is there an effective project-management process, with cost and timing goals, for new product start-ups?	O	O
18	Is a supplier certification process—with measures for quality, delivery, and cost performance—displayed?	O	O
19	Have key product characteristics been identified, and are fail-safe methods used to forestall propagation of defects?	O	O
20	Would you buy the products this operation produces?	O	O

Total number of yeses ____

Rating Sheet

Rating Leanness

RPA Rating Sheet

Team members use the RPA rating sheet to assess a plant in 11 categories on a scale from "poor" (1) to "excellent" (9) to "best in class" (11). The total score for all categories will fall between 11 (poor in all categories) and 121 (the best in the world in all categories), with an average score of 55. Factors to consider to rate a plant in each category are described in Chapter 9; a more detailed list of evaluative factors appears on the Web at www.bus.umich.edu/rpa. The rating sheet also guides team members to questions in the RPA questionnaire (Exhibit 9B.1) that relate specifically to each category.

When plants are rated every year, the ratings for most tend to improve. Ratings are usually shared with plants, and motivated managers first improve their plants in the categories that receive the lowest ratings.

Plant: _____

Tour date: _____

Rated by: _____

		RATINGS						
CATEGORIES	RELATED QUESTIONS IN RPA QUESTIONNAIRE	POOR (1)	BELOW AVERAGE (3)	AVERAGE (5)	ABOVE AVERAGE (7)	EXCELLENT (9)	BEST IN CLASS (11)	CATEGORY SCORE
1 Customer satisfaction	1, 2, 20							
2 Safety, environment, cleanliness, and order	3–5, 20							
3 Visual management system	2, 4, 6–10, 20							
4 Scheduling system	11, 20							
5 Use of space, movement of materials, and product line flow	7, 12, 13, 20							
6 Levels of inventory and work in process	7, 11, 20							
7 Teamwork and motivation	6, 9, 14, 15, 20							
8 Condition and maintenance of equipment and tools	16, 20							
9 Management of complexity and variability	8, 17, 20							
10 Supply chain integration	18, 20							
11 Commitment to quality	15, 17, 19, 20							

Total score for 11 categories _____
(*max* = 121)

section

SUPPLY CHAIN DESIGN

3

WITHOUT SUPPLIERS, NEITHER A GENERAL NOR A SOLDIER IS GOOD FOR ANYTHING

 CLERCHUS OF SPARTA, IN 401 B.C., RECOGNIZED THE VALUE of supply in his speech to the small Greek army he led in a civil war with Artaxerxes II. His army of 14,000 was 1,300 miles from Greece when the Battle of Cunaxa began. The survival of the Greek army depended not only on its discipline, training, and morale but also on its supply chain.

Today the survival of most firms depends on intelligent supply chain decisions. Never have so much technology and brainpower been applied to improving supply chain performance. Point-of-sale scanners, electronic data interchange, and the Internet let all stages of the supply chain hear the customer's voice and react to it.

This section starts with a briefing on electronic commerce showing how firms are taking full advantage of the Internet to become more responsive and to better penetrate customer markets.

Chapter 10 is a high-level view of the latest concepts that relate to supply chain strategy. Such ideas as outsourcing, postponement, and global product sourcing are discussed. Capacity management is critical to success in running a global supply chain. Not only must the amount of production, distribution, and other capacity be correct, but it also must be positioned in the right locations to be effective. Capacity management and facility location are the topics of Chapter 11 in this section. We conclude the section with a tactical view of lean production systems. Here we discuss the details of working with vendors to coordinate our activities along the supply chain. In addition, we look at how internal processes are designed to support the just-in-time approach while still operating in a lean manner.

chapter

SUPPLY CHAIN STRATEGY

10 WHY HAVING AN EFFECTIVE SUPPLY CHAIN MATTERS

 A recent study by Acenture, INSEAD, and Stanford University has documented a strong direct relationship between supply chain operations and corporate financial performance. The bottom line is that supply chain leaders are rewarded by the stock market with substantially higher growth in stock values than companies with lesser performance in supply chain management.

The study used data from more than 600 "Global 3,000" companies across 24 industries covering 1995 to 2000. Companies were classified as supply chain "leaders" or "laggards," based on their performance compared with the others

on inventory turns, cost of goods sold as a percentage of revenue, and return on assets. The study then calculated the financial performance for each company based on its change in stock market capitalization during the study period, compared with other companies in its industry. It's difficult to argue with the stock market as the ultimate arbiter of company value for this purpose.

The impact was dramatic: The compound average annual growth in market capitalization of the leaders was 10 to 30 percentage points higher than the laggards. The results applied across the board—for 21 of the 24 industries the supply chain leaders had higher stock value growth over the six-year period. Companies all try to beat the Dow or the S&P 500 averages and are happy if they are ahead by a couple of percentage points on a consistent basis. The supply chain leaders beat the market by an annual average of 26 points during the period 1995–1997 and 7 points during 1998–2000.

Is it possible for a company's financial value to grow without being a supply chain leader? Sure. Fifteen percent of the "laggards" had top-tier market

Source: Accenture research report, available at http://www.accenture.com.

cap growth. But the reality is that most supply chain laggards were also underperformers in the stock market.

Armed with these results, is it easy to become a supply chain leader? Of course not. It takes processes, people, technology, leadership, discipline, and maybe a little luck. It requires knowing what to do and how to do it. It stands to reason that if you can build your product to order rather than carry inventory, closely match store requirements to actual customer sales trends, restock the shelves quickly, minimize the amount of end-of-season markdown merchandise, or reduce the property, plant, and equipment assets needed to generate a dollar's worth of profit, then you will earn an outsized return from the market. →

SUPPLY CHAIN STRATEGY

Supply chain

Global

Service

Supply chain management is a hot topic in business today. The idea is to apply a total systems approach to managing the entire flow of information, materials, and services from raw materials suppliers through factories and warehouses to the end customer. The term **supply chain** comes from a picture of how organizations are linked together as viewed from a particular company. Exhibit 10.1 depicts a global supply chain for both manufacturing and service companies. Note the linkage between suppliers that provide inputs, manufacturing and service support operations that transform the inputs into products and services, and the distribution and local service providers that localize the product. Localization can involve just the delivery of the product or some more involved process that tailors the product or service to the needs of the local market.

So why is supply chain management such a popular topic these days? The answer is that many companies are achieving significant competitive advantage by the way they configure and manage their supply chain operations. Dell Computer, for example, skips the distribution and retail steps typical of a manufacturing company's supply chain. Dell takes orders for its computers from customers over the Internet and manufactures directly to the orders. The computers are never sent to distribution centers and are never displayed in a retail store. Customers are able to get the latest models at very competitive prices in only five or six days using this approach.

Keep in mind that a good supply chain design for Dell may not work for a company like Campbell Soup. If Campbell Soup were to eliminate distribution centers from their supply chain, the costs associated with transporting their products to grocery stores would be excessive. Imagine ordering cans of chicken noodle soup over the Internet directly from the manufacturer. It's an interesting idea, but the cost to transport that individual can of soup is higher than the cost of the soup. The grocery store is needed as the intermediary so that the shipping cost can be reduced through truckload shipments.

Our purpose in this chapter is to show how supply chains should be structured to meet the needs of different products and customer groups. We begin by developing some terminology that will be useful for measuring supply chain performance; then we look strategically at different supply chain designs and the trade-offs involved. Following this, we describe strategies that are important to large companies operating in global markets. These strategies involve outsourcing of work and postponing assembly in the supply chain.

MEASURING SUPPLY CHAIN PERFORMANCE

One view of the supply chain is centered on the inventories that are positioned in the system. Exhibit 10.2 shows how hamburger meat and potatoes are stored in various locations in a typical fast-food restaurant chain. Here we see the steps that the beef and potatoes move through on their way to the local retail store and then to the customer. At each step inventory is carried, and this inventory has a particular cost to the company. Inventory serves

The Supply Chain Network

exhibit 10.1

Inventory in the Supply Chain—Fast-Food Restaurant

exhibit 10.2

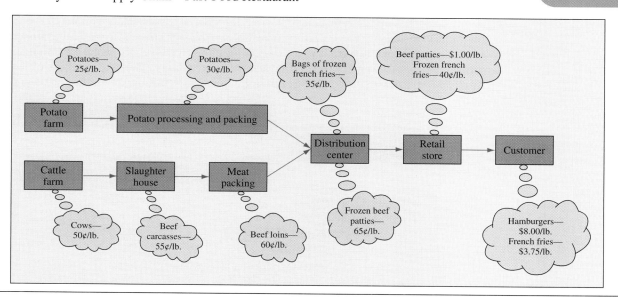

as a buffer, thus allowing each stage to operate independently of the others. For example, the distribution center inventory allows the system that supplies the retail stores to operate independently of the meat and potato packing operations. Because the inventory at each stage ties up money, it is important that the operations at each stage are synchronized to minimize the size of these buffer inventories. The efficiency of the supply chain can be measured based on the size of the inventory investment in the supply chain. The inventory investment is measured relative to the total cost of the goods that are provided through the supply chain.

Two common measures to evaluate supply chain efficiency are *inventory turnover* and *weeks-of-supply*. These essentially measure the same thing and mathematically are the inverse of one another. **Inventory turnover** is calculated as follows:

Inventory turnover

[10.1]
$$\text{Inventory turnover} = \frac{\text{Cost of goods sold}}{\text{Average aggregate inventory value}}$$

Cost of goods sold

Average aggregate inventory value

The **cost of goods sold** is the annual cost for a company to produce the goods or services provided to customers; it is sometimes referred to as the *cost of revenue*. This does not include the selling and administrative expenses of the company. The **average aggregate inventory value** is the total value of all items held in inventory for the firm valued at cost. It includes the raw material, work-in-process, finished goods, and distribution inventory considered owned by the company.

Good inventory turnover values vary by industry and the type of products being handled. At one extreme, a grocery store chain may turn inventory over 100 times per year. Values of six to seven are typical for manufacturing firms.

Weeks of supply

In many situations, particularly when distribution inventory is dominant, **weeks of supply** is the preferred measure. This is a measure of how many weeks' worth of inventory is in the system at a particular point in time. The calculation is as follows:

[10.2]
$$\text{Weeks of supply} = \left(\frac{\text{Average aggregate inventory value}}{\text{Cost of goods sold}} \right) \times 52 \text{ weeks}$$

When company financial reports cite inventory turnover and weeks of supply, we can assume that the measures are being calculated firmwide. We show an example of this type of calculation in the example that follows using Dell Computer data. These calculations, though, can be done on individual entities within the organization. For example, we might be interested in the production raw materials inventory turnover or the weeks of supply associated with the warehousing operation of a firm. In these cases, the cost would be that associated with the total amount of inventory that runs through the specific inventory. In some very-low-inventory operations, days or even hours are a better unit of time for measuring supply.

A firm considers inventory an investment because the intent is for it to be used in the future. Inventory ties up funds that could be used for other purposes, and a firm may have to borrow money to finance the inventory investment. The objective is to have the proper amount of inventory and to have it in the correct locations in the supply chain. Determining the correct amount of inventory to have in each position requires a thorough analysis of the supply chain coupled with the competitive priorities that define the market for the company's products.

EXAMPLE 10.1: Inventory Turnover Calculation

Dell Computer reported the following information in its 1999 annual report (all amounts are expressed in millions):

Net revenue (fiscal year 1999)	$18,243
Cost of revenue (fiscal year 1999)	14,137
Cost of production materials (fiscal year 1999)	6,423
Production materials on hand (25 January 1999)	234
Work-in-process and finished goods on hand (25 January 1999)	39
Production materials—days of supply	6 days

THE RAW MATERIAL, STRAWBERRIES, FOR TOM'S OF MAINE ARE SAMPLED BY A QA TEAM TO VERIFY QUALITY. INGREDIENTS ARE COMBINED, PROCESSED, THEN SENT TO FILLING STATIONS FOR PACKAGING AND SHIPPING TO ONE OF THE 35,000 STORES THROUGHOUT NORTH AMERICA RETAILING THEIR PRODUCTS.

The cost of revenue corresponds to what we call cost of goods sold. One might think that U.S. companies, at least, would use a common accounting terminology, but this is not true. The inventory turnover calculation is

$$\text{Inventory turnover} = \frac{14{,}137}{234 + 39} = 51.78 \text{ turns per year}$$

This is amazing performance for a high-tech company, but it explains much of why the company is such a financial success.

The corresponding weeks of supply calculation is

$$\text{Weeks of supply} = \left(\frac{234 + 39}{14{,}137}\right) \times 52 = 1 \text{ week} \;\bullet$$

SUPPLY CHAIN DESIGN STRATEGY

The Dell Company example is unique and interesting. Through a combination of innovative product design, an Internet order-taking process, an innovative assembly system, and amazing cooperation from its suppliers, Dell Computer has been able to create a supply chain that is extremely efficient. Dell Computer now has become the benchmark company for the computer industry.

A key to the success of Dell Computer is the fact that customers order over the Internet and are willing to wait at least a week for the delivery of their computer systems. Most consumers do not buy computers this way; rather, they go to Wal-Mart or Staples or some other discount store and purchase a computer from the available stock in the store. Often the computer is bundled with other services that offer rebates enticing the customer to buy the package, thus reducing the overall cost of the computer and the service.

Marshall Fisher[1] argues that in many cases there are adversarial relations between supply chain partners as well as dysfunctional industry practices such as a reliance on price promotions. Consider the common food industry practice of offering price promotions every January on a product. Retailers respond to the price cut by stocking up, in some cases buying a year's supply—a practice the industry calls *forward buying*. Nobody wins in the deal. Retailers have to pay to carry the year's supply, and the shipment bulge adds cost throughout the supplier's system. For example, the supplier plants must go on overtime starting in October to meet the bulge. Even the vendors that supply the manufacturing plants are affected because they must quickly react to the large surge in raw material requirements.

exhibit 10.3   Increasing Variability of Orders up the Supply Chain

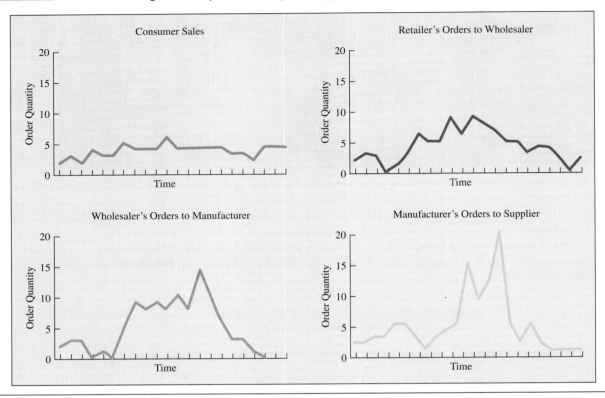

Bullwhip effect

The impact of these types of practices has been studied at companies such as Procter & Gamble. Exhibit 10.3 shows typical order patterns faced by each node in a supply chain that consists of a manufacturer, a distributor, a wholesaler, and a retailer. In this case, the demand is for disposable baby diapers. The retailer's orders to the wholesaler display greater variability than the end-consumer sales; the wholesaler's orders to the manufacturer show even more oscillations; and, finally, the manufacturer's orders to its suppliers are the most volatile. This phenomenon of variability magnification as we move from the customer to the producer in the supply chain is often referred to as the **bullwhip effect**. The effect indicates a lack of synchronization among supply chain members. Even a slight change in consumer sales ripples backward in the form of magnified oscillations upstream, resembling the result of a flick of a bullwhip handle. Because the supply patterns do not match the demand patterns, inventory accumulates at various stages, and shortages and delays occur at others. This bullwhip effect has been observed by many firms in numerous industries, including Campbell Soup and Procter & Gamble in consumer products; Hewlett-Packard, IBM, and Motorola in electronics; General Motors in automobiles; and Eli Lilly in pharmaceuticals.

Campbell Soup has a program called *continuous replenishment* that typifies what many manufacturers are doing to smooth the flow of materials through their supply chain. Here is how the program works. Campbell establishes electronic data interchange (EDI) links with retailers and offers an "everyday low price" that eliminates discounts. Every morning, retailers electronically inform the company of their demand for all Campbell products and of the level of inventories in their distribution centers. Campbell uses that information to forecast future demand and to determine which products require replenishment based on upper and lower inventory limits previously established with each supplier. Trucks leave the Campbell shipping plant that afternoon and arrive at the retailers' distribution centers with the required replenishments the same day. Using this system, Campbell can cut the retailers' inventories, which under the old system averaged four weeks of supply, to about two weeks of supply.

This solves some problems for Campbell Soup, but what are the advantages for the retailer? Most retailers figure that the cost to carry the inventory of a given product for a year equals at least 25 percent of what they paid for the product. A two-week inventory reduction represents a cost savings equal to nearly 1 percent of sales. The average retailer's profits equal about 2 percent of sales, so this saving is enough to increase profits by 50 percent. Because the retailer makes more money on Campbell products delivered through continuous replenishment, it has an incentive to carry a broader line of them and to give them more shelf space. Campbell Soup found that after it introduced the program, sales of its products grew twice as fast through participating retailers as they did through other retailers.

Fisher has developed a framework to help managers understand the nature of demand for their products and then devise the supply chain that can best satisfy that demand. Many aspects of a product's demand are important—for example, product life cycle, demand predictability, product variety, and market standards for lead times and service. Fisher has found that products can be categorized as either primarily functional or primarily innovative. Because each category requires a distinctly different kind of supply chain, the root cause of supply chain problems is a mismatch between the type of product and type of supply chain.

Functional products include the staples that people buy in a wide range of retail outlets, such as grocery stores and gas stations. Because such products satisfy basic needs, which do not change much over time, they have stable, predictable demand and long life cycles. But their stability invites competition, which often leads to low profit margins. Specific criteria suggested by Fisher for identifying functional products include the following: product life cycle of more than two years, contribution margin of 5 to 20 percent, only 10 to 20 product variations, an average forecast error at time of production of only 10 percent, and a lead time for make-to-order products of from six months to one year.

To avoid low margins, many companies introduce innovations in fashion or technology to give customers an additional reason to buy their products. Fashionable clothes and personal computers are good examples. Although innovation can enable a company to achieve higher profit margins, the very newness of the innovative products makes demand for them unpredictable. These **innovative products** typically have a life cycle of just a few months. Imitators quickly erode the competitive advantage that innovative products enjoy, and companies are forced to introduce a steady stream of newer innovations. The short life cycles and the great variety typical of these products further increase unpredictability.

Exhibit 10.4 summarizes the differences between functional and innovative products.

Hau Lee[2] expands on Fisher's ideas by focusing on the "supply" side of the supply chain. While Fisher has captured important demand characteristics, Lee points out that there are uncertainties revolving around the supply side that are equally important drivers for the right supply chain strategy.

Lee defines a *stable supply process* as one where the manufacturing process and the underlying technology are mature and the supply base is well established. In contrast, an *evolving*

Functional products *(margin)*

Innovative products *(margin)*

Demand and Supply Uncertainty Characteristics

exhibit 10.4

DEMAND CHARACTERISTICS		SUPPLY CHARACTERISTICS	
FUNCTIONAL	INNOVATIVE	STABLE	EVOLVING
Low demand uncertainty	High demand uncertainty	Less breakdowns	Vulnerable to breakdowns
More predictable demand	Difficult to forecast	Stable and higher yields	Variable and lower yields
Stable demand	Variable demand	Less quality problems	Potential quality problems
Long product life	Short selling season	More supply sources	Limited supply sources
Low inventory cost	High inventory cost	Reliable suppliers	Unreliable suppliers
Low profit margin	High profit margin	Less process changes	More process changes
Low product variety	High product variety	Less capacity constraints	Potential capacity constrained
Higher volume	Low volume	Easier to change over	Difficult to change over
Low stockout cost	High stockout cost	Flexible	Inflexible
Low obsolescence	High obsolescence	Dependable lead times	Variable lead time

exhibit 10.5

Hau Lee's Uncertainty Framework—Examples and Types of Supply Chain Needed

		DEMAND UNCERTAINTY	
		LOW (FUNCTIONAL PRODUCTS)	HIGH (INNOVATIVE PRODUCTS)
SUPPLY UNCERTAINTY	LOW (STABLE PROCESS)	Grocery, basic apparel, food, oil and gas **Efficient Supply Chain**	Fashion apparel, computers, popular music **Responsive Supply Chain**
	HIGH (EVOLVING PROCESS)	Hydroelectric power, some food produce **Risk-Hedging Supply Chain**	Telecom, high-end computers, semiconductor **Agile Supply Chain**

supply process is where the manufacturing process and the underlying technology are still under early development and are rapidly changing. As a result the supply base may be limited in both size and experience. In a stable supply process, manufacturing complexity tends to be low or manageable. Stable manufacturing processes tend to be highly automated, and long-term supply contracts are prevalent. In an evolving supply process, the manufacturing process requires a lot of fine-tuning and is often subject to breakdowns and uncertain yields. The supply base may not be reliable, as the suppliers themselves are going through process innovations. Exhibit 10.4 summarizes some of the differences between stable and evolving supply processes.

Lee argues that while functional products tend to have a more mature and stable supply process, that is not always the case. For example, the annual demand for electricity and other utility products in a locality tend to be stable and predictable, but the supply of hydroelectric power, which relies on rainfall in a region, can be erratic year by year. Some food products also have a very stable demand, but the supply (both quantity and quality) of the products depends on yearly weather conditions. Similarly, there are also innovative products with a stable supply process. Fashion apparel products have a short selling season and their demand is highly unpredictable. However, the supply process is very stable, with a reliable supply base and a mature manufacturing process technology. Exhibit 10.5 gives some examples of products that have different demand and supply uncertainties.

According to Lee, it is more challenging to operate a supply chain that is in the right column of Exhibit 10.5 than in the left column, and similarly it is more challenging to operate a supply chain that is in the lower row of Exhibit 10.5 than in the upper row. Before setting up a supply chain strategy, it is necessary to understand the sources of the underlying uncertainties and explore ways to reduce these uncertainties. If it is possible to move the uncertainty characteristics of the product from the right column to the left or from the lower row to the upper, then the supply chain performance will improve.

Lee characterizes four types of supply chain strategies as shown in Exhibit 10.5. Information technologies play an important role in shaping such strategies.

- **Efficient supply chains.**   These are supply chains that utilize strategies aimed at creating the highest cost efficiency. For such efficiencies to be achieved, non-value-added activities should be eliminated, scale economies should be pursued, optimization techniques should be deployed to get the best capacity utilization in production and distribution, and information linkages should be established to ensure the most efficient, accurate, and cost-effective transmission of information across the supply chain.
- **Risk-hedging supply chains.**   These are supply chains that utilize strategies aimed at pooling and sharing resources in a supply chain so that the risks in supply disruption can be shared. A single entity in a supply chain can be vulnerable to supply disruptions, but if there is more than one supply source or if alternative supply resources are available, then the risk of disruption is reduced. A company may, for example, increase the safety stock of its key component to hedge against the risk of supply disruption, and by sharing the safety stock with other companies who also need this key component, the cost of maintaining this safety stock can be shared. This type of strategy is common in

retailing, where different retail stores or dealerships share inventory. Information technology is important for the success of these strategies since real-time information on inventory and demand allows the most cost-effective management and transshipment of goods between partners sharing the inventory.

- **Responsive supply chains.**   These are supply chains that utilize strategies aimed at being responsive and flexible to the changing and diverse needs of the customers. To be responsive, companies use build-to-order and mass customization processes as a means to meet the specific requirements of customers.
- **Agile supply chains.**   These are supply chains that utilize strategies aimed at being responsive and flexible to customer needs, while the risks of supply shortages or disruptions are hedged by pooling inventory and other capacity resources. These supply chains essentially have strategies in place that combine the strengths of "hedged" and "responsive" supply chains. They are agile because they have the ability to be responsive to the changing, diverse, and unpredictable demands of customers on the front end, while minimizing the back-end risks of supply disruptions.

Demand and supply uncertainty is a good framework for understanding supply chain strategy. Innovative products with unpredictable demand and an evolving supply process face a major challenge. Because of shorter and shorter product life cycles, the pressure for dynamically adjusting and adopting a company's supply chain strategy is great. In the following we explore the concepts of outsourcing, global sourcing, mass customization, and postponement. These are important tools for coping with demand and supply uncertainty.

OUTSOURCING

Outsourcing is the act of moving some of a firm's internal activities and decision responsibility to outside providers. The terms of the agreement are established in a contract. Outsourcing goes beyond the more common purchasing and consulting contracts because not only are the activities transferred, but also resources that make the activities occur, including people, facilities, equipment, technology, and other assets, are transferred. The responsibilities for making decisions over certain elements of the activities are transferred as well. Taking complete responsibility for this is a specialty of contract manufacturers such as Flextronics and Solectron. In the electronics industry, for example, 11 percent of manufacturing is performed by such contract manufacturers, many of whom manage the full supply chain, even including distribution and repair.[3]

The reasons why a company decides to outsource can vary greatly. Exhibit 10.6 lists 20 examples of reasons to outsource and the accompanying benefits. Outsourcing allows a firm to focus on activities that represent its core competencies. Thus, the company can create a competitive advantage while reducing cost. An entire function may be outsourced, or some elements of an activity may be outsourced, with the rest kept in-house. For example, some of the elements of information technology may be strategic, some may be critical, and some may be performed less expensively by a third party. Identifying a function as a potential outsourcing target, and then breaking that function into its components, allows decision makers to determine which activities are strategic or critical and should remain in-house and which can be outsourced like commodities. As an example, outsourcing the logistics function will be discussed.

There has been dramatic growth in outsourcing in the logistics area. **Logistics** is a term that refers to the management functions that support the complete cycle of material flow: from the purchase and internal control of production materials; to the planning and control of work-in-process; to the purchasing, shipping, and

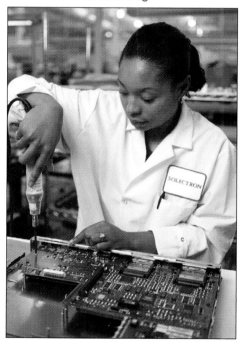

Outsourcing

SOLECTRON HAS PARTNERSHIPS WITH MANY COMPANIES IN HIGH-TECH ELECTRONICS, INCLUDING CISCO SYSTEMS, ERICSSON, HEWLETT-PACKARD, IBM, MICROSOFT, MOTOROLA, NORTEL NETWORKS, SONY AND SUN MICROSYSTEMS. SOLECTRON HAS RECEIVED MORE THAN 450 QUALITY AND SERVICE AWARDS FROM ITS CUSTOMERS IN ADDITION TO WINNING TWO MALCOLM BALDRIGE AWARDS.

exhibit 10.6

Reasons to Outsource and the Benefits

ORGANIZATIONALLY DRIVEN REASONS

- Enhance effectiveness by focusing on what you do best.
- Increase flexibility to meet changing business conditions, demand for products and services, and technologies.
- Transform the organization.
- Increase product and service value, customer satisfaction, and shareholder value.

IMPROVEMENT-DRIVEN REASONS

- Improve operating performance (increase quality and productivity, shorten cycle times, and so on).
- Obtain expertise, skills, and technologies that are not otherwise available.
- Improve management and control.
- Improve risk management.
- Acquire innovative ideas.
- Improve credibility and image by associating with superior providers.

FINANCIALLY DRIVEN REASONS

- Reduce investments in assets and free up these resources for other purposes.
- Generate cash by transferring assets to the provider.

REVENUE-DRIVEN REASONS

- Gain market access and business opportunities through the provider's network.
- Accelerate expansion by tapping into the provider's developed capacity, processes, and systems.
- Expand sales and production capacity during periods when such expansion cannot be financed.
- Commercially exploit existing skills.

COST-DRIVEN REASONS

- Reduce costs through superior provider performance and the provider's lower cost structure.
- Turn fixed costs into variable costs.

EMPLOYEE-DRIVEN REASONS

- Give employees a stronger career path.
- Increase commitment and energy in noncore areas.

Logistics

distribution of the finished product. The emphasis on lean inventory means there is less room for error in deliveries. Trucking companies such as Ryder have started adding the logistics aspect to their businesses—changing from merely moving goods from point A to point B, to managing all or part of all shipments over a longer period, typically three years, and replacing the shipper's employees with their own. Logistics companies now have complex computer tracking technology that reduces the risk in transportation and allows the logistics company to add more value to the firm than it could if the function were performed in-house. Third-party logistics providers track freight using electronic data interchange technology and a satellite system to tell customers exactly where its drivers are and when deliveries will be made. Such technology is critical in some environments where the delivery window may be only 30 minutes long.

Federal Express has one of the most advanced systems available for tracking items being sent through its services. The system is available to all customers over the Internet. It tells the exact status of each item currently being carried by the company. Information on the exact time a package is picked up, when it is transferred between hubs in the company's network, and when it is delivered is available on the system. You can access this system at the FedEx Web site (www.fedex.com). Select your country on the initial screen and then select "Track Shipments" in the Track box in the lower part of the page. Of course, you will need the actual tracking number for an item currently in the system to get information. Federal Express has integrated its tracking system with many of its customers' in-house information systems.

Another example of innovative outsourcing in logistics involves Hewlett-Packard. Hewlett-Packard turned over its inbound raw materials warehousing in Vancouver, Washington, to Roadway Logistics. Roadway's 140 employees operate the warehouse 24 hours a day, seven days a week, coordinating the delivery of parts to the warehouse and managing storage. Hewlett-Packard's 250 employees were transferred to other company activities. Hewlett-Packard reports savings of 10 percent in warehousing operating costs.

One of the drawbacks to outsourcing is the layoffs that often result. Even in cases where the outsourcing partner hires former employees, they are often hired back at lower wages with fewer benefits. Outsourcing is perceived by many unions as an effort to circumvent union contracts.   *Drawbacks*

In theory, outsourcing is a no-brainer. Companies can unload noncore activities, shed balance sheet assets, and boost their return on capital by using third-party service providers. But in reality, things are more complicated. "It's really hard to figure out what's core and what's noncore today," says Jane Linder, senior research fellow and associate director of Accenture's Institute for Strategic Change in Cambridge, Massachusetts. "When you take another look tomorrow, things may have changed. On September 9, 2001, airport security workers were noncore; on September 12, 2001, they were core to the federal government's ability to provide security to the nation. It happens every day in companies as well."[4]

Exhibit 10.7 is a useful framework to help managers make appropriate choices for the structure of supplier relationships. The decision goes beyond the notion that "core competencies" should be maintained under the direct control of management of the firm and that other activities should be outsourced. In this framework, a continuum that ranges from vertical integration to arm's-length relationships forms the basis for the decision.

An activity can be evaluated using the following characteristics: required coordination, strategic control, and intellectual property. Required coordination refers to how difficult it is to ensure that the activity will integrate well with the overall process. Uncertain activities that require much back-and-forth exchange of information should not be outsourced whereas

A Framework for Structuring Supplier Relationships   exhibit 10.7

	VERTICAL INTEGRATION (DO NOT OUTSOURCE)	ARM'S-LENGTH RELATIONSHIPS (OUTSOURCE)
Coordination	"Messy" interfaces; adjacent tasks involve a high degree of mutual adaptation, exchange of implicit knowledge, and learning-by-doing. Requisite information is highly particular to the task.	Standardized interfaces between adjacent tasks; requisite information is highly codified and standardized (prices, quantities, delivery schedules, etc.).
Strategic control	Very high: significant investments in highly durable relationship-specific assets needed for optimal execution of tasks. Investments cannot be recovered if relationship terminates: • Collocation of specialized facilities • Investment in brand equity • Large proprietary learning curves • Long-term investments in specialized R&D programs	Very low: assets applicable to businesses with a large number of other potential customers or suppliers.
Intellectual property	Unclear or weak intellectual property protection Easy-to-imitate technology "Messy" interfaces between different technological components	Strong intellectual property protection Difficult-to-imitate technology "Clean" boundaries between different technological components

SOURCE: ROBERT HAYES, GARY PISANO, DAVID UPTON, AND STEVEN WHEELWRIGHT, *OPERATIONS STRATEGY AND TECHNOLOGY: PURSUING THE COMPETITIVE EDGE* (NEW YORK: JOHN WILEY & SONS, 2005), P. 137. COPYRIGHT © 2005 JOHN WILEY & SONS. REPRINTED BY PERMISSION.

activities that are well understood and highly standardized can easily move to business partners who specialize in the activity. Strategic control refers to the degree of loss that would be incurred if the relationship with the partner were severed. There could be many types of losses that would be important to consider including specialized facilities, knowledge of major customer relationships, and investment in research and development. A final consideration is the potential loss of intellectual property though the partnership.

Global

Intel is an excellent example of a company that recognized the importance of this type of decision framework in the mid-1980s. During the early 1980s, Intel found itself being squeezed out of the market for the memory chips that it had invented by Japanese competitors such as Hitachi, Fujitsu, and NEC. These companies had developed stronger capabilities to develop and rapidly scale up complex semiconductor manufacturing processes. It was clear by 1985 that a major Intel competency was in its ability to design complex integrated circuits, not in manufacturing or developing processes for more standardized chips. As a result, faced with growing financial losses, Intel was forced to exit the memory chip market.

Learning a lesson from the memory market, Intel shifted its focus to the microprocessor market, a device that it had invented in the late 1960s. To keep from repeating the mistake with memory chips, Intel felt it was essential to develop strong capabilities in process development and manufacturing. A pure "core competency" strategy would have suggested that Intel focus on the design of microprocessors and use outside partners to manufacture them. Given the close connection between semiconductor product development and process development, however, relying on outside parties for manufacturing would likely have created costs in terms of longer development lead times. Over the late-1980s Intel invested heavily in building world-class capabilities in process development and manufacturing. These capabilities are one of the chief reasons it has been able to maintain approximately 90 percent of the personal computer microprocessor market, despite the ability of competitors like AMD to "clone" Intel designs relatively quickly. Expanding its capabilities beyond its original core capability of product design has been a critical ingredient in Intel's sustained success.

In some cases, companies leave themselves vulnerable to market coup by former partners when they outsource. Such was the case with the German consumer electronics company Blaupunkt, notes Ed Frey, a vice president at Booz Allen Hamilton. To beef up the product line it offered to its dealers, Blaupunkt decided to add VCRs and contracted the work out to Panasonic (once a lowly circuit-board stuffer). Later, with the Blaupunkt reputation attached to its products, Panasonic approached the dealers directly and, presto, it had a ready-made distribution network for its own product line. "In effect, all Blaupunkt did was give access to its dealer network to Panasonic," says Frey.

Good advice is to keep control of—or acquire—activities that are true competitive differentiators or leave the potential to yield a competitive advantage, and to outsource the rest. It is important to make a distinction between "core" and "strategic" activities. Core activities are key to the business, but do not confer a competitive advantage, such as a bank's information technology operations. Strategic activities are a key source of competitive advantage. Because the competitive environment can change rapidly, companies need to monitor the situation constantly, and adjust accordingly. As an example, Coca-Cola, which decided to stay out of the bottling business in the early 1900s, partnered instead with independent bottlers and quickly built market share. The company reversed itself in the 1980s when bottling became a key competitive element in the industry.

DESIGN FOR LOGISTICS

Design for logistics

The logistics interface with procurement and manufacturing, as well as with engineering and marketing, can be greatly enhanced by incorporating a concept known as **design for logistics** into the early phases of product development. This concept involves consideration of material procurement and distribution costs during the product design phase. Given the heavy emphasis on minimizing inventory and handling in efficient supply chains, how a product is designed and the design of the components and materials themselves can have a significant impact on the cost to deliver the product. In particular, product packaging and transportation requirements need to be incorporated into the design process. For example, if inbound components are packaged in containers with a standard quantity of 50, but only 30 components are needed to meet production requirements, then waste will occur. Additionally, product and component design must have consideration of transportation and internal materials handling methods to ensure that cost-efficient, damage-free logistics performance can be achieved. Similar design considerations must be made for the finished product itself.

VALUE DENSITY (VALUE PER UNIT OF WEIGHT)

A common and important decision is how an item should be shipped. The way an item is shipped is referred to as the **transportation mode**. There are five basic modes of transportation: highway, rail, water, pipeline, and air. Each mode has its own advantages and limitations, as shown in Exhibit 10.8.

Transportation mode

Although it may seem oversimplified, the value of an item per pound of weight—**value density**—is an important measure when deciding where items should be stocked geographically and how they should be shipped. Consider a company like Intel that makes microprocessor chips for personal computers. The company must decide whether to ship microprocessors to customers by ground or air carrier. Analysis shows that the time saved by air shipment can be justified if the shipping cost is appropriate. The decision involves a trade-off: the reduced transit time and the resulting reduced inventory investment compared to the increase in shipping costs. In the following section, details of the trade-off analysis are provided. Keep in mind that this is just an example of the type of analysis that would be typical in this type of supply chain decision. The basic methodology of building a spreadsheet that allows the trade-off to be studied is sound and can be applied no matter what exact details are needed to explore the alternatives.

Value density

EXAMPLE 10.2: Evaluating the Trade-Off between Air and Ground Package Shipping

We can approach the problem by examining a specific situation. Consider the cost of shipping from Bloomington, Indiana, to Littleton, Massachusetts. Assume that the inventory carrying cost rate is 30 percent per year of the product value. This cost rate captures the cost of capital, insurance, warehouse cost, and so on. We use this cost rate to determine the actual cost to carry an item in inventory for a year given the value of an item. For example, an item that costs $100 would cost $30 to carry in inventory for a year if the carrying cost rate were 30 percent. Our alternative transportation modes are highway service provided by United Parcel Service (UPS), which takes eight days to ship from Bloomington to Littleton, and Federal Express, which offers a two-day air service. Exhibit 10.9 indicates the cost to ship 1 to 10 pounds from Bloomington to Littleton using the alternative services.

Modes of Transportation and Their Advantages and Limitations

exhibit 10.8

- **Highway (trucking)**—flexibility because items can be delivered to almost any location in a continent. Transit times are good, and rates are usually reasonable for small quantities and over short distances.
- **Rail**—low cost, but transit times are long and may be subject to variability.
- **Water**—very high capacity and very low cost, but transit times are very slow, and large areas of the world are not directly accessible to water carriers.
- **Pipeline**—highly specialized and limited to liquids, gases, or solids in slurry form. No packaging is needed, and the costs per mile are low. The initial cost to build the pipeline is very high.
- **Air**—fast but most expensive.

exhibit 10.9

Product Density Shipping Cost Comparison

Excel: Value Density

				Days saved = 6	
Carrying cost rate = 0.3					
SHIPPING WEIGHT (POUNDS)	UNITED PARCEL SERVICE: 8-DAY GROUND SERVICE	FEDERAL EXPRESS: 2-DAY AIR SERVICE	COST SAVINGS WITH UPS	BREAK-EVEN PRODUCT VALUE	BREAK-EVEN PRODUCT VALUE (PER POUND)
1	$3.30	$18.25	$14.95	$3,031.53	$3,031.53
2	$3.60	$20.50	16.90	3,426.94	1,713.47
3	$3.85	$22.50	18.65	3,781.81	1,260.60
4	$4.10	$24.50	20.40	4,136.67	1,034.17
5	$4.30	$26.75	22.45	4,552.36	910.47
6	$4.50	$28.75	24.25	4,917.36	819.56
7	$4.65	$30.75	26.10	5,292.50	756.07
8	$4.75	$32.75	28.00	5,677.78	709.72
9	$4.85	$34.75	29.90	6,063.06	673.67
10	$5.00	$36.75	31.75	6,438.19	643.82

SOLUTION

The problem involves equating the cost of transportation via air to the cost of highway shipment plus the cost of carrying inventory for the additional six days. Logically, we can make the general statement that expensive items can be sent by air using Federal Express, whereas lower-value items can be shipped by the less expensive highway service offered by UPS.

$$\text{Shipping cost saving} = \text{Air shipping cost} - \text{Regular highway shipping cost}$$

At break-even, the cost savings are equal to inventory carrying cost.

$$\text{Shipping cost savings} = \text{Inventory carrying cost} = \frac{\text{Item value} \times 0.30 \times 6 \text{ days}}{365 \text{ days per year}}$$

The carrying cost is calculated by multiplying the value of the item (at cost) times the yearly carrying cost percentage (30 percent) times the proportion of the year that the item is being carried—which in this case is 6 out of 365 days. Solving for item value,

$$\text{Item value} = \frac{365 \times \text{Shipping cost savings}}{0.30 \times 6}$$

The different cost savings in the fourth column of our spreadsheet in Exhibit 10.9 are calculated using our item value equation for each shipping weight. This gives the product value in the fifth column. Dividing by the package weight gives the break-even product value per pound in the last column. The exhibit indicates that any item whose value is greater than that shown in the last column should be shipped by air. For example, a five-pound shipment of integrated circuits whose average value is more than $910.47 per pound should be shipped by Federal Express. ●

GLOBAL SOURCING

Global

⬭⬭⬭◯   We are in the middle of a major change in the global economy. Great opportunities are available because of the collapse of communism in the Eastern Bloc, the issuance of the euro currency, and new markets in Turkey, India, South Africa, and so on. We have seen the results of agreements such as the North American Free Trade Agreement and the General Agreement on Tariffs and Trade. China is a huge market and is now a powerful trading partner.

The Breakthrough box titled "Supply Chain Management, Hong Kong Style" gives great insight into how global sourcing works in the quickly changing and competitive fashion industry.

Managers face an interesting predicament. Let's take the example of Nike, the maker of high-quality tennis shoes. For Nike a key raw material is leather, which is available from many sources around the world. The lowest-cost leather, though, might be available in South America while the least expensive labor is in China, locations that are on opposite sides of the globe. These locations are far removed from the major markets for the shoes in the United States, Europe, and Japan. To make matters worse, those customers in the United States, Europe, and Japan do not even agree on what they want.

Companies that face such diverse sourcing, production, and distribution decisions need to weigh the costs associated with materials, transportation, production, warehousing, and distribution to develop a comprehensive network designed to minimize costs. Of course, this network must be designed with consideration of outsourcing alternatives as described earlier in this chapter. Technical Note 11, "Facility Location," describes techniques useful for minimizing these costs.

MASS CUSTOMIZATION

The term **mass customization** has been used to describe the ability of a company to deliver highly customized products and services to different customers around the world.[5] The key to mass-customizing effectively is postponing the task of differentiating a product for a specific customer until the latest possible point in the supply network. In order to do this, companies must rethink and integrate the designs of their products, the processes used to make and deliver those products, and the configuration of the entire supply network. By adopting such a comprehensive approach, companies can operate at maximum efficiency and quickly meet customers' orders with a minimum amount of inventory.

Mass customization

Three organization design principles together form the basic building blocks of an effective mass customization program.

Principle 1: *A product should be designed so it consists of independent modules that can be assembled into different forms of the product easily and inexpensively.* Hewlett-Packard decided to use a modular product design to allow its DeskJet printers to be easily customized for the European and Asian markets. The company decided to customize the printers at its local distribution centers

LAND ROVER OWNERS ARE AMONG THE MOST ACTIVE CUSTOMIZERS OF VEHICLES. DEFENDERS ARE POPULAR WORLDWIDE AMONG INDIVIDUAL CUSTOMERS, AND THEY ARE ALSO OFTEN CUSTOMIZED FOR MILITARY, MEDICAL AND RESCUE APPLICATIONS.

rather than at its factories. For example, instead of customizing the DeskJets at its factory in Singapore before shipping them to Europe, Hewlett-Packard has its European distribution center near Stuttgart, Germany, perform this job. The company designed the new printer with a country-specific external power supply that the customer plugs in when setting up the printer. The distribution center not only customizes the product but also purchases the materials that differentiate it (the power supplies, packaging, and manuals). As a result of this redesign, manufacturing costs are slightly higher than when the factories customized the printers, but the total manufacturing, shipping, and inventory costs dropped by 25 percent.

Global

Principle 2: *Manufacturing and service processes should be designed so that they consist of independent modules that can be moved or rearranged easily to support different*

BREAKTHROUGH

SUPPLY CHAIN MANAGEMENT, HONG KONG STYLE

The following are comments by Victor Fung, the Chairman of Li & Fung—the largest export trading company in Hong Kong and an innovator in the development of supply chain management. On behalf of its customers, primarily American and European retailers, Li & Fung works with an ever-expanding network of suppliers around the globe, sourcing clothing and other consumer goods ranging from toys to fashion accessories to luggage.

Question: How do you define the difference between what Li & Fung does today—supply chain management—and the trading business founded by your grandfather in 1906?

Fung: When my grandfather started the company in Canton, 90 years ago during the Ching dynasty, his "value added" was that he spoke English. In those days, it took three months to get to China by boat from the West; a letter would take a month. No one at the Chinese factories spoke English, and the American merchants spoke no Chinese. As an interpreter, my grandfather's commission was 15 percent.

Continuing through my father's generation, Li & Fung was basically a broker, charging a fee to put buyers and sellers together. But as an intermediary, the company was squeezed between the growing power of the buyers and the factories. Our margins slipped to 10 percent, then 5 percent, then 3 percent. When I returned to Hong Kong in 1976 my friends warned me that in 10 years buying agents like Li & Fung would be extinct. "Trading is a sunset industry," they all said.

My brother and I felt we could turn the business into something different, and so we took it through several stages of development. In the first stage, we acted as what I would call a regional sourcing agent and extended our geographic reach by establishing offices in Taiwan, Korea, and Singapore. Our knowledge of the region had value for customers. Most big buyers could manage their own sourcing if they needed to deal with only Hong Kong—they'd know which 10 factories to deal with and wouldn't need any help.

But dealing with the whole region was more complex. In textiles, quotas govern world trade. Knowing which quotas have been used up in Hong Kong, for example, tells you when you have to start buying from Taiwan.

Understanding products was also more complex. We knew that in Taiwan the synthetics were better, but that Hong Kong was the place to go for cottons. We could provide a package from the whole region rather than a single product from Hong Kong.

By working with a larger number of countries, we were able to assemble components; we call this "assortment packing." Say I sell a tool kit to a major discount chain. I could buy the spanners from one country and the screwdrivers from another and put together a product package. That has some value in it—not great value, but some.

In the second stage, we took the company's sourcing-agent strategy one step further and became a manager and deliverer of manufacturing programs. In the old model, the customer

distribution network designs. The way neighborhood hardware and paint stores match paint colors on their premises is a good example. Instead of making a broad range of different paints to meet customers' specific requirements, factories make generic paint and a variety of color pigments, which hardware and paint stores stock. The stores use a chromatograph to analyze a customer's paint sample and to determine the paint-and-pigment mixture that will match it. This process provides customers with a virtually unlimited number of consistent choices and, at the same time, significantly reduces the inventory of paint that the stores need to stock in order to match every customer's desired color on demand. **Process postponement** is the term used to describe delay of the process step that differentiates the product to as late in the supply chain as possible. The key to postponement, in this case, was separating the production of the paint and the mixing of the pigment and paint and creating a low-cost chromatograph.

Process postponement

would say, "This is the item I want. Please go out and find the best place to buy it for me." The new model works this way. The Limited, one of our big customers, comes to us and says, "For next season, this is what we're thinking about—this type of look, these colors, these quantities. Can you come up with a production program?"

Starting with their designers' sketches, we research the market to find the right type of yarn and dye swatches to match the colors. We take product concepts and realize them in prototypes. Buyers can then look at the samples and say, "No, I don't really like that, I like this. Can you do more of this?" We then create an entire program for the season, specifying the product mix and the schedule. We contract for all the resources. We work with factories to plan and monitor production so we can ensure quality and on-time delivery.

This strategy of delivering manufacturing programs carried us through the 1980s, but that decade brought us a new challenge—and led to our third stage. As the Asian tigers emerged, Hong Kong became an increasingly expensive and uncompetitive place to manufacture. For example, we completely lost the low-end transistor radio business to Taiwan and Korea. What saved us was that China began to open up to trade, allowing Hong Kong to fix its cost problem by moving the labor-intensive portion of production across the border into Southern China.

So for transistor radios we created little kits—plastic bags filled with all the components needed to build a radio. Then we shipped the kits to China for assembly. After the labor-intensive work was completed, the finished goods came back to Hong Kong for final testing and inspection. If you missed a screw you were in trouble: the whole line stopped cold.

Breaking up the value chain as we did was a novel concept at the time. We call it "dispersed manufacturing." This method of manufacturing soon spread to other industries, giving Hong Kong a new lease on life and also transforming our economy. Between 1979 and 1997, Hong Kong's position as a trading entity moved from number 12 in the world to number 8. All our manufacturing moved into China, and Hong Kong became a huge service economy with 84 percent of its gross domestic product coming from services.

This Hong Kong model of borderless manufacturing has become a new paradigm for the region. Today Asia consists of multiple networks of dispersed manufacturing—high-cost hubs that do the sophisticated planning for regional manufacturing. Bangkok works with the Indochinese peninsula, Taiwan with the Philippines, Seoul, and Northern China. Dispersed manufacturing is what's behind the boom in Asia's trade and investment statistics in the 1990s—companies moving raw materials and semifinished parts around Asia. But the region is still very dependent on the ultimate sources of demand, which are in North America and Western Europe. They start the whole cycle going.

Principle 3: *The supply network—the positioning of inventory and the location, number, and structure of service, manufacturing, and distribution facilities—should be designed to provide two capabilities. First, it must be able to supply the basic product to the facilities performing the customization in a cost-effective manner. Second, it must have the flexibility and the responsiveness to take individual customers' orders and deliver the finished, customized good quickly.* To support mass customization, an agile supply network is needed. A company with many product options benefits little from having many distribution centers around the world if those centers perform only the tasks of warehousing and distribution. The investments in inventory that are required to support all the options would be enormous. The example of the paint production process just described is ideal because the paint manufacturing company now has a ready source of capacity to handle the final mixing step: the local paint stores. The generic paint can be shipped in bulk and the final product produced while the customer is in the store. The manufacturing economics change radically when a company redesigns its products and processes into modules so that the final customization steps take place on receipt of a customer's order. It becomes cost-effective to have more distribution centers or stores as in the case of the paint example, each of which stocks basic products and performs the final steps in the customization process.

Having distribution centers perform light manufacturing or assembly can help a company both comply with the local-content rules that are prevalent in emerging markets and respond to customers who are unwilling to wait for a customized product to be shipped from a factory in another region. In this way, a company enjoys the best of both worlds: on the one hand, it can concentrate its manufacturing of critical parts in a few sites around the world so that it can achieve economies of scale, and on the other hand, it can maintain a local presence.

Making decisions like these is not easy. It involves people from at least five areas of the company: marketing, research and development, manufacturing, distribution, and finance. These five groups must play the following roles to support an effective mass customization program:

Cross Functional

- Marketing must determine the extent to which mass customization is needed to fulfill customers' requirements.
- Research and development must redesign the product so that it can be customized at the most efficient point in the supply network.
- Manufacturing and distribution must coordinate both the supply and redesign of materials and situate manufacturing or assembly processes in the most efficient locations.
- Finance must provide activity-based cost information and financial analyses of the alternatives.

Each group at any company has its own measures of performance. Marketing, for example, is evaluated on revenue growth, research and development on a product's functionality and the cost of its components, and manufacturing and distribution on the cost of assembling and delivering a product to the customer. The different measures focus the groups on different objectives. Marketing wants to offer as many product options as possible to attract more customers; research and development wants to offer the product with the greatest possible functionality at the lowest possible cost; and manufacturing and distribution want to make one product at a stable volume. If the groups are not properly coordinated, their attempts to optimize their own performance may hurt the company's ability to create the most efficient supply network that can deliver a customized product at the lowest cost. Negotiations among these groups are critical, with the goal being to decide to do what is best for the company as a whole.

A supply chain links all of the stages together from raw materials through production to the consumer. The supply chain is coordinated with an electronic information system. Many options define the logic of these systems; in all cases, the frequency and speed of communicating information through the chain has a great effect on inventory levels, efficiencies, and costs. For large manufacturing companies, the new enterprise resource planning systems, discussed in Section Four, are now being used extensively.

Managing the supply chain is being shifted, to a large extent, to the vendor. Purchasing contracts are now tied to delivery schedules; we look at the coordination needed to do this when we study lean production systems in Chapter 12. Electronic information flow has shifted routine activities to the vendor by allowing direct access to point-of-sales data and giving responsibility for forecasting and delivery of product directly to the vendor. Today such relationships tend to be long-term, but one can speculate whether the relationships will be long-term in the future.

CONCLUSION

Supply chain management is important in business today. The term *supply chain* comes from a picture of how organizations are linked together as viewed from a particular company. Many companies have enjoyed significant success due to unique ways in which they have organized their supply chains. Dell Computer, for example, skips the distribution and retail steps typical of a manufacturing company's supply chain. However, a good supply chain design for one company may not work for another. This chapter shows how supply chains should be structured to meet the needs of different products and customer groups.

Measures of supply chain efficiency are inventory turnover and weeks of supply. Efficient processes should be used for functional products and responsive processes for innovative products. This alignment of supply chain strategy and product characteristics is extremely important to the operational success of a company.

Companies that face diverse sourcing, production, and distribution decisions need to weigh the costs associated with materials, transportation, production, warehousing, and distribution to develop a comprehensive network designed to minimize costs.

KEY TERMS

Supply chain How organizations are linked together as viewed from a particular company.

Inventory turnover and **weeks of supply** Measures of supply chain efficiency that are mathematically the inverse of one another.

Cost of goods sold The annual cost for a company to produce the goods or services provided to customers.

Average aggregate inventory value The total value of all items held in inventory for the firm valued at cost.

Weeks of supply A measure of how many weeks' worth of inventory is in the system at a particular point in time.

Bullwhip effect The variability in demand is magnified as we move from the customer to the producer in the supply chain.

Functional products Staples that people buy in a wide range of retail outlets, such as grocery stores and gas stations.

Innovative products Products such as fashionable clothes and personal computers that typically have a life cycle of just a few months.

Outsourcing Moving some of a firm's internal activities and decision responsibility to outside providers.

Logistics Management functions that support the complete cycle of material flow: from the purchase and internal control of production materials; to the planning and control of work-in-process; to the purchasing, shipping, and distribution of the finished product.

Design for logistics This concept involves consideration of material procurement and distribution costs during the product design phase.

Transportation mode How an item is shipped.

Value density The value of an item per pound of weight.

Mass customization The ability of a company to deliver highly customized products and services to different customers around the world.

Process postponement Delay of the process step that differentiates a product to as late in the supply chain as possible.

FORMULA REVIEW

[10.1]
$$\text{Inventory turnover} = \frac{\text{Cost of goods sold}}{\text{Average aggregate inventory value}}$$

[10.2]
$$\text{Weeks of supply} = \left(\frac{\text{Average aggregate inventory value}}{\text{Cost of goods sold}} \right) \times 52 \text{ weeks}$$

REVIEW AND DISCUSSION QUESTIONS

1   What recent changes have caused supply chain management to gain importance?
2   With so much productive capacity and room for expansion in the United States, why would a company based in the United States choose to purchase items from a foreign firm? Discuss the pros and cons.

3   Describe the differences between functional and innovative products.

4   What are characteristics of efficient, responsive, risk-hedging, and agile supply chains? Can a supply chain be both efficient and responsive? Risk-hedging and agile? Why or why not?

5   As a supplier, which factors about a buyer (your potential customer) would you consider to be important in setting up a long-term relationship?

6   For the value density problem in Example 10.2, what would the effect be if a competing firm offers you a similar service for 10 percent less than Federal Express's rates?

7   What are the advantages of using the postponement strategy?

8   Describe how outsourcing works. Why would a firm want to outsource?

9   What is so different about Li & Fung's approach to working with their customers? Would this approach work with functional products like toothpaste and basketballs?

10 What are the basic building blocks of an effective mass customization program? What kind of companywide cooperation is required for a successful mass customization program?

Excel: Chapter 10-Problem 1

PROBLEMS

1   Calculate the break-even product value of using Express Mail (overnight delivery) versus Parcel Post (three-day delivery) for sending a package from Peoria, Illinois, to Memphis, Tennessee. The following table contains the appropriate costs. Assume that inventory carrying cost is 25 percent per year of the product value and that there are 365 days per year.

SHIPPING COST: U.S. POSTAL SERVICE; PEORIA, IL, TO MEMPHIS, TN

WEIGHT (LBS.)	COST (OVERNIGHT)	COST (3-DAY)
2	$15.00	$2.87
3	17.25	3.34
4	19.40	3.78
5	21.55	4.10
6	25.40	4.39
7	26.45	4.67
8	27.60	4.91
9	28.65	5.16

2   Using the data from the Dell Computer annual report given in Example 10.1, determine how Dell calculated the six days' supply of raw materials. Do you think six days' supply is a valid representation of the amount of raw material Dell has on hand at the end of the year?

3   The McDonald's fast-food restaurant on campus sells an average of 4,000 quarter-pound hamburgers each week. Hamburger patties are resupplied twice a week, and on average the store has 350 pounds of hamburger in stock. Assume that the hamburger costs $1.00 a pound. What is the inventory turnover for the hamburger patties? On average, how many days of supply are on hand?

4   The U.S. Airfilter company has hired you as a supply chain consultant. The company makes air filters for residential heating and air-conditioning systems. These filters are made in a single plant located in Louisville, Kentucky, in the United States. They are distributed to retailers through wholesale centers in 100 locations in the United States, Canada, and Europe. You have collected the following data relating to the value of inventory in the U.S. Airfilter supply chain:

	QUARTER 1 (JANUARY THROUGH MARCH)	QUARTER 2 (APRIL THROUGH JUNE)	QUARTER 3 (JULY THROUGH SEPTEMBER)	QUARTER 4 (OCTOBER THROUGH DECEMBER)
SALES (TOTAL QUARTER):				
UNITED STATES	300	350	405	375
CANADA	75	60	75	70
EUROPE	30	33	20	15
COST OF GOODS SOLD (TOTAL QUARTER)	280	295	340	350

Excel: U.S. Airfilter

	QUARTER 1 (JANUARY THROUGH MARCH)	QUARTER 2 (APRIL THROUGH JUNE)	QUARTER 3 (JULY THROUGH SEPTEMBER)	QUARTER 4 (OCTOBER THROUGH DECEMBER)
RAW MATERIALS AT THE LOUISVILLE PLANT (END-OF-QUARTER)	50	40	55	60
WORK-IN-PROCESS AND FINISHED GOODS AT THE LOUISVILLE PLANT (END-OF-QUARTER)	100	105	120	150
DISTRIBUTION CENTER INVENTORY (END-OF-QUARTER):				
UNITED STATES	25	27	23	30
CANADA	10	11	15	16
EUROPE	5	4	5	5

ALL AMOUNTS IN MILLIONS OF U.S. DOLLARS

a. What is the average inventory turnover for the firm?

b. If you were given the assignment to increase inventory turnover, what would you focus on? Why?

c. The company reported that it used $500M worth of raw material during the year. On average, how many weeks of supply of raw material are on hand at the factory?

INTERNET ENRICHMENT EXERCISES

1 Using the United Parcel Service Web site at http://www.ups.com and the Federal Express site at http://www.fedex.com, compare rates for shipping a three-pound package, that you will wrap yourself, from New York City to Los Angeles, California. This is a wedding anniversary gift for your parents and is valued at about $100. Your parents' wedding anniversary is in two weeks and you have already purchased and packed the gift. Which service should you use? Why?

2 You are at work in your New York City office and need to send a repair part to a Los Angeles manufacturing plant. The part is a small computer control module weighing only one pound and is valued at about $25. The machine that needs the part is not operating, and it has been estimated that for every hour the machine is not operating, the company loses $150. Which service should you use? Why?

Internet

CASE: SAMYEONG CABLE COMPANY*

INTRODUCTION

Though it was not the first time for President Choi, Oh Gil of Samyeong Cable Company to attend the annual seminar held for Hyundai's Supplier Cooperation Program, with around 500 suppliers in attendance, there was something in the air that made him feel uneasy. He reasoned that it must be due to the fierce competition between the suppliers that had arisen in the last two or three years.

The uneasiness at the seminar was clarified by the information given by President Park, Byung Jae of Hyundai, who was especially concerned with Hyundai's supplier relationships. Compared to Japan, Korean firms had only half the productivity and were also far behind those of the United States. With regard to quality of supply, the disparity was even worse.

President Park, who had just become the CEO of Hyundai Motor Company, had strongly asserted that to make up for the inferior status of Korean firms in the world market, the suppliers' role was the most important factor and was the key to achieving world class success. The motor vehicle industry is one of the key industries from which to assess the competitiveness of the nation. To improve the competitiveness, it required the whole economic-value chain of suppliers and buyers to improve. It could not be done by just Hyundai, Kia, or another company alone. Figures 1–4 provide some comparative information gathered by Hyundai.

After showing these alarming figures, President Park of Hyundai announced that there would be some appraisal of the suppliers. Hyundai would select those few firms that met Hyundai's criteria by their capability and performance to compete in the world market.

Figure 1

Quality—IQS (defect cases for 100 cars in 3 months)

Figure 2

Wage Increases

Figure 3

Revenue per Worker

Figure 4

Value Added per Worker

* Japanese data came from 127 Japanese automakers.

The manual that showed how this process was to be conducted was distributed to all participants at the seminar.

In the seminar President Park of Hyundai had shown some examples of the world class leaders in the motor vehicle industry such as GM, Toyota, and others in their supplier development program, and announced that Hyundai would adopt some unique programs to cope with the fierce competition.

After the seminar, President Choi of Samyeong returned to his own business to assess its competitiveness. With a careful evaluation of his factory, he found that some major changes were needed at his company. His assessment was conducted in three areas: productivity, quality, and cost, which were the central theme of the seminar and the factors that Hyundai would use in evaluating their suppliers. However, after realising that major changes were necessary, he was at an impasse in trying to understand what to do and where to begin.

BACKGROUND OF THE SAMYEONG CABLE COMPANY

Samyeong Cable Company was established in 1969 at Songdong Ku, Seoul, to produce control cables, speedometer cables, and filter elements mostly for motor vehicles, e.g., for Hyundai Motor Co. and other large motor companies such as Kia and Daewoo. A brief history will show how this company has grown and expanded along with the Korean economic boom.

In May 1973, the company name was changed to Samyeong Cable Co., Ltd. It was quite a small company, producing cables largely through manual means. In May 1974, Samyeong was selected by the Consumer Protective Association as a firm that needed encouragement to expand. In July 1978, Samyeong was designated as a specialised manufacturer for automotive cables by the government. This gave Samyeong an opportunity to catch up technologically and to be one of the most technologically competitive firms in the cable industry.

In October 1979, Samyeong moved to a new plant in the Banwol industrial complex, Ansan City, to accommodate the growth in size of the company and in December 1982, it was designated as a "firm of modernisation and rationalisation of medium industry" by the government.

Since March 1987, Chrysler Corporation in the U.S. has approved Samyeong Cable Company as an OEM supplier of hood latch cables. Samyeong has globalised its markets and technological sources. In January 1988, an appreciation medal was awarded to Samyeong by Hyundai Motor Service Co., Ltd., for being an excellent quality supplier. The Industrial Bank of Korea awarded Samyeong Cable Company in December 1989 for being an excellent firm. However, it experienced a major labour dispute in 1989 that severely disappointed the founding president Hahm, Jae Sun who sold his 50 percent share of the Samyeong company to the current President Choi, Oh Gil (age of 52). Subsequently, President Choi took control over the company in 1991.

In April 1990, Samyeong was approved by Rockwell International B.C.S. Australia as an OEM supplier for door regulator cables. In September 1991 a three-year validation of technological aid contract was concluded with YAZAKI Corporation, Japan, for automotive ignition cables. Ignition cables were the only automotive cables where Samyeong did not have their own technology and most of their development efforts have been in this area.

Samyeong Co. established the Technology Research Institute in Chonan in December 1991 with other small–medium firms of about the same size as Samyeong and in the same industry. The new factory for Samyeong was also located in Chonan so that it could take full advantage of the location.

In December 1992, Samyeong established a joint corporation named Shenyan Samyeong Leather Products Co., Ltd., to diversify the company. In February 1993, Samyeong established a trading corporation, Ohsung Korea Co., Ltd., in Seoul to facilitate their exports. In February 1994 it established another joint corporation, named Beijing Samyeong Cable Co., Ltd., with Beijing Cable Co., Ltd., in China. And in November 1994, Samyeong was awarded a prize for excellent trading performance by the South Korean government.

In December 1994 Samyeong constructed a second plant on the site of 13,392m^2 in Chonan and this was where the case began. The new owner, President Choi, Oh Gil, was a qualified CPA and an MBA graduate. He was previously the president of Dong Shin Pharmaceutical Company. Although it was the first time for President Choi to be the owner of a company, he had experience in senior management positions in other companies. The most important thing in this case was the adoption of new management techniques that he had learned from business school and from his experience in other fields. Unlike the former owner, President Choi had a more rational and innovative management style, which brought many organisational and technological changes to Samyeong. After he had taken over control of Samyeong, it had been continuously expanding in size, in sales volume, and production facilities. With President Choi's new management style, the company changed its culture to a more innovative and challenging one. This organisational change enabled the company to cope with the rapidly changing business environment.

The company's revenue of 8.7 billion won in 1991 grew to 22 billion in 1995; the total number of the workers was 313. Its foreign export was predicted to be $7 million in 1995 and most of that was to Rockwell Co. in Australia and China.

FACTORS SETTING THE CONTEXT OF CHANGE

Supplier Relationship Strategy of Hyundai   Since Hyundai was the major purchaser from Samyeong, and Samyeong supplied mostly to Hyundai, it is necessary to carefully look at how Hyundai managed its supplier relationships. Hyundai usually double- or triple-sourced its supply of components to guarantee delivery reliability and had its own measures to evaluate each supplier and assign the amount to be purchased from each supplier. (This was the primary method used to control the suppliers.) So it was important for the suppliers to fit in with Hyundai's evaluation process.

For control cables, Hyundai had two major supplier companies, namely Samyeong and Daedong. This was due to Hyundai's double-sourcing policy that was sometimes varied depending on the items and the level of their suppliers' technological capability. The major characteristic and problem of automotive cables were that, compared to other automotive products, rapid design changes were required as well as worker care. Samyeong was the only source for Hyundai for ignition cables, which were imported from Japan or the U.S. Other than that, most of the products were produced with their own technology.

President Park of Hyundai believed that the basis for supplier selection should be the long-term capability of the suppliers rather than the products being purchased at any one time. The bargaining power of Hyundai as a buyer was actually greater than that of the suppliers as seller, as the buyer purchased through competitive-based sourcing among multiple suppliers. This might guarantee low purchase prices on specific occasions. However, it made the relationship adversarial and short-term with the suppliers, resulting in higher overall costs than would be achieved by taking a long-term view.

Figure 5

A Shifting Paradigm for the Buyer–Seller Relationship

	BASIS FOR SUPPLIER SELECTION	
	PRODUCT-/COMMODITY-BASED	CAPABILITY-BASED
Adversarial Bargaining Power Buyer > Seller	Short-term/operational Price-/quality-based Multiple sourcing	Long-term/strategic Capability-based Competitive Multiple sourcing
Cooperative Partnership-like Buyer = Seller	Nonprice based Operational emphasis Management assistance Technical advice	Strategic emphasis Single sourcing Continuous improvement Cost, quality, delivery

Capability-based single-sourcing had been considered as a way of protecting Hyundai from direct conflict with the suppliers who wanted to sell more specific products to Hyundai. This system provided the suppliers with opportunities to compete with their fellow suppliers in improving their capability on a long-term basis rather than compete in selling specific products. Hyundai could also take advantage of this system in eventually selecting the highest capability suppliers from among the multiple suppliers who participated in Hyundai's supplier relationship program. Eventually, the most capable single supplier for each product was selected. This was made possible through the implementation of an appropriate evaluation system.

Figure 5 illustrates a model of the buyer–seller relationship. This is the original model that Hyundai has pursued in its supplier relationships.

Through this kind of relationship, Hyundai aimed to disseminate its strategic objectives to its suppliers. Hyundai's position should be at the lower right corner, which was ideal for Hyundai to project its corporate strategy onto its suppliers. In this kind of partnership-like relationship, continual improvement is crucial to sustain the relationship. It was also advantageous to cope with the constantly changing environment. For Hyundai, the major problem was that the capabilities of their suppliers were far behind that of other world leaders in the industry. Since the parts that were sourced from suppliers would determine the quality of the final products, this implied many important production activities in Hyundai were related to supplier management.

Supplier Development Program In an attempt to develop their suppliers' strategic capability in better responding to changes, Hyundai set up a supplier development program as shown in Figure 6. At the first stage of the supplier development process, they would outline the objectives of the supplier-relationship development program by which they rate the suppliers and determine the areas requiring improvement. Then Hyundai would organise the advisory team to be dispatched to specific suppliers. The development teams would usually stay at the supplier's plant until the problems were solved. Hyundai established three department units: technical assistance, cooperation development, and parts and components development, all of which reported directly to the president.

Hyundai's major difference from Japanese and U.S. firms was that Hyundai had a permanent department that utilised several ad hoc working teams made up of the necessary experts from different functional areas. Also, the developmental activities could be triggered by supplier evaluation results or by the company's long-term development objectives. For the following three campaigns: CR30

overall cost reduction campaign, Productivity "2 by 2" campaign, and Quality Management "100 ppm" campaign (which will be described later), Hyundai supported their suppliers with ad hoc member teams (which consisted of personnel from other departments) and taught their suppliers the operation of the new technology with the necessary support so that they could adopt the campaigns successfully.

Hyundai used delivery reliability as the most important factor, and then cost, quality, and flexibility. Hyundai assigned their suppliers into five groups (A, B1, B2, C, D) with the A and B groups being autonomously managed and supported. The competition among suppliers had encouraged them to improve their capabilities from "D" to "A" grades where an "A" graded supplier would be treated with rewards in terms of financing, purchase volume, management aid, and many other incentives and fringe benefits that are not awarded to lower grade suppliers. (Hyundai's supplier rating report is in Appendix 1.)

Companies in the C and D groups would be kept under tight control but not actively supported by Hyundai. Most of the transactions were normally associated with companies in the A and B groups, where most of the supporting investment was carried out. As shown in Figure 6, the supplier ratings are determined after the evaluation stage and again after the implementation stage of the development action plans. Table 1 shows the rankings of all of Hyundai's suppliers.

Following the process of supplier development, Hyundai would designate their consensus development action plans by acronyms such as CR30, 2 by 2, and 100 ppm. President Park, Hyundai's CEO, targeted the cooperative single sourcing system through the capability-based competition among Hyundai's multiple suppliers. Usually, Japanese carmakers could select one supplier relatively easily because the suppliers were already competent, while Korean companies had no reservoir of competent suppliers yet. Basically, grade "A" supplier status was what Hyundai wanted its suppliers to achieve.

Experience in Labour Disputes However, single sourcing, in spite of all the expected benefits, had sometimes been found to be vulnerable to unexpected difficulties that caused the suppliers to not be able to supply their parts on time. These difficulties were mainly caused by labour disputes, which were catastrophic to the whole operation of Hyundai. Therefore, the company needed to take protective measures against them. [See Figure 7.] Following are some examples of Hyundai's actual experiences in 1993 and 1994.

The labour dispute was the most serious problem that Hyundai had encountered and was also a major problem where supplier management was concerned. A small labour dispute in a supplier company

Supplier Development Decision Process

Figure 6

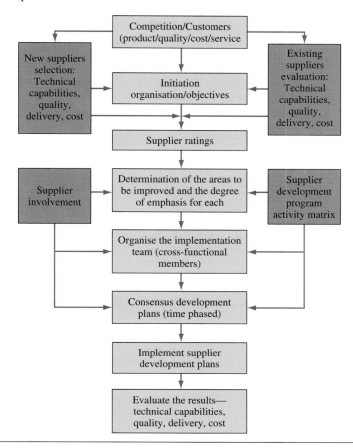

The Rank Classification of Hyundai Suppliers

Table 1

	A CLASS	B CLASS-1	B CLASS-2	C CLASS	D CLASS
Total Number of 92 Suppliers in Passenger Car Part	14	29 Samyeong	28	14	7

Example of Multiple Sourcing

Figure 7

In case of labour disputes or other problems with delivery in Supplier 2, Suppliers 1 and 3 back up Supplier 2.

could damage the whole of Hyundai's process, as had been proved in the case of Apollo Company. The effect was the same as having a dispute in Hyundai since Hyundai could not get the parts to run their production process. It was a big issue in the Korean economy at the time and provided a more realistic view of the supplier chain model. The dispute caused some corrective devices to be added to the supplier relationship program operated by Hyundai.

Contingent Supply Backup System   Since then, Hyundai has utilised single sourcing but distinguishes it with contingent supply backups. This "contingent supply backup system" stipulates that the suppliers designated to a specific model of car were always kept ready to supply the parts to Hyundai for other models if the designated supplier had difficulty in supplying. This was done by preparing lines, tools, and molds to make parts for other models and keeping them available so that the affected parts could be supplied at short notice.

For example, Hyundai had contracts with three different suppliers to acquire seatbelts for the Excel, Sonata, and Grandeur models, but it is still single sourcing from one supplier for each model. In the case of a labour dispute, Hyundai could quickly move to another company and ask them to supply the seatbelts for other vehicle models. It was also easy for the supplier of Excel seatbelts to change its design to supply the Grandeur model since the supplier possessed the capability to produce the other designs. Hyundai had obliged the suppliers to keep the molds, castings, and other necessary items with which they could quickly produce other models.

CONTENT AND SUBSTANCE OF CHANGE

Following the supplier rating stage, Hyundai designated the consensus development action plans for their suppliers by the acronyms "CR30," "2 by 2," and "100 ppm"—programs for cost, productivity, and quality, respectively. Hyundai supported their suppliers with seminars, working manuals, and supporting teams that stayed with the supplier company to coach the production personnel.

CR30—An Overall Cost Reduction Campaign   CR30 was an abbreviation for 30 percent cost reduction. CR30 came into existence in order to countermatch the world leaders like GM, Chrysler, and Toyota, who adopted the "2/3/4" strategy. Here 2 referred to an improvement in the function of the car by 2 times; 3 referred to cost reduction by 1/3 in three years; and 4 aimed for a reduction in weight of the car by 1/4. The objective of CR30 was to identify the parts and components costs that were not competitive with those of the competing companies and help the suppliers of the parts and components to cut down their manufacturing cost by 30 percent. CR30 started in 1987 followed by "2 by 2" in 1991 and "100 ppm" in 1993. CR30 was run in parallel with the other two programs but managed separately. CR30 was utilised by Hyundai Motor Company as an important device for manufacturing cost control of the supplied parts and components. In the supplier relationship, Hyundai was known as a mother company and its suppliers were known as collaboration companies. They exchanged important cost information with each other in order to better control the whole process of manufacturing the cars along the supply chain.

Productivity Campaign: "2 by 2"   The CR30 program was followed by a productivity increase program called "2 by 2," which aimed to double the productivity within two years. This program commenced in July 1994 and targeted to finish in year 1996. The campaign was executed in two phases: the first phase was 1994–1995 and the second, 1995–1996. The year 1993 was to initi-

ate the program to introduce the structure of the campaign and to train people so that the program could begin. The "2 by 2" program was initially introduced by Hyundai in order to absorb the rapid wage increase over productivity increase due to the labour unrest during the 1988–1992 period in Korea. The worker productivity at Hyundai Motor Company then was considered to be only 37 percent of that of Toyota, which had more than one hundred years of experience in car manufacturing. The "2 by 2" campaign was considered beneficial to both Hyundai and its suppliers.

Quality Management by "100 ppm"   President Park, Byung Jae, of Hyundai, who was the founding father of the supplier-relationship development program at Hyundai Motor Company, initiated this campaign in 1990 when he returned to the Ulsan plant for the second time. During that time, he was under pressure because the Hyundai cars were relatively inferior in terms of quality in comparison to their competitors in the world market. The average incoming defect rate of supply parts in Korea was about one thousand times higher than that at Toyota. Hyundai was still using the percentage defect rate as measures instead of parts per million, which had been long adopted by Japanese companies. President Park thought that achieving quality improvements on par with the Japanese levels would provide Hyundai an epoch, an initial turning point in the modernisation of the Hyundai operation. He figured cost, quality, after-sales service, and other competitive priority factors measured by carmakers seemed to be built on a quality foundation. He then decided to launch a "100 ppm" campaign as the cornerstone for innovation in Hyundai's operation along with the CR30 program for cost and the "2 by 2" program for productivity improvement.

At first, "100 parts per million" as a defect rate measure is 10,000 times finer when compared to percent. The "100 ppm" campaign achieved a surprising result, in that Hyundai qualified about 40 suppliers out of 450 by the end of 1995, which was four years after the campaign started. The "100 ppm" campaign was then spread over all industrial companies and the Korean government also promoted this campaign as a national program through public organisations.

PROCESS OF TRANSITION

CR30—An Overall Cost Reduction Campaign   Every year during October through March, both parties in the supplier relationship would update the prices of the supplied parts through a bargaining process. Samyeong had to prepare cost data for itself very thoroughly for the price bargaining so that it could convince Hyundai to agree with its price requests.

After the bargaining process and agreement on the price level, Hyundai would decide whether or not they would embark on a managerial and engineering help program with the supplier in order to achieve further cost reductions. After a price bargaining session in March 1995, Hyundai dispatched a three-man advisory team to Samyeong for the CR30 program. Samyeong had already formed a task force and was ready to start working together with the Hyundai staff. The Samyeong CR30 team investigated its manufacturing lines, supply chain from their own vendors, and product structures, etc., as per the Hyundai staff advice. Both teams jointly prepared the CR30 procedure for Samyeong according to the predetermined guideline manual that was recommended by Hyundai. The procedure included the following areas of analysis:

1   **Objective setting.** The target of cost reduction was expanded to the specific areas of material cost (45 percent), labour cost (30 percent), and overhead cost (20 percent) in two years.

2 **Structural and functional analysis of parts.** According to the attributes operationalised in the objective setting, the parts were analysed in a cross-structure and function matrix of value engineering.

3 **Production process analysis.** Manufacturing processes were analysed and motion study techniques were implemented to eliminate inefficient activities.

4 **Aggregate execution plan.** Integrating all the previous stages of analysis enabled an improvement plan to be drawn up. Elimination, combination, change, and simplification were recommended for departments, components, materials, processes, activities, etc., and were detailed in an action program. As a result, the CR30 program came up with some very successful innovations.

The first example was the standardisation of the "Eye End" gear shift cables. These cables used to be designed and produced for different car models so that the production lot sizes were inevitably small, causing higher production costs. The Samyeong CR30 team reduced the number of designs by almost two-thirds, resulting in common intermediate models of cable to fit all kinds of Hyundai cars. This required a lot of change of the related parts and systems of cars. The second example was the change in processing from lathe work to cold forging of metal parts. The forging work was also automated. Ignition cables were also developed by Samyeong's own R & D group in order to replace the imported ignition cables from Japan.

Productivity Campaign: "2 by 2"   In launching the "2 by 2" campaign, Hyundai categorised the "2 by 2" target companies into two groups. The first group was considered as practice models and the best companies. The companies in the second group would receive intensive care to improve their productivity. Hyundai's "2 by 2" promotion centre provided the suppliers with basic guidelines through workshops for the CEOs and the "2 by 2" program managers of the suppliers. In addition, Hyundai operated every other month "mini exchange meetings" that consisted of five to nine supplying companies grouped by item and region. The meetings required the presence of the CEOs and senior managers from the suppliers that were in charge of the "2 by 2" programs. The meetings were designed to provide the managers with an opportunity to exchange their successful experiences in the program. The "2 by 2 circuit study meeting" was another means to promote and encourage the companies to get involved in the program as actively as possible.

The concentrated care program was another major device to help the less successful suppliers by sending Hyundai staff to assist them. Hyundai equipped their "2 by 2" suppliers with a productivity improvement tool with which to increase productivity. The numerator of their productivity definition formula (output/input) consisted of the factors utilisation, yield rate, automation ratio, safety, space utilisation, office automation, information network, etc., each of which was measured and encouraged to increase. The denominator included lead time, set-up time, cycle time, stock level, rework, defect rate, line breakdown, lot size, etc., each of which was, on the other hand, encouraged to decrease.

Like any other suppliers, Samyeong entered the "2 by 2" campaign with seven major action programs. They embraced the above factors and included the following:

1 Worker consciousness of the "2 by 2" productivity improvement program.

2 Layout improvement and line-balancing.

3 Automation.

4 Set-up time reduction.

5 Waste elimination.

6 Value analysis of product design.

7 5S.

Samyeong adopted a top-down organisation improvement by which the senior management assigned the productivity improvement targets by level and department. The line workers were empowered to make improvements to assist their motivation and the managers applied their own initiatives to set examples for the workers.

President Choi of Samyeong asserted that employee work ethic and consciousness were the most critical elements in order to achieve the "2 by 2" productivity improvement. He also relied heavily on a suggestion system. In 1994 Samyeong solicited around 5,000 suggestions from the workers. "ATTACK100" was the catch phrase for the company to design small group activities, which was equivalent to the Japanese QC Circle. "100" implied "Do it perfectly" on the production line. President Choi often sent middle managers and engineers to Japan to benchmark Samyeong with Japanese companies.

The in-house and outside training programs were also considered important to motivate the employees in Samyeong. The production layout changed from I-shape to U-shape and benefited the company in driving out unnecessary lead time and work in process. The workers could concentrate on their work with much less tension than before. Following are three examples of improvement in processes suggested by Samyeong workers:

1 Simultaneous process of stripping and flaring of the inner wire through automation.

2 Automating the formerly manual process for the parking brake cable conduit.

3 Automation of the inspection process for the parking brake inner wire for the model J-3.

Samyeong identified seven kinds of waste to be removed from the production lines. These included overstocking, moving costs, defects, work methods, waiting time caused by line unbalance, and bottlenecks. The changes in the production layout and automation of production lines had significant contribution in resolving the long-term built-in wastes, especially overstocking and bottlenecks in the production lines. Samyeong controlled the lines by adopting a system called "my machine," which protected the machines and lines as a whole from breakdown and poor operation. The "my machine system" assigned every worker to one machine so that the person could be in charge of the particular machine and be responsible for maintaining his/her machine in the best condition. The company provided the workers about one hour, twice a week, for "my machine day meeting" where they shared their experiences among themselves.

The Japanese 5S technique was incorporated to keep the machines and lines clean and in order. Samyeong rotated the line managers among the different lines once a month so that employees could easily communicate across departments and understand the recent functions operations in the lines and plant as a whole.

A "visual control system" was also imported into Samyeong in motivating the employees to accept changes in the operations and management of the department and the entire plant. All kinds of necessary performance information, such as worker absenteeism, production rate, productivity, defect rates, accidents, and so forth, were measured by date, by department, and even by individual worker. The performance measures were then posted on the walls so that the information was clearly visible to the employees.

The actual performance of the "2 by 2" program was subject to an open evaluation by Hyundai monthly, quarterly, and annually. Hyundai would then compare the actual performances with the plans and targets, and evaluation was measured in terms of the line level, department level, and the whole company. "Productivity" or "value added" was measured in SPH (sales per hour) per worker and per capita monthly sales. Value added was defined as sales less material cost. The calculation of the three measures was based on utilisation factor, production rate, input man-hours (direct or indirect), and material consumption. This new measurement of the organisation became more active and dynamic in the production area.

Quality Management by "100 ppm" In December 1991, Samyeong adopted the "100 ppm" program in order to improve the quality of its products. According to Hyundai's recommendation, Samyeong started the "100 ppm" program by targeting three quality dimensions: quality in the factory, quality at the supplier level, and quality at the buyer level, which included after-sales service of complete cars. Samyeong made an attempt to be qualified in 1994 but failed. Samyeong continued its effort in the new plant in Chonan City and eventually succeeded in 1995 and was named as the 35th "100 ppm" supplier of Hyundai Motor Company. Hyundai provided very thorough procedures that the supplier should follow to implement their "100 ppm" programs as effectively as possible. Samyeong took advantage of the Hyundai procedure in establishing its brand new plant in Chonan. The company tried to follow the Hyundai procedure as closely as possible because of the potential time saving, especially when compared to the old Samyeong plant located in Ansan. From the beginning of the new plant project, Samyeong requested Hyundai to provide a supplier support team to assist in setting up the lines and management systems. Samyeong's "100 ppm" organisation was under the direct supervision of President Choi and information was reported by the plant superintendents.

The Hyundai "100 ppm" procedure consisted of six major components in sequence. They are as follows:

1st Stage: Initiation and Preparation
- Identify the 100 ppm target items.
- 100 percent inspection for all finished products.
- Set up the organisation and motivate the employees by education and promotion devices such as badge wearing, placards, case study meetings, ceremony award system, and QC circles.
- 3X5S system that is to stabilize the quality by fixing the lot size, containers, and location of operations and the classical Japanese 5S.

2nd Stage: Typology of Defect
- Analyse the causes of defects and identify the types of defect.
- Identify the target processes to improve.
- Set up inspection measures.

3rd Stage: Troubleshooting
- Analyse the parameters for the production lines of the target items.
- Identify the limiting factors causing the trouble from four dimensions such as equipment, materials, working method, and operators. Interviews are recommended for operators.

- Correlative analysis of the tendency of defects and the limiting factors of the four items.
- Draw out the defect causes from the correlation analysis.

4th Stage: Development of the Three-Dimensional Measures
- First measure is to improve the line and then standardise the method by which the line was corrected.
- Second measure is to follow up the corrected process done above.
- Third measure is to audit carefully the quality of the products, so an auditing system is prepared.
- Planning the implementation in terms of ppm for a schedule over a time period.

5th Stage: Implementation onto the Floor
- Put the target lines under control as planned in the 4th stage.
- Set up work method, the procedure to follow the work method, and 3C 5S rules.
- Evaluate and correct the lines until the quality level reaches the target level.

6th Stage: Completion of Improvement
- Self company evaluation and Hyundai Motor Company evaluation are required to get acceptance at completion.
- Follow-up activity is very important to keep the lines under control.

For example, in the case of speedometer cables, they found that the friction between the core pin and the driver gear caused noise. It was due to the attachment of a key joint that was not qualified, and there was too much agitation between the core and core pin recorded on October 10, October 25, and December 10, respectively. They solved the problem by first looking over the design of the driver gear as a related part of the core pin, then adopted CAE (which is NISA reading software for design processes) to improve the process.

OPERATION OF NEW PRACTICES

CR30—An Overall Cost Reduction Campaign Although cost reduction was the most critical item to both Hyundai and its suppliers, the CR30 program was not sufficient to clearly confine its scope and extent. Cost reduction was a long-ranging and comprehensive task to carry out. President Choi of Samyeong thought that even though Hyundai had proved helpful to Samyeong in launching the CR30 program, the time spent between Hyundai staff and Samyeong was not sufficient to cover all of the issues. The problems remained very complex. President Choi of Samyeong remarked that:

> The Hyundai task team members seemed to be overly anxious to dig out some factors as quickly as possible by which they could easily show off their achievement of cost reduction at Samyeong . . . That tendency might cause us just to look at the purchase price of materials from our vendors as a cost reduction source instead of looking at other possible attributes in the overall operation such as waste in production lines, inventory system, physical distribution, inadequate design, wage increases, high overhead cost, physical distribution cost, and so on.

He continued:

> The purchase price of materials from our vendors has a great impact on the relationship we have with our vendors . . . Those second-tier vendors are not so developed technologically and managerially so we have to do something that is helpful to them, but we are not yet ready to help them reduce their cost . . . So we, Samyeong, take the pressure between Hyundai, our buyer, and our vendors.

Productivity Campaign: "2 by 2"   Samyeong's adoption of the programs to achieve "2 by 2" began at the cable manufacturing section. It was because there were more design changes in cable manufacturing than any other automotive products in Samyeong, and the product life cycle of the cable was rather short, about three to four years. In view of this, the rapid design changes and short product life cycle imposed certain limitations when implementing automation. However, Samyeong achieved the automation of 1,000 items out of their total of 2,000 items. Figure 8 shows how rapidly SPH improved over time. Almost 60 percent of SPH measures have been improved.

As shown in Figure 9, the SPH or productivity increased steadily as targeted by Hyundai and Samyeong for the first year after the launch of the program. The result was mainly contributed by process and work analysis and VE techniques, which resulted in increasing the automation of the inner wire flaring, coating, stripping, and flaring processes.

Quality Management by "100 ppm"   To qualify as a "100 ppm" supplier, the identified company had to meet the "100 ppm" level of quality in three areas: (1) the production process, (2) finished products, and (3) outside the company. Requirements (1) and (2) were

for a two-month guarantee after improvement. Requirement (3) applied to Hyundai Motor Company incoming inspections for three months after delivery, and to after-service parts for six months after delivery in domestic maintenance, and one year after overseas shipping. The "100 ppm" auditing was a point system; the 100 points achievement was equivalent to 1–20 ppm of finished products and 0–100 ppm of work in process. The lowest score was 55 points, which was equivalent to 10,001 ppm or higher of finished products and 30,001 ppm or higher of work in process.

Samyeong finally passed the 100 ppm completion of improvement evaluation in October 1995, after three consequent internal audits by Hyundai. For instance, the final quality level of speedometer cables improved from 19,556 ppm in July 1994 down to 700 ppm in April 1995. The progression in quality is presented in Figure 10.

CONCLUSION

This case study has examined three campaigns in an integrated way within Samyeong Cable Company, namely

1 CR30 overall cost reduction campaign.
2 Productivity "2 by 2" campaign.
3 Quality management "100 ppm" campaign.

SPH (sales per hour) per Person of Parking Brake Cable

Figure 8

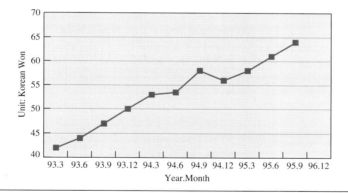

SPH of Samyeong (in total)

Figure 9

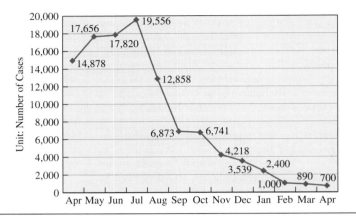

Figure 10   Number of After-Sales Service Three Months after Sales for Speedometer Cable (in 1994)

Surprisingly, there wasn't any significant political battle or resistance from the workers throughout implementation of the new systems. This is due to the following factors.

Firstly, Hyundai placed great effort in working with its supplier companies to achieve its strategic goals through its suppliers. Even though it was a cooperative relationship between Hyundai and Samyeong, Hyundai was the driver of change and Samyeong followed in a cooperative manner. Through a well-designed model of supplier management and strong support, which was delivered by a flexibly manned team, Hyundai was able to aggressively lead the suppliers in the direction that they wanted. This could not have been achieved if there was resistance from the suppliers. Hyundai managed to retain a good relationship with its partners due to this well-designed model. The most unique attribute of Hyundai's supplier development program was that the relationship strived for long-term single sourcing with flexibility. This protected Hyundai from being exposed to inefficient suppliers and helped to develop the supplier's capability without confrontation in any hostile way.

Secondly, even though Hyundai's supplier management program was initially difficult for supplier companies to adopt new and advanced technology such as 100 ppm because of their small size, they could easily get access to the new technology from Hyundai at a low price. This was partly because of Hyundai's supplier management policy, and also because of the suppliers' positive reaction to the programs conducted by Hyundai.

Thirdly, the CEO of the supplier company provided strong support. Samyeong's new owner, President Choi, was a well-educated professional manager who was able to implement new management techniques effectively compared to many Korean companies, especially the small and medium ones, which were managed by their owners with little experience in advanced management styles. In this case, President Choi, who had a strong background in management theory and application experiences, drove the company to adopt a new management style and changed the culture of the firm. Additionally, Samyeong's new factory in Chonan also had the geographic advantage of being close to the co-research centre for the cable industry, which was also established at Chonan.

This case implies that for small and medium companies that cannot afford to develop new technology that requires large capital investment, it would be better to adopt the technology through their buying firm's expense and experience. In the case of Hyundai being the buying firm, it is true that in order to achieve their own strategic goal, it was important to have their supplier companies well managed in a cooperative manner, especially in complex industries like the auto industry.

APPENDIX 1: HYUNDAI'S SUPPLIER RATING REPORT

	EVALUATION PARTS	POINTS
Managerial (20%)	Stability	4
	Growth	4
	Activity	4
	Revenue	4
	Productivity	4
	Others	Varies
Technological development (25%)	A80	5
	Product development capability	15
	Manufacturing capability	5
Production management (25%)	Production planning	3
	2 by 2	5
	Field management	3
	SS	5
	Task management	3
	Fire prevention	1.5
	Computerised degree	1.5
	Defect rates	3
Quality management (25%)	Quality insurance	3
	Outsourcing	3
	Process management	3
	Product management	3
	Reliability	3
	Suggestion systems	2
	Domestic A/S	3
	Foreign A/S	5
Incentives (5%)	Patents	2
	100 ppm	1
	ISO	1
	Exports	1

APPENDIX 2: IMPROVEMENT CASE OF Y3-PARKING BRAKE INNER WIRE

Before:

Problem: Inconsistent length of the product due to conduit shrinking.

After:

Effects: Saving 162,000 wons a month by low defects and low cost.
Investment: 50,000 wons.
Time taken: 0.3 month.

*THIS CASE WAS DEVELOPED FOR USE IN CLASSROOM DISCUSSION AND IS NOT INTENDED TO NECESSARILY ILLUSTRATE APPROPRIATE OR INAPPROPRIATE MANAGEMENT PRACTICES. CASE AUTHOR: KEE YOUNG KIM, YONSEI UNIVERSITY, 1996. SIMON POON, A DOCTORAL STUDENT IN THE GRADUATE SCHOOL OF MANAGEMENT AT MACQUARIE UNIVERSITY, WAS THE RESEARCH ASSOCIATE WHO REWROTE THE CASE IN 2000. THE FUNDING FOR THIS CASE PRODUCTION WAS PROVIDED BY THE AUSTRALIAN FEDERAL GOVERNMENT'S DEPARTMENT OF INDUSTRY, SCIENCE AND RESOURCES.

SELECTED BIBLIOGRAPHY

Bowersox, D. J.; D. J. Closs; and M. B. Cooper. *Supply Chain and Logistics Management.* New York: Irwin/McGraw-Hill, 2002.

Burt, D. N.; D. W. Dobler; and S. L. Starling. *World Class Supply Management^SM: The Key to Supply Chain Management.* 7th ed. New York: McGraw-Hill/Irwin, 2003.

Chopra, S., and P. Meindl. *Supply Chain Management: Strategy, Planning, and Operations.* 2nd ed. Upper Saddle River, NJ: Prentice Hall, 2003.

Greaver II, M. F. *Strategic Outsourcing: A Structured Approach to Outsourcing Decisions and Initiatives.* New York: American Management Association, 1999.

Handfield, R. B., and E. L. Nichols Jr. *Introduction to Supply Chain Management.* Upper Saddle River, NJ: Prentice Hall, 1999.

Hayes, R.; G. Pisano; D. Upton; and S. Wheelwright. *Operations Strategy and Technology: Pursuing the Competitive Edge.* New York: John Wiley & Sons, 2005.

Simchi-Levi, D.; P. Kaminski; and E. Simchi-Levi. *Supply Chain Management.* 2nd ed. New York: McGraw-Hill, 2003.

Vollmann, T.; W. L. Berry; D. C. Whybark; and F. R. Jacobs. *Manufacturing Planning and Control Systems for Supply Chain Management: The Definitive Guide for Professionals.* New York: McGraw-Hill/Irwin, 2004.

FOOTNOTES

1 M. L. Fisher, "What Is the Right Supply Chain for Your Product?" *Harvard Business Review,* March–April 1997, pp. 105–16.

2 Hau L. Lee, "Aligning Supply Chain Strategies with Product Uncertainties," *California Management Review* 44, no. 3 (Spring 2002), pp. 105–19. Copyright © 2002 by the Regents of the University of California. By permission of the Regents.

3 "Have Factory Will Travel," *The Economist,* February 12–18, 2000, pp. 61–62.

4 Adapted from Martha Craumer, "How to Think Strategically about Outsourcing," *Harvard Management Update,* May 2002, p. 4.

5 This section is adapted from E. Feitzinger and H. Lee, "Mass Customization at Hewlett-Packard: The Power of Postponement," *Harvard Business Review,* January–February 1997, pp. 116–21.

chapter

STRATEGIC CAPACITY MANAGEMENT

11
PHARMACEUTICAL COMPANIES HAVE CHALLENGING CAPACITY-PLANNING DECISIONS

Manufacturing capacity decision making in pharmaceuticals is extremely complex given the number of options a company faces. It is an expensive gamble due to the high capital cost of manufacturing facilities in the industry and the opportunity cost of restricting investment in other projects. Consider a new biotech product in Phase II (this is the second out of three steps required to prove that the product is safe and works) with very high potential sales. The company needed to secure capacity immediately but was unsure about how

much to obtain. Possible uncertainty over patent infringement problems, the organization's marketing ability, and competitor response meant that the range of sales projections varied by 600 percent and the probability of actually launching the products was estimated to be only 45 percent. It looked like a £200 million gamble.

So how did the consulting company working with the biotech company handle this problem? They used the exact tools that we discuss in this chapter. They considered the following:

- What is the expected value of the drug under different supply scenarios? What happens if production capacity is constrained?

- What is the expected return on investment for different manufacturing options? Options included in-house production and outsourcing.
- What is best between "hijacking" (sharing) another product's capacity and keeping a fixed capacity constraint?

These are challenging problems that are addressed at the top levels of the firm. →

Manufacturing and service capacity investment decisions can be very complex. Consider some of the following difficult questions that need to be addressed:

- How long will it take to bring new capacity on stream? How does this match with the time that it takes to develop a new product?
- What will be the impact of not having sufficient capacity for a promising product?
- Should the firm use third-party contract manufacturers? How much of a premium will the contract manufacturer charge for providing flexibility in manufacturing volume?

In this chapter, we look at these tough strategic capacity decisions. We begin by discussing the nature of capacity from an OM perspective.

CAPACITY MANAGEMENT IN OPERATIONS

Capacity

Service

Cross Functional

A dictionary definition of **capacity** is "the ability to hold, receive, store, or accommodate." In a general business sense, it is most frequently viewed as the amount of output that a system is capable of achieving over a specific period of time. In a service setting, this might be the number of customers that can be handled between noon and 1:00 P.M. In manufacturing, this might be the number of automobiles that can be produced in a single shift.

When looking at capacity, operations managers need to look at both resource inputs *and* product outputs. The reason is that, for planning purposes, real (or effective) capacity depends on what is to be produced. For example, a firm that makes multiple products inevitably can produce more of one kind than of another with a given level of resource inputs. Thus, while the managers of an automobile factory may state that their facility has 10,000 labor hours available per year, they are also thinking that these labor hours can be used to make either 50,000 two-door models or 40,000 four-door models (or some mix of the two- and four-door models). This reflects their knowledge of what their current technology and labor force inputs can produce and the product mix that is to be demanded from these resources.

An operations management view also emphasizes the time dimension of capacity. That is, capacity must also be stated relative to some period of time. This is evidenced in the common distinction drawn between long-range, intermediate-range, and short-range capacity planning. (See the box "Time Horizons for Capacity Planning.")

Finally, capacity planning itself has different meaning to individuals at different levels within the operations management hierarchy. The vice president of manufacturing is concerned with aggregate capacity of all factories within the firm. The vice president's concern relates mainly to the financial resources required to support these factories. You will study this process when you cover capital budgeting during your finance course.

The plant manager (PM) is concerned with the capacity of the individual plant. The PM must decide how best to use this capacity to meet the anticipated demand for products. Because short-term demand may greatly exceed short-term capacity during peak demand periods, the PM must determine when and how much inventory to build in anticipation of these peaks. We will deal with this topic in depth when we cover sales and operations planning in Chapter 14. Today many firms are using information systems to coordinate the use of plant capacity across multiple sites. This results in the optimal use of manufacturing and distribution resources.

TIME HORIZONS FOR CAPACITY PLANNING

Capacity planning is generally viewed in three time durations:

Long range—greater than one year. Where productive resources (such as buildings, equipment, or facilities) take a long time to acquire or dispose of, long-range capacity planning requires top management participation and approval.

Intermediate range—monthly or quarterly plans for the next 6 to 18 months. Here, capacity may be varied by such alterna-tives as hiring, layoffs, new tools, minor equipment purchases, and subcontracting.

Short range—less than one month. This is tied into the daily or weekly scheduling process and involves making adjust-ments to eliminate the variance between planned and actual output. This includes alternatives such as overtime, personnel transfers, and alternative production routings.

The first-level supervisor is concerned with capacity of the equipment and staff mix in his or her department. This person will work out detailed schedules to accommodate the daily flow of work. We will study this scheduling process in Chapter 17.

Although there is no one person with the job title "capacity manager," there are several managerial positions charged with the effective use of capacity. *Capacity* is a relative term; in an operations management context, it may be defined as *the amount of resource inputs avail-able relative to output requirements over a particular period of time.* Note that this definition makes no distinction between efficient and inefficient use of capacity. In this respect, it is consistent with how the federal Bureau of Economic Analysis defines *maximum practical capacity* used in its surveys: "That output attained within the normal operating schedule of shifts per day and days per week including the use of high-cost inefficient facilities."[1]

The objective of **strategic capacity planning** is to provide an approach for determining the overall capacity level of capital-intensive resources—facilities, equipment, and overall labor force size—that best supports the company's long-range competitive strategy. The capacity level selected has a critical impact on the firm's response rate, its cost structure, its inventory policies, and its management and staff support requirements. If capacity is inadequate, a company may lose customers through slow service or by allowing competitors to enter the market. If capacity is excessive, a company may have to reduce prices to stimu-late demand; underutilize its workforce; carry excess inventory; or seek additional, less pro-fitable products to stay in business.

Strategic capacity planning

JELLY BELLY CANDY COMPANY, HEADQUARTERED IN FAIRFIELD, CALIFORNIA, PRODUCES 100,000 POUNDS OF JELLY BELLY BEANS PER DAY, APPROXIMATELY 347 BEANS PER SECOND. IT TAKES 7 TO 21 DAYS OF CURING ON THESE TRAYS TO MAKE A JELLY BELLY BEAN.

PRODUCTION CAPACITY IS AFFECTED BY FACILITIES, EQUIPMENT, PROCESSING METHODS, LABOR, AND SUPPLIES. THE CAPACITY OF THIS ORANGE JUICE PLANT ALSO HAS TO BE MANAGED FOR SEASONAL EFFECTS ON BOTH RESOURCE SUPPLIES AND CUSTOMER DEMAND.

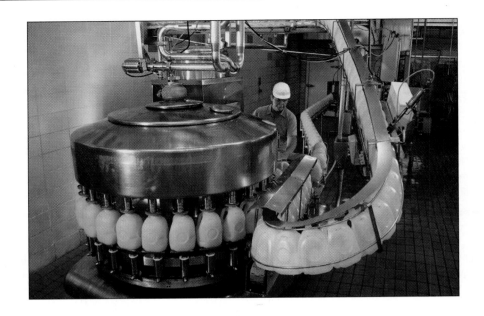

CAPACITY PLANNING CONCEPTS

Best operating level

The term *capacity* implies an attainable rate of output, for example, 300 cars per day, but says nothing about how long that rate can be sustained. Thus, we do not know if this 300 cars per day is a one-day peak or a six-month average. To avoid this problem, the concept of **best operating level** is used. This is the level of capacity for which the process was designed and thus is the volume of output at which average unit cost is minimized. Determining this minimum is difficult because it involves a complex trade-off between the allocation of fixed overhead costs and the cost of overtime, equipment wear, defect rates, and other costs.

Capacity utilization rate

An important measure is the **capacity utilization rate,** which reveals how close a firm is to its best operating point (that is, design capacity):

$$\text{Capacity utilization rate} = \frac{\text{Capacity used}}{\text{Best operating level}}$$

The capacity utilization rate is expressed as a percentage and requires that the numerator and denominator be measured in the same units and time periods (such as machine hour/day, barrels of oil/day, dollar of output/day).

ECONOMIES AND DISECONOMIES OF SCALE

The basic notion of economies of scale is that as a plant gets larger and volume increases, the average cost per unit of output drops. This is partially due to lower operating and capital cost, because a piece of equipment with twice the capacity of another piece typically does not cost twice as much to purchase or operate. Plants also gain efficiencies when they become large enough to fully utilize dedicated resources for tasks such as material handling, computer equipment, and administrative support personnel.

At some point, the size of a plant becomes too large and diseconomies of scale become a problem. These diseconomies may surface in many different ways. For example, maintaining the demand required to keep the large facility busy may require significant discounting of the product. The U.S. automobile manufacturers continually face this problem. Another typical example involves using a few large-capacity pieces of equipment. Minimizing equipment downtime is essential in this type of operation. M&M Mars, for example, has highly automated, high-volume equipment to make M&Ms. A single packaging line moves 2.6 million M&Ms each hour. Even though direct labor to operate the equipment is very low, the labor required to maintain the equipment is high.

The Experience Curve

exhibit 11.1

a. Costs per unit produced fall by a specific percentage each time cumulative production doubles. This relationship can be expressed through a linear scale as shown in this graph of a 70 percent learning curve:

b. It can also be expressed through logarithms:

In many cases, the size of a plant may be influenced by factors other than the internal equipment, labor, and other capital expenditures. A major factor may be the cost to transport raw materials and finished product to and from the plant. A cement factory, for example, would have a difficult time serving customers more than a few hours from its plant. Analogously, automobile companies such as Ford, Honda, Nissan, and Toyota have found it advantageous to locate plants within specific international markets. The anticipated size of these intended markets will largely dictate the size of the plants.

Jaguar, the luxury automobile producer, recently found they had too many plants. Jaguar was employing 8,560 workers in three plants that produced 126,122 cars, about 14 cars per employee. In comparison, Volvo's plant in Torslanda, Sweden, was more than twice as productive, building 158,466 cars with 5,472 workers, or 29 cars per employee. By contrast, BMW AG's Mini unit made 174,000 vehicles at a single British plant with just 4,500 workers (39 cars per employee).

Global

THE EXPERIENCE CURVE

A well-known concept is the experience curve. As plants produce more, they gain experience in the best production methods, which reduce their costs of production in a predictable manner. Every time a plant's cumulative production doubles, its production costs decline by a specific percentage depending on the nature of the business. Exhibit 11.1 demonstrates the effect of an experience curve on the production costs of hamburgers.

The experience curve percentage varies across industries. To apply this concept to the restaurant industry, consider a hypothetical fast-food chain that has produced 5 million hamburgers. Given a current variable cost of $0.55 per burger, what will the cost per burger be when cumulative production reaches 10 million burgers? If the firm has a 90 percent experience curve, costs will fall to 90 percent of $0.55, or $0.495, when accumulated production reaches 10 million. At 1 billion hamburgers, the variable cost drops to less than $0.25.

Note that sales volume becomes an important issue in achieving cost savings. If firm A serves twice as many hamburgers daily as firm B, it will accumulate "experience" twice as fast. (Additional discussion of experience or learning curves is provided in Technical Note 4.)

WHERE ECONOMIES OF SCALE MEET THE EXPERIENCE CURVE

The astute reader will realize that larger plants can have a two-way cost advantage over their competitors. Not only does a larger plant gain from economies of scale, but it will also produce more, giving it experience curve advantages as well. Companies often use this dual advantage as a competitive strategy by first building a large plant with substantial economies of scale, and then using its lower costs to price aggressively and increase sales volume. The increased volume moves them down the experience curve more quickly than their competitors, allowing the company to lower prices further, gaining still more volume. However, two criteria must be met for this strategy to succeed: (1) The product must fit customers' needs and (2) the demand must be sufficiently large to support the volume.

CAPACITY FOCUS

The concept of the focused factory holds that a production facility works best when it focuses on a fairly limited set of production objectives.[2] This means, for example, that a firm should not expect to excel in every aspect of manufacturing performance: cost, quality, flexibility, new product introductions, reliability, short lead times, and low investment. Rather, it should select a limited set of tasks that contribute the most to corporate objectives. However, given the breakthroughs in manufacturing technology, there is an evolution in factory objectives toward trying to do everything well. How do we deal with these apparent contradictions? One way is to say that if the firm does not have the technology to master multiple objectives, then a narrow focus is the logical choice. Another way is to recognize the practical reality that not all firms are in industries that require them to use their full range of capabilities to compete.

Capacity focus   The **capacity focus** concept can also be operationalized through the mechanism of plants within plants— or *PWPs*. A focused plant may have several PWPs, each of which may have separate suborganizations, equipment and process policies, workforce management policies, production control methods, and so forth for different products—even if they are made under the same roof. This, in effect, permits finding the best operating level for each department of the organization and thereby carries the focus concept down to the operating level.

CAPACITY FLEXIBILITY

Capacity flexibility means having the ability to rapidly increase or decrease production levels, or to shift production capacity quickly from one product or service to another. Such flexibility is achieved through flexible plants, processes, and workers, as well as through strategies that use the capacity of other organizations.

Flexible Plants   Perhaps the ultimate in plant flexibility is the *zero-changeover-time* plant. Using movable equipment, knockdown walls, and easily accessible and reroutable utilities, such a plant can quickly adapt to change. An analogy to a familiar service business captures the flavor well: a plant with equipment "that is easy to install and easy to tear down and move—like the Ringling Bros.–Barnum and Bailey Circus in the old tent-circus days."[3]

Flexible Processes   Flexible processes are epitomized by flexible manufacturing systems on the one hand and simple, easily set up equipment on the other. Both of these technological approaches permit rapid low-cost switching from one product line to another, enabling what are sometimes referred to as **economies of scope.** (By definition, economies of scope exist when multiple products can be produced at a lower cost in combination than they can separately.)

Economies of scope

Flexible Workers   Flexible workers have multiple skills and the ability to switch easily from one kind of task to another. They require broader training than specialized workers and need managers and staff support to facilitate quick changes in their work assignments.

CAPACITY PLANNING

CONSIDERATIONS IN ADDING CAPACITY

Many issues must be considered when adding capacity. Three important ones are maintaining system balance, frequency of capacity additions, and the use of external capacity.

Maintaining System Balance   In a perfectly balanced plant, the output of stage 1 provides the exact input requirement for stage 2. Stage 2's output provides the exact input requirement for stage 3, and so on. In practice, however, achieving such a "perfect" design is usually both impossible and undesirable. One reason is that the best operating levels for each stage generally differ. For instance, department 1 may operate most efficiently over a range of 90 to 110 units per month, whereas department 2, the next stage in the process, is most efficient at 75 to 85 units per month, and department 3 works best over a range of 150 to 200 units per month. Another reason is that variability in product demand and the processes themselves generally leads to imbalance except in automated production lines, which, in essence, are just one big machine.

There are various ways of dealing with imbalance. One is to add capacity to stages that are bottlenecks. This can be done by temporary measures such as scheduling overtime, leasing equipment, or purchasing additional capacity through subcontracting. A second way is through the use of buffer inventories in front of the bottleneck stage to ensure that it always has something to work on. (This is a central feature of the synchronous manufacturing approach detailed in Chapter 18.) A third approach involves duplicating the facilities of one department on which another is dependent.

Frequency of Capacity Additions   There are two types of costs to consider when adding capacity: the cost of upgrading too frequently and that of upgrading too infrequently. Upgrading capacity too frequently is expensive. Direct costs include removing and replacing old equipment and training employees on the new equipment. In addition, the new equipment must be purchased, often for considerably more than the selling price of the old. Finally, there is the opportunity cost of idling the plant or service site during the changeover period.

Conversely, upgrading capacity too infrequently is also expensive. Infrequent expansion means that capacity is purchased in larger chunks. Any excess capacity that is purchased must be carried as overhead until it is utilized. (Exhibit 11.2 illustrates frequent versus infrequent capacity expansion.)

External Sources of Capacity   In some cases, it may be cheaper to not add capacity at all, but rather to use some existing external source of capacity. Two common

exhibit 11.2

Frequent versus Infrequent Capacity Expansion

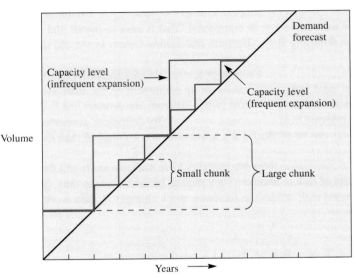

strategies used by organizations are outsourcing and sharing capacity. An example of outsourcing is Japanese banks in California subcontracting check-clearing operations. An example of sharing capacity is two domestic airlines flying different routes with different seasonal demands exchanging aircraft (suitably repainted) when one's routes are heavily used and the other's are not. A new twist is airlines sharing routes—using the same flight number even though the airline company may change through the route. Outsourcing is covered in more depth in Chapter 10.

DETERMINING CAPACITY REQUIREMENTS

In determining capacity requirements, we must address the demands for individual product lines, individual plant capabilities, and allocation of production throughout the plant network. Typically this is done according to the following steps:

1. Use forecasting techniques (see Chapter 13) to predict sales for individual products within each product line.
2. Calculate equipment and labor requirements to meet product line forecasts.
3. Project labor and equipment availabilities over the planning horizon.

Capacity cushion

Often the firm then decides on some **capacity cushion** that will be maintained between the projected requirements and the actual capacity. A capacity cushion is an amount of capacity in excess of expected demand. For example, if the expected annual demand on a facility is $10 million in products per year and the design capacity is $12 million per year, it has a 20 percent capacity cushion. A 20 percent capacity cushion equates to an 83 percent utilization rate (100%/120%).

When a firm's design capacity is less than the capacity required to meet its demand, it is said to have a negative capacity cushion. If, for example, a firm has a demand of $12 million in products per year but can produce only $10 million per year, it has a negative capacity cushion of 16.7 percent.

We now apply these three steps to an example.

EXAMPLE 11.1: Determining Capacity Requirements

The Stewart Company produces two flavors of salad dressings: Paul's and Newman's. Each is available in bottles and single-serving plastic bags. Management would like to determine equipment and labor requirements for the next five years.

SOLUTION

Step 1. Use forecasting techniques to predict sales for individual products within each product line. The marketing department, which is now running a promotional campaign for Newman's dressing, provided the following forecast demand values (in thousands) for the next five years. The campaign is expected to continue for the next two years.

	YEAR				
	1	2	3	4	5
PAUL'S					
Bottles (000s)	60	100	150	200	250
Plastic bags (000s)	100	200	300	400	500
NEWMAN'S					
Bottles (000s)	75	85	95	97	98
Plastic bags (000s)	200	400	600	650	680

Step 2. Calculate equipment and labor requirements to meet product line forecasts. Currently, three machines that can package up to 150,000 bottles each per year are available. Each machine requires two operators and can produce bottles of both Newman's and Paul's dressings. Six bottle machine operators are available. Also, five machines that can package up to 250,000 plastic bags each per year are available. Three operators are required for each machine, which can produce plastic bags of both Newman's and Paul's dressings. Currently, 20 plastic bag machine operators are available.

Total product line forecasts can be calculated from the preceding table by adding the yearly demand for bottles and plastic bags as follows:

	YEAR				
	1	2	3	4	5
Bottles	135	185	245	297	348
Plastic bags	300	600	900	1,050	1,180

We can now calculate equipment and labor requirements for the current year (year 1). Because the total available capacity for packaging bottles is 450,000/year (3 machines × 150,000 each), we will be using 135/450 = 0.3 of the available capacity for the current year, or 0.3 × 3 = 0.9 machine. Similarly, we will need 300/1,250 = 0.24 of the available capacity for plastic bags for the current year, or 0.24 × 5 = 1.2 machines. The number of crew required to support our forecast demand for the first year will consist of the crew required for the bottle and the plastic bag machines.

The labor requirement for year 1's bottle operation is

$$0.9 \text{ bottle machine} \times 2 \text{ operators} = 1.8 \text{ operators}$$
$$1.2 \text{ bag machines} \times 3 \text{ operators} = 3.6 \text{ operators}$$

Step 3. Project labor and equipment availabilities over the planning horizon. We repeat the preceding calculations for the remaining years:

	YEAR				
	1	2	3	4	5
PLASTIC BAG OPERATION					
Percentage capacity utilized	24	48	72	84	94
Machine requirement	1.2	2.4	3.6	4.2	4.7
Labor requirement	3.6	7.2	10.8	12.6	14.1
BOTTLE OPERATION					
Percentage capacity utilized	30	41	54	66	77
Machine requirement	.9	1.23	1.62	1.98	2.31
Labor requirement	1.8	2.46	3.24	3.96	4.62

A positive capacity cushion exists for all five years because the available capacity for both operations always exceeds the expected demand. The Stewart Company can now begin to develop the intermediate-range or sales and operations plan for the two production lines. (See Chapter 14 for a discussion of sales and operations planning.) ●

USING DECISION TREES TO EVALUATE CAPACITY ALTERNATIVES

A convenient way to lay out the steps of a capacity problem is through the use of decision trees. The tree format helps not only in understanding the problem but also in finding a solution. A *decision tree* is a schematic model of the sequence of steps in a problem and the conditions and consequences of each step. In recent years, a few commercial software packages have been developed to assist in the construction and analysis of decision trees. These packages make the process quick and easy.

Decision trees are composed of decision nodes with branches to and from them. Usually squares represent decision points and circles represent chance events. Branches from decision points show the choices available to the decision maker; branches from chance events show the probabilities for their occurrence.

In solving decision tree problems, we work from the end of the tree backward to the start of the tree. As we work back, we calculate the expected values at each step. In calculating the expected value, the time value of money is important if the planning horizon is long.

Once the calculations are made, we prune the tree by eliminating from each decision point all branches except the one with the highest payoff. This process continues to the first decision point, and the decision problem is thereby solved.

We now demonstrate an application to capacity planning for Hackers Computer Store. The exhibits used to solve this problem were generated using a program called DATA by TreeAge Software. (A demonstration version of the software, capable of solving the problems given in this chapter, is included on the book DVD.)

**Program DATA
TreeAge
Software**

Service

EXAMPLE 11.2: Decision Trees

The owner of Hackers Computer Store is considering what to do with his business over the next five years. Sales growth over the past couple of years has been good, but sales could grow substantially if a major electronics firm is built in his area as proposed. Hackers' owner sees three options. The first is to enlarge his current store, the second is to locate at a new site, and the third is to simply wait and do nothing. The decision to expand or move would take little time, and, therefore, the store would not lose revenue. If nothing were done the first year and strong growth occurred, then the decision to expand would be reconsidered. Waiting longer than one year would allow competition to move in and would make expansion no longer feasible.

The assumptions and conditions are as follows:

1. Strong growth as a result of the increased population of computer fanatics from the new electronics firm has a 55 percent probability.
2. Strong growth with a new site would give annual returns of $195,000 per year. Weak growth with a new site would mean annual returns of $115,000.
3. Strong growth with an expansion would give annual returns of $190,000 per year. Weak growth with an expansion would mean annual returns of $100,000.
4. At the existing store with no changes, there would be returns of $170,000 per year if there is strong growth and $105,000 per year if growth is weak.
5. Expansion at the current site would cost $87,000.
6. The move to the new site would cost $210,000.
7. If growth is strong and the existing site is enlarged during the second year, the cost would still be $87,000.
8. Operating costs for all options are equal.

SOLUTION

We construct a decision tree to advise Hackers' owner on the best action. Exhibit 11.3 shows the decision tree for this problem. There are two decision points (shown with the square nodes) and three chance occurrences (round nodes).

Decision Tree for Hackers Computer Store Problem

exhibit 11.3

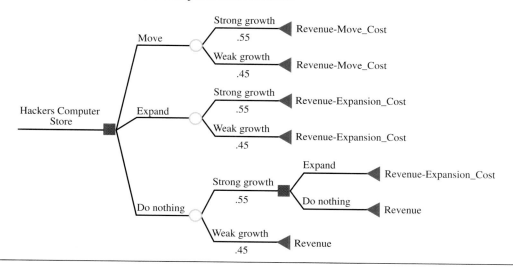

Decision Tree Analysis Using DATA (TreeAge Software, Inc.)

exhibit 11.4

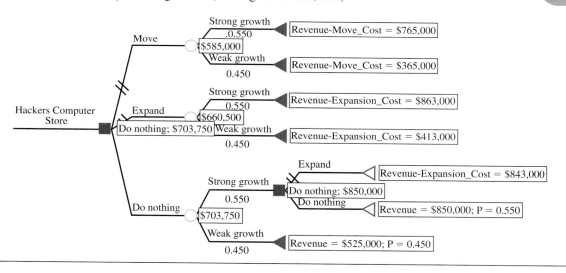

The values of each alternative outcome shown on the right of the diagram in Exhibit 11.4 are calculated as follows:

ALTERNATIVE	REVENUE	COST	VALUE
Move to new location, strong growth	$195,000 × 5 yrs	$210,000	$765,000
Move to new location, weak growth	$115,000 × 5 yrs	$210,000	$365,000
Expand store, strong growth	$190,000 × 5 yrs	$87,000	$863,000
Expand store, weak growth	$100,000 × 5 yrs	$87,000	$413,000
Do nothing now, strong growth, expand next year	$170,000 × 1 yr + $190,000 × 4 yrs	$87,000	$843,000
Do nothing now, strong growth, do not expand next year	$170,000 × 5 yrs	$0	$850,000
Do nothing now, weak growth	$105,000 × 5 yrs	$0	$525,000

Working from the rightmost alternatives, which are associated with the decision of whether to expand, we see that the alternative of doing nothing has a higher value than the expansion alternative.

exhibit 11.5

Decision Tree Analysis Using Net Present Value Calculations

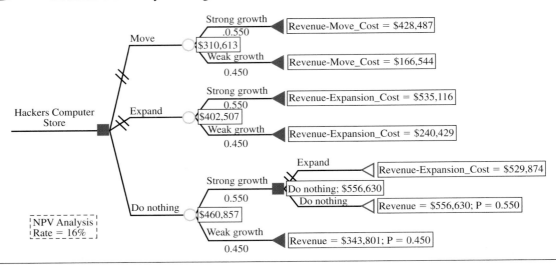

We therefore eliminate the expansion in the second year alternatives. What this means is that if we do nothing in the first year and we experience strong growth, then in the second year it makes no sense to expand.

Now we can calculate the expected values associated with our current decision alternatives. We simply multiply the value of the alternative by its probability and sum the values. The expected value for the alternative of moving now is $585,000. The expansion alternative has an expected value of $660,500, and doing nothing now has an expected value of $703,750. Our analysis indicates that our best decision is to do nothing (both now and next year)!

Due to the five-year time horizon, it may be useful to consider the time value of the revenue and cost streams when solving this problem. Details concerning the calculation of the discounted monetary values are given in Supplement A ("Financial Analysis"). For example, if we assume a 16 percent interest rate, the first alternative outcome (move now, strong growth) has a discounted revenue valued at $428,487 ($195,000 × 3.274293654) minus the $210,000 cost to move immediately. Exhibit 11.5 shows the analysis considering the discounted flows. Details of the calculations are given below. Present value table G.3 (in Appendix G) can be used to look up the discount factors. In order to make our calculations agree with those completed by the computer program, we have used discount factors that are calculated to 10 digits of precision (it is easy to do this with Excel). The only calculation that is a little tricky is the one for revenue when we do nothing now and expand at the beginning of next year. In this case, we have a revenue stream of $170,000 the first year, followed by four years at $190,000. The first part of the calculation (170,000 × .862068966) discounts the first-year revenue to present. The next part (190,000 × 2.798180638) discounts the next four years to the start of year two. We then discount this four-year stream to present value. The computer program used to generate Exhibit 11.5 performed the calculations automatically.

ALTERNATIVE	REVENUE	COST	VALUE
Move to new location, strong growth	$195,000 × 3.274293654	$210,000	$428,487
Move to new location, weak growth	$115,000 × 3.274293654	$210,000	$166,544
Expand store, strong growth	$190,000 × 3.274293654	$87,000	$535,116
Expand store, weak growth	$100,000 × 3.274203654	$87,000	$240,429
Do nothing now, strong growth, expand next year	$170,000 × .862068966 $190,000 × 2.798180638 × .862068966	$87,000 × .862068966	$529,874
Do nothing now, strong growth, do not expand next year	$170,000 × 3.274293654	$0	$556,630
Do nothing now, weak growth	$105,000 × 3.274293654	$0	$343,801

PLANNING SERVICE CAPACITY

CAPACITY PLANNING IN SERVICE VERSUS MANUFACTURING

Although capacity planning in services is subject to many of the same issues as manufacturing capacity planning, and facility sizing can be done in much the same way, there are several important differences. Service capacity is more time- and location-dependent, it is subject to more volatile demand fluctuations, and utilization directly impacts service quality.

Service

Time   Unlike goods, services cannot be stored for later use. The capacity must be available to produce a service when it is needed. For example, a customer cannot be given a seat that went unoccupied on a previous airline flight if the current flight is full. Nor could the customer purchase a seat on a particular day's flight and take it home to be used at some later date.

Location   The service capacity must be located near the customer. In manufacturing, production takes place, and then the goods are distributed to the customer. With services, however, the opposite is true. The capacity to deliver the service must first be distributed to the customer (either physically or through some communications medium such as the telephone); then the service can be produced. A hotel room or rental car that is available in another city is not much use to the customer—it must be where the customer is when that customer needs it.

Volatility of Demand   The volatility of demand on a service delivery system is much higher than that on a manufacturing production system for three reasons. First, as just mentioned, services cannot be stored. This means that inventory cannot smooth the demand as in manufacturing. The second reason is that the customers interact directly with the production system—and these customers often have different needs, will have different levels of experience with the process, and may require different numbers of transactions. This contributes to greater variability in the processing time required for each customer and hence greater variability in the minimum capacity needed. The third reason for the greater volatility in service demand is that it is directly affected by consumer behavior. Influences on customer behavior ranging from the weather to a major event can directly affect demand for different services. Go to any restaurant near your campus during spring break and it will probably be almost empty. Or try to book a room at a local hotel during homecoming weekend. This behavioral effect can be seen over even shorter time frames such as the lunch-hour rush at a bank's drive-through window or the sudden surge in pizza orders during halftime on Superbowl Sunday. Because of this volatility, service capacity is often planned in increments as small as 10 to 30 minutes, as opposed to the one-week increments more common in manufacturing.

CAPACITY UTILIZATION AND SERVICE QUALITY

Planning capacity levels for services must consider the day-to-day relationship between service utilization and service quality. Exhibit 11.6 shows a service situation cast in waiting line terms (arrival rates and service rates).[4] As noted by Haywood-Farmer and Nollet, the best operating point is near 70 percent of the maximum capacity. This is "enough to keep servers busy but allows enough time to serve customers individually and keep enough capacity in reserve so as not to create too many managerial headaches."[5] In the critical zone, customers are processed through the system, but service quality declines. Above the critical zone, the line builds up and it is likely that many customers may never be served.

exhibit 11.6

Relationship between the Rate of Service Utilization (ρ) and Service Quality

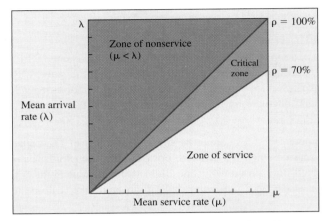

SOURCE: J. HAYWOOD-FARMER AND J. NOLLET, *SERVICES PLUS: EFFECTIVE SERVICE MANAGEMENT* (BOUCHERVILLE, QUEBEC, CANADA: G. MORIN PUBLISHER LTD., 1991). P. 59.

MULTIMEDIA CONTACT CENTER SOFTWARE SUCH AS SOLIDUS ECARE FROM ERICSSON ALLOWS DISPERSED CUSTOMER SERVICE ORGANIZATIONS TO BEHAVE AS A SINGLE UNIT. THE SOFTWARE ROUTES CALLS TO AGENTS BASED ON THEIR SKILL SETS, BLENDING CALLS WITH E-MAIL, WEB-CHAT, WEB BROWSING WITH CUSTOMERS, AND AUTOMATED RESPONSES FOR FREQUENTLY ASKED QUESTIONS. THIS FLEXIBILITY EFFECTIVELY EXPANDS CAPACITY OF CUSTOMER SERVICE.

Haywood-Farmer and Nollet also note that the optimal utilization rate is very context specific. Low rates are appropriate when both the degree of uncertainty and the stakes are high. For example, hospital emergency rooms and fire departments should aim for low utilization because of the high level of uncertainty and the life-or-death nature of their activities. Relatively predictable services such as commuter trains or service facilities without customer contact, such as postal sorting operations, can plan to operate much nearer 100 percent utilization. Interestingly, there is a third group for which high utilization is desirable. All sports teams like sellouts, not only because of the virtually 100 percent contribution margin of each customer, but because a full house creates an atmosphere that pleases customers, motivates the home team to perform better, and boosts future ticket sales. Stage performances and bars share this phenomenon. On the other hand, many airline passengers feel that a flight is too crowded when the seat next to theirs is occupied. Airlines capitalize on this response to sell more business-class seats.[6]

CONCLUSION

Service

Strategic capacity planning involves an investment decision that must match resource capabilities to a long-term demand forecast. As discussed in this chapter, factors to be taken into account in selecting capacity additions for both manufacturing and services include

- The likely effects of economies of scale.
- The effects of experience curves.
- The impact of changing facility focus and balance among production stages.
- The degree of flexibility of facilities and the workforce.

For services in particular, a key consideration is the effect of capacity changes on the quality of the service offering. In the next technical note, we discuss the related issue of where to locate the firm's facilities.

KEY TERMS

Capacity The amount of output that a system is capable of achieving over a specific period of time.

Strategic capacity planning Determining the overall capacity level of capital-intensive resources that best supports the company's long-range competitive strategy.

Best operating level The level of capacity for which the process was designed and the volume of output at which average unit cost is minimized.

Capacity utilization rate Measures how close a firm is to its best operating level.

Capacity focus Can be operationalized through the plants-within-plants concept, where a plant has several suborganizations specialized for different products—even though they are under the same roof. This permits finding the best operating level for each suborganization.

Economies of scope Exist when multiple products can be produced at a lower cost in combination than they can separately.

Capacity cushion Capacity in excess of expected demand.

SOLVED PROBLEM

E-Education is a new start-up that develops and markets MBA courses offered over the Internet. The company is currently located in Chicago and employs 150 people. Due to strong growth the company needs additional office space. The company has the option of leasing additional space at its current location in Chicago for the next two years, but after that will need to move to a new building. Another option the company is considering is moving the entire operation to a small Midwest town immediately. A third option is for the company to lease a new building in Chicago immediately. If the company chooses the first option and leases new space at its current location, it can, at the end of two years, either lease a new building in Chicago or move to the small Midwest town.

The following are some additional facts about the alternatives and current situation:

1. The company has a 75 percent chance of surviving the next two years.
2. Leasing the new space for two years at the current location in Chicago would cost $750,000 per year.
3. Moving the entire operation to a Midwest town would cost $1 million. Leasing space would run only $500,000 per year.
4. Moving to a new building in Chicago would cost $200,000, and leasing the new building's space would cost $650,000 per year.
5. The company can cancel the lease at any time.
6. The company will build its own building in five years, if it survives.
7. Assume all other costs and revenues are the same no matter where the company is located.

What should E-Education do?

Solution

Step 1: Construct a decision tree that considers all of E-Education's alternatives. The following shows the tree that has decision points (with the square nodes) followed by chance occurrences (round nodes). In the case of the first decision point, if the company survives, two additional decision points need consideration.

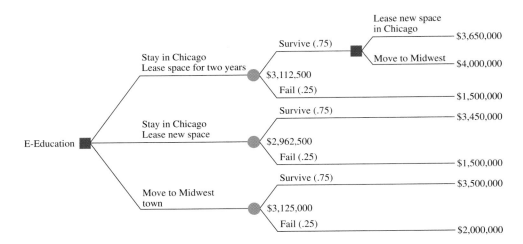

Step 2: Calculate the values of each alternative as follows:

ALTERNATIVE	CALCULATION	VALUE
Stay in Chicago, lease space for two years, survive, lease new building in Chicago	(750,000) × 2 + 200,000 + (650,000) × 3 =	$3,650,000
Stay in Chicago, lease space for two years, survive, move to Midwest	(750,000) × 2 + 1,000,000 + (500,000) × 3 =	$4,000,000
Stay in Chicago, lease space for two years, fail	(750,000) × 2 =	$1,500,000
Stay in Chicago, lease new building in Chicago, survive	200,000 + (650,000) × 5 =	$3,450,000
Stay in Chicago, lease new building in Chicago, fail	200,000 + (650,000) × 2 =	$1,500,000
Move to Midwest, survive	1,000,000 + (500,000) × 5 =	$3,500,000
Move to Midwest, fail	1,000,000 + (500,000) × 2 =	$2,000,000

Working from our rightmost alternatives, the first two alternatives end in decision nodes. Because the first option, staying in Chicago and leasing space for two years, is the lowest cost, this is what we would do if for the first two years we decide to stay in Chicago. If we fail after the first two years, represented by the third alternative, the cost is only $1,500,000. The expected value of the first option of staying in Chicago and leasing space for the first two years is .75 × 3,650,000 + .25 × 1,500,000 = $3,112,500.

The second option, staying in Chicago and leasing a new building now, has an expected value of .75 × 3,450,000 + .25 × 1,500,000 = $2,962,500.

Finally, the third option of moving to the Midwest immediately has an expected value of .75 × 3,500,000 + .25 × 2,000,000 = $3,125,000.

From this, it looks like the best alternative is to stay in Chicago and lease a new building immediately.

REVIEW AND DISCUSSION QUESTIONS

1   What capacity problems are encountered when a new drug is introduced to the market?
2   List some practical limits to economies of scale; that is, when should a plant stop growing?
3   What are some capacity balance problems faced by the following organizations or facilities?
   a. An airline terminal.
   b. A university computing center.
   c. A clothing manufacturer.

4   What are some major capacity considerations in a hospital? How do they differ from those of a factory?

5   Management may choose to build up capacity in anticipation of demand or in response to developing demand. Cite the advantages and disadvantages of both approaches.

6   What is capacity balance? Why is it hard to achieve? What methods are used to deal with capacity imbalances?

7   What are some reasons for a plant to maintain a capacity cushion? How about a negative capacity cushion?

8   At first glance, the concepts of the focused factory and capacity flexibility may seem to contradict each other. Do they really?

PROBLEMS

1   AlwaysRain Irrigation, Inc., would like to determine capacity requirements for the next four years. Currently two production lines are in place for bronze and plastic sprinklers. Three types of sprinklers are available in both bronze and plastic: 90-degree nozzle sprinklers, 180-degree nozzle sprinklers, and 360-degree nozzle sprinklers. Management has forecast demand for the next four years as follows:

YEARLY DEMAND

	1 (IN 000S)	2 (IN 000S)	3 (IN 000S)	4 (IN 000S)
Plastic 90	32	44	55	56
Plastic 180	15	16	17	18
Plastic 360	50	55	64	67
Bronze 90	7	8	9	10
Bronze 180	3	4	5	6
Bronze 360	11	12	15	18

Both production lines can produce all the different types of nozzles. Each bronze machine requires two operators and can produce up to 12,000 sprinklers. The plastic injection molding machine requires four operators and can produce up to 200,000 sprinklers. Three bronze machines and only one injection molding machine are available. What are the capacity requirements for the next four years?

2   Suppose that AlwaysRain Irrigation's marketing department will undertake an intense ad campaign for the bronze sprinklers, which are more expensive but also more durable than the plastic ones. Forecast demand for the next four years is

YEARLY DEMAND

	1 (IN 000S)	2 (IN 000S)	3 (IN 000S)	4 (IN 000S)
Plastic 90	32	44	55	56
Plastic 180	15	16	17	18
Plastic 360	50	55	64	67
Bronze 90	11	15	18	23
Bronze 180	6	5	6	9
Bronze 360	15	16	17	20

What are the capacity implications of the marketing campaign?

3   In anticipation of the ad campaign, AlwaysRain bought an additional bronze machine. Will this be enough to ensure that enough capacity is available?

4   Suppose that operators have enough training to operate both the bronze machines and the injection molding machine for the plastic sprinklers. Currently AlwaysRain has 10 such employees. In anticipation of the ad campaign described in Problem 2, management approved the purchase of two additional bronze machines. What are the labor requirement implications?

5   Expando, Inc., is considering the possibility of building an additional factory that would produce a new addition to their product line. The company is currently considering two options. The first is a small facility that it could build at a cost of $6 million. If demand for new products is low,

the company expects to receive $10 million in discounted revenues (present value of future revenues) with the small facility. On the other hand, if demand is high, it expects $12 million in discounted revenues using the small facility. The second option is to build a large factory at a cost of $9 million. Were demand to be low, the company would expect $10 million in discounted revenues with the large plant. If demand is high, the company estimates that the discounted revenues would be $14 million. In either case, the probability of demand being high is .40, and the probability of it being low is .60. Not constructing a new factory would result in no additional revenue being generated because the current factories cannot produce these new products. Construct a decision tree to help Expando make the best decision.

6   A builder has located a piece of property that she would like to buy and eventually build on. The land is currently zoned for four homes per acre, but she is planning to request new zoning. What she builds depends on approval of zoning requests and your analysis of this problem to advise her. With her input and your help, the decision process has been reduced to the following costs, alternatives, and probabilities:

Cost of land: $2 million.

Probability of rezoning: .60.

If the land is rezoned, there will be additional costs for new roads, lighting, and so on, of $1 million.

If the land is rezoned, the contractor must decide whether to build a shopping center or 1,500 apartments that the tentative plan shows would be possible. If she builds a shopping center, there is a 70 percent chance that she can sell the shopping center to a large department chain for $4 million over her construction cost, which excludes the land; and there is a 30 percent chance that she can sell it to an insurance company for $5 million over her construction cost (also excluding the land). If, instead of the shopping center, she decides to build the 1,500 apartments, she places probabilities on the profits as follows: There is a 60 percent chance that she can sell the apartments to a real estate investment corporation for $3,000 each over her construction cost; there is a 40 percent chance that she can get only $2,000 each over her construction cost. (Both exclude the land cost.)

If the land is not rezoned, she will comply with the existing zoning restrictions and simply build 600 homes, on which she expects to make $4,000 over the construction cost on each one (excluding the cost of land).

Draw a decision tree of the problem and determine the best solution and the expected net profit.

C A S E :   INTERNATIONAL DECORATIVE GLASS*

In June 1996, Delta, British Columbia, remained overcast and rainy. Frank Lattimer, vice president operations of International Decorative Glass (IDG), mused that it really didn't matter, as there would be little time for golf this year. Rapidly increasing demand for decorative glass panels by steel door manufacturers in the United States, IDG's primary market, had its two production facilities in Delta and Shuenyi, China, scrambling to keep up.

Lattimer had been asked to develop a recommendation for capacity expansion for consideration by the board of directors. The board had emphasized the need to move quickly as sales were increasing faster than IDG's ability to meet them. Although either existing plant could be expanded, IDG also had recently been approached about considering further off-shore sourcing in the rapidly developing country of Vietnam. Frank knew that any decision would have significant ramifications for the company's long-term positioning and ability to meet its ambitious goals for growth.

THE INDUSTRY

Decorative glass panels typically are inserted into residential steel doors and were increasingly being used by builders and home renovators to add architectural interest and a customized appearance to doorways. Growth in the industry was being fueled by the general trend away from wooden exterior doors to steel doors. Forestry restrictions, lumber prices, energy efficiency, and increasing criminal activity all contributed to the growing demand for retrofitting wood doors with steel replacements, often with decorative glass panels. In addition, the lower price of steel doors relative to the traditional wood door, with wholesale prices starting as low as C$300, further eroded market share in new home construction. Decorative glass was now being incorporated into 10 percent of new home construction.

The total North American sales for decorative glass panels was conservatively estimated at $2 billion in 1995 (all figures are reported in Canadian dollars), and the market showed signs of continued strong growth. Industry experts predicted that annual sales could reach $4.5 billion in the U.S. alone, within five years. Canada's weighting of the North American market was disproportionately high, at 15 percent, reflecting the somewhat earlier development of the market there for these panels. By 1996, panels were found in approximately 85 percent of steel doors in Western Canadian homes.

Manufacturers in Canada tended to be more vertically integrated than their U.S. counterparts, with plants fabricating both the steel door and the decorative panel. Locally, British Columbia's supply capacity grew well past the sustainable growth rate during the late 1980s and early 1990s as new market entrants scrambled to ramp up production capability to capitalize on the residential construction boom. The result was steadily eroding margins, followed quickly by industry consolidation, with high cost producers closing or being absorbed by more competitive operations. In spite of these changes, Canadian industry continued to be characterized by oversupply, underutilized capacity, and commodity pricing. Lattimer had recently completed a basic competitive assessment of several key Canadian competitors as part of IDG's business plan (Exhibit 1).

By contrast, U.S. manufacturers of decorative glass panels acted as original equipment manufacturers (OEMs) for large residential steel door fabricators and retail chains. The industry was quite fragmented, with the largest three producers in the U.S. each having less than 6 percent of the total market. Unfortunately, information on these producers was limited (Exhibit 2). Manufacturers ship panels to predetermined central warehousing and assembly points where their panels are fitted into the steel doors and distributed by the door fabricators through their retail channels. In general, the U.S. marketplace demanded high quality, fast service, and, increasingly, low price.

At this time, the U.S., unlike Canada, was rapidly growing and underserved. In addition, Canadian manufacturers generally were about three years ahead of their U.S. counterparts in product functionality and design and, thus, able to develop strategic partnerships with steel door manufacturers. An undervalued currency also provided Canadian suppliers, such as IDG, with an initial competitive advantage. Combined, these factors created a significant market opportunity for any Canadian supplier who could meet rigorous quality standards and maintain a high level of customer responsiveness to design customized panels.

Early attempts by Canadian firms to develop their export sales quickly revealed that a customer would pay only so much for quality, service, and product differentiation, and price was becoming an increasingly important driver in the purchase decision. In response, manufacturers on both sides of the border began to source production of the glass panels at lower cost to facilities located abroad. Because labor represented a large portion of cost of goods sold, production was increasingly being moved to countries with low labor costs, such as Mexico, Thailand, and China. At this time, only a few

Summary of Major Canadian Competitors

Exhibit 1

	COMPANY		
	ACCENT	JCX GLASS	ROSEVIEW
Target Market	Small regional distributors	Anyone who calls	Small regional distributors
Supply	Custom—None Volume—Langley, B.C., and Tacoma, WA	Custom—None Volume—New Westminster, B.C., Georgia Buy from China	Custom—None Volume—Surrey, B.C.
Positioning	Good quality	Copy designs of others	Design leader Lower quality
Cost Base	• 2 locations, 38,000 sq. ft. • Heavy overheads • Nonunion • Small orders, but purchase materials in volume; thus very high raw material & finished goods inventory • Efficient production system	• 2 locations, 105,000 sq. ft. • Heavy overheads • 1 year left on collective agreement • Volume purchase • Finished goods inventory of $3.2 million • Efficient production system	• One location, 38,000 sq. ft. • Heavy overheads • Nonunion • High raw material costs • Finished goods inventory of $1.6 million
Sales (est. 1995)	• $11 million • Down, some of their lowest months	• $14 million • Up 39%	• $3 million • Down
Warranty	1 year	10 year	1 year
CAD	Yes	No	No
MRP	Some implementation	Some implementation	No
Reputation/Customer Relations	Very good in Pacific Northwest with the "old boys" network	Generally poor, can let the customer down	Generally poor, always lets customer down
Management	Good, but have lost their spark and desire	Aggressive, but weak in the middle management	Generally weak

| Exhibit 2 | Summary of Major U.S. Competitors |

	COMPANY			
	SPANNER DOOR	WESTERN DESIGN	BILLINGS	NEW ENGLAND GLASS
Target Market	National (U.S.)	National (U.S.)	National (U.S.)	Eastern (U.S.)
Positioning	Good quality Simple, high volume panels	Broad product line	Broad product line; focus on high volume commodities, although some lower volume panels	Fast delivery, high quality
Supply	Good operations in Mexico, with long-term commitment	Plants in Mexico and Thailand	No offshore production	High cost producer; focus on automation
Est. 1995 Sales	$120 million	$85 million	$60 million	$25 million
Reputation/Customer Relations		Extensive distribution system	Product line is narrower than IDG	Strong, dependable supplier
Management		Three top managers have left recently		

Canadian manufacturers had been able to address all of these challenges successfully.

PRODUCTION OF DECORATIVE GLASS PANELS

The production process for decorative glass panels was quite standardized, with little variation among firms and plants. As might be expected with a product that until recently was considered a "craft," the process was very labor intensive, with the equivalent of up to two-person days required for each panel. Production equipment was generally quite flexible and could be purchased from several suppliers.

Decorative glass panels consist of multiple glass panes of different sizes, colors, and grades assembled between soldered brass rods to form a decorative picture. The production of the panels used a multistep process that cut and formed the glass and brass components and assembled the parts into sealed decorative glass units that could withstand the harsh exposure needed for exterior doors.

The manufacturing process began with the cutting of raw glass sheets of various colors and finishes into pieces of the precise shape and size needed for the final design. Some of these pieces were then bevelled to give a more attractive final appearance. The specialized cutting and bevelling of the glass pieces were the most capital-intensive steps in the production process.

In a separate area, brass rods were cut and shaped into segments that ultimately serve to hold and separate the glass pieces. The correct set of glass pieces and brass rods were grouped into panel-specific "kits." These kits were assembled and soldered into predetermined patterns that formed semifinished panels. Several cleaning and touch-up steps followed.

Next, clear solid glass panes were added to each side of the inlay, creating a "sandwich" that protected the more delicate decorative inlay. Swizzle, a sealant material, was added around the edge to insulate and protect the panel from water damage. The panel was then put through an automated sealing machine, washed, and inserted into a frame. Finally, the finished panel was labeled and packaged for shipment. These operations typically were performed in small batches of panels.

THE COMPANY

Located near Vancouver, British Columbia, IDG was founded in 1984 by Michael Jeffrey, decorative glass designer and entrepreneur. Initially, the company started as an integrated manufacturer of steel doors and decorative glass panels, and IDG enjoyed modest prosperity through the 1980s as the housing market boomed in that province. During this period, numerous firms entered the market, hoping to share in the prosperity of the industry. As real estate development slowed and even stagnated in the early 1990s, and the competitive basis shifted to cost, Jeffrey realized that the company was losing money in their manufacturing of steel doors. He felt that IDG could significantly enhance profitability by concentrating exclusively on decorative glass panels.

Jeffrey also recognized the need for a senior operations and business development person to make the operations more competitive in that market. Lattimer was hired in 1991 with the mandate to grow the international market, to improve cost efficiency, to set up a fully integrated management information system, and to create a corporate structure and culture that would support continued expansion. To meet these objectives, contacts and sales were further developed with several U.S. steel door manufacturers, the largest being Midwest. Lattimer also gained concessions in wage rates and flexibility in staffing requirements during collective bargaining with the union. Finally, a management information system, including materials requirements planning (MRP), was installed and brought on line to improve access to timely information and to raise customer responsiveness.

Historically, IDG's sales had been driven by custom orders for the glass panels. However, with recent efforts to increase sales volume, an increasing number of higher volume orders were being pursued, although often at much lower margins. In spite of labor concessions, high wage rates and limited flexibility continued to make IDG's plant in Delta increasingly less cost competitive. To reduce production costs, Lattimer was forced to explore alternative, offshore sources of production.

CENTURY GLASS

In January 1995, IDG began sourcing some of its high-volume, low-skill production through a strategic partnership with Century Glass, located in Shuenyi, approximately an hour's drive outside of Beijing, China. This manufacturing facility was developed solely to meet the production needs of IDG, although the actual plant was owned and operated by the father of a former employee, Jianwei (Jerry) Lo. Lo had returned to China to set up the joint venture with IDG.

When IDG first arrived, the Shuenyi facility was little more than a deserted warehouse, situated across the highway from the village of 2,000 people where Lo had been born. The Lo family was well respected in the area, even though they came from modest means relative to Canadian standards. There was no electricity, telephone, or plumbing in the village, and fresh water was unavailable.

With minimal infrastructure in place, power requirements, communication, and capital equipment challenges all needed to be addressed. Cogeneration power supplies and inverters were supplied by IDG; satellite and cellular phones were used until Century received a land line (faxes were sent from Beijing in the interim). Basic production equipment needed to cut glass sheets and brass rods were sourced locally; however, one large panel sealing machine was imported from Korea. Practically everything else at the facility was built by the local work force. Approximately one-third of the workers lived in four-person dormitory rooms located on the premises, and the production plant also included space for the workers to grow their own food in the courtyard.

Family ties of the Los facilitated the shipment of goods, as Chinese bureaucracy was legendary. Jerry's uncle was the police chief of the local district and, thus, extremely well connected politically; IDG benefited from the association. The movement of raw materials into China and finished goods out of China, via Tientsin to the Gulf of Chihli, was expedited through Jerry's uncle.

Because of differences in proximity to the market and cost structure, the Chinese production facility concentrated on producing high-volume, low-cost glass panels for IDG. These panels were then shipped in bulk to the Delta production facility for final processing, followed by packaging and shipment to U.S. or Canadian customers. The additional processing in Canada resulted in a change in product classification under the North American Free Trade Agreement (NAFTA), which allowed the finished product to be imported duty-free into the U.S. market. (By contrast, if complete, sealed panels were imported directly from China into the U.S., a 60 percent duty would apply.)

For some customers, the standardized panels produced at Shuenyi were modified and further assembled at Delta to form larger, more complex, customized panels. By necessity, these arrangements required a long lead time, currently 18 to 20 weeks (Exhibit 3), well above that of the Delta plant, where lead times averaged one month.

Initial start-up problems in 1995 centered on logistics and quality. Rather than allow IDG's reputation for excellent customer service to suffer by missing delivery dates, orders of panels were, at times, air freighted to Delta from China, at an extra cost of $250,000 in the first year. These problems were gradually overcome as typical production lead times were reduced to their current levels. Low yields and high waste/breakage also plagued the start-up. However, as the skill levels of the local work force improved, yields increased dramatically. By mid-1996, finished panel yields consistently surpassed 99 percent, although in-process breakage and other losses remained a problem.

Current Status   By June 1996, Century Glass produced 80 percent of IDG's panels, representing 60 percent of revenues. The remaining somewhat more specialized, lower volume panels were produced by 70 employees in the Delta plant. The Century plant was operating close to capacity, with approximately 100 employees producing 8,000 panels per month. Dorms were overcrowded and people were elbow-to-elbow in the manufacturing area.

The joint venture agreement specified that IDG purchase all materials, own all inventories, and specify all finished product standards. The production arrangement with Century stipulated a fixed charge per employee and a variable cost per finished panel. Specifically, IDG paid $140 per employee, per month. In addition, IDG also paid Century a product transfer price of $4 for each panel that met IDG's rigorous quality standards for finished panels. Employment levels could be varied as needed to match sales volumes. Employees worked seven eight-hour days per week, every week. This was high by Chinese standards, where the five- or six-day work week was more common.

By comparison, in Canada, unionized employees received $9.75 per hour per 40-hour work week. Combined, these differences in labor translated into a significant cost advantage for Shuenyi, without accounting for the operational advantages of increased labor flexibility. Relative product costs are illustrated in Exhibit 4.

Labor savings were offset to some degree by a higher working capital investment necessary to finance larger inventories and longer payment cycles. For example, inventory turnover at Century Glass was only two turns per year in 1995, whereas Delta averaged six. In addition, banks refused to finance or factor raw material and work-in-process (WIP) inventories located in, or in transit to or from, China as the risk of recouping funds in the case of insolvency was considered too high. This risk varied by country. Some developing countries, such as Mexico, were viewed as less risky, while others, such as India, offered government guarantees for export-oriented manufacturers.

The Lo family was anxious to keep 100 percent of IDG's business at their facility. However, Lattimer was very concerned about

---

Order Cycle Time for Production at Shuenyi Plant

Exhibit 3

Raw materials ordered and received for shipment	2–4 weeks
Components in transit to China facility	5 weeks
Raw materials conversion to WIP and semi-finished goods	4 weeks
Subassemblies shipped to Canada	5 weeks
Final assembly completed at Delta, B.C., facility	2 weeks
Finished goods shipped to customer	1/2 week
Total time	18–20 weeks

Exhibit 4

Typical Production Costs

	PRODUCTION LOCATION	
PRODUCT	SHUENYI	DELTA
#677, OVAL-SAN MARINO		
Materials	95.19	92.97
Labor	6.61	69.44
Freight	7.82	1.25
Total direct costs	$109.62	$163.66
#936, 22" × 36" PANEL		
Materials	44.27	44.27
Labor	3.18	40.27
Freight	7.08	1.25
Total direct costs	$54.53	$85.79
#445, 7-1/2" × 18-1/2" PANEL		
Materials	15.51	15.51
Labor	1.10	10.13
Freight	1.08	0.50
Total direct costs	$17.69	$26.14

Exhibit 5

International Decorative Glass

INCOME STATEMENT
AS OF SEPTEMBER 30
(ALL FIGURES REPORTED AS $000s)

	1995	1994
Sales	$5,404	$3,634
Cost of sales	4,365	2,610
Gross profit	1,039	1,024
Expenses		
Administration and marketing	388	413
Travel and promotion	97	44
Rent and assessment	120	138
Amortization of debt	48	55
Bank charges and interest	141	48
Interest on long-term debt	18	17
Other expenses	182	258
Subtotal	994	973
Income (loss) from operations	45	51
Other income	28	0
Income (loss) before taxes	73	51
Income taxes		
Current	24	0
Deferred	(6)	11
Net income (loss) for the year	$55	$40

having only a single supplier in China, where political risks were perceived to be significant for such a large portion of their production. For example, the repatriation of Hong Kong in 1997, adverse trade tensions, and possible trade restrictions between China, the U.S., and Canada all indicated that a move to establish another production source might have strategic and operational merits.

FINANCIAL RESULTS

IDG's revenue growth had been impressive since 1990, increasing from $2.6 million to $5.4 million for fiscal 1995. Financial results for the last two years are summarized in Exhibits 5 and 6. Revenues were projected to reach $10.5 million this year, with 95 percent of sales being made in the U.S. As noted earlier, margins

International Decorative Glass

Exhibit 6

BALANCE SHEET
AS OF SEPTEMBER 30
(ALL FIGURES REPORTED AS $000s)

	1995	1994
Current		
Cash	$ 1	$ 2
Accounts receivable	1,513	474
Income taxes recoverable	15	22
Inventories	1,422	988
Prepaid expenses	54	28
	3,005	1,514
Capital assets	233	296
	3,238	1,810
Current		
Bank loans	1,435	593
Accounts payable	886	482
Income taxes payable	17	0
Current portion of long-term debt	32	39
	2,370	1,114
Long-term debt	152	177
Deferred income taxes	13	20
Due to (from) affiliated company	522	372
	3,057	1,683
Share capital	0.1	0.1
Contributed surplus	45	45
Retained earnings	136	82
	$3,238	$1,810

had eroded during the early 1990s as residential construction slowed and competition increased. Sales levels had risen significantly in 1995 as new production capacity became available at Shuenyi. However, profitability fell as a result of poor initial yields and air freight shipment costs at this new plant. Looking forward, Lattimer expected margins to increase as productivity further improved in Shuenyi.

Both Jeffrey and Lattimer strongly felt that the market for strong growth by IDG was there. IDG had already been turning away business as they struggled to meet existing customer commitments from their two production facilities. Current plans called for revenue growth to $30 million by the year 2000. Critical to achieving these long-term results was an increase in production capacity to match the forecasted sales volumes.

This aggressive growth necessitated access to additional capital to finance investment in new capacity and additional working capital. In August 1995, IDG approached a venture capital firm, Working Opportunity Fund, for $2 million of equity financing. The structure of the investment was negotiated, due diligence conducted, and the deal finalized in November of that year. In addition, IDG paid down its line-of-credit from the bank by financing its inventory in China with a guarantee from Canada's Export Development Corporation. This effectively reduced IDG's investment in working capital and made the sourcing of manufacturing to Asian facilities increasingly attractive.

Combined, these additional sources of capital enabled IDG to increase its operating flexibility and further develop its presence in the U.S. market.

CAPACITY EXPANSION

Lattimer had narrowed the options for expansion of production to three alternatives. Expansion was possible at either existing plant. In addition, another strategic partnership could be developed in another low labor-cost country, similar to IDG's earlier decision to expand into China. After exploring options in other developing nations with low labor costs, Lattimer, in consultation with senior management, had narrowed the candidate list of countries to one: Vietnam. This country offered a critical advantage in Lattimer's mind over other developing nations: a potential local partner, Dan Kim. Kim's firm currently supplied raw glass to IDG, and Kim had approached Lattimer about establishing a manufacturing joint venture.

Expansion in Delta At this time, companywide capacity could be doubled by investing a relatively modest amount of capital, $30,000, in the Delta plant. Labor costs would rise based on existing wage levels. Given the close proximity of this plant to the U.S. market, the existing production planning system could be further leveraged and customer responsiveness further improved.

Expansion in Shuenyi   Because production at the Shuenyi plant was already very tight, any expansion would involve a significant increase of middle management and support staff, and an expanded production planning system, mirroring the earlier MRP investment made in Delta. Existing arrangements for labor would be maintained, where IDG would pay a flat monthly fee per person, plus a variable rate per panel.

Although some of the existing production equipment still had excess capacity, additional equipment would be needed. In total, an estimated capital investment of $30,000 would be needed in new cutting equipment to double companywide capacity. Incremental manufacturing overhead costs would be approximately $150,000 per year. Direct labor costs would increase proportionately with production volumes. These costs did not include either a desperately needed new building or additional inventory carrying charges. Timing for ramp-up to this volume level would be approximately six to eight months.

The most significant concerns with expansion at Shuenyi were related to further dependence on a single supplier and issues related to political risks associated with production in China. Trade uncertainties between China and the U.S. also aggravated long-term planning efforts. Management was apprehensive that existing tensions could escalate over any, or all, of repatriation of Hong Kong in 1997, intellectual property rights (software piracy and patents), dissident protests, strained relations with Taiwan, and a general trade imbalance.

Smaller manufacturers that supply the U.S. market, like IDG, inadvertently have been punished by short-term high tariffs, customs delays, and other nontariff barriers. Although quite unlikely now, the worst case scenario would be a ban on importation from China. Unfortunately, because of the general income levels in China and construction norms, there was little local market for IDG's products at this time, although it did look promising in the longer term.

Foreign Operations in Vietnam   Vietnam had only recently begun to exhibit the economic growth characteristic of other countries in Asia-Pacific. Like many developing countries, infrastructure at this time was terribly inadequate. Lattimer estimated that development was at least five years behind China, and conditions were even more challenging than those first faced by IDG when they established their joint venture in China.

In recent years, Vietnam had been plagued by internal political problems, and foreign investors were apprehensive to invest. This situation now was beginning to change, as the U.S. had moved to reestablish diplomatic relations with the Socialist Republic of Vietnam in 1995. In turn, this thawing of the political climate had encouraged foreign investment, which had grown rapidly as a result. Vietnam also had a strategic location for reexport to other markets in Asia.

Although a Communist state, the central government had instituted the beginnings of "Doi Moi" or "open door" policy as early as 1986. The objectives of Doi Moi were to develop export-oriented production capabilities that create jobs and generate foreign currency, to develop import substitutes, to stimulate production using natural resources, to acquire foreign technology, and to strengthen Vietnam's infrastructure. Incentives offered included: the option to establish wholly owned foreign subsidiaries; favorable corporate income tax and tax holidays; waivers on import/export duties; and full repatriation of profits and capital.

With 75 million citizens and a labor force of 32 million, Vietnam had the second lowest wage rate in the Pacific Rim. Only about 11 percent of the working population was employed in manufacturing, another 19 percent in the service sector, and the remainder in agriculture. Inflation was high, at 14 percent in 1995, partially because of the devaluation of the "new dong" as the government had allowed the currency to float in world markets for the first time. The primary industries of Vietnam included food processing, textiles, machinery, mining, cement, chemical fertilizers, tires, oil, and glass. Vietnamese companies already supplied some of the standard glass and bevelled glass components used by IDG.

Generally, the labor force was energetic, disciplined, and hard working, although unemployment remained high, at 20 percent. English and French were widely spoken but literacy was relatively low, at 88 percent. Unfortunately, basic human rights and freedoms had received little attention. There was widespread conflict between local and central governing bodies, extensive corruption, and exhaustive bureaucracy at both levels.

Production of Decorative Glass Panels in Vietnam   The State Committee for Cooperation and Investment (SCCI) identified seven areas of the Vietnam economy where foreign investment would receive preferential tax treatment. Of particular relevance to IDG, labor-intensive manufacturing was one such area. The SCCI would assist the new venture in whatever way they could, typically through the development of contacts with customers and suppliers, as well as guiding the investor through the government bureaucracy that approved any business venture.

The Vietnamese government also had legislated five approaches for establishing a business venture in the country. Of the five, the international business community and the government widely favored the joint venture approach. Under this approach, a foreign firm such as IDG would sign a contract with one or more Vietnamese parties to create a new legal entity with limited liability. Foreign capital had to constitute at least 30 percent of the new entity's total capital. A foreign investor could then leverage the local partner's contacts, knowledge of the local market, and access to land and resources.

The Vietnamese had a saying; "*Nhap gia tuy tuc,*" which means, "When you come into a new country, you have to follow the culture." Clearly, identification of a strong local partner would be critical for meeting the cultural norms in Vietnam and ensuring the success of any investment by IDG; this had been a major obstacle for many other foreign firms.

Lattimer saw many parallels with the earlier joint venture into China. That investment had succeeded largely as a result of IDG's strategic partnership with Century Glass and the Lo family. IDG had been able to limit their investment risk to supplying capital equipment for the facility and inventories. By contrast, other decorative glass suppliers operating in China were paying higher costs and making larger investments in plant and infrastructure. The partnership with Century also had provided IDG with additional political clout and allowed them to bypass much of the Chinese bureaucracy.

One obvious choice for a local partner was IDG's bevelled glass supplier, managed by Dan Kim. Kim operated a glass plant in Da Nang, which was well under capacity and had an oversupply of qualified labor. Kim had approached both IDG and government authorities and essentially paved the way for IDG to begin joint venture operations within a 6- to 12-month time frame. Labor and product transfer prices were likely to be significantly lower than either the Delta or Shuenyi plants, with these costs being approximately half those of Shuenyi. Additional overhead costs were

Production Equipment Required for Start-up in Vietnam (all figures reported as $000s)

Exhibit 7

PRODUCTION EQUIPMENT	COST
Electrical back-up generator	$ 13
Air compressor	2
Glass equipment	
Two-shape cutter (pneumatic, from Korea)	7
Shape cutter (CNC, from Canada)	110
Glass washer	60
Brass equipment	
Roll-former	55
Roll-forming dies	22
Circle rollers (large and small)	5
Saws (4)/blades/sharpeners	4
Bevelling equipment	
Straight-line beveller	125
Curved bevelling machines (12)	30
Miscellaneous equipment	
Small forklift	7
Pallet jack	2
Computer, fax, etc.	3
Hand tools, tables, etc.	5
Total capital equipment	$449

estimated at $50,000 annually. Finally, a significant investment would be needed in new equipment to reach the same, company-wide production volume possible with the other options (Exhibit 7). Lattimer wondered whether he might be able to extract more favorable terms for any joint venture relationship, such as shifting responsibilities for financing inventories to Kim.

THE DECISION

As Lattimer was putting together his proposal for the board, he reflected on a conversation he had with Jerry Lo last month. Lo had indicated that Century would soon expect their piecework compensation to increase from $4 to $7 per finished panel. While seemingly a small fraction of total production costs, Lattimer worried that further requests for increases would follow unless other alternatives

were developed. He also was only too aware that with up to $1 million invested in inventory at Century at any given time, IDG was in a very precarious position. Single sourcing had given Century a level of bargaining power that might limit IDG's future options and cost competitiveness.

Lo had become agitated as Lattimer described IDG's exploration of additional manufacture sourcing arrangements, but had to agree it made sense from IDG's perspective. Lattimer reassured Lo that IDG wanted to add capacity, not replace it. This discussion had reinforced the need to delicately handle IDG's existing relationships. Any recommendation for locating new production capacity would have to take into account the skilled Canadian work force, Century Glass and the Lo family, and Dan Kim's offer for an expanded relationship in Vietnam.

*JIM BARKER PREPARED THIS CASE UNDER THE SUPERVISION OF PROFESSORS ROBERT KLASSEN AND PAUL BEAMISH SOLELY TO PROVIDE MATERIAL FOR CLASS DISCUSSION. THE AUTHORS DO NOT INTEND TO ILLUSTRATE EITHER EFFECTIVE OR INEFFECTIVE HANDLING OF A MANAGERIAL SITUATION. THE AUTHORS MAY HAVE DISGUISED CERTAIN NAMES AND OTHER IDENTIFYING INFORMATION TO PROTECT CONFIDENTIALITY.

IVEY MANAGEMENT SERVICES PROHIBITS ANY FORM OF REPRODUCTION, STORAGE, OR TRANSMITTAL WITHOUT ITS WRITTEN PERMISSION. THIS MATERIAL IS NOT COVERED UNDER AUTHORIZATION FROM CANCOPY OR ANY REPRODUCTION RIGHTS ORGANIZATION. TO ORDER COPIES OR REQUEST PERMISSION TO REPRODUCE MATERIALS, CONTACT IVEY PUBLISHING, IVEY MANAGEMENT SERVICES, C/O RICHARD IVEY SCHOOL OF BUSINESS, THE UNIVERSITY OF WESTERN ONTARIO, LONDON, ONTARIO, CANADA, N6A 3K7; PHONE (519) 661-3208; FAX (519) 661-3882; E-MAIL CASES@IVEY.UWO.CA. COPYRIGHT © 1997, IVEY MANAGEMENT SERVICES.

THE RICHARD IVEY SCHOOL OF BUSINESS GRATEFULLY ACKNOWLEDGES THE GENEROUS SUPPORT OF THE RICHARD AND JEAN IVEY FUND IN THE DEVELOPMENT OF THIS CASE AS PART OF THE RICHARD AND JEAN IVEY FUND ASIAN CASE SERIES.

SELECTED BIBLIOGRAPHY

Amran, M., and N. Kulatilaka. "Disciplined Decisions: Aligning Strategy with the Financial Markets." *Harvard Business Review,* January–February 1999, pp. 95–104.

Bakke, N. A., and R. Hellberg. "The Challenges of Capacity Planning." *International Journal of Production Economics* 30–31 (1993), pp. 243–64.

Correll, J. G., and N. W. Edson. *Gaining Control: Capacity Management and Scheduling.* 2nd ed. New York: Wiley, 1998.

Hammesfahr, R. D. Jack; J. A. Pope; and A. Ardalan. "Strategic Planning for Production Capacity." *International Journal of Operations and Production Management* 13, no. 5 (1993), pp. 41–53.

Meyer, C. *Fast Cycle Time: How to Align Purpose, Strategy and Structure for Speed.* New York: Free Press, 1993.

Giffi, C.; A. V. Roth; and G. M. Seal, eds. *Competing in World-Class Manufacturing: National Center for Manufacturing Sciences.* Homewood, IL: Business One Irwin, 1990.

Govil, M., and J. Proth. *Supply Chain Design and Management.* Burlington, MA: Academic Press, 2001.

Yu-Lee, R. T. *Essentials of Capacity Management.* New York: Wiley, 2002.

FOOTNOTES

1 In gathering capacity statistics, the Bureau of Economic Analysis asks two questions of surveyed firms: (1) At what percentage of manufacturing capacity did your company operate in (month and year)? (2) At what percentage of (month and year) manufacturing capacity would your company have preferred to operate in order to achieve maximum profits or other objective? See "Survey of Current Business," an annual publication of the *U.S. Department of Commerce Journal.*

2 W. Skinner, "The Focused Factory," *Harvard Business Review,* May–June 1974, pp. 113–21.

3 See R. J. Schonberger, "The Rationalization of Production," *Proceedings of the 50th Anniversary of the Academy of Management* (Chicago: Academy of Management, 1986), pp. 64–70.

4 Waiting lines are discussed in Technical Note 7.

5 J. Haywood-Farmer and J. Nollet, *Services Plus: Effective Service Management* (Boucherville, Quebec, Canada: G. Morin Publisher Ltd., 1991), p. 58.

6 Ibid.

7 Shouldice Hospital is at http://www.shouldice.com. The Web site has much additional information concerning the history of the hospital and current hernia operation procedures.

technical note eleven
FACILITY LOCATION

STARBUCKS GENERAL APPROACH TO SITE SELECTION

⊙⊙○ Starbucks has achieved a phenomenal rate of growth due in part to location analysis and site selection criteria. In some heavily populated areas such as New York City, it seems that there is a Starbucks every few blocks. And indeed, on Manhattan's upper west side, there are eight Starbucks within a one square mile area between West 66th and West 86th streets!

In its early years, a small group of Starbucks executives made site selection decisions based on largely subjective analysis. Now, the company uses spatial modeling and extensive analysis of demographic information to identify and analyze potential locations.

SPATIAL MODELING

Unlike many other retail chains, Starbucks does not accept credit cards or checks because most of their customers pay cash. Starbucks conducts periodic store intercept studies to aid

Source: www.geoplace.com.

ALCOA'S PORTLAND, VICTORIA, AUSTRALIA PLANT IS ONE OF OVER TWO DOZEN SMELTERS PRODUCING PRIMARY ALUMINUM FOR ALCOA GLOBALLY. THE CREATION OF PARKLANDS AROUND THE PLANT SITE HAS EARNED IT THE TITLE, "SMELTER IN THE PARK," AND THE ONLY CERTIFICATION AS A VIABLE HABITAT GRANTED OUTSIDE THE U.S. BY THE WILDLIFE HABITAT ENHANCEMENT COUNCIL.

in location analysis and site selection. Maps are used to calculate walktime trade areas. The number of potential customers in an area, say a 10-square-block area of a given business district, is utilized to calculate how many people could walk to a store within two minutes, how many people could walk to a store within four minutes, and so forth. As walktime increases, the number of potential customers decreases. A similar approach is used in analyzing suburban locations when drive time is the consideration. Maps also are used—based on consumer proximity figures plus demographics data (e.g., disposable income figures)—to pinpoint hotspots for gourmet coffee consumption.

DEMOGRAPHICS

Starbucks has historically targeted higher-income geographic areas. Now it is looking for more moderate-income neighborhoods as well as neighborhoods undergoing gentrification. They are also moving into new tourist destination zones such as Baltimore's inner harbor and downtown Miami, Florida.

International site selection is proving to be more challenging due to the lack of available data. Translation of data, terms, and boundaries from foreign data formatting into domestic site selection criterion formats can be challenging. For example, a "county" in Japan and in England is not the same as a county in the United States. Adding to the challenge, Claritas, a widely used vendor of demographics data, does not yet have one central global clearinghouse of international data. Likewise, ESRI (another popular vendor of demographics data) doesn't have information available for many nondomestic markets. →

Where should a plant or service facility be located? This is a top question on the strategic agendas of contemporary manufacturing and service firms, particularly in this age of global markets and global production. Dramatic changes in international trade agreements have made the world truly a "global factory," allowing companies greater flexibility in their location choices. In practice, however, the question of location is very much linked to two competitive imperatives:

1. The need to produce close to the customer due to time-based competition, trade agreements, and shipping costs.
2. The need to locate near the appropriate labor pool to take advantage of low wage costs and/or high technical skills.

This technical note discusses these and other issues in facility location decisions. Examples cover different industries with a global perspective. We present typical techniques involved in facility location analysis and two cases on global location decisions.

ISSUES IN FACILITY LOCATION

Global

The problem of facility location is faced by both new and existing businesses, and its solution is critical to a company's eventual success. An important element in designing a company's supply chain is the location of its facilities. For instance, 3M has moved a significant part of its corporate activity, including R&D, to the more temperate climate of Austin, Texas. Toys "Я" Us has opened a new location in Japan as a part of its global strategy. Disney chose Paris, France, for its European theme park, and BMW assembles the Z3 sports car in South Carolina. Manufacturing and service companies' location decisions are guided by a variety of criteria defined by competitive imperatives. Criteria that influence manufacturing plant and warehouse location planning are discussed next.

Proximity to Customers   For example, Japan's NatSteel Electronics has built its two largest plants in Mexico and Hungary to be closer to major markets in the United States and Europe—whose buyers want their goods delivered yesterday. Such proximity also helps ensure that customer needs are incorporated into products being developed and built.

Business Climate   A favorable business climate can include the presence of similar-sized businesses, the presence of companies in the same industry, and, in the case of international locations, the presence of other foreign companies. Probusiness government legislation and local government intervention to facilitate businesses locating in an area via subsidies, tax abatements, and other support are also factors.

Total Costs   The objective is to select a site with the lowest total cost. This includes regional costs, inbound distribution costs, and outbound distribution costs. Land, construction, labor, taxes, and energy costs make up the regional costs. In addition, there are hidden costs that are difficult to measure. These involve (1) excessive moving of preproduction material between locations before final delivery to the customers and (2) loss of customer responsiveness arising from locating away from the main customer base.

Infrastructure   Adequate road, rail, air, and sea transportation are vital. Energy and telecommunications requirements also must be met. In addition, the local government's willingness to invest in upgrading infrastructure to the levels required may be an incentive to select a specific location.

Quality of Labor   The educational and skill levels of the labor pool must match the company's needs. Even more important are the willingness and ability to learn.

Suppliers   A high-quality and competitive supplier base makes a given location suitable. The proximity of important suppliers' plants also supports lean production methods.

Other Facilities   The location of other plants or distribution centers of the same company may influence a new facility's location in the network. Issues of product mix and capacity are strongly interconnected to the location decision in this context.

Free trade zone

Global

Free Trade Zones A foreign trade zone or a **free trade zone** is typically a closed facility (under the supervision of the customs department) into which foreign goods can be brought without being subject to the normal customs requirements. There are about 260 such free trade zones in the United States today. Such specialized locations also exist in other countries. Manufacturers in free trade zones can use imported components in the final product and delay payment of customs duties until the product is shipped into the host country.

Political Risk The fast-changing geopolitical scenes in numerous nations present exciting, challenging opportunities. But the extended phase of transformation that many countries are undergoing makes the decision to locate in those areas extremely difficult. Political risks in both the country of location and the host country influence location decisions.

Government Barriers Barriers to enter and locate in many countries are being removed today through legislation. Yet many nonlegislative and cultural barriers should be considered in location planning.

Trading blocs

Trading Blocs The Central America Free Trade Agreement (CAFTA) is one of the new **trading blocs** in our hemisphere. Such agreements influence location decisions, both within and outside trading bloc countries. Firms typically locate, or relocate, within a bloc to take advantage of new market opportunities or lower total costs afforded by the trading agreement. Other companies (those outside the trading bloc countries) decide on locations within the bloc so as not to be disqualified from competing in the new market. Examples include the location of various Japanese auto manufacturing plants in Europe before 1992 as well as recent moves by many communications and financial services companies into Mexico in a post-NAFTA environment.

Environmental Regulation The environmental regulations that impact a certain industry in a given location should be included in the location decision. Besides measurable cost implications, these regulations influence the relationship with the local community.

Host Community The host community's interest in having the plant in its midst is a necessary part of the evaluation process. Local educational facilities and the broader issue of quality of life are also important.

Global

Competitive Advantage An important decision for multinational companies is the nation in which to locate the home base for each distinct business. Porter suggests that a company can have different home bases for distinct businesses or segments. Competitive advantage is created at a home base where strategy is set, the core product and process technology are created, and a critical mass of production takes place. So a company should move its home base to a country that stimulates innovation and provides the best environment for global competitiveness.[1] This concept can also be applied to domestic companies seeking to gain sustainable competitive advantage. It partly explains the southeastern states' recent emergence as the preferred corporate destination within the United States (that is, their business climate fosters innovation and low-cost production).

PLANT LOCATION METHODS

 As we will see, there are many techniques available for identifying potential sites for plants or other types of facilities. The process required to narrow the decision down to a particular area can vary significantly depending on the type of business we are in and the competitive pressures that must be considered. As we have discussed, there are often many different criteria that need to be considered when selecting from the set of feasible sites.

In this section, we sample three different types of techniques that have proven to be very useful to many companies. The first is the *factor-rating system* that allows us to consider many different types of criteria using simple point-rating scales. Next, we consider the *transportation method* of linear programming, a powerful technique for estimating the cost of using a network of plants and warehouses. Following this, we consider the *centroid method,* a technique often used by communications companies (cell phone providers) to locate their transmission towers. Finally, we consider how service firms such as McDonald's and State Farm Insurance use statistical techniques to find desirable locations for their facilities.

FACTOR-RATING SYSTEMS

Factor-rating systems are perhaps the most widely used of the general location techniques because they provide a mechanism to combine diverse factors in an easy-to-understand format.

By way of example, a refinery assigned the following range of point values to major factors affecting a set of possible sites:

	RANGE
Fuels in region	0 to 330
Power availability and reliability	0 to 200
Labor climate	0 to 100
Living conditions	0 to 100
Transportation	0 to 50
Water supply	0 to 10
Climate	0 to 50
Supplies	0 to 60
Tax policies and laws	0 to 20

Each site was then rated against each factor, and a point value was selected from its assigned range. The sums of assigned points for each site were then compared. The site with the most points was selected.

A major problem with simple point-rating schemes is that they do not account for the wide range of costs that may occur within each factor. For example, there may be only a few hundred dollars' difference between the best and worst locations on one factor and several thousands of dollars' difference between the best and the worst on another. The first factor may have the most points available to it but provide little help in making the location decision; the second may have few points available but potentially show a real difference in the value of locations. To deal with this problem, it has been suggested that points possible for each factor be derived using a weighting scale based on standard deviations of costs rather than simply total cost amounts. In this way, relative costs can be considered.

TRANSPORTATION METHOD OF LINEAR PROGRAMMING

The **transportation method** is a special linear programming method. (Note that linear programming is developed in detail in Technical Note 2.) It gets its name from its application to problems involving transporting products from several sources to several destinations. The two common objectives of such problems are either (1) minimize the cost of shipping *n* units to *m* destinations or (2) maximize the profit of shipping *n* units to *m* destinations.

Factor-rating systems

Transportation method

Interactive Operations Management

EXAMPLE TN11.1: U.S. Pharmaceutical Company

Suppose the U.S. Pharmaceutical Company has four factories supplying the warehouses of four major customers and its management wants to determine the minimum-cost shipping schedule for its monthly output to these customers. Factory supply, warehouse demands, and shipping costs per case for these drugs are shown in Exhibit TN11.1.

The transportation matrix for this example appears in Exhibit TN11.2, where supply availability at each factory is shown in the far right column and the warehouse demands are shown in the bottom row.

exhibit TN11.1

Data for U.S. Pharmaceutical Transportation Problem

FACTORY	SUPPLY	WAREHOUSE	DEMAND	FROM	SHIPPING COSTS PER CASE (IN DOLLARS)			
					To COLUMBUS	To ST. LOUIS	To DENVER	To LOS ANGELES
Indianapolis	15	Columbus	10	Indianapolis	$25	$35	$36	$60
Phoenix	6	St. Louis	12	Phoenix	55	30	25	25
New York	14	Denver	15	New York	40	50	80	90
Atlanta	11	Los Angeles	9	Atlanta	30	40	66	75

exhibit TN11.2

Transportation Matrix for U.S. Pharmaceutical Problem

From \ To	Columbus	St. Louis	Denver	Los Angeles	Factory supply
Indianapolis	25	35	36	60	15
Phoenix	55	30	25	25	6
New York	40	50	80	90	14
Atlanta	30	40	66	75	11
Destination requirements	10	12	15	9	46 / 46

The shipping costs are shown in the small boxes within the cells. For example, the cost to ship one unit from the Indianapolis factory to the customer warehouse in Columbus is $25.

**Tutorial:
Excel Solver**

SOLUTION

This problem can be solved by using Microsoft® Excel's® Solver function. Exhibit TN11.3 shows how the problem can be set up in the spreadsheet. Cells B6 through E6 contain the requirement for each customer warehouse. Cells F2 through F5 contain the amount that can be supplied from each plant. Cells B2 through E5 are the cost of shipping one unit for each potential plant and warehouse combination.

Cells for the solution of the problem are B9 through E12. These cells can initially be left blank when setting up the spreadsheet. Column cells F9 through F12 are the sum of each row indicating how much is actually being shipped from each factory in the candidate solution. Similarly, row cells B13 through E13 are sums of the amount being shipped to each customer in the candidate solution. The Excel® Sum function can be used to calculate these values.

The cost of the candidate solution is calculated in cells B16 through E19. Multiplying the amount shipped in the candidate solution by the cost per unit of shipping over that particular route makes this calculation. For example, multiplying B2 by B9 in cell B16 gives the cost of shipping between Indianapolis and Columbus for the candidate solution. The total cost shown in cell F20 is the sum of all these individual costs.

To solve the problem, the Excel® Solver application needs to be accessed. The Solver is found by selecting Tools and then Solver from the Excel® menu. A screen similar to what is shown below should appear. If you cannot find Solver at that location, the required add-in might not have been added when

Excel® Screen Showing the U.S. Pharmaceutical Problem

Microsoft Excel - US Pharmaceutical.xls

File Edit View Insert Format Tools Data Window Help

F20 = =SUM(B16:E19)

	A	B	C	D	E	F
1	**From/To**	Columbus	St. Louis	Denver	Los Angeles	**Factory Supply**
2	Indianapolis	25	35	36	60	15
3	Phoenix	55	30	25	25	6
4	New York	40	50	80	90	14
5	Atlanta	30	40	66	75	11
6	**Requirements**	10	12	15	9	
7						
8	**Candidate Solution**					**Total Shipped**
9	Indianapolis	0	0	15	0	15
10	Phoenix	0	0	0	6	6
11	New York	10	4	0	0	14
12	Atlanta	0	8	0	3	11
13	**Total Supplied**	10	12	15	9	
14						
15	**Cost Calculations**					
16	Indianapolis	0	0	540	0	
17	Phoenix	0	0	0	150	
18	New York	400	200	0	0	
19	Atlanta	0	320	0	225	
20					**Total Cost**	$1,835
21						
22						

US Pharmaceutical

Ready   NUM

Excel: US Pharmaceutical.xls

Excel® was initially installed on your computer. Solver can easily be added if you have your original Excel® installation disk.

Solver parameters now need to be set. First set the target cell. This is the cell where the total cost associated with the solution is calculated. In our sample problem, this is cell F20. Next we need to indicate that we are minimizing this cell. Selecting the "Min" button does this. The location of our solution is indicated in the "Changing Cells." These cells are B9 through E12 in our example.

Next we need to indicate the constraints for our problem. For our transportation problem we need to be sure that customer demand is met and that we do not exceed the capacity of our manufacturing plants. To ensure that demand is met, click on "Add" and highlight the range of cells where we have calculated the total amount being shipped to each customer. This range is B13 to E13 in our example. Next select "=" indicating that we want the amount shipped to equal demand. Finally, on the right side enter the range of cells where the actual customer demand is stated in our spreadsheet. This range is B6 to E6 in our example.

The second set of constraints that ensures that the capacity of our manufacturing plants is not exceeded is entered similarly. The range of cells that indicated how much is being shipped from each factory is F9 to F12. These values need to be less than or equal to (<=) the capacity of each factory, which is in cells F2 to F5. To set up the Solver, a few options need to be set as well. Click on the "Options" button and the following screen should appear:

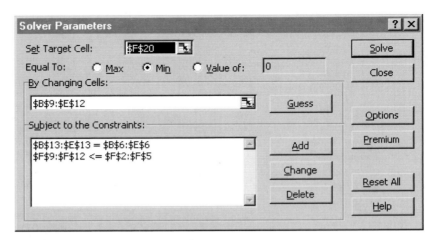

Excel® Screen shots from Microsoft® Excel © 2001 Microsoft Corporation.

Two options need to be set for solving transportation problems. First we need "Assume Linear Model." This tells the Solver that there are no nonlinear calculations in our spreadsheet. This is important because the Solver can use a very efficient algorithm to calculate the optimal solution to this problem if this condition exists. Next the "Assume Non-Negative" box needs to be checked. This tells Solver that the values in our solution need to be greater than or equal to zero. In transportation problems, shipping negative quantities does not make any sense. Click "OK" to return to the main Solver box, and then click "Solve" to actually solve the problem. Solver will notify you that it found a solution. Indicate that you want that solution saved. Finally, click OK to go back to the main spreadsheet. The solution should be in cells B9 to E12.

The transportation method can be used to solve many different types of problems if it is applied innovatively. For example, it can be used to test the cost impact of different candidate locations on the entire production–distribution network. To do this we might add a new row that contains the unit shipping cost from a factory in a new location, say, Dallas, to the existing set of customer warehouses, along with the total amount it could supply. We could then solve this particular matrix for minimum total cost. Next we would replace the factory located in Dallas in the same row of the matrix with a factory at a different location, Houston, and again solve for minimum total cost. Assuming the factories in Dallas and Houston would be identical in other important respects, the location resulting in the lowest total cost for the network would be selected.

For additional information about using the Solver, see Technical Note 2, "Linear Programming Using the Excel Solver." ●

CENTROID METHOD

Centroid method

The **centroid method** is a technique for locating single facilities that considers the existing facilities, the distances between them, and the volumes of goods to be shipped. The technique is often used to locate intermediate or distribution warehouses. In its simplest form, this

Grid Map for Centroid Example

- Plant
- Distributor

**Excel:
Centroid_method.xls**

method assumes that inbound and outbound transportation costs are equal, and it does not include special shipping costs for less than full loads.

Another major application of the centroid method today is the location of communication towers in urban areas. Examples include radio, TV, and cell phone towers. In this application the goal is to find sites that are near clusters of customers, thus ensuring clear radio signals.

The centroid method begins by placing the existing locations on a coordinate grid system. The choice of coordinate systems is entirely arbitrary. The purpose is to establish relative distances between locations. Using longitude and latitude coordinates might be helpful in international decisions. Exhibit TN11.4 shows an example of a grid layout.

The centroid is found by calculating the X and Y coordinates that result in the minimal transportation cost. We use the formulas

$$C_x = \frac{\sum d_{ix} V_i}{\sum V_i} \qquad C_y = \frac{\sum d_{iy} V_i}{\sum V_i}$$

where

$C_x = X$ coordinate of the centroid
$C_y = Y$ coordinate of the centroid
$d_{ix} = X$ coordinate of the ith location
$d_{iy} = Y$ coordinate of the ith location
$V_i = $ Volume of goods moved to or from the ith location

**Interactive
Operations
Management**

EXAMPLE TN11.2: HiOctane Refining Company

The HiOctane Refining Company needs to locate an intermediate holding facility between its refining plant in Long Beach and its major distributors. Exhibit TN11.4 shows the coordinate map. The amount of gasoline shipped to or from the plant and distributors appears in Exhibit TN11.5.

In this example, for the Long Beach location (the first location), $d_{1x} = 325$, $d_{1y} = 75$, and $V_1 = 1,500$.

SOLUTION

Using the information in Exhibits TN11.4 and TN11.5, we can calculate the coordinates of the centroid:

$$C_x = \frac{(325 \times 1,500) + (400 \times 250) + (450 \times 450) + (350 \times 350) + (25 \times 450)}{1,500 + 250 + 450 + 350 + 450}$$

$$= \frac{923,750}{3,000} = 307.9$$

**Excel:
Centriod_method.xls**

Shipping Volumes, Centroid Example

LOCATIONS	GALLONS OF GASOLINE PER MONTH (000,000)
Long Beach	1,500
Anaheim	250
LaHabra	450
Glendale	350
Thousand Oaks	450

$$C_y = \frac{(75 \times 1,500) + (150 \times 250) + (350 \times 450) + (400 \times 350) + (450 \times 450)}{1,500 + 250 + 450 + 350 + 450}$$

$$= \frac{650,000}{3,000} = 216.7$$

This gives management the *X* and *Y* coordinates of approximately 308 and 217, respectively, and provides an initial starting point to search for a new site. By examining the location of the calculated centroid on the grid map, we can see that it might be more cost-efficient to ship directly between the Long Beach plant and the Anaheim distributor than to ship via a warehouse near the centroid. Before a location decision is made, management would probably recalculate the centroid, changing the data to reflect this (that is, decrease the gallons shipped from Long Beach by the amount Anaheim needs and remove Anaheim from the formula). ●

LOCATING SERVICE FACILITIES

Service

Because of the variety of service firms and the relatively low cost of establishing a service facility compared to one for manufacturing, new service facilities are far more common than new factories and warehouses. Indeed, there are few communities in which rapid population growth has not been paralleled by concurrent rapid growth in retail outlets, restaurants, municipal services, and entertainment facilities.

LESS THAN TWO MILES FROM TWIN CITIES INTERNATIONAL AIRPORT, WITH FOUR MAJOR HIGHWAYS INTERSECTING THE 78-ACRE PROPERTY, BLOOMINGTON'S MALL OF AMERICA HAS BECOME GLOBALLY RECOGNIZED AS THE LARGEST ENTERTAINMENT AND RETAIL COMPLEX IN THE UNITED STATES. SERVING OVER 28 MILLION PEOPLE WITHIN A ONE-DAY DRIVE AS WELL AS MANY MORE AS A DESTINATION, THE MALL EMPLOYS MORE THAN 12,000 PEOPLE AND TOTAL TRAFFIC IS BETWEEN 35 AND 42 MILLION VISITS YEARLY. VISITORS SPEND AN AVERAGE OF THREE HOURS IN THE MALL, WHICH IS THREE TIMES THE NATIONAL AVERAGE FOR SHOPPING MALLS.

GEOGRAPHIC INFORMATION SYSTEMS (GIS), SHOWN HERE FROM MAPINFO, ARE USED BY RETAILERS, FINANCIAL SERVICES GROUPS, AND OTHERS IN THE SITE SELECTION PROCESS. MAPPING INFORMATION ON POTENTIAL SITES SUCH AS DEMOGRAPHICS, COMPETITORS, AND SO ON ALLOWS INFORMATION TO BE SEEN IN A SINGLE, COMPREHENSIVE VIEW FOR MORE INFORMED DECISION MAKING.

COPYRIGHT © 2002 MAPINFO CORPORATION, TROY, NEW YORK.

Services typically have multiple sites to maintain close contact with customers. The location decision is closely tied to the market selection decision. If the target market is college-age groups, locations in retirement communities—despite desirability in terms of cost, resource availability, and so forth—are not viable alternatives. Market needs also affect the number of sites to be built and the size and characteristics of the sites. Whereas manufacturing location decisions are often made by minimizing costs, many service location decision techniques maximize the profit potential of various sites. Next we present a multiple regression model that can be used to help select good sites.

EXAMPLE TN11.3: Screening Location Sites at La Quinta Motor Inns

Selecting good sites is crucial to a hotel chain's success. Of the four major marketing considerations (price, product, promotion, and location), location and product have been shown to be most important for multisite firms. As a result, hotel chain owners who can pick good sites quickly have a distinct competitive advantage.

Exhibit TN11.6 shows the initial list of variables included in a study to help La Quinta Motor Inns screen potential locations for its new hotels.[2] Data were collected on 57 existing La Quinta Inns. Analysis of the data identified the variables that correlated with operating profit in 1983 and 1986. (See Exhibit TN11.7.)

SOLUTION

A *regression model* (see Chapter 13) was constructed. Its final form was

Profitability = 39.05 − 5.41 × State population per inn (1,000)

$\qquad$ + 5.86 × Price of the inn

$\qquad$ − 3.91 × Square root of the median income of the area (1,000)

$\qquad$ + 1.75 × College students within four miles

The model shows that profitability is affected by market penetration, positively affected by price, negatively affected by higher incomes (the inns do better in lower-median-income areas), and positively affected by colleges nearby.

Independent Variables Collected for the Initial Model-Building Stage

CATEGORY	NAME	DESCRIPTION
Competitive	INNRATE	Inn price
	PRICE	Room rate for the inn
	RATE	Average competitive room rate
	RMS 1	Hotel rooms within 1 mile
	RMSTOTAL	Hotel rooms within 3 miles
	ROOMSINN	Inn rooms
Demand generators	CIVILIAN	Civilian personnel on base
	COLLEGE	College enrollment
	HOSP1	Hospital beds within 1 mile
	HOSPTOTL	Hospital beds within 4 miles
	HVYIND	Heavy industrial employment
	LGTIND	Light industrial acreage
	MALLS	Shopping mall square footage
	MILBLKD	Military base blocked
	MILITARY	Military personnel
	MILTOT	MILITARY + CIVILIAN
	OFC1	Office space within 1 mile
	OFCTOTAL	Office space within 4 miles
	OFCCBD	Office space in Central Business District
	PASSENGR	Airport passengers enplaned
	RETAIL	Scale ranking of retail activity
	TOURISTS	Annual tourists
	TRAFFIC	Traffic count
	VAN	Airport van
Demographic	EMPLYPCT	Unemployment percentage
	INCOME	Average family income
	POPULACE	Residential population
Market awareness	AGE	Years inn has been open
	NEAREST	Distance to nearest inn
	STATE	State population per inn
	URBAN	Urban population per inn
Physical	ACCESS	Accessibility
	ARTERY	Major traffic artery
	DISTCBD	Distance to downtown
	SIGNVIS	Sign visibility

A Summary of the Variables That Correlated with Operating Margin in 1983 and 1986

VARIABLE	1983	1986
ACCESS	.20	
AGE	.29	.49
COLLEGE		.25
DISTCBD		−.22
EMPLYPCT	−.22	−.22
INCOME		−.23
MILTOT		.22
NEAREST	−.51	
OFCCBD	.30	
POPULACE	.30	.35
PRICE	.38	.58
RATE		.27
STATE	−.32	−.33
SIGNVIS	.25	
TRAFFIC	.32	
URBAN	−.22	−.26

La Quinta implemented the model on a spreadsheet and routinely uses the spreadsheet to screen potential real estate acquisitions. The founder and president of La Quinta has accepted the model's validity and no longer feels obligated to personally select the sites.

This example shows that a specific model can be obtained from the requirements of service organizations and used to identify the most important features in site selection. ●

CONCLUSION

◯◯◯◯ Facility location decisions are a key element in any firm's overall strategic plan. Dramatic changes in the global geopolitical environment, coupled with rapid advances in technology, have placed a premium on making location decisions in a matter of weeks rather than months, as has been the case in the recent past. As a final comment, much of the location "action" is in deciding where to locate support functions rather than factories or retail outlets. In these situations, the need for special capabilities of the workforce is often far more important than other cost factors. For example, IBM Business Consulting Services stated that a dominant factor in deciding where to locate the software application group of its client, a U.S. investment bank, was the availability of a large pool of multilingual workers.

KEY TERMS

Free trade zones A closed facility (under the supervision of government customs officials) into which foreign goods can be brought without being subject to the payment of normal import duties.

Trading bloc A group of countries that agree on a set of special arrangements governing the trading of goods between member countries. Companies may locate in places affected by the agreement to take advantage of new market opportunities.

Factor-rating system An approach for selecting a facility location by combining a diverse set of factors. Point scales are developed for each criterion. Each potential site is then evaluated on each criterion and the points are combined to calculate a rating for the site.

Transportation method A special linear programming method that is useful for solving problems involving transporting products from several sources to several destinations.

Centroid method A technique for locating single facilities that considers the existing facilities, the distances between them, and the volumes of goods to be shipped.

FORMULA REVIEW

Centroid

$$C_x = \frac{\sum d_{ix} V_i}{\sum V_i} \qquad C_y = \frac{\sum d_{iy} V_i}{\sum V_i}$$

SOLVED PROBLEM

Cool Air, a manufacturer of automotive air conditioners, currently produces its XB-300 line at three different locations: Plant A, Plant B, and Plant C. Recently management decided to build all compressors, a major product component, in a separate dedicated facility, Plant D.

Using the centroid method and the information displayed in Exhibits TN11.8 and TN11.9, determine the best location for Plant D. Assume a linear relationship between volumes shipped and shipping costs (no premium charges).

Solution

$$d_{1x} = 150 \qquad d_{1y} = 75 \qquad V_1 = 6,000$$
$$d_{2x} = 100 \qquad d_{2y} = 300 \qquad V_2 = 8,200$$
$$d_{3x} = 275 \qquad d_{3y} = 380 \qquad V_3 = 7,000$$

$$C_x = \frac{\sum d_{ix} V_i}{\sum V_i} = \frac{(150 \times 6,000) + (100 \times 8,200) + (275 \times 7,000)}{6,000 + 8,200 + 7,000} = 172$$

Plant Location Matrix

**Excel:
Centroid_method.xls**

Quantity of Compressors Required by Each Plant

PLANT	COMPRESSORS REQUIRED PER YEAR
A	6,000
B	8,200
C	7,000

$$C_y = \frac{\sum d_{iy} V_i}{\sum V_i} = \frac{(75 \times 6{,}000) + (300 \times 8{,}200) + (380 \times 7{,}000)}{21{,}200} = 262.7$$

Plant D$[C_x, C_y]$ = D[172, 263]

REVIEW AND DISCUSSION QUESTIONS

1   What motivations typically cause firms to initiate a facilities location or relocation project?
2   List five major reasons why a new electronic components manufacturing firm should move into your city or town.
3   How do facility location decisions differ for service facilities and manufacturing plants?
4   What are the pros and cons of relocating a small or midsized manufacturing firm (that makes mature products) from the United States to Mexico in the post-NAFTA environment?
5   If you could locate your new software development company anywhere in the world, which place would you choose, and why?

PROBLEMS

1   Refer to the information given in the solved problem. Suppose management decides to shift 2,000 units of production from Plant B to Plant A. Does this change the proposed location of Plant D, the compressor production facility? If so, where should Plant D be located?
2   A small manufacturing facility is being planned that will feed parts to three heavy manufacturing facilities. The locations of the current plants with their coordinates and volume requirements are given in the following table:

PLANT LOCATION	COORDINATES (x, y)	VOLUME (PARTS PER YEAR)
Peoria	300, 320	4,000
Decatur	375, 470	6,000
Joliet	470, 180	3,000

Use the centroid method to determine the best location for this new facility.

3 Bindley Corporation has a one-year contract to supply motors for all washing machines produced by Rinso Ltd. Rinso manufactures the washers at four locations around the country: New York, Fort Worth, San Diego, and Minneapolis. Plans call for the following numbers of washing machines to be produced at each location:

New York	50,000
Fort Worth	70,000
San Diego	60,000
Minneapolis	80,000

Bindley has three plants that can produce the motors. The plants and production capacities are

Boulder	100,000
Macon	100,000
Gary	150,000

Due to varying production and transportation costs, the profit Bindley earns on each 1,000 units depends on where they were produced and where they were shipped. The following table gives the accounting department estimates of the dollar profit per unit. (Shipment will be made in lots of 1,000.)

	SHIPPED TO			
PRODUCED AT	NEW YORK	FORT WORTH	SAN DIEGO	MINNEAPOLIS
Boulder	7	11	8	13
Macon	20	17	12	10
Gary	8	18	13	16

Given profit maximization as a criterion, Bindley would like to determine how many motors should be produced at each plant and how many motors should be shipped from each plant to each destination.

a. Develop a transportation grid for this problem.

b. Find the optimal solution using Microsoft® Excel.

4 Rent'R Cars is a multisite car rental company in the city. It is trying out a new "return the car to the location most convenient for you" policy to improve customer service. But this means that the company has to constantly move cars around the city to maintain required levels of vehicle availability. The supply and demand for economy cars, and the total cost of moving these vehicles between sites, are shown below.

From \ To	D	E	F	G	Supply
A	$9	$8	$6	$5	50
B	9	8	8	0	40
C	5	3	3	10	75
Demand	50	60	25	30	165 / 165

a. Find the solution that minimizes moving costs using Microsoft® Excel.

b. What would you have to do to the costs to assure that *A* always sends a car to *D* as part of the optimal solution?

CASE: APPLICHEM—THE TRANSPORTATION PROBLEM

Applichem management is faced with the difficult problem of allocating to its customers the capacity of manufacturing plants that are located around the world. Management has long recognized that the manufacturing plants differ greatly in efficiency but has had little success in improving the operations of the inefficient plants. At this time, management has decided to focus on how best to use the capacity of its plants given the differences in manufacturing costs that currently exist. They recognize that this study may result in the significant reduction of output or possibly the shutting down of one or more of the existing plants.

Applichem makes a product called Release-ease. Plastics molding manufacturers use this chemical product. Plastic parts are made by injecting hot plastic into a mold made in the shape of the part. After the plastic has sufficiently cooled, the fresh part is removed from the mold and the mold is then reused to make subsequent parts. Release-ease is a dry powder, applied as part of the manufacturing process, that makes it easy to remove the part from the mold.

Applichem has made the product since the early 1950s, and demand has been consistent over time. A recent study by Applichem's market research team has indicated that demand for Release-ease should be fairly steady for the next five years. Although Applichem does have some competition, particularly in the European markets, management feels that as long as they can provide a quality product at a competitive cost, customers should stick with Applichem. Release-ease sells at an average price of $1.00 per pound.

The company owns plants capable of making Release-ease in the following cities: Gary, Indiana; Windsor, Ontario, Canada; Frankfurt, Germany; Mexico City, Mexico; Caracas, Venezuela; and Osaka, Japan. Although the plants are focused on meeting demand for the immediate surrounding regions, there is considerable exporting and importing of product for various reasons. The following table contains data on how demand has been met during the past year:

PRODUCT MADE AND SHIPPED DURING PAST YEAR (×100,000 POUNDS)

FROM/TO	MEXICO	CANADA	VENEZUELA	EUROPE	UNITED STATES	JAPAN
Mexico City	3.0		6.3			7.9
Windsor, Ontario		2.6				
Caracas			4.1			
Frankfurt			5.6	20.0	12.4	
Gary					14.0	
Osaka						4.0

Differences in the technologies used in the plants and in local raw material and labor costs created significant differences in the cost to produce Release-ease in the various locations. These costs may change dramatically due to currency valuation and labor law changes in some of the countries. This is especially true in Mexico and Venezuela. The capacity of each plant also differs at each location, and management has no interest in increasing capacity anywhere at this time. The following table gives details on the costs to produce and capacity of each plant:

PLANT PRODUCTION COSTS AND CAPACITY

PLANT	PRODUCTION COST (PER 1,000 LBS)	PLANT CAPACITY (×100,000 LBS)
Mexico City	95.01	22.0
Windsor, Ontario	97.35	3.7
Caracas	116.34	4.5
Frankfurt	76.69	47.0
Gary	102.93	18.5
Osaka	153.80	5.0

In considering how best to use the capacity of its plants, Applichem management needs to consider the cost of shipping product from one customer region to another. Applichem now commonly ships product in bulk around the world, but it is expensive. The costs involved are not only the transportation costs but also import duties that are assessed by customs in some countries. Applichem is committed to meeting demand, though, and sometimes this is done even though profit might not be made on all orders.

The following table details the demand in each country, the cost to transport product from each plant to each country, and the current import duty rate levied by each country. (These percentages do not reflect current duties.) Import duty is calculated on the approximate production plus transportation cost of product brought into the country. (For example, if the production and shipping cost for 1,000 pounds of Release-ease shipped into Venezuela were $100, the import duty would be $100 × .5 = $50.)

TRANSPORTATION COST (PER 1,000 LBS), IMPORT DUTIES, AND DEMANDS FOR RELEASE-EASE

PLANT/COUNTRY	MEXICO	CANADA	VENEZUELA	EUROPE	UNITED STATES	JAPAN
Mexico City	0	11.40	7.00	11.00	11.00	14.00
Windsor, Ontario	11.00	0	9.00	11.50	6.00	13.00
Caracas	7.00	10.00	0	13.00	10.40	14.30
Frankfurt	10.00	11.50	12.50	0	11.20	13.30
Gary	10.00	6.00	11.00	10.00	0	12.50
Osaka	14.00	13.00	12.50	14.20	13.00	0
Total demand (×100,000 lbs)	3.0	2.6	16.0	20.0	26.4	11.9
Import duty	0.0%	0.0%	50.0%	9.5%	4.5%	6.0%

QUESTIONS

Given all these data, set up a spreadsheet (Applichem.xls is a start) and answer the following questions for management:

Excel:
Applichem.xls

1. Evaluate the cost associated with the way Applichem's plant capacity is currently being used.
2. Determine the optimal use of Applichem's plant capacity using the Solver in Excel.
3. What would you recommend that Applichem management do? Why?

SOURCE: THIS CASE IS ROUGHLY BASED ON DATA CONTAINED IN "APPLICHEM (A)," HARVARD BUSINESS SCHOOL, 9-685-051.

CASE: THE PLANT LOCATION PUZZLE[3]

⦶⦶⦶ Ann Reardon made her way across the crowded tradeshow floor, deep in thought and oblivious to the noisy activity all around her. As CEO of the Eldora Company (EDC) for the previous 13 years, she had led her organization through a period of extraordinary success. While larger bicycle makers had moved their manufacturing operations overseas to take advantage of lower labor costs, Eldora had stuck with a domestic manufacturing strategy, keeping its plant on the same campus as its corporate offices in Boulder, Colorado. Ann felt that her strategy of keeping all the parts of the company in the same location, although unconventional, had contributed greatly to cooperation among various departments and, ultimately, to the company's growth: EDC had become the largest and most profitable bicycle company in the United States. Yet her manufacturing vice president, Sean Andrews, was now urging her to build a plant in China.

"Look at the number of companies here," he had said that morning, as they helped several other EDC staffers stack brochures on the exhibit table and position the company's latest models around the perimeter of their area. Manufacturing heads rarely attended trade shows; in fact, this was Sean's first, but he had wanted to attend, and Ann had supported his interest. "There are too many players in this market," he had said. "I've been saying this for two months now, and you know the forecasters' numbers back me up. But if they weren't enough to convince you, just look around. The industry is reaching the saturation point here in the States. We have to break into Asia."

"Leave it alone, Sean," Ann had replied. "I know this is something you're pushing; you've said so in the past. But let's set up a time to talk about it in detail later. This isn't the time or the place."

Now, three hours later, with the show in full swing, Ann understood why Sean had been compelled to speak up again. Having all their competitors in the same room at the same time was a powerful visual reminder of how the industry had changed. She thought about what Sean had said about the U.S. market. In 1992 EDC's sales and earnings had hit record levels. The company now produced almost 30 percent of the bicycles sold in the United States. U.S. mass-market bicycle sales were growing by only 2 percent per year, while the Asian market for those same bikes was nearly doubling annually. And Eldora could not competitively serve those markets from its U.S. manufacturing facility. Two of the largest bike manufacturers in the world, located in rapidly growing Asian markets, enjoyed a significant labor and distribution cost advantage.

She stopped at a mountain bike display set up by a fast-growing young bike company. Mountain bikes with front suspension were the latest trend—the added support and cushion allowed riders to better absorb the shocks inherent in off-road riding without slowing down or losing balance. Most of these bikes were still prohibitively expensive. But Eldora, too, had an entry in this product category, retailing for about $190, and Ann was proud of it. For years, the company had concentrated its efforts on inexpensive bicycles, which retailed through mass merchandisers for between $100 and $200. Eldora's prices were slightly higher than other low-end competitors, but large retailers were willing to pay the premium because EDC had consistently been able to offer many state-of-the-art styles and features with quick, timely deliveries that competitors building overseas couldn't match.

One of the reasons the company had been so successful was that Boulder, Colorado, was a bicyclists' mecca. Eldora employees at all levels shared a genuine love of bicycling and eagerly pursued knowledge of the industry's latest trends and styles. Someone was always suggesting a better way to position the hand brakes or a new toe grip that allowed for better traction and easier dismounts. And Eldora never had a shortage of people willing to test out the latest prototypes.

Another reason was that all marketing staff, engineers, designers, and manufacturing personnel worked on one campus, within a 10-minute walk of one another. Ann had bet big on that strategy, and it had paid off. Communication was easy, and changes in styles, production plans, and the like could be made quickly and efficiently. Mountain bikes, for example, had gone from 0 percent to more than 50 percent of the market volume since 1988, and Eldora had met the increased demand with ease. And when orders for cross-bikes—a mountain/road bike hybrid that had enjoyed a spurt of popularity—began to fall off, Eldora had been able to adjust its production run with minimal disruption.

EDC had also benefited from its foray into the high-end market (bicycles retailing for between $400 and $700) 12 years earlier. One of Ann's first moves as CEO had been to enter into a joint venture with Rinaldi, a high-end Italian bicycle manufacturer that at the time was specializing in racing models. As part of the agreement, EDC had begun importing Rinaldi bikes under the brand name Summit and selling them through specialty bike dealers. Similarly, Rinaldi had begun marketing EDC bikes in Europe. That arrangement had had lasting rewards: Although racing bikes were no longer very popular, EDC's offerings had taken off. About 20 percent of EDC's sales were now made outside the United States (primarily in Europe and Canada) through this and other agreements.

The relationships with Rinaldi and the specialty bike shops also helped keep EDC management aware of the latest industry trends over the years. Most recently, those trends had included a move toward more exotic frame materials like aluminum and carbon fiber and more advanced components, including the new front-fork suspension systems. Ann examined another rival's brochure touting a soon-to-be-released high-end model with these advances. EDC engineers were clearly ahead of the curve.

Her satisfaction was quickly tempered with thoughts of foreign sales performance. Between 1987 and 1991, EDC's foreign sales had grown at an annual rate of over 80 percent. But during the previous two years they had been flat.

Sean appeared at Ann's side, jolting her out of her thoughts and into the reality of her surroundings. "Dale just finished up the first round of retailers' meetings," he said. "We'd like to get some lunch back over at the hotel and talk about our options." Dale Stewart was Eldora's marketing vice president. His views of what was best for the company often differed from Sean's, but the two had an amiable working relationship and enjoyed frequent spirited verbal sparring matches.

"You won't let this go, will you," Ann said, throwing up her hands in a gesture of surrender. "Fine, let's talk. But you know I won't make a decision until we've had a more formal round of discussions back in Boulder next month."

Over sandwiches, Sean made his case. "Our primary markets in North America and western Europe represent less than a quarter of the worldwide demand. Of the 200 million bicycles made in the world last year, 40 million were sold in China, 30 million in India, and 9 million in Japan. Historically, bikes sold in Asia's developing markets were low-end products used as primary modes of transportation. But the economic picture is changing fast. There's a growing middle class. Suddenly people have disposable income. Many consumers there are now seeking higher quality and trendier styles. Mountain bikes with suspension are in. And cross-bikes are still holding their own. In fact, the demand in these markets for the product categories we produce has been doubling annually, and the growth rates seem sustainable.

"If we're going to compete in Asia, though, we need a local plant. My staff has evaluated many locations there. We've looked at wage rates, proximity to markets, and materials costs, and we feel that China is our best bet. We'd like to open a plant there as soon as possible, and start building our position."

Dale jumped in. "Two of our largest competitors, one from China, one from Taiwan, have been filling the demand so far," he said. "In 1990, 97 percent of the volume produced by these companies was for export. In 1994, they are projecting that 45 percent of their production will be for local markets. We can't compete with them from here. About 20 percent of our product cost is labor, and the hourly wages of the manufacturing workforce in these countries are between 5 percent and 15 percent of ours. It also costs us an additional 20 percent in transportation and duties to get our bicycles to these markets."

He glanced at Sean quickly and continued. "But here's where I disagree with Sean. I think we need a short-term solution. These companies have a big lead on us, and the more I think about it, the more I believe we need to put a direct sales operation in Asia first."

"Dale, you're crazy," Sean said, pouring himself some ice water from the pitcher on the table. "What good would an Asian sales operation do without a manufacturing plant? I know we source components in Asia now, but we could save another 10 percent of those parts if we were located there. Then we would really be bringing Eldora to Asia. If we want to compete there, we have to play from our greatest strength—quality. If we did it your way, you wouldn't be selling Eldora bikes. You'd just be selling some product with our label on it. You wouldn't get the quality. You wouldn't build the same kind of reputation we have here. It wouldn't really be Eldora. Over the long term, it couldn't work."

"We're building bicycles, not rocket ships," Dale countered. "There are lots of companies in Asia that could provide us with a product very quickly if we gave them our designs and helped them with their production process. We could outsource production in the short term until we made more permanent arrangements." He turned to Ann. "We could even outsource the product permanently, despite what Sean says. What do we know about building and running a plant in China? All I know is we're losing potential share even as we sit here. The trading companies aren't giving our products the attention they deserve, and they also aren't giving us the information we need on the features that consumers in these markets want. A sales operation would help us learn the market even as we're entering it. Setting up a plant first would take too long. We need to be over there now, and opening a sales operation is the quickest way."

Ann cut in. "Dale has a good point, Sean," she said. "We've been successful here in large part because our entire operation is in Boulder, on one site. We've had complete control over our own flexible manufacturing operation, and that's been a key factor in our ability to meet rapid change in the local market. How would we address the challenges inherent in manufacturing in a facility halfway around the world? Would you consider moving there? And for how long?

"Also, think about our other options. If the biggest issue keeping us out of these markets right now is cost, then both of you are ignoring a few obvious alternatives. Right now, only our frame-building operation is automated. We could cut labor costs significantly by automating more processes. And why are you so bent on China? Frankly, when I was there last month touring facilities, a lot of what I saw worried me. You know, that day I was supposed to tour a production facility, there was a power failure. Judging by the reactions of the personnel in the plant the next day, these outages are common. The roads to the facility are in very poor condition. And wastewater and cleaning solvents are regularly dumped untreated into the waterways. We could operate differently if we located there, but what impact would that have on costs?

"Taiwan has a better-developed infrastructure than China. What about making that our Asian base? And I've heard that Singapore offers attractive tax arrangements to new manufacturing operations. Then there's Mexico. It's closer to home, and aside from distribution costs, the wage rates are similar to Asia's and many of the other risks would be minimized. You both feel strongly about this, I know, but this isn't a decision we can make based on enthusiasm." Ann crumpled up her sandwich wrapper and drank the last of her soda. "Let's get back over to the exhibits. I'm attending the IT seminar at 1:30. We'll schedule a formal meeting on this subject soon. I was going to say next month, but how about bumping it up two weeks?"

Walking back to the convention center with Dale and Sean, Ann realized that she wasn't just frustrated because she didn't know which course EDC should pursue. She was concerned that she really didn't know which aspects of the decision were important and which were irrelevant. Should she establish a division in China? If so, which functions should she start with? Manufacturing? Marketing? And what about engineering? Or should she consider a different location? Would China's low labor costs offset problems caused by a poor infrastructure?

Growth had always been vitally important to Eldora, both in creating value to shareholders and in providing a work environment that could attract and retain the most talented people. Now it appeared that Ann would have to choose between continued growth and a domestic-only manufacturing strategy that had served her well. Ann knew the plant location decision she had made years earlier had been critical to the company's success, and she felt the company's next move would be just as crucial.

QUESTIONS

1 What is the competitive environment facing EDC?
2 What are EDC's strengths in manufacturing?
3 Should EDC establish a manufacturing division in Asia?
4 What plan of action would you recommend to Ann Reardon?

SELECTED BIBLIOGRAPHY

Ballou, R. H. *Business Logistics Management.* 4th ed. Upper Saddle River, NJ: Prentice Hall, 1998.

Drezner, Z., and H. Hamacher. *Facility Location: Applications and Theory.* Berlin: Springer Verlag, 2002.

Khumawala, B. M., and D. C. Whybark. *The Use of Economic Logic in Facility Location.* West Lafayette, IN: Institute for Research in the Behavioral, Economic, and Management Sciences, Krannert School, Purdue University, 1975.

Klamroth, K. *Single Facility Location Problems with Barriers.* Berlin: Springer-Verlag Telos, 2002.

Pasto, D. J., and R. L. Francis. *Facility Layout and Location: Analytical Approach.* Upper Saddle River, NJ: Prentice Hall, 1998.

Sule, D. R. *Manufacturing Facilities: Location, Planning and Design.* Boston: PWS Publishing Company, 1994.

FOOTNOTES

1 M. E. Porter, "The Competitive Advantage of Nation," *Harvard Business Review,* March–April 1990.

2 S. E. Kimes and J. A. Fitzsimmons, "Selecting Profitable Hotel Sites at La Quinta Motor Inn," *Interfaces* 20 (March–April 1990), pp. 12–20.

3 This is a broad top-management–oriented strategy case designed to elicit debate.

chapter

LEAN PRODUCTION

12

THE LEAN SERVICE MACHINE

Jefferson Pilot Financial, a full-service life insurance and annuities company, exemplifies how manufacturing company lean concepts can be successfully applied to service companies.

The processing of insurance policy applications at Jefferson Pilot Financial (JPF) is remarkably similar to assembly-line manufacturing processes. Like the series of steps in an automobile assembly line, JPF insurance policies go through a series of steps from initial application input to application risk assessment (known as underwriting in the insurance industry) to policy application acceptance or policy application decline. The challenge was to

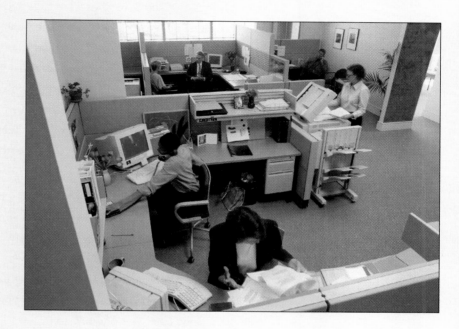

make this assembly line flow with high volume and high quality to meet customer demand. Among the lean concepts they adopted were placing linked processes near one another, standardizing procedures, eliminating loop-backs, setting a common tempo, balancing loads, and posting performance results.

PLACING LINKED PROCESSES NEAR ONE ANOTHER

Teams were physically relocated so that those involved in the successive steps of processing applications were placed in closer proximity to one another. This not only fostered continuous flow but also enhanced increased interaction between people in different work units.

STANDARDIZING PROCEDURES

Each worker had his or her own way of filing applications in progress. This resulted in bottlenecks and wasted time when fellow workers had to look high

Source: Summarized from Cynthia K. Swank, "The Lean Service Machine," *Harvard Business Review* 81, no. 10 (October 2003), pp. 123–29.

and low for particular applications when someone was out sick or on vacation. A uniform way of filing and storing applications (e.g., alphabetically and in the same drawer at each work station) was implemented.

ELIMINATING LOOP-BACKS

JPF had historically separated applications into pools of those that required physician statements and those that did not. Applications were further divided by the first letter of the applicant's last name such that last names beginning with the letters P, D, or S were assigned to employees X, Y and Z. Batches were large and could take a day—or more—to move from one processing unit to the next processing unit of JPF employees. Excess work-in-process "inventory" existed, as did excess idle time among workers. A mistake discovered down the line resulted in a "loop-back" to the individual worker where the mistake originated. Such loop-backs led to bottlenecks and further delays. All teams are now assigned equal-size batches of incoming applications regardless of which letter of the alphabet an applicant's last name begins with. A loop-back now goes to a team such that one worker on a team corrects a mistake while the other workers continue to process new applications, resulting in a continuous flow of work.

SETTING A COMMON TEMPO

Takt time

Work flow was smoothed out by pacing the work according to customer demand. This is called **takt time**, a German word for meter. For example, new business needed to process 10 applications per hour, or a takt time of one every six minutes. All workers in the process would have to meet this pace to assure meeting the work-flow demand, and studies were done to find the best ways of doing so.

BALANCING LOADS

Applications requiring physician statements were separated from applications not requiring physician statements and each of these two types of applications was assigned to a different group. Segregating "easy" applications from more complex applications resulted in dramatic increases in efficiency. For example, the turnaround time for processing policy applications that did not require a physician's statement was reduced by 84 percent.

POSTING PERFORMANCE RESULTS

Productivity results are now continuously updated on a new whiteboard conspicuously hung out for all to see. Workers now feel that their work is being more objectively evaluated, teamwork has increased, morale has gone up, productivity has increased, and costs have been driven down. Total labor costs, for example, were reduced by 26 percent.

The lean production outcomes at JPF resulted in an astounding 60 percent increase in new annualized life insurance premiums in just two years. And what did JPF customers think? JPF clients, who formerly had to wait one to two months, could now receive approved policies in less than three weeks! →

HISTORICAL NOTE

JIT gained worldwide prominence in the 1970s, but some of its philosophy can be traced to the early 1900s in the United States. Henry Ford used JIT concepts as he streamlined his moving assembly lines to make automobiles. For example, to eliminate waste, he used the bottom of the packing crates for car seats as the floor board of the car. Although elements of JIT were being used by Japanese industry as early as the 1930s, it was not fully refined until the 1970s, when Tai-ichi Ohno of Toyota Motors used JIT to take Toyota's cars to the forefront of delivery time and quality.

In the 1990s, many companies adopted the term *lean* in place of JIT to emphasize the goal of systematically eliminating waste throughout their operations. JIT has come to refer mainly to the production scheduling aspects, such as pull systems, that underlie the lean philosophy.

The most significant production management approach of the past 50 years is lean[1] or just in time (JIT) production. This chapter relates the logic of lean production; its evolution in Japan at Toyota; how it is implemented; and its current applications in manufacturing and at service companies such as Jefferson Pilot Financial described in the opening vignette. (See the box "Historical Note" for additional information.)

LEAN LOGIC

Lean production is an integrated set of activities designed to achieve high-volume production using minimal inventories of raw materials, work-in-process, and finished goods. Parts arrive at the next workstation "just in time" and are completed and move through the process quickly. Lean is also based on the logic that nothing will be produced until it is needed. Exhibit 12.1 illustrates the process. Production need is created by actual demand for the product. When an item is sold, in theory, the market pulls a replacement from the last position in the system—final assembly in this case. This triggers an order to the factory production line, where a worker then pulls another unit from an upstream station in the flow to replace the unit taken. This upstream station then pulls from the next station further upstream and so on back to the release of raw materials. To enable this pull process to work smoothly, lean production demands high levels of quality at each stage of the process, strong vendor relations, and a fairly predictable demand for the end product. See Exhibit 12.2 for other features of lean production.

Lean production

Lean Production Pull System

exhibit 12.1

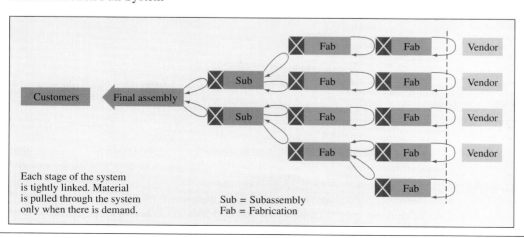

Customers   Final assembly

Sub   Fab   Fab   Vendor

Each stage of the system is tightly linked. Material is pulled through the system only when there is demand.

Sub = Subassembly
Fab = Fabrication

exhibit 12.2
Features of Lean Production

WHAT IT IS	WHAT IT DOES
■ Management philosophy ■ "Pull" system through the plant	■ Attacks waste (time, inventory, scrap) ■ Exposes problems and bottlenecks ■ Achieves streamlined production

WHAT IT REQUIRES	WHAT IT ASSUMES
■ Employee participation ■ Industrial engineering/basics ■ Continuing improvement ■ Total quality control ■ Small lot sizes	■ Stable environment

THE TOYOTA PRODUCTION SYSTEM

In this section we develop the philosophy and elements of lean production developed in Japan and embodied in the Toyota Production System—the benchmark for lean manufacturing. The Toyota Production System was developed to improve quality and productivity and is predicated upon two philosophies that are central to the Japanese culture: elimination of waste and respect for people.[2]

Global

Value stream mapping

ELIMINATION OF WASTE

Waste, as defined by Toyota's president, Fujio Cho, is "anything other than the minimum amount of equipment, materials, parts, and workers (working time) which are absolutely essential to production." (An expanded lean definition advanced by Fujio Cho identifies seven prominent types of waste to be eliminated from the value stream: (1) waste from overproduction, (2) waste of waiting time, (3) transportation waste, (4) inventory waste, (5) processing waste, (6) waste of motion, and (7) waste from product defects.[3]) See the box "Value Stream Mapping" for a general approach to eliminating waste.

This definition of lean leaves no room for surplus or safety stock. No safety stocks are allowed because if you cannot use it now, you do not need to make it now; that would be waste. Hidden inventory in storage areas, transit systems, carousels, and conveyors is a key target for inventory reduction. (Note that, in practice, safety stock will be required to deal with inherent process variability as discussed in the process analysis chapter.)

The seven elements that address elimination of waste are

1. Focused factory networks.
2. Group technology.
3. Quality at the source.
4. JIT production.
5. Uniform plant loading.
6. Kanban production control system.
7. Minimized setup times.

Focused Factory Networks The Japanese build small specialized plants rather than large vertically integrated manufacturing facilities. (Toyota has 12 plants located in and around Toyota City and other areas of Aichi Prefecture.) They find large operations and their bureaucracies difficult to manage and not in line with their management styles. Plants designed for one purpose can be constructed and operated more economically. The bulk of Japanese plants, some 60,000, have between 30 and 1,000 workers.

VALUE STREAM MAPPING

Value stream mapping is becoming widely used as a means of eliminating waste in a process. The value stream is a network of steps from beginning to end that provides the result for the customer. (An example of the value stream mapping approach is presented at the end of the chapter.)

Some activities add value to the result, some do not add value, and, sometimes, the process stops with no activity at all.

VALUE STREAM PRINCIPLES

1   Keep the value stream moving at maxium velocity.
2   Eliminate waste that stops, slows down, or diverts the value stream.

3   Concentrate on removing waste rather than speeding up value-adding operations.
4   Look for waste in the factory, office, physical, procedural, and technical operations.

SOURCE: SUPERFACTORY LEARNING CENTER, http://www.superfactory.com/.

Group Technology   Group technology (GT) is a philosophy in which similar parts are grouped into families, and the processes required to make the parts are arranged in a specialized work cell. Instead of transferring jobs from one department to another to specialized workers, GT considers all operations required to make a part and groups those machines together. Exhibit 12.3 illustrates the difference between the clusters of various machines grouped into work centers for parts versus departmental layouts. The group technology cells eliminate

Group technology

exhibit 12.3   Group Technology versus Departmental Specialty

movement and queue (waiting) time between operations, reduce inventory, and reduce the number of employees required. Workers, however, must be flexible to run several machines and processes. Due to their advanced skill level, these workers have increased job security. (Group technology cells are described in more depth in Technical Note 6.)

Quality at the source

Quality at the Source   Quality at the source means do it right the first time and, when something goes wrong, stop the process or assembly line immediately. Factory workers become their own inspectors, personally responsible for the quality of their output. Workers concentrate on one part of the job at a time so quality problems are uncovered. If the pace is too fast, if the worker finds a quality problem, or if a safety issue is discovered, the worker is obligated to push a button to stop the line and turn on a visual signal. People from other areas respond to the alarm and the problem. Workers are empowered to do their own maintenance and housekeeping until the problem is fixed.

JIT Production   JIT means producing what is needed when needed and no more. Anything over the minimum amount necessary is viewed as waste, because effort and material expended for something not needed now cannot be utilized now. This is in contrast to relying on extra material just in case something goes wrong.

JIT is typically applied to repetitive manufacturing, which is when the same or similar items are made one after another. JIT does not require large volumes and can be applied to any repetitive segments of a business regardless of where they appear. Under JIT the ideal lot size is one. Although workstations may be geographically dispersed, the Japanese minimize transit time and keep transfer quantities small—typically one-tenth of a day's production. Vendors even ship several times a day to their customers to keep lot sizes small and inventory low. The goal is to drive all inventory queues to zero, thus minimizing inventory investment and shortening lead times.

When inventory levels are low, quality problems become very visible. Exhibit 12.4 illustrates this idea. If the water in a pond represents inventory, the rocks represent problems that could occur in a firm. A high level of water hides the problems (rocks). Management assumes everything is fine, but as the water level drops in an economic downturn, problems are presented. If you deliberately force the water level down (particularly in good economic times), you can expose and correct problems before they cause worse problems. JIT manufacturing exposes problems otherwise hidden by excess inventories and staff.

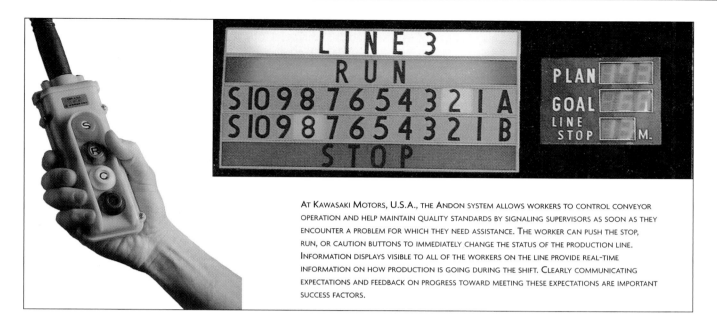

AT KAWASAKI MOTORS, U.S.A., THE ANDON SYSTEM ALLOWS WORKERS TO CONTROL CONVEYOR OPERATION AND HELP MAINTAIN QUALITY STANDARDS BY SIGNALING SUPERVISORS AS SOON AS THEY ENCOUNTER A PROBLEM FOR WHICH THEY NEED ASSISTANCE. THE WORKER CAN PUSH THE STOP, RUN, OR CAUTION BUTTONS TO IMMEDIATELY CHANGE THE STATUS OF THE PRODUCTION LINE. INFORMATION DISPLAYS VISIBLE TO ALL OF THE WORKERS ON THE LINE PROVIDE REAL-TIME INFORMATION ON HOW PRODUCTION IS GOING DURING THE SHIFT. CLEARLY COMMUNICATING EXPECTATIONS AND FEEDBACK ON PROGRESS TOWARD MEETING THESE EXPECTATIONS ARE IMPORTANT SUCCESS FACTORS.

Inventory Hides Problems

exhibit 12.4

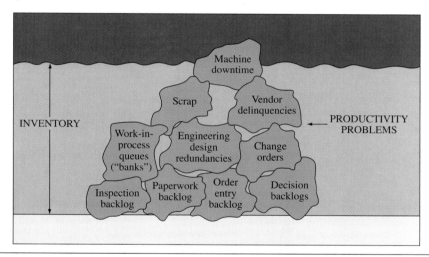

Uniform Plant Loading   Smoothing the production flow to dampen the reaction waves that normally occur in response to schedule variations is called **uniform plant loading** (or, in Japanese, **heijunka**). When a change is made in a final assembly, the changes are magnified throughout the line and the supply chain. The only way to eliminate the problem is to make adjustments as small as possible by setting a firm monthly production plan for which the output rate is frozen. (This is how a company addresses the need for a stable demand environment noted in Exhibit 12.2.)

Toyota found they could do this by building the same mix of products every day in small quantities. Thus, they always have a total mix available to respond to variations in demand. A Toyota example is shown in Exhibit 12.5. Monthly car style quantities are reduced to daily quantities (assuming a 20-day month) in order to compute a model *cycle time* (defined here as the time between two identical units being completed on the line). The cycle time figure is used to adjust resources to produce the precise quantity needed. The speed of equipment or

Uniform plant loading (heijunka)

exhibit 12.5

Toyota Example of Mixed-Model Production Cycle in a Japanese Assembly Plant

MODEL	MONTHLY QUANTITY	DAILY QUANTITY	MODEL CYCLE TIME (MINUTES)
Sedan	5,000	250	2
Hardtop	2,500	125	4
Wagon	2,500	125	4

Sequence: Sedan, hardtop, sedan, wagon, sedan, hardtop, sedan, wagon, and so on (one minute apart).

exhibit 12.6

Flow of Two Kanbans

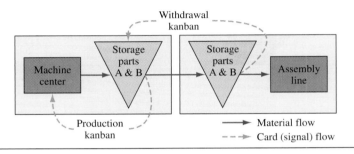

of the production line is adjusted so only the needed quantity is produced each day. JIT strives to produce on schedule, on cost, and on quality. (Additional discussion of mixed-model assembly is provided in Technical Note 6.)

Kanban

Kanban pull system

Interactive Operations Management

Kanban Production Control Systems   A kanban control system uses a signaling device to regulate JIT flows. **Kanban** means "sign" or "instruction card" in Japanese. In a paperless control system, containers can be used instead of cards. The cards or containers make up the **kanban pull system.** The authority to produce or supply additional parts comes from downstream operations. Consider Exhibit 12.6, where we show an assembly line that is supplied with parts by a machine center. The machine center makes two parts, A and B. These two parts are stored in containers that are located next to the assembly line and next to the machine center. Each container next to the assembly line has a withdrawal kanban, and each container next to the machine center has a production kanban. This is often referred to as a two-card kanban system.

When the assembly line takes the first part A from a full container, a worker takes the withdrawal kanban from the container, and takes the card to the machine center storage area. In the machine center area, the worker finds a container of part A, removes the production kanban, and replaces it with the withdrawal kanban. Placement of this card on the container authorizes the movement of the container to the assembly line. The freed production kanban is placed on a rack by the machine center, which authorizes the production of another lot of material. A similar process is followed for part B. The cards on the rack become the dispatch list for the machine center. Cards are not the only way to signal the need for production of a part; other visual methods are possible, as shown in Exhibit 12.7.

The following are some other possible approaches:

Kanban squares.   Some companies use marked spaces on the floor or on a table to identify where material should be stored. When the square is empty, like the one shown in the photo on page 477, the supplying operations are authorized to produce; when the square is full, no parts are needed.

Diagram of Outbound Stockpoint with Warning Signal Marker

exhibit 12.7

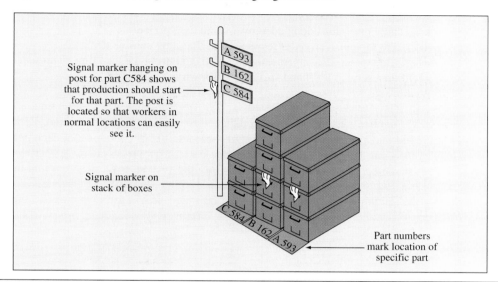

Signal marker hanging on post for part C584 shows that production should start for that part. The post is located so that workers in normal locations can easily see it.

Signal marker on stack of boxes

A 593
B 162
C 584

C 584 / B 162 / A 593

Part numbers mark location of specific part

Container system.   Sometimes the container itself can be used as a signal device. In this case, an empty container on the factory floor visually signals the need to fill it. The amount of inventory is adjusted by simply adding or removing containers.

Colored golf balls.   At a Kawasaki engine plant, when a part used in a sub-assembly is down to its queue limit, the assembler rolls a colored golf ball down a pipe to the replenishment machine center. This tells the operator which part to make next. Many variations have been developed on this approach.

The kanban pull approach can be used not only within a manufacturing facility but also between manufacturing facilities (pulling engines and transmissions into an automobile assembly operation, for example) and between manufacturers and external suppliers.

Determining the Number of Kanbans Needed   Setting up a kanban control system requires determination of the number of kanban cards (or containers) needed. In a two-card system, we are finding the number of sets of withdrawal and production cards. The kanban cards represent the number of containers of material that flow back and forth between the supplier and the user areas. Each container represents the minimum production lot size to be supplied. The number of containers, therefore, directly controls the amount of work-in-process inventory in the system.

Accurately estimating the lead time needed to produce a container of parts is the key to determining the number of containers. This lead time is a function of the processing time for the container, any waiting time during the production process, and the time required to transport the material to the user. Enough kanbans are needed to cover the expected demand during this lead time plus some additional amount for safety stock. The number of kanban card sets is

$$k = \frac{\text{Expected demand during lead time} + \text{Safety stock}}{\text{Size of the container}}$$

[12.1]

$$= \frac{DL(1 + S)}{C}$$

where

k = Number of kanban card sets

D = Average number of units demanded over some time period

L = Lead time to replenish an order (expressed in the same units as demand)

S = Safety stock expressed as a percentage of demand during the lead time (This can be based on a service level and variance as shown in Chapter 15.)

C = Container size

Observe that a kanban system does not produce zero inventory; rather, it controls the amount of material that can be in process at a time—the number of containers of each item. The kanban system can be easily adjusted to fit the current way the system is operating, because card sets can be easily added or removed from the system. If the workers find that they are not able to consistently replenish the item on time, an additional container of material, with the accompanying kanban cards, can be added. If it is found that excess containers of material accumulate, card sets can be easily removed, thus reducing the amount of inventory.

EXAMPLE 12.1: Determining the Number of Kanban Card Sets

Arvin Automotive, a company that makes muffler assemblies for the Big Three, is committed to the use of kanban to pull material through its manufacturing cells. Arvin has designed each cell to fabricate a specific family of muffler products. Fabricating a muffler assembly involves cutting and bending pieces of pipe that are welded to a muffler and a catalytic converter. The mufflers and catalytic converters are pulled into the cell based on current demand. The catalytic converters are made in a specialized cell.

Catalytic converters are made in batches of 10 units and are moved in special hand carts to the fabrication cells. The catalytic converter cell is designed so that different types of catalytic converters can be made with virtually no setup loss. The cell can respond to an order for a batch of catalytic converters in approximately four hours. Because the catalytic converter cell is right next to the muffler assembly fabrication cell, transportation time is virtually zero.

The muffler assembly fabrication cell averages approximately eight assemblies per hour. Each assembly uses the same catalytic converter. Due to some variability in the process, management has decided to have safety stock equivalent to 10 percent of the needed inventory.

How many kanban sets are needed to manage the replenishment of the catalytic converters?

SOLUTION

In this case, the lead time for replenishment of the converters (L) is four hours. The demand (D) for the catalytic converters is eight per hour. Safety stock (S) is 10 percent of the expected demand, and the container size (C) is 10 units.

$$k = \frac{8 \times 4(1 + .1)}{10} = \frac{35.2}{10} = 3.52$$

In this case, we would need four kanban card sets, and we would have four containers of converters in the system. In all cases, when we calculate k, we will round the number up because we always need to work with full containers of parts. ●

Minimized Setup Times   Because small lot sizes are the norm, machines must be quickly set up to produce the mixed models on the line. In a widely cited example from the late 1970s, Toyota teams of press operators producing car hoods and fenders were able to change an 800-ton press in 10 minutes, compared with the average of six hours for U.S.

workers and four hours for German workers. (Now, however, such speed is common in most U.S. auto plants.) To achieve such setup time reduction, setups are divided into internal and external activities. Internal setups must be done while a machine is stopped. External setups can be done while the machine is running. Other time-saving devices such as duplicate tool holders also are used to speed setups.

RESPECT FOR PEOPLE

Respect for people is a key to the Toyota Production System. They have traditionally strived to assure lifetime employment for permanent positions and to maintain level payrolls even when business conditions deteriorate. Permanent workers (about one-third of the total workforce of Japan) have job security and tend to be more flexible, remain with a company, and do all they can to help a firm achieve its goals. (The recent recession in Japan has caused many Japanese companies to move away from this ideal.)

Company unions at Toyota as well as elsewhere in Japan exist to foster a cooperative relationship with management. All employees receive two bonuses a year in good times. Employees know that if the company performs well, they will get a bonus. This encourages workers to improve productivity. Management views workers as assets, not as human machines. Automation and robotics are used extensively to perform dull or routine jobs so employees are free to focus on important improvement tasks.

Global

Toyota relies heavily on subcontractor networks. Indeed, more than 90 percent of all Japanese companies are part of the supplier network of small firms. Some suppliers are specialists in a narrow field, usually serving multiple customers. Firms have long-term partnerships with their suppliers and customers. Suppliers consider themselves part of a customer's family.

The Four Rules   The Toyota Production System does a better job than any of its competitors in controlling variability and creating learning opportunities from its processes. Underlying its approach are the four unwritten rules identified by Spear and Bowen, presented in the Breakthrough box on the next page.

A recent study by Christer Karlsson of the Stockholm School of Economics points out that the lean ideas found here are not universally used in all manufacturing companies in Japan. Rather, they are applied situationally and where appropriate. However, the fundamental ideas of elimination of waste and respect for workers are still foundations of the exceptional productivity of most Japanese manufacturing companies.[4]

LEAN IMPLEMENTATION REQUIREMENTS

This section is structured around the model shown in Exhibit 12.8. It discusses ways to accomplish lean production. These suggestions are geared to repetitive production systems—those that make the same products again and again. Also, bear in mind that these elements are linked: Any changes in part of the production system impact other features of the system.

LEAN LAYOUTS AND DESIGN FLOWS

Lean requires the plant layout to be designed to ensure balanced work flow with a minimum of work-in-process inventory. Each workstation is part of a production line, whether or not a physical line actually exists. Capacity is balanced using the same logic for an assembly line, and operations are linked through a pull system. In addition, the system designer must visualize how all aspects of the internal and external logistics system tie to the layout.

BREAKTHROUGH

THE FOUR RULES

The tacit knowledge that underlies the Toyota Production System can be captured in four basic rules. These rules guide the design, operation, and improvement of every activity, connection, and pathway for every product and service. The rules are as follows:

Rule 1. All work shall be highly specified as to content, sequence, timing, and outcome.

Rule 2. Every customer–supplier connection must be direct, and there must be an unambiguous yes-or-no way to send requests and receive responses.

Rule 3. The pathway for every product and service must be simple and direct.

Rule 4. Any improvement must be made in accordance with the scientific method, under the guidance of a teacher, at the lowest possible level in the organization.

All the rules require that activities, connections, and flow paths have built-in tests to signal problems automatically. It is the continual response to problems that makes this seemingly rigid system so flexible and adaptable to changing circumstances.

---

exhibit 12.8   How to Accomplish Lean Production

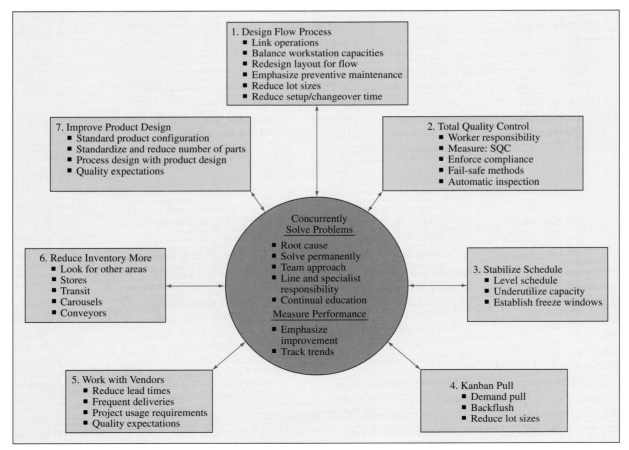

THIS DIAGRAM IS MODELED AFTER THE ONE USED BY HEWLETT-PACKARD'S BOISE PLANT TO ACCOMPLISH ITS LEAN PRODUCTION PROGRAM.

Preventive maintenance is emphasized to ensure that flows are not interrupted by downtime or malfunctioning equipment. Preventive maintenance involves periodic inspection and repair designed to keep a machine reliable. Operators perform much of the maintenance because they are most familiar with their machines and because machines are easier to repair, as lean operations favor several simple machines rather than one large complex one.

Preventive maintenance

The reductions in setup and changeover times previously discussed are necessary to achieve a smooth flow. Exhibit 12.9 shows the relationship between lot size and setup costs. Under a traditional approach, setup cost is treated as a constant, and the optimal order quantity is shown as six. Under the kanban approach, setup cost is treated as a variable and the optimal order quantity is reduced. In the exhibit, the order quantity has been reduced from six to two under lean methods by employing setup-time–saving procedures. This organization will ultimately strive for a lot size of one.

LEAN APPLICATIONS FOR LINE FLOWS

Exhibit 12.10 illustrates a pull system in a simple line flow. In a pure lean environment, no employee does any work until the product has been pulled from the end of the line by the market. The product could be a final product or a component used in later production. When a product is pulled, a replenishment unit is pulled from upstream operations. In the exhibit, an item of finished goods is pulled from F, the finished goods inventory. The inventory clerk then goes to processing station E and takes replacement product to fill the void. This pattern continues up the line to worker A, who pulls material from the raw material inventory. The rules of the flow layout require employees to keep completed units at their workstation, and if someone takes the completed work away, the employee must move upstream in the flow to get additional work to complete.

Relationship between Lot Size and Setup Cost

exhibit 12.9

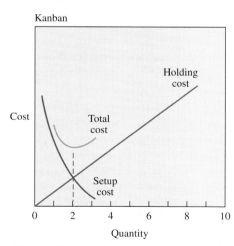

Definitions: *Holding cost* includes the costs of storing inventory and the cost of money tied up in inventory. *Setup cost* includes the wage costs attributable to workers making the setup, and various administrative and supplies costs. (These are defined in total in Chapter 15, "Inventory Control.")

Lean in a Line Flow Layout

exhibit 12.10

PLANT TOUR: ARVIN MERITOR, INC

Arvin was founded in 1919 and has been a supplier of complete exhaust systems for the original equipment market since 1929. Arvin has had great success achieving excellence with its Arvin Total Quality Production System (ATQPS). The JIT production system is just a part of its team approach; Arvin NAA is involved early in the vehicle design with its customers.

Teams meet frequently to assess progress, solve problems, and make decisions. At Arvin, employees work in teams, learn in teams, and succeed in teams. Suggestions and ideas from teams and individuals are the fuel of continuous improvement.

TEAM PRODUCTION

Each manufacturing cell is laid out to assure visual communications among operators, a smooth flow of materials, timely delivery of components, and responsive shipment of finished products.

LEAN APPLICATIONS FOR JOB SHOPS

Although job shops are characterized by low volume and high variety, lean can be used if demand can be stabilized to permit repetitive manufacture. Stabilizing demand is usually easier to accomplish when the demand is from a downstream production stage rather than an end customer. (The logic is that internal customers can smooth their input requirements far more easily than a distributor or individual purchaser.)

Factory machining centers, paint shops, and shirt making are examples of job-shop–type operations that process parts and components before they reach final production stages. By way of example, consider the production system in Exhibit 12.11. If a work center produces nine different parts used by several product varieties that are produced just in time, the work center keeps containers of completed output of all nine parts at the center to be picked up by users. Operators could make periodic rounds throughout the facility (hourly or more frequently) to pick up empty containers and drop them off at the corresponding upstream work center and to pick up full containers. In Exhibit 12.11, automatic guided vehicles pick up and deliver part numbers M_5 and M_8 to lines 2 and 3 for processing. These handling procedures can be manual or automated, but either way, these periodic pickups and drop-offs allow the system to operate in a just-in-time mode.

TQC (TOTAL QUALITY CONTROL)

Total quality control (TQC)   Lean and TQC have merged in theory and practice. **Total quality control (TQC)** is the practice of building quality into the process and not identifying quality by inspection. It also refers to the theory of employees assuming responsibility for the quality of their own work. When

Team-devised color coding facilitates quick changeover, improving flexibility and quality and promoting production of small lots to meet customer needs precisely. Visual controls remove ambiguity and assure quality at the source.

. . . and to external customers, too.

Arvin Meritor's disciplined "pull system" uses production leveling and kanban signals to produce small, efficient lots delivered just in time to internal customers . . .

A Lean Job Shop Layout Showing the Materials-Handling Vehicle Route Connecting Machine Centers and Line Operations

exhibit 12.11

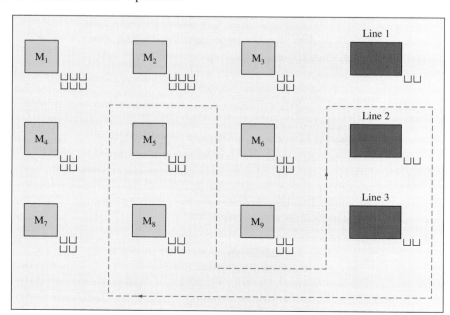

employees are responsible for quality, lean works at its best because only good-quality products are pulled through the system. When all products are good, no "just-in-case" extra inventory is needed. Thus organizations can achieve high quality and high productivity. By using statistical quality control methods and training workers to maintain quality, inspections can be reduced to the first and last units produced. If they are perfect, we can assume the other units between these points are perfect as well.

A foundation of quality is improved product design. Standard product configurations, fewer parts, and standardized parts are important elements in lean production. These design modifications reduce variability in the end item or in the materials that go into the product. Besides improving the producibility of a product, product design activities can facilitate the processing of engineering changes. (Total quality management and statistical quality control are described in Chapter 8 and Technical Note 8.)

A STABLE SCHEDULE

Level schedule

As noted earlier, lean production requires a stable schedule over a lengthy time horizon. This is accomplished by level scheduling, freeze windows, and underutilization of capacity. A **level schedule** is one that requires material to be pulled into final assembly in a pattern uniform enough to allow the various elements of production to respond to pull signals. It does not necessarily mean that the usage of every part on an assembly line is identified hour by hour for days on end; it does mean that a given production system equipped with flexible setups and a fixed amount of material in the pipelines can respond.[5]

Freeze window

Backflush

The term **freeze window** refers to that period of time during which the schedule is fixed and no further changes are possible. An added benefit of the stable schedule is seen in how parts and components are accounted for in a pull system. Here, the concept of **backflush** measurement is used to periodically explode an end item's bill of materials (the parts that go into each product) to calculate how many of each part went into the final product(s). This eliminates much of the shop-floor data collection activity, which is required if each part must be tracked and accounted for during production.

Underutilization and overutilization of capacity are controversial features of lean production. Conventional approaches use safety stocks and early deliveries as a hedge against production problems like poor quality, machine failures, and unanticipated bottlenecks in traditional manufacturing. Under lean production, excess labor, machines, and overtime provide the hedge. The excess capacity in labor and equipment that results is much cheaper than carrying excess inventory. When demand is greater than expected, overtime must be used. Often part-time labor is used when additional capacity is needed. During idle periods, personnel can be put to work on other activities such as special projects, work group activities, and workstation housekeeping.

WORK WITH SUPPLIERS

Service

Just as customers and employees are key components of lean systems, suppliers are also important to the process. If a firm shares its projected usage requirements with its vendors, they have a long-run picture of the demands that will be placed on their production and distribution systems. Some vendors are linked online with a customer to share production scheduling and input needs data. This permits them to develop level production systems. Confidence in the supplier or vendor's delivery commitment allows reductions of buffer inventories. Maintaining stock at a lean level requires frequent deliveries during the day. Some suppliers even deliver to a location on the production line and not at a receiving dock. When vendors adopt quality practices, incoming receiving inspections of their products can be bypassed.

Building a Lean Supply Chain   As we discussed in Chapter 11, a supply chain is the sum total of organizations involved—from raw materials firms through tiers of suppliers to original equipment manufacturers, onward to the ultimate distribution and delivery of the finished product to the customer. Womack and Jones, in their seminal work *Lean Thinking,* provide the following guidelines for implementing a lean supply chain:[6]

- Value must be defined jointly for each product family along with a target cost based on the customer's perception of value.
- All firms along the value stream must make an adequate return on their investments related to the value stream.
- The firms must work together to identify and eliminate *muda (waste)* to the point where the overall target cost and return-on-investment targets of each firm are met.
- When cost targets are met, the firms along the stream will immediately conduct new analyses to identify remaining *muda* and set new targets.
- Every participating firm has the right to examine every activity in every firm relevant to the value stream as part of the joint search for waste.

To summarize: To be lean, everyone's got to be on the same page!

LEAN SERVICES

Many lean techniques have been successfully applied by service firms. Just as in manufacturing, the suitability of each technique and the corresponding work steps depend on the characteristics of the firm's markets, production and equipment technology, skill sets, and corporate culture. Service firms are not different in this respect. Here are 10 of the more successful applications.

Service

Organize Problem-Solving Groups Honeywell is extending its quality circles from manufacturing into its service operations. Other corporations as diverse as First Bank/Dallas, Standard Meat Company, and Miller Brewing Company are using similar approaches to improve service. British Airways used quality circles as a fundamental part of its strategy to implement new service practices.

Upgrade Housekeeping Good housekeeping means more than winning the clean broom award. It means that only the necessary items are kept in a work area, that there is a place for everything, and that everything is clean and in a constant state of readiness. The employees clean their own areas.

Service organizations such as McDonald's, Disneyland, and Speedi-Lube have recognized the critical nature of housekeeping. Their dedication to housekeeping has meant that service processes work better, the attitude of continuous improvement is easier to develop, and customers perceive that they are receiving better service.

Upgrade Quality The only cost-effective way to improve quality is to develop reliable process capabilities. Process quality is quality at the source—it guarantees first-time production of consistent and uniform products and services.

McDonald's is famous for building quality into its service delivery process. It literally "industrialized" the service delivery system so that part-time, casual workers could provide the same eating experience anywhere in the world. Quality doesn't mean producing the best; it means consistently producing products and services that give the customers their money's worth.

Clarify Process Flows Clarification of flows, based on JIT themes, can dramatically improve the process performance. Here are examples.

First, Federal Express Corporation changed air flight patterns from origin-to-destination to origin-to-hub, where the freight is transferred to an outbound plane heading for the destination. This revolutionized the air transport industry. Second, the order-entry department of a manufacturing firm converted from functional subdepartments to customer-centered work groups and reduced the order processing lead time from eight to two days. Third, a county government used the JIT approach to cut the time to record a deed transfer by 50 percent.

GATEGOURMET IS ONE OF THE TOP AIRLINE FOOD CATERERS. THE COMPANY SERVES OVER 208 MILLION PASSENGERS THROUGH 140 FLIGHT KITCHENS, LOCATED IN 31 COUNTRIES. THE COMPANY USES SPECIAL EQUIPMENT TO MAKE THE PROCESS OF LOADING FOOD ONTO AIRPLANES QUICK.

Finally, Supermaids sends in a team of house cleaners, each with a specific responsibility, to clean each house quickly with parallel processes. Changes in process flows can literally revolutionize service industries.

Revise Equipment and Process Technologies   Revising technologies involves evaluation of the equipment and processes for their ability to meet the process requirements, to process consistently within tolerance, and to fit the scale and capacity of the work group.

Speedi-Lube converted the standard service station concept to a specialized lubrication and inspection center by changing the service bays from drive-in to drive-through and by eliminating the hoists and instead building pits under the cars where employees have full access to the lubrication areas on the vehicle.

A hospital reduced operating room setup time so that it had the flexibility to perform a wider range of operations without reducing the operating room availability.

Level the Facility Load   Service firms synchronize production with demand. They have developed unique approaches to leveling demand so they can avoid making customers wait for service. McDonald's offers a special breakfast menu in the morning. Retail stores use take-a-number systems. The post office charges more for next-day delivery. These are all examples of the service approach for creating uniform facility loads.

Eliminate Unnecessary Activities   A step that does not add value is a candidate for elimination. A step that does add value may be a candidate for reengineering to improve the process consistency or to reduce the time to perform the tasks.

A hospital discovered that significant time was spent during an operation waiting for an instrument that was not available when the operation began. It developed a checklist of instruments required for each category of operation. Speedi-Lube eliminated steps, but it also added steps that did not improve the lubrication process but did make customers feel more assured about the work being performed.

Reorganize Physical Configuration   Work area configurations frequently require reorganization during a lean implementation. Often manufacturers accomplish this by setting up manufacturing cells to produce items in small lots, synchronous to demand. These cells amount to microfactories inside the plant.

Most service firms are far behind manufacturers in this area. However, a few interesting examples do come out of the service sector. Some hospitals—instead of routing patients all over the building for tests, exams, X-rays, and injections—are reorganizing their services into work groups based on the type of problem. Teams that treat only trauma are common, but other work groups have been formed to treat less immediate conditions like hernias. These amount to microclinics within the hospital facility.

Introduce Demand-Pull Scheduling   Due to the nature of service production and consumption, demand-pull (customer-driven) scheduling is necessary for operating a service business. Moreover, many service firms are separating their operations into "back room" and "customer contact" facilities. This approach creates new problems in coordinating schedules between the facilities. The original Wendy's restaurants were set up so cooks could see cars enter the parking lot. They put a preestablished number of hamburger patties onto the grill for each car. This pull system was designed to have a fresh patty on the grill before the customer even placed an order.

Develop Supplier Networks   The term *supplier networks* in the lean context refers to the cooperative association of suppliers and customers working over the long term for mutual benefit. Service firms have not emphasized supplier networks for materials because the service costs are often predominantly labor. Notable exceptions must include service organizations like McDonald's, one of the biggest food products purchasers in the world, which has been developing lean practices. Manpower and other employment agencies have established lean-type relationships with a temporary employment service and a trade school to develop a reliable source of trained assemblers.

CONCLUSION

As we have seen lean production has proven its value to thousands of companies throughout the world. The Toyota version, however, has been modified successfully by other auto producers such as Nissan and Honda, and now is being challenged by BMW. (See the box titled "BMW Moves beyond Just-in-Time Production.") Lean production is an encompassing philosophy considering product design, process design, equipment and facilities design, supply chain coordination, job design, and productivity improvement. If there is one "key" to successful implementation of lean or its variants, it's adopting a holistic approach, which according to a study by UK's McKinsey Production Centre, "transforms not just the technical production system, but also the company's management system using a comprehensive change management process."[7]

KEY TERMS

Takt time A German word for musical meter. It refers to pacing work according to customer demand.

Lean production Integrated activities designed to achieve high-volume, high-quality production using minimal inventories of raw materials, work-in-process, and finished goods.

Value stream mapping A graphical way to analyze where value is or isn't being added as material flows though a process.

Group technology A philosophy in which similar parts are grouped into families, and the processes required to make the parts are arranged in a specialized work cell.

Quality at the source Philosophy of making factory workers personally responsible for the quality of their output. Workers are expected to make the part correctly the first time and to stop the process immediately if there is a problem.

Uniform plant loading (heijunka) Smoothing the production flow to dampen schedule variation.

Kanban and the kanban pull system An inventory or production control system that uses a signaling device to regulate flows.

Preventive maintenance Periodic inspection and repair designed to keep equipment reliable.

Total quality control (TQC) The practice of building quality into the process and not identifying quality by inspection.

Level schedule A schedule that pulls material into final assembly at a constant rate.

Freeze window The period of time during which the schedule is fixed and no further changes are possible.

Backflush Calculating how many of each part were used in production and using these calculations to adjust actual on-hand inventory balances. This eliminates the need to actually track each part used in production.

BMW MOVES BEYOND JUST-IN-TIME PRODUCTION

The department managers, engineers, and computer software developers at BMW AG's U.S. factory are about to drop-kick the auto plant into a new era. Call it the "post-just-in-time" era. "Don't forget the suppliers," says Helmut Leube, president of BMW Manufacturing Corp. in Spartanburg County, South Carolina. "Please don't underestimate the role of our suppliers in this effort." As Leube explains it, "this effort" is a shift from the lean, just-in-time production that automakers have championed since the 1980s to delivery-on-demand.

The South Carolina plant and other BMW plants worldwide are attempting to make ordering a vehicle from a BMW factory and getting that vehicle on the day it is promised as easy as possible. Easy probably is the wrong word. To build this flexibility into its factory system, BMW is making major changes, including a $300 million capital expense program that just completed an overhaul of its nearly eight-year-old body shop. The manufacturing changes are as diverse as procedures in the Spartanburg plant and ordering tools for dealerships.

The following changes are under way.

Vehicles are being gradually redesigned to reduce variations in sheet metal. The changes will reduce dramatically the number of body structure differences. The upcoming 3-series, for example, will decline from 16 body variations to two. the redesigned Z3 that goes into production in South Carolina late this year will have eight body variations instead of 12.

HOLD THAT VIN

BMW is changing its standard global factory procedure of assigning vehicles to customers. Until now, when a BMW factory received an order for a car, it stamped a VIN number onto a freshly welded body. That vehicle remained assigned to the same customer as it moved through body assembly, paint, and final assembly. Now, once the overhaul is complete, BMW assigns the VIN later. Bodies will be constructed and painted before the production control department claims it for a customer order. That delay will give customers more time to change their minds. It also will give the manufacturer more scheduling freedom. The company is adopting a computer ordering system at dealerships in Europe. Shoppers there will work with retailers to configure the vehicle wanted and receive the date of delivery. The delivery date will return on the screen five seconds after making the order. When the order is submitted, it will go to BMW's central office in Munich, Germany, where orders will be calculated nightly and distributed to factories worldwide.

STILL LEAN?

To use a system that BMW considers more efficient, the plant is taking some steps that appear to be less efficient. The Spartanburg plant will double the size of its vehicle stacking center—a giant mechanism that can temporarily shelve half of a shift's worth of cars at once. Its role is to solve scheduling glitches caused by vehicles out of sync with the production schedule. Some changes also will be made to allow more parts to stand along the assembly line. This should reduce scheduling glitches caused by a series of cars passing down the line out of order while the worker is loaded with parts for different cars.

DON'T FORGET THE SUPPLIERS

BMW must make this system work throughout its supply chain. That means it must design a computer system that tracks customer orders from dealerships around the world to parts makers in South Carolina and Germany. BMW is working the bugs out of a system that will go online in the fall in preparation for sales of the redesigned Z3 in November.

If all goes as planned, BMW will be able to request a production change from suppliers only a few hours before the parts are needed on the BMW line. Suppliers are accustomed to locking their production plans weeks ahead of delivery. The challenge begins with production forecasting. Normally, the manufacturer would be able to forecast its production needs and notify suppliers six months in advance with only about 60 percent accuracy, Leube explains. Six weeks ahead of production, the forecast is still only about 80 percent accurate. The forecast becomes 100 percent accurate four days ahead of production.

BMW wants to be so accurate it can do two things: first, lock into 100 percent accurate production plans much earlier; second, take advantage of that accuracy to liberate suppliers to make more last-minute changes. In other words, the supplier will have the confidence in the forecasts to build most of its parts ahead of schedule. And by doing so, it will have the flexibility to make late schedule changes to accommodate customer requests without throwing off the overall schedule.

The new global ordering system will allow this to happen, with sales orders processed nightly and communicated to the factory planning departments, Leube says.

CROSS-FUNCTIONING

The changes also required a new method of managing the Spartanburg plant, says Doug Bartow, vice president of paint for the subsidiary. It wasn't just a matter of getting new software to track the more complex schedule, Bartow says. "It was a matter of creating a new way of managing it," he says. "Ontime delivery is a very cross-functional effort. You have to have people who can move between the departments to solve problems."

Spartanburg created a job title of indicator champion. This person might identify a delay in final assembly, for example, and track its cause to a problem in the paint shop. The champion has the authority to sort issues in various departments to solve schedule problems.

BRAND IDENTITY CRITICAL

Why go through so much factory change just to allow showroom customers a few more days to change their minds?

In BMW's strategy, it is a brand identity issue. Ninety-eight percent of all of the cars BMW's German factories build are customer orders. In North America, the number is 60 percent. Though it is unusual by U.S. standards, BMW wants to increase that share. BMW believes shoppers who are confident about getting exactly what they want when they expect it are more likely to buy this way. That requires a more controlled factory and scheduling system, Leube says. "We're not talking about the 20-day car," he says. "Some customers will need their car much sooner than 20 days, and we will be able to handle that. But other customers won't need it nearly so fast."

Leube says there will be gains at the manufacturing level. A precise schedule will lead to a more stable and profitable supplier base, he reasons. Reducing product complexity also will allow a plant to increase production on new products. With fewer variations, the plant can move toward full-line speed faster, Leube says.

"It's certainly challenging," he says. "But BMW is a company that wants to be able to respond at the latest possible moment. And this is how we will get there."

BMW'S NEW ORDERING SYSTEM WILL ENABLE IT TO REQUEST A PRODUCTION CHANGE FROM SUPPLIERS ONLY A FEW HOURS BEFORE THE PARTS ARE NEEDED ON THE LINE AT THE AUTOMAKER'S PLANT IN SOUTH CAROLINA.

FORMULA REVIEW

Determining the number of kanbans

[12.1]

$$k = \frac{DL(1 + S)}{C}$$

SOLVED PROBLEM

A local hospital wants to set up a kanban system to manage its supply of blood with the regional blood bank. The regional blood bank delivers blood to the hospital each day with a one-day order lead time (an order placed by 6 P.M. today will be delivered tomorrow afternoon). Internally, the hospital purchasing group places orders for blood each day at 5 P.M. Blood is measured by the pint and is shipped in containers that contain six pints. For a particular blood type, the hospital uses an average of 12 pints per day. Due to the critical nature of a blood shortage, the hospital wants to carry a safety stock of two days' expected supply. How many kanban card sets should the hospital prepare?

Solution

This problem is typical of how a real application might look. Using the data given, the variables for this problem are as follows:

$D = 12$ pints per day (average demand)
$L = 1$ day (lead time)
$S = 200$ percent (safety stock, as a fraction this is 2.0)
$C = 6$ pints (container size)

$$k = \frac{DL(1 + S)}{C} = \frac{12(1 + 2)}{6} = 6$$

This indicates that we need to prepare six kanban card sets. Each time a new container of blood (containing six pints) is opened, the card will be sent to purchasing and another six pints of blood will be ordered. When the blood is received, the card will be attached to the new container and moved to the blood storage area.

REVIEW AND DISCUSSION QUESTIONS

1 What lean principles are being used by Arvin Meritor (see the box on pages 482 and 483)? Use the categories in Exhibit 12.8 to develop your answer.
2 Is it possible to achieve zero inventories? Why or why not?
3 Stopping waste is a vital part of lean. Using value stream mapping, identify some sources of waste in your home or dorm and discuss how they may be eliminated.
4 Discuss lean in a job shop layout and in a line layout.
5 Why must lean have a stable schedule?
6 Will lean work in service environments? Why or why not?
7 Discuss ways to use lean to improve one of the following: a pizza restaurant, a hospital, or an auto dealership.
8 What objections might a marketing manager have to uniform plant loading?
9 What are the implications for cost accounting of lean production?
10 What are the roles of suppliers and customers in a lean system?
11 Explain how cards are used in a kanban system.
12 In which ways, if any, are the following systems analogous to kanban: returning empty bottles to the supermarket and picking up filled ones; running a hot dog stand at lunchtime; withdrawing money from a checking account; raking leaves into bags?
13 Why is lean hard to implement in practice?
14 Explain the relationship between quality and productivity under the lean philosophy.
15 Why would a JIT advocate have a problem with the system proposed for the BMW AG's U.S. factory (discussed in the box "BMW Moves beyond Just-in-Time Production")?

PROBLEMS

1. A supplier of instrument gauge clusters uses a kanban system to control material flow. The gauge cluster housings are transported five at a time. A fabrication center produces approximately 10 gauges per hour. It takes approximately two hours for the housing to be replenished. Due to variations in processing times, management has decided to keep 20 percent of the needed inventory as safety stock. How many kanban card sets are needed?

2. Transmissions are delivered to the fabrication line four at a time. It takes one hour for transmissions to be delivered. Approximately four vehicles are produced each hour, and management has decided that 50 percent of expected demand should be maintained as safety stock. How many kanban card sets are needed?

3. A bottling plant fills 2,400 bottles every two hours. The lead time is 40 minutes and a container accommodates 120 bottles. The safety stock is 10 percent of expected demand. How many kanban cards are needed?

4. Refer to Example 12.1 as the basis for this problem. Arvin Meritor hires a team of consultants. The consultants suggest a partial robotic automation as well as an increase in safety stock to 0.125. Arvin Automotive implements these suggestions. The result is an increase in efficiency in both the fabrication of muffler assembly and in the making of catalytic converters. The muffler assembly fabrication cell now averages 16 assemblies per hour and the lead time has been decreased to two hours' response time for a batch of 10 catalytic converters. How many kanban cards are now needed?

5. Arvin Meritor is so pleased with the outcome from the consultants' previous suggestions that the consultants are invited back for more consulting work. The consultants now suggest a more complete robotic automation of the making of muffler assemblies and also a reduction in container size to eight per container. Arvin Meritor implements these suggestions and the result is that the muffler assembly fabrication cell now averages approximately 32 assemblies per hour, and the catalytic converter assembly cell can now respond to an order for a batch of catalytic converters in one hour. The safety stock remains at .125. How many kanban cards are needed?

6. Refer to Technical Note 6, "Facility Layout," page 254, Problem 1 regarding the Cyprus Citrus Cooperative. Use the layout provided on that page to (*a*) value stream map the business and its processes as they are now and (*b*) develop and analyze a future state mapping of how locations can be rearranged and which processes, if any, can be combined to result in a leaner work environment. Assume that there is currently a 2-hour lag time between the first three processes, a 12-hour lag time between the fourth and fifth processes, and a 4-hour lag time between the office supervisor's final approval and the transmission of instructions to the shipping department to ship the order. Further assume that each order takes, on average, six minutes at each process along the way. Workers at the Cypress Citrus Cooperative work three shifts, 24 hours a day, seven days a week.

CASE: IMPLEMENTATION OF A JIT PULL SYSTEM AT DUCT MANUFACTURING CENTRE*

In one summer morning in July 1995, Nancy Wallace, the general manager at that time, was in a conference room with her management team (no longer referred to as Deltaforce), reflecting on the progress at the Duct Manufacturing Centre (DMC) of Turbine Systems Corporation. Nancy had been general manager of DMC for four months. Also attending were general managers of several other business units within Turbine Systems who were interested in DMC's progress. Nancy reviewed:

With the help of Marshall Atherton, our factory superintendent, I plan first to provide a retrospective on business at DMC. I'm sure that our guests from sister business units can relate to the difficulties of managing during an economic downturn. Since you are particularly interested in our pull system, Pam Petersen, an industrial engineering manager, will then discuss the details of these efforts that have spanned almost four years. Roy Doctor, an area supervisor, will then discuss prospects for process improvement, and I plan to conclude by summarizing the challenges we face over the next several years.

Despite the adversities of an economic downturn and "revolving door" transfers of our general managers, a great deal has been accomplished since we embarked on the re-engineering effort five years ago. Today we are viewed as one of the most progressive business units in the Turbine Systems Corporation. We are in a modern factory, and thanks to our process improvement teams, we have a cellular layout that has facilitated dramatic performance improvements. During the period April 1990 to April 1995, our WIP inventory has been reduced from 46,000 part numbers to 4,500 in (Exhibit 1). Manufacturing flow time has decreased on average from 25 days per part to 6 days (Exhibit 2).

We attribute much of the credit for these improvements to an emphasis on speed. Just-in-time was an initiative started by one of my predecessors, Lance Lipscomb, and supported by the three general managers that followed. Flow time compression was difficult at first, but

Exhibit 1   Work-in-Process Inventory

Exhibit 2   Flow Time

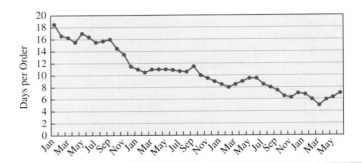

Exhibit 3   Cost per Part (excludes equipment depreciation, material, and purchased parts)

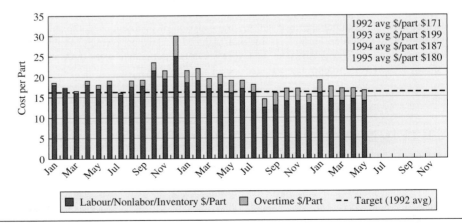

after a few years we began to make progress. A reduction in flow time of only a few days per part was achieved during the period April 1990 to July 1992. The first pull system was implemented late in 1992, but aborted three months later. Much of the compression in flow time occurred in 1993 when we finally began to realize the benefits of good housekeeping, reduced batch sizes, improved quality, staff collocation, and moving the stock room and heat treat into the new building. Another pull system was implemented in January 1995. The second system overcame the blockage difficulties encountered during the first effort. Performance continued to improve because of the effectiveness of this system as well as our program to standardize and simplify the part routings.

Yet we are not satisfied with our progress toward JIT. I share the view with my predecessors that flow time reduction provides the engine for productivity improvement. I sense that we have reached another plateau with respect to flow time, and this, in turn, will limit our ability to improve performance in terms of cost, delivery, and quality. (Refer to Exhibits 3, 4, and 5.) The turnover in leadership hasn't helped, and economic conditions in the turbine business have been poor for several years. There is no question that we are understaffed. Despite these factors, we can continue to improve. We need to fine-tune the mechanics of the pull system to our complex shop environment and we also must continue to make process and layout improvements. Our "pull team," with some of our best and brightest people, is working on these issues.

Late Deliveries

Quality

I am sure that you share my concern about the effects of the new MRP II system the corporation is installing. I appreciate that DMC has been chosen as the first implementation site within the corporation for a complex manufacturing application, but the scope of activities and the time line for implementation are quite ambitious. The transition will be difficult. Additionally, I am concerned about the compatibility of MRP as a "push system" for order release with our "pull system" for shop-floor control.

A lot has changed since Lance Lipscomb held Nancy's position three years ago. Nancy was the third general manager since Lance was transferred in September 1993; i.e., four in fourteen months. These leadership changes were due in large part to a corporate directive to share knowledge among business units. The DMC earned the reputation as being progressive and innovative, and the corporation was anxious to share with the other business units the advanced manufacturing techniques, technologies, and management practices they had applied.

Marshall Atherton, the factory superintendent, described some of the difficulties encountered by DMC over the last three years:

Each general manager had his or her priorities, and it was difficult for the employees to maintain momentum and stability with respect to prior initiatives. This was exacerbated by declining economic conditions during

the last three years. Since Lance departed, demand for turbine systems has declined, and corporate responded by requiring each business unit to reduce costs.

Payroll reductions contributed the most to achieving the cost targets since most other line items in our budget, such as depreciation, could not be adjusted. Exhibit 6 depicts the change since 1992 in headcount relative to demand. Note that during this period headcount was reduced by 28 percent while the demand dropped by only 5 percent.

Nancy Wallace (general manager) interjected:

We feel that the corporation's system for budgeting and accounting is partially responsible for the diminution in the work force. We treat depreciation as an uncontrollable expense much like the federal government treats entitlements. The remaining portion of the budget that is considered controllable must endure large reductions to cover the mandated compression in the overall budget. The problem is compounded by our income-reporting system that overstates the level of depreciation. I appreciate the tax advantages of using a short useful life of five years for our equipment, but most of our equipment has a much longer productive life. This accounting system causes distortions in headcount decisions and it inhibits our ability to make the capital improvements I believe we need to reach a higher level of productivity. Maybe if we work collectively on this issue we can convince corporate to improve their managerial accounting system.

| Exhibit 6 | 1995 Baseline Operating Plan: Total Headcount |

Unfortunately, reductions in headcount have been offset to a certain extent by rising labour rates. Because of seniority policies and skill levels, many of the people that have remained have the highest paying jobs. Furthermore, our payroll expense has grown to cover salary inflation and extraordinarily large increases in benefits (from 42 percent of direct labour in 1990 to 55 percent today).

Marshall Atherton (factory superintendent) added:

This downsizing has placed a strain on the work force. While our people have become more productive to compensate for the lower headcount and the increased labour rates, there has also been an increased demand for non–work statement activities such as training. With current economic conditions, we cannot afford the level of training and education provided during the tenure of Lance Lipscomb. Yet with the layoffs, the percentage of time spent on non–work statement activities has actually increased.

Product complexity has also increased over the last few years. Some of our new work statements are considerably more complex than prior jobs because of the introduction by our parent company of a new generation of turbine systems.

Balancing cost and delivery has proven difficult in recent months. Because we are undermanned, we have been spending money on overtime to keep up with delivery dates. This has compromised our budget and has been particularly hard on the work force. Some people have been working seven days a week since last fall. Morale could be better and productivity has dropped due to burn-out.

The First Pull System   To develop pull systems, Deltaforce established separate teams of operators and support people for the three areas within DMC: hard metals, soft metals, and detail. Marshall Atherton explained the history of the effort:

Since the general managers of the sister divisions have expressed particular interest in our just-in-time efforts, we plan to focus on the features of our pull systems. In complex shop environments such as ours and yours, we feel you would benefit most by learning the details.

Pull systems for the three areas were inaugurated late in 1992, but the one in detail was soon abandoned. The two pull systems that remained were essentially the same with the exception of the form of the work authorization document, commonly known as the Kanban. Teams representing hard metals wanted an electronic authorization system while the team for soft metals decided to use Kanban cards as the authorization. The soft metals team reasoned that their physical identification

system would be more reliable because it was not subject to computer failure.

Both pull systems departed from traditional JIT practice in two respects: (1) Kanban cards were transferred between some but not all operations, and (2) for those operations governed by Kanban, finished work was stored at the previous operation rather than at the next one. First, Kanban transactions were established between cells but not within them. For example, Kanban cards were not used to control work between operations performed within the titanium cell that makes ducts between 2 1/2 inches and 4 inches in diameter, but were used between titanium and other cells such as cleaning, final assembly, penetrant inspect, and pressure test. The reasoning was as follows. Regulation of the flow between these cells was sufficient to control work-in-process inventory levels. Because of labour substitutions within cells but not across them, the benefits of limiting queues within cells would be more than offset by the disruptive effects from the additional transactions. The idea was to base the intra-cell Kanban limits on historical WIP levels and then to adjust them with experience.

The second departure from conventional JIT discipline was that both of the remaining teams decided to store jobs at the cells where they had just been completed rather than to move them to the next cells in the routings. The finished jobs were placed in containers arranged by destination, although the operator would transport the Kanban cards to the next cell and file them in first-come, first-served order. Only a prescribed number of Kanban cards were allotted between a cell and its destination cells. When all the cards resided at the destination cells (leaving none at the feeder cell to authorize work), this signaled the feeder operation to stop all activity. The teams favoured keeping the work behind because they believed the workers would be less tempted to process work out of order if they pulled a Kanban card in sequence and then asked a dispatcher to retrieve the job for them at the feeder cell.

Unfortunately, the two pull systems that remained were aborted in March 1993 after only three months of use. During the three-month period, jobs began to finish behind-schedule at an alarming rate, and shop personnel began to circumvent the system by increasing the Kanban limits and processing work out of order. Yet it was not clear why the pull systems were ineffective in controlling the workflow. George Stinebuck, the general manager who followed Lance Lipscomb, formed the "pull team" in 1994 to learn from the successes and mistakes of the last pull system and to design a new one.

Efforts by the Pull Team   What went awry with the pull systems and how to ameliorate them were questions that Pam Petersen (industrial engineering manager) and her fellow pull team members attempted to answer. Pam described the investigation:

> The literature on JIT was not helpful because it covered only very simple flow processes. We traced our difficulties to complexity as manifested in the form of procedural problems, part variety, routing cycles, and workload variability.
>
> We have a complex process, but we added a layer of complexity by operating different systems in each area. Between January and March of 1993, the detail area, the one that feeds the other two areas, continued to use a push system, while hard and soft metals implemented pull systems. And the two pull systems used different types of work authorizations. As the pull team, we viewed standardization of procedures as an important aspect of our mission.
>
> Systems aside, we had a complicated business. In hard metals alone, we had more than 1,100 different part numbers at the time the first pull system was aborted. To illustrate the challenges created by this part variety for our pull systems, consider the two part routings shown in Exhibit 7. Jobs for each part type pass through a titanium cell but then the first job goes to X-ray while the one that follows is routed next to final assembly. With this first pull system, each feeder cell has a Kanban limit. Suppose that at titanium, the second job has not yet been started, but the first job destined for X-ray has just been completed. Also suppose that there is a backlog of three jobs at X-ray, but final assembly currently has no jobs to process. The system requires that the job just completed be kept behind at titanium, and that the last remaining Kanban authorization card (of a total allotment of four) be filed at X-ray. In this case, the Kanban limit of four has been reached between titanium and its two destination cells, and all four finished titanium jobs are destined for X-ray. This renders the titanium cell idle, thus blocking the second job (waiting at titanium and destined for final assembly). Thus, a bottleneck at X-ray has effectively blocked work at titanium and starved work at final assembly. Workers, conscious of the deadlines on orders, naturally reacted to situations like this by increasing Kanban limits and choosing jobs in an order counter to the first-come, first-served discipline.
>
> Routing cycles and load variability compounded the workflow problems. Many of our parts revisit operations in their routings. The cleaning cell is a good example. We must have the cleanest parts in town because we clean them after every operation. At any rate, because of the merging and diverging flows and the loops in the routings, we cannot consider ourselves a flow shop in the strictest sense.
>
> Workload variability occurs both in the service and arrival processes. Variability in the service times for parts at a particular resource is a function of the plethora of different types of parts that are routed to it.
>
> We attribute the variability in the arrival pattern to routing differences, erratic customer demand, and schedule changes. The demand for our duct parts destined for finished goods is unstable because of lumpiness in customer master schedules, batching in their processes, and new product introductions. The remaining demand, comprised of rush orders for equipment down in the field and of spares for an increasingly aging fleet of turbine systems, is even more volatile.
>
> In addition, we have on average five schedule revisions per order per month. Schedule changes due to internally generated discrepancies such as scrap are minor compared to external changes by our customers and vendors. We suspect that our antiquated MRP [materials requirements planning] system contributes to this problem. We have noticed that with a schedule change, there tends to follow several more changes for the same part. We hope that the new MRP system will dampen these schedule oscillations. Much to our dismay, the current MRP system allows organizations within Turbine Systems but outside the DMC to adjust the lead times for our internal tasks.

Roy Doctor, an area supervisor and fellow pull team member, commented on the effects of this variability:

> With erratic workloads, we need excess capacity in our pull system to provide good service, but capacity is scarce in these days of downsizing and tight budgets.

Pam Petersen proceeded to summarize the pull team's approach:

> We launched a six-month effort in June 1994 to study and simplify the part flows. After two months we realized that while the DMC produced in excess of 4,000 part types, many followed the same routings through the factory. In numerous cases, parts with quite different configurations had the same sequence. In addition, many of the part routings that differed could be simplified and standardized.

First Kanban Card System

Exhibit 7

We discovered a great deal of latitude in the planning systems and individual predilections that determined the manner in which ducts were made. Through an extensive effort by our Manufacturing Engineering group, we were able to determine preferred manufacturing methods. For example, the penetrant inspect and X-ray operations could be sequenced either way; some planners chose one sequence while others chose the reverse ordering. These planning variations spawned many unnecessary part routings.

We developed an orientation document called the Planning Convention Book as well as a series of decision trees that formalized the preferred practices. Through training, the planners were able to simplify and condense existing parts, and for new work statements, they knew when the routings for existing families or new families were appropriate.

The New Pull System   Between December 1994 and June 1995, Manufacturing Engineering at DMC was able to prune the product line from over 4,000 part numbers to 3,526, and to establish a representative set of 1,099 families. This was accomplished despite the introduction of many parts to satisfy new turbine system offerings. (Recall that a family describes a set of part numbers that follows the same routing.) The part numbers and families are identified as of June 1995 by the areas below:

AREA	# PART NUMBERS	# FAMILIES
Hard metals	817	325
Soft metals	849	413
Detail	1,860	361
Totals	3,526	1,099

The pull team discovered that although a particular family may contain many part numbers, it might not be very active because the parts it embodied were for turbine systems that were customer unique or obsolete. Conversely, another family may contain one part number but is needed on every turbine system the corporation currently builds. Pam Petersen explained:

It became clear that to prevent blockage and starvation in our new pull system, we needed to devote special attention to the active families. A Pareto chart (Exhibit 8) reveals that 70 percent of the work processed in

the hard metals area is represented by only 60 primary families (of the 325 total). We found similar patterns in the soft metals and detail areas.

We decided to design the pull system around two types of families: primary and miscellaneous. Primary families represent 70 percent of the volume while the miscellaneous designation covers the remainder. We use separate types of Kanban cards (and associated queue limits) for each primary family plus the miscellaneous category.

Members of the pull team proceeded to explain the pull system discipline. Pam began:

Regardless of the family, the cards associated with jobs destined for a cell are filed in one box according to first-come, first-served discipline. Differences between the families are recognized by a numerical designation on the cards. Primary families are treated slightly differently than the miscellaneous family.

Kanban limits for each primary family are established by allowing only a prescribed number of cards between cells; a job in a primary family cannot be started in a cell without a Kanban card that authorizes the work. Suppose that family A has a prescribed intrastage limit of four and visits three cells, cleaning, titanium, and X-ray, respectively. Four cards for each adjacent pair of cells would be distributed. This limit ensures that there would be at most four jobs for family A: between order release and cleaning, between cleaning and titanium, and between titanium and X-ray. A job for family A that had been released by MRP could not be started at cleaning without an available, family-specific Kanban card that authorizes the work. (A card would not be available at cleaning, for instance, if all four cards for that family were filed in the box at titanium. This indicates that four A jobs were already cleaned, sitting in the container for titanium and thus, not yet started in titanium. When one of the jobs is transferred and finished by titanium, the associated Kanban card would be returned to cleaning and designated as available.)

Roy Doctor described nuances of the pull system:

If we were to make every family in the factory primary, the number of Kanban types and associated WIP would be staggering. Obviously, we needed the miscellaneous category, but changes in the pull system were required to make it work. Since the part types within miscellaneous have different routings, we couldn't create Kanban transfers between all affected cells without experiencing proliferation. The breakthrough came when we recognized that almost all parts within miscellaneous share certain but not all flows between cells. Hence, we were able to gain

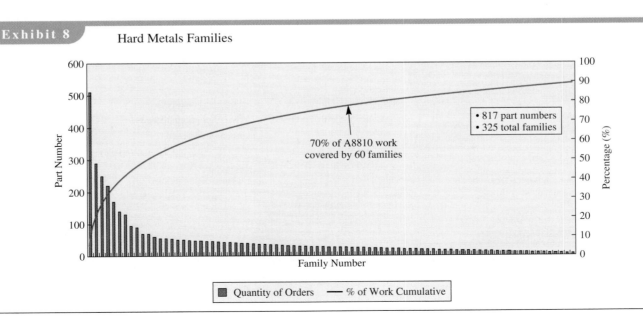

Exhibit 8   Hard Metals Families

70% of A8810 work covered by 60 families

- 817 part numbers
- 325 total families

Part Number / Family Number / Percentage (%)

■ Quantity of Orders   — % of Work Cumulative

Revised Kanban Card System

Exhibit 9

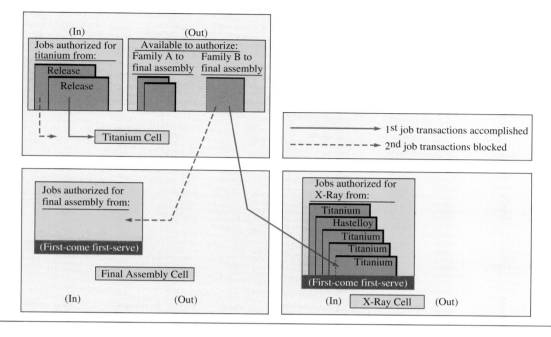

control over miscellaneous by regulating the common flows and ignoring the unique ones. (Recall that even for primary families, we do not control flows between every operation, just between the cells.)

Pam cited other benefits with the new system:

Let's return to the previous example where two jobs pass through a titanium cell but then the first job goes to X-ray while the one that follows is routed next to final assembly. Suppose the first job is in family A and the one sequenced behind it is in family B. Note that in Exhibit 9 we now have separate Kanban cards and limits governing their flows; the limit reached at X-ray prohibits further flow to X-ray by members of family A but does not stop work on the job in family B destined for final assembly. Hence, the system avoids the previous problems of blockage at the titanium cell and of starvation at the final assembly cell.

Roy Doctor interjected:

Of course, the miscellaneous category with its routing variety could still cause trouble, but because of the infrequent usage, this seldom occurs. Initially, we considered offloading some of the miscellaneous part types, but decided not to do so. Besides being inappropriate in the short term due to declining business, we realized that much of the work classified at the tail of the distribution is bread-and-butter work for us. We have distinctive competencies to perform this work, and we do not wish to create by default these skills in our competitors. Instead, we have had a concentrated effort to define better, more standard manufacturing processes. In August 1994 we had only 1.7 part numbers per family, whereas today we have 4.6. Offload should be a last resort.

As was the case with the first pull systems, Kanban cards within the new system are exchanged between cells, not within them, and we maintain work at the previous cell rather than at the next one in the routing. However, there are differences between the first and second pull systems. We have already described how the new system treats part families. Another difference is that we now deal with cycling by issuing separate Kanban cards between cells for each pair of operations. Hence, when a job travels between two cells on more than one occasion, separate Kanban cards govern their flow.

We have also developed a formal means for expediting hot parts through their routings. Kanbans for equipment down in the field are automatically placed at the front of the Kanban boxes at each cell. And in emergencies, the factory superintendent directs parts to be hand-carried through the shop, if necessary interrupting other jobs in process.

Finally, we decided to have the operators retrieve the jobs they intend to work on rather than asking a dispatcher to move the jobs, as was the case with the initial pull systems. This allows the operators to regularly visit their internal suppliers and customers, and this increases awareness of the whole manufacturing chain.

Despite the progress with the new pull system, vexing questions remain as to how to effectively set the Kanban limits. Following the classic reorder point formula, we calculate, for each family, the average usage and the standard deviation; we set the limit as the mean plus one standard deviation times the square root of the lead time at the destination cell.[†] However, this approach for establishing family limits has its weaknesses. It does not recognize the interactions among parts within the same family or across families that are treated by the same resources.[‡] The individual limits should have a cascading effect on overall inventory levels in the cells. (This is similar in effect to the quality assurance problem of cascading tolerances on an assembly despite tight control of specifications for the individual parts that go into the assembly.)

We have other questions about the limits. For a primary family, should we set the same limits between every adjacent pair of cells in its routing or should the limits differ? How should a bottleneck or nonbottleneck affect these limits?

Informal systems have again emerged. Supervisors regulate the work in their cells because they feel there should be some overall control of WIP. They know from experience how much work the cells need to operate. The supervisors will not permit jobs to be pulled, despite Kanban authorization to do so, if there is insufficient capacity to perform the work.

The operators also have an informal system. Because work is kept at the previous cell rather than at the next one in the routing, bottlenecks at subsequent cells become visible to the workers at the prior cells. They can see the jobs piling up in a container for a particular destination. Even if the Kanban limit has not been reached for the destination with a lot of work in the container, the operator might choose jobs destined for less busy cells where they could soon be processed.

Pam spoke next:

We in the pull team feel that the measures instituted by the supervisors and workers have merit, but we are concerned that they will eventually compromise the pull system. We recognize this as a complex queuing problem, and we are investigating queuing and simulation as a means to resolve it. The appendix [to this case] describes our preliminary findings regarding queuing and simulation. You will note that our research tends to support the merits of the informal approaches practiced by the supervisors and workers.

Process and Layout Challenges   The layout proposed in 1992 for the new building was significantly better than the previous one, but in many cases the resulting cells were too far apart for workers to help across cells. Roy Doctor commented on the potential for improvement:

I recall a quote from the famous architect, Mies van der Rohe. He said that, "God is in the details." From my perspective, process improvement drives speed; flow time does not drop by itself. In 1992 there were too many routings for the parts to be built within self-contained areas. Yet with the progress we have made on routing simplification and families, we have definite opportunities for process improvements that will have a positive impact on flow time.

I mentioned before that we need more capacity in our pull system to provide good service, but capacity is scarce these days. While worker flexibility would enable us to gain effective capacity, we have encountered several obstacles. The cleaning cell provides an example of how our parts revisit operations in their routings. There is merit to hand-cleaning the parts within self-contained cells rather than transferring them across the shop. Provisions for the space and handling of the special cleaning agents poses difficulties, but I think it can be done. Flow time would benefit in three respects. First, fewer people would be involved since the mechanic would clean the parts. Second, travel distance would be reduced. Finally, more cleaning units would obviate the need with the current cleaning configuration for batching to save setups.

Cooperation across cells often is not practiced even when it is possible. The three titanium cells corresponding to different duct diameters provide a case in point. Operators within the cells have developed a sense of ownership and are reluctant to help elsewhere despite the similarity in tasks. Establishing separate managers for the titanium cells also helped to forge this sense of ownership. In many respects, the workers are so proud of the cells they helped design for the new building that the layout has become somewhat of a sacred cow.

To further complicate matters, many ducts cycle through welding and mechanical operations several times before finishing, yet the two types of operations are governed by different unions. Perhaps we could eventually resolve the need for separate certifications and job classifications.

In retrospect, we would have been better served by designing small versions of the large penetrant inspect and pressure test equipment for which we currently have separate cells. Penetrant inspect involves the examination under ultraviolet light of weld areas on the ducts for inconsistencies in a thin coating of translucent powder. The pressure test forces water into the ducts at twice the prescribed tolerance to uncover leaks in the weld joints. Neither operation is technologically complex, however. Rather than creating separate, centralized cells for this large equipment, we could have replicated and placed the smaller versions in various, self-contained cells.

It would be nice to eliminate a few days of flow time while parts travel from the detail area into stores and then into hard or soft metals. This delay in the storeroom allows us to kit the finished detail parts, thus compensating for variability inherent in the detail process. The bending process is an art, not a science, because of variations in the alloy mix and the temper of the metals. Perhaps with better control of the bending process and better part coordination, we could dispense with our stock room.

Future Direction   Nancy Wallace closed the session with the following observations:

Improvement is a continuous proposition. The DMC has clearly benefited from the reengineering efforts begun five years ago. We attribute much of the progress at DMC to cascade education, TQM, team decision making, and an emphasis on speed. We even benefited from the endeavour to implement the first pull system in that workers began to understand its mechanics and appreciate how it enforces limits on the inventory. Recognition of the strong work flows through our shop has enabled us to design a better pull system and begin to consider prospects for process improvements.

We could further compress our flow time from six days to two. Our production process is still far too complex, and we need to get people on the shop floor more involved in decision making. There is still a command and control environment at DMC. Management and especially support personnel need to hone their people skills. We need to be more effective in the way we solicit employee suggestions and respond to employee concerns. We have a long way to go in changing the roles of management from fire fighters and expediters to coaches and cheerleaders.

The worst is behind us with respect to layoffs and transfers, but we obviously have a lot of issues with which to contend. The most important task for me is to prioritize these initiatives.

APPENDIX: ANALYSIS OF ALTERNATIVE KANBAN SYSTEMS
USING QUEUING AND SIMULATION

An Alternative Kanban System   We propose a variation of the first and second systems implemented at DMC. We suggest for the proposed system that the Kanban cards be destination-specific rather than family/destination-specific (as is the case with the current system). We illustrate the proposed system in Exhibits 10A, 10B, and 10C. We proposed separate Kanban cards and limits governing the flows between: (1) feeder cells and X-ray, and (2) feeder cells and final assembly. Hence, the proposed system requires an aggregate limit for each cell serving as a destination in the part routings.

Another departure from the prior pull systems is that in the proposed system, the Kanban card would not be automatically returned to a feeder cell once a job is completed at the destination cell. This is because with multiple feeder cells, the operator at the destination would not know where to return the Kanban without some (most likely, inefficient) allocation system. Instead, the available Kanban would remain at the destination. The operator at a feeder cell would be alerted that at least one Kanban is available at the destination cell, and that he or she should go there to pick up one card as a work authorization. (Perhaps the availability of work authorization(s) could be transmitted by computer, or by a visual signal using a light on the ceiling above the destination cell.)

To illustrate, let us return to the previous example; this time suppose that there are three jobs rather than two. Exhibit 10A indicates that the first job (in family A) goes from titanium to X-ray; Exhibit 10B shows that the second job (in family B) goes from titanium to final assembly; and Exhibit 10C shows that the third job (in family C) is routed from hastelloy to X-ray.

The first event occurs when the operator in titanium is free (see Exhibit 10A). He finds two authorized cards representing jobs waiting to be processed at titanium; he chooses the one that arrived first, a job that is routed to X-ray after titanium. He checks to see that there is an available card at X-ray, he retrieves the card from X-ray, and he gets the parts for the job that are waiting to be processed at titanium. After completing that job at titanium, he designates as available in titanium the card that had authorized the work in titanium, and he designates as authorized in X-ray the card that had been identified as available.

Proposed Kanban Card System

Proposed Kanban Card System

The second event occurs when the operator in titanium again becomes free (see Exhibit 10B). He finds one authorized card for a job waiting to be processed at titanium, a job that is routed to final assembly after titanium. He checks to see that there is an available card at final assembly, he retrieves the card from final assembly, and he gets the parts for the job that are waiting to be processed at titanium. After completing that job at titanium, he designates as avail-

able in titanium the card that had authorized the work in titanium, and he designates as authorized in final assembly the card that had been identified as available.

The third event occurs when the operator in hastelloy becomes free (see Exhibit 10C). She finds an authorized card for a job waiting to be processed at hastelloy, a job that is routed to X-ray after hastelloy. She checks to see if there is an available card at X-ray. Since there

Exhibit 10C   Proposed Kanban System

are none available in X-ray, she for the moment abandons the idea of working on that job. She checks for the next job that is authorized in hastelloy. Since there are no others in the box designated as authorized, she has been rendered idle until the next job is authorized in hastelloy or an available card appears at X-ray. Hence, the limit at X-ray has prohibited further flow to X-ray regardless of the feeder cell, but did not block work in feeder cells destined for final assembly.

There are four potential advantages of the proposed system over the current one. First, this system should substantially reduce the number of Kanban limits compared to the current system where a limit is needed for every family and destination. We expect this to ameliorate the problems of cascading inventories due to the multiple limits at each stage. Second, queuing will enable us to derive analytically the queue limits for each cell. Third, the proposed system addresses the concerns of the foremen and operators that have begun to follow informal rules sometimes counter to the rules of the current system. The foremen should be pleased to find that the system is regulating the aggregate flow through the cell, and the operators in feeder cells should find that the limits would keep them from sending too much work to a destination if it is a bottleneck. Finally, queuing analysis permits us to achieve desired flow time allowances by deriving the required capacity levels at the cells. In this respect, queuing analysis could determine headcount as well as appropriate cross-training patterns.

However, these four conjectures may or may not be realized in actual practice because of certain assumptions inherent in queuing analysis (such as independent, homogeneous arrivals and independent services). We next describe an animated simulation program designed to compare under more realistic operating conditions the performance of the current and proposed systems.

Simulation Analysis   We simulate a shop with three families and three cells. Two of the families are primary and the third is classified as miscellaneous. Parts within primary family A are routed from

titanium to cleaning to titanium to X-ray. Parts within primary family B are routed from titanium to cleaning to X-ray to titanium to cleaning. Parts in the miscellaneous family M begin at titanium or cleaning, follow a random routing through the remaining cells, and end with a common sequence of tasks, titanium then cleaning. Following standard practice at DMC, parts within titanium cycle between the mechanic and weld booths. In addition, parts within the cleaning cell are batched in lots of four to maintain high utilization of the vats of cleaning solution. (Different part types can be batched together during cleaning. Once submerged, the cleaning cycle is constant at three minutes regardless of the part type.)

To emulate a large number of part types within each family, an exponential distribution (with a mean of three minutes) is used to generate the service times for each operation except cleaning, which has a constant time. The interarrival times of jobs entering the shop are also exponentially distributed with a mean of 12 minutes. Parts and people travel at a fixed rate of 25 feet per minute; the average travel time between operations is less than one minute.

Two alternative Kanban systems are evaluated, the current one with limits for each family/destination and the proposed one with limits for each destination cell. In the current system, the Kanban limits for the families and destinations are derived using the reorder point formula (mean plus standard deviation times the square root of the lead time at the destination cell). In the proposed system, the Kanban limits for the destination cells are derived using queuing analysis. The queuing analysis is based on the mean service and interarrival times.

The results of one replication for the alternative systems are shown in Exhibit 11. The simulation results indicate that for the same level of resources, the proposed system yields on average 58 percent more output, 55 percent less flow time, and 72 percent less inventory than the current system. The proposed system shows promise for improving performance at DMC, although more experimentation is warranted.

Promodel Simulation Results

Exhibit 11

CURRENT SYSTEM					PROPOSED SYSTEM	
FAMILY	FROM	TO	LIMIT		STATION	LIMIT
A	Titanium	Clean	20		Titanium	8
A	Clean	Titanium	16		Clean	8
A	Titanium	X-ray	20		X-ray	8
B	Titanium	Clean, first step	20			
B	Clean	X-ray	16			
B	X-ray	Titanium	17			
B	Titanium	Clean, last step	20			
Misc.	Titanium	Clean, last step	20			

MEASUREMENT	CURRENT SYSTEM	PROPOSED SYSTEM	IMPROVEMENT
Average inventory	50	14	72%
Average flow time (hours)	11	5	55
Total three-day output	38	60	58

*THIS CASE WAS DEVELOPED FOR USE IN CLASSROOM DISCUSSION AND IS NOT INTENDED TO NECESSARILY ILLUSTRATE APPROPRIATE OR INAPPROPRIATE MANAGEMENT PRACTICES. CASE AUTHOR: THOMAS G. SCHMITT, UNIVERSITY OF WASHINGTON, 1996. THE FUNDING FOR THIS CASE PRODUCTION WAS PROVIDED BY THE AUSTRALIAN FEDERAL GOVERNMENT'S DEPARTMENT OF INDUSTRY, SCIENCE AND RESOURCES.

†REFER TO VOLLMANN, BERRY, WHYBARK, AND JACOBS, *MANUFACTURING PLANNING AND CONTROL SYSTEMS*, FIFTH EDITION (NEW YORK: MCGRAW-HILL).

‡THE FORMULA ASSUMES THAT: (1) THE VARIANCE OF DEMAND FOR EACH PART TYPE WITHIN A FAMILY IS THE SAME, (2) THE COVARIANCE IN DEMAND BETWEEN PART TYPES WITHIN A FAMILY IS ZERO, I.E., THE DEMAND FOR EACH IS INDEPENDENT OF THE OTHERS, AND (3) THE LEAD TIME IS CONSTANT AND EQUAL FOR EACH PART TYPE. THE LAST ASSUMPTION PRECLUDES THE CONSIDERATION OF THE DYNAMIC QUEUING EFFECTS WE WOULD EXPECT TO SEE WHEN PART TYPES WITHIN OR AMONG FAMILIES ARE TREATED BY THE SAME RESOURCES.

SELECTED BIBLIOGRAPHY

Allen, M. "Picture-Perfect Manufacturing [Using Value Stream Mapping]." *Modern Machine Shop Magazine Online*, August 2004.

Bremner, B., and C. Dawson. "Can Anything Stop Toyota: An Inside Look at How It's Reinventing the Auto Industry." *BusinessWeek*, November 17, 2003, pp. 114–22.

George, M. L. *Lean Six Sigma.* New York: McGraw-Hill, 2002.

Gross, J. M., and K. R. McInnis. *Kanban Made Simple: Demystifying and Applying Toyota's Legendary Manufacturing Process.* New York: AMACOM, 2003.

Hogg, D. "There's Simply Common Sense Behind Lean." *Manufacturing Engineering*, 131, no. 5 (November 2003), pp. 14–21.

Monden, Y. *Toyota Production System: An Integrated Approach to Just-in-Time.* Atlanta, GA: Institute of Industrial Engineers, 1998.

Phelps, T.; M. Smith; and T. Hoenes. "Building a Lean Supply Chain." *Manufacturing Engineering* 132, no. 5 (May 2004), pp. 107–13.

Shingo, S. *A Revolution in Manufacturing: The SMED System.* Tokyo: Japan Management Association, 1983.

Womack, J. P., and D. T. Jones. *Lean Thinking: Banish Waste and Create Wealth in Your Corporation.* New York: Simon & Schuster, 1996.

Womack, J. P.; D. T. Jones; and D. Roos. *The Machine That Changed the World.* New York: R. A. Rawston Associates, 1990.

FOOTNOTES

1 J. P. Womack, D. T. Jones, and D. Roos, *The Machine That Changed the World* (New York: R. A. Rawston Associates, 1990).

2 K. A. Wantuck, *The Japanese Approach to Productivity* (Southfield, MI: Bendix Corporation, 1983).

3 K. Suzaki, *The New Manufacturing Challenge: Techniques for Continuous Improvement* (New York: Free Press, 1987), pp. 7–25.

4 C. Karlsson, *Japanese Production Management in Sunrise or Sunset* (Stockholm, Sweden: Stockholm School of Economics, EFI/The Economic Research Institute. 1999).

5 R. H. Hall, *Zero Inventories* (Homewood, IL: Dow Jones-Irwin, 1983), p. 64.

6 J. P. Womack and D. T. Jones, *Lean Thinking* (New York: Simon & Shuster, 1996), p. 277.

7 "Lean Not Working? You've Got It Wrong!" *Works Management*, no. 7 (July 2002), p. 7.

8 J. Lovelle, "Mapping the Value Stream," *IIE Solutions* 33, no. 2 (February 2001), pp. 26–33.

section

PLANNING AND CONTROLLING THE SUPPLY CHAIN

4

IN RUNNING A BUSINESS, COMPUTERS CAN DO MORE THAN JUST WORD PROCESSING AND E-MAIL

RUNNING A BUSINESS REQUIRES A GREAT PLANNING system. What do we expect to sell in the future? How many people should we hire to handle the Christmas rush? How much inventory do we need? What should we make today? These are all questions that managers need to answer every day. This section discusses different approaches to answering these questions. Computers running comprehensive software packages can help. For a manager, it is important to understand the best way to solve these planning problems, so the right software can be purchased and configured correctly. Often a good spreadsheet is all that is needed.

managerial briefing
ENTERPRISE RESOURCE PLANNING SYSTEMS

INFORMATION CRISIS—THE MISSING DESK

"Okay, Jerry, what's up?"

"I'll tell you what's up! $20,000 is what's up. We've lost the desk for that lawyer in Atlanta. You remember, the one that was supposed to ship a couple of weeks ago. He called me yesterday and said enough is enough. He reminded me of all the delays we had since he first placed the order. I reminded him of all the changes he wanted made. He reminded me that the last notice he got after the final change was that the desk would be there no later than last week. Well, he didn't believe us, so he postponed some big cocktail party until this week so the desk would be there. I stopped reminding him of stuff and said I'd find out what was going on." Jerry was not happy.

"What did you find out?"

"Nothing. I went out in the shop yesterday evening and couldn't find the thing. I tried to call you at home but I guess you didn't get enough vacation."

Source: F. R. Jacobs and D. C. Whybark, *Why ERP? A Primer on SAP Implementation* (New York: Irwin/McGraw-Hill, 2000), pp. 10–11.

"Wait a minute, going over to the in-laws to swap the pictures of sand we each took at the beach isn't exactly an extended vacation. How the heck can we lose a lawyer's desk?" Billy was not happy.

"I don't know, and neither did the two guys I talked to from the shop. They said it was still sitting there yesterday. What is going on anyway?" asked Jerry.

"Well, I remember now. There was a delay because of the last-minute change in some of the hardware that the guy wanted. Remember, we found out the vendor couldn't ship that until last week, and then we needed some time to make sure the finish was okay. When we ran the MRP system to check the schedules, I learned that the desk wouldn't ship until late last week, but it didn't go. It must have gone yesterday, late. I'll check and let you know."

Back in his office, Billy pulled up the record for the desk and found the order was closed out. He went back to the history file and learned that it indeed had been shipped late yesterday and was off the production books. Why the sales people didn't know it had shipped was a mystery to him. He called the trucking company and asked them where the shipment was. Expecting to be told they would check and call back, he was pleasantly surprised to be told immediately that the shipment was picked up late yesterday, it had gone to Raleigh where another Atlanta-bound shipment was picked up, and the truck was now on the outer beltway of Atlanta. The clerk apologized and said that it might be midday before the delivery could be made. They had to drop off the other shipment first. Finally, the clerk took Billy's number and said he would call if there was any delay in getting the shipment to the customer by noon.

"Why can't we do that?" wondered Billy.

He called Jerry and told him to tell the lawyer to go ahead with his party. Then he asked why the shipment never got picked up in the sales system. Jerry replied, "It looks like it never got entered yesterday. It's probably still on someone's desk. I'll check and see, but I'm really more worried about our not knowing of the delay two weeks ago when you did."

"I wonder if this is a problem that comes from lack of integration," mused Billy as he set about learning about how many forecasts the company had for next month. →

The missing desk tale depicts a typical situation in a company where information is not integrated. An **enterprise resource planning (ERP)** system, when implemented correctly, links all the areas of the business. Manufacturing knows about new orders as soon as they are entered in the system. Sales knows the exact status of a customer order. Purchasing knows what manufacturing needs to the minute, and the accounting system is updated as all the relevant transactions occur. The potential benefits are huge. Savings in the redundant posting of information alone can save a company millions of dollars a year. The real value, though, is in the new ways that a company can do business. Many redundant jobs can simply be eliminated. The time taken to do the remaining jobs can be reduced significantly due to the quick availability of information. With a well-designed ERP system, new ways to run the business are possible. Of course, this is not without cost. ERP systems are complex and expensive and may require major changes in processes.

The purpose of this managerial briefing is to provide an overview of what an ERP system is and why it can benefit a company. The current ERP vendors have set new standards in information integration. In this briefing, we focus on a company called SAP AG and their flagship product R/3. Our intent is not to endorse the SAP R/3 product as the only software product that a firm should consider; rather, this is a good benchmark for comparing other competing products.

Enterprise resource planning (ERP)

Cross Functional

Major Developers of Enterprise Resource Planning Software

VENDOR	SPECIAL SOFTWARE FEATURES	WEB SITE
American Software	Comprehensive selection; focus on supply chain management	http://www.amsoftware.com
SSA Global Technologies	Comprehensive selection of software for discrete and process manufacturing	http://www.baan.com
i2 Technologies	Forecasting; flow manufacturing	http://www.i2.com
Manugistics	Optimization of logistics functions	http://www.manugistics.com
Oracle/PeopleSoft	Comprehensive system; major database vendor	http://www.oracle.com http://www.peoplesoft.com
SAP	Integrated client/server system	http://www.sap.com

Exhibit MB13.1 lists the major developers of ERP software. In a sense, it can be argued that SAP AG was in the right place at the right time.

In the early 1990s, many large companies realized that it was time to update their existing information systems to take advantage of new technologies. Programs written in programming languages such as COBOL, PL1, RPG, and assembler were becoming increasingly expensive to maintain. Further, the mainframe computer technology was not cost-effective compared to the ever more powerful and inexpensive microprocessor-based computers. Change was inevitable, and SAP offered a comprehensive solution.

SAP AG'S R/3

Cross Functional

SAP AG, a German firm, is the world leader in providing ERP software. Its flagship product is known as R/3. The software is designed to operate in a three-tier client/server configuration. As shown in Exhibit MB13.2, the core of the system is a high-speed network of database servers. These database servers are special computers designed to efficiently handle a large database of information. The applications, which consist of the software modules discussed in the next section, can be run on separate computers. The applications are networked around the database cluster and have independent access to it. Users communicate with the applications through the front-end servers.

The R/3 applications are fully integrated so that data are shared between all applications. If, for example, an employee posts a shipping transaction in the Sales and Distribution module, the transaction is immediately seen by Accounts Payable in the Financial Accounting module and by Inventory Management in the Materials Management module. The Manufacturing and Logistics module has applications that support virtually all of the topics discussed in this book.

Much of the success of the product is due to the comprehensive coverage of business applications. In a sense, SAP has changed the face of information technology. We now have the enterprisewide integrated system we only dreamed of a few years ago. Companies can consider the automation of their basic business processes as if it were a utility like electricity or water: Hook it up and get back to the real, challenging business at hand.

Of course, it is not really this simple. The problem is that many of the applications do not line up with the way a company operates. The SAP consultants argue that the modules are designed around industry "best practices." But this, in many cases, means that a firm wishing to use SAP needs to change its practices to those implemented by the SAP programmers.

Three-Tier Client/Server Configuration

R/3 Application Modules

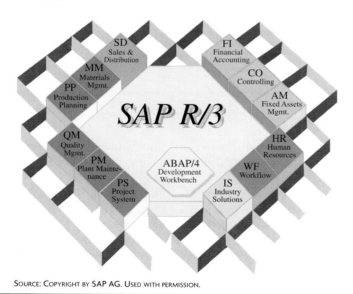

SOURCE: COPYRIGHT BY SAP AG. USED WITH PERMISSION.

R/3 APPLICATION MODULES

R/3 is built around a comprehensive set of application modules that can be used either alone or in combination. Exhibit MB13.3 shows the major modules of R/3. The modules can be used to support processes that span different functional areas in the firm. Because the modules are integrated and use a common database, transactions processed in one area immediately update all other areas. For example, if an order is received from a customer via the Internet, accounting, production scheduling, and purchasing immediately know about the order and the impact it has on their areas.

**Cross
Functional**

BREAKTHROUGH

R/3's OPEN INFORMATION WAREHOUSE

Any modern database will let you easily formulate an SQL query like "What sales did my company have in Italy in 1997?" A report generated in response to such a query could look like this:

REGION	Q1	Q2	Q3	Q4	TOTAL
Umbria	1000	1200	800	2000	5000
Toscana	2000	2600	1600	2800	9000
Calabria	400	300	150	450	1300
Total	3400	4100	2550	5250	15300

But things get more complex if, for instance, we then want to use this answer as the basis for *drilling down* to look at the sales for different quarters and sales representatives in the various regions. Drilling down means descending through an existing hierarchy to bring out more and more detail.

In the following example, we drill down through the sales hierarchy (sales representatives in Toscana). Signore Corleone's sales do not appear to have been affected by the holiday season in the third quarter.

SALES	Q1	Q2	Q3	Q4	TOTAL
S. Paolo	500	600	300	500	1900
S. Vialli	700	600	200	700	2200
S. Ferrari	600	700	400	700	2400
S. Corleone	200	700	700	900	2500
Total	2000	2600	1600	2800	9000

At this point, you can switch to another dimension—for instance, from sales representative to product sold. This is often referred to as *slice and dice*.

PRODUCT	Q1	Q2	Q3	Q4	TOTAL
X-11	2000	2500	1500	3550	9550
Z-12	1400	1600	1050	1700	5750
Total	3400	4100	2550	5250	15300

From the standpoint of a data analyst, it can now be useful to check sales of particular products in each region. SAP R/3 allows the end user to do this easily using the data warehouse approach implemented within the system.

SOURCE: THIS EXAMPLE WAS TAKEN FROM C. HEINRICH AND M. HOFMANN, "DECISION SUPPORT FROM THE SAP OPEN INFORMATION WAREHOUSE," SAP WEB SITE, http://www.sap.com.

A significant feature that improves access to information in the system is the *data warehouse*. See the Breakthrough box titled "R/3's Open Information Warehouse" for an example of how this works.

In our review of the application modules that make up R/3 (see Exhibit MB13.3), the emphasis is placed on what these modules actually do, not on the technical aspects of how they communicate with one another. The technical aspects of how SAP has implemented this software are interesting, particularly if you are a student in the information systems area. Much information on the technical aspects of the software is available from the SAP Web page (http://www.sap.com).

SAP organizes the R/3 modules in a variety of ways in its documents. In general, there are four major elements to the organization: financial accounting, human resources, manufacturing and logistics, and sales and distribution. We describe these four elements in terms of functionality, but these descriptions are by no means complete. SAP indicates that modules are updated twice a year, based upon changes in business practices, technological advances, and the requirements of their customers.

FINANCIAL ACCOUNTING

Financial accounting

The **financial accounting** segment of R/3 includes three major categories of functionality needed to run the financial accounts for a company: financials (FI), controlling (CO), and asset management (AM). FI includes accounts payable, accounts receivable, general ledger, and capital investments. Also included in the FI category are the procedures to post accounts; close

HILLERICH AND BRADSBY, THE MANUFACTURER OF LOUISVILLE SLUGGER BASEBALL BATS, AS WELL AS GOLF AND HOCKEY EQUIPMENT, MANAGES ITS BUSINESS WITH AN ERP SYSTEM UTILIZING SAP R/3. AFTER IMPLEMENTATION, H & B NOW SHIPS 80 PERCENT OF ALL ORDERS ON TIME, COMPARED WITH ONLY 40 PERCENT PREVIOUSLY.

the books for the month and year; prepare financial statements, including the balance sheet; and perform planning functions. Naturally, the system provides the capability to document processes, prepare reports, archive certain data, and make additions and changes to the financial data as necessary.

As with all the modules in the R/3 system, the user will find all information current and integrated. Thus, an individual manufacturing plant or sales organization can run a profit-and-loss report at any time during the month and be shown the most up-to-date information. This, of course, depends upon having set up the company hierarchy in such a way that the plant or sales group is designated as a profit-and-loss center.

The controlling category includes costing; cost center, profit center, and enterprise accounting and planning; internal orders; open item management; posting and allocation; profitability analysis; and a variety of reporting functions. It also includes a project system to track activity and costs related to major corporate projects, such as the implementation of an R/3 system. This is not the same thing as a project management system, which can be found in the manufacturing modules.

Also included is a module to add activity-based costing (ABC) to other types of costing approaches. ABC is recognized as an effective approach to model the flow of costs between cost objects. Activity costs can then be allocated to business processes.

The asset management category includes the ability to manage all types of corporate assets, including fixed assets, leased assets, and real estate. It also includes the capital investment management module, which provides the ability to manage, measure, and oversee capital investment programs. Treasury capabilities are offered, including the ability to manage cash and funds belonging to the corporation.

HUMAN RESOURCES (HR)

The **human resources** (HR) segment contains the full set of capabilities needed to manage, schedule, pay, and hire the people who make a company run. It includes payroll, benefits administration, applicant data administration, personnel development planning, workforce planning, schedule and shift planning, time management, and travel expense accounting.

Human resources

Because the structure of most companies shifts frequently, one function in the human resources category provides the ability to represent organizational charts, including organizational units, jobs, positions, workplaces, and tasks. Thus, the user can represent and plan matrix organization, split responsibilities, and temporary project groups.

Capturing data from the human resources module, the SAP Business Workflow (WF) system allows management to define and manage the flow of work required in a cross-functional business process. Process owners find this useful for monitoring activities that have deadlines either by individual or by position.

MANUFACTURING AND LOGISTICS

Manufacturing and logistics

The **manufacturing and logistics** segment is the largest and most complex of the module categories. It can be divided into five major components: materials management (MM), plant maintenance (PM), quality management (QM), production planning and control (PP), and a project management system (PS). Each component is divided into a number of subcomponents. Materials management covers all tasks within the supply chain, including consumption-based planning, purchasing, vendor evaluation, and invoice verification. It also includes inventory and warehouse management to manage stock until usage dictates the cycle should begin again. Electronic kanban/just-in-time delivery is supported.

Plant maintenance supports the activities associated with planning and performing repairs and preventive maintenance. Completion and cost reports are available. Maintenance activities can be managed and measured.

The quality management capability plans and implements procedures for inspection and quality assurance. It is built on the ISO 9001 standard for quality management. It is integrated with the procurement and production processes so that the user can identify inspection points both for incoming materials and for products during the manufacturing process.

Production planning and control supports both discrete and process manufacturing processes. Repetitive and configure-to-order approaches are provided. This set of modules supports all phases of manufacturing, providing capacity leveling and requirements planning, material requirements planning, product costing, bills of material explosion and implosion, CAD dialog interface, and engineering change management. The system allows users to link rework orders to production schedules. Orders can be generated from internal sales orders or from links to a World Wide Web site.

The project management system lets the user set up, manage, and evaluate large, complex projects. Whereas the financial costing project system focuses on costs, the manufacturing project system is used for planning and monitoring dates and resources. The system walks the user through the typical project steps: concept, rough-cut planning, detailed planning, approval, execution, and closing. It manages a sequence of activities, each with its interrelationships to the others. Activities are defined as tasks that take time, are processed without interruption, require resources, and incur costs. Projects are measured based on projected and actual dates and results. The system provides the capability to manage availability, budget, capacity and cost planning, project status, and time scheduling.

SALES AND DISTRIBUTION (SD)

Sales and distribution

The **sales and distribution** (SD) set of modules provides customer management; sales order management; configuration management; distribution, export controls, shipping, and transportation management; and billing, invoicing, and rebate processing. Because this, like the other modules, can be implemented globally, the user can manage the sales process worldwide. For example, an order may be received in Hong Kong. If the products are not available locally, they may be internally procured from warehouses in other parts of the world and shipped to arrive together at the Hong Kong customer's site.

In sales and distribution, products or services are sold to customers. In implementing the SD module (as in other modules), the company structure must be represented in the system so that, for example, R/3 knows where and when to recognize revenue. It is possible to

Global

Logistics Integration Overview

SOURCE: COPYRIGHT BY SAP AG. USED WITH PERMISSION.

represent the structure of the firm from the point of view of accounting, materials manage-ment, or sales and distribution. These structures can also be combined.

When a sales order is entered, it automatically includes the correct information on pricing, promotions, availability, and shipping options. Batch order processing is available for special-ized industries such as food, pharmaceutical, or chemical. Users can reserve inventory for spe-cific customers, request production of subassemblies, or enter orders that are assemble-to-order, build-to-order, or engineer-to-order as well as special customized orders. Exhibit MB13.4 depicts the complex data linkages between modules needed to integrate information managed by the system.

The modules included with the R/3 system are built on what SAP considers best practices. SAP has a research and development group that continually looks for better ways to carry out a particular process or subprocess. System upgrades are designed to reflect the newest best practices.

mySAP.COM—INTEGRATED E-BUSINESS PLATFORM

SAP's strategy is to build a set of business software solutions around the application modules. Each of these solutions is designed for a specific purpose. The solutions can all be implemented using an Internet interface known as mySAP, thus making it possible for users to have the full functionality of the SAP software without requiring the deployment of any special software to the users. The user only needs a functioning Web browser to use the system. To further simplify implementation, a company can even totally outsource the running of the SAP software by using a provider that specializes in serving mySAP over the Internet.

To illustrate how the topics covered in the chapters in this section of the book are imple-mented by SAP, we focus on the mySAP Supply Chain Management (SCM) product. SAP, just as we have organized the topics in these chapters, organizes its software into planning scenarios that represent the basic needs of the organization. Within mySAP SCM, the plan-ning scenarios are called "collaborative demand planning," "sales and operations planning," and "collaborative supply and distribution planning."

mySAP SCM Demand Planning is basically a toolkit of statistical forecasting techniques and planning features that helps the user create accurate estimates of future requirements. These techniques are the topic of Chapter 13, "Forecasting." The software gives visibility to all levels of detail using the data warehouse technology described in the Breakthrough box (p. 502). The software includes time series techniques, such as exponential smoothing complete with trend and seasonal indexes. Causal analyses where factors such as price, number of stores, or demographics are considered are included in the tools. SAP also offers a set of collaborative planning tools implemented through Internet forms as part of the package. Collaborative forecasting is a topic discussed in Chapter 13 together with the time series and causal techniques.

Sales and Operations Planning is the entire process of integrating sales and marketing plans with plans for producing products and delivering services. In Chapter 14 we cover this topic and show a technique for bringing the demand and operations information together in a spreadsheet format. SAP uses what they call the Supply Chain Cockpit that consists of a graphical instrument panel that is configured to allow the user to view and manage key elements of the supply chain.

A key element of SAP's Sales and Operations Planning is the Advanced Planner and Optimizer (APO) functions that are available. APO is a library of advanced, highly configurable planning and optimization algorithms to provide task-specific, industry-specific, and even company-specific optimization. In the case of this book, we built custom spreadsheets for each planning problem and then used the Microsoft Excel® Solver to aid in finding solutions to these problems. Our approach works well for smaller problems like those we cover in the book. Large applications, as would be encountered in a real firm, require more powerful techniques. APO is the software that SAP uses to formulate and solve these problems. SAP also supports the exporting of data to Microsoft Excel, allowing user-developed applications to be used.

The final element of mySAP SCM is the collaborative supply and distribution planning functions. These functions allow the user to create plans for purchasing, manufacturing, distributing inventory, and transporting material. The software supports different types of strategies such as make to stock, make to order, and assemble to order. Being an integrated system, SAP gives a real-time view of plans. When plans change and when actual transactions are executed, the impact on the system is immediately known. Actual planning is supported by a simulation mode where what-if scenarios can be quickly run. In the book, simulation is covered in Technical Note 17. In addition, techniques from the APO library also can be used to optimize certain decisions.

In this book, we cover the details related to these functions in Chapters 15 and 16. Planning safety stock is discussed in Chapter 15 together with the logic for targeting inventory levels throughout the supply chain. SAP implements the logic on an item and individual location basis using the same logic as described in the book. The special case of manufacturing inventory is covered in Chapter 16. The book describes material requirements planning logic in detail through relatively simple examples. In SAP this logic is implemented in a manner that can support the simultaneous planning of thousands of items.

IMPLEMENTING ERP SYSTEMS

SAP has some strong competition. Companies such as Oracle, i2 Technologies, and PeopleSoft (now owned by Oracle) have aggressively gone after the market. SAP, though, is the market leader with over 44,500 sites and over 10,000,000 users worldwide. Implementation of ERP is costly, with the actual cost of the software typically one-third or less of the total cost. Large companies, such as Chevron Corp. and Bristol-Myers Squibb, typically earmark $250 million or more to implement an ERP system.

Implementing these systems does not always work out. A survey conducted by the Harvard Business School revealed that a large percentage of executives had negative feelings toward ERP software.[1] In particular, they felt that (1) ERP technology could not support their businesses, (2) their organizations could not make changes needed to extract benefits from the new systems, and (3) ERP implementation might actually damage their businesses. The same

BREAKTHROUGH

mySAP:ERP

SAP has a special version of their software for small and medium-sized firms. mySAP:ERP provides features and functions for operational analysis to help optimize total customer satisfaction. The offering includes features that support the following business activities:

- **Procurement monitoring.** Monitor purchasing operations and provide a detailed analysis of purchasing activities and procurement processes.
- **Inventory and warehouse management.** Assess your organization's actual stock situation based on quantity- and value-based criteria. Analyze warehouse activities such as the physical flow of materials and workloads.
- **Manufacturing reporting.** Provide various standard reports and analyses detailing production-related information.
- **Order fulfillment analysis.** Evaluate and improve order fulfillment using key performance indicators (KPIs) for transportation and order management, strategic performance measurements or the distribution statistics needed for supply chain optimization, and operative performance measurements that capture the day-to-day information used for process optimization.

- **Customer service analysis.** Monitor financial trends, costs, and revenues per customer, as well as service contracts and operations. The solution also supports installed-base analysis and provides both customer analytics and warranty analytics.
- **Program and project management.** Monitor and control project data, evaluate projects, and enable design-to-cost engineering to optimize product costs.
- **Quality management.** Plan, collect, settle, and evaluate quality-related costs. The solution includes quality management features that provide data to determine standard or user-defined quality scores.
- **Enterprise asset management.** Perform strategic evaluations, including mean time to repair (MTTR) and mean time between repair (MTBR) analyses.
- **Sales planning.** Set sales targets by using multiple dimensions and key figures, integrate and consolidate sales planning with marketing or service plans, and optimize your supply chain through offline account planning. The solution enables territory management according to regions, product lines, or other variables, as well as opportunity planning and analysis and partner planning.
- **Sales analysis.** Provide your sales organizations with an accurate overview of current sales performance and an overview of sales force effectiveness.

survey indicated that many companies implementing ERP had overrun cost and schedule targets and had not achieved the benefits sought.

Despite the reservations about ERP, most companies surveyed by Harvard were going ahead with ERP initiatives. The most popular reasons cited included a desire to standardize and improve processes, to improve systems integration, and to improve information quality. Even though there is evidence of many problems with implementing ERP systems, firms continue in their ERP efforts because of the opportunity for substantial reward. SAP is now targeting small and medium-sized firms with their mySAP:ERP product described in the Breakthrough box.

CONCLUSION

The reason for including this managerial briefing at this point in the book is so you can see that the techniques described in this section are now commonly available and widely implemented in companies. In the following sections we discuss such forecasting tools as moving averages and exponential smoothing, inventory control tools such as material requirements planning, and scheduling using earliest due-date logic. All of these techniques are included in the leading ERP packages. One might think that there is no need to learn how these techniques actually work; all that needs to be done is fire up the ERP system and let it make all the decisions. If it were that simple, we would all be out of work.

In reality, there are many ways to implement these different techniques, and different techniques are applicable to different types of firms. R/3, for example, has three ways that forecasts can be calculated (discussed in Chapter 13) and five different lot-sizing rules for batch production (discussed in Chapter 16). So many different decisions need to be made to properly use any system.

To select from the many ERP systems that are available, one needs to evaluate the strengths and weaknesses of each offering. i2 Technologies has a very strong forecasting capability and is known for flow manufacturing scheduling. In Chapter 13 the different types of forecasting systems are discussed in some depth, giving you the ability to evaluate whether the unique characteristics of the i2 offering match what is needed by your firm. Similarly, in Chapter 16, all the different lot-sizing rules are studied, and the flow manufacturing concept is compared to traditional material requirements planning (MRP). Given this information, you can evaluate whether i2 would be good for your company.

In our writing this managerial briefing, one temptation was to include an extensive comparison of the various ERP systems available. (A great source of the most current information is the Operations Management Center at http://www.mhhe.com/pom). The problem with doing this and publishing it in a textbook is that by the time the book is printed the comparison would be out of date. Business software technology is moving at an amazing rate. Every day a new package becomes available with some slick trick that supposedly makes it better than the rest. To make matters worse, each vendor likes to tag names to things to give the appearance of something new. In reality, there are not many new ideas; conventional techniques are typically repackaged in new ways. Sometimes more efficient ways to implement these techniques are developed. Understanding the conventional approaches is an important first step to being able to keep up with this rapidly expanding area of software technology.

K E Y   T E R M S

Enterprise resource planning (ERP) A computer system that integrates application programs in accounting, sales, manufacturing, and the other functions in a firm. This integration is accomplished through a database shared by all the application programs.

Financial accounting A segment of R/3 that includes the financials, controlling, and asset management functionality needed to run the financial accounts for a company. Financials include accounts payable, accounts receivable, general ledger, capital investments, and the procedures to close the books for the month and year.

Human resources A segment with the capabilities needed to manage, schedule, pay, and hire the people who work for the company. This includes payroll, benefits administration, applicant data administration, personnel development planning, workforce planning, schedule and shift planning, time management, and travel expense accounting.

Manufacturing and logistics Contains five major components: materials management, plant maintenance, quality management, production planning and control, and project management.

Sales and distribution A segment that includes customer, sales order, and configuration management; distribution export controls; shipping and management; and billing, order, and rebate processing.

R E V I E W   A N D   D I S C U S S I O N   Q U E S T I O N S

1   What key technological features of SAP R/3 set it apart from conventional business accounting/planning/control software?

2   SAP R/3 allows the human resources, financial accounting, and manufacturing and logistics modules to be implemented separately. How would this change impact the implementation process?

3   A feature that many companies are considering is taking customer orders via Web sites. Put yourself in the place of the person at Ford Motor Company considering this approach to taking customer orders for the Ford Explorer sport utility vehicle. What information would you need to collect from the customer? What information would you give the customer regarding the order? How would the information be used within Ford Motor Company? What major problems would you anticipate need solving prior to implementing the system? If this project is successful—that is, customers find ordering their Explorer over the Web preferable to negotiating with a dealer—what are the long-term implications to Ford Motor Company?

SELECTED BIBLIOGRAPHY

ASAP World Consultancy et al. *Using SAP R/3*. Indianapolis, IN: Que, 1996.

Bancroft, N. *Implementing SAP R/3: How to Introduce a Large System into a Large Organization*. Greenwich, CT: Manning, 1996.

Curran, T.; G. Keller; and A. Ladd. *Business Blueprint: Understanding SAP's R/3 Reference Model*. Upper Saddle River, NJ: Prentice Hall, 1998.

Davenport, T. H. "Putting the Enterprise into the System." *Harvard Business Review*, July–August 1998.

Hernâandez, J. A. *The SAP R/3 Handbook*. New York: McGraw-Hill, 1997.

Jacobs, F. R., and D. C. Whybark. *Why ERP? A Primer on SAP Implementation*. New York: Irwin/McGraw-Hill, 2000.

Norris, G. *E-Business and ERP: Transforming the Enterprise*. New York: Wiley, 2000.

Shtub, A. *Enterprise Resource Planning: The Dynamics of Operations Management*. Boston: Kluwer Academic Publishers, 1999.

Wallace, T. F., and M. H. Kremzar. *ERP: Making It Happen: The Implementers' Guide to Success with Enterprise Resource Planning*. New York: Wiley, 2001.

FOOTNOTE

1 C. X. Escalle and M. Cotteleer, "Enterprise Resource Planning (ERP)," 9-699-020, Harvard Business School, February 11, 1999, p. 3.

chapter

FORECASTING

13

Wal-Mart's size and power in the retail industry is having a huge influence in the database industry. Wal-Mart manages one of the world's largest data warehouses with more than 35 terabytes of data. Wal-Mart's formula for success—getting the right product on the appropriate shelf at the lowest price—owes much to the company's multimillion-dollar investment in data warehousing. Wal-Mart has more detail than most of its competitors on what's going on by product, by store, and by day.

The systems track point of sale data at each store, inventory levels by store, products in transit, market statistics, customer demographics, finance, product returns, and supplier performance. The data are used for three broad areas of

decision support: analyzing trends, managing inventory, and understanding customers. What emerges are "personality traits" for each of Wal-Mart's 3,000 or so outlets, which Wal-Mart managers use to determine product mix and presentation for each store.

Data mining is next. Wal-Mart has developed a demand-forecasting application that looks at individual items for individual stores to decide the seasonal sales profile of each item. The system keeps a year's worth of data on the sales of 100,000 products and predicts which items will be needed in each store.

Wal-Mart is now doing market-basket analysis. Data are collected on items that make up a shopper's total purchase so that the company can analyze relationships and patterns in customer purchases. The data warehouse is made available over the Web to its store managers and suppliers.→

Cross Functional

Forecasts are vital to every business organization and for every significant management decision. Forecasting is the basis of corporate long-run planning. In the functional areas of finance and accounting, forecasts provide the basis for budgetary planning and cost control. Marketing relies on sales forecasting to plan new products, compensate sales personnel, and make other key decisions. Production and operations personnel use forecasts to make periodic decisions involving process selection, capacity planning, and facility layout, as well as for continual decisions about production planning, scheduling, and inventory.

Bear in mind that a perfect forecast is usually impossible. Too many factors in the business environment cannot be predicted with certainty. Therefore, rather than search for the perfect forecast, it is far more important to establish the practice of continual review of forecasts and to learn to live with inaccurate forecasts. This is not to say that we should not try to improve the forecasting model or methodology, but that we should try to find and use the best forecasting method available, *within reason.*

When forecasting, a good strategy is to use two or three methods and look at them for the commonsense view. Will expected changes in the general economy affect the forecast? Are there changes in industrial and private consumer behaviors? Will there be a shortage of essential complementary items? Continual review and updating in light of new data are basic to successful forecasting. In this chapter we look at *qualitative* and *quantitative* forecasting and concentrate primarily on several quantitative time series techniques. We cover in some depth moving averages, linear regression, trends, seasonal ratios (including deseasonalization), and focused forecasting. We also discuss sources and measurement of errors.

DEMAND MANAGEMENT

⊙⊙⊙○   The purpose of demand management is to coordinate and control all sources of demand so the productive system can be used efficiently and the product delivered on time.

Where does demand for a firm's product or service come from, and what can a firm do to manage it? There are two basic sources of demand: dependent demand and independent demand. **Dependent demand** is the demand for a product or service caused by the demand for other products or services. For example, if a firm sells 1,000 tricycles, then 1,000 front wheels and 2,000 rear wheels are needed. This type of internal demand needs not a forecast, just a tabulation. As to how many tricycles the firm might sell, this is called **independent demand** because its demand cannot be derived directly from that of other products.[1] We discuss dependence and independence more fully in Chapters 15 and 16.

Dependent demand

Independent demand

There is not much a firm can do about dependent demand. It must be met (although the product or service can be purchased rather than produced internally). But there is a lot a firm can do about independent demand—if it wants to. The firm can

1. **Take an active role to influence demand.**   The firm can apply pressure on its sales force, it can offer incentives both to customers and to its own personnel, it can wage campaigns to sell products, and it can cut prices. These actions can increase demand. Conversely, demand can be decreased through price increases or reduced sales efforts.
2. **Take a passive role and simply respond to demand.**   There are several reasons a firm may not try to change demand but simply accept what happens. If a firm is running at full capacity, it may not want to do anything about demand. Other reasons are a firm may be powerless to change demand because of the expense to advertise; the market may be fixed in size and static; or demand is beyond its control (such as in the case of sole supplier). There are other competitive, legal, environmental, ethical, and moral reasons that market demand is passively accepted.

A great deal of coordination is required to manage these dependent, independent, active, and passive demands. These demands originate both internally and externally in the form of new product sales from marketing, repair parts for previously sold products from product service, restocking from the factory warehouses, and supply items for manufacturing. In this chapter, our primary interest is in forecasting for independent items.

A GTE LABORATORIES ENGINEER EXAMINES A PRINT GENERATED BY GRANET, A GRAPHICS-BASED SOFTWARE TOOL DEVELOPED BY GTE TO HELP ENGINEERS WORLDWIDE PLAN CELLULAR NETWORKS AND FORECAST THEIR PERFORMANCE.

TYPES OF FORECASTING

Forecasting can be classified into four basic types: *qualitative, time series analysis, causal relationships,* and *simulation.*

Qualitative techniques are subjective or judgmental and are based on estimates and opinions. **Time series analysis,** the primary focus of this chapter, is based on the idea that data relating to past demand can be used to predict future demand. Past data may include several components, such as trend, seasonal, or cyclical influences, and are described in the following section. Causal forecasting, which we discuss using the linear regression technique, assumes that demand is related to some underlying factor or factors in the environment. Simulation models allow the forecaster to run through a range of assumptions about the condition of the forecast. Exhibit 13.1 describes a variety of the four basic types of forecasting models. In this chapter we discuss the first four time series analysis methods in the exhibit and the first of the causal techniques.

Time series analysis

COMPONENTS OF DEMAND

In most cases, demand for products or services can be broken down into six components: average demand for the period, a trend, seasonal element, cyclical elements, random variation, and autocorrelation. Exhibit 13.2 illustrates a demand over a four-year period, showing the average, trend, and seasonal components and randomness around the smoothed demand curve.

Cyclical factors are more difficult to determine because the time span may be unknown or the cause of the cycle may not be considered. Cyclical influence on demand may come from such occurrences as political elections, war, economic conditions, or sociological pressures.

Random variations are caused by chance events. Statistically, when all the known causes for demand (average, trend, seasonal, cyclical, and autocorrelative) are subtracted from total demand, what remains is the unexplained portion of demand. If we cannot identify the cause of this remainder, it is assumed to be purely random chance.

Autocorrelation denotes the persistence of occurrence. More specifically, the value expected at any point is highly correlated with its own past values. In waiting line theory, the length of a waiting line is highly autocorrelated. That is, if a line is relatively long at one time, then shortly after that time, we would expect the line still to be long.

When demand is random, it may vary widely from one week to another. Where high autocorrelation exists, demand is not expected to change very much from one week to the next.

exhibit 13.1

Forecasting Techniques and Common Models

I. Qualitative	Subjective; judgmental. Based on estimates and opinions.
Grass roots	Derives a forecast by compiling input from those at the end of the hierarchy who deal with what is being forecast. For example, an overall sales forecast may be derived by combining inputs from each salesperson who is closest to his or her own territory.
Market research	Sets out to collect data in a variety of ways (surveys, interviews, and so on) to test hypotheses about the market. This is typically used to forecast long-range and new product sales.
Panel consensus	Free open exchange at meetings. The idea is that discussion by the group will produce better forecasts than any one individual. Participants may be executives, salespeople, or customers.
Historical analogy	Ties what is being forecast to a similar item. Important in planning new products where a forecast may be derived by using the history of a similar product.
Delphi method	Group of experts responds to questionnaire. A moderator compiles results and formulates a new questionnaire that is submitted to the group. Thus, there is a learning process for the group as it receives new information and there is no influence of group pressure or dominating individuals.
II. Time series analysis	Based on the idea that the history of occurrences over time can be used to predict the future.
Simple moving average	A time period containing a number of data points is averaged by dividing the sum of the point values by the number of points. Each, therefore, has equal influence.
Weighted moving average	Specific points may be weighted more or less than the others, as seen fit by experience.
Exponential smoothing	Recent data points are weighted more with weighting declining exponentially as data become older.
Regression analysis	Fits a straight line to past data generally relating the data value to time. Most common fitting technique is least squares.
Box Jenkins technique	Very complicated but apparently the most accurate statistical technique available. Relates a class of statistical models to data and fits the model to the time series by using Bayesian posterior distributions.
Shiskin time series	(Also called X-11.) Developed by Julius Shiskin of the Census Bureau. An effective method to decompose a time series into seasonals, trends, and irregular. It needs at least three years of history. Very good in identifying turning points, for example, in company sales.
Trend projections	Fits a mathematical trend line to the data points and projects it into the future.
III. Causal	Tries to understand the system underlying and surrounding the item being forecast. For example, sales may be affected by advertising, quality, and competitors.
Regression analysis	Similar to least squares method in time series but may contain multiple variables. Basis is that forecast is caused by the occurrence of other events.
Econometric models	Attempts to describe some sector of the economy by a series of interdependent equations.
Input/output models	Focuses on sales of each industry to other firms and governments. Indicates the changes in sales that a producer industry might expect because of purchasing changes by another industry.
Leading indicators	Statistics that move in the same direction as the series being forecast but move before the series, such as an increase in the price of gasoline indicating a future drop in the sale of large cars.
IV. Simulation models	Dynamic models, usually computer-based, that allow the forecaster to make assumptions about the internal variables and external environment in the model. Depending on the variables in the model, the forecaster may ask such questions as, what would happen to my forecast if price increased by 10 percent? What effect would a mild national recession have on my forecast?

Historical Product Demand Consisting of a Growth Trend and Seasonal Demand

exhibit 13.2

**Excel:
Components
of Demand.xls**

Common Types of Trends

exhibit 13.3

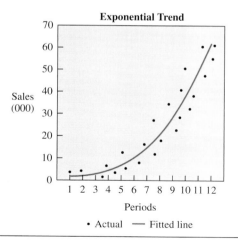

Trend lines are the usual starting point in developing a forecast. These trend lines are then adjusted for seasonal effects, cyclical elements, and any other expected events that may influence the final forecast. Exhibit 13.3 shows four of the most common types of trends. A linear trend is obviously a straight continuous relationship. An S-curve is typical of a product growth and maturity cycle. The most important point in the S-curve is where the trend changes from slow growth to fast growth, or from fast to slow. An asymptotic trend starts with the highest demand growth at the beginning but then tapers off. Such a curve could happen when a firm enters an existing market with the objective of saturating and capturing a large share of the market. An exponential curve is common in products with explosive growth. The exponential trend suggests that sales will continue to increase—an assumption that may not be safe to make.

A widely used forecasting method plots data and then searches for the standard distribution (such as linear, S-curve, asymptotic, or exponential) that fits best. The attractiveness of this method is that because the mathematics for the curve are known, solving for values for future time periods is easy.

Sometimes our data do not seem to fit any standard curve. This may be due to several causes essentially beating the data from several directions at the same time. For these cases, a simplistic but often effective forecast can be obtained by simply plotting data.

QUALITATIVE TECHNIQUES IN FORECASTING

GRASS ROOTS

As stated in Exhibit 13.1, *grass roots* forecasting builds the forecast by adding successively from the bottom. The assumption here is that the person closest to the customer or end use of the product knows its future needs best. Though this is not always true, in many instances it is a valid assumption, and it is the basis for this method.

Forecasts at this bottom level are summed and given to the next higher level. This is usually a district warehouse, which then adds in safety stocks and any effects of ordering quantity sizes. This amount is then fed to the next level, which may be a regional warehouse. The procedure repeats until it becomes an input at the top level, which, in the case of a manufacturing firm, would be the input to the production system.

MARKET RESEARCH

Firms often hire outside companies that specialize in *market research* to conduct this type of forecasting. You may have been involved in market surveys through a marketing class. Certainly you have not escaped telephone calls asking you about product preferences, your income, habits, and so on.

Market research is used mostly for product research in the sense of looking for new product ideas, likes and dislikes about existing products, which competitive products within a

A NUMBER OF FIRMS, INCLUDING THE GILMORE RESEARCH GROUP, NOW OFFER MARKETERS SOFTWARE OR DATABASES TO HELP THEM MORE ACCURATELY FORECAST SALES FOR SPECIFIC MARKET AREAS, PRODUCTS, OR SEGMENTS.

particular class are preferred, and so on. Again, the data collection methods are primarily surveys and interviews.

PANEL CONSENSUS

In a *panel consensus,* the idea that two heads are better than one is extrapolated to the idea that a panel of people from a variety of positions can develop a more reliable forecast than a narrower group. Panel forecasts are developed through open meetings with free exchange of ideas from all levels of management and individuals. The difficulty with this open style is that lower employee levels are intimidated by higher levels of management. For example, a salesperson in a particular product line may have a good estimate of future product demand but may not speak up to refute a much different estimate given by the vice president of marketing. The Delphi technique (which we discuss shortly) was developed to try to correct this impairment to free exchange.

When decisions in forecasting are at a broader, higher level (as when introducing a new product line or concerning strategic product decisions such as new marketing areas), the term *executive judgment* is generally used. The term is self-explanatory: a higher level of management is involved.

HISTORICAL ANALOGY

In trying to forecast demand for a new product, an ideal situation would be where an existing product or generic product could be used as a model. There are many ways to classify such analogies—for example, complementary products, substitutable or competitive products, and products as a function of income. Again, you have surely gotten a deluge of mail advertising products in a category similar to a product purchased via catalog, the Internet, or mail order. If you buy a DVD through the mail, you will receive more mail about new DVDs and DVD players. A causal relationship (listed in Exhibit 13.1, Part III) would be that demand for compact discs is caused by demand for DVD players. An analogy would be forecasting the demand for digital videodisc players by analyzing the historical demand for VCRs. The products are in the same general category of electronics and may be bought by consumers at similar rates. A simpler example would be toasters and coffee pots. A firm that already produces toasters and wants to produce coffee pots could use the toaster history as a likely growth model.

DELPHI METHOD

As we mentioned under panel consensus, a statement or opinion of a higher-level person will likely be weighted more than that of a lower-level person. The worst case is where lower-level people feel threatened and do not contribute their true beliefs. To prevent this problem, the *Delphi method* conceals the identity of the individuals participating in the study. Everyone has the same weight. Procedurally, a moderator creates a questionnaire and distributes it to participants. Their responses are summed and given back to the entire group along with a new set of questions.

The Delphi method was developed by the Rand Corporation in the 1950s. The step-by-step procedure is

1. Choose the experts to participate. There should be a variety of knowledgeable people in different areas.
2. Through a questionnaire (or e-mail), obtain forecasts (and any premises or qualifications for the forecasts) from all participants.
3. Summarize the results and redistribute them to the participants along with appropriate new questions.
4. Summarize again, refining forecasts and conditions, and again develop new questions.
5. Repeat Step 4 if necessary. Distribute the final results to all participants.

The Delphi technique can usually achieve satisfactory results in three rounds. The time required is a function of the number of participants, how much work is involved for them to develop their forecasts, and their speed in responding.

SOURCE: J. H. WILSON AND D. ALLISON-KOERBER, "COMBINING SUBJECTIVE AND OBJECTIVE FORECASTS IMPROVES RESULTS," *JOURNAL OF BUSINESS FORECASTING*, FALL 1992, P. 4.

exhibit 13.4   A Guide to Selecting an Appropriate Forecasting Method

FORECASTING METHOD	AMOUNT OF HISTORICAL DATA	DATA PATTERN	FORECAST HORIZON
Simple moving average	6 to 12 months, weekly data are often used	Data should be stationary (i.e., no trend or seasonality)	Short to medium
Weighted moving average and simple exponential smoothing	5 to 10 observations needed to start	Data should be stationary	Short
Exponential smoothing with trend	5 to 10 observations needed to start	Stationary and trend	Short
Linear regression	10 to 20 observations; for seasonality, at least 5 observations per season	Stationary, trend, and seasonality	Short to medium

TIME SERIES ANALYSIS

Interactive Operations Management

Time series forecasting models try to predict the future based on past data. For example, sales figures collected for the past six weeks can be used to forecast sales for the seventh week. Quarterly sales figures collected for the past several years can be used to forecast future quarters. Even though both examples contain sales, different forecasting time series models would likely be used.

Exhibit 13.4 shows the time series models discussed in the chapter and some of their characteristics. Terms such as *short, medium,* and *long* are relative to the context in which they are used. However, in business forecasting *short-term* usually refers to under three months; *medium-term,* three months to two years; and *long-term,* greater than two years. In general, the short-term models compensate for random variation and adjust for short-term changes (such as consumers' responses to a new product). Medium-term forecasts are useful for seasonal effects, and long-term models detect general trends and are especially useful in identifying major turning points.

Which forecasting model a firm should choose depends on

1. Time horizon to forecast.
2. Data availability.
3. Accuracy required.
4. Size of forecasting budget.
5. Availability of qualified personnel.

In selecting a forecasting model, there are other issues such as the firm's degree of flexibility. (The greater the ability to react quickly to changes, the less accurate the forecast needs to be.) Another item is the consequence of a bad forecast. If a large capital investment decision is to be based on a forecast, it should be a good forecast.

SIMPLE MOVING AVERAGE

When demand for a product is neither growing nor declining rapidly, and if it does not have seasonal characteristics, a moving average can be useful in removing the random fluctuations for forecasting. Although *moving averages* are frequently centered, it is more convenient to use past data to predict the following period directly. To illustrate, a centered five-month average of January, February, March, April, and May gives an average centered on March. However, all five months of data must already exist. If our objective is to forecast for June, we must project our moving average—by some means—from March to June. If the average is not centered but is at the forward end, we can forecast more easily, though we may lose some accuracy. Thus, if we want to forecast June with a five-month moving average, we can take the average of January, February, March, April, and May. When June passes, the forecast for July would be the average of February, March, April, May, and June. This is how Exhibits 13.5 and 13.6 were computed.

Forecast Demand Based on a Three- and a Nine-Week Simple Moving Average

exhibit 13.5

WEEK	DEMAND	3 WEEK	9 WEEK	WEEK	DEMAND	3 WEEK	9 WEEK
1	800			16	1,700	2,200	1,811
2	1,400			17	1,800	2,000	1,800
3	1,000			18	2,200	1,833	1,811
4	1,500	1,067		19	1,900	1,900	1,911
5	1,500	1,300		20	2,400	1,967	1,933
6	1,300	1,333		21	2,400	2,167	2,011
7	1,800	1,433		22	2,600	2,233	2,111
8	1,700	1,533		23	2,000	2,467	2,144
9	1,300	1,600		24	2,500	2,333	2,111
10	1,700	1,600	1,367	25	2,600	2,367	2,167
11	1,700	1,567	1,467	26	2,200	2,367	2,267
12	1,500	1,567	1,500	27	2,200	2,433	2,311
13	2,300	1,633	1,556	28	2,500	2,333	2,311
14	2,300	1,833	1,644	29	2,400	2,300	2,378
15	2,000	2,033	1,733	30	2,100	2,367	2,378

**Excel:
Forecasting**

Moving Average Forecast of Three- and Nine-Week Periods versus Actual Demand

exhibit 13.6

**Excel:
Forecasting**

Although it is important to select the best period for the moving average, there are several conflicting effects of different period lengths. The longer the moving average period, the more the random elements are smoothed (which may be desirable in many cases). But if there is a trend in the data—either increasing or decreasing—the moving average has the adverse characteristic of lagging the trend. Therefore, while a shorter time span produces more oscillation, there is a closer following of the trend. Conversely, a longer time span gives a smoother response but lags the trend.

The formula for a simple moving average is

[13.1]
$$F_t = \frac{A_{t-1} + A_{t-2} + A_{t-3} + \cdots + A_{t-n}}{n}$$

where

F_t = Forecast for the coming period
n = Number of periods to be averaged
A_{t-1} = Actual occurrence in the past period
$A_{t-2}, A_{t-3},$ and A_{t-n} = Actual occurrences two periods ago, three periods ago, and so on up to n periods ago

Exhibit 13.6, a plot of the data in Exhibit 13.5, shows the effects of various lengths of the period of a moving average. We see that the growth trend levels off at about the 23rd week. The three-week moving average responds better in following this change than the nine-week average, although overall, the nine-week average is smoother.

The main disadvantage in calculating a moving average is that all individual elements must be carried as data because a new forecast period involves adding new data and dropping the earliest data. For a three- or six-period moving average, this is not too severe. But plotting a 60-day moving average for the usage of each of 20,000 items in inventory would involve a significant amount of data.

WEIGHTED MOVING AVERAGE

Whereas the simple moving average gives equal weight to each component of the moving average database, a weighted moving average allows any weights to be placed on each element, providing, of course, that the sum of all weights equals 1. For example, a department store may find that in a four-month period, the best forecast is derived by using 40 percent of the actual sales for the most recent month, 30 percent of two months ago, 20 percent of three months ago, and 10 percent of four months ago. If actual sales experience was

MONTH 1	MONTH 2	MONTH 3	MONTH 4	MONTH 5
100	90	105	95	?

the forecast for month 5 would be

$$F_5 = 0.40(95) + 0.30(105) + 0.20(90) + 0.10(100)$$

$$= 38 + 31.5 + 18 + 10$$

$$= 97.5$$

The formula for a weighted moving average is

[13.2]
$$F_t = w_1 A_{t-1} + w_2 A_{t-2} + \cdots + w_n A_{t-n}$$

where

$w_1 =$ Weight to be given to the actual occurrence for the period $t - 1$
$w_2 =$ Weight to be given to the actual occurrence for the period $t - 2$
$w_n =$ Weight to be given to the actual occurrence for the period $t - n$
$n =$ Total number of periods in the forecast

Although many periods may be ignored (that is, their weights are zero) and the weighting scheme may be in any order (for example, more distant data may have greater weights than more recent data), the sum of all the weights must equal 1.

$$\sum_{i=1}^{n} w_i = 1$$

Suppose sales for month 5 actually turned out to be 110. Then the forecast for month 6 would be

$$F_6 = 0.40(110) + 0.30(95) + 0.20(105) + 0.10(90)$$

$$= 44 + 28.5 + 21 + 9$$

$$= 102.5$$

Choosing Weights   Experience and trial and error are the simplest ways to choose weights. As a general rule, the most recent past is the most important indicator of what to expect in the future, and, therefore, it should get higher weighting. The past month's revenue or plant capacity, for example, would be a better estimate for the coming month than the revenue or plant capacity of several months ago.

However, if the data are seasonal, for example, weights should be established accordingly. Bathing suit sales in July of last year should be weighted more heavily than bathing suit sales in December (in the Northern Hemisphere).

The weighted moving average has a definite advantage over the simple moving average in being able to vary the effects of past data. However, it is more inconvenient and costly to use than the exponential smoothing method, which we examine next.

EXPONENTIAL SMOOTHING

In the previous methods of forecasting (simple and weighted moving averages), the major drawback is the need to continually carry a large amount of historical data. (This is also true for regression analysis techniques, which we soon will cover.) As each new piece of data is added in these methods, the oldest observation is dropped, and the new forecast is calculated. In many applications (perhaps in most), the most recent occurrences are more indicative of the future than those in the more distant past. If this premise is valid—that the importance of data diminishes as the past becomes more distant—then **exponential smoothing** may be the most logical and easiest method to use.

Exponential smoothing

The reason this is called exponential smoothing is that each increment in the past is decreased by $(1 - \alpha)$. If α is 0.05, for example, weights for various periods would be as follows (α is defined below):

	WEIGHTING AT $\alpha = 0.05$
Most recent weighting $= \alpha(1 - \alpha)^0$	0.0500
Data one time period older $= \alpha(1 - \alpha)^1$	0.0475
Data two time periods older $= \alpha(1 - \alpha)^2$	0.0451
Data three time periods older $= \alpha(1 - \alpha)^3$	0.0429

Therefore, the exponents 0, 1, 2, 3, . . . , and so on give it its name.

Exponential smoothing is the most used of all forecasting techniques. It is an integral part of virtually all computerized forecasting programs, and it is widely used in ordering inventory in retail firms, wholesale companies, and service agencies.

Exponential smoothing techniques have become well accepted for six major reasons:

1. Exponential models are surprisingly accurate.
2. Formulating an exponential model is relatively easy.
3. The user can understand how the model works.
4. Little computation is required to use the model.
5. Computer storage requirements are small because of the limited use of historical data.
6. Tests for accuracy as to how well the model is performing are easy to compute.

In the exponential smoothing method, only three pieces of data are needed to forecast the future: the most recent forecast, the actual demand that occurred for that forecast period, and a **smoothing constant alpha (α)**. This smoothing constant determines the level of smoothing and the speed of reaction to differences between forecasts and actual occurrences. The value for the constant is determined both by the nature of the product and by the manager's sense of what constitutes a good response rate. For example, if a firm produced a standard item with relatively stable demand, the reaction rate to differences between actual and forecast demand would tend to be small, perhaps just 5 or 10 percentage points. However, if the firm were experiencing growth, it would be desirable to have a higher reaction rate, perhaps 15 to 30 percentage points, to give greater importance to recent growth experience. The more rapid the growth, the higher the reaction rate should be. Sometimes users of the simple moving average switch to exponential smoothing but like to keep the forecasts about the same as the simple moving average. In this case, α is approximated by $2 \div (n + 1)$, where n is the number of time periods.

Smoothing constant alpha (α)

The equation for a single exponential smoothing forecast is simply

[13.3]
$$F_t = F_{t-1} + \alpha(A_{t-1} - F_{t-1})$$

where

F_t = The exponentially smoothed forecast for period t
F_{t-1} = The exponentially smoothed forecast made for the prior period
A_{t-1} = The actual demand in the prior period
α = The desired response rate, or smoothing constant

This equation states that the new forecast is equal to the old forecast plus a portion of the error (the difference between the previous forecast and what actually occurred).[2]

To demonstrate the method, assume that the long-run demand for the product under study is relatively stable and a smoothing constant (α) of 0.05 is considered appropriate. If the exponential method were used as a continuing policy, a forecast would have been made for last month.[3] Assume that last month's forecast (F_{t-1}) was 1,050 units. If 1,000 actually were demanded, rather than 1,050, the forecast for this month would be

$$F_t = F_{t-1} + \alpha(A_{t-1} - F_{t-1})$$
$$= 1,050 + 0.05(1,000 - 1,050)$$
$$= 1,050 + 0.05(-50)$$
$$= 1,047.5 \text{ units}$$

Because the smoothing coefficient is small, the reaction of the new forecast to an error of 50 units is to decrease the next month's forecast by only $2\frac{1}{2}$ units.

Single exponential smoothing has the shortcoming of lagging changes in demand. Exhibit 13.7 presents actual data plotted as a smooth curve to show the lagging effects of the

exhibit 13.7

Exponential Forecasts versus Actual Demand for Units of a Product over Time Showing the Forecast Lag

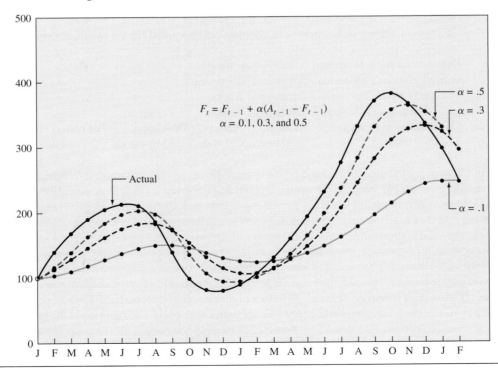

exponential forecasts. The forecast lags during an increase or decrease but overshoots when a change in direction occurs. Note that the higher the value of alpha, the more closely the forecast follows the actual. To more closely track actual demand, a trend factor may be added. Adjusting the value of alpha also helps. This is termed *adaptive forecasting*. Both trend effects and adaptive forecasting are briefly explained in following sections.

Trend Effects in Exponential Smoothing

Remember that an upward or downward trend in data collected over a sequence of time periods causes the exponential forecast to always lag behind (be above or below) the actual occurrence. Exponentially smoothed forecasts can be corrected somewhat by adding in a trend adjustment. To correct the trend, we need two smoothing constants. Besides the smoothing constant α, the trend equation also uses a **smoothing constant delta (δ).** The delta reduces the impact of the error that occurs between the actual and the forecast. If both alpha and delta are not included, the trend overreacts to errors.

Smoothing constant delta (δ)

To get the trend equation going, the first time it is used the trend value must be entered manually. This initial trend value can be an educated guess or a computation based on observed past data.

The equation to compute the forecast including trend (FIT) is

[13.4]
$$\text{FIT}_t = F_t + T_t$$

[13.5]
$$F_t = \text{FIT}_{t-1} + \alpha(A_{t-1} - \text{FIT}_{t-1})$$

[13.6]
$$T_t = T_{t-1} + \delta(F_t - \text{FIT}_{t-1})$$

where

F_t = The exponentially smoothed forecast for period t
T_t = The exponentially smoothed trend for period t
FIT_t = The forecast including trend for period t
FIT_{t-1} = The forecast including trend made for the prior period
A_{t-1} = The actual demand for the prior period
α = Smoothing constant
δ = Smoothing constant

EXAMPLE 13.1: Forecast Including Trend

Assume an initial starting F_t of 100 units, a trend of 10 units, an alpha of .20, and a delta of .30. If actual demand turned out to be 115 rather than the forecast 100, calculate the forecast for the next period.

SOLUTION

Adding the starting forecast and the trend, we have

$$\text{FIT}_{t-1} = F_{t-1} + T_{t-1} = 100 + 10 = 110$$

The actual A_{t-1} is given as 115. Therefore,

$$F_t = \text{FIT}_{t-1} + \alpha(A_{t-1} - \text{FIT}_{t-1})$$
$$= 110 + .2(115 - 110) = 111.0$$
$$T_t = T_{t-1} + \delta(F_t - \text{FIT}_{t-1})$$
$$= 10 + .3(111 - 110) = 10.3$$
$$\text{FIT}_t = F_t + T_t = 111.0 + 10.3 = 121.3$$

If, instead of 121.3, the actual turned out to be 120, the sequence would be repeated and the forecast for the next period would be

$$F_{t+1} = 121.3 + .2(120 - 121.3) = 121.04$$

$$T_{t+1} = 10.3 + .3(121.04 - 121.3) = 10.22$$

$$\text{FIT}_{t+1} = 121.04 + 10.22 = 131.26 \;\bullet$$

Choosing the Appropriate Value for Alpha   Exponential smoothing requires that the smoothing constant alpha (α) be given a value between 0 and 1. If the real demand is stable (such as demand for electricity or food), we would like a small alpha to lessen the effects of short-term or random changes. If the real demand is rapidly increasing or decreasing (such as in fashion items or new small appliances), we would like a large alpha to try to keep up with the change. It would be ideal if we could predict which alpha we should use. Unfortunately, two things work against us. First, it would take some passage of time to determine the alpha that would best fit our actual data. This would be tedious to follow and revise. Second, because demands do change, the alpha we pick this week may need to be revised soon. Therefore, we need some automatic method to track and change our alpha values.

There are two approaches to controlling the value of alpha. One uses various values of alpha. The other uses a tracking signal.

1. **Two or more predetermined values of alpha.**   The amount of error between the forecast and the actual demand is measured. Depending on the degree of error, different values of alpha are used. If the error is large, alpha is 0.8; if the error is small, alpha is 0.2.

2. **Computed values for alpha.**   A tracking alpha computes whether the forecast is keeping pace with genuine upward or downward changes in demand (as opposed to random changes). In this application, the tracking alpha is defined as the exponentially smoothed actual error divided by the exponentially smoothed absolute error. Alpha changes from period to period within the possible range of 0 to 1.

FORECAST ERRORS

In using the word *error,* we are referring to the difference between the forecast value and what actually occurred. In statistics, these errors are called *residuals.* As long as the forecast value is within the confidence limits, as we discuss later in "Measurement of Error," this is not really an error. But common usage refers to the difference as an error.

Demand for a product is generated through the interaction of a number of factors too complex to describe accurately in a model. Therefore, all forecasts certainly contain some error. In discussing forecast errors, it is convenient to distinguish between *sources of error* and the *measurement of error.*

SOURCES OF ERROR

Errors can come from a variety of sources. One common source that many forecasters are unaware of is projecting past trends into the future. For example, when we talk about statistical errors in regression analysis, we are referring to the deviations of observations from our regression line. It is common to attach a confidence band (that is, statistical control limits) to the regression line to reduce the unexplained error. But when we then use this regression line as a forecasting device by projecting it into the future, the error may not be correctly defined by the projected confidence band. This is because the confidence interval is based on past data; it may not hold for projected data points and therefore cannot be used with the same confidence. In fact, experience has shown that the actual errors tend to be greater than those predicted from forecast models.

Errors can be classified as bias or random. *Bias errors* occur when a consistent mistake is made. Sources of bias include the failure to include the right variables; the use of the wrong relationships among variables; employing of the wrong trend line; a mistaken shift in the seasonal demand from where it normally occurs; and the existence of some undetected secular trend. *Random errors* can be defined as those that cannot be explained by the forecast model being used.

MEASUREMENT OF ERROR

Several common terms used to describe the degree of error are *standard error, mean squared error* (or *variance*), and *mean absolute deviation*. In addition, tracking signals may be used to indicate any positive or negative bias in the forecast.

Standard error is discussed in the section on linear regression in this chapter. Because the standard error is the square root of a function, it is often more convenient to use the function itself. This is called the mean square error or variance.

The **mean absolute deviation (MAD)** was in vogue in the past but subsequently was ignored in favor of standard deviation and standard error measures. In recent years, MAD has made a comeback because of its simplicity and usefulness in obtaining tracking signals. MAD is the average error in the forecasts, using absolute values. It is valuable because MAD, like the standard deviation, measures the dispersion of some observed value from some expected value.

Mean absolute deviation (MAD)

MAD is computed using the differences between the actual demand and the forecast demand without regard to sign. It equals the sum of the absolute deviations divided by the number of data points, or, stated in equation form,

[13.7]
$$\text{MAD} = \frac{\sum_{i=1}^{n} |A_t - F_t|}{n}$$

where

t = Period number
A = Actual demand for the period
F = Forecast demand for the period
n = Total number of periods
$|\ |$ = A symbol used to indicate the absolute value disregarding positive and negative signs

When the errors that occur in the forecast are normally distributed (the usual case), the mean absolute deviation relates to the standard deviation as

$$1 \text{ standard deviation} = \sqrt{\frac{\pi}{2}} \times \text{MAD, or approximately } 1.25 \text{ MAD}$$

Conversely,

$$1 \text{ MAD} = 0.8 \text{ standard deviation}$$

The standard deviation is the larger measure. If the MAD of a set of points was found to be 60 units, then the standard deviation would be 75 units. In the usual statistical manner, if control limits were set at plus or minus 3 standard deviations (or ±3.75 MADs), then 99.7 percent of the points would fall within these limits.

A **tracking signal** is a measurement that indicates whether the forecast average is keeping pace with any genuine upward or downward changes in demand. As used in forecasting, the tracking signal is the *number* of mean absolute deviations that the forecast value is above or below the actual occurrence. Exhibit 13.8 shows a normal distribution with a mean of 0 and a MAD equal to 1. Thus, if we compute the tracking signal and find it equal to minus 2, we can see that the forecast model is providing forecasts that are quite a bit above the mean of the actual occurrences.

Tracking signal

exhibit 13.8   A Normal Distribution with Mean = 0 and MAD = 1

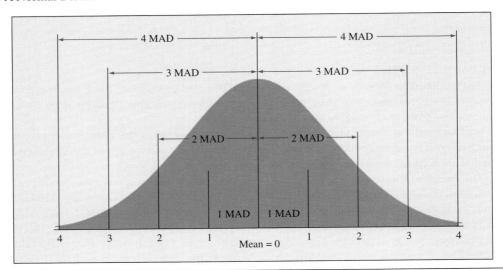

A tracking signal (TS) can be calculated using the arithmetic sum of forecast deviations divided by the mean absolute deviation:

[13.8]
$$TS = \frac{RSFE}{MAD}$$

where

   RSFE = The running sum of forecast errors, considering the nature of the error. (For example, negative errors cancel positive errors and vice versa.)
   MAD = The average of all the forecast errors (disregarding whether the deviations are positive or negative). It is the average of the absolute deviations.

Exhibit 13.9 illustrates the procedure for computing MAD and the tracking signal for a six-month period where the forecast had been set at a constant 1,000 and the actual demands that occurred are as shown. In this example, the forecast, on the average, was off by 66.7 units and the tracking signal was equal to 3.3 mean absolute deviations.

We can get a better feel for what the MAD and tracking signal mean by plotting the points on a graph. Though this is not completely legitimate from a sample-size standpoint, we plotted each month in Exhibit 13.10 to show the drift of the tracking signal. Note that it drifted from minus 1 MAD to plus 3.3 MADs. This happened because actual demand was greater than the forecast in four of the six periods. If the actual demand does not fall below the forecast to offset the continual positive RSFE, the tracking signal would continue to rise and we would conclude that assuming a demand of 1,000 is a bad forecast.

Acceptable limits for the tracking signal depend on the size of the demand being forecast (high-volume or high-revenue items should be monitored frequently) and the amount of personnel time available (narrower acceptable limits cause more forecasts to be out of limits and therefore require more time to investigate). Exhibit 13.11 shows the area within the control limits for a range of 1 to 4 MADs.

In a perfect forecasting model, the sum of the actual forecast errors would be 0; the errors that result in overestimates should be offset by errors that are underestimates. The tracking signal would then also be 0, indicating an unbiased model, neither leading nor lagging the actual demands.

Often MAD is used to forecast errors. It might then be desirable to make the MAD more sensitive to recent data. A useful technique to do this is to compute an exponentially smoothed

exhibit 13.9

Computing the Mean Absolute Deviation (MAD), the Running Sum of Forecast Errors (RSFE), and the Tracking Signal (TS) from Forecast and Actual Data

MONTH	DEMAND FORECAST	ACTUAL	DEVIATION	RSFE	ABS. DEV.	SUM OF ABS. DEV.	MAD*	$TS = \dfrac{RSFE^{\dagger}}{MAD}$
1	1,000	950	−50	−50	50	50	50	−1
2	1,000	1,070	+70	+20	70	120	60	.33
3	1,000	1,100	+100	+120	100	220	73.3	1.64
4	1,000	960	−40	+80	40	260	65	1.2
5	1,000	1,090	+90	+170	90	350	70	2.4
6	1,000	1,050	+50	+220	50	400	66.7	3.3

*For month 6, MAD = 400 ÷ 6 = 66.7.

†For month 6, $TS = \dfrac{RSFE}{MAD} = \dfrac{220}{66.7} = 3.3$ MADs.

**Excel:
Forecasting**

---

exhibit 13.10

A Plot of the Tracking Signals Calculated in Exhibit 13.9

**Excel:
Forecasting**

---

exhibit 13.11

The Percentages of Points Included within the Control Limits for a Range of 1 to 4 MADs

	CONTROL LIMITS	
NUMBER OF MADS	RELATED NUMBER OF STANDARD DEVIATIONS	PERCENTAGE OF POINTS LYING WITHIN CONTROL LIMITS
±1	0.798	57.048
±2	1.596	88.946
±3	2.394	98.334
±4	3.192	99.856

MAD as a forecast for the next period's error range. The procedure is similar to single exponential smoothing, covered earlier in this chapter. The value of the MAD forecast is to provide a range of error. In the case of inventory control, this is useful in setting safety stock levels.

$$MAD_t = \alpha|A_{t-1} - F_{t-1}| + (1 - \alpha)MAD_{t-1}$$

where

MAD_t = Forecast MAD for the *t*th period
α = Smoothing constant (normally in the range of 0.05 to 0.20)
A_{t-1} = Actual demand in the period $t - 1$
F_{t-1} = Forecast demand for period $t - 1$

LINEAR REGRESSION ANALYSIS

Regression can be defined as a functional relationship between two or more correlated variables. It is used to predict one variable given the other. The relationship is usually developed from observed data. The data should be plotted first to see if they appear linear or if at least parts of the data are linear. *Linear regression* refers to the special class of regression where the relationship between variables forms a straight line.

The linear regression line is of the form $Y = a + bX$, where Y is the value of the dependent variable that we are solving for, a is the Y intercept, b is the slope, and X is the independent variable. (In time series analysis, X is units of time.)

Linear regression is useful for long-term forecasting of major occurrences and aggregate planning. For example, linear regression would be very useful to forecast demands for product families. Even though demand for individual products within a family may vary widely during a time period, demand for the total product family is surprisingly smooth.

Linear regression forecasting

The major restriction in using **linear regression forecasting** is, as the name implies, that past data and future projections are assumed to fall about a straight line. Although this does limit its application, sometimes, if we use a shorter period of time, linear regression analysis can still be used. For example, there may be short segments of the longer period that are approximately linear.

Linear regression is used both for time series forecasting and for causal relationship forecasting. When the dependent variable (usually the vertical axis on a graph) changes as a result of time (plotted as the horizontal axis), it is time series analysis. If one variable changes because of the change in another variable, this is a causal relationship (such as the number of deaths from lung cancer increasing with the number of people who smoke).

We use the following example to demonstrate linear least squares regression analysis.

EXAMPLE 13.2: Least Squares Method

A firm's sales for a product line during the 12 quarters of the past three years were as follows:

QUARTER	SALES	QUARTER	SALES
1	600	7	2,600
2	1,550	8	2,900
3	1,500	9	3,800
4	1,500	10	4,500
5	2,400	11	4,000
6	3,100	12	4,900

The firm wants to forecast each quarter of the fourth year—that is, quarters 13, 14, 15, and 16.

SOLUTION

The least squares equation for linear regression is

[13.9]
$$Y = a + bx$$

where

Y = Dependent variable computed by the equation
y = The actual dependent variable data point (used below)
a = Y intercept
b = Slope of the line
x = Time period

Least Squares Regression Line

exhibit 13.12

**Excel:
Forecasting**

The least squares method tries to fit the line to the data *that minimizes the sum of the squares of the vertical distance* between each data point and its corresponding point on the line. If a straight line is drawn through the general area of the points, the difference between the point and the line is $y - Y$. Exhibit 13.12 shows these differences. The sum of the squares of the differences between the plotted data points and the line points is

$$(y_1 - Y_1)^2 + (y_2 - Y_2)^2 + \cdots + (y_{12} - Y_{12})^2$$

The best line to use is the one that minimizes this total.

As before, the straight line equation is

$$Y = a + bx$$

Previously we determined a and b from the graph. In the least squares method, the equations for a and b are

[13.10]
$$a = \bar{y} - b\bar{x}$$

[13.11]
$$b = \frac{\sum xy - n\bar{x} \cdot \bar{y}}{\sum x^2 - n\bar{x}^2}$$

where

$a = Y$ intercept
$b =$ Slope of the line
$\bar{y} =$ Average of all ys
$\bar{x} =$ Average of all xs
$x = x$ value at each data point
$y = y$ value at each data point
$n =$ Number of data points
$Y =$ Value of the dependent variable computed with the regression equation

exhibit 13.13

Least Squares Regression Analysis

**Excel:
Forecasting**

(1)x	(2)y	(3)xy	(4)x^2	(5)y^2	(6)Y
1	600	600	1	360,000	801.3
2	1,550	3,100	4	2,402,500	1,160.9
3	1,500	4,500	9	2,250,000	1,520.5
4	1,500	6,000	16	2,250,000	1,880.1
5	2,400	12,000	25	5,760,000	2,239.7
6	3,100	18,600	36	9,610,000	2,599.4
7	2,600	18,200	49	6,760,000	2,959.0
8	2,900	23,200	64	8,410,000	3,318.6
9	3,800	34,200	81	14,440,000	3,678.2
10	4,500	45,000	100	20,250,000	4,037.8
11	4,000	44,000	121	16,000,000	4,397.4
12	4,900	58,800	144	24,010,000	4,757.1
78	33,350	268,200	650	112,502,500	

$\bar{x} = 6.5$ $b = 359.6153$

$\bar{y} = 2{,}779.17$ $a = 441.6666$

Therefore $Y = 441.66 + 359.6x$

$S_{yx} = 363.9$

Exhibit 13.13 shows these computations carried out for the 12 data points in the problem. Note that the final equation for Y shows an intercept of 441.6 and a slope of 359.6. The slope shows that for every unit change in X, Y changes by 359.6.

Strictly based on the equation, forecasts for periods 13 through 16 would be

$$Y_{13} = 441.6 + 359.6(13) = 5{,}116.4$$

$$Y_{14} = 441.6 + 359.6(14) = 5{,}476.0$$

$$Y_{15} = 441.6 + 359.6(15) = 5{,}835.6$$

$$Y_{16} = 441.6 + 359.6(16) = 6{,}195.2$$

The standard error of estimate, or how well the line fits the data, is[4]

[13.12]
$$S_{yx} = \sqrt{\frac{\sum_{i=1}^{n}(y_i - Y_i)^2}{n - 2}}$$

The standard error of estimate is computed from the second and last columns of Exhibit 13.13:

$$S_{yx} = \sqrt{\frac{(600 - 801.3)^2 + (1{,}550 - 1{,}160.9)^2 + (1{,}500 - 1{,}520.5)^2 + \cdots + (4{,}900 - 4{,}757.1)^2}{10}}$$

$$= 363.9$$

Microsoft® Excel has a very powerful regression tool designed to perform these calculations. To use the tool, a table is needed that contains data relevant to the problem (see Exhibit 13.14). The tool is part of the Data Analysis ToolPak that is accessed from the Tools menu (you may need to add this to your Tools options by using the Add-In option under Tools).

To use the tool, first input the data in two columns in your spreadsheet, then access the Regression option from the Tools → Data Analysis menu. Next, specify the Y Range, which is B2:B13, and the X-Range, which is A2:A13 in our exmple. Finally, an Output Range is specified. This is where you

Excel Regression Tool

exhibit 13.14

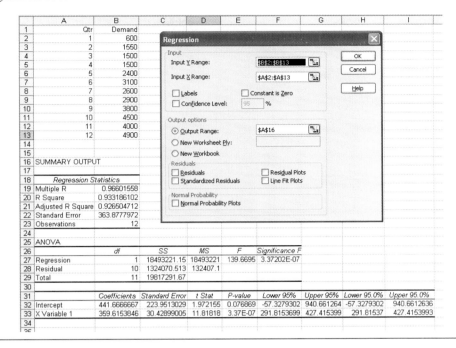

would like the results of the regression analysis placed in your spreadsheet. In the example A16 is entered. There is some information provided that goes beyond what we have covered, but what you are looking for is the Intercept and X Variable coefficients that correspond to the intercept and slope values in the linear equation. These are in rows 32 and 33 in Exhibit 13.14. ●

We discuss the possible existence of seasonal components in the next section on decomposition of a time series.

DECOMPOSITION OF A TIME SERIES

A *time series* can be defined as chronologically ordered data that may contain one or more components of demand: trend, seasonal, cyclical, autocorrelation, and random. *Decomposition* of a time series means identifying and separating the time series data into these components. In practice, it is relatively easy to identify the trend (even without mathematical analysis, it is usually easy to plot and see the direction of movement) and the seasonal component (by comparing the same period year to year). It is considerably more difficult to identify the cycles (these may be many months or years long), autocorrelation, and random components. (The forecaster usually calls random anything left over that cannot be identified as another component.)

When demand contains both seasonal and trend effects at the same time, the question is how they relate to each other. In this description, we examine two types of seasonal variation: *additive* and *multiplicative*.

Additive Seasonal Variation   Additive seasonal variation simply assumes that the seasonal amount is a constant no matter what the trend or average amount is.

$$\text{Forecast including trend and seasonal} = \text{Trend} + \text{Seasonal}$$

Exhibit 13.15A shows an example of increasing trend with constant seasonal amounts.

exhibit 13.15   Additive and Multiplicative Seasonal Variation Superimposed on Changing Trend

A. Additive Seasonal

B. Multiplicative Seasonal

**Excel:
Forecasting.xls**

COMPANIES SUCH AS TORO MANUFACTURE LAWNMOWERS AND SNOW BLOWERS TO MATCH SEASONAL DEMAND. USING THE SAME EQUIPMENT AND ASSEMBLY LINES PROVIDES BETTER CAPACITY UTILIZATION, WORKFORCE STABILITY, PRODUCTIVITY, AND REVENUE.

Multiplicative Seasonal Variation   In multiplicative seasonal variation, the trend is multiplied by the seasonal factors.

$$\text{Forecast including trend and seasonal} = \text{Trend} \times \text{Seasonal factor}$$

Exhibit 13.15B shows the seasonal variation increasing as the trend increases because its size depends on the trend.

The multiplicative seasonal variation is the usual experience. Essentially, this says that the larger the basic amount projected, the larger the variation around this that we can expect.

Seasonal Factor (or Index)   A seasonal factor is the amount of correction needed in a time series to adjust for the season of the year.

We usually associate *seasonal* with a period of the year characterized by some particular activity. We use the word *cyclical* to indicate other than annual recurrent periods of repetitive activity.

The following examples show how seasonal indexes are determined and used to forecast (1) a simple calculation based on past seasonal data and (2) the trend and seasonal index from a hand-fit regression line. We follow this with a more formal procedure for the decomposition of data and forecasting using least squares regression.

EXAMPLE 13.3: Simple Proportion

Assume that in past years, a firm sold an average of 1,000 units of a particular product line each year. On the average, 200 units were sold in the spring, 350 in the summer, 300 in the fall, and 150 in the winter. The seasonal factor (or index) is the ratio of the amount sold during each season divided by the average for all seasons.

SOLUTION

In this example, the yearly amount divided equally over all seasons is $1,000 \div 4 = 250$. The seasonal factors therefore are

	PAST SALES	AVERAGE SALES FOR EACH SEASON (1,000/4)	SEASONAL FACTOR
Spring	200	250	200/250 = 0.8
Summer	350	250	350/250 = 1.4
Fall	300	250	300/250 = 1.2
Winter	150	250	150/250 = 0.6
Total	1,000		

Using these factors, if we expected demand for next year to be 1,100 units, we would forecast the demand to occur as

	EXPECTED DEMAND FOR NEXT YEAR	AVERAGE SALES FOR EACH SEASON (1,100/4)		SEASONAL FACTOR		NEXT YEAR'S SEASONAL FORECAST
Spring		275	×	0.8	=	220
Summer		275	×	1.4	=	385
Fall		275	×	1.2	=	330
Winter		275	×	0.6	=	165
Total	1,100					

The seasonal factor may be periodically updated as new data are available. The following example shows the seasonal factor and multiplicative seasonal variation.

EXAMPLE 13.4: Computing Trend and Seasonal Factor from a Hand-Fit Straight Line

Here we must compute the trend as well as the seasonal factors.

SOLUTION

We solve this problem by simply hand fitting a straight line through the data points and measuring the trend and intercept from the graph. Assume the history of data is

QUARTER	AMOUNT	QUARTER	AMOUNT
I—2004	300	I—2005	520
II—2004	200	II—2005	420
III—2004	220	III—2005	400
IV—2004	530	IV—2005	700

exhibit 13.16

A Plot of Quarterly Demand History

exhibit 13.17

Computing a Seasonal Factor from the Actual Data and Trend Line

QUARTER	ACTUAL AMOUNT	FROM TREND EQUATION $T_t = 170 + 55t$	RATIO OF ACTUAL ÷ TREND	SEASONAL FACTOR (AVERAGE OF SAME QUARTERS IN BOTH YEARS)
2004				
I	300	225	1.33	I—1.25
II	200	280	.71	II—0.78
III	220	335	.66	III—0.69
IV	530	390	1.36	IV—1.25
2005				
I	520	445	1.17	
II	420	500	.84	
III	400	555	.72	
IV	700	610	1.15	

First, we plot as in Exhibit 13.16 and then visually fit a straight line through the data. (Naturally, this line and the resulting equation are subject to variation.) The equation for the line is

$$\text{Trend}_t = 170 + 55t$$

Our equation was derived from the intercept 170 plus a rise of $(610 - 170) \div 8$ periods. Next we can derive a seasonal index by comparing the actual data with the trend line as in Exhibit 13.17. The seasonal factor was developed by averaging the same quarters in each year.

We can compute the 2006 forecast including trend and seasonal factors (FITS) as follows:

$$\text{FITS}_t = \text{Trend} \times \text{Seasonal}$$

$$\text{I—2006 FITS}_9 = [170 + 55(9)]1.25 = 831$$

$$\text{II—2006 FITS}_{10} = [170 + 55(10)]0.78 = 562$$

$$\text{III—2006 FITS}_{11} = [170 + 55(11)]0.69 = 535$$

$$\text{IV—2006 FITS}_{12} = [170 + 55(12)]1.25 = 1,038$$

Decomposition Using Least Squares Regression   Decomposition of a time series means finding the series' basic components of trend, seasonal, and cyclical. Indexes are calculated for seasons and cycles. The forecasting procedure then reverses the process by projecting the trend and adjusting it by the seasonal and cyclical indexes, which were determined in the decomposition process. More formally, the process is

1. Decompose the time series into its components.
   a. Find seasonal component.
   b. Deseasonalize the demand.
   c. Find trend component.
2. Forecast future values of each component.
   a. Project trend component into the future.
   b. Multiply trend component by seasonal component.

Note that the random component is not included in this list. We implicitly remove the random component from the time series when we average as in Step 1. It is pointless to attempt a projection of the random component in Step 2 unless we have information about some unusual event, such as a major labor dispute, that could adversely affect product demand (and this would not really be random).

Exhibit 13.18 shows the decomposition of a time series using least squares regression and the same basic data we used in our earlier examples. Each data point corresponds to using a

Deseasonalized Demand

exhibit 13.18

(1) PERIOD (x)	(2) QUARTER	(3) ACTUAL DEMAND (y)	(4) AVERAGE OF THE SAME QUARTERS OF EACH YEAR	(5) SEASONAL FACTOR	(6) DESEASONALIZED DEMAND (y_d) COL. (3) ÷ COL. (5)	(7) x^2 (COL. 1)^2	(8) $x \times y_d$ COL. (1) × COL. (6)
1	I	600	(600 + 2,400 + 3,800)/3 = 2,266.7	0.82	735.7	1	735.7
2	II	1,550	(1,550 + 3,100 + 4,500)/3 = 3,050	1.10	1,412.4	4	2,824.7
3	III	1,500	(1,500 + 2,600 + 4,000)/3 = 2,700	0.97	1,544.0	9	4,631.9
4	IV	1,500	(1,500 + 2,900 + 4,900)/3 = 3,100	1.12	1,344.8	16	5,379.0
5	I	2,400		0.82	2,942.6	25	14,713.2
6	II	3,100		1.10	2,824.7	36	16,948.4
7	III	2,600		0.97	2,676.2	49	18,733.6
8	IV	2,900		1.12	2,599.9	64	20,798.9
9	I	3,800		0.82	4,659.2	81	41,932.7
10	II	4,500		1.10	4,100.4	100	41,004.1
11	III	4,000		0.97	4,117.3	121	45,290.1
12	IV	4,900		1.12	4,392.9	144	52,714.5
78		33,350		12.03	33,350.1*	650	265,706.9

$$\bar{x} = \frac{78}{12} = 6.5 \qquad b = \frac{\sum xy_d - n\bar{x}\bar{y}_d}{\sum x^2 - n\bar{x}^2} = \frac{265,706.9 - 12(6.5)2,779.2}{650 - 12(6.5)^2} = 342.2$$

$$\bar{y}_d = 33,350/12 = 2,779.2 \qquad a = \bar{y}_d - b\bar{x} = 2,779.2 - 342.2(6.5) = 554.9$$

Therefore $Y = a + bx = 554.9 + 342.2x$

*Column 3 and column 6 totals should be equal at 33,350. Differences are due to rounding. Column 5 was rounded to two decimal places.

single three-month quarter of the three-year (12-quarter) period. Our objective is to forecast demand for the four quarters of the fourth year.

Step 1. Determine the seasonal factor (or index).   Exhibit 13.18 summarizes the calculations needed. Column 4 develops an average for the same quarters in the three-year period. For example, the first quarters of the three years are added together and divided by three. A seasonal factor is then derived by dividing that average by the general average for all 12 quarters $\left(\dfrac{33{,}350}{12}, \text{ or } 2{,}779\right)$. These are entered in column 5. Note that the seasonal factors are identical for similar quarters in each year.

Step 2. Deseasonalize the original data.   To remove the seasonal effect on the data, we divide the original data by the seasonal factor. This step is called the deseasonalization of demand and is shown in column 6 of Exhibit 13.18.

Step 3. Develop a least squares regression line for the deseasonalized data.   The purpose here is to develop an equation for the trend line Y, which we then modify with the seasonal factor. The procedure is the same as we used before:

$$Y = a + bx$$

where

   y_d = Deseasonalized demand (see Exhibit 13.18)
   x = Quarter
   Y = Demand computed using the regression equation $Y = a + bx$
   a = Y intercept
   b = Slope of the line

The least squares calculations using columns 1, 7, and 8 of Exhibit 13.18 are shown in the lower section of the exhibit. The final deseasonalized equation for our data is $Y = 554.9 + 342.2x$. This straight line is shown in Exhibit 13.19.

Step 4. Project the regression line through the period to be forecast.   Our purpose is to forecast periods 13 through 16. We start by solving the equation for Y at each of these periods (shown in step 5, column 3).

Step 5. Create the final forecast by adjusting the regression line by the seasonal factor.   Recall that the Y equation has been deseasonalized. We now reverse the procedure by

---

exhibit 13.19

Straight Line Graph of Deseasonalized Equation

**Excel:
Forecasting.xls**

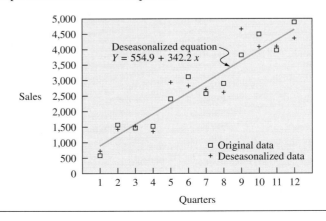

exhibit 13.20

Prediction Intervals for Linear Trend

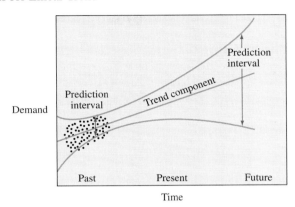

multiplying the quarterly data we derived by the seasonal factor for that quarter:

PERIOD	QUARTER	Y FROM REGRESSION LINE	SEASONAL FACTOR	FORECAST ($Y \times$ SEASONAL FACTOR)
13	1	5,003.5	0.82	4,102.87
14	2	5,345.7	1.10	5,880.27
15	3	5,687.9	0.97	5,517.26
16	4	6,030.1	1.12	6,753.71

Our forecast is now complete. The procedure is generally the same as what we did in the hand-fit previous example. In the present example, however, we followed a more formal procedure and computed the least squares regression line as well.

Error Range   When a straight line is fitted through data points and then used for forecasting, errors can come from two sources. First, there are the usual errors similar to the standard deviation of any set of data. Second, there are errors that arise because the line is wrong. Exhibit 13.20 shows this error range. Instead of developing the statistics here, we will briefly show why the range broadens. First, visualize that one line is drawn that has some error in that it slants too steeply upward. Standard errors are then calculated for this line. Now visualize another line that slants too steeply downward. It also has a standard error. The total error range, for this analysis, consists of errors resulting from both lines as well as all other possible lines. We included this exhibit to show how the error range widens as we go further into the future.

CAUSAL RELATIONSHIP FORECASTING

To be of value for the purpose of forecasting, any independent variable must be a leading indicator. For example, we can expect that an extended period of rain will increase sales of umbrellas and raincoats. The rain causes the sale of rain gear. This is a **causal relationship**, where one occurrence causes another. If the causing element is known far enough in advance, it can be used as a basis for forecasting.

Causal relationship

The first step in causal relationship forecasting is to find those occurrences that are really the causes. Often leading indicators are not causal relationships, but in some indirect way, they may suggest that some other things might happen. Other noncausal relationships just seem to exist as a coincidence. One study some years ago showed that the amount of alcohol sold in Sweden was directly proportional to teachers' salaries. Presumably this was a spurious (false) relationship. The following shows one example of a forecast using a causal relationship.

exhibit 13.21   Causal Relationship: Sales to Housing Starts

**Excel:
Forecasting**

EXAMPLE 13.5: Forecasting Using a Causal Relationship

The Carpet City Store in Carpenteria has kept records of its sales (in square yards) each year, along with the number of permits for new houses in its area.

	NUMBER OF HOUSING STARTS	
YEAR	PERMITS	SALES (IN SQ. YDS.)
1997	18	13,000
1998	15	12,000
1999	12	11,000
2000	10	10,000
2001	20	14,000
2002	28	16,000
2003	35	19,000
2004	30	17,000
2005	20	13,000

Carpet City's operations manager believes forecasting sales is possible if housing starts are known for that year. First, the data are plotted in Exhibit 13.21, with

$x =$ Number of housing start permits
$y =$ Sales of carpeting

Because the points appear to be in a straight line, the manager decides to use the linear relationship $Y = a + bx$. We solve this problem by hand fitting a line. We could also solve for this equation using least squares regression as we did earlier.

SOLUTION

Projecting the hand-fit line causes it to intercept the Y axis at about 7,000 yards. This could be interpreted as the demand when no new houses are built; that is, probably as replacement for old carpeting. To estimate the slope, two points are selected, such as

YEAR	x	y
2000	10	10,000
2004	30	17,000

From algebra the slope is calculated as

$$b = \frac{y(2004) - y(2000)}{x(2004) - x(2000)} = \frac{17,000 - 10,000}{30 - 10} = \frac{7,000}{20} = 350$$

The manager interprets the slope as the average number of square yards of carpet sold for each new house built in the area. The forecasting equation is therefore

$$Y = 7,000 + 350x$$

Now suppose that there are 25 permits for houses to be built in 2006. The 2006 sales forecast would therefore be

$$7,000 + 350(25) = 15,750 \text{ square yards}$$

In this problem, the lag between filing the permit with the appropriate agency and the new homeowner coming to Carpet City to buy carpet makes a causal relationship feasible for forecasting. ●

MULTIPLE REGRESSION ANALYSIS

Another forecasting method is multiple regression analysis, in which a number of variables are considered, together with the effects of each on the item of interest. For example, in the home furnishings field, the effects of the number of marriages, housing starts, disposable income, and the trend can be expressed in a multiple regression equation as

$$S = B + B_m(M) + B_h(H) + B_i(I) + B_t(T)$$

where

S = Gross sales for year
B = Base sales, a starting point from which other factors have influence
M = Marriages during the year
H = Housing starts during the year
I = Annual disposable personal income
T = Time trend (first year = 1, second = 2, third = 3, and so forth)

B_m, B_h, B_i, and B_t represent the influence on expected sales of the numbers of marriages and housing starts, income, and trend.

Forecasting by multiple regression is appropriate when a number of factors influence a variable of interest—in this case, sales. Its difficulty lies with the mathematical computation. Fortunately, standard computer programs for multiple regression analysis are available, relieving the need for tedious manual calculation.

Microsoft Excel® supports the time series analysis techniques described in this section. These functions are available under the Tools → Data Analysis menu. Analysis tools for exponential smoothing, moving averages, and regression are available.

FOCUS FORECASTING

Focus forecasting

⚪⚪⚪⚪ Focus forecasting is the creation of Bernie Smith.[5] Smith uses it primarily in finished goods inventory management. Smith substantiates strong arguments that statistical approaches used in forecasting do not give the best results. He states that simple techniques that work well on past data also prove the best in forecasting the future.

METHODOLOGY OF FOCUS FORECASTING

Focus forecasting simply tries several rules that seem logical and easy to understand to project past data into the future. Each of these rules is used in a computer simulation program to actually project demand and then measure how well that rule performed when compared to what actually happened. Therefore, the two components of the focus forecasting system are (1) several simple forecasting rules and (2) computer simulation of these rules on past data.

These are simple, commonsense rules made up and then tested to see whether they should be kept. Examples of simple forecasting rules could include

1. Whatever we sold in the past three months is what we will probably sell in the next three months.
2. What we sold in the same three-month period last year, we will probably sell in that three-month period this year. (This would account for seasonal effects.)
3. We will probably sell 10 percent more in the next three months than we sold in the past three months.
4. We will probably sell 50 percent more over the next three months than we did for the same three months of last year.
5. Whatever percentage change we had for the past three months this year compared to the same three months last year will probably be the same percentage change that we will have for the next three months of this year.

These forecasting rules are not hard and fast. If a new rule seems to work well, it is added. If one has not been working well, it is deleted.

The second part of the process is computer simulation. To use the system, a data history should be available—for example, 18 to 24 months of data. The simulation process then uses each forecasting rule to predict some recent past data. The rule that did best in predicting the past is the rule used to predict the future. Example 13.6 is an exercise used by Smith.[6]

EXAMPLE 13.6: Demand in Units for a Broiler Pan

The following table shows unit demand for a broiler pan over an 18-month period. (Try to guess what demand might be for July, August, and September this year, and compare your guess to the actual data presented later.)

	LAST YEAR	THIS YEAR		LAST YEAR	THIS YEAR
January	6	72	July	167	
February	212	90	August	159	
March	378	108	September	201	
April	129	134	October	153	
May	163	92	November	76	
June	96	137	December	30	

SOLUTION

For brevity, we use only two rules to demonstrate the method: 1 and 5. In practice, they would all be used.

Using focus forecasting, we first try forecasting rule 1—whatever we sold in the past three months is what we will probably sell in the next three months. (We are using the terms *demands* and *sales* interchangeably, assuming that demands culminate in actual sales.) We first test this rule on the past three months:

$$\text{Forecast (April, May, June)} = \text{Demand (January + February + March)}$$
$$= 72 + 90 + 108 = 270$$

Because what actually occurred was 363 (134 + 92 + 137), the forecast was 270/363 = 74 percent. In other words, it was 26 percent low.

Let's try another, say, rule 5—whatever percentage change we had over last year in the past three months will probably be our percentage change over last year in the next three months.

Forecast (April + May + June)

$$= \frac{\text{Demand (January + February + March) this year}}{\text{Demand (January + February + March) last year}}$$

$$\times \text{ Demand (April + May + June) last year}$$

$$= \frac{72 + 90 + 108}{6 + 212 + 378} \times (129 + 163 + 96)$$

$$= \frac{270}{596}(388) = 175.77$$

What actually occurred during April, May, and June this year was 363, so the forecast was 175/363, or only 48 percent of the actual demand.

Because rule 1 was better in predicting the past three months, we use that rule in predicting July, August, and September of this year. Rule 1 says that whatever we sold in the past three months is what we will probably sell in the next three months.

$$\text{Forecast (July + August + September)} = \text{Demand (April + May + June)}$$
$$= 134 + 92 + 137 = 363$$

The actual demand for the period was 357, as seen in the table, which shows the completed demand history for this year and serves as a basis for comparison.

	LAST YEAR	THIS YEAR		LAST YEAR	THIS YEAR
January	6	72	July	167	120
February	212	90	August	159	151
March	378	108	September	201	86
April	129	134	October	153	113
May	163	92	November	76	97
June	96	137	December	30	40

Forecasts made using focus forecasting logic are then reviewed and modified (if necessary) by buyers or inventory control personnel who have responsibility over these items. When they see the forecasts made by the computer, they know which method was used and can either accept it or change the forecast if they do not agree. Smith says that about 8 percent of the forecasts are changed by the buyers because they know something that the computer does not (such as the cause of a previous large demand, or that the next forecast is too high because a competitor is introducing a competing product).

Smith states that in all the forecast simulations he has run using variations of exponential smoothing (including adaptive smoothing), focus forecasting gave significantly better results.

WEB-BASED FORECASTING: COLLABORATIVE PLANNING, FORECASTING, AND REPLENISHMENT (CPFR)[7]

Collaborative Planning, Forecasting, and Replenishment (CPFR)

◯◯◯◯◯ Proposed in 1995, **Collaborative Planning, Forecasting, and Replenishment (CPFR)** has evolved into a Web-based tool used to coordinate demand forecasting, production and purchase planning, and inventory replenishment between supply chain trading partners. CPFR is being used as a means of integrating all members of an *n*-tier supply chain, including manufacturers, distributors, and retailers. As depicted in Exhibit 13.22, the ideal point of collaboration utilizing CPFR is the retail-level demand forecast, which is successively used to synchronize forecasts, production, and replenishment plans upstream through the supply chain.

Although the methodology is applicable to any industry, CPFR applications to date have largely focused on the food, apparel, and general merchandise industries. The potential benefits of sharing information for enhanced planning visibility in any supply chain are enormous. Various estimates for cost savings attributable to improved supply chain coordination have been proposed, including $30 billion annually in the food industry alone.[8]

CPFR's objective is to exchange selected internal information on a shared Web server in order to provide for reliable, longer-term future views of demand in the supply chain. CPFR uses a cyclic and iterative approach to derive consensus supply chain forecasts. It consists of the following five steps.

> **Step 1. Creation of a front-end partnership agreement.** This agreement specifies (1) objectives (e.g., inventory reductions, lost sale elimination, lower product obsolescence) to be gained through collaboration, (2) resource requirements (e.g., hardware, software, performance metrics) necessary for the collaboration, and (3) expectations of confidentiality concerning the prerequisite trust necessary to share sensitive company information, which represents a major implementation obstacle.

> **Step 2. Joint business planning.** Typically partners create partnership strategies, design a joint calendar identifying the sequence and frequency of planning activities to follow that affect product flows, and specify exception criteria for handling planning variances between the trading partners' demand forecasts.

> **Step 3. Development of demand forecasts.** Forecast development may follow preexisting company procedures. Retailers should play a critical role as shared *point-of-sale* (POS) data permit the development of more accurate and timely expectations (compared with extrapolated warehouse withdrawals or aggregate store orders) for both retailers and vendors. Given the frequency of forecast generation and the potential for vast numbers of items requiring forecast preparation, a simple forecast procedure such as a moving average is commonly used within CPFR. Simple techniques are easily used in conjunction with expert knowledge of promotional or pricing events to modify forecast values accordingly.

> **Step 4. Sharing forecasts.** Retailer (order forecasts) and vendor (sales forecasts) then electronically post their latest forecasts for a list of products on a shared, dedicated server.

---

exhibit 13.22

n-Tier Supply Chain with Retail Activities

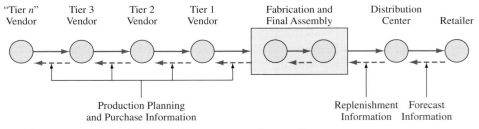

Note: Solid arrows represent material flows; dashed arrows represent information flows.

The server examines pairs of corresponding forecasts and issues an exception notice for any forecast pair where the difference exceeds a preestablished safety margin (e.g., 5 percent). If the safety margin is exceeded, planners from both firms may collaborate electronically to derive a consensus forecast.

Step 5. Inventory replenishment.   Once the corresponding forecasts are in agreement, the order forecast becomes an actual order, which commences the replenishment process. Each of these steps is then repeated iteratively in a continuous cycle, at varying times, by individual products and the calendar of events established between trading partners. For example, partners may review the front-end partnership agreement annually, evaluate the joint business plans quarterly, develop forecasts weekly to monthly, and replenish daily.

The early exchange of information between trading partners provides for reliable, longer-term future views of demand in the supply chain. The forward visibility based upon information sharing leads to a variety of benefits within supply chain partnerships.

As with most new corporate initiatives, there is skepticism and resistance to change. One of the largest hurdles hindering collaboration is the lack of trust over complete information sharing between supply chain partners. The conflicting objective between the profit-maximizing vendor and cost-minimizing customer gives rise to adversarial supply chain relationships. Sharing sensitive operating data may enable one trading partner to take advantage of the other. Similarly, there is the potential loss of control as a barrier to implementation. Some companies are rightfully concerned about the idea of placing strategic data such as financial reports, manufacturing schedules, and inventory values online. Companies open themselves to security breaches. The front-end partnership agreements, nondisclosure agreements, and limited information access may help overcome these fears.

CONCLUSION

Developing a forecasting system is not easy. However, it must be done because forecasting is fundamental to any planning effort. In the short run, a forecast is needed to predict the requirements for materials, products, services, or other resources to respond to changes in demand. Forecasts permit adjusting schedules and varying labor and materials. In the long run, forecasting is required as a basis for strategic changes, such as developing new markets, developing new products or services, and expanding or creating new facilities.

For long-term forecasts that lead to heavy financial commitments, great care should be taken to derive the forecast. Several approaches should be used. Causal methods such as regression analysis or multiple regression analysis are beneficial. These provide a basis for discussion. Economic factors, product trends, growth factors, and competition, as well as myriad other possible variables, need to be considered and the forecast adjusted to reflect the influence of each.

Short- and intermediate-term forecasting (such as required for inventory control as well as staffing and material scheduling) may be satisfied with simpler models, such as exponential smoothing with perhaps an adaptive feature or a seasonal index. In these applications, thousands of items are usually being forecast. The forecasting routine should therefore be simple and run quickly on a computer. The routines should also detect and respond rapidly to definite short-term changes in demand while at the same time ignoring the occasional spurious demands. Exponential smoothing, when monitored by management to control the value of alpha, is an effective technique.

Web-based collaborative forecasting systems that use combinations of the forecasting methods will be the wave of the future in many industries. Information sharing between trading partners with direct links into each firm's ERP system ensures rapid and error-free information, at very low cost.

In summary, forecasting is tough. A perfect forecast is like a hole in one in golf: great to get but we should be satisfied just to get close to the cup—or, to push the analogy, just to land on the green. The ideal philosophy is to create the best forecast that you reasonably can and then hedge by maintaining flexibility in the system to account for the inevitable forecast error.

KEY TERMS

Dependent demand Requirements for a product or service caused by the demand for other products or services. This type of internal demand does not need a forecast, but can be calculated based on the demand for the other products or services.

Independent demand Demand that cannot be directly derived from the demand for other products.

Time series analysis A type of forecast in which data relating to past demand are used to predict future demand.

Exponential smoothing A time series forecasting technique in which each increment of past demand data is decreased by $(1 - \alpha)$.

Smoothing constant alpha (α) The parameter in the exponential smoothing equation that controls the speed of reaction to differences between forecasts and actual demand.

Smoothing constant delta (δ) An additional parameter used in an exponential smoothing equation that includes an adjustment for trend.

Mean absolute deviation (MAD) The average forecast error using absolute values of the error of each past forecast.

Tracking signal A measure that indicates whether the forecast average is keeping pace with any genuine upward or downward changes in demand.

Linear regression forecasting A forecasting technique that assumes that past data and future projections fall around a straight line.

Causal relationship A situation in which one event causes another. If the event is far enough in the future, it can be used as a basis for forecasting.

Focus forecasting An approach to forecasting in which several different techniques are tried in a computer simulation and the best technique or combination of techniques is used to make the actual forecast.

Collaborative Planning, Forecasting, and Replenishment (CPFR) An Internet tool to coordinate forecasting, production, and purchasing in a firm's supply chain.

FORMULA REVIEW

Simple moving average

[13.1]
$$F_t = \frac{A_{t-1} + A_{t-2} + A_{t-3} + \cdots + A_{t-n}}{n}$$

Weighted moving average

[13.2]
$$F_t = w_1 A_{t-1} + w_2 A_{t-2} + \cdots + w_n A_{t-n}$$

Single exponential smoothing

[13.3]
$$F_t = F_{t-1} + \alpha(A_{t-1} - F_{t-1})$$

Exponential smoothing with trend

[13.4]
$$\text{FIT}_t = F_t + T_t$$

[13.5]
$$F_t = \text{FIT}_{t-1} + \alpha(A_{t-1} - \text{FIT}_{t-1})$$

[13.6]
$$T_t = T_{t-1} + \delta(F_t - \text{FIT}_{t-1})$$

Mean absolute deviation

[13.7]
$$\text{MAD} = \frac{\sum_{i=1}^{n} |A_t - F_t|}{n}$$

Tracking signal

[13.8]
$$\text{TS} = \frac{\text{RSFE}}{\text{MAD}}$$

Least squares regression

[13.9] $$Y = a + bx$$

[13.10] $$a = \bar{y} - b\bar{x}$$

[13.11] $$b = \frac{\sum xy - n\bar{x} \cdot \bar{y}}{\sum x^2 - n\bar{x}^2}$$

Standard error of estimate

[13.12] $$S_{yx} = \sqrt{\frac{\sum_{i=1}^{n}(y_i - Y_i)^2}{n - 2}}$$

SOLVED PROBLEMS

SOLVED PROBLEM 1

Sunrise Baking Company markets doughnuts through a chain of food stores. It has been experiencing over- and underproduction because of forecasting errors. The following data are its demand in dozens of doughnuts for the past four weeks. Doughnuts are made for the following day; for example, Sunday's doughnut production is for Monday's sales, Monday's production is for Tuesday's sales, and so forth. The bakery is closed Saturday, so Friday's production must satisfy demand for both Saturday and Sunday.

**Excel:
Forecasting**

	4 WEEKS AGO	3 WEEKS AGO	2 WEEKS AGO	LAST WEEK
Monday	2,200	2,400	2,300	2,400
Tuesday	2,000	2,100	2,200	2,200
Wednesday	2,300	2,400	2,300	2,500
Thursday	1,800	1,900	1,800	2,000
Friday	1,900	1,800	2,100	2,000
Saturday				
Sunday	2,800	2,700	3,000	2,900

Make a forecast for this week on the following basis:
a. Daily, using a simple four-week moving average.
b. Daily, using a weighted average of 0.40, 0.30, 0.20, and 0.10 for the past four weeks.
c. Sunrise is also planning its purchases of ingredients for bread production. If bread demand had been forecast for last week at 22,000 loaves and only 21,000 loaves were actually demanded, what would Sunrise's forecast be for this week using exponential smoothing with $\alpha = 0.10$?
d. Suppose, with the forecast made in c, this week's demand actually turns out to be 22,500. What would the new forecast be for the next week?

Solution

a. Simple moving average, four-week.

Monday $\dfrac{2,400 + 2,300 + 2,400 + 2,200}{4} = \dfrac{9,300}{4} = 2,325$ doz.

Tuesday $= \dfrac{8,500}{4} = 2,125$ doz.

Wednesday $= \dfrac{9,500}{4} = 2,375$ doz.

Thursday $= \dfrac{7,500}{4} = 1,875$ doz.

Friday $= \dfrac{7,800}{4} = 1,950$ doz.

Saturday and Sunday $= \dfrac{11,400}{4} = 2,850$ doz.

b. Weighted average with weights of .40, .30, .20, and .10.

	(.10)		(.20)		(.30)		(.40)		
Monday	220	+	480	+	690	+	960	=	2,350
Tuesday	200	+	420	+	660	+	880	=	2,160
Wednesday	230	+	480	+	690	+	1,000	=	2,400
Thursday	180	+	380	+	540	+	800	=	1,900
Friday	190	+	360	+	630	+	800	=	1,980
Saturday and Sunday	280	+	540	+	900	+	1,160	=	2,880
	1,300	+	2,660	+	4,110	+	5,600	=	13,670

c. Exponentially smoothed forecast for bread demand

$$F_t = F_{t-1} + \alpha(A_{t-1} - F_{t-1})$$

$$= 22{,}000 + 0.10(21{,}000 - 22{,}000)$$

$$= 22{,}000 - 100 = 21{,}900 \text{ loaves}$$

d. Exponentially smoothed forecast

$$F_{t+1} = 21{,}900 + .10(22{,}500 - 21{,}900)$$

$$= 21{,}900 + .10(600) = 21{,}960 \text{ loaves}$$

SOLVED PROBLEM 2

Here are the actual demands for a product for the past six quarters. Using focus forecasting rules 1 through 5, find the best rule to use in predicting the third quarter of this year.

	QUARTER			
	I	II	III	IV
Last year	1,200	700	900	1,100
This year	1,400	1,000		

Solution

Rule 1: Next three months' demand = Last three months' demand.

Testing this on the last three months, $F_{II} = A_I$; therefore $F_{II} = 1{,}400$.

Actual demand was 1,000, so $\dfrac{1{,}000}{1{,}400} = 71.4\%$.

Rule 2: This quarter's demand equals demand in the same quarter last year.
The forecast for the second quarter this year will therefore be 700, the amount for that quarter last year.

Actual demand was 1,000, and $\dfrac{1{,}000}{700} = 142.9\%$.

Rule 3: 10 percent more than last quarter.

$$F_{II} = 1{,}400 \times 1.10 = 1{,}540$$

Actual was 1,000, and $\dfrac{1{,}000}{1{,}540} = 64.9\%$.

Rule 4: 50 percent more than same quarter last year.

$$F_{II} = 700 \times 1.50 = 1{,}050$$

Actual was 1,000, and $\dfrac{1{,}000}{1{,}050} = 95.2\%$.

Rule 5: Same rate of increase or decrease as last three months.

$$\frac{1,400}{1,200} = 1.167$$

$$F_{II} = 700 \times 1.167 = 816.7$$

Actual was 1,000, so $\dfrac{1,000}{816.7} = 122.4\%$.

Rule 4 was the closest in predicting the recent quarter—95.2 percent or just 4.8 percent under. Using this rule (50 percent more than the same quarter last year), we would forecast the third quarter this year as 50 percent more than the third quarter last year, or

$$\text{This year } F_{III} = 1.50 \, A_{III} \qquad \text{(last year)}$$

$$F_{III} = 1.50(900) = 1,350 \text{ units}$$

SOLVED PROBLEM 3

A specific forecasting model was used to forecast demand for a product. The forecasts and the corresponding demand that subsequently occurred are shown below. Use the MAD and tracking signal technique to evaluate the accuracy of the forecasting model.

**Excel:
Forecasting**

	ACTUAL	FORECAST
October	700	660
November	760	840
December	780	750
January	790	835
February	850	910
March	950	890

Solution

Evaluate the forecasting model using MAD and tracking signal.

	ACTUAL DEMAND	FORECAST DEMAND	ACTUAL DEVIATION	CUMULATIVE DEVIATION (RSFE)	ABSOLUTE DEVIATION
October	700	660	40	40	40
November	760	840	−80	−40	80
December	780	750	30	−10	30
January	790	835	−45	−55	45
February	850	910	−60	−115	60
March	950	890	60	−55	60
				Total dev. =	315

$$\text{MAD} = \frac{315}{6} = 52.5$$

$$\text{Tracking signal} = \frac{-55}{52.5} = -1.05$$

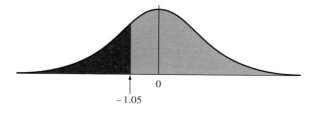

There is not enough evidence to reject the forecasting model, so we accept its recommendations.

**Excel:
Forecasting**

SOLVED PROBLEM 4

Here are quarterly data for the past two years. From these data, prepare a forecast for the upcoming year using decomposition.

PERIOD	ACTUAL	PERIOD	ACTUAL
1	300	5	416
2	540	6	760
3	885	7	1191
4	580	8	760

Solution

(Note that the values you obtain may be slightly different due to rounding. The values given here were obtained using an Excel spreadsheet.)

(1) PERIOD x	(2) ACTUAL Y	(3) PERIOD AVERAGE	(4) SEASONAL FACTOR	(5) DESEASONALIZED DEMAND
1	300	358	0.527	568.99
2	540	650	0.957	564.09
3	885	1,038	1.529	578.92
4	580	670	0.987	587.79
5	416		0.527	789.01
6	760		0.957	793.91
7	1,191		1.529	779.08
8	760		0.987	770.21
Total	5,432	2,716	8.0	
Average	679	679	1	

Column 3 is seasonal average. For example, the first-quarter average is

$$\frac{300 + 416}{2} = 358$$

Column 4 is the quarter average (column 3) divided by the overall average (679). Column 5 is the actual data divided by the seasonal index. To determine x^2 and xy we can construct a table as follows:

PERIOD x	DESEASONALIZED DEMAND (y_d)	x^2	xy
1	568.99	1	569.0
2	564.09	4	1128.2
3	578.92	9	1736.7
4	587.79	16	2351.2
5	789.01	25	3945.0
6	793.91	36	4763.4
7	779.08	49	5453.6
8	770.21	64	6161.7
Sums 36	5,432	204	26,108.8
Average 4.5	679		

Now we calculate regression results for deseasonalized data.

$$b = \frac{(26108) - (8)(4.5)(679)}{(204) - (8)(4.5)^2} = 39.64$$

$$a = \overline{Y} - b\overline{x}$$

$$a = 679 - 39.64(4.5) = 500.6$$

Therefore, the deseasonalized regression results are

$$Y = 500.6 + 39.64x$$

PERIOD	TREND FORECAST		SEASONAL FACTOR		FINAL FORECAST
9	857.4	×	0.527	=	452.0
10	897.0	×	0.957	=	858.7
11	936.7	×	1.529	=	1431.9
12	976.3	×	0.987	=	963.4

REVIEW AND DISCUSSION QUESTIONS

1 What is the difference between dependent and independent demand?
2 Examine Exhibit 13.4 and suggest which model you might use for (*a*) bathing suit demand, (*b*) demand for new houses, (*c*) electrical power usage, (*d*) new plant expansion plans.
3 What is the logic in the least squares method of linear regression analysis?
4 Explain the procedure to create a forecast using the decomposition method of least squares regression.
5 Give some very simple rules you might use to manage demand for a firm's product. (An example is "limited to stock on hand.")
6 What strategies are used by supermarkets, airlines, hospitals, banks, and cereal manufacturers to influence demand?
7 All forecasting methods using exponential smoothing, adaptive smoothing, and exponential smoothing including trend require starting values to get the equations going. How would you select the starting value for, say, F_{t-1}?
8 From the choice of simple moving average, weighted moving average, exponential smoothing, and linear regression analysis, which forecasting technique would you consider the most accurate? Why?
9 Give some examples that have a multiplicative seasonal trend relationship.
10 What is the main disadvantage of daily forecasting using regression analysis?
11 What are the main problems with using adaptive exponential smoothing in forecasting?
12 How is a seasonal index computed from a regression line analysis?
13 Discuss the basic differences between the mean absolute deviation and the standard deviation.
14 What implications do forecast errors have for the search for ultrasophisticated statistical forecasting models?
15 What are the strongest selling points of focused forecasting?
16 Causal relationships are potentially useful for which component of a time series?

PROBLEMS

1 Demand for stereo headphones and CD players for joggers has caused Nina Industries to grow almost 50 percent over the past year. The number of joggers continues to expand, so Nina expects demand for headsets to also expand, because, as yet, no safety laws have been passed to prevent joggers from wearing them. Demand for the stereo units for last year was as follows:

MONTH	DEMAND (UNITS)	MONTH	DEMAND (UNITS)
January	4,200	July	5,300
February	4,300	August	4,900
March	4,000	September	5,400
April	4,400	October	5,700
May	5,000	November	6,300
June	4,700	December	6,000

a. Using least squares regression analysis, what would you estimate demand to be for each month next year? Using a spreadsheet, follow the general format in Exhibit 13.13. Compare your results to those obtained by using the forecast spreadsheet function.
b. To be reasonably confident of meeting demand, Nina decides to use three standard errors of estimate for safety. How many additional units should be held to meet this level of confidence?

2   Historical demand for a product is

	DEMAND
January	12
February	11
March	15
April	12
May	16
June	15

a. Using a weighted moving average with weights of 0.60, 0.30, and 0.10, find the July forecast.
b. Using a simple three-month moving average, find the July forecast.
c. Using single exponential smoothing with $\alpha = 0.2$ and a June forecast $= 13$, find the July forecast. Make whatever assumptions you wish.
d. Using simple linear regression analysis, calculate the regression equation for the preceding demand data.
e. Using the regression equation in *d*, calculate the forecast for July.

3   The following tabulations are actual sales of units for six months and a starting forecast in January.
a. Calculate forecasts for the remaining five months using simple exponential smoothing with $\alpha = 0.2$.
b. Calculate MAD for the forecasts.

	ACTUAL	FORECAST
January	100	80
February	94	
March	106	
April	80	
May	68	
June	94	

4   Zeus Computer Chips, Inc., used to have major contracts to produce the 386- and 486-type chips. The market has been declining during the past three years because of the pentium-type chips, which it cannot produce, so Zeus has the unpleasant task of forecasting next year. The task is unpleasant because the firm has not been able to find replacement chips for its product lines. Here is demand over the past 12 quarters:

2003		2004		2005	
I	4,800	I	3,500	I	3,200
II	3,500	II	2,700	II	2,100
III	4,300	III	3,500	III	2,700
IV	3,000	IV	2,400	IV	1,700

Use the decomposition technique to forecast the four quarters of 2006.

5   Sales data for two years are as follows. Data are aggregated with two months of sales in each "period."

MONTHS	SALES	MONTHS	SALES
January–February	109	January–February	115
March–April	104	March–April	112
May–June	150	May–June	159
July–August	170	July–August	182
September–October	120	September–October	126
November–December	100	November–December	106

a. Plot the data.

b. Fit a simple linear regression model to the sales data.

c. In addition to the regression model, determine multiplicative seasonal index factors. A full cycle is assumed to be a full year.

d. Using the results from parts *b* and *c*, prepare a forecast for the next year.

6 The tracking signals computed using past demand history for three different products are as follows. Each product used the same forecasting technique.

	TS 1	TS 2	TS 3
1	−2.70	1.54	0.10
2	−2.32	−0.64	0.43
3	−1.70	2.05	1.08
4	−1.1	2.58	1.74
5	−0.87	−0.95	1.94
6	−0.05	−1.23	2.24
7	0.10	0.75	2.96
8	0.40	−1.59	3.02
9	1.50	0.47	3.54
10	2.20	2.74	3.75

Discuss the tracking signals for each and what the implications are.

7 The following table shows the past two years of quarterly sales information. Assume that there are both trend and seasonal factors and that the seasonal cycle is one year. Use time series decomposition to forecast quarterly sales for the next year.

QUARTER	SALES	QUARTER	SALES
1	160	5	215
2	195	6	240
3	150	7	205
4	140	8	190

8 Tucson Machinery, Inc., manufactures numerically controlled machines, which sell for an average price of $0.5 million each. Sales for these NCMs for the past two years were as follows:

QUARTER	QUANTITY (UNITS)	QUARTER	QUANTITY (UNITS)
2004		2005	
I	12	I	16
II	18	II	24
III	26	III	28
IV	16	IV	18

a. Hand fit a line (or do a regression using Excel®).

b. Find the trend and seasonal factors.

c. Forecast sales for 2006.

9 Not all the items in your office supply store are evenly distributed as far as demand is concerned, so you decide to forecast demand to help plan your stock. Past data for legal-sized yellow tablets for the month of August are

Week 1	300	Week 3	600
Week 2	400	Week 4	700

a. Using a three-week moving average, what would you forecast the next week to be?

b. Using exponential smoothing with $\alpha = 0.20$, if the exponential forecast for week 3 was estimated as the average of the first two weeks [(300 + 400)/2 = 350], what would you forecast week 5 to be?

10 Given the following history, use focus forecasting to forecast the third quarter of this year. Use three focus forecasting strategies.

	JAN	FEB	MAR	APR	MAY	JUN	JUL	AUG	SEP	OCT	NOV	DEC
Last year	100	125	135	175	185	200	150	140	130	200	225	250
This year	125	135	135	190	200	190						

11 Here are the actual tabulated demands for an item for a nine-month period (January through September). Your supervisor wants to test two forecasting methods to see which method was better over this period.

MONTH	ACTUAL	MONTH	ACTUAL
January	110	June	180
February	130	July	140
March	150	August	130
April	170	September	140
May	160		

a. Forecast April through September using a three-month moving average.
b. Use simple exponential smoothing with an alpha of .3 to estimate April through September.
c. Use MAD to decide which method produced the better forecast over the six-month period.

12 A particular forecasting model was used to forecast a six-month period. Here are the forecasts and actual demands that resulted:

	FORECAST	ACTUAL
April	250	200
May	325	250
June	400	325
July	350	300
August	375	325
September	450	400

Find the tracking signal and state whether you think the model being used is giving acceptable answers.

13 Harlen Industries has a simple forecasting model: Take the actual demand for the same month last year and divide that by the number of fractional weeks in that month. This gives the average weekly demand for that month. This weekly average is used as the weekly forecast for the same month this year. This technique was used to forecast eight weeks for this year, which are shown below along with the actual demand that occurred.

The following eight weeks show the forecast (based on last year) and the demand that actually occurred:

WEEK	FORECAST DEMAND	ACTUAL DEMAND	WEEK	FORECAST DEMAND	ACTUAL DEMAND
1	140	137	5	140	180
2	140	133	6	150	170
3	140	150	7	150	185
4	140	160	8	150	205

a. Compute the MAD of forecast errors.
b. Using the RSFE, compute the tracking signal.
c. Based on your answers to *a* and *b*, comment on Harlen's method of forecasting.

14 The following table contains the demand from the last 10 months:

MONTH	ACTUAL DEMAND	MONTH	ACTUAL DEMAND
1	31	6	36
2	34	7	38
3	33	8	40
4	35	9	40
5	37	10	41

  a. Calculate the single exponential smoothing forecast for these data using an α of .30 and an initial forecast (F_1) of 31.
  b. Calculate the exponential smoothing with trend forecast for these data using an α of .30, a δ of .30, an initial trend forecast (T_1) of 1, and an initial exponentially smoothed forecast (F_1) of 30.
  c. Calculate the mean absolute deviation (MAD) for each forecast. Which is best?

15 In this problem, you are to test the validity of your forecasting model. Here are the forecasts for a model you have been using and the actual demands that occurred:

WEEK	FORECAST	ACTUAL
1	800	900
2	850	1,000
3	950	1,050
4	950	900
5	1,000	900
6	975	1,100

Use the method stated in the text to compute the MAD and tracking signal. Then decide whether the forecasting model you have been using is giving reasonable results.

16 Assume that your stock of sales merchandise is maintained based on the forecast demand. If the distributor's sales personnel call on the first day of each month, compute your forecast sales by each of the three methods requested here.

	ACTUAL
June	140
July	180
August	170

  a. Using a simple three-month moving average, what is the forecast for September?
  b. Using a weighted moving average, what is the forecast for September with weights of .20, .30, and .50 for June, July, and August, respectively?
  c. Using single exponential smoothing and assuming that the forecast for June had been 130, forecast sales for September with a smoothing constant alpha of .30.

17 Historical demand for a product is as follows:

	DEMAND
April	60
May	55
June	75
July	60
August	80
September	75

  a. Using a simple four-month moving average, calculate a forecast for October.
  b. Using single exponential smoothing with $\alpha = 0.2$ and a September forecast $= 65$, calculate a forecast for October.
  c. Using simple linear regression, calculate the trend line for the historical data. Say the X axis is April $= 1$, May $= 2$, and so on, while the Y axis is demand.
  d. Calculate a forecast for October.

18   Sales by quarter for last year and the first three quarters of this year were as follows:

	QUARTER			
	I	II	III	IV
Last year	23,000	27,000	18,000	9,000
This year	19,000	24,000	15,000	

Using the focus forecasting procedure described in the text, forecast expected sales for the fourth quarter of this year.

19   The following table shows predicted product demand using your particular forecasting method along with the actual demand that occurred:

FORECAST	ACTUAL
1,500	1,550
1,400	1,500
1,700	1,600
1,750	1,650
1,800	1,700

a. Compute the tracking signal using the mean absolute deviation and running sum of forecast errors.

b. Discuss whether your forecasting method is giving good predictions.

20   Your manager is trying to determine what forecasting method to use. Based upon the following historical data, calculate the following forecast and specify what procedure you would utilize.

MONTH	ACTUAL DEMAND	MONTH	ACTUAL DEMAND
1	62	7	76
2	65	8	78
3	67	9	78
4	68	10	80
5	71	11	84
6	73	12	85

a. Calculate the simple three-month moving average forecast for periods 4–12.

b. Calculate the weighted three-month moving average using weights of 0.50, 0.30, and 0.20 for periods 4–12.

c. Calculate the single exponential smoothing forecast for periods 2–12 using an initial forecast (F_1) of 61 and an α of 0.30.

d. Calculate the exponential smoothing with trend component forecast for periods 2–12 using an initial trend forecast (T_1) of 1.8, an initial exponential smoothing forecast (F_1) of 60, an α of 0.30, and a δ of 0.30.

e. Calculate the mean absolute deviation (MAD) for the forecasts made by each technique in periods 4–12. Which forecasting method do you prefer?

21   Use regression analysis on deseasonalized demand to forecast demand in summer 2006, given the following historical demand data:

YEAR	SEASON	ACTUAL DEMAND
2004	Spring	205
	Summer	140
	Fall	375
	Winter	575
2005	Spring	475
	Summer	275
	Fall	685
	Winter	965

22   Here are the data for the past 21 months for actual sales of a particular product:

	2004	2005
January	300	275
February	400	375
March	425	350
April	450	425
May	400	400
June	460	350
July	400	350
August	300	275
September	375	350
October	500	
November	550	
December	500	

Develop a forecast for the fourth quarter using three different focus forecasting rules. (Note that to correctly use this procedure, the rules are first tested on the third quarter; the best-performing one is used to forecast the fourth quarter.) Do the problem using quarters, as opposed to forecasting separate months.

23   Actual demand for a product for the past three months was

Three months ago	400 units
Two months ago	350 units
Last month	325 units

a. Using a simple three-month moving average, make a forecast for this month.
b. If 300 units were actually demanded this month, what would your forecast be for next month?
c. Using simple exponential smoothing, what would your forecast be for this month if the exponentially smoothed forecast for three months ago was 450 units and the smoothing constant was 0.20?

24   After using your forecasting model for six months, you decide to test it using MAD and a tracking signal. Here are the forecast and actual demands for the six-month period:

PERIOD	FORECAST	ACTUAL
May	450	500
June	500	550
July	550	400
August	600	500
September	650	675
October	700	600

a. Find the tracking signal.
b. Decide whether your forecasting routine is acceptable.

25   Here are earnings per share for two companies by quarter from the first quarter of 2002 through the second quarter of 2005. Forecast earnings per share for the rest of 2005 and 2006. Use exponential smoothing to forecast the third period of 2005, and the time series decomposition method to forecast the last two quarters of 2005 and all four quarters of 2006. (It is much easier to solve this problem on a computer spreadsheet so you can see what is happening.)

	EARNINGS PER SHARE		
	QUARTER	COMPANY A	COMPANY B
2002	I	$1.67	$0.17
	II	2.35	0.24
	III	1.11	0.26
	IV	1.15	0.34

(continued)

	QUARTER	COMPANY A	COMPANY B
2003	I	1.56	0.25
	II	2.04	0.37
	III	1.14	0.36
	IV	0.38	0.44
2004	I	0.29	0.33
	II	−0.18 (loss)	0.40
	III	−0.97 (loss)	0.41
	IV	0.20	0.47
2005	I	−1.54 (loss)	0.30
	II	0.38	0.47

  a. For the exponential smoothing method, choose the first quarter of 2002 as the beginning forecast. Make two forecasts: one with $\alpha = 0.10$ and one with $\alpha = 0.30$.

  b. Using the MAD method of testing the forecasting model's performance, plus actual data from 2002 through the second quarter of 2005, how well did the model perform?

  c. Using the decomposition of a time series method of forecasting, forecast earnings per share for the last two quarters of 2005 and all four quarters of 2006. Is there a seasonal factor in the earnings?

  d. Using your forecasts, comment on each company.

26 The following are sales revenues for a large utility company for 1995 through 2005. Forecast revenue for 2006 through 2009. Use your own judgment, intuition, or common sense concerning which model or method to use, as well as the period of data to include.

	REVENUE (MILLIONS)			REVENUE (MILLIONS)
1995	$4,865.9		2001	$5,094.4
1996	5,067.4		2002	5,108.8
1997	5,515.6		2003	5,550.6
1998	5,728.8		2004	5,738.9
1999	5,497.7		2005	5,860.0
2000	5,197.7			

27 Mark Price, the new productions manager for Speakers and Company, needs to find out which variable most affects the demand for their line of stereo speakers. He is uncertain whether the unit price of the product or the effects of increased marketing are the main drivers in sales and wants to use regression analysis to figure out which factor drives more demand for their particular market. Pertinent information was collected by an extensive marketing project that lasted over the past 10 years and was reduced to the data that follow:

YEAR	SALES/UNIT (THOUSANDS)	PRICE/UNIT	ADVERTISING ($000)
1994	400	280	600
1995	700	215	835
1996	900	211	1,100
1997	1,300	210	1,400
1998	1,150	215	1,200
1999	1,200	200	1,300
2000	900	225	900
2001	1,100	207	1,100
2002	980	220	700
2003	1,234	211	900
2004	925	227	700
2005	800	245	690

  a. Perform a regression analysis based on these data using Excel®. Answer the following questions based on your results.

  b. Which variable, price or advertising, has a larger effect on sales and how do you know?

c. Predict average yearly speaker sales for Speakers and Company based on the regression results if the price was $300 per unit and the amount spent on advertising (in thousands) was $900.

28   Assume an initial starting F_t of 300 units, a trend of 8 units, an alpha of .30, and a delta of .40. If actual demand turned out to be 288, calculate the forecast for the next period.

SELECTED BIBLIOGRAPHY

De Lurgio, S. *Forecasting Principles and Applications.* New York: Irwin/McGraw-Hill, 1998.

Diebold, F. X. *Elements of Forecasting.* 2nd ed. Cincinnati, OH: South-Western College Publishing, 2000.

Hanke, J. E.; A. G. Reitsch; and D. W. Wichem. *Business Forecasting.* 7th ed. Upper Saddle River, NJ : Prentice Hall, 2001.

Makridakis, S; S. C. Wheelwright; and R. J. Hyndman. *Forecasting: Methods for Management.* New York: John Wiley & Sons, 1998.

FOOTNOTES

1 In addition to dependent and independent demands, other relationships include complementary products and causal relationships where demand for one causes the demand for another.

2 Some writers prefer to call F_t a smoothed average.

3 When exponential smoothing is first introduced, the initial forecast or starting point may be obtained by using a simple estimate or an average of preceding periods such as the average of the first two or three periods.

4 An equation for the standard error that is often easier to compute is $S_{yx} = \sqrt{\dfrac{\sum y^2 - a\sum y - b\sum xy}{n-2}}$

5 B. T. Smith, *Focus Forecasting: Computer Techniques for Inventory Control* (Boston: CBI Publishing, 1984).

6 We use this exercise because it includes real data from the records of American Hardware Supply Company, where Smith was inventory manager. This forecasting exercise has been played by many people: buyers for American Hardware, inventory consultants, and numerous participants at national meetings of the American Production and Inventory Control Society. Further, data for the remainder of the year exist that allow for checking the results.

7 Special thanks to Gene Fliedner for help with this section. Gene Fliedner, "Hierarchical Forecasting: Issues and Use Guidelines," *Industrial Management & Data Systems* 101, no. 1 (2001), pp. 5–12.

8 Marshall L. Fisher, "What Is the Right Supply Chain for Your Product?" *Harvard Business Review*, March–April 1997, pp. 105–16.

chapter

AGGREGATE SALES AND OPERATIONS PLANNING

14

Let's eavesdrop on an executive staff meeting at the Acme Widget Company. The participants are not happy campers.

President: This shortage situation is terrible. When will we ever get our act together? Whenever business gets good, we run out of product and our customer service is lousy.

VP Operations: I'll tell you when. When we start to get some decent forecasts from the Sales Department . . .

VP Sales (interrupting): Wait a minute. We forecasted this upturn.

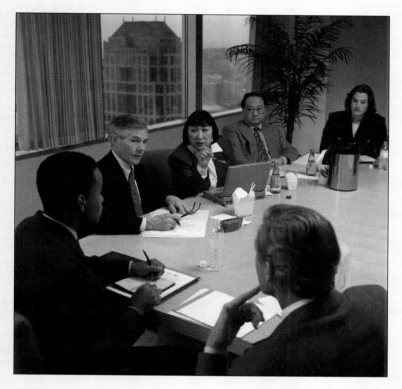

VP Operations: . . . in time to do something about it. Yeah, we got the revised forecast—four days after the start of the month. By then it was too late.

VP Sales: I could have told you months ago. All you had to do was ask.

VP Finance: I'd like to be in on those conversations. We've been burned more than once by building inventories for a business upturn that doesn't happen. Then we get stuck with tons of inventory and run out of cash.

And the beat goes on. Back orders, dissatisfied customers, high inventories, late shipments, finger-pointing, cash-flow problems, demand and supply out of balance, missing the business plan. This is the norm in many companies.

Source: Adapted from Thomas F. Wallace, *Sales and Operations Planning: The How-To Handbook* (Cincinnati, OH: T. F. Wallace & Co., 2000), p. 3. Copyright © 2000 Thomas Wallace. Used with permission.

It does not, however, have to be that way. Today many companies are using a business process called sales and operations planning (S&OP) to help avoid such problems. To learn what it is, and how to make it work, read on. →

Aggregate operations plan

In this chapter, we focus on the **aggregate operations plan,** which translates annual and quarterly business plans into broad labor and output plans for the intermediate term (3 to 18 months). The objective of the aggregate operations plan is to minimize the cost of resources required to meet demand over that period.

WHAT IS SALES AND OPERATIONS PLANNING?

⊙⊙⊙◯ Sales and operations planning is a process to help give better customer service, lower inventory, shorten customer lead times, stabilize production rates, and give top management a handle on the business. The process is built on teamwork between sales, operations, finance, and product development. The process is designed to help a company get demand and supply in balance and to keep them in balance over time. Balancing supply and demand is essential to running a business well.

The sales and operations planning process consists of a series of meetings, finishing with a high-level meeting where key intermediate-term decisions are made. The end goal is an agreement between various departments on the best course of action to achieve the optimal balance between supply and demand. The idea is to put the operational plan in line with the business plan.

This balance must occur at an aggregate level and also at the detailed individual product level. By *aggregate* we mean at the level of major groups of products. Over time, we need to ensure that we have enough total capacity. Since demand is often quite dynamic, it is important that we monitor our expected needs 3 to 18 months or further in the future. When planning this far into the future, it is difficult to know exactly how many of a particular product we will need, but we should be able to know how a larger group of similar products should sell. The term *aggregate* refers to this group of products. Given that we have enough aggregate capacity, our individual product schedulers, working within aggregate capacity constraints, can handle the daily and weekly launching of individual product orders to meet short-term demand.

OVERVIEW OF SALES AND OPERATIONS PLANNING ACTIVITIES

Sales and operations planning

⊙⊙⊙◯ Exhibit 14.1 positions sales and operations planning relative to other major operations planning activities presented in the text. The term **sales and operations planning** has been coined by companies to refer to the process that helps companies keep demand and supply in balance. In operations management we have traditionally called this process *aggregate planning*. The new terminology is meant to capture the importance of cross-functional work. Typically this activity involves general management, sales, operations, finance, and product development.

Within sales and operations planning, marketing develops a sales plan that extends through the next 3 to 18 months. This sales plan typically is in units of aggregate product groups and is often tied into sales incentive programs and other marketing activities. The operations side develops an operations plan as an output of the process, which we discuss in depth in this chapter. By focusing on aggregate product and sales volumes, the marketing and operations functions are able to develop plans for how demand will be met. This is a particularly difficult task when there are significant changes in demand over time due to market trends, seasonality, or other factors.

Aggregation on the supply side is by product families and on the demand side by groups of customers. Individual product production schedules and matching customer orders can be handled more readily as a result of the sales and operations planning process. Typically, sales

Cross Functional

Overview of Major Operations Planning Activities

exhibit 14.1

and operations planning occurs on a monthly cycle. Sales and operations planning links the company's strategic plans and business plan to its detailed processes. These detailed processes include master scheduling, material requirements planning, and order entry for manufacturing firms and weekly and daily workforce and customer scheduling in service firms.

In Exhibit 14.1 the time dimension is shown as long, intermediate, and short range. **Long-range planning** is generally done annually, focusing on a horizon greater than one year. **Intermediate-range planning** usually covers a period from 3 to 18 months, with time increments that are weekly, monthly, or sometimes quarterly. **Short-range planning** covers a period from one day or less to six months, with the time increment daily or weekly.

Process planning deals with determining the specific technologies and procedures required to produce a product or service. (See Chapters 6 and 7.) Strategic capacity planning deals with determining the long-term capabilities (such as the size and scope) of the production systems. (See Chapter 11.) Sales and operations planning involves taking the sales plan from marketing and developing an aggregate operations plan that balances demand and supply. For services and manufacturing, the aggregate operations plan is essentially the same, the major exception being manufacturing's use of inventory buildups and cutback to smooth production (as we will discuss shortly). After the aggregate operations plan is developed, manufacturing and service planning activities are generally quite different.

The aggregate operations plan should be updated at least every quarter (13 weeks). Many companies now update them every four weeks. In manufacturing, the planning process can be summarized as follows: The production control group inputs existing or forecast orders into a **master production schedule (MPS)**. The MPS generates the amounts and dates of specific items required for each order. **Rough-cut capacity planning** then verifies that production and warehouse facilities, equipment, and labor are available and that key vendors have allocated sufficient capacity to provide materials when needed. As Chapter 16 details, **material requirements planning (MRP)** takes the end product requirements from the MPS and breaks

Long-range planning

Intermediate-range planning

Short-range planning

Master production schedule (MPS)

Rough-cut capacity planning

Material requirements planning (MRP)

Capacity requirements planning

Order scheduling

Service

them down into their component parts and subassemblies to create a materials plan. This plan specifies when production and purchase orders must be placed for each part and subassembly to complete the products on schedule. Most MRP systems also allocate production capacity to each order. (This is called **capacity requirements planning.**) The final planning activity is daily or weekly **order scheduling** of jobs to specific machines, production lines, or work centers. (See Chapter 17 for details.)

In services, once the aggregate staffing level is determined, the focus is on workforce and customer scheduling during the week or even hour by hour during the day. Workforce schedules are a function of the hours the service is available to a customer, the particular skills needed at particular times over the relevant period, and so on. Many service jobs have unique time and legal restrictions affecting scheduling that typical manufacturing work lacks. Airline flight crews are a good example of such constraints that make their scheduling far more complicated than scheduling manufacturing personnel. (Again, see Chapter 17.) Customer (or demand) scheduling deals with setting appointments and reservations for customers to use the service, and assigning priorities when they arrive at the service facility. These obviously range from formal reservation systems to simple sign-up sheets.

We now turn our attention back to manufacturing.

THE AGGREGATE OPERATIONS PLAN

The aggregate operations plan is concerned with setting production rates by product group or other broad categories for the intermediate term (3 to 18 months). Note again from Exhibit 14.1 that the aggregate plan precedes the master schedule. *The main purpose of the aggregate plan is to specify the optimal combination of production rate, workforce level, and inventory on hand.* **Production rate** refers to the number of units completed per unit of time (such as per hour or per day). **Workforce level** is the number of workers needed for production (production = production rate × workforce level). **Inventory on hand** is unused inventory carried over from the previous period.

Production rate

Workforce level

Inventory on hand

Here is a formal statement of the aggregate planning problem: Given the demand forecast F_t for each period t in the planning horizon that extends over T periods, determine the production level P_t, inventory level I_t, and workforce level W_t for periods $t = 1, 2, \ldots, T$ that minimize the relevant costs over the planning horizon.

The form of the aggregate plan varies from company to company. In some firms, it is a formalized report containing planning objectives and the planning premises on which it is based. In other companies, particularly smaller ones, the owner may make simple calculations of workforce needs that reflect a general staffing strategy.

The process by which the plan itself is derived also varies. One common approach is to derive it from the corporate annual plan, as shown in Exhibit 14.1. A typical corporate plan

JOHN DEERE MANUFACTURES FRONT-MOUNTED MOWERS AND BACK-MOUNTED MOWERS ON THE SAME LINE, ALLOWING MORE RESPONSIVE MATCHING OF OPERATIONS TO DEMAND.

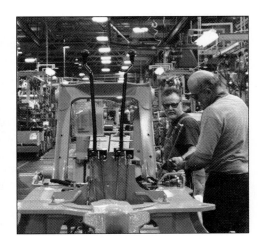

contains a section on manufacturing that specifies how many units in each major product line need to be produced over the next 12 months to meet the sales forecast. The planner takes this information and attempts to determine how best to meet these requirements with available resources. Alternatively, some organizations combine output requirements into equivalent units and use this as the basis for the aggregate plan. For example, a division of General Motors may be asked to produce a certain number of cars of all types at a particular facility. The production planner would then take the average labor hours required for all models as a basis for the overall aggregate plan. Refinements to this plan, specifically model types to be produced, would be reflected in shorter-term production plans.

Another approach is to develop the aggregate plan by simulating various master production schedules and calculating corresponding capacity requirements to see if adequate labor and equipment exist at each work center. If capacity is inadequate, additional requirements for overtime, subcontracting, extra workers, and so forth are specified for each product line and combined into a rough-cut plan. This plan is then modified by cut-and-try or mathematical methods to derive a final and (one hopes) lower-cost plan.

PRODUCTION PLANNING ENVIRONMENT

Exhibit 14.2 illustrates the internal and external factors that constitute the production planning environment. In general, the external environment is outside the production planner's direct control, but in some firms, demand for the product can be managed. Through close cooperation between marketing and operations, promotional activities and price cutting can be used to build demand during slow periods. Conversely, when demand is strong, promotional activities can be curtailed and prices raised to maximize the revenues from those products or services that the firm has the capacity to provide. The current practices in managing demand will be discussed later in the section titled "Yield Management."

Complementary products may work for firms facing cyclical demand fluctuations. For instance, lawnmower manufacturers will have strong demand for spring and summer, but weak demand during fall and winter. Demands on the production system can be smoothed out by producing a complementary product with high demand during fall and winter, and low demand during spring and summer (for instance, snowmobiles, snowblowers, or leafblowers). With services, cycles are more often measured in hours than months. Restaurants with strong demand during lunch and dinner will often add a breakfast menu to increase demand during the morning hours.

But even so, there are limits to how much demand can be controlled. Ultimately, the production planner must live with the sales projections and orders promised by the marketing

Cross Functional

Service

Required Inputs to the Production Planning System

exhibit 14.2

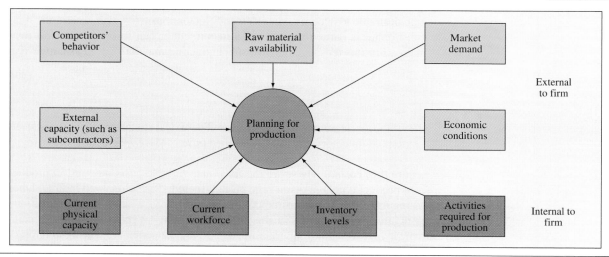

function, leaving the internal factors as variables that can be manipulated in deriving a production plan. A new approach to facilitate managing these internal factors is termed *accurate response*. This entails refined measurement of historical demand patterns blended with expert judgment to determine when to begin production of particular items. The key element of the approach is clearly identifying those products for which demand is relatively predictable from those for which demand is relatively unpredictable.[1]

The internal factors themselves differ in their controllability. Current physical capacity (plant and equipment) is usually nearly fixed in the short run; union agreements often constrain what can be done in changing the workforce; physical capacity cannot always be increased; and top management may limit the amount of money that can be tied up in inventories. Still, there is always some flexibility in managing these factors, and production planners can implement one or a combination of the **production planning strategies** discussed here.

Production planning strategies

Production Planning Strategies   There are essentially three production planning strategies. These strategies involve trade-offs among the workforce size, work hours, inventory, and backlogs.

1. **Chase strategy.**   Match the production rate to the order rate by hiring and laying off employees as the order rate varies. The success of this strategy depends on having a pool of easily trained applicants to draw on as order volumes increase. There are obvious motivational impacts. When order backlogs are low, employees may feel compelled to slow down out of fear of being laid off as soon as existing orders are completed.
2. **Stable workforce—variable work hours.**   Vary the output by varying the number of hours worked through flexible work schedules or overtime. By varying the number of work hours, you can match production quantities to orders. This strategy provides workforce continuity and avoids many of the emotional and tangible costs of hiring and firing associated with the chase strategy.
3. **Level strategy.**   Maintain a stable workforce working at a constant output rate. Shortages and surpluses are absorbed by fluctuating inventory levels, order backlogs, and lost sales. Employees benefit from stable work hours at the costs of potentially decreased customer service levels and increased inventory costs. Another concern is the possibility of inventoried products becoming obsolete.

When just one of these variables is used to absorb demand fluctuations, it is termed a **pure strategy**; two or more used in combination constitute a **mixed strategy.** As you might suspect, mixed strategies are more widely applied in industry.

Pure strategy

Mixed strategy

Subcontracting   In addition to these strategies, managers also may choose to subcontract some portion of production. This strategy is similar to the chase strategy, but hiring and laying off are translated into subcontracting and not subcontracting. Some level of subcontracting can be desirable to accommodate demand fluctuations. However, unless the relationship with the supplier is particularly strong, a manufacturer can lose some control over schedule and quality. For this reason, extensive subcontracting may be viewed as a high-risk strategy.

RELEVANT COSTS

Four costs are relevant to the aggregate production plan. These relate to the production cost itself as well as the cost to hold inventory and to have unfilled orders. More specifically, these are

1. **Basic production costs.**   These are the fixed and variable costs incurred in producing a given product type in a given time period. Included are direct and indirect labor costs and regular as well as overtime compensation.
2. **Costs associated with changes in the production rate.**   Typical costs in this category are those involved in hiring, training, and laying off personnel. Hiring temporary help is a way of avoiding these costs.

IT'S ALL IN THE PLANNING

You're sitting anxiously in the suddenly assembled general manager's staff meeting. Voices are nervously subdued. The rumor mill is in high gear about another initiative-of-the-month about to be loosed among the leery survivors of the last purge. The meeting begins. Amid the tricolor visuals and 3D spreadsheets, the same old message is skeptically received by managers scrambling for politically correct responses in an endless game of shoot the messenger.

This is a familiar scene in corporations around the world. But interestingly, firms such as Advanced Optical Components, a division of Finisar, formerly VCSEL, have learned how to manage the process of successfully matching supply and demand. Advanced Optical Components has developed a new semiconductor laser used in computing, networking, and sensing applications. Forecasting and managing production capacity is a unique challenge for companies with a stream of new and innovative products coming to market. Using a monthly sales and operations planning process, Advanced Optical Components has been able to improve their short- and long-term forecasting

accuracy from 60 percent to consistently hitting 95 percent or better. The specific steps within their plan focus the executive team on (1) the demand opportunities for current and new products and (2) the constraints on the organization's ability to produce product to meet this demand. The plan, developed in a monthly sales and operations planning executive meeting, ensures that demand is synchronized with supply, so customers get the product they want, when they want it, while inventory and costs are kept to a minimum.

Advanced Optical Components managers indicated that a critical step was getting the general manager to champion the process. The second step was achieving a complete understanding of required behavior from the team, including committing to a balanced and synchronized demand/supply plan, being accountable for meeting the performance standards, having open and honest communication, not promising what cannot be delivered, and making the decisions needed to address the identified opportunities and constraints.

SOURCE: ADAPTED FROM http://www.themanufacturer.com, SEPTEMBER 2004.

3. **Inventory holding costs.** A major component is the cost of capital tied up in inventory. Other components are storing, insurance, taxes, spoilage, and obsolescence.
4. **Backordering costs.** Usually these are very hard to measure and include costs of expediting, loss of customer goodwill, and loss of sales revenues resulting from backordering.

Budgets To receive funding, operations managers are generally required to submit annual, and sometimes quarterly, budget requests. The aggregate plan is key to the success of the budgeting process. Recall that the goal of the aggregate plan is to minimize the total production-related costs over the planning horizon by determining the optimal combination of workforce levels and inventory levels. Thus, the aggregate plan provides justification for the requested budget amount. Accurate medium-range planning increases the likelihood of (1) receiving the requested budget and (2) operating within the limits of the budget.

In the next section we provide examples of medium-range planning in both manufacturing and service settings. These examples illustrate the trade-offs associated with different production planning strategies.[2]

AGGREGATE PLANNING TECHNIQUES

Interactive Operations Management

Companies commonly use simple cut-and-try charting and graphic methods to develop aggregate plans. A cut-and-try approach involves costing out various production planning alternatives and selecting the one that is best. Elaborate spreadsheets are developed to facilitate the decision process. Sophisticated approaches involving linear programming and simulation are often incorporated into these spreadsheets. In the following, we demonstrate a spreadsheet approach to evaluate four strategies for meeting demand for the CA&J Company. Later we discuss more sophisticated approaches using linear programming.

A CUT-AND-TRY EXAMPLE: THE CA&J COMPANY

A firm with pronounced seasonal variation normally plans production for a full year to capture the extremes in demand during the busiest and slowest months. But we can illustrate the general principles involved with a shorter horizon. Suppose we wish to set up a production plan for the CA&J Company for the next six months. We are given the following information:

DEMAND AND WORKING DAYS

	JANUARY	FEBRUARY	MARCH	APRIL	MAY	JUNE	TOTALS
Demand forecast	1,800	1,500	1,100	900	1,100	1,600	8,000
Number of working days	22	19	21	21	22	20	125

COSTS

Materials	$100.00/unit
Inventory holding cost	$1.50/unit/month
Marginal cost of stockout	$5.00/unit/month
Marginal cost of subcontracting	$20.00/unit ($120 subcontracting cost less $100 material savings)
Hiring and training cost	$200.00/worker
Layoff cost	$250.00/worker
Labor hours required	5/unit
Straight-time cost (first eight hours each day)	$4.00/hour
Overtime cost (time and a half)	$6.00/hour

INVENTORY

Beginning inventory	400 units
Safety stock	25% of month demand

In solving this problem, we can exclude the material costs. We could have included this $100 cost in all our calculations, but if we assume that a $100 cost is common to each demanded unit, then we need only concern ourselves with the marginal costs. Because the subcontracting cost is $120, our true cost for subcontracting is just $20 because we save the materials.

Note that many costs are expressed in a different form than typically found in the accounting records of a firm. Therefore, do not expect to obtain all these costs directly from such records, but obtain them indirectly from management personnel, who can help interpret the data.

Inventory at the beginning of the first period is 400 units. Because the demand forecast is imperfect, the CA&J Company has determined that a *safety stock* (buffer inventory) should be

Cross Functional

Aggregate Production Planning Requirements

exhibit 14.3

	JANUARY	FEBRUARY	MARCH	APRIL	MAY	JUNE
Beginning inventory	400	450	375	275	225	275
Demand forecast	1,800	1,500	1,100	900	1,100	1,600
Safety stock (.25 × Demand forecast)	450	375	275	225	275	400
Production requirement (Demand forecast + Safety stock − Beginning inventory)	1,850	1,425	1,000	850	1,150	1,725
Ending inventory (Beginning inventory + Production requirement − Demand forecast)	450	375	275	225	275	400

established to reduce the likelihood of stockouts. For this example, assume the safety stock should be one-quarter of the demand forecast. (Chapter 15 covers this topic in depth.)

Before investigating alternative production plans, it is often useful to convert demand forecasts into *production requirements,* which take into account the safety stock estimates. In Exhibit 14.3, note that these requirements implicitly assume that the safety stock is never actually used, so that the ending inventory each month equals the safety stock for that month. For example, the January safety stock of 450 (25 percent of January demand of 1,800) becomes the inventory at the end of January. The production requirement for January is demand plus safety stock minus beginning inventory (1,800 + 450 − 400 = 1,850).

Now we must formulate alternative production plans for the CA&J Company. Using a spreadsheet, we investigate four different plans with the objective of finding the one with the lowest total cost.

Plan 1. Produce to exact monthly production requirements using a regular eight-hour day by varying workforce size.

Plan 2. Produce to meet expected average demand over the next six months by maintaining a constant workforce. This constant number of workers is calculated by finding the average number of workers required each day over the horizon. Take the total production requirements and multiply by the time required for each unit. Then divide by the total time that one person works over the horizon [(8,000 units × 5 hours per unit) ÷ (125 days × 8 hours per day) = 40 workers]. Inventory is allowed to accumulate, with shortages filled from next month's production by backordering. Negative beginning inventory balances indicate that demand is backordered. In some cases, sales may be lost if demand is not met. The lost sales can be shown with a negative ending inventory balance followed by a zero beginning inventory balance in the next period. Notice that in this plan we use our safety stock in January, February, March, and June to meet expected demand.

Plan 3. Produce to meet the minimum expected demand (April) using a constant workforce on regular time. Subcontract to meet additional output requirements. The number of workers is calculated by locating the minimum monthly production requirement and determining how many workers would be needed for that month [(850 units × 5 hours per unit) ÷ (21 days × 8 hours per day) = 25 workers] and subcontracting any monthly difference between requirements and production.

Plan 4. Produce to meet expected demand for all but the first two months using a constant workforce on regular time. Use overtime to meet additional output requirements. The number of workers is more difficult to compute for this plan, but the goal is to finish June with an ending inventory as close as possible to the June safety stock. By trial and error it can be shown that a constant workforce of 38 workers is the closest approximation.

The next step is to calculate the cost of each plan. This requires the series of simple calculations shown in Exhibit 14.4. Note that the headings in each row are different for each plan because each is a different problem requiring its own data and calculations.

The final step is to tabulate and graph each plan and compare their costs. From Exhibit 14.5 we can see that using subcontractors resulted in the lowest cost (Plan 3). Exhibit 14.6 shows the

exhibit 14.4
Costs of Four Production Plans

**Excel:
Aggregate
Planning**

PRODUCTION PLAN 1: EXACT PRODUCTION; VARY WORKFORCE							
	JANUARY	FEBRUARY	MARCH	APRIL	MAY	JUNE	TOTAL
Production requirement (from Exhibit 14.3)	1,850	1,425	1,000	850	1,150	1,725	
Production hours required (Production requirement × 5 hr./unit)	9,250	7,125	5,000	4,250	5,750	8,625	
Working days per month	22	19	21	21	22	20	
Hours per month per worker (Working days × 8 hrs./day)	176	152	168	168	176	160	
Workers required (Production hours required/Hours per month per worker)	53	47	30	25	33	54	
New workers hired (assuming opening workforce equal to first month's requirement of 53 workers)	0	0	0	0	8	21	
Hiring cost (New workers hired × $200)	$0	$0	$0	$0	$1,600	$4,200	$5,800
Workers laid off	0	6	17	5	0	0	
Layoff cost (Workers laid off × $250)	$0	$1,500	$4,250	$1,250	$0	$0	$7,000
Straight-time cost (Production hours required × $4)	$37,000	$28,500	$20,000	$17,000	$23,000	$34,500	$160,000
						Total cost	$172,800

PRODUCTION PLAN 2: CONSTANT WORKFORCE; VARY INVENTORY AND STOCKOUT							
	JANUARY	FEBRUARY	MARCH	APRIL	MAY	JUNE	TOTAL
Beginning inventory	400	8	−276	−32	412	720	
Working days per month	22	19	21	21	22	20	
Production hours available (Working days per month × 8 hr./day × 40 workers)*	7,040	6,080	6,720	6,720	7,040	6,400	
Actual production (Production hours available/5 hr./unit)	1,408	1,216	1,344	1,344	1,408	1,280	
Demand forecast (from Exhibit 14.3)	1,800	1,500	1,100	900	1,100	1,600	
Ending inventory (Beginning inventory + Actual production − Demand forecast)	8	−276	−32	412	720	400	
Shortage cost (Units short × $5)	$0	$1,380	$160	$0	$0	$0	$1,540
Safety stock (from Exhibit 14.3)	450	375	275	225	275	400	
Units excess (Ending inventory − Safety stock) only if positive amount	0	0	0	187	445	0	
Inventory cost (Units excess × $1.50)	$0	$0	$0	$281	$668	$0	$948
Straight-time cost (Production hours available × $4)	$28,160	$24,320	$26,880	$26,880	$28,160	$25,600	$160,000
						Total cost	$162,488

* (Sum of production requirement in Exhibit 14.3 × 5 hr./unit)/(Sum of production hours available × 8 hr./day) = (8,000 × 5)/(125 × 8) = 40.

PRODUCTION PLAN 3: CONSTANT LOW WORKFORCE; SUBCONTRACT							
	JANUARY	FEBRUARY	MARCH	APRIL	MAY	JUNE	TOTAL
Production requirement (from Exhibit 14.3)	1,850	1,425	1,000	850	1,150	1,725	
Working days per month	22	19	21	21	22	20	
Production hours available (Working days × 8 hrs./day × 25 workers)*	4,400	3,800	4,200	4,200	4,400	4,000	

*Minimum production requirement. In this example, April is minimum of 850 units. Number of workers required for April is (850 × 5)/(21 × 8) = 25.

(continued)

(Concluded)

exhibit 14.4

PRODUCTION PLAN 3: CONSTANT LOW WORKFORCE; SUBCONTRACT (*CONCLUDED*)

	JANUARY	FEBRUARY	MARCH	APRIL	MAY	JUNE	TOTAL
Actual production (Production hours available/5 hr. per unit)	880	760	840	840	880	800	
Units subcontracted (Production requirement − Actual production)	970	665	160	10	270	925	
Subcontracting cost (Units subcontracted × $20)	$19,400	$13,300	$3,200	$200	$5,400	$18,500	$60,000
Straight-time cost (Production hours available × $4)	$17,600	$15,200	$16,800	$16,800	$17,600	$16,000	$100,000
						Total cost	$160,000

PRODUCTION PLAN 4: CONSTANT WORKFORCE; OVERTIME

	JANUARY	FEBRUARY	MARCH	APRIL	MAY	JUNE	TOTAL
Beginning inventory	400	0	0	177	554	792	
Working days per month	22	19	21	21	22	20	
Production hours available (Working days × 8 hr./day × 38 workers)*	6,688	5,776	6,384	6,384	6,688	6,080	
Regular shift production (Production hours available/5 hrs. per unit)	1,338	1,155	1,277	1,277	1,338	1,216	
Demand forecast (from Exhibit 14.3)	1,800	1,500	1,100	900	1,100	1,600	
Units available before overtime (Beginning inventory + Regular shift production − Demand forecast). This number has been rounded to the nearest integer.	−62	−345	177	554	792	408	
Units overtime	62	375	0	0	0	0	
Overtime cost (Units overtime × 5 hr./unit × $6/hr.)	$1,860	$10,350	$0	$0	$0	$0	$12,210
Safety stock (from Exhibit 14.3)	450	375	275	225	275	400	
Units excess (Units available before overtime − Safety stock) only if positive amount	0	0	0	329	517	8	
Inventory cost (Units excessive × $1.50)	$0	$0	$0	$494	$776	$12	$1,281
Straight-time cost (Production hours available × $4)	$26,752	$23,104	$25,536	$25,536	$26,752	$24,320	$152,000
						Total cost	$165,491

*Workers determined by trial and error. See text for explanation.

effects of the four plans. This is a cumulative graph illustrating the expected results on the total production requirement.

Note that we have made one other assumption in this example: The plan can start with any number of workers with no hiring or layoff cost. This usually is the case because an aggregate plan draws on existing personnel, and we can start the plan that way. However, in an actual application, the availability of existing personnel transferable from other areas of the firm may change the assumptions.

Each of these four plans focused on one particular cost, and the first three were simple pure strategies. Obviously, there are many other feasible plans, some of which would use a combination of workforce changes, overtime, and subcontracting. The problems at the end of this chapter include examples of such mixed strategies. In practice, the final plan chosen would come from searching a variety of alternatives and future projections beyond the six-month planning horizon we have used.

Excel: Aggregate Planning

Comparison of Four Plans

COST	PLAN 1: EXACT PRODUCTION; VARY WORKFORCE	PLAN 2: CONSTANT WORKFORCE; VARY INVENTORY AND STOCKOUT	PLAN 3: CONSTANT LOW WORKFORCE; SUBCONTRACT	PLAN 4: CONSTANT WORKFORCE; OVERTIME
Hiring	$ 5,800	$ 0	$ 0	$ 0
Layoff	7,000	0	0	0
Excess inventory	0	948	0	1,281
Shortage	0	1,540	0	0
Subcontract	0	0	60,000	0
Overtime	0	0	0	12,210
Straight time	160,000	160,000	100,000	152,000
	$172,800	$162,488	$160,000	$165,491

Four Plans for Satisfying a Production Requirement over the Number of Production Days Available

Keep in mind that the cut-and-try approach does not guarantee finding the minimum-cost solution. However, spreadsheet programs, such as Microsoft Excel®, can perform cut-and-try cost estimates in seconds and have elevated this kind of what-if analysis to a fine art. More sophisticated programs can generate much better solutions without the user having to intercede, as in the cut-and-try method.

AGGREGATE PLANNING APPLIED TO SERVICES: TUCSON PARKS AND RECREATION DEPARTMENT

Service

Charting and graphic techniques are also useful for aggregate planning in service applications. The following example shows how a city's parks and recreation department could use the alternatives of full-time employees, part-time employees, and subcontracting to meet its commitment to provide a service to the city.

Tucson Parks and Recreation Department has an operation and maintenance budget of $9,760,000. The department is responsible for developing and maintaining open space, all public recreational programs, adult sports leagues, golf courses, tennis courts, pools, and so forth. There are 336 full-time-equivalent employees (FTEs). Of these, 216 are full-time permanent personnel who provide the administration and year-round maintenance to all areas. The remaining 120 FTE positions are staffed with part-timers; about three-quarters of them are used during the summer and the remaining quarter in the fall, winter, and spring seasons. The three-fourths (or 90 FTE positions) show up as approximately 800 part-time summer jobs: lifeguards, baseball umpires, and instructors in summer programs for children. Eight hundred part-time jobs came from 90 FTEs because many last only for a month or two, while the FTEs are a year long.

Currently, the only parks and recreation work subcontracted amounts to less than $100,000. This is for the golf and tennis pros and for grounds maintenance at the libraries and veterans' cemetery.

Because of the nature of city employment, the probable bad public image, and civil service rules, the option to hire and fire full-time help daily or weekly to meet seasonal demand is out of the question. However, temporary part-time help is authorized and traditional. Also, it is virtually impossible to have regular (full-time) staff for all the summer jobs. During the summer months, the approximately 800 part-time employees are staffing many programs that occur simultaneously, prohibiting level scheduling over a normal 40-hour week. A wider variety of skills are required (such as umpires, coaches, lifeguards, and teachers of ceramics, guitar, karate, belly dancing, and yoga) than can be expected from full-time employees.

Three options are open to the department in its aggregate planning:

1. The present method, which is to maintain a medium-level full-time staff and schedule work during off-seasons (such as rebuilding baseball fields during the winter months) and to use part-time help during peak demands.
2. Maintain a lower level of staff over the year and subcontract all additional work presently done by full-time staff (still using part-time help).
3. Maintain an administrative staff only and subcontract all work, including part-time help. (This would entail contracts to landscaping firms and pool maintenance companies as well as to newly created private firms to employ and supply part-time help.)

The common unit of measure of work across all areas is full-time equivalent jobs or employees. For example, assume in the same week that 30 lifeguards worked 20 hours each, 40 instructors worked 15 hours each, and 35 baseball umpires worked 10 hours each. This is equivalent to $(30 \times 20) + (40 \times 15) + (35 \times 10) = 1{,}550 \div 40 = 38.75$ FTE positions for that week. Although a considerable amount of workload can be shifted to off-season, most of the work must be done when required.

Full-time employees consist of three groups: (1) the skeleton group of key department personnel coordinating with the city, setting policy, determining budgets, measuring performance, and so forth; (2) the administrative group of supervisory and office personnel who are responsible for or whose jobs are directly linked to the direct-labor workers; and (3) the direct-labor workforce of 116 full-time positions. These workers physically maintain the department's areas of responsibility, such as cleaning up, mowing golf greens and ballfields, trimming trees, and watering grass.

Cost information needed to determine the best alternative strategy is

Full-time direct-labor employees	
Average wage rate	$4.45 per hour
Fringe benefits	17% of wage rate
Administrative costs	20% of wage rate
Part-time employees	
Average wage rate	$4.03 per hour
Fringe benefits	11% of wage rate
Administrative costs	25% of wage rate
Subcontracting all full-time jobs	$1.6 million
Subcontracting all part-time jobs	$1.85 million

June and July are the peak demand seasons in Tucson. Exhibits 14.7 and 14.8 show the high requirements for June and July personnel. The part-time help reaches 576 FTE positions (although, in actual numbers, this is approximately 800 different employees). After a low fall and winter staffing level, the demand shown as "full-time direct" reaches 130 in March (when grounds are reseeded and fertilized) and then increases to a high of 325 in July. The present

---

exhibit 14.7

Actual Demand Requirement for Full-Time Direct Employees and Full-Time Equivalent (FTE) Part-Time Employees

**Excel:
Aggregate
Planning**

	JAN.	FEB.	MAR.	APR.	MAY	JUNE	JULY	AUG.	SEPT.	OCT.	NOV.	DEC.	TOTAL
Days	22	20	21	22	21	20	21	21	21	23	18	22	252
Full-time employees	66	28	130	90	195	290	325	92	45	32	29	60	
Full-time days*	1,452	560	2,730	1,980	4,095	5,800	6,825	1,932	945	736	522	1,320	28,897
Full-time equivalent part-time employees	41	75	72	68	72	302	576	72	0	68	84	27	
FTE days	902	1,500	1,512	1,496	1,512	6,040	12,096	1,512	0	1,564	1,512	594	30,240

*Full-time days are derived by multiplying the number of days in each month by the number of workers.

---

exhibit 14.8

Monthly Requirement for Full-Time Direct-Labor Employees (Other Than Key Personnel) and Full-Time Equivalent Part-Time Employees

**Excel:
Aggregate
Planning**

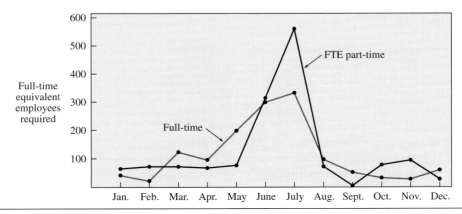

Three Possible Plans for the Parks and Recreation Department

exhibit 14.9

Alternative 1: Maintain 116 full-time regular direct workers. Schedule work during off-seasons to level workload throughout the year. Continue to use 120 full-time equivalent (FTE) part-time employees to meet high demand periods.

COSTS	DAYS PER YEAR (EXHIBIT 14.7)	HOURS (EMPLOYEES × DAYS × 8 HOURS)	WAGES (FULL-TIME, $4.45; PART-TIME, $4.03)	FRINGE BENEFITS (FULL-TIME, 17%; PART-TIME, 11%)	ADMINISTRATIVE COST (FULL-TIME, 20%; PART-TIME, 25%)
116 full-time regular employees	252	233,856	$1,040,659	$176,912	$208,132
120 part-time employees	252	241,920	974,938	107,243	243,735
Total cost = $2,751,619			$2,015,597	$284,155	$451,867

Excel: Aggregate Planning

Alternative 2: Maintain 50 full-time regular direct workers and the present 120 FTE part-time employees. Subcontract jobs releasing 66 full-time regular employees. Subcontract cost, $1,100,000.

COST	DAYS PER YEAR (EXHIBIT 14.7)	HOURS (EMPLOYEES × DAYS × 8 HOURS)	WAGES (FULL-TIME, $4.45; PART-TIME, $4.03)	FRINGE BENEFITS (FULL-TIME, 17%; PART-TIME, 11%)	ADMINISTRATIVE COST (FULL-TIME, 20%; PART-TIME, 25%)	SUBCONTRACT COST
50 full-time employees	252	100,800	$ 448,560	$ 76,255	$ 89,712	
120 FTE part-time employees	252	241,920	974,938	107,243	243,735	
Subcontracting cost						$1,100,000
Total cost = $3,040,443			$1,423,498	$183,498	$333,447	$1,100,000

Alternative 3: Subcontract all jobs previously performed by 116 full-time regular employees. Subcontract cost $1,600,000. Subcontract all jobs previously performed by 120 FTE part-time employees. Subcontract cost $1,850,000.

COST	SUBCONTRACT COST
0 full-time employees	
0 part-time employees	
Subcontract full-time jobs	$1,600,000
Subcontract part-time jobs	1,850,000
Total cost	$3,450,000

method levels this uneven demand over the year to an average of 116 full-time year-round employees by early scheduling of work. As previously mentioned, no attempt is made to hire and lay off full-time workers to meet this uneven demand.

Exhibit 14.9 shows the cost calculations for all three alternatives. Exhibit 14.10 compares the total costs for each alternative. From this analysis, it appears that the department is already using the lowest-cost alternative (Alternative 1).

LEVEL SCHEDULING

In this chapter we looked at four primary strategies for production planning: vary workforce size to meet demand, work overtime and part-time, vary inventory through excesses and shortages, and subcontract.

A level schedule holds production constant over a period of time. It is something of a combination of the strategies we have mentioned here. For each period, it keeps the workforce constant and inventory low, and depends on demand to pull products through. Level production has a number of advantages, which makes it the backbone of JIT production:

1. The entire system can be planned to minimize inventory and work-in-process.
2. Product modifications are up-to-date because of the low amount of work-in-process.

**Excel:
Aggregate
Planning**

exhibit 14.10

Comparison of Costs for All Three Alternatives

	ALTERNATIVE 1: 116 FULL-TIME DIRECT-LABOR EMPLOYEES, 120 FULL-TIME EQUIVALENT PART-TIME EMPLOYEES	ALTERNATIVE 2: 50 FULL-TIME DIRECT-LABOR EMPLOYEES, 120 FULL-TIME EQUIVALENT PART-TIME EMPLOYEES, SUBCONTRACTING	ALTERNATIVE 3: SUBCONTRACTING JOBS FORMERLY PERFORMED BY 116 DIRECT-LABOR FULL-TIME EMPLOYEES AND 120 FTE PART-TIME EMPLOYEES
Wages	$2,015,597	$ 1,423,498	—
Fringe benefits	284,155	183,498	—
Administrative costs	451,867	333,447	—
Subcontracting, full-time jobs		1,100,000	$1,600,000
Subcontracting, part-time jobs			1,850,000
Total	$2,751,619	$3,040,443	$3,450,000

3. There is a smooth flow throughout the production system.
4. Purchased items from vendors can be delivered when needed, and, in fact, often directly to the production line.

Toyota Motor Corporation, for example, creates a yearly production plan that shows the total number of cars to be made and sold. The aggregate production plan creates the system requirements to produce this total number with a level schedule. The secret to success in the Japanese level schedule is *production smoothing*. The aggregate plan is translated into monthly and daily schedules that *sequence* products through the production system. The procedure is essentially this: Two months in advance, the car types and quantities needed are established. This is converted to a detailed plan one month ahead. These quantities are given to subcontractors and vendors so that they can plan on meeting Toyota's needs. The monthly needs of various car types are then translated into daily schedules. For example, if 8,000 units of car type A are needed in one month, along with 6,000 type B, 4,000 type C, and 2,000 type D, and if we assume the line operates 20 days per month, then this would be translated to a daily output of 400, 300, 200, and 100, respectively. Further, this would be sequenced as four units of A, three of B, two of C, and one of D each 9.6 minutes of a two-shift day (960 minutes).

Each worker operates a number of machines, producing a sequence of products. To use this level scheduling technique,

1. Production should be repetitive (assembly-line format).
2. The system must contain excess capacity.
3. Output of the system must be fixed for a period of time (preferably a month).
4. There must be a smooth relationship among purchasing, marketing, and production.
5. The cost of carrying inventory must be high.
6. Equipment costs must be low.
7. The workforce must be multiskilled.

For more about level scheduling, see uniform plant loading in Chapter 12 on lean production systems. Also see the discussion on mixed-model line balancing in Technical Note 6 on layout.

MATHEMATICAL TECHNIQUES

Linear Programming The general model of linear programming is appropriate to aggregate planning if the cost and variable relationships are linear and demand can be treated as deterministic (see Technical Note 2). For the special case where hiring and firing are not considerations, the more easily formulated transportation model can be applied in a manner similar to the location problem in Technical Note 11.

The application of a transportation matrix to aggregate planning is illustrated by the solved problem in Exhibit 14.11. This formulation is termed a *period model* because it relates

Aggregate Planning by the Transportation Method of Linear Programming

exhibit 14.11

PRODUCTION PERIODS (SOURCES)		SALES PERIODS 1	2	3	4	ENDING INVENTORY	UNUSED CAPACITY	TOTAL CAPACITY
Beginning inventory		50 [0]	[5]	[10]	[15]	[20]	[0]	50
1	Regular time	700 [50]	[55]	[60]	[65]	[70]	[0]	700
1	Overtime	50 [75]	[80]	[85]	[90]	50 [95]	250 [0]	350
2	Regular time	X	700 [50]	[55]	[60]	[65]	[0]	700
2	Overtime	X	100 [75]	[80]	[85]	150 [90]	[0]	250
3	Regular time	X	X	700 [50]	[55]	[60]	[0]	700
3	Overtime	X	X	100 [75]	[80]	150 [85]	[0]	250
4	Regular time	X	X	X	700 [50]	[55]	[0]	700
4	Overtime	X	X	X	100 [75]	150 [80]	[0]	250
Total requirements		800	800	800	800	500	250	3,950

Additional Factors That Can Be Included in the Transportation Method for Aggregate Planning

exhibit 14.12

1 **Multiproduct production.** When more than one product shares common facilities, additional columns are included corresponding to each product. For each month, the number of columns will equal the number of products, and the cost entry in each cell will equal the cost for the corresponding product.

2 **Backordering.** The backorder time and the cost of backordering can be included by treating the assignments marked with an X in Exhibit 14.11 as feasible. If a product demanded in period 1 is delivered in period 2, this is equivalent to meeting period 1's demand with production in period 2. For, say, a $10 unit cost associated with such a backorder, the cost entry in the cell corresponding to period 2 regular time row and period 1 column will be $60 ($10 plus the $50 cost of regular-time production in period 2).

3 **Lost sales.** When stockouts are allowed and a part of the demand is not met, the firm incurs opportunity cost equal to the lost revenue. This can be included in the matrix by adding a "lost sales" row for each period. The cost entry in the cell will be equal to lost revenue per unit.

4 **Perishability.** When perishability does not permit the sale of a product after it has been in stock for a certain period, the corresponding cells in the matrix are treated as infeasible. If the product in Exhibit 14.11 cannot be sold after it has been in stock for two periods, the cells occupying the intersection of period 1 rows and columns beyond period 3 will be infeasible.

5 **Subcontracting.** This can be included by adding a "subcontracting" row for each period. Cost values in each cell would be the unit cost to subcontract plus any inventory holding cost (incremented in the same fashion as regular time and overtime costs).

production demand to production capacity by periods.[3] In this case, there are four subperiods with demand forecast as 800 units in each. The total capacity available is 3,950 or an excess capacity of 750 (3,950 − 3,200). However, the bottom row of the matrix indicates a desire for 500 units in inventory at the end of the planning period, so unused capacity is reduced to 250. The left side of the matrix indicates the means by which production is made available over the planning period (that is, beginning inventory and regular and overtime work during each period). An X indicates a period where production cannot be backlogged. That is, you cannot produce in, say, Period 3 to meet demand in Period 2. (This is feasible if the situation allows backorders.) Finally, the costs in each cell are incremented by a holding cost of $5 for each period. Thus, if one produces on regular time in Period 1 to satisfy demand for Period 4, there will be a $15 holding cost. Overtime is, of course, more expensive to start with, but holding costs in this example are not affected by whether production is on regular time or overtime. The solution shown is an optimal one.

The transportation matrix is remarkably versatile and can incorporate a variety of aggregate planning factors as described in Exhibit 14.12.

Observations on Linear Programming and Mathematical Techniques   Linear programming is appropriate when the cost and variable relationships are linear or can be cut into approximately linear segments. Much of this is being done using the Solver Option in Microsoft Excel as described in Technical Note 2. The basic issue is management's attitude toward models in general. Those companies where modeling is a way of life are likely to try the more sophisticated methods; in those where it is not, we would suspect that graphic and charting approaches would be used. Somewhere in the middle ground lie companies that have substantial experience in data processing and use the computer primarily for detailed scheduling. In these firms, we would expect to see experimentation with alternative cut-and-try plans in developing aggregate plans.

Recently, companies such as SAP and Oracle have begun offering advanced planning options as part of their enterprise resource planning systems. This software provides a toolkit of powerful problem-solving applications and includes functions for solving linear programming and other types of mathematical programming problems. We expect that many companies will develop applications that use these tools and that "optimization" will become common practice.

YIELD MANAGEMENT

Yield management

Service

Why is it that the guy sitting next to you on the plane paid half the price you paid for your ticket? Why was a hotel room you booked more expensive when you booked it six months in advance than when you checked in without a reservation (or vice versa)? The answers lie in the practice known as yield management. **Yield management** can be defined as the process of allocating the right type of capacity to the right type of customer at the right price and time to maximize revenue or yield. Yield management can be a powerful approach to making demand more predictable, which is important to aggregate planning.

Yield management has existed as long as there has been limited capacity for serving customers. However, its widespread scientific application began with American Airlines' computerized reservation system (SABRE), introduced in the mid-1980s. The system allowed the airline to change ticket prices on any routes instantaneously as a function of forecast demand. Peoples' Express, a no-frills, low-cost competitor airline, was one of the most famous victims of American's yield management system. Basically, the system enabled hour-by-hour updating on competing routes so that American could match or better prices wherever Peoples' Express was flying. The president of Peoples' Express realized that the game was lost when his mother flew on American to Peoples' hub for a lower price than Peoples' could offer!

AIR CARRIERS SUCH AS SINGAPORE AIRLINES UTILIZE YIELD MANAGEMENT STRATEGIES TO MAXIMIZE REVENUE FOR THE CAPACITY THEY HAVE.

From an operational perspective, yield management is most effective when

1. Demand can be segmented by customer.
2. Fixed costs are high and variable costs are low.
3. Inventory is perishable.
4. Product can be sold in advance.
5. Demand is highly variable.

Hotels illustrate these five characteristics well. They offer one set of rates during the week for the business traveler and another set during the weekend for the vacationer. The variable costs associated with a room (such as cleaning) are low in comparison to the cost of adding rooms to the property. Available rooms cannot be transferred from night to night, and blocks of rooms can be sold to conventions or tours. Finally, potential guests may cut short their stay or not show up at all.

Most organizations (such as airlines, rental car agencies, cruise lines, and hotels) manage yield by establishing decision rules for opening or closing rate classes as a function of expected demand and available supply. The methodologies for doing this can be quite sophisticated. A common approach is to forecast demand over the planning horizon and then use marginal analysis to determine the rates that will be charged if demand is forecast as being above or below set control limits around the forecast mean.

OPERATING YIELD MANAGEMENT SYSTEMS

A number of interesting issues arise in managing yield. One is that pricing structures must appear logical to the customer and justify the different prices. Such justification, commonly called *rate fences,* may have either a physical basis (such as a room with a view) or a non-physical basis (like unrestricted access to the Internet). Pricing should also relate to addressing specific capacity problems. If capacity is sufficient for peak demand, price reductions stimulating off-peak demand should be the focus. If capacity is insufficient, offering deals to customers who arrive during nonpeak periods (or creating alternative service locations) may enhance revenue generation.

A second issue is handling variability in arrival or starting times, duration, and time between customers. This entails employing maximally accurate forecasting methods (the greater the accuracy in forecasting demand, the more likely yield management will succeed); coordinated policies on overbooking, deposits, and no-show or cancellation penalties; and well-designed service processes that are reliable and consistent.

A third issue relates to managing the service process. Some strategies include scheduling additional personnel to meet peak demand; increasing customer coproduction; creating adjustable capacity; utilizing idle capacity for complementary services; and cross-training employees to create reserves for peak periods.

The fourth and perhaps most critical issue is training workers and managers to work in an environment where overbooking and price changes are standard occurrences that directly impact the customer. Companies have developed creative ways for mollifying overbooked customers. A golf course company offers $100 putters to players who have been overbooked at a popular tee time. Airlines, of course, frequently give overbooked passengers free tickets for other flights.

The essence of yield management is the ability to manage demand. Kimes and Chase suggest that two strategic levers can be used to accomplish this goal: pricing and duration control.[4] If these two levers are thought of in matrix form (see Exhibit 14.13) with price being either fixed or variable and duration being either predictable or unpredictable, then traditional applications of yield management have been by firms located in the variable price/predictable duration quadrant. This type of matrix provides a framework for a firm to identify its position and the necessary actions to manage yield. For example, an action controlling duration would be to convert the service offering from an event of indeterminate time to an offering that is time-based. This improves reservation planning and hence allocation of resources. An example would be having diners reserve a fixed block of time for dining at a restaurant (e.g., 7–8 P.M.) rather than an open-ended table reservation for 7 P.M.

exhibit 14.13   Price/Service Duration Matrix: Positioning of Selected Service Industries

		Price	
		Fixed	Variable
Duration	Predictable	**Quadrant 1:** Movies Stadiums/arenas Convention centers	**Quadrant 2:** Hotels Airlines Rental cars Cruise lines
	Unpredictable	**Quadrant 3:** Restaurants Golf courses Internet service providers	**Quadrant 4:** Continuing care hospitals

SOURCE: S. KIMES AND R. B. CHASE, "THE STRATEGIC LEVERS OF YIELD MANAGEMENT," JOURNAL OF SERVICE RESEARCH 1, NO. 2 (1998), PP. 298–308. COPYRIGHT © 1998 BY SAGE PUBLISHERS. USED BY PERMISSION OF SAGE PUBLICATIONS, INC.

CONCLUSION

Sales and operations planning and the aggregate plan translate corporate strategic and capacity plans into broad categories of workforce size, inventory quantity, and production levels.

Demand variations are a fact of life, so the planning system must include sufficient flexibility to cope with such variations. Flexibility can be achieved by developing alternative sources of supply, cross-training workers to handle a wide variety of orders, and engaging in more frequent replanning during high-demand periods.

Decision rules for production planning should be adhered to once they have been selected. However, they should be carefully analyzed prior to implementation by checks such as simulation of historical data to see what really would have happened if the decision rules had operated in the past.

Yield management is an important tool that can be used to shape demand patterns so a firm can operate more efficiently.

KEY TERMS

Aggregate operations plan Translating annual and quarterly business plans into labor and production output plans for the intermediate term. The objective is to minimize the cost of resources required to meet demand.

Sales and operations planning A term that refers to the process that helps companies keep demand and supply in balance. The terminology is meant to capture the importance of cross-functional work.

Long-range planning Activity typically done annually and focusing on a horizon of a year or more.

Intermediate-range planning Activity that usually covers a period from 3 to 18 months with weekly, monthly, or quarterly time increments.

Short-range planning Planning that covers a period less than six months with either daily or weekly increments of time.

Master production schedule (MPS) A schedule of the amounts and times when specific items will be manufactured, typically using weekly increments of time.

Rough-cut capacity planning Verification that sufficient capacity exists to meet a master production schedule.

Material requirements planning (MRP) Given the master production schedule, a procedure that generates specific schedules for component parts and subassemblies.

Capacity requirements planning Allocation of production resource capacity to specific orders.

Order scheduling Final planning of the use of specific machines, production lines, or work centers to produce orders.

Production rate The number of units completed per unit of time.

Workforce level The number of production workers needed each period.

Inventory on hand Unused inventory carried from a previous period.

Production planning strategies Plans that involve trade-offs among workforce size, work hours, inventory, and backlogs.

Pure strategy A plan that uses just one of the options available for meeting demand. Typical options include chasing demand, using a stable workforce with overtime or part-time work, and constant production with shortages and overages absorbed by inventory.

Mixed strategy A plan that combines options available for meeting demand.

Yield management Allocating the right type of capacity to the right type of customer at the right price and time to maximize revenue or yield.

SOLVED PROBLEM

Jason Enterprises (JE) produces video telephones for the home market. Quality is not quite as good as it could be at this point, but the selling price is low and Jason can study market response while spending more time on R&D.

At this stage, however, JE needs to develop an aggregate production plan for the six months from January through June. You have been commissioned to create the plan. The following information should help:

Excel: Aggregate Planning Solved Problem

DEMAND AND WORKING DAYS

	JANUARY	FEBRUARY	MARCH	APRIL	MAY	JUNE	TOTALS
Demand forecast	500	600	650	800	900	800	4,250
Number of working days	22	19	21	21	22	20	125

COSTS

Materials	$100.00/unit
Inventory holding cost	$10.00/unit/month
Marginal cost of stockout	$20.00/unit/month
Marginal cost of subcontracting	$100.00/unit ($200 subcontracting cost less $100 material savings)
Hiring and training cost	$50.00/worker
Layoff cost	$100.00/worker
Labor hours required	4/unit
Straight-time cost (first eight hours each day)	$12.50/hour
Overtime cost (time and a half)	$18.75/hour

INVENTORY

Beginning inventory	200 units
Safety stock required	0% of month demand

What is the cost of each of the following production strategies?

a. Produce exactly to meet demand; vary workforce (assuming opening workforce equal to first month's requirements).

b. Constant workforce; vary inventory and allow shortages only (assuming a starting workforce of 10).

c. Constant workforce of 10; use subcontracting.

Solution

AGGREGATE PRODUCTION PLANNING REQUIREMENTS

	JANUARY	FEBRUARY	MARCH	APRIL	MAY	JUNE	TOTAL
Beginning inventory	200	0	0	0	0	0	
Demand forecast	500	600	650	800	900	800	

(continued)

AGGREGATE PRODUCTION PLANNING REQUIREMENTS (*CONCLUDED*)

	JANUARY	FEBRUARY	MARCH	APRIL	MAY	JUNE	TOTAL
Safety stock (0.0 × Demand forecast)	0	0	0	0	0	0	
Production requirement (Demand forecast + Safety stock − Beginning inventory)	300	600	650	800	900	800	
Ending inventory (Beginning inventory + Production requirement − Demand forecast)	0	0	0	0	0	0	

PRODUCTION PLAN 1: EXACT PRODUCTION; VARY WORKFORCE

	JANUARY	FEBRUARY	MARCH	APRIL	MAY	JUNE	TOTAL
Production requirement	300	600	650	800	900	800	
Production hours required (Production requirement × 4 hr./unit)	1,200	2,400	2,600	3,200	3,600	3,200	
Working days per month	22	19	21	21	22	20	
Hours per month per worker (Working days × 8 hrs./day)	176	152	168	168	176	160	
Workers required (Production hours required/Hours per month per worker)	7	16	15	19	20	20	
New workers hired (assuming opening workforce equal to first month's requirement of 7 workers)	0	9	0	4	1	0	
Hiring cost (New workers hired × $50)	$0	$450	$0	$200	$50	$0	$700
Workers laid off	0	0	1	0	0	0	
Layoff cost (Workers laid off × $100)	$0	$0	$100	$0	$0	$0	$100
Straight-time cost (Production hours required × $12.50)	$15,000	$30,000	$32,500	$40,000	$45,000	$40,000	$202,500
							Total cost $203,300

PRODUCTION PLAN 2: CONSTANT WORKFORCE; VARY INVENTORY AND STOCKOUT

	JANUARY	FEBRUARY	MARCH	APRIL	MAY	JUNE	TOTAL
Beginning inventory	200	140	−80	−310	−690	−1150	
Working days per month	22	19	21	21	22	20	
Production hours available (Working days per month × 8 hr./day × 10 workers)*	1,760	1,520	1,680	1,680	1,760	1,600	
Actual production (Production hours available/4 hr./unit)	440	380	420	420	440	400	
Demand forecast	500	600	650	800	900	800	
Ending inventory (Beginning inventory + Actual production − Demand forecast)	140	−80	−310	−690	−1150	−1550	
Shortage cost (Units short × $20)	$0	$1,600	$6,200	$13,800	$23,000	$31,000	$75,600
Safety stock	0	0	0	0	0	0	
Units excess (Ending inventory − Safety stock; only if positive amount)	140	0	0	0	0	0	
Inventory cost (Units excess × $10)	$1,400	$0	$0	$0	$0	$0	$1,400
Straight-time cost (Production hours available × $12.50)	$22,000	$19,000	$21,000	$21,000	$22,000	$20,000	$125,000
							Total cost $202,000

*Assume a constant workforce of 10.

PRODUCTION PLAN 3: CONSTANT WORKFORCE; SUBCONTRACT

	JANUARY	FEBRUARY	MARCH	APRIL	MAY	JUNE	TOTAL
Production requirement	300	460[†]	650	800	900	800	
Working days per month	22	19	21	21	22	20	
Production hours available (Working days × 8 hrs./day × 10 workers)*	1,760	1,520	1,680	1,680	1,760	1,600	
Actual production (Production hours available/4 hr. per unit)	440	380	420	420	440	400	
Units subcontracted (Production requirements − Actual production)	0	80	230	380	460	400	
Subcontracting cost (Units subcontracted × $100)	$0	$8,000	$23,000	$38,000	$46,000	$40,000	$155,000
Straight-time cost (Production hours available × $12.50)	$22,000	$19,000	$21,000	$21,000	$22,000	$20,000	$125,000

Total cost $280,000

*Assume a constant workforce of 10.
[†]600 − 140 units of beginning inventory in February.

SUMMARY

PLAN DESCRIPTION	HIRING	LAYOFF	SUBCONTRACT	STRAIGHT TIME	SHORTAGE	EXCESS INVENTORY	TOTAL COST
1. Exact production; vary workforce	$700	$100		$202,500			$203,300
2. Constant workforce; vary inventory and shortages				$125,000	$75,600	$1,400	$202,000
3. Constant workforce; subcontract			$155,000	$125,000			$280,000

REVIEW AND DISCUSSION QUESTIONS

1 What is the major difference between aggregate planning in manufacturing and aggregate planning in services?
2 What are the basic controllable variables of a production planning problem? What are the four major costs?
3 Distinguish between pure and mixed strategies in production planning.
4 Define level scheduling. How does it differ from the pure strategies in production planning?
5 Compare the best plans in the CA&J Company and the Tucson Parks and Recreation Department. What do they have in common?
6 How does forecast accuracy relate, in general, to the practical application of the aggregate planning models discussed in the chapter?
7 In which way does the time horizon chosen for an aggregate plan determine whether it is the best plan for the firm?
8 Review the opening vignette. How does sales and operations planning help resolve product shortage problems?
9 How would you apply yield management concepts to a barbershop? A soft drink vending machine?

PROBLEMS

1 For the solved problem, devise the least costly plan you can. You may choose your starting workforce level.
2 Assume that Alexandra Industries has purchased Jason Enterprises (see the solved problem) and has instituted Japanese-style management in which workers are guaranteed a job for life (with no layoffs). Based on the data in Problem 1 (and additional information provided here), develop a production plan using the transportation method of linear programming. To keep things simple, plan for the first three months only and convert costs from hours to units in your model. Additional information: overtime is limited to 11 units per month per worker, and up to 5 units per month may be subcontracted at a cost of $100 per unit.

3   Develop a production plan and calculate the annual cost for a firm whose demand forecast is fall, 10,000; winter, 8,000; spring, 7,000; summer, 12,000. Inventory at the beginning of fall is 500 units. At the beginning of fall you currently have 30 workers, but you plan to hire temporary workers at the beginning of summer and lay them off at the end of the summer. In addition, you have negotiated with the union an option to use the regular workforce on overtime during winter or spring if overtime is necessary to prevent stockouts at the end of those quarters. Overtime is *not* available during the fall. Relevant costs are: hiring, $100 for each temp; layoff, $200 for each worker laid off; inventory holding, $5 per unit-quarter; backorder, $10 per unit; straight time, $5 per hour; overtime, $8 per hour. Assume that the productivity is 0.5 unit per worker hour, with eight hours per day and 60 days per season.

4   Plan production for a four-month period: February through May. For February and March, you should produce to exact demand forecast. For April and May, you should use overtime and inventory with a stable workforce; *stable* means that the number of workers needed for March will be held constant through May. However, government constraints put a maximum of 5,000 hours of overtime labor per month in April and May (zero overtime in February and March). If demand exceeds supply, then backorders occur. There are 100 workers on January 31. You are given the following demand forecast: February, 80,000; March, 64,000; April, 100,000; May, 40,000. Productivity is four units per worker hour, eight hours per day, 20 days per month. Assume zero inventory on February 1. Costs are hiring, $50 per new worker; layoff, $70 per worker laid off; inventory holding, $10 per unit-month; straight-time labor, $10 per hour; overtime, $15 per hour; backorder, $20 per unit. Find the total cost of this plan.

5   Plan production for the next year. The demand forecast is spring, 20,000; summer, 10,000; fall, 15,000; winter, 18,000. At the beginning of spring you have 70 workers and 1,000 units in inventory. The union contract specifies that you may lay off workers only once a year, at the beginning of summer. Also, you may hire new workers only at the end of summer to begin regular work in the fall. The number of workers laid off at the beginning of summer and the number hired at the end of summer should result in planned production levels for summer and fall that equal the demand forecasts for summer and fall, respectively. If demand exceeds supply, use overtime in spring only, which means that backorders could occur in winter. You are given these costs: hiring, $100 per new worker; layoff, $200 per worker laid off; holding, $20 per unit-quarter; backorder cost, $8 per unit; straight-time labor, $10 per hour; overtime, $15 per hour. Productivity is 0.5 unit per worker hour, eight hours per day, 50 days per quarter. Find the total cost.

6   DAT, Inc., needs to develop an aggregate plan for its product line. Relevant data are

Production time	1 hour per unit	Beginning inventory	500 units
Average labor cost	$10 per hour	Safety stock	One-half month
Workweek	5 days, 8 hours each day	Shortage cost	$20 per unit per month
Days per month	Assume 20 work days per month	Carrying cost	$5 per unit per month

The forecast for next year is

JAN.	FEB.	MAR.	APR.	MAY	JUNE	JULY	AUG.	SEPT.	OCT.	NOV.	DEC.
2,500	3,000	4,000	3,500	3,500	3,000	3,000	4,000	4,000	4,000	3,000	3,000

Management prefers to keep a constant workforce and production level, absorbing variations in demand through inventory excesses and shortages. Demand not met is carried over to the following month.

Develop an aggregate plan that will meet the demand and other conditions of the problem. Do not try to find the optimum; just find a good solution and state the procedure you might use to test for a better solution. Make any necessary assumptions.

7   Old Pueblo Engineering Contractors creates six-month "rolling" schedules, which are recomputed monthly. For competitive reasons (they would need to divulge proprietary design criteria, methods, and so on), Old Pueblo does not subcontract. Therefore, its only options to meet customer requirements are (1) work on regular time; (2) work on overtime, which is limited to 30 percent of regular time; (3) do customers' work early, which would cost an additional $5 per hour per month; and (4) perform customers' work late, which would cost an additional $10 per hour per month penalty, as provided by their contract.

Old Pueblo has 25 engineers on its staff at an hourly rate of $30. The overtime rate is $45. Customers' hourly requirements for the six months from January to June are

JANUARY	FEBRUARY	MARCH	APRIL	MAY	JUNE
5,000	4,000	6,000	6,000	5,000	4,000

Develop an aggregate plan using the transportation method of linear programming. Assume 20 working days in each month.

8   Alan Industries is expanding its product line to include new models: Model A, Model B, and Model C. These are to be produced on the same production equipment, and the objective is to meet the demands for the three products using overtime where necessary. The demand forecast for the next four months, in required hours, is

PRODUCT	APRIL	MAY	JUNE	JULY
Model A	800	600	800	1,200
Model B	600	700	900	1,100
Model C	700	500	700	850

Because the products deteriorate rapidly, there is a high loss in quality and, consequently, a high carryover cost into subsequent periods. Each hour's production carried into future months costs $3 per productive hour of Model A, $4 for Model B, and $5 for Model C.

Production can take place during either regular working hours or overtime. Regular time is paid at $4 when working on Model A, $5 for Model B, and $6 for Model C. Overtime premium is 50 percent.

The available production capacity for regular time and overtime is

	APRIL	MAY	JUNE	JULY
Regular time	1,500	1,300	1,800	1,700
Overtime	s700	650	900	850

a. Set up the problem in matrix form and show appropriate costs.

b. Show a feasible solution.

9   Shoney Video Concepts produces a line of videodisc players to be linked to personal computers for video games. Videodiscs have much faster access time than tape. With such a computer/video link, the game becomes a very realistic experience. In a simple driving game where the joystick steers the vehicle, for example, rather than seeing computer graphics on the screen, the player is actually viewing a segment of a videodisc shot from a real moving vehicle. Depending on the action of the player (hitting a guard rail, for example), the disc moves virtually instantaneously to that segment and the player becomes part of an actual accident of real vehicles (staged, of course).

Shoney is trying to determine a production plan for the next 12 months. The main criterion for this plan is that the employment level is to be held constant over the period. Shoney is continuing in its R&D efforts to develop new applications and prefers not to cause any adverse feeling with the local workforce. For the same reason, all employees should put in full workweeks, even if this is not the lowest-cost alternative. The forecast for the next 12 months is

MONTH	FORECAST DEMAND	MONTH	FORECAST DEMAND
January	600	July	200
February	800	August	200
March	900	September	300
April	600	October	700
May	400	November	800
June	300	December	900

Manufacturing cost is $200 per set, equally divided between materials and labor. Inventory storage cost is $5 per month. A shortage of sets results in lost sales and is estimated to cost an overall $20 per unit short.

The inventory on hand at the beginning of the planning period is 200 units. Ten labor hours are required per videodisc player. The workday is eight hours.

Develop an aggregate production schedule for the year using a constant workforce. For simplicity, assume 22 working days each month except July, when the plant closes down for three weeks' vacation (leaving seven working days). Assume that total production capacity is greater than or equal to total demand.

10   Develop a production schedule to produce the exact production requirements by varying the workforce size for the following problem. Use the example in the chapter as a guide (Plan 1).

The monthly forecasts for Product X for January, February, and March are 1,000, 1,500, and 1,200, respectively. Safety stock policy recommends that half of the forecast for that month be defined as safety stock. There are 22 working days in January, 19 in February, and 21 in March. Beginning inventory is 500 units.

Manufacturing cost is $200 per unit, storage cost is $3 per unit per month, standard pay rate is $6 per hour, overtime rate is $9 per hour, cost of stockout is $10 per unit per month, marginal cost of subcontracting is $10 per unit, hiring and training cost is $200 per worker, layoff cost is $300 per worker, and worker productivity is 0.1 unit per hour. Assume that you start off with 50 workers and that they work 8 hours per day.

11   Helter Industries, a company that produces a line of women's bathing suits, hires temporaries to help produce its summer product demand. For the current four-month rolling schedule, there are three temps on staff and 12 full-time employees. The temps can be hired when needed and can be used as needed, whereas the full-time employees must be paid whether they are needed or not. Each full-time employee can produce 205 suits, while each part-time employee can produce 165 suits per month.

Demand for bathing suits for the next four months is as follows:

MAY	JUNE	JULY	AUGUST
3,200	2,800	3,100	3,000

Beginning inventory in May is 403 complete (a complete two-piece includes both top and bottom) bathing suits. Bathing suits cost $40 to produce and carrying cost is 24 percent per year. Develop an aggregate plan using the transportation method of linear programming.

Excel: Bradford Manufacturing

CASE: BRADFORD MANUFACTURING—PLANNING PLANT PRODUCTION

THE SITUATION

You are the operations manager for a manufacturing plant that produces pudding food products. One of your important responsibilities is to prepare an aggregate plan for the plant. This plan is an important input into the annual budget process. The plan provides information on production rates, manufacturing labor requirements, and projected finished goods inventory levels for the next year.

You make those little boxes of pudding mix on packaging lines in your plant. A packaging line has a number of machines that are linked by conveyors. At the start of the line the pudding is mixed; it is then placed in small packets. These packets are inserted into the small pudding boxes, which are collected and placed in cases that hold 48 boxes of pudding. Finally, 160 cases are collected and put on a pallet. The pallets are staged in a shipping area from which they are sent to four distribution centers. Over the years, the technology of the packaging lines has improved so that all the different flavors can be made in relatively small batches with no setup time to switch between flavors. The plant has 15 of these lines, but currently only 10 are being used. Six employees are required to run each line.

The demand for this product fluctuates from month to month. In addition, there is a seasonal component, with peak sales before Thanksgiving, Christmas, and Easter each year. To complicate matters, at the end of the first quarter of each year the marketing group runs a promotion in which special deals are made for large purchases. Business is going well, and the company has been experiencing a general increase in sales.

The plant sends product to four large distribution warehouses strategically located in the United States. Trucks move product daily. The amounts shipped are based on maintaining target inventory levels at the warehouses. These targets are calculated based on anticipated weeks of supply at each warehouse. Current targets are set at two weeks of supply.

In the past, the company has had a policy of producing very close to what it expects sales to be because of limited capacity for storing finished goods. Production capacity has been adequate to support this policy.

Forecast Demand by Quarter (1,000 Case Units)

Quarter	1st (1–13)	2nd (14–26)	3rd (27–39)	4th (40–52)	1st (Next Year)
Demand	2,000	2,200	2,500	2,650	2,220

A sales forecast for next year has been prepared by the marketing department. The forecast is based on quarterly sales quotas, which are used to set up an incentive program for the salespeople. Sales are mainly to the large U.S. retail grocers. The pudding is shipped to the grocers from the distribution warehouses based on orders taken by the salespeople.

Your immediate task is to prepare an aggregate plan for the coming year. The technical and economic factors that must be considered in this plan are shown next.

TECHNICAL AND ECONOMIC INFORMATION

1 Currently the plant is running 10 lines with no overtime. Each line requires six people to run. For planning purposes, the lines are run for 7.5 hours each normal shift. Employees, though, are paid for eight hours' work. It is possible to run up to two hours of overtime each day, but it must be scheduled for a week at a time, and all the lines must run overtime when it is scheduled. Workers are paid $20.00/hour during a regular shift and $30.00/hour on overtime. The standard production rate for each line is 450 cases/hour.

2 The marketing forecast for demand is as follows: Q1— 2,000; Q2—2,200; Q3—2,500; Q4—2,650; and Q1 (next year)—2,200. These numbers are in 1,000-case units. Each number represents a 13-week forecast.

3 Management has instructed manufacturing to maintain a two-week supply of pudding inventory in the warehouses. The two-week supply should be based on future expected sales. The following are ending inventory target levels for each quarter: Q1—338; Q2—385; Q3—408; Q4—338.

4 Inventory carrying cost is estimated by accounting to be $1.00 per case per year. This means that if a case of pudding is held in inventory for an entire year, the cost to just carry that case in inventory is $1.00. If a case is carried for only one week, the cost is $1.00/52, or $.01923. The cost is pro-

portional to the time carried in inventory. There are 200,000 cases in inventory at the beginning of Q1 (this is 200 cases in the 1,000-case units that the forecast is given in).

5 If a stockout occurs, the item is backordered and shipped at a later date. The cost when a backorder occurs is $2.40 per case due to the loss of goodwill and the high cost of emergency shipping.

6 The human resource group estimates that it costs $5,000 to hire and train a new production employee. It costs $3,000 to lay off a production worker.

QUESTIONS

1 Prepare an aggregate plan for the coming year, assuming that the sales forecast is perfect. Use the spreadsheet "Bradford Manufacturing" from this book's DVD. In the spreadsheet an area has been designated for your aggregate plan solution. Supply the number of packaging lines to run and the number of overtime hours for each quarter. You will need to set up the cost calculations in the spreadsheet.

You may want to try using the Excel Solver to find a solution. You will need to "unprotect" the spreadsheet to run the Solver (Tools > Protection > Unprotect). You will also need to set the "not-negativity" box in the "options" area. Remember that your final solution needs an integer number of lines and an integer number of overtime hours for each quarter. (Solutions that require 8.9134 lines and 1.256 hours of overtime are not feasible.)

2 Review your solution carefully and be prepared to defend it. Bring a printout of your solution to class. If you have a notebook computer, bring it to class with a copy of your completed spreadsheet. Your instructor may run a simulation in class using your solution.

SELECTED BIBLIOGRAPHY

Brandimarte, P., and A. Villa (eds.). *Modeling Manufacturing Systems: From Aggregate Planning to Real-Time Control.* New York: Springer, 1999.

Fisher, M. L.; J. H. Hammond; W. R. Obermeyer; and A. Raman. "Making Supply Meet Demand in an Uncertain World." *Harvard Business Review* 72, no. 3 (May–June 1994), pp. 83–93.

Narasimhan, S.; D. W. McLeavey; and P. J. Billington. *Production Planning and Inventory Control.* Englewood Cliffs, NJ: Prentice Hall, 1995.

Silver, E. A.; D. F. Pyke; and R. Peterson. *Inventory Management and Production Planning and Scheduling.* New York: Wiley, 1998.

Smith-Daniels, V.; S. Scheweikhar; and D. Smith-Daniels. "Capacity Management in Health Care Services: Review and Future Research Directions." *Decision Sciences* 19 (1988), pp. 889–919.

Vollmann, T. E.; W. L. Berry; D. C. Whybark; and F. R. Jacobs. *Manufacturing Planning and Control for Supply Chain Management.* 5th ed. New York: Irwin/McGraw-Hill, 2004.

Wallace, T. F. *Sales and Operations Planning: The How-To Handbook.* Cincinnati, OH: T. F. Wallace & Company, 2000.

Whybark, D. C., and G. Vartag. *Global Manufacturing Practices: A Worldwide Survey of Practices in Production Planning and Control.* New York: Elsevier, 1993.

FOOTNOTES

1 M. L. Fisher, J. H. Hammond, W. R. Obermeyer, and A. Raman, "Making Supply Meet Demand in an Uncertain World," *Harvard Business Review* 72, no. 3 (May–June 1994), p. 84.

2 For an interesting application of aggregate planning in nonprofit humanitarian organizations, see C. Sheu and J. G. Wacker, "A Planning and Control Framework for Nonprofit Humanitarian Organizations," *International Journal of Operations and Production Management* 14, no. 4 (1994), pp. 64–77.

3 The analogy used here to the standard transportation problem is that (1) production periods are factories and sales periods are warehouses, (2) wages and holding costs are the transportation costs, and (3) ending inventory and unused capacity are dummy warehouses.

4 S. Kimes and R. B. Chase, "The Strategic Levers of Yield Management," *Journal of Service Research* 1, no. 2 (1998), pp. 298–308.

chapter

INVENTORY CONTROL

15

NEW "ONLINE CATEGORY MANAGERS" SOLVE RETAILER PROBLEMS

 CircuitCity.com executives have found an innovative way to add music compact discs, videos, and DVDs to their online offerings of consumer electronics and avoid taking on huge new inventories. To add movies alone, they were looking at carrying upwards of 55,000 video and DVD titles if their online selection was to meet the average Web shoppers' expectations—compared with the 500 to 3,000 titles stocked in the typical bricks-and-mortar Circuit City store. Further, the home-electronics giant's distribution model was based on making bulk shipments of relatively small numbers of titles to its stores, not

on shipping thousands of individual copies to homes and offices. Experience has found that Web customers tend to go a lot more for the back-catalog stuff, not necessarily the latest hits, so to serve the online customers the selection needs to be comprehensive.

The solution? The "online category manager," a third-party distributor specializing in a particular product category, such as videos, compact discs, or sporting goods. These specialists, often operating behind the scenes, have become increasingly common in Internet retailing as stores such as Circuit City seek to broaden their online offerings without incurring the inventory costs and distribution headaches that come with selling on the Web. With category managers, Web shoppers do not necessarily realize they're dealing with a third party. The sites tend to mirror the look of the retailer sites and to follow the retailers' cues when it comes to promotions and other marketing matters. Retailers generally pay initial fees to integrate their e-commerce systems, but in return they're freed from incurring the larger costs traditionally associated with adding a new product line, or the risks of carrying potentially huge new inventories. In most cases, category managers own the product inventory.

Circuit City, for example, does not buy any movie or music titles from its online category manager until an online sale is made at CircuitCity.com. Circuit City then pays its manager and makes its profit from the higher price it charges the Web customer. The relationship enables CircuitCity.com to set the prices that customers pay. In addition, Circuit City accepts returns at its bricks-and-mortar stores, heading off any complaints or confusion for customers. This relationship allows Circuit City to focus on what it's best at, which is the electronics side of the business. →

You should visualize inventory as stacks of money sitting on forklifts, on shelves, and in trucks and planes while in transit. That's what inventory is—money. For many businesses, inventory is the largest asset on the balance sheet at any given time, even though it is often not very liquid. It is a good idea to try to get your inventory down as far as possible.

A few years ago, Heineken, the Netherlands beer company, figured it could save a whole bunch of money on inventory-in-transit if it could just shorten the forecasting lead time. They expected two things to happen. First, they expected to reduce the need for inventory in the pipeline, therefore cutting down the amount of money devoted to inventory itself. Second, they figured that with a shorter forecasting time, forecasts would be more accurate, reducing emergencies and waste. The Heineken system, called HOPS, cut overall inventory in the system from 16 to 18 weeks to 4 to 6 weeks—a huge drop in time, and a big gain in cash. Forecasts were more accurate, and there was another benefit, too.

Heineken found that its salespeople were suddenly more productive. That is because they were not dealing with all those calls where they had to check on inventory or solve bad forecasting problems, or change orders that were already in process. Instead, they could concentrate on good customer service and helping distributors do better. It was a "win" all the way around.

The key here involves doing things that decrease your inventory order cycle time and increase the accuracy of your forecast. Look for ways to use automated systems and electronic communication to substitute the rapid movement of electrons for the cumbersome movement of masses of atoms.

The economic benefit from inventory reduction is evident from the following statistics: The average cost of inventory in the United States is 30 to 35 percent of its value. For example, if a firm carries an inventory of $20 million, it costs the firm more than $6 million per year. These costs are due to obsolescence, insurance, opportunity costs, and so forth. If the amount of inventory could be reduced to $10 million, for instance, the firm would save over

$3 million, which goes directly to the bottom line. That is, the savings from reduced inventory results in increased profit.

In this chapter we present standard inventory models designed to help management keep the cost down while still meeting production and customer service requirements. Also included are special-purpose models, such as price-break, as well as the ABC technique. In addition, we discuss inventory accuracy and show applications of the models in department stores and auto parts supply.

One particularly interesting application that we discuss is the use of a single-period inventory model in "yield management" situations. Yield management has been discussed in Chapter 14, but solving the problems needed to apply the concept was left to this chapter, since the problem is similar to inventory problems. Yield management is useful for decisions related to overbooking hotel rooms, airline flights, and similar service situations.

There are conflicting views concerning the teaching of classical inventory models. On one side, articles claim that economic order quantity (EOQ) models are invalid. The other side defends their use. We believe both sides are correct—from within their own arenas. Although you must be careful in their application, there certainly are situations in manufacturing where EOQ models can be successfully used. Just-in-time manufacturing (JIT), for example, is based on the classical production–consumption inventory model discussed here. Classical models are quite valid for the many thousands of companies engaged in product and parts distribution.

Concerning JIT and safety stocks, recall that JIT *does* have safety stock. It shows up as the size of containers and the number of containers between each station in a production sequence. Further, all manufacturers that supply parts cannot have similar JIT schedules. A manufacturer with a JIT system utilizing twice-per-day deliveries by a supplier to the production line might be surprised that the supplier produces those supplies a month's worth at a time using an EOQ formula! How we compute inventory requirements depends on many factors; all methods are valid given the correct set of circumstances. Therefore, we should become familiar with them all.

DEFINITION OF INVENTORY

Inventory is the stock of any item or resource used in an organization. An *inventory system* is the set of policies and controls that monitor levels of inventory and determine what levels should be maintained, when stock should be replenished, and how large orders should be.

By convention, *manufacturing inventory* generally refers to items that contribute to or become part of a firm's product output. Manufacturing inventory is typically classified

Inventory ✓

CANNONDALE BICYCLE CORP'S FLEXIBLE PRODUCTION SYSTEM. A VARIETY OF PREMADE FRAME MODELS ARE AVAILABLE INVENTORY FOR QUICK ACCESS. SINCE FRAMES ARE THE LARGEST LEAD ITEM IN THEIR CUSTOMIZATION PROCESS, THIS ALLOWS FOR QUICK ASSEMBLY TO ORDER OF HANDCRAFTED BIKES.

into *raw materials, finished products, component parts, supplies,* and *work-in-process.* In services, *inventory* generally refers to the tangible goods to be sold and the supplies necessary to administer the service.

The basic purpose of inventory analysis in manufacturing and stockkeeping services is to specify (1) when items should be ordered and (2) how large the order should be. Many firms are tending to enter into longer-term relationships with vendors to supply their needs for perhaps the entire year. This changes the "when" and "how many to order" to "when" and "how many to deliver."

PURPOSES OF INVENTORY

[handwritten: Why inventories are needed?]

All firms (including JIT operations) keep a supply of inventory for the following reasons:

1. **To maintain independence of operations.** A supply of materials at a work center allows that center flexibility in operations. For example, because there are costs for making each new production setup, this inventory allows management to reduce the number of setups.

Independence of workstations is desirable on assembly lines as well. The time that it takes to do identical operations will naturally vary from one unit to the next. Therefore, it is desirable to have a cushion of several parts within the workstation so that shorter performance times can compensate for longer performance times. This way the average output can be fairly stable.

2. **To meet variation in product demand.** If the demand for the product is known precisely, it may be possible (though not necessarily economical) to produce the product to exactly meet the demand. Usually, however, demand is not completely known, and a safety or buffer stock must be maintained to absorb variation.

3. **To allow flexibility in production scheduling.** A stock of inventory relieves the pressure on the production system to get the goods out. This causes longer lead times, which permit production planning for smoother flow and lower-cost operation through larger lot-size production. High setup costs, for example, favor producing a larger number of units once the setup has been made.

4. **To provide a safeguard for variation in raw material delivery time.** When material is ordered from a vendor, delays can occur for a variety of reasons: a normal variation in shipping time, a shortage of material at the vendor's plant causing backlogs, an unexpected strike at the vendor's plant or at one of the shipping companies, a lost order, or a shipment of incorrect or defective material.

5. **To take advantage of economic purchase order size.** There are costs to place an order: labor, phone calls, typing, postage, and so on. Therefore, the larger each order is, the fewer the orders that need be written. Also, shipping costs favor larger orders—the larger the shipment, the lower the per-unit cost.

For each of the preceding reasons (especially for items 3, 4, and 5), be aware that inventory is costly and large amounts are generally undesirable. Long cycle times are caused by large amounts of inventory and are undesirable as well.

INVENTORY COSTS

In making any decision that affects inventory size, the following costs must be considered.

1. **Holding (or carrying) costs.** This broad category includes the costs for storage facilities, handling, insurance, pilferage, breakage, obsolescence, depreciation, taxes, and the

opportunity cost of capital. Obviously, high holding costs tend to favor low inventory levels and frequent replenishment.

2. **Setup (or production change) costs.**   To make each different product involves obtaining the necessary materials, arranging specific equipment setups, filling out the required papers, appropriately charging time and materials, and moving out the previous stock of material.

If there were no costs or loss of time in changing from one product to another, many small lots would be produced. This would reduce inventory levels, with a resulting savings in cost. One challenge today is to try to reduce these setup costs to permit smaller lot sizes. (This is the goal of a JIT system.)

3. **Ordering costs.**   These costs refer to the managerial and clerical costs to prepare the purchase or production order. Ordering costs include all the details, such as counting items and calculating order quantities. The costs associated with maintaining the system needed to track orders are also included in ordering costs.

4. **Shortage costs.**   When the stock of an item is depleted, an order for that item must either wait until the stock is replenished or be canceled. There is a trade-off between carrying stock to satisfy demand and the costs resulting from stockout. This balance is sometimes difficult to obtain, because it may not be possible to estimate lost profits, the effects of lost customers, or lateness penalties. Frequently, the assumed shortage cost is little more than a guess, although it is usually possible to specify a range of such costs.

Establishing the correct quantity to order from vendors or the size of lots submitted to the firm's productive facilities involves a search for the minimum total cost resulting from the combined effects of four individual costs: holding costs, setup costs, ordering costs, and shortage costs. Of course, the timing of these orders is a critical factor that may impact inventory cost.

INDEPENDENT VERSUS DEPENDENT DEMAND

In inventory management, it is important to understand the difference between dependent and independent demand. The reason is that entire inventory systems are predicated on whether demand is derived from an end item or is related to the item itself.

Briefly, the distinction between **independent and dependent demand** is this: In independent demand, the demands for various items are unrelated to each other. For example, a workstation may produce many parts that are unrelated but meet some external demand requirement. In dependent demand, the need for any one item is a direct result of the need for some other item, usually a higher-level item of which it is part.

Independent and dependent demand

In concept, dependent demand is a relatively straightforward computational problem. Needed quantities of a dependent-demand item are simply computed, based on the number needed in each higher-level item in which it is used. For example, if an automobile company plans on producing 500 cars per day, then obviously it will need 2,000 wheels and tires (plus spares). The number of wheels and tires needed is *dependent* on the production levels and is not derived separately. The demand for cars, on the other hand, is *independent*—it comes from many sources external to the automobile firm and is not a part of other products; it is unrelated to the demand for other products.

To determine the quantities of independent items that must be produced, firms usually turn to their sales and market research departments. They use a variety of techniques, including customer surveys, forecasting techniques, and economic and sociological trends, as we discussed in Chapter 13 on forecasting. Because independent demand is uncertain, extra units must be carried in inventory. This chapter presents models to determine how many units need to be ordered, and how many extra units should be carried to reduce the risk of stocking out.

Cross Functional

INVENTORY SYSTEMS

An inventory system provides the organizational structure and the operating policies for maintaining and controlling goods to be stocked. The system is responsible for ordering and receipt of goods: timing the order placement and keeping track of what has been ordered, how much, and from whom. The system also must follow up to answer such questions as, Has the supplier received the order? Has it been shipped? Are the dates correct? Are the procedures established for reordering or returning undesirable merchandise?

This section divides systems into single-period systems and multiple-period systems. The classification is based on whether the decision is just a one-time purchasing decision where the purchase is designed to cover a fixed period of time and the item will not be reordered, or the decision involves an item that will be purchased periodically where inventory should be kept in stock to be used on demand. We begin with a look at the one-time purchasing decision and the single-period inventory model.

A SINGLE-PERIOD INVENTORY MODEL

Certainly, an easy example to think about is the classic single-period "newsperson" problem. For example, consider the problem that the newsperson has in deciding how many newspapers to put in the sales stand outside a hotel lobby each morning. If the person does not put enough papers in the stand, some customers will not be able to purchase a paper and the newsperson will lose the profit associated with these sales. On the other hand, if too many papers are placed in the stand, the newsperson will have paid for papers that were not sold during the day, lowering profit for the day.

Actually, this is a very common type of problem. Consider the person selling T-shirts promoting a championship basketball or football game. This is especially difficult, since the person must wait to learn what teams will be playing. The shirts can then be printed with the proper team logos. Of course, the person must estimate how many people will actually want the shirts. The shirts sold prior to the game can probably be sold at a premium price, whereas those sold after the game will need to be steeply discounted.

A simple way to think about this is to consider how much risk we are willing to take for running out of inventory. Let's consider that the newsperson selling papers in the sales stand had collected data over a few months and had found that on average each Monday 90 papers were sold with a standard deviation of 10 papers (of course, this assumes that the papers had never run out). With these data, our newsperson could simply state a service rate that is felt

SOUVENIR HATS SOLD AT THE 104TH U.S. OPEN AT SHINNECOCK HILLS GOLF CLUB, SOUTHHAMPTON, NEW YORK, IN 2004. INVENTORY MUST BE CAREFULLY PLANNED FOR SPECIAL EVENTS WHERE ONE BATCH HAS TO MATCH DEMAND IN A SMALL SALES WINDOW.

to be acceptable. For example, the newsperson might want to be 80 percent sure of not running out of papers each Monday.

Recall from your study of statistics, assuming that the probability distribution associated with the sales of the paper is normal, then if we stocked exactly 90 papers each Monday morning, the risk of stocking out would be 50 percent, since 50 percent of the time we expect demand to be less than 90 papers and 50 percent of the time we expect demand to be greater than 90. To be 80 percent sure of not stocking out, we need to carry a few more papers. From the "cumulative standard normal distribution" table given in Appendix E, we see that we need approximately .85 standard deviation of extra papers to be 80 percent sure of not stocking out. A quick way to find the exact number of standard deviations needed for a given probability of stocking out is with the NORMSINV(probability) function in Microsoft Excel (NORMSINV(.8) = .84162). Given our result from Excel, which is more accurate than what we can get from the tables, the number of extra papers would be .84162 × 10 = 8.416, or 9 papers (there is no way to sell .4 paper!).

To make this more useful, it would be good to actually consider the potential profit and loss associated with stocking either too many or too few papers on the stand. Let's say that our newspaper person pays $.20 for each paper and sells the papers for $.50. In this case the marginal cost associated with underestimating demand is $.30, the lost profit. Similarly, the marginal cost of overestimating demand is $.20, the cost of buying too many papers. The optimal stocking level, using marginal analysis, occurs at the point where the expected benefits derived from carrying the next unit are less than the expected costs for that unit. Keep in mind that the specific benefits and costs depend on the problem.

In symbolic terms, define

C_o = Cost per unit of demand overestimated
C_u = Cost per unit of demand underestimated

By introducing probabilities, the expected marginal cost equation becomes

$$P(C_o) \leq (1 - P)C_u$$

where P is the probability that the unit will not be sold and $1 - P$ is the probability of it being sold, because one or the other must occur. (The unit is sold or is not sold.)[1]

Then, solving for P, we obtain

[15.1]
$$P \leq \frac{C_u}{C_o + C_u}$$

This equation states that we should continue to increase the size of the order so long as the probability of selling what we order is equal to or less than the ratio $C_u/(C_o + C_u)$.

Returning to our newspaper problem, our cost of overestimating demand (C_o) is $.20 per paper and the cost of underestimating demand (C_u) is $.30. The probability therefore is .3/(.2 + .3) = .6. Now, we need to find the point on our demand distribution that corresponds to the cumulative probability of .6. Using the NORMSINV function to get the number of standard deviations (commonly referred to as the Z-score) of extra newspapers to carry, we get .253, which means that we should stock .253(10) = 2.53 or 3 extra papers. The total number of papers for the stand each Monday morning, therefore, should be 93 papers.

This model is very useful and, as we will see in our solved sample problem, can even be used for many service sector problems, such as the number of seats to book on a full airline flight or the number of reservations to book on a full night at a hotel.

EXAMPLE 15.1: Hotel Reservations

A hotel near the university always fills up on the evening before football games. History has shown that when the hotel is fully booked, the number of last-minute cancellations has a mean of 5 and standard deviation of 3. The average room rate is $80. When the hotel is overbooked, policy is to find a room in a nearby hotel and to pay for the room for the customer. This usually costs the hotel approximately $200 since rooms booked on such late notice are expensive. How many rooms should the hotel overbook?

SOLUTION

The cost of underestimating the number of cancellations is $80 and the cost of overestimating cancellations is $200.

$$P \leq \frac{C_u}{C_o + C_u} = \frac{\$80}{\$200 + \$80} = .2857$$

Using NORMSINV(.2857) from Excel® gives a Z-score of $-.56599$. The negative value indicates that we should overbook by a value less than the average of 5. The actual value should be $-.56599(3) = 1.69797$, or 2 reservations less than 5. The hotel should overbook three reservations on the evening prior to a football game.

Another common method for analyzing this type of problem is with a discrete probability distribution found using actual data and marginal analysis. For our hotel, consider that we have collected data and our distribution of no-shows is as follows:

NUMBER OF NO-SHOWS	PROBABILITY	CUMULATIVE PROBABILITY
0	.05	.05
1	.08	.13
2	.10	.23
3	.15	.38
4	.20	.58
5	.15	.73
6	.11	.84
7	.06	.90
8	.05	.95
9	.04	.99
10	.01	1.00

Using these data, a table showing the impact of overbooking is created. Total expected cost of each overbooking option is then calculated by multiplying each possible outcome by its probability and summing the weighted costs. The best overbooking strategy is the one with minimum cost.

Excel: Inventory Control.xls

NUMBER OF RESERVATIONS OVERBOOKED

No-Shows	Probability	0	1	2	3	4	5	6	7	8	9	10
0	0.05	0	200	400	600	800	1,000	1,200	1,400	1,600	1,800	2,000
1	0.08	80	0	200	400	600	800	1,000	1,200	1,400	1,600	1,800
2	0.1	160	80	0	200	400	600	800	1,000	1,200	1,400	1,600
3	0.15	240	160	80	0	200	400	600	800	1,000	1,200	1,400
4	0.2	320	240	160	80	0	200	400	600	800	1,000	1,200
5	0.15	400	320	240	160	80	0	200	400	600	800	1,000
6	0.11	480	400	320	240	160	80	0	200	400	600	800
7	0.06	560	480	400	320	240	160	80	0	200	400	600
8	0.05	640	560	480	400	320	240	160	80	0	200	400
9	0.04	720	640	560	480	400	320	240	160	80	0	200
10	0.01	800	720	640	560	480	400	320	240	160	80	0
Total cost		337.6	271.6	228	212.4	238.8	321.2	445.6	600.8	772.8	958.8	1,156

From the table, the minimum total cost is when three extra reservations are taken. This approach using discrete probability is useful when valid historic data are available. ●

Single-period inventory models are useful for a wide variety of service and manufacturing applications. Consider the following:

1. **Overbooking of airline flights.** It is common for customers to cancel flight reservations for a variety of reasons. Here the cost of underestimating the number of cancellations is the revenue lost due to an empty seat on a flight. The cost of overestimating cancellations is the awards, such as free flights or cash payments, that are given to customers unable to board the flight.

2. **Ordering of fashion items.** A problem for a retailer selling fashion items is that often only a single order can be placed for the entire season. This is often caused by long lead times and limited life of the merchandise. The cost of underestimating demand is the lost profit due to sales not made. The cost of overestimating demand is the cost that results when it is discounted.

3. **Any type of one-time order.** For example, ordering T-shirts for a sporting event or printing maps that become obsolete after a certain period of time.

MULTIPERIOD INVENTORY SYSTEMS

There are two general types of multiperiod inventory systems: fixed–order quantity models (also called the *economic order quantity,* EOQ, and **Q-model**) and fixed–time period models (also referred to variously as the *periodic* system, *periodic review* system, *fixed-order interval* system, and **P-model**). Multiperiod inventory systems are designed to ensure that an item will be available on an ongoing basis throughout the year. Usually the item will be ordered multiple times throughout the year where the logic in the system dictates the actual quantity ordered and the timing of the order.

Fixed–order quantity models (Q-models)

Fixed–time period models (P-models)

The basic distinction is that fixed–order quantity models are "event triggered" and fixed–time period models are "time triggered." That is, a fixed–order quantity model initiates an order when the event of reaching a specified reorder level occurs. This event may take place at any time, depending on the demand for the items considered. In contrast, the fixed–time period model is limited to placing orders at the end of a predetermined time period; only the passage of time triggers the model.

To use the fixed–order quantity model (which places an order when the remaining inventory drops to a predetermined order point, R), the inventory remaining must be continually monitored. Thus, the fixed–order quantity model is a *perpetual* system, which requires that every time a withdrawal from inventory or an addition to inventory is made, records must be updated to reflect whether the reorder point has been reached. In a fixed–time period model, counting takes place only at the review period. (We will discuss some variations of systems that combine features of both.)

Some additional differences tend to influence the choice of systems (also see Exhibit 15.1):

- The fixed–time period model has a larger average inventory because it must also protect against stockout during the review period, T; the fixed–order quantity model has no review period.
- The fixed–order quantity model favors more expensive items because average inventory is lower.
- The fixed–order quantity model is more appropriate for important items such as critical repair parts because there is closer monitoring and therefore quicker response to potential stockout.
- The fixed–order quantity model requires more time to maintain because every addition or withdrawal is logged.

Exhibit 15.2 shows what occurs when each of the two models is put into use and becomes an operating system. As we can see, the fixed–order quantity system focuses on order quantities and reorder points. Procedurally, each time a unit is taken out of stock, the withdrawal is logged and the amount remaining in inventory is immediately compared to the

exhibit 15.1

Fixed–Order Quantity and Fixed–Time Period Differences

FEATURE	Q-MODEL FIXED–ORDER QUANTITY MODEL	P-MODEL FIXED–TIME PERIOD MODEL
Order quantity	Q—constant (the same amount ordered each time)	q—variable (varies each time order is placed)
When to place order	R—when inventory position drops to the reorder level	T—when the review period arrives
Recordkeeping	Each time a withdrawal or addition is made	Counted only at review period
Size of inventory	Less than fixed–time period model	Larger than fixed–order quantity model
Time to maintain	Higher due to perpetual recordkeeping	
Type of items	Higher-priced, critical, or important items	

exhibit 15.2

Comparison of Fixed–Order Quantity and Fixed–Time Period Reordering Inventory Systems

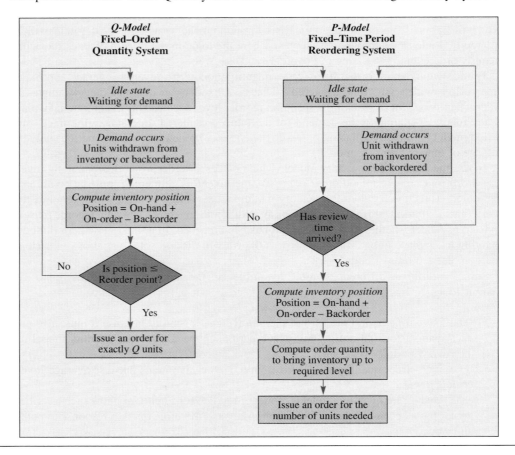

reorder point. If it has dropped to this point, an order for Q items is placed. If it has not, the system remains in an idle state until the next withdrawal.

In the fixed–time period system, a decision to place an order is made after the stock has been counted or reviewed. Whether an order is actually placed depends on the inventory position at that time.

FIXED–ORDER QUANTITY MODELS

 Fixed–order quantity models attempt to determine the specific point, R, at which an order will be placed and the size of that order, Q. The order point, R, is always a specified number of units. An order of size Q is placed when the inventory available (currently in stock and on order) reaches the point R. **Inventory position** is defined as the on-hand plus on-order minus backordered quantities. The solution to a fixed–order quantity model may stipulate something like this: When the inventory position drops to 36, place an order for 57 more units.

Inventory position

The simplest models in this category occur when all aspects of the situation are known with certainty. If the annual demand for a product is 1,000 units, it is precisely 1,000—not 1,000 plus or minus 10 percent. The same is true for setup costs and holding costs. Although the assumption of complete certainty is rarely valid, it provides a good basis for our coverage of inventory models.

Exhibit 15.3 and the discussion about deriving the optimal order quantity are based on the following characteristics of the model. These assumptions are unrealistic, but they represent a starting point and allow us to use a simple example.

- Demand for the product is constant and uniform throughout the period.
- Lead time (time from ordering to receipt) is constant.
- Price per unit of product is constant.
- Inventory holding cost is based on average inventory.
- Ordering or setup costs are constant.
- All demands for the product will be satisfied. (No backorders are allowed.)

The "sawtooth effect" relating Q and R in Exhibit 15.3 shows that when the inventory position drops to point R, a reorder is placed. This order is received at the end of time period L, which does not vary in this model.

In constructing any inventory model, the first step is to develop a functional relationship between the variables of interest and the measure of effectiveness. In this case, because we are concerned with cost, the following equation pertains:

Tutorial: EOQ

$$\text{Total annual cost} = \text{Annual purchase cost} + \text{Annual ordering cost} + \text{Annual holding cost}$$

or

[15.2]
$$TC = DC + \frac{D}{Q}S + \frac{Q}{2}H$$

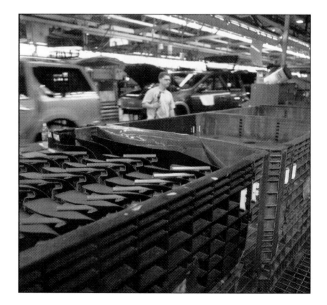

exhibit 15.3

Basic Fixed–Order Quantity Model

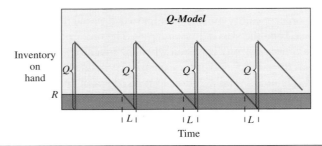

exhibit 15.4

Annual Product Costs, Based on Size of the Order

where

TC = Total annual cost

D = Demand (annual)

C = Cost per unit

Q = Quantity to be ordered (the optimal amount is termed the *economic order quantity*—EOQ—or Q_{opt})

S = Setup cost or cost of placing an order

R = Reorder point

L = Lead time

H = Annual holding and storage cost per unit of average inventory (often holding cost is taken as a percentage of the cost of the item, such as $H = iC$, where i is the percent carrying cost)

On the right side of the equation, DC is the annual purchase cost for the units, $(D/Q)S$ is the annual ordering cost (the actual number of orders placed, D/Q, times the cost of each order, S), and $(Q/2)H$ is the annual holding cost (the average inventory, $Q/2$, times the cost per unit for holding and storage, H). These cost relationships are graphed in Exhibit 15.4.

The second step in model development is to find that order quantity Q_{opt} at which total cost is a minimum. In Exhibit 15.4, the total cost is minimal at the point where the slope of the curve is zero. Using calculus, we take the derivative of total cost with respect to Q and set this equal to zero. For the basic model considered here, the calculations are

Interactive Operations Management

$$TC = DC + \frac{D}{Q}S + \frac{Q}{2}H$$

$$\frac{dTC}{dQ} = 0 + \left(\frac{-DS}{Q^2}\right) + \frac{H}{2} = 0$$

[15.3]

$$Q_{opt} = \sqrt{\frac{2DS}{H}}$$

Because this simple model assumes constant demand and lead time, no safety stock is necessary, and the reorder point, R, is simply

[15.4]
$$R = \bar{d}L$$

where

$\bar{d}$ = Average daily demand (constant)
L = Lead time in days (constant)

EXAMPLE 15.2: Economic Order Quantity and Reorder Point

Find the economic order quantity and the reorder point, given

Annual demand $(D) = 1,000$ units
Average daily demand $(\bar{d}) = 1,000/365$
Ordering cost $(S) = \$5$ per order
Holding cost $(H) = \$1.25$ per unit per year
Lead time $(L) = 5$ days
Cost per unit $(C) = \$12.50$

What quantity should be ordered?

**Excel:
Inventory
Control.xls**

SOLUTION

The optimal order quantity is

$$Q_{\text{opt}} = \sqrt{\frac{2DS}{H}} = \sqrt{\frac{2(1,000)5}{1.25}} = \sqrt{8,000} = 89.4 \text{ units}$$

The reorder point is

$$R = \bar{d}L = \frac{1,000}{365}(5) = 13.7 \text{ units}$$

Rounding to the nearest unit, the inventory policy is as follows: When the inventory position drops to 14, place an order for 89 more.

The total annual cost will be

$$TC = DC + \frac{D}{Q}S + \frac{Q}{2}H$$

$$= 1,000(12.50) + \frac{1,000}{89}(5) + \frac{89}{2}(1.25)$$

$$= \$12,611.81$$

Note that in this example, the purchase cost of the units was not required to determine the order quantity and the reorder point because the cost was constant and unrelated to order size. ●

ESTABLISHING SAFETY STOCK LEVELS

The previous model assumed that demand was constant and known. In the majority of cases, though, demand is not constant but varies from day to day. Safety stock must therefore be maintained to provide some level of protection against stockouts. Safety stock can be defined   **Safety stock** as the amount of inventory carried in addition to the expected demand. In a normal distribution, this would be the mean. For example, if our average monthly demand is 100 units and we expect next month to be the same, if we carry 120 units, then we have 20 units of safety stock.

Safety stock can be determined based on many different criteria. A common approach is for a company to simply state that a certain number of weeks of supply be kept in safety stock. It is better, though, to use an approach that captures the variability in demand.

For example, an objective may be something like "set the safety stock level so that there will only be a 5 percent chance of stocking out if demand exceeds 300 units." We call this approach to setting safety stock the probability approach.

The Probability Approach   Using the probability criterion to determine safety stock is pretty simple. With the models described in this chapter, we assume that the demand over a period of time is normally distributed with a mean and a standard deviation. *Again, remember that this approach considers only the probability of running out of stock, not how many units we are short.* To determine the probability of stocking out over the time period, we can simply plot a normal distribution for the expected demand and note where the amount we have on hand lies on the curve.

Let's take a few simple examples to illustrate this. Say we expect demand to be 100 units over the next month, and we know that the standard deviation is 20 units. If we go into the month with just 100 units, we know that our probability of stocking out is 50 percent. Half of the months we would expect demand to be greater than 100 units; half of the months we would expect it to be less than 100 units. Taking this further, if we ordered a month's worth of inventory of 100 units at a time and received it at the beginning of the month, over the long run we would expect to run out of inventory in six months of the year.

If running out this often was not acceptable, we would want to carry extra inventory to reduce this risk of stocking out. One idea might be to carry an extra 20 units of inventory for the item. In this case, we would still order a month's worth of inventory at a time, but we would schedule delivery to arrive when we still have 20 units remaining in inventory. This would give us that little cushion of safety stock to reduce the probability of stocking out. If the standard deviation associated with our demand was 20 units, we would then be carrying one standard deviation worth of safety stock. Looking at the Cumulative Standard Normal Distribution (Appendix E), and moving one standard deviation to the right of the mean, gives a probability of .8413. So approximately 84 percent of the time we would not expect to stock out, and 16 percent of the time we would. Now if we order every month, we would expect to stock out approximately two months per year ($.16 \times 12 = 1.92$). For those using Excel, given a z value, the probability can be obtained with the NORMSDIST function.

It is common for companies using this approach to set the probability of not stocking out at 95 percent. This means we would carry about 1.64 standard deviations of safety stock, or 33 units ($1.64 \times 20 = 32.8$) for our example. Once again, keep in mind that this does not mean that we would order 33 units extra each month. Rather, it means that we would still order a month's worth each time, but we would schedule the receipt so that we could expect to have 33 units in inventory when the order arrives. In this case, we would expect to stock out approximately .6 month per year, or that stockouts would occur in 1 of every 20 months.

FIXED–ORDER QUANTITY MODEL WITH SAFETY STOCK

A fixed–order quantity system perpetually monitors the inventory level and places a new order when stock reaches some level, R. The danger of stockout in this model occurs only during the lead time, between the time an order is placed and the time it is received. As shown in Exhibit 15.5, an order is placed when the inventory position drops to the reorder point, R. During this lead time L, a range of demands is possible. This range is determined either from an analysis of past demand data or from an estimate (if past data are not available).

The amount of safety stock depends on the service level desired, as previously discussed. The quantity to be ordered, Q, is calculated in the usual way considering the demand, shortage cost, ordering cost, holding cost, and so forth. A fixed–order quantity model can be used

Fixed–Order Quantity Model

exhibit 15.5

to compute Q, such as the simple Q_{opt} model previously discussed. The reorder point is then set to cover the expected demand during the lead time plus a safety stock determined by the desired service level. Thus, *the key difference between a fixed–order quantity model where demand is known and one where demand is uncertain is in computing the reorder point. The order quantity is the same in both cases.* The uncertainty element is taken into account in the safety stock.

The reorder point is

[15.5]
$$R = \bar{d}L + z\sigma_L$$

where

R = Reorder point in units
$\bar{d}$ = Average daily demand
L = Lead time in days (time between placing an order and receiving the items)
z = Number of standard deviations for a specified service probability
σ_L = Standard deviation of usage during lead time

The term $z\sigma_L$ is the amount of safety stock. Note that if safety stock is positive, the effect is to place a reorder sooner. That is, R without safety stock is simply the average demand during the lead time. If lead time usage was expected to be 20, for example, and safety stock was computed to be 5 units, then the order would be placed sooner, when 25 units remained. The greater the safety stock, the sooner the order is placed.

Computing $\bar{d}$, σ_L, and z   Demand during the replenishment lead time is really an estimate or forecast of expected use of inventory from the time an order is placed to when it is received. It may be a single number (for example, if the lead time is a month, the demand may be taken as the previous year's demand divided by 12), or it may be a summation of expected demands over the lead time (such as the sum of daily demands over a 30-day lead time). For the daily demand situation, d can be a forecast demand using any of the models in Chapter 13 on forecasting. For example, if a 30-day period was used to calculate d, then a simple average would be

[15.6]
$$\bar{d} = \frac{\sum_{i=1}^{n} d_i}{n}$$

$$= \frac{\sum_{i=1}^{30} d_i}{30}$$

where n is the number of days.

The standard deviation of the daily demand is

[15.7]
$$\sigma_d = \sqrt{\frac{\sum_{i=1}^{n}(d_i - \bar{d})^2}{n}}$$

$$= \sqrt{\frac{\sum_{i=1}^{30}(d_i - \bar{d})^2}{30}}$$

Because σ_d refers to one day, if lead time extends over several days, we can use the statistical premise that the standard deviation of a series of independent occurrences is equal to the square root of the sum of the variances. That is, in general,

[15.8]
$$\sigma_L = \sqrt{\sigma_1^2 + \sigma_2^2 + \cdots + \sigma_L^2}$$

For example, suppose we computed the standard deviation of demand to be 10 units per day. If our lead time to get an order is five days, the standard deviation for the five-day period, because each day can be considered independent, is

$$\sigma_5 = \sqrt{(10)^2 + (10)^2 + (10)^2 + (10)^2 + (10)^2} = 22.36$$

Next we need to find z, the number of standard deviations of safety stock.

Suppose we wanted our probability of not stocking out during the lead time to be .95. The z value associated with a 95 percent probability of not stocking out is 1.64 (see Appendix D or use the Excel NORMSINV function). Given this, safety stock is calculated as follows:

[15.9]
$$SS = z\sigma_L$$

$$= 1.64 \times 22.36$$

$$= 36.67$$

We now compare two examples. The difference between them is that in the first, the variation in demand is stated in terms of standard deviation over the entire lead time, while in the second, it is stated in terms of standard deviation per day.

EXAMPLE 15.3: Economic Order Quantity

Consider an economic order quantity case where annual demand $D = 1,000$ units, economic order quantity $Q = 200$ units, the desired probability of not stocking out $P = .95$, the standard deviation of demand during lead time $\sigma_L = 25$ units, and lead time $L = 15$ days. Determine the reorder point. Assume that demand is over a 250-workday year.

SOLUTION

In our example, $\bar{d} = \frac{1000}{250} = 4$, and lead time is 15 days. We use the equation

$$R = \bar{d}L + z\sigma_L$$

$$= 4(15) + z(25)$$

In this case z is 1.64.

Completing the solution for R, we have

$$R = 4(15) + 1.64(25) = 60 + 41 = 101 \text{ units}$$

This says that when the stock on hand gets down to 101 units, order 200 more. ●

EXAMPLE 15.4: Order Quantity and Reorder Point

Daily demand for a certain product is normally distributed with a mean of 60 and standard deviation of 7. The source of supply is reliable and maintains a constant lead time of six days. The cost of placing the order is $10 and annual holding costs are $0.50 per unit. There are no stockout costs, and unfilled orders are filled as soon as the order arrives. Assume sales occur over the entire 365 days of the year. Find the order quantity and reorder point to satisfy a 95 percent probability of not stocking out during the lead time.

**Excel:
Inventory
Control.xls**

SOLUTION

In this problem we need to calculate the order quantity Q as well as the reorder point R.

$\bar{d} = 60 \qquad S = \$10$

$\sigma_d = 7 \qquad H = \$0.50$

$D = 60(365) \qquad L = 6$

daily demand   Annual demand

$\sqrt{\dfrac{2 * 60 * 365 * 10}{0.50}}$

The optimal order quantity is

$$Q_{\text{opt}} = \sqrt{\frac{2DS}{H}} = \sqrt{\frac{2(60)365(10)}{0.50}} = \sqrt{876{,}000} = 936 \text{ units}$$

To compute the reorder point, we need to calculate the amount of product used during the lead time and add this to the safety stock.

The standard deviation of demand during the lead time of six days is calculated from the variance of the individual days. Because each day's demand is independent[2]

$$\sigma_L = \sqrt{\sum_{i=1}^{L} \sigma_d^2} = \sqrt{6(7)^2} = 17.15$$

Once again, z is 1.64.

$$R = \bar{d}L + z\sigma_L = 60(6) + 1.64(17.15) = 388 \text{ units}$$

To summarize the policy derived in this example, an order for 936 units is placed whenever the number of units remaining in inventory drops to 388. ●

FIXED–TIME PERIOD MODELS

  In a fixed–time period system, inventory is counted only at particular times, such as every week or every month. Counting inventory and placing orders periodically is desirable in situations such as when vendors make routine visits to customers and take orders for their complete line of products, or when buyers want to combine orders to save transportation costs. Other firms operate on a fixed time period to facilitate planning their inventory count; for example, Distributor X calls every two weeks and employees know that all Distributor X's product must be counted.

Fixed–time period models generate order quantities that vary from period to period, depending on the usage rates. These generally require a higher level of safety stock than a fixed–order quantity system. The fixed–order quantity system assumes continual tracking of inventory on hand, with an order immediately placed when the reorder point is reached. In contrast, the standard fixed–time period models assume that inventory is counted only at the time specified for review. It is possible that some large demand will draw the stock down to zero right after an order is placed. This condition could go unnoticed until the next review period. Then the new order, when placed, still takes time to arrive. Thus, it is possible to be out of stock throughout the entire review period, T, and order lead time, L. Safety stock, therefore,

exhibit 15.6

Fixed–Time Period Inventory Model

must protect against stockouts during the review period itself as well as during the lead time from order placement to order receipt.

FIXED–TIME PERIOD MODEL WITH SAFETY STOCK

In a fixed–time period system, reorders are placed at the time of review (T), and the safety stock that must be reordered is

[15.10] $$\text{Safety stock} = z\sigma_{T+L}$$

Exhibit 15.6 shows a fixed–time period system with a review cycle of T and a constant lead time of L. In this case, demand is randomly distributed about a mean $\bar{d}$. The quantity to order, q, is

[15.11]
$$
\begin{array}{ccc}
\dfrac{\text{Order}}{\text{quantity}} & = & \begin{array}{c}\text{Average demand}\\\text{over the}\\\text{vulnerable period}\end{array} + \begin{array}{c}\text{Safety}\\\text{stock}\end{array} - \begin{array}{c}\text{Inventory currently}\\\text{on hand (plus on}\\\text{order, if any)}\end{array}
\end{array}
$$

$$q \quad = \quad \bar{d}(T+L) \quad + \quad z\sigma_{T+L} \quad - \quad I$$

where

$q =$ Quantity to be ordered
$T =$ The number of days between reviews
$L =$ Lead time in days (time between placing an order and receiving it)
$\bar{d} =$ Forecast average daily demand
$z =$ Number of standard deviations for a specified service probability
$\sigma_{T+L} =$ Standard deviation of demand over the review and lead time
$I =$ Current inventory level (includes items on order)

Note: The demand, lead time, review period, and so forth can be any time units such as days, weeks, or years so long as they are consistent throughout the equation.

In this model, demand ($\bar{d}$) can be forecast and revised each review period if desired or the yearly average may be used if appropriate. We assume that demand is normally distributed.

The value of z is dependent on the probability of stocking out and can be found using Appendix D or by using the Excel® NORMSINV function.

**Excel:
Inventory
Control.xls**

EXAMPLE 15.5: Quantity to Order

Daily demand for a product is 10 units with a standard deviation of 3 units. The review period is 30 days, and lead time is 14 days. Management has set a policy of satisfying 98 percent of demand from items in stock. At the beginning of this review period, there are 150 units in inventory.

How many units should be ordered?

SOLUTION

The quantity to order is

$$q = \bar{d}(T + L) + z\sigma_{T+L} - I$$
$$= 10(30 + 14) + z\sigma_{T+L} - 150$$

Before we can complete the solution, we need to find σ_{T+L} and z. To find σ_{T+L}, we use the notion, as before, that the standard deviation of a sequence of independent random variables equals the square root of the sum of the variances. Therefore, the standard deviation during the period $T + L$ is the square root of the sum of the variances for each day:

[15.12]
$$\sigma_{T+L} = \sqrt{\sum_{i=1}^{T+L} \sigma_d^2}$$

Because each day is independent and σ_d is constant,

$$\sigma_{T+L} = \sqrt{(T + L)\sigma_d^2} = \sqrt{(30 + 14)(3)^2} = 19.90$$

The z value for $P = .98$ is 2.05.
  The quantity to order, then, is

$$q = \bar{d}(T + L) + z\sigma_{T+L} - I = 10(30 + 14) + 2.05(19.90) - 150 = 331 \text{ units}$$

To ensure a 98 percent probability of not stocking out, order 331 units at this review period. ●

INVENTORY CONTROL AND SUPPLY CHAIN MANAGEMENT

It is important for managers to realize that how they run items using inventory control logic relates directly to the financial performance of the firm. A key measure that relates to company performance is inventory turn. Recall that inventory turn is calculated as follows:

$$\text{Inventory turn} = \frac{\text{Cost of goods sold}}{\text{Average inventory value}}$$

So what is the relationship between how we manage an item and the inventory turn for that item? Here, let us simplify things and consider just the inventory turn for an individual item or a group of items. First, if we look at the numerator, the cost of goods sold for an individual item relates directly to the expected yearly demand (D) for the item. Given a cost per unit (C) for the item, the cost of goods sold is just D times C. Recall this is the same as what was used in our EOQ equation. Next, consider average inventory value. Recall from EOQ that the average inventory is $Q/2$, which is true if we assume that demand is constant. When we bring uncertainty into the equation, safety stock is needed to manage the risk created by demand variability. The fixed–order quantity model and fixed–time period model both have equations for calculating the safety stock required for a given probability of stocking out. In both models, we assume that when going through an order cycle, half the time we need to use the safety stock and half the time we do not. So on average, we expect the safety stock (SS) to be on hand. Given this, the average inventory is equal to the following:

[15.13]
$$\text{Average inventory value} = (Q/2 + SS)C$$

The inventory turn for an individual item then is

[15.14]
$$\text{Inventory turn} = \frac{DC}{(Q/2 + SS)C} = \frac{D}{Q/2 + SS}$$

EXAMPLE 15.6: Average Inventory Calculation—Fixed–Order Quantity Model

Suppose the following item is being managed using a fixed–order quantity model with safety stock.

    Annual demand $(D) = 1{,}000$ units
    Order quantity $(Q) = 300$ units
    Safety stock $(SS) = 40$ units

What are the average inventory level and inventory turn for the item?

SOLUTION

$$\text{Average inventory} = Q/2 + SS = 300/2 + 40 = 190 \text{ units}$$

$$\text{Inventory turn} = \frac{D}{Q/2 + SS} = \frac{1{,}000}{190} = 5.263 \text{ turns per year} \quad \bullet$$

EXAMPLE 15.7: Average Inventory Calculation—Fixed–Time Period Model

Consider the following item that is being managed using a fixed–time period model with safety stock.

    Weekly demand $(d) = 50$ units
    Review cycle $(T) = 3$ weeks
    Safety stock $(SS) = 30$ units

What are the average inventory level and inventory turn for the item?

SOLUTION

Here we need to determine how many units we expect to order each cycle. If we assume that demand is fairly steady, then we would expect to order the number of units that we expect demand to be during the review cycle. This expected demand is equal to dT if we assume that there is no trend or seasonality in the demand pattern.

$$\text{Average inventory} = dT/2 + SS = 50(3)/2 + 30 = 105 \text{ units}$$

$$\text{Inventory turn} = \frac{52d}{dT/2 + SS} = \frac{50(52)}{105} = 24.8 \text{ turns per year}$$

assuming there are 52 weeks in the year. $\bullet$

PRICE-BREAK MODELS

Price-break models deal with the fact that, generally, the selling price of an item varies with the order size. This is a discrete or step change rather than a per-unit change. For example, wood screws may cost $0.02 each for 1 to 99 screws, $1.60 per 100, and $13.50 per 1,000. To determine the optimal quantity of any item to order, we simply solve for the economic order quantity for each price and at the point of price change. But not all of the economic order quantities determined by the formula are feasible. In the wood screw example, the Q_{opt} formula might tell us that the optimal decision at the price of 1.6 cents is to order 75 screws. This would be impossible, however, because 75 screws would cost 2 cents each.

In general, to find the lowest-cost order quantity, we need to calculate the economic order quantity for each possible price and check to see whether the quantity is feasible. It is possible that the economic order quantity that is calculated is either higher or lower than the range to which the price corresponds. Any feasible quantity is a potential candidate order quantity. We also need to calculate the cost at each of the price-break quantities, since we know that price is feasible at these points and the total cost may be lowest at one of these values.

The calculations can be simplified a little if holding cost is based on a percentage of unit price (they will be in all the examples and problems given in this book). In this case, we only need to look at a subset of the price-break quantities. The following two-step procedure can be used:

Step 1. Sort the prices from lowest to highest, and then, beginning with the lowest price, calculate the economic order quantity for each price level until a feasible economic order quantity is found. By feasible we mean that the price is in the correct corresponding range.

Step 2. If the first feasible economic order quantity is for the lowest price, this quantity is best and you are finished. Otherwise, calculate the total cost for the first feasible economic order quantity (you did these from lowest to highest price) and also calculate the total cost at each price break lower than the price associated with the first feasible economic order quantity. This is the lowest order quantity at which you can take advantage of the price break. The optimal Q is the one with the lowest cost.

Looking at Exhibit 15.7, we see that order quantities are solved from right to left, or from the lowest unit price to the highest, until a valid Q is obtained. Then the order quantity at each *price break* above this Q is used to find which order quantity has the least cost—the computed Q or the Q at one of the price breaks.

Curves for Three Separate Order Quantity Models in a Three-Price-Break Situation (orange line depicts feasible range of purchases)

exhibit 15.7

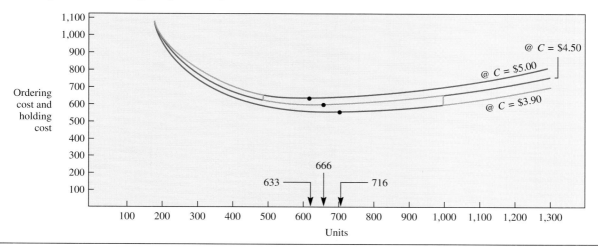

EXAMPLE 15.8: Price Break

Consider the following case, where

$D = 10{,}000$ units (annual demand)

$S = \$20$ to place each order

$i = 20$ percent of cost (annual carrying cost, storage, interest, obsolescence, etc.)

$C = $ Cost per unit (according to the order size; orders of 0 to 499 units, \$5.00 per unit; 500 to 999, \$4.50 per unit; 1,000 and up, \$3.90 per unit)

What quantity should be ordered?

SOLUTION

The appropriate equations from the basic fixed-quantity case are

$$TC = DC + \frac{D}{Q}S + \frac{Q}{2}iC$$

and

[15.15]
$$Q = \sqrt{\frac{2DS}{iC}}$$

Solving for the economic order size, we obtain

$$@~C = \$3.90, \quad Q = 716 \quad \text{Not feasible}$$
$$@~C = \$4.50, \quad Q = 667 \quad \text{Feasible, cost} = \$45{,}600$$
$$\text{Check } Q = 1{,}000, \quad \text{Cost} = \$39{,}590 \quad \text{Optimal solution}$$

In Exhibit 15.7, which displays the cost relationship and order quantity range, note that most of the order quantity–cost relationships lie outside the feasible range and that only a single, continuous range results. This should be readily apparent because, for example, the first order quantity specifies buying 633 units at \$5.00 per unit. However, if 633 units are ordered, the price is \$4.50, not \$5.00. The same holds true for the third order quantity, which specifies an order of 716 units at \$3.90 each. This \$3.90 price is not available on orders of less than 1,000 units.

Exhibit 15.8 itemizes the total costs at the economic order quantities and at the price breaks. The optimal order quantity is shown to be 1,000 units. ●

exhibit 15.8

Relevant Costs in a Three-Price-Break Model

	$Q = 633$ WHERE $C = \$5$	$Q = 667$ WHERE $C = \$4.50$	$Q = 716$ WHERE $C = \$3.90$	PRICE BREAK 1,000
Holding cost $\left(\frac{Q}{2}iC\right)$		$\frac{667}{2}(0.20)4.50$ $= \$300.15$		$\frac{1{,}000}{2}(0.20)3.90$ $= \$390$
Ordering cost $\left(\frac{D}{Q}S\right)$	Not feasible	$\frac{10{,}000(20)}{667}$ $= \$299.85$	Not feasible	$\frac{10{,}000(20)}{1{,}000}$ $= \$200$
Holding and ordering cost		\$600.00		\$590
Item cost (DC)		10,000(4.50)		10,000(3.90)
Total cost		\$45,600		\$39,590

One practical consideration in price-break problems is that the price reduction from volume purchases frequently makes it seemingly economical to order amounts larger than the Q_{opt}. Thus, when applying the model, we must be particularly careful to obtain a valid estimate of product obsolescence and warehousing costs.

— × —

MISCELLANEOUS SYSTEMS AND ISSUES

Obtaining actual order, setup, carrying, and shortage costs is difficult—sometimes impossible. Even the assumptions are sometimes unrealistic. For example, Exhibit 15.9 compares ordering costs that are assumed linear to the real case where every addition of a staff person causes a step increase in cost.

All inventory systems are plagued by two major problems: maintaining adequate control over each inventory item and ensuring that accurate records of stock on hand are kept. In this section we present three simple systems often used in practice (an optional replenishment system, a one-bin system, and a two-bin system), ABC analysis (a method for analyzing inventory based on value), and cycle counting (a technique for improving inventory record accuracy).

THREE SIMPLE INVENTORY SYSTEMS

Optional Replenishment System   An optional replenishment system forces reviewing the inventory level at a fixed frequency (such as weekly) and ordering a replenishment supply if the level has dropped below some amount. In Exhibit 15.1, this is a *P*-model. For example, the maximum inventory level (which we will call *M*) can be computed based on demand, ordering costs, and shortage costs. Because it takes time and costs money to place an order, a minimum order of size *Q* can be established. Then, whenever this item is reviewed, the inventory position (we will call it *I*) is subtracted from the replenishment level (*M*). If that number (call it *q*) is equal to or greater than *Q*, order *q*. Otherwise, forget it until the next review period. Stated formally,

$$q = M - I$$
$$\text{If} \quad q \geq Q, \quad \text{order } q.$$

Otherwise, do not order any.

Two-Bin System   In a two-bin system, items are used from one bin, and the second bin provides an amount large enough to ensure that the stock can be replenished. In Exhibit 15.1, this is a *Q*-model. Ideally, the second bin would contain an amount equal to the reorder point (*R*) calculated earlier. As soon as the second bin supply is brought to the first bin, an order is placed to replenish the second bin. Actually, these bins can be located together. In fact, there

---

Cost to Place Orders versus the Number of Orders Placed: Linear Assumption and Normal Reality

exhibit 15.9

Assumption	Reality
Ordering costs	
Number of orders	Number of orders

could be just one bin with a divider between. The key to a two-bin operation is to separate the inventory so that part of it is held in reserve until the rest is used first.

One-Bin System   A one-bin inventory system involves periodic replenishment no matter how few are needed. At fixed periods (such as weekly), the inventory is brought up to its predetermined maximum level. The one bin is always replenished, and it therefore differs from the optional replenishment system, which reorders only when the inventory used is greater than some minimum amount. This is a *P*-model in Exhibit 15.1.

ABC INVENTORY PLANNING

Maintaining inventory through counting, placing orders, receiving stock, and so on takes personnel time and costs money. When there are limits on these resources, the logical move is to try to use the available resources to control inventory in the best way. In other words, focus on the most important items in inventory.

In the nineteenth century Villefredo Pareto, in a study of the distribution of wealth in Milan, found that 20 percent of the people controlled 80 percent of the wealth. This logic of the few having the greatest importance and the many having little importance has been broadened to include many situations and is termed the *Pareto principle.*[3] This is true in our everyday lives (most of our decisions are relatively unimportant, but a few shape our future) and is certainly true in inventory systems (where a few items account for the bulk of our investment).

Any inventory system must specify when an order is to be placed for an item and how many units to order. Most inventory control situations involve so many items that it is not practical to model and give thorough treatment to each item. To get around this problem, the ABC classification scheme divides inventory items into three groupings: high dollar volume (A), moderate dollar volume (B), and low dollar volume (C). Dollar volume is a measure of importance; an item low in cost but high in volume can be more important than a high-cost item with low volume.

ABC Classification   If the annual usage of items in inventory is listed according to dollar volume, generally, the list shows that a small number of items account for a large dollar volume and that a large number of items account for a small dollar volume. Exhibit 15.10 illustrates the relationship.

The ABC approach divides this list into three groupings by value: A items constitute roughly the top 15 percent of the items, B items the next 35 percent, and C items the last 50 percent. From observation, it appears that the list in Exhibit 15.10 may be meaningfully grouped with A including 20 percent (2 of the 10), B including 30 percent, and C including 50 percent. These points show clear delineations between sections. The result of this segmentation is shown in Exhibit 15.11 and plotted in Exhibit 15.12.

exhibit 15.10	Annual Usage of Inventory by Value

ITEM NUMBER	ANNUAL DOLLAR USAGE	PERCENTAGE OF TOTAL VALUE
22	$ 95,000	40.69%
68	75,000	32.13
27	25,000	10.71
03	15,000	6.43
82	13,000	5.57
54	7,500	3.21
36	1,500	0.64
19	800	0.34
23	425	0.18
41	225	0.10
	$233,450	100.0%

ABC Grouping of Inventory Items

exhibit 15.11

CLASSIFICATION	ITEM NUMBER	ANNUAL DOLLAR USAGE	PERCENTAGE OF TOTAL
A	22, 68	$170,000	72.9%
B	27, 03, 82	53,000	22.7
C	54, 36, 19, 23, 41	10,450	4.4
		$233,450	10.0%

ABC Inventory Classification (inventory value for each group versus the group's portion of the total list)

exhibit 15.12

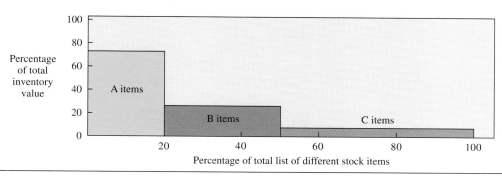

Segmentation may not always occur so neatly. The objective, though, is to try to separate the important from the unimportant. Where the lines actually break depends on the particular inventory under question and on how much personnel time is available. (With more time, a firm could define larger A or B categories.)

The purpose of classifying items into groups is to establish the appropriate degree of control over each item. On a periodic basis, for example, class A items may be more clearly controlled with weekly ordering, B items may be ordered biweekly, and C items may be ordered monthly or bimonthly. Note that the unit cost of items is not related to their classification. An A item may have a high dollar volume through a combination of either low cost and high usage or high cost and low usage. Similarly, C items may have a low dollar volume because of either low demand or low cost. In an automobile service station, gasoline would be an A item with daily or weekly replenishment; tires, batteries, oil, grease, and transmission fluid may be B items and ordered every two to four weeks; and C items would consist of valve stems, windshield wiper blades, radiator caps, hoses, fan belts, oil and gas additives, car wax, and so forth. C items may be ordered every two or three months or even be allowed to run out before reordering because the penalty for stockout is not serious.

Sometimes an item may be critical to a system if its absence creates a sizable loss. In this case, regardless of the item's classification, sufficiently large stocks should be kept on hand to prevent runout. One way to ensure closer control is to designate this item an A or a B, forcing it into the category even if its dollar volume does not warrant such inclusion.

INVENTORY ACCURACY AND CYCLE COUNTING

Inventory records usually differ from the actual physical count; inventory accuracy refers to how well the two agree. Companies such as Wal-Mart (see the Breakthrough box titled "Inventory on a Grand Scale") understand the importance of inventory accuracy and expend considerable effort ensuring it. The question is, How much error is acceptable? If the record shows a balance of 683 of part X and an actual count shows 652, is this within reason? Suppose the actual count shows 750, an excess of 67 over the record; is this any better?

BREAKTHROUGH

INVENTORY ON A GRAND SCALE

Inventory at Wal-Mart is precision on a gargantuan scale, like a maneuver of the Atlantic Fleet or a dam project in the Yangtze River.

In his ruling on Wal-Mart's tax court case, Judge David Laro provided a behind-the-scenes look at the operation. Its effectiveness, he says, has led "many other companies, both domestic and foreign" to seek Wal-Mart's advice on inventory taking.

Preparation alone takes four to six weeks. Forty-five days in advance, the chain's internal audit department sends a preparation kit to each store. It contains detailed instructions, including 13 schedules.

Involved in the inventory are a team of 18 to 40 independent counters and representatives of the company's operations division and departments of loss prevention and internal audit.

At randomly selected stores, employees of Ernst & Young, independent auditors for Wal-Mart, are present to test accuracy by recounting.

An inventory is taken between 8 A.M. and 6 P.M., while the store—some of which are 24-hour operations—is open to customers. Immediately after the inventory is completed, the physical count team reconciles its findings with the book inventory. The results are reviewed later by the internal audit department.

Inventories are taken every 11 to 13 months, and most occur from March through September: inventory is never taken in November or December, when it would interfere with the Christmas season, or in the first week in January, when employees are recuperating and busy with exchanges and returns.

The job can be made no easier by the facts that Wal-Mart's inventory turns over 4.5 times a year (competitors average about 2.8 turns) and its stores carry between 60,000 and 90,000 specific types of merchandise.

Between physical counts, Wal-Mart employs a perpetual system that records, at the time of sale, the cost and quantity of goods sold. This "reveals the cost and/or quantity of goods sold since the beginning of the current period and . . . of goods that are on hand at any given time."

SOURCE: W. RIGGLE, "INVENTORY ON A GRAND SCALE," *SUPERMARKET BUSINESS*, FEBRUARY 1997, P. 45. COPYRIGHT © 1997. REPRODUCED WITH PERMISSION.

Every production system must have agreement, within some specified range, between what the record says is in inventory and what actually is in inventory. There are many reasons why records and inventory may not agree. For example, an open stockroom area allows items to be removed for both legitimate and unauthorized purposes. The legitimate removal may have been done in a hurry and simply not recorded. Sometimes parts are misplaced, turning up months later. Parts are often stored in several locations, but records may be lost or the location recorded incorrectly. Sometimes stock replenishment orders are recorded as received, when in fact they never were. Occasionally, a group of parts is recorded as removed from inventory, but the customer order is canceled and the parts are replaced in inventory without canceling the record. To keep the production system flowing smoothly without parts shortages and efficiently without excess balances, records must be accurate.

How can a firm keep accurate, up-to-date records? The first general rule is to keep the storeroom locked. If only storeroom personnel have access, and one of their measures of performance for personnel evaluation and merit increases is record accuracy, there is a strong motivation to comply. Every location of inventory storage, whether in a locked storeroom or on the production floor, should have a recordkeeping mechanism. A second way is to convey the importance of accurate records to all personnel and depend on them to assist in this effort. (This all boils down to this: Put a fence that goes all the way to the ceiling around the storage area so that workers cannot climb over to get parts; put a lock on the gate and give one person the key. Nobody can pull parts without having the transaction authorized and recorded.)

Another way to ensure accuracy is to count inventory frequently and match this against records. A widely used method is called *cycle counting*.

Cycle counting **Cycle counting** is a physical inventory-taking technique in which inventory is counted frequently rather than once or twice a year. The key to effective cycle counting and, therefore, to accurate records lies in deciding which items are to be counted, when, and by whom.

Virtually all inventory systems these days are computerized. The computer can be programmed to produce a cycle count notice in the following cases:

1. When the record shows a low or zero balance on hand. (It is easier to count fewer items.)
2. When the record shows a positive balance but a backorder was written (indicating a discrepancy).
3. After some specified level of activity.
4. To signal a review based on the importance of the item (as in the ABC system) such as in the following table:

Annual Dollar Usage	Review Period
$10,000 or more	30 days or less
$3,000–$10,000	45 days or less
$250–3,000	90 days or less
Less than $250	180 days or less

The easiest time for stock to be counted is when there is no activity in the stockroom or on the production floor. This means on the weekends or during the second or third shift, when the facility is less busy. If this is not possible, more careful logging and separation of items are required to count inventory while production is going on and transactions are occurring.

The counting cycle depends on the available personnel. Some firms schedule regular stockroom personnel to do the counting during lulls in the regular working day. Other companies hire private firms that come in and count inventory. Still other firms use full-time cycle counters who do nothing but count inventory and resolve differences with the records. Although this last method sounds expensive, many firms believe that it is actually less costly than the usual hectic annual inventory count generally performed during the two- or three-week annual vacation shutdown.

The question of how much error is tolerable between physical inventory and records has been much debated. Some firms strive for 100 percent accuracy, whereas others accept 1, 2, or 3 percent error. The accuracy level often recommended by experts is ± 0.2 percent for A items, ± 1 percent for B items, and ± 5 percent for C items. Regardless of the specific accuracy decided on, the important point is that the level be dependable so that safety stocks may be provided as a cushion. Accuracy is important for a smooth production process so that customer orders can be processed as scheduled and not held up because of unavailable parts.

INVENTORY CONTROL IN SERVICES

To demonstrate how inventory control is conducted in service organizations, we have selected two areas to describe: a department store and an automobile service agency.

Service

Stockkeeping unit (SKU)

Department Store Inventory Policy   The common term used to identify an inventory item is the **stockkeeping unit (SKU)**. The SKU identifies each item, its manufacturer, and its cost. The number of SKUs becomes large even for small departments. For example, if towels carried in a domestic items department are obtained from three manufacturers in three quality levels, three sizes (hand towel, face towel, and bath towel), and four colors, there are 108 different items ($3 \times 3 \times 3 \times 4$). Even if towels are sold only in sets of three pieces (hand towel, face towel, and bath towel), the number of SKUs needed to identify the towel sets is $3 \times 3 \times 1 \times 4 = 36$. Depending on the store, a housewares department may carry 3,000 to 4,000 SKUs, and a linen and domestic items department may carry 5,000 to 6,000.

Such large numbers mean that individual economic order quantities cannot be calculated for each item by hand. How, then, does a department keep tabs on its stock and place orders for replenishment?

Generally, housewares are divided into staple and promotional items. Within these major divisions, further classifications are used, such as cookware and tableware. Also, items are frequently classified by price, as $5 items, $4, $3, and so forth.

The housewares department usually purchases from a distributor rather than directly from a manufacturer. The use of a distributor, who handles products from many manufacturers, has the advantage of fewer orders and faster shipping time (shorter lead time). Further, the distributor's sales personnel may visit the housewares department weekly and count all the items they supply to this department. Then, in line with the replenishment level that has been established by the buyer, the distributor's salesperson places orders for the buyer. This saves the department time in counting inventory and placing orders. The typical lead time for receipt of stock from a housewares distributor is two or three days. The safety stock, therefore, is quite low, and the buyer establishes the replenishment level so as to supply only enough items for the two- to three-day lead time, plus expected demand during the period until the distributor's salesperson's next visit.

Note that a formal method of estimating stockout and establishing safety stock levels is usually not followed because the number of items is too great. Instead, the total value of items in the department is monitored. Thus, replenishment levels are set by dollar allocation.

Through planning, each department has an established monthly value for inventory. By tabulating inventory balance, monthly sales, and items on order, an "open-to-buy" figure is determined. ("Open-to-buy" is the unspent portion of the budget.) This dollar amount is the sum available to the buyer for the following month. When an increase in demand is expected (Christmas, Mother's Day, and so forth), the allocation of funds to the department is increased, resulting in a larger open-to-buy position. Then the replenishment levels are raised in line with the class of goods, responding to the demand increases, thereby creating a higher stock of goods on hand.

In practice, the open-to-buy funds are largely spent during the first days of the month. However, the buyer tries to reserve some funds for special purchases or to restock fast-moving items. Promotional items in housewares are controlled individually (or by class) by the buyer.

Maintaining an Auto Replacement Parts Inventory   A firm in the automobile service business purchases most of its parts supplies from a small number of distributors. Franchised new-car dealers purchase the great bulk of their supplies from the auto manufacturer. A dealer's demand for auto parts originates primarily from the general public and other departments of the agency, such as the service department or body shop. The problem, in this case, is to determine the order quantities for the several thousand items carried.

A franchised auto agency of medium size may carry a parts inventory valued in the area of $500,000. Because of the nature of this industry, alternate uses of funds are plentiful, so opportunity costs are high. For example, dealers may lease cars, carry their own contracts, stock a larger new-car inventory, or open sidelines such as tire shops, trailer sales, or recreational vehicle sales—all with potentially high returns. This creates pressure to carry a low inventory level of parts and supplies while still meeting an acceptable service level.

Although some dealers still order their inventory by hand, most use computers and software packages provided by car manufacturers. For both manual and computerized systems, an ABC classification works well. Expensive and high-turnover supplies are counted and ordered frequently; low-cost items are ordered in large quantities at infrequent intervals. A common drawback of frequent order placement is the extensive amount of time needed to physically put the items on the shelves and log them in. (However, this restocking procedure does not greatly add to an auto agency's cost because parts department personnel generally do this during slow periods.)

A great variety of computerized systems are currently in use. In a monthly reordering system, for example, the items to be ordered are counted and the number on hand is entered into the computer. By subtracting the number on hand from the previous month's inventory and adding the orders received during the month, the usage rate is determined. Some programs use exponential smoothing forecasts, whereas others use a weighted-average method. For the weighted-average method, the computer program stores the usage rate for, say, four previous months. Then, with the application of a set of weighting factors, a forecast is made in the same manner as described in Chapter 13. This works as follows: Suppose usage of a part during January, February, March, and April was 17, 19, 11, and 23, respectively, and the set of corresponding weights was 0.10, 0.20, 0.30, and 0.40. Thus, the forecast for May is $0.10(17) + 0.20(19) + 0.30(11) + 0.40(23)$, or 18 units. If safety stock were included and equal to one-month demand, then 36 units would be ordered (one-month demand plus one-month safety stock) less whatever is on hand at the time of order placement. This simple two-month rule allows for forecast usage during the lead time plus the review period, with the balance providing the safety stock.

The computer output provides a useful reference file, identifying the item, cost, order size, and the number of units on hand. The output itself constitutes the purchase order and is sent to the distributor or factory supply house. The simplicity in this is attractive because, once the forecast weighting is selected, all that needs to be done is to input the number of units of each item on hand. Thus, negligible computation is involved, and very little preparation is needed to send the order out.

CONCLUSION

This chapter introduced the two main classes of demand: (1) independent demand, referring to the external demand for a firm's end product, and (2) dependent demand, usually referring—within the firm—to the demand for items created because of the demand for more complex items of which they are a part. Most industries have items in both classes. In manufacturing, for example, independent demand is common for finished products, service and repair parts, and operating supplies; and dependent demand is common for those parts and materials needed to produce the end product. In wholesale and retail sales of consumer goods, most demand is independent—each item is an end item, with the wholesaler or retailer doing no further assembly or fabrication.

Independent demand, the focus of this chapter, is based on statistics. In the fixed–order quantity and fixed–time period models, the influence of service level was shown on safety stock and reorder point determinations. Two special-purpose models—the price-break and single-period models—were also presented.

To distinguish among item categories for analysis and control, the ABC method was offered. The importance of inventory accuracy was also noted, and cycle counting was described. Finally, brief descriptions of inventory procedures in a department store and an auto parts shop illustrated some of the simpler ways nonmanufacturing firms control their inventory.

In this chapter we also pointed out that inventory reduction requires a knowledge of the operating system. It is not simply a case of selecting an inventory model off the shelf and plugging in some numbers. In the first place, a model might not even be appropriate. In the second case, the numbers might be full of errors or even based on erroneous data. Determining order quantities is often referred to as a trade-off problem; that is, trading off holding costs for setup costs. Note that companies really want to reduce both.

The simple fact is that firms have very large investments in inventory, and the cost to carry this inventory runs from 25 to 35 percent of the inventory's worth annually. Therefore, a major goal of most firms today is to reduce inventory.

A caution is in order, though. The formulas in this chapter try to minimize cost. Bear in mind that a firm's objective should be something like "making money"—so be sure that reducing inventory cost does, in fact, support this. Usually, correctly reducing inventory lowers cost, improves quality and performance, and enhances profit.

KEY TERMS

Inventory The stock of any item or resource used in an organization.

Independent demand The demands for various items are unrelated to each other.

Dependent demand The need for any one item is a direct result of the need for some other item, usually an item of which it is a part.

Fixed–order quantity model (or Q-model) An inventory control model where the amount requisitioned is fixed and the actual ordering is triggered by inventory dropping to a specified level of inventory.

Fixed–time period model (or P-model) An inventory control model that specifies inventory is ordered at the end of a predetermined time period. The interval of time between orders is fixed and the order quantity varies.

Inventory position The amount on-hand plus on-order minus back-ordered quantities. In the case where inventory has been allocated for special purposes, the inventory position is reduced by these allocated amounts.

Safety stock The amount of inventory carried in addition to the expected demand.

Cycle counting A physical inventory-taking technique in which inventory is counted on a frequent basis rather than once or twice a year.

Stockkeeping unit (SKU) A common term used to identify an inventory item.

FORMULA REVIEW

Single-period model. Cumulative probability of not selling the last unit. Ratio of marginal cost of underestimating demand and marginal cost of overestimating demand.

[15.1]
$$P \le \frac{C_u}{C_o + C_u}$$

Q-model. Total annual cost for an ordered Q, a per-unit cost C, setup cost S, and per-unit holding cost H.

[15.2]
$$TC = DC + \frac{D}{Q}S + \frac{Q}{2}H$$

Q-model. Optimal (or economic) order quantity.

[15.3]
$$Q_{opt} = \sqrt{\frac{2DS}{H}}$$

Q-model. Reorder point R based on average daily demand $\bar{d}$ and lead time L in days.

[15.4]
$$R = \bar{d}L$$

Q-model. Reorder point providing a safety stock of $z\sigma_L$.

[15.5]
$$R = \bar{d}L + z\sigma_L$$

Average daily demand over a period of n days.

[15.6]
$$\bar{d} = \frac{\sum_{i=1}^{n} d_i}{n}$$

Standard deviation of demand over a period of n days.

[15.7]
$$\sigma_d = \sqrt{\frac{\sum_{i=1}^{n} (d_i - \bar{d})^2}{n}}$$

[Handwritten margin notes:]

Ordering cost for a year $= \dfrac{D * S}{Q_{opt}}$

Storage cost for a year $= \dfrac{Q_{opt} * H}{2}$

Standard deviation of a series of independent demands.

[15.8]
$$\sigma_s = \sqrt{\sigma_1^2 + \sigma_2^2 + \cdots + \sigma_i^2}$$

Q-model. Safety stock calculation.

[15.9]
$$SS = z\sigma_L$$

P-model. Safety stock calculation.

[15.10]
$$SS = z\sigma_{T+L}$$

P-model. Optimal order quantity in a fixed-period system with a review period of T days and lead time of L days.

[15.11]
$$q = \bar{d}(T + L) + z\sigma_{T+L} - I$$

P-model. Standard deviation of a series of independent demands over the review period T and lead time L.

[15.12]
$$\sigma_{T+L} = \sqrt{\sum_{i=1}^{T+L} \sigma_{d_i}^2}$$

[15.13]
$$\text{Average inventory value} = (Q/2 + SS)C$$

[15.14]
$$\text{Inventory turn} = \frac{DC}{(Q/2 + SS)C} = \frac{D}{Q/2 + SS}$$

Q-model. Optimal order quantity based on an order cost S, holding cost as a percentage (i) of the unit cost (C).

[15.15]
$$Q = \sqrt{\frac{2DS}{iC}}$$

SOLVED PROBLEMS

SOLVED PROBLEM 1

A product is priced to sell at $100 per unit, and its cost is constant at $70 per unit. Each unsold unit has a salvage value of $20. Demand is expected to range between 35 and 40 units for the period; 35 definitely can be sold and no units over 40 will be sold. The demand probabilities and the associated cumulative probability distribution (P) for this situation are shown below.

NUMBER OF UNITS DEMANDED	PROBABILITY OF THIS DEMAND	CUMULATIVE PROBABILITY
35	.10	.10
36	.15	.25
37	.25	.50
38	.25	.75
39	.15	.90
40	.10	1.00

Excel:
Inventory
Control

How many units should be ordered?

Solution

The cost of underestimating demand is the loss of profit, or $C_u = \$100 - \$70 = \$30$ per unit. The cost of overestimating demand is the loss incurred when the unit must be sold at salvage value, $C_o = \$70 - \$20 = \$50$.

The optimal probability of not being sold is

$$P \leq \frac{C_u}{C_o + C_u} = \frac{30}{50 + 30} = \underline{.375}$$

From the distribution data above, this corresponds to the 37th unit.

The following is a full marginal analysis for the problem. Note that the minimum cost is when 37 units are purchased.

		NUMBER OF UNITS PURCHASED					
UNITS DEMANDED	PROBABILITY	35	36	37	38	39	40
35	0.1	0	50	100	150	200	250
36	0.15	30	0	50	100	150	200
37	0.25	60	30	0	50	100	150
38	0.25	90	60	30	0	50	100
39	0.15	120	90	60	30	0	50
40	0.1	150	120	90	60	30	0
Total cost		75	53	43	53	83	125

SOLVED PROBLEM 2

Items purchased from a vendor cost $20 each, and the forecast for next year's demand is 1,000 units. If it costs $5 every time an order is placed for more units and the storage cost is $4 per unit per year, what quantity should be ordered each time?

a. What is the total ordering cost for a year?
b. What is the total storage cost for a year?

Solution

The quantity to be ordered each time is

$$Q = \sqrt{\frac{2DS}{H}} = \sqrt{\frac{2(1,000)5}{4}} = 50 \text{ units}$$

a. The total ordering cost for a year is

$$\frac{D}{Q}S = \frac{1,000}{50}(\$5) = \$100$$

b. The storage cost for a year is

$$\frac{Q}{2}H = \frac{50}{2}(\$4) = \$100$$

SOLVED PROBLEM 3

Daily demand for a product is 120 units, with a standard deviation of 30 units. The review period is 14 days and the lead time is 7 days. At the time of review, 130 units are in stock. If only a 1 percent risk of stocking out is acceptable, how many units should be ordered?

**Excel:
Inventory
Control**

Solution

$$\sigma_{T+L} = \sqrt{(14+7)(30)^2} = \sqrt{18,900} = 137.5$$

$$z = 2.33$$

$$q = \bar{d}(T+L) + z\sigma_{T+L} - I$$

$$= 120(14+7) + 2.33(137.5) - 130$$

$$= 2,710 \text{ units}$$

SOLVED PROBLEM 4

**Excel:
Inventory
Control**

A company currently has 200 units of a product on hand that it orders every two weeks when the salesperson visits the premises. Demand for the product averages 20 units per day with a standard deviation of 5 units. Lead time for the product to arrive is seven days. Management has a goal of a 95 percent probability of not stocking out for this product.

The salesperson is due to come in late this afternoon when 180 units are left in stock (assuming that 20 are sold today). How many units should be ordered?

Solution

Given $I = 180$, $T = 14$, $L = 7$, $\bar{d} = 20$

$$\sigma_{T+L} = \sqrt{21(5)^2} = 23$$
$$z = 1.64$$
$$q = \bar{d}(T + L) + z\sigma_{T+L} - I$$
$$= 20(14 + 7) + 1.64(23) - 180$$
$$q = 278 \text{ units}$$

REVIEW AND DISCUSSION QUESTIONS

1 Distinguish between dependent and independent demand in a McDonald's restaurant, in an integrated manufacturer of personal copiers, and in a pharmaceutical supply house.
2 Distinguish between in-process inventory, safety stock inventory, and seasonal inventory.
3 Discuss the nature of the costs that affect inventory size.
4 Under which conditions would a plant manager elect to use a fixed–order quantity model as opposed to a fixed–time period model? What are the disadvantages of using a fixed–time period ordering system?
5 Discuss the general procedure for determining the order quantity when price breaks are involved. Would there be any differences in procedure if holding cost were a fixed percentage of price rather than a constant amount?
6 What two basic questions must be answered by an inventory-control decision rule?
7 Discuss the assumptions that are inherent in production setup cost, ordering cost, and carrying costs. How valid are they?
8 "The nice thing about inventory models is that you can pull one off the shelf and apply it so long as your cost estimates are accurate." Comment.
9 Which type of inventory system would you use in the following situations?
   a. Supplying your kitchen with fresh food.
   b. Obtaining a daily newspaper.
   c. Buying gas for your car.
   To which of these items do you impute the highest stockout cost?
10 Why is it desirable to classify items into groups, as the ABC classification does?
11 What kind of policy or procedure would you recommend to improve the inventory operation in a department store? What advantages and disadvantages does your system have vis-à-vis the department store inventory operation described in this chapter?

PROBLEMS

1 The local supermarket buys lettuce each day to ensure really fresh produce. Each morning any lettuce that is left from the previous day is sold to a dealer that resells it to farmers who use it to feed their animals. This week the supermarket can buy fresh lettuce for $4.00 a box. The lettuce is sold for $10.00 a box and the dealer that sells old lettuce is willing to pay $1.50 a box. Past history says that tomorrow's demand for lettuce averages 250 boxes with a standard deviation of 34 boxes. How many boxes of lettuce should the supermarket purchase tomorrow?
2 Next week, Super Discount Airlines has a flight from New York to Los Angeles that will be booked to capacity. The airline knows from past history that an average of 25 customers (with a standard deviation of 15) cancel their reservation or do not show for the flight. Revenue from a ticket on the flight is $125. If the flight is overbooked, the airline has a policy of getting the customer on the next available flight and giving the person a free round-trip ticket on a future flight. The cost of this free round-trip ticket averages $250. Super Discount considers the cost of flying the plane from New York to Los Angeles a sunk cost. By how many seats should Super Discount overbook the flight?
3 Ray's Satellite Emporium wishes to determine the best order size for its best-selling satellite dish (model TS111). Ray has estimated the annual demand for this model at 1,000 units. His cost to carry one unit is $100 per year per unit, and he has estimated that each order costs $25 to place. Using the EOQ model, how many should Ray order each time?
4 Dunstreet's Department Store would like to develop an inventory ordering policy of a 95 percent probability of not stocking out. To illustrate your recommended procedure, use as an example the ordering policy for white percale sheets.

   Demand for white percale sheets is 5,000 per year. The store is open 365 days per year. Every two weeks (14 days) inventory is counted and a new order is placed. It takes 10 days for the sheets to be delivered. Standard deviation of demand for the sheets is five per day. There are currently 150 sheets on hand.

How many sheets should you order?

5   Charlie's Pizza orders all of its pepperoni, olives, anchovies, and mozzarella cheese to be shipped directly from Italy. An American distributor stops by every four weeks to take orders. Because the orders are shipped directly from Italy, they take three weeks to arrive.

Charlie's Pizza uses an average of 150 pounds of pepperoni each week, with a standard deviation of 30 pounds. Charlie's prides itself on offering only the best-quality ingredients and a high level of service, so it wants to ensure a 98 percent probability of not stocking out on pepperoni.

Assume that the sales representative just walked in the door and there are currently 500 pounds of pepperoni in the walk-in cooler. How many pounds of pepperoni would you order?

6   Given the following information, formulate an inventory management system. The item is demanded 50 weeks a year.

Item cost	$10.00	Standard deviation of weekly demand	25 per week
Order cost	$250.00		
Annual holding cost (%)	33% of item cost	Lead time	1 week
Annual demand	25,750	Service probability	95%
Average demand	515 per week		

a. State the order quantity and reorder point.
b. Determine the annual holding and order costs.
c. If a price break of $50 per order was offered for purchase quantities of over 2,000, would you take advantage of it? How much would you save annually?

7   Lieutenant Commander Data is planning to make his monthly (every 30 days) trek to Gamma Hydra City to pick up a supply of isolinear chips. The trip will take Data about two days. Before he leaves, he calls in the order to the GHC Supply Store. He uses chips at an average rate of five per day (seven days per week) with a standard deviation of demand of one per day. He needs a 98 percent service probability. If he currently has 35 chips in inventory, how many should he order? What is the most he will ever have to order?

8   Jill's Job Shop buys two parts (Tegdiws and Widgets) for use in its production system from two different suppliers. The parts are needed throughout the entire 52-week year. Tegdiws are used at a relatively constant rate and are ordered whenever the remaining quantity drops to the reorder level. Widgets are ordered from a supplier who stops by every three weeks. Data for both products are as follows:

ITEM	TEGDIW	WIDGET
Annual demand	10,000	5,000
Holding cost (% of item cost)	20%	20%
Setup or order cost	$150.00	$25.00
Lead time	4 weeks	1 week
Safety stock	55 units	5 units
Item cost	$10.00	$2.00

a. What is the inventory control system for Tegdiws? That is, what is the reorder quantity and what is the reorder point?
b. What is the inventory control system for Widgets?

9   Demand for an item is 1,000 units per year. Each order placed costs $10; the annual cost to carry items in inventory is $2 each.
a. In what quantities should the item be ordered?
b. Supposing a $100 discount on each order is given if orders are placed in quantities of 500 or more. Should orders be placed in quantities of 500, or should you stick to the decision you made in *a*?

10   The annual demand for a product is 15,600 units. The weekly demand is 300 units with a standard deviation of 90 units. The cost to place an order is $31.20, and the time from ordering to receipt is four weeks. The annual inventory carrying cost is $0.10 per unit. Find the reorder point necessary to provide a 98 percent service probability.

Suppose the production manager is asked to reduce the safety stock of this item by 50 percent. If she does so, what will the new service probability be?

11   Daily demand for a product is 100 units, with a standard deviation of 25 units. The review period is 10 days and the lead time is 6 days. At the time of review there are 50 units in stock. If 98 percent service probability is desired, how many units should be ordered?

12   Item X is a standard item stocked in a company's inventory of component parts. Each year the firm, on a random basis, uses about 2,000 of item X, which costs $25 each. Storage costs, which include insurance and cost of capital, amount to $5 per unit of average inventory. Every time an order is placed for more item X, it costs $10.

    a. Whenever item X is ordered, what should the order size be?

    b. What is the annual cost for ordering item X?

    c. What is the annual cost for storing item X?

13   Annual demand for a product is 13,000 units; weekly demand is 250 units with a standard deviation of 40 units. The cost of placing an order is $100, and the time from ordering to receipt is four weeks. The annual inventory carrying cost is $0.65 per unit. To provide a 98 percent service probability, what must the reorder point be?

    Suppose the production manager is told to reduce the safety stock of this item by 100 units. If this is done, what will the new service probability be?

14   A particular raw material is available to a company at three different prices, depending on the size of the order:

Less than 100 pounds	$20 per pound
100 pounds to 1,000 pounds	$19 per pound
More than 1,000 pounds	$18 per pound

    The cost to place an order is $40. Annual demand is 3,000 units. Holding (or carrying) cost is 25 percent of the material price.

    What is the economic order quantity to buy each time?

15   In the past, Taylor Industries has used a fixed–time period inventory system that involved taking a complete inventory count of all items each month. However, increasing labor costs are forcing Taylor Industries to examine alternative ways to reduce the amount of labor involved in inventory stockrooms, yet without increasing other costs, such as shortage costs. Here is a random sample of 20 of Taylor's items.

ITEM NUMBER	ANNUAL USAGE	ITEM NUMBER	ANNUAL USAGE
1	$ 1,500	11	$13,000
2	12,000	12	600
3	2,200	13	42,000
4	50,000	14	9,900
5	9,600	15	1,200
6	750	16	10,200
7	2,000	17	4,000
8	11,000	18	61,000
9	800	19	3,500
10	15,000	20	2,900

    a. What would you recommend Taylor do to cut back its labor cost? (Illustrate using an ABC plan.)

    b. Item 15 is critical to continued operations. How would you recommend it be classified?

16   Gentle Ben's Bar and Restaurant uses 5,000 quart bottles of an imported wine each year. The effervescent wine costs $3 per bottle and is served only in whole bottles because it loses its bubbles quickly. Ben figures that it costs $10 each time an order is placed, and holding costs are 20 percent of the purchase price. It takes three weeks for an order to arrive. Weekly demand is 100 bottles (closed two weeks per year) with a standard deviation of 30 bottles.

    Ben would like to use an inventory system that minimizes inventory cost and will provide a 95 percent service probability.

    a. What is the economic quantity for Ben to order?

    b. At what inventory level should he place an order?

17   Retailers Warehouse (RW) is an independent supplier of household items to department stores. RW attempts to stock enough items for a 98 percent service probability.

A stainless steel knife set is one item it stocks. Demand (2,400 sets per year) is relatively stable over the entire year. Whenever new stock is ordered, a buyer must assure that numbers are correct for stock on hand and then phone in a new order. The total cost involved to place an order is about $5. RW figures that holding inventory in stock and paying for interest on borrowed capital, insurance, and so on adds up to about $4 holding cost per unit per year.

Analysis of the past data shows that the standard deviation of demand from retailers is about four units per day for a 365-day year. Lead time to get the order is seven days.

a. What is the economic order quantity?

b. What is the reorder point?

18   Daily demand for a product is 60 units with a standard deviation of 10 units. The review period is 10 days, and lead time is 2 days. At the time of review there are 100 units in stock. If 98 percent service probability is desired, how many units should be ordered?

19   University Drug Pharmaceuticals orders its antibiotics every two weeks (14 days) when a salesperson visits from one of the pharmaceutical companies. Tetracycline is one of its most prescribed antibiotics, with average daily demand of 2,000 capsules. The standard deviation of daily demand was derived from examining prescriptions filled over the past three months and was found to be 800 capsules. It takes five days for the order to arrive. University Drug would like to satisfy 99 percent of the prescriptions. The salesperson just arrived, and there are currently 25,000 capsules in stock.

How many capsules should be ordered?

20   Sally's Silk Screening produces specialty T-shirts that are primarily sold at special events. She is trying to decide how many to produce for an upcoming event. During the event itself, which lasts one day, Sally can sell T-shirts for $20 apiece. However, when the event ends, any unsold T-shirts are sold for $4 apiece. It costs Sally $8 to make a specialty T-shirt. Using Sally's estimate of demand that follows, how many T-shirts should she produce for the upcoming event?

DEMAND	PROBABILITY
300	.05
400	.10
500	.40
600	.30
700	.10
800	.05

21   Famous Albert prides himself on being the Cookie King of the West. Small, freshly baked cookies are the specialty of his shop. Famous Albert has asked for help to determine the number of cookies he should make each day. From an analysis of past demand he estimates demand for cookies as

DEMAND	PROBABILITY OF DEMAND
1,800 dozen	0.05
2,000	0.10
2,200	0.20
2,400	0.30
2,600	0.20
2,800	0.10
3,000	0.05

Each dozen sells for $0.69 and costs $0.49, which includes handling and transportation. Cookies that are not sold at the end of the day are reduced to $0.29 and sold the following day as day-old merchandise.

a. Construct a table showing the profits or losses for each possible quantity.

b. What is the optimal number of cookies to make?

c. Solve this problem by using marginal analysis.

22   Sarah's Muffler Shop has one standard muffler that fits a large variety of cars. Sarah wishes to establish a reorder point system to manage inventory of this standard muffler. Use the following

information to determine the best order size and the reorder point:

Annual demand	3,500 mufflers	Ordering cost	$50 per order
Standard deviation of daily demand	6 mufflers per working day	Service probability	90%
Item cost	$30 per muffler	Lead time	2 working days
Annual holding cost	25% of item value	Working days	300 per year

23 Alpha Products, Inc., is having a problem trying to control inventory. There is insufficient time to devote to all its items equally. Here is a sample of some items stocked, along with the annual usage of each item expressed in dollar volume.

ITEM	ANNUAL DOLLAR USAGE	ITEM	ANNUAL DOLLAR USAGE
a	$ 7,000	k	$80,000
b	1,000	l	400
c	14,000	m	1,100
d	2,000	n	30,000
e	24,000	o	1,900
f	68,000	p	800
g	17,000	q	90,000
h	900	r	12,000
i	1,700	s	3,000
j	2,300	t	32,000

a. Can you suggest a system for allocating control time?

b. Specify where each item from the list would be placed.

24 After graduation, you decide to go into a partnership in an office supply store that has existed for a number of years. Walking through the store and stockrooms, you find a great discrepancy in service levels. Some spaces and bins for items are completely empty; others have supplies that are covered with dust and have obviously been there a long time. You decide to take on the project of establishing consistent levels of inventory to meet customer demands. Most of your supplies are purchased from just a few distributors that call on your store once every two weeks.

You choose, as your first item for study, computer printer paper. You examine the sales records and purchase orders and find that demand for the past 12 months was 5,000 boxes. Using your calculator you sample some days' demands and estimate that the standard deviation of daily demand is 10 boxes. You also search out these figures:

Cost per box of paper: $11.

Desired service probability: 98 percent.

Store is open every day.

Salesperson visits every two weeks.

Delivery time following visit is three days.

Using your procedure, how many boxes of paper would be ordered if, on the day the salesperson calls, 60 boxes are on hand?

25 A distributor of large appliances needs to determine the order quantities and reorder points for the various products it carries. The following data refer to a specific refrigerator in its product line:

Cost to place an order	$100
Holding cost	20 percent of product cost per year
Cost of refrigerator	$500 each
Annual demand	500 refrigerators
Standard deviation during lead time	10 refrigerators
Lead time	7 days

Consider an even daily demand and a 365-day year.

a. What is the economic order quantity?

b. If the distributor wants a 97 percent service probability, what reorder point, R, should be used?

26   It is your responsibility, as the new head of the automotive section of Nichols Department Store, to ensure that reorder quantities for the various items have been correctly established. You decide to test one item and choose Michelin tires, XW size 185 × 14 BSW. A perpetual inventory system has been used, so you examine this as well as other records and come up with the following data:

Cost per tire	$35 each
Holding cost	20 percent of tire cost per year
Demand	1,000 per year
Ordering cost	$20 per order
Standard deviation of daily demand	3 tires
Delivery lead time	4 days

Because customers generally do not wait for tires but go elsewhere, you decide on a service probability of 98 percent. Assume the demand occurs 365 days per year.
   a. Determine the order quantity.
   b. Determine the reorder point.

27   UA Hamburger Hamlet (UAHH) places a daily order for its high-volume items (hamburger patties, buns, milk, and so on). UAHH counts its current inventory on hand once per day and phones in its order for delivery 24 hours later. Determine the number of hamburgers UAHH should order for the following conditions:

Average daily demand	600
Standard deviation of demand	100
Desired service probability	99%
Hamburger inventory	800

28   CU, Incorporated (CUI), produces copper contacts that it uses in switches and relays. CUI needs to determine the order quantity, Q, to meet the annual demand at the lowest cost. The price of copper depends on the quantity ordered. Here are price-break and other data for the problem:

Price of copper	$0.82 per pound up to 2,499 pounds
	$0.81 per pound for orders between 2,500 and 5,000 pounds
	$0.80 per pound for orders greater than 5,000 pounds
Annual demand	50,000 pounds per year
Holding cost	20 percent per unit per year of the price of the copper
Ordering cost	$30

Which quantity should be ordered?

29   DAT, Inc., produces digital audiotapes to be used in the consumer audio division. DAT lacks sufficient personnel in its inventory supply section to closely control each item stocked, so it has asked you to determine an ABC classification. Here is a sample from the inventory records:

ITEM	AVERAGE MONTHLY DEMAND	PRICE PER UNIT	ITEM	AVERAGE MONTHLY DEMAND	PRICE PER UNIT
1	700	$6.00	6	100	10.00
2	200	4.00	7	3,000	2.00
3	2,000	12.00	8	2,500	1.00
4	1,100	20.00	9	500	10.00
5	4,000	21.00	10	1,000	2.00

Develop an ABC classification for these 10 items.

30   A local service station is open 7 days per week, 365 days per year. Sales of 10W40 grade premium oil average 20 cans per day. Inventory holding costs are $0.50 per can per year. Ordering costs are $10 per order. Lead time is two weeks. Backorders are not practical—the motorist drives away.
   a. Based on these data, choose the appropriate inventory model and calculate the economic order quantity and reorder point. Describe in a sentence how the plan would work. Hint: Assume demand is deterministic.

b. The boss is concerned about this model because demand really varies. The standard deviation of demand was determined from a data sample to be 6.15 cans per day. The manager wants a 99.5 percent service probability. Determine a new inventory plan based on this information and the data in *a*. Use Q_{opt} from *a*.

31 Dave's Auto Supply custom mixes paint for its customers. The shop performs a weekly inventory count of the main colors that are used for mixing paint. Determine the amount of white paint that should be ordered using the following information:

Average weekly demand	20 gallons
Standard deviation of demand	5 gallons/week
Desired service probability	98%
Current inventory	25 gallons
Lead time	1 week

CASE: HEWLETT-PACKARD—SUPPLYING THE DESKJET PRINTER IN EUROPE

The DeskJet printer was introduced in 1988 and has become one of Hewlett-Packard's (HP's) most successful products. Sales have grown steadily, reaching a level of over 600,000 units in 1990. Unfortunately, inventory growth has tracked sales growth closely. HP's distribution centers are filled with pallets of the DeskJet printer. Worse yet, the organization in Europe claims that inventory levels there need to be raised even further to maintain satisfactory product availability.

THE DESKJET SUPPLY CHAIN
The network of suppliers, manufacturing sites, distribution centers (DCs), dealers, and customers for the DeskJet product make up the DeskJet supply chain (see Exhibit 15.13). HP in Vancouver does manufacturing. There are two key stages in the manufacturing process: (1) printed circuit assembly and test (PCAT) and (2) final assembly and test (FAT). PCAT involves the assembly and testing of electronic components (like integrated circuits, read-only memories, and raw printed circuit boards) to make logic boards used in the printer. FAT involves the assembly of other subassemblies (like motors, cables, keypads, plastic chassis, gears, and the printed circuit assemblies from PCAT) to produce a working printer, as well as the final testing of the printer. The components needed for PCAT and

FAT are sourced from other HP divisions as well as from external suppliers worldwide.

Selling the DeskJet in Europe requires customizing the printer to meet the language and power supply requirements of the local countries, a process known as "localization." Specifically, the localization of the DeskJet of different countries involves assembling the appropriate power supply module, which reflects the correct voltage requirements (110 or 220) and power cord plug, and packaging it with the working printer and a manual written in the appropriate language. Currently, the final test is done with the actual power supply module included with the printer. Hence, the finished products of the factory are "localized" versions of the printer destined for all the different countries. For the European Market six different versions are currently produced. These are designated A, AA, AB, AQ, AU, and AY as indicated in the Bills of Materials shown in Exhibit 15.14.

The total factory throughput time through the PCAT and FAT stages is about one week. The transportation time from Vancouver to the European DC is five weeks. The long shipment time to Europe is due to ocean transit and the time to clear customs and duties at port of entry. The plant sends a weekly shipment of printers to the DC in Europe.

HP DeskJet Supply Chain

exhibit 15.13

Key: IC Mfg—Integrated Circuit Manufacturing
     PCAT—Printed Circuit Assembly and Test
     FAT—Final Assembly and Test
     Print Mech Mfg—Print Mechanism Manufacturing

exhibit 15.14   HP DeskJet Bill of Materials

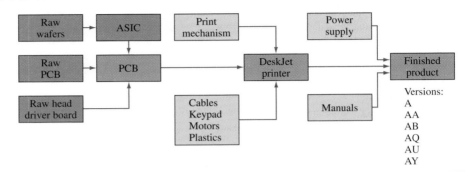

exhibit 15.15   DeskJet Demand Data from Europe

Excel: HP Deskjet

EUROPE OPTIONS	NOV.	DEC.	JAN.	FEB.	MAR.	APR.	MAY.	JUN.	JUL.	AUG.	SEP.	OCT.
A	80	—	60	90	21	48	—	9	20	54	84	42
AB	20,572	20,895	19,252	11,052	19,864	20,316	13,336	10,578	6,095	14,496	23,712	9,792
AU	4,564	3,207	7,485	4,908	5,295	90	—	5,004	4,385	5,103	4,302	6,153
AA	400	255	408	645	210	87	432	816	430	630	456	273
AQ	4,008	2,196	4,761	1,953	1,008	2,358	1,676	540	2,310	2,046	1,797	2,961
AY	248	450	378	306	219	204	248	484	164	363	384	234
Total	29,872	27,003	32,344	18,954	26,617	23,103	15,692	17,431	13,405	22,692	30,735	19,455

The printer industry is highly competitive. Resellers want to carry as little inventory as possible. Consequently there has been increasing pressure for HP as a manufacturer to provide high levels of availability at the DC. In response, management has decided to stock the DCs so that a high level of availability is maintained.

THE INVENTORY SERVICE CRISIS

To limit the amount of inventory throughout the DeskJet supply chain and at the same time provide the high level of service needed has been quite a challenge to Vancouver's management. The manufacturing group has been very successful in reducing the uncertainties caused by delivery to the European DC. Forecasting demand in Europe, though, is a significant problem. It has become common to have product shortages for model demands from some countries, while inventory of other models keeps piling up. In the past, the target inventory levels at the DCs were based on safety stocks that were a result of some judgmental rule of thumb. Specifically, target inventory levels, equal to one-month average sales, were set for each model carried in the DC. Now, however, it seems that the increasing difficulty of getting accurate forecasts means the safety stock rules should be revisited.

HP has put together a team of employees to help implement a scientifically based safety stock system that will be responsive to forecast errors and replenishment lead times. They are to recommend a method for calculating appropriate safety stock levels for the various DeskJet models carried in the European DC. The team has a good sample of demand data that can be used for developing the safety stock methodology (see Exhibit 15.15). HP hopes this new methodology will solve the inventory and service problem.

One issue that continually comes up is the choice of inventory carrying cost to be used in safety stock analyses. Estimates within the company range from 12 percent (HP's cost of debt plus some warehousing expenses) to 60 percent (based on the ROI expected of new product development projects). Management has decided to use 25 percent for this study. Assume that all printers cost an average of approximately $250 each to produce and ship to Europe. Another issue is the choice of safety stock probability for the model. The company has decided to use a probability of 98 percent, a number that marketing feels is appropriate.

THE DISTRIBUTION PROCESS

The DCs have traditionally envisioned their process as a simple, straight-line, standardized process. There are four process stops:

1 Receive (complete) products from various suppliers and stock them.
2 Pick the various products needed to fill a customer order.
3 Shrink-wrap the complete order and label it.
4 Ship the order via the appropriate carrier.

The DeskJet printer fits well into the standard process. In contrast, other products, such as personal computers and monitors, require special processing called "integration," which includes addition of an appropriate keyboard and manual for the destination country. Although this extra processing does not require much extra labor, it is difficult to accommodate in the standard process and disrupts the material flow. There is considerable frustration within DC management regarding the support of assembly processes. In general, DC management stresses the DCs' role as warehouses and the need to continue to do what they are best at—distribution.

Top management, though, feels that integration of the product at the warehouse is extremely valuable because it allows generic products to be sent to the DC with final configuration of the product done just prior to shipment to the customer. Rather than the factory making products specific to a country, generic products could be produced and shipped to Europe. Management is very interested in studying the value of this approach as it could be applied to the DeskJet printers.

QUESTIONS

1 Develop an inventory model for managing the DeskJet printers in Europe assuming that the Vancouver plant continues to produce the six models sold in Europe. Using the data in Exhibit 15.15, apply your model and calculate the expected yearly investment in DeskJet printer inventory in the Europe DC.

2 Compare your results from question 1 to the current policy of carrying one month's average inventory at the DC.

3 Evaluate the idea of supplying generic printers to the Europe DC and integrating the product by packaging the power supply and the instruction manual at the DC just prior to delivery to the European resellers. Focus on the impact on DC inventory investment in this analysis.

4 What is your recommendation to HP?

SELECTED BIBLIOGRAPHY

Brooks, R. B., and L. W. Wilson. *Inventory Record Accuracy: Unleashing the Power of Cycle Counting.* Essex Junction, VT: Oliver Wight, 1993.

Silver, E.; D. Pyke; and R. Peterson. *Decision Systems for Inventory Management and Production Planning and Control.* 3rd ed. New York: Wiley, 1998.

Sipper, D., and R. L. Bulfin Jr. *Production Planning, Control, and Integration.* New York: McGraw-Hill, 1997.

Tersine, R. J. *Principles of Inventory and Materials Management.* 4th ed. New York: North-Holland, 1994.

Vollmann, T. E.; W. L. Berry; D. C. Whybark; and F. R. Jacobs. *Manufacturing Planning and Control Systems for Supply Chain Management.* 5th ed. New York: McGraw-Hill, 2004.

Wild, T. *Best Practices in Inventory Management.* New York: Wiley, 1998.

Zipkin, P. H. *Foundations of Inventory Management.* New York: Irwin/ McGraw-Hill, 2000.

FOOTNOTES

1 P is actually a cumulative probability because the sale of the nth unit depends not only on exactly n being demanded but also on the demand for any number greater than n.

2 As previously discussed, the standard deviation of a sum of independent variables equals the square root of the sum of the variances.

3 The Pareto principle is also widely applied in quality problems through the use of Pareto charts. (See Chapter 8.)

chapter

MATERIAL REQUIREMENTS PLANNING

16 FROM PUSH TO PULL

In the 1980s manufacturing led the national economy in the move from batch-oriented data processing systems to online transaction processing systems. The focus was MRP (initially material requirements planning, evolving to manufacturing resource planning), which later evolved into enterprise resource planning (ERP). It has been a long ride, and anyone who has been there for the duration deserves a rest.

However, the winds of change are blowing again as yet another new paradigm comes roaring through manufacturing. Specifically, we are speaking of the change in our economy from a build-to-stock to a build-to-order model of doing business.

The weak link in the build-to-stock model is inventory management, and this can be traced to an even weaker link, reliance upon sales forecasts. A build-to-order model begins with the order, not the forecast. The old problem of coordinating the procurement of parts, production of the product, and shipping the product still exists.

Today the term *flow management* is used to describe new hybrid production planning systems that combine the information integration and planning capability of MRP with the response of a JIT kanban system. Major ERP software vendors such as Oracle, SAP, and i2 Technologies are selling these new systems.

Essentially, the idea with flow management is to produce a constantly changing mix of products, a mix that is based on current orders, using a stream of parts that are supplied just-in-time. It's important not to be tricked into thinking that all these new words really represent something new. Actually, flow manufacturing just combines things that have been used for years. In this case the combination is JIT kanban logic, MRP logic for planning material requirements, and client–server ERP. →

Material requirements planning (MRP)

Manufacturing resource planning (MRP II)

Cross Functional

As Virginia Slims ads used to say, "You've come a long way, baby." So has material requirements planning (MRP) come a long way. From humble beginnings computing the schedules and amounts of materials required, MRP has grown to become fully integrated, interactive, real-time systems capable of multisite global applications. In this chapter we go back to the beginning and introduce the basic MRP system and take you through the logic and calculations of scheduling and materials ordering.

Material requirements planning (MRP) systems have been installed almost universally in manufacturing firms, even those considered small. The reason is that MRP is a logical, easily understandable approach to the problem of determining the number of parts, components, and materials needed to produce each end item. MRP also provides the schedule specifying when each of these materials, parts, and components should be ordered or produced.

The original MRP planned only materials. However, as computer power grew and applications expanded, so did the breadth of MRP. Soon it considered resources as well as materials and was called **MRP II,** standing for **manufacturing resource planning.** A complete MRP program included 20 or so modules controlling the entire system from order entry through scheduling, inventory control, finance, accounting, accounts payable, and so on. Today MRP impacts the entire system and includes just-in-time, kanban, and computer-integrated manufacturing (CIM).

All firms maintain a bill of materials (BOM) file, which is simply the sequence of everything that goes into the final product. It can be called a *product structure tree,* a *schematic,* or a *flow diagram,* which shows the order of creating the item. Also maintained by all firms is an inventory file. This database contains specifications about each item, where it is purchased or produced, and how long it takes. MRP in its basic form is a computer program determining how much of each item is needed and when it is needed to complete a specified number of units in a specific time period. MRP does this by reaching into the bill of materials file and inventory records file to create a time schedule and the number of units needed at each step in the process.

MRP is based on dependent demand. Dependent demand is caused by the demand for a higher-level item. Tires, wheels, and engines are dependent demand items based on the demand for automobiles.

Determining the number of dependent demand items needed is essentially a straightforward multiplication process. If one Part A takes five parts of B to make, then five parts of A require 25 parts of B. The basic difference in independent demand covered in the previous chapter and dependent demand covered in this chapter is as follows: If Part A is sold outside

SARA LEE HOUSEHOLD AND PERSONAL CARE OVERHAULED THEIR BUSINESS SYSTEMS AND IMPLEMENTED AN MRP II SYSTEM ALONG WITH THE LOGOL FORECASTING PACKAGE. SINCE THE INTEGRATION, INVENTORY ACCURACY OF RAW MATERIALS HAS IMPROVED TO 99.8%, AND FINISHED GOODS INVENTORY ACCURACY ROSE FROM 20% TO 98.5%, WHICH HAS SAVED THE COMPANY 50% ON INVENTORY INVESTMENT AND HELPED BRING THEIR CUSTOMER SATISFACTION LEVELS TO A SOARING 99.5%.

the firm, the amount of Part A that we sell is uncertain. We need to create a forecast using past data or do something like a market analysis. Part A is an independent item. However, Part B is a dependent part and its use depends on Part A. The number of B needed is simply the number of A times five. As a result of this type of multiplication, the requirements of other dependent demand items tend to become more and more lumpy as we go farther down into the product creation sequence. Lumpiness means that the requirements tend to bunch or lump rather than having an even dispersal. This is also caused by the way manufacturing is done. When manufacturing occurs in lots, items needed to produce the lot are withdrawn from inventory in quantities (perhaps all at once) rather than one at a time.

The main purpose of this chapter is to explain MRP more thoroughly and to demonstrate its use. We show that just-in-time (JIT) systems and MRP are not necessarily competing ways for production but can work effectively together.

WHERE MRP CAN BE USED

MRP is most valuable in industries where a number of products are made in batches using the same productive equipment. The list in Exhibit 16.1 includes examples of different industry types and the expected benefit from MRP. As you can see in the exhibit, MRP is most valuable to companies involved in assembly operations and least valuable to those in fabrication. One more point to note: MRP does not work well in companies that produce a low number of units annually. Especially for companies producing complex, expensive products requiring advanced research and design, experience has shown that lead times tend to be too long and too uncertain, and the product configuration too complex. Such companies need the control features that network scheduling techniques offer. These project management methods are covered in Chapter 3.

Industry Applications and Expected Benefits of MRP

exhibit 16.1

INDUSTRY TYPE	EXAMPLES	EXPECTED BENEFITS
Assemble-to-stock	Combines multiple component parts into a finished product, which is then stocked in inventory to satisfy customer demand. Examples: watches, tools, appliances.	High
Fabricate-to-stock	Items are manufactured by machine rather than assembled from parts. These are standard stock items carried in anticipation of customer demand. Examples: piston rings, electrical switches.	Low
Assemble-to-order	A final assembly is made from standard options that the customer chooses. Examples: trucks, generators, motors.	High
Fabricate-to-order	Items are manufactured by machine to customer order. These are generally industrial orders. Examples: bearings, gears, fasteners.	Low
Manufacture-to-order	Items are fabricated or assembled completely to customer specification. Examples: turbine generators, heavy machine tools.	High
Process	Includes industries such as foundries, rubber and plastics, specialty paper, chemicals, paint, drug, food processors.	Medium

A SIMPLE MRP EXAMPLE

Before discussing details of an MRP system, we briefly explain how quantities are calculated, lead times are offset, and order releases and receipts are established.

Suppose that we are to produce Product T, which is made of two parts U and three parts V. Part U, in turn, is made of one part W and two parts X. Part V is made of two parts W and two parts Y. Exhibit 16.2 shows the product structure tree of Product T. By simple computation, we calculate that if 100 units of T are required, we need

$$
\begin{aligned}
\text{Part U:} \quad & \left. 2 \times \text{number of Ts} = \quad 2 \times 100 \right\} = 200 \\
\text{Part V:} \quad & \left. 3 \times \text{number of Ts} = \quad 3 \times 100 \right\} = 300 \\
\text{Part W:} \quad & \begin{array}{l} 1 \times \text{number of Us} = \quad 1 \times 200 \\ +2 \times \text{number of Vs} = \quad +2 \times 300 \end{array} \Big\} = 800 \\
\text{Part X:} \quad & 2 \times \text{number of Us} = \quad 2 \times 200 \quad = 400 \\
\text{Part Y:} \quad & 2 \times \text{number of Vs} = \quad 2 \times 300 \quad = 600
\end{aligned}
$$

exhibit 16.2

Product Structure Tree for Product T

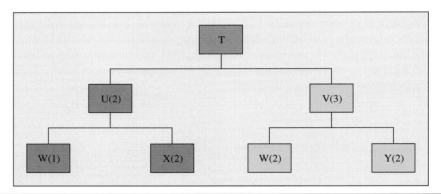

exhibit 16.3

Material Requirements Plan for Completing 100 Units of Product T in Period 7

		Week							
		1	2	3	4	5	6	7	
T	Required date							100	T lead time = 1 week
	Order placement						100		
U	Required date						200		U lead time = 2 weeks
	Order placement				200				
V	Required date						300		V lead time = 2 weeks
	Order placement				300				
W	Required date				800				W lead time = 3 weeks
	Order placement	800							
X	Required date				400				X lead time = 1 week
	Order placement			400					
Y	Required date				600				Y lead time = 1 week
	Order placement			600					

Now consider the time needed to obtain these items, either to produce the part internally or to obtain it from an outside vendor. Assume, now, that T takes one week to make; U, 2 weeks; V, 2 weeks; W, 3 weeks; X, 1 week; and Y, 1 week. If we know when Product T is required, we can create a schedule chart specifying when all materials must be ordered and received to meet the demand for T. Exhibit 16.3 shows which items are needed and when. We have thus created a material requirements plan based on the demand for Product T, the knowledge of how T is made, and the time needed to obtain each part.

From this simple illustration, it is apparent that developing a material requirements plan manually for thousands or even hundreds of items would be impractical—a great deal of computation is needed, and a tremendous amount of data must be available about the inventory status (number of units on hand, on order, and so forth) and about the product structure (how the product is made and how many units of each material are required). Because we are compelled to use a computer, our emphasis from here on in this chapter is to discuss the files needed for a computer program and the general makeup of the system. However, the basic logic of the program is essentially the same as that for our simple example.

MASTER PRODUCTION SCHEDULE

⭕⭕⭕⭕ Generally, the master schedule deals with end items. If the end item is quite large or quite expensive, however, the master schedule may schedule major subassemblies or components instead.

All production systems have limited capacity and limited resources. This presents a challenging job for the master scheduler. Although the aggregate plan provides the general range of operation, the master scheduler must specify exactly what is to be produced. These decisions are made while responding to pressures from various functional areas, such as the sales department (meet the customer's promised due date), finance (minimize inventory), management (maximize productivity and customer service, minimize resource needs), and manufacturing (have level schedules and minimize setup time).

To determine an acceptable feasible schedule to be released to the shop, trial master production schedules are run through the MRP program. The resulting planned order releases (the detailed production schedules) are checked to make sure that resources are available and that the completion times are reasonable. What appears to be a feasible master schedule may turn out to require excessive resources once the product explosion has taken place and materials, parts, and components from lower levels are determined. If this does happen (the usual case), the master production schedule is then modified with these limitations and the MRP program is run again. To ensure good master scheduling, the master scheduler (the human being) must

- Include all demands from product sales, warehouse replenishment, spares, and interplant requirements.
- Never lose sight of the aggregate plan.
- Be involved with customer order promising.
- Be visible to all levels of management.
- Objectively trade off manufacturing, marketing, and engineering conflicts.
- Identify and communicate all problems.

Cross Functional

The upper portion of Exhibit 16.4 shows an aggregate plan for the total number of mattresses planned per month, without regard for mattress type. The lower portion shows a master production schedule specifying the exact type of mattress and the quantity planned for production by week. The next level down (not shown) would be the MRP program that develops detailed schedules showing when cotton batting, springs, and hardwood are needed to make the mattresses.

To again summarize the planning sequence, the aggregate operations plan, discussed in Chapter 14, specifies product groups. It does not specify exact items. The next level down in

exhibit 16.4

The Aggregate Plan and the Master Production Schedule for Mattresses

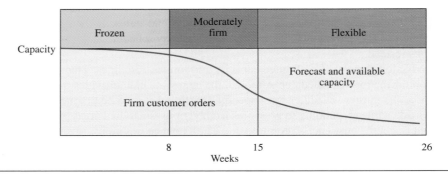

Aggregate Production
Plan for Mattresses

Month	1	2
Mattress production	900	950

Master Production
Schedule for
Mattress Models

	1	2	3	4	5	6	7	8
Model 327	200			400		200	100	
Model 538		100	100		150		100	
Model 749			100			200		200

exhibit 16.5

Master Production Schedule Time Fences

	Frozen	Moderately firm	Flexible
Capacity			

Firm customer orders

Forecast and available capacity

8   15   26

Weeks

Master production schedule (MPS)

the planning process is the master production schedule. The **master production schedule (MPS)** is the time-phased plan specifying how many and when the firm plans to build each end item. For example, the aggregate plan for a furniture company may specify the total volume of mattresses it plans to produce over the next month or next quarter. The MPS goes the next step down and identifies the exact size mattresses and their qualities and styles. All of the mattresses sold by the company would be specified by the MPS. The MPS also states period by period (usually weekly) how many and when each of these mattress types is needed.

Still further down the disaggregation process is the MRP program, which calculates and schedules all raw materials, parts, and supplies needed to make the mattress specified by the MPS.

TIME FENCES

The question of flexibility within a master production schedule depends on several factors: production lead time, commitment of parts and components to a specific end item, relationship between the customer and vendor, amount of excess capacity, and the reluctance or willingness of management to make changes.

The purpose of time fences is to maintain a reasonably controlled flow through the production system. Unless some operating rules are established and adhered to, the system could be chaotic and filled with overdue orders and constant expediting.

Exhibit 16.5 shows an example of a master production schedule time fence. Management defines *time fences* as periods of time having some specified level of opportunity for the customer to make changes. (The customer may be the firm's own marketing department, which may be considering product promotions, broadening variety, or the like.) Note in the exhibit that for the next eight weeks, this particular master schedule is frozen. Each firm has its own time fences and operating rules. Under these rules, *frozen* could be defined as anything from absolutely no changes in one company to only the most minor of changes in another. *Moderately firm* may allow changes in specific products within a product group so long as parts are available. *Flexible* may allow almost any variations in products, with the provisions that capacity remains about the same and that there are no long lead time items involved.

Some firms use a feature known as **available to promise** for items that are master scheduled. This feature identifies the difference between the number of units currently included in the master schedule and firm customer orders. For example, assume the master schedule indicates that 100 units of Model 538 mattress are going to be made during week seven. If firm customer orders now only indicate that 65 of those mattresses have actually been sold, the sales group has another 35 mattresses "available to promise" for delivery during that week. This can be a powerful tool for coordinating sales and production activities.

Available to promise

MATERIAL REQUIREMENTS PLANNING (MRP) SYSTEMS

As we stated previously, based on a *master schedule* derived from a *production plan*, a *material requirements planning (MRP) system* creates schedules identifying the specific parts and materials required to produce end items, the exact numbers needed, and the dates when orders for these materials should be released and be received or completed within the production cycle. MRP systems use a computer program to carry out these operations. Most firms have used computerized inventory systems for years, but they were independent of the scheduling system; MRP links them together.

PURPOSES OF MRP

The main purposes of a basic MRP system are to control inventory levels, assign operating priorities for items, and plan capacity to load the production system. The *theme* of MRP is "getting the right materials to the right place at the right time."

SOLUTIA INC. UNDERWENT A SUCCESSFUL CERTIFICATION PROCESS TO ACHIEVE CLASS A OPERATIONAL EXCELLENCE THROUGH MRP II. AMONG THE MANY RESULTS OF THE INTEGRATION, THE RESTRUCTURED INVENTORY SYSTEM GETS THE RIGHT PRODUCT TO THE RIGHT PLACE AT THE RIGHT TIME. ON-TIME DELIVERY AGAINST FIRST PROMISE IS NOW CONSISTENTLY AT 95% VERSUS 90% IN 2000.

The *objectives* of inventory management under an MRP system are the same as under any inventory management system: to improve customer service, minimize inventory investment, and maximize production operating efficiency.

The *philosophy* of material requirements planning is that materials should be expedited (hurried) when their lack would delay the overall production schedule, and de-expedited (delayed) when the schedule falls behind and postpones their need. Traditionally, and perhaps still typically, when an order is behind schedule, significant effort is spent trying to get it back on schedule. However, the opposite is not always true; when an order, for whatever reason, has its completion date delayed, the appropriate adjustments are not made in the schedule. This results in a one-sided effort—later orders are hurried, but early orders are not rescheduled for later. Aside from perhaps using scarce capacity, it is preferable not to have raw materials and work-in-process before the actual need because inventories tie up finances, clutter up stockrooms, prohibit design changes, and prevent the cancellation or delay of orders.

MATERIAL REQUIREMENTS PLANNING SYSTEM STRUCTURE

The material requirements planning portion of manufacturing activities most closely interacts with the master schedule, bill of materials file, inventory records file, and the output reports as shown in Exhibit 16.6.

Each facet of Exhibit 16.6 is detailed in the following sections, but essentially, the MRP system works as follows: Orders for products are used to create a master production schedule, which states the number of items to be produced during specific time periods. A bill of materials file identifies the specific materials used to make each item and the correct quantities of

exhibit 16.6

Overall View of the Inputs to a Standard Material Requirements Planning Program and the Reports Generated by the Program

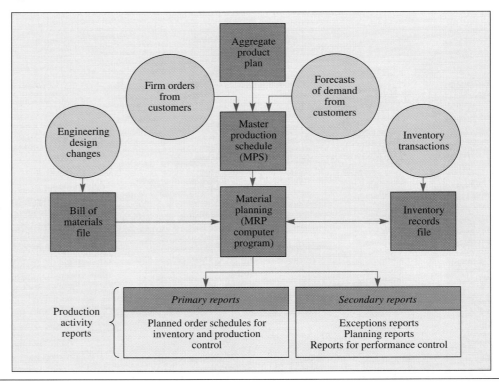

each. The inventory records file contains data such as the number of units on hand and on order. These three sources—master production schedule, bill of materials file, and inventory records file—become the data sources for the material requirements program, which expands the production schedule into a detailed order scheduling plan for the entire production sequence.

DEMAND FOR PRODUCTS

Product demand for end items comes primarily from two main sources. The first is known customers who have placed specific orders, such as those generated by sales personnel, or from interdepartment transactions. These orders usually carry promised delivery dates. There is no forecasting involved in these orders—simply add them up. The second source is forecast demand. These are the normal independent-demand orders; the forecasting models presented in Chapter 13 can be used to predict the quantities. The demand from the known customers and the forecast demand are combined and become the input for the master production schedule.

In addition to the demand for end products, customers also order specific parts and components either as spares or for service and repair. These demands are not usually part of the master production schedule; instead, they are fed directly into the material requirements planning program at the appropriate levels. That is, they are added in as a gross requirement for that part or component.

BILL OF MATERIALS FILE

The **bill of materials (BOM)** file contains the complete product description, listing not only the materials, parts, and components but also the sequence in which the product is created. This BOM file is one of the three main inputs to the MRP program. (The other two are the master schedule and the inventory records file.)

Bill of materials (BOM)

The BOM file is often called the *product structure file* or *product tree* because it shows how a product is put together. It contains the information to identify each item and the quantity used per unit of the item of which it is a part. To illustrate this, consider Product A shown in Exhibit 16.7. Product A is made of two units of Part B and three units of Part C. Part B is

THE CATWEB NAVIGATOR FROM IBM GIVES USERS THE ABILITY TO GENERATE IN REAL TIME THE ASSEMBLED BILL OF MATERIALS OF THE DISPLAYED 3D MODEL.

exhibit 16.7

Bill of Materials (Product Structure Tree) for Product A

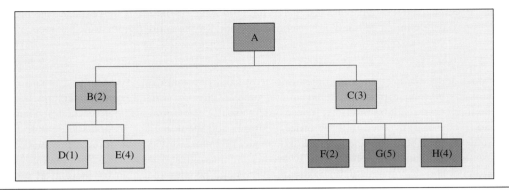

exhibit 16.8

Parts List in an Indented Format and in a Single-Level List

INDENTED PARTS LIST			SINGLE-LEVEL PARTS LIST	
A			A	
	B(2)			B(2)
		D(1)		C(3)
		E(4)	B	
	C(3)			D(1)
		F(2)		E(4)
		G(5)	C	
		H(4)		F(2)
				G(5)
				H(4)

made of one unit of Part D and four units of Part E. Part C is made of two units of Part F, five units of Part G, and four units of Part H.

Bills of materials often list parts using an indented structure. This clearly identifies each item and the manner in which it is assembled because each indentation signifies the components of the item. A comparison of the indented parts in Exhibit 16.8 with the item structure in Exhibit 16.7 shows the ease of relating the two displays. From a computer standpoint, however, storing items in indented parts lists is very inefficient. To compute the amount of each item needed at the lower levels, each item would need to be expanded ("exploded") and summed. A more efficient procedure is to store parts data in simple single-level lists. That is, each item and component is listed showing only its parent and the number of units needed per unit of its parent. This avoids duplication because it includes each assembly only once. Exhibit 16.8 shows both the indented parts list and the single-level parts list for Product A.

A *modular* bill of materials is the term for a buildable item that can be produced and stocked as a subassembly. It is also a standard item with no options within the module. Many end items that are large and expensive are better scheduled and controlled as modules (or subassemblies). It is particularly advantageous to schedule subassembly modules when the same subassemblies appear in different end items. For example, a manufacturer of cranes can combine booms, transmissions, and engines in a variety of ways to meet a customer's needs. Using a modular bill of materials simplifies the scheduling and control and also makes it easier to forecast the use of different modules. Another benefit in using modular bills is that if the same item is used in a number of products, then the total inventory investment can be minimized.

A *super* bill of materials includes items with fractional options. (A super bill can specify, for example, 0.3 of a part. What that means is that 30 percent of the units produced contain that part and 70 percent do not.) Modular and super bills of materials are often referred to as planning bills of materials since they simplify the planning process.

Low-Level Coding   If all identical parts occur at the same level for each end product, the total number of parts and materials needed for a product can be computed easily. Consider Product L shown in Exhibit 16.9a. Notice that Item N, for example, occurs both as an input to L and as an input to M. Item N, therefore, needs to be lowered to level 2 (Exhibit 16.9b) to bring all Ns to the same level. If all identical items are placed at the same level, it becomes a simple matter for the computer to scan across each level and summarize the number of units of each item required.

INVENTORY RECORDS FILE

The inventory records file can be quite lengthy. Exhibit 16.10 shows the variety of information contained in the inventory records. The MRP program accesses the *status* segment of the record according to specific time periods (called *time buckets* in MRP slang). These records are accessed as needed during the program run.

Product L Hierarchy in (a) Expanded to the Lowest Level of Each Item in (b)

exhibit 16.9

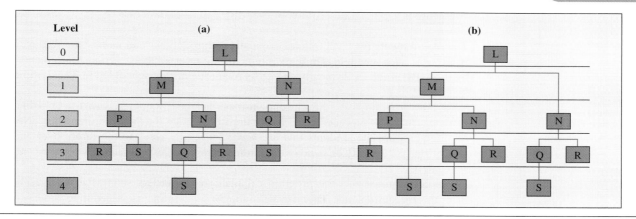

The Inventory Status Record for an Item in Inventory

exhibit 16.10

Item master data segment	Part no.		Description			Lead time		Std. cost		Safety stock			
	Order quantity			Setup	Cycle		Last year's usage			Class			
	Scrap allowance		Cutting data		Pointers		Etc.						
Inventory status segment	Allocated		Control balance	Period									Totals
				1	2	3	4	5	6	7	8		
	Gross requirements												
	Scheduled receipts												
	On hand												
	Planned order releases												
Subsidiary data segment	Order details												
	Pending action												
	Counters												
	Keeping track												

As we will see, the MRP program performs its analysis from the top of the product structure downward, calculating requirements level by level. There are times, however, when it is desirable to identify the parent item that caused the material requirement. The MRP program allows the creation of a *peg record* file either separately or as part of the inventory record file. Pegging requirements allows us to retrace a material requirement upward in the product structure through each level, identifying each parent item that created the demand.

Inventory Transactions File　　The inventory status file is kept up to date by posting inventory transactions as they occur. These changes occur because of stock receipts and disbursements, scrap losses, wrong parts, canceled orders, and so forth.

MRP Computer Program

The material requirements planning program operates using information from the inventory records, the master schedule, and the bill of materials. The process of calculating the exact requirements for each item managed by the system is often referred to as the "explosion" process. Working from the top level downward in the bill of materials, requirements from parent items are used to calculate the requirements for component items. Consideration is taken of current on-hand balances, and orders that are scheduled for receipt in the future.

The following is a general description of the MRP explosion process:

1. The requirements for level 0 items, typically referred to as "end items," are retrieved from the master schedule. These requirements are referred to as "gross requirements" by the MRP program. Typically, the gross requirements are scheduled in weekly time buckets.
2. Next, the program uses the current on-hand balance, together with the schedule of orders that will be received in the future to calculate the "net requirements." Net requirements are the amounts that are needed week by week in the future over and above what is currently on hand or committed to through an order already released and scheduled.
3. Using net requirements the program calculates when orders should be received to meet these requirements. This can be a simple process of just scheduling orders to arrive according to the exact net requirements or a more complicated process where requirements are combined for multiple periods. This schedule of when orders should arrive is referred to as "planned-order receipts."
4. Since there is typically a lead time associated with each order, the next step is to find a schedule for when orders are actually released. Offsetting the "planned-order receipts" by the required lead time does this. This schedule is referred to as the "planned-order release."
5. After these four steps have been completed for all the level zero items, the program moves to level 1 items.
6. The gross requirements for each level 1 item are calculated from the planned-order release schedule for the parents of each level 1 item. Any additional independent demand also needs to be included in the gross requirements.
7. After the gross requirements have been determined, net requirements, planned-order receipts, and planned-order releases are calculated as described in steps 2–4 above.
8. This process is then repeated for each level in the bill of materials.

The process of doing these calculations is much simpler than the description, as you will see in the example that follows. Typically, the explosion calculations are performed each week or whenever changes have been made to the master schedule. Some MRP programs have the option of generating immediate schedules, called *net change* schedules. **Net change systems** are "activity" driven and requirements and schedules are updated whenever a transaction is processed that has an impact on the item. Net change enables the system to reflect in "real time" the exact status of each item managed by the system.

Net change systems

AN EXAMPLE USING MRP

⊚⊚⊚⊚ Ampere, Inc., produces a line of electric meters installed in residential buildings by electric utility companies to measure power consumption. Meters used on single-family homes are of two basic types for different voltage and amperage ranges. In addition to complete meters, some subassemblies are sold separately for repair or for changeovers to a different voltage or power load. The problem for the MRP system is to determine a production schedule to identify each item, the period it is needed, and the appropriate quantities. The schedule is then checked for feasibility, and the schedule is modified if necessary.

FORECASTING DEMAND

Demand for the meters and components originates from two sources: regular customers that place firm orders and unidentified customers that make the normal random demands for these items. The random requirements were forecast using one of the usual techniques described in Chapter 13 and past demand data. Exhibit 16.11 shows the requirements for meters A and B and Subassembly D for a three-month period (months three through five). There are some "other parts" used to make the meters. In order to keep our example manageable, we are not including them in this example.

DEVELOPING A MASTER PRODUCTION SCHEDULE

For the meter and component requirements specified in Exhibit 16.11, assume that the quantities to satisfy the known and random demands must be available during the first week of the month. This assumption is reasonable because management (in our example) prefers to produce meters in a single batch each month rather than a number of batches throughout the month.

Exhibit 16.12 shows the trial master schedule that we use under these conditions, with demand for months 3, 4, and 5 listed in the first week of each month, or as Weeks 9, 13, and 17. For brevity, we will work with demand through Week 9. The schedule we develop should be

exhibit 16.11

Future Requirements for Meters A and B and Subassembly D Stemming from Specific Customer Orders and from Random Sources

	METER A		METER B		SUBASSEMBLY D	
MONTH	KNOWN	RANDOM	KNOWN	RANDOM	KNOWN	RANDOM
3	1,000	250	410	60	200	70
4	600	250	300	60	180	70
5	300	250	500	60	250	70

exhibit 16.12

A Master Schedule to Satisfy Demand Requirements as Specified in Exhibit 16.11

	Week								
	9	10	11	12	13	14	15	16	17
Meter A	1,250				850				550
Meter B	470				360				560
Subassembly D	270				250				320

exhibit 16.13   Product Structure for Meters A and B

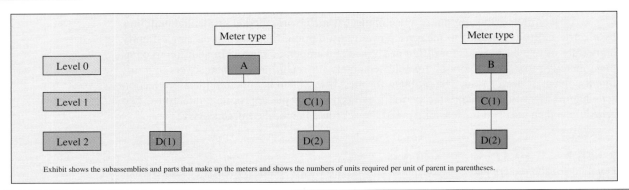

Exhibit shows the subassemblies and parts that make up the meters and shows the numbers of units required per unit of parent in parentheses.

exhibit 16.14   Indented Parts List for Meter A and Meter B, with the Required Number of Items per Unit of Parent Listed in Parentheses

	METER A			METER B	
A			B		
	D(1)				
	C(1)			C(1)	
		D(2)			D(2)

examined for resource availability, capacity availability, and so on, and then revised and run again. We will stop with our example at the end of this one schedule, however.

BILL OF MATERIALS (PRODUCT STRUCTURE) FILE

The product structure for meters A and B is shown in Exhibit 16.13 in the typical way using low-level coding, in which each item is placed at the lowest level at which it appears in the structure hierarchy. Meters A and B consist of a common subassembly C and some parts that include part D. To keep things simple, we will focus on only one of the parts, part D, which is a transformer.

From the product structure, notice that part D (the transformer) is used in subassembly C (which is used in both meters A and B). In the case of meter A, an additional part D (transformer) is needed. The "2" in parentheses next to D when used to make a C indicates that two D's are required for every C that is made. The product structure, as well as the indented parts list in Exhibit 16.14, indicates how the meters are actually made. First subassembly C is made and potentially these are carried in inventory. In a final assembly process, meters A and B are put together and in the case of meter A an additional part D is used.

INVENTORY RECORDS (ITEM MASTER) FILE

The inventory records data would be similar to that shown in Exhibit 16.10. As shown earlier in the chapter, additional data such as vendor identity, cost, and lead time would also be included in these data. For this example, the pertinent data include the on-hand inventory at the start of the program run, safety stock requirements, and the current status of orders that have already been released (see Exhibit 16.15). Safety stock is a minimum amount of inventory that we always want to keep on hand for an item. For example, for subassembly C, we never want the inventory to get below 5 units. We also see that we have an order for 10 units of meter B that is scheduled for receipt at the beginning of Week 5. Another order for 100 units of part D (the transformer) is scheduled to arrive at the beginning of Week 4.

Number of Units on Hand and Lead Time Data That Would Appear on the Inventory Record File

exhibit 16.15

ITEM	ON-HAND INVENTORY	LEAD TIME (WEEKS)	SAFETY STOCK	ON ORDER
A	50	2	0	
B	60	2	0	10 (week 5)
C	40	1	5	
D	200	1	20	100 (week 4)

Material Requirements Planning Schedule for Meters A and B, and Subassemblies C and D

exhibit 16.16

Item		Week					
		4	5	6	7	8	9
A LT = 2 weeks On hand = 50 Safety stock = 0 Order qty = lot-for-lot	Gross requirements						1250
	Scheduled receipts						
	Projected available balance	50	50	50	50	50	50
	Net requirements						1200
	Planned order receipts						1200
	Planned order releases				1200		
B LT = 2 weeks On hand = 60 Safety stock = 0 Order qty = lot-for-lot	Gross requirements						470
	Scheduled receipts		10				
	Projected available balance	60	60	70	70	70	70
	Net requirements						400
	Planned order receipts						400
	Planned order releases				400		
C LT = 1 week On hand = 40 Safety stock = 5 Order qty = 2000	Gross requirements				400+ 1200		
	Scheduled receipts						
	Projected available balance	35	35	35	35	435	435
	Net requirements				1565		
	Planned order receipts				2000		
	Planned order releases			2000			
D LT = 1 week On hand = 200 Safety stock = 20 Order qty = 5000	Gross requirements			4000	1200		270
	Scheduled receipts	100					
	Projected available balance	180	280	280	1280	80	80
	Net requirements			3720			190
	Planned order receipts			5000			5000
	Planned order releases		5000			5000	

PERFORMING THE MRP CALCULATIONS (LOGIC OF THE MRP COMPUTER PROGRAM)

Conditions are now set to perform the MRP calculations: End-item requirements have been presented in the master production schedule, while the status of inventory and the order lead times are available, and we also have the pertinent product structure data. The MRP calculations (often referred to as an explosion) are done level by level, in conjunction with the inventory data and data from the master schedule.

Exhibit 16.16 shows the details of these calculations. The following analysis explains the logic in detail. We will limit our analysis to the problem of meeting the gross requirements for 1,250 units of meter A, 470 units of meter B, and 270 units of transformer D, all in Week 9.

An MRP record is kept for each item managed by the system. The record contains *gross requirements, scheduled receipts, projected available balance, net requirements, planned order receipts,* and *planned order releases* data. *Gross requirements* are the total amount required for a particular item. These requirements can be from external customer demand and also from demand calculated due to manufacturing requirements. *Scheduled receipts* represent orders that have already been released and that are scheduled to arrive as of the beginning of the period. Once the paperwork on an order has been released, what was prior to that event a "planned" order now becomes a *scheduled receipt. Projected available balance* is the amount of inventory that is expected as of the beginning of a period. This can be calculated as follows:

$$\text{Projected available balance}_{t} = \text{Projected available balance}_{t-1} - \text{Gross requirements}_{t-1} + \text{Scheduled receipts}_{t-1} + \text{Planned order receipts}_{t-1} - \text{Safety stock}$$

A *net requirement* is the amount needed when the *projected available* balance plus the *scheduled receipts* in a period are not sufficient to cover the *gross requirement.* The *planned order receipt* is the amount of an order that is required to meet a net requirement in the period. Finally, the *planned order release* is the planned order receipt offset by the lead time.

Beginning with meter A, the projected available balance is 50 units and there are no net requirements until Week 9. In Week 9, an additional 1,200 units are needed to cover the demand of 1,250 generated from the order scheduled through the master schedule. The order quantity is designated "lot-for-lot," which means that we can order the exact quantity needed to meet net requirements. An order, therefore, is planned for receipt of 1,200 units for the beginning of Week 9. Since the lead time is two weeks, this order must be released at the beginning of Week 7.

Meter B is similar to A, although an order for 10 units is scheduled for receipt in period 5. We project that 70 units will be available in week 6. There is a net requirement for 400 additional units to meet the gross requirement of 470 units in Week 9. This requirement is met with an order for 400 units that must be released at the beginning of Week 7.

Item C is the subassembly used in both meters A and B. We only need additional C's when either A or B is being made. Our analysis of A indicates that an order for 1,200 will be released in Week 7. An order for 400 B's will also be released in Week 7, so total demand for C is 1,600 units in Week 7. The projected available balance is the 40 units on hand minus the safety stock of 5 units that we have specified, or 35 units. In Week 7, the net requirement is 1,565 units. The order policy for C indicates an order quantity of 2,000 units, so an order receipt for 2,000 is planned for Week 7. This order needs to be released in Week 6 due to the one-week lead time. Assuming this order is actually processed in the future, the projected available balance is 435 units in Weeks 8 and 9.

Item D, the transformer, has demand from three different sources. The demand in Week 6 is due to the requirement to put D's into subassembly C. In this case two D's are needed for every C, or 4,000 units (the product structure indicates this two-to-one relationship). In the seventh week, 1,200 D's are needed for the order for 1,200 A's that are scheduled to be released in Week 7. Another 270 units are needed in Week 9 to meet the independent demand that is scheduled through the master schedule. Projected available balance coming into Week 4 is 180 units (200 on hand minus the safety stock of 20 units), 280 units in Weeks 2 and 3. There is a net requirement for an additional 3,720 units in Week 6, so we plan to receive an order for 5,000 units (the order quantity). This results in a projected balance of 1,280 in Week 7, of which 1,200 are used to meet demand. Eighty units are projected to be available in Weeks 8 and 9. Due to the demand for 270 in Week 9, a net requirement of 190 units in Week 9 results in planning the receipt of an additional 5,000-unit order in Week 9.

IMPROVEMENTS IN THE MRP SYSTEM

⊚⊚⊚ MRP, as it was originally introduced and as we have discussed it so far in this chapter, considered only materials. Revising the schedule because of capacity considerations was done external to the MRP software program. Often, the schedule needs revision because of capacity constraints requiring the MRP program to be run again. (The Nichols case at the end of this chapter requires that the schedule be revised manually in Question 2 of the case.) The response to all other elements and resource requirements were not part of the system. Later refinements included the capacity of the work centers as part of the software program. Feedback of information was also introduced. We give an example of capacity planning at a work center and a closed-loop system. Following that we discuss MRP II systems.

COMPUTING WORK CENTER LOAD

The place to start in computing capacity requirements is right from the routing sheets for the jobs scheduled to be processed. Exhibit 6.7 in Chapter 6 shows the routing sheet for a plug assembly. Note that the routing sheet specifies where a job is to be sent, the particular operations involved, and the standard setup time and run time per piece. These are the types of figures used to compute the total work at each work center.

While the routing sheet is a "job view" that follows a particular job around the productive facility, a work center file is the view seen from a work center. Each work center is generally a functionally defined center so that jobs routed to it require the same type of work and the same equipment. From the work center view, if there is adequate capacity, the issue is just sequencing because all jobs will be done on time. (We discuss priority scheduling rules in Chapter 17.) If there is insufficient capacity, however, the problem must be resolved because some jobs will be late unless the schedule is adjusted.

Exhibit 16.17 shows a work center that has various jobs assigned to it. Note that the capacity per week was computed at the bottom of the exhibit at 161.5 hours. The jobs scheduled for the three weeks result in two weeks planned under work center capacity and one week over capacity.

Workload for Work Center A

exhibit 16.17

WEEK	JOB NO.	UNITS	SETUP TIME	RUN TIME PER UNIT	TOTAL JOB TIME	TOTAL FOR WEEK
10	145	100	3.5	.23	26.5	
	167	160	2.4	.26	44.0	
	158	70	1.2	.13	10.3	
	193	300	6.0	.17	57.0	137.8
11	132	80	5.0	.36	33.8	
	126	150	3.0	.22	36.0	
	180	180	2.5	.30	56.5	
	178	120	4.0	.50	64.0	190.3
12	147	90	3.0	.18	19.2	
	156	200	3.5	.14	31.5	
	198	250	1.5	.16	41.5	
	172	100	2.0	.12	14.0	
	139	120	2.2	.17	22.6	128.8

COMPUTING WORK CENTER CAPACITY

The available capacity in standard hours is 161.5 hours per five-day week, calculated as (2 machines) × (2 shifts) (10 hours/shift) (85% machine utilization) (95% efficiency).

exhibit 16.18   Scheduled Workload for Work Center A

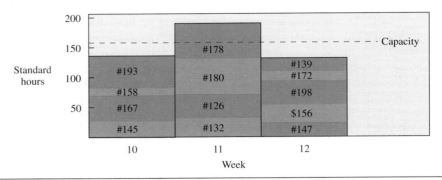

Exhibit 16.17 uses the terms *utilization* and *efficiency.* In this exhibit, utilization refers to the actual time that the machines are used. Efficiency refers to how well the machine is performing while it is being used. Efficiency is usually defined as a comparison to a defined standard output or an engineering design rate. For instance, a machine used for six hours of an eight-hour shift is utilized 6/8, or 75 percent. If the standard output for that machine is defined as 200 parts per hour and an average of 250 parts are made, then efficiency is 125 percent. Note that in these definitions, efficiency can be more than 100 percent, but utilization cannot.

Exhibit 16.18 shows a loading representation of Work Center A for the three weeks. The scheduled work exceeds capacity for Week 11. There are several options available:

1. Work overtime.
2. Select an alternative work center that could perform the task.
3. Subcontract to an outside shop.
4. Try to schedule part of the work of Week 11 earlier into Week 10, and delay part of the work into Week 12.
5. Renegotiate the due date and reschedule.

An MRP program with a capacity requirements planning module allows rescheduling to try to level capacity. Two techniques used are backward scheduling and forward scheduling—the fourth option on the preceding list. The objective of the master scheduler is to try to spread the load in Exhibit 16.18 more evenly to remain within the available capacity.

CLOSED-LOOP MRP

Closed-loop MRP

When the material requirements planning (MRP) system has information feedback from its module outputs, this is termed **closed-loop MRP**. Closed-loop MRP is defined as

> A system built around material requirements that includes the additional planning functions of sales and operations (production planning, master production scheduling, and capacity requirements planning). Once this planning phase is complete and the plans have been accepted as realistic and attainable, the execution functions come into play. These include the manufacturing control functions of input-output (capacity) measurement, detailed scheduling and dispatching, as well as anticipated delay reports from both the plant and suppliers, supplier scheduling, etc. The term "closed-loop" implies that not only is each of these elements included in the overall system, but also that feedback is provided by the execution functions so that the planning can be kept valid at all times.[1]

Exhibit 16.19 shows a closed-loop MRP system. The closed loop means that questions and output data are looped back up the system for verification and, if necessary, modification.

Closed-Loop MRP System Showing Feedback

exhibit 16.19

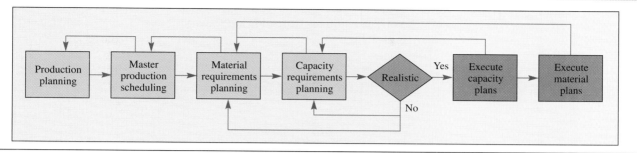

Recognize that the input to the MRP system is the master production schedule, as was stated earlier in the chapter. The MRP program does an explosion of all the parts, components, and other resources needed to meet this schedule. The capacity requirements planning module then checks the MRP output to see if sufficient capacity exists. If it does not, feedback to the MRP module indicates that the schedule needs to be modified. Continuing through the MRP system, orders are released to the production system by executing the capacity and material plans. From that point on, it is a matter of monitoring, data collection, completing the order, and evaluating results. Any changes in production, capacity, or material are fed back into the system.

MRP II (MANUFACTURING RESOURCE PLANNING)

An expansion of the material requirements planning system to include other portions of the productive system was natural and to be expected. One of the first to be included was the purchasing function. At the same time, there was a more detailed inclusion of the production system itself—on the shop floor, in dispatching, and in the detailed scheduling control. MRP had already included work center capacity limitations, so it was obvious that the name *material requirements planning* was no longer adequate to describe the expanded system. Someone (probably Ollie Wight) introduced the name *manufacturing resource planning (MRP II)* to reflect the idea that more and more of the firm was becoming involved in the program. To quote Wight,

> The fundamental manufacturing equation is:
>
> > What are we going to make?
> > What does it take to make it?
> > What do we have?
> > What do we have to get?[2]

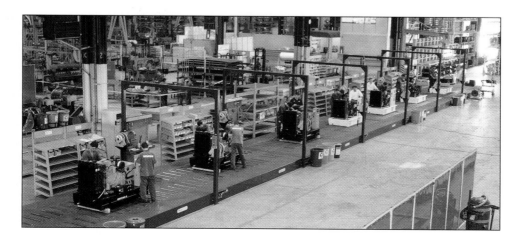

CATERPILLAR WAS AN EARLY INNOVATOR WITH MRP II IN THE 1980s.

The initial intent for MRP II was to plan and monitor all of the resources of a manufacturing firm—manufacturing, marketing, finance, and engineering—through a closed-loop system generating financial figures. The second important intent of the MRP II concept was that it simulates the manufacturing system allowing better visibility of what should occur in the future and better planning.

FLOW MANUFACTURING: EMBEDDING JIT INTO MRP

MRP and JIT each have benefits. The question is, Can they work together successfully, and how would one go about combining them? As stated earlier in the chapter, most major manufacturing firms use MRP. Of the firms using MRP, many in repetitive manufacturing also use JIT techniques. Although JIT is best suited to repetitive manufacturing, MRP

exhibit 16.20

Controlling Production Processes with MRP Alone and MRP/JIT Combined

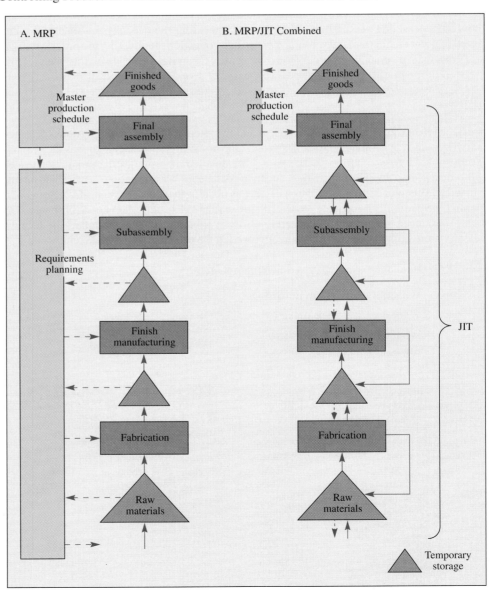

is used in everything from custom job shops to assembly-line production. A challenge arises in integrating the shop-floor improvement approaches of JIT with an MRP-based planning and control system. The MRP/JIT combination creates what might be considered a hybrid manufacturing system. As discussed in the opening vignette, the term **flow manufacturing** is now being used by many software vendors to describe new software modules that combine MRP and JIT logic.

Flow manufacturing

Exhibit 16.20 shows a master production schedule with an MRP system on the left. MRP systems can help create the master production schedule. From that point on, it remains a pure MRP system. Scheduling resources such as inventory are continuously controlled and monitored.

The right side of Exhibit 16.20 shows a master production schedule at the top feeding a JIT system. Computer control has been severed, and the JIT portion operates as its own separate pull method drawing from preceding stages. MRP may well be used to help create the master production schedule, but MRP's involvement stops there.

LOT SIZING IN MRP SYSTEMS

The determination of lot sizes in an MRP system is a complicated and difficult problem. Lot sizes are the part quantities issued in the planned order receipt and planned order release sections of an MRP schedule. For parts produced in-house, lot sizes are the production quantities of batch sizes. For purchased parts, these are the quantities ordered from the supplier. Lot sizes generally meet part requirements for one or more periods.

Most lot-sizing techniques deal with how to balance the setup or order costs and holding costs associated with meeting the net requirements generated by the MRP planning process. Many MRP systems have options for computing lot sizes based on some of the more commonly used techniques. It should be obvious, though, that the use of lot-sizing techniques increases the complexity in generating MRP schedules. When fully exploded, the numbers of parts scheduled can be enormous.

Next we explain four lot-sizing techniques using a common example. The lot-sizing techniques presented are lot-for-lot (L4L), economic order quantity (EOQ), least total cost (LTC), and least unit cost (LUC).

Consider the following MRP lot-sizing problem; the net requirements are shown for eight scheduling weeks:

Cost per item				$10.00			
Order or setup cost				$47.00			
Inventory carrying cost/week				0.5%			
Weekly net requirements:							
1	2	3	4	5	6	7	8
50	60	70	60	95	75	60	55

LOT-FOR-LOT

Lot-for-lot (L4L) is the most common technique. It

- Sets planned orders to exactly match the net requirements.
- Produces exactly what is needed each week with none carried over into future periods.
- Minimizes carrying cost.
- Does not take into account setup costs or capacity limitations.

Exhibit 16.21 shows the lot-for-lot calculations. The net requirements are given in column 2. Because the logic of lot-for-lot says the production quantity (column 3) will exactly match the required quantity (column 2), there will be no inventory left at the end (column 4).

exhibit 16.21   Lot-for-Lot Run Size for an MRP Schedule

(1) WEEK	(2) NET REQUIREMENTS	(3) PRODUCTION QUANTITY	(4) ENDING INVENTORY	(5) HOLDING COST	(6) SETUP COST	(7) TOTAL COST
1	50	50	0	$0.00	$47.00	$ 47.00
2	60	60	0	0.00	47.00	94.00
3	70	70	0	0.00	47.00	141.00
4	60	60	0	0.00	47.00	188.00
5	95	95	0	0.00	47.00	235.00
6	75	75	0	0.00	47.00	282.00
7	60	60	0	0.00	47.00	329.00
8	55	55	0	0.00	47.00	376.00

Without any inventory to carry over into the next week, there is zero holding cost (column 5). However, lot-for-lot requires a setup cost each week (column 6). Incidentally, there is a setup cost each week because this is a work center where a variety of items are worked on each week. This is not a case where the work center is committed to one product and sits idle when it is not working on that product (in which case only one setup would result). Lot-for-lot causes high setup costs.

ECONOMIC ORDER QUANTITY

In Chapter 15 we already discussed the EOQ model that explicitly balances setup and holding costs. In an EOQ model, either fairly constant demand must exist or safety stock must be kept to provide for demand variability. The EOQ model uses an estimate of total annual demand, the setup or order cost, and the annual holding cost. EOQ was not designed for a system with discrete time periods such as MRP. The lot-sizing techniques used for MRP assume that part requirements are satisfied at the start of the period. Holding costs are then charged only to the ending inventory for the period, not to the average inventory as in the case of the EOQ model. EOQ assumes that parts are used continuously during the period. The lot sizes generated by EOQ do not always cover the entire number of periods. For example, the EOQ might provide the requirements for 4.6 periods. Using the same data as in the lot-for-lot example, the economic order quantity is calculated as follows:

$$\text{Annual demand based on the 8 weeks} = D = \frac{525}{8} \times 52 = 3{,}412.5 \text{ units}$$

$$\text{Annual holding cost} = H = 0.5\% \times \$10 \times 52 \text{ weeks} = \$2.60 \text{ per unit}$$

$$\text{Setup cost} = S = \$47 \text{ (given)}$$

$$\therefore \text{EOQ} = \sqrt{\frac{2DS}{H}} = \sqrt{\frac{2(3{,}412.5)(\$47)}{\$2.60}} = 351 \text{ units}$$

Exhibit 16.22 shows the MRP schedule using an EOQ of 351 units. The EOQ lot size in Week 1 is enough to meet requirements for Weeks 1 through 5 and a portion of Week 6. Then, in Week 6 another EOQ lot is planned to meet the requirements for Weeks 6 through 8. Notice that the EOQ plan leaves some inventory at the end of Week 8 to carry forward into Week 9.

LEAST TOTAL COST

The least total cost method (LTC) is a dynamic lot-sizing technique that calculates the order quantity by comparing the carrying cost and the setup (or ordering) costs for various lot sizes and then selects the lot in which these are most nearly equal.

Economic Order Quantity Run Size for an MRP Schedule

exhibit 16.22

WEEK	NET REQUIREMENTS	PRODUCTION QUANTITY	ENDING INVENTORY	HOLDING COST	SETUP COST	TOTAL COST
1	50	351	301	$15.05	$47.00	$ 62.05
2	60	0	241	12.05	0.00	74.10
3	70	0	171	8.55	0.00	82.65
4	60	0	111	5.55	0.00	88.20
5	95	0	16	0.80	0.00	89.00
6	75	351	292	14.60	47.00	150.60
7	60	0	232	11.60	0.00	162.20
8	55	0	177	8.85	0.00	171.05

Least Total Cost Run Size for an MRP Schedule

exhibit 16.23

WEEKS	QUANTITY ORDERED	CARRYING COST	ORDER COST	TOTAL COST	
1	50	$ 0.00	$ 47.00	$ 47.00	
1–2	110	3.00	47.00	50.00	
1–3	180	10.00	47.00	57.00	
1–4	240	19.00	47.00	66.00	1st order
1–5	335	38.00	47.00	85.00 ← Least total cost	
1–6	410	56.75	47.00	103.75	
1–7	470	74.75	47.00	121.75	
1–8	525	94.00	47.00	141.00	
6	75	0.00	47.00	47.00	
6–7	135	3.00	47.00	50.00	2nd order
6–8	190	8.50	47.00	55.50 ← Least total cost	

WEEK	NET REQUIREMENTS	PRODUCTION QUANTITY	ENDING INVENTORY	HOLDING COST	SETUP COST	TOTAL COST
1	50	335	285	$14.25	$47.00	$ 61.25
2	60	0	225	11.25	0.00	72.50
3	70	0	155	7.75	0.00	80.25
4	60	0	95	4.75	0.00	85.00
5	95	0	0	0.00	0.00	85.00
6	75	190	115	5.75	47.00	137.75
7	60	0	55	2.75	0.00	140.50
8	55	0	0	0.00	0.00	140.05

The top half of Exhibit 16.23 shows the least cost lot size results. The procedure to compute least total cost lot sizes is to compare order costs and holding costs for various numbers of weeks. For example, costs are compared for producing in Week 1 to cover the requirements for Week 1; producing in Week 1 for Weeks 1 and 2; producing in Week 1 to cover Weeks 1, 2, and 3, and so on. The correct selection is the lot size where the ordering costs and holding costs are approximately equal. In Exhibit 16.23 the best lot size is 335 because a $38 carrying cost and a $47 ordering cost are closer than $56.75 and $47 ($9 versus $9.75). This lot size covers requirements for Weeks 1 through 5. Unlike EOQ, the lot size covers only whole numbers of periods.

Based on the Week 1 decision to place an order to cover five weeks, we are now located in Week 6, and our problem is to determine how many weeks into the future we can provide for from here. Exhibit 16.23 shows that holding and ordering costs are closest in the quantity that covers requirements for Weeks 6 through 8. Notice that the holding and ordering costs here are far apart. This is because our example extends only to Week 8. If the planning horizon were longer, the lot size planned for Week 6 would likely cover more weeks into the future beyond Week 8. This brings up one of the limitations of both LTC and LUC (discussed below). Both techniques are influenced by the length of the planning horizon. The bottom half of Exhibit 16.23 shows the final run size and total cost.

LEAST UNIT COST

The least unit cost method is a dynamic lot-sizing technique that adds ordering and inventory carrying cost for each trial lot size and divides by the number of units in each lot size, picking the lot size with the lowest unit cost. The top half of Exhibit 16.24 calculates the unit cost for ordering lots to meet the needs of Weeks 1 through 8. Note that the minimum occurred when the quantity 410, ordered in Week 1, was sufficient to cover Weeks 1 through 6. The lot size planned for Week 7 covers through the end of the planning horizon.

The least unit cost run size and total cost are shown in the bottom half of Exhibit 16.24.

CHOOSING THE BEST LOT SIZE

Using the lot-for-lot method, the total cost for the eight weeks is $376; the EOQ total cost is $171.05; the least total cost method is $140.50; and the least unit cost is $153.50. The lowest cost was obtained using the least total cost method of $140.50. If there were more than eight weeks, the lowest cost could differ.

The advantage of the least unit cost method is that it is a more complete analysis and would take into account ordering or setup costs that might change as the order size increases. If the ordering or setup costs remain constant, the lowest total cost method is more attractive because it is simpler and easier to compute; yet it would be just as accurate under that restriction.

---

exhibit 16.24   Least Unit Cost Run Size for an MRP Schedule

WEEKS	QUANTITY ORDERED	CARRYING COST	ORDER COST	TOTAL COST	UNIT COST	
1	50	$ 0.00	$ 47.00	$ 47.00	$0.9400	
1–2	110	3.00	47.00	50.00	0.4545	
1–3	180	10.00	47.00	57.00	0.3167	
1–4	240	19.00	47.00	66.00	0.2750	
1–5	335	38.00	47.00	85.00	0.2537	1st order
1–6	410	56.75	47.00	103.75	0.2530 ← Least unit cost	
1–7	470	74.75	47.00	121.75	0.2590	
1–8	525	94.00	47.00	141.00	0.2686	
7	60	0.00	47.00	47.00	0.7833	2nd order
7–8	115	2.75	47.00	49.75	0.4326 ← Least unit cost	

WEEK	NET REQUIREMENTS	PRODUCTION QUANTITY	ENDING INVENTORY	HOLDING COST	SETUP COST	TOTAL COST
1	50	410	360	$18.00	$ 47.00	$ 65.00
2	60	0	300	15.00	0.00	80.00
3	70	0	230	11.50	0.00	91.50
4	60	0	170	8.50	0.00	100.00
5	95	0	75	3.75	0.00	103.75
6	75	0	0	0	0	103.75
7	60	115	55	2.75	47.00	153.50
8	55	0	0	0	0	$153.50

CONCLUSION

Since the 1970s, MRP has grown from its purpose of determining simple time schedules to its present advanced types that tie together all major functions of an organization. During its growth and its application, MRP's disadvantages as a scheduling mechanism have been well recognized. This is largely because MRP tries to do too much in light of the dynamic, often jumpy system in which it is trying to operate.

MRP is recognized, however, for its excellent databases and linkages within the firm. MRP also does a good job in helping to produce master schedules. Many firms in repetitive manufacturing are installing JIT systems to link with the MRP system. JIT takes the master production schedule as its pulling force but does not use MRP's generated schedule. Results indicate that this is working very well.

Many newer MRP-type software programs have been developed since the early 1990s. These allow more open exchange of data than the earlier systems, embrace a larger part of the firm's operation (such as multiple sites, global customers, languages, and currency rates), and operate in real time.

Over the longer term, experts predict that e-business will force manufacturers to abandon the MRP or work order business model, a model that depends on accurate forecasts. Flow manufacturing, in which a company aims to minimize its working inventory and drive production by actual demand, should dominate.

MRP's service applications have not fared well, even though it seems that they should have. The MRP approach would appear to be valuable in producing services because service scheduling consists of identifying the final service and then tracing back to the resources needed, such as equipment, space, and personnel. Consider, for example, a hospital operating room planning an open-heart surgery. The master schedule can establish a time for the surgery (or surgeries, if several are scheduled). The BOM could specify all required equipment and personnel—MDs, nurses, anesthesiologist, operating room, heart/lung machine, defibrillator, and so forth. The inventory status file would show the availability of the resources and commit them to the project. The MRP program could then produce a schedule showing when various parts of the operation are to be started, expected completion time, required materials, and so forth. Checking this schedule would allow "capacity planning" in answering such questions as "Are all the materials and personnel available?" and "Does the system produce a feasible schedule?"

Service

We still believe that MRP systems will eventually find their way into service applications. But after a number of years of believing this, we have not seen development and implementation. One reason is that even service managers who are aware of it believe that MRP is just a manufacturing tool. Also, service managers tend to be people-oriented and skeptical of tools from outside their industry.

KEY TERMS

Material requirements planning (MRP) The logic for determining the number of parts, components, and materials needed to produce a product. MRP also provides the schedule specifying when each of these materials, parts, and components should be ordered or produced.

Manufacturing resource planning (MRP II) An expanded version of MRP that integrates finance, accounting, accounts payable, and other business processes into the production scheduling and inventory control functions that are part of a basic MRP system.

Master production schedule (MPS) A time-phased plan specifying how many and when the firm plans to build each end item.

Available to promise A feature of MRP systems that identifies the difference between the number of units currently included in the master schedule and actual (firm) customer orders.

Bill of materials (BOM) A computer file that contains the complete product description, listing the materials, parts, and components and the sequence in which the product is created.

Net change system An MRP system that calculates the impact of a change in the MRP data (the inventory status, BOM, or master schedule) immediately. This is a common feature in current systems.

Closed-loop MRP The use of actual data from the production system to continually update the MRP system. This feedback is provided so that planning can be kept valid at all times.

Flow manufacturing Hybrid production planning systems that combine the information integration and planning capabilities of MRP with the response of a JIT kanban system.

S O L V E D   P R O B L E M S

SOLVED PROBLEM 1

Product X is made of two units of Y and three of Z. Y is made of one unit of A and two units of B. Z is made of two units of A and four units of C.

    Lead time for X is one week; Y, two weeks; Z, three weeks; A, two weeks; B, one week; and C, three weeks.

a. Draw the bill of materials (product structure tree).
b. If 100 units of X are needed in week 10, develop a planning schedule showing when each item should be ordered and in what quantity.

Solution

a.

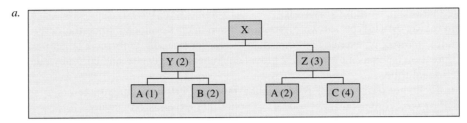

b.

		3	4	5	6	7	8	9	10
X	LT = 1							100	100
Y	LT = 2					200		200	
Z	LT = 3				300			300	
A	LT = 2			600	200	600	200		
B	LT = 1					400	400		
C	LT = 3	1200			1200				

SOLVED PROBLEM 2

Product M is made of two units of N and three of P. N is made of two units of R and four units of S. R is made of one unit of S and three units of T. P is made of two units of T and four units of U.

a. Show the bill of materials (product structure tree).
b. If 100 M are required, how many units of each component are needed?
c. Show both a single-level parts list and an indented parts list.

Solution

a.

```
                    M
          ┌─────────┴─────────┐
        N (2)               P (3)
      ┌───┴───┐          ┌────┴────┐
    R (2)   S (4)      T (2)     U (4)
   ┌──┴──┐
 S (1)  T (3)
```

b. M = 100   S = 800 + 400 = 1,200
    N = 200   T = 600 + 1,200 = 1,800
    P = 300   U = 1,200
    R = 400

c.

SINGLE-LEVEL PARTS LIST	INDENTED PARTS LIST

SINGLE-LEVEL PARTS LIST

M
  N (2)
  P (3)
N
  R (2)
  S (4)
R
  S (1)
  T (3)
P
  T (2)
  U (4)

INDENTED PARTS LIST

M
 N(2)
  R(2)
   S (1)
   T (3)
  S (4)
 P (3)
  T (2)
  U (4)

REVIEW AND DISCUSSION QUESTIONS

1 Discuss the meaning of MRP terms such as *planned order release* and *scheduled order receipts.*
2 Many practitioners currently update MRP weekly or biweekly. Would it be more valuable if it were updated daily? Discuss.
3 What is the role of safety stock in an MRP system?
4 How does MRP relate to CIM? (See Supplement B.)
5 Contrast the significance of the term *lead time* in the traditional EOQ context and in an MRP system.
6 Discuss the importance of the master production schedule in an MRP system.
7 "MRP just prepares shopping lists. It does not do the shopping or cook the dinner." Comment.
8 What are the sources of demand in an MRP system? Are these dependent or independent, and how are they used as inputs to the system?
9 State the types of data that would be carried in the bill of materials file and the inventory record file.

PROBLEMS

1 Semans is a manufacturer that produces bracket assemblies. Demand for bracket assemblies (X) is 130 units. The following is the BOM in indented form:

ITEM			DESCRIPTION	USAGE
X			Bracket assembly	1
	A		Wall board	4
	B		Hanger subassembly	2
		D	Hanger casting	3
		E	Ceramic knob	1
	C		Rivet head screw	3
		F	Metal tong	4
		G	Plastic cap	2

Below is a table indicating current inventory levels:

Item	X	A	B	C	D	E	F	G
Inventory	25	16	60	20	180	160	1000	100

 a. Using Excel, create the MRP using the product tree structure.
 b. What are the net requirements of each item in the MPS?

2 In the following MRP planning schedule for Item J, indicate the correct net requirements, planned order receipts, and planned order releases to meet the gross requirements. Lead time is one week.

	WEEK NUMBER					
ITEM J	0	1	2	3	4	5
Gross requirements			75		50	70
On-hand			40			
Net requirements						
Planned order receipt						
Planned order release						

3   Repeat Solved Problem 1 using current on-hand inventories of 20 X, 40 Y, 30 Z, 50 A, 100 B, and 900 C.

4   Assume that Product Z is made of two units of A and four units of B. A is made of three units of C and four D. D is made of two units of E.

   Lead times for purchase or fabrication of each unit to final assembly are: Z takes two weeks; A, B, C, and D take one week each; and E takes three weeks.

   Fifty units are required in Period 10. (Assume that there is currently no inventory on hand of any of these items.)

   a. Show the bill of materials (product structure tree).

   b. Develop an MRP planning schedule showing gross and net requirements and order release and order receipt dates.

5   *Note:* For Problems 5 through 10, to simplify data handling to include the receipt of orders that have actually been placed in previous periods, the following six-level scheme can be used. (A number of different techniques are used in practice, but the important issue is to keep track of what is on hand, what is expected to arrive, what is needed, and what size orders should be placed.) One way to calculate the numbers is as follows:

WEEK
Gross requirements
Scheduled receipts
On hand from prior period
Net requirements
Planned order receipt
Planned order release

One unit of A is made of three units of B, one unit of C, and two units of D. B is composed of two units of E and one unit of D. C is made of one unit of B and two units of E. E is made of one unit of F.

   Items B, C, E, and F have one-week lead times; A and D have lead times of two weeks.

   Assume that lot-for-lot (L4L) lot sizing is used for Items A, B, and F; lots of size 50, 50, and 200 are used for Items C, D, and E, respectively. Items C, E, and F have on-hand (beginning) inventories of 10, 50, and 150, respectively; all other items have zero beginning inventory. We are scheduled to receive 10 units of A in Week 2, 50 units of E in Week 1, and also 50 units of F in Week 1. There are no other scheduled receipts. If 30 units of A are required in Week 8, use the low-level-coded bill of materials to find the necessary planned order releases for all components.

6   One unit of A is made of two units of B, three units of C, and two units of D. B is composed of one unit of E and two units of F. C is made of two units of F and one unit of D. E is made of two units of D. Items A, C, D, and F have one-week lead times; B and E have lead times of two weeks. Lot-for-lot (L4L) lot sizing is used for Items A, B, C, and D; lots of size 50 and 180 are used for Items E and F, respectively. Item C has an on-hand (beginning) inventory of 15; D has an on-hand inventory of 50; all other items have zero beginning inventory. We are scheduled to receive 20 units of Item E in Week 2; there are no other scheduled receipts.

   Construct simple and low-level-coded bills of materials (product structure tree) and indented and summarized parts list.

   If 20 units of A are required in Week 8, use the low-level-coded bill of materials to find the necessary planned order releases for all components. (See the note in Problem 5.)

7   One unit of A is made of one unit of B and one unit of C. B is made of four units of C and one unit each of E and F. C is made of two units of D and one unit of E. E is made of three units of F. Item C has a lead time of one week; Items A, B, E, and F have two-week lead times; and Item D has a lead time of three weeks. Lot-for-lot lot sizing is used for Items A, D, and E; lots of size 50, 100, and 50 are used for Items B, C, and F, respectively. Items A, C, D, and E have on-hand

(beginning) inventories of 20, 50, 100, and 10, respectively; all other items have zero beginning inventory. We are scheduled to receive 10 units of A in Week 1, 100 units of C in Week 1, and 100 units of D in Week 3; there are no other scheduled receipts. If 50 units of A are required in Week 10, use the low-level-coded bill of materials (product structure tree) to find the necessary planned order releases for all components. (See the note in Problem 5.)

8   One unit of A is made of two units of B and one unit of C. B is made of three units of D and one unit of F. C is composed of three units of B, one unit of D, and four units of E. D is made of one unit of E. Item C has a lead time of one week; Items A, B, E, and F have two-week lead times; and Item D has a lead time of three weeks. Lot-for-lot lot sizing is used for Items C, E, and F; lots of size 20, 40, and 160 are used for Items A, B, and D, respectively. Items A, B, D, and E have on-hand (beginning) inventories of 5, 10, 100, and 100, respectively; all other items have zero beginning inventories. We are scheduled to receive 10 units of A in Week 3, 20 units of B in Week 7, 40 units of F in Week 5, and 60 units of E in Week 2; there are no other scheduled receipts. If 20 units of A are required in Week 10, use the low-level-coded bill of materials (product structure tree) to find the necessary planned order releases for all components. (See the note in Problem 5.)

9   One unit of A is composed of 2 units of B and three units of C. Each B is composed of one unit of F. C is made of one unit of D, one unit of E, and two units of F. Items A, B, C, and D have 20, 50, 60, and 25 units of on-hand inventory. Items A, B, and C use lot-for-lot (L4L) as their lot-sizing technique, while D, E, and F require multiples of 50, 100, and 100, respectively, to be purchased. B has scheduled receipts of 30 units in Period 1. No other scheduled receipts exist. Lead times are one period for Items A, B, and D, and two periods for Items C, E, and F. Gross requirements for A are 20 units in Period 1, 20 units in Period 2, 60 units in Period 6, and 50 units in Period 8. Find the planned order releases for all items.

10 Each unit of A is composed of one unit of B, two units of C, and one unit of D. C is composed of two units of D and three units of E. Items A, C, D, and E have on-hand inventories of 20, 10, 20, and 10 units, respectively. Item B has a scheduled receipt of 10 units in Period 1, and C has a scheduled receipt of 50 units in Period 1. Lot-for-lot (L4L) is used for Items A and B. Item C requires a minimum lot size of 50 units. D and E are required to be purchased in multiples of 100 and 50, respectively. Lead times are one period for Items A, B, and C, and two periods for Items D and E. The gross requirements for A are 30 in Period 2, 30 in Period 5, and 40 in Period 8. Find the planned order releases for all items.

11 The MRP gross requirements for Item A are shown here for the next 10 weeks. Lead time for A is three weeks and setup cost is $10. There is a carrying cost of $0.01 per unit per week. Beginning inventory is 90 units.

	WEEK									
	1	2	3	4	5	6	7	8	9	10
Gross requirements	30	50	10	20	70	80	20	60	200	50

Use the least total cost or the least unit cost lot-sizing method to determine when and for what quantity the first order should be released.

12 (This problem is intended as a very simple exercise to go from the aggregate plan to the master schedule to the MRP.) Gigamemory Storage Devices, Inc., produces CD-ROMs (read only memory) and WORMs (write once read many) for the computer market. Aggregate demand for the WORMs for the next two quarters is 2,100 units and 2,700 units. Assume that demand is distributed evenly for each month of the quarter.

There are two models of the WORM: an internal model and an external model. The drive assemblies in both are the same, but the electronics and housing are different. Demand is higher for the external model and currently is 70 percent of aggregate demand.

The bill of materials and the lead times follow. One drive assembly and one electronic and housing unit go into each WORM.

The MRP system is run monthly. Currently, 200 external WORMs and 100 internal WORMs are in stock. Also in stock are 250 drive assemblies, 50 internal electronic and housing units, and 125 external electronic and housing units.

Problem: Show the aggregate plan, the master production schedule, and the full MRP with the gross and net requirements and planned order releases.

13 Product A is an end item and is made from two units of B and four of C. B is made of three units of D and two of E. C is made of two units of F and two of E.

A has a lead time of one week. B, C, and E have lead times of two weeks, and D and F have lead times of three weeks.

a. Show the bill of materials (product structure tree).

b. If 100 units of A are required in Week 10, develop the MRP planning schedule, specifying when items are to be ordered and received. There are currently no units of inventory on hand.

14 Product A consists of two units of Subassembly B, three units of C, and one unit of D. B is composed of four units of E and three units of F. C is made of two units of H and three units of D. H is made of five units of E and two units of G.

a. Construct a simple bill of materials (product structure tree).

b. Construct a product structure tree using low-level coding.

c. Construct an indented parts list.

d. To produce 100 units of A, determine the numbers of units of B, C, D, E, F, G, and H required.

15 The MRP gross requirements for Item X are shown here for the next 10 weeks. Lead time for A is two weeks, and setup cost is $9. There is a carrying cost of $0.02 per unit per week. Beginning inventory is 70 units.

	WEEK									
	1	2	3	4	5	6	7	8	9	10
Gross requirements	20	10	15	45	10	30	100	20	40	150

Use the least total cost or the least unit cost lot-sizing method to determine when and for what quantity the first order should be released.

16 Audio Products, Inc., produces two AM/FM/CD players for cars. The radio/CD units are identical, but the mounting hardware and finish trim differ. The standard model fits intermediate and full-size cars, and the sports model fits small sports cars.

Audio Products handles the production in the following way. The chassis (radio/CD unit) is assembled in Mexico and has a manufacturing lead time of two weeks. The mounting hardware is purchased from a sheet steel company and has a three-week lead time. The finish trim is purchased from a Taiwan electronics company with offices in Los Angeles as prepackaged units consisting of knobs and various trim pieces. Trim packages have a two-week lead time. Final assembly time may be disregarded because adding the trim package and mounting are performed by the customer.

Audio Products supplies wholesalers and retailers, who place specific orders for both models up to eight weeks in advance. These orders, together with enough additional units to satisfy the small number of individual sales, are summarized in the following demand schedule:

	WEEK							
MODEL	1	2	3	4	5	6	7	8
Standard model				300				400
Sports model					200			100

There are currently 50 radio/CD units on hand but no trim packages or mounting hardware.

Prepare a material requirements plan to meet the demand schedule exactly. Specify the gross and net requirements, on-hand amounts, and the planned order release and receipt periods for the radio/CD chassis, the standard trim and sports car model trim, and the standard mounting hardware and the sports car mounting hardware.

17 An item has a setup cost of $100 and a weekly holding cost of $0.50 per unit. Given the following net requirements, what should the lot sizes be using lot-for-lot (L4L), economic order

quantity (EOQ), and least total cost (LTC)? Also, what is the total cost associated with each lot-sizing technique?

WEEK	NET REQUIREMENTS	WEEK	NET REQUIREMENTS
1	10	5	20
2	30	6	40
3	10	7	50
4	50	8	30

18   Brown and Brown Electronics manufactures a line of digital videodisc (DVD) players. Although there are differences among the various products, there are a number of common parts within each player. The bill of materials, showing the number of each item required, lead times, and the current inventory on hand for the parts and components, follows:

ITEM	NUMBER CURRENTLY IN STOCK	LEAD TIME (WEEKS)
DVD Model A	30	1
DVD Model B	50	2
Subassembly C	75	1
Subassembly D	80	2
Subassembly E	100	1
Part F	150	1
Part G	40	1
Raw Material H	200	2
Raw Material I	300	2

Brown and Brown created a forecast that it plans to use as its master production schedule, producing exactly to schedule. Part of the MPS shows a demand for 700 units of Model A and 1,200 units of Model B in Week 10.

Develop an MRP schedule to meet the demand.

**Excel:
Nichols.xls**

CASE: NICHOLS COMPANY

This particular December day seemed bleak to Joe Williams, president of Nichols Company (NCO). He sat in his office watching the dying embers in his fireplace, hoping to clear his mind. Suddenly there came a tapping by someone gently rapping, rapping at his office door. "Another headache," he muttered, "tapping at my office door. Only that and nothing more."*

The intruder was Barney Thompson, director of marketing. "A major account has just canceled a large purchase of A units because we are backordered on tubing. This can't continue. My sales force is out beating the bushes for customers, and our production manager can't provide the product."

For the past several months, operations at NCO have been unsteady. Inventory levels have been high, while at the same time, there have been stockouts. This has resulted in late deliveries, complaints, and cancellations. To compound the problem, overtime has been excessive.

HISTORY

Nichols Company was started by Joe Williams and Susan Schaap, both with MBAs from the University of Arizona. Much has happened since Williams and Schaap formed the company. Schaap has left the company and is working in real estate

exhibit 16.25

Bills of Materials for Products A, B, and C

exhibit 16.26

Work Center Routings for Products and Components

ITEM	WORK CENTER NUMBER	STANDARD TIME (HOURS PER UNIT)	ITEM	WORK CENTER NUMBER	STANDARD TIME (HOURS PER UNIT)
Product A	1	0.20	Component E	2	0.15
	4	0.10		4	0.05
Product B	2	0.30	Component F	2	0.15
	4	0.08		3	0.20
Product C	3	0.10	Component G	1	0.30
	4	0.05		2	0.10
Component D	1	0.15	Component H	1	0.05
	4	0.10		3	0.10

exhibit 16.27

Inventory Levels and Lead Times for Each Item on the Bill of Materials at the Beginning of Week I

PRODUCT/COMPONENT	ON HAND (UNITS)	LEAD TIME (WEEKS)
Product A	100	1
Product B	200	1
Product C	175	1
Component D	200	1
Component E	195	1
Component F	120	1
Component G	200	1
Component H	200	1
Raw Material I	300	1

development in Queensland, Australia. Under the direction of Williams, NCO has diversified to include a number of other products.

NCO currently has 355 full-time employees directly involved in manufacturing the three primary products: A, B, and C. Final assembly takes place in a converted warehouse adjacent to NCO's main plant.

THE MEETING

Williams called a meeting the next day to get input on the problems facing NCO and to lay the groundwork for some solutions. Attending the meeting, besides himself and Barney Thompson, were Allison Bright of production and inventory control, Trevor Hansen of purchasing, and Margaret Wu of accounting.

The meeting lasted all morning. Participation was vocal and intense.

Bright said, "The forecasts that marketing sends us are always way off. We are constantly having to expedite one product or another to meet current demand. This runs up our overtime."

Thompson said, "Production tries to run too lean. We need a large inventory of finished goods. If I had the merchandise, my salespeople could sell 20 percent more product."

Wu said, "No way! Our inventory is already uncomfortably high. We can't afford the holding costs, not to mention how fast technology changes around here causing even more inventory, much of it obsolete."

Bright said, "The only way I can meet our stringent cost requirement is to buy in volume."

Forecast Demand for Weeks 4 to 27

exhibit 16.28

WEEK	PRODUCT A	PRODUCT B	PRODUCT C	WEEK	PRODUCT A	PRODUCT B	PRODUCT C
1				15	1,900	1,900	1,500
2				16	2,200	2,300	2,300
3				17	2,000	2,300	2,300
4	1,500	2,200	1,200	18	1,700	2,100	2,000
5	1,700	2,100	1,400	19	1,600	1,900	1,700
6	1,150	1,900	1,000	20	1,400	1,800	1,800
7	1,100	1,800	1,500	21	1,100	1,800	2,200
8	1,000	1,800	1,400	22	1,000	1,900	1,900
9	1,100	1,600	1,100	23	1,400	1,700	2,400
10	1,400	1,600	1,800	24	1,400	1,700	2,400
11	1,400	1,700	1,700	25	1,500	1,700	2,600
12	1,700	1,700	1,300	26	1,600	1,800	2,400
13	1,700	1,700	1,700	27	1,500	1,900	2,500
14	1,800	1,700	1,700				

At the end of the meeting, Williams had lots of input but no specific plan. What do you think he should do? Use Exhibits 16.25 through 16.28 showing relevant data to answer the specific questions at the end of the case.

QUESTIONS

Use Microsoft® Excel to solve the Nichols Company case. (Note that if you start from scratch, it will take several hours to answer Question 1, about the same for Question 2, and perhaps double that for Question 3. A spreadsheet is on the DVD included with this book to help with this problem.)

Simplifying assumption: To get the program started, some time is needed at the beginning because MRP backloads the system. For simplicity, assume that the forecasts (and therefore demands) are zero for Periods 1 through 3. Also assume that the starting inventory specified in Exhibit 16.27 is available from Week 1. For the master production schedule, use only End Items A, B, and C.

To modify production quantities, adjust only Products A, B, and C. Do not adjust the quantities of D, E, F, G, H, and I. These should be linked so that changes in A, B, and C automatically adjust them.

1   Disregarding machine center limitations, develop an MRP schedule and also capacity profiles for the four machine centers.

2   Work center capacities and costs follow. Repeat Question 1 creating a *feasible* schedule (within the capacities of the machine centers) and compute the relevant costs. Do this by adjusting the MPS only. Try to minimize the total cost of operation for the 27 weeks.

3   Suppose end items had to be ordered in multiples of 100 units, components in multiples of 500 units, and raw materials in multiples of 1,000 units. How would this change your schedule?

	CAPACITY	COST
Work Center 1	6,000 hours available	$20 per hour
Work Center 2	4,500 hours available	$25 per hour
Work Center 3	2,400 hours available	$35 per hour
Work Center 4	1,200 hours available	$65 per hour

Inventory carrying cost	
End Items A, B, and C	$2.00 per unit per week
Components D, E, F, G, and H	$1.50 per unit per week
Raw Material I	$1.00 per unit per week

Backorder cost	
End Items A, B, and C	$20 per unit per week
Components D, E, F, G, and H	$14 per unit per week
Raw Material I	$8 per unit per week

*WITH APOLOGIES TO E. A. P. (EDGAR ALLAN POE).

SELECTED BIBLIOGRAPHY

Drexl, A., and E. Kimms (eds.). *Beyond Manufacturing Resource Planning (MRP II): Advanced Models and Methods for Production Planning.* New York: Springer, 1998.

Orlicky, J. *Materials Requirements Planning.* New York: McGraw-Hill, 1975. (This is the classic book on MRP.)

Sheikh, K. *Manufacturing Resource Planning (MRP II) with Introduction to ERP, SCM, and CRM.* New York: McGraw-Hill, 2002.

Vollmann, T. E.; W. L. Berry; D. C. Whybark; and F. R. Jacobs. *Manufacturing Planning and Control Systems for Supply Chain Management.* 5th ed. Burr Ridge, IL: McGraw-Hill, 2004.

FOOTNOTES

1 Dictionary definitions are reprinted with the permission of APICS, Inc., *APICS Dictionary,* 8th ed., 1995.

2 O. Wight, *The Executive's Guide to Successful MRP II* (Williston, VT: Oliver Wight, 1982), pp. 6, 17.

chapter

OPERATIONS SCHEDULING

17

HOSPITALS CUT *ER* WAITS—NEW "FAST TRACK" UNITS, HIGH-TECH IDs SPEED VISITS; SEE A DOCTOR IN 17 MINUTES

Two years ago, Oakwood Hospital and Medical Center in Dearborn, Michigan, promised that anybody taken to the emergency department would be seen by a doctor within 30 minutes—or they would get a written apology and two free movie passes. It sounded like a cheap marketing ploy. Some employees cringed.

Today, the 30-minute guarantee is a huge success. All four of Oakwood Healthcare System's hospitals have rolled it out. Patient satisfaction levels have soared. And only 0.9 percent of last year's 191,000 emergency room patients

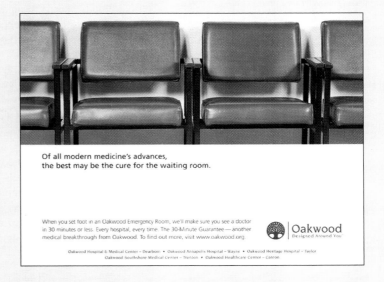

(about 1,700 people) asked for free tickets. "We're down to 17 minutes on average" between arrival and a physician's examination, says Corinne Victor, administrator of emergency services. "In October or November, we'll start offering a 15-minute guarantee." It's just one hospital system's response to the huge and prolonged problem of overcrowded emergency departments. Some 62 percent of U.S. emergency rooms report being "at" or "over" capacity, according to a survey by the American College of Emergency Physicians, a trade group. On average, it takes 47 minutes before a doctor sees a patient in a U.S. emergency room, according to studies by VHA Inc., an alliance of community hospitals. But that's nothing compared with the hours upon hours that some patients end up waiting.

But the seemingly intractable problems of emergency room crowding are starting to spawn numerous attempts at solutions. Some of them, such as Oakwood's, are actually starting to work. A growing number of hospitals are putting patients with relatively minor ailments—those who previously would be left to languish in the waiting room—into "fast track" units to get them in and out of emergency beds quickly. Others are using sophisticated computer systems to give administrators a complete up-to-the-minute status report on

Source: Adapted from "Hospitals Cut ER Waits," Bernard Wysocki Jr., *The Wall Street Journal*, July 3, 2002. Copyright © 2002 Dow Jones & Company, Inc. Used with permission.

every patient in every emergency bed. In Long Beach, California, Memorial Health Services has issued 500,000 medical identification cards—anyone can get them through the hospital's Web site (www.memorialcare.com)—that can be swiped into a computer to speed up patient registrations and produce instant vital information to emergency doctors and nurses. About 75 other hospitals have expressed interest in licensing the card system. To make good on its promise to slash ER waiting times, Oakwood had to reengineer its billing, records, and laboratory operations; upgrade its technical staff; and replace its emergency physician group with a new crew who would pitch in with longer hours. →

Keep in mind that work flow equals cash flow, and scheduling lies at the heart of the process. A schedule is a timetable for performing activities, utilizing resources, or allocating facilities. In this chapter we discuss short-run scheduling and control of orders with an emphasis on work centers. We also introduce some basic approaches to short-term scheduling of workers in services.

MANUFACTURING EXECUTION SYSTEMS

Operations scheduling is at the heart of what is currently referred to as Manufacturing Execution Systems (MES). An MES is an information system that schedules, dispatches, tracks, monitors, and controls production on the factory floor. Such systems also provide real-time linkages to MRP systems, product and process planning, as well as systems that extend beyond the factory including supply chain management, ERP, sales, and service management. There are a number of software specialty houses that develop and implement MESs as part of a suite of software tools.

THE NATURE AND IMPORTANCE OF WORK CENTERS

Work center

A **work center** is an area in a business in which productive resources are organized and work is completed. The work center may be a single machine, a group of machines, or an area where a particular type of work is done. These work centers can be organized according to function in a job-shop configuration; or by product in a flow, assembly line, or group technology cell (GT cell) configuration. Recall from the discussion in Technical Note 6 that many firms have moved from the job-shop configuration to GT cells. Exhibit TN6.14 showed an example of job-shop and GT cell configurations from Rockwell Telecommunications Division.

In the case of the job shop, jobs need to be routed between functionally organized work centers to complete the work. When a job arrives at a work center—for example, the drilling department in a factory that makes custom-printed circuit boards—it enters a queue to wait for a drilling machine that can drill the required holes. Scheduling, in this case, involves determining the order for running the jobs, and also assigning a machine that can be used to make the holes.

A characteristic that distinguishes one scheduling system from another is how capacity is considered in determining the schedule. Scheduling systems can use either infinite or finite loading. **Infinite loading** occurs when work is assigned to a work center simply based on what is needed over time. No consideration is given directly to whether there is sufficient capacity at the resources required to complete the work, nor is the actual sequence of the work as done by each resource in the work center considered. Often, a simple check is made of key resources to see if they are overloaded in an aggregate sense, as demonstrated in Chapter 16

Infinite loading

in Exhibit 16.18. This is done by calculating the amount of work required over a period (usually a week) using setup and run time standards for each order. When using an infinite loading system, lead time is estimated by taking a multiple of the expected operation time (setup and run time) plus an expected queuing delay caused by material movement and waiting for the order to be worked on.

A **finite loading** approach actually schedules in detail each resource using the setup and run time required for each order. In essence, the system determines exactly what will be done by each resource at every moment during the working day. If an operation is delayed due to a part(s) shortage, the order will sit in queue and wait until the part is available from a preceding operation. Theoretically, all schedules are feasible when finite loading is used.

Finite loading

Another characteristic that distinguishes scheduling systems is whether the schedule is generated forward or backward in time. For this forward–backward dimension, the most common is forward scheduling. **Forward scheduling** refers to the situation in which the system takes an order and then schedules each operation that must be completed forward in time. A system that forward schedules can tell the earliest date that an order can be completed. Conversely, **backward scheduling** starts from some date in the future (possibly a due date) and schedules the required operations in reverse sequence. The backward schedule tells when an order must be started in order to be done by a specific date.

Forward scheduling

Backward scheduling

A material requirements planning (MRP) system is an example of an infinite, backward scheduling system for materials. With simple MRP, each order has a due date sometime in the future. In this case, the system calculates parts needs by backward scheduling the time that the operations will be run to complete the orders. The time required to make each part (or batch of parts) is estimated based on historical data. The scheduling systems addressed in this chapter are intended for the processes required to actually make those parts and subassemblies.

Thus far, the term *resources* has been used in a generic sense. In practice, we need to decide what we are going to actually schedule. Commonly, processes are referred to as either machine limited or labor limited. In a **machine-limited process**, equipment is the critical resource that is scheduled. Similarly, in a **labor-limited process**, people are the key resource that is scheduled. Most actual processes are either labor limited or machine limited but, luckily, not both.

Machine-limited process

Labor-limited process

Exhibit 17.1 describes the scheduling approaches typically used for different manufacturing processes. Whether capacity is considered depends on the actual process. Available computer technology allows generation of very detailed schedules, such as scheduling each job on each machine and assigning a specific worker to the machine at a specific point in time. Systems that capture the exact state of each job and each resource are also

INTELLIGENT INSTRUMENTATION, A TEXAS INSTRUMENTS COMPANY, PRODUCES LAN POINT CE.NET VEHICLE MOUNT DATA COLLECTION TERMINALS. COMPANIES SUCH AS EVERREADY BATTERY USE THIS TOOL IN THEIR FULFILLMENT AND SHIPPING PROCESSES. THIS INSURES FIFO INVENTORY MANAGEMENT CONTROL AND FASTER OPERATIONS.

exhibit 17.1

Types of Manufacturing Processes and Scheduling Approaches

TYPE	PRODUCT	CHARACTERISTICS	TYPICAL SCHEDULING APPROACH
Continuous process	Chemicals, steel, wire and cables, liquids (beer, soda), canned goods	Full automation, low labor content in product costs, facilities dedicated to one product	Finite forward scheduling of the process; machine limited
High-volume manufacturing	Automobiles, telephones, fasteners, textiles, motors, household fixtures	Automated equipment, partial automated handling, moving assembly lines, most equipment in line	Finite forward scheduling of the line (a production rate is typical); machine limited; parts are pulled to the line using just-in-time (kanban) system
Mid-volume manufacturing	Industrial parts, high-end consumer products	GT cells, focused minifactories	Infinite forward scheduling typical: priority control; typically labor limited, but often machine limited; often responding to just-in-time orders from customers or MRP due dates
Low-volume job shops	Custom or prototype equipment, specialized instruments, low-volume industrial products	Machining centers organized by manufacturing function (not in line), high labor content in product cost, general-purpose machinery with significant changeover time, little automation of material handling, large variety of product	Infinite, forward scheduling of jobs: usually labor limited, but certain functions may be machine limited (a heat-treating process or a precision machining center, for example); priorities determined by MRP due dates

available. Using bar-coding technology, these systems can efficiently capture all of this detailed information.

TYPICAL SCHEDULING AND CONTROL FUNCTIONS

The following functions must be performed in scheduling and controlling an operation:

1. Allocating orders, equipment, and personnel to work centers or other specified locations. Essentially, this is short-run capacity planning.
2. Determining the sequence of order performance (that is, establishing job priorities).

Dispatching

3. Initiating performance of the scheduled work. This is commonly termed **dispatching** of orders.
4. Shop-floor control (or production activity control) involving
   a. Reviewing the status and controlling the progress of orders as they are being worked on.
   b. Expediting late and critical orders.[1]

A simple work-center scheduling process is shown in Exhibit 17.2. At the start of the day, the scheduler (in this case, a production control person assigned to this department) selects and

Typical Scheduling Process

exhibit 17.2

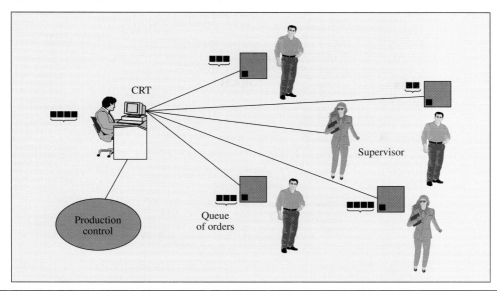

sequences available jobs to be run at individual workstations. The scheduler's decisions would be based on the operations and routing requirements of each job, the status of existing jobs at each work center, the queue of work before each work center, job priorities, material availability, anticipated job orders to be released later in the day, and work-center resource capabilities (labor and/or machines).

To help organize the schedule, the scheduler would draw on job status information from the previous day, external information provided by central production control, process engineering, and so on. The scheduler would also confer with the supervisor of the department about the feasibility of the schedule, especially workforce considerations and potential bottlenecks. The details of the schedule are communicated to workers via dispatch lists shown on computer terminals, in hard-copy printouts, or by posting a list of what should be worked on in central areas. Visible schedule boards are highly effective ways to communicate the priority and current status of work.

OBJECTIVES OF WORK-CENTER SCHEDULING

The objectives of work-center scheduling are to (1) meet due dates, (2) minimize lead time, (3) minimize setup time or cost, (4) minimize work-in-process inventory, and (5) maximize machine or labor utilization. It is unlikely, and often undesirable, to simultaneously satisfy all of these objectives. For example, keeping all equipment and/or employees busy may result in having to keep too much inventory. Or, as another example, it is possible to meet 99 out of 100 of your due dates but still have a major schedule failure if the one due date that was missed was for a critical job or key customer. The important point, as is the case with other production activities, is to maintain a systems perspective to assure that work-center objectives are in sync with the operations strategy of the organization.

JOB SEQUENCING

The process of determining the job order on some machine or in some work center is known as **sequencing** or priority sequencing. **Priority rules** are the rules used in obtaining a job sequence. These can be very simple, requiring only that jobs be sequenced according to one piece of data, such as processing time, due date, or order of arrival. Other rules, though equally simple, may require several pieces of information, typically to derive an index number such as the least-slack rule and the critical-ratio rule (both defined later). Still others,

Sequencing

Priority rules

exhibit 17.3   Priority Rules for Job Sequencing

1 **FCFS** (first-come, first-served). Orders are run in the order they arrive in the department.

2 **SOT** (shortest operating time). Run the job with the shortest completion time first, next-shortest second, and so on. This is sometimes also referred to as SPT (shortest processing time). Often this rule is combined with a lateness rule to prevent jobs with longer times being delayed too long.

3 **EDD** (earliest due date first). Run the job with the earliest due date first.

4 **STR** (slack time remaining). This is calculated as the time remaining before the due date minus the processing time remaining. Orders with the shortest slack time remaining (STR) are run first.

   STR = Time remaining before due date − Remaining processing time

5 **STR/OP** (slack time remaining per operation). Orders with the shortest slack time per number of operations are run first.

   STR/OP = STR/Number of remaining operations

6 **CR** (critical ratio). This is calculated as the difference between the due date and the current date divided by the number of work days remaining. Orders with the smallest CR are run first.

7 **LCFS** (last-come, first-served). This rule occurs frequently by default. As orders arrive, they are placed on the top of the stack; the operator usually picks up the order on top to run first.

8 **Random** order or whim. The supervisors or the operators usually select whichever job they feel like running.

Interactive Operations Management

such as Johnson's rule (also discussed later), apply to job scheduling on a sequence of machines and require a computational procedure to specify the order of performance. Eight of the more common priority rules are shown in Exhibit 17.3.

The following standard measures of schedule performance are used to evaluate priority rules:

1. Meeting due dates of customers or downstream operations.
2. Minimizing the flow time (the time a job spends in the process).
3. Minimizing work-in-process inventory.
4. Minimizing idle time of machines or workers.

PRIORITY RULES AND TECHNIQUES

SCHEDULING *n* JOBS ON ONE MACHINE

Let's look at some of the eight priority rules compared in a static scheduling situation involving four jobs on one machine. (In scheduling terminology, this class of problems is referred to as an "*n* job—one-machine problem" or simply "*n*/1.") The theoretical difficulty of scheduling problems increases as more machines are considered rather than as more jobs must be processed; therefore, the only restriction on *n* is that it be a specified, finite number. Consider the following example.

EXAMPLE 17.1: *n* Jobs on One Machine

Mike Morales is the supervisor of Legal Copy-Express, which provides copy services for downtown Los Angeles law firms. Five customers submitted their orders at the beginning of the week. Specific scheduling data are as follows:

JOB (IN ORDER OF ARRIVAL)	PROCESSING TIME (DAYS)	DUE DATE (DAYS HENCE)
A	3	5
B	4	6
C	2	7
D	6	9
E	1	2

All orders require the use of the only color copy machine available; Morales must decide on the processing sequence for the five orders. The evaluation criterion is minimum flow time. Suppose that

Morales decides to use the FCFS rule in an attempt to make Legal Copy-Express appear fair to its customers.

SOLUTION

FCFS RULE: The FCFS rule results in the following flow times:

FCFS SCHEDULE

JOB SEQUENCE	PROCESSING TIME (DAYS)	DUE DATE (DAYS HENCE)	FLOW TIME (DAYS)
A	3	5	$0 + 3 = 3$
B	4	6	$3 + 4 = 7$
C	2	7	$7 + 2 = 9$
D	6	9	$9 + 6 = 15$
E	1	2	$15 + 1 = 16$

Total flow time $= 3 + 7 + 9 + 15 + 16 = 50$ days

Mean flow time $= \dfrac{50}{5} = 10$ days

Comparing the due date of each job with its flow time, we observe that only Job A will be on time. Jobs B, C, D, and E will be late by 1, 2, 6, and 14 days, respectively. On average, a job will be late by $(0 + 1 + 2 + 6 + 14)/5 = 4.6$ days. ●

SOLUTION

SOT RULE: Let's now consider the SOT rule. Here Morales gives the highest priority to the order that has the shortest processing time. The resulting flow times are

SOT SCHEDULE

JOB SEQUENCE	PROCESSING TIME (DAYS)	DUE DATE (DAYS HENCE)	FLOW TIME (DAYS)
E	1	2	$0 + 1 = 1$
C	2	7	$1 + 2 = 3$
A	3	5	$3 + 3 = 6$
B	4	6	$6 + 4 = 10$
D	6	9	$10 + 6 = 16$

Total flow time $= 1 + 3 + 6 + 10 + 16 = 36$ days

Mean flow time $= \dfrac{36}{5} = 7.2$ days

SOT results in a lower average flow time than the FCFS rule. In addition, Jobs E and C will be ready before the due date, and Job A is late by only one day. On average, a job will be late by $(0 + 0 + 1 + 4 + 7)/5 = 2.4$ days. ●

SOLUTION

EDD RULE: If Morales decides to use the EDD rule, the resulting schedule is

EDD SCHEDULE

JOB SEQUENCE	PROCESSING TIME (DAYS)	DUE DATE (DAYS HENCE)	FLOW TIME (DAYS)
E	1	2	$0 + 1 = 1$
A	3	5	$1 + 3 = 4$
B	4	6	$4 + 4 = 8$
C	2	7	$8 + 2 = 10$
D	6	9	$10 + 6 = 16$

Total completion time $= 1 + 4 + 8 + 10 + 16 = 39$ days

Mean flow time $= 7.8$ days

In this case Jobs B, C, and D will be late. On average, a job will be late by $(0 + 0 + 2 + 3 + 7)/5 = 2.4$ days. ●

SOLUTION

LCFS, RANDOM, and STR RULES: Here are the resulting flow times of the LCFS, random, and STR rules:

JOB SEQUENCE	PROCESSING TIME (DAYS)	DUE DATE (DAYS HENCE)	FLOW TIME (DAYS)	SLACK
LCFS SCHEDULE				
E	1	2	$0 + 1 = 1$	
D	6	9	$1 + 6 = 7$	
C	2	7	$7 + 2 = 9$	
B	4	6	$9 + 4 = 13$	
A	3	5	$13 + 3 = 16$	

Total flow time = 46 days
Mean flow time = 9.2 days
Average lateness = 4.0 days

JOB SEQUENCE	PROCESSING TIME (DAYS)	DUE DATE (DAYS HENCE)	FLOW TIME (DAYS)	SLACK
RANDOM SCHEDULE				
D	6	9	$0 + 6 = 6$	
C	2	7	$6 + 2 = 8$	
A	3	5	$8 + 3 = 11$	
E	1	2	$11 + 1 = 12$	
B	4	6	$12 + 4 = 16$	

Total flow time = 53 days
Mean flow time = 10.6 days
Average lateness = 5.4 days

JOB SEQUENCE	PROCESSING TIME (DAYS)	DUE DATE (DAYS HENCE)	FLOW TIME (DAYS)	SLACK
STR SCHEDULE				
E	1	2	$0 + 1 = 1$	$2 - 1 = 1$
A	3	5	$1 + 3 = 4$	$5 - 3 = 2$
B	4	6	$4 + 4 = 8$	$6 - 4 = 2$
D	6	9	$8 + 6 = 14$	$9 - 6 = 3$
C	2	7	$14 + 2 = 16$	$7 - 2 = 5$

Total flow time = 43 days
Mean flow time = 8.6 days
Average lateness = 3.2 days   ●

COMPARISON OF PRIORITY RULES

Here are some of the results summarized for the rules that Morales examined:

RULE	TOTAL FLOW TIME (DAYS)	MEAN FLOW TIME (DAYS)	AVERAGE LATENESS (DAYS)
FCFS	50	10	4.6
SOT	36	7.2	2.4
EDD	39	7.8	2.4
LCFS	46	9.2	4.0
Random	53	10.6	5.4
STR	43	8.6	3.2

Here, SOT is better than the other rules in terms of mean flow time. Moreover, it can be shown mathematically that the SOT rule yields an optimal solution in the $n/1$ case for mean waiting time and average tardiness as well. In fact, so powerful is this simple rule that it has been termed "the most important concept in the entire aspect of sequencing."[2] It does have its shortcomings, however. The main one is that longer jobs may never be started if short jobs keep arriving at the scheduler's desk. To avoid this, companies may invoke what is termed a *truncated* SOT rule whereby jobs waiting for a specified time period are automatically moved to the front of the line.

SCHEDULING *n* JOBS ON TWO MACHINES

The next step up in complexity is the $n/2$ flow-shop case, where two or more jobs must be processed on two machines in a common sequence. As in the $n/1$ case, there is an approach that leads to an optimal solution according to certain criteria. The objective of this approach, termed **Johnson's rule** or *Johnson's method* (after its developer), is to minimize the flow time from the beginning of the first job until the finish of the last. Johnson's rule consists of the following steps:

Johnson's rule

1. List the operation time for each job on both machines.
2. Select the shortest operation time.
3. If the shortest time is for the first machine, do the job first; if it is for the second machine, do the job last. In the case of a tie, do the job on the first machine.
4. Repeat Steps 2 and 3 for each remaining job until the schedule is complete.

EXAMPLE 17.2: *n* Jobs on Two Machines

We can illustrate this procedure by scheduling four jobs through two machines.

SOLUTION

Step 1: List operation times.

JOB	OPERATION TIME ON MACHINE 1	OPERATION TIME ON MACHINE 2
A	3	2
B	6	8
C	5	6
D	7	4

Steps 2 and 3: Select the shortest operation time and assign. Job A is shortest on Machine 2 and is assigned first and performed last. (Once assigned, Job A is no longer available to be scheduled.)

Step 4: Repeat Steps 2 and 3 until completion of the schedule. Select the shortest operation time among the remaining jobs. Job D is second-shortest on Machine 2, so it is performed second to last. (Remember, Job A is last.) Now Jobs A and D are not available for scheduling. Job C is the shortest on Machine 1 among the remaining jobs. Job C is performed first. Now only Job B is left with the shortest operation time on Machine 1. Thus, according to Step 3, it is performed first among the remaining, or second overall. (Job C was already scheduled first.)

In summary, the solution sequence is C → B → D → A, and the flow time is 25 days, which is a minimum. Also minimized are total idle time and mean idle time. The final schedule appears in Exhibit 17.4.

These steps result in scheduling the jobs having the shortest time in the beginning and end of the schedule. As a result, the concurrent operating time for the two machines is maximized, thus minimizing the total operating time required to complete the jobs. ●

Johnson's method has been extended to yield an optimal solution for the $n/3$ case. When flow-shop scheduling problems larger than $n/3$ arise (and they generally do), analytical solution procedures leading to optimality are not available. The reason for this is that even

exhibit 17.4

Optimal Schedule of Jobs Using Johnson's Rule

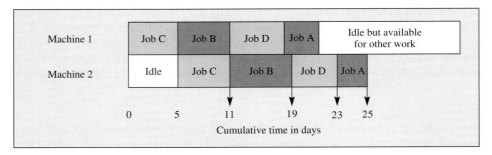

Schedule Obtained Using the LEKIN Scheduling System (see DVD)

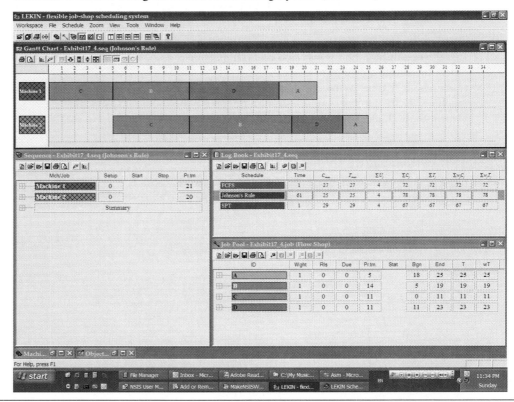

though the jobs may arrive in static fashion at the first machine, the scheduling problem becomes dynamic, and waiting lines start to form in front of machines downstream. At this point it becomes a multistage queuing problem, which is generally solved using simulation techniques such as those discussed in the technical note after this chapter.

SCHEDULING A SET NUMBER OF JOBS ON THE SAME NUMBER OF MACHINES

Some job shops have enough of the right kinds of machines to start all jobs at the same time. Here the problem is not which job to do first, but rather which particular assignment of individual jobs to individual machines will result in the best overall schedule. In such cases, we can use the assignment method.

Assignment method

The **assignment method** is a special case of the transportation method of linear programming. It can be applied to situations where there are *n* supply sources and *n* demand uses (such as five jobs on five machines) and the objective is to minimize or maximize some measure of effectiveness. This technique is convenient in applications involving allocation of jobs to

Assignment Matrix Showing Machine Processing Costs for Each Job

exhibit 17.5

JOB	MACHINE				
	A	B	C	D	E
I	$5	$6	$4	$8	$3
II	6	4	9	8	5
III	4	3	2	5	4
IV	7	2	4	5	3
V	3	6	4	5	5

work centers, people to jobs, and so on. The assignment method is appropriate in solving problems that have the following characteristics:

1. There are n "things" to be distributed to n "destinations."
2. Each thing must be assigned to one and only one destination.
3. Only one criterion can be used (minimum cost, maximum profit, or minimum completion time, for example).

EXAMPLE 17.3: Assignment Method

Suppose that a scheduler has five jobs that can be performed on any of five machines ($n = 5$). The cost of completing each job–machine combination is shown in Exhibit 17.5. The scheduler would like to devise a minimum-cost assignment. (There are 5!, or 120, possible assignments.)

SOLUTION

This problem may be solved by the assignment method, which consists of four steps (note that this also can be solved using the Excel Solver):

1. Subtract the smallest number in each *row* from itself and all other numbers in that row. (There will then be at least one zero in each row.)
2. Subtract the smallest number in each *column* from all other numbers in that column. (There will then be at least one zero in each column.)
3. Determine if the *minimum* number of lines required to cover each zero is equal to n. If so, an optimal solution has been found, because job machine assignments must be made at the zero entries, and this test proves that this is possible. If the minimum number of lines required is less than n, go to Step 4.
4. Draw the least possible number of lines through all the zeros. (These may be the same lines used in Step 3.) Subtract the smallest number not covered by lines from itself and all other uncovered numbers, and add it to the number at each intersection of lines. Repeat Step 3.

For the example problem, the steps listed in Exhibit 17.6 would be followed.

Note that even though there are two zeros in three rows and three columns, the solution shown in Exhibit 17.6 is the only one possible for this problem because Job III must be assigned to Machine C to meet the "assign to zero" requirement. Other problems may have more than one optimal solution, depending, of course, on the costs involved. ●

The nonmathematical rationale of the assignment method is one of minimizing opportunity costs.[3] For example, if we decided to assign Job I to Machine A instead of to Machine E, we would be sacrificing the opportunity to save $2 ($5 − $3). The assignment algorithm in effect performs such comparisons for the entire set of alternative assignments by means of row and column reduction, as described in Steps 1 and 2. It makes similar comparisons in Step 4. Obviously, if assignments are made to zero cells, no opportunity cost, with respect to the entire matrix, occurs.

exhibit 17.6   Procedure to Solve an Assignment Matrix

Step 1: Row reduction—the smallest number is subtracted from each row.

JOB	A	B	C	D	E
I	2	3	1	5	0
II	2	0	5	4	1
III	2	1	0	3	2
IV	5	0	2	3	1
V	0	3	1	2	2

Step 2: Column reduction—the smallest number is subtracted from each column.

JOB	A	B	C	D	E
I	2	3	1	3	0
II	2	0	5	2	1
III	2	1	0	1	2
IV	5	0	2	1	1
V	0	3	1	0	2

Step 3: Apply line test—the number of lines to cover all zeros is 4; because 5 are required, go to step 4.

JOB	A	B	C	D	E
I	2	3	1	3	0
II	2	0	5	2	1
III	2	1	0	1	2
IV	5	0	2	1	1
V	0	3	1	0	2

Step 4: Subtract smallest uncovered number and add to intersection of lines. Using lines drawn in Step 3, smallest uncovered number is 1.

JOB	A	B	C	D	E
I	1	3	0	2	0
II	1	0	4	1	1
III	2	2	0	1	3
IV	4	0	1	0	1
V	0	4	1	0	3

Optimal solution—by "line test."

JOB	A	B	C	D	E
I	1	3	0	2	0
II	1	0	4	1	1
III	2	2	0	1	3
IV	4	0	1	0	1
V	0	4	1	0	3

Optimal assignments and their costs.

Job I to Machine E	$ 3
Job II to Machine B	4
Job III to Machine C	2
Job IV to Machine D	5
Job V to Machine A	3
Total cost	$17

SCHEDULING *n* JOBS ON *m* MACHINES

Complex job shops are characterized by multiple machine centers processing a variety of different jobs arriving at the machine centers intermittently throughout the day. If there are n jobs to be processed on m machines and all jobs are processed on all machines, then there are $(n!)^m$ alternative schedules for this job set. Because of the large number of schedules that exist for even small job shops, computer simulation (see Technical Note 17) is the only practical way to determine the relative merits of different priority rules in such situations.

Which Priority Rule Should Be Used?   We believe that the needs of most manufacturers are reasonably satisfied by a relatively simple priority scheme that embodies the following principles:

1. It should be dynamic, that is, computed frequently during a job to reflect changing conditions.
2. It should be based in one way or another on slack (the difference between the work remaining to be done on a job and the time remaining to do it).

Newer approaches combine simulation with human schedulers to create schedules.

SHOP-FLOOR CONTROL

Scheduling job priorities is just one aspect of **shop-floor control** (now often called **production activity control**). The *APICS Dictionary* defines a *shop-floor control system* as

Shop-floor (production activity) control

> A system for utilizing data from the shop floor as well as data processing files to maintain and communicate status information on shop orders and work centers.

The major functions of shop-floor control are

1. Assigning priority of each shop order.
2. Maintaining work-in-process quantity information.
3. Conveying shop-order status information to the office.
4. Providing actual output data for capacity control purposes.
5. Providing quantity by location by shop order for WIP inventory and accounting purposes.
6. Measuring efficiency, utilization, and productivity of manpower and machines.

GANTT CHARTS

Smaller job shops and individual departments of large ones employ the venerable Gantt chart to help plan and track jobs. As described in Chapter 3, the Gantt chart is a type of bar chart that plots tasks against time. Gantt charts are used for project planning as well as to coordinate a number of scheduled activities. The example in Exhibit 17.7 indicates that Job A is behind schedule by about four hours, Job B is ahead of schedule, and Job C has been completed, after a delayed start for equipment maintenance. Note that whether the job is ahead of schedule or behind schedule is based on where it stands compared to where we are now. In Exhibit 17.7 we are at the end of Wednesday, and Job A should have been completed. Job B has already had some of Thursday's work completed.

TOOLS OF SHOP-FLOOR CONTROL

The basic tools of shop-floor control are

1. The *daily dispatch list,* which tells the supervisor which jobs are to be run, their priority, and how long each will take. (See Exhibit 17.8a.)
2. Various *status and exception reports,* including
   a. The anticipated delay report, made out by the shop planner once or twice a week and reviewed by the chief shop planner to see if there are any serious delays that could affect the master schedule. (See Exhibit 17.8b.)
   b. Scrap reports.
   c. Rework reports.
   d. Performance summary reports giving the number and percentage of orders completed on schedule, lateness of unfilled orders, volume of output, and so on.
   e. Shortage list.

Gantt Chart

exhibit 17.7

Gantt Chart Symbols

Job	Monday	Tuesday	Wednesday	Thursday	Friday
A					
B					
C	Maintenance				

	Start of an activity
	End of an activity
	Schedule allowed activity time
	Actual work progress
	Point in time where chart is reviewed
	Time set aside for nonproduction activities; e.g., repairs, routine maintenance, material outages

exhibit 17.8 Some Basic Tools of Shop-Floor Control

A. Dispatch List

Work center 1501—Day 205

Start date	Job #	Description	Run time
201	15131	Shaft	11.4
203	15143	Stud	20.6
205	15145	Spindle	4.3
205	15712	Spindle	8.6
207	15340	Metering rod	6.5
208	15312	Shaft	4.6

B. Anticipated Delay Report

Dept. 24 April 8

Part #	Sched. date	New date	Cause of delay	Action
17125	4/10	4/15	Fixture broke	Toolroom will return on 4/15
13044	4/11	5/1	Out for plating— plater on strike	New lot started
17653	4/11	4/14	New part holes don't align	Engineering laying out new jig

C. Input/Output Control Report

Work center 0162

Week ending	505	512	519	526
Planned input	210	210	210	210
Actual input	110	150	140	130
Cumulative deviation	−100	−160	−230	−310
Planned output	210	210	210	210
Actual output	140	120	160	120
Cumulative deviation	−70	−160	−210	−300

3. An *input/output control report,* which is used by the supervisor to monitor the workload–capacity relationship for each workstation. (See Exhibit 17.8c.)

INPUT/OUTPUT CONTROL

Input/output (I/O) control

Input/output (I/O) control is a major feature of a manufacturing planning and control system. Its major precept is that the planned work input to a work center should never exceed the planned work output. When the input exceeds the output, backlogs build up at the work center, which in turn increases the lead time estimates for jobs upstream. Moreover, when jobs pile up at the work center, congestion occurs, processing becomes inefficient, and the flow of work to downstream work centers becomes sporadic. (The water flow analogy to shop capacity control in Exhibit 17.9 illustrates the general phenomenon.) Exhibit 17.8c shows an I/O report for a downstream work center. Looking first at the lower or output half of the report, we see that output is far below plan. It would seem that a serious capacity problem exists for this work center. However, a look at the input part of the plan makes it apparent that the serious capacity problem exists at an upstream work center feeding this work center. The control process would entail finding the cause of upstream problems and adjusting

Shop Capacity Control Load Flow

exhibit 17.9

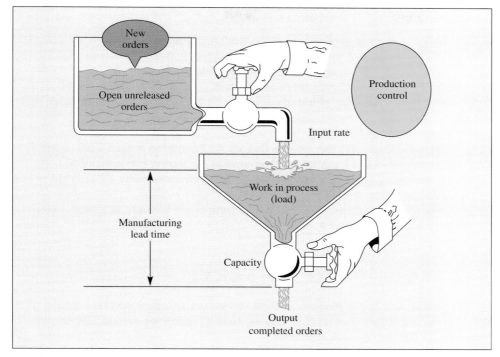

SOURCE: "TRAINING AID—SHOP FLOOR CONTROL," UNDATED. REPRINTED WITH PERMISSION OF APICS—THE EDUCATIONAL SOCIETY FOR RESOURCE MANAGEMENT, FALLS CHURCH, VA.

capacity and inputs accordingly. The basic solution is simple: Either increase capacity at the bottleneck station or reduce the input to it. (Input reduction at bottleneck work centers, incidentally, is usually the first step recommended by production control consultants when job shops get into trouble.)

DATA INTEGRITY

Shop-floor control systems in most modern plants are now computerized, with job status information entered directly into a computer as the job enters and leaves a work center. Many plants have gone heavily into bar coding and optical scanners to speed up the reporting process and to cut down on data entry errors. As you might guess, the key problems in shop-floor control are data inaccuracy and lack of timeliness.

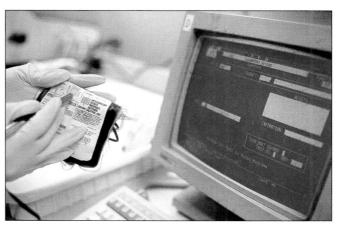

When these occur, data fed back to the overall planning system are wrong, and incorrect production decisions are made. Typical results are excess inventory, stockout problems, or both; missed due dates; and inaccuracies in job costing.

Of course, maintaining data integrity requires that a sound data-gathering system be in place; but more important, it requires adherence to the system by everybody interacting with it. Most firms recognize this, but maintaining what is variously referred to as *shop discipline, data integrity,* or *data responsibility* is not always easy. And despite periodic drives to publicize the importance of careful shop-floor reporting by creating data integrity task forces, inaccuracies can still creep into the system in many ways: A line worker drops a part under the workbench and pulls a replacement from stock without recording either transaction. An inventory clerk makes an error in a cycle count. A manufacturing engineer fails to note a change in the routing of a part. A department supervisor decides to work jobs in a different order than specified in the dispatch list.

PRINCIPLES OF WORK-CENTER SCHEDULING

Much of our discussion of work-center scheduling systems can be summarized in the following principles:

1. There is a direct equivalence between work flow and cash flow.
2. The effectiveness of any shop should be measured by speed of flow through the shop.
3. Schedule jobs as a string, with process steps back to back.
4. Once started, a job should not be interrupted.
5. Speed of flow is most efficiently achieved by focusing on bottleneck work centers and jobs.
6. Reschedule every day.
7. Obtain feedback each day on jobs that are not completed at each work center.
8. Match work-center input information to what the worker can actually do.
9. When seeking improvement in output, look for incompatibility between engineering design and process execution.
10. Certainty of standards, routings, and so forth is not possible in a shop, but always work toward achieving it.

PERSONNEL SCHEDULING IN SERVICES

Service

The scheduling problem in most service organizations revolves around setting weekly, daily, and hourly personnel schedules. In this section we present simple analytical approaches for developing such schedules.

SCHEDULING CONSECUTIVE DAYS OFF

A practical problem encountered in many services is setting schedules so that employees can have two consecutive days off. The importance of the problem stems from the fact that the Fair Labor Standards Act requires overtime pay for any work hours (by hourly workers) in excess of 40 hours per week. Obviously, if two consecutive days off cannot be scheduled each week for each employee, the likelihood of unnecessary overtime is quite high. In addition, most people probably prefer two consecutive days off per week. The following heuristic procedure is designed for this problem.

Objective   Find the schedule that minimizes the number of five-day workers with two consecutive days off, subject to the demands of the daily staffing schedule.

Procedure   Starting with the total number of workers required for each day of the week, create a schedule by adding one worker at a time. This is a two-step procedure:

Step 1. Assign the first worker to all of the days that require staffing. Do this by simply recopying the total requirements for each day. (This gives us an easy way to keep track of the number of workers needed each day.) A positive number means that the worker has been assigned to work that day.

Because the first worker may have been assigned to all seven days, circle the two consecutive days with the lowest numbers. These will be considered for days off. The lowest pair is the one where the highest number in the pair is equal to or lower than the highest number in any other pair. This ensures that the days with the highest requirements are covered by staff. (Monday and Sunday may be chosen even though they are at opposite ends of the array of days.) In case of ties, choose the days-off pair with the lowest requirement on an adjacent day. This day may be before or after the pair. If a tie still remains, choose the first of the available tied pairs. (Do not bother using further tie-breaking rules, such as second-lowest adjacent days.)

Step 2. For Worker 2, subtract 1 from each of the days not circled with positive numbers and enter this in the Worker 2 row. This indicates that one less worker is required on these days because the first worker has just been assigned to them.

The two steps are repeated for the second worker, the third worker, and so forth, until no more workers are required to satisfy the schedule.

EXAMPLE 17.4: Scheduling Days Off

NUMBER OF WORKERS REQUIRED

	M	Tu	W	Th	F	S	Su
	4	3	4	2	3	1	2
Worker 1	4	3	4	2	3	(1	2)
Worker 2	3	2	3	1	(2	1)	2
Worker 3	2	1	2	0	2	(1	1)
Worker 4	1	(0	1)	0	1	1	1
Worker 5	0	0	1	0	0	0	0

SOLUTION

This solution consists of five workers covering 19 worker days, although slightly different assignments may be equally satisfactory.

The schedule is Worker 1 assigned S–Su off, Worker 2 F–S off, Worker 3 S–Su off, Worker 4 Tu–W off, and Worker 5 works only on Wednesday because there are no further requirements for the other days. Note that Workers 3 and 4 are also off on Thursday. ●

SCHEDULING DAILY WORK TIMES

We now show how bank clearinghouses and back-office operations of large bank branches establish daily work times. Basically, management wants to derive a staffing plan that (1) requires the fewest workers to accomplish the daily workload and (2) minimizes the variance between actual and planned output.

In structuring the problem, bank management defines inputs (checks, statements, investment documents, and so forth) as *products,* which are routed through different processes or *functions* (receiving, sorting, encoding, and so forth).

To solve the problem, a daily demand forecast is made by product for each function. This is converted to labor hours required per function, which in turn is converted to workers required per function. These figures are then tabled, summed, and adjusted by an absence and vacation factor to give planned hours. Then they are divided by the number of hours in

RESTAURANTS AND OTHER SERVICES SCHEDULE EMPLOYEES BASED ON PEAK TIMES, BUT MUST ALSO AVOID OVERSTAFFING. FOR EXAMPLE, THESE WINE STEWARDS WOULD BE SCHEDULED ONLY FOR EVENINGS, BUT FOR LONGER SHIFTS ON LATE WEEK OR WEEKEND NIGHTS.

BREAKTHROUGH

EMPLOYEE SCHEDULING SOFTWARE APPLIED TO SECURITY

ScheduleSource Inc. of Broomfield, Colorado, offers an integrated suite of tools for workforce management named TeamWork. At the heart of TeamWork is a customizable and automated employee scheduling system. The benefits of TeamWork software include features such as Web-based, optimized schedules; zero conflict scheduling; time and attendance recordkeeping; e-mail notifications; audit trail; advanced reporting; and accessibility from anywhere anytime. The way it works is this:

Step 1: Define labor requirements.

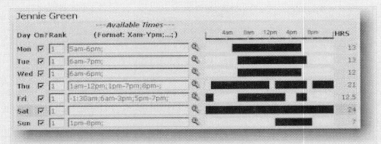

Step 2: Establish employee availability.

Step 3: Assign employees to particular skill sets and rank an employee's skill set level from 1 to 10 (1 being novice, 5 being average, and 10 being superlative).

Step 4: The TeamWork software automatically builds a schedule.

ScheduleSource customers include the Transportation Security Administration (TSA). Over an initial five-month period beginning in July 2002, ScheduleSource was successfully implemented to generate schedules for more than 44,000 federal airport security personnel at 429 airports. Over 30,000,000 individual shifts were scheduled in the airport security deployment.

the workday to yield the number of workers required. This yields the daily staff hours required. (See Exhibit 17.10.) This becomes the basis for a departmental staffing plan that lists the workers required, workers available, variance, and managerial action in light of variance. (See Exhibit 17.11.) Individual workers can be assigned using the days off scheduling procedure described in Example 17.4.

Daily Staff Hours Required to Schedule Daily Work Times

exhibit 17.10

PRODUCT	DAILY VOLUME	RECEIVE		PREPROCESS		MICROFILM		VERIFY		TOTALS
		P/H	H_{std}	P/H	H_{std}	P/H	H_{std}	P/H	H_{std}	H_{std}
Checks	2,000	1,000	2.0	600	3.3	240	8.3	640	3.1	16.7
Statements	1,000	—	—	600	1.7	250	4.0	150	6.7	12.4
Notes	200	30	6.7	15	13.3		—			20.0
Investments	400	100	4.0	50	8.0	200	2.0	150	2.7	16.7
Collections	500	300	1.7			300	1.7	60	8.4	11.8
Total hours required			14.4		26.3		16.0		20.9	77.6
Times 1.25 (absences and vacations)			18.0		32.9		20.0		26.1	
Divided by 8 hours equals staff required			2.3		4.1		2.5		3.3	12.2

Note: P/H indicates production rate per hour; H_{std} indicates required hours.

Staffing Plan

exhibit 17.11

FUNCTION	STAFF REQUIRED	STAFF AVAILABLE	VARIANCE (±)	MANAGEMENT ACTIONS
Receive	2.3	2.0	−0.3	Use overtime.
Preprocess	4.1	4.0	−0.1	Use overtime.
Microfilm	2.5	3.0	+0.5	Use excess to verify.
Verify	3.3	3.0	−0.3	Get 0.3 from microfilm.

SCHEDULING HOURLY WORK TIMES

Services such as restaurants face changing requirements from hour to hour. More workers are needed for peak hours, and fewer are needed in between. Management must continuously adjust to this changing requirement. This kind of personnel scheduling situation can be approached by applying a simple rule, the *"first-hour"* principle. This procedure can be best explained using the following example. Assume that each worker works continuously for an eight-hour shift. The first-hour rule says that for the first hour, we assign a number of workers equal to the requirement in that period. For each subsequent period, assign the exact number of additional workers to meet the requirements. When in a period one or more workers come to the end of their shifts, add more workers only if they are needed to meet the requirement. The following table shows the worker requirements for the first 12 hours in a 24-hour restaurant:

	PERIOD											
	10 A.M.	11 A.M.	NOON	1 P.M.	2 P.M.	3 P.M.	4 P.M.	5 P.M.	6 P.M.	7 P.M.	8 P.M.	9 P.M.
Requirement	4	6	8	8	6	4	4	6	8	10	10	6

The schedule shows that four workers are assigned at 10 A.M., two are added at 11 A.M., and another two are added at noon to meet the requirement. From noon to 5 P.M. we have eight workers on duty. Note the overstaffing between 2 P.M. and 6 P.M. The four workers assigned at 10 A.M. finish their eight-hour shifts by 6 P.M., and four more workers are added to start their shifts. The two workers starting at 11 A.M. leave by 7 P.M., and the number of workers available drops to six. Therefore, four new workers are assigned at 7 P.M. At 9 P.M., there are 10 workers on duty, which is more than the requirement, so no worker is added. This procedure continues as new requirements are given.

	PERIOD											
	10 A.M.	11 A.M.	NOON	1 P.M.	2 P.M.	3 P.M.	4 P.M.	5 P.M.	6 P.M.	7 P.M.	8 P.M.	9 P.M.
Requirement	4	6	8	8	6	4	4	6	8	10	10	6
Assigned	4	2	2	0	0	0	0	0	4	4	2	0
On duty	4	6	8	8	8	8	8	8	8	10	10	10

Another option is splitting shifts. For example, the worker can come in, work for four hours, then come back two hours later for another four hours. The impact of this option in scheduling is essentially similar to that of changing lot size in production. When workers start working, they have to log in, change uniforms, and probably get necessary information from workers in the previous shift. This preparation can be considered as the "setup cost" in a production scenario. Splitting shifts is like having smaller production lot sizes and thus more preparation (more setups). This problem can be solved by linear programming methods described in the Nanda and Browne bibliographic reference.

CONCLUSION

In manufacturing job shops, scheduling now relies heavily on simulation to estimate the flow of work through the system to determine bottlenecks and adjust job priorities. Various software packages are available to do this. In services, the focus is typically on employee scheduling using mathematical tools that can be used to set work schedules in light of expected customer demand. No matter what the scheduling situation is, it is important to avoid suboptimization—a schedule that works well for one part of the organization but creates problems for other parts or, most important, for the customer.

KEY TERMS

Work center An area in a business in which productive resources are organized and work is completed.

Infinite loading Work is assigned to a work center based on what is needed over time. Capacity is not considered.

Finite loading Each resource is scheduled in detail using the setup and run time required for each order. The system determines exactly what will be done by each resource at every moment during the working day.

Forward scheduling Schedules from now into the future to tell the earliest that an order can be completed.

Backward scheduling Starts from some date in the future (typically the due date) and schedules the required operations in reverse sequence. Tells the latest time when an order can be started so that it is completed by a specific date.

Machine-limited process Equipment is the critical resource that is scheduled.

Labor-limited process People are the key resource that is scheduled.

Dispatching The activity of initiating scheduled work.

Sequencing The process of determining which job to start first on a machine or work center.

Priority rules The logic used to determine the sequence of jobs in a queue.

Johnson's rule A sequencing rule used for scheduling any number of jobs on two machines. The rule is designed to minimize the time required to complete all the jobs.

Assignment method A special case of the transportation method of linear programming that is used to allocate a specific number of jobs to the same number of machines.

Shop-floor (production activity) control A system for utilizing data from the shop floor to maintain and communicate status information on shop orders and work centers.

Input/output (I/O) control Work being released into a work center should never exceed the planned work output. When the input exceeds the output, backlogs build up at the work center that increase the lead time.

SOLVED PROBLEM

Joe's Auto Seat Cover and Paint Shop is bidding on a contract to do all the custom work for Smiling Ed's used car dealership. One of the main requirements in obtaining this contract is rapid delivery time, because Ed—for reasons we shall not go into here—wants the cars facelifted and back on his lot in a hurry. Ed has said that if Joe can refit and repaint five cars that Ed has just received in 24 hours or less, the contract will be his. Following is the time (in hours) required in the refitting shop and the paint shop for each of the five cars. Assuming that cars go through the refitting operations before they are repainted, can Joe meet the time requirements and get the contract?

CAR	REFITTING TIME (HOURS)	REPAINTING TIME (HOURS)
A	6	3
B	0	4
C	5	2
D	8	6
E	2	1

Solution

This problem can be viewed as a two-machine flow shop and can be easily solved using Johnson's rule. The final schedule is B–D–A–C–E. Using the LEKIN software (see DVD):

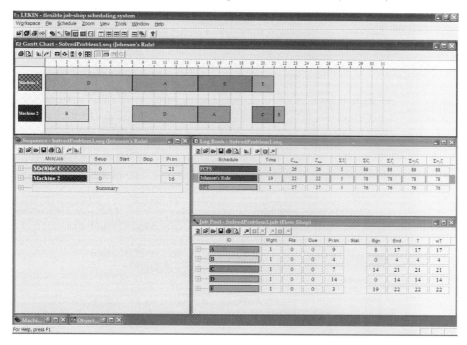

Manually, the problem is solved as follows:

	ORIGINAL DATA		JOHNSON'S RULE	
CAR	REFITTING TIME (HOURS)	REPAINTING TIME (HOURS)	ORDER OF SELECTION	POSITION IN SEQUENCE
A	6	3	4	3
B	0	4	1	1
C	5	2	3	4
D	8	6	5	2
E	2	1	2	5

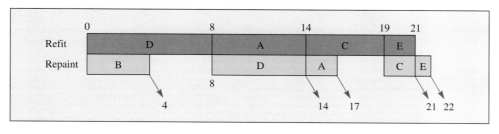

REVIEW AND DISCUSSION QUESTIONS

1 What are the objectives of work-center scheduling?
2 Distinguish between a job shop, a GT cell, and a flow shop.
3 What practical considerations are deterrents to using the SOT rule?
4 What priority rule do you use in scheduling your study time for midterm examinations? If you have five exams to study for, how many alternative schedules exist?
5 The SOT rule provides an optimal solution in a number of evaluation criteria. Should the manager of a bank use the SOT rule as a priority rule? Why?
6 Data integrity is a big deal in industry. Why?
7 Why does batching cause so much trouble in job shops?
8 What job characteristics would lead you to schedule jobs according to "longest processing time first"?
9 Why is managing bottlenecks so important in job-shop scheduling?
10 Under what conditions is the assignment method appropriate?
11 How might planning for a special customer affect the personnel schedule in a service?

PROBLEMS

1 Christine has three cars that must be overhauled by her ace mechanic, Megan. Given the following data about the cars, use least slack per remaining operation to determine Megan's scheduling priority for each:

CAR	CUSTOMER PICK-UP TIME (HOURS HENCE)	REMAINING OVERHAUL TIME (HOURS)	REMAINING OPERATION
A	10	4	Painting
B	17	5	Wheel alignment, painting
C	15	1	Chrome plating, painting, seat repair

2 A hotel has to schedule its receptionists according to hourly loads. Management has identified the number of receptionists needed to meet the hourly requirement, which changes from day to day. Assume each receptionist works a four-hour shift. Given the following staffing requirement in a certain day, use the first-hour principle to find the personnel schedule:

	PERIOD											
	8 A.M.	9 A.M.	10 A.M.	11 A.M.	NOON	1 P.M.	2 P.M.	3 P.M.	4 P.M.	5 P.M.	6 P.M.	7 P.M.
Requirement	2	3	5	8	8	6	5	8	8	6	4	3
Assigned												
On duty												

3 Seven jobs must be processed in two operations: A and B. All seven jobs must go through A and B in that sequence—A first, then B. Determine the optimal order in which the jobs should be sequenced through the process using these times:

JOB	PROCESS A TIME	PROCESS B TIME
1	9	6
2	8	5
3	7	7
4	6	3
5	1	2
6	2	6
7	4	7

4   Jumbo's Restaurant is trying to create a consecutive-days-off schedule that uses the fewest workers. Use the following information to create a five-days-on, two-days-off schedule:

	DAY						
	M	TU	W	TH	F	S	SU
Requirements	2	2	1	3	3	4	2

5   The following list of jobs in a critical department includes estimates of their required times:

JOB	REQUIRED TIME (DAYS)	DAYS TO DELIVERY PROMISE	SLACK
A	8	12	4
B	3	9	6
C	7	8	1
D	1	11	10
E	10	−10 (late)	−20
F	6	10	4
G	5	−8 (late)	−13
H	4	6	2

a. Use the shortest operation time rule to schedule these jobs.

What is the schedule?
What is the mean flow time?

b. The boss does not like the schedule in *a.* Jobs E and G must be done first, for obvious reasons. (They are already late.) Reschedule and do the best you can while scheduling Jobs E and G first and second, respectively.

What is the new schedule?
What is the new mean flow time?

6   The following matrix shows the costs in thousands of dollars for assigning Individuals A, B, C, and D to Jobs 1, 2, 3, and 4. Solve the problem showing your final assignments in order to minimize cost.

INDIVIDUALS	JOBS			
	1	2	3	4
A	7	9	3	5
B	3	11	7	6
C	4	5	6	2
D	5	9	10	12

7   A manufacturing facility has five jobs to be scheduled into production. The following table gives the processing times plus the necessary wait times and other necessary delays for each of the jobs. Assume that today is April 3 and the jobs are due on the dates shown:

JOB	DAYS OF ACTUAL PROCESSING TIME REQUIRED	DAYS OF NECESSARY DELAY TIME	TOTAL TIME REQUIRED	DATE JOB DUE
1	2	12	14	April 30
2	5	8	13	April 21
3	9	15	24	April 28
4	7	9	16	April 29
5	4	22	26	April 27

Determine *two* schedules, stating the order in which the jobs are to be done. Use the critical ratio priority rule for one. You may use any other rule for the second schedule as long as you state what it is.

8 An accounting firm, Debits 'R Us, would like to keep its auditing staff to a maximum of five people and still satisfy the staffing needs and the policy of two days off per week. Given the following requirements, is this possible? What should the schedule be?

Requirements (Monday through Sunday): 3, 2, 3, 5, 4, 3, 4.

9 The Glendale Electronics Store employs five people. Customer traffic is highest on the weekend and is lowest during midweek. Accordingly, demand for employee help is given in the following table. Make an employee work schedule that will meet staffing requirements and guarantee each employee two consecutive days off per week.

| | DAY | | | | | | |
	MONDAY	TUESDAY	WEDNESDAY	THURSDAY	FRIDAY	SATURDAY	SUNDAY
Requirements	4	3	2	3	4	5	4
Adams							
Chang							
Klein							
Ramirez							
Sampson							

10 Jobs A, B, C, D, and E must go through Processes I and II in that sequence (Process I first, then Process II). Use Johnson's rule to determine the optimal sequence in which to schedule the jobs to minimize the total required time.

JOB	REQUIRED PROCESSING TIME ON I	REQUIRED PROCESSING TIME ON II
A	4	5
B	16	14
C	8	7
D	12	11
E	3	9

11 In a job shop, six machinists were uniquely qualified to operate any one of the five machines in the shop. The job shop had considerable backlog, and all five machines were kept busy at all times. The one machinist not operating a machine was usually occupied doing clerical or routine maintenance work. Given the value schedule below for each machinist on each of the five machines, develop an optimal assignment. (Hint: Add a dummy column with zero cost values, and solve using the assignment method.)

| | MACHINE | | | | |
MACHINIST	1	2	3	4	5
A	65	50	60	55	80
B	30	75	125	50	40
C	75	35	85	95	45
D	60	40	115	130	110
E	90	85	40	80	95
F	145	60	55	45	85

12 Joe has achieved a position of some power in the institution in which he currently resides and works. In fact, things have gone so well that he has decided to divide the day-to-day operations of his business activities among four trusted subordinates: Big Bob, Dirty Dave, Baby Face Nick, and Tricky Dick. The question is how he should do this in order to take advantage of his associates'

unique skills and to minimize the costs from running all areas for the next year. The following matrix summarizes the costs that arise under each possible combination of men and areas:

	AREA			
ASSOCIATE	1	2	3	4
Big Bob	$1,400	$1,800	$ 700	$1,000
Dirty Dave	600	2,200	1,500	1,300
Baby Face Nick	800	1,100	1,200	500
Tricky Dick	1,000	1,800	2,100	1,500

13 Joe has now been released from his government job. Based on his excellent performance, he was able to land a job as production scheduler in a brand-new custom refinishing auto service shop located near the border. Techniques have improved in the several years he was out of circulation, so processing times are considerably faster. This system is capable of handling 10 cars per day. The sequence now is customizing first, followed by repainting.

CAR	CUSTOMIZING TIME (HOURS)	PAINTING (HOURS)	CAR	CUSTOMIZING TIME (HOURS)	PAINTING (HOURS)
1	3.0	1.2	6	2.1	0.8
2	2.0	0.9	7	3.2	1.4
3	2.5	1.3	8	0.6	1.8
4	0.7	0.5	9	1.1	1.5
5	1.6	1.7	10	1.8	0.7

In what sequence should Joe schedule the cars?

14 The following table contains information regarding jobs that are to be scheduled through one machine:

JOB	PROCESSING TIME (DAYS)	DUE DATE
A	4	20
B	12	30
C	2	15
D	11	16
E	10	18
F	3	5
G	6	9

a. What is the first-come, first-served (FCFS) schedule?
b. What is the shortest operating time (SOT) schedule?
c. What is the slack time remaining (STR) schedule?
d. What is the earliest due date (EDD) schedule?
e. What are the mean flow times for each of the schedules above?

15 Schedule the following six jobs through two machines in sequence to minimize the flow time using Johnson's rule:

	OPERATIONS TIME	
JOB	MACHINE 1	MACHINE 2
A	5	2
B	16	15
C	1	9
D	13	11
E	17	3
F	18	7

16   Martina's Bar and Grill wishes to create a consecutive-days-off schedule for its wait staff. Even though business is heaviest on Friday and Saturday, part-time workers are difficult to find in this area. Create a five-days-on, two-days-off schedule using the fewest workers possible given the following wait staff requirements for each day of the week:

	DAY						
	M	TU	W	TH	F	S	SU
Requirements	5	2	3	4	8	9	3

17   The following wait staff are needed at a restaurant. Use the first-hour principle to generate a personnel schedule. Assume a four-hour shift.

	PERIOD										
	11 A.M.	NOON	1 P.M.	2 P.M.	3 P.M.	4 P.M.	5 P.M.	6 P.M.	7 P.M.	8 P.M.	9 P.M.
Requirements	4	8	5	3	2	3	5	7	5	4	2
Assigned											
On duty											

18   The following matrix contains the costs (in dollars) associated with assigning Jobs A, B, C, D, and E to Machines 1, 2, 3, 4, and 5. Assign jobs to machines to minimize costs.

	MACHINES				
JOBS	1	2	3	4	5
A	6	11	12	3	10
B	5	12	10	7	9
C	7	14	13	8	12
D	4	15	16	7	9
E	5	13	17	11	12

19   Bill Edstrom, managing partner at a biomedical consulting firm, has requested your expert advice in devising the best schedule for him for the following consulting projects, starting on 2/2/05:

	DESCRIPTION OF CONSULTATION		CALL RECEIVED		DUE DATE (CLOSE OF BUSINESS)
TASK	LENGTH	COMPANY	DATE	TIME	
I	3 days	Novartis Corp.	February 1, 2005	9 a.m.	February 5, 2005
II	1 day	Reardon Biotech Corp.	February 1, 2005	10 a.m.	February 7, 2005
III	2 days	Vertex Pharmaceuticals	February 1, 2005	11 a.m.	February 7, 2005
IV	2 days	OSI Pharmaceuticals	February 1, 2005	1 p.m.	February 7, 2005

The consulting firm charges a flat rate of $4,000 per day. All four firms impose fines for lateness. Reardon Biotech charges a $500-per-day fine for each day that the completion of the consulting work is past the due date; Vertex Pharmaceuticals, Novartis, and OSI Pharmaceuticals all charge a fine of $1,500 per day for each day late.

Prepare alternative schedules based on the following priority rules: SOT, FCFS, EDD, STR, and another rule—longest processing time (LPT), which orders jobs according to longest assigned first, second longest assigned second, and so on. For the sake of simplicity, assume that consulting work is performed seven days a week. Which rule provides Bill with the best schedule? Why?

CASE: KEEP PATIENTS WAITING? NOT IN MY OFFICE

⬭⬭⬭⬭ Good doctor–patient relations begin with both parties being punctual for appointments. This is particularly important in my specialty—pediatrics. Mothers whose children have only minor problems don't like them to sit in the waiting room with really sick ones, and the sick kids become fussy if they have to wait long.

But lateness—no matter who's responsible for it—can cause problems in any practice. Once you've fallen more than slightly behind, it may be impossible to catch up that day. And although it's unfair to keep someone waiting who may have other appointments, the average office patient cools his heels for almost 20 minutes, according to one recent survey. Patients may tolerate this, but they don't like it.

I don't tolerate that in my office, and I don't believe you have to in yours. I see patients *exactly* at the appointed hour more than 99 times out of 100. So there are many GPs (grateful patients) in my busy solo practice. Parents often remark to me, "We really appreciate your being on time. Why can't other doctors do that too?" My answer is "I don't know, but I'm willing to tell them how I do it."

BOOKING APPOINTMENTS REALISTICALLY

The key to successful scheduling is to allot the proper amount of time for each visit, depending on the services required, and then stick to it. This means that the physician must pace himself carefully, receptionists must be corrected if they stray from the plan, and patients must be taught to respect their appointment times.

By actually timing a number of patient visits, I found that they break down into several categories. We allow half an hour for any new patient, 15 minutes for a well-baby checkup or an important illness, and either 5 or 10 minutes for a recheck on an illness or injury, an immunization, or a minor problem like warts. You can, of course, work out your own time allocations, geared to the way you practice.

When appointments are made, every patient is given a specific time, such as 10:30 or 2:40. It's an absolute no-no for anyone in my office to say to a patient, "Come in 10 minutes" or "Come in a half-hour." People often interpret such instructions differently, and nobody knows just when they'll arrive.

There are three examining rooms that I use routinely, a fourth that I reserve for teenagers, and a fifth for emergencies. With that many rooms, I don't waste time waiting for patients, and they rarely have to sit in the reception area. In fact, some of the younger children complain that they don't get time to play with the toys and puzzles in the waiting room before being examined, and their mothers have to let them play awhile on the way out.

On a light day I see 20 to 30 patients between 9 A.M. and 5 P.M. But our appointment system is flexible enough to let me see 40 to 50 patients in the same number of hours if I have to. Here's how we tighten the schedule:

My two assistants (three on the busiest days) have standing orders to keep a number of slots open throughout each day for patients with acute illnesses. We try to reserve more such openings in the winter months and on the days following weekends and holidays, when we're busier than usual.

Initial visits, for which we allow 30 minutes, are always scheduled on the hour or the half-hour. If I finish such a visit sooner than planned, we may be able to squeeze in a patient who needs to be seen immediately. And, if necessary, we can book two or three visits

in 15 minutes between well checks. With these cushions to fall back on, I'm free to spend an extra 10 minutes or so on a serious case, knowing that the lost time can be made up quickly.

Parents of new patients are asked to arrive in the office a few minutes before they're scheduled in order to get the preliminary paperwork done. At that time the receptionist informs them, "The doctor always keeps an accurate appointment schedule." Some already know this and have chosen me for that very reason. Others, however, don't even know that there *are* doctors who honor appointment times, so we feel that it's best to warn them on the first visit.

FITTING IN EMERGENCIES

Emergencies are the excuse doctors most often give for failing to stick to their appointment schedules. Well, when a child comes in with a broken arm or the hospital calls with an emergency Caesarean section, naturally I drop everything else. If the interruption is brief, I may just scramble to catch up. If it's likely to be longer, the next few patients are given the choice of waiting or making new appointments. Occasionally my assistants have to reschedule all appointments for the next hour or two. Most such interruptions, though, take no more than 10 to 20 minutes, and the patients usually choose to wait. I then try to fit them into the spaces we've reserved for acute cases that require last-minute appointments.

The important thing is that emergencies are never allowed to spoil my schedule for the whole day. Once a delay has been adjusted for, I'm on time for all later appointments. The only situation I can imagine that would really wreck my schedule is simultaneous emergencies in the office and at the hospital—but that has never occurred.

When I return to the patient I've left, I say, "Sorry to have kept you waiting, I had an emergency—a bad cut" (or whatever). A typical reply from the parent: "No problem, Doctor. In all the years I've been coming here, you've never made me wait before. And I'd surely want you to leave the room if *my* kid were hurt."

Emergencies aside, I get few walk-ins, because it's generally known in the community that I see patients only by appointment except in urgent circumstances. A nonemergency walk-in is handled as a phone call would be. The receptionist asks whether the visitor wants advice or an appointment. If the latter, he or she is offered the earliest time available for nonacute cases.

TAMING THE TELEPHONE

Phone calls from patients can sabotage an appointment schedule if you let them. I don't. Unlike some pediatricians, I don't have a regular telephone hour, but my assistants will handle calls from parents at any time during office hours. If the question is a simple one, such as "How much aspirin do you give a one-year-old?" the assistant will answer it. If the question requires an answer from me, the assistant writes it in the patient's chart and brings it to me while I'm seeing another child. I write the answer in—or she enters it in the chart. Then she relays it to the caller.

What if the caller insists on talking with me directly? The standard reply is "The doctor will talk with you personally if it won't take more than one minute. Otherwise you'll have to make an appointment and come in." I'm rarely called to the phone in such cases, but if the mother is very upset, I prefer to talk with her. I don't always limit her to one minute; I may let the conversation run two or three. But the caller knows I've left a patient to talk with her, so she tends to keep it brief.

DEALING WITH LATECOMERS

Some people are habitually late; others have legitimate reasons for occasional tardiness, such as a flat tire or "He threw up on me." Either way, I'm hard-nosed enough not to see them immediately if they arrive at my office more than 10 minutes behind schedule, because to do so would delay patients who arrived on time. Anyone who is less than 10 minutes late is seen right away, but is reminded of what the appointment time was.

When it's exactly 10 minutes past the time reserved for a patient and he hasn't appeared at the office, a receptionist phones his home to arrange a later appointment. If there's no answer and the patient arrives at the office a few minutes later, the receptionist says pleasantly, "Hey, we were looking for you. The doctor's had to go ahead with his other appointments, but we'll squeeze you in as soon as we can." A note is then made in the patient's chart showing the date, how late he was, and whether he was seen that day or given another appointment. This helps us identify the rare chronic offender and take stronger measures if necessary.

Most people appear not to mind waiting if they know they themselves have caused the delay. And I'd rather incur the anger of the rare person who *does* mind than risk the ill will of the many patients who would otherwise have to wait after coming in on schedule. Although I'm prepared to be firm with parents, this is rarely necessary. My office in no way resembles an army camp. On the contrary, most people are happy with the way we run it, and tell us so frequently.

COPING WITH NO-SHOWS

What about the patient who has an appointment, doesn't turn up at all, and can't be reached by telephone? Those facts, too, are noted in the chart. Usually there's a simple explanation, such as being out of town and forgetting about the appointment. If it happens a second time, we follow the same procedure. A third-time offender, though, receives a letter reminding him that time was set aside for

him and he failed to keep three appointments. In the future, he's told, he'll be billed for such wasted time.

That's about as tough as we ever get with the few people who foul up our scheduling. I've never dropped a patient for doing so. In fact, I can't recall actually billing a no-show; the letter threatening to do so seems to cure them. And when they come back—as nearly all of them do—they enjoy the same respect and convenience as my other patients.

QUESTIONS

1   What features of the appointment scheduling system were crucial in capturing "many grateful patients"?

2   What procedures were followed to keep the appointment system flexible enough to accommodate the emergency cases, and yet be able to keep up with the other patients' appointments?

3   How were the special cases such as latecomers and no-shows handled?

4   Prepare a schedule starting at 9 A.M. for the following patients of Dr. Schafer:
Johnny Appleseed, a splinter on his left thumb.
Mark Borino, a new patient.
Joyce Chang, a new patient.
Amar Gavhane, 102.5 degree (Fahrenheit) fever.
Sarah Goodsmith, an immunization.
Tonya Johnston, well-baby checkup.
JJ Lopez, a new patient.
Angel Ramirez, well-baby checkup.
Bobby Toolright, recheck on a sprained ankle.
Rebecca White, a new patient.
Doctor Schafer starts work promptly at 9 A.M. and enjoys taking a 15-minute coffee break around 10:15 or 10:30 A.M.

Apply the priority rule that maximizes scheduling efficiency. Indicate whether or not you see an exception to this priority rule that might arise. Round up any times listed in the case study (e.g., if the case study stipulates 5 or 10 minutes, then assume 10 minutes for the sake of this problem).

SOURCE: W. B. SCHAFER, "KEEP PATIENTS WAITING? NOT IN MY OFFICE," *MEDICAL ECONOMICS*, MAY 12, 1986, PP. 137–41. COPYRIGHT © BY MEDICAL ECONOMICS. REPRINTED BY PERMISSION. MEDICAL ECONOMICS IS A COPYRIGHTED PUBLICATION OF ADVANSTAR COMMUNICATIONS, INC. ALL RIGHTS RESERVED.

SELECTED BIBLIOGRAPHY

Baker, K. R. *Introduction to Sequencing and Scheduling*. 2004. (Current edition is available from author.)

Blochlige, I. "Modeling Staff Scheduling Problems: A Tutorial." *European Journal of Operational Research* 158, no. 3 (November 1, 2004), p. 533.

Brucker, P. *Scheduling Algorithms*. Berlin: Spring Verlag, 2001.

Ernst, A. T.; H. Jiang; M. Krishnamoorthy; B. Owens; and D. Sier. "An Annotated Bibliography of Personal Scheduling and Rostering." *Annals of Operations Research* 127, nos. 1–4 (March 2004), pp. 21–25.

Gang, Y.; J. Pachon; B. Thengvall; D. Chandler; and A. Wilson. "Optimizing Pilot Planning and Training for Continental Airlines." *Interfaces* 34, no. 4 (July/August 2004), pp. 253–65.

Hollman, L. *Call Center Magazine* 16, no. 4 (April 2003), pp. 28–38.

Kirchmier, B., and G. I. Plenert. *Finite Capacity Scheduling*. New York: Wiley, 2002.

Nanda, R., and J. Browne. *Introduction to Employee Scheduling*. New York: Van Nostrand Reinhold, 1992.

Pinedo, M. *Scheduling: Theory, Algorithms, and Systems*. 2nd ed. Upper Saddle River, NJ: Prentice Hall, 2002.

Sule, D. R. *Industrial Scheduling*. Boston: PWS Publishing Company, 1997.

FOOTNOTES

1 Despite the fact that expediting is frowned on by production control specialists, it is nevertheless a reality of life. In fact, a typical entry-level job in production control is that of expeditor or "stock chaser." In some companies, a good expeditor—one who can negotiate a critical job through the system or can scrounge up materials that nobody thought were available—is a prized possession.

2 R. W. Conway, W. L. Maxwell, and L. W. Miller, *Theory of Scheduling* (Reading, MA: Addison-Wesley, 1967), p. 26. This is a classic book on the subject.

3 The underlying rationale of the procedure of adding and subtracting the smallest cell values is as follows: Additional zeros are entered into the matrix by subtracting an amount equal to one of the cells from all cells. Negative numbers, which are not permissible, occur in the matrix. To get rid of the negative numbers, an amount equal to the maximum negative number must be added to each element of the row or column in which it occurs. This results in adding this amount twice to any cell that lies at the intersection of a row and a column that were both changed. The net result is that the lined rows and columns revert to their original amounts, and the intersections increase by the amount subtracted from the uncovered cells. (The reader may wish to prove this by solving the example without using lines.)

technical note seventeen
SIMULATION

Service

Simulation has become a standard tool in business. In manufacturing, simulation is used to determine production schedules, inventory levels, and maintenance procedures; to plan capacity, resource requirements, and processes; and more. In services, simulation is widely used to analyze waiting lines and schedule operations. Often, when a mathematical technique fails, we turn to simulation.

DEFINITION OF SIMULATION

Although the term *simulation* can have various meanings depending on its application, in business, it generally refers to using a computer to perform experiments on a model of a real system. Examples of other types of simulation are airplane flight simulators, video games, and virtual reality animation. Simulation experiments may be undertaken before a real system is operational, to aid in its design, to see how the system might react to changes in its operating rules, or to evaluate the system's response to changes in its structure. Simulation is particularly appropriate to situations in which the size or complexity of the problem makes the use of optimizing techniques difficult or impossible. Thus, job shops, which are characterized by complex queuing problems, have been studied extensively via simulation, as have certain types of inventory, layout, and maintenance problems (to name but a few). Simulation can also be used in conjunction with traditional statistical and management science techniques.

In addition, simulation is useful in training managers and workers in how the real system operates, in demonstrating the effects of changes in system variables, in real-time control, and in developing new ideas about how to run the business.

SIMULATION METHODOLOGY

Exhibit TN17.1 is a flowchart of the major phases in a simulation study. In this section, we develop each phase with particular reference to the key factors noted at the right of the chart.

Major Phases in a Simulation Study

PROBLEM DEFINITION

Problem definition for purposes of simulation differs little from problem definition for any other tool of analysis. Essentially, it entails specifying the objectives and identifying the relevant controllable and uncontrollable variables of the system to be studied. Consider the example of a fish market. The objective of the market's owner is maximizing the profit on sales of fish. The relevant controllable variable (that is, under the control of the decision maker) is the ordering rule; the relevant uncontrollable variables are the daily demand levels for fish and the amount of fish sold. Other possible objectives could also be specified, such as to maximize profit from the sale of lobsters or to maximize sales revenue.

CONSTRUCTING A SIMULATION MODEL

A feature that distinguishes simulation from techniques such as linear programming or queuing theory is the fact that a simulation model must be custom built for each problem situation. (A linear programming model, in contrast, can be used in a variety of situations with only a restatement of the values for the objective function and constraint equations.) There are simulation languages that make the model building easier, however. We discuss this subject later in this technical note. The unique nature of each simulation model means that the procedures discussed later for building and executing a model represent a synthesis of various approaches to simulation and are guidelines rather than rigid rules.

Parameters

Variables

Specification of Variables and Parameters   The first step in constructing a simulation model is determining which properties of the real system should be fixed (called **parameters**) and which should be allowed to vary throughout the simulation run (called **variables**). In a fish market, the variables are the amount of fish ordered, the amount demanded, and the amount sold; the parameters are the cost of the fish and the selling price of the fish. In most simulations, the focus is on the status of the variables at different points in time, such as the number of pounds of fish demanded and sold each day.

Decision rules

Specification of Decision Rules   **Decision rules** (or operating rules) are sets of conditions under which the behavior of the simulation model is observed. These rules are either directly or indirectly the focus of most simulation studies. In many simulations, decision rules are priority rules (for example, which customer to serve first, which job to process first). In certain situations these can be quite involved, taking into account a large number of variables in the system. For example, an inventory ordering rule could be stated in such a way that the amount to order would depend on the amount in inventory, the amount previously ordered but not received, the amount backordered, and the desired safety stock.

Distributions

Specification of Probability Distributions   Two categories of **distributions** can be used for simulation: empirical frequency distributions and standard mathematical distributions. An empirical distribution is derived from observing the relative frequencies of some event such as arrivals in a line or demand for a product. In other words, it is a custom-built demand distribution that is relevant only to a particular situation. It might appear like the one shown on the left side of Exhibit TN17.2. Such distributions have to be determined by direct observation or detailed analysis of records. (We show how to use these later in the waiting line simulation example.) But often demand, for example, can reasonably be assumed to closely approximate a standard mathematical distribution such as the normal or Poisson. This greatly simplifies data collection and computerization.

EXAMPLE TN17.1: Relating Random Numbers to a Standard Distribution

To illustrate how to relate random numbers to a standard distribution, suppose that daily demand for newspapers from a vending machine is normally distributed with a mean of 55 and standard deviation of 10. (This distribution is shown on the right side of Exhibit TN17.2.) Under this assumption, the generation of daily demand would employ a table of randomly distributed normal numbers (or deviates) in conjunction with the statistical formula $D_n = \bar{x} + Z_n\sigma$ (terms defined later).[1]

Actual Distribution of Demand and Normal Distribution with the Same Mean

Randomly Distributed Normal Numbers

1.23481	−1.66161	1.49673	−.26990	−.23812	.34506
1.54221	.02629	1.22318	.52304	.18124	.20790
.19126	1.18250	1.00826	.24826	−1.35882	.70691
−.54929	−.87214	−2.75470	−1.19941	−1.45402	.16760
1.14463	−.23153	1.11241	1.08497	−.28185	−.17022
−.63248	−.04776	−.55806	.04496	1.16515	2.24938
−.29988	.31052	−.49094	−.00926	−.28278	−.95339
−.32855	−.93166	−.04187	−.94171	1.64410	−.96893
.35331	.56176	−.98726	.82752	.32468	.36915
.72576					
.04406					

SOLUTION

1. Draw a five- or six-digit number from Exhibit TN17.3. The entries in this table are randomly developed deviate values that pertain to a normal distribution having a mean of 0 and a standard deviation of 1. The term *deviate* refers to the number of standard deviations some value is from the mean and, in this case, represents the number of standard deviations that any day's demand is from the mean demand. In the preceding formula for D_n, it would be the value for Z on day n. If we are simulating Day 1 and using the first entry in Exhibit TN17.3, then $Z_1 = 1.23481$. A negative deviate value means simply that the particular level of demand will be less than the mean, not that demand will be a negative value.

2. Substitute the value of Z_1, along with the predetermined values for x and σ, into the formula

$$D_n = \bar{x} + Z_n \sigma$$

where

D_n = Demand on day n
$\bar{x}$ = Mean demand (55 in this example)
σ = Estimated standard deviation (10 in this example)
z_n = Number of standard deviations from the mean on day n

Thus $D_n = 55 + (1.23481)(10)$.

3.   Solve for D_n:

$$D_n = 55 + 12.3481$$
$$D_n = 67.3481$$

4.   Repeat Steps 1 to 3, using different normal deviates from the table until the desired number of days have been simulated. ●

Time incrementing

Specification of Time-Incrementing Procedure   In a simulation model, time can be advanced by one of two methods: (1) fixed-time increments or (2) variable-time increments. Under both methods of **time incrementing,** the concept of a simulated clock is important. In the fixed-time increment method, uniform clock-time increments (such as minutes, hours, or days) are specified, and the simulation proceeds by fixed intervals from one time period to the next. At each point in clock time, the system is scanned to determine if any events are to occur. If they are, the events are simulated, and time is advanced; if they are not, time is still advanced by one unit.

In the variable-time increment method, clock time is advanced by the amount required to initiate the next event.

Which method is most appropriate? Experience suggests that the fixed-time increment is desirable when events of interest occur with regularity or when the number of events is large, with several commonly occurring in the same time period. The variable-time increment method is generally desirable, taking less computer run time, when there are relatively few events occurring within a considerable amount of time. It ignores time intervals where nothing happens and immediately advances to the next point when some event does take place.

SPECIFYING VALUES OF VARIABLES AND PARAMETERS

A variable, by definition, changes in value as the simulation progresses, but it must be given an initial starting value. The value of a parameter, remember, stays constant; however, it may be changed as different alternatives are studied in other simulations.

Determining Starting Conditions   Determining starting conditions for variables is a major tactical decision in simulation. This is because the model is biased by the set of initial starting values until the model has settled down to a steady state. To cope with this problem, analysts have followed various approaches, such as (1) discarding data generated during the early parts of the run, (2) selecting starting conditions that reduce the duration of the warm-up period, or (3) selecting starting conditions that eliminate bias. To employ any of these alternatives, however, the analyst must have some idea of the range of output data expected. Therefore, in one sense, the analyst biases results. On the other hand, one of the unique features of simulation is that it allows judgment to enter into the design and analysis of the simulation; so if the analyst has some information that bears on the problem, it should be included.

Run length (run time)

Determining Run Length   The length of the simulation run (run length or run time) depends on the purpose of the simulation. Perhaps the most common approach is to continue the simulation until it has achieved equilibrium. In the fish market example, this would mean that simulated fish sales correspond to their historical relative frequencies. Another approach is to run the simulation for a set period, such as a month, a year, or a decade, and see if the conditions at the end of the period appear reasonable. A third approach is to set run length so that a sufficiently large sample is gathered for purposes of statistical hypothesis testing. This alternative is considered further in the next section.

EVALUATING RESULTS

The types of conclusions that can be drawn from a simulation depend, of course, on the degree to which the model reflects the real system, but they also depend on the design of the simulation in a statistical sense. Indeed, many analysts view simulation as a form of hypothesis testing, with each simulation run providing one or more pieces of sample data that are amenable to formal analysis through inferential statistical methods. Statistical procedures commonly used in evaluating simulation results include analysis of variance, regression analysis, and *t* tests.

In most situations, the analyst has other information available with which to compare the simulation results: past operating data from the real system, operating data from the performance of similar systems, and the analyst's own intuitive understanding of the real system's operation. Admittedly, however, information obtained from these sources is probably not sufficient to validate the conclusions derived from the simulation. Thus, the only true test of a simulation is how well the real system performs after the results of the study have been implemented.

VALIDATION

In this context, *validation* refers to testing the computer program to ensure that the simulation is correct. Specifically, it is a check to see whether the computer code is a valid translation of the flowchart model and whether the simulation adequately represents the real system. Errors may arise in the program from mistakes in the coding or from mistakes in logic. Mistakes in coding are usually easily found because the program is most likely not executed by the computer. Mistakes in logic, however, present more of a challenge. In these cases, the program runs but fails to yield correct results.

To deal with this problem, the analyst has three alternatives: (1) have the program print out all calculations and verify these calculations by separate computation, (2) simulate present conditions and compare the results with the existing system, or (3) pick some point in the simulation run and compare its output to the answer obtained from solving a relevant mathematical model of the situation at that point. Even though the first two approaches have obvious drawbacks, they are more likely to be employed than the third, because if we had a relevant mathematical model in mind, we would probably be able to solve the problem without the aid of simulation.

PROPOSING A NEW EXPERIMENT

Based on the simulation results, a new simulation experiment may be in order. We might like to change many of the factors: parameters, variables, decision rules, starting conditions, and run length. As for parameters, we might be interested in replicating the simulation with several different costs or prices of a product to see what changes would occur. Trying different decision rules would obviously be in order if the initial rules led to poor results or if these runs yielded new insights into the problem. (The procedure of using the same stream of random numbers is a good general approach in that it sharpens the differences among alternatives and permits shorter runs.) Also, the values from the previous experiment may be useful starting conditions for subsequent simulations.

Finally, whether trying different run lengths constitutes a new experiment rather than a replication of a previous experiment depends on the types of events that occur in the system operation over time. It might happen, for example, that the system has more than one stable level of operation and that reaching the second level is time dependent. Thus, while the first series of runs of, say, 100 periods shows stable conditions, doubling the length of the series may provide new and distinctly different but equally stable conditions. In this case, running the simulation over 200 time periods could be thought of as a new experiment.

COMPUTERIZATION

When using a computer model, we reduce the system to be studied to a symbolic representation to be run on a computer. Although it is beyond this book's scope to detail the technical aspects of computer modeling, some that bear directly on simulation are

1.   Computer language selection.
2.   Flowcharting.

3. Coding.
4. Data generation.
5. Output reports.
6. Validation.

We say more about simulation programs and languages at the end of this technical note.

Output Reports   General-purpose languages permit the analyst to specify any type of output report (or data) desired, providing one is willing to pay the price in programming effort. Special-purpose languages have standard routines that can be activated by one or two program statements to print out such data as means, variances, and standard deviations. Regardless of language, however, our experience has been that too much data from a simulation can be as dysfunctional to problem solving as too little data; both situations tend to obscure important, truly meaningful information about the system under study.

SIMULATING WAITING LINES

Waiting lines that occur in series and parallel (such as in assembly lines and job shops) usually cannot be solved mathematically. However, because waiting lines are often easily simulated on a computer, we have chosen a two-stage assembly line as our second simulation example.

EXAMPLE: A TWO-STAGE ASSEMBLY LINE

Consider an assembly line that makes a product of significant physical size, such as a refrigerator, stove, car, boat, TV, or furniture. Exhibit TN17.4 shows two workstations on such a line.

The size of the product is an important consideration in assembly-line analysis and design because the number of products that can exist at each workstation affects worker performance. If the product is large, then the workstations are dependent on each other. Exhibit TN17.4, for example, shows Bob and Ray working on a two-stage line where Bob's output in Station 1 is fed to Ray in Station 2. If the workstations are adjacent so that there is no room for items in between, then Bob, by working slowly, would cause Ray to wait. Conversely, if Bob completes a product quickly (or if Ray takes longer to finish the task), then Bob must wait for Ray.

In this simulation, assume that Bob, the first worker on the line, can pull over a new item to work on whenever needed. We concentrate our analysis on the interaction between Bob and Ray.

---

exhibit TN17.4   Two Workstations on an Assembly Line

Station 1   Station 2

Bob   Ray

Objective of the Study   We would like to answer a number of questions about the assembly line from this study. A partial list would be

- What is the average performance time of each worker?
- What is the output rate of product through this line?
- How much time does Bob wait for Ray?
- How much time does Ray wait for Bob?
- If the space between the two stations were increased so that items could be stored there and give workers some independence, how would this affect output rates, wait times, and so on?

Data Collection   To simulate this system, we need the performance times of Bob and Ray. One way to collect these data is to divide the range of performance times into segments, and then observe each worker. A simple check or tally mark in each of these segments results in a useful histogram of data.

Exhibit TN17.5 shows the data collection form used to observe the performances of Bob and Ray. To simplify the procedure, performance time was divided into 10-second intervals. Bob was observed for 100 repetitions of the work task, and Ray was observed just 50 times. The number of observations does not have to be the same, but the more there are and the smaller the size of the time segments, the more accurate the study will be. The trade-off is that more observations and smaller segments take more time and more people (as well as more time to program and run a simulation).

Exhibit TN17.6 contains the random number intervals assigned that correspond to the same ratio as the actual observed data. For example, Bob had 4 out of 100 times at 10 seconds. Therefore, if we used 100 numbers, we would assign 4 of those numbers as corresponding to 10 seconds. We could have assigned any four numbers, for example, 42, 18, 12, and 93. However, these would be a nuisance to search for, so we assign consecutive numbers, such as 00, 01, 02, and 03.

There were 50 observations of Ray. There are two ways we could assign random numbers. First, we could use just 50 numbers (say, 00–49) and ignore any numbers over that. However, this is wasteful because we would discard 50 percent of all the numbers from the list. Another choice would be to double the frequency number. For example, rather than assign, say, numbers 0–03 to account for the 4 observations out of 50 that took 10 seconds, we could assign numbers 00–07 to represent 8 observations out of 100, which is double the observed number but the same frequency. Actually, for this example and the speed of computers, the savings of time by doubling is insignificant.

Exhibit TN17.7 shows a hand simulation of 10 items processed by Bob and Ray. The random numbers used were from Appendix B, starting at the first column of two numbers and working downward.

Data Collection Form for Worker Observation

SECONDS TO COMPLETE TASK	BOB	TOTALS	RAY	TOTALS
5–14.99	IIII	4	IIII	4
15–24.99	JHT I	6	JHT	5
25–34.99	JHT JHT	10	JHT I	6
35–44.99	JHT JHT JHT JHT	20	JHT II	7
45–54.99	JHT JHT JHT JHT JHT JHT JHT JHT	40	JHT JHT	10
55–64.99	JHT JHT I	11	JHT III	8
65–74.99	JHT	5	JHT I	6
75–84.99	III	4	IIII	4
		100		50

Random Number Intervals for Bob and Ray

SECONDS	TIME FREQUENCIES FOR BOB (OPERATION 1)	RN INTERVALS	TIME FREQUENCIES FOR RAY (OPERATION 2)	RN INTERVALS
10	4	00–03	4	00–07
20	6	04–09	5	08–17
30	10	10–19	6	18–29
40	20	20–39	7	30–43
50	40	40–79	10	44–63
60	11	80–90	8	64–79
70	5	91–95	6	80–91
80	4	96–99	4	92–99
	100		50	

Simulation of Bob and Ray—Two-Stage Assembly Line

ITEM NUMBER	BOB						RAY				
	RANDOM NUMBER	START TIME	PERFORMANCE TIME	FINISH TIME	WAIT TIME	STORAGE SPACE	RANDOM NUMBER	START TIME	PERFORMANCE TIME	FINISH TIME	WAIT TIME
1	56	00	50	50		0	83	50	70	120	50
2	55	50	50	100	20	0	47	120	50	170	
3	84	120	60	180		0	08	180	20	200	10
4	36	180	40	220		0	05	220	10	230	20
5	26	220	40	260		0	42	260	40	300	30
6	95	260	70	330		0	95	330	80	410	30
7	66	330	50	380	30	0	17	410	20	430	
8	03	410	10	420	10	0	21	430	30	460	
9	57	430	50	480		0	31	480	40	520	20
10	69	480	50	530		0	90	530	70	600	10
			470		60				430		170

Assume that we start out at time 00 and run it in continuous seconds (not bothering to convert this to hours and minutes). The first random number is 56 and corresponds to Bob's performance at 50 seconds on the first item. The item is passed to Ray, who starts at 50 seconds. Relating the next random number, 83, to Exhibit TN17.6, we find that Ray takes 70 seconds to complete the item. In the meantime, Bob starts on the next item at time 50 and takes 50 seconds (random number 55), finishing at time 100. However, Bob cannot start on the third item until Ray gets through with the first item at time 120. Bob, therefore, has a wait time of 20 seconds. (If there was storage space between Bob and Ray, this item could have been moved out of Bob's workstation, and Bob could have started the next item at time 100.) The remainder of the exhibit was calculated following the same pattern: obtaining a random number, finding the corresponding processing time, noting the wait time (if any), and computing the finish time. Note that with no storage space between Bob and Ray, there was considerable waiting time for both workers.

We can now answer some questions and make some statements about the system. For example,

The output time averages 60 seconds per unit (the complete time 600 for Ray divided by 10 units).

Utilization of Bob is $\frac{470}{530} = 88.7$ percent.

Utilization of Ray is $\frac{430}{550} = 78.2$ percent (disregarding the initial startup wait for the first item of 50 seconds).

The average performance time for Bob is $\frac{470}{10} = 47$ seconds.

The average performance time for Ray is $\frac{430}{10} = 43$ seconds.

We have demonstrated how this problem would be solved in a simple manual simulation. A sample of 10 is really too small to place much confidence in, so this problem should be run on a computer for several thousand iterations. (We extend this same problem further in the next section of this technical note.)

It is also vital to study the effect of item storage space between workers. The problem would be run to see what the throughput time and worker utilization times are with no storage space between workers. A second run should increase this storage space to one unit, with the corresponding changes noted. Repeating the runs for two, three, four, and so on offers management a chance to compute the additional cost of space compared with the increased use. Such increased space between workers may require a larger building, more materials and parts in the system, material handling equipment, and a transfer machine, plus added heat, light, building maintenance, and so on.

These would also be useful data for management to see what changes in the system would occur if one worker position was automated. The assembly line could be simulated using data from the automated process to see if such a change would be cost justified.

SPREADSHEET SIMULATION

As we have stated throughout this book, spreadsheets such as Microsoft® Excel are very useful for a variety of problems. Exhibit TN17.8 shows Bob and Ray's two-stage assembly line on an Excel® spreadsheet. The procedure follows the same pattern as our manual display in Exhibit TN17.7.

The total simulation on Excel® passed through 1,200 iterations (shown in Exhibits TN17.10 and TN17.11); that is, 1,200 parts were finished by Ray. Simulation, as an analytic tool, has an advantage over quantitative methods in that it is dynamic, whereas analytic methods show long-run average performance. As you can see in Exhibits TN17.9 and TN17.10, there is an unmistakable startup (or transient) phase. We could even raise some questions about the long-term operation of the line because it does not seem to have settled to a constant (steady state) value, even after the 1,200 items. Exhibit TN17.9 shows 100 items that pass through the Bob and Ray two-stage system. Notice the wide variation in time for the first units completed. These figures are the average time that units take. It is a cumulative number; that is, the first unit takes the time generated by the random numbers. The average time for two units is the average time of the sum of the first and second units. The average time for three units is the average time for the sum of the first three units, and so on. This display could have almost any starting shape, not necessarily what we have shown. It all depends on the stream of random numbers. What we can be sure of is that the times do oscillate for a while until they settle down as units are finished and smooth the average.

Exhibit TN17.10 shows the average time that parts spend in the system. At the start, the display shows an increasing amount of time in the system. This can be expected because the system started empty and there are no interruptions for parts passing from Bob to Ray. Often parts enter the system and may have to wait between stages as work-in-process; this causes delays for subsequent parts and adds to the waiting time. As time goes on, however, stability should occur unless the capacity of the second stage is less than the first stage's. In our present case, we did not allow space between them. Therefore, if Bob finished first, he had to wait for Ray. If Ray finished first, he had to wait for Bob.

Exhibit TN17.11 shows the results of simulating Bob and Ray completing 1,200 units of product. Compare these figures to those that we obtained simulating 10 items by hand. Not too bad, is it? The average performance time for Bob is shown as 46.48 seconds. This is close to the

Bob and Ray Two-Stage Assembly Line on Microsoft Excel®

Excel: Two-Stage Assembly.xls

		BOB					RAY						AVERAGE TIME IN SYSTEM
ITEM	RN	START TIME	PERF. TIME	FINISH TIME	WAIT TIME	RN	START TIME	PERF. TIME	FINISH TIME	WAIT TIME	AVERAGE TIME/UNIT	TOTAL TIME	
1	93	0	70	70	0	0	70	10	80	70	80.0	80	80.0
2	52	70	50	120	0	44	120	50	170	40	85.0	100	90.0
3	15	120	30	150	20	72	170	60	230	0	76.7	110	96.7
4	64	170	50	220	10	35	230	40	270	0	67.5	100	97.5
5	86	230	60	290	0	2	290	10	300	20	60.0	70	92.0
6	20	290	40	330	0	82	330	70	400	30	66.7	110	95.0
7	83	330	60	390	10	31	400	40	440	0	62.9	110	97.1
8	89	400	60	460	0	13	460	20	480	20	60.0	80	95.0
9	69	460	50	510	0	53	510	50	560	30	62.2	100	95.6
10	41	510	50	560	0	48	560	50	610	0	61.0	100	96.0
11	32	560	40	600	10	13	610	20	630	0	57.3	70	93.6
12	1	610	10	620	10	67	630	60	690	0	57.5	80	92.5
13	11	630	30	660	30	91	690	70	760	0	58.5	130	95.4
14	2	690	10	700	60	76	760	60	820	0	58.6	130	97.9
15	11	760	30	790	30	41	820	40	860	0	57.3	100	98.0
16	55	820	50	870	0	34	870	40	910	10	56.9	90	97.5
17	18	870	30	900	10	28	910	30	940	0	55.3	70	95.9
18	39	910	40	950	0	53	950	50	1000	10	55.6	90	95.6
19	13	950	30	980	20	41	1000	40	1040	0	54.7	90	95.3
20	7	1000	20	1020	20	21	1040	30	1070	0	53.5	70	94.0
21	29	1040	40	1080	0	54	1080	50	1130	10	53.8	90	93.8
22	58	1080	50	1130	0	39	1130	40	1170	0	53.2	90	93.6
23	95	1130	70	1200	0	70	1200	60	1260	30	54.8	130	95.2
24	27	1200	40	1240	20	60	1260	50	1310	0	54.6	110	95.8
25	59	1260	50	1310	0	93	1310	80	1390	0	55.6	130	97.2
26	85	1310	60	1370	20	51	1390	50	1440	0	55.4	130	98.5
27	12	1390	30	1420	20	35	1440	40	1480	0	54.8	90	98.1
28	34	1440	40	1480	0	51	1480	50	1530	0	54.6	90	97.9
29	60	1480	50	1530	0	87	1530	70	1600	0	55.2	120	98.6
30	97	1530	80	1610	0	29	1610	30	1640	10	54.7	110	99.0

Excel: LineSim.xls

weighted average of what you would expect in the long run. For Bob it is $(10 \times 4 + 20 \times 6 + 30 \times 10 \text{ etc.})/100 = 45.9$ seconds. Ray's expected time is $(10 \times 4 + 20 \times 5 + 30 \times 6 \text{ etc.})/50 = 46.4$ seconds.

The two-stage assembly line simulation is a good example of a specially designed spreadsheet for analyzing this problem. More general simulation programs built within Excel® are available. John McClain, professor of operations management at Cornell University, has developed two simulation spreadsheets that can be used to demonstrate a variety of common systems. These spreadsheets have been included on this book's DVD ROM.

The first spreadsheet, titled "LineSim.xls," is designed to analyze a simple serial production line. This is a system with a series of machines; the output of one machine goes to a storage

TN17.9—Average Time per Unit of Output
(Finish Time/Number of Units)

TN17.10—Average Time the Product Spends
in the System

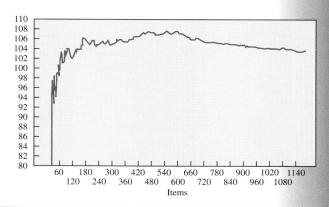

Results of Simulating 1,200 Units Processed by Bob and Ray

	BOB	RAY	UNIT
Utilization	0.81	0.85	
Average wait time	10.02	9.63	
Average performance time	46.48	46.88	
Average time per unit			57.65
Average time in system			103.38

area, which is the input to the next machine. The spreadsheet can be easily configured for different numbers of machines, different buffer sizes, and numerous processing time distributions. In addition, machine breakdowns and repairs can be modeled. The second spreadsheet, "CellSim.xls," is similar but allows machines to be arranged more generally. We thank Professor McClain for making these spreadsheets available.

Excel: CellSim.xls

SIMULATION PROGRAMS AND LANGUAGES

Simulation models can be classified as *continuous* or *discrete*. Continuous models are based on mathematical equations and therefore are continuous, with values for all points in time. In contrast, discrete simulation occurs only at specific points. For example, customers arriving at a bank teller's window would be discrete simulation. The simulation jumps from point to point; the arrival of a customer, the start of a service, the ending of service, the arrival of the next customer, and so on. Discrete simulation also can be triggered to run by units of time (daily, hourly, minute by minute). This is called *event simulation;* points in between either have no value to our simulation or cannot be computed because of the lack of some sort of mathematical relationship to link the succeeding events. Operations management applications almost exclusively use discrete (event) simulation.

BREAKTHROUGH

ANIMATION AND SIMULATION SOFTWARE

Call centers are a good application for simulation. They are easy to model and information is available about the service time, arrival rates, renege times, and the paths that the calls take through the center. In this call center, there are four types of calls arriving at random intervals and four types of agents who are able to answer the calls. Each agent type is specialized in a particular call type. However, some agents are able to answer calls of different types.

This was quickly modeled using Extend, a product of Imagine That! company. The product makes extensive use of animation so that the user can actually watch the call center operate. You can learn more about this product at http://www.imaginethatinc.com.

Service

Simulation programs also can be categorized as general-purpose and special-purpose. General-purpose software allow programmers to build their own models. Examples are SLAM II, SIMSCRIPT II.5, SIMAN, GPSS/H, GPSS/PC, PC-MODEL, and RESQ. Special-purpose software simulation programs are specially built to simulate specific applications, such as Extend and SIMFACTORY. In a specialized simulation for manufacturing, for example, provisions in the model allow for specifying the number of work centers, their description, arrival rates, processing time, batch sizes, quantities of work in process, available resources including labor, sequences, and so on. Additionally, the program may allow the observer to watch the animated operation and see the quantities and flows throughout the system as the simulation is running. Data are collected, analyzed, and presented in a form most suitable for that type of application. The software package called Extend is featured in the Breakthrough box titled "Animation and Simulation Software."

Many software simulation programs are available. How, then, do you choose a program from a long list? The first step is to understand the different types of simulation. Then it becomes a matter of reviewing programs on the market to find one that fits your specific needs. (See the Breakthrough box titled "Hospital Overcrowding Solutions Are Found with Simulation" for a successful application of a commercial program.)

As a last comment on simulation programs, do not rule out spreadsheets for simulation. As you noticed, we simulated Bob and Ray on a spreadsheet in the preceding section. Spreadsheets are becoming quite user-friendly and are adding many features, such as allowing random number generation and asking what-if questions. The simplicity in using a spreadsheet for simulation may well compensate for any needed reduction in the complexity of the problem in order to use the spreadsheet.

@RISK is an add-in program that works with Microsoft Excel®. The program adds many useful simulation-related functions to the spreadsheet. Using @RISK automates the process of taking random values from a specified distribution function, automates the recalculation of the spreadsheet with the new random values, and captures output values and statistics. @RISK simplifies the process of building and running spreadsheet simulations.[2]

BREAKTHROUGH

HOSPITAL OVERCROWDING SOLUTIONS ARE FOUND WITH SIMULATION

Thanks to increased life expectancy through improved health care coupled with shifting population demographics, hospitals everywhere are becoming increasingly overcrowded. Limited health care budgets are forcing hospitals to explore creative solutions. But creative solutions can be risky, so they need to be carefully evaluated. From the standpoint of cost, the earlier a solution can be evaluated and either accepted or rejected, the better.

Along these lines, the outpatient laboratory at Bay Medical Center was experiencing serious capacity constraints. Adding to its difficulties, a renovation designed to improve efficiency actually added to the overcrowding problem. Dave Nall, a management engineer for Bay Medical Center, ran a study to evaluate several alternatives and make recommendations designed to reduce bottlenecks and improve patient flow through the outpatient laboratory. The objective of this study was to develop and evaluate alternative ways of reducing overcrowding at the outpatient laboratory.

SOLUTION

The key technology employed by Dave in conducting this analysis was computer simulation. Dave had used computer simulation numerous times in the past and had found that it was an efficient way to both gain insight into the problem and evaluate the solutions.

Through discussions with managers responsible for the outpatient laboratory, Dave built a network describing the patient's flow through the laboratory as it was currently configured. Then data were collected on the times required for patients to receive the various services they might need as well as the travel time between rooms where the services were provided. From this information, Dave constructed a computer simulation of the baseline laboratory configuration.

Dave then modified the computer simulation and used it to study issues relating to three categories of solutions to outpatient laboratory overcrowding: (1) changing staff, including both medical and administrative staff; (2) utilizing another clinic as an overflow laboratory; and (3) possible redesign of the laboratory facility itself.

With respect to staffing, the computer simulation verified that the medical staff currently employed was indeed the

optimal number. However, Dave found that the administrative functions, if anything, were overstaffed and that a staff reduction could take place with no appreciable reduction in patient service. Staffing was not the key problem. With respect to the option of utilizing another laboratory for overflow, there were significant opportunities for improving throughput if other patients could be enticed to use another laboratory. Although the simulation did not tell him how to get the patients to use an alternative laboratory, it did allow Dave to quantify the benefits of implementing

policies that would increase alternative laboratory usage by 5 percent, 10 percent, and so on. With respect to redesign of the existing outpatient laboratory, Dave determined that, with a relatively minor redesign of the facility and a procedural change, the laboratory would become significantly more productive. Increased productivity would, of course, lead to better patient service.

BENEFITS

Individually, no one could have accurately guessed the impact of the different ways of addressing overcrowding at the outpatient laboratory at Bay Medical Center. Through the results of the simulation analysis and the insights gained, Dave was able to assess the relative merits of each alternative as well as predict their impact. With a small investment in Dave's time, Bay Medical Center was able to make informed decisions with an understanding of both costs and benefits. As a result, the right decisions were made, money was saved, and patients were better served.

SOURCE: MICRO ANALYSIS AND DESIGN MICRO SAINT SIMULATION SOFTWARE. © 2004 MICRO ANALYSES & DESIGN. USED WITH PERMISSION.

DESIRABLE FEATURES OF SIMULATION SOFTWARE

Simulation software takes a while to learn to use. Once specific software is learned, the tendency is to stay with it for a long time, so the choice must be made carefully. Simulation software should

1. Be capable of being used interactively as well as allowing complete runs.
2. Be user-friendly and easy to understand.
3. Allow modules to be built and then connected. In this way models can be worked on separately without affecting the rest of the system.
4. Allow users to write and incorporate their own routines; no simulation program can provide for all needs.
5. Have building blocks that contain built-in commands (such as statistical analysis or decision rules for where to go next).
6. Have macro capability, such as the ability to develop machining cells.
7. Have material flow capability. Operations involve the movement of material and people; the program should be able to model trucks, cranes, conveyers, and so on.
8. Output standard statistics such as cycle times, utilizations, and wait times.
9. Allow a variety of data analysis alternatives for both input and output data.
10. Have animation capabilities to display graphically the product flow through the system.
11. Permit interactive debugging of the model so the user can trace flows through the model and more easily find errors.[3]

ADVANTAGES AND DISADVANTAGES OF SIMULATION

The following is not intended as a comprehensive list of reasons why one should elect to use or not use simulation as a technique. Rather, we state some of the generally accepted advantages and disadvantages.

ADVANTAGES

1. Developing the model of a system often leads to a better understanding of the real system.
2. Time can be compressed in simulation; years of experience in the real system can be compressed into seconds or minutes.
3. Simulation does not disrupt ongoing activities of the real system.
4. Simulation is far more general than mathematical models and can be used where conditions are not suitable for standard mathematical analysis.
5. Simulation can be used as a game for training experience.
6. Simulation provides a more realistic replication of a system than mathematical analysis.
7. Simulation can be used to analyze transient conditions, whereas mathematical techniques usually cannot.
8. Many standard packaged models, covering a wide range of topics, are available commercially.
9. Simulation answers what-if questions.

DISADVANTAGES

1. Although a great deal of time and effort may be spent to develop a model for simulation, there is no guarantee that the model will, in fact, provide good answers.

2. There is no way to prove that a simulation model's performance is completely reliable. Simulation involves numerous repetitions of sequences that are based on randomly generated occurrences. An apparently stable system can, with the right combination of events—however unlikely—explode.
3. Depending on the system to be simulated, building a simulation model can take anywhere from an hour to 100 worker years. Complicated systems can be very costly and take a long time.
4. Simulation may be less accurate than mathematical analysis because it is randomly based. If a given system can be represented by a mathematical model, it may be better to use than simulation.
5. A significant amount of computer time may be needed to run complex models.
6. The technique of simulation, while making progress, still lacks a standardized approach. Therefore, models of the same system built by different individuals may differ widely.

CONCLUSION

We could make the statement that anything that can be done mathematically can be done with simulation. However, simulation is not always the best choice. Mathematical analysis, when appropriate to a specific problem, is usually faster and less expensive. Also, it is usually provable as far as the technique is concerned, and the only real question is whether the system is adequately represented by the mathematical model.

Simulation, however, has nothing fixed; there are no boundaries to building a model or making assumptions about the system. Expanding computer power and memory have pushed out the limits of what can be simulated. Further, the continued development of simulation languages and programs—both general-purpose programs (SIMAN, SLAM) and special-purpose programs (Extend, Process Model, SIMFACTORY, Optima!)—have made the entire process of creating simulation models much easier.

KEY TERMS

Parameters Properties of a simulation model that are fixed.

Variables Properties of a simulation model that are allowed to vary throughout the simulation run. The results of the simulation are analyzed through these variables.

Decision rules Logic that controls the behavior of a simulation.

Distributions The probability distributions that are used to model the random events in a simulation.

Time incrementing The process of moving through time in a simulation.

Run length (or run time) The duration of a simulation in simulated time or number of events.

SOLVED PROBLEMS

SOLVED PROBLEM 1

To use an old statistical example for simulation, if an urn contains 100 balls, of which 10 percent are green, 40 percent are red, and 50 percent are spotted, develop a simulation model of the process of drawing balls at random from the urn. Each time a ball is drawn and its color noted, it is replaced. Use the following random numbers as you desire.

Simulate drawing 10 balls from the urn. Show which numbers you have used.

26768	66954	83125	08021
42613	17457	55503	36458
95457	03704	47019	05752
95276	56970	84828	05752

Solution

Assign random numbers to the balls to correspond to the percentage present in the urn.

	RANDOM NUMBER
10 green balls	00–09
40 red balls	10–49
50 spotted balls	50–99

Many possible answers exist, depending on how the random numbers were assigned and which numbers were used from the list provided in the problem.

For the random number sequence above and using the first two numbers of those given, we obtain

RN	COLOR	RN	COLOR
26	Red	17	Red
42	Red	3	Green
95	Spotted	56	Spotted
95	Spotted	83	Spotted
66	Spotted	55	Spotted

For the 10 there were 1 green, 3 red, and 6 spotted balls—a good estimate based on a sample of only 10!

SOLVED PROBLEM 2

A rural clinic receives a delivery of fresh plasma once each week from a central blood bank. The supply varies according to demand from other clinics and hospitals in the region but ranges between four and nine pints of the most widely used blood type, type O. The number of patients per week requiring this blood varies from zero to four, and each patient may need from one to four pints. Given the following delivery quantities, patient distribution, and demand per patient, what would be the number of pints in excess or short for a six-week period? Use simulation to derive your answer. Consider that plasma is storable and there is currently none on hand.

		PATIENT DISTRIBUTION			
DELIVERY QUANTITIES		PATIENTS PER WEEK REQUIRING BLOOD		DEMAND PER PATIENT	
PINTS PER WEEK	PROBABILITY		PROBABILITY	PINTS	PROBABILITY
4	0.15	0	0.25	1	0.40
5	0.20	1	0.25	2	0.30
6	0.25	2	0.30	3	0.20
7	0.15	3	0.15	4	0.10
8	0.15	4	0.05		
9	0.10				

Solution

First develop a random number sequence; then simulate.

DELIVERY			NUMBER OF PATIENTS			PATIENT DEMAND		
PINTS	PROBABILITY	RANDOM NUMBER	BLOOD	PROBABILITY	RANDOM NUMBER	PINTS	PROBABILITY	NUMBER
4	.15	00–14	0	.25	00–24	1	.40	00–39
5	.20	15–34	1	.25	25–49	2	.30	40–69
6	.25	35–59	2	.30	50–79	3	.20	70–89
7	.15	60–74	3	.15	80–94	4	.10	90–99
8	.15	75–89	4	.05	95–99			
9	.10	90–99						

Week No.	Beginning Inventory	Quantity Delivered		Total Blood on Hand	Patients Needing Blood		Patient	Quantity Needed		Number of Pints Remaining
		RN	Pints		RN	Patients		RN	Pints	
1	0	74	7	7	85	3	First	21	1	6
							Second	06	1	5
							Third	71	3	2
2	2	31	5	7	28	1		96	4	3
3	3	02	4	7	72	2	First	12	1	6
							Second	67	2	4
4	4	53	6	10	44	1		23	1	9
5	9	16	5	14	16	0				14
6	14	40	6	20	83	3	First	65	2	18
							Second	34	1	17
							Third	82	3	14
7	14									

At the end of six weeks, there were 14 pints on hand.

REVIEW AND DISCUSSION QUESTIONS

1   Why is simulation often called a technique of last resort?
2   What roles does statistical hypothesis testing play in simulation?
3   What determines whether a simulation model is valid?
4   Must you use a computer to get good information from a simulation? Explain.
5   What methods are used to increment time in a simulation model? How do they work?
6   What are the pros and cons of starting a simulation with the system empty? With the system in equilibrium?
7   Distinguish between known mathematical distributions and empirical distributions. What information is needed to simulate using a known mathematical distribution?
8   What is the importance of run length in simulation? Is a run of 100 observations twice as valid as a run of 50? Explain.

PROBLEMS

1   CLASSROOM SIMULATION: FISH FORWARDERS
This is a competitive exercise designed to test players' skills at setting inventory ordering rules over a 10-week planning horizon. Maximum profit at the end determines the winner.

Fish Forwarders supplies fresh shrimp to a variety of customers in the New Orleans area. It orders cases of shrimp from fleet representatives at the beginning of each week to meet a demand from its customers at the middle of the week. Shrimp are subsequently delivered to Fish Forwarders and then, at the end of the week, to its customers.

Both the supply of shrimp and the demand for shrimp are uncertain. The supply may vary as much as ±10 percent from the amount ordered, and by contract, Fish Forwarders must purchase this supply. The probability associated with this variation is −10 percent, 30 percent of the time; 0 percent, 50 percent of the time; and +10 percent, 20 percent of the time. Weekly demand for shrimp is normally distributed with a mean of 800 cases and standard deviation of 100 cases.

A case of shrimp costs Fish Forwarders $30 and sells for $50. Any shrimp not sold at the end of the week are sold to a cat-food company at $4 per case. Fish Forwarders may, if it chooses, order the shrimp flash-frozen by the supplier at dockside, but this raises the cost of a case by $4 and, hence, costs Fish Forwarders $34 per case.

Procedure for play. The game requires that each week a decision be made as to how many cases to order of regular shrimp and of flash-frozen shrimp. The number ordered may be any amount. The instructor plays the role of referee and supplies the random numbers. The steps in playing the game are as follows:

a.   Decide on the order amount of regular shrimp or flash-frozen shrimp and enter the figures in column 3 of the worksheet. (See Exhibit TN17.12.) Assume that there is no opening inventory of flash-frozen shrimp.

Simulation Worksheet

(1)	(2)	(3) Orders placed		(4) Orders received		(5) Available (regular and flash-frozen)	(6) Demand (800 + 100Z)	(7) Sales (minimum of demand or available)	(8) Excess		(9) Shortages
Week	Flash-frozen inventory	Regular	Flash-frozen	Regular	Flash-frozen				Regular	Flash	
1											
2											
3											
4											
5											
6											
7		MARDI GRAS					*				
8											
9											
10											
Total											

*Flash-frozen only.

b. Determine the amount that arrives and enter it under "Orders received." To accomplish this, the referee draws a random number from a uniform random number table (such as that in Appendix B) and finds its associated level of variation from the following random number intervals: 00 to 29 = −10 percent, 30 to 79 = 0 percent, and 80 to 99 = +10 percent. If the random number is, say, 13, the amount of variation will be −10 percent. Thus, if you decide to order 1,000 regular cases of shrimp and 100 flash-frozen cases, the amount you would actually receive would be $1,000 − 0.10(1,000)$, or 900 regular cases, and $100 − 0.10(100)$, or 90 flash-frozen cases. (Note that the variation is the same for both regular and flash-frozen shrimp.) These amounts are then entered in column 4.

c. Add the amount of flash-frozen shrimp in inventory (if any) to the quantity of regular and flash-frozen shrimp just received and enter this amount in column 5. This would be 990, using the figures provided earlier.

d. Determine the demand for shrimp. To accomplish this, the referee draws a random normal deviate value from Exhibit TN17.3 or Appendix C and enters it into the equation at the top of column 6. Thus, if the deviate value is −1.76, demand for the week is $800 + 100(−1.76)$, or 624.

e. Determine the amount sold. This will be the lesser of the amount demanded (column 6) and the amount available (column 5). Thus, if a player has received 990 and demand is 624, the quantity entered will be 624 (with $990 − 624$, or 366 left over).

f. Determine the excess. The amount of excess is simply that quantity remaining after demand for a given week is filled. Always assume that regular shrimp are sold before the flash-frozen. Thus, if we use the 366 figure obtained in *e*, the excess would include all the original 90 cases of flash-frozen shrimp.

g. Determine shortages. This is simply the amount of unsatisfied demand each period, and it occurs only when demand is greater than sales. (Because all customers use the shrimp within the week in which they are delivered, backorders are not relevant.) The amount of shortage (in cases of shrimp) is entered in column 9.

Profit determination. Exhibit TN17.13 is provided for determining the profit achieved at the end of play. The values to be entered in the table are obtained by summing the relevant columns of Exhibit TN17.12 and making the calculations.

Assignment. Simulate operations for a total of 10 weeks. It is suggested that a 10-minute break be taken at the end of Week 5, allowing the players to evaluate how they may improve their performance. They might also wish to plan an ordering strategy for the week of Mardi Gras, when no shrimp will be supplied.

Profit from Fish Forwarders' Operations

Revenue from sales ($50 × Col. 7)	$_____
Revenue from salvage ($4 × Col. 8 reg.)	$_____
Total revenue	$_____
Cost of regular purchases ($30 × Col. 4 reg.)	$_____
Cost of flash-frozen purchases ($34 × Col. 4 flash)	$_____
Cost of holding flash-frozen shrimp ($2 × Col. 8 flash)	$_____
Cost of shortages ($20 × Col. 9)	$_____
Total cost	$_____
Profit	$_____

2 The manager of a small post office is concerned that the growing township is overloading the one-window service being offered. Sample data are collected on 100 individuals who arrive for service:

TIME BETWEEN ARRIVALS (MINUTES)	FREQUENCY		SERVICE TIME (MINUTES)	FREQUENCY
1	8		1.0	12
2	35		1.5	21
3	34		2.0	36
4	17		2.5	19
5	6		3.0	7
	100		3.5	5
				100

Using the following random number sequence, simulate six arrivals; estimate the average customer waiting time and the average idle time for clerks.

RN: 08, 74, 24, 34, 45, 86, 31, 32, 45, 21, 10, 67, 60, 17, 60, 87, 74, 96

3 Thomas Magnus, a private investigator, has been contacted by a potential client in Kamalo, Molokai. The call came just in time because Magnus is down to his last $10. Employment, however, is conditional on Magnus's meeting the client at Kamalo within eight hours. Magnus, presently at the Masters' residence in Kipahulu, Maui, has three alternative ways to get to Kamalo. Magnus may

a. Drive to the native village of Honokahua and take an outrigger to Kamalo.
b. Drive to Honokahua and swim the 10 miles across Pailolo Channel to Kamalo.
c. Drive to Hana and ask his friend T. C. to fly him by helicopter to Kamalo.

If option *a* is chosen, driving times to Honokahua are given in Distribution 1. Once at Honokahua, Magnus must negotiate with the friendly Tai natives. Negotiations always include a few Mai Tais, so if Magnus begins to negotiate, swimming becomes impossible. Negotiations center on how much each of the three outrigger crew members will be paid. Negotiation time, crew pay, and outrigger travel time are in Distributions 3, 4, and 5, respectively. You may assume each crew member is paid the same amount. If crew pay totals more than $10, Magnus is out of luck—trip time may then be taken to be infinity.

If option *b* is chosen, driving times to Honokahua and swimming times are given in Distributions 1 and 6.

If option *c* is chosen, driving times to Hana are given in Distribution 2. T. C., however, is at the airport only 10 percent of the time. If T. C. is not at the airport, Magnus will wait for him to arrive. Magnus's waiting time is given by Distribution 8. T. C. may refuse to fly for the $10 Magnus has available; Magnus puts the probability of T. C. refusing to fly for $10 at 30 percent. You may assume negotiation time is zero. If T. C. refuses, Magnus will drive to Honokahua via Kipahulu and swim to Kamalo. Helicopter flying times are given in Distribution 7.

Simulate each of the three alternative transportation plans *twice* and, based on your simulation results, calculate the average trip time for each plan. Use the following random numbers in the order they appear; do not skip any random numbers.

RN: 7, 3, 0, 4, 0, 5, 3, 5, 6, 1, 6, 6, 4, 8, 4, 9, 0, 7, 7, 1, 7, 0, 6, 8, 8, 7, 9, 0, 1, 2, 9, 7, 3, 2, 3, 8, 6, 0, 6, 0, 5, 9, 7, 9, 6, 4, 7, 2, 8, 7, 8, 1, 7, 0, 5

DISTRIBUTION 1: TIME TO DRIVE FROM KIPAHULU TO HONOKAHUA (HOURS)

TIME	PROBABILITY	RN
1	.2	0–1
1.5	.6	2–7
2	.2	8–9

DISTRIBUTION 2: TIME TO DRIVE FROM KIPAHULU TO HANA AND VICE VERSA (HOURS)

TIME	PROBABILITY	RN
.5	.2	0–1
1	.7	2–8
1.5	.1	9

DISTRIBUTION 3: NEGOTIATION TIME (HOURS)

TIME	PROBABILITY	RN
1	.2	0–1
1.5	.3	2–4
2	.3	5–7
2.5	.2	8–9

DISTRIBUTION 4: OUTRIGGER PAY PER CREW MEMBER

PAY	PROBABILITY	RN
$2	.3	0–2
3	.3	3–5
4	.4	6–9

DISTRIBUTION 5: OUTRIGGER TRAVEL TIME FROM HONOKAHUA TO KAMALO (HOURS)

TIME	PROBABILITY	RN
3	.1	0
4	.5	1–5
5	.4	6–9

DISTRIBUTION 6: TIME TO SWIM FROM HONOKAHUA TO KAMALO (HOURS)

TIME	PROBABILITY	RN
5	.2	0–1
6	.6	2–7
7	.2	8–9

DISTRIBUTION 7: TIME TO FLY FROM HANA TO KAMALO (HOURS)

TIME	PROBABILITY	RN
1	.1	0
1.5	.7	1–7
2	.2	8–9

DISTRIBUTION 8: MAGNUS'S WAITING TIME AT AIRPORT (HOURS)

TIME	PROBABILITY	RN
1	.1	0
2	.2	1–2
3	.4	3–6
4	.3	7–9

4   A bank of machines in a manufacturing shop breaks down according to the following interarrival time distribution. The time it takes one repairperson to complete the repair of a machine is given

in the service time distribution:

INTERARRIVAL TIME (HOURS)	P(X)	RN		SERVICE TIME (HOURS)	P(X)	RN
.5	.30	0–29		.5	.25	0–24
1.0	.22	30–51		1.0	.20	25–44
1.5	.16	52–67		2.0	.25	45–69
2.0	.10	68–77		3.0	.15	70–84
3.0	.14	78–91		4.0	.10	85–94
4.0	.08	92–99		5.0	.05	95–99
	1.00				1.00	

Simulate the breakdown of five machines. Calculate the average machine downtime using two repairpersons and the following random number sequence. (Both repairpersons cannot work on the same machine.)

RN: 30, 81, 02, 91, 51, 08, 28, 44, 86, 84, 29, 08, 37, 34, 99

5   Jennifer Jones owns a small candy store she operates herself. A study was made observing the time between customers coming into the store and the time that Jones took to serve them. The following data were collected from 100 customers observed:

INTERARRIVAL TIME (MINUTES)	NUMBER OF OBSERVATIONS		SERVICE TIME (MINUTES)	NUMBER OF OBSERVATIONS
1	5		1	10
2	10		2	15
3	10		3	15
4	15		4	20
5	15		5	15
6	20		6	10
7	10		7	8
8	8		8	4
9	5		9	2
10	2		10	1

Simulate the system (all of the arrivals and services) until 10 customers pass through the system and are serviced.

How long does the average customer spend in the system? Use Appendix B to obtain random numbers.

6   A professional football coach has six running backs on his squad. He wants to evaluate how injuries might affect his stock of running backs. A minor injury causes a player to be removed from the game and miss only the next game. A major injury puts the player out of action for the rest of the season. The probability of a major injury in a game is 0.05. There is at most one major injury per game. The probability distribution of minor injuries per game is

NUMBER OF INJURIES	PROBABILITY
0	.2
1	.5
2	.22
3	.05
4	.025
5	.005
	1.000

Injuries seem to happen in a completely random manner, with no discernible pattern over the season. A season is 10 games.

Using the following random numbers, simulate the fluctuations in the coach's stock of running backs over the season. Assume that he hires no additional running backs during the season.

RN: 044, 392, 898, 615, 986, 959, 558, 353, 577, 866, 305, 813, 024, 189, 878, 023, 285, 442, 862, 848, 060, 131, 963, 874, 805, 105, 452

7   At Tucson Mills, minor breakdowns of machines occur frequently. The occurrence of break-downs and the service time to fix the machines are randomly distributed. Management is concerned with minimizing the cost of breakdowns. The cost per hour for the machines to be down is $40. The cost of service repairpersons is $12 per hour. A preliminary study has produced the following data on times between successive breakdowns and their service times:

RELATIVE FREQUENCY OF BREAKDOWNS

Time between breakdowns (in minutes)	4	5	6	7	8	9
Relative frequency	.10	.30	.25	.20	.10	.05

RELATIVE FREQUENCY OF SERVICE TIMES

Service time (in minutes)	4	5	6	7	8	9
Relative frequency	.10	.40	.20	.15	.10	.05

Simulate 30 breakdowns under two conditions: with one service repairperson and with two service repairpersons.

Use the following random number sequence to determine time between breakdowns:

RN: 85, 16, 65, 76, 93, 99, 65, 70, 58, 44, 02, 85, 01, 97, 63, 52, 53, 11, 62, 28, 84, 82, 27, 20, 39, 70, 26, 21, 41, 81

Use the following random number sequence to determine service times:

RN: 68, 26, 85, 11, 16, 26, 95, 67, 97, 73, 75, 64, 26, 45, 01, 87, 20, 01, 19, 36, 69, 89, 81, 81, 02, 05, 10, 51, 24, 36

a. Using the results of the simulations, calculate
  (1) The total idle time for the service repairpersons under each condition.
  (2) The total delay caused by waiting for a service repairperson to begin working on a breakdown.
b. Determine the lowest-cost approach.

8   Jethro's service station has one gasoline pump. Because everyone in Kornfield County drives big cars, there is room at the station for only three cars, including the car at the pump. Cars arriving when three cars are already at the station drive on to another station. Use the following probability distributions to simulate the arrival of four cars to Jethro's station:

INTERARRIVAL TIME (MINUTES)	P(X)	RN	SERVICE TIME (MINUTES)	P(X)	RN
10	.40	0–39	5	.45	0–44
20	.35	40–74	10	.30	45–74
30	.20	75–94	15	.20	75–94
40	.05	95–99	20	.05	95–99

Use the following random numbers sequence:

RN: 99, 00, 73, 09, 38, 53, 72, 91

How many cars go to another station? What is the average time a car spends at the station?

9 You have been hired as a consultant by a supermarket chain to answer a basic question: How many items per customer should be permitted in the fast checkout line? This is no trivial question for the chain's management; your findings will be the basis for corporate policy for all 2,000 stores. The vice president of operations has given you one month to do the study and two assistants to help you gather the data.

In starting this study, you decide to avoid queuing theory as the tool for analysis (because of your concern about the reliability of its assumptions) and instead opt for simulation. Given the following data, explain in detail how you would go about your analysis stating (1) the criteria you would use in making your recommendation, (2) what additional data you would need to set up your simulation, (3) how you would gather the preliminary data, (4) how you would set up the problem for simulation, and (5) which factors would affect the applicability of your findings to all of the stores.

Store locations	The United States and Canada
Hours of operation	16 per day
Average store size	9 checkout stands including fast checkout
Available checkers	7 to 10 (some engage in stocking activities when not at a checkout stand)

10 The saga of Joe from Chapter 17 (Problem 13, page 687) continues. Joe has the opportunity to do a big repair job for a local motorcycle club. (Their cycles were accidentally run over by a garbage truck.) The compensation for the job is good, but it is vital that the total repair time for the five cycles be less than 40 hours. (The leader of the club has stated that he would be very distressed if the cycles were not available for a planned rally.) Joe knows from experience that repairs of this type often entail several trips between processes for a given cycle, so estimates of time are difficult to provide. Still, Joe has the following historical data about the probability that a job will start in each process, processing time in each process, and transitional probabilities between each pair of processes:

Process	Probability of Job Starting in Process	Processing Time Probability (Hours)			Probability of Going from Process to Other Processes or Completion (Out)			
		1	2	3	Frame	Engine Work	Painting	Out
Frame repair	0.5	0.2	0.4	0.4	—	0.4	0.4	0.2
Engine work	0.3	0.6	0.1	0.3	0.3	—	0.4	0.3
Painting	0.2	0.3	0.3	0.4	0.1	0.1	—	0.8

Given this information, use simulation to determine the repair times for each cycle. Display your results on a Gantt chart showing an FCFS schedule. (Assume that only one cycle can be worked on at a time in each process.) Based on your simulation, what do you recommend Joe do next?

11 "Eat at Helen's" has decided to add a drive-up window to the restaurant. Due to limited capital, there is enough space for only two cars in the drive-up window lane (one being served and one waiting). Helen would like to know how many customers are bypassing her restaurant due to the limited space in the drive-up window lane. Simulate 10 cars as they attempt to use the drive-up window using the following distributions and random numbers:

Time between Arrivals (Minutes)	Probability	Service Time (Minutes)	Probability
1	0.40	1	0.20
2	0.30	2	0.40
3	0.15	3	0.40
4	0.15		

Use the following two-digit random numbers for this problem:

Arrivals: 37, 60, 79, 21, 85, 71, 48, 39, 31, 35
Service: 66, 74, 90, 95, 29, 72, 17, 55, 15, 36

12   Jane's Auto World has a policy of placing an order for 27 of the most popular model whenever inventory reaches 20. Lead time on delivery is two weeks, and 25 automobiles are currently on hand. Simulate 15 weeks' worth of sales using the following probabilities that were derived from historical information:

SALES PER WEEK	PROBABILITY	SALES PER WEEK	PROBABILITY
5	.05	10	.20
6	.05	11	.20
7	.10	12	.10
8	.10	13	.05
9	.10	14	.05

Use the following random numbers for sales: 23, 59, 82, 83, 61, 00, 48, 33, 06, 32, 82, 51, 54, 66, 55.

Does this policy appear to be appropriate? Explain.

ADVANCED CASE: UNDERSTANDING THE IMPACT OF VARIABILITY ON THE CAPACITY OF A PRODUCTION SYSTEM

Excel: LinesSim.xls

This exercise, which uses LineSim.xls, is an opportunity to study the impact that variability in processing time has on the capacity of a simple serial production system. Much more complex systems could be studied, but our hope is that by studying this simple system, you will gain insight that can be applied to more complex systems.

The system we are studying is similar to the two-stage assembly line discussed in this technical note; here we look at a three-stage assembly line. In practice, assembly lines have many more workstations, but completing an exercise with more workstations would take considerably longer. If you do not believe that your results can be generalized to a larger system, feel free to expand your study.

For this study we use the Serial Line Simulator (LineSim.xls) that is included on this book's DVD-ROM. This Microsoft Excel® spreadsheet simulates a simple serial production line. We are indebted to John McClain at the Johnson Graduate School of Management, Cornell University, for allowing us to use his innovative spreadsheet.

GOAL OF THIS EXERCISE

Our goal in this exercise is that you learn firsthand how variability can impact the performance of multistage production systems. A common approach used to reduce the impact of variability is through some type of buffering mechanism. To be more specific, in our system variability exists in the amount of time that it takes to perform work at a workstation. In analyzing the system we use the average time to complete each unit, so sometimes it takes longer and sometimes less time. It probably seldom takes exactly the average time.

When there is variability, production engineers put buffer stations between each workstation. These buffers allow the variability to be smoothed so that the variability in one workstation has less impact on the other workstations. An interesting question to study with simulation is if these buffers are eliminated, or if there are 100 units between each workstation, how would this change the performance of the system?

DETAILS OF THE EXERCISE

Start with the spreadsheet as Professor McClain configures it initially. Click the "Design" tab, and note that we have a three-station assembly line. The stations are named "Joe," "Next's," and "M2." There is a buffer area downstream from "Joe" with a capacity of one unit, and another downstream from "Next's" with a capacity of one unit. The way this simulation is designed, "Joe" will always have something to work on, and "M2" can always deposit finished work in a storage area.

Notice that the processing time distribution is Shifted Exponential with a mean of 5 and a standard deviation of 5. The shape of this distribution, described in the "Instructions" tab, shows that there is much process time variation. Answer the following question before going on to the next part of the exercise:

Question 1: How many units would you expect to be able to produce over 100 time periods?

Click the "Run" tab and, using the default values for "Run-In Time," "Run Length," and "Repetitions," run the simulation. Tabulate the average utilization at each machine based on the five repetitions, and tabulate the mean and standard deviation of the output of the system (these data are in the "Machine" worksheet).

Question 2: How many units did you actually produce per 100 time periods? Explain any difference between your simulation result and your estimate made in Question 1.

Next map the impact that increased buffer inventory has on the output of the system. You can change the buffer behind "Joe" and "Next" by changing the inventory cell designated "Joe's Inventory" (this is on the "Design" worksheet) and then clicking "Make Storage Areas Like #1."

Question 3: Create a graph that shows the impact of changing the buffer stock on the output of the system. Consider buffer levels that vary from 0 to a maximum of 20 units. What can you conclude from your experiment?

Finally, experiment with the impact of a bottleneck in the system.

Question 4: What would be the impact on system performance if "M2" had a processing time that averaged 6 time units? (Assume that "Joe" and "Next" still run at an average

of 5.) What happens to the inventory after "Joe" and "Next"? Does varying the size of these inventories have any impact?

Question 5: What happens if instead of "M2" being the bottleneck, "Joe" is the bottleneck? Do the buffers at "Joe" and "Next" have any impact?

Keep your answers brief; your entire report, including graphs, should be no longer than two double-spaced pages.

SELECTED BIBLIOGRAPHY

Evans, J. R., and D. L. Olson. *Introduction to Simulation and Risk Analysis.* Upper Saddle River, NJ: Prentice Hall, 1998.

Harrington, H. J., and K. Tumay. *Simulation Modeling Methods.* New York: McGraw-Hill, 1999.

Kelton, W. D.; R. P. Sadowski; and D. J. Sturvock. *Simulation with Arena.* New York: McGraw-Hill, 2003.

Law, A. M., and W. D. Kelton. *Simulation Modeling and Analysis.* New York: McGraw-Hill, 2000.

Pritsker, A. A. *Introduction to Simulation and SLAM II.* New York: Wiley, 1995.

Winston, W. L. *Simulation Modeling Using @RISK.* Belmont, CA: Wadsworth, 2000.

FOOTNOTES

1 The basic formula is $Z = \frac{x-\mu}{\sigma}$, which when restated in terms of x appears as $x = \mu + Z\sigma$. We then substituted D_n for x and $\bar{x}$ for μ to relate the method more directly to the sample problem.

2 See W. L. Winston, *Simulation Modeling Using @RISK* (Belmont, CA: Wadsworth, 2000). @RISK is a product of Palisade Corporation (http://www.palisade.com).

3 S. W. Haider and J. Banks, "Simulation Software Products for Analyzing Manufacturing Systems," *Industrial Engineering* 18, no. 7 (July 1986), pp. 98–103.

chapter

SYNCHRONOUS MANUFACTURING AND THEORY OF CONSTRAINTS

18

Scene: Alex Rogo is the plant manager at the Barrington Plant of UniWare, a Division of UniCo. He has had a lot of trouble with his plant in keeping schedules, reducing inventory, improving quality, and cutting costs, among other problems. Bill Peach, division vice president, just visited him and gave him three months to improve, or else the plant will be closed.

Alex's son Dave and his Boy Scout troop are taking a 20-mile overnight hike (10 miles to Devil's Gulch where they will camp for the night, returning the following morning). Alex had been coaxed by his wife and son to accompany the troop. They are now on the hike and way behind schedule. The line of scouts is spread way out with the fastest kids in front; Herbie, the slowest, lags way

behind in the rear. Alex is trying to figure out how he can make the Boy Scouts stay together and move faster.

Up front, you've got Andy, who wants to set a speed record. And here you are stuck behind Fat Herbie, the slowest kid in the woods. After an hour, the kid in front—if he's really moving at three miles per hour—is going to be two miles ahead, which means you're going to have to run two miles to catch up with him.

Alex is thinking, "If this were my plant, Peach wouldn't even give me three months. I'd already be on the street by now. The demand was for us to cover 10 miles in five hours, and we've only done half of that. Inventory is racing out of sight. The carrying costs on that inventory would be rising. We'd be ruining the company."

"Okay," I say. "Everybody join hands."

They all look at each other.

"Come on! Just do it!" I tell them. "And don't let go."

Then I take Herbie by the hand and, as if I'm dragging a chain, I go up the trail, snaking past the entire line. Hand in hand, the rest of the troop follows.

Source: E. M. Goldratt and J. Cox, *The Goal: A Process of Ongoing Improvement*, 2nd rev. ed. (Great Barrington, MA: North River Press, 1992), pp. 114–18.

I pass Andy and keep walking. When I'm twice the distance of the lineup, I stop. What I've done is turn the entire troop around so that the boys have exactly the opposite order they had before.

"Now listen up!" I say. "This is the order you're going to stay in until we reach where we're going. Understood? Nobody passes anybody.

"The idea of this hike is not to see who can get there the fastest. The idea is to get there together. We're not a bunch of individuals out here. We're a team."

So we start off again. And it works. No kidding. Everybody stays together behind Herbie. I've gone to the back of the line so I can keep tabs, and I keep waiting for the gaps to appear, but they don't.

"Mr. Rogo, can't we put somebody faster up front?" asks a kid ahead of me.

"Listen, if you guys want to go faster, then you have to figure out a way to let Herbie go faster," I tell them.

One of the kids in the rear says, "Hey, Herbie, what have you got in your pack?"

Herbie stops and turns around. I tell him to come to the back of the line and take off his pack. As he does, I take the pack from him—and nearly drop it.

"Herbie, this thing weighs a ton," I say. "What have you got in here?"

"Nothing much," says Herbie.

I open it up and reach in. Out comes a six-pack of soda. Next are some cans of spaghetti. Then come a box of candy bars, a jar of pickles, and two cans of tuna fish. Beneath a raincoat and rubber boots and a bag of tent stakes, I pull out a large iron skillet.

"Herbie, look, you've done a great job of lugging this stuff so far. But we have to make you able to move faster," I say. "If we take some of the load off you, you'll be able to do a better job at the front of the line."

Herbie finally seems to understand.

Again we start walking. But this time, Herbie can really move. Relieved of most of the weight in his pack, it's as if he's walking on air. We're flying now, doing twice the speed as a troop that we did before. And we still stay together. Inventory is down. Throughput is up.

Dave and I share the same tent that night. We're lying inside it, both of us tired. Dave is quiet for a while. Then he speaks up.

He says, "You know, Dad, I was really proud of you today."

"You were? How come?"

"The way you figured out what was going on and kept everyone together, and put Herbie in front."

"Thanks," I tell him. "Actually, I learned a lot of things today."

"You did?"

"Yeah, stuff that I think is going to help me straighten out the plant," I say.

"Really? Like what?"

"Are you sure you want to hear about it?"

"Sure I am," he claims.

This is the beginning of Alex's successful turnaround of his plant—applying simple principles to the plant's operation. →

The story of Herbie is an analogy to the problems facing plant manager Alex Rogo and comes from a best-selling novel, *The Goal,* by Dr. Eli Goldratt.[1] Around 1980, Goldratt contended that manufacturers were not doing a good job in scheduling and in controlling their resources and inventories. To solve this problem, Goldratt and his associates at a company named Creative Output developed software that scheduled jobs through manufacturing processes, taking into account limited facilities, machines, personnel, tools, materials, and any other constraints that would affect a firm's ability to adhere to a schedule.

This was called *optimized production technology (OPT)*. The schedules were feasible and accurate and could be run on a computer in a fraction of the time needed by an MRP system. This was because the scheduling logic was based on the separation of bottleneck and nonbottleneck operations. To explain the principles behind the OPT scheduling logic, Goldratt described nine production scheduling rules (see Exhibit 18.1). After approximately 100 large firms had installed this software, Goldratt went on to promote the logic of the approach rather than the software.

In broadening his scope, Goldratt has developed his "Theory of Constraints" (TOC), which has become popular as a problem-solving approach that can be applied to many business areas. Exhibit 18.2 lists the "Five Focusing Steps of TOC." His Goldratt Institute (http://www.goldratt.com) teaches courses in improving production, distribution, and project management. The common thread through all of these courses is Goldratt's TOC concepts.

In this chapter we focus on Goldratt's approach to manufacturing. To correctly treat the topic, we decided to approach it in the same way that Goldratt did: that is, first defining some basic issues about firms—purposes, goals, and performance measures—and then dealing with scheduling, providing buffer inventories, the influences of quality, and the interactions with marketing and accounting.

Underlying Goldratt's work is the notion of **synchronous manufacturing**, which refers to the entire production process working in harmony to achieve the profit goal of the firm.

Synchronous manufacturing

Goldratt's Rules of Production Scheduling

exhibit 18.1

1 Do not balance capacity—balance the flow.
2 The level of utilization of a nonbottleneck resource is determined not by its own potential but by some other constraint in the system.
3 Utilization and activation of a resource are not the same.
4 An hour lost at a bottleneck is an hour lost for the entire system.
5 An hour saved at a nonbottleneck is a mirage.
6 Bottlenecks govern both throughput and inventory in the system.
7 The transfer batch may not and many times should not be equal to the process batch.
8 A process batch should be variable both along its route and in time.
9 Priorities can be set only by examining the system's constraints. Lead time is a derivative of the schedule.

Goldratt's Theory of Constraints (TOC)

exhibit 18.2

1 Identify the system constraints. (No improvement is possible unless the constraint or weakest link is found.)
2 Decide how to exploit the system constraints. (Make the constraints as effective as possible.)
3 Subordinate everything else to that decision. (Align every other part of the system to support the constraints even if this reduces the efficiency of nonconstraint resources.)
4 Elevate the system constraints. (If output is still inadequate, acquire more of this resource so it no longer is a constraint.)
5 If, in the previous steps, the constraints have been broken, go back to Step 1, but do not let inertia become the system constraint. (After this constraint problem is solved, go back to the beginning and start over. This is a continuous process of improvement: identifying constraints, breaking them, and then identifying the new ones that result.)

When manufacturing is truly synchronized, its emphasis is on total system performance, not on localized measures such as labor or machine utilization.

GOAL OF THE FIRM

⌖⌖⌖◯ Goldratt has a very straightforward idea of the goal of a firm:

THE GOAL OF A FIRM IS TO MAKE MONEY.

Goldratt argues that although an organization may have many purposes—providing jobs, consuming raw materials, increasing sales, increasing share of the market, developing technology, or producing high-quality products—these do not guarantee long-term survival of the firm. They are means to achieve the goal, not the goal itself. If the firm makes money—and only then—it will prosper. When a firm has money, it can place more emphasis on other objectives.

PERFORMANCE MEASUREMENTS

⌖⌖⌖◯ To adequately measure a firm's performance, two sets of measurements must be used: one from the financial point of view and the other from the operations point of view.

Cross Functional

FINANCIAL MEASUREMENTS

We have three measures of the firm's ability to make money:

1. *Net profit*—an absolute measurement in dollars.
2. *Return on investment*—a relative measure based on investment.
3. *Cash flow*—a survival measurement.

All three measurements must be used together. For example, a *net profit* of $10 million is important as one measurement, but it has no real meaning until we know how much investment it took to generate that $10 million. If the investment was $100 million, this is a 10 percent *return on investment. Cash flow* is important because cash is necessary to pay bills for day-to-day operations; without cash, a firm can go bankrupt even though it is very sound in normal accounting terms. A firm can have a high profit and a high return on investment but still be short on cash if, for example, profit is invested in new equipment or tied up in inventory.

OPERATIONAL MEASUREMENTS

Financial measurements work well at the higher level, but they cannot be used at the operational level. We need another set of measurements that will give us guidance:

Throughput

Inventory

Operating expenses

1. **Throughput**—the rate at which money is generated by the system through sales.
2. **Inventory**—all the money that the system has invested in purchasing things it intends to sell.
3. **Operating expenses**—all the money that the system spends to turn inventory into throughput.

Throughput is specifically defined as goods *sold.* An inventory of finished goods is not throughput, but inventory. Actual sales must occur. It is specifically defined this way to prevent the system from continuing to produce under the illusion that the goods *might* be sold. Such action simply increases costs, builds inventory, and consumes cash. Inventory that is carried (whether work-in-process or finished goods) is valued only at the cost of the

Operational Goal

exhibit 18.3

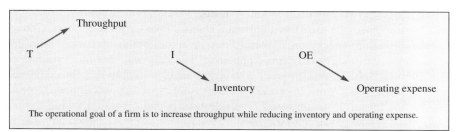

The operational goal of a firm is to increase throughput while reducing inventory and operating expense.

materials it contains. Labor cost and machine hours are ignored. (In traditional accounting terms, money spent is called *value added.*)

Although this is often an arguable point, using only the raw material cost is a conservative view. When the value-added method (which includes all costs of production) is used, inventory is inflated and presents some serious income and balance sheet problems. Consider, for example, work-in-process or finished-goods inventory that has become obsolete, or for which a contract was canceled. It is a difficult management decision to declare large amounts of inventory as scrap because it is often carried on the books as an asset even though it may really have no value. Using just raw materials cost also avoids the problem of determining which costs are direct and which are indirect.

Operating expenses include production costs (such as direct labor, indirect labor, inventory carrying costs, equipment depreciation, and materials and supplies used in production) and administrative costs. The key difference here is that there is no need to separate direct and indirect labor.

As shown in Exhibit 18.3, the objective of a firm is to treat all three measurements simultaneously and continually; this achieves the goal of making money.

From an operations standpoint, the goal of the firm is to

> INCREASE THROUGHPUT WHILE SIMULTANEOUSLY REDUCING INVENTORY AND REDUCING OPERATING EXPENSE.

PRODUCTIVITY

Typically, **productivity** is measured in terms of output per labor hour. However, this measurement does not ensure that the firm will make money (for example, when extra output is not sold but accumulates as inventory). To test whether productivity has increased, we should ask these questions: Has the action taken increased throughput? Has it decreased inventory? Has it decreased operational expense? This leads us to a new definition:

Productivity

> PRODUCTIVITY IS ALL THE ACTIONS THAT BRING A COMPANY CLOSER TO ITS GOALS.

UNBALANCED CAPACITY

Historically (and still typically in most firms) manufacturers have tried to balance capacity across a sequence of processes in an attempt to match capacity with market demand. However, this is the wrong thing to do—*unbalanced capacity* is better. The vignette at the beginning of this chapter is an example of unbalanced capacity. Some Boy Scouts were fast walkers, whereas Herbie was very slow. The challenge is to use this difference advantageously.

Consider a simple process line with several stations, for example. Once the output rate of the line has been established, production people try to make the capacities of all stations the same. This is done by adjusting machines or equipment used, workloads, skill and type of labor assigned, tools used, overtime budgeted, and so on.

In synchronous manufacturing thinking, however, making all capacities the same is viewed as a bad decision. Such a balance would be possible only if the output times of all stations were constant or had a very narrow distribution. A normal variation in output times causes downstream stations to have idle time when upstream stations take longer to process. Conversely, when upstream stations process in a shorter time, inventory builds up between the stations. The effect of the statistical variation is cumulative. The only way that this variation can be smoothed is by increasing work-in-process to absorb the variation (a bad choice because we should be trying to reduce work-in-process) or increasing capacities downstream to be able to make up for the longer upstream times. The rule here is that capacities within the process sequence should not be balanced to the same levels. Rather, attempts should be made to balance the flow of product through the system. When flow is balanced, capacities are unbalanced. This idea is further explained in the next section.

DEPENDENT EVENTS AND STATISTICAL FLUCTUATIONS

The term *dependent events* refers to a process sequence. If a process flows from A to B to C to D, and each process must be completed before passing on to the next step, then B, C, and D are dependent events. The ability to do the next process is dependent on the preceding one.

Statistical fluctuation refers to the normal variation about a mean or average. When statistical fluctuations occur in a dependent sequence without any inventory between workstations, there is no opportunity to achieve the average output. When one process takes longer than the average, the next process cannot make up the time. We follow through an example of this to show what could happen.

Suppose that we wanted to process five items that could come from the two distributions in Exhibit 18.4. The processing sequence is from A to B with no space for inventory in between. Process A has a mean of 10 hours and a standard deviation of 2 hours. This means that we would expect 95.5 percent of the processing time to be between 6 hours and 14 hours (plus or minus 2 sigma). Process B has a constant processing time of 10 hours.

We see that the last item was completed in 66 hours, for an average of 13.2 hours per item, although the expected time of completion was 60, for an average of 12 hours per item (taking into account the waiting time for the first unit by Process B).

exhibit 18.4

Processing and Completion Times, Process A to Process B

ITEM NUMBER	START TIME	PROCESSING TIME	FINISH TIME	ITEM NUMBER	START TIME	PROCESSING TIME	FINISH TIME
1	0 hrs	14 hrs	14 hrs	1	14 hrs	10 hrs	24 hrs
2	14	12	26	2	26	10	36
3	26	10	36	3	36	10	46
4	36	8	44	4	46	10	56
5	44	6	50	5	56	10	66
	Average = 10 hours				Average = 10 hours		

Here the flow is from Process A to Process B. Process A has a mean of 10 hours and a standard deviation of 2 hours; Process B has a constant 10-hour processing time.

Processing and Completion Times, Process B to Process A   **exhibit 18.5**

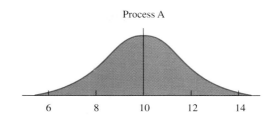

| | | PROCESSING | | | | | PROCESSING | |
ITEM NUMBER	START TIME	TIME	FINISH TIME	ITEM NUMBER	START TIME	TIME	FINISH TIME
1	o hrs	10 hrs	10 hrs	1	10 hrs	6 hrs	16 hrs
2	10	10	20	2	20	8	28
3	20	10	30	3	30	10	40
4	30	10	40	4	40	12	52
5	40	10	50	5	52	14	66
	Average = 10 hours				Average = 10 hours		

This is similar to Exhibit 18.4. However, the processing sequence has been reversed as well as the order of Process A's times.

Suppose we reverse the processes—B feeds A. To illustrate the possible delays, we also reverse A's performance times. (See Exhibit 18.5.) Again, the completion time of the last item is greater than the average (13.2 hours rather than 12 hours). Process A and Process B have the same average performance time of 10 hours, and yet performance is late. In neither case could we achieve the expected average output rate. Why? Because the time lost when the second process is idle cannot be made up.

This example is intended to challenge the theory that capacities should be balanced to an average time. *Rather than capacities being balanced, the flow of product through the system should be balanced.*

BOTTLENECKS AND CAPACITY-CONSTRAINED RESOURCES

A **bottleneck** is defined as any resource whose capacity is less than the demand placed upon it. A bottleneck is a constraint within the system that limits throughput. It is that point in the manufacturing process where flow thins to a narrow stream. A bottleneck may be a machine, scarce or highly skilled labor, or a specialized tool. Observations in industry have shown that most plants have very few bottleneck operations.

Bottleneck

If there is no bottleneck, then excess capacity exists and the system should be changed to create a bottleneck (such as more setups or reduced capacity), which we will discuss later.

Capacity is defined as the available time for production. This excludes maintenance and other downtime. A **nonbottleneck** is any resource whose capacity is greater than the demand placed on it. A nonbottleneck, therefore, should not be working constantly because it can produce more than is needed. A nonbottleneck contains idle time.

Nonbottleneck

A **capacity-constrained resource (CCR)** is one whose utilization is close to capacity and could be a bottleneck if it is not scheduled carefully. For example, a CCR may be receiving work in a job-shop environment from several sources. If these sources schedule their flow in a way that causes occasional idle time for the CCR in excess of its unused capacity time, the CCR becomes a bottleneck when the surge of work arrives at a later time. This can happen if batch sizes are changed or if one of the upstream operations is not working for some reason and does not feed enough work to the CCR.

Capacity-constrained resource (CCR)

BASIC MANUFACTURING BUILDING BLOCKS

All manufacturing processes and flows can be simplified to four basic configurations, as shown in Exhibit 18.6. In Exhibit 18.6A, product that flows through Process X feeds into Process Y. In B, Y is feeding X. In C, Process X and Process Y are creating subassemblies, which are then combined, say, to feed the market demand. In D, Process X and Process Y are independent of each other and are supplying their own markets. The last column in the exhibit shows possible sequences of nonbottleneck resources, which can be grouped and displayed as Y to simplify the representation.

The value in using these basic building blocks is that a production process can be greatly simplified for analysis and control. Rather than track and schedule all of the steps in a production sequence through nonbottleneck operations, for example, attention can be placed at the beginning and end points of the building block groupings.

---

exhibit 18.6   The Basic Building Blocks of Manufacturing Derived by Grouping Process Flows

DESCRIPTION	BASIC BUILDING BLOCKS SIMPLIFIED BY GROUPING NONBOTTLENECKS	ORIGINAL REPRESENTATION
A. Bottleneck feeding nonbottleneck	X ⟶ Y ⟶ Market	(Y) X ⟶ A ⟶ B ⟶ C ⟶ D ⟶ Market
B. Nonbottleneck feeding bottleneck	Y ⟶ X ⟶ Market	(Y) A ⟶ B ⟶ C ⟶ D ⟶ X ⟶ Market
C. Output of bottleneck and nonbottleneck assembled into a product	X ⟶ Final Assembly ⟶ Market, Y ⟶	X ⟶ Final Assembly ⟶ Market, (Y) A ⟶ B ⟶ C ⟶ D ⟶
D. Bottleneck and nonbottleneck have independent markets for their output	X ⟶ Market, Y ⟶ Market	(Y) A ⟶ B ⟶ C ⟶ D, X ⟶ Market, Market

X is a bottleneck.
Y is a nonbottleneck (has excess capacity).

METHODS FOR CONTROL

Exhibit 18.7 shows how bottleneck and nonbottleneck resources should be managed.

Resource X and Resource Y are work centers that can produce a variety of products. Each of these work centers has 200 hours available per month. For simplicity, assume that we are dealing with only one product and we will alter the conditions and makeup for four different situations. Each unit of X takes one hour of production time and the market demand is 200 units per month. Each unit of Y takes 45 minutes of production time and the market demand is also 200 units per month.

Exhibit 18.7A shows a bottleneck feeding a nonbottleneck. Product flows from Work Center X to Work Center Y. X is the bottleneck because it has a capacity of 200 units (200 hours/1 hour per unit) and Y has a capacity of 267 units (200 hours/45 minutes per unit). Because Y has to wait for X and Y has a higher capacity than X, no extra product accumulates in the system. It all flows through to the market.

Exhibit 18.7B is the reverse of A, with Y feeding X. This is a nonbottleneck feeding a bottleneck. Because Y has a capacity of 267 units and X has a capacity of only 200 units, we should produce only 200 units of Y (75 percent of capacity) or else work-in-process will accumulate in front of X.

Exhibit 18.7C shows that the products produced by X and Y are assembled and then sold to the market. Because one unit from X and one unit from Y form an assembly, X is the bottleneck with 200 units of capacity and, therefore, Y should not work more than 75 percent or else extra parts will accumulate.

In Exhibit 18.7D, equal quantities of product from X and Y are demanded by the market. In this case we can call these products "finished goods" because they face independent demands. Here Y has access to material independent of X and, with a higher capacity than needed to satisfy the market, it can produce more product than the market will take. However, this would create an inventory of unneeded finished goods.

Product Flow through Bottlenecks and Nonbottlenecks

exhibit 18.7

A.

X → Y → Market

200 units of product (200 hours)   200 units of product (150 hours)

$$X \text{ used } \frac{200}{200} = 100\%$$

$$Y \text{ used } \frac{150}{200} = 75\%$$

B. | WIP |

Y → X → Market

Y can be used only 75% of the time or work-in-process will build up.

C. Market

Assembly | Spare parts |

X   Y

Y can be used only 75% of the time or spare parts will accumulate.

D. Market   Market

| FG |

X   Y

Y can be used only 75% of the time or finished goods inventory will build up.

X is a bottleneck; Y is a nonbottleneck. Both X and Y have 200 hours available.

The four situations just discussed demonstrate bottleneck and nonbottleneck resources and their relationships to production and market demand. They show that the industry practice of using resource utilization as a measure of performance can encourage the overuse of nonbottlenecks and result in excess inventories.

TIME COMPONENTS

The following kinds of time make up production cycle time:

1. *Setup time*—the time that a part spends waiting for a resource to be set up to work on this same part.
2. *Processing time*—the time that the part is being processed.
3. *Queue time*—the time that a part waits for a resource while the resource is busy with something else.
4. *Wait time*—the time that a part waits not for a resource but for another part so that they can be assembled together.
5. *Idle time*—the unused time; that is, the cycle time less the sum of the setup time, processing time, queue time, and wait time.

For a part waiting to go through a bottleneck, queue time is the greatest. As we discuss later in this chapter, this is because the bottleneck has a fairly large amount of work to do in front of it (to make sure that it is always working). For a nonbottleneck, wait time is the greatest. The part is just sitting there waiting for the arrival of other parts so that an assembly can take place.

Schedulers are tempted to save setup times. Suppose that the batch sizes are doubled to save half the setup times. Then, with a double batch size, all of the other times (processing time, queue time, and wait time) increase twofold. Because these times are doubled while saving only half of the setup time, the net result is that the work-in-process is approximately doubled, as is the investment in inventory.

FINDING THE BOTTLENECK

There are two ways to find the bottleneck (or bottlenecks) in a system. One is to run a capacity resource profile; the other is to use our knowledge of the particular plant, look at the system in operation, and talk with supervisors and workers.

A capacity resource profile is obtained by looking at the loads placed on each resource by the products that are scheduled through them. In running a capacity profile, we assume that the data are reasonably accurate, although not necessarily perfect. As an example, consider that products have been routed through Resources M1 through M5. Suppose that our first computation of the resource loads on each resource caused by these products shows the following:

M1	130 percent of capacity
M2	120 percent of capacity
M3	105 percent of capacity
M4	95 percent of capacity
M5	85 percent of capacity

For this first analysis, we can disregard any resources at lower percentages because they are nonbottlenecks and should not be a problem. With this list in hand, we should physically go to the facility and check all five operations. Note that M1, M2, and M3 are overloaded; that is, they are scheduled above their capacities. We would expect to see large quantities of inventory in front of M1. If this is not the case, errors must exist somewhere—perhaps in the bill of materials or in the routing sheets. Let's say that our observations and discussions with shop personnel showed that there were errors in M1, M2, M3, and M4. We tracked them down, made the appropriate corrections, and ran the capacity profile again:

M2	115 percent of capacity
M1	110 percent of capacity
M3	105 percent of capacity
M4	90 percent of capacity
M5	85 percent of capacity

M1, M2, and M3 are still showing a lack of sufficient capacity, but M2 is the most serious. If we now have confidence in our numbers, we use M2 as our bottleneck. If the data contain too many errors for a reliable data analysis, it may not be worth spending time (it could take months) making all the corrections.

SAVING TIME

Recall that a bottleneck is a resource whose capacity is less than the demand placed on it. Because we focus on bottlenecks as restricting *throughput* (defined as *sales*), a bottleneck's capacity is less than the market demand. There are a number of ways we can save time on a bottleneck (better tooling, higher-quality labor, larger batch sizes, reduction in setup times, and so forth), but how valuable is the extra time? Very, very valuable!

> AN HOUR SAVED AT THE BOTTLENECK ADDS AN EXTRA HOUR TO THE ENTIRE PRODUCTION SYSTEM.

How about time saved on a nonbottleneck resource?

> AN HOUR SAVED AT A NONBOTTLENECK IS A MIRAGE AND ONLY ADDS AN HOUR TO ITS IDLE TIME.

Because a nonbottleneck has more capacity than the system needs for its current throughput, it already contains idle time. Implementing any measures to save more time does not increase throughput but only serves to increase its idle time.

AVOID CHANGING A NONBOTTLENECK INTO A BOTTLENECK

When nonbottleneck resources are scheduled with larger batch sizes, this action could create a bottleneck that we certainly would want to avoid. Consider the case in Exhibit 18.8, where Y_1, Y_2, and Y_3 are nonbottleneck resources. Y_1 currently produces Part A, which is routed to Y_3, and Part B, which is routed to Y_2. To produce Part A, Y_1 has a 200-minute setup time and a processing time of 1 minute per part. Part A is currently produced in batches of 500 units. To produce Part B, Y_1 has a setup time of 150 minutes and 2 minutes' processing time per part. Part B is currently produced in batches of 200 units. With this sequence, Y_2 is utilized 70 percent of the time and Y_3 is utilized 80 percent of the time.

Because setup time is 200 minutes for Y_1 on Part A, both worker and supervisor mistakenly believe that more production can be gained if fewer setups are made. Let's assume that the batch size is increased to 1,500 units and see what happens. The illusion is that we have saved 400 minutes of setup. (Instead of three setups taking 600 minutes to produce three batches of 500 units each, there is just one setup with a 1,500-unit batch.)

The problem is that the 400 minutes saved served no purpose, but this delay did interfere with the production of Part B because Y_1 produces Part B for Y_2. The sequence before any changes were made was Part A (700 minutes), Part B (550 minutes), Part A (700 minutes), Part B (550 minutes), and so on. Now, however, when the Part A batch is increased to

exhibit 18.8

Nonbottleneck Resources

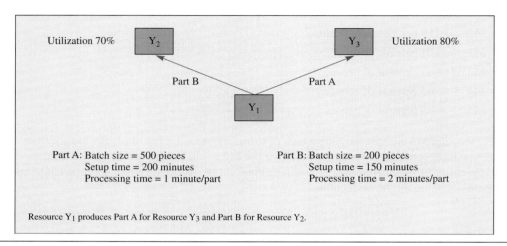

Utilization 70%   Y$_2$ Y$_3$ Utilization 80%

Part B   Part A

Y$_1$

Part A: Batch size = 500 pieces
Setup time = 200 minutes
Processing time = 1 minute/part

Part B: Batch size = 200 pieces
Setup time = 150 minutes
Processing time = 2 minutes/part

Resource Y$_1$ produces Part A for Resource Y$_3$ and Part B for Resource Y$_2$.

1,500 units (1,700 minutes), Y$_2$ and Y$_3$ could well be starved for work and have to wait more time than they have available (30 percent idle time for Y$_2$ and 20 percent for Y$_3$). The new sequence would be Part A (1,700 minutes), Part B (1,350 minutes), and so on. Such an extended wait for Y$_2$ and Y$_3$ could be disruptive. Y$_2$ and Y$_3$ could become temporary bottlenecks and lose throughput for the system.

DRUM, BUFFER, ROPE

Drum, Buffer, Rope Tutorial

Interactive Operations Management

Every production system needs some control point or points to control the flow of product through the system. If the system contains a bottleneck, the bottleneck is the best place for control. This control point is called the *drum* because it strikes the beat that the rest of the system (or those parts that it influences) uses to function. Recall that a *bottleneck* is defined as a resource that does not have the capacity to meet demand. Therefore, a bottleneck is working all the time, and one reason for using it as a control point is to make sure that the operations upstream do not overproduce and build up excess work-in-process inventory that the bottleneck cannot handle.

If there is no bottleneck, the next-best place to set the drum would be a capacity-constrained resource (CCR). A capacity-constrained resource, remember, is one that is operating near capacity but, on the average, has adequate capability as long as it is not incorrectly scheduled (for example, with too many setups, causing it to run short of capacity, or producing too large a lot size, thereby starving downstream operations).

If neither a bottleneck nor a CCR is present, the control point can be designated anywhere. The best position would generally be at some divergent point where the output of the resource is used in several downstream operations.

Dealing with the bottleneck is most critical, and our discussion focuses on ensuring that the bottleneck always has work to do. Exhibit 18.9 shows a simple linear flow A through G. Suppose that Resource D, which is a machine center, is a bottleneck. This means that the capacities are greater both upstream and downstream from it. If this sequence is not controlled, we would expect to see a large amount of inventory in front of Work Center D and very little anywhere else. There would be little finished goods inventory because (by the definition of the term *bottleneck*) all the product produced would be taken by the market.

There are two things that we must do with this bottleneck:

1. Keep a *buffer* inventory in front of it to make sure that it always has something to work on. Because it is a bottleneck, its output determines the throughput of the system.
2. Communicate back upstream to A what D has produced so that A provides only that amount. This keeps inventory from building up. This communication is called the *rope*. It can be formal (such as a schedule) or informal (such as daily discussion).

exhibit 18.9

Linear Flow of Product with a Bottleneck

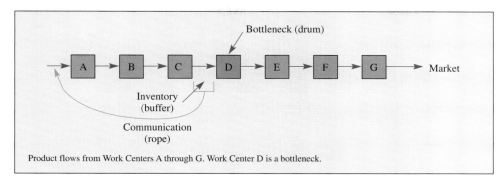

Product flows from Work Centers A through G. Work Center D is a bottleneck.

exhibit 18.10

Capacity Profile of Work Center D (Showing Assigned Jobs A through P over a Period of Four 24-Hour Days)

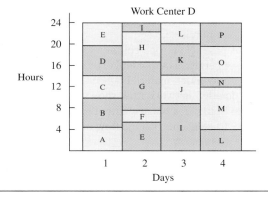

The buffer inventory in front of a bottleneck operation is a *time buffer*. We want to make sure that Work Center D always has work to do, and it does not matter which of the scheduled products are worked on. We might, for example, provide 96 hours of inventory in the buffer as shown in the sequence A through P in Exhibit 18.10. Jobs A through about half of E are scheduled during the 24 hours of Day 1; Jobs E through a portion of Job I are scheduled during the second 24-hour day; Jobs I through part of L are scheduled during the third 24-hour day; and Jobs L through P are scheduled during the fourth 24-hour day, for a total of 96 hours. This means that through normal variation, or if something happens upstream and the output has been temporarily stalled, D can work for another 96 hours, protecting the throughput. (The 96 hours of work, incidentally, include setups and processing times contained in the job sheets, which usually are based on engineering standard times.)

We might ask, How large should the time buffer be? The answer: As large as it needs to be to ensure that the bottleneck continues to work. By examining the variation of each operation, we can make a guess. Theoretically, the size of the buffer can be computed statistically by examining past performance data, or the sequence can be simulated. In any event, precision is not critical. We could start with an estimate of the time buffer as one-fourth of the total lead time of the system. Say, the sequence A to G in our example (Exhibit 18.9) took a total of 16 days. We could start with a buffer of four days in front of D. If, during the next few days or weeks, the buffer runs out, we need to increase the buffer size. We do this by releasing extra material to the first operation, A. On the other hand, if we find that our buffer never drops below three days, we might want to hold back releases to A and reduce the time buffer to three days. Experience is the best determination of the final buffer size.

exhibit 18.11

Linear Flow of Product with a Capacity-Constrained Resource

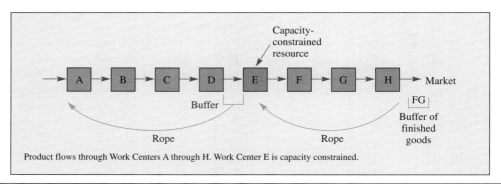

Product flows through Work Centers A through H. Work Center E is capacity constrained.

If the drum is not a bottleneck but a CCR (and thus it can have a small amount of idle time), we might want to create two buffer inventories: one in front of the CCR and the second at the end as finished goods. (See Exhibit 18.11.) The finished-goods inventory protects the market, and the time buffer in front of the CCR protects throughput. For this CCR case, the market cannot take all that we can produce, so we want to ensure that finished goods are available when the market does decide to purchase.

We need two ropes in this case: (1) a rope communicating from finished-goods inventory back to the drum to increase or decrease output and (2) a rope from the drum back to the material release point, specifying how much material is needed.

Exhibit 18.12 is a more detailed network flow showing one bottleneck. Inventory is provided not only in front of that bottleneck but also after the nonbottleneck sequence of processes that feed the subassembly. This ensures that the flow of product is not slowed down by having to wait after it leaves the bottleneck.

IMPORTANCE OF QUALITY

An MRP system allows for rejects by building a larger batch than actually needed. A JIT system cannot tolerate poor quality because JIT success is based on a balanced capacity. A defective part or component can cause a JIT system to shut down, thereby losing throughput of the total system. Synchronous manufacturing, however, has excess capacity throughout the system, except for the bottleneck. If a bad part is produced upstream of the bottleneck, the result is that there is a loss of material only. Because of the excess capacity, there is still time to do another operation to replace the one just scrapped. For the bottleneck, however, extra time does not exist, so there should be a quality control inspection just prior to the bottleneck to ensure that the bottleneck works only on good product. Also, there needs to be assurance downstream from the bottleneck that the passing product is not scrapped—that would mean lost throughput.

BATCH SIZES

In an assembly line, what is the batch size? Some would say "one" because one unit is moved at a time; others would say "infinity" because the line continues to produce the same item. Both answers are correct, but they differ in their point of view. The first answer, "one," in an assembly line focuses on the *part* transferred one unit at a time. The second focuses on the *process*. From the point of view of the resource, the process batch is infinity because it is continuing to run the same units. Thus, in an assembly line, we have a *process batch* of infinity (or all the units until we change to another process setup) and a *transfer batch* of one unit.

Setup costs and carrying costs were treated in depth in Chapter 15 ("Inventory Control"). In the present context, setup costs relate to the process batch and carrying costs relate to the transfer batch.

Network Flow with One Bottleneck

exhibit 18.12

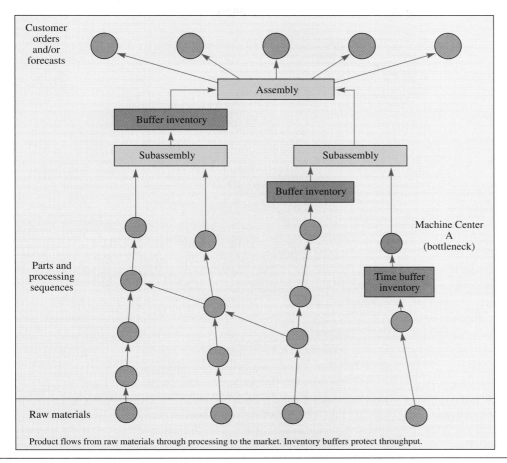

Product flows from raw materials through processing to the market. Inventory buffers protect throughput.

A process batch is of a size large enough or small enough to be processed in a particular length of time. From the point of view of a resource, two times are involved: setup time and processing run time (ignoring downtime for maintenance or repair). Larger process batch sizes require fewer setups and therefore can generate more processing time and more output. For bottleneck resources, larger batch sizes are desirable. For nonbottleneck resources, smaller process batch sizes are desirable (by using up the existing idle time), thereby reducing work-in-process inventory.

Transfer batches refer to the movement of part of the process batch. Rather than wait for the entire batch to be finished, work that has been completed by that operation can be moved to the next downstream workstation so that it can begin working on that batch. A transfer batch can be equal to a process batch, but it should not be larger under a properly designed system. This could occur only if a completed process batch was held until sometime later when a second batch was processed. If this later time was acceptable in the beginning, then both jobs should be combined and processed together at the later time.

The advantage of using transfer batches that are smaller than the process batch quantity is that the total production time is shorter so the amount of work-in-process is smaller. Exhibit 18.13 shows a situation where the total production lead time was reduced from 2,100 to 1,310 minutes by (1) using a transfer batch size of 100 rather than 1,000 and (2) reducing the process batch sizes of Operation 2.

How to Determine Process Batch and Transfer Batch Sizes

Logic would suggest that the master production schedule (however it was developed) be analyzed as to its effect on various work centers. In an MRP system, this means that the master

exhibit 18.13   Effect of Changing the Process Batch Sizes on Production Lead Time for a Job Order of 1,000 Units

production schedule should be run through the MRP and the CRP (capacity requirements planning program) to generate a detailed load on each work center. Srikanth states that from his experience, there are too many errors in the manufacturing database to do this.[2] He suggests using the alternative procedure of first identifying the probable CCRs and bottlenecks. There should be only one (or a few), and they should be reviewed by managers so that they understand which resources are actually controlling their plant. These resources set the drumbeat.

Rather than try to adjust the master production schedule to change resource loads, it is more practical to control the flow at each bottleneck or CCR to bring the capacities in line. The process batch sizes and transfer batch sizes are changed after comparing past performances in meeting due dates.

Smaller transfer batches give lower work-in-process inventory but faster product flow (and consequently shorter lead time). More material handling is required, however. Larger transfer batches give longer lead times and higher inventories, but there is less material handling. Therefore, the transfer batch size is determined by a trade-off of production lead times, inventory reduction benefits, and costs of material movement.

When trying to control the flow at CCRs and bottlenecks, there are four possible situations:

1. A bottleneck (no idle time) with no setup time required when changing from one product to another.
2. A bottleneck with setup time required to change from one product to another.
3. A capacity-constrained resource (CCR with a small amount of idle time) with no setup time required to change from one product to another.
4. A CCR with setup time required when changing from one product to another.

In the first case (a bottleneck with no setup time to change products), jobs should be processed in the order of the schedule so that delivery is on time. Without setups, only the sequence is important. In the second case, when setups are required, larger batch sizes combine separate similar jobs in the sequence. This means reaching ahead into future time periods. Some jobs will therefore be done early. Because this is a bottleneck resource, larger batches save setups and thereby increase throughput. (The setup time saved is used for processing.) The larger process batches may cause the early-scheduled jobs to be late. Therefore, frequent small transfer batches are necessary to try to shorten the lead time.

Situations 3 and 4 include a CCR without a setup and a CCR with setup time requirements. Handling the CCR would be similar to handling a nonbottleneck, though more carefully. That is, a CCR has some idle time. It would be appropriate here to cut the size of some of the process batches so that there can be more frequent changes of product. This would decrease lead time, and jobs would be more likely to be done on time. In a make-to-stock situation, cutting process batch sizes has a much more profound effect than increasing the number of transfer batches. This is because the resulting product mix is much greater, leading to reduced WIP and production lead time.

HOW TO TREAT INVENTORY

The traditional view of inventory is that its only negative impact on a firm's performance is its carrying cost. We now realize inventory's negative impact also comes from lengthening lead times and creating problems with engineering changes. (When an engineering change on a product comes through, which commonly occurs, product still within the production system often must be modified to include the changes. Therefore, less work-in-process reduces the number of engineering changes to be made.)

Fox and Goldratt propose to treat inventory as a loan given to the manufacturing unit. The value of the loan is based only on the purchased items that are part of the inventory. As we stated earlier, inventory is treated in this chapter as material cost only, without any accounting-type value added from production. If inventory is carried as a loan to manufacturing, we need a way to measure how long the loan is carried. One measurement is dollar days.

Dollar Days   A useful performance measurement is the concept of *dollar days,* a measurement of the value of inventory and the time it stays within an area. To use this measure, we could simply multiply the total value of inventory by the number of days inventory spends within a department.

Suppose Department X carries an average inventory of $40,000, and, on the average, the inventory stays within the department five days. In dollar days, Department X is charged with $40,000 times five days, or $200,000 dollar days of inventory. At this point, we cannot say the $200,000 is high or low, but it does show where the inventory is located. Management can then see where it should focus attention and determine acceptable levels. Techniques can be instituted to try to reduce the number of dollar days while being careful that such a measure does not become a local objective (that is, minimizing dollar days) and hurt the global objectives (such as increasing ROI, cash flow, and net profit).

Dollar days could be beneficial in a variety of ways. Consider the current practice of using efficiencies or equipment utilization as a performance measurement. To get high utilization, large amounts of inventory are held to keep everything working. However, high inventories would result in a high number of dollar days, which would discourage high levels of work-in-process. Dollar day measurements could also be used in other areas:

- Marketing—to discourage holding large amounts of finished-goods inventory. The net result would be to encourage sale of finished products.
- Purchasing—to discourage placing large purchase orders that on the surface appear to take advantage of quantity discounts. This would encourage just-in-time purchasing.
- Manufacturing—to discourage large work-in-process and producing earlier than needed. This would promote rapid flow of material within the plant.
- Project management—to quantify a project's limited resource investments as a function of time. This promotes the proper allocation of resources to competing projects. See the Breakthrough box on "Critical Chain Project Management" for Goldratt ideas for scheduling projects.

Cross Functional

BREAKTHROUGH

CRITICAL CHAIN PROJECT MANAGEMENT

Critical Chain Project Management is the name of the approach that Eli Goldratt developed for scheduling and managing projects. The approach borrows many ideas from those used for manufacturing processes. The conventional critical path method was covered in Chapter 3 and Goldratt goes beyond those ideas by considering resource constraints and special time buffers in the project. The following are specific ideas included in his Critical Chain Project Management approach:

1 Schedules are level-loaded based on the limitations of available resources (constraints). This produces the "critical chain"—the longest set of sequential tasks (due to both task dependency and resource contention)—which dictates the shortest overall project duration.

2 Time buffers are inserted at strategic locations in the plan—at the end of the critical chain and at every point where a task interests the critical chain—to absorb the adverse effects of uncertainty without damaging performance. To create the buffers, some of the slack time built into tasks in planning is repositioned to these strategic locations.

3 Projects are "pipelined" or staged based on resource availability to combat the cascade effect of shared resources across projects and create viable multiproject plans.

4 Buffer management is used to dynamically set task priorities in execution. As uncertainty changes the original plan, tasks are prioritized based on the buffer burn rate (the amount of buffer consumed versus the percent of the work complete). Tasks with critical buffer penetration take precedence over those with lower burn rates.

Learn more about Critical Chain Project Management at http://www.tocc.com.

COMPARING SYNCHRONOUS MANUFACTURING TO MRP AND JIT

MRP uses *backward scheduling* after having been fed a master production schedule. MRP schedules production through a bill of materials explosion in a backward manner—working backward in time from the desired completion date. As a secondary procedure, MRP, through its capacity resource planning module, develops capacity utilization profiles of work centers. When work centers are overloaded, either the master production schedule must be adjusted or enough slack capacity must be left unscheduled in the system so that work can be smoothed at the local level (by work center supervisors or the workers themselves). Trying to smooth capacity using MRP is so difficult and would require so many computer runs that capacity overloads and underloads are best left to local decisions, such as at the machine centers. An MRP schedule becomes invalid just days after it was created.

The synchronous manufacturing approach uses *forward scheduling* because it focuses on the critical resources. These are scheduled forward in time, ensuring that loads placed on them are within capacity. The noncritical (or nonbottleneck) resources are then scheduled to support the critical resources. (This can be done backward to minimize the length of time that inventories are held.) This procedure ensures a feasible schedule. To help reduce lead time and work-in-process, in synchronous manufacturing the process batch size and transfer batch size are varied—a procedure that MRP is not able to do.

Comparing JIT to synchronous manufacturing, JIT does an excellent job in reducing lead times and work-in-process, but it has several drawbacks:

1. JIT is limited to repetitive manufacturing.
2. JIT requires a stable production level (usually about a month long).
3. JIT does not allow very much flexibility in the products produced. (Products must be similar with a limited number of options.)

4. JIT still requires work-in-process when used with kanban so that there is "something to pull." This means that completed work must be stored on the downstream side of each workstation to be pulled by the next workstation.

5. Vendors need to be located nearby because the system depends on smaller, more frequent deliveries.

Because synchronous manufacturing uses a schedule to assign work to each workstation, there is no need for more work-in-process other than that being worked on. The exception is for inventory specifically placed in front of a bottleneck to ensure continual work, or at specific points downstream from a bottleneck to ensure flow of product.

Concerning continual improvements to the system, JIT is a trial-and-error procedure applied to a real system. In synchronous manufacturing, the system can be programmed and simulated on a computer because the schedules are realistic (can be accomplished) and computer run time is short.

RELATIONSHIP WITH OTHER FUNCTIONAL AREAS

The production system must work closely with other functional areas to achieve the best operating system. This section briefly discusses accounting and marketing—areas where conflicts can occur, and where cooperation and joint planning should occur.

Cross Functional

ACCOUNTING'S INFLUENCE

Sometimes we are led into making decisions to suit the measurement system rather than to follow the firm's goals. Consider the following example: Suppose that two old machines are currently being used to produce a product. The processing time for each is 20 minutes per part and, because each has the capacity of three parts per hour, they have the combined capacity of six per hour, which exactly meets the market demand of six parts per hour. Suppose that engineering finds a new machine that produces parts in 12 minutes rather than 20. However, the capacity of this one machine is only five per hour, which does not meet the market demand. Logic would seem to dictate that the supervisor should use an old machine to make up the lacking one unit per hour. However, the system does not allow this. The standard has been changed from the 20 minutes each to 12 minutes each and performance would look very bad on paper because the variance would be 67 percent $[(20 - 12)/12]$ for units made on the old machines. The supervisor, therefore, would work the new machine on overtime.

Problems in Cost Accounting Measurements   Cost accounting is used for performance measurement, cost determinations, investment justification, and inventory valuation. Two sets of accounting performance measurements are used for evaluation: (1) global measurements, which are financial statements showing net profit, return on investment, and cash flow (with which we agree); and (2) local cost accounting measurements showing efficiencies (as variances from standard) or utilization rate (hours worked/hours present).

From the cost accounting (local measurement) viewpoint, then, performance has traditionally been based on cost and full utilization. This logic forces supervisors to activate their workers all the time, which leads to excessive inventory. The cost accounting measurement system can also instigate other problems. For example, attempting to use the idle time to increase utilization can create a bottleneck, as we discussed earlier in this chapter. Any measurement system should support the objectives of the firm and not stand in the way. Fortunately, the cost accounting measurement philosophy is changing.

MARKETING AND PRODUCTION

Marketing and production should communicate and conduct their activities in close harmony. In practice, however, they act very independently. There are many reasons for this. The difficulties range from differences in personalities and cultures to unlike systems of merits and rewards in the two functions. Marketing people are judged on the growth of the company in terms of sales, market share, and new products introduced. Marketing is sales oriented. Manufacturing people are evaluated on cost and utilization. Therefore, marketing wants a variety of products to increase the company's position, whereas manufacturing is trying to reduce cost.

Data used for evaluating marketing and manufacturing are also quite different. Marketing data are "soft" (qualitative); manufacturing data are "hard" (quantitative). The orientation and experiences of marketing and production people also differ. Those in marketing management have likely come up through sales and a close association with customers. Top manufacturing managers have likely progressed through production operations and therefore have plant performance as a top objective.

Cultural differences can also be important in contrasting marketing and manufacturing personnel. Marketing people tend to have a greater ego drive and are more outgoing. Manufacturing personnel tend to be more meticulous and perhaps more introverted (at least less extroverted than their marketing counterparts).

The solution to coping with these differences is to develop an equitable set of measurements to evaluate performance in each area and to promote strong lines of communication so that they both contribute to reaching the firm's goals.

We now present two examples to show that different objectives and measurement criteria can lead to the wrong decisions. These examples also show that, even though you may have all the data required, you still may not be able to solve the problem—unless you know how!

EXAMPLE 18.1: What to Produce?

In this first example, three products (A, B, and C) are sold in the market at $50, $75, and $60 per unit, respectively. The market will take all that can be supplied.

Three work centers (X, Y, and Z) process the three products as shown in Exhibit 18.14. Processing times for each work center are also shown. Note that each work center works on all three products. Raw materials, parts, and components are added at each work center to produce each product. The per unit cost of these materials is shown as RM.

Which product or products should be produced?

SOLUTION

Three different objectives could exist that lead to different conclusions:

1. Maximize sales revenue because marketing personnel are paid commissions based on total revenue.
2. Maximize per unit gross profit.
3. Maximize total gross profit.

In this example we use gross profit as selling price less materials. We could also include other expenses such as operating expenses, but we left them out for simplicity. (We include operating expenses in our next example.)

Objective 1: Maximize sales commission. Sales personnel in this case are unaware of the processing time required so, therefore, they will try to sell only B at $75 per unit and none of A or C. Maximum revenue is determined by the limiting resource as follows:

PRODUCT	LIMITING RESOURCE	TIME REQUIRED	NUMBER PRODUCED PER HOUR	SELLING PRICE	SALES REVENUE PER HOUR
A	Y	10 min	6	$50	$300
B	X	6 min	10	75	750
C	Z	5 min	12	60	720

Prices and Production Requirements for Three Products and Three Work Centers

exhibit 18.14

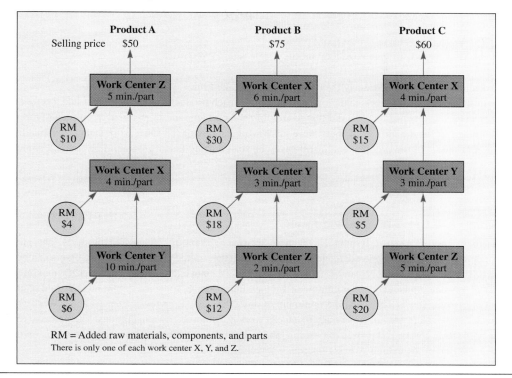

Objective 2: Maximize per unit gross profit.

(1) PRODUCT	(2) SELLING PRICE	(3) RAW MATERIAL COST	(4) GROSS PROFIT PER UNIT (2) − (3)
A	$50	$20	$30
B	$75	$60	$15
C	$60	$40	$20

The decision would be to sell only Product A, which has a $30 per unit gross profit.

Objective 3: Maximize total gross profit. We can solve this problem by finding either total gross profit for the period or the rate at which profit is generated. We use rate to solve the problem both because it is easier and because it is a more appropriate measure. We use profit per hour as the rate.

Note that each product has a different work center that limits its output. The rate at which the product is made is then based on this bottleneck work center.

(1) PRODUCT	(2) LIMITING WORK CENTER	(3) PROCESSING TIME PER UNIT (MINUTES)	(4) PRODUCT OUTPUT RATE (PER HOUR)	(5) SELLING PRICE	(6) RAW MATERIAL COST	(7) PROFIT PER UNIT	(8) PROFIT PER HOUR (4) × (7)
A	Y	10	6	$50	$20	$30	$180
B	X	6	10	75	60	15	150
C	Z	5	12	60	40	20	240

From our calculations, Product C provides the highest profit of $240 per hour. Note that we get three different answers:

1. We choose B to maximize sales revenue.
2. We choose A to maximize profit per unit.
3. We choose C to maximize total profit.

Choosing Product C is obviously the correct answer for the firm.

In this example, all work centers were required for each product and each product had a different work center as a constraint. We did this to simplify the problem and to ensure that only one product would surface as the answer. If there were more work centers or the same work center constraint in different products, the problem could still easily be solved using linear programming (as in Technical Note 2). ●

EXAMPLE 18.2: How Much to Produce?

In this example, shown in Exhibit 18.15, there are two workers producing four products. The plant works three shifts. The market demand is unlimited and takes all the products that the workers can produce. The only stipulation is that the ratio of products sold cannot exceed 10 to 1 between the maximum sold of any one product and the minimum of another. For example, if the maximum number sold of any one of the products is 100 units, the minimum of any other cannot be fewer than 10 units. Workers 1 and 2, on each shift, are not cross-trained and can work only on their own operations. The time and raw material (RM) costs are shown in the exhibit, and a summary of the costs and times involved is on the lower portion of the exhibit. Weekly operating expenses are $3,000.

What quantities of A, B, C, and D should be produced?

---

exhibit 18.15   Production Requirements and Selling Price of Four Products

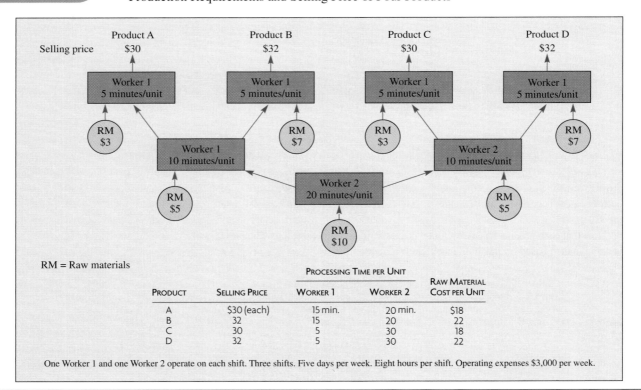

PRODUCT	SELLING PRICE	PROCESSING TIME PER UNIT		RAW MATERIAL COST PER UNIT
		WORKER 1	WORKER 2	
A	$30 (each)	15 min.	20 min.	$18
B	32	15	20	22
C	30	5	30	18
D	32	5	30	22

One Worker 1 and one Worker 2 operate on each shift. Three shifts. Five days per week. Eight hours per shift. Operating expenses $3,000 per week.

SOLUTION

As in the previous example, there are three answers to this question, depending on each of the following objectives:

1. Maximize revenue for sales personnel who are paid on commission.
2. Maximize per unit gross profit.
3. Maximize the utilization of the bottleneck resource (leading to maximum gross profit).

Objective 1: Maximize sales commission on sales revenue. Sales personnel prefer to sell B and D (selling price $32) rather than A and C (selling price $30). Weekly operating expenses are $3,000.

The ratio of units sold will be: 1A : 10B : 1C : 10D.

Worker 2 on each shift is the bottleneck and therefore determines the output. Note that if this truly is a bottleneck with an unlimited market demand, this should be a seven-day-per-week operation, not just a five-day workweek.

$$5 \text{ days per week} \times 3 \text{ shifts} \times 8 \text{ hours} \times 60 \text{ minutes} = 7,200 \text{ minutes per week available}$$

Worker 2 spends these times on each unit:

$$\text{A} \quad 20 \text{ minutes} \qquad \text{B} \quad 20 \text{ minutes} \qquad \text{C} \quad 30 \text{ minutes} \qquad \text{D} \quad 30 \text{ minutes}$$

The ratio of output units is 1 : 10 : 1 : 10. Therefore,

$$1x(20) + 10x(20) + 1x(30) + 10x(30) = 7,200$$

$$550x = 7,200$$

$$x = 13.09$$

Therefore, the numbers of units produced are

$$\text{A} = 13 \qquad \text{B} = 131 \qquad \text{C} = 13 \qquad \text{D} = 131$$

Total revenue is

$$13(30) + 131(32) + 13(30) + 131(32) = \$9,164 \text{ per week}$$

For comparison with Objectives 2 and 3, we will compute gross profit per week.

Gross profit per week (selling price less raw material less weekly expenses) is

$$13(30 - 18) + 131(32 - 22) + 13(30 - 18) + 131(32 - 22) - 3,000$$

$$= 156 + 1,310 + 156 + 1,310 - 3,000$$

$$= (\$68) \text{ loss.}$$

Objective 2: Maximize per unit gross profit.

	GROSS PROFIT	=	SELLING PRICE	−	RAW MATERIAL COST
A	12	=	30	−	18
B	10	=	32	−	22
C	12	=	30	−	18
D	10	=	32	−	22

A and C have the maximum gross profit, so the ratio will be 10 : 1 : 10 : 1 for A, B, C, and D. Worker 2 is the constraint and has

$$5 \text{ days} \times 3 \text{ shifts} \times 8 \text{ hours} \times 60 \text{ minutes} = 7,200 \text{ minutes available per week}$$

As before, A and B take 20 minutes, while C and D take 30 minutes. Thus

$$10x(20) + 1x(20) + 10x(30) + 1x(30) = 7,200$$

$$550x = 7,200$$

$$x = 13$$

Therefore, the number of units produced is

$$A = 131 \qquad B = 13 \qquad C = 131 \qquad D = 13$$

Gross profit (selling price less raw materials less $3,000 weekly expense) is

$$131(30 - 18) + 13(32 - 22) + 131(30 - 18) + 13(32 - 22) - 3,000$$
$$= 1,572 + 130 + 1,572 + 130 - 3,000$$
$$= \$404 \text{ profit}$$

Objective 3: Maximize the use of the bottleneck resource, Worker 2. For every hour Worker 2 works, the following numbers of products and gross profits result:

(1) PRODUCT	(2) PRODUCTION TIME	(3) UNITS PRODUCED PER HOUR	(4) SELLING PRICE EACH	(5) RAW MATERIAL COST PER UNIT	(6) GROSS PROFIT PER HOUR (3) × [(4) − (5)]
A	20 minutes	3	$30	$18	$36
B	20	3	32	22	30
C	30	2	30	18	24
D	30	2	32	22	20

Product A generates the greatest gross profit per hour of Worker 2 time, so the ratio is 10 : 1 : 1 : 1 for A, B, C, and D.

Available time for Worker 2 is the same as before:

$$3 \text{ shifts} \times 5 \text{ days} \times 8 \text{ hours} \times 60 \text{ minutes} = 7,200 \text{ minutes}$$

Worker 2 should produce 10 As for every 1 B, 1 C, and 1 D. Worker 2's average production rate is

$$10x(20) + 1x(20) + 1x(30) + 1x(30) = 7,200$$
$$280x = 7,200$$
$$x = 25.7$$

Therefore, the number of units that should be produced is

$$A = 257 \qquad B = 25.7 \qquad C = 25.7 \qquad D = 25.7$$

Gross profit (price less raw materials less $3,000 weekly expenses) is

$$257(30 - 18) + 25.7(32 - 22) + 25.7(30 - 18) + 25.7(32 - 22) - 3,000$$
$$= 3,084 + 257 + 308.4 + 257 - 3,000$$
$$= \$906.40$$

In summary, using three different objectives to decide how many of each product to make gave us three different results:

1. Maximizing sales commission resulted in a $68 loss in gross profit.
2. Maximizing gross profit gave us a profit of $404.
3. Maximizing the use of the capacity-constrained worker gave us the best gross profit, $906.40. ●

Both examples demonstrate that production and marketing need to interact. Marketing should sell the most profitable use of available capacity. However, to plan capacity, production needs to know from marketing what products could be sold.

CONCLUSION

⊙⊙⊙⊙ The measurement system within a firm should encourage the increase of net profits, return on investment, and cash flow. The firm can accomplish this if, at the operations level, it rewards performance based on the amount of throughput, inventory, and operating expense created. This is essential for a firm's success.

To control throughput, inventory, and operating expense, the system must be analyzed to find bottlenecks and capacity-constrained resources. Only then can the company define a drum for control, buffers to ensure throughput, and ropes for communicating the correct information to the correct locations, while minimizing work-in-process everywhere else. Without this focus, problems are not correctly diagnosed and solution procedures are impossible.

Goldratt defined nine rules (Exhibit 18.1) to help guide the logic of an operating system and to identify the important points. These are basic to any operating system.

The underlying philosophy presented in this chapter—the vital importance of concentrating on system limitations imposed by capacity-constrained resources—has led Goldratt to broaden his view of the importance of system limitations and to develop his five-step "general theory of constraints."[3] (See Exhibit 18.2.)

Although the terms *bottleneck* and *constraint* can mean essentially the same thing, Goldratt uses *constraint* in the broadest sense to mean anything that limits the performance of a system and slows or prevents it from continuing to move toward its goal.

This general theory of constraints directs companies to find what is stopping them from moving toward their goals and find ways to get around this limitation. If, in a manufacturing environment, the limitation is insufficient capacity, then ways to break the constraint might be overtime, specialized tools, supporting equipment, exceptionally skilled workers, subcontracting, redesigning product or process, alternative routings, and so on. Point 5 (Exhibit 18.2) warns against letting biases in thinking prevent the search for further exploitation of constraints. For example, if a search and exploitation of a constraint has been conducted under the limitation of cost, make sure that this cost measure is not carried into the next search. Start clean each time.

One last summary comment on this chapter, which also serves well as a summary comment for this book: The key to competitive advantage through operations is for the firm to operate as a synchronized system, with all parts working in concert. Companies that do this effectively are well on their way to achieving the fundamental goal of the firm—profitability.

Cross Functional

KEY TERMS

Synchronous manufacturing A production process coordinated to work in harmony to achieve the goals of the firm.

Throughput The rate at which money is generated by the system through sales (Goldratt's definition).

Inventory All the money that the system has invested in purchasing things it intends to sell (Goldratt's definition).

Operating expenses All the money that the system spends to turn inventory into throughput (Goldratt's definition).

Productivity All the actions that bring a company closer to its goals (Goldratt's definition).

Bottleneck Any resource whose capacity is less than the demand placed upon it (Goldratt's definition).

Nonbottleneck Any resource whose capacity is greater than the demand placed on it (Goldratt's definition).

Capacity-constrained resource (CCR) A resource whose utilization is close to capacity and could be a bottleneck if not scheduled carefully (Goldratt's definition).

SOLVED PROBLEM

Here is the process flow for Products A, B, and C. Products A, B, and C sell for $20, $25, and $30, respectively. There are only one Resource X and one Resource Y, which are used to produce A, B, and C for the numbers of minutes stated on the diagram. Raw materials are needed at the process steps as shown, with the costs in dollars per unit of raw material. (One unit is used for each product.)

The market will take all that you can produce.

a. Which product would you produce to maximize gross margin per unit?

b. If sales personnel are paid on commission, which product or products would they sell and how many could they sell?

c. Which and how many product or products should you produce to maximize gross profit for one week?

d. From *c*, how much gross profit would there be for the week?

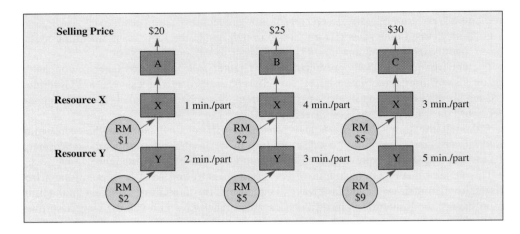

Solution

a. Maximizing gross margin per unit:

	GROSS MARGIN	=	SELLING PRICE	−	RAW MATERIAL COST
A	17	=	20	−	3
B	18	=	25	−	7
C	16	=	30	−	14

Product B will be produced.

b. Maximizing sales commission: Sales personnel would sell the highest-priced product, C (unless they knew the market and capacity limitations). If we assume the market will take all that we can make, then we would work 7 days/week, 8 hours/day. Y is the constraint in producing C. The number of C we can make in a week is

$$C = \frac{8 \text{ hours/day} \times 7 \text{ days/week} \times 60 \text{ minutes/hour}}{5 \text{ minutes/part}}$$

$$= 672 \text{ units}$$

c. To maximize profit, we need to compare profits per hour for each product:

(1)	(2)	(3)	(4)	(5)	(6)	(7)
			NUMBER OF UNITS			GROSS PROFIT
	CONSTRAINT	PRODUCTION TIME ON	OUTPUT	SELLING	RM	PER HOUR
PRODUCT	RESOURCE	RESOURCE	PER HOUR	PRICE ($)	COST ($)	(4) × (5 − 6)
A	Y	2	30	20	3	$510
B	X	4	15	25	7	270
C	Y	5	12	30	14	192

If the constraining resource were the same for all three products, our problem would be solved and the answer would be to produce just A, and as many as possible. However, X is the constraint for B, so the answer could be a combination of A and B. To test this, we can see that the value of each hour of Y while producing B is

$$\frac{60 \text{ minutes/hour}}{3 \text{ minutes/unit}} \times (\$25 - 7) = \$360/\text{hour}$$

This is less than the $510 per hour producing A, so we would produce only A. The number of units of A produced during the week is

$$\frac{60 \text{ minutes/hour} \times 24 \text{ hours/day} \times 7 \text{ days/week}}{2 \text{ minutes/unit}} = 5{,}040$$

d. Gross profit for the week is $5{,}040 \times \$17 = \$85{,}680$.
   Solved using profit per hour: $\$510 \times 24 \times 7 = \$85{,}680$.

REVIEW AND DISCUSSION QUESTIONS

1. State the global performance measurements and operational performance measurements and briefly define each of them. How do these differ from traditional accounting measurements?
2. Discuss process batches and transfer batches. How might you determine what the sizes should be?
3. Compare and contrast JIT, MRP, and synchronized manufacturing, stating their main features, such as where each is or might be used, amounts of raw materials and work-in-process inventories, production lead times and cycle times, and methods for control.
4. Compare the importance and relevance of quality control in JIT, MRP, and synchronous manufacturing.
5. Discuss what is meant by forward loading and backward loading.
6. Define and explain the cause or causes of a moving bottleneck.
7. Explain how a nonbottleneck can become a bottleneck.
8. What are the functions of inventory in MRP, JIT, and synchronous manufacturing scheduling?
9. Define *process batch* and *transfer batch* and their meaning in each of these applications: MRP, JIT, and bottleneck or constrained resource logic.
10. Discuss how a production system is scheduled using MRP logic, JIT logic, and synchronous manufacturing logic.
11. Discuss the concept of "drum–buffer–rope."
12. From the standpoint of the scheduling process, how are resource limitations treated in an MRP application? How are they treated in a synchronous manufacturing application?
13. What are operations people's primary complaints against the accounting procedures used in most firms? Explain how such procedures can cause poor decisions for the total company.
14. Most manufacturing firms try to balance capacity for their production sequences. Some believe that this is an invalid strategy. Explain why balancing capacity does not work.
15. Discuss why transfer batches and process batches many times may not and should not be equal.

PROBLEMS

1. For the four basic configurations that follow, assume that the market is demanding product that must be processed by both Resource X and Resource Y for Cases I, II, and III. For Case IV, both resources supply separate but dependent markets; that is, the number of units of output from both X and Y must be equal.

   Plans are being made to produce a product that requires 40 minutes on Resource X and 30 minutes on Resource Y. Assume that there is only one of each of these resources, and that market demand is 1,400 units per month.

   How many hours of production time would you schedule for X and Y? What would happen if both were scheduled for the same number of hours?

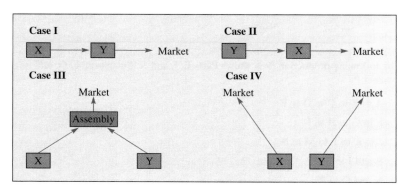

2   Following are the process flow sequences for three products: A, B, and C. There are two bottleneck operations—on the first leg and fourth leg—marked with an X. Boxes represent processes, which may be either machine or manual. Suggest the location of the drum, buffer, and ropes.

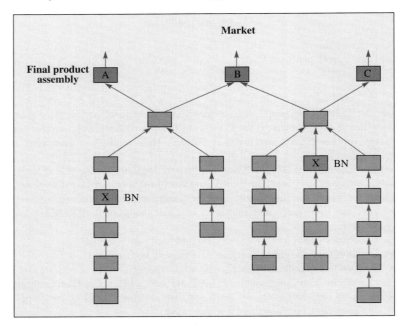

3   The accompanying figure shows a production network model with the parts and processing sequences. State clearly on the figure (1) where you would place inventory; (2) where you would perform inspection; and (3) where you would emphasize high-quality output. (Note: Operations may be shown either as rectangles as in Problem 2 or as circles as in Problem 3.)

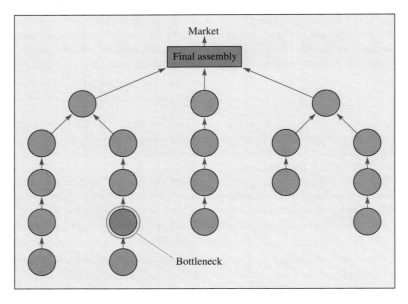

4   The following production flow shows Parts E, I, and N; Subassembly O; and final assembly for Product P:

    A to B to C to D to E

    F to G to H to I

    J to K to L to M to N

    E and I to O

    N and O to P

B involves a bottleneck operation, and M involves a CCR.
a. Draw the process flow.
b. Where would you locate buffer inventories?
c. Where would you place inspection points?
d. Where would you stress the importance of quality production?

5 Here are average process cycle times for several work centers. State which are bottlenecks, nonbottlenecks, and capacity-constrained resources.

Processing time		Setup time

Processing time	Setup	Idle

Processing time	Setup	Idle

Processing time	Setup	Idle

Processing time	Setup	Idle

6 The following diagram shows the flow process, raw material costs, and machine processing time for three products: A, B, and C. There are three machines (W, X, and Y) used in the production of these products; the times shown are in required minutes of production per unit. Raw material costs are shown in cost per unit of product. The market will take all that can be produced.
a. Assuming that sales personnel are paid on a commission basis, which product should they sell?
b. On the basis of maximizing gross profit per unit, which product should be sold?
c. To maximize total profit for the firm, which product should be sold?

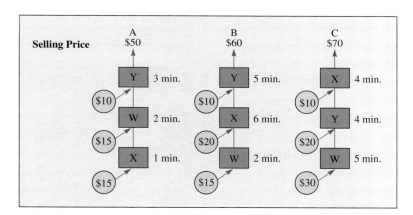

7 Willard Lock Company is losing market share because of horrendous due-date performance and long delivery lead times. The company's inventory level is high and includes many finished goods that do not match the short-term orders. Material control analysis shows that purchasing has ordered on time, the vendors have delivered on time, and the scrap/rework rates have been as expected. However, the buildable mix of components and subassemblies does not generally match the short-term and past-due requirements at final assembly. End-of-month expediting and overtime are the rule, even though there is idle time early in the month. Overall efficiency figures are around 70 percent for the month. These figures are regarded as too low.

   You have just been hired as a consultant and must come up with recommendations. Help the firm understand its problems. Specifically state some actions that it should take.

8 The M–N plant manufactures two different products: M and N. Selling prices and weekly market demands are shown in the following diagram. Each product uses raw materials with costs as shown. The plant has three different machines: A, B, and C. Each performs different tasks and can work on only one unit of material at a time.

   Process times for each task are shown in the diagram. Each machine is available 2,400 minutes per week. There are no "Murphys" (major opportunities for the system to foul up). Setup and transfer times are zero. Demand is constant.

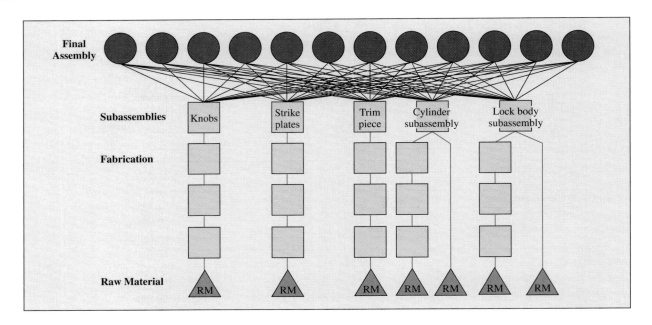

Operating expenses (including labor) total a constant $12,000 per week. Raw materials are not included in weekly operating expenses.

a. Where is the constraint in this plant?

b. What product mix provides the highest profit?

c. What is the maximum weekly profit this plant can earn?

CASE: SOLVE THE OPT QUIZ—A CHALLENGE IN SCHEDULING

Are you looking for a real scheduling challenge? This is a problem that was proposed by Dr. Eli Goldratt in a promotion for a factory-scheduling package called OPT (Optimized Production Technology). At the time Dr. Goldratt offered a $5,000 prize for the best schedule! See how good a schedule you can develop by applying the concepts described in this chapter to this problem.

THE TASK

The goal is to ship the most units, given the conditions listed below. Provide schedules on a Gantt chart for each of the three machines for the eight-week period to show how you reached your result.

CONDITIONS

1 There is one and only one of each of the three machines (A, B, and C).

2 A machine setup of 60 minutes occurs whenever a machine is switched from one operation to another.

3 The eight-week period consists of five-day weeks and 24-hour days with no breaks.

4 There is an unlimited supply of raw materials.

5 There is no inventory in the system at the beginning of the eight-week period.

6 To calculate the value of work-in-process and finished-parts inventory, assume each part has a value of $100 the moment

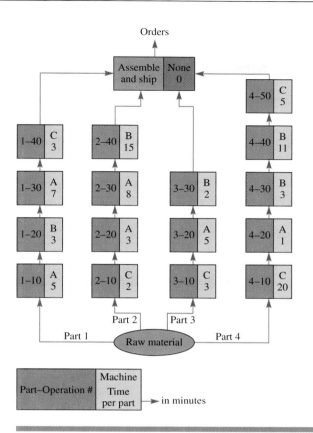

Orders

it starts at the first operation. Once a set of four parts reaches assembly, the parts are assembled and shipped immediately. Raw material and completed units should not be included in the inventory calculation.

MINIMUM REQUIRED FOR A SOLUTION

1   The raw material value of work-in-process and finished-parts inventory may not exceed $50,000 at any given time.
2   The minimum shipments of end items must be at least 140 units each week and at least 680 units by the end of the first four-week period.

Good luck!

SELECTED BIBLIOGRAPHY

Goldratt, E. *Critical Chain.* Croton-on-Hudson, NY: North River Press, 1997.

———. *The Haystack Syndrome: Sifting Information Out of the Data Ocean.* Croton-on-Hudson, NY: North River Press, 1990.

———. *Necessary but Not Sufficient.* Croton-on-Hudson, NY: North River Press, 2000.

———. *Theory of Constraints.* Croton-on-Hudson, NY: North River Press, 2000.

Goldratt, E. M., and J. Cox. *The Goal: Process of Ongoing Improvement.* 2nd rev. ed. Croton-on-Hudson, NY: North River Press, 1992.

Srikanth, M., and M. Umble. *Synchronous Management: Profit Based Manufacturing for the 21st Century.* Guilford, CT: Spectrum Publishing, 1997.

FOOTNOTES

1 Most of this chapter is based on the writings and teaching of Dr. Eliyahu M. Goldratt. Dr. Goldratt founded the Avraham Y. Goldratt Institute. The Institute's Web site is at http://www.rogo.com. We thank Dr. Goldratt for his permission to freely use his concepts, definitions, and other material.

2 M. L. Srikanth, *The Drum–Buffer–Rope System of Material Control* (New Haven, CT: Spectrum Management Group, 1987), pp. 25–37.

3 E. M. Goldratt, *The General Theory of Constraints* (New Haven, CT: Avraham Y. Goldratt Institute, 1989).

FINANCIAL ANALYSIS

Cross Functional

In this supplement we review basic concepts and tools of financial analysis for OM. These include the types of cost (fixed, variable, sunk, opportunity, avoidable), risk and expected value, and depreciation (straight line, sum-of-the-years'-digits, declining balance, double-declining balance, and depreciation-by-use). We also discuss activity-based costing and cost-of-capital calculations. Our focus is on capital investment decisions.

CONCEPTS AND DEFINITIONS

We begin with some basic definitions.

Fixed Costs   A *fixed cost* is any expense that remains constant regardless of the level of output. Although no cost is truly fixed, many types of expense are virtually fixed over a wide range of output. Examples are rent, property taxes, most types of depreciation, insurance payments, and salaries of top management.

Variable Costs   *Variable costs* are expenses that fluctuate directly with changes in the level of output. For example, each additional unit of sheet steel produced by USX requires a specific amount of material and labor. The incremental cost of this additional material and labor can be isolated and assigned to each unit of sheet steel produced. Many overhead expenses are also variable because utility bills, maintenance expense, and so forth vary with the production level.

Exhibit SA.1 illustrates the fixed and variable cost components of total cost. Note that total cost increases at the same rate as variable costs because fixed costs are constant.

Sunk Costs   *Sunk costs* are past expenses or investments that have no salvage value and therefore should not be taken into account in considering investment alternatives. Sunk costs could also be current costs that are essentially fixed, such as rent on a building. For example, suppose an ice cream manufacturing firm occupies a rented building and is considering making sherbet in the same building. If the company enters sherbet production, its cost accountant will assign some of the rental expense to the sherbet operation. However, the building rent remains unchanged and therefore is not a relevant expense to be considered in making the decision. The rent is *sunk;* that is, it continues to exist and does not change in amount regardless of the decision.

Opportunity Costs   *Opportunity cost* is the benefit *forgone,* or advantage *lost,* that results from choosing one action over the *best-known alternative* course of action.

exhibit SA.1

Fixed and Variable Cost Components of Total Cost

Suppose a firm has $100,000 to invest, and two alternatives of comparable risk present themselves, each requiring a $100,000 investment. Investment A will net $25,000; Investment B will net $23,000. Investment A is clearly the better choice, with a $25,000 net return. If the decision is made to invest in B instead of A, the opportunity cost of B is $2,000, which is the benefit forgone.

Avoidable Costs   *Avoidable costs* include any expense that is *not* incurred if an investment is made but that *must* be incurred if the investment is *not* made. Suppose a company owns a metal lathe that is not in working condition but is needed for the firm's operations. Because the lathe must be repaired or replaced, the repair costs are avoidable if a new lathe is purchased. Avoidable costs reduce the cost of a new investment because they are not incurred if the investment is made. Avoidable costs are an example of how it is possible to "save" money by spending money.

Expected Value   Risk is inherent in any investment because the future can never be predicted with absolute certainty. To deal with this uncertainty, mathematical techniques such as expected value can help. Expected value is the expected outcome multiplied by the probability of its occurrence. Recall that in the preceding example the expected outcome of Alternative A was $25,000 and B, $23,000. Suppose the probability of A's actual outcome is 80 percent while B's probability is 90 percent. The expected values of the alternatives are determined as follows:

$$\begin{array}{c} \text{Expected} \\ \text{outcome} \end{array} \times \begin{array}{c} \text{Probability that actual} \\ \text{outcome will be the} \\ \text{expected outcome} \end{array} = \begin{array}{c} \text{Expected} \\ \text{value} \end{array}$$

Investment A: $25,000 \times 0.80 = $20,000
Investment B: $23,000 \times 0.90 = $20,700

Investment B is now seen to be the better choice, with a net advantage over A of $700.

Economic Life and Obsolescence   When a firm invests in an income-producing asset, the productive life of the asset is estimated. For accounting purposes, the asset is depreciated over this period. It is assumed that the asset will perform its function during this time and then be considered obsolete or worn out, and replacement will be required. This view of asset life rarely coincides with reality.

Assume that a machine expected to have a productive life of 10 years is purchased. If at any time during the ensuing 10 years a new machine is developed that can perform the same task more efficiently or economically, the old machine has become obsolete. Whether or not it is "worn out" is irrelevant.

The *economic life* of a machine is the period over which it provides the best method for performing its task. When a superior method is developed, the machine has become obsolete. Thus, the stated *book value* of a machine can be a meaningless figure.

Depreciation   Depreciation is a method for allocating costs of capital equipment. The value of any capital asset—buildings, machinery, and so forth—decreases as its useful life is expended. *Amortization* and *depreciation* are often used interchangeably. Through convention, however, *depreciation* refers to the allocation of cost due to the physical or functional deterioration of *tangible* (physical) assets, such as buildings or equipment, whereas *amortization* refers to the allocation of cost over the useful life of *intangible* assets, such as patents, leases, franchises, and goodwill.

Depreciation procedures may not reflect an asset's true value at any point in its life because obsolescence may at any time cause a large difference between true value and book value. Also, because depreciation rates significantly affect taxes, a firm may choose a particular method from the several alternatives with more consideration for its effect on taxes than its ability to make the book value of an asset reflect the true resale value.

Next we describe five commonly used methods of depreciation.

STRAIGHT-LINE METHOD

Under this method, an asset's value is reduced in uniform annual amounts over its estimated useful life. The general formula is

$$\text{Annual amount to be depreciated} = \frac{\text{Cost} - \text{Salvage value}}{\text{Estimated useful life}}$$

A machine costing $10,000, with an estimated salvage value of $0 and an estimated life of 10 years, would be depreciated at the rate of $1,000 per year for each of the 10 years. If its estimated salvage value at the end of the 10 years is $1,000, the annual depreciation charge is

$$\frac{\$10,000 - \$1,000}{10} = \$900$$

SUM-OF-THE-YEARS'-DIGITS (SYD) METHOD

The purpose of the SYD method is to reduce the book value of an asset rapidly in early years and at a lower rate in the later years of its life.

Suppose that the estimated useful life is five years. The numbers add up to 15: $1 + 2 + 3 + 4 + 5 = 15$. Therefore, we depreciate the asset by $5 \div 15$ after the first year, $4 \div 15$ after the second year, and so on, down to $1 \div 15$ in the last year.

DECLINING-BALANCE METHOD

This method also achieves an accelerated depreciation. The asset's value is decreased by reducing its book value by a constant percentage each year. The percentage rate selected is often the one that just reduces book value to salvage value at the end of the asset's estimated life. In any case, the asset should never be reduced below estimated salvage value. Use of the declining-balance method and allowable rates are controlled by Internal Revenue Service regulations. As a simplified illustration, the preceding example is used in the next table with an arbitrarily selected rate of 40 percent. Note that depreciation is based on full cost, *not* cost minus salvage value.

YEAR	DEPRECIATION RATE	BEGINNING BOOK VALUE	DEPRECIATION CHARGE	ACCUMULATED DEPRECIATION	ENDING BOOK VALUE
1	0.40	$17,000	$6,800	$ 6,800	$10,200
2	0.40	10,200	4,080	10,880	6,120
3	0.40	6,120	2,448	13,328	3,672
4	0.40	3,672	1,469	14,797	2,203
5		2,203	203	15,000	2,000

In the fifth year, reducing book value by 40 percent would have caused it to drop below salvage value. Consequently, the asset was depreciated by only $203, which decreased book value to salvage value.

DOUBLE-DECLINING-BALANCE METHOD

Again, for tax advantages, the double-declining-balance method offers higher depreciation early in the life span. This method uses a percentage twice the straight line for the life span of the item but applies this rate to the undepreciated original cost. The method is the same as the declining-balance method, but the term *double-declining balance* means double the straight-line rate. Thus, equipment with a 10-year life span would have a straight-line depreciation rate of 10 percent per year, and a double-declining-balance rate (applied to the undepreciated amount) of 20 percent per year.

DEPRECIATION-BY-USE METHOD

The purpose of this method is to depreciate a capital investment in proportion to its use. It is applicable, for example, to a machine that performs the same operation many times. The life of the machine is estimated not in years but rather in the total number of operations it may reasonably be expected to perform before wearing out. Suppose that a metal-stamping press has an estimated life of one million stamps and costs $100,000. The charge for depreciation per stamp is then $100,000 ÷ 1,000,000, or $0.10. Assuming a $0 salvage value, the depreciation charges are as shown in the following table:

YEAR	TOTAL YEARLY STAMPS	COST PER STAMP	YEARLY DEPRECIATION CHARGE	ACCUMULATED DEPRECIATION	ENDING BOOK VALUE
1	150,000	0.10	$15,000	$15,000	$85,000
2	300,000	0.10	30,000	45,000	55,000
3	200,000	0.10	20,000	65,000	35,000
4	200,000	0.10	20,000	85,000	15,000
5	100,000	0.10	10,000	95,000	5,000
6	50,000	0.10	5,000	100,000	0

The depreciation-by-use method is an attempt to gear depreciation charges to actual use and thereby coordinate expense charges with productive output more accurately. Also, because a machine's resale value is related to its remaining productive life, it is hoped that book value will approximate resale value. The danger, of course, is that technological improvements will render the machine obsolete, in which case book value will not reflect true value.

ACTIVITY-BASED COSTING

To know how much it costs to make a certain product or deliver a service, some method of allocating overhead costs to production activities must be applied. The traditional approach is to allocate overhead costs to products on the basis of direct labor dollars or hours. By dividing the total estimated overhead costs by total budgeted direct labor hours, an overhead rate can be established. The problem with this approach is that direct labor as a percentage of total costs has fallen dramatically over the past decade. For example, introduction of advanced manufacturing technology and other productivity improvements has driven direct labor to as low as 7 to 10 percent of total manufacturing costs in many industries. As a result, overhead rates of 600 percent or even 1,000 percent are found in some highly automated plants.

This traditional accounting practice of allocating overhead to direct labor can lead to questionable investment decisions; for example, automated processes may be chosen over labor-intensive processes based on a comparison of projected costs. Unfortunately, overhead does not disappear when the equipment is installed, and overall costs may actually be lower with the labor-intensive process. It also can lead to wasted effort because an inordinate amount of time is spent tracking direct labor hours. For example, one plant spent 65 percent of computer costs tracking information about direct labor transactions even though direct labor accounted for only 4 percent of total production costs.[1]

Activity-based costing techniques have been developed to alleviate these problems by refining the overhead allocation process to more directly reflect actual proportions of overhead consumed by the production activity. Causal factors, known as *cost drivers,* are identified and used as the means for allocating overhead. These factors might include machine hours, beds occupied, computer time, flight hours, or miles driven. The accuracy of overhead allocation, of course, depends on the selection of appropriate cost drivers.

Activity-based costing involves a two-stage allocation process, with the first stage assigning overhead costs to *cost activity pools.* These pools represent activities such as performing machine setups, issuing purchase orders, and inspecting parts. In the second stage, costs are assigned from these pools to activities based on the number or amount of pool-related activity required in their completion. Exhibit SA.2 compares traditional cost accounting and activity-based costing.

Consider the example of activity-based costing in Exhibit SA.3. Two products, A and B, are produced using the same number of direct labor hours. The same number of direct labor hours produces 5,000 units of Product A and 20,000 units of Product B. Applying traditional costing, identical overhead costs would be charged to each product. By applying exhibit SA.2

Traditional and Activity-Based Costing

exhibit SA.3

Overhead Allocations by an Activity Approach

BASIC DATA

	TRACEABLE COSTS	EVENTS OF TRANSACTIONS		
ACTIVITY		TOTAL	PRODUCT A	PRODUCT B
Machine setups	$230,000	5,000	3,000	2,000
Quality inspections	160,000	8,000	5,000	3,000
Production orders	81,000	600	200	400
Machine-hours worked	314,000	40,000	12,000	28,000
Material receipts	90,000	750	150	600
Number of units produced		25,000	5,000	20,000
	$875,000			

OVERHEAD RATES BY ACTIVITY

ACTIVITY	(a) TRACEABLE COSTS	(b) TOTAL EVENTS OR TRANSACTIONS	(a) ÷ (b) RATE PER EVENT OR TRANSACTION
Machine setups	$230,000	5,000	$46/setups
Quality inspections	160,000	8,000	$20/inspection
Production orders	81,000	600	$135/order
Machine-hours worked	314,000	40,000	$7.85/hour
Material receipts	90,000	750	$120/receipt

OVERHEAD COST PER UNIT OF PRODUCT

	PRODUCT A		PRODUCT B	
	EVENTS OR TRANSACTIONS	AMOUNT	EVENTS OR TRANSACTIONS	AMOUNT
Machine setups, at $46/setup	3,000	$138,000	2,000	$92,000
Quality inspections, at $20/inspection	5,000	100,000	3,000	60,000
Product orders, at $135/order	200	27,000	400	54,000
Machine-hours worked, at $7.85/hour	12,000	94,200	28,000	219,800
Material receipts, at $120/receipt	150	18,000	600	72,000
Total overhead cost assigned		$377,200		$497,800
Number of units produced		5,000		20,000
Overhead cost per unit, $\frac{\text{Total overhead}}{\text{No. of units}}$		$75.44		$24.89

SEE R. GARRISON, *MANAGERIAL ACCOUNTING*, 10TH ED. (NEW YORK: MCGRAW-HILL, 2002).

activity-based costing, traceable costs are assigned to specific activities. Because each product required a different amount of transactions, different overhead amounts are allocated to these products from the pools.

As stated earlier, activity-based costing overcomes the problem of cost distortion by creating a cost pool for each activity or transaction that can be identified as a cost driver, and by assigning overhead cost to products or jobs on a basis of the number of separate activities required for their completion. Thus, in the previous situation, the low-volume product would be assigned the bulk of the costs for machine setup, purchase orders, and quality inspections, thereby showing it to have high unit costs compared to the other product.

Finally, activity-based costing is sometimes referred to as *transactions costing*. This transactions focus gives rise to another major advantage over other costing methods: It improves the traceability of overhead costs and thus results in more accurate unit cost data for management.

THE EFFECTS OF TAXES

Tax rates and the methods of applying them occasionally change. When analysts evaluate investment proposals, tax considerations often prove to be the deciding factor because depreciation expenses directly affect taxable income and therefore profit. The ability to write off depreciation in early years provides an added source of funds for investment. Before 1986, firms could employ an investment tax credit, which allowed a direct reduction in tax liability. But tax laws change, so it is crucial to stay on top of current tax laws and try to predict future changes that may affect current investments and accounting procedures.

CHOOSING AMONG INVESTMENT PROPOSALS

The capital investment decision has become highly rationalized, as evidenced by the variety of techniques available for its solution. In contrast to pricing or marketing decisions, the capital investment decision can usually be made with a higher degree of confidence because the variables affecting the decision are relatively well known and can be quantified with fair accuracy.

Investment decisions may be grouped into six general categories:

1. Purchase of new equipment or facilities.
2. Replacement of existing equipment or facilities.
3. Make-or-buy decisions.
4. Lease-or-buy decisions.
5. Temporary shutdowns or plant abandonment decisions.
6. Addition or elimination of a product or product line.

Investment decisions are made with regard to the lowest acceptable rate of return on investment. As a starting point, the lowest acceptable rate of return may be considered to be the cost of investment capital needed to underwrite the expenditure. Certainly an investment will not be made if it does not return at least the cost of capital.

Investments are generally ranked according to the return they yield in excess of their cost of capital. In this way, a business with only limited investment funds can select investment alternatives that yield the highest net returns. (*Net return* is the earnings an investment yields after gross earnings have been reduced by the cost of the funds used to finance the investment.) In general, investments should not be made unless the return in funds exceeds the marginal cost of investment capital. (*Marginal cost* is the incremental cost of each new acquisition of funds from outside sources.)

DETERMINING THE COST OF CAPITAL

The cost of capital is calculated from a weighted average of debt and equity security costs. This average will vary depending on the financing strategy employed by the company. The most common sources of financing are short-term debt, long-term debt, and equity securities. A bank loan is an example of short-term debt. Bonds normally provide long-term debt. Finally, stock is a common form of equity financing. In the following, we give a short example of each form of financing, and then show how they are combined to find the weighted average cost of capital.

The cost of short-term debt depends on the interest rate on the loan and whether the loan is discounted. Remember that interest is a tax-deductible expense for a company.

$$\text{Cost of short-term debt} = \frac{\text{Interest paid}}{\text{Proceeds received}}$$

If a bank discounts a loan, interest is deducted from the face of the loan to get the proceeds. When a compensating balance is required (that is, a percentage of the face value of the loan is held by the bank as collateral), proceeds are also reduced. In either case, the effective or real interest rate on the loan is higher than the face interest rate owing to the proceeds received from the loan being less than the amount (face value) of the loan.

EXAMPLE OF SHORT-TERM DEBT

A company takes a $150,000, one-year, 13 percent loan. The loan is discounted, and a 10 percent compensating balance is required. The effective interest rate is computed as follows:

$$\frac{13\% \times \$150,000}{\$115,500} = \frac{\$19,500}{\$115,500} = 16.89\%$$

Proceeds received equal

Face of loan	$150,000
Less interest	(19,500)
Compensating balance (10% × $150,000)	(15,000)
Proceeds	$115,500

Notice how the effective cost of the loan is significantly greater than the stated interest rate.

Long-term debt is normally provided through the sale of corporate bonds. The real cost of bonds is obtained by computing two types of yield: simple (face) yield and yield to maturity (effective interest rate). The first involves an easy approximation, but the second is more accurate. The nominal interest rate equals the interest paid on the face (maturity value) of the bond and is always stated on a per-annum basis. Bonds are generally issued in $1,000 denominations and may be sold above face value (at a premium) or below (at a discount, termed original issue discount, or OID). A bond is sold at a discount when the interest rate is below the going market rate. In this case, the yield will be higher than the nominal interest rate. The opposite holds for bonds issued at a premium.

The issue price of a bond is the par (or face value) times the premium (or discount).

$$\text{Simple yield} = \frac{\text{Nominal interest}}{\text{Issue price of bond}}$$

$$\text{Yield to maturity} = \frac{\text{Nominal interest} + \dfrac{\text{Discount (or premium)}}{\text{Years}}}{\dfrac{\text{Issue price} + \text{Maturity value}}{2}}$$

EXAMPLE OF LONG-TERM DEBT

A company issues a $400,000, 12 percent, 10-year bond for 97 percent of face value. Yield computations are as follows:

$$\text{Nominal annual payment} = 12\% \times \$400,000$$
$$= \$48,000$$

$$\text{Bond proceeds} = 97\% \times \$400,000$$
$$= \$388,000$$

$$\text{Bond discount} = 3\% \times \$400{,}000$$
$$= \$12{,}000$$

$$\text{Simple yield} = \frac{12\% \times \$400{,}000}{97\% \times \$400{,}000} = \frac{\$48{,}000}{\$388{,}000} = 12.4\%$$

$$\text{Yield to maturity} = \frac{\$48{,}000 + \dfrac{\$12{,}000}{10}}{\dfrac{\$388{,}000 + \$400{,}000}{2}} = \frac{\$48{,}000 + \$1{,}200}{\$394{,}000} = 12.5\%$$

Note that because the bonds were sold at a discount, the yield exceeds the nominal interest rate (12 percent). Bond interest is tax deductible to the corporation.

The actual cost of equity securities (stocks) comes in the form of dividends, which are not tax deductible to the corporation.

$$\text{Cost of common stock} = \frac{\text{Dividends per share}}{\text{Value per share}} + \text{Growth rate of dividends}$$

Here the value per share equals the market price per share minus flotation costs (that is, the cost of issuing securities, such as brokerage fees and printing costs). It should be noted that this valuation does not consider what the investor expects in market price appreciation. This expectation is based on the expected growth in earnings per share and the relative risk taking by purchasing the stock. The capital asset pricing model (CAPM) can be used to capture this impact.[2]

EXAMPLE OF THE COST OF COMMON STOCK
A company's dividend per share is $10, net value is $70 per share, and the dividend growth rate is 5 percent.

$$\text{Cost of the stock} = \frac{\$10}{\$70} + 0.05 = 19.3\%$$

To compute the weighted average cost of capital, we consider the percentage of the total capital that is being provided by each financing alternative. We then calculate the after-tax cost of each financing alternative. Finally, we weight these costs in proportion to their use.

EXAMPLE OF CALCULATING THE WEIGHTED AVERAGE COST OF CAPITAL
Consider a company that shows the following figures in its financial statements:

Short-term bank loan (13%)	$1 million
Bonds payable (16%)	$4 million
Common stock (10%)	$5 million

For our example, assume that each of the percentages given above represents the cost of the source of capital. In addition to the above, we need to consider the tax rate of the firm because the interest paid on the bonds and on the short-term loan is tax deductible. Assume a corporate tax rate of 40 percent.

	PERCENT	AFTER-TAX COST	WEIGHTED AVERAGE COST
Short-term bank loan	10%	13% × 60% = 7.8%	.78%
Bonds payable	40%	16% × 60% = 9.6%	3.84%
Common stock	50%	10%	5%
Total	100%		9.62%

Keep in mind that in developing this section we have made many assumptions in these calculations. When these ideas are applied to a specific company, many of these assumptions may change. The basic concepts, though, are the same; keep in mind that the goal is to simply calculate the after-tax cost of the capital used by the company. We have shown the cost of capital for the entire company, though often only the capital employed for a specific project is used in the calculation.

INTEREST RATE EFFECTS

There are two basic ways to account for the effects of interest accumulation. One is to compute the total amount created over the time period into the future as the *compound value*. The other is to remove the interest rate effect over time by reducing all future sums to present-day dollars, or the *present value*.

Compound Value of a Single Amount   Albert Einstein was quoted as saying that compound interest is the eighth wonder of the world. After reviewing this section showing compound interest's dramatic growth effects over a long time, you might wish to propose a new government regulation: On the birth of a child, the parents must put, say, $1,000 into a retirement fund for that child, available at age 65. This might reduce the pressure on Social Security and other state and federal pension plans. Although inflation would decrease the value significantly, there would still be a lot left over. At 14 percent return on investment, our $1,000 would increase to $500,000 after subtracting the $4.5 million for inflation. That is still a 500-fold increase. (Many mutual funds today have long-term performances in excess of 14 percent per year.)

Spreadsheets and calculators make such computation easy. The box titled "Using a Spreadsheet" shows the most useful financial functions. However, many people still refer to tables for compound values. Using Appendix G, Table G.1 (compound sum of $1), for example, we see that the value of $1 at 10 percent interest after three years is $1.331. Multiplying this figure by $10 gives $13.31.

Compound Value of an Annuity   An *annuity* is the receipt of a constant sum each year for a specified number of years. Usually an annuity is received at the end of a period and does not earn interest during that period. Therefore, an annuity of $10 for three years would bring in $10 at the end of the first year (allowing the $10 to earn interest if invested for the remaining two years), $10 at the end of the second year (allowing the $10 to earn interest for the remaining one year), and $10 at the end of the third year (with no time to earn interest). If the annuity receipts were placed in a bank savings account at 5 percent interest, the total or compound value of the $10 at 5 percent for the three years would be

YEAR	RECEIPT AT END OF YEAR		COMPOUND INTEREST FACTOR $(1 + i)^n$		VALUE AT END OF THIRD YEAR
1	$10.00	×	$(1 + 0.05)^2$	=	$11.02
2	10.00	×	$(1 + 0.05)^1$	=	10.50
3	10.00	×	$(1 + 0.05)^0$	=	10.00
					$31.52

The general formula for finding the compound value of an annuity is

$$S_n = R[(1 + i)^{n-1} + (1 + i)^{n-2} + \cdots + (1 + i)^1 + 1]$$

where

S_n = Compound value of an annuity
R = Periodic receipts in dollars
n = Length of the annuity in years

USING A SPREADSHEET

We hope that you are all doing these calculations using a spreadsheet program. Even though the computer makes these calculations simple, it is important that you understand what the computer is actually doing. Further, you should check your calculations manually to make sure that you have the formulas set up correctly in your spreadsheet. There are many stories of the terrible consequences of making a wrong decision based on a spreadsheet with errors!

For your quick reference, the following are the financial functions you will find most useful. These are from the Microsoft Excel help screens.

PV (rate, nper, pmt)—Returns the present value of an investment. The present value is the total amount that a series of future payments is worth now. For example, when you borrow money, the loan amount is the present value to the lender. Rate is the interest rate per period. For example, if you obtain an automobile loan at a 10 percent annual interest rate and make monthly payments, your interest rate per month is 10%/12, or .83%. You would enter 10%/12, or .83%, or .0083, in the formula as the rate. Nper is the total number of payment periods in an annuity. For example, if you get a four-year car loan and make monthly payments, your loan has 4*12 (or 48) periods. You would enter 48 into the formula for nper. Pmt is the payment made each period and cannot change over the life of the annuity. Typically, this includes principal and interest but no other fees or taxes. For example, the monthly payment on a $10,000, four-year car loan at 12 percent is $263.33. You would enter 263.33 into the formula as pmt.

FV (rate, nper, pmt)—Returns the future value of an investment based on periodic, constant payments and a constant interest rate. Rate is the interest rate per period. Nper is the total number of payment periods in an annuity. Pmt is the payment made each period; it cannot change over the life of the annuity. Typically, pmt contains principal and interest but no other fees or taxes.

NPV (rate, value1, value2, . . .)—Returns the net present value of an investment based on a series of periodic cash flows and a discount rate. The net present value of an investment is today's value of a series of future payments (negative values) and income (positive values). Rate is the rate of discount over the length of one period. Value1, value2, . . . must be equally spaced in time and occur at the end of each period.

IRR(values)—Returns the internal rate of return for a series of cash flows represented by the numbers in values. (*Values* is defined below.) These cash flows do not have to be even, as they would be for an annuity. The internal rate of return is the interest rate received for an investment consisting of payments (negative values) and income (positive values) that occur at regular periods. *Values* is an array or a reference to cells that contain numbers for which you want to calculate the internal rate of return. Values must contain at least one positive value and one negative value to calculate the internal rate of return. IRR uses the order of values to interpret the order of cash flows. Be sure to enter your payment and income values in the sequence you want.

Applying this formula to the preceding example, we get

$$S_n = R[(1 + i)^2 + (1 + i) + 1]$$
$$= \$10[(1 + 0.05)^2 + (1 + 0.05) + 1] = \$31.52$$

In Appendix G, Table G.2 lists the compound value factor of $1 for 5 percent after three years as 3.152. Multiplying this factor by $10 yields $31.52.

In a fashion similar to our previous retirement investment example, consider the beneficial effects of investing $2,000 each year, just starting at the age of 21. Assume investments in AAA-rated bonds are available today yielding 9 percent. From Table G.2 in Appendix G, after 30 years (at age 51) the investment is worth 136.3 times $2,000, or $272,600. Fourteen years later (at age 65) this would be worth $963,044 (using a hand calculator, because the table goes only to 30 years, and assuming the $2,000 is deposited at the end of each year)! But what 21-year-old thinks about retirement?

Present Value of a Future Single Payment   Compound values are used to determine future value after a specific period has elapsed; present value (PV) procedures accomplish just the reverse. They are used to determine the current value of a sum or stream of receipts expected to be received in the future. Most investment decision techniques use present value concepts rather than compound values. Because decisions affecting the future are made in the present, it is better to convert future returns into their present value at the time the decision is being made. In this way, investment alternatives are placed in better perspective in terms of current dollars.

An example makes this more apparent. If a rich uncle offers to make you a gift of $100 today or $250 after 10 years, which should you choose? You must determine whether the $250 in 10 years will be worth more than the $100 now. Suppose that you base your decision on the rate of inflation in the economy and believe that inflation averages 10 percent per year. By deflating the $250, you can compare its relative purchasing power with $100 received today. Procedurally, this is accomplished by solving the compound formula for the present sum, P, where V is the future amount of $250 in 10 years at 10 percent. The compound value formula is

$$V = P(1 + i)^n$$

Dividing both sides by $(1 + i)^n$ gives

$$P = \frac{V}{(1 + i)^n}$$

$$= \frac{250}{(1 + 0.10)^{10}} = \$96.39$$

This shows that, at a 10 percent inflation rate, $250 in 10 years will be worth $96.39 today. The rational choice, then, is to take the $100 now.

The use of tables is also standard practice in solving present value problems. With reference to Appendix G, Table G.3, the present value factor for $1 received 10 years hence is 0.386. Multiplying this factor by $250 yields $96.50.

Present Value of an Annuity The present value of an annuity is the value of an annual amount to be received over a future period expressed in terms of the present. To find the value of an annuity of $100 for three years at 10 percent, find the factor in the present value table that applies to 10 percent in *each* of the three years in which the amount is received and multiply each receipt by this factor. Then sum the resulting figures. Remember that annuities are usually received at the end of each period.

YEAR	AMOUNT RECEIVED AT END OF YEAR		PRESENT VALUE FACTOR AT 10%		PRESENT VALUE
1	$100	×	0.909	=	$ 90.90
2	100	×	0.826	=	82.60
3	100	×	0.751	=	75.10
Total receipts	$300		Total present value	=	$248.60

The general formula used to derive the present value of an annuity is

$$A_n = R\left[\frac{1}{(1 + i)} + \frac{1}{(1 + i)^2} + \cdots + \frac{1}{(1 + i)^n}\right]$$

where

A_n = Present value of an annuity of n years
R = Periodic receipts
n = Length of the annuity in years

Applying the formula to the preceding example gives

$$A_n = \$100\left[\frac{1}{(1 + 0.10)} + \frac{1}{(1 + 0.10)^2} + \frac{1}{(1 + 0.10)^3}\right]$$

$$= \$100(2.487) = \$248.70$$

In Appendix G, Table G.4 contains present values of an annuity for varying maturities. The present value factor for an annuity of $1 for three years at 10 percent (from Appendix G, Table G.4) is 2.487. Given that our sum is $100 rather than $1, we multiply this factor by $100 to arrive at $248.70.

When the stream of future receipts is uneven, the present value of each annual receipt must be calculated. The present values of the receipts for all years are then summed to arrive at total present value. This process can sometimes be tedious, but it is unavoidable.

Discounted Cash Flow   The term *discounted cash flow* refers to the total stream of payments that an asset will generate in the future discounted to the present time. This is simply present value analysis that includes all flows: single payments, annuities, and all others.

METHODS OF RANKING INVESTMENTS

Net Present Value   The net present value method is commonly used in business. With this method, decisions are based on the amount by which the present value of a projected income stream exceeds the cost of an investment.

A firm is considering two alternative investments. The first costs $30,000 and the second, $50,000. The expected yearly cash income streams are shown in this table:

	CASH INFLOW	
YEAR	ALTERNATIVE A	ALTERNATIVE B
1	$10,000	$15,000
2	10,000	15,000
3	10,000	15,000
4	10,000	15,000
5	10,000	15,000

To choose between Alternatives A and B, find which has the higher net present value. Assume an 8 percent cost of capital.

ALTERNATIVE A		ALTERNATIVE B	
3.993 (PV factor)		3.993 (PV factor)	
× $10,000	= $39,930	× $15,000	= $59,895
Less cost of investment =	30,000	Less cost of investment =	50,000
Net present value	= $ 9,930	Net present value	= $ 9,895

Investment A is the better alternative. Its net present value exceeds that of Investment B by $35 ($9,930 − $9,895 = $35).

Payback Period   The payback method ranks investments according to the time required for each investment to return earnings equal to the cost of the investment. The rationale is that the sooner the investment capital can be recovered, the sooner it can be reinvested in new revenue-producing projects. Thus, supposedly, a firm will be able to get the most benefit from its available investment funds.

Consider two alternatives requiring a $1,000 investment each. The first will earn $200 per year for six years; the second will earn $300 per year for the first three years and $100 per year for the next three years.

If the first alternative is selected, the initial investment of $1,000 will be recovered at the end of the fifth year. The income produced by the second alternative will total $1,000 after only four years. The second alternative will permit reinvestment of the full $1,000 in new revenue-producing projects one year sooner than the first.

Though the payback method is declining in popularity as the sole measure in investment decisions, it is still frequently used in conjunction with other methods to indicate the time commitment of funds. The major problems with payback are that it does not consider income beyond the payback period and it ignores the time value of money. A method that ignores the time value of money must be considered questionable.

Internal Rate of Return   The internal rate of return may be defined as the interest rate that equates the present value of an income stream with the cost of an investment. There is no procedure or formula that may be used directly to compute the internal rate of return—it must be found by interpolation or iterative calculation.

Suppose we wish to find the internal rate of return for an investment costing $12,000 that will yield a cash inflow of $4,000 per year for four years. We see that the present value factor sought is

$$\frac{\$12,000}{\$4,000} = 3.000$$

and we seek the interest rate that will provide this factor over a four-year period. The interest rate must lie between 12 and 14 percent because 3.000 lies between 3.037 and 2.914 (in the fourth row of Appendix G, Table G.4). Linear interpolation between these values, according to the equation

$$I = 12 + (14 - 12)\frac{(3.037 - 3.000)}{(3.037 - 2.914)}$$

$$= 12 + 0.602 = 12.602\%$$

gives a good approximation to the actual internal rate of return.

When the income stream is discounted at 12.6 percent, the resulting present value closely approximates the cost of investment. Thus, the internal rate of return for this investment is 12.6 percent. The cost of capital can be compared with the internal rate of return to determine the net rate of return on the investment. If, in this example, the cost of capital were 8 percent, the net rate of return on the investment would be 4.6 percent.

The net present value and internal rate of return methods involve procedures that are essentially the same. They differ in that the net present value method enables investment alternatives to be compared in terms of the dollar value in excess of cost, whereas the internal rate of return method permits comparison of rates of return on alternative investments. Moreover, the internal rate of return method occasionally encounters problems in calculation, as multiple rates frequently appear in the computation.

Ranking Investments with Uneven Lives   When proposed investments have the same life expectancy, comparison among them, using the preceding methods, will give a reasonable picture of their relative value. When lives are unequal, however, there is the question of how to relate the two different time periods. Should replacements be considered the same as the original? Should productivity for the shorter-term unit that will be replaced earlier be considered higher? How should the cost of future units be estimated?

No estimate dealing with investments unforeseen at the time of decision can be expected to reflect a high degree of accuracy. Still, the problem must be dealt with, and some assumptions must be made in order to determine a ranking.

SAMPLE PROBLEMS: INVESTMENT DECISIONS

EXAMPLE SA.1: An Expansion Decision

William J. Wilson Ceramic Products, Inc., leases plant facilities in which firebrick is manufactured. Because of rising demand, Wilson could increase sales by investing in new equipment to expand output. The selling price of $10 per brick will remain unchanged if output and sales increase. Based on engineering and cost estimates, the accounting department provides management with the following cost estimates based on an annual increased output of 100,000 bricks:

Cost of new equipment having an expected life of five years	$500,000
Equipment installation cost	20,000
Expected salvage value	0
New operation's share of annual lease expense	40,000
Annual increase in utility expenses	40,000
Annual increase in labor costs	160,000
Annual additional cost for raw materials	400,000

The sum-of-the-years'-digits method of depreciation will be used, and taxes are paid at a rate of 40 percent. Wilson's policy is not to invest capital in projects earning less than a 20 percent rate of return. Should the proposed expansion be undertaken?

SOLUTION

Compute the cost of investment:

Acquisition cost of equipment	$500,000
Equipment installation costs	20,000
Total cost of investment	$520,000

Determine yearly cash flows throughout the life of the investment.

The lease expense is a sunk cost. It will be incurred whether or not the investment is made and is therefore irrelevant to the decision and should be disregarded. Annual production expenses to be considered are utility, labor, and raw materials. These total $600,000 per year.

Annual sales revenue is $10 \times 100,000$ units of output, which totals $1,000,000. Yearly income before depreciation and taxes is thus $1,000,000 gross revenue, less $600,000 expenses, or $400,000.

Next, determine the depreciation charges to be deducted from the $400,000 income each year using the SYD method (sum-of-years'-digits $= 1 + 2 + 3 + 4 + 5 = 15$):

YEAR	PROPORTION OF $500,000 TO BE DEPRECIATED		DEPRECIATION CHARGE
1	5/15 × $500,000	=	$166,667
2	4/15 × 500,000	=	133,333
3	3/15 × 500,000	=	100,000
4	2/15 × 500,000	=	66,667
5	1/15 × 500,000	=	33,333
	Accumulated depreciation		$500,000

Find each year's cash flow when taxes are 40 percent. Cash flow for only the first year is illustrated:

Earnings before depreciation and taxes		$400,000
Deduct: Taxes at 40% (40% × 400,000)	$160,000	
Tax benefit of depreciation expense (0.4 × 166,667)	66,667	93,333
Cash flow (first year)		$306,667

Determine the present value of the cash flow. Because Wilson demands at least a 20 percent rate of return on investments, multiply the cash flows by the 20 percent present value factor for each year. The factor for each respective year must be used because the cash flows are not an annuity.

YEAR	PRESENT VALUE FACTOR		CASH FLOW		PRESENT VALUE
1	0.833	×	$306,667	=	$255,454
2	0.694	×	293,333	=	203,573
3	0.579	×	280,000	=	162,120
4	0.482	×	266,667	=	128,533
5	0.402	×	253,334	=	101,840
	Total present value of cash flows (discounted at 20%) =				$851,520

Now find whether net present value is positive or negative:

Total present value of cash flows	$851,520
Total cost of investment	520,000
Net present value	$331,520

Net present value is positive when returns are discounted at 20 percent. Wilson will earn an amount in excess of 20 percent on the investment. The proposed expansion should be undertaken. ●

EXAMPLE SA.2: A Replacement Decision

For five years Bennie's Brewery has been using a machine that attaches labels to bottles. The machine was purchased for $4,000 and is being depreciated over 10 years to a $0 salvage value using straight-line depreciation. The machine can be sold now for $2,000. Bennie can buy a new labeling machine for $6,000 that will have a useful life of five years and cut labor costs by $1,200 annually. The old machine will require a major overhaul in the next few months at an estimated cost of $300. If purchased, the new machine will be depreciated over five years to a $500 salvage value using the straight-line method. The company will invest in any project earning more than the 12 percent cost of capital. The tax rate is 40 percent. Should Bennie's Brewery invest in the new machine?

SOLUTION

Determine the cost of investment:

Price of the new machine		$6,000
Less: Sale of old machine	$2,000	
Avoidable overhaul costs	300	2,300
Effective cost of investment		$3,700

Determine the increase in cash flow resulting from investment in the new machine:

Yearly cost savings = $1,200

Differential depreciation

  Annual depreciation on old machine:

$$\frac{Cost - Salvage}{Expected\ life} = \frac{\$4,000 - \$0}{10} = \$400$$

  Annual depreciation on new machine:

$$\frac{Cost - Salvage}{Expected\ life} = \frac{\$6,000 - \$500}{5} = \$1,100$$

  Differential depreciation = $1,100 − $400 = $700

Yearly net increase in cash flow into the firm:

Cost savings		$1,200
Deduct: Taxes at 40%	$480	
Add: Advantage of increase in depreciation (0.4 × $700)	280	200
Yearly increase in cash flow		$1,000

Determine total present value of the investment:

  The five-year cash flow of $1,000 per year is an annuity.

  Discounted at 12 percent, the cost of capital, the present value is

  3.605 × $1,000 = $3,605

  The present value of the new machine, if sold at its salvage value of $500 at the end of the fifth year, is

  0.567 × $500 = $284

  Total present value of the expected cash flows is

  $3,605 + $284 = $3,889

Determine whether net present value is positive:

Total present value	$3,889
Cost of investment	3,700
Net present value	$189

Bennie's Brewery should make the purchase because the investment will return slightly more than the cost of capital.

Note: The importance of depreciation has been shown in this example. The present value of the yearly cash flow resulting from operations is

$$(\text{Cost savings} - \text{Taxes}) \times (\text{Present value factor})$$

$$(\$1,200 - \$480) \qquad \times \qquad (3.605) \qquad = \$2,596$$

This figure is $1,104 less than the $3,700 cost of the investment. Only a very large depreciation advantage makes this investment worthwhile. The total present value of the advantage is $1,009:

$$(\text{Tax rate} \times \text{Differential depreciation}) \times (\text{PV factor})$$

$$(0.4 \times \$700) \qquad\qquad \times \quad (3.605) \quad = \$1,009 \; \bullet$$

EXAMPLE SA.3: A Make-or-Buy Decision

The Triple X Company manufactures and sells refrigerators. It makes some of the parts for the refrigerators and purchases others. The engineering department believes it might be possible to cut costs by manufacturing one of the parts currently being purchased for $8.25 each. The firm uses 100,000 of these parts each year. The accounting department compiles the following list of costs based on engineering estimates:

Fixed costs will increase by $50,000.

Labor costs will increase by $125,000.

Factory overhead, currently running $500,000 per year, may be expected to increase 12 percent.

Raw materials used to make the part will cost $600,000.

Given the preceding estimates, should Triple X make the part or continue to buy it?

SOLUTION

Find the total cost incurred if the part were manufactured:

Additional fixed costs	$ 50,000
Additional labor costs	125,000
Raw materials cost	600,000
Additional overhead costs = 0.12 × $500,000	60,000
Total cost to manufacturer	$835,000

Find the cost per unit to manufacture:

$$\frac{\$835,000}{100,000} = \$8.35 \text{ per unit}$$

Triple X should continue to buy the part. Manufacturing costs exceed the present cost to purchase by $0.10 per unit. $\bullet$

SELECTED BIBLIOGRAPHY

Bodie, Z.; A. Kane; and A. Marcus. *Investments.* 3rd ed. Burr Ridge, IL: Richard D. Irwin, 1996.

Helfert, E. *Techniques of Financial Analysis: A Modern Approach.* 9th ed. New York: Irwin/McGraw-Hill, 1997.

Poterba, J. M., and L. H. Summers. "A CEO Survey of U.S. Companies' Time Horizons and Hurdle Rates." *Sloan Management Review,* Fall 1995, pp. 43–53.

FOOTNOTES

1 T. Johnson and R. Kaplan, *Relevance Lost: The Rise and Fall of Management Accounting* (Boston: Harvard Business School Press, 1987), p. 188.

2 A description of capital asset pricing is included in many finance textbooks; see, for example, Z. Bodie, A. Kane, and A. Marcus, *Investments,* 3rd ed. (Burr Ridge, IL: Richard D. Irwin, 1996), pp. 236–65.

OPERATIONS TECHNOLOGY

Much of the recent growth in productivity has come from the application of operations technology. In services this comes primarily from soft technology—information processing. In manufacturing it comes from a combination of soft and hard (machine) technologies. Given that most readers of this book have covered information technologies in services in MIS courses, our focus in this supplement is on manufacturing.

TECHNOLOGIES IN MANUFACTURING

Although technological changes have occurred in almost every industry, many may be unique to an industry. For instance, a prestressed concrete block is a technological advance unique to the construction industry. Major developments in the design of automobiles will result in cars that are made from recyclable parts. (See Exhibit SB.1 for a description of the materials and process technologies that are being developed.)

Some technological advances in recent decades have had a significant, widespread impact on manufacturing firms in many industries. These advances, which are the topic of this section, can be categorized in two ways: hardware systems and software systems.

Hardware technologies have generally resulted in greater automation of processes; they perform labor-intensive tasks originally performed by humans. Examples of these major types of hardware technologies are numerically controlled machine tools, machining centers, industrial robots, automated materials handling systems, and flexible manufacturing systems. These are all computer-controlled devices that can be used in the manufacturing of products.

Automobile Recycling

exhibit SB.1

Refrigerant from air conditioners is routinely recovered, cleaned, and reused in other cars.

Coolant is purified so that it can be used once again.

Batteries are replaced periodically; the lead plates, acid, and even plastic cases are usually recycled.

Oil is replaced frequently but typically can be recycled as fuel oil.

Bumpers can be disassembled and recycled into new bumpers.

Catalytic converters contain valuable amounts of platinum and thodium, although extracting these elements has proved difficult.

Transmissions and other mechanical components of the engine and drivetrain are often refurbished.

Wheels are commonly used as replacements or can be recycled for scrap steel.

Plastic interiors are the troubling parts to recycle, but innovative methods are having success.

Body parts such as doors are kept as replacements or recycled for scrap steel.

Tires may be used for scrap rubber, or can be ground up and burned as fuel.

Automobile recycling is one of the most successful examples of reuse of manufactured product. About 75 percent of a typical car can be recycled in the form of refurbished parts, useful fluids, and scrap materials. This process can, however, be taken further. New methods to separate and recycle plastic components, for example, offer the possibility of removing even more material from the waste stream and returning it to the manufacturing cycle.

FIGURE FROM R. A. FROSCH, "THE INDUSTRIAL ECOLOGY," *SCIENTIFIC AMERICAN*, SEPTEMBER 1995, P. 18. ILLUSTRATION © 1995 BY KARL GUDE. USED WITH PERMISSION.

Software-based technologies aid in the design of manufactured products and in the analysis and planning of manufacturing activities. These technologies include computer-aided design and automated manufacturing planning and control systems. Each of these technologies will be described in greater detail in the following sections.

Hardware Systems   *Numerically controlled (NC) machines* are comprised of (1) a typical machine tool used to turn, drill, or grind different types of parts and (2) a computer that controls the sequence of processes performed by the machine. NC machines were first adopted by U.S. aerospace firms in the 1960s, and they have since proliferated to many other industries. In more recent models, feedback control loops determine the position of the machine tooling during the work, constantly compare the actual location with the programmed location, and correct as needed. This is often called *adaptive control.*

Machining centers represent an increased level of automation and complexity relative to NC machines. Machining centers not only provide automatic control of a machine, they may also carry many tools that can be automatically changed depending on the tool required for each operation. In addition, a single machine may be equipped with a shuttle system so that a finished part can be unloaded and an unfinished part loaded while the machine is working on a part. To help you visualize a machining center, we have included a diagram in Exhibit SB.2.

Industrial robots are used as substitutes for workers for many repetitive manual activities and tasks that are dangerous, dirty, or dull. A robot is a programmable, multifunctional machine that may be equipped with an end effector. Examples of end effectors include a gripper to pick things up or a tool such as a wrench, a welder, or a paint sprayer. Exhibit SB.3 examines the human motions a robot can reproduce. Advanced capabilities have been designed into robots to allow vision, tactile sensing, and hand-to-hand coordination. In addition, some models can

exhibits SB.2 & 3

SB.2—The CNC Machining Center

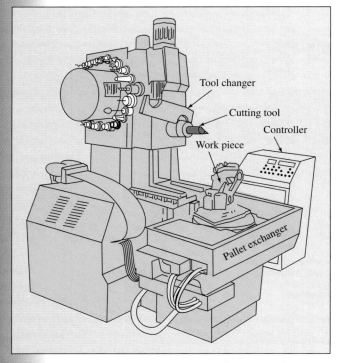

SOURCE: J. T. BLACK, *THE DESIGN OF THE FACTORY WITH A FUTURE* (NEW YORK: MCGRAW-HILL, 1991), P. 39, WITH PERMISSION OF THE MCGRAW-HILL COMPANIES.

SB.3—Typical Robot Axes of Motion

SOURCE: L. V. OTTINGER, "ROBOTICS FOR THE IE: TERMINOLOGY, TYPES OF ROBOTS," *INDUSTRIAL ENGINEERING*, NOVEMBER 1981, P. 30.

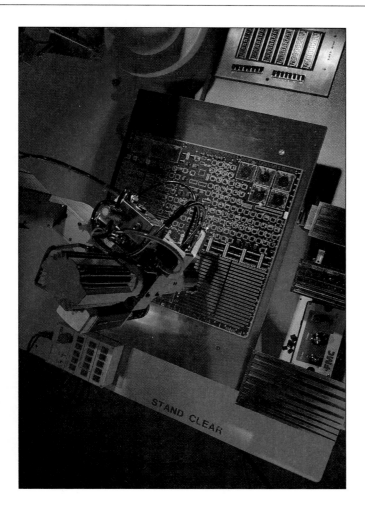

be "taught" a sequence of motions in a three-dimensional pattern. As a worker moves the end of the robot arm through the required motions, the robot records this pattern in its memory and repeats it on command. Newer robotic systems can conduct quality control inspections and then transfer, via mobile robots, those parts to other robots downstream. As shown in the box "Formula for Evaluating a Robot Investment," robots are often justified based on labor savings.

Automated materials handing (AMH) systems improve efficiency of transportation, storage, and retrieval of materials. Examples are computerized conveyors and automated storage and retrieval systems (AS/RS) in which computers direct automatic loaders to pick and place items. Automated guided vehicle (AGV) systems use embedded floor wires to direct driverless vehicles to various locations in the plant. Benefits of AMH systems include quicker material movement, lower inventories and storage space, reduced product damage, and higher labor productivity.

These individual pieces of automation can be combined to form *manufacturing cells* or even complete *flexible manufacturing systems (FMS)*. A manufacturing cell might consist of a robot and a machining center. The robot could be programmed to automatically insert and remove parts from the machining center, thus allowing unattended operation. An FMS is a totally automated manufacturing system that consists of machining centers with automated loading and unloading of parts, an automated guided vehicle system for moving parts between machines, and other automated elements to allow unattended production of parts. In an FMS, a comprehensive computer control system is used to run the entire system.

A good example of an FMS is the Cincinnati Milacron facility in Mt. Orab, Ohio, which has been in operation for over 20 years. Exhibit SB.4 is a layout of this FMS. In this system, parts are loaded onto standardized fixtures (these are called "risers"), which are mounted on pallets that can be moved by the AGVs. Workers load and unload tools and parts onto the

FORMULA FOR EVALUATING A ROBOT INVESTMENT

Many companies use the following modification of the basic payback formula in deciding if a robot should be purchased:

$$P = \frac{I}{L - E + q(L + Z)}$$

where

P = Payback period in years

I = Total capital investment required in robot and accessories

L = Annual labor costs replaced by the robot (wage and benefit costs per worker times the number of shifts per day)

E = Annual maintenance cost for the robot

q = Fractional speedup (or slowdown) factor

Z = Annual depreciation

Example:

I = $50,000

L = $60,000 (two workers × $20,000 each working one of two shifts; overhead is $10,000 each)

E = $9,600 ($2/hour × 4,800 hours/year)

q = 1.5 (robot works 150 percent as fast as a worker)

Z = $10,000

then

$$P = \frac{\$50,000}{\$60,000 - \$9,600 + 1.5(\$60,000 + \$10,000)}$$

$$= 1/3 \text{ year.}$$

ONE OF THE FOUR LARGE MACHINING CENTERS (SEE EXHIBIT SB.4) THAT ARE PART OF THE FLEXIBLE MANUFACTURING SYSTEMS AT CINCINNATI MILACRON'S MT. ORAB, OHIO, PLANT.

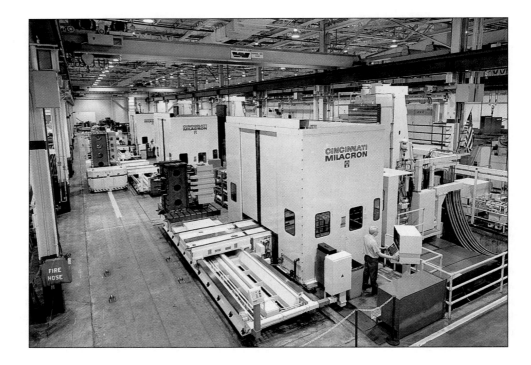

standardized fixtures at the workstations shown on the right side of the diagram. Most of this loading and unloading is done during a single shift. The system can operate virtually unattended for the other two shifts each day.

Within the system there are areas for the storage of tools (Area 7) and for parts (Area 5). This system is designed to machine large castings used in the production of the machine tools made by Cincinnati Milacron. The machining is done by the four CNC machining centers (Area 1). When the machining has been completed on a part, it is sent to the parts washing station (Area 4), where it is cleaned. The part is then sent to the automated inspection station (Area 6) for a quality check. The system is capable of producing hundreds of different parts.

Software Systems   *Computer-aided design (CAD)* is an approach to product and process design that utilizes the power of the computer. CAD covers several automated

The Cincinnati Milacron Flexible Manufacturing System

Key:

1 Four Milacron T-30 CNC Machining Centers.
2 Four tool interchange stations, one per machine, for tool storage chain delivery via computer-controlled cart.
3 Cart maintenance station. Coolant monitoring and maintenance area.
4 Parts wash station, automatic handling.
5 Automatic Workchanger (10 pallets) for online pallet queue.
6 One inspection module—horizontal type coordinate measuring machine.
7 Three queue stations for tool delivery chains.
8 Tool delivery chain load/unload stations.
9 Four part load/unload stations.
10 Pallet/fixture build station.
11 Control center, computer room (elevated).
12 Centralized chip/coolant collection/recovery system (----flume path).
13 Three computer-controlled carts, with wire-guided path.
⌒ Cart turnaround station (up to 360° around its own axis)

SOURCE: TOUR BROCHURE FROM THE PLANT.

technologies, such as *computer graphics* to examine the visual characteristics of a product and *computer-aided engineering (CAE)* to evaluate its engineering characteristics. Rubbermaid used CAD to refine dimensions of its ToteWheels to meet airline requirements for checked baggage. CAD also includes technologies associated with the manufacturing process design, referred to as *computer-aided process planning (CAPP)*. CAPP is used to design the computer part programs that serve as instructions to computer-controlled machine tools, and to design the programs used to sequence parts through the machine centers and other processes (such as the washing and inspection) needed to complete the part. These programs are referred to as *process plans*. Sophisticated CAD systems also are able to do on-screen tests, replacing the early phases of prototype testing and modification.

CAD has been used to design everything from computer chips to potato chips. Frito-Lay, for example, used CAD to design its O'Grady's double-density, ruffled potato chip. The problem in designing such a chip is that if it is cut improperly, it may be burned on the outside and soggy on the inside, be too brittle (and shatter when placed in the bag), or display other characteristics that make it unworthy for, say, a guacamole dip. However, through the use of CAD, the proper angle and number of ruffles were determined mathematically; the O'Grady's model passed its stress test in the infamous Frito-Lay "crusher" and made it to your grocer's shelf.

CAD is now being used to custom design swimsuits. Measurements of the wearer are fed into the CAD program, along with the style of suit desired. Working with the customer, the designer modifies the suit design as it appears on a human-form drawing on the computer screen. Once the design is decided upon, the computer prints out a pattern, and the suit is cut and sewn on the spot.

Automated manufacturing planning and control systems (MP&CS) are simply computer-based information systems that help plan, schedule, and monitor a manufacturing operation. They obtain information from the factory floor continuously about work status, material arrivals, and so on, and they release production and purchase orders. Sophisticated manufacturing and planning control systems include order-entry processing, shop-floor control, purchasing, and cost accounting.

COMPUTER-INTEGRATED MANUFACTURING (CIM)

All of these automation technologies are brought together under *computer-integrated manufacturing (CIM)*. CIM is the automated version of the manufacturing process, where the three major manufacturing functions—product and process design, planning and control, and the manufacturing process itself—are replaced by the automated technologies just described. Further, the traditional integration mechanisms of oral and written communication are replaced by computer technology. Such highly automated and integrated manufacturing also goes under other names: *total factory automation* and the *factory of the future.*

All of the CIM technologies are tied together using a network and integrated database. For instance, data integration allows CAD systems to be linked to *computer-aided manufacturing (CAM),* which consists of numerical-control parts programs; and the manufacturing planning and control system can be linked to the automated material handling systems to facilitate parts pick list generation. Thus, in a fully integrated system, the areas of design, testing, fabrication, assembly, inspection, and material handling are not only automated but also integrated with each other and with the manufacturing planning and scheduling function.

EVALUATION OF TECHNOLOGY INVESTMENTS

Modern technologies such as flexible manufacturing systems or computerized order processing systems represent large capital investments. Hence, a firm has to carefully assess its financial and strategic benefits from a technology before acquiring it. Evaluating such investments is especially hard because the purpose of acquiring new technologies is not just to reduce labor costs but also to increase product quality and variety, to shorten production lead times, and to increase the flexibility of an operation. Some of these benefits are intangible relative to labor cost reduction, so justification becomes difficult. Further, rapid technological change renders new equipment obsolete in just a few years, making the cost–benefit evaluation more complex.

But never assume that new automation technologies are always cost-effective. Even when there is no uncertainty about the benefits of automation, it may not be worthwhile to adopt it. For instance, many analysts predicted that integrated CAD/CAM systems would be the answer to all manufacturing problems. But a number of companies investing in such systems lost money in the process. The idea was to take a lot of skilled labor out of the process of tooling up for new or redesigned products and to speed up the process. However, it can take less time to mill complex, low-volume parts than to program the milling machine, and programmer time is more expensive than the milling operator time. Also, it may not always be easy to transfer all the expert knowledge and experience that a milling operator has gained over the years into a computer program. CAD/CAM integration software has attained sufficient levels of quality and cost effectiveness that it is now routinely utilized even in high-variety low-volume manufacturing environments.

BENEFITS OF TECHNOLOGY INVESTMENTS

The typical benefits from adopting new manufacturing technologies are both tangible and intangible. The tangible benefits can be used in traditional modes of financial analysis, such as discounted cash flow, to make sound investment decisions. Specific benefits can be summarized as follows:

COST REDUCTION

Labor costs.   Replacing people with robots, or enabling fewer workers to run semi-automatic equipment.

Material costs.   Using existing materials more efficiently, or enabling the use of high-tolerance materials.

Inventory costs.   Fast changeover equipment allowing for JIT inventory management.

Quality costs.   Automated inspection and reduced variation in product output.

Maintenance costs.   Self-adjusting equipment.

OTHER BENEFITS

Increased product variety.   Scope economies due to flexible manufacturing systems.

Improved product features.   Ability to make things that could not be made by hand (e.g., microprocessors).

Shorter cycle times.   Faster setups and changeovers.

Greater product output.

Risks in Adopting New Technologies   Although there may be many benefits in acquiring new technologies, several types of risk accompany the acquisition of new technologies. These risks have to be evaluated and traded off against the benefits before the technologies are adopted. Some of these risks are described next.

TECHNOLOGICAL RISKS

An early adopter of a new technology has the benefit of being ahead of the competition, but he or she also runs the risk of acquiring an untested technology whose problems could disrupt the firm's operations. There is also the risk of obsolescence, especially with electronics-based technologies where change is rapid and when the fixed cost of acquiring new technologies or the cost of upgrades is high. Also, alternative technologies may become more cost-effective in the future, negating the benefits of a technology today.

OPERATIONAL RISKS

There could also be risks in applying a new technology to a firm's operations. Installation of a new technology generally results in significant disruptions, at least in the short run, in the form of plantwide reorganization, retraining, and so on. Further risks are due to the delays and errors introduced in the production process and the uncertain and sudden demands on various resources.

ORGANIZATIONAL RISKS

Firms may lack the organizational culture and top management commitment required to absorb the short-term disruptions and uncertainties associated with adopting a new technology. In such organizations, there is a risk that the firm's employees or managers may quickly abandon the technology when there are short-term failures or will avoid major changes by simply automating the firm's old, inefficient process and therefore not obtain the benefits of the new technology.

ENVIRONMENTAL OR MARKET RISKS

In many cases, a firm may invest in a particular technology only to discover a few years later that changes in some environmental or market factors make the investment worthless. For instance, in environmental issues auto firms have been reluctant to invest in technology for making electric cars because they are uncertain about future emission standards of state and federal governments, the potential for decreasing emissions from gasoline-based cars, and the potential for significant improvements in battery technology. Typical examples of market risks are fluctuations in currency exchange rates and interest rates.

CONCLUSION

Technology has played the dominant role in the productivity growth of most nations and has provided the competitive edge to firms that have adopted it early and implemented it successfully. Although each of the manufacturing and information technologies described here is a powerful tool by itself and can be adopted separately, their benefits grow exponentially when they are integrated with each other. This is particularly the case with CIM technologies.

With more modern technologies, the benefits are not entirely tangible and many benefits may be realized only on a long-term basis. Thus, typical cost accounting methods and standard financial analysis may not adequately capture all the potential benefits of technologies such as CIM. Hence, we must take into account the strategic benefits in evaluating such investments. Further, because capital costs for many modern technologies are substantial, the various risks associated with such investments have to be carefully assessed.

Implementing flexible manufacturing systems or complex decision support systems requires a significant commitment for most firms. Such investments may even be beyond the reach of small to medium-sized firms. However, as technologies continue to improve and are adopted more widely, their costs may decline and place them within the reach of smaller firms. Given the complex, integrative nature of these technologies, the total commitment of top management and all employees is critical for the successful implementation of these technologies.

REVIEW AND DISCUSSION QUESTIONS

1 Do robots have to be trained? Explain.

2 How does the axiom used in industrial selling "You don't sell the product; you sell the company" pertain to manufacturing technology?

3 List three analytical tools (other than financial analysis) covered elsewhere in the book that can be used to evaluate technological alternatives.

4 The Belleville, Ontario, Canada, subsidiary of Atlanta-based Interface Inc., one of the world's largest makers of commercial flooring, credits much of its profitability to "green manufacturing" or "eco-efficiency." What do you believe these terms mean, eh? And how could such practices lead to cost reduction?

5 Give two examples each of recent process and product technology innovations.

6 What is the difference between an NC machine and a machining center?

7 The major auto companies are planning to invest millions of dollars in developing new product and process technologies required to make electric cars. Describe briefly why they are investing in these technologies. Discuss the potential benefits and risks involved in these investments.

SELECTED BIBLIOGRAPHY

Black, J. T. *The Design of the Factory with a Future.* New York: McGraw-Hill, 1991.

Chang, T.; R. A. Wysk; and H. Wang. *Computer-Aided Manufacturing.* Upper Saddle Creek, NJ: Prentice Hall, 1997.

Cohen, M., and U. Apte. *Manufacturing Automation.* New York: Irwin/McGraw-Hill, 1997.

Gaynor, G. H. *Achieving the Competitive Edge through Integrated Technology Management.* New York: McGraw-Hill, 1991.

Groover, M. P. *Fundamentals of Modern Manufacturing.* 2nd ed. New York: Wiley, 2001.

Hyer, N., and U. Wemmerlöv. *Reorganizing the Factory: Competing through Cellular Manufacturing.* Portland: OR; Productivity Press, 2002.

Melnyk, S. A., and R. Narasimhan. *Computer Integrated Manufacturing.* Homewood, IL: Irwin Professional Publishing, 1992.

Negroponte, N. *Being Digital.* New York: Vantage Books, 1995.

ANSWERS TO SELECTED PROBLEMS

Chapter 2

1   Productivity (hours)
    Deluxe   0.20
    Limited   0.20
    Productivity (dollars)
    Deluxe   133.33
    Limited   135.71

Technical Note 2

2   Optimal combination is $B = 10$, $A = 15$, and $Z = 70$.
4   a. $600A + 900B \leq 3,600$
       $600A + 900B \geq 1,800$
       $200A + 700B \leq 1,400$
       $400A + 100B \geq 400$
       $A \leq 2$
       Minimize $.75A + .15B$
    b. $A = 0.54$
       $B = 1.85$
       Obj $= 0.68$

Chapter 3

3   b. A-C-F-G-I and A-D-F-G-I
    c. C: one week
       D: one week
       G: one week
    d. Two paths: A-C-F-G-I; and A-D-F-G-I; 16 weeks
6   a. Critical path is A-E-G-C-D
    b. 26 weeks
    c. No difference in completion date
8   a. Critical path is A-C-D-F-G
    b.

Day	Cost	Activity
First	$1,000	A
Second	1,200	C
Third	1,500	D (or F)
Fourth	1,500	F (or D)
	$5,200	

Chapter 4

5   a. 5,600 components
    b. 8,000; drilling operation
    c. 9,600; final assembly operation
    d. $1.81, $1.79

Technical Note 4

3   LR labor, 80%
    LR parts, 90%
    Labor $= 11,556$ hours
    Parts $= $330,876$
7   4,710 hours
11 a. 3rd $= 35.1$ hours
    b. Average $= 7.9$ hours each; well worth it

Chapter 5

1   Traditional method 20 min. setup $+ 10 \times 2 =$ 40 min. total scan/retrieve system. 1 min. setup $+ 10 \times 5 = 51$ min. total. Traditional method is best.
3   a. The market can be served only at 3 gals/hr. In 50 hours bathtub will overflow.

Technical Note 5

3   a. 1.35 minutes
    b. 1.51 minutes
    c. $48. The worker would not make the bonus.
7   a. NT $= .9286$ minute/part
    b. ST $= 1.0679$ minutes/part
    c. Daily output $= 449.50$
       Day's wages $= 44.49

Chapter 6

4   a. 20,000 books
    b. higher
    c. lower
10 80 units/hour

Technical Note 6

3   b. 120 seconds
    d. 87.5%
9   a. 33.6 seconds
    b. 3.51 therefore 4 workstations
    d. AB, DF, C, EG, H
    e. Efficiency $= 70.2\%$
    f. Reduce cycle time to 32 seconds and work $6\frac{2}{3}$ minutes overtime
    g. 1.89 hours overtime; may be better to rebalance

Technical Note 7

5   $W_s = 4.125$ minutes
    $L'_q = 4.05$ cars
    $L_s = 4.95$ car
9   a. $L = .22$ waiting
    b. $W = .466$ hour
    c. $D = .362$
10 a. 2 people
    b. 6 minutes
    c. .2964
    d. 67%
    e. 0.03375 hour
17 a. 0.833
    b. 5 documents
    c. 0.2 hour
    d. 0.4822
    e. $L_1 =$ tends to infinity

Technical Note 8

1   *a.* Not inspecting cost = \$20/hr. Cost to inspect = \$9/hr. Therefore, inspect.

     b. \$.18 each

     c. \$.22 per unit

6    $\overline{\overline{X}} = 999.1$

     $UCL = 1014.965$

     $LCL = 983.235$

     $\overline{R} = 21.733$

     $UCL = 49.551$

     $LCL = 0$

     Process is in control

9   *a.* $n = 31.3$ (round sample size to 32)

     b. Random sample 32; reject if more than 8 are defective.

12    $\overline{\overline{X}} = .499$

     $UCL = .520$

     $LCL = .478$

     $R = .037$

     $UCL = .078$

     $LCL = .000$

     Process is in control

Chapter 10

1   2 lbs (\$8,854.90), 3 lbs (\$10,154.30)

     4 lbs (\$11,402.60), 5 lbs (\$12,738.50)

     6 lbs (\$15,337.30), 7 lbs (\$15,899.40)

     8 lbs (\$16,563.70), 9 lbs (\$17,147.70)

Chapter 11

3   No. Must consider demand in fourth year.

5   Expected NPV—Small

     \$4.8 million

     Expected NPV—Large

     \$2.6 million

Technical Note 11

1    $C_X = 176.7$

     $C_Y = 241.5$

2    $C_X = 374$

     $C_Y = 357$

Chapter 12

1   5 kanban card sets

Chapter 13

3   *a.* February 84

     March 86

     April 90

     May 88

     June 84

     b. MAD = 15

7

QUARTER	FORECAST
9	232
10	281
11	239
12	231

11   *a.* April to September = 130, 150, 160, 170, 160, 150

     b. April to September = 136, 146, 150, 159, 153, 146

     c. Exponential smoothing performed better.

15   MAD = 104

     TS = 3.1

     The high TS value indicates the model is unacceptable.

19   *a.* MAD = 90

     TS = −1.67

     b. Model okay since tracking is −1.67

Chapter 14

3   Total cost = \$413,600

6   Total cost = \$413,750

Chapter 15

5    $q = 713$

8   *a.* $Q = 1,225$

     $R = 824$

     b. $q = 390 -$ Inventory on hand

12   *a.* $Q = 89$

     b. \$224.72

     c. \$222.50

15   *a.* A (4, 13, 18);

     B (2, 5, 8, 10, 11, 14, 16);

     C (remainder)

     b. Classify as A.

18    $q = 691$

27   729 hamburgers

28   5,000 pounds

Chapter 16

4

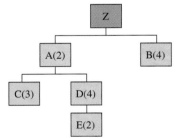

11   Least total cost method: Order 250 units in Period 1 for Periods 1–8;

     Least unit cost method: Order 450 units in Period 1 for Periods 1–9.

14   *c.* .A
      .B(2)
          .E(4)
          .F(3)
      .C(3)
          .D(3)
          .H(2)
              .E(5)
              .G(2)
      .D(1)

d.

Level 0	100 units of A
Level 1	200 units of B
	300 units of C
Level 2	600 units of F
	600 units of H
	1000 units of D
Level 3	3800 units of E
	1200 units of G

Chapter 17

3   Job order: 5, 6, 7, 3, 1, 2, 4
6   A to 3, B to 1, C to 4, D to 2; cost = $17,000
7   Critical ratio schedule: 5, 3, 2, 4, 1
    Earliest due date, job priority: 2, 5, 3, 4, 1
    Shortest processing time (including delay time): 2, 1, 4, 3, 5
10   E, A, B, D, C
15   C, B, D, F, E, A

Technical Note 17

2   Average customer waiting time = $\frac{1}{6}$ minute
    Average teller idle time = $\frac{4}{6}$ minute

7   *a.*

Condition 1	Condition 2
(1) Idle 18 min.	76 + 134 = 210 min.
(2) Delay 87 min.	0 min.

b.

Condition 1	Condition 2
Cost of repairperson	
$ 38.80	$ 77.20
Cost of machine down	
175.33	$117.33
$214.13	$194.53 (Total Cost)

    Lowest cost is Condition 2.
11   One car bypasses.

Chapter 18

1   Case I: X used = 933.3 hours
                Y used = 700 hours
    Case II: Y = 700 hours
                X = 933.3 hours
    Case III: X = 933.3 hours
                Y = 700 hours
    Case IV: X = 933.3 hours
                Y = 700 hours
    Otherwise:
    Case I: No problem
    Case II: Excess WIP
    Case III: Excess spare parts
    Case IV: Excess finished goods
8   *a.* Machine B is the constraint.
    b. All of M; as many N as possible
    c. $600 (100 M and 30 N)

UNIFORMLY DISTRIBUTED RANDOM DIGITS

56970	10799	52098	04184	54967	72938	50834	23777	08392
83125	85077	60490	44369	66130	72936	69848	59973	08144
55503	21383	02464	26141	68779	66388	75242	82690	74099
47019	06683	33203	29603	54553	25971	69573	83854	24715
84828	61152	79526	29554	84580	37859	28504	61980	34997
08021	31331	79227	05748	51276	57143	31926	00915	45821
36458	28285	30424	98420	72925	40729	22337	48293	86847
05752	96045	36847	87729	81679	59126	59437	33225	31280
26768	02513	58454	56958	20575	76746	40878	06846	32828
42613	72456	43030	58085	06766	60227	96414	32671	45587
95457	12176	65482	25596	02678	54592	63607	82096	21913
95276	67524	63564	95958	39750	64379	46059	51666	10433
66954	53574	64776	92345	95110	59448	77249	54044	67942
17457	44151	14113	02462	02798	54977	48340	66738	60184
03704	23322	83214	59337	01695	60666	97410	55064	17427
21538	16997	33210	60337	27976	70661	08250	69509	60264
57178	16730	08310	70348	11317	71623	55510	64750	87759
31048	40058	94953	55866	96283	40620	52087	80817	74533
69799	83300	16498	80733	96422	58078	99643	39847	96884
90595	65017	59231	17772	67831	33317	00520	90401	41700
33570	34761	08039	78784	09977	29398	93896	78227	90110
15340	82760	57477	13898	48431	72936	78160	87240	52710
64079	07733	36512	56186	99098	48850	72527	08486	10951
63491	84886	67118	62063	74958	20946	28147	39338	32109
92003	76568	41034	28260	79708	00770	88643	21188	01850
52360	46658	66511	04172	73085	11795	52594	13287	82531
74622	12142	68355	65635	21828	39539	18988	53609	04001
04157	50070	61343	64315	70836	82857	35335	87900	36194
86003	60070	66241	32836	27573	11479	94114	81641	00496
41208	80187	20351	09630	84668	42486	71303	19512	50277
06433	80674	24520	18222	10610	05794	37515	48619	62866
39298	47829	72648	37414	75755	04717	29899	78817	03509
89884	59651	67533	68123	17730	95862	08034	19473	63971
61512	32155	51906	61662	64430	16688	37275	51262	11569
99653	47635	12506	88535	36553	23757	34209	55803	96275
95913	11085	13772	76638	48423	25018	99041	77529	81360
55804	44004	13122	44115	01601	50541	00147	77685	58788
35334	82410	91601	40617	72876	33967	73830	15405	96554
57729	88646	76487	11622	96297	24160	09903	14047	22917
86648	89317	63677	70119	94739	25875	38829	68377	43918
30574	06039	07967	32422	76791	30725	53711	93385	13421
81307	13114	83580	79974	45929	85113	72268	09858	52104
02410	96385	79067	54939	21410	86980	91772	93307	34116
18969	87444	52233	62319	08598	09066	95288	04794	01534
87863	80514	66860	62297	80198	19347	73234	86265	49096
08397	10538	15438	62311	72844	60203	46412	65943	79232
28520	45247	58729	10854	99058	18260	38765	90038	94209
44285	09452	15867	70418	57012	72122	36634	97283	95943
86299	22510	33571	23309	57040	29285	67870	21913	72958
84842	05748	90894	61658	15001	94005	36308	41161	37341

NORMALLY DISTRIBUTED RANDOM DIGITS

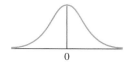

0

An entry in the table is the value z from a normal distribution with a mean of 0 and a standard deviation of 1.

1.98677	1.23481	−.28360	.99217	−.87919	−.21600
−.59341	1.54221	−.65806	1.08372	1.68560	1.14899
.11340	.19126	−.65084	.12188	.02338	−.61545
.89783	−.54929	−.03663	−1.89506	.15158	−.20061
−.50790	1.14463	1.30917	1.26528	.09459	.16423
−1.63968	−.63248	.21482	−1.16241	−.60015	−.55233
1.14081	−.29988	−.48053	−1.21397	−.34391	−1.84881
−.43354	−.32855	.67115	.52289	−1.42796	−.14181
.05707	.35331	.20470	.01847	1.71086	−1.44738
.77153	.72576	−.29833	.26139	1.25845	−.35468
−1.38286	.04406	−.75499	.61068	.61903	−.96845
1.60166	−1.66161	.70886	−.20302	−.28373	2.07219
−.48781	.02629	−.34306	2.00746	−1.12059	.07943
−1.10632	1.18250	−.60065	.09737	.63297	1.00659
.77000	−.87214	−.63584	−.39546	−.72776	.45594
−.56882	−.23153	−2.03852	−.28101	.30384	−.14246
.27721	−.04776	.11740	−.17211	1.63483	1.34221
−.40251	−.31052	−1.04834	−.23243	−1.52224	.85903
1.27086	−.93166	−.03766	1.21016	.13451	.81941
1.14464	.56176	.89824	1.54670	1.48411	.14422
.04172	1.49672	−.15490	.77084	−.29064	2.87643
−.36795	1.22318	−1.05084	−1.05409	.82052	.09670
1.94110	1.00826	−.85411	−1.31341	−1.85921	.74578
.14946	−2.75470	−.10830	1.02845	.69291	−.78579

APPENDIX D

AREAS OF THE STANDARD NORMAL DISTRIBUTION

An entry in the table is the proportion under the entire curve that is between $z = 0$ and a positive value of z. Areas for negative values of z are obtained by symmetry. Using Microsoft Excel® these probabilities are generated with the equation:

$$\text{NORMSDIST}\,(z) - .5$$

z	.00	.01	.02	.03	.04	.05	.06	.07	.08	.09
0.0	.0000	.0040	.0080	.0120	.0160	.0199	.0239	.0279	.0319	.0359
0.1	.0398	.0438	.0478	.0517	.0557	.0596	.0636	.0675	.0714	.0753
0.2	.0793	.0832	.0871	.0910	.0948	.0987	.1026	.1064	.1103	.1141
0.3	.1179	.1217	.1255	.1293	.1331	.1368	.1406	.1443	.1480	.1517
0.4	.1554	.1591	.1628	.1664	.1700	.1736	.1772	.1808	.1844	.1879
0.5	.1915	.1950	.1985	.2019	.2054	.2088	.2123	.2157	.2190	.2224
0.6	.2257	.2291	.2324	.2357	.2389	.2422	.2454	.2486	.2517	.2549
0.7	.2580	.2611	.2642	.2673	.2703	.2734	.2764	.2794	.2823	.2852
0.8	.2881	.2910	.2939	.2967	.2995	.3023	.3051	.3078	.3106	.3133
0.9	.3159	.3186	.3212	.3238	.3264	.3289	.3315	.3340	.3365	.3389
1.0	.3413	.3438	.3461	.3485	.3508	.3531	.3554	.3577	.3599	.3621
1.1	.3643	.3665	.3686	.3708	.3729	.3749	.3770	.3790	.3810	.3830
1.2	.3849	.3869	.3888	.3907	.3925	.3944	.3962	.3980	.3997	.4015
1.3	.4032	.4049	.4066	.4082	.4099	.4115	.4131	.4147	.4162	.4177
1.4	.4192	.4207	.4222	.4236	.4251	.4265	.4279	.4292	.4306	.4319
1.5	.4332	.4345	.4357	.4370	.4382	.4394	.4406	.4418	.4429	.4441
1.6	.4452	.4463	.4474	.4484	.4495	.4505	.4515	.4525	.4535	.4545
1.7	.4554	.4564	.4573	.4582	.4591	.4599	.4608	.4616	.4625	.4633
1.8	.4641	.4649	.4656	.4664	.4671	.4678	.4686	.4693	.4699	.4706
1.9	.4713	.4719	.4726	.4732	.4738	.4744	.4750	.4756	.4761	.4767
2.0	.4772	.4778	.4783	.4788	.4793	.4798	.4803	.4808	.4812	.4817
2.1	.4821	.4826	.4830	.4834	.4838	.4842	.4846	.4850	.4854	.4857
2.2	.4861	.4864	.4868	.4871	.4875	.4878	.4881	.4884	.4887	.4890
2.3	.4893	.4896	.4898	.4901	.4904	.4906	.4909	.4911	.4913	.4916
2.4	.4918	.4920	.4922	.4925	.4927	.4929	.4931	.4932	.4934	.4936
2.5	.4938	.4940	.4941	.4943	.4945	.4946	.4948	.4949	.4951	.4952
2.6	.4953	.4955	.4956	.4957	.4959	.4960	.4961	.4962	.4963	.4964
2.7	.4965	.4966	.4967	.4968	.4969	.4970	.4971	.4972	.4973	.4974
2.8	.4974	.4975	.4976	.4977	.4977	.4978	.4979	.4979	.4980	.4981
2.9	.4981	.4982	.4982	.4983	.4984	.4984	.4985	.4985	.4986	.4986
3.0	.4987	.4987	.4987	.4988	.4988	.4989	.4989	.4989	.4990	.4990

AREAS OF THE CUMULATIVE STANDARD NORMAL DISTRIBUTION[1]

An entry in the table is the proportion under the curve cumulated from the negative tail.

z	G(z)	z	G(z)	z	G(z)
−4.00	0.00003	−1.30	0.09680	1.40	0.91924
−3.95	0.00004	−1.25	0.10565	1.45	0.92647
−3.90	0.00005	−1.20	0.11507	1.50	0.93319
−3.85	0.00006	−1.15	0.12507	1.55	0.93943
−3.80	0.00007	−1.10	0.13567	1.60	0.94520
−3.75	0.00009	−1.05	0.14686	1.65	0.95053
−3.70	0.00011	−1.00	0.15866	1.70	0.95543
−3.65	0.00013	−0.95	0.17106	1.75	0.95994
−3.60	0.00016	−0.90	0.18406	1.80	0.96407
−3.55	0.00019	−0.85	0.19766	1.85	0.96784
−3.50	0.00023	−0.80	0.21186	1.90	0.97128
−3.45	0.00028	−0.75	0.22663	1.95	0.97441
−3.40	0.00034	−0.70	0.24196	2.00	0.97725
−3.35	0.00040	−0.65	0.25785	2.05	0.97982
−3.30	0.00048	−0.60	0.27425	2.10	0.98214
−3.25	0.00058	−0.55	0.29116	2.15	0.98422
−3.20	0.00069	−0.50	0.30854	2.20	0.98610
−3.15	0.00082	−0.45	0.32636	2.25	0.98778
−3.10	0.00097	−0.40	0.34458	2.30	0.98928
−3.05	0.00114	−0.35	0.36317	2.35	0.99061
−3.00	0.00135	−0.30	0.38209	2.40	0.99180
−2.95	0.00159	−0.25	0.40129	2.45	0.99286
−2.90	0.00187	−0.20	0.42074	2.50	0.99379
−2.85	0.00219	−0.15	0.44038	2.55	0.99461
−2.80	0.00256	−0.10	0.46017	2.60	0.99534
−2.75	0.00298	−0.05	0.48006	2.65	0.99598
−2.70	0.00347	0.00	0.50000	2.70	0.99653
−2.65	0.00402	0.05	0.51994	2.75	0.99702
−2.60	0.00466	0.10	0.53983	2.80	0.99744
−2.55	0.00539	0.15	0.55962	2.85	0.99781
−2.50	0.00621	0.20	0.57926	2.90	0.99813
−2.45	0.00714	0.25	0.59871	2.95	0.99841
−2.40	0.00820	0.30	0.61791	3.00	0.99865
−2.35	0.00939	0.35	0.63683	3.05	0.99886
−2.30	0.01072	0.40	0.65542	3.10	0.99903
−2.25	0.01222	0.45	0.67364	3.15	0.99918
−2.20	0.01390	0.50	0.69146	3.20	0.99931
−2.15	0.01578	0.55	0.70884	3.25	0.99942
−2.10	0.01786	0.60	0.72575	3.30	0.99952
−2.05	0.02018	0.65	0.74215	3.35	0.99960
−2.00	0.02275	0.70	0.75804	3.40	0.99966
−1.95	0.02559	0.75	0.77337	3.45	0.99972
−1.90	0.02872	0.80	0.78814	3.50	0.99977
−1.85	0.03216	0.85	0.80234	3.55	0.99981
−1.80	0.03593	0.90	0.81594	3.60	0.99984
−1.75	0.04006	0.95	0.82894	3.65	0.99987
−1.70	0.04457	1.00	0.84134	3.70	0.99989
−1.65	0.04947	1.05	0.85314	3.75	0.99991
−1.60	0.05480	1.10	0.86433	3.80	0.99993
−1.55	0.06057	1.15	0.87493	3.85	0.99994
−1.50	0.06681	1.20	0.88493	3.90	0.99995
−1.45	0.07353	1.25	0.89435	3.95	0.99996
−1.40	0.08076	1.30	0.90320	4.00	0.99997
−1.35	0.08851	1.35	0.91149		

[1] Using Microsoft Excel®, these probabilities are generated with the NORMSDIST(z) function.

NEGATIVE EXPONENTIAL DISTRIBUTION: VALUES OF e^{-x}[1]

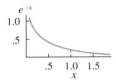

X	e^{-x} (VALUE)	X	e^{-x} (VALUE)	X	e^{-x} (VALUE)	X	e^{-x} (VALUE)
0.00	1.00000	0.50	0.60653	1.00	0.36788	1.50	0.22313
0.01	0.99005	0.51	.60050	1.01	.36422	1.51	.22091
0.02	.98020	0.52	.59452	1.02	.36060	1.52	.21871
0.03	.97045	0.53	.58860	1.03	.35701	1.53	.21654
0.04	.96079	0.54	.58275	1.04	.35345	1.54	.21438
0.05	.95123	0.55	.57695	1.05	.34994	1.55	.21225
0.06	.94176	0.56	.57121	1.06	.34646	1.56	.21014
0.07	.93239	0.57	.56553	1.07	.34301	1.57	.20805
0.08	.92312	0.58	.55990	1.08	.33960	1.58	.20598
0.09	.91393	0.59	.55433	1.09	.33622	1.59	.20393
0.10	.90484	0.60	.54881	1.10	.33287	1.60	.20190
0.11	.89583	0.61	.54335	1.11	.32956	1.61	.19989
0.12	.88692	0.62	.53794	1.12	.32628	1.62	.19790
0.13	.87809	0.63	.53259	1.13	.32303	1.63	.19593
0.14	.86936	0.64	.52729	1.14	.31982	1.64	.19398
0.15	.86071	0.65	.52205	1.15	.31664	1.65	.19205
0.16	.87514	0.66	.51685	1.16	.31349	1.66	.19014
0.17	.84366	0.67	.51171	1.17	.31037	1.67	.18825
0.18	.83527	0.68	.50662	1.18	.30728	1.68	.18637
0.19	.82696	0.69	.50158	1.19	.30422	1.69	.18452
0.20	.81873	0.70	.49659	1.20	.30119	1.70	.18268
0.21	.81058	0.71	.49164	1.21	.29820	1.71	.18087
0.22	.80252	0.72	.48675	1.22	.29523	1.72	.17907
0.23	.79453	0.73	.48191	1.23	.29229	1.73	.17728
0.24	.78663	0.74	.47711	1.24	.28938	1.74	.17552
0.25	.77880	0.75	.47237	1.25	.28650	1.75	.17377
0.26	.77105	0.76	.46767	1.26	.28365	1.76	.17204
0.27	.76338	0.77	.46301	1.27	.28083	1.77	.17033
0.28	.75578	0.78	.45841	1.28	.27804	1.78	.16864
0.29	.74826	0.79	.45384	1.29	.27527	1.79	.16696
0.30	.74082	0.80	.44933	1.30	.27253	1.80	.16530
0.31	.73345	0.81	.44486	1.31	.26982	1.81	.16365
0.32	.72615	0.82	.44043	1.32	.26714	1.82	.16203
0.33	.71892	0.83	.43605	1.33	.26448	1.83	.16041
0.34	.71177	0.84	.43171	1.34	.26185	1.84	.15882
0.35	.70469	0.85	.42741	1.35	.25924	1.85	.15724
0.36	.69768	0.86	.42316	1.36	.25666	1.86	.15567
0.37	.69073	0.87	.41895	1.37	.25411	1.87	.15412
0.38	.68386	0.88	.41478	1.38	.25158	1.88	.15259
0.39	.67706	0.89	.41066	1.39	.24908	1.89	.15107
0.40	.67032	0.90	.40657	1.40	.24660	1.90	.14957
0.41	.66365	0.91	.40252	1.41	.24414	1.91	.14808
0.42	.65705	0.92	.39852	1.42	.24171	1.92	.14661
0.43	.65051	0.93	.39455	1.43	.23931	1.93	.14515
0.44	.64404	0.94	.39063	1.44	.23693	1.94	.14370
0.45	.63763	0.95	.38674	1.45	.23457	1.95	.14227
0.46	.63128	0.96	.38289	1.46	.23224	1.96	.14086
0.47	.62500	0.97	.37908	1.47	.22993	1.97	.13946
0.48	.61878	0.98	.37531	1.48	.22764	1.98	.13807
0.49	.61263	0.99	.37158	1.49	.22537	1.99	.13670
0.50	.60653	1.00	.36788	1.50	.22313	2.00	.13534

[1] Using Microsoft Excel®, these values are calculated with the equation: $1 - $ EXPONDIST(x, 1, TRUE).

INTEREST TABLES

Compound Sum of $1[1]

YEAR	1%	2%	3%	4%	5%	6%	7%	8%	9%
1	1.010	1.020	1.030	1.040	1.050	1.060	1.070	1.080	1.090
2	1.020	1.040	1.061	1.082	1.102	1.124	1.145	1.166	1.188
3	1.030	1.061	1.093	1.125	1.158	1.191	1.225	1.260	1.295
4	1.041	1.082	1.126	1.170	1.216	1.262	1.311	1.360	1.412
5	1.051	1.104	1.159	1.217	1.276	1.338	1.403	1.469	1.539
6	1.062	1.126	1.194	1.265	1.340	1.419	1.501	1.587	1.677
7	1.072	1.149	1.230	1.316	1.407	1.504	1.606	1.714	1.828
8	1.083	1.172	1.267	1.369	1.477	1.594	1.718	1.851	1.993
9	1.094	1.195	1.305	1.423	1.551	1.689	1.838	1.999	2.172
10	1.105	1.219	1.344	1.480	1.629	1.791	1.967	2.159	2.367
11	1.116	1.243	1.384	1.539	1.710	1.898	2.105	2.332	2.580
12	1.127	1.268	1.426	1.601	1.796	2.012	2.252	2.518	2.813
13	1.138	1.294	1.469	1.665	1.886	2.133	2.410	2.720	3.066
14	1.149	1.319	1.513	1.732	1.980	2.261	2.579	2.937	3.342
15	1.161	1.346	1.558	1.801	2.079	2.397	2.759	3.172	3.642
16	1.173	1.373	1.605	1.873	2.183	2.540	2.952	3.426	3.970
17	1.184	1.400	1.653	1.948	2.292	2.693	3.159	3.700	4.328
18	1.196	1.428	1.702	2.026	2.407	2.854	3.380	3.996	4.717
19	1.208	1.457	1.754	2.107	2.527	3.026	3.617	4.316	5.142
20	1.220	1.486	1.806	2.191	2.653	3.207	3.870	4.661	5.604
25	1.282	1.641	2.094	2.666	3.386	4.292	5.427	6.848	8.623
30	1.348	1.811	2.427	3.243	4.322	5.743	7.612	10.063	13.268

YEAR	10%	12%	14%	15%	16%	18%	20%	24%	28%
1	1.100	1.120	1.140	1.150	1.160	1.180	1.200	1.240	1.280
2	1.210	1.254	1.300	1.322	1.346	1.392	1.440	1.538	1.638
3	1.331	1.405	1.482	1.521	1.561	1.643	1.728	1.907	2.067
4	1.464	1.574	1.689	1.749	1.811	1.939	2.074	2.364	2.684
5	1.611	1.762	1.925	2.011	2.100	2.288	2.488	2.932	3.436
6	1.772	1.974	2.195	2.313	2.436	2.700	2.986	3.635	4.398
7	1.949	2.211	2.502	2.660	2.826	3.185	3.583	4.508	5.629
8	2.144	2.476	2.853	3.059	3.278	3.759	4.300	5.590	7.206
9	2.358	2.773	3.252	3.518	3.803	4.435	5.160	6.931	9.223
10	2.594	3.106	3.707	4.046	4.411	5.234	6.192	8.594	11.806
11	2.853	3.479	4.226	4.652	5.117	6.176	7.430	10.657	15.112
12	3.138	3.896	4.818	5.350	5.936	7.288	8.916	13.216	19.343
13	3.452	4.363	5.492	6.153	6.886	8.599	10.699	16.386	24.759
14	3.797	4.887	6.261	7.076	7.988	10.147	12.839	20.319	31.691
15	4.177	5.474	7.138	8.137	9.266	11.974	15.407	25.196	40.565
16	4.595	6.130	8.137	9.358	10.748	14.129	18.488	31.243	51.923
17	5.054	6.866	9.276	10.761	12.468	16.672	22.186	38.741	66.461
18	5.560	7.690	10.575	12.375	14.463	19.673	26.623	48.039	85.071
19	6.116	8.613	12.056	14.232	16.777	23.214	31.948	59.568	108.89
20	6.728	9.646	13.743	16.367	19.461	27.393	38.338	73.864	139.38
25	10.835	17.000	26.462	32.919	40.874	62.669	95.396	216.542	478.90
30	17.449	29.960	50.950	66.212	85.850	143.371	237.376	634.820	1645.5

[1] Using Microsoft Excel®, these are calculated with the equation: $(1 + interest)^{years}$.

table G.2

Sum of an Annuity[2] of $1 for N Years

YEAR	1%	2%	3%	4%	5%	6%	7%	8%
1	1.000	1.000	1.000	1.000	1.000	1.000	1.000	1.000
2	2.010	2.020	2.030	2.040	2.050	2.060	2.070	2.080
3	2.030	3.060	3.019	3.122	3.152	3.184	3.215	3.246
4	4.060	4.122	4.184	4.246	4.310	4.375	4.440	4.506
5	5.101	5.204	5.309	5.416	5.526	5.637	5.751	5.867
6	6.152	6.308	6.468	6.633	6.802	6.975	7.153	7.336
7	7.214	7.434	7.662	7.898	8.142	8.394	8.654	8.923
8	8.286	8.583	8.892	9.214	9.549	9.897	10.260	10.637
9	9.369	9.755	10.159	10.583	11.027	11.491	11.978	12.488
10	10.462	10.950	11.464	12.006	12.578	13.181	13.816	14.487
11	11.567	12.169	12.808	13.486	14.207	14.972	15.784	16.645
12	12.683	13.412	14.192	15.026	15.917	16.870	17.888	18.977
13	13.809	14.680	15.618	16.627	17.713	18.882	20.141	21.495
14	14.947	15.974	17.086	18.292	19.599	21.051	22.550	24.215
15	16.097	17.293	18.599	20.024	21.579	23.276	25.129	27.152
16	17.258	18.639	20.157	21.825	23.657	25.673	27.888	30.324
17	18.430	20.012	21.762	23.698	25.840	28.213	30.840	33.750
18	19.615	21.412	23.414	25.645	28.132	30.906	33.999	37.450
19	20.811	22.841	25.117	27.671	30.539	33.760	37.379	41.446
20	22.019	24.297	26.870	29.778	33.066	36.786	40.995	45.762
25	28.243	32.030	36.459	41.646	47.727	54.865	63.249	73.106
30	34.785	40.568	47.575	56.085	66.439	79.058	94.461	113.283

YEAR	9%	10%	12%	14%	16%	18%	20%	24%
1	1.000	1.000	1.000	1.000	1.000	1.000	1.000	1.000
2	2.090	2.100	2.120	2.140	2.160	2.180	2.200	2.240
3	3.278	3.310	3.374	3.440	3.506	3.572	3.640	3.778
4	4.573	4.641	4.770	4.921	5.066	5.215	5.368	5.684
5	5.985	6.105	6.353	6.610	6.877	7.154	7.442	8.048
6	7.523	7.716	8.115	8.536	8.977	9.442	9.930	10.980
7	9.200	9.487	10.089	10.730	11.414	12.142	12.916	14.615
8	11.028	11.436	12.300	13.233	14.240	15.327	16.499	19.123
9	13.021	13.579	14.776	16.085	17.518	19.086	20.799	24.712
10	15.193	15.937	17.549	19.337	21.321	23.521	25.959	31.643
11	17.560	18.531	20.655	23.044	25.733	28.755	32.150	40.238
12	20.141	21.384	24.133	27.271	30.850	34.931	39.580	50.985
13	22.953	24.523	28.029	32.089	36.786	42.219	48.497	64.110
14	26.019	27.975	32.393	37.581	43.672	50.818	59.196	80.496
15	29.361	31.772	37.280	43.842	51.660	60.965	72.035	100.815
16	33.003	35.950	42.753	50.980	60.925	72.939	87.442	126.011
17	36.974	40.545	48.884	59.118	71.673	87.068	105.931	157.253
18	41.301	45.599	55.750	68.394	84.141	103.740	128.117	195.994
19	46.018	51.159	63.440	78.969	98.603	123.414	154.740	244.033
20	51.160	57.275	72.052	91.025	115.380	146.628	186.688	303.601
25	84.701	93.347	133.334	181.871	249.214	342.603	471.981	898.092
30	136.308	164.494	241.333	356.787	530.312	790.948	1181.882	2640.916

[2] Using Microsoft Excel®, these are calculated with the function: FV(interest, years, −1).

Present Value of $1[3]

YEAR	1%	2%	3%	4%	5%	6%	7%	8%	9%	10%	12%	14%	15%
1	.990	.980	.971	.962	.952	.943	.935	.926	.917	.909	.893	.877	.870
2	.980	.961	.943	.925	.907	.890	.873	.857	.842	.826	.797	.769	.756
3	.971	.942	.915	.889	.864	.840	.816	.794	.772	.751	.712	.675	.658
4	.961	.924	.889	.855	.823	.792	.763	.735	.708	.683	.636	.592	.572
5	.951	.906	.863	.822	.784	.747	.713	.681	.650	.621	.567	.519	.497
6	.942	.888	.838	.790	.746	.705	.666	.630	.596	.564	.507	.456	.432
7	.933	.871	.813	.760	.711	.665	.623	.583	.547	.513	.452	.400	.376
8	.923	.853	.789	.731	.677	.627	.582	.540	.502	.467	.404	.351	.327
9	.914	.837	.766	.703	.645	.592	.544	.500	.460	.424	.361	.308	.284
10	.905	.820	.744	.676	.614	.558	.508	.463	.422	.386	.322	.270	.247
11	.896	.804	.722	.650	.585	.527	.475	.429	.388	.350	.287	.237	.215
12	.887	.788	.701	.625	.557	.497	.444	.397	.356	.319	.257	.208	.187
13	.879	.773	.681	.601	.530	.469	.415	.368	.326	.290	.229	.182	.163
14	.870	.758	.661	.577	.505	.442	.388	.340	.299	.263	.205	.160	.141
15	.861	.743	.642	.555	.481	.417	.362	.315	.275	.239	.183	.140	.123
16	.853	.728	.623	.534	.458	.394	.339	.292	.252	.218	.163	.123	.107
17	.844	.714	.605	.513	.436	.371	.317	.270	.231	.198	.146	.108	.093
18	.836	.700	.587	.494	.416	.350	.296	.250	.212	.180	.130	.095	.081
19	.828	.686	.570	.475	.396	.331	.276	.232	.194	.164	.116	.083	.070
20	.820	.673	.554	.456	.377	.312	.258	.215	.178	.149	.104	.073	.061
25	.780	.610	.478	.375	.295	.233	.184	.146	.116	.092	.059	.038	.030
30	.742	.552	.412	.308	.231	.174	.131	.099	.075	.057	.033	.020	.015

YEAR	16%	18%	20%	24%	28%	32%	36%	40%	50%	60%	70%	80%	90%
1	.862	.847	.833	.806	.781	.758	.735	.714	.667	.625	.588	.556	.526
2	.743	.718	.694	.650	.610	.574	.541	.510	.444	.391	.346	.309	.277
3	.641	.609	.579	.524	.477	.435	.398	.364	.296	.244	.204	.171	.146
4	.552	.516	.482	.423	.373	.329	.292	.260	.198	.153	.120	.095	.077
5	.476	.437	.402	.341	.291	.250	.215	.186	.132	.095	.070	.053	.040
6	.410	.370	.335	.275	.227	.189	.158	.133	.088	.060	.041	.029	.021
7	.354	.314	.279	.222	.178	.143	.116	.095	.059	.037	.024	.016	.011
8	.305	.266	.233	.179	.139	.108	.085	.068	.039	.023	.014	.009	.006
9	.263	.226	.194	.144	.108	.082	.063	.048	.026	.015	.008	.005	.003
10	.227	.191	.162	.116	.085	.062	.046	.035	.017	.009	.005	.003	.002
11	.195	.162	.135	.094	.066	.047	.034	.025	.012	.006	.003	.002	.001
12	.168	.137	.112	.076	.052	.036	.025	.018	.008	.004	.002	.001	.001
13	.145	.116	.093	.061	.040	.027	.018	.013	.005	.002	.001	.001	.000
14	.125	.099	.078	.049	.032	.021	.014	.009	.003	.001	.001	.000	.000
15	.108	.084	.065	.040	.025	.016	.010	.006	.002	.001	.000	.000	.000
16	.093	.071	.054	.032	.019	.012	.007	.005	.002	.001	.000	.000	
17	.080	.060	.045	.026	.015	.009	.005	.003	.001	.000	.000		
18	.069	.051	.038	.021	.012	.007	.004	.002	.001	.000	.000		
19	.060	.043	.031	.017	.009	.005	.003	.002	.000	.000			
20	.051	.037	.026	.014	.007	.004	.002	.001	.000	.000			
25	.024	.016	.010	.005	.002	.001	.000	.000					
30	.012	.007	.004	.002	.001	.000	.000						

[3] Using Microsoft Excel®, these are calculated with the equation: $(1 + \text{interest})^{-\text{years}}$.

table G.4

Present Value of an Annuity of $1[4]

YEAR	1%	2%	3%	4%	5%	6%	7%	8%	9%	10%
1	0.990	0.980	0.971	0.962	0.952	0.943	0.935	0.926	0.917	0.909
2	1.970	1.942	1.913	1.886	1.859	1.833	1.808	1.783	1.759	1.736
3	2.941	2.884	2.829	2.775	2.723	2.673	2.624	2.577	2.531	2.487
4	3.902	3.808	3.717	3.630	3.546	3.465	3.387	3.312	3.240	3.170
5	4.853	4.713	4.580	4.452	4.329	4.212	4.100	3.993	3.890	3.791
6	5.795	5.601	5.417	5.242	5.076	4.917	4.766	4.623	4.486	4.355
7	6.728	6.472	6.230	6.002	5.786	5.582	5.389	5.206	5.033	4.868
8	7.652	7.325	7.020	6.733	6.463	6.210	6.971	5.747	5.535	5.335
9	8.566	8.162	7.786	7.435	7.108	6.802	6.515	6.247	5.985	5.759
10	9.471	8.983	8.530	8.111	7.722	7.360	7.024	6.710	6.418	6.145
11	10.368	9.787	9.253	8.760	8.306	7.887	7.449	7.139	6.805	6.495
12	11.255	10.575	9.954	9.385	8.863	8.384	7.943	7.536	7.161	6.814
13	12.134	11.348	10.635	9.986	9.394	8.853	8.358	7.904	7.487	7.103
14	13.004	12.106	11.296	10.563	9.899	9.295	8.745	8.244	7.786	7.367
15	13.865	12.849	11.938	11.118	10.380	9.712	9.108	8.559	8.060	7.606
16	14.718	13.578	12.561	11.652	10.838	10.106	9.447	8.851	8.312	7.824
17	15.562	14.292	13.166	12.166	11.274	10.477	9.763	9.122	8.544	8.022
18	16.398	14.992	13.754	12.659	11.690	10.828	10.059	9.372	8.756	8.201
19	17.226	15.678	14.324	13.134	12.085	11.158	10.336	9.604	8.950	8.365
20	18.046	16.351	14.877	13.590	12.462	11.470	10.594	9.818	9.128	8.514
25	22.023	19.523	17.413	15.622	14.094	12.783	11.654	10.675	9.823	9.077
30	25.808	22.397	19.600	17.292	15.373	13.765	12.409	11.258	10.274	9.427

YEAR	12%	14%	16%	18%	20%	24%	28%	32%	36%
1	0.893	0.877	0.862	0.847	0.833	0.806	0.781	0.758	0.735
2	1.690	1.647	1.605	1.566	1.528	1.457	1.392	1.332	1.276
3	2.402	2.322	2.246	2.174	2.106	1.981	1.868	1.766	1.674
4	3.037	2.914	2.798	2.690	2.589	2.404	2.241	2.096	1.966
5	3.605	3.433	3.274	3.127	2.991	2.745	2.532	2.345	2.181
6	4.111	3.889	3.685	3.498	3.326	3.020	2.759	2.534	2.339
7	4.564	4.288	4.039	3.812	3.605	3.242	2.937	2.678	2.455
8	4.968	4.639	4.344	4.078	3.837	3.421	3.076	2.786	2.540
9	5.328	4.946	4.607	4.303	4.031	3.566	3.184	2.868	2.603
10	5.650	5.216	4.833	4.494	4.193	3.682	3.269	2.930	2.650
11	5.988	5.453	5.029	4.656	4.327	3.776	3.335	2.978	2.683
12	6.194	5.660	5.197	4.793	4.439	3.851	3.387	3.013	2.708
13	6.424	5.842	5.342	4.910	4.533	3.912	3.427	3.040	2.727
14	6.628	6.002	5.468	5.008	4.611	3.962	3.459	3.061	2.740
15	6.811	6.142	5.575	5.092	4.675	4.001	3.483	3.076	2.750
16	6.974	6.265	5.669	5.162	4.730	4.033	3.503	3.088	2.758
17	7.120	6.373	5.749	5.222	4.775	4.059	3.518	3.097	2.763
18	7.250	6.467	5.818	5.273	4.812	4.080	3.529	3.104	2.767
19	7.366	6.550	5.877	5.316	4.844	4.097	3.539	3.109	2.770
20	7.469	6.623	5.929	5.353	4.870	4.110	3.546	3.113	2.772
25	7.843	6.873	6.097	5.467	4.948	4.147	3.564	3.122	2.776
30	8.055	7.003	6.177	5.517	4.979	4.160	3.569	3.124	2.778

[4] Using Microsoft Excel®, these are calculated with the function: PV(interest, years, −1).

NAME INDEX

SUBJECT INDEX